69 10 13.

PSYCHOLOGY

The Brain, the Person, the World

Stephen M. Kosslyn
Harvard University

Robin S. Rosenberg
Adjunct Faculty
Lesley College

Allyn and Bacon
Boston ▲ London ▲ Toronto ▲ Sydney ▲ Tokyo ▲ Singapore

Executive Editor, Psychology: Rebecca Pascal
Senior Development Editor: Sue Gleason
Series Editorial Assistant: Whitney Brown
Senior Marketing Manager: Caroline Croley
Editorial Production Supervisor: Susan McIntyre
Editorial Production Service: Andrea Cava
Composition Buyer: Linda Cox
Manufacturing Buyer: Megan Cochran
Cover Administrator: Linda Knowles
Design and Electronic Composition: Shelley Davidson
Photo Research: Sarah Evertson, ImageQuest

All chapter opener art images and the Looking at Levels icon were created by
Diane Fenster (www.diane_fenster.com).

Library of Congress Cataloging-in-Publication Data
Kosslyn, Stephen Michael, 1948–
   Psychology: the brain, the person, the world / Stephen M. Kosslyn,
    Robin S. Rosenberg.
    p. cm.
   Includes bibliographical references and indexes.
   ISBN 0-205-27465-X (alk. paper)
   1. Psychology. I. Rosenberg, Robin S. II. Title.

BF121 .K59 2000
150—dc21

00-061058

To Nathaniel, David, and Justin,
for showing us how psychology really works.

CONTENTS

3 SENSATION AND PERCEPTION
How the World Enters the Mind   88

4 CONSCIOUSNESS   128

5 LEARNING   164

6 MEMORY
Living With Yesterday 198

7 LANGUAGE AND THINKING 234

8 TYPES OF INTELLIGENCE
What Does It Mean to Be Smart?   272

11 PSYCHOLOGY OVER THE LIFE SPAN
Growing Up, Growing Older, Growing Wiser   386

12 STRESS, HEALTH, AND COPING   431

15 SOCIAL PSYCHOLOGY Meeting of the Minds   552

PREFACE

Does the field of psychology really need another introductory psychology text-book? This is what we, as coauthors, asked each other as we started to consider writing this book. One of us is a cognitive neuroscientist and the other a clinical psychologist. In working together, we began to see how our different areas of psychology were dovetailing. We had both come to view psychology in terms of events that occur at different levels of analysis: the brain (biological factors), the person (beliefs, desires, and feelings), the group (social, cultural, and environmental factors), and their inter-actions. This view of psychology is exciting because it can be applied to all psychological phenomena and can offer a way to organize a diverse range of theories and discoveries. We realized that this was an important way of teaching psychology. Different fields of psychology are interconnected, although they are not often presented this way in textbooks.

We also wanted to show students that applying the results of psychological research can make learning and remembering easier—not just for this course, but for any course, from economics to art history, and for the demands of life in general. We wanted to do more than just tell students how psychology can help them to be better learners—we wanted to apply these principles in this book, and teach students how to use these principles for themselves. A detailed explanation of this idea is found in the introduction, "Using Psychology to Learn Psychology," on pages 1–5.

ORGANIZATION OF THIS TEXTBOOK

Our goal was to write a textbook that would better integrate the field of psychology and engage students. We felt we could do this by exploring both how psychology can be viewed from various levels of analysis and how psychological principles can be applied to enhance learning. Both of these themes are reflected in the overall organization of the text and its individual chapters.

Most comprehensive psychology textbooks have anywhere from 16 to 22 chapters; ours has 15. When using textbooks with more chapters, introductory psychology instructors often end up skipping parts in the interest of time, or requiring students to read multiple chapters per week. Neither option is ideal; both are likely to result in only a superficial grasp of the field as a whole. Because introductory psychology is intended to be a survey of the entire field, we believed that a more compact book would allow students to sample all the areas of psychology. We have carefully chosen both core and cutting-edge concepts, theories, and findings, to give students a deeper understanding of the field.

To achieve a more compact book, we have combined several topics that we think are best covered in a more integrated manner. For example, Chapter 1 includes both an introduction to the field of psychology and an overview of the methods used in psychological research. To understand any science, students need to learn about the kinds of questions that are asked and the methods for answering them. By considering the methods, students get a concrete sense of the shape of the science as it stands today. Appendix A (Statistics) and Appendix B (How to Read, Critically Evaluate, and Write Research Papers) further enhance this coverage and can be assigned at any time in the course.

Chapter 3 covers both sensation and perception. These two topics are strongly related, and recent brain research suggests that the same brain systems underlie both types of phenomena. Combining the two topics in one chapter makes it easier for students to see how sensation and perception work to achieve the same ends, specifically, the identification of stimuli and the representation of spatial relations.

Similarly, Chapter 9 discusses the essentials of emotion and motivation in one chapter. The reason for including the two topics in one chapter is straightforward: Emotion is a major factor that motivates us. Unlike most other textbooks, ours introduces emotion first. By beginning the chapter with emotion, we are able to show how dramatic breakthroughs in the study of emotion (which have occurred, in part, because of discoveries about the brain) can illuminate aspects of human motivation.

We include a single chapter on social psychology, Chapter 15. This chapter is further divided into two sections: social cognition and social behavior, the traditional domains of the field. Again, by including both topics in a single chapter, we are better able to show how they are related. Students learn how cognition about other people's beliefs, desires, and feelings plays a key role in our social interactions.

In addition to providing more detailed information about research methods used in psychology, Appendix B walks students through the American Psychological Association (APA) format for research articles. This appendix helps students understand not only the APA format for a research paper, but also how a research study is designed to answer a particular question (or questions) of interest, and whether the data support a particular answer to the question. Appendix B also helps students to organize their own research papers and to know what should be included in each section. Finally, this appendix also helps students think critically about psychological studies that they may read or learn about through television, print, and online resources.

PEDAGOGICAL FEATURES

The introduction, "Using Psychology to Learn Psychology," is a roadmap devoted exclusively to the pedagogical features of this book; we ask students to read this introduction before they turn to Chapter 1. It will not only explain how to make the most of their time and effort in reading this text, but it will also teach them general principles that they can apply to their other courses. Each chapter of the text follows the format described in the introduction, which is based, in part, on psychological findings about how people best learn and remember information.

Chapter Story

Each chapter begins with a different story about a person or a set of people. The story is then elaborated on throughout the chapter, providing a framework for the chapter's discussion of relevant psychological theories and research. These stories serve several purposes. They allow students to see how the psychological material covered in the chapter might apply to people outside of a psychological laboratory. This also makes the material more interesting and applicable to their lives, thus facilitating learning and remembering. In addition, the story integrates the various topics contained within a chapter, creating a coherent, thematic whole. Finally, the story itself provides retrieval cues to help students remember the material. For instance, Chapter 5, the chapter on learning principles, portrays a couple, Maria and Chris. As readers learn more about Maria's and Chris's relationship over the course of the chapter, they also learn more about learning principles and their applications. Because readers are likely to remember the couple's relationship, they will also remember a lot about learning principles.

The chapter story is continued at the beginning of each section. This fosters integration with the rest of the chapter and introduces each section's topic in an applied context.

Learning Objectives

At the beginning of each section, after the continuation of the story, we provide learning objective questions that highlight the most important points to be discussed, learned, and remembered. These questions are then answered at the end of the section (see *Consolidate!* below).

Looking at Levels

Near the end of each section, we take some aspect of its content—a theory, a research study, the application of a psychological phenomenon—and consider it from three levels of analysis: the brain, the person, and the group, as well as interactions among events at each level. For instance, the section on sleep in Chapter 4 examines jet lag from the point of view of the brain (what happens at the biological level), the person (how jet lag affects the person's beliefs, desires, and feelings), and the group (how it affects interactions with others). We then show how events at the three levels affect one another. The events in the brain, for instance, clearly affect social interactions—if you're jet lagged, you will be slower and possibly more irritable in your interactions with others.

The information in the "Looking at Levels" feature serves to integrate knowledge about the brain; personal beliefs, desires, and feelings; and group interactions within each chapter, rather than relegating such information to only one or two chapters. This feature also provides an opportunity to integrate information across chapters, leading to more effective learning and remembering.

Consolidate!

At the end of each section are answers to the learning objective questions posed at the beginning. These answers also review the most important aspects of the material. All of this will help *consolidate* learning (hence the name of the feature).

Minidemonstrations

Most chapters have what we call *minidemonstrations*: demonstrations of psychological phenomena for students to try alone or with others. Trying out these brief exercises will (1) provide another modality of learning about the phenomenon—experiencing, not merely reading about it; (2) make the material more vivid, thereby enhancing attention and memory; and (3) bring psychological principles to life for students through their participation. The minidemonstrations include:

Introspection (pp. 13–14)
Simulated participation in a research study (pp. 34–35)
Measuring neural conduction time (p. 49)
The Stroop effect (p. 91)
Pop-out (p. 95)
Finding your blind spot (p. 99)
Seeing afterimages (p. 100)
Demonstration of channels (p. 102)
Motion cues (p. 106)

Recognition and identification (pp. 108–109)
Meditation (p. 149)
Modality-specific memory (p. 205)
Lincoln's head on a penny (p. 211)
False memory (pp. 221–222)
Building mnemonics (p. 229)
Discovering syntax (p. 238)
Mental imagery (pp. 250–251)
Prototypes (pp. 253–254)
The hiking monk problem (p. 257)
The candle problem (p. 257)
Mental simulation (p. 258)
The triangle problem (pp. 260, 262)
Wason and Johnson-Laird's card task (p. 265)
Mental models (p. 265)
Representativeness (p. 266)
Divergent thinking (p. 303)
"Fake" personality reading (p. 351)
Assessment of stages of change (p. 446)
Myths about suicide (p. 486)
Progressive muscle relaxation (p. 523)
Cognitive dissonance (p. 559)

A Deeper Level: Recap and Thought Questions

Several features at the end of the chapter help students further consolidate what they have learned and provide an opportunity for additional learning by applying the material to new situations.

SUMMARY At the close of each chapter is a section-by-section review of the material. These summaries highlight the key points that students should know after a thorough reading of the material. This feature helps consolidate the core material even further in memory.

STORY QUESTIONS AND ANSWERS This feature poses questions about the characters in the chapter story, followed by answers. The questions and answers show students how to apply each section's psychological principles and research to life outside the psychology laboratory, using the chapter story as an extended example.

THINK IT THROUGH Additional critical thinking questions called "Think It Through" are also provided for each section of the chapter. These questions ask students to apply the material to real-world settings and require them to think deeply about the material. Such active processing enhances memory.

Illustration Program: Showing and Telling

Many of the most important studies are not only described in the text, but are also visually demonstrated in step-by-step illustrations. These multimodal presentations enhance learning in several ways. First, the panel illustrations walk through each study, allowing the reader to understand its details more fully. Second, the clear, uncomplicated illustrations use perceptual principles to convey information effectively. Third, this dual-mode format allows for both visual and verbal learning; students can recall either the words in the text *or* the illustrations when remembering the study. Finally, working through these displays leads to active processing—and better remembering. Examples include a study on alcohol and sexual aggression (p. 156), Watson's famous experiment with Little Albert (p. 169), Garcia's taste aversion conditioning

(p. 174), the training of dolphins at Sea World (p. 184), Bandura's Bobo doll experiment (p. 192), Kosslyn's imagery scanning experiment (p. 250), the Schacter-Singer experiment (p. 318), and systematic desensitization (p. 524).

Like the illustrations, the evocative chapter opening artwork may serve the function of "priming" readers with ideas and expectations about what will come in the chapter.

First-Person Accounts of Psychological Disorders

Chapter 13, Psychological Disorders, provides an opportunity to understand the major disorders not only from the psychologist's perspective, but also from the point of view of people experiencing those disorders. Discussion of each of the major disorders includes first-person accounts from individuals who have struggled with a disorder, which describe the ways it affected their lives. These accounts, entitled " . . . From the Inside," allow students to see beneath the clinical description—to understand how psychological disorders affect real people.

INSTRUCTOR AND STUDENT SUPPLEMENTS

Instructor Resources

INSTRUCTOR'S RESOURCE MANUAL Written by Gary Piggremat at the Devry Institute of Technology, Columbus, this helpful teaching aid includes for each chapter: chapter-at-a-glance table, chapter overview, chapter outline, list of teaching objectives, list of key terms with page references, discussion questions, classroom demonstrations, student activities, list of media and internet resources, and Web activities.

TEST BANK Prepared by Wendy Domjan at the University of Texas, Austin, this resource includes 125–140 questions per chapter in multiple-choice and essay formats. Each question is rated for difficulty and categorized as factual, conceptual, or applied. Page references to the text are provided for each question. Wendy Domjan is also the author of the Practice Test booklet, available free to your students when ordered with a new textbook. The practice tests are made up of a completely separate set of 25 multiple-choice questions per chapter. Domjan's authorship of both test supplements ensures consistency between testing and practice.

TEST BANK II This resource will provide an additional 100 questions per chapter in multiple-choice and essay formats. Each question will be rated for difficulty and as factual, conceptual, or applied. Page references will also be provided for each question. Test Bank II will be published for the fall semester of 2001 to ensure an ample number of questions for use over multiple semesters.

ALLYN AND BACON TEST MANAGER — COMPUTERIZED TEST BANK (Available for Windows, CD-ROM and disk, and Macintosh disk; DOS disk available upon request.) Allyn and Bacon Test Manager is an integrated suite of testing and assessment tools for Windows and Macintosh. You can use Test Manager to create professional-looking exams in just minutes by building tests from the existing database of questions, editing questions, or adding your own. Course management features include a class roster, gradebook, and item analysis. Test Manager also has everything you need to create and administer online tests. For first-time users, there is a guided tour of the entire Test Manager system and screen wizards to walk you through each area.

CALL-IN AND FAX TESTING One toll-free call to our testing center will have a finished, ready-to-duplicate test on its way to you within 48 hours, via mail or fax.

ALLYN AND BACON TRANSPARENCIES FOR INTRODUCTORY PSYCHOLOGY, 2001 A full set of color acetate transparencies is available to enhance classroom lectures and discussions. These images include those from the Kosslyn and Rosenberg text and other sources, to support and extend teaching and learning.

KOSSLYN AND ROSENBERG POWERPOINT PRESENTATION CD-ROM This book-specific presentation provides detailed outlines of key points for each chapter, supported by charts, graphs, diagrams, and other visuals from the textbook. Resources from the Kosslyn and Rosenberg companion Website are also integrated for easy access to this Website from your classroom. This material is also available in a Web format accessible at www.abacon.com/ppt.

ALLYN AND BACON DIGITAL MEDIA ARCHIVE CD-ROM FOR PSYCHOLOGY, VERSION 2.0 Allyn and Bacon provides an array of media products to help liven up your classroom presentations. The Digital Media Archive provides charts, graphs, tables, and figures electronically on one cross-platform CD-ROM. The Digital Media Archive also provides video and audio clips along with the electronic images that can be easily integrated into your lectures. This helpful resource extends the coverage found on the Kosslyn and Rosenberg PowerPoint Presentation CD-ROM.

ALLYN AND BACON MIND MATTERS CD-ROM FACULTY GUIDE This helpful instructor resource offers detailed overviews of each unit of the Mind Matters CD-ROM (described below), supplemented by additional test questions and chapter-by-chapter references correlating content from the CD-ROM with the Kosslyn and Rosenberg textbook. This in-depth guide makes it easy to integrate the Allyn and Bacon Mind Matters CD-ROM into your syllabus. Visit the Allyn and Bacon Mind Matters Website at www.abacon.com/mindmatters to download samples of this helpful resource.

ALLYN AND BACON INTERACTIVE VIDEO AND VIDEO PACKAGE *Psychology: The Brain, the Person, the World* is supported by a unique interactive video containing brief video clips based on content in each chapter of the text. Each video clip contains contextualizing information and critical thinking questions, further relating the video content to that in the textbook chapter. A wide variety of additional videos are also available upon adoption of the Kosslyn and Rosenberg textbook. Please contact your local Allyn and Bacon publisher's representative for more information.

COURSE MANAGEMENT SYSTEMS Course Management Systems combine Allyn and Bacon's premium online content with enhanced class management tools such as syllabus building, quizzing and grading, and results reporting. To find out which systems are available with the Kosslyn and Rosenberg text, visit the Kosslyn and Rosenberg Website at http://www.abacon.com/kosslyn for more information.

Student Resources

STUDENT STUDY GUIDE WITH PRACTICE TESTS This study guide, written by Marjorie Hardy of Eckerd College, contains a wide variety of helpful study tools including, for each chapter: "Before You Read" preview sections with chapter summaries; "As You Read" self-tests; "A Deeper Level" thought questions that focus on critical thinking; glossary term identification exercises; "After You Read" multiple-choice post-tests; and Web resources. Marjorie Hardy is also the author of the text-specific Kosslyn and Rosenberg Website content, ensuring consistency in practice and review across the Study Guide and Web resources.

PRACTICE TEST BOOKLET If students want extra help preparing for exams (and who doesn't?), this booklet, written by Test Bank author Wendy Domjan, provides sample multiple-choice tests for each chapter, allowing students to practice what they have learned using a simulated classroom quiz. The booklet also includes answers and page references to the text. Available packaged free with new copies of the Kosslyn and Rosenberg textbook.

ALLYN AND BACON MIND MATTERS CD-ROM This student CD-ROM features in-depth units on the history of psychology, research methodology, biopsychology, learning, memory, sensation, and perception. Each unit includes self-contained modules that cover core psychological concepts through a combination of text, graphics, humor, activities, and extensive assessment. This resource is available packaged with new copies of the Kosslyn and Rosenberg textbook and is supported by an in-depth faculty guide (see above).

PSYCHOLOGY ON THE NET, 2001 Updated to reflect the most current URLs related to the study of psychology, this easy-to-read guide helps point you and your students in the right direction when looking at the tremendous array of information related to psychology on the Internet. Available free packaged with new copies of the Kosslyn and Rosenberg textbook (value package option only).

Online Supplements for Students and Instructors

SUPERSITE FOR KOSSLYN AND ROSENBERG This premiere Website offers access to *The Psychology Place*,™ an extensive Web resource for introductory psychology that benefits both students and instructors. Instructors enjoy an extensive selection of teaching resources, access to recent research news, Web investigations, a wide variety of scientifically accurate and appropriate Web resources, integration of online investigative and collaborative learning activities, communication with other instructors, and the ability to share teaching ideas and challenges by participating in the Op Ed Forum. Students receive a 6-month subscription that provides access to a wide range of helpful resources, including extensive learning activities, news updates, research reports, Web links, and animations.

This extensive site is organized by chapter in the Kosslyn and Rosenberg textbook and is supported by additional text-specific resources including audio and video clips, learning objectives, chapter summaries, interactive online quizzes, and additional Web links to relevant psychology sites, to reinforce learning. Please visit www.abacon.com/kosslyn or contact your local Allyn and Bacon publisher's representative for more information.

KOSSLYN AND ROSENBERG E-BOOK An e-book is an electronic (digital) version of the print textbook. The e-book duplicates the print textbook, following the exact page format and page numbering of the print book.

Why would a student want to purchase an e-book rather than a print textbook? The e-book is an option for students. Students who prefer the print textbook can buy the textbook from the bookstore as they always have. However, students who want to have their textbook content in electronic form can now purchase the content electronically. The e-book offers students:

▶ The convenience of buying their text content 24 hours a day, 7 days a week. For students who generally don't buy a textbook, or suddenly decide they need to have textbook content, the e-book offers an immediate option for purchase. Students will also have the ability to print pages from the e-book.

▶ A new way to study. For students who use their computers frequently, the e-book gives them access not only to rich textbook content, but also to powerful study tools that let them highlight, take notes, and quickly search for information.

How does a student purchase an e-book? Visit the Kosslyn and Rosenberg Website at http://www.abacon.com/kosslyn for ordering information. At our Website, students will be instructed on how to use a credit card to purchase their e-book. The textbook they buy is downloaded onto their computer; the student then owns, housed on his or her own computer, a copy of the electronic textbook.

Additional Resources

HOW TO THINK STRAIGHT ABOUT PSYCHOLOGY, 6TH EDITION This well-known critical thinking manual by Keith Stanovich helps students become educated consumers of psychological information, particularly those topics they may encounter in the media or self-help literature.

DIVERSITY ACTIVITIES FOR PSYCHOLOGY This student manual, developed by Valerie Whittlesey, offers a wide variety of hands-on activities to help incorporate issues of diversity into your classroom. Activities are correlated with all major areas of psychological research, making it easy to assign this supplement with the Kosslyn and Rosenberg textbook.

ASK DR. MIKE: FREQUENTLY ASKED QUESTIONS ABOUT PSYCHOLOGY Developed by Mike Atkinson, author of the popular "Ask Dr. Mike" column on the Psychology Place™ Website, this manual contains a collection of commonly asked student questions with in-depth answers, organized by major topics in the introductory psychology course.

EVALUATING PSYCHOLOGICAL INFORMATION: SHARPENING YOUR CRITICAL THINKING SKILLS, 3RD EDITION Developed by James Bell, this workbook focuses on helping students to evaluate psychological research systematically and to improve their critical thinking skills.

TOOLS OF CRITICAL THINKING This critical thinking text by David A. Levy provides tools and skills for approaching all forms of problem solving, particularly in psychology.

HANDBOOK FOR PSYCHOLOGY This helpful handbook, created by Drew Appleby, provides students with a wide array of information ranging from majoring in psychology to graduate school and job opportunities with a psychology degree.

HOW TO WRITE PSYCHOLOGY PAPERS, 2ND EDITION Les Parrot provides a brief overview for writing APA-style psychology papers, including information on overcoming paper panic, using the Internet, preparing a working reference list, avoiding plagarism, and using inclusive language. This book extends and elaborates on the material in Appendix B.

ACKNOWLEDGMENTS

We want to give a heartfelt thanks to the many reviewers who read earlier versions of one or more chapters, sometimes the entire book. This is by far a better book for their efforts:

Sharon Akimoto
Carleton College

Jeff Anastasi
Francis Marion University

Joe Bean
Shorter College

James Benedict
James Madison University

James F. Calhoun
University of Georgia

Brad Carothers
Evergreen Valley College

James Carroll
Central Michigan University

M. B. Casey
St. Mary's College of Maryland

Dave Christian
University of Idaho

George A. Cicala
University of Delaware

Gerald S. Clack
Loyola University of New Orleans

Verne C. Cox
University of Texas, Arlington

Nancy Dickson
Tennessee Technical College

William O. Dwyer
University of Memphis

Valeri Farmer-Dougan
Illinois State University

William Ford
Bucks County Community College

Mary Gauvain
University of California, Riverside

Dan Gilbert
Harvard University

Peter Graf
University of British Columbia

Peter Gram
Pensacola Junior College

Karl Haberlandt
Trinity College

Richard Hackman
Harvard University

Richard Haier
University of California, Irvine

Marjorie Hardy
Eckerd College

Bruce Henderson
Western Carolina University

James Hilton
University of Michigan

Rick Ingram
San Diego State University

John H. Krantz
Hanover College

Richard Lippa
California State University, Fresno

Walter J. Lonner
Western Washington University

Michael Markham
Florida International University

Pam McAuslan
University of Michigan, Dearborn

David G. McDonald
University of Missouri

Rafael Mendez
Bronx Community College

Sarah Murray
Kwantlen University College

Paul Ngo
Saint Norbert College

Thomas R. Oswald
Northern Iowa Area Community College

Carol Pandey
Los Angeles Pierce College

Robert J. Pellegrini
San Jose State University

Dorothy C. Piontkowski
San Francisco State University

Brad Redburn
Johnson County Community College

Cheryl Rickabaugh
University of Redlands

Alan Salo
University of Maine, Presque Isle

Jim Schirillo
Wake Forest University

Michael Scoles
University of Central Arkansas

Michael Shaughnessy
Eastern New Mexico University

Nancy Simpson
Trident Technical College

Linda J. Skinner
Middle Tennessee State University

Michael Spiegler
Providence College

Don Stanley
North Harris College

Bruce B. Svare
State University of New York at Albany

Thomas Thielan
College of St. Catherine

Paul E. Turner
Lipscomb University

Lori Van Wallendael
University of North Carolina, Charlotte

Frank J. Vattano
Colorado State University

Rich Velayo
Pace University

Rick Wesp
East Stroudsburg University

We also profited enormously from conversations with our friends and colleagues, particularly Nalini Ambady, Mark Baxter, Alain Berthoz, John Cacioppo, David Caplan, Alfonso Caramazza, Patrick Cavanagh, Verne Caviness, Christopher Chabris, Jonathan Cohen, Suzanne Corkin, Francis Crick, Richard Davidson, Susan Edbril, Jeffrey Epstein, Michael Friedman, Al Galaburda, Giorgio Ganis, Jeremy Gray, Anne Harrington, Marc Hauser, Kenneth Hugdahl, Steven Hyman, Jerome Kagan, Denis Le Bihan, Fred Mast, Richard McNally, Merrill Mead-Fox, Ken Nakayama, Kevin O'Regan, Alvaro Pascual-Leone, Steven Pinker, Scott Rauch, Melissa Robbins, Robert Rose, Steven Rosenberg, Daniel Schacter, Jeanne Serafin, Lisa Shin, Dan Simons, Edward E. Smith, Elizabeth Spelke, David Spiegel, Larry Squire, Eve vanCauter, and Laura Weisberg. We thank Maya and Alain Berthoz, Maryvonne Caraftan, Tom Cohen, Michel Denis, Elizabeth Hickling, Christian and Denis Le Bihan, Josette and Jacques Lautrey, Bernard Mazoyer, and Nathalie Tzurio for their hospitality during our year in France, which made it possible and enjoyable to work productively there. We also thank the staff at the Collège de France for their help, in too many ways to list. And to our parents (Bunny, Stanley, Rhoda, and Duke), and our children (Nathaniel, David, and Justin), a huge thanks for your patience with our work-filled weekends and evenings, and for your love, support, and good humor. You have sustained us.

Other people have been instrumental in making this book a reality. These include Andrea Volfova (for her good-humored assistance and incisive comments), Jennifer Shephard, Bill Thompson, David Hurvitz, Steve Stose, Cinthia Guzman, Nicole Rosenberg, and Deborah Bell for their patience and willingness to help us dig out references and check facts, especially via long-distance communication during the year we were in France. The idea for the book developed over years of working with the Sophomore Tutors and Assistant to the Head Tutor, Shawn Harriman, at Harvard University, and we want to thank them all; helping them grapple with the concept of levels of analysis led us to make this book clearer. We are particularly indebted to two of them, Laurie Santos and Jason Mitchell, who read an early draft of the book and offered copious and wise comments.

The professionals at Allyn and Bacon have been instrumental in bringing this book to you. From our first meeting with Sean Wakely, Bill Barke, Joyce Nilsen, Sandi Kirshner, and Marcie Mealia, we were sold on Allyn and Bacon's team. Moreover, we are indebted to our Senior Development Editor, Sue Gleason, and Executive Editor, Rebecca Pascal, for their assistance and unflagging support through the long process of bringing this project to fruition. Consulting editors Kathy Field and Hannah Rubenstein helped us make the words work together well. Editorial Production Supervisor Susan McIntyre's careful attention to the artwork and manuscript has enhanced the book's clarity, as have the thoughtful and probing comments of Andrea Cava and Kathryn Daniel. There are not enough words of praise to give Nancy Brooks for her editorial assistance; Nancy likes to claim that less is more, but the more of her help we got, the better the book became. Caroline Croley and Deidre Jacobson were very creative in their marketing and advertising.

And finally, to you the reader, thank you for taking the time and effort to read this preface to its conclusion. We hope that this book helps you learn about psychology, about yourselves, and about the world.

ABOUT THE AUTHORS

STEPHEN M. KOSSLYN

Stephen Kosslyn is Professor of Psychology at Harvard University and Associate Psychologist in the Department of Neurology at Massachusetts General Hospital. He received his B.A. from UCLA and his Ph.D. from Stanford University, both in psychology. His first academic position was at Johns Hopkins University, where he was appointed Assistant Professor. He joined the Harvard faculty in 1977 as Associate Professor, and left in 1980 to take a Research Career Development Award. After a brief stay at Brandeis and a visit to Johns Hopkins in 1983, Kosslyn returned to Harvard as a Full Professor. His research has focused primarily on the nature of visual mental imagery and visual communication, and he has published 5 books and over 200 papers on these topics. Kosslyn has received numerous honors, including the National Academy of Sciences Initiatives in Research Award, the Prix Jean-Louis Signoret, and election to the American Academy of Arts and Sciences and the Society of Experimental Psychologists. He is currently "head tutor," supervising graduate students who teach a year-long introductory psychology course using levels of analysis, and chairs the Committee on Undergraduate Instruction at Harvard. He is currently on the editorial boards of many professional journals; is a Fellow of the American Psychological Association, American Psychological Society, and American Association for the Advancement of Science; and has served on several National Research Council committees to advise the government on new technologies. Kosslyn has been a guest on local National Public Radio stations, CBS radio, CNN news, and *Nova*, and has been quoted in many newspapers and magazines.

ROBIN S. ROSENBERG

Robin Rosenberg is a clinical psychologist in private practice and has taught introductory psychology at Lesley College. She is certified in clinical hypnosis and is a member of the Academy for Eating Disorders. She received her B.A. in psychology from New York University, and her M.A. and Ph.D. in clinical psychology from the University of Maryland, College Park. She did her clinical internship at Massachusetts Mental Health Center and had a postdoctoral fellowship at Harvard Community Health Plan before joining the staff at Newton-Wellesley Hospital's Outpatient Services, where she worked for a number of years before leaving to expand her private practice. She specializes in treating people with eating disorders, depression, and anxiety and is interested in the integration of different therapy approaches. She was the founder and coordinator of the New England Society for Psychotherapy Integration and has given numerous professional talks on various topics related to the treatment of people with eating disorders, as well as popular talks on relapse prevention and on developing a healthy relationship with food, and with one's body.

PSYCHOLOGY

USING PSYCHOLOGY TO LEARN PSYCHOLOGY

Scientific psychology has made massive leaps and bounds in recent decades. Its impressive progress has given us a window into ourselves that could scarcely have been imagined in earlier years, and the view from that window provides insights into the ways we learn and remember. The structure of this book reflects those insights. In fact, its organization is built on specific psychological principles that will help you to make the material your own, yours to remember and build on.

ORGANIZATION, ORGANIZATION, ORGANIZATION

It seems only common sense that the more you know about something, the easier it is to learn even more about it. But wait a minute: If you're filling your head with stuff—facts, relationships, ideas—won't you have *less* room available for new material?

This is what researchers who study memory call the "paradox of the expert." They have learned that instead of filling up, our memory storage capacity seems to *increase* as more material is stored. How can this be? Part of becoming an expert in an area is developing an efficient way to organize information about it; and the better the organization, the easier it is to learn new things in that area.

When you first start learning psychology, you face what seems like a random collection of theories and facts. But as you learn more and more, you begin to see how the facts interconnect—perhaps because you learn, for instance, that the same parts of the brain are activated during different behaviors. As you read on, facts begin to "fall into place," and each new fact becomes easier to learn and remember than the previous ones.

The organization of this book gives you the framework you need to begin categorizing and learning more quickly. Each chapter deals with a particular area of psychological discovery and begins with a story, which serves multiple purposes in learning. First, the story helps you see how events in the "real world," which may be much like events in your life or in the lives of those around you, arise from the working of psychological principles. Thus new facts are fitted with the facts of your own experiences, making it easier for you to organize the new material and thus to learn it. Second, the opening story runs like a thread through the chapter, as an illustration of the various topics discussed and as a connection to a real-world situation. Third, because each chapter has its own story, each story becomes a reminder that will help you remember the material in that chapter.

Each major section within a chapter begins with an aspect of a story and learning objectives questions, targeting the general ideas to be explored in that section. At the end of each section is a *Consolidate!* summary that answers those learning objective questions. At the end of the chapter is a summary called *A Deeper Level: Recap and Thought Questions* that revisits the major themes of the chapter, helping you to see the overall picture that was painted in each section. Here, too, you will find questions and answers that link back to the chapter story, as well as *Think It Through* questions, hypothetical situations that invite you to think about the broader implications of what you have learned—and thereby to understand the material better.

CONNECTIONS ACROSS TOPICS

In these pages we will consider a wide range of human mental processes and behavior. Our explorations—and thus the chapters of this book—are tied together by a specific and fruitful kind of analysis we apply to all of them. In every chapter, in every area of psychological activity, we consider the contributions of events in the *brain*, of *personal beliefs, desires, and feelings*, and of *group interactions*. A direct example: Events in the brain might be the chemicals produced by fatigue or excitement, which affect your ability to understand what you read in this book; your personal goals and interests may motivate you to undertake the study of psychology; and interactions among your group of friends can further spark your interest and help you study effectively.

French philosopher René Descartes's famous observation, "I think, therefore I am," can be appropriately paraphrased for us as "I think, therefore I have a brain." In other words, we cannot fully consider how and why we behave as we do without knowing how the brain works (and, sometimes, doesn't work). The way the brain operates is a facet of all psychological phenomena, and we ignore it at the peril of missing key insights into why we think, feel, and behave as we do. In every chapter, for every topic, you will see how events in the brain, along with personal beliefs, desires, and feelings, and group interactions, are relevant to our understanding of ourselves. Looking at events at these three "levels" helps you to organize and integrate the material *within* each chapter and *across* all the chapters. At the end of each major section within a chapter is *Looking at Levels,* which presents a high-interest issue and examines it by considering events at all three levels, illustrating how they constantly interact.

LEARNING WITHOUT STRAINING

One of the most interesting findings about memory is that you don't have to *try* to store something in memory; you only have to "process" the material thoroughly. For instance, if—without a conscious attempt to memorize—you talk about the possible reasons why people who have more genes in common have more similar IQs, the simple act of considering these factors will probably cause you to learn them. A key aim of this book is to lead you to process the material thoroughly. This is accomplished in various ways: through the figures, the minidemonstrations and exercises described in the text, the *Consolidate!* and *Think It Through* sections, and the headings that include memorable phrases to help you integrate the material with what you already know.

ILLUSTRATIONS: SHOWING AND TELLING

In a review of 46 experiments comparing the effectiveness of learning from text alone and learning from text with pictures, Levie and Lentz (1982) found that 45 of them showed that pictures do help. In some situations, an effective picture can literally double your chances of remembering the information. Moreover, Alan Paivio (1971) showed that when people can store both verbal and pictorial information, they can later remember the material far better than when they can store only verbal information. For example, if you are learning vocabulary in a foreign language, having a picture that illustrates the meaning along with the definition will boost your memory.

Thus, many of the important studies described in this book are presented in multi-panel displays, with the events in each panel explained in detail. This device gives you a double-barreled shot of learning—with the combined effectiveness of both verbal and pictorial modalities.

But not just any picture will do. Levie and Lentz also found that if the illustrations are not relevant, they don't help; a later survey (Levin et al., 1987) found that pictures that are purely decorative actually get in the way of learning. The figures in this book take this finding to heart. Illustrations are particularly effective when they teach according to the principle "seeing is believing."

A major difficulty with many visual displays is information overload. The point is illustrated in Figure 1. We cannot take in too much information at a time (that's why telephone numbers and most license plates have only 7 or 8 digits or characters). A method we use to avoid this problem is designing displays in accordance with the principles of perceptual organization. You are overloaded not by the number of elements that are present, but by the number of *perceptual units* they form. For example, you can take in two flocks of geese

For better or worse (given what can be done with computers these days), seeing is often believing.

heading south for the winter as easily as two individual geese flying solo—but if the flocks disband, and 80 birds fly randomly through the sky, your ability to track them would be overwhelmed.

Psychological research has also shown that an effective visual display doesn't require you to search and memorize any more than is absolutely necessary to understand the message. A well-designed VCR has the "power" and "play" buttons in obvious locations and prominent enough so you can spot them immediately. If a dis-

FIGURE 1
Avoiding Information Overload

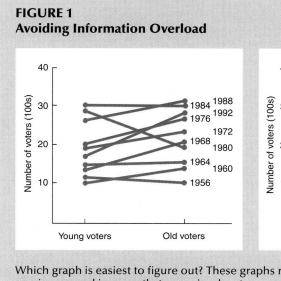

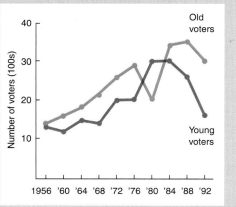

Which graph is easiest to figure out? These graphs represent the same data, but only one is arranged in a way that your visual system can organize easily. (From Kosslyn, 1994a.)

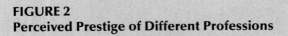

FIGURE 2
Perceived Prestige of Different Professions

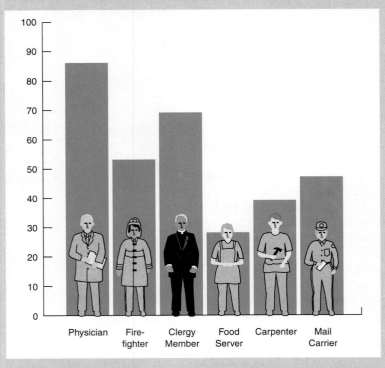

Because your visual system draws your attention to aspects of the world that are different from their surroundings, you are immediately drawn to the person in black. This would be appropriate only if the discussion focused on the clergy member. The same principles are at work when you look at the world and when you look at an illustration. (Adapted from Holmes, 1984. Data from National Opinion Research Center, 1994.)

play is too complex, you won't bother to try to unravel it; and why should you? The illustrations in this book have been designed to guide your eye through them systematically. It is known, for example, that sharp changes along a visual dimension, such as the use of a color, pop out and reflexively grab the viewer's attention. Properties such as this (look at Figure 2) are used appropriately throughout this text to define the more important parts of displays.

In this way, we accomplish two aims. First, the material in the illustrations aids learning, instead of getting in its way. Second, the helpfulness of the design is itself an example of the utility of psychological findings, providing a practical demonstration. These illustrations both show and tell.

IN SUM . . .

Table 1 summarizes the many tools built into the structure of this book to smooth the occasionally rough path of learning. The most important learning tools of all, of course, are the excitement inherent in the ideas and the connections you will make with your own experience. What you learn here can be applied to all learning, not just psychology or literature or physics, but also on the job and in life in general. We hope you will find yourself thinking about these ideas at odd moments away from class, away from this book. If you do, the book has been a success.

TABLE 1

Summary of Learning Tools

Chapter Outline

- Provides an overall framework for learning.
- Headings include memorable phrases to help you integrate the material with what you already know.

Chapter Story

- Relevance to real world allows new information to be integrated with prior knowledge.
- Integrates topics throughout the chapter.
- Provides retrieval cues.

Chapter Sections

- Learning objective questions provide a structure for each section, highlighting the most important points to be discussed.
- Expansion of the opening story at the outset of each section relates back to the story, thereby fostering integration and introducing specific topics.
- Sections "chunk" material into easily learned units.

Glossary

- Key terms are defined in the margin, highlighting essential information.
- Related terms are often grouped together, promoting conceptual links.

Consolidate!

- Reinforces the main points of each section.
- Connects back to the section learning objective questions, providing answers.

A Deeper Level

- Shows connections among the material discussed in the chapter sections, thereby providing an overall organization for the chapter's main messages.
- Questions about the opening story are posed and answered, providing a connection to real-world contexts.
- *Think It Through* exercises require thinking deeply about the material, thereby enhancing memory.

Levels of Analysis

- Integrates information about the brain; personal beliefs, desires, and feelings; and group interactions within chapters.
- Integrates information across chapters.
- *Looking at Levels* sections reinforce integration of the different types of events (the brain, the person, the group).

Minidemonstrations

- Active learning increases comprehension by integrating information with common experience.
- Active learning increases memory by leading you to think more deeply about the material.

Illustrations: Showing and Telling

- Multipanel displays encourage both visual and verbal learning.
- Clear, uncomplicated illustrations use psychological principles of effective communication.

1 THE SCIENCE OF PSYCHOLOGY

Yesterday and Today

On a balmy spring day in 1997, a young man was playing golf. Nothing unusual about that. But when this young man sank his final putt, the watching crowd let out a roar, and he looked for his parents and embraced them, fighting back tears. The occasion was the PGA Masters Tournament, and the young man was Tiger Woods.

Think of the magnitude of his victory: At 21, Woods was the youngest golfer ever to win the Masters, by the greatest margin over his nearest opponent and with a score that broke the tournament record. And golf's newest champion, in a sport that had long been effectively closed to all but whites, was of Asian, black, white, and Native American ancestry. If you could discern and explain the events that led up to this dramatic moment, you would be a very insightful psychologist.

But where would you begin? You could look at Tiger Woods's hand–eye coordination, his concentration and focus, his ability to judge distances and calculate factors of wind, temperature, and humidity.

You could look at his personality—his reaction to racist hate mail (as a college student at Stanford University, he even kept one particularly vile letter taped to his wall), his religious beliefs (he was raised in his mother's faith, Buddhism), his demeanor during play, his discipline in training.

You could look at his relationships with the social world around him—his family, his competitors, his fans.

Is this psychology? Indeed it is. Psychology asks and, in scientific ways, attempts to answer questions about why and how people think, feel, and behave as they do. Because we are all human and so have much in common, sometimes the answers are universal. But we are also, like snowflakes, all different, and psychology helps to explain our uniqueness. In this chapter we show you how to look at and answer such questions by methods used in current research and (because the inquiry into what makes us tick has a history) how psychologists over the past century have approached them.

Psychology is about mental processes and behavior, both exceptional and ordinary.

PSYCHOLOGICAL SCIENCE: GETTING TO KNOW YOU

Virtually everything any of us does, thinks, or feels falls within the sphere of psychology. You may observe psychology in action when you watch people interacting in a classroom or at a party, or notice that a friend is in a really terrible mood. Psychology is at work when you daydream as you watch the clouds drift by, when you have trouble recalling someone's name, even when you're asleep.

▶ 1. Psychology can illuminate all aspects of a person's life, but what *is* psychology?

▶ 2. What is the concept of "levels of analysis," and how can you use it to understand psychology?

What Is Psychology?

Although it may seem complex and wide-ranging, the field you are studying in this textbook can be defined in one simple sentence: *Psychology is the science of mental processes and behavior*. Let's look at the key words in this definition.

First, *science*. From the Latin *scire*, "to know," science avoids mere opinions, intuitions, and guesses, and strives to nail down facts—to *know* them—by using objective evidence to answer questions such as, What makes the sun shine? Why does garlic make your breath smell strong? How is Tiger Woods able to direct his swings so superbly? Science uses logic to reason about the possible causes of a phenomenon and then tests the resulting ideas by collecting additional facts, which will either support the ideas or refute them, and thus nudge the scientist further along the road to the answer.

Second, *mental processes*. **Mental processes** are what your brain is doing not only when you engage in "thinking" activities such as storing memories, recognizing objects, and using language, but also when you feel depressed, jump for joy, or savor the experience of being in love. How can we find objective facts about mental processes, which are hidden and internal? One way, which has a long history in psy-

Psychology: The science of mental processes and behavior.

Mental processes: What the brain does when a person stores, recalls, or uses information, or has specific feelings.

chology, is to work backward, observing what people do and inferring from outward signs what is going on "inside." Another, as new as the latest technological advances in neuroscience, is to use brain-scanning techniques to take pictures of the living brain that show its physical changes as it works.

Third, *behavior*. By **behavior** we mean the outwardly observable acts of a person, either alone or in a group. Behavior consists of physical movements, voluntary or involuntary, of the limbs, facial muscles, or other parts of the body. A particular behavior is often preceded by mental processes such as a perception of the current situation (how far the golf ball must travel) and a decision about what to do next (how forcefully to swing the club). A behavior may also be governed by the relationship between the individual and a group. Tiger Woods might not have performed the way he did in 1997 had he been playing in 1920, when many in the crowd would not have wanted a nonwhite person to win. So there are layers upon layers: An individual's mental processes affect his or her behavior, and these processes are affected by the surrounding group (the members of which, in turn, have their own individual mental processes and behaviors).

The goals of psychology are not simply to *describe* and *explain* mental processes and behavior, but also to *predict* and *control* them. As an individual, you'd probably like to be able to predict what kind of person would make a good spouse for you, or which politician would make sound decisions in crisis situations. As a society, we all would greatly benefit by knowing how people learn most effectively, how to control addictive and destructive behaviors, and how to cure mental illness.

Levels of Analysis: The Complete Psychology

The areas you might explore to answer questions about Tiger Woods's success—his coordination and focus, his beliefs and attitudes, his relationships with his parents and his audience—occur at three levels of scale, each of which provides a field for analysis. First, at the level of the *brain*, we can ask questions about his visualization techniques, hand–eye coordination, and concentration. Second, at the level of the whole *person*, we can ask how his beliefs and goals may have motivated him. And third, at the level of the *group*, we can investigate the roles of his parents and the reactions of crowds. At any moment in Tiger Woods's day, or yours, events are happening at all three levels: brain, person, and group. Of course, a person is not just a larger-scale brain, and a group is not a larger-scale person. But looking at the individual at a microlevel (the brain) and a macrolevel (in relation to a group) reveals much that would be hidden were we to look at only one level. The concept of levels of analysis has long held a central role in science in general (Anderson, 1998; Nagel, 1979; Schaffner, 1967) and in the field of psychology in particular (Fodor, 1968, 1983; Kosslyn & Koenig, 1995; Looren de Jong, 1996; Marr, 1982; Putnam, 1973).

EVENTS LARGE AND SMALL. Imagine that it's the first day of class. You are standing at the front of the room, gazing over the lecture hall full of students (see Figure 1.1 on page 10). Focus on a single student sitting near the middle of the room. Like a camera lens, zoom in so that the student's head fills your field of view. Zoom in even closer, to a small spot on the forehead, and shift an inch forward and zoom closer yet, to visualize the inside of the brain. As you continue to zoom in, magnification increases, and groups of brain cells appear. Finally, you home in on a single brain cell (which you will examine close up in the next chapter).

Now, reverse the journey: Zoom back until you see the entire person, whose psychology you would describe in terms of his or her beliefs, desires, and feelings, not just as a container of brain cells. Continue zooming back, to the point where you can take in the entire view, the full lecture hall. Now you see the world surrounding that particular student—the 20 or 30 other students, the color of the walls, the height and width of the room, the arrangement of chairs into rows, the sunlight streaming in.

Behavior: The outwardly observable acts of an individual, alone or in a group.

FIGURE 1.1
Levels of Analysis

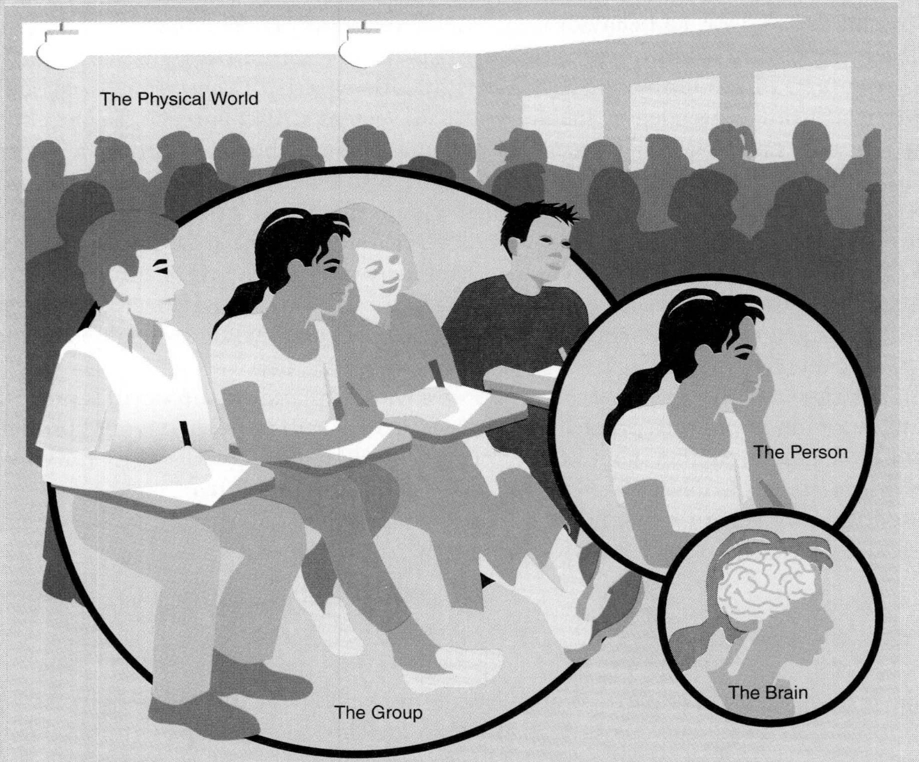

Levels of analysis differ in the size of the events being considered, ranging from very large to very small.

At the **level of the brain,** psychologists focus on very small things. At this level we consider not only the activity of the brain but also the structure and properties of the organ itself—brain cells and their connections, the chemical soup in which they exist (including the hormones that alter the way the brain operates) and the genes that give rise to them. At the level of the brain, you are able to hear and understand a lecture because the appropriate cells are firing and making various connections. At the level of the brain, a psychologist might want to design an experiment that would test the effectiveness of Tiger Woods's techniques for focusing his attention on his swing.

The brain is only part of the story, though. As we've said, brains are not people. People have beliefs (such as ideas, knowledge, expectations), desires (such as hopes, goals, needs), and feelings (such as fears, guilts, attractions). The brain is in many ways a canvas on which life's experiences are painted. To talk about the picture itself, we must shift to another level of analysis. At the **level of the person,** psychologists focus on a larger unit, the person as a whole and his or her beliefs, desires, and feelings. At this level we consider the *content* of mental processes, not just their internal mechanics. At the level of the person, you are in a psychology class because you hope it will be interesting, because you want to learn about people, and perhaps because you know that the course is a graduation requirement. At the level of the person, a psychologist might want to investigate the factors—among them, possibly, Tiger Woods's Buddhist faith—behind the strong sense of inner calm he displays under pressure.

"No man is an island," the poet John Donne wrote. We all live in *social environments* that vary over time and space and that are populated by our friends and professors, our parents, the other viewers in a movie theater, the other drivers on a busy

Level of the brain: Events that involve the structure and properties of the organ itself—brain cells and their connections, the chemical soup in which they exist, and the genes.

Level of the person: Events that involve the nature of beliefs, desires, and feelings—the *content* of the mind, not just its internal mechanics.

highway. Our lives are intertwined with other people's lives, and from birth to old age, we take our cues from other people around us. The relationships that arise within groups make them more than simply a collection of individuals. Mental processes and behavior characterize groups as well as individuals. Street gangs and reading clubs both have distinct identities based on shared beliefs and practices that are passed on to succeeding generations of members as *culture,* which has been defined as the "language, beliefs, values, norms, behaviors, and even material objects that are passed from one generation to the next" (Henslin, 1999). Thus, at the **level of the group,** psychologists focus on units even larger than the brain or the person, looking at the ways collections of people (as few as one other person, as many as a society) shape individual mental processes and behavior. As you shift in your seat in the lecture hall, you are not alone: Other students' reactions, their questions, their irritating habits or encouraging comments, affect the way you experience the course. At the level of the group, a psychologist might want to examine the role of a supportive and enthusiastic audience in helping Tiger Woods birdie instead of bogey.

Events that occur at every level of analysis—brain, person, and group—are intimately tied to conditions in the physical world. All our mental processes and behaviors take place within, and are influenced by, a specific *physical environment.* A windy day at the golf course changes the way Tiger Woods plays a shot; if the classroom is too hot, you may have trouble focusing on the lecture. The group is only part of the world; to understand the events at each level of analysis, we must always relate them to the physical world that surrounds us.

ALL TOGETHER NOW. Events at the different levels not only occur at the same time, they are constantly interacting. As you sit in the lecture hall, the signals among your brain cells that enable you to understand the lecture, and the new connections among your brain cells that enable you to remember it, are happening because your desire to pass the course has put you in the room: That is, events at the level of the person are affecting events at the level of the brain. But as you listen to the lecture, your neighbor's knuckle cracking is really getting to you, and you're finding it hard to concentrate: Events at the level of the group are affecting events at the level of the brain. Because you really want to hear this stuff, you're wondering how to get your neighbor to cut it out, and you decide to shoot a few dirty looks his way: Events at the level of the person are affecting events at the level of the group (which, as we've seen, affect events at the level of the brain). And all of this is going on within the physical environment of the room, where the sunlight that had seemed warm and welcoming is now pretty hot, and you're getting drowsy, and you're *really* irritated, and you finally change your seat. . . . And round and round. Events at the three levels of analysis, in a specific physical context, are constantly changing and influencing one another. To understand fully what's going on in life situations, you need to look at all three.

> **Level of the group:** Events that involve relationships between people (e.g., love, competition, cooperation), relationships among groups, and culture. Events at the level of the group are one aspect of the environment; the other aspect is the physical environment itself (the time, temperature, and other physical stimuli).

LOOKING AT LEVELS

Drought Among the Maasai

The Maasai, a native people of Kenya and Tanzania, keep herds of cattle, following them as they graze across the plains of East Africa. Rather than feeding their infants on a fixed schedule, Maasai mothers feed them whenever they cry or otherwise make their need known. At the height of a 10-year drought in the early 1970s, many cattle died; some families lost 98% of their herds. With cow's milk scarce, the infants were more dependent on their mothers' milk. Psychiatrist Marten deVries (1984), who was studying the Maasai children when the drought began, had been following the development of a group of 48 infants. He had focused on 20 of them, characterizing half as "easy" and half as "difficult"; easy babies were calm and cooperative, difficult ones testy and demanding. As the drought intensified, deVries

Interactions among events at the different levels of analysis can explain why, during a drought, "easy" babies died but "difficult" babies survived.

tried to track down these 20 babies, now 6 to 8 months old. He expected that the "difficult" babies would stress their caregivers even more than usual and hence these babies would suffer behavioral impairments and ill health. To his surprise, he found the opposite: More of the easy babies had died (five of the seven he could find, compared to only one of the six difficult babies). Despite the small number of cases, the results were highly suggestive. Apparently the difficult babies demanded to be fed more often, boosting their mothers' milk supply (frequent breast-feeding stimulates milk production), even though the mothers were malnourished. The less demanding, easy babies died when their mothers' milk supplies dwindled.

The deaths of the easy babies illustrate the crucial role played by events at each of the three levels of analysis and their interactions within a physical context. Temperament is at least in part biologically determined, a topic we explore in Chapters 10 and 11. The child's temperament *(level of the brain)* regulated the mother's behavior; her behavior, based on her belief that she should feed her child only when it fussed *(level of the person)*, in turn affected how her body functioned. Finally, in the Maasai culture *(level of the group)*, babies are cared for by an extended family, and thus the stress presented by difficult babies does not fall on the mother only, as is common in our society. Thus, a difficult baby was not as stressful as he or she would be for a single caretaker. Moreover, because the Maasai are nomads *(level of the group)*, they were dependent on the naturally available supplies of water (they didn't farm or irrigate). As a result, the physical environment—that is, the drought—was disastrous for them.

Note that we cannot understand what happened to the babies by considering only the physical environment. Although the drought set the stage for the psychological drama that followed, it did not determine the outcome. Nor can we understand what happened if we consider events only at a single level. To understand fully why more difficult babies than easy babies survived the drought, we must consider how events at all three levels interacted. Only by investigating the interactions among the babies' temperaments, the mothers' beliefs about feeding, and the Maasai's culture can we understand the psychological factors that led to the deaths of the easy children.

CONSOLIDATE!

► 1. *Psychology can illuminate all aspects of a person's life, but what is psychology?* Psychology is the science of mental processes and behavior. Science is a way of answering questions that relies on, first, using logic to reason about the possible causes of a phenomenon and, then, collecting new facts to test the resulting ideas. Psychology focuses on both the internal events that underlie our thoughts, feelings, and behavior and the behavior itself.

► 2. *What is the concept of "levels of analysis," and how can you use it to understand psychology?* Any psychological phenomenon can best be understood by considering events at three levels of analysis: the brain (its functioning and its structure), the person (his or her beliefs, desires, and feelings), and the group (social interactions and cultural influences). All these events occur in the context of the physical world. Events at the different levels are constantly interacting, and thus it is impossible to explain mental processes or behavior adequately in terms of only a single level of analysis.

PSYCHOLOGY THEN AND NOW

How do you think psychologists 50 or 100 years ago might have interpreted Tiger Woods's performance? Would they have focused on the same things as psychologists do today? One hallmark of the sciences is that rather than casting aside earlier findings, researchers use them as stepping stones to the next set of discoveries. Reviewing how psychology has developed over time will help us understand where we are today. In the century or so during which psychology has taken shape as a formal discipline, the issues under investigation have changed, the focus has shifted from one level of analysis to another, and events at each level have often been viewed as operating separately or occurring in isolation.

▶ 1. How has psychology evolved over time?

▶ 2. What are the different types of psychology, and what do different types of psychologists do?

The Evolution of a Science

In one form or another, psychology has probably always been with us. People have apparently always been curious about why they and others think, feel, and behave the way they do. In contrast, the history of psychology as a scientific field is relatively brief, spanning little more than a century. The roots of psychology lie in philosophy (the use of logic and speculation to understand the nature of reality, experience, and values) on the one hand and physiology (the study of the biological workings of the body, including the brain) on the other. From philosophy, psychology borrowed theories of the nature of mental processes and behavior (for example, the idea that thinking relies on a series of mental images). From physiology, psychologists learned to recognize the role of the brain in giving rise to mental processes and behavior and acquired tools to investigate these processes. These twin influences of philosophy and physiology remain in force today, shaped and sharpened by developments over time.

EARLY DAYS: STRUCTURALIST, FUNCTIONALIST, AND GESTALT PSYCHOLOGY.
The earliest scientific psychologists were not much interested in why we behave as we do. Instead, these pioneers focused their efforts on understanding the operation of perception (the ways in which we sense the world), memory, and problem solving—events at what we now think of as the level of the brain. Wilhelm Wundt (1832–1920), usually considered the founder of scientific psychology, set up the first psychology laboratory in 1879 in Leipzig, Germany. The work of Wundt and his colleagues led to **structuralism,** the first formal movement in psychology. The structuralists sought to identify the "building blocks" of consciousness. Part of Wundt's research led him to characterize two types of elements of consciousness. The first comprised sensations, which arise from the eyes, ears, and other sense organs; the second consisted of feelings, such as fear, anger, and love. The goal of this school of psychology was to describe the rules that determine how particular sensations or feelings may occur at the same time or in sequence, combining in various ways into mental *structures.* Edward Titchener (1867–1927), an American student of Wundt, broadened the structuralist approach to apply it to the nature of concepts and thinking in general.

The structuralists developed and tested their theories partly with objective techniques, such as measures of the time it takes to respond to different sensations. Their primary research tool, however, was **introspection,** which means literally "looking within." Here is an example of introspection: Try to recall how many windows and doors are in your room. Are you aware of "seeing" the room in a mental image, of scanning along the walls and counting the windows and doors? Introspection is the technique of noticing your mental processes as, or immediately after, they occur.

Structuralism: The school of psychology that sought to identify the basic elements of experience and to describe the rules and circumstances under which these elements combine to form mental *structures.*

Introspection: The process of "looking within."

Had the structuralists been asked to analyze Tiger Woods's golf success—how, for example, he perceives distances, fairway terrain, and wind direction—they probably would have trained him to use introspection to describe his mental processes. By 1913, however, another German scientist, Oswald Kulpe, had discovered that not all mental processes are accompanied by mental imagery. In fact, if you asked Tiger Woods how he manages to swing a golf club so well, he probably wouldn't be able to tell you. Contemporary researchers have discovered that as our expertise in a skill increases, we are correspondingly less able to use introspection to describe it, an apparent paradox that reflects the use of implicit memories (see Chapter 6).

Let's say that although you are able to use introspection as a tool to recall the numbers of windows and doors in your room, your best friend doesn't seem to be able to do the same. How could you prove that mental images actually exist and objects can indeed be visualized? For the early psychologists, this was the core of the problem. Barring the ability to read minds, there was no way to resolve disagreements about the nature of introspection. If the only way you can gather evidence is through a process that cannot be verified, you cannot establish the evidence it yields as fact. This is precisely what happened when the structuralists tried to use introspection as a scientific tool. Their observations could not be objectively repeated with the same results, and thus their theorizing based on introspective reports fell apart.

Rather than trying to chart the elements of mental processes, the adherents of **functionalism** sought to understand how our minds help us to adapt to the world around us—in short, how to *function* in it. As psychology historian Edwin G. Boring (1950) put it, the structuralists were interested in "the psychology of the *Is*," whereas the functionalists were interested in the "*Is-for*." Whereas the structuralists asked *what* are mental processes and *how* do they operate, the functionalists wanted to know *why* humans think, feel, and behave as we do. The functionalists, many of whom were Americans, shared the urge to gather knowledge that could be put to immediate use. Sitting in a room introspecting simply didn't seem worthwhile to them. The functionalists' interest lay in the methods by which people learn and in how goals and beliefs are shaped by environment. As such, their interests spanned the levels of the person and the group.

The functionalists were strongly influenced by Charles Darwin (1809–1882), whose theory of natural selection in evolution stressed that some individual organisms in every species, from ants to oaks, possess characteristics that enable them to survive and reproduce more fruitfully than others. The phrase "survival of the fittest," often quoted in relation to natural selection, doesn't quite capture the key idea. (For one thing, these days "the fittest" implies the muscle-bound star of the health club rather than its older meaning of something "fit for" or "suited to" its situation.) The idea of natural selection is that certain inborn characteristics make particular individuals more fit for their environments, enabling them to have more offspring that survive, and they in turn have more offspring, and so on, until the characteristics that led them to flourish are spread through the whole population. Darwin called the inborn characteristics that help an organism survive and produce many offspring *adaptations*. (Chapter 2 covers Darwin's theory more fully.)

The functionalists applied Darwin's theory to mental characteristics. For example, William James (1842–1910), who set up the first psychology laboratory in the United States at Harvard University, studied the ways in which consciousness helps an individual survive and adapt to an environment. The functionalists likely would have tried to discover how Tiger Woods's goals and beliefs enable him to press on in the face of adversity such as losing an important match or receiving hate mail.

The functionalists made several enduring contributions to psychology. Their emphasis on Darwin's theory of natural selection and its link between human and nonhuman animals led them to theorize that human psychology is related to the psychology of animals. This insight meant that the observation of animals could provide clues to human behavior. The functionalist focus on issues of society, such as improving methods of education, also spawned research that continues today.

Functionalism: The school of psychology that sought to understand the ways that the mind helps individuals *function,* or adapt to the world.

Although their work began in earnest nearly 50 years later, the Gestalt psychologists, like the structuralists, were interested in consciousness, particularly as it arises during perception (and thus also focused on events at the level of the brain). But instead of trying to dissect the elements of experience, **Gestalt psychology**—taking its name from the German word *Gestalt*, which means "whole"—emphasized the overall patterns of thoughts or experience. Based in Germany, scientists such as Max Wertheimer (1880–1943) and his colleagues noted that much of the content of our thoughts comes from what we perceive and, further, from inborn tendencies to structure what we see in certain ways.

Have you ever glanced up to see a flight of birds heading south for the winter? If so, you probably didn't pay attention to each individual bird but instead focused on the flock. In Gestalt terms, the flock was a *perceptual unit*, a whole formed from individual parts. The Gestalt psychologists developed over 100 perceptual laws, or principles, that describe how our eyes and brains organize the world. For example, both because the birds are near one another (the law of proximity) and because they are moving in the same direction (the law of common fate), we perceive them as a single unit. Gestaltists believed that these principles are a result of the most basic workings of the brain and that they affect how we all think. Most of these principles illustrate the dictum that "the whole is more than the sum of its parts." When you see the birds in flight, the flock has a size and shape that cannot be predicted from the size and shape of the birds viewed one at a time. To Gestalt psychologists, just as the flock is an entity that is more than a collection of individual birds, our patterns of thought are more than the simple sum of individual images or ideas. Gestaltists would want to know how Tiger Woods can take in the overall layout of each hole, or even 18-hole course, and plan his strategy accordingly.

Today the study of perception has grown beyond the province of Gestalt psychology alone and is now a central focus of psychology, as well it should be. Perception is, after all, our gateway to the world; if our perceptions are not accurate, our corresponding thoughts and feelings will be based on a distorted view of reality. The research of the Gestaltists addressed how the brain works, and today Gestaltism has become integrated into studies of the brain itself.

PSYCHODYNAMIC THEORY: MORE THAN MEETS THE EYE. Sigmund Freud (1856–1939), a Viennese physician specializing in neurology (the study and treatment of diseases of the brain and nervous system), developed detailed and subtle theories of how thoughts and feelings affect our actions. These theories address mental processes and behavior less at the level of the brain and more at the level of the person (and, to some extent, the level of the group). We consider Freud and theorists who followed in his footsteps in Chapter 10; here we touch briefly on key points of his theory.

Freud stressed the notion that many mental processes are **unconscious,** that is, they are outside our conscious awareness and beyond our ability to bring to awareness at will. Freud believed that we have many unconscious sexual, and sometimes aggressive, urges. Even young infants, Freud wrote, are highly sexual beings, a notion that disturbed many of his contemporaries, and disturbs many of us. On a conscious level, Freud argued, we find these urges unacceptable and so banish them to the unconscious. According to Freud, unconscious thoughts and feelings build up until, eventually and inevitably, they demand release as thoughts, feelings, or actions.

Freud developed what has since been called a **psychodynamic theory.** From the Greek words *psyche*, or "mind," and *dynamo*, meaning "power," the term refers to the continual push-and-pull interaction among conscious and unconscious forces. Freud believed that it was these interactions that produced abnormal behaviors, such as obsessively washing one's hands until they crack and bleed. According to Freud, such hand-washing might be traced to unacceptable unconscious sexual or aggressive impulses bubbling up to consciousness (the "dirt" perceived on the hands) and that washing symbolically serves to remove the "dirt." Freud interpreted many statements and events symbolically, often assigning a sexual meaning to them. For example, he

Gestalt psychology: An approach to understanding mental processes that focuses on the idea that the whole is more than the sum of its parts.

Unconscious: Outside conscious awareness and not able to be brought to consciousness at will.

Psychodynamic theory: A theory of how thoughts and feelings affect behavior; refers to the continual push-and-pull interaction among conscious and unconscious forces.

Behaviorism: The school of psychology that focuses on how a specific stimulus (object, person, or event) evokes a specific response (behavior in reaction to the stimulus).

believed that long, thin objects often represented the penis and that objects with holes in them symbolized the vagina. What would followers of psychodynamic theory say about Tiger Woods? The long skinny club that he wields so effectively might be considered a symbol for a penis, and a Freudian would probably ask Woods about his earliest memories and experiences and try with him to analyze the sexual or aggressive urges that led to his intense interest in golf.

Others modified Freud's theory in various ways, for example, by de-emphasizing sex in favor of other sources of unconscious conflicts; Alfred Adler (1870–1937), for instance, stressed the role of feelings of inferiority. Psychodynamic theories have attracted many passionate followers. Rather than deriving from objective scientific studies, however, their guiding principles rest on subjective interpretations of what patients say and do. As such, critics charge, there is no objective way to verify whether a given interpretation is correct: as Freud (a cigar smoker) himself remarked, "Sometimes a cigar is only a cigar." Psychodynamic theory can usually explain any given observation or research result as easily as its opposite, and thus it becomes impossible to evaluate the theory, obviously a serious drawback. Nevertheless, the key idea of psychodynamic theory, that behavior is driven by mental processes that are often hidden from conscious awareness, has proven invaluable; also invaluable is its focus on the level of the person. In addition, psychodynamic theories led to entirely new approaches to treating psychological problems, which have since been modified and refined (see Chapter 14). For instance, Freud's theory led to *psychoanalysis,* in which a therapist listens to a patient talk about his or her childhood, relationships, and dreams, and attempts to help the patient understand the unconscious bases of his or her thoughts, feelings, and behavior.

BEHAVIORISM: THE POWER OF THE ENVIRONMENT. By the early part of the twentieth century, a new generation of psychologists calling themselves behaviorists began to question a key assumption shared by their predecessors, that psychologists should study hidden mental processes. Because they found the theories of mental processes so difficult to pin down, American psychologists such as Edward Lee Thorndike (1874–1949), John B. Watson (1878–1958), and Clark L. Hull (1884– 1952) rejected the idea that psychology should focus on these unseen phenomena. Instead, these followers of **behaviorism** concluded that psychology should concentrate on understanding directly observable behavior.

Some behaviorists were willing to talk about internal stimuli such as motivation, but only those stimuli that were directly reflected in behavior (such as running quickly to catch a bus). Later behaviorists, among them B. F. Skinner (1904–1990), urged that psychology move away from the study of internal processes altogether, arguing that they played no role at all in causing behavior. Skinner and his followers went so far as to argue that there is no such thing as mental processes, that people don't really have "thoughts." For instance, rather than saying that someone treats dogs well because she "likes" them ("liking" being an unobservable mental process), these behaviorists would say that she approaches dogs, protects them from harm, pets them, and otherwise treats them well because such responses have come to be associated with the stimulus of perceiving a dog. Behaviorists thus cut out the middleman of mental processes: The behaviors that are generally regarded as reflections of the internal state of "liking" can instead be viewed as direct responses to particular stimuli. Because of their concern with the content of the stimulus–response associations, the behaviorists focused on events at the level of the person.

The behaviorists pointed out that responses usually produce consequences, either negative or positive, which in turn affect how the organism responds the next

THE FAR SIDE   By GARY LARSON

© 1988 FarWorks, Inc

B·28

"Stimulus, response! Stimulus, response! Don't you ever think?"

time it encounters the same stimulus. Say you put money in a vending machine (a response to the stimulus of seeing the machine) and the machine dispenses a tasty candy bar; chances are good that you will repeat the behavior in the future. If, on the other hand, the machine serves up a stale candy bar with a torn wrapper, you will be less inclined to use this or another machine like it again (see Chapter 5 for a detailed discussion of how consequences affect learning).

How might the behaviorists explain Tiger Woods's success? A key idea in behaviorism is *reinforcement,* the strengthening or supporting consequences that result from a given behavior. A reward, such as payment for a job, is a common type of reinforcement. If the consequences of a behavior are reinforcing, we are likely to repeat the behavior. Conversely, if a behavior produces an undesirable outcome ("punishment"), we are less likely to do it again. From his earliest days, Tiger Woods received an extraordinary amount of reinforcement for playing well, at first from his father and then from an increasingly larger affirming public. It was this reinforcement, the behaviorists would argue, that spurred him to repeat those acts that brought desirable consequences, while shunning behaviors (including ineffective golfing techniques) that did not help him play well.

The behaviorists developed many principles that describe the conditions in which specific stimuli lead to specific responses, many of which have stood up well in later investigations (as you will see in Chapter 5). For example, they found that individuals respond more frequently when the desirable outcomes are intermittent than when those "rewards" occur every time. Thus if Tiger were hitting golf balls one after the other onto a putting green, he would be more likely to play longer and hit more balls if he had sunk only some of them than if he had sunk every shot. On the other hand, as you will see, many of the behaviorists' objections to the study of mental processes have since been refuted by subsequent research.

HUMANISTIC PSYCHOLOGY. Partly as a reaction to the mechanistic theories of the Freudians and behaviorists, which viewed people as driven either by the content of their mental processes or by external stimuli, in the late 1950s and early 1960s a new psychology emerged. According to **humanistic psychology,** people have positive values, free will, and a deep inner creativity, which in combination allow us to choose life-fulfilling paths to personal growth. The humanistic approach (focused on the level of the person) rests on the ideas that the "client" (no longer the "patient") must be respected as equal to the therapist and that each person has dignity and self-worth.

Psychologists such as Carl Rogers (1902–1987) and Abraham Maslow (1908–1970) developed therapies based on these theories. Rogers's *client-centered therapy* incorporated Maslow's theory that people have an urge to *self-actualize*—that is, to develop to their fullest potentials—and that given the right environment this development will in time occur. Rather than serving as an expert in a position of authority, the client-centered therapist provides a "mirror" in the form of an unconditionally supportive and positive environment. How might humanistic psychologists explain Tiger Woods's psychology? No doubt they would point to him as someone who is striving to reach his full potential. They might question, however, whether in the long run his intense focus on golf will prove entirely satisfying, especially if he ignores other aspects of life.

Humanistic psychology continues to attract followers today, but it is no longer a major force in the field. Nevertheless, many of the therapies now in use reflect the influence of humanistic thinking (as we discuss in Chapter 14).

THE COGNITIVE REVOLUTION. The tension between psychological approaches—on the one hand, structuralism, functionalism, and psychoanalytic psychology, which studied unobservable mental processes, and on the other, behaviorism, which addressed only directly observable behavior—was resolved by an unlikely source: the computer. The computer led to the *cognitive revolution* of the late 1950s and early 1960s; its proponents looked to the computer as a model for the way human

Humanistic psychology: The school of psychology that assumes people have positive values, free will, and deep inner creativity, the combination of which leads them to choose life-fulfilling paths to personal growth.

mental processes work. This movement came into full flower in the mid-1970s, led by, among others, psychologist/computer scientists Herbert A. Simon and Alan Newell (Simon went on to win a Nobel Prize, in part for this work) and linguist Noam Chomsky. (Gardner [1985] provides a detailed history of the cognitive revolution.)

The cognitive revolution produced a new way to conceive of mental events, giving birth to **cognitive psychology,** which attempts to characterize the nature of human *information processing,* that is, the way information is stored and operated on internally (Neisser, 1967). In this view, mental processes are like computer software (programs), and the brain is like the hardware (the machine itself). Cognitive psychologists believe that just as different types of software can be discussed without ever considering how the hardware works, mental processes can be discussed without regard to the structure of the brain.

Computers showed, once and for all, why it is important that there be a science of the unobservable events that take place in the head, not just a science of directly observable behavior. Consider, for example, how you might react if your word-processing program produced *italics* whenever you entered the command for **boldface.** Noticing the software's "behavior" is only the first step in fixing this error: You need to dig deeper in order to find out where the program has gone wrong. This would involve seeing what internal events are triggered by the command and how those events affect what the program does. So, too, for people. If somebody is acting odd, we must go beyond the essential step of noticing the unusual behavior; we also need to think about what is happening inside and consider what is causing the problem. Indeed, the cognitive revolution led to new ways of conceptualizing and treating mental disorders, such as depression. For example, Albert Ellis (b. 1913) and Aaron Beck (b. 1921) claimed that people's distressing feelings or symptoms are caused by irrational and distorted ways of thinking about their interactions with others, themselves, and their surroundings. Beck showed that symptoms such as anxiety and depression could be addressed by attacking the problems in thinking.

Cognitive psychology defined many of the questions that are still being pursued in psychology, such as how information is stored when we perform a given task, and it continues to develop subtle experimental methods to study hidden mental processes. Principles of cognitive psychology have been used to compare abilities across cultures, in part to sort out which aspects of our psychologies arise from inherent properties of the brain (common to all people) and which are a product of our particular social experiences (Cole, 1996; Cole et al., 1997).

The theories and research methods developed by cognitive psychologists have also proven crucial in the recent development of **cognitive neuroscience,** which blends cognitive psychology and neuroscience (the study of the brain). Cognitive neuroscientists argue that "the mind is what the brain does" (Kosslyn & Koenig, 1995) and hope to discover the nature, organization, and operation of mental processes by studying the brain. This is one of the most exciting areas of psychology today, in part because new brain-scanning technologies have allowed us, for the first time in history, to observe human brains at work.

The cognitive neuroscience approach considers events at the three levels of analysis, but with a primary focus on the brain. Cognitive neuroscientists seeking to explain Tiger Woods's golfing achievements would likely investigate how different parts of his brain function while he plays golf, looking to discover the way his brain processes information. For example, how does the visual input he receives standing at the tee allow him to judge distance to the pin? They would also compare Woods's brain function with that of less accomplished golfers and would even program computers to mimic the way his brain works during play.

EVOLUTIONARY PSYCHOLOGY. One of the most recent developments in the field, **evolutionary psychology,** first made its appearance in the late 1980s. This school of thought has a heritage—with a twist—in the work of the functionalists and their emphasis on Darwin's theory of natural selection. Central to the approach is

Cognitive psychology: The approach in psychology that attempts to characterize how information is stored and operated on internally.

Cognitive neuroscience: A blending of cognitive psychology and neuroscience (the study of the brain) that aims to specify how the brain stores and processes information.

Evolutionary psychology: The approach in psychology that assumes that certain cognitive strategies and goals are so important that natural selection has built them into our brains.

the idea that certain cognitive strategies and goals are so important that natural selection has built them into our brains. But instead of proposing that evolution has selected specific behaviors per se (as earlier evolutionary theorists, including Charles Darwin himself, believed), these theorists believe that general cognitive strategies (such as using deception to achieve one's goals) and certain goals (such as finding attractive mates) are inborn. This approach is currently being developed by researchers such as Lida Cosmides and John Tooby (1996), David Buss (1994, 1999), and Steven Pinker (1994, 1997; see also Barkow et al., 1992; Plotkin, 1994, 1997). For example, these theorists claim that we have the ability to lie because our ancestors who could lie had an advantage: They could trick their naïve companions into giving up resources. These more devious ancestors had more children who survived than their nonlying contemporaries, and their lying children had more children, and so on, until the ability to lie was inborn in all members of our species. Notice that lying is not a specific behavior; it is a strategy that can be expressed by many behaviors, all of them deceitful.

How can you test a theory about the history of human psychology? Fossils will tell you little. Instead, some researchers seek evidence for evolutionary developments in contemporary humans. Probably the best source of evidence for theories in evolutionary psychology is *cultural universality,* instances of the same practice occurring in all cultures. If people even in remote areas with very different cultures show the same tendencies, it is likely that the tendencies are not the result of learning. In fact, people in all cultures have been found to share certain concepts and practices, including lying, telling stories, gossiping, using proper names, expressing emotions with facial expressions, fearing snakes, dancing, making music, giving gifts, making medicines; the list goes on and on (Brown, 1991). Being human is more than having a certain type of body; it is also having a certain type of brain and mind that works in certain ways.

However, even these sorts of concepts and practices are not entirely predetermined by built-in mechanisms. For example, Buunk and colleagues (1996) asked German, Dutch, and American men and women if they would be more upset if their mates had sex with someone else or if they became emotionally involved with another person. These researchers found that men claimed that they would be generally more upset if their mate had sex with someone else than if she became emotionally involved, but women responded oppositely. However, this difference was larger in the United States than in European countries, suggesting that culture can play a role in modulating or modifying evolutionarily relevant behaviors.

Evolutionary psychologists compare human abilities with those of animals, particularly nonhuman primates (Hauser, 1996). For example, by studying the way animals communicate, researchers try to infer which abilities formed the basis of human language. By studying animals, researchers hope to discover the abilities of our common ancestors and, from those data, develop theories about the way they may have been refined over the course of evolution. When asked about what might underlie Tiger Woods's achievements, an evolutionary psychologist might note that although our species did not evolve to play golf, the abilities that arose via natural selection for hunting game and avoiding predators could also be used in other ways, including sports.

But evidence of universality or shared abilities in nonhuman animals and humans does not tell us *why* those characteristics are present. Are they really adaptations? Evolutionary theories are notoriously difficult to test because we don't know what our ancestors were like and how they evolved. Just because we are born with certain tendencies and characteristics does not mean that these are evolutionarily selected adaptations. As Stephen Jay Gould and Richard Lewontin (1979) point out, at least some of our modern characteristics are simply by-products of other characteristics that were in fact selected. Your nose evolved to warm air and direct scents; and once you have a nose, you can use it to hold up your eyeglasses. But just as nobody would claim that the nose evolved to hold up glasses, nobody should claim that all the cur-

TABLE 1.1

Schools of Psychological Thought

Dates based on Boring (1950).

NAME	LANDMARK EVENTS	KEY IDEAS
Structuralism	Wundt founds first psychology laboratory, 1879	Use introspection to discover the elements of mental processes and rules for combining them.
Functionalism	James's *Principles of Psychology* published, 1890	Study why thoughts, feelings, and behavior occur, how they are adaptive.
Gestalt psychology	Wertheimer's paper on perceived movement, 1912	Focus on overall patterns of thoughts or experience; "the whole is more than the sum of its parts."
Psychodynamic theory	Freud publishes *The Ego and the Id*, 1927	Conflicts among conscious and unconscious forces underlie many thoughts, feelings, and behaviors.
Behaviorism	Watson's paper *Psychology as the Behaviorist Views It*, 1913; Skinner's *The Behavior of Organisms*, 1938	Behavior is the appropriate focus of psychology, and it can be understood by studying stimuli, responses, and the consequences of responses.
Humanistic psychology	Maslow publishes *Motivation and Personality*, 1954	Nonscientific approach; belief that people have positive values, free will, and deep inner creativity.
Cognitive psychology	Neisser's book *Cognitive Psychology* gives the "school" its name, 1967	Mental processes are like information processing in a computer.
Cognitive neuroscience	First issue of the *Journal of Cognitive Neuroscience* appears, 1989	"The mind is what the brain does."
Evolutionary psychology	Barkow, Cosmides, and Tooby edit *The Adapted Mind*, 1992	Mental strategies and goals are often inborn, the result of natural selection.

rent functions of the brain resulted from natural selection. The various schools of psychological thought are summarized in Table 1.1.

The Psychological Way: What Today's Psychologists Do

As the field of psychology developed, different schools of thought focused on different aspects of mental processes and behavior, and their varying influences are felt in what today's psychologists do. And just what is that?

There are many types of psychologists and many ways to apply psychology in practice. Here we consider three major types of psychologists: those who help people deal with personal problems or stress, those who study mental processes and behavior scientifically, and those who seek to solve specific practical problems, such as helping athletes perform better.

CLINICAL AND COUNSELING PSYCHOLOGY: A HEALING PROFESSION.
Andrea is a **clinical psychologist** who specializes in treating people with eating disorders. Many of Andrea's clients have a disorder called *anorexia nervosa*, characterized by refusal to maintain a healthy weight. Others, who have a disorder called *bulimia nervosa*, eat and then force themselves to vomit or take laxatives immediately afterward. Andrea sees such patients once or twice a week, for 50 minutes per session.

Clinical psychologist: The type of psychologist who provides psychotherapy and is trained to administer and interpret psychological tests.

During these sessions, Andrea's job is usually to discover why behaviors that are so destructive in the long run seem so desirable to the patient in the short run. She then helps her patients phase out the destructive behaviors and replace them with more adaptive behaviors—for instance, responding to anxiety after eating by taking a quick walk around the block instead of vomiting. Depending on the setting in which Andrea works (probably a private office, clinic, or hospital), she will spend varying portions of her day with patients; meeting with other psychologists to discuss how to be more helpful to patients; supervising psychotherapists in training; going out into the community, perhaps lecturing about eating disorders at high school assemblies; and doing paperwork, including writing notes on each patient, submitting forms to insurance companies for payment, and reading professional publications to keep up with new findings and techniques.

Andrea has been trained to provide **psychotherapy,** which involves listening and talking to patients and helping them discover the causes of, and solutions to, their difficulties; she also administers and interprets psychological tests, which can help in diagnosis and planning the appropriate treatment. *Clinical neuropsychologists* are clinical psychologists who work specifically with tests designed to diagnose the effects of brain damage on thoughts, feelings, and behavior and to indicate which parts of the brain are impaired following trauma. Other clinical psychologists work with organizations such as corporations to help company groups function more effectively; for example, a psychologist might advise a company about reducing stress among workers in a particular unit, or teach relaxation techniques to all employees. Some clinical psychologists have a Ph.D. (doctor of philosophy) degree, awarded by a university psychology department; these graduate programs teach students not only how to do psychotherapy and psychological testing, but also how to conduct and interpret psychological research. A clinical psychologist may also have a Psy.D. (doctor of psychology), a graduate degree from a program with less emphasis on research.

If Andrea had been trained as a **counseling psychologist,** she would have learned to help people deal with issues we all face, such as choosing a career, marrying, raising a family, and performing at work. Counseling psychologists often provide career counseling and vocational testing to help people decide which occupations best suit their interests and abilities. They sometimes provide psychotherapy, but these professionals may have a more limited knowledge of therapeutic techniques than clinical psychologists. They may have a Ph.D. (often from a program that specifically trains them in this area) or often an Ed.D. (doctor of education) degree granted by a school of education.

Psychotherapy: Talking and listening to patients about their problems and helping them to see the causes and—more important—to find solutions.

Counseling psychologist: The type of psychologist who is trained to help people with issues that naturally arise during the course of life.

There are many kinds of psychotherapy, and different training prepares therapists in different ways. Psychiatrists, for example, typically would not treat families, but clinical psychologists and social workers—as well as other mental health professionals— might.

Andrea could also have become a **psychiatrist.** If she had gone this route, her training and competence would have differed from that of the other mental health professionals. First, as a physician with an M.D. (doctor of medicine) degree, a psychiatrist has extensive medical training and can prescribe drugs, whereas in general psychologists cannot (some psychologists in understaffed rural areas have had intensive training about medications for mental illnesses and have been given limited prescribing privileges). Second, a medical doctor, unlike a clinical psychologist, has typically not been trained to interpret and understand psychological research or psychological testing.

There are two other types of clinical mental health practitioners who are not psychologists, and her interest in clinical work might have led Andrea to choose either of those professions: social work or psychiatric nursing. If she had earned an M.S.W. (master of social work) degree, as a **social worker** she would typically focus on helping families and individuals by psychotherapy, and she also would teach clients how to use the social service system in their community. A **psychiatric nurse** holds a master's degree in nursing (M.S.N, master of science in nursing) as well as a certificate of clinical specialization (C.S.) in psychiatric nursing. A psychiatric nurse provides psychotherapy, usually in a hospital or clinic, or in private practice, and works closely with medical doctors to monitor and administer medications; in some cases, a psychiatric nurse can prescribe medications.

ACADEMIC PSYCHOLOGY: TEACHING AND RESEARCH. James is a professor of psychology at a large state university. Most mornings he prepares lectures, which he delivers three times a week. He also has morning office hours, when students can come by to ask questions about their program of courses in the department or their progress in one of James's classes. Once a week at noon he has a committee meeting; this week the committee on computer technology is discussing how best to structure

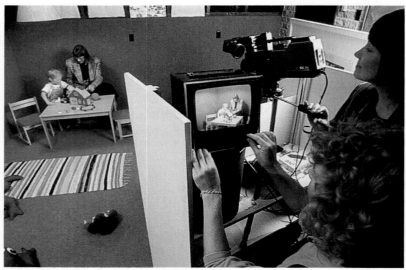

Developmental psychologists often take special care to prevent their presence from affecting the child's behavior in any way.

the department computer network. His afternoons are taken up mostly with research. (If he worked at a smaller college, he might spend more time teaching and less time on research; alternatively, if he worked at a hospital, he might spend the lion's share of his time doing research and very little time teaching.) James's specialty is *developmental psychology*, the study of how thinking, feeling, and behaving develop with age and experience. Today his research work takes place at a laboratory preschool at the university, where he and his assistants are testing the ways children become attached to objects such as dolls and blankets. James also must find time to write papers for publication in professional journals, and he regularly writes grant proposals requesting funding for his research, so that he can pay students to help him test the children in his studies. He also writes letters of recommendation, grades papers and tests, and reads journal articles to keep up with current research in his and related fields. James tries to eat lunch with colleagues at least twice a week to keep up-to-date on departmental events and the work going on at the university in other areas of psychology.

Although the activities of most **academic psychologists** are similar in that they all teach and conduct research, the kinds of research vary widely. Different types of psychologists focus on different types of questions. For example, if James had become a *cognitive psychologist* (one who studies thinking, memory, and related topics), he might ask, "How was Tiger Woods able to hit the ball with the appropriate force in the correct direction?" but not "What was the role of the audience, and would it have been different if the tournament had been held 50 years ago?" If he had become a *social psychologist* (one who studies how people think and feel about themselves and other people, and how groups function), he might ask the second question, but not the first. And in neither case would he ask, "What aspects of Tiger Woods's character help him deal with the extreme stress he faces?" That question would interest a *personality psychologist* (one who studies individual differences in preferences and inclinations).

Because psychology is a science, it rests on objective tests of its theories and ideas. It is through research that we learn how to diagnose people's problems and how to cure them; it is through research that we determine what kind of career will make good use of a particular person's talents; it is through research that we understand how to present material so that students can understand and remember it most effectively. Theories about such issues can come from anywhere, but there is no way to know if an idea is right or wrong except by testing it scientifically, through research.

There are at least as many different types of academic psychologists as there are separate sections in this book. In fact, this book represents a harvest of their research. Thousands of researchers are working on the topics covered in each chapter, and it is through their efforts that we have learned enough that a book like this can be written.

APPLIED PSYCHOLOGY: BETTER LIVING THROUGH PSYCHOLOGY. Maria works in the software development department of a high-tech company; she is a *human factors psychologist*, a professional who works to improve products so that people can use them more intuitively and effectively. Maria begins her day by testing several versions of menus to be used with a computer program under development. She wants to know which commands the software users will expect to find listed under the headings on the menu bar at the top of the screen. She has designed a study in which she asks people to find specific commands and records by computer where they look for the commands and how long it takes to find them. Maria often has lunch in the company cafeteria, but today she is eating at her desk, studying the results from the morning's testing session. Puzzled by what she sees, Maria suddenly realizes that the way she has labeled the commands is affecting how people think of them. She quickly begins to set up another series of tests on the computer. After lunch, she attends a talk by a visiting scientist about his new research, some of which may prove useful in her project: The subject is the nature of memory, and she takes careful notes. Afterward, she has a weekly meeting of the project team. Today the person who is designing the screen icons reports that he has run into difficulty; he describes the problem to the team, and various members ask questions and make suggestions. After this meeting, Maria goes to her office and works for an hour on a written progress report, then spends another hour on an article she is writing for a technical journal.

Applied psychologists use the principles and theories of psychology in practical areas such as education, industry, and marketing. An applied psychologist may hold a Ph.D. or, sometimes, only a master's degree in an area of psychology (in North America a master's degree typically requires two years of postgraduate study instead of the four to six for a Ph.D.). Applied psychologists not only work on improving products and procedures but also conduct research aimed at solving specific practical problems. Working in applied psychology, a *developmental psychologist* may be employed by or consult with the product development department of a toy company. Using her knowledge of children, she can help design toys that would be appropriate for particular age levels; she would then bring children to a playroom at the company to see how they play with new toys. A *physiological psychologist* studies the brain and brain/body interactions and may work at a company that makes drugs or brain-scanning machines. A *social psychologist* may help lawyers decide which possible jurors should be rejected. A *personality psychologist* may design a new test to help select suitable personnel for a job. An

Applied psychologist: The type of psychologist who studies how to improve products and procedures and conducts research to help solve specific practical problems.

Applied psychologists have many roles, one of which is to help attorneys decide which potential jurors are likely to be sympathetic or hostile to the defendant.

FIGURE 1.2
What Psychologists Do
Percentages of psychologists working in different specialty areas.

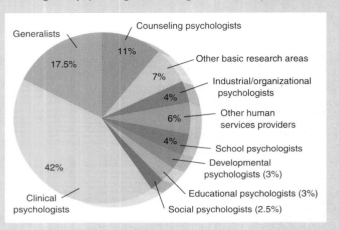

- Generalists 17.5%
- Counseling psychologists 11%
- Other basic research areas 7%
- Industrial/organizational psychologists 4%
- Other human services providers 6%
- School psychologists 4%
- Developmental psychologists (3%)
- Educational psychologists (3%)
- Social psychologists (2.5%)
- Clinical psychologists 42%

industrial/organizational (I/O) psychologist focuses on using psychology in the workplace; he or she might help an employer create a more comfortable and effective work environment so as to increase worker productivity or might redesign work spaces to promote more effective employee communication. A *sport psychologist* works with athletes to help them improve their performances, by helping them learn to concentrate better, deal with stress, and practice more efficiently (Tiger Woods works with a sport psychologist). An *educational* or *school psychologist* works with educators (and sometimes families), devising ways to improve the cognitive, emotional, and social development of children at school.

The relative numbers of the various types of psychologists are illustrated in Figure 1.2, and their occupations are summarized in Table 1.2.

TABLE 1.2

What Psychologists Do

Clinical psychologist	Administers and interprets psychological tests; provides psychotherapy.
Clinical neuropsychologist	Diagnoses effects of brain damage on thoughts, feelings, and behavior, and diagnoses the locus of damage.
Counseling psychologist	Helps people with issues that arise during everyday life (career, marriage, family, work).
Developmental psychologist	Researches and teaches the development of mental processes and behavior with age.
Cognitive psychologist	Researches and teaches the nature of thinking, memory, and related aspects of mental processes.
Social psychologist	Researches and teaches how people think and feel about themselves and other people and how groups function.
Personality psychologist	Researches and teaches individual differences in preferences and inclinations.
Physiological psychologist	Researches and teaches the nature of the brain and brain/body interactions.
Industrial/organizational psychologist	Applies psychology in the workplace.
Sport psychologist	Applies psychology to improve athletic performance.
Educational or School psychologist	Applies psychology to improve cognitive, emotional, and social development of schoolchildren.

LOOKING AT LEVELS

A Science of the Obvious?

Science is an attempt to cajole Mother Nature into giving up her secrets. Over the years, the science of psychology has made many such attempts at unveiling the secrets of mental processes and behavior by means of the various approaches just reviewed. In the process, research psychologists of various persuasions are sometimes accused of merely demonstrating the obvious.

For example, the old saw that familiarity breeds contempt states the obvious—or does it? Let's see how a social psychologist would approach testing the obvious in this case. Robert Zajonc (1968, 1970) was interested in the factors that lead us to like something or someone. He found, repeatedly, that people like previously seen things *better* than unfamiliar ones; research shows that familiarity breeds not contempt but affinity (Bornstein, 1989). This is called the *mere-exposure effect*. At the level of the brain, the repeated presentation of a picture allows it to be taken in with less effort, which at the level of the person leads to positive feelings and preferences (Bornstein & D'Agostino, 1994). These effects can in turn alter behavior, including behavior toward other people (the level of the group).

In a later study, Leone and Galley (Bornstein, 1987) demonstrated that the mere-exposure effect is not just a laboratory curiosity. They showed participants photographs of one of two faces, flashing them so briefly that the faces could not be identified. Following this, the participant met with the person in the photograph and a third person, ostensibly to decide whether the author of some poems was a man or a woman. As arranged beforehand, the two other people disagreed, and the participant had to be the tie-breaker. The participants tended to side with the person whose face they had seen in the photograph, even though they were unaware they had seen it. The mere-exposure effect was at work here across levels, an event in the brain affecting a preference (level of the person) that in turn affected a social interaction (level of the group).

So, not all results from psychological research are obvious, and in fact you will see many such examples of discoveries that are not obvious as you continue in this book. The following section explores in more detail just how studies can be conducted to discover new and sometimes surprising facts about mental processes and behavior.

CONSOLIDATE!

▶ 1. *How has psychology evolved over time?* Wundt, Titchener, and the other structuralists aimed to understand the elements of mental processes and how they are organized; this approach relied largely on introspection ("looking within"), which turned out to be not very reliable and not always valid—people often have no idea how their mental processes work, at least not in ways they can easily report. The functionalists rejected this approach as disconnected from real-world concerns and focused instead on how mental processes adapt to help us survive in the natural world; their pragmatic concerns led them to apply psychology to education and other social activities. In contrast, the Gestalt psychologists, who reacted to the attempt to dissect mental processes into isolated elements, studied the way the brain organizes material into overarching patterns. Freud and his colleagues shifted attention primarily to the level of the person; their psychodynamic theories were concerned largely with the operation of unconscious mental processes and primitive impulses (often related to sex) in dictating what people think, feel, and do. The behaviorists denounced the assumption, shared by all their pre-

decessors, that mental processes should be the focus of psychology; they urged us to stick with what we could see—stimuli, responses, and the consequences of responses. But this view turned out to be too limiting. The humanists, in part reacting against the scientific approach, developed psychotherapies that relied on respect for individuals and their potentials. Elements of the various strands came together in the cognitive revolution, and many researchers who study cognition today conceive of mental processes as "what the brain does." Evolutionary psychology treats many goals and cognitive strategies as adaptive results of natural selection.

▶ 2. *What are the different types of psychology, and what do different types of psychologists do?* Clinical and counseling psychologists administer diagnostic tests and help people with their problems; academic psychologists teach and do research; and applied psychologists trained in various areas of psychology seek to solve specific practical problems, such as making better products and improving procedures in the workplace.

THE SCIENCE OF PSYCHOLOGY: DESIGNED TO BE VALID

You could probably speculate for hours about how Tiger Woods came to be such a superb golfer. Let's say, however, that you really want to *know* why some people are able to perform at high levels in spite of extraordinary pressure. How could you find out for sure?

► 1. What is the scientific method?

► 2. What research tools can psychologists use to study mental processes and behavior scientifically?

► 3. What should you look for when deciding whether to accept a study's conclusions?

The Scientific Method

The **scientific method** is a way to gather facts that will lead to the formulation and validation of a theory. It involves *specifying a problem; systematically observing events; forming a hypothesis of the relation between variables; collecting new observations to test the hypothesis; using such evidence to formulate and support a theory; and finally, testing the theory.*

Let's take a closer look at the scientific method, one step at a time. First, what do we mean by "specifying a problem"? Science tries to answer questions, any one of which may be rephrased as a "problem." Despite the way the word is often used in ordinary conversation, a problem is not necessarily bad: It is simply a question you want to answer, or a puzzle you want to solve. A scientist might notice what seems to be a consistent pattern, for example, and wonder if it reflects a connection or a coincidence. For example, a scientist might notice that many cultures have an afternoon siesta or "tea time" and wonder whether humans have a biological rhythm that makes us sluggish at that time of day. Speaking metaphorically, a scientist might notice a nail sticking above the boards and ask why it is different from other nails. Even as a child, Tiger Woods's abilities and discipline made him stand out from other children. Why? Was there something different about his brain? about the way he was being raised?

Second, consider the idea of "systematically observing events." Scientists are not content to rely on impressions or interpretations. They want to know the facts, as free from any particular notions of their significance as possible. Facts are established by collecting **data,** which are careful observations or numerical measurements of a phenomenon. Properly collected data can be **replicated,** that is, found again by the original investigator or someone else. Scientists often prefer quantitative data (numerical measurements), such as how many seconds it takes a rat to run a maze, how many people gather at the scene of an accident, how many times in a row Tiger Woods can sink a 10-foot putt. In addition to numerical data, scientists rely on systematic observations, which simply document that a certain event occurs—for example, that brain damage can cause someone to fail to name fruits and vegetables while still able to name other objects (Hart et al., 1985). But unless numbers are involved, it is often difficult to sort the observation from the interpretation. Thus scientists prefer to have careful observation produce numbers (for example, the number of fruits and vegetables that could be named out of a possible 100).

Third, what do we mean by "events"? An event in the scientific sense is the occurrence of a particular phenomenon. Scientists study two kinds of events: those that are themselves directly observable (such as how many times in an hour a mother strokes her infant) and those that, like thoughts or emotions, can only be inferred. For example, when people smile without really meaning it, the muscles used are not the same ones that produce a sincere smile (Ekman, 1985). It is possible to observe directly which set of muscles is in use, and the recorded data would distinguish between the two kinds of contractions. But the researcher's interest goes beyond the directly observable contractions to the link with inner (and invisible) thoughts and feelings. By studying what's observable (the muscles), researchers can learn about the unobservable (the mental state of the smiler).

Fourth, what about "forming a hypothesis of the relation between variables"? A **hypothesis** is a tentative idea that might explain a set of observations. Say you are inspired by Tiger Woods's example and decide to take golf lessons. On the course, you notice a particularly good player and ask her for tips. She says that when she's

Scientific method: The scientific method involves specifying a problem; systematically observing events; forming a hypothesis of the relation between variables; collecting new observations to test the hypothesis; using such evidence to formulate and support a theory; and finally, testing the theory.

Data: Careful observations or numerical measurements.

Replicate: To repeat a study and obtain the same results as were found previously.

off the course, she often practices her swings mentally, imagining herself whacking the ball straight down the fairway or out of the sand trap; she assures you that the mental practice has improved her game. Well, maybe there's a connection between two **variables**—aspects of the situation that are liable to change, that can vary. Here the variables are the time spent visualizing giving the ball a good whack and the golf score. The idea appeals to you, in part because it means that you can practice even at night, or whenever you are bored, or when the course is covered with snow. But it's a hypothesis only. Before you go to the trouble of imagining yourself playing, over and over and over, you ought to test the hypothesis to find out whether it's correct.

Thus, you must go about "collecting new observations to test the hypothesis." Are there reliable studies that bear on the expert golfer's testimony? In fact, much research has been conducted on mental practice, and many studies have documented that it actually does improve performance. In a typical study, people are divided into two groups, and the performance of both groups is assessed. One group then uses mental practice for a specified period, while the other makes no preparation. Then the performance of both groups is assessed again. Usually, the people who engage in mental practice show greater improvement (Doheny, 1993; Driskell et al., 1994; Druckman & Swets, 1988; White & Hardy, 1995; Yagueez et al., 1998).

Now consider "using such evidence to formulate and support a theory." A **theory** consists of a set of principles that are supposed to explain a set of observations; in other words, the theory is an answer to the question being asked. In our example, the idea that mental practice leads to better performance is a hypothesis, not a theory. A theory might explain that mental practice works because the brain activity that allows you to perform an action is also induced when you practice mentally, and thus after mental practice, the appropriate processes are more efficient when you later engage in the actual behavior. Hypotheses and theories both produce **predictions**, expectations about specific events that should occur in particular circumstances if the hypothesis or theory is correct.

Finally, what do we mean by "testing the theory"? A theory is only a tentative answer; it must be tested. The theory of mental practice predicts that the parts of the brain used to produce a behavior—in our example, swinging a golf club—are activated by merely imagining the behavior. This prediction has also been tested by using new brain-scanning techniques to observe what happens in the brain when an individual imagines moving. And, in fact, parts of the brain used in controlling actual movements have been found to be activated when the movements are only imagined (Jeannerod, 1994, 1995; Kosslyn et al., 1998; Parsons, 1987, 1994; Parsons & Fox, 1998). Each time a theory makes a correct prediction, the theory is supported, and each time it fails to make a correct prediction, the theory is weakened. If enough of its predictions are unsupported, the theory must be rejected and the data explained in some other way. A good theory is *falsifiable*; that is, it makes predictions it cannot "squirm out of." A falsifiable theory can be rejected if the predictions are not confirmed.

Having examined all the steps of the scientific method, you can now use it to evaluate a claim. Say you've heard that putting a crystal under your bed will focus cosmic energies and improve your athletic ability. Should you believe this? First, you specify the problem, phrasing it as a question: Can crystals under beds improve performance? Second, you systematically observe events: Perhaps you notice that on days after the members of a golf team place crystals under their beds, they do perform better. Third, from those data you form a hypothesis: Something about the crystals themselves, not the beliefs of the players who use them or any other factors, is responsible for the improvement. Fourth, you test the hypothesis: Before some of Tiger Woods's games, you sneak a crystal under his bed, making sure he never knows when it is there and when it isn't; then you observe whether he plays better on post-crystal days. Fifth, if the hypothesis is supported and Woods *does* play a better game on days after a crystal was under his bed, you would need a theory to explain how the crystal works (for example,

Hypothesis: A tentative idea that might explain a set of observations.

Variable: An aspect of a situation that can vary, or change.

Theory: A statement of a set of underlying principles that are supposed to explain a set of observations.

Prediction: Expectation about specific events that should occur in particular circumstances if a theory or hypothesis is correct.

Would putting a crystal under your bed improve your ability to dance? The scientific method will let you find out.

Independent variable: The aspect of the experimental situation that is intentionally varied.

Dependent variable: The aspect of the experimental situation that is measured as an independent variable is changed; the value of the dependent variable *depends on* the value of the independent variable.

Effect: The difference in the dependent variable that is due to changes in the independent variable.

you might hypothesize that it somehow alters the magnetic field of the earth). Finally, you would test the theory: You might put the crystal in a magnetically shielded box and see whether the crystal still raises Tiger's level of play.

The Psychologist's Toolbox: Techniques of Scientific Research

Although all sound investigations rely on the scientific method, the different areas of psychology often pose and answer questions differently. Psychologists use a variety of research tools, each with its own advantages and disadvantages.

EXPERIMENTAL DESIGN. Much psychological research relies on conducting experiments, controlled situations in which variables are manipulated. The variables in a situation—for example, "time spent in mental practice" and "change in golf score"—are the aspects of a situation that can vary. The experimenter deliberately alters one aspect of a situation, which is called the **independent variable,** and measures another, called the **dependent variable.** In other words, the value of the dependent variable *depends on* the value of the independent variable (see Figure 1.3). In our mental practice/golf improvement example, the amount of time participants in the experiment spent in mental practice was the independent variable (it was deliberately varied), and the golf score was the dependent variable (it was measured). By examining the link between independent and dependent variables, a researcher hopes to discover exactly which factor is causing an **effect,** the difference in the dependent

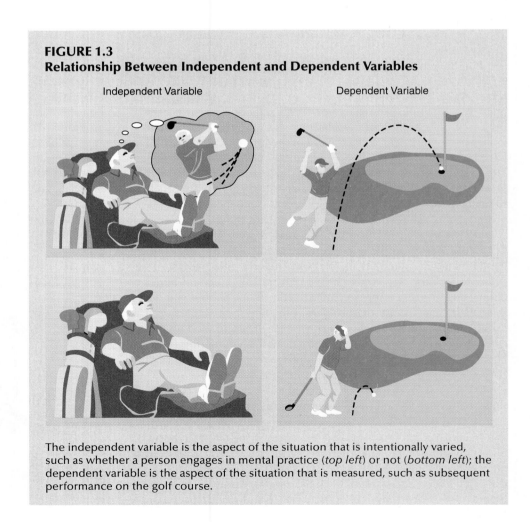

FIGURE 1.3
Relationship Between Independent and Dependent Variables

Independent Variable   Dependent Variable

The independent variable is the aspect of the situation that is intentionally varied, such as whether a person engages in mental practice (*top left*) or not (*bottom left*); the dependent variable is the aspect of the situation that is measured, such as subsequent performance on the golf course.

28   CHAPTER 1   THE SCIENCE OF PSYCHOLOGY: YESTERDAY AND TODAY

variable that results from a change in the independent variable. In our golf example, the effect is the degree of improvement from the first assessment of performance (before mental practice) to the second assessment (after mental practice).

Once researchers have found a relation between two variables, they need to test that relation to rule out other possible explanations for it. Say we had tested only one group, the one that used mental practice. The fact that these players improved would not necessarily show that mental practice works. Why? Perhaps simply practicing during the first test session (before the mental practice) is enough to cause an improvement by the second test session. Or perhaps people are simply more relaxed at the time of the second test session, and that is why they perform better. **Confounds,** or **confounding variables,** are other possible aspects of the situation that have become entangled with the aspects that you have chosen to vary. Confounds thus lead to results that are ambiguous, that do not have a clear-cut interpretation.

One way to disentangle confounds is to use a **control group.** A control group is a second group that is treated identically in the course of the experiment *except* with regard to the one variable you want to study. A good control group holds constant—or controls—all the variables in the experimental group except the one of interest. In the mental practice experiments, the experimental group does mental practice; the control group does not. If the kinds of people assigned to the two groups differ markedly, say, in age, gender, or previous athletic experience (or all three), those factors could be confounds that would mask a clear reading of the experiment's results, because any difference in the group's golf play could have been caused by those elements. In a properly conducted experiment, therefore, participants are assigned *randomly,* that is, by chance, to the experimental and the control groups, so that no biases can sneak into the composition of the groups.

Similarly, you can use a **control condition,** either for a single person or for a group of people. Instead of testing a separate control group, you test the same group another time, keeping everything the same as in the experimental condition except for the single independent variable of interest. You are using a control condition when on some nights you *don't* put a crystal under Tiger Woods's bed. To avoid confounding the order of testing with the condition (experimental versus control), you would test half the people in the control condition first and half in the experimental condition first, or would carefully balance the order of conditions for a single person.

A particularly dramatic example of a confounding variable in everyday life was present during the Victorian age. At this time in history, some women were considered frail and delicate creatures, at least partly because they seemed prone to fainting spells. Did they faint because of their "inner natures" or for some other reason? Consider the fact that many of these women wore extremely tight corsets to give them tiny waists. In fact, the corsets were so tight that women could only take shallow breaths—if they took a deep breath, they ran the risk of being stabbed by the whale bone "stays" in the corset. These stays were thin and very sharp, and not only could cause a bloody wound, but also could puncture a lung! One consequence of continued shallow breathing is dizziness—hence the fainting spells common among stylish Victorian women. These fainting spells were viewed as evidence of a weak nature and frail constitution. How could you design an experiment to show conclusively that the corsets were to blame? How do you think views of women would have been different if men had worn tight corsets too?

During Victorian times, some women were considered frail and delicate. However, there were confounding variables, such as the fact that their corsets were so tight, they couldn't take a deep breath.

Quasi-Experimental Design. One element of a true experiment is that the assignment of participants to the different groups is random. But in the real world, it is not always possible to achieve randomness, and so sometimes designs must be *quasi-experimental* (*quasi* means "as if" in Latin). Say you want to discover whether the effects of mental practice are different for people of different ages, so you decide to test four groups of people: teenagers, college students, middle-aged people, and the elderly. Obviously you cannot assign people to the different age groups randomly. You should

Confound (or confounding variable): Independent variable that varies along with the one of interest and could affect what is measured.

Control group: A group that is treated exactly the same way as the experimental group, except for the one aspect of the situation under study—the independent variable—and so holds constant, or controls, all of the other variables.

Control condition: Like a control group, but administered to the same participants who receive the experimental condition.

control for as many variables (such as health and education level) as you can in order to make the groups as similar as possible; however, the real world does not always cooperate, and it may be necessary to use special statistical techniques after you have established the groups to remove the effects of potential confounds. Similarly, if you want to track changes over time (for example, the happiness of single mothers as their children grow older), it is not possible to assign people randomly to the groups as time goes by because you are taking measurements only from people you have measured before. In all these examples, participants are not assigned randomly to groups, and such quasi-experiments rely on comparing multiple groups or multiple sets of measurements taken over time, attempting to eliminate potential confounds as much as possible.

CORRELATIONAL RESEARCH. Experiments and quasi-experiments allow researchers to zero in on exactly what variables cause what effects. But sometimes it is not possible to do an experiment or even a quasi-experiment, particularly if you are interested in studying large groups or if it is difficult (or unethical) to manipulate the variables. Let's say you want to answer this question: Does intelligence increase with body size? Not only is there a problem in assigning randomly to groups people who have different levels of intelligence, but it is also unethical to manipulate a person's body size. For a question like this, not even a quasi-experiment can be performed.

In such situations, researchers use another method to study the relations among variables, a method that relies on the idea of **correlation.** Correlation is a relationship in which changes in the measurements of one variable are matched by changes in the measurements of another variable. Thus, a correlation is an index of how closely related two measured variables are. Figure 1.4 illustrates three predicted correlations between variables. The more tightly the numbers cluster around the line, the higher the correlation. A *positive correlation* means that the values of one variable increase as the values of another variable increase. Conversely, a *negative correlation* means that the values of one variable increase as the values of another decrease. If we had plotted "sickness" instead of "health" in the middle panel, the line would have gone down—and the correlation we plotted would have been −.4 instead of +.4.

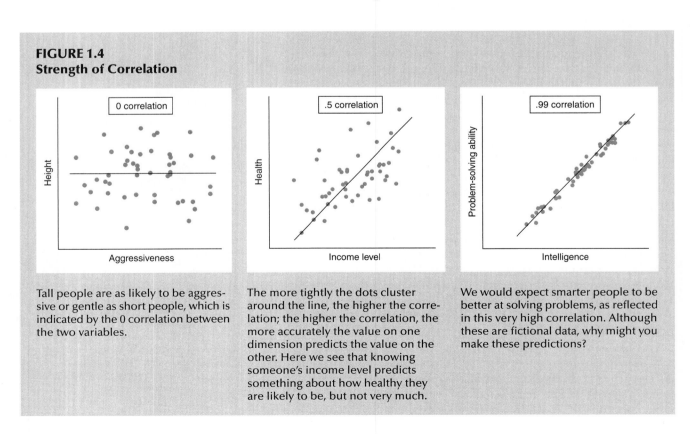

FIGURE 1.4
Strength of Correlation

Tall people are as likely to be aggressive or gentle as short people, which is indicated by the 0 correlation between the two variables.

The more tightly the dots cluster around the line, the higher the correlation; the higher the correlation, the more accurately the value on one dimension predicts the value on the other. Here we see that knowing someone's income level predicts something about how healthy they are likely to be, but not very much.

We would expect smarter people to be better at solving problems, as reflected in this very high correlation. Although these are fictional data, why might you make these predictions?

Correlational research involves measuring at least two things about each of a set of individuals or groups (or measuring the same individuals or groups at a number of different times), and looking at the way one set of measurements goes up or down in tandem with another set of measurements; correlations always compare one pair of measures at a time. For example, researchers have found that the lower the level of a chemical called monoamine oxidase (MAO) in the blood, the more the person will tend to seek thrills (such as sky diving and bungee jumping) (Zuckerman, 1995). Thus there is a negative correlation between the two measures: as MAO levels go down, thrill seeking goes up.

The main advantage of correlational research is that it allows researchers to compare variables that cannot be manipulated directly. The main disadvantage is that correlations indicate only that two variables tend to vary together, not that one causes the other. Does the correlation between MAO levels and thrill seeking mean that a low level of MAO *causes* the behavior? No. We don't know whether MAO level causes the behavior or vice versa—or if some other chemical, personality trait, or social factor causes the levels of both MAO and thrill seeking to vary. Remember: *Correlation does not equal causation.* Nevertheless, the existence of correlations does allow us to make predictions.

NATURALISTIC OBSERVATION. Essential to the scientific method is careful observation, and some researchers specialize in collecting data from real-world settings. As we noted earlier, observation—usually—precedes the formulation of a testable hypothesis; in fact, a set of careful observations often suggests a hypothesis. Some comparative psychologists use this method to study animal behavior in the wild and, say, consider to what degree it resembles human behavior; developmental psychologists use observation to study children interacting with caregivers; social psychologists use it to study people in shopping malls. This work is not simply the collecting of impressions, but of specific documented observations that can be repeated by others. For example, researchers observing caregivers found that they change their language and speech patterns when talking to young children, using short sentences and speaking in a high pitch. This speech modification, originally dubbed "motherese," is now often called *child-directed speech* (Morgan & Demuth, 1996; Snow, 1991, 1999).

Although naturalistic observation is an essential part of science, it does not provide explanations. You cannot control for confounded variables, and you cannot change the variables to see what the critical factor in a particular mental process or behavior might be. The discovery of motherese does not tell us whether caregivers use it in order to help children understand them, or to entertain them, or simply to imitate other caregivers they have heard. In science, observing an event is only the first step.

CASE STUDIES. Sometimes nature performs unique experiments that change an independent variable in a novel way. For example, accidents can cause damage to specific parts of the brain that affects the victim's thoughts, feelings, or behavior; depending on which part of the brain has been damaged, different abnormalities occur. A **case study** focuses on a single instance of a situation, examining it in detail. Many neuropsychologists study individual brain-damaged patients in depth to discover which abilities are "knocked out" following certain types of damage (in Chapter 2 you will read about a young soldier who, after suffering brain injury, had bizarre visual impairments). A psychologist who studies abnormal behavior might study a reported case of multiple personalities to discover whether there's anything to the idea (books such as *Sybil* and *The Three Faces of Eve* describe such cases in great detail), and a cognitive psychologist may investigate how an unusually gifted memory expert is able to retain huge amounts of information almost perfectly.

Unlike naturalistic observation, case studies permit experimentation (such as testing the ability of the memory expert to recall lists of familiar versus unfamiliar things, or to remember words versus pictures) and can help us understand the particular situation in detail. Nevertheless, as with other forms of research, we must always be cautious about *generalizing* from the one case; that is, we must be careful in assuming

Case study: A scientific study that examines a single instance of a situation in detail.

that the findings in the case study extend to all other similar cases. Any particular person may be unusual for many reasons and so may not be at all representative of people in general.

SURVEYS. A **survey** is a search for information, usually in the form of a set of questions put to the participants about their beliefs, attitudes, preferences, or activities. Surveys are a relatively inexpensive way to collect a lot of data fairly quickly, and they are popular among psychologists who study personality and social interactions. Surveys provide data that can be used to formulate or test a hypothesis. However, as with introspection, the value of surveys is limited by what people are capable of reporting accurately. You would not use a survey to ask people how their brains work, or to report subtle behaviors, such as body language, that they may engage in unconsciously. Moreover, even if they are capable of answering, people may not always respond honestly; as we note in Chapter 9, this is especially a problem when the survey touches on sensitive personal issues, such as sex. And even if people do respond honestly, what they say does not always reflect what they do. We cite a classic example in Chapter 15 in which restaurant managers were asked whether they would serve Chinese people; although most said they would not, when Chinese people had actually come to their restaurants, virtually all served them without question (La Piere, 1934). Finally, not everyone who is asked to respond does in fact fill in the survey. Because a particular factor (such as income or age) may incline some people, but not others, to respond, it is difficult to know if you are justified in generalizing from the respondents to the rest of the group of interest.

Survey questions have to be carefully worded so that they don't lead the respondent to answer in a certain way and yet still get at the data of interest. In the survey mentioned earlier in which the respondents had to decide which was worse, a mate having sex with or becoming emotionally involved with someone else, people who disliked both possibilities equally had no way to say so, and the forced choice would not reflect their true position. Similarly, the nature of the response scale affects what people say. In one survey, patients rating their symptoms were given a scale that ranged from "twice a month or less" to "several times a day," which provides "room" to indicate high rates of occurrence. With this scale, 62% said that they had symptoms more than twice a month. But when the scale was changed to range from "never" to "more than twice a month," which emphasizes the lower ranges of occurrence, only 39% said that they had symptoms more than twice a month (Schwarz & Scheuring, 1992, as cited in Schwarz, 1999). And even the order in which questions are asked can affect how people respond to any given question (Schwarz, 1999).

In short, when you see the results of a survey in the news, ask yourself whether people are capable of reporting what they think about the topic, whether they would be likely to report honestly, whether their opinions are likely to predict their behavior, whether the sample was representative of the group of interest, and whether the wording invited particular responses—if so, none of the other variables matters.

META-ANALYSIS. Science is a community effort. Usually many people are conducting studies on the same problem, each one painting additional strokes onto an emerging picture. **Meta-analysis** is a technique that allows researchers to combine results from different studies. This is particularly useful when results have been mixed, with some studies showing an effect and some not. Meta-analysis can determine whether a relationship exists among variables that transcends any one study, a strand that cuts across the entire set of findings.

Sometimes results that are not evident in any individual study become obvious in a meta-analysis. Why? Studies almost always involve observing or testing a **sample** from the **population**; the sample is the group that is measured or observed, and the population is the entire set of relevant people or animals (perhaps defined in terms of age, gender, race). The crucial fact is that there is always variation in the population. Just as people vary in height and weight, they also vary in their behavioral tendencies, cognitive abilities, and personality characteristics. Thus, samples taken from the population

Survey: A set of questions, typically about beliefs, attitudes, preferences, or activities.

Meta-analysis: A technique that combines the results from different studies to discover patterns in the data.

Sample: The group from which a researcher obtains measures or observations.

Population: The entire set of relevant people or animals.

TABLE 1.3

Summary of Research Methods

Experimental design	Participants are assigned randomly to groups, and the effects of manipulating one or more independent variables on a dependent variable are studied.
Quasi-experimental design	Experiments in which participants are not assigned to groups randomly.
Correlational research	Relations among different variables are documented, but causation cannot be inferred.
Naturalistic observation	Observed events are carefully documented.
Case study	A single instance of a situation is analyzed in depth.
Survey	Investigation requires participants to answer specific questions.
Meta-analysis	The results of many studies are combined in a single overall analysis to discover underlying general patterns in the data.

will vary, and if a sample is relatively small, the luck of the draw could obscure an overall difference that actually exists in the population. For example, if you stopped the first two males and first two females you saw in a shopping mall and measured their heights, the females might actually be taller than the males. The problem of variation in samples is particularly severe when the difference of interest—the effect—is not great. If men averaged 8 feet tall and women 4 feet tall, small samples would not be a problem; you would quickly figure out the usual height difference between men and women. But if men averaged 5 feet 10 inches and women averaged 5 feet 9 inches, you would need to measure many men and women before you were assured of finding the difference. Meta-analysis is a way of combining the samples from many studies, giving you the ability to detect even subtle differences or relations among variables (Rosenthal, 1991). Table 1.3 summarizes the major methods used by psychologists.

Be a Critical Consumer of Psychology

No technique is always used perfectly, so you must be a critical consumer of all science, including the science of psychology. Metaphorically speaking, there are no good psychologists on salt-free diets—we take everything with at least a grain of salt! Whenever you read a report of a psychological finding in a newspaper, a journal article, or a book (including this one), look for aspects of the study that could lead to alternative explanations. You already know about the possibility of confounds; here are a few other issues that can cloud the interpretation of experiments.

RELIABILITY: COUNT ON IT! Not all data are created equal; some are better than others. One way to evaluate data is in terms of **reliability**. Reliability means consistency. A reliable car is one you can count on to behave consistently in the same way, starting even on cold mornings and not dropping random parts on the highway. A reliable study is one that can be replicated, that is, repeated with the same results. When you read a result, find out if it has been replicated; if it has, then you can have greater confidence that the findings are reliable.

VALIDITY: WHAT DOES IT REALLY MEAN? Something is said to be *valid* if it is well grounded in the facts, if its claims are justifiable. A study may be reliable but not valid. **Validity** means that a study provides a true measure of what it is *meant* to measure.

To understand the concept of validity, it is useful to see what it is like to be a participant in a study. So, before reading further, try this exercise. Table 1.4 on page 34 contains a list of words. Decide whether the first word names a living object or a nonliving one (circle the word "living" at the right if it is living; otherwise move to the next word); then decide whether the second word begins with the letter *t* (circle the words "begins

Reliability: A study is reliable if it yields the same results when repeated.

Validity: A measure is valid if it does in fact measure what it is supposed to measure.

with *t*" if it does; otherwise move to the next word); then decide whether the third word names a living or a nonliving object, whether the fourth word begins with the letter *t*, and so on, alternating judgments as you go down the list. Please do this now.

<table>
<tr><td>TABLE 1.4</td><td colspan="5">What's in a Word?</td></tr>
<tr><td></td><td colspan="5">Circle the word on the right if the word on the left has the named property; otherwise, move on to the next word. After you finish the list, read on.</td></tr>
<tr><td></td><td>salmon</td><td>living</td><td>trout</td><td>living</td></tr>
<tr><td></td><td>tortoise</td><td>begins with t</td><td>donkey</td><td>begins with t</td></tr>
<tr><td></td><td>airplane</td><td>living</td><td>teapot</td><td>living</td></tr>
<tr><td></td><td>toad</td><td>begins with t</td><td>house</td><td>begins with t</td></tr>
<tr><td></td><td>guitar</td><td>living</td><td>table</td><td>living</td></tr>
<tr><td></td><td>goat</td><td>begins with t</td><td>terrain</td><td>begins with t</td></tr>
<tr><td></td><td>timber</td><td>living</td><td>tiger</td><td>living</td></tr>
<tr><td></td><td>automobile</td><td>begins with t</td><td>rosebush</td><td>begins with t</td></tr>
<tr><td></td><td>snake</td><td>living</td><td>bacteria</td><td>living</td></tr>
<tr><td></td><td>tent</td><td>begins with t</td><td>carpet</td><td>begins with t</td></tr>
<tr><td></td><td>toast</td><td>living</td><td>staple</td><td>living</td></tr>
<tr><td></td><td>television</td><td>begins with t</td><td>tricycle</td><td>begins with t</td></tr>
<tr><td></td><td>wagon</td><td>living</td><td>lawn</td><td>living</td></tr>
<tr><td></td><td>tarantula</td><td>begins with t</td><td>ocean</td><td>begins with t</td></tr>
<tr><td></td><td>toadstool</td><td>living</td><td>tuna</td><td>living</td></tr>
<tr><td></td><td>elephant</td><td>begins with t</td><td>terrier</td><td>begins with t</td></tr>
</table>

When you have finished marking the list, take out a piece of paper and (without looking!) write down as many of the words as you can. How many words from the list were you able to remember?

The standard result from this kind of study is that people will remember more words after making a living/nonliving judgment than after making a *t*/non-*t* judgment (for example, see Craik & Tulving, 1975). This result is usually interpreted to mean that the more we think about (or "process") the material, as we must in order to make the living/nonliving decision, the better we remember it; for the *t* words, we only need think of the sound of the letter, not about the named object at all. In fact, if we are forced to think about something in detail but don't consciously try to learn it, we end up remembering it about as well as if we *did* try to learn it (we discuss this curiosity more in Chapter 6).

Does this demonstration of differences in memory following differences in judgment really bear out this interpretation? What if you remembered the words you judged as living/nonliving better because you had to read the whole word to make the required judgment, but you only looked at the first letter of the other words to decide whether they began with *t*? If this were the case, your better memory of words in the living/nonliving category would have nothing to do with "thinking about it more." Therefore, the experiment would not be valid—it would not be measuring what the investigator designed it to measure.

When you read a result, always try to think of as many interpretations for it as you can; you may be surprised at how easy this can be. And if you can think of an alternative interpretation, see whether you can think of a control group or condition that would allow you to tell who was right, you or the author of the study.

BIAS: PLAYING WITH LOADED DICE. Sometimes beliefs, expectations, or habits alter how participants in a study respond or affect how a researcher sets up or conducts a study, thus influencing its outcome. This leaning toward a particular result, whether conscious or unconscious, is called **bias,** and it can take many forms. One form of bias is **response bias,** in which people have a tendency to respond in a particular way regardless of their actual knowledge or beliefs. For example, many people tend to say yes more than no, particularly in some Asian cultures (such as Japanese). This sort of bias toward responding in "acceptable" ways is a devilish problem for survey research. Another form of bias is **sampling bias,** which occurs when the participants or items are not chosen at random but instead are selected so that an attribute is over- or underrepresented. Back to the shopping mall: What if you measured the males outside a toy store (and so were likely to be measuring little boys), but measured the women outside a fashion outlet for tall people (and so were likely to find especially tall women)? Or, what if the words in the living/nonliving group in Table 1.4 were interesting words such as *centipede* and *boomerang* and the words in the *t*/non-*t* group were bland words such as *toe* and *broom*? Or, perhaps the living/nonliving words were more emotionally charged than the *t*/non-*t* words, or were more familiar. What if only language majors were tested, or only people who read a lot and have terrific vocabularies? Could we assume that all people would respond the same way? Take another look at Table 1.4; can you spot any potential confounds?

Possibly the most famous example of sampling bias occurred in the 1948 U.S. presidential election, between Harry Truman and Thomas Dewey. From the responses in telephone interviews, the Chicago *Tribune* concluded on election night that Dewey had won and ran a headline to that effect that appeared the next morning—much to President-elect Truman's glee. What had happened? Sampling bias. Dewey was a Republican, and in those days more Republicans than Democrats had telephones. The biased survey sample led to the wrong conclusion.

EXPERIMENTER EXPECTANCY EFFECTS: "MAKING IT HAPPEN." Clever Hans, a horse that lived in Germany in the early 1890s, apparently could add (Rosenthal, 1976). When a questioner (one of several) called out two numbers to add, say, "6 plus 4," Hans would tap out the correct answer with his hoof. Was Hans a genius horse? Was he psychic? No. Despite appearances, Hans wasn't really adding. He *seemed* to be able to add, and even to spell out words (with one additional tap for each letter in the alphabet), but he responded only if his questioner stood in his line of sight and knew the answer. The questioner, who *expected* Hans to begin tapping, always looked at Hans's feet right after asking the question—thereby cuing Hans to start tapping. When Hans had tapped out the right number, the questioner always looked up—cuing Hans to stop tapping. Although in fact Hans could neither add nor spell, he was a pretty bright horse: He was not trained to do this; he "figured it out" on his own.

The cues offered by Hans's questioners were completely unintentional; they had no wish to mislead (and in fact some of them were probably doubters). But unintentional cues such as these lead to **experimenter expectancy effects,** which occur when an investigator's expectations lead him or her (consciously or unconsciously) to treat participants in a way that encourages them to produce the expected results.

A good experiment uses a **double blind design.** Not only is the participant "blind" to (unaware of) the predictions of the study and so unable consciously or unconsciously to serve up the expected results, but also the experimenter is "blind" to the condition assigned to the participant and thus unable to induce the expected results. What would have happened if a questioner of Clever Hans had not known the answer to the question?

PSYCHOLOGY AND PSEUDOPSYCHOLOGY: WHAT'S FLAKY AND WHAT ISN'T? Are you a fire sign? Do you believe your Zodiac sign matters? So many people apparently do that the opening page for the Excite! search engine on the World Wide Web provides your horoscope every day. But astrology, along with palm reading and tea-leaf reading and all their relatives, is not a branch of psychology; it is **pseudopsychology.**

Bias: Occurs when previous beliefs, expectations, or habits alter the participants' responses or affect the design or conduct of a study.

Response bias: A tendency to respond in a particular way regardless of knowledge or beliefs relevant to performing the task correctly.

Sampling bias: Occurs when the participants or items are not chosen at random, so that an attribute is over- or underrepresented.

Experimenter expectancy effects: Occurs when an investigator's expectations lead him or her (consciously or unconsciously) to treat participants in a way that induces the expected results.

Double blind design: An experimental procedure in which the participant is "blind" to (unaware of) the predictions of the study (and so cannot try, consciously or unconsciously, to produce the predicted results), and the experimenter is "blind" to the condition assigned to the participant (and so cannot induce the predicted results).

Pseudopsychology: Theories or statements that look like psychology but are in fact superstition or unsupported opinion pretending to be science.

Pseudopsychology is not just "bad psychology," which rests on poorly documented observations or badly designed studies and thus has questionable foundations. Pseudopsychology is not psychology at all. It may look and sound like psychology, but it is superstition or unsupported opinion pretending to be science.

Some people claim to have supernormal "psychic" powers, such as the ability to read minds. These claims can be treated as hypotheses, but until they are supported by clear-cut research results, they cannot be regarded as psychology.

But appearances can be misleading. Consider extrasensory perception (ESP). Is this pseudopsychology? ESP refers to a collection of mental abilities that do not rely on the ordinary senses or abilities. Telepathy, for instance, is the ability to read minds. This sounds not only wonderful but magical. No wonder people are fascinated by the possibility that they, too, may have latent, untapped, extraordinary abilities. The evidence that such abilities really exist is shaky, as discussed in Chapter 3. But the mere fact that many experiments on ESP have come up empty does not mean that the experiments themselves are bad or "unscientific." One can conduct a perfectly good experiment, guarding against confounds, bias, and expectancy effects, even on ESP. Such research is not pseudopsychology.

Let's say you want to study telepathy. You might arrange to test pairs of participants, with one member of each pair acting as "sender" and the other as "receiver." The sender and receiver both would look at hands of playing cards that contained the same four cards. The sender would focus on one card (say, an ace), and would "send" the receiver a mental image of the chosen card. The receiver's job would be to guess which card the sender is seeing. By chance alone, with only four cards to choose from, the receiver would guess right about 25% of the time. So the question is, can the receiver do *better* than mere guesswork? In this study, you would measure the percentage of times the receiver picks the right card, and compare this to what you would expect from guessing alone.

But wait! What if the sender, like the questioners of Clever Hans, provided visible cues (accidentally or on purpose) which have nothing to do with ESP, perhaps smiling when "sending" an ace, grimacing when "sending" a two. A better experiment would have sender and receiver in different rooms, thus controlling for such possible confounds. Furthermore, what if people have an unconscious bias to prefer red over black cards, which leads both sender and receiver to select them more often than would be dictated by chance? This difficulty can be countered by including a control condition, in which a receiver guesses cards when the sender is not actually sending. Such guesses will reveal response biases (such as a preference for red cards), which exist independently of messages sent via ESP.

Whether ESP can be considered a valid, reliable phenomenon will depend on the results of such studies. If they conclusively show that there is nothing to it, then people who claim to have ESP or to understand it will be trying to sell a bill of goods—and engaging in pseudopsychology. But as long as proper studies are under way, we cannot dismiss it as pseudopsychology.

LOOKING AT LEVELS

Who Catches Colds?

Mental processes obviously affect the body: Not only can we move if we decide to, but if we imagine something upsetting or threatening, our palms will begin to sweat (Hugdahl, 1995b). Many people believe that mental processes also affect physical health. How could we study this idea rigorously?

One way of investigating the problem depends on knowing who in a group has been exposed to a cold virus, and Cohen and his collaborators found a way to do just that (Cohen et al., 1991). To set up their independent variable, they asked volunteers to squirt into their nostrils a spray that did or did not contain a cold virus (all participants, who were randomly assigned to one of two groups, were warned that there might be a cold virus in their sprays). Half the participants got the "live" spray;

this was the experimental group. The other half had no cold virus in their sprays; this was the control group. To guard against expectancy effects, each participant was blind to the treatment he or she received.

So far this sounds like a true experiment, with participants being assigned randomly to conditions that were defined by manipulating an independent variable (virus versus no virus). However, the researchers also assessed the values of many other independent variables, which varied naturally over the groups of participants. For example, they measured whether the people often felt guilty and whether they had frequent interactions with other people. When these other variables were considered, the assignment of subjects to conditions was in fact not random, and the study was therefore a quasi-experiment.

These researchers looked for factors that were correlated with characteristics of those in the experimental group who caught a cold (only a few in the control group caught colds, through "natural" causes). They found that the more stress (a variable that has effects at the level of the brain) a participant reported before exposure to the cold virus, the more likely he or she was to catch a cold after receiving the virus. They also looked closely at different causes of stress. The causes that best predicted whether somebody would get a cold were (1) how uncontrollable and unpredictable they rated their lives to be (a condition defined by socially created events, at the level of the group) and (2) how likely they were to experience negative feelings such as guilt, anger, or being upset (events that usually occurred because of their desires and beliefs, at the level of the person) (Cohen et al., 1993). A key fact about stress is that the actual event itself isn't as important as how we *interpret*, and what we *believe* about, the situation (an event at the level of the person); that is, what is stressful to one person may be invigorating, or even boring, to another (discussed further in Chapter 12). But this was not all there was to it. People who interacted with many kinds of people (level of the group)—friends, neighbors, relatives, colleagues, fellow members of social or religious organizations—were half as likely to catch a cold as those who were socially isolated (Cohen, Doyle et al., 1997). Social isolation is as strong a risk factor for catching colds as are smoking, stress, and vitamin C deficiency.

Thus, your immune system (which is controlled by your brain, as we explain in the next chapter) is affected not only by your perceptions of stress, but also by the availability of other people in your life. The interactions go in both directions. If you are sick all the time, you will have different social interactions than if you are not sick. And if you have social support, your perceptions of stress may change—people can help you enjoy the rigors of a freezing winter, for example, by giving you something to look forward to (say, snowboarding or a sleigh ride). So even something as basic as whether a virus causes you to catch cold can be understood well only if scientific research considers events at the three different levels and how they interact.

CONSOLIDATE!

▶ 1. *What is the scientific method?* The scientific method is a way to gain objective knowledge that involves specifying a problem; systematically observing events; forming a hypothesis of the relation between variables; collecting new observations to test the hypothesis; using such evidence to formulate and support a theory; and finally, testing the theory.

▶ 2. *What research tools can psychologists use to study mental processes and behavior scientifically?* Psychologists use experimental designs, assigning participants randomly to groups and studying the

effects of one or more independent variables on a dependent variable; quasi-experimental designs, similar to experimental designs except that participants are not randomly assigned to groups; correlational research, in which the relations among different variables are documented but causation cannot be inferred; naturalistic observation, involving careful documentation of events; case studies, detailed analyses of a single instance of a situation; surveys, in which participants are asked sets of specific questions; and meta-analysis, a consideration of the results of many studies in a single overall analysis.

(continued)

CONSOLIDATE! *continued*

▶ 3. *What should you look for when deciding whether to accept a study's conclusions?* The measures taken must be reliable (repeatable), valid (assess what they are supposed to), unbiased, free of experimental ex-pectancy effects (leading participants to respond in specific ways), well designed (eliminating confounds and having appropriate controls), and properly inter-preted (alternative accounts are ruled out).

ETHICS: DOING IT RIGHT

Let's say that Tiger Woods wants to learn how to overcome pain so that he can practice hard even when he is hurt, but that practicing when injured might cause long-term damage to his body. Would it be ethical for a sport psychologist to teach Tiger—or anyone else—techniques for continuing to work out through damaging pain? Or, what if Tiger developed a "block" that impaired his playing. Would it be ethical for a therapist to treat him with new, unproven techniques?

▶ 1. What are proper ethics in research with humans and animals?

▶ 2. What are proper ethics in clinical practice?

Ethics in Research

Following World War II, people were horrified to learn that the Nazis had performed ghastly experiments on human beings. The war trials in Nuremberg led directly to the first set of rules, subscribed to by many nations, outlawing these sorts of experiments.

Sometimes the actions of psychologists also call for a set of rules, especially when participants' rights conflict with a research method or clinical treatment. Certain meth-ods are obviously unethical; everybody knows not to cause people in experiments to become addicted to drugs to see how easily they can overcome the addiction, and not to beat people to help them overcome a psychological problem. But most situations are not so clear-cut.

RESEARCH WITH PEOPLE: HUMAN GUINEA PIGS? In 1996 some New York psychiatrists were tapping the spines of severely depressed teenagers at regular inter-vals in order to see if the presence of certain chemicals in the spinal fluid could predict whether particular teens would attempt suicide. As required by law, the youths' par-ents had given permission for the researchers to draw the fluids. However, this study was one of at least ten that a court in New York brought to a screeching halt on December 5, 1996 (*New York Times,* page A1). The New York State Appeals Court found that the existing rules for the treatment of children and the mentally ill were unconstitutional because they did not properly protect these participants from abuse by researchers. However, the researchers claimed that without these studies they would never be able to develop the most effective drugs for treating serious impairments, some of which might lead to suicide. Do the potential benefits of such studies outweigh the pain they cause?

New York was more lax in its policies than many other states. California, Con-necticut, Massachusetts, and Illinois do not allow researchers to conduct experi-ments in which the gain is not outweighed by the pain, or that have risks but do not benefit a participant directly, unless the participants themselves (not someone else for them) provide **informed consent.** Informed consent means that before agreeing to take part, potential participants in a study must be told what they will be asked to do and must be advised of the possible risks and benefits of the procedure. They are also told that they can withdraw from the study at any time without being penalized. Only after

Informed consent: The re-quirement that a potential par-ticipant in a study be told what he or she will be asked to do and possible risks and benefits of the study before agreeing to take part.

an individual clearly understands this information and gives consent by signature can he or she take part in a study.

Any study that uses funds from the U.S. government or from most private funding sources must be approved by an Institutional Review Board (IRB) at the university, hospital, or other institution that sponsors or hosts the study. The IRB monitors all research projects at that institution, not just those of psychologists. An IRB usually includes not only scientists but also physicians, clergy, and representatives from the local community. The IRB considers the potential risks and benefits of each research proposal and decides whether the study can be performed. In many universities and hospitals, researchers are asked to discuss their projects with the board, to explain in more detail what they are doing and why.

Concerns about the ethical treatment of human participants lead most IRBs to insist that participants be **debriefed,** that is, interviewed after the study about their experience. The purpose of debriefing is to ensure that they are having no negative reactions as a result of their participation and that they have understood the purposes of the study. Deceiving participants with false or misleading information is frowned on and approved only when the participants will not be harmed and the knowledge gained clearly outweighs the use of dishonesty.

Debriefing: An interview after a study to ensure that the participant has no negative reactions as a result of participation and understands why the study was conducted.

RESEARCH WITH ANIMALS. Animals are studied in some types of psychological research, particularly studies that focus on understanding the brain. Animals, of course, can't give informed consent, don't volunteer, and can't decide to withdraw from the study if they get nervous or uncomfortable. But this doesn't mean animals are not protected. Animal studies, like human ones, must have the stamp of approval of an IRB. The IRB makes sure the animals are housed properly (in cages that are large enough and cleaned often enough) and that they are not mistreated. Researchers are not allowed to cause animals pain unless that is explicitly what is being studied—and even then, they must justify in detail the potential benefits to humans (and possibly to animals, by advancing veterinary medicine) of inflicting pain.

In large parts of India, animals are not eaten (some are even considered sacred). Many in that culture may believe that animal research is not appropriate.

Is it ethical to test animals at all? This is not an easy question to answer. Researchers who study animals argue that their research is ethical. They point out that although there are substitutes for eating meat and wearing leather, there is no substitute for the use of animals in certain kinds of research. So if the culture allows the use of animals for food and clothing, it is not clear why animals should not be studied in laboratories if the animals do not suffer and the findings produce important knowledge. This is not a cut-and-dried issue, however, and thoughtful people disagree. As the new brain-scanning technologies improve (see Chapter 2), the need for some types of animal studies may diminish.

Ethics in Clinical Practice

Imagine a Dr. Smith who has developed a new type of therapy that she claims is particularly effective for patients who are afraid of some social situations, such as public speaking or meeting strangers. You are a therapist who has a patient struggling with such difficulties and not responding to conventional therapy. You haven't been trained in Smith therapy, but you want to help your patient. Should you try Smith therapy? According to the American Psychological Association guidelines (see Table 1.5 on page 40), the answer is clear: No. If you have not been trained appropriately or are not learning the therapy under supervision, you have no business delivering it.

This sort of ethical decision is relatively straightforward. But the process of psychotherapy sometimes requires careful stepping through emotional and ethical mine-

TABLE 1.5

General Ethical Principles of Psychologists and Code of Conduct

Source: *From APA (1992), with portions abridged and adapted; for a complete description, see http://www.apa.org/ethics/code.html.*

PRINCIPLE A: COMPETENCE

Psychologists provide only those services and use only those techniques for which they are qualified by education, training, or experience.

PRINCIPLE B: INTEGRITY

Psychologists are honest, fair, and respectful of others in the science, teaching, and practice of psychology. In describing or reporting their qualifications, services, products, fees, research, or teaching, they do not make statements that are false, misleading, or deceptive. Psychologists avoid improper and potentially harmful dual relationships (e.g., improper friendships or sexual relationships).

PRINCIPLE C: PROFESSIONAL AND SCIENTIFIC RESPONSIBILITY

Psychologists uphold professional standards of conduct, clarify their professional roles and obligations, accept appropriate responsibility for their behavior, and adapt their methods to the needs of different populations.

PRINCIPLE D: RESPECT FOR PEOPLE'S RIGHTS AND DIGNITY

Psychologists accord appropriate respect to the fundamental rights, dignity, and worth of all people. They respect the rights of individuals to privacy, confidentiality, self-determination, and autonomy; psychologists do not knowingly participate in or condone unfair discriminatory practices.

PRINCIPLE E: CONCERN FOR OTHERS' WELFARE

Psychologists seek to contribute to the welfare of those with whom they interact professionally. In their professional actions, psychologists weigh the welfare and rights of their patients or clients, students, supervisees, human research participants, and other affected persons, and the welfare of animal subjects of research.

PRINCIPLE F: SOCIAL RESPONSIBILITY

Psychologists are aware of their professional and scientific responsibilities to the community and the society in which they work and live. They apply and make public their knowledge of psychology in order to contribute to human welfare.

fields. Psychologists are bound by their states' laws of confidentiality and may not communicate about a patient without specific permission from the patient, except in certain extreme cases, as when a life or (in some states) property is at stake. Therapists have gone to jail rather than reveal personal information about their patients. Indeed, difficult cases sometimes cause new laws to be written. A patient at the University of California told a psychologist at the student health center that he wanted to kill someone and named the person. The campus police were told; they interviewed the patient and let him go. The patient then killed his target. The dead woman's parents sued the university for "failure to warn." The case eventually wound its way to California's highest court. One issue was whether the therapist had the right to divulge confidential information from therapy sessions. The court ruled that a therapist is obligated to use reasonable care to protect a potential victim. More specifically, in California (and in most other states now), if a patient has told his or her psychologist that he or she plans to harm a specific other person, and the psychologist has reason to believe the patient can and will follow through with that plan, the psychologist must take steps to protect the target person from harm, even though doing so may violate the patient's confidentiality. Similar guidelines apply to cases of potential suicide.

Further, a therapist cannot engage in sexual relations with a patient or mistreat a patient physically or emotionally. The American Psychological Association has developed many detailed ethical guidelines based on the principles listed in Table 1.5.

Gambling With a Mind

Schizophrenia is a devastating brain disease that often cripples a person's ability to function in the world. Research has found that its victims benefit greatly if medicated as soon as possible after the onset of the disease (DeQuardo, 1998; Johnstone, 1998; Wyatt et al., 1998). Given this finding, we have an ethical dilemma: When new treatments are created, how can we justify trying them when we know that delaying the treatments already *known* to be effective will cause long-term negative effects for the patient?

You've seen earlier how the levels approach helps us to understand psychological events, and now you can see that it also guides us in asking appropriate questions. Focusing on the level of the brain, you would consider how likely it is that a new drug or treatment will be better than available treatments. If a well-supported theory of brain functioning leads you to be confident that a new drug will be better than the available ones, it would be easier to justify trying it. At the level of the person, you must consider whether delaying effective treatment will change how the person can function in everyday life. If the possible changes would be drastic (for example, leading the person to lose a job), a strong note of caution should temper your deliberations. At the level of the group, you might ask how the new drug might affect the person's family. Would it make him or her more irritable? less responsive? And of course, you must think about how events at the different levels could interact: If the treatment makes the patient more irritable, how will the reactions of the family affect the sufferer? Considering such concerns, what is *your* view on this dilemma?

CONSOLIDATE!

▶ *1. What are proper ethics in research with humans and animals?* For humans, informed consent is necessary before a person can participate in a study (informed consent requires that the person appreciate the potential risks and benefits); in the vast majority of cases, studies must be approved in advance by an Institutional Review Board (IRB); participants must be debriefed after the study, to ensure that they have no negative reactions and to confirm their understanding of the purpose of the study. Animals must be treated humanely; animal studies must be approved in advance by the IRB; animals cannot be caused pain or discomfort unless that is what is being studied (and even then, researchers must justify the potential benefits to humans or animals).

▶ *2. What are proper ethics in clinical practice?* Although guidelines vary across states, in general, strict confidentiality is observed unless a specific other person may be harmed, suicide appears to be a real possibility, or (in some states) another's property may be damaged. Therapists must not take advantage of their special relationships with patients in any way.

A DEEPER LEVEL ■ ➞

Recap and Thought Questions

▶ **Psychological Science: Getting to Know You**

Psychology is the science of mental processes and behavior. The goals of psychology are to describe, explain, predict, and control mental processes and behavior. Psychology can best be understood by studying events at different levels of analysis: (1) The level of the brain, where we examine the activity of certain brain systems, structural differences in people's brains; and effects of various chemicals (such as hormones) on mental processes and behavior. (2) The level of the person, where we study the contents of mental processes, not just the machine that gives rise to them. The contents of our memories, beliefs, goals, feelings, and the like are part and parcel of who we are. (3) The level of the group—both our previous and our present social interactions. Events at the different levels are interdependent and are always interacting.

How can we think about what makes Tiger Woods special and what his exceptional abilities tell us about people in general? The best approach would consider events at the different levels of analysis. For example, at the level of the brain, we would ask if there were something special about the parts of Tiger Woods's brain that control movement. At the level of the person, we would note that he was raised to have certain goals and beliefs, and we could consider how they contributed to his current success. At the level of the group, it is clear that his relationships, particularly with his parents, were crucial factors in shaping his development. These factors affect us all.

> **Think It Through.** Can you think of any dangers in adopting a scientific understanding of psychology? Think about criminals. How would you react if it could be shown conclusively that all criminals have an abnormal structure in a certain part of their brains? If this were true, what should we do with this knowledge? Or, what if it could be shown that criminals have perfectly normal brains, but they all had weak parents who didn't give them enough discipline as kids? Neither of these single-perspective views is likely to be correct, but what if one level of analysis turns out to be more important than the others?

▶ Psychology Then and Now

Psychology began as the study of mental processes, such as those that underlie perception, memory, and reasoning. The structuralists tried to understand such processes; their goal was to identify the elements of consciousness and the rules by which these elements are combined into mental structures. One of their primary methods, introspection ("looking within"), turned out to be unreliable and not always valid. The functionalists rejected the goal of identifying mental processes and how they operated in favor of seeking explanations for thoughts, feelings, and behavior. The functionalists were interested in how mental processes adapt to help people survive in the natural world. In contrast, the Gestalt psychologists also reacted against the structuralists, but they were more disturbed by the emphasis on breaking mental processes into distinct elements. The Gestaltists studied the way the brain organizes material into overall patterns, both in perception and in thinking. All of these approaches focused primarily on events at the level of the brain. Freud and his colleagues shifted focus to events at the level of the person (and, to some extent, the level of the group). Their psychodynamic theories of the mind were concerned largely with the operation of unconscious mental processes and primitive impulses (often related to sex) in dictating what we think, feel, and do. The behaviorists rejected the assumption that psychol-

ogy should focus on mental processes; they urged us to stick with what we could see—stimuli, responses, and the consequences of responses. The humanists, in part reacting against the scientific approach, were interested in developing treatments of psychological problems that relied on respect for individuals and their potentials. Elements of the various strands came together in the cognitive revolution, which began by thinking of the mind by analogy to a computer program; in this view, mental processing is information processing. Today, cognitive neuroscientists study the relation between events at all three levels of analysis, with an emphasis on how the brain gives rise to thoughts, feelings, and behavior. Evolutionary psychology treats many goals and cognitive strategies as adaptations that are the results of natural selection.

The three types of psychologists are distinguished by their training, work settings, and types of work. Clinical and counseling psychologists administer and interpret psychological tests, provide psychotherapy, offer career and vocational counseling, and help people with specific psychological problems. Academic psychologists teach and do research, in addition to helping to run their universities, colleges, or institutions. Applied psychologists use the findings and theories of psychology to solve practical problems.

If Tiger Woods were being studied by adherents of a single psychological "school," which would be least likely to produce useful insights? most likely? When asked to account for his remarkable skill, Tiger Woods professes to have no conscious knowledge about how he plays so well. Thus, introspection would not be a useful tool for studying his abilities, and it is similarly unlikely that a structuralist approach would yield much of interest. In contrast, both behavioral (studying his responses to particular stimuli, social and physical) and cognitive (studying the way his brain processes information) approaches would be more likely to be fruitful. The quality of the results, however, would be only as good as the quality of the research designs.

> **Think It Through.** Which "school" of psychology is most interesting to you? Can you think of any ways in which combining ideas or approaches from the different schools might be helpful?
>
> If you were (or are) an athlete and began to freeze up whenever you played, what kind of psychologist would you seek? Would your choice be different if you already had a clear understanding of why you "choke"?
>
> Would the White House be a more effective place if the president had a chief psychologist? If so, which sort of psychologist would be most helpful? (Don't assume it would necessarily be a clinical psychologist.) Why?

▶ The Science of Psychology: Designed to Be Valid

The science of psychology relies on the scientific method, which involves specifying a problem; systematically observing events; forming a hypothesis of the relation between variables; collecting new observations to test the hypothesis; using such data to formulate and support a theory; and finally, testing the theory. Psychologists test hypotheses and look for relations among variables using a variety of tools, including (1) experiments, in which the effect of manipulating one or more independent variables on the value of a dependent variable is measured, and participants are assigned randomly to groups; (2) quasi-experiments, in which participants are not assigned to groups randomly; (3) correlational studies, in which the relation between pairs of variables is assessed, but shifts in one variable cannot be assumed to cause shifts in the other; (4) naturalistic observation, which involves careful observation and documentation of events; (5) case studies, which are detailed investigations of a single instance of a situation (the detailed exploration of Tiger Woods's story would be a case study); (6) surveys, in which participants answer sets of specific questions; and (7) meta-analyses, which combine the results of many studies in an attempt to discover common threads.

When reading reports of studies, you should be alert to the following: evidence that the data are reliable, which means that they can be obtained again; evidence that the data are valid, which means that they measure what they are supposed to measure; possible contamination from confounds, which are other independent variables that change along with the one of interest; biases, including a general tendency to respond in a particular way (response bias) and the nonrandom selection of participants or experimental materials (sampling bias); and experimenter expectancy effects, which are factors that convey the investigator's expectations to the participants, leading them to respond in the desired ways. In addition, the results should be appropriately interpreted—no leap of logic should be required to get from the data to the investigator's conclusions. Pseudopsychology differs from psychology not necessarily in its content, but in how it is supported by data.

What methods would be most appropriate for studying Tiger Woods? A case study is clearly appropriate, as we have presented the story of Woods that way, but many other methods could be used within that context. We could not only ask him questions about his beliefs and goals, but also compare his performance on attention and motor tasks to that of a matched control group. We could also correlate his feelings and other characteristics, such as the amount of sleep he had, or the amount of food or liquids he ingested on a given day, with his performance.

> **Think It Through.** Say that you read a report by Dr. Sales, an applied psychologist, that watching television commercials with the sound muted actually makes people remember the commercials better. What questions would you want to ask about the study before you would accept the results? Suppose this were a correlational study: The more people used their mute buttons during commercials, the better their memories. What possible confounding factors might account for this result? (Hint: Do you think people who mute the sound a lot watch the same amount of TV as people who tolerate the sound?) If you were going to write to an advertising firm and offer to design a better study (for a hefty fee, of course), what would you do to improve it?

▶ Ethics: Doing It Right

Research with humans or nonhuman animals at universities, hospitals, and most industrial settings requires approval from an Institutional Review Board (IRB). For research with humans, the IRB will insist that the study include informed consent, which is information in advance about the possible risks and benefits of participation; debriefing, which is an interview after the study to ensure that the participant had no negative reactions and did in fact understand the purpose of the study; and lack of deception, unless the deception is harmless and absolutely necessary. For research with animals, the IRB requires that the animals be treated well (for example, housed in clean cages) and that pain be inflicted only if that is what is studied and is justified by the benefits from the research. In clinical practice, psychotherapists have clear ethical guidelines to follow, which include maintaining confidentiality unless a specific other person (or, in some states, property) is clearly in danger or suicide is a genuine concern. In addition, therapists cannot use techniques that they have not been trained to use or engage in inappropriate personal behavior with patients.

Would it be ethical to study Tiger Woods as if he were some kind of guinea pig? It would not be ethical to treat him or anyone else simply as an object to be studied. Studying Tiger Woods, or anyone else, is appropriate only after informed consent has been given, and only if the participant suffers no adverse affects from participating.

> **Think It Through.** You are an academic psychologist doing research on whether sugar makes chimps more active and less able to concentrate on tasks. So far, your student who is carrying out the research has found that sugar clearly leads to increased activity and difficulty on cognitive tasks requiring concentration. A new student joins the project to help with the research, and she tells you that the animals appear to be agitated, have difficulty sleeping, and at times appear to be in pain. The study is otherwise going well. What should you do? When you write up the study for publication, how will you address this issue?
> You are a clinical psychologist who has a patient with a severe eating disorder. You've heard about a new, promising drug. What should you do? What should you not do?

2 THE BRAIN

The Psychological Organ

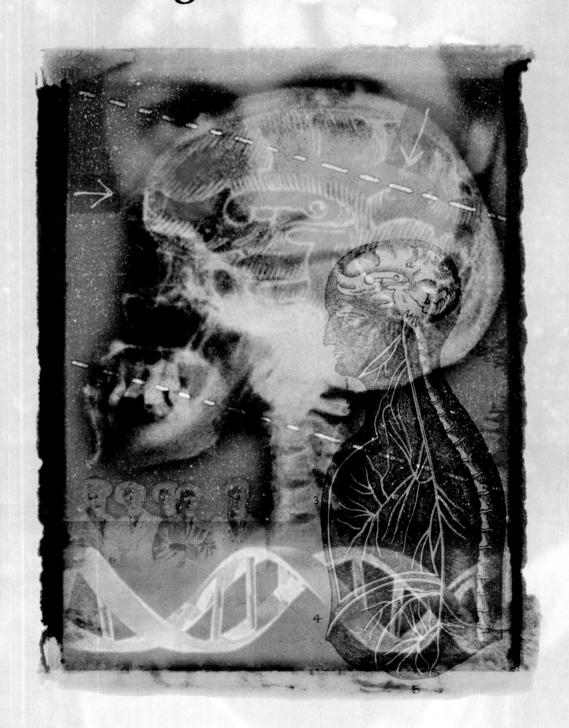

As the hard jets of water massaged the 25-year-old soldier while he showered, colorless and odorless fumes of carbon monoxide, which are known to cause brain damage, slowly seeped into the stall. Unaware that he was gradually being poisoned, the soldier continued his routine until he eventually passed out.

After the soldier was discovered and revived, doctors examined him. The young man could get around with ease, but he presented a host of bizarre symptoms. He was unable to name objects by sight, but as soon as he touched them, he could say what they were. He could identify things by smell and sound, he could name colors or identify them by pointing to a color named by someone else, and he had no difficulty recognizing familiar people when they spoke. But he couldn't identify these same people by sight alone. In fact, when he looked at his own face in the mirror, he thought he was looking at his doctor. When he was shown a rubber eraser, he identified it as "a small ball"; when shown a safety pin, he said it was "like a watch or nail clipper." When the doctors asked the soldier to inspect a picture of a nude woman and show where her eyes were, he pointed to her breasts (Benson & Greenberg, 1969).

Clearly, something was wrong with the young soldier's vision, but the problem had nothing to do with his eyes; it had to do with his brain. He couldn't get knowledge by way of his sense of sight. Why? Though he retained some aspects of his vision, he had lost others—he seemed unable to recognize what he clearly could see. The fumes the soldier had inhaled had affected his brain, but how? What, exactly, had gone wrong? To consider these questions, you need to understand how the brain works.

As you have seen, events at the level of the brain can influence many aspects of behavior, in ways not immediately apparent. If you should break your hand, you will have trouble holding a pencil: The effect of the accident is direct and mechanical. If you were in any doubt before your mishap about the role of muscle and bone in grasping and holding, you're in no doubt now, when those abilities are distinctly impaired because muscles are torn and bones fractured. But although it is a physical organ like muscle and bone, the brain is unique: It is also a *psychological* organ, ultimately responsible for our moods of despair and elation, our sense of well-being and our sense that something's wrong, our perception of the outside world and our awareness of its meaning. The effects of an accident in the brain are no less real than a broken hand, but the path to them is less obvious (and, indeed, until recently was invisible). It is this path, through a thicket of sometimes difficult names and processes, that we must trace if we are to gain a meaningful understanding of who we are and why we behave as we do.

So, how does it work, this mysterious brain? What is it made up of; what are its building blocks? Can we ever see the brain at work? How could we find out exactly which parts of the soldier's brain were damaged? Do all our brains respond the same way to the same environmental influences? Or do different people, with different genetic makeups and life experiences, respond differently? Let's start finding out.

Brain Circuits: Making Connections

The carbon monoxide fumes that the soldier breathed interfered with his brain's ability to use oxygen, causing him to pass out. Unfortunately, he inhaled enough of these fumes that some brain cells probably died; ordinarily, brain cells begin to succumb after a few minutes without oxygen. But just saying that brain cells "died" isn't much of an explanation—that would be a little like saying that a building fell down because its molecules were rearranged. Why did the death of these cells have the effects it did?

▶ 1. How do neurons work? What could cause neurons to die?

▶ 2. How do chemicals allow neurons to communicate? What happens if healthy neurons can no longer communicate?

The Neuron: A Powerful Computer

All brain activity hinges on the workings of brain cells, or **neurons.** There are three types of neurons. Some, the **sensory neurons,** respond to input from the senses; others, the **motor neurons,** send signals to muscles to control movement; finally, **interneurons** stand between the neurons that register what's out there and those that control movement (or, they stand between other interneurons). Most of the neurons in the brain are interneurons.

Neurons differ in their size, shape, and function. Some typically excite other neurons to send signals; others typically inhibit them. Some major types of neurons are

Neuron: A cell that receives signals from other neurons or sense organs, processes these signals, and sends the signals to other neurons, muscles, or bodily organs; the basic unit of the nervous system.

Sensory neuron: A neuron that responds to input from sense organs.

Motor neuron: A neuron that sends signals to muscles to control movement.

Interneuron: A neuron that is connected to other neurons, not to sense organs or muscles.

FIGURE 2.1
Examples of Types of Neurons

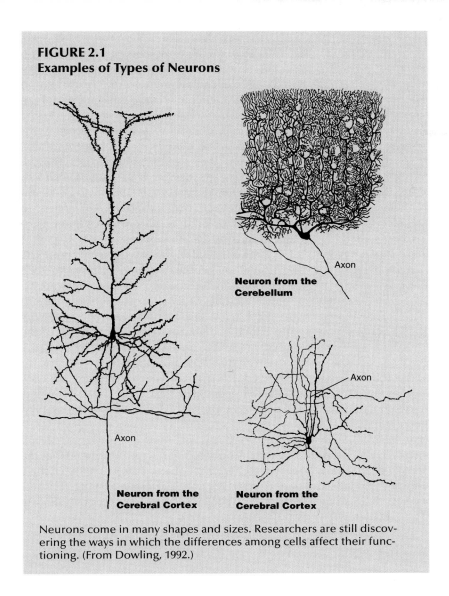

Neuron from the Cerebellum

Axon

Axon

Neuron from the Cerebral Cortex

Neuron from the Cerebral Cortex

Axon

Neurons come in many shapes and sizes. Researchers are still discovering the ways in which the differences among cells affect their functioning. (From Dowling, 1992.)

shown in Figure 2.1. Just as you can use stone to build either a hut or a palace, the same neural building blocks can build very different brains. For example, most mammals, from horses to humans, largely share the same types of neurons. But as you will see, what made Secretariat a horse and you a human is the number of neurons and how they are arranged and connected.

The average human brain contains about 100 billion neurons, plus ten times as many **glial cells** (the name comes from the Greek word for "glue"), which fill the gaps between neurons. Glial cells facilitate the communication between neurons, clean up the remains of dead neurons, and generally help in the care and feeding of neurons.

Neurons would not be much good if they did not affect other neurons or the rest of the body—how useful would your home telephone be if nobody else had one? **Brain circuits** are sets of neurons that affect one another. When one neuron in a circuit is triggered by another neuron, it in turn triggers others, and so on, causing a chain reaction. Neurons often receive and put together many inputs at the same time. The result can be the awareness that a sumptuous dessert is on the table, a command to the muscles to turn up the volume of a stereo, a sudden memory of an assignment due yesterday, a flash of feeling for an attractive classmate—anything we perceive, think, feel, or do.

Glial cell: A cell that fills the gaps between neurons, influences the communication among them, and generally helps in the care and feeding of neurons.

Brain circuit: A set of neurons that affect one another.

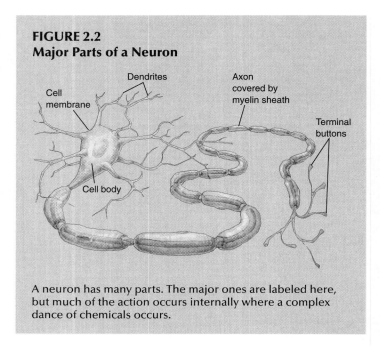

FIGURE 2.2
Major Parts of a Neuron

Dendrites

Cell
membrane

Axon
covered by
myelin sheath

Terminal
buttons

Cell body

A neuron has many parts. The major ones are labeled here, but much of the action occurs internally where a complex dance of chemicals occurs.

Cell body: The middle part of a cell, which contains the nucleus.

Cell membrane: The skin of a cell.

Channel: A small hole in the outer skin of cells that can open and close.

Axon: The sending end of the neuron, or the long cable extending from the cell body.

Terminal button: A structure at the end of axons that, when the neuron is triggered, releases chemicals into the space between neurons.

Dendrite: The twiggy part of a neuron that receives messages from the axons of other neurons.

Ion: An atom that has a positive or negative charge.

Action potential: A shifting change in charge that moves down the axon to the end, causing the terminal buttons to release a chemical signal.

All-or-none law: States that if the neuron is sufficiently stimulated, it fires, sending the action potential all the way down the axon and releasing chemicals from the terminal buttons; either the action potential occurs or it doesn't.

STRUCTURE OF A NEURON: THE INS AND OUTS. To understand psychological events, you need to know a few facts about the structure of the neuron. As you can see in Figure 2.2, each neuron has a receiving end, a sending end, and a part in the middle.

The part in the middle is called the **cell body.** Like all cells, it has a nucleus, which regulates the cell's functions, and a **cell membrane,** which is the skin of the cell. The membrane has very small holes, or pores, called **channels.** The channels open and close: When they are open, different chemicals in the surrounding fluid flow into the cell, and substances inside the cell flow out.

The sending end of the neuron is the **axon,** the long, cablelike structure extending from the cell body, along which signals travel to other neurons, muscles, or bodily organs. Most axons divide into many branches so that a neuron can send a message to more than one place at a time. At the end of the axon are **terminal buttons,** little knoblike structures that release chemicals into the space between neurons when the neuron has been triggered. Most neurons communicate this way, releasing chemicals that affect other neurons, usually at their receiving end. (A few neurons, such as some of those in the eye, communicate via electrical impulses, but this electrical communication is rare.)

Each neuron has only one sending end—that is, only one axon—but a neuron may have many receiving ends. These are the **dendrites;** their name is derived from the Greek word *dendron,* meaning "tree," which makes sense when you look at their shape, in Figure 2.2. The dendrites receive messages from the axons of other neurons. Although sometimes axons connect directly to the cell body of another neuron, the connection is usually made from axon to dendrite.

NEURAL IMPULSES: THE BRAIN IN ACTION. When a neuron receives enough stimulation from other neurons, some of the channels in the cell membrane open, allowing a complex exchange of **ions** (atoms that are positively or negatively charged). This exchange works its way down to the end of the axon, finally causing the terminal buttons to open, releasing chemicals that will affect other neurons. The shifting change in charge that moves down the axon is known as an **action potential.** This process, the basis of the neural communication that permits us to live in the world and respond to it, is illustrated in Figure 2.3.

Notice that the action potential obeys an **all-or-none law.** If enough stimulation reaches the neuron, it fires. In other words the sequence of shifting charges sends the action potential all the way down the axon, releasing chemicals from the terminal buttons. Either the action potential occurs or it doesn't. Many neurons can fire hundreds of times a second because chemical reactions reset the neuron so it can fire again if it receives adequate stimulation.

When you feel like stretching, does it seem as if no sooner has the thought occurred to you than your limbs are in motion—as if the physical response to the idea is instantaneous? Many people have this sense, and it comes as a surprise to realize just how slow our neurons actually are. In fact, in the fastest neurons, impulses travel only about 120 meters per second, compared with 300,000,000 meters per second for the speed of light. Even compared with the impulses traveling in a computer, our neurons are extremely slow. To convince yourself that neurons require a measurable amount of time to work, try the simple exercise described in Figure 2.4 with some friends (developed by Rozin & Jonides, 1977).

FIGURE 2.3
Ion Flow That Produces an Action Potential

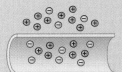 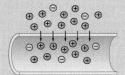 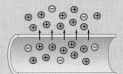 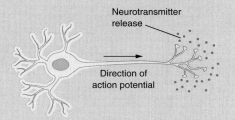

Neurotransmitter release

Direction of action potential

At rest, there are lots of sodium (Na⁺) and chloride (Cl⁻) ions outside the cell membrane, and lots of potassium (K⁺) and anion (A⁻) ions inside.

An action potential is triggered when the neuron is stimulated strongly, causing the ions to change their balance on the outside and inside of the neuron.

Positive sodium ions from the outside rush in, pushing out ions from the inside.

When the ion exchanges reach the end of the axon, they cause transmitters to be released from the terminal buttons.

Neurons would operate even more slowly were it not for the fact that most axons are covered with **myelin,** a fatty substance that helps impulses travel down the axon more efficiently. Multiple sclerosis (MS) is one of several disorders that illustrates the importance of myelin. MS causes myelin to deteriorate, which makes impulses stumble as they move down the axon. People with MS experience impaired sensation in their limbs, loss of vision, and paralysis. Could myelin loss have caused the young soldier's problem? Probably not: His visual problem was selective, whereas myelin loss creates overall problems in seeing.

Myelin: A fatty substance that helps impulses travel down the axon more efficiently.

FIGURE 2.4
Measuring Neural Conduction Time

Sit in a row with some friends, with each person using his or her left arm to grasp the ankle of the person on his or her left. The person at the head of the line, the leader, says "Go" and starts a stopwatch at the same time he or she squeezes the ankle of the person to his or her left; as soon as that person feels the squeeze, he or she squeezes the ankle of the next person to the left; and so on. When the last person feels the squeeze, he or she says "Done." The leader records the time.

Now repeat the exercise, but each of you should grasp not the ankle but the shoulder of the person to your left. Less time is required for the squeezes to make their way down the row when shoulders are squeezed than when ankles are squeezed. Why? Because the impulses have farther to travel when the ankle is squeezed. By subtracting the difference in times and estimating the average distance from ankle to shoulder for each row, you can actually estimate neural transmission time! This exercise should be done several times, first ankle, then shoulder, then shoulder, and then ankle; this procedure helps to control for the effects of practice in general.

Neurotransmitters and Neuromodulators: Bridging the Gap

When just one neuron in your brain fires, it might be sending a chemical message to thousands of other neurons. Each neuron is typically connected to about 10,000 others (and some neurons are connected to up to 100,000 others; Shepherd, 1999). The number of possible connections among neurons is shockingly large. In fact, Thompson (1993) has estimated that the number of possible connections in your brain is greater than the number of atoms in the universe! There are about 100,000,000,000 neurons in the brain, and if each could be connected to an average of even 10,000 others (varying which ones are connected in all combinations), the numbers of ways your brain can be "connected up" becomes . . . well, astronomical!

How do neurons actually communicate? What are the connections between them like? The site where communication between neurons occurs is the **synapse**, where an axon of one neuron sends a signal to the membrane of another neuron. In most cases, the sending and receiving neurons are not hooked up physically but are separated by a gap called the **synaptic cleft**, shown in Figure 2.5.

CHEMICAL MESSAGES: SIGNALS AND MODULATORS. As their name suggests, the chemicals that send signals, crossing from the terminal buttons across the synaptic clefts, are the **neurotransmitters**. The **neuromodulators** are chemicals that modulate, or alter, the effects of the neurotransmitters.

Imagine that you are using a pair of tin cans with a string between them as a walkie-talkie. When you speak into one can and your friend holds the other up to her ear, sound waves transmit the message. The gap from your mouth to one of the cans, and from the other can to her ear, is crossed by these waves, which carry the message. Neurotransmitters play the same role as the sound waves, allowing the message to cross the gap.

In contrast to the neurotransmitters, neuromodulators would produce the effect of tightening or loosening the string connecting the cans. When the string is drawn tight, the message is transmitted more effectively from one can to the other; when it is slackened, the sound must be louder to be heard. Other substances (which are not, strictly speaking, called neuromodulators) can affect what happens at the gap itself, for example, by affecting how quickly the neurotransmitters are removed from the synaptic cleft. Imagine that the room holding the linked tin cans has very thin air, with fewer molecules to vibrate. In this case, a louder sound would be needed to cause the bottoms of the tin cans to vibrate. On the other hand, if the air pressure were greater, a softer sound could convey the signal.

Glial cells, the cells that fill the gaps between neurons, also influence what goes on at the synaptic cleft. These cells control the amount of neurotransmitters that can reach a neuron. Some of them apparently produce substances that increase or decrease a neuron's sensitivity to inputs from other neurons (Newman & Zahs, 1998).

RECEPTORS: ON THE RECEIVING END. What do the neurotransmitters do once they cross the gap? That depends. Each neuron has **receptors**, specialized sites on the dendrites or cell bodies that respond to specific neurotransmitters or neuromodulators. The receptor sites are the places where "messenger molecules" of the released chemicals—neurotransmitters or neuromodulators—attach themselves. A good anal-

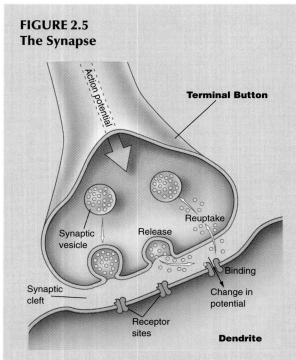

**FIGURE 2.5
The Synapse**

Impulses cross between neurons at the synapse. Chemicals released at the terminal buttons cross the synaptic cleft, where they bind to receptors and trigger events in the receiving neuron.

Synapse: The place where an axon of one neuron meets the membrane (on a dendrite or cell body) of another neuron.

Synaptic cleft: The gap between the axon of one neuron and the membrane of another, across which communication occurs.

Neurotransmitter: A chemical that sends signals from the terminal buttons on one neuron to the dendrites or cell body of another.

Neuromodulator: A chemical that alters the effects of neurotransmitters.

ogy here is an ordinary lock set: The lock is the receptor, which is opened by the key-like action of a particular neurotransmitter or neuromodulator.

When neurotransmitters or neuromodulators become attached to receptors, they are said to *bind*. After binding, they can have one of two general types of effects. They can be *excitatory*, making the receiving neuron more likely to fire an action potential. Or they can be *inhibitory*, making the receiving neuron less easily triggered. Because the typical axon divides into many branches and each neuron has many dendrites, there are many binding sites, so the neuron can receive thousands of different inputs from different sending neurons at the same time. The exciting and inhibiting inputs to each receiving neuron add up or cancel one another out, and their sum determines whether and when the neuron fires an action potential down its axon.

There are many types of neurotransmitters, neuromodulators, and receptors. Each particular neuron produces a small number of transmitters or modulators, and each neuron can have many types of receptors. The same neurotransmitter or neuromodulator can have very different effects, depending on which receptors are present.

In fact, the same neurotransmitter can have opposite effects on a neuron depending on which type of receptor accepts it, and the same chemical that can act as a neurotransmitter (sending a signal) in one context can act as a neuromodulator (altering a signal) in another (Dowling, 1992). For example, acetylcholine (ACh) can act as a neurotransmitter to slow down the heart, and can also function as a neuromodulator to help us store new memories. We will return to these substances repeatedly throughout the book, particularly when we consider the factors contributing to mental illness.

Not all of a given neurotransmitter released by the terminal buttons is taken up by receptors; some of it remains in the gap. Special chemical reactions are required to reabsorb—or **reuptake**—the excess neurotransmitter back into the *vesicles* (which store a neurotransmitter) of the sending neuron.

Binding and reuptake are chemical reactions, and like all chemical reactions, they require energy to work. Our bodies need energy, derived from nutrients and oxygen, simply to stay alive; the more active we are, the more energy we need. The same principle applies at the cellular level, for our neurons. Brain cells that fire more frequently require more nutrients and more oxygen. Techniques that provide pictures of the brain's activity, which we will look at shortly, depend on this fact: The images produced in brain scans are in fact graphical representations of the varying amounts of nutrients and oxygen used in various parts of the brain as someone performs different tasks—such as reading, speaking, dreaming, or reasoning. By taking such measurements, researchers track which parts of the brain are working harder during particular tasks. The results are helping researchers figure out just what different parts of the brain do.

UNBALANCED BRAIN: COPING WITH BAD CHEMICALS. By piecing together the story of how neurons communicate, scientists are not only developing a clear picture of how the brain works but also are learning how its functioning can go awry and how they can use drugs to repair it. Drugs that affect the way the brain works either increase or decrease the effectiveness of neural activity. Some of these drugs are **agonists,** which mimic the effects of a neurotransmitter or neuromodulator by activating a particular type of receptor. Other drugs may actually increase the amount of a neurotransmitter, sometimes by slowing down its reuptake. Depression, for example, is currently treated by several types of drugs that affect neurotransmitters and neuromodulators, including **selective serotonin-reuptake inhibitors (SSRIs),** which block the reuptake of the neurotransmitter serotonin. (Prozac, Zoloft, and Paxil are all SSRIs.) Still other drugs interfere with the effect of a neurotransmitter or neuromodulator. Some of these drugs are **antagonists,** which block a particular receptor. (As a memory aid, think of an "antagonist" at a party who is "blocking you" from meeting a charmer across the room.)

Could the young soldier whose vision was so strangely disrupted have had malfunctioning neurotransmitters or neuromodulators? Could such a disturbance have produced the highly selective impairments he experienced after inhaling the carbon

Receptor: A site on the dendrite or cell body where a messenger molecule attaches itself; like a lock that is opened by one key, a receptor receives only one type of neurotransmitter or neuromodulator.

Reuptake: The process by which surplus neurotransmitter is reabsorbed back into the sending neuron so that the neuron can effectively fire again.

Agonist: A chemical that mimics the effects of a neurotransmitter (sometimes by preventing reuptake).

Selective serotonin-reuptake inhibiter (SSRI): A chemical that blocks the reuptake of the neurotransmitter serotonin.

Antagonist: A chemical that blocks the effect of a neurotransmitter (sometimes by blocking a receptor or enhancing the reuptake mechanism).

monoxide fumes? It's possible, if just the right combinations of chemicals were disrupted. However, this scenario is unlikely. Because most neurotransmitters and neuromodulators are used widely throughout the brain, not solely in the parts of the brain involved in visual perception, we would expect their disruption to create more widespread difficulties, such as in hearing, understanding language, walking, and other functions.

We have every reason to think, however, that the soldier's difficulty with visual recognition had something to do with the operations of neurons. To understand why only some neurons were disrupted but not others, we need to look further and consider the structure of the brain. Now that you know the essentials of how neurons work, and how they affect each other via neurotransmitters and neuromodulators, you are ready to examine how neurons work within different brain structures and how their functioning can break down. First, however, let's pause to review how the effects of neurotransmitter and neuromodulator activity can ripple outward from the brain and body to profoundly change a person's life.

LOOKING AT LEVELS

Parkinson's Disease

The connection between brain and behavior is seen in the devastating effects of *Parkinson's disease*, a classic brain disorder. Named after the British physician James Parkinson, who first described the disorder in 1817, Parkinson's afflicts about half a million Americans, from every slice of life—from celebrity Michael J. Fox to the lady next door. The hands of people with Parkinson's disease shake; they may move sluggishly, with a stooped posture and shuffling walk; their limbs often seem frozen in position and resist attempts to bend them.

A piano tuner named John had to stop working because he developed Parkinson's disease. He had difficulty controlling his movements, and his behavior changed as well. He became so listless that he rarely left his house. He missed meals. And he started to contract various minor illnesses, which worsened his other symptoms.

All these changes, physical and behavioral, were caused directly or indirectly by the death of particular neurons in John's brain. In the brains of people with Parkinson's disease, cells that produce the neurotransmitter *dopamine* have died. Dopamine plays a key role in the areas of the brain that are involved in planning movements. When patients take a drug that helps produce dopamine, L-Dopa, symptoms decrease, often for a long period of time.

When John's neurons no longer produced enough dopamine, the working of his brain was affected and his muscle control impaired. Events at the level of the brain interacted with events at the level of the person: Shaky hands made it almost impossible for him to tune pianos, so John had to retire. After he gave up the work he loved, he became depressed. He began to think of himself as diseased, and he began interpreting all his behaviors in terms of his disease and predicting his future behaviors in that light. As a consequence, he lost interest in going out. Now events at the level of the person affected events at the level of the group: He stopped seeing many people, who in turn stopped seeing, and helping, him. The events in his brain influenced his feelings about himself and his relationships with other people.

Events at the different levels interact in both directions: The brain-based symptoms of shaking hands and shuffling gait became worse when John was ill from other causes, which occurred more often than before because he stopped taking care of himself; and the lack of social interactions led to his physical health deteriorating even further, making him more depressed and less likely to seek out the company of others. If John had been a member of a close-knit family, he might have had more support and suffered less lonliness and depression.

▶ *1. How do neurons work? What could cause neurons to die?* Neurons receive input from other neurons (which themselves may be connected to a sense organ), on either their dendrites or their cell bodies. If the sum of all the inputs is strong enough, the neuron fires, sending a rapid exchange of ions across the cell membrane. This exchange works its way down the axon, until the terminal buttons release a neurotransmitter (which sends a signal) or a neuromodulator (which alters the effect of a signal). This chemical crosses the synaptic cleft to the dendrites or cell bodies of other neurons.

▶ *2. How do chemicals allow neurons to communicate? What happens if healthy neurons can no longer communicate?* Neurons have receptors, which are like locks that can be opened by certain keys; the keys are the neurotransmitters and the neuromodulators. Depending on the properties of the particular receptors, these chemicals can excite the neuron to fire or inhibit it from firing. Agonists mimic the action of neurotransmitters or neuromodulators, whereas antagonists block their effects.

STRUCTURE AND FUNCTION: AN ORCHESTRA WITH MANY MEMBERS

Consider some additional problems experienced by the young soldier who was poisoned while taking a shower. When researchers showed him a blue page on which white letters were printed, he thought he was looking at a "beach scene"—the blue was water and the white letters were "people seen on the beach from an airplane." He could visually pick out similar objects when they were placed in front of him, but only if they were of a similar color and size. His doctors found that he could be trained to name a few everyday objects by sight as children are taught to recognize sight words on *Sesame Street* without actually reading them, but this training broke down when the color or size of the objects changed. The young man learned to name a red toothbrush as "toothbrush," but he couldn't properly name a green toothbrush, and when he was shown a red pencil, he called it "my toothbrush."

The results of the entire series of tests made it clear that the soldier could see and understand color and size, but not shape. He had *some* sense of shape, though; he didn't call the pencil a "shoe" or a "basketball" but a "toothbrush." To understand what had gone wrong in the soldier's brain, you need to know what the different parts of the nervous system do.

▶ 1. What are the major parts of the nervous system that can sustain damage?

▶ 2. What is the cerebral cortex? What are the major cortical and subcortical systems, and what do they do?

▶ 3. How do the functions of the two sides of the brain differ?

▶ 4. What parts of the brain lie under the cerebral cortex? What do these subcortical structures do?

Overview: The Wonderful Wet Machine

A brain living in a vat wouldn't be of much use to anyone—it would be like a computer with no keyboard or monitor. To do its job, the brain needs both to receive input from the body and the outside world and to be able to act on these inputs. To understand the brain's job, then, you must see what it receives and what it sends out.

Spinal cord: The flexible rope of nerves that runs inside the backbone, or spinal column.

Central nervous system (CNS): The spinal cord and the brain.

Sensory neurons of spinal cord: Neurons in the back of the spinal cord that carry information about touch and the state of internal organs to the brain.

Motor neurons of spinal cord: Neurons in the front inside part of the spinal cord that carry commands from the brain to the muscles.

Reflex: An automatic response to an event.

THE CRANIAL NERVES: CABLES TO COMMAND CENTRAL. The brain sends and receives information from the 12 cranial nerves, so named because they connect to the brain through holes in the cranium, the part of the skull that encloses the brain. These nerves control specific muscles, such as those responsible for eye movements; glands, such as the salivary glands; and internal organs, such as the heart and stomach. The cranial nerves also receive information from sense organs, such as the eyes, ears, nose, and those in the skin. Damage to a cranial nerve can cut off key inputs or outputs from the brain. If you weren't wearing a seat belt in an automobile accident, for example, your head might slam into the steering wheel. This could cause your brain to slosh forward and scrape along the underside of your skull. The scraping could disrupt the functioning of your olfactory nerves, and thus impair your ability to smell. This may not sound like a severe problem, but as you will see in the following chapter, smell plays a major role in taste—and food would never taste the same again.

THE SPINAL CORD: FLEXING AND REFLEXING. The largest conduit for information going to and from the brain is the **spinal cord,** the flexible rope of nerves that runs inside the backbone, or *spinal column.* In fact, so intimately connected is the spinal cord to the brain that the two together are called the **central nervous system (CNS).** At each of 31 places, spinal nerves emerge from the spinal cord in pairs, one on the left and one on the right, as Figure 2.6 shows. Through these nerves the spinal cord plays a key role in sending the brain's commands to the body and in turn allowing the brain to register information about the state of the body. The spinal cord also allows us, through our sense of touch, to gain information about the world.

As illustrated in Figure 2.6, **sensory neurons** at the back of the cord carry information about touch and the state of internal organs to the brain, and **motor neurons** in the inside front part of the cord carry commands from the brain to the muscles.

The spinal cord isn't simply a set of cables that relays commands and information between brain and body. The spinal cord itself can initiate some aspects of our behavior, such as reflexes. A **reflex** is an automatic response to an event, an action that does not require thought. Even a simple reflex requires hundreds of neurons. How do reflexes work? When sensory neurons in the skin detect a sharp thorn, for example, they send signals that stimulate sensory neurons in the spinal cord. These neurons in turn are connected to interneurons in the spinal cord, as shown in Figure 2.7. When you jerk away from something that pricks you, interneurons have sent signals to motor neurons, which then cause the muscles to jerk, pulling your finger away from the source of pain. This arrangement allows you to respond immediately, bypassing the brain—it wouldn't pay to be lost in thought every time a threat appeared.

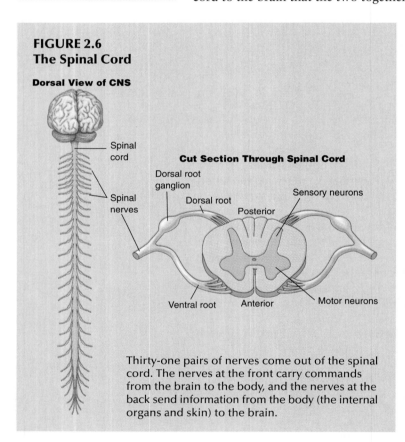

**FIGURE 2.6
The Spinal Cord**

Dorsal View of CNS

Spinal cord

Spinal nerves

Cut Section Through Spinal Cord

Dorsal root ganglion

Dorsal root

Posterior

Sensory neurons

Ventral root   Anterior   Motor neurons

Thirty-one pairs of nerves come out of the spinal cord. The nerves at the front carry commands from the brain to the body, and the nerves at the back send information from the body (the internal organs and skin) to the brain.

If the point of reflexes is to get things done in a hurry, why aren't the sensory neurons directly connected to motor neurons? Why the intermediary? Because interneurons provide a particular benefit: They allow the brain to send signals to *prevent* a reflex response. Perhaps you are handing a beautiful red rose to a good friend as a gift and accidentally prick your finger. Instead of flinging the rose away, you grit your teeth and continue to hold it. You are able to do this because the part of your

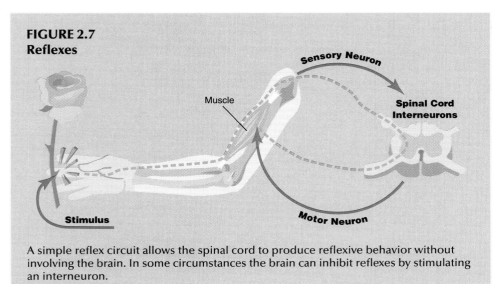

FIGURE 2.7
Reflexes

Sensory Neuron

Muscle

Spinal Cord
Interneurons

Stimulus

Motor Neuron

A simple reflex circuit allows the spinal cord to produce reflexive behavior without involving the brain. In some circumstances the brain can inhibit reflexes by stimulating an interneuron.

brain that is involved in formulating goals and intentions knows not to flub this gesture and sends a signal to the interneurons to stop the motor neurons from firing.

THE PERIPHERAL NERVOUS SYSTEM: A MOVING STORY. As shown in Figure 2.8, the CNS (which consists of the brain and the spinal cord) hooks into the **peripheral nervous system (PNS).** The PNS links the central nervous system to the organs of the body. The PNS has two parts: the autonomic nervous system and the skeletal (or somatic) system. The **autonomic nervous system (ANS)** controls the smooth muscles in the body and some glandular functions. Smooth muscles, so called because they look smooth under a microscope, are found in the heart, blood vessels, stomach lining, and intestines. Many of the activities that the ANS controls, such as

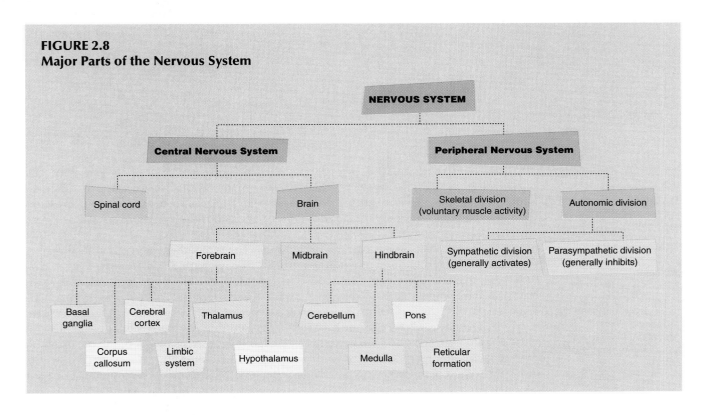

FIGURE 2.8
Major Parts of the Nervous System

NERVOUS SYSTEM

Central Nervous System

Peripheral Nervous System

Spinal cord

Brain

Skeletal division (voluntary muscle activity)

Autonomic division

Forebrain

Midbrain

Hindbrain

Sympathetic division (generally activates)

Parasympathetic division (generally inhibits)

Basal ganglia

Cerebral cortex

Thalamus

Cerebellum

Pons

Corpus callosum

Limbic system

Hypothalamus

Medulla

Reticular formation

FIGURE 2.9
The Sympathetic and Parasympathetic Nervous Systems' Effects on the Body

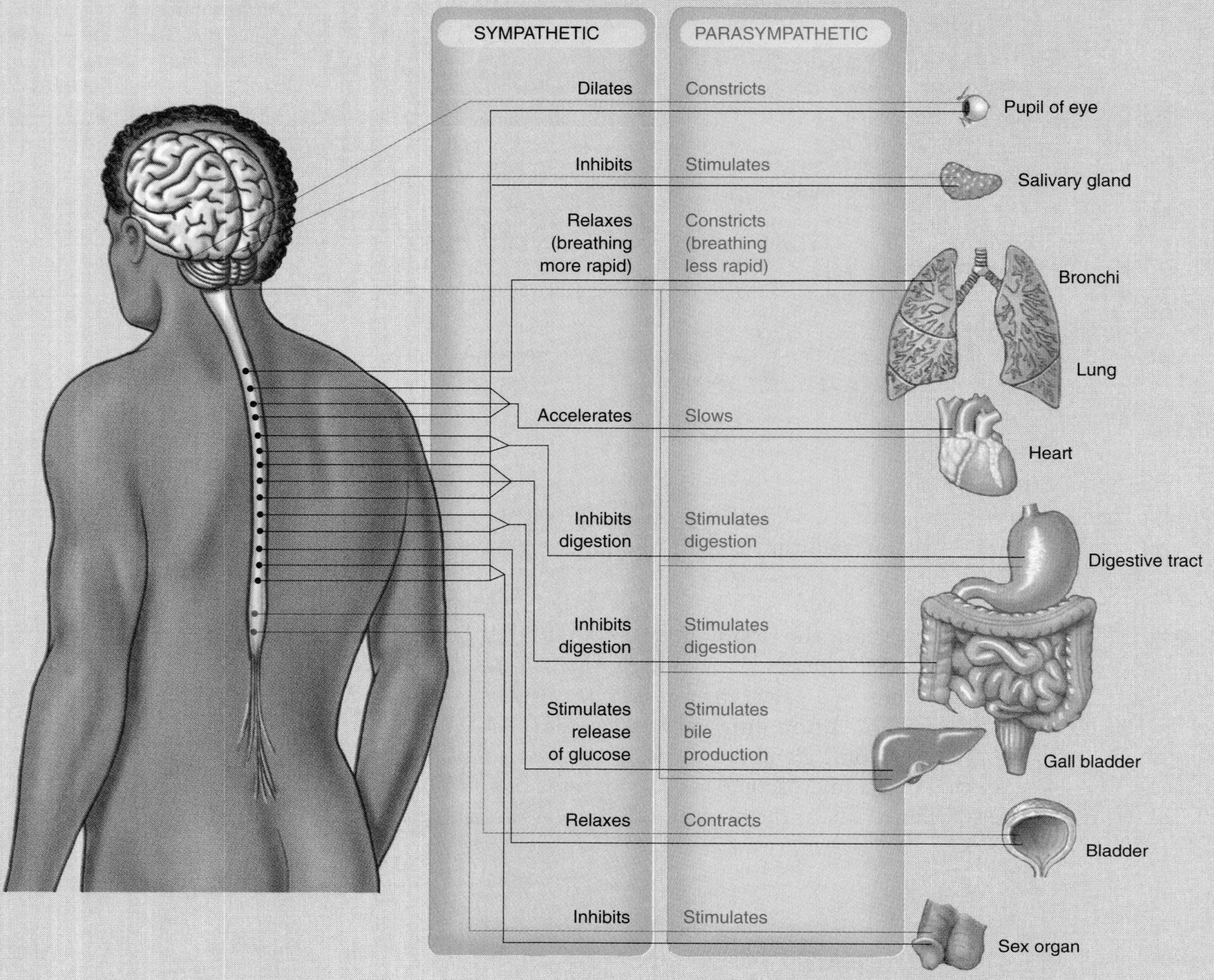

The two major branches of the ANS are the sympathetic and parasympathetic nervous systems. In general the sympathetic nervous system prepares the body to fight or flee, and the parasympathetic dampens down the sympathetic nervous system.

Skeletal system: Consists of nerves that are attached to striated muscles and bones.

Sympathetic nervous system: Part of the ANS that readies an animal to fight or to flee by speeding up the heart, increasing breathing rate to deliver more oxygen, dilating the pupils, producing sweat, increasing salivation, inhibiting activity in the stomach, and relaxing the bladder.

digestion and circulation, are self-regulating and are usually not under conscious control. In contrast, the **skeletal system** consists of nerves that are attached to voluntary muscles; these muscles are also known as striated muscles because under a microscope they appear "striated," or striped. If you clench your fist and "make a muscle," you are using this system.

The ANS itself has two major divisions. The **sympathetic nervous system** readies an animal (including you and the authors) to cope with an emergency. This system usually comes into play in response to a threat in the environment, perhaps a near-accident when you are driving in heavy traffic. As Figure 2.9 shows, the sympathetic system speeds up the heart, increases the breathing rate to provide more oxygen, dilates the pupils for greater light sensitivity and thus sharper vision, produces sweat slightly (giving your hand a better grip), slightly increases salivation, inhibits stomach activity, and relaxes the bladder. If your heart is pounding and your palms are sweaty, it's a good bet that your sympathetic system has kicked in. The overall effect of these changes is to prepare your body to react—to fight or to flee. More oxygen flows into your muscles, your vision is improved, and the rest of your body is ready to support physical exertion. The visual difficulties that plagued the young soldier also threatened the smooth operation of his sympathetic nervous system, a vital system for soldiers. Even if his sympathetic nervous system were to remain perfectly intact after carbon monoxide poisoning, because he no longer accurately recognizes objects and people, he cannot react appropriately to danger.

Fight-or-flight situations are not the only conditions that activate the sympathetic nervous system. This system also operates in circumstances that may be less extreme but nonetheless threatening, such as getting ready to give an important speech, having a conversation with a touchy authority figure, or rushing to avoid being late for an important meeting. People prone to excessive amounts of anxiety tend to have sympathetic nervous systems that overshoot the mark and get the body too revved up. They might hyperventilate (that is, breathe in too much oxygen), sweat profusely, or experience a pounding heart when there is no apparent threat. These and other unpleasant physical symptoms of anxiety occur whenever the sympathetic nervous system responds too strongly. Sweat makes your skin conduct electricity more readily, and researchers take advantage of this fact by measuring skin conductance to study arousal.

The **parasympathetic nervous system** lies, figuratively, "next to" the sympathetic system (*para* is Greek for "next to" or "alongside") and tends to counteract its effects (see Figure 2.9). The sympathetic system speeds things up, and the parasympathetic system slows them down. Heart rate slows, pupils contract, salivation increases massively, digestion is stimulated, the bladder contracts. Whereas the sympathetic system tends to affect all the organs at the same time and can be thought of as increasing arousal in general, the parasympathetic system tends to affect organs one at a time or in small groups.

The sympathetic and parasympathetic systems don't exactly have a push-and-pull relationship; they don't always work against each other. For example, an erection is caused by the parasympathetic system, but the sympathetic system controls ejaculation. If a man is too tense about sex, the sympathetic system will override the parasympathetic system, and (metaphorically speaking) desire will remain solely in the young man's heart.

THE VISIBLE BRAIN: LOBES AND LANDMARKS. You've worked your way down through the spinal cord and have seen its marvelous abilities to control some behaviors. But these behaviors are very limited when viewed in light of all we can do. To understand the range of human abilities, you need to turn to the other part of the central nervous system, the brain itself.

Imagine that you could see through someone's hair and scalp, even through the skull itself. The first thing you would see under the skull are the **meninges,** three protective layered membranes that cover the brain (*meningitis* is an infection of these membranes). Under this lies a network of blood vessels on the surface of the brain itself. Viewing the brain from above—looking down through the top of the head—you can see that the brain is divided into two halves, left and right, separated by a deep fissure down the middle. Each half-brain is called a **cerebral hemisphere** (*cerebrum* is Latin for "brain") because each is shaped roughly like half a sphere. Curiously, each hemisphere receives information from, and controls the muscles of, the opposite side of the body. For example, if you are right-handed, your left hemisphere controls your hand as you write.

Each hemisphere is divided into four major parts, or **lobes:** the occipital lobe, at the back of the brain; the temporal lobe, which lies below the temples, in front of the ears, where sideburns begin to grow down; the parietal lobe, in the upper middle/rear of the brain, above the occipital lobe; and the frontal lobe, behind the forehead (see

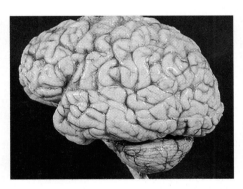

Most of your brain is water; the average brain weighs about 3 pounds, but if the water were removed, it would weigh only 10 ounces; this extra material (which includes proteins and fats, as well as various types of ions) are the parts of the neurons, glial cells, and everything else that gives the brain a structure.

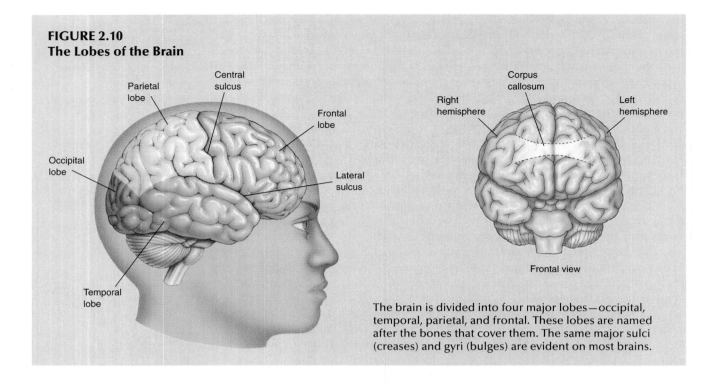

FIGURE 2.10
The Lobes of the Brain

Parietal lobe

Central sulcus

Frontal lobe

Occipital lobe

Lateral sulcus

Temporal lobe

Corpus callosum

Right hemisphere

Left hemisphere

Frontal view

The brain is divided into four major lobes—occipital, temporal, parietal, and frontal. These lobes are named after the bones that cover them. The same major sulci (creases) and gyri (bulges) are evident on most brains.

Figure 2.10). The two halves of the brain are connected by the **corpus callosum,** which contains somewhere between 250 to 300 million nerve fibers (some other smaller connections exist between the two halves of the brain, but they are less important).

Now, peer deeper. Immediately under the network of blood vessels on the surface of the brain is the convoluted, pinkish-gray surface of the brain itself: This is the **cerebral cortex** (*cortex* means "rind" or "shell" in Latin). This is where most of the brain's mental processes take place. Although the cerebral cortex is only about 2 millimeters thick, it is brimming with the cell bodies of neurons, giving the cortex its characteristic color and its nickname, "gray matter." Looking directly at the surface of the brain, you can see that the cortex has many creases and bulges, as shown in Figure 2.10. The creases are called **sulci** (the singular is sulcus), and the areas that bulge up between the sulci are the **gyri** (singular, gyrus). The cortex, so vital to our functioning, is crumpled up this way so that more of it can be stuffed into the skull.

Now peel back the cortex and look beneath it. Here you see lots of white fibers packed together. This material is actually myelinated axons, mostly from the neurons in the cortex; it is white because that is the color of the fatty white myelin insulation that surrounds the axons and, not surprisingly, these fibers are called "white matter." Below the white matter, in the very center of the brain, are hollow areas, called **ventricles,** where fluid is stored (the same fluid that fills the core of the spinal column). On either side and beneath the ventricles are the **subcortical** ("under the cortex") **structures** of the inner brain; these contain gray matter and are very similar to the organs of many animals that are much simpler than humans.

STRUCTURE AND FUNCTION: NO DOTTED LINES. So far we've focused on the structure, or physical makeup, of the brain. But what do the various parts of the brain do? Consider a bike: You can point to its parts and discuss their physical structures (for example, a chain connects a metal gear to the back wheel), and you can discuss how the parts work (what the chain does). So too with the brain: You can point to the brain and discuss its physical parts, and you can describe how parts of the brain function. The question of how specific brain structures function is at center stage in psychology today, and the question is much easier to ask than to answer. Be-

Corpus callosum: The huge band of nerve fibers that connects the two halves of the brain.

Cerebral cortex: The convoluted pinkish-gray surface of the brain, where most mental processes take place.

Sulcus: A fold in the cerebral cortex.

Gyrus: A bulge between sulci in the cerebral cortex that forms a crease.

Ventricle: A hollow area in the center of the brain that stores fluid.

Subcortical structure: An "inner brain" organ that contains gray matter, located under the cerebral cortex.

cause the functioning of the brain is so complicated, researchers have approached it using a strategy of divide and conquer. The same approach is helpful when reviewing key facts about the brain. Thus, just as you would explore a castle one room at a time, you will be given a tour of the brain one part at a time. Dividing the brain into parts makes understanding what each one does much easier. Then you will be ready to explore the relationships among these parts.

Already, though, there is a problem. When it comes to its functioning, the brain isn't like the diagram of a cow in a butcher's shop; there are no dotted lines to show the different cuts of beef, the distinct regions that do different things. But in spite of the missing dotted lines, there are physical hints we can use to identify the brain's functional parts. Think of two stone walls; from a distance they may look the same—the same height, same color. But as you move up close, you can see they are different, both because they are made up of different kinds of stones and because the stones are arranged differently. Similarly, under the microscope, parts of the brain appear different because they contain different types of neurons and these cells are organized differently. Brain areas that differ in terms of the arrangement of their neurons have often turned out to have distinct functions.

In addition, normal human brains do have certain major physical landmarks that help us to recognize parts that carry out different functions. Particular sulci and gyri, the creases and bulges in the cerebral cortex, for example, often consist of groups of neurons with well-defined functions. Unlike the creases and bulges that occur randomly when you crumple up a sheet of paper, some sulci and gyri occur for a reason. There are major connections between areas that tend to work together, and as the brain develops and the cortex expands, these firm connections force the cortex to fold in certain ways (Van Essen, 1997).

Let's focus more closely on some of these regions of the human brain.

The Cerebral Cortex: The Seat of the Mind

Most of the neurons in the brain are located in the lobes of the cerebral cortex, and it is here that most thinking takes place. These different areas of the cortex, the lobes of each cerebral hemisphere, have different functions, and we discuss them one at a time. But always remember that the lobes do not function in isolation; they usually work in concert with one another.

OCCIPITAL LOBES: LOOKING GOOD. The **occipital lobes** are concerned entirely with different aspects of vision, and most of the fibers from the eyes lead to these lobes. If somebody were to hit you in the back of the head with a brick (an experiment we do not recommend), the "stars" you are likely to see appear because of the impact on this area. The occipital lobes contain many separate areas that work together to specify visual properties such as shape, color, and motion. Damage to these lobes results in partial or complete blindness. Because each half of the brain receives sensory information from the opposite side, if a surgeon has to remove the left occipital lobe (perhaps to take out a brain tumor), the patient will not be able to see things to his or her right side when looking ahead. Even a small hole in the occipital cortex disrupts vision, producing a blind spot (the effect would be something like what you would see if a black dot were glued onto your contact lens).

Because of the way the major arteries feed blood to the back of the brain, poisoning by carbon monoxide (which displaces oxygen) often leads to scattered cell death in the occipital lobe. Our young soldier probably suffered damage to the occipital lobes, perhaps in addition to injury to other parts of the brain. Such damage often affects visual perception, making the entire world seem fuzzy and making it difficult to organize information. Still, this probably does not sufficiently explain all of the soldier's vision problems; if this were all there was to it, why would he confuse white letters with sunbathers on the beach?

Occipital lobe: The brain lobe at the back of the head; concerned entirely with different aspects of vision.

FIGURE 2.11
Shattered Vision

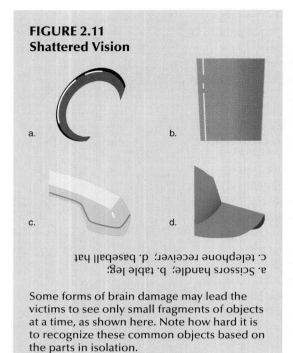

a. Scissors handle; b. table leg;
c. telephone receiver; d. baseball hat

Some forms of brain damage may lead the victims to see only small fragments of objects at a time, as shown here. Note how hard it is to recognize these common objects based on the parts in isolation.

Temporal lobe: The brain lobe under the temples, in front of the ears, where sideburns begin to grow down; among its many functions are visual memory and hearing.

Parietal lobe: The brain lobe at the top, center/rear of the head, involved in registering spatial location, attention, and motor control.

Somatosensory strip: The gyrus, located immediately behind the central sulcus, that registers sensation on the body and is organized by body part.

Frontal lobe: The brain lobe located behind the forehead; the seat of planning, memory search, motor control, and reasoning, as well as numerous other functions.

Motor strip: The gyrus, located immediately in front of the central sulcus, that controls fine movements and is organized by body part; also called *primary motor cortex*.

TEMPORAL LOBES: UP TO THEIR EARS IN WORK. The **temporal lobes,** which lie in front of the ears and roughly where sideburns start, play a key role in many functions, including processing sound, storing new memories, and comprehending language. Sounds are processed in the top part of the temporal lobes; visual memories of shapes are stored in the bottom. Animals that have had their temporal lobes removed are not blind (we know this because they don't bump into things), but they can no longer recognize objects by sight; their visual memories are gone. They are said to be "mindblind," a phenomenon Sigmund Freud termed *agnosia*. The soldier may have had damage in either one or both temporal lobes or in the connections from an occipital lobe to one or both temporal lobes. If the connections were damaged, only a small amount of information might now reach the part of the temporal lobes where visual memories of shapes are stored, and he might be able to take in only fragments of what he sees. This diagnosis would go a long way toward explaining his problem. For example, in order to see a letter, he would have to look at one segment at a time (a vertical line, then a curved line, and so on), which isn't good enough to recognize the shape of a letter as whole. The world might look to the soldier like the images in Figure 2.11.

PARIETAL LOBES: INNER SPACE. When you recall where you left your keys, how to drive to a friend's house, or what's over your left shoulder, your **parietal lobes** (see Figure 2.10) are at work. Right now, your parietal lobes are playing a role in allowing you to define the distance between your face and the book and to shift attention to each of these words; they are even helping control your eye movements. The parietal lobes are also involved when you do arithmetic and when you think about the relationships among objects in space. Albert Einstein (1945) claimed that he reasoned by imagining objects in space, which is interesting in light of the fact that his parietal lobes were found to be about 15% larger than normal (Witelson et al., 1999). His unusual parietal lobes may have contributed to his genius.

Part of each parietal lobe, right behind the central sulcus (which runs across the brain, roughly at right angles to the fissure between the hemispheres (see Figure 2.12), is the **somatosensory strip.** This area registers sensation on your body. In fact, sensa-

FIGURE 2.12
The "Homunculus" of the Somatosensory Strip

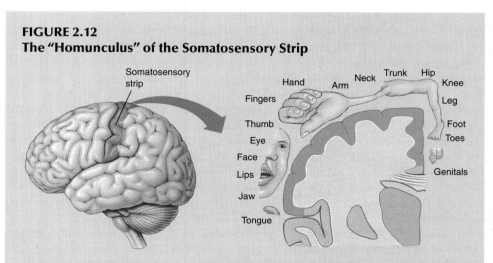

The somatosensory strip is organized so that different parts of the body are registered by adjacent portions of cortex; the size of the picture indicates the amount of tissue dedicated to that part of the body.

tions from each part of your body are registered in a specific section of this strip of cortex. Tickling your toes, for example, activates neurons in the cortex next to the area devoted to stimulation from your ankle, as you can see in Figure 2.12. Larger areas of the cortex correspond to areas of the body that are more sensitive (notice the amount of space devoted to lips and hands).

The parietal lobes also play a role in consciousness, a topic explored in depth in Chapter 4. Patients who suffer damage to a parietal lobe may exhibit a curious deficit known as *unilateral visual neglect.* They aren't blind, but they typically ignore (that is, they "neglect") everything on the side opposite that of the damage— if the damage is in the right parietal lobe, they ignore everything on their left sides (see Figure 2.13). When they shave, for instance, they shave only half the face; when they dress, they put clothes on only

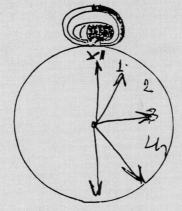
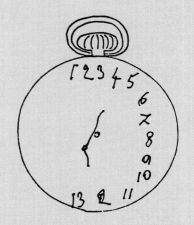

FIGURE 2.13
Visual Unilateral Neglect

When patients who suffered from left-sided unilateral visual neglect are asked to draw a clock, they ignore the left side and try to cram all the numbers into the side to which they pay attention. Here are drawings from two such patients. (From Bisiach et al., 1981.)

half the body (pulling their shirt over only one arm, pants over only one leg). If only a simple stimulus is present in the ignored side of space (for example, an examiner wiggles a finger on that side), they can sometimes see this; but when stimuli are present in both sides of space (the examiner wiggles fingers to the left and right sides of the patient at the same time), they ignore those on the "bad" side. Many of these patients also have *anosognosia,* a lack of awareness that anything is wrong. Indeed, in one case a doctor showed such a patient her neglected arm and asked her what it was. The patient replied that the doctor had a third arm; she thought that her own arm was part of the doctor's body (Gerstmann, 1942, p. 892); similar cases are not uncommon (Aglioti et al., 1996; Yamadori, 1997).

FRONTAL LOBES: LEADERS OF THE PACK. Probably the most dramatic difference between the appearance of a human brain and a monkey brain is how much the human brain bulges out in front. The size and development of the **frontal lobes** are one of the features that make us uniquely human. The frontal lobes are critically involved in speech, the search for specific memories, reasoning (including the use of memory in reasoning), and emotions. These crucial lobes also contain the **motor strip** (also called the *primary motor cortex*), which is located in the gyrus immediately in front of the central sulcus. The motor strip controls fine movements and, as with the somatosensory strip, is organized in terms of parts of the body. Relatively large areas of this strip of cortex are dedicated to those parts of the body that we control with precision, such as the hands and mouth.

Hints about the functions of the frontal lobes, like other parts of the brain, have emerged from studies of patients with brain damage. Phineas Gage, the foreman of a gang of workers building a railroad in Vermont late in the nineteenth century, is perhaps the most famous case of a patient with damage to the frontal lobes. Gage's unfortunate loss was psychology's gain, as researchers were able to observe the consequences of damage to this vital area of the brain. The story began when Gage became distracted as he was packing blasting powder into a hole in a rock. When the metal bar he was using to pack in the powder accidentally hit the rock, it created a spark, which set off the powder. The metal bar, like a spear shot from a cannon, went right through the front part of his head, flew high in the air, and landed

A computer-reconstructed picture of the path taken by the metal bar as it passed through Phineas Gage's skull.

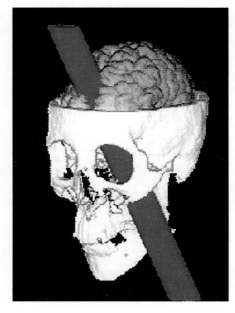

Split-brain patient: A person whose corpus callosum has been severed for medical reasons, so that neuronal impulses no longer pass from one hemisphere to the other.

about 30 meters behind him. Miraculously, Gage lived, but he was a changed man. Previously, he had been responsible and organized; he now led a disorderly life. He couldn't stick to any decision, had little self-control, and his formerly decent language was now laced with profanity (Macmillan, 1986, 1992). Like Phineas Gage, people with damage to the frontal regions of the brain have difficulty reasoning.

The frontal lobes are also involved in emotion. The left frontal lobe plays a special role in *approach* (positive) emotions, whereas the right plays a special role in *withdrawal* (negative) emotions (Davidson, 1993). As you can see, the frontal lobe is a vast piece of cortical real estate, with many functions; we will return to it repeatedly in this book.

The Dual Brain: Thinking With Both Barrels

Researchers have long suspected that the two cerebral hemispheres, left and right, play distinct roles in cognition. This idea has even made it into the popular culture; Saab, for example, once advertised that its cars satisfied both the left and right brains (implying that other cars were seriously lacking, by half). What do the hemispheres do differently?

Split-Brain Research: A Deep Disconnect. The most compelling evidence to date that the two half-brains perform distinct functions has come from looking at the effects of severing the connection between the two hemispheres. When this is done, neuronal impulses no longer pass from one hemisphere to the other. Patients who have undergone this surgery are called **split-brain patients.** Why would such drastic surgery be performed? This procedure has been used to help patients with severe, otherwise untreatable epilepsy. *Epilepsy* is a disease that causes parts of the brain to go into spasm, leading to bodily convulsions; in severe form, it prevents sufferers from leading a normal life. Cutting the corpus callosum prevents the spasm that originates in one hemisphere from reaching the other hemisphere, and thus the whole brain does not become involved in the convulsions and their severity is thereby lessened. Ida McKinley, the wife of President William McKinley, apparently experienced such seizures. During these spells, she lost consciousness but nevertheless remained upright in her chair. When others were present, President McKinley would put a handkerchief over her face and continue his conversation (Seuling, 1978).

FIGURE 2.14
The Eyes, Optic Chiasm, and Cerebral Hemispheres

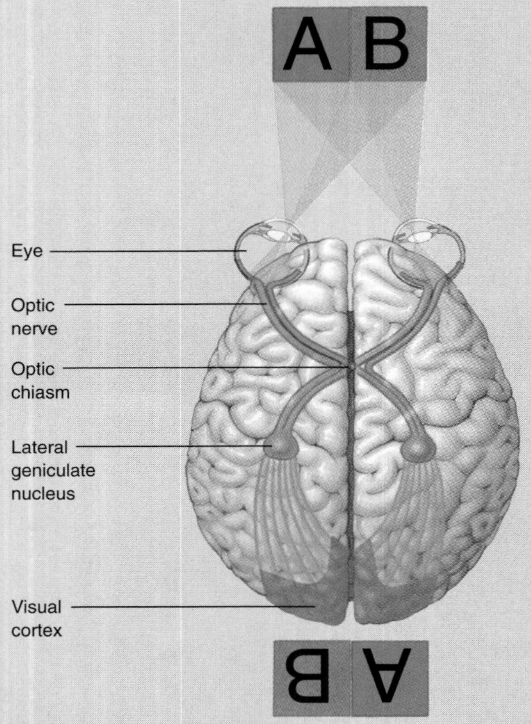

A B
Eye
Optic nerve
Optic chiasm
Lateral geniculate nucleus
Visual cortex
B A

The backs of the eyes are actually parts of the brain pushed forward during development; the left half of each eye is connected only to the left cerebral hemisphere, whereas the right half of each eye is connected only to the right cerebral hemisphere.

Although it is easy to see how cutting the corpus callosum would decrease the severity of epileptic convulsion, the full effects of this procedure on mental processes cannot be understood without discussing vision. As shown in Figure 2.14, the left half of each eye is connected directly to the left hemisphere, but not to the right hemisphere; similarly, the right half of each eye is connected directly, and only, to the right hemisphere. (Note, it's not that the left eye is connected only to the left hemisphere, and the right only to the right.) Thus, if you stare straight ahead, objects to the left are seen first by the right brain, and those to the right are seen first by the left brain. If the corpus callosum is cut,

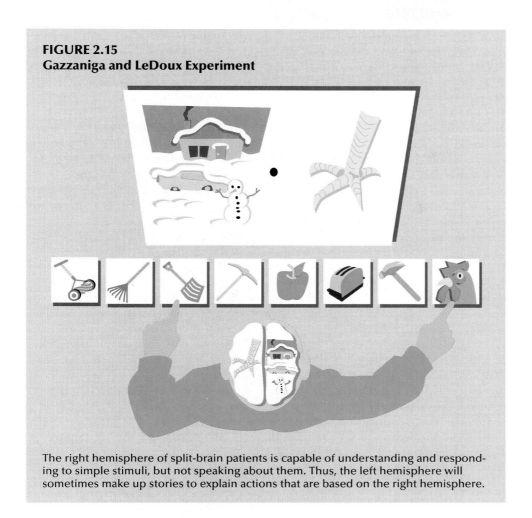

FIGURE 2.15
Gazzaniga and LeDoux Experiment

The right hemisphere of split-brain patients is capable of understanding and responding to simple stimuli, but not speaking about them. Thus, the left hemisphere will sometimes make up stories to explain actions that are based on the right hemisphere.

the input stays in the hemisphere that receives the information; in normal people, it also crosses over to the other side.

What are the practical effects of this division? One way to find out is to present pictures or words to the left or right side (fast enough so that the participant can't move his or her eyes to look directly at them). In a classic study of a split-brain patient, illustrated in Figure 2.15, Gazzaniga and LeDoux (1978) presented a picture of a snow scene to the right hemisphere (which controls the left hand) and, at the same time, a picture of a chicken's claw to the left hemisphere (which controls the right hand and, usually, speech). The patient was then shown several other pictures and asked to choose which of them was implied by the stimulus. The patient used his right hand (controlled by the left hemisphere) to select a picture of a chicken, and his left hand (controlled by the right hemisphere) to select a picture of a shovel. The investigators then asked the patient what he had seen. "I saw a claw and I picked a chicken," he replied. Because the left hemisphere controls almost all of speech, it described what the left hemisphere saw. The patient continued: "And you have to clean out the chicken shed with a shovel." The left hemisphere did not actually know what the right hemisphere had seen, so it made up a story. The left hemisphere, in right-handed people (and most left-handed people), not only controls most aspects of language but also plays a crucial role in interpreting the world, in making up stories, and in many forms of reasoning (Gazzaniga, 1995; LeDoux et al., 1977).

HEMISPHERIC SPECIALIZATION: NOT JUST FOR THE DEEPLY DISCONNECTED.
The methods used to study split-brain patients can also be used to study brain function in normal people. Because the corpus callosum is intact in normal people,

information sent first to one hemisphere moves quickly to the other—but this takes a measurable amount of time, and it is possible that the information is of slightly poorer quality after it has crossed to the other hemisphere (Springer & Deutsch, 1994). Normal participants will make a judgment faster if information is delivered initially to the hemisphere that is better at making that kind of judgment (Hellige, 1993; Hellige & Sergent, 1986; Sergent & Hellige, 1986).

Perhaps you've wondered whether you are a "left-brain person" or a "right-brain person." It's often said that the left brain is analytical and verbal, whereas the right brain is intuitive and perceptual. In fact, these generalizations must be made with caution. For example, the left brain is actually better than the right at some types of perception (such as determining whether one object is above or below another; Hellige & Michimata, 1989; Kosslyn et al., 1989), and the right brain is better than the left at some aspects of language (such as making the pitch of the voice rise at the end of a question or understanding humor; Bihrle et al., 1986; Brownell et al., 1984; Ellis & Young, 1987). Moreover, the abilities of the two hemispheres often differ only in degree, not in kind. One hemisphere may be better than the other at some particular task (such as noticing the relations of objects in space), but both can do the job to some extent (Hellige, 1993). A major exception to this generalization is language. As you will see in Chapter 7, many aspects of language are carried out by a single hemisphere, usually the left.

Although researchers have not yet been able to pinpoint precisely all of the ways in which the two hemispheres differ, they do know that in normal people the two hemispheres work together. The hemispheres appear to have adopted the strategy of division of labor, with both operating at the same time to carry out different aspects of a task. For example, in perception, the left hemisphere captures the details of a shape while the right captures the overall shape (Delis et al., 1986; Robertson & Delis, 1986; Robertson et al., 1988); in language comprehension, the left hemisphere registers the literal meaning of a message while the right extracts metaphors and allusions (Brownell et al., 1984).

Could it be that the young soldier with difficulties in visual recognition had suffered a functional deficit in his right hemisphere that prevented him from being able to see the overall shapes of objects? The right temporal lobe in particular appears to play a key role in recognizing overall shapes (Ivry & Robertson, 1998). After such damage, he would have had to rely on his left hemisphere, which tends to register details only, not overall shape.

Beneath the Cortex: The Inner Brain

Some parts of the brain lie deep beneath the cortex and so are called *subcortical*. These parts are often similar to the corresponding parts of other animals' brains, which leads some people to think that subcortical areas are somehow simpler than the more recently evolved parts of the brain. Not so. These areas often carry out extraordinarily complex tasks. Moreover, the inner brain is intimately connected with the cortex. Although the examiners of the young soldier did not mention this, it is likely that the soldier became lethargic after his accident—as is typical of people who have suffered brain damage. But why would brain damage cause someone to be less vigorous? The answer lies in the connections between the cortex and inner parts of the brain that are concerned with motivation and emotion. The most important of these subcortical areas are illustrated in Figure 2.16. Together with the cortex, most of these structures are considered to be part of the **forebrain** (so called because in a four-legged, horizontal animal such as a rat, these areas are at the front); but given their great variety of function, this traditional category is not very useful.

Forebrain: The cortex, thalamus, limbic system, and basal ganglia.

Thalamus: A subcortical region that receives inputs from sensory and motor systems and plays a crucial role in attention; often thought of as a switching center.

THALAMUS: CROSSROADS OF THE BRAIN. The **thalamus** is often compared with a switching center but could also be likened to an airline hub where planes converge and then take off for far-flung destinations. The sensory systems, such as vision

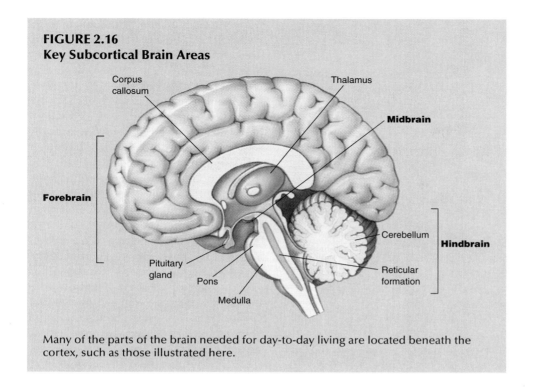

FIGURE 2.16
Key Subcortical Brain Areas

Corpus callosum

Thalamus

Midbrain

Forebrain

Cerebellum

Hindbrain

Pituitary gland

Pons

Reticular formation

Medulla

Many of the parts of the brain needed for day-to-day living are located beneath the cortex, such as those illustrated here.

and hearing, and the motor systems that control muscles send fibers to the thalamus, which routes their signals to other parts of the brain. The intricate connections of the thalamus appear to explain a puzzling phenomenon reported by patients who have had a limb amputated. These people sometimes have the sensation that the limb is still there; they feel a *phantom limb*. Davis and her colleagues (1998) studied the thalamus in such patients and found that mild electrical stimulation of the thalamus produced sensations that seemed to come from the missing limb. Moreover, phantom limb sensations can be painful, and mild electrical stimulation of the thalamus has been found to relieve the pain.

The thalamus has many separate parts composed of clusters of neurons, each of which is called a *nucleus*. The *lateral geniculate nuclei (LGN)*, one in each hemisphere, direct input from the eyes to the visual areas in the occipital lobes, whereas the *medial geniculate nuclei (MGN)* direct input from the ears to the auditory areas in the temporal lobes. (These names are not so formidable when you know what they really mean. *Medial* means nearer the midline of a body or structure, *lateral* means nearer the side; *geniculate*, from the Latin word for "knee," refers to their bent shape.) If the LGNs in the young soldier had been destroyed, he would have had no conscious experience of sight at all; partial damage, however, might have produced some of the symptoms he exhibited.

The thalamus is also involved in attention; as a matter of fact, at this very second your thalamus is allowing you to fix your attention on each word you read. The thalamus is also involved in sleep control. The thalamus plays such a critical role in daily life that if it is badly damaged, the patient will die, even if the cortex remains untouched.

HYPOTHALAMUS: THERMOSTAT AND MORE. The **hypothalamus** sits under the thalamus, as illustrated in Figure 2.17. The small size of this structure shouldn't fool you: It is absolutely critical for controlling many bodily functions, such as eating and drinking; keeping body temperature, blood pressure, and heart rate within the proper limits; and governing sexual behavior. The hypothalamus also regulates hormones, such as those that prepare an animal to fight or to flee when confronted by danger. Again, if visual recognition is impaired, as in the case of our young soldier, this organ would not receive the information it needs to function properly. If confronted

Hypothalamus: A brain structure that sits under the thalamus and plays a central role in controlling eating and drinking, and in regulating the body's temperature, blood pressure, and heart rate.

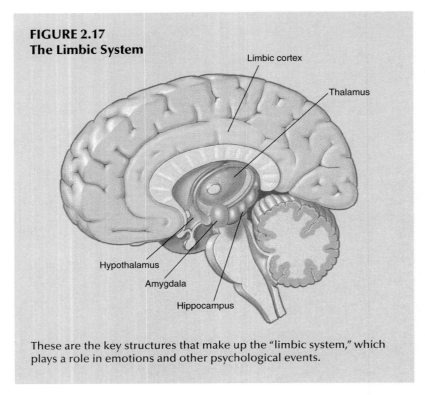

FIGURE 2.17
The Limbic System

Limbic cortex

Thalamus

Hypothalamus

Amygdala

Hippocampus

These are the key structures that make up the "limbic system," which plays a role in emotions and other psychological events.

by an enemy in the field, the soldier would not be able to register the information required to cause the right chemicals to flow into his bloodstream to marshal the body's resources for fight or flight.

Like the thalamus, the hypothalamus consists of clusters of neurons. Some of these can produce pain if stimulated by electrical current; others produce hunger or thirst; still others produce pleasure. In a now-famous experiment with rats, James Olds and his student Peter Milner (1954) electrically stimulated part of a rat's hypothalamus whenever it pressed a bar. The rodent found the electrical reward of pressing the bar so enticing that it continued to press it for hours. Stimulated this way, rats would press the bar thousands of times an hour; if given a choice of two bars to press—one producing food and the other, electrical stimulation—the rats consistently "chose" to press the bar for electrical stimulation (Valenstein, 1973). As a result of this well-documented finding (German & Bowden; 1974; Koob, 1999; Robbins & Everitt, 1999), this hypothalamic area has sometimes been called the "pleasure center."

Just how accurate the term "pleasure center" is has been brought into question, however. Noting the apparent gratification rats get when the hypothalamus is stimulated, researchers turned their attention to humans. Would wires placed in this area of the human brain produce similar results? As it happens, science fiction writer Larry Niven based a series of stories on just this idea, calling the characters addicted to such brain stimulation "wireheads." In spite of Mr. Niven's efforts to base his stories on actual discoveries, real experiments with humans about to have brain surgery have yielded no evidence suggesting that stimulating the hypothalamus produces such pure pleasure (LeDoux, 1996). Various explanations have been offered for this observed difference in rats and humans. One explanation is that the rat's brain registers pleasure differently from ours. Another is that the stimulation the rats received indirectly stimulated, via connecting fibers, some other areas that in fact produce pleasure (Gallistel, 1983; Robbins & Everitt, 1999). Yet another line of reasoning is that the rats weren't really experiencing pleasure; for all we know, the current might have produced a sensation more like the craving for water that follows eating salty potato chips. The bottom line, at least at present, is that we really don't know how rats feel, and it is premature to think of the hypothalamus as a "pleasure center" in the brain.

HIPPOCAMPUS: REMEMBER IT. The **hippocampus** is a structure that looks something like a seahorse (at least to some people), and hence its name, from the Greek *hippokampos,* a mythological "seahorse" monster. This structure plays a key role in allowing us to store new information in the brain's memory banks. The role of the hippocampus was vividly illustrated by the case of patient H.M., who had his hippocampus (and nearby structures) removed in an effort to control his epilepsy. After the operation, his doctors noticed something unexpected: H.M. could no longer learn new things (Milner et al., 1968). His memory for events that occurred a year or so before the operation seemed normal, but he was stuck at that stage of his life. Each day began truly anew, with no memory of what had occurred earlier—in fact, he

Hippocampus: A subcortical structure that plays a key role in allowing new information to be stored in the brain's memory banks.

could not even remember what had happened a few minutes ago, let alone hours or days. Later, more careful study (Squire, 1987) revealed that, in fact, he also could not remember events that had occurred in the year or so before the operation. H.M. does not seem particularly aware of his deficit, and when one of us interviewed him years after the operation, he was in good spirits and remarkably comfortable with himself. When asked about the meanings of words that were coined after his operation, he gamely offered definitions, suggesting, for example, that a jacuzzi is a "new kind of dance." He didn't seem to notice what was missing in his life. (Perhaps this is a case of the left hemisphere telling stories to fill in gaps, as Gazzaniga and LeDoux noted in their study of a split-brain patient.)

Patients such as H.M. led researchers eventually to discover that the hippocampus plays a key role in storing new information in memory. If the young soldier had damage to the occipital or temporal systems that register visual input, these areas would not feed the proper information to the hippocampus—and thus he would not be able to store in memory the stimuli he saw.

AMYGDALA: INNER FEELINGS. The **amygdala** is an almond-shaped structure (its name means "almond" in ancient Greek) near the hippocampus. The amygdala plays a special role in emotions such as fear and anger. Damasio and his colleagues (1994) described a patient who had a rare disorder that destroyed both of her amygdalae (there is one in each hemisphere); this patient not only had difficulty expressing emotion but also had lost the ability to read emotions in the facial exressions of other people. The young soldier probably couldn't register emotions very well either—he couldn't even tell when he was seeing a face. Damasio's patient could recognize faces, but not the emotions on them.

The hypothalamus and amygdala play crucial roles as bridges between the CNS and the PNS. Indeed, both are key components of the **limbic system,** shown in Figure 2.17. The limbic system has long been thought of as being involved in the basics of emotion and motivation: fighting, fleeing, feeding, and sex. But each of the structures in this "system" is now known to have distinct roles that do not involve these functions (for example, the hippocampus is crucially important in storing new memories); further, other brain structures, outside this set, also play a role in emotion. For these reasons, some researchers regard the very concept of a "limbic system" as out of date (LeDoux, 1996).

BASAL GANGLIA: GETTING IN THE HABIT. The **basal ganglia,** positioned to the outer sides of the thalami, are involved in planning and producing movement. These structures have rich connections with parts of the frontal lobes that are also involved in controlling movement. Neurons in part of the basal ganglia have been found to fire right before an animal makes an intentional movement (Iansek & Porter, 1980). Moreover, people with Parkinson's disease, which produces trembling and impairs movement, often have abnormal basal ganglia; the functioning of this structure depends crucially on dopamine.

The basal ganglia also play a critical role in a particular type of learning: forming a habit. When you learn to put your foot on the brake automatically at a red light, the basal ganglia are busy connecting the stimulus (the light) with your response (moving your foot). As discussed in Chapters 5 and 6, this system is distinct from the one used to learn facts (the one, that, presumably, is at work right now, as you read this page).

BRAINSTEM: THE BRAIN'S WAKEUP CALL. As illustrated in Figure 2.16, at the base of the brain are structures that feed into, and receive information from, the spinal cord. These structures are often collectively called the **brainstem.** The **medulla,** at the lowest part of the lower brainstem (see Figure 2.16), is important in the automatic control of breathing, swallowing, and blood circulation. The brainstem also contains a number of small structures together called the **reticular formation,** which has two main parts. The "ascending" part, the *reticular activating system (RAS),* plays a

Amygdala: A subcortical structure that plays a special role in fear and is involved in other sorts of emotions, such as anger.

Limbic system: A set of brain areas, including the hippocampus, amygdala, and other areas, that has long been thought of as being involved in fighting, fleeing, feeding, and sex.

Basal ganglia: Subcortical structures that play a role in planning and producing movement.

Brainstem: The set of neural structures at the base of the brain, including the medulla and pons.

Medulla: The lowest part of the lower brainstem, which plays a central role in automatic control of breathing, swallowing, and blood circulation.

Reticular formation: Two-part structure in the brainstem; the "ascending" part plays a key role in keeping a person awake and alert; the "descending" part is important in producing autonomic nervous system reactions.

key role in keeping you awake and making you perk up when something interesting happens. The RAS produces neuromodulators (as do several other specialized structures deep in the brain) that affect the operation of many other parts of the brain. Neurons of the RAS have long axons that reach up to other parts of the brain and alter the functioning of distant neurons. Some of these structures play a critical role in sleep, arousal, and attention; when the connections from these structures to the cerebral cortex are disrupted, the cortex may receive less activating input from these subcortical structures. It is this kind of disruption in particular that would have caused the soldier to be sluggish following the damage to his brain. The "descending" part of the reticular formation receives input from the hypothalamus and is important in producing autonomic nervous system reactions. It is also involved in connecting impulses from muscles not under voluntary control to those under voluntary control (such as those used in swallowing and speech).

The **pons** is a bridge (*pons* is Latin for "bridge") connecting the brainstem and the cerebellum; it is involved with a variety of functions, ranging from sleep to control of muscles used to form facial expressions.

CEREBELLUM: WALKING TALL. The **cerebellum** is concerned in part with physical coordination. If your cerebellum were damaged, you might walk oddly and have trouble standing normally and keeping an upright posture. In addition, however, damage to some parts of the cerebellum might disrupt your ability to estimate time or to pay attention properly. The surface area of the cerebellum is nearly the same as that of the entire cerebral cortex, and hence it will not be surprising if this structure turns out to be involved in many cognitive functions. The medulla, pons, and cerebellum are often grouped together as the **hindbrain,** because they lie at the rear end of the brain of a horizontal animal such as a rat; the other brainstem structures form the **midbrain,** which lies between the hindbrain and forebrain.

The Neuroendocrine System: It's Hormonal

You now know that the central nervous system can affect the body not only by moving muscles voluntarily, but also by moving muscles automatically and by influencing the autonomic nervous system. In addition, some structures in the brain affect the body by producing (or causing to be produced) certain chemicals. For example, something happens during puberty that changes a child's body into an adult's and changes the child's behavior as well. Charming boys and sweet girls can become sullen and rebellious, moody and impulsive. That "something" is hormones. **Hormones** are chemicals that are produced by glands and can act as neuromodulators. The CNS hooks into the **neuroendocrine system,** which makes hormones that affect many bodily functions. The CNS not only regulates this system, but also receives information from it—which in turn alters the way the CNS operates.

Figure 2.18 shows the locations of the major *endocrine glands;* endocrine glands secrete substances into the bloodstream, as opposed to other glands, such as sweat glands, that excrete substances outside the body. Some hormones affect sexual development and functioning. Among these, **testosterone** causes boys to develop facial hair and other external sexual characteristics, as well as to build up muscle, and **estrogen** causes girls to develop breasts and is involved in the menstrual cycle. Some hormones affect the levels of salt and sugar in the blood, and others help the body cope with stressful situations. The outer layer of the adrenal glands produces **cortisol,** which helps the body cope with the extra energy demands of stress by breaking down protein and fat and converting them to sugar; the sugar provides energy to the body, increases blood flow, and allows you to respond more vigorously and for a longer period of time.

A part of the brain called the **pituitary gland** is particularly interesting because its hormones actually control the other glands; for this reason it has sometimes been called the "master gland." But master or not, this gland is still controlled by the brain,

Pons: A bridge between the brainstem and the cerebellum that plays a role in functions ranging from sleep to control of facial muscles.

Cerebellum: A large structure at the base of the brain that is concerned in part with physical coordination, estimating time, and paying attention.

Hindbrain: The medulla, pons, and cerebellum.

Midbrain: Brainstem structures that connect the forebrain and hindbrain, including the reticular formation.

Hormone: A chemical produced by glands that can act as a neuromodulator.

Neuroendocrine system: The system regulated by the CNS, that makes hormones that affect many bodily functions; also provides the CNS with information.

Testosterone: The hormone that causes males to develop facial hair and other sex characteristics and to build up muscle volume.

Estrogen: The hormone that causes breasts to develop and is involved in the menstrual cycle.

Cortisol: A hormone produced by the outer layer of the adrenal glands that helps the body cope with the extra energy demands of stress by breaking down and converting protein and fat to sugar.

Pituitary gland: So-called "master gland" that regulates other glands but is itself controlled by the brain, primarily via connections from the hypothalamus.

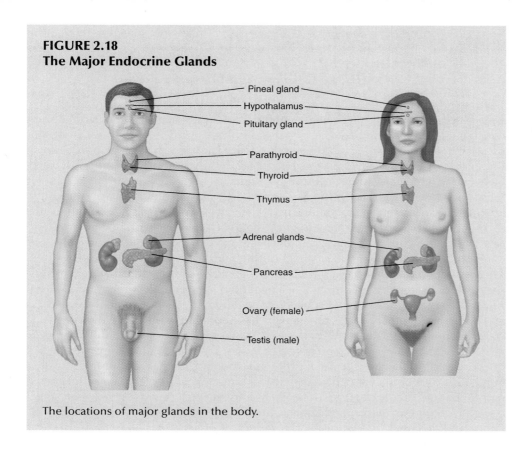

FIGURE 2.18
The Major Endocrine Glands

Pineal gland
Hypothalamus
Pituitary gland
Parathyroid
Thyroid
Thymus
Adrenal glands
Pancreas
Ovary (female)
Testis (male)

The locations of major glands in the body.

primarily via connections from the hypothalamus. If information from the world isn't interpreted properly by the young soldier's cortex, it won't have the normal effect on the hypothalamus, which in turn will not produce the normal hormonal response. Thus, the charms of the opposite sex will be wasted on this unfortunate man.

The Immune System: A Healthy Brain in a Healthy Body

Finally, the brain plays a major role in regulating the **immune system,** which protects the body from disease by producing chemicals and specific types of cells to fight invasions by foreign organisms. A field called *psychoneuroimmunology* has emerged to focus on the ways in which mental and emotional states affect the immune system. For example, researchers have found that elderly traditional Chinese are more likely to die right after the Chinese New Year than just before it, whereas orthodox Jews show no difference in mortality rates during this period. However, the pattern is exactly reversed around the High Holy Days, the most important days in the Jewish year; it is now the Jews who hold on until the holidays are over and Chinese who are unaffected (Phillips & Smith, 1990; Phillips et al., 1992). What does this have to do with the immune system? People probably live longer because their bodies are fighting off whatever ailment is killing them. In fact, Spiegel and his colleagues (Spiegel, 1994, 1997) have found that women with breast cancer who take part in groups that offer emotional support live longer than those who do not—and this effect may occur because these same people have more of a type of blood cell (part of the immune system) that removes foreign bodies (Spiegel et al., 1998). As you will see in Chapter 12, there is no question about it: The brain affects the immune system. Researchers know that the hypothalamus has something to do with this, but the details of how are just now being discovered.

Immune system: The system that protects the body from disease by developing chemicals and specific types of cells to fight against foreign organisms.

Brain Damage and Divorce

At this point, it should be clear that damage to various parts of the brain can have wide-ranging effects on the victim's life. Damage to the left side of the brain can disrupt the ability to produce and understand language. Damage to the right side can disrupt speech patterns, making the voice flat and robotic. The lore in neurology wards (which to our knowledge has never been studied directly) is that more patients with right-hemisphere damage than left-hemisphere damage end up divorced. The reason? It seems that even though the left-hemisphere damage may disrupt language (sometimes leaving the patient able to mutter little more than a few words), this is less troublesome to an intimate relationship than losing the ability to express emotional nuance.

Think about this possibility from the perspective of the three levels of analysis. A damaged brain can leave some aspects of thinking, feeling, and behavior impaired. This disruption can alter basic aspects of personality—of the self. Emotional expressiveness, for example, is an aspect of personality so important that it may have crucial roles at the level of the group: People respond differently if emotional expressiveness is lacking than if other aspects of behavior have been altered by brain damage. Such considerations lead us to predict that right-hemisphere damage will in fact impede intimate relationships. However, note that even if intimate relationships are harmed or even destroyed by the absence of expressed emotion, in other relationships, such as in business, this particular deficit may be less catastrophic than losing one's memory, perception, or language abilities. The likely consequences of brain damage on someone's life depend on the kind of damage, the sort of person he or she was prior to the injury, and the kinds of relationships at the center of his or her life.

CONSOLIDATE!

▶ *1. What are the major parts of the nervous system that can sustain damage?* All parts of our nervous systems are vulnerable, from the cranial nerves, to the spinal cord, to the brain itself or the peripheral nervous system.

▶ *2. What is the cerebral cortex? What are the major cortical systems, and what do they do?* The cortex is a thin (about 2 mm) layer of neurons on the surface of the brain. Most cognitive functions depend crucially on the cortex. The major cortical systems are organized into the functions of the four major lobes. The occipital lobe is the first part of the cortex to process visual input in detail. The temporal lobe receives inputs from the occipital lobe and is the seat of visual memories. It is also involved in language comprehension and hearing, storing new memories, and some aspects of consciousness. The parietal lobe also receives inputs from the occipital lobe, and registers size, three-dimensionality, and location in space. This lobe, also involved in arithmetic, attention, and motor control, includes the somatosensory strip, which registers sensation from parts of the body. Different regions of the somatosensory strip register input from different parts of the body, with larger areas devoted to more sensitive parts of the body. The pari-

etal lobe plays a role in consciousness. The frontal lobes are involved in producing speech, searching for memories, reasoning, and making decisions. The frontal lobes contain the motor strip, which controls fine motor movements. The motor strip is organized so that larger areas are devoted to parts of the body that we can control more precisely.

▶ *3. How do the functions of the two sides of the brain differ?* The left hemisphere plays a larger role in language, and the right hemisphere plays a larger role in spatial attention and nonverbal functions. Moreover, the left hemisphere may play a selective role in "approach" emotions and the right in "withdrawal" emotions. The left brain appears to play a critical role in inventing stories to make sense of the world. However, these differences are usually matters of degree, and both hemispheres often can perform all functions to some extent. A major exception to this generalization is that most aspects of language are restricted to a single hemisphere (typically the left).

▶ *4. What parts of the brain lie under the cerebral cortex? What do these subcortical structures do?* The thalamus is often thought of as a switching center; its many separate parts handle connections to and from distinct parts of the brain. Attention depends on por-

(continued)

tions of the thalamus. The hypothalamus controls many bodily functions, such as eating, drinking, and sex. It is also critically involved in regulating hormones. The hippocampus plays a key role in storing new memories in the brain, and the amygdala is involved in fear and other emotions. The hippocampus, amygdala, and other structures make up the limbic system, which is essential for fighting, fleeing, feeding, and sex. The basal ganglia are important in planning and producing movements, as well as in learning new habits. The brainstem contains a number of structures, many of which are crucial for alertness, sleep, and arousal; damage to these structures would cause sluggishness. The cerebellum is noteworthy because its cortex is about as large as the cortex covering the outer brain (the cerebral cortex) and thus may prove to have important roles in cognitive processes. This structure is involved in motor control, timing, and attention.

PROBING THE BRAIN

Having toured the major parts of the brain and noted their major functions, you can make a pretty good guess about what areas of the brain were damaged when the soldier suffered carbon monoxide poisoning. We cannot know for sure, given the limitations of the tests available at the time of his accident, in 1966. Today, however, doctors can obtain impressive high-quality images of a living brain. These images can show damage to particular brain structures and record brain activity, or the disruption of it, in specific areas.

▶ 1. What can researchers learn about the brain's function by studying behavior following brain damage?

▶ 2. What techniques allow us to record the activity of neurons in the brain as they function?

▶ 3. How can different parts of the brain be stimulated to see whether they are working properly?

▶ 4. What is neuroimaging?

The Damaged Brain: What's Missing?

The first evidence that different parts of the brain do different things came from *natural experiments*, accidents in which people suffered damage to the brain. Such damage typically produces a region of impaired tissue, called a **lesion**. The most frequent source of damage is a **stroke**, which occurs when blood, with its life-sustaining nutrients and oxygen, fails to reach part of the brain (usually because a clot clogs up a crucial blood vessel) causing neurons in the affected area to die. In such cases, researchers study the patients in two ways: First, they are interested in the way function breaks down: which abilities tend to be impaired together and which tend to be impaired separately. Such data provide clues about the way information is stored (for example, by category, such as fruits versus vegetables) (Hart et al., 1985), and how it is processed (for example, reading by converting text to sounds versus recognizing the written word directly) (Shallice & Warrington, 1980). Second, researchers try to relate the *location* of the damage to subsequent behavioral problems. Say, for example, that the young soldier had a lesion in the right temporal lobe and thereafter was unable to perceive overall shapes. The link between the two events offers a hint about one function of this area of the brain.

Although natural experiments can offer important clues about brain functioning, they have several serious limitations. Most important, natural experiments are rarely very neat. The damage caused by a stroke, for example, can extend over a

Lesion: A region of impaired tissue.

Stroke: A result of the failure of blood (with its life-giving nutrients and oxygen) to reach part of the brain, causing neurons in that area to die.

large part of the brain, affecting more than one area and disrupting more than one function. This can make it difficult to relate the disruption in a particular function to the operation of a specific part of the brain. Also, because of the position of the blood vessels, some areas of the brain tend to be the ones damaged by stroke, whereas others are generally spared. So looking at the results of stroke is likely to tell researchers about only certain parts of the brain. Furthermore, stroke victims are usually older people, and often they have not led healthy lives (they've smoked, eaten high-cholesterol foods, not exercised); thus, they are not a representative sample of the population as a whole.

Such drawbacks have led some researchers to turn to *lesioning studies*. In these experiments, researchers remove specific parts of the brains of animals and observe the consequences on behavior. But because animals are not people, we must be cautious in generalizing from animal brains to human brains. And even when researchers know the precise site of brain damage in an animal, or a human (for example, following brain surgery to remove a tumor), drawing conclusions from lesioning studies can be tricky. We cannot assume that the behavior disrupted after brain damage is normally under the control of the damaged area. Think of the problem this way: If sugar and salt are missing from bread dough, the dough won't rise even though it's neither sugar nor salt that makes the dough rise; it's yeast. But yeast depends on sugar and salt to do its stuff. And damage to the brain disrupts not only the area that is directly injured but also parts of the brain that receive information from the damaged areas (Caramazza, 1984, 1986, 1992; Kosslyn & Intriligator, 1992; Shallice, 1988)—and the resulting deficits could reflect dysfunction in those other parts. For example, one of us saw a patient who had a lesion in the left frontal lobe in a location usually associated with language difficulties and found that this man also had visual problems. The lesion did not directly affect the visual areas, but it disrupted connections from the frontal lobe to the back of the brain, causing decreased brain activity in the visual areas (Kosslyn, Daly et al., 1993).

Lesioning techniques not only provide valuable hints about the function of specific parts of the brain, but they also have a special place in testing theories of brain function. If the theory specifies that an area has a particular function, then damage to that area should disrupt all tasks that require that function. However, lesioning studies do not provide a complete picture of brain function, and thus this technique has been supplemented by other methods.

Recording Techniques: The Music of the Cells

Rather than having to rely on the indirect evidence supplied by damaged brains, researchers can now make use of several methods to record the activity of normal brains. Neurons are never totally "off" (they maintain a baseline level of firing even when you sleep or are resting), but their rate of firing depends on what the brain is doing. Neurons that are used in a given task fire more frequently than those not involved in its performance, and this activity can be recorded.

To some extent, brain activity can be measured by making an electromagnetic recording. In one version of this technique, an **electroencephalograph** (**EEG**) machine records electrical current produced by the brain, as shown in Figure 2.19. When neurons fire, they produce electrical fields. When many neurons are firing together, these fields can be detected by electrodes (small metal disks that pick up electrical activity) placed on the scalp. Researchers can record electrical activity in response to a particular stimulus, or can record the activity over time; the result is a tracing of these "brain waves" of electrical fluctuation called an **electroencephalogram** (see Figure 2.19). Psychologists have used this technique to learn much about the brain. It is through EEGs, for example, that they learned that people go through distinct stages of sleep marked by different types of brain activity (see Chapter 4 for a detailed discussion of these stages).

Electroencephalograph (EEG): A machine that records electrical current produced by the brain.

Electroencephalogram: A recording from the scalp of electrical activity over time, which produces a tracing of pulses at different frequencies.

FIGURE 2.19
The Electroencephalograph

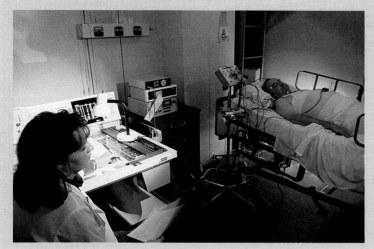

Relaxed/rest

Task performance

The top image shows an EEG during relaxed rest, whereas the bottom image shows an EEG during performance of a task; clearly, the brain is more active when an individual is performing a task than when he or she is relaxed.

This equipment allows researchers to record electrical activity on the scalp, which reflects electrical activity in the brain.

Although EEGs have shed light on brain activity, particularly the time course of changes, the technique poses a major problem: The electrodes placed on the scalp cannot detect the precise locations of the electrical currents in the brain. The electrical current is distorted when it passes through the skull and current travels across the surface of the brain and the scalp. Another technique, **magnetoencephalography (MEG),** avoids these difficulties by recording magnetic waves, which are not distorted as they pass through the skull and do not travel across the scalp. Just as running a current through a wire produces a magnetic field, neural firings produce a magnetic field. Rapid changes in neural firing can be detected with this technique. However, many neurons must be lined up the same way to produce a detectable magnetic field, and thus this technique is not sensitive to activity in all parts of the brain. In addition, neither EEG nor MEG is very sensitive to subcortical activity.

Researchers can avoid the problems associated with EEG and MEG by recording neural activity directly. In this technique, called *single-cell recording*, tiny probes called **microelectrodes** can be placed in individual cells in the brain; these record the firing rates of neurons. A typical microelectrode is at most only 1/10 as wide as a human hair (and some are only 1/100 as wide!). Usually researchers hook up the wires from microelectrodes to amplifiers and speakers rather than to a screen, so they can hear neuronal activity (as clicking sounds) rather than watch a monitor; their eyes are then free to guide the placement of the electrodes. Microelectrodes are sometimes put in human brains before brain surgery in order to find out what a part of the brain does before it is cut. Studies with microelectrodes have yielded some fascinating results. For example, when people look at words, some neurons respond to specific words but not others (Heit et al., 1988).

This technique also has its limitations, particularly in the range of what it shows. If there were a neuron that responded only to huge gray moving objects, it would probably never be found—unless, of course, an elephant happened to visit the hospital while the tests were being performed. Direct recording can help determine which neurons are active during a particular task, but only very clever experimentation can help researchers use this information to figure out exactly what the neurons do.

Magnetoencephalography (MEG): Measurement of the magnetic waves emitted during brain activity.

Microelectrode: A tiny probe inserted into the brain to record electrical activity.

Stimulation: Tickling the Neurons

Transcranial magnetic stimulation (TMS): Researchers stimulate the brain from the outside, by putting a wire coil on a person's head and delivering a magnetic pulse. The magnetic fields are so strong that they make neurons under the coil fire.

Neuroimaging: Brain scanning techniques that produce a picture of the structure or functioning of neurons.

Computer-assisted tomography (CT, formerly **CAT):** A neuroimaging technique that produces a three-dimensional image of brain structure using X rays.

To come closer to detecting just what neurons do, researchers can also stimulate them and observe the results. Three kinds of stimulation studies have been used to find out what parts of the human brain do.

In one technique, mild electricity is delivered to parts of the participant's brain, and the person is then asked to report what he or she experiences. Wilder Penfield and his colleagues (Penfield & Perot, 1963; Penfield & Rasmussen, 1950) pioneered this method with patients who were about to undergo brain operations. Penfield reported that people experience different images, memories, and feelings depending on the area in the brain that is stimulated. A problem with this method, however, is that researchers cannot be sure whether actual memories are activated or whether the participants are making up stories.

In a second, recently developed method, **transcranial magnetic stimulation (TMS),** researchers stimulate the brain by putting a wire coil on a person's head and discharging a large current through the coil, thus creating a magnetic field. This magnetic field is so strong that it causes a large cluster of neurons under it to fire. Using this technique, researchers can make a person's fingers move by shifting the coil over the parts of the brain that control the fingers (in the motor strip) and producing on/off magnetic pulses (Pascual-Leone et al., 1997; Pascual-Leone et al., 1998). Similarly, if such pulses are directed to the occipital lobe, both visual perception and visual mental imagery can be temporarily impaired (Kosslyn et al., 1999). A difficulty with this technique is that when neurons are stimulated, they in turn stimulate other neurons, and it is sometimes hard to know which set of neurons is responsible for the observed effects.

In the third type of stimulation study, electrodes are placed on the surface of a human brain or inside it (in preparation for brain surgery), and researchers observe which activities are disrupted when current is applied (Ojemann, 1983; Ojemann et al., 1989). Like TMS, this method is limited because stimulating particular neurons can lead to the activation of remote neurons, and these other neurons could produce the observed effects.

Neuroimaging: Picturing the Living Brain

Today if you had an emergency like the young soldier's, you would probably be rushed to a hospital and immediately have your brain scanned. Your doctors would order the procedure to determine both the structural damage (which areas were physically affected) and the functional deficits (which areas were performing below par). Because they yield an actual picture of neuronal structure and function, scanning techniques are referred to as **neuroimaging.** It is fair to say that neuroimaging techniques have transformed psychology, allowing researchers to answer questions that were hopelessly out of reach before the mid-1980s (Cabeza & Nyberg, 2000; Posner & Raichle, 1994).

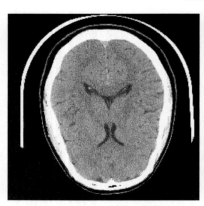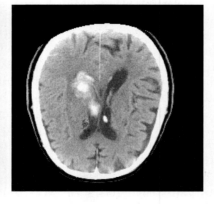

On the left, a computer-assisted tomography (CT) scan, and on the right, a magnetic resonance imaging (MRI) scan. The invention of MRI has provided much higher resolution images of structures of the brain.

VISUALIZING BRAIN STRUCTURE. The oldest neuroimaging techniques involve taking pictures of brain structures using X rays. The invention of the computer allowed scientists to construct machines for **computer-assisted tomography (CT,** formerly **CAT).** In this technique, a series of X rays builds up a three-dimensional image, slice by slice (*tomography* comes from a Greek word meaning "section"). More recently, **magnetic resonance imaging (MRI)** has been developed to take even sharper pictures of the structure of the brain. To understand how MRI works, consider how an opera singer can hit a note that will break a glass. This happens because the glass resonates with the sound waves so that it shakes at the same frequency as the note—shakes so hard that it shatters. Different materials resonate to different frequencies; the note that cracks a thin glass may not be the same as one that cracks a thicker, leaded glass. Similarly, different atoms in the brain resonate to different frequencies of magnetic fields. In MRI, a background magnetic field lines up all the atoms in the brain (or whatever organ is being scanned). A second magnetic field, oriented differently from the background field, is turned on and off many times a second; at certain pulse rates, particular atoms resonate and line up with this second field. When the second field is turned off, the atoms that were lined up with it swing back to align with the background field. As they swing back, they create a signal that can be picked up and converted into an image. The image shows the presence or absence of the substance of interest; in the brain, MRI often assesses the density of water in a region, which differs for gray versus white matter.

Magnetic resonance imaging (MRI): A technique that uses magnetic properties of atoms to take sharp pictures of the structure of the brain.

VISUALIZING BRAIN FUNCTION. CT scans and MRIs give amazing views of the physical structure of the living brain; but for images that reflect the brain in action, researchers need other types of brain scans, ones that track the amount of blood, oxygen, or nutrients moving to particular parts of the brain. When you take a shower or wash a load of laundry, water is drawn into the plumbing pipes from the water main. Similarly, when a part of the brain is working, it draws more blood. This fact was dramatically demonstrated by the case of Walter K (as described by Posner & Raichle, 1994). After a brain operation accidentally altered the shape of the bone over the back of his head, he noticed an odd humming noise coming from inside his head, which he thought became louder when he was using his eyes. His physician, John Fulton, took Walter's report seriously. He listened carefully to the back of Walter K's head when his eyes were opened and when they were closed. Fulton too heard the sound, which became louder when Walter was looking carefully at something; the noise did not occur when Walter was listening carefully, or when he was smelling tobacco or vanilla. Fulton measured the sound coming from his patient's head and demonstrated conclusively that when Walter was looking carefully at something (for example, when he was reading a newspaper), the noise level increased. Why? Because the back of the brain is used in vision, and the noise, audible after the bone structure

A positron emission tomography (PET) machine.

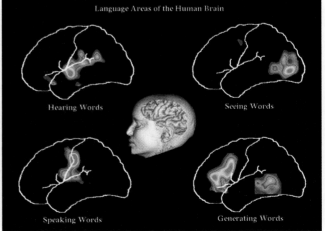

Brighter colors indicate regions of greater blood flow in the brain while the participant performed a particular task (from Posner & Raichle, 1994).

Positron emission tomography (PET): A neuroimaging technique that uses small amounts of radiation to track blood or energy consumption in the brain.

Functional magnetic resonance imaging (fMRI): A type of MRI that usually detects the amount of oxygen being brought to a particular place in the brain.

at the back of Walter's head changed, was the sound of the blood moving into the occipital lobe whenever it was needed for visual tasks.

One of the most important techniques for measuring blood flow or energy consumption in the brain is **positron emission tomography (PET)**. Small amounts of radiation are introduced into the blood, which is then taken up into different brain areas in proportion to how hard the neurons are working. The amount of radiation emitted at different parts of the head is recorded, and a computer uses this information to build three-dimensional images of the brain. In these images, brighter colors indicate places where there was more radiation, and thus greater brain activity. PET scanning has shown that different parts of the frontal lobes are used when you speak your native language and when you speak a language learned after childhood (even though you may be fluent in the second language) (Kim et al., 1997). This finding may explain why, in bilingual people, a stroke can wipe out one language and leave the other intact. The main drawbacks with this technique are that it requires radiation, it takes at least 40 seconds or so to build up an image, and it can cost as much as $2,000 to test a single person.

Probably the most popular type of neuroimaging today is **functional magnetic resonance imaging (fMRI)**. The most common sort of fMRI reveals function by detecting the amount of oxygen that is being brought to a particular place in the brain. When a part of the brain is working hard, the blood that is drawn in brings with it more oxygen than can be used up right away; so oxygen in that area piles up. The iron in the red blood cells carrying oxygen affects the surrounding water differently than the iron in the red blood cells that no longer have oxygen. The most common form of fMRI uses this difference to detect the regions where oxygen is piling up, which indicates where more brain activity is occurring. Unlike PET, fMRIs do not require the introduction of radioactivity into the brain. Moreover, it is possible to build an image of events that occur in only a few seconds. The main drawbacks of this technique are that the MRI machines are noisy and require the participant to lie very still within a narrow tube, a situation some people find uncomfortable.

LOOKING AT LEVELS

The Musical Brain

Because even medium-size hospitals have MRI machines for medical diagnosis, many researchers have been able to use these machines to explore all manner of human abilities. Part of the motor strip in the right half of the brain controls the fingers of the left hand. MRI has shown that this part of the brain is larger in orchestra members who play string instruments than in nonmusicians (Elber et al., 1995; Schlaug et al., 1995). Apparently brain areas that are used a lot actually grow larger, probably because of the formation of additional connections among neurons. Consider this finding from the levels perspective: the size of brain areas—the physical structure of your brain—depends in part on what you do! If you have musical talent and interest (characteristics at the level of the person) and have the opportunity to develop musical ability, your brain can be altered by the experience. If your playing is smiled upon by others (the level of the group), you will be even more motivated to continue practicing—and changing your brain. And once your brain is altered, your playing improves—leading to more praise from others. Even the structure of your brain can be fully understood only from the levels perspective. Lest you think that these findings apply only to musicians, consider the fact that taxi drivers have been found to have unusually large hippocampi—and the longer a driver has worked, the larger they are (Maguire et al., 2000).

▶ **1. What can researchers learn about the brain's function by studying behavior following brain damage?** By looking at altered performance after brain damage, researchers can gain hints about how information is stored and processed and about what functions are carried out by particular parts of the brain. They can also test a theory of the specific functions caried out by a particular part of the brain—if the theory is correct, then all patients with damage to that part should have specific deficits.

▶ **2. What techniques allow us to record the activity of neurons in the brain as they function?** Electroencephalography (EEG) records "brain waves"—fluctuations of electrical fields from the brain. This technique relies on electrodes placed on the skull and can record, for example, electrical variations immediately after someone has received a stimulus or made a decision. Magnetoencephalography (MEG) detects faint magnetic fields, also an index of neural activity; such fields, unlike electrical ones, do not travel over the surface of the brain or scalp and are not distorted as they pass through the skull. Researchers can also use microelectrodes to record neural activity directly, in both humans and animals.

▶ **3. How can different parts of the brain be stimulated to see whether they are working properly?** Transcranial magnetic stimulation (TMS) can be used to stimulate large clusters of neurons by pulsing magnetic fields into the brain. More precise stimulation can be achieved by placing electrodes on the surface of the brain, or actually into specific neurons, and applying small amounts of electric current.

▶ **4. What is neuroimaging?** Neuroimaging techniques allow researchers to visualize the structure and function of the brain. At present, four major techniques are used: computer-assisted tomography (CT), which uses X rays to obtain images of the structure of the brain; magnetic resonance imaging (MRI), which uses the effects of different magnetic fields to produce sharp pictures of the brain; positron emission tomography (PET), which relies on small amounts of radioactivity to track neural activity; and functional magnetic resonance imaging (fMRI), which tracks the movement of oxygen-bearing red blood cells in the brain as a task is performed.

GENES, BRAIN, AND ENVIRONMENT: THE BRAIN IN THE WORLD

Why was the brain of the young soldier vulnerable to such damage from carbon monoxide fumes? Could he have done anything in advance to prepare his brain to survive such an event? Could he have done anything after the accident to speed his recovery? Let's consider the factors of environment and heredity that shape our brains so that they operate in particular ways and not in others, and the degree to which parts of the brain can change their functions if need be.

▶ 1. Can "bad genes" make you more vulnerable to the environment? How do genes and the environment interact as the brain develops and functions?

▶ 2. What does *heritability* mean?

▶ 3. How has evolution shaped the functions of the brain?

Genes as Blueprints: Born to Be Wild?

Figure 2.20 on page 78 illustrates the **deoxyribonucleic acid, or DNA,** molecule that contains our genes. A **gene** is a stretch of DNA that produces a specific protein (including enzymes), which in turn forms building blocks of our bodies (including our brains) or drives the processes that allow us to live. Genes affect us from the instant of conception and are in turn affected by the environment surrounding us at every phase of our lives.

Deoxyribonucleic acid, or DNA: The molecule that contains genes.

Gene: A stretch of DNA that produces a specific protein, which in turn forms the building blocks of our bodies (including our brains) or drives the processes that allow us to live.

FIGURE 2.20
The Secret of DNA

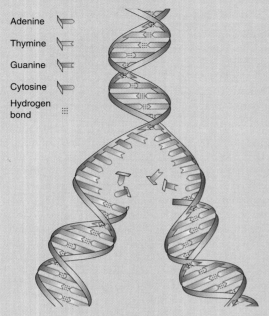

Adenine
Thymine
Guanine
Cytosine
Hydrogen bond

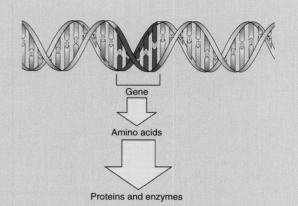

Gene

Amino acids

Proteins and enzymes

What, exactly, is a gene? Let's begin with a chromosome, which is a long, twisted molecule of deoxyribonucleic acid, or DNA, contained in the nucleus of all cells. Every cell of the human body (except for sex cells) has 23 pairs of chromosomes. The two strands in the DNA molecule are separated by pairs of four types of bases. The base adenine (A) always hooks up with thymine (T), and guanine (G) always hooks up with cytosine (C). Thus, if the helix is unzipped down the middle, the extra bases floating about will hook up correctly to form two complete copies of the original molecule. This is how this amazing molecule is able to reproduce itself.

The particular ordering of pairs of bases codes genes; a gene is a segment along the strand of DNA that produces amino acids, which in turn are converted into proteins and enzymes. Everything else in our bodies (including our brains) is built of these molecules.

GENETIC PROGRAMS: THE GENES MATTER. Genes affect not only obvious traits—such as eye color, height, and other physical features—but also behavior. That this is so is clear if you think about other animals. Consider dogs, for example. According to Plomin and his colleagues (1997), historically many dogs were genetically bred to behave in certain ways. Terriers were bred to crawl down holes and flush out small animals, labrador retrievers to carry game such as ducks in their mouths, and so on. It is apparent that breeds of dogs differ in their intelligence and temperament, and yet all are members of the same species; they can interbreed. The variations among the different breeds are due to their genes.

In some organisms, such as yeast, researchers have *mapped* the genes in detail. To "map" a gene is to discover the particular base pairs along the DNA molecule that constitute the gene. In the single-celled organism paramecium (that wiggly oblong creature you may have labored to get into focus under a microscope in high school biology class), at least 20 genes are known to affect one aspect of its behavior—withdrawal. Scientists have found that **mutations,** or physical changes, of various genes produce different behaviors. The mutations are often given amusing names, which makes them easy to remember (we talk about mnemonics in Chapter 6). For example, "pawn" mutant paramecia can only swim forward, like a chess pawn; "paranoiac" mutants tend to swim backward (apparently wary of everything in front of them); and "sluggish" mutants are, well, sluggish.

Mutation: A physical change of a gene.

It is staggering to discover the degree of understanding scientists have achieved over the way genes work. Consider a startling result reported in late 1996 by Ryner and her colleagues. These researchers identified a single gene that can change the sexual behavior of fruit flies. Usually, fruit flies engage in a "courtship dance" before they mate. The male follows the female, uses his forelegs to tap her body, produces a "song" by vibrating his wings, then licks her genitals, curls his abdomen, and tries to mate with her (Ferveur et al., 1995; Hall, 1994 [cited in Ryner et al., 1996]). By altering one gene, scientists produced male fruit flies that performed this courtship dance for other males. In fact, when a group of males with this gene were together, they lined up in a long chain, each male both being courted by and courting other males. The gene that produced this behavior affects only about 500 of the 100,000 neurons in the insect's head. A small genetic change, affecting a relatively small number of neurons, had a big effect. The affected neurons apparently coordinate many other neurons, which in turn produce the behavior. The far-reaching power of relatively small genetic changes can be seen dramatically by comparing chimpanzees with humans: About 99% of the genetic material in both species is identical.

TUNING GENETIC PROGRAMS: THE ENVIRONMENT MATTERS.

There can be no question that genes play a major role in shaping our abilities. But it is critical to point out that genes *cannot* program the structure of the brain entirely in advance. Your brain contained far more connections at birth than it does now. As you interacted with the environment, certain neural connections were used over and over again, while others were used hardly at all. Connections between neurons in parts of the brain that are used frequently survive, while others, which are not useful, are pruned away (Huttenlocher, in press). **Pruning** is a process whereby certain neural connections are eliminated (Cowan et al., 1984; Huttenlocher, in press): As the saying goes, "Use it or lose it." In short, the genes define the possibilities for brain circuits, but interactions with the environment lead some connections to persist and others to disappear.

Pruning is only one of the ways in which your brain changes as you experience the world. Connections are also added. In fact, researchers have found that if rats are raised in enriched environments, with lots of toys and things to do, their brains actually become heavier than those of rats raised in average environments. The additional weight comes about in large part because more blood flows to the cortex (Jones & Greenough, 1996), and in part because new connections are formed (Black et al., 1998; Comery et al., 1995; Diamond et al., 1972; Greenough & Chang, 1985; Greenough et al., 1987; Nelson, 1999; Turner & Greenough, 1985). The environment not only helps to select among connections established by the genes; it can also cause new connections to form.

In fact, even adult brains are capable of dramatic reorganization. If a finger is lost or immobilized, the part of the brain that used to register its input is soon taken over by inputs from other fingers (Merzenich, Kaas, Wall, Nelson, Sur, 1983; additional evidence is provided by Ramachandran, 1993; Ramachandran et al., 1992; Xerri et al., 1999). Moreover, if two fingers are surgically connected, the brain regions that register them start to function as a unit, but this unit splits up if the fingers are then surgically separated (Clark et al., 1988; Das & Gilbert, 1995; Kaas, 1995; Mogilner et al., 1993; Wang et al., 1995). We also now know that adult brains can create new neurons, at least in some regions (Gould et al., 1999). Thus, genes are not destiny; they don't fix our characteristics forevermore. Interactions with the environment can alter both the structure and the function of the brain.

GENES AND ENVIRONMENT: A SINGLE SYSTEM.

How do interactions with the environment alter the brain? Some people think of genes as blueprints for the body, providing the instructions on how to build organs, but this notion captures only part of the gene story. For one thing, rather than being filed away in a dusty drawer once their instructions have been followed, many genes keep working throughout your life.

Pruning: A process whereby certain connections among neurons are eliminated.

Some songbirds learn the songs of their particular species only by hearing other birds sing them. Mello and colleagues (1992) showed that the process of learning a song begins when certain genes are turned on when the bird first hears the song, which in turn regulates the effects of other genes that actually produce the learning.

They are the reason some people go bald, others develop high cholesterol, still others get varicose veins. Even more important, genes are not simply time bombs that are set at birth and ready to explode at the proper hour. Many genes change their operation constantly, sometimes producing proteins and sometimes not. Genes work by coding the production of proteins that affect the workings of the cells in your body, including those in your brain; a protein that is produced at the "instruction" of the genes is said to be *expressed.* Hyman suggested to one of us the following illuminating example: Say you want bigger biceps, so you go to the gym and start lifting weights. After the first week, all you have to show for your time and sweat is aching arms. But after a few weeks, the muscles begin to firm up and soon may even begin to bulge. What has happened? When you first lifted weights, you actually damaged the muscles, and the damage caused the release of certain chemicals. Those chemicals then—and this is the important part—*turned on* genes in the muscle cells. By "turn on" we mean that the proteins coded by the genes were expressed. These proteins were used to build up the damaged muscles. If the damage stops, so do the chemicals that signal the genes to turn on, and the genes will no longer produce those extra proteins. So, you need to lift increasingly heavier weights to keep building more muscle. No pain, no gain.

The important point to remember is that many genes are constantly being turned on and off, as needed, to produce new substances. As you read this, for example, terminal buttons are releasing neurotransmitters that enable you to understand the printed words. Genes are turned on to replenish the buttons' supply of neurotransmitter. Similarly, genes regulate the flow of neuromodulators, and it is the genes that lead to new connections among cells during learning of new material.

Exercise does more than build muscles; it also turns on genes in the brain that build better neurons. Neeper and colleagues (1995, 1996) showed that exercise turns on genes that produce a chemical called brain-derived neurotrophic factor (BDNF). BDNF protects neurons and helps them continue to function properly.

The efficiency of a neuron depends on the way its genes are operating. Just as interacting with the environment (such as lifting weights) can lead to bulging muscles, interacting with the environment can set your brain to operate more or less efficiently. And depending on how your brain is working, you behave differently. By regulating the brain, genes affect behavior.

It is commonplace today for scientists to stress that both genes and environment are important. This is true, but simply stated, it misses the mark. Genes and environment cannot really be considered as separate factors; they are instead *different aspects of a single system.* In much the same way as you can focus separately on the brushstrokes, texture, composition, and color of a painting, you can discuss genes and the environment as discrete entities. But, as with a painting, to appreciate the "whole picture," you must consider genes and environment together (Gottlieb, 1998).

ENVIRONMENT AND GENES: A TWO-WAY STREET. Genes can affect the environment, and the environment can regulate the genes. Remember, we are talking about a single system here. Plomin and colleagues (1997), Scarr and McCartney (1983), and others distinguish three ways that the genes and environment interact. First, **passive interaction** occurs when the parents' or sibling's genetically shaped tendencies produce an environment that is passively received by the child. An example: Parents with higher intelligence tend to read more, and thus have more books in the house. Given that parents with higher intelligence tend to have children with higher intelligence, this means that children with higher intelligence will tend to be born into

Passive interaction: Occurs when the parents' or sibling's genetically shaped tendencies produce an environment that is passively received by the child.

environments with more books (see Plomin, 1995). Second, **evocative** (or **reactive**) **interaction** occurs when our genetically influenced characteristics draw out behaviors from other people. We might call this the "blondes have more fun" effect. As it happens, responses to this stereotype vary, at least in U.S. culture. Some people react to blondes more positively than to brunettes. Others, however, may think blondes are less substantial people than are brunettes. Third, genes and environment interact when people deliberately choose to put themselves in specific situations and aggressively avoid others. Such **active interaction** involves constructing situations or shaping and modifying existing ones in ways that are comfortable for existing genetic tendencies. A timid child, for instance, may avoid loud parties and amusement parks, instead seeking out peaceful settings and quiet pastimes.

Behavioral Genetics

Researchers in the field of **behavioral genetics** try to determine how much of the differences among people's abilities are due to their different genetic makeups and how much to differences in their environments. The environment varies at different times and places, so this is a difficult question indeed. Throughout this book, we talk about the relative contributions of genes and the environment to differences in mental processes or behavior. Here we need to stress a crucial point: Any conclusions about the relative contributions of genes and environment can apply only to the specific circumstances in which they were measured. To see why, let's say you have two types of apple trees, one bred to produce large apples and one bred to produce small ones. If you plant the seeds with "big apple genes" in the shade, in rocky soil, and scrimp on water, they will probably produce apples even smaller than those produced by seeds with "small apple genes" planted in better circumstances. The point of this example is simple, and vitally important: The effects of the genes vary in different environments. Genes cannot be described in isolation; they can be characterized only in relation to the specific environments in which they operate. Statements about relative contributions of genes and environments therefore apply only to the situation at hand and have no bearing on different circumstances.

HERITABILITY, NOT INHERITABILITY. Researchers in behavioral genetics focus on estimating the "heritability" of various characteristics, ranging from intelligence to personality, as they occur in specific environments. **Heritability** is perhaps an unfortunate term. It does not indicate the amount of a characteristic or trait that is inherited, but rather how much of the variability in that characteristic in a population is due to genetics. Height in Western countries is about 90% heritable. This statement means that 90% of the *variability* among the heights of these people is genetically determined, not that *your* height was determined 90% by your genes and 10% by your environment. In fact, the possible differences in height owing to diet may actually be greater than the differences owing to genes; but *in a specific environment* (for example, one in which diet is constant), heritability indicates the contribution of the genes to variations. If the environment were different, the heritability might be different too.

TWIN STUDIES: ONLY SHARED GENES? At first glance, the simplest way to study whether variability in a characteristic is inherited might seem to involve comparing the characteristics of parents and their children. But this method doesn't sort out the effects of genes and the environment. On the one hand, the parents and kids share a common household, which could *increase* the correlation. But factors such as different ages and occupations, and the likelihood that parents and children spend much of their days in different environments, could *decrease* the correlation. Because of these confounding variables, we can gain greater insight by studying brothers and sisters who are about the same age. But because even small age differences can make

Evocative (or reactive) interaction: Occurs when genetically influenced characteristics draw out behaviors from other people.

Active interaction: Occurs when people choose, partly based on genetic tendencies, to put themselves in specific situations and to avoid others.

Behavioral genetics: The field in which researchers attempt to determine how much of the differences among people are due to their genes and how much to the environment.

Heritability: The degree to which variability in a characteristic is due to genetics.

a big difference in certain environments (such as school), it is best to study twins, people who are exactly the same age.

Twin studies compare the two types of twins, identical and fraternal. Identical twins start life when a single egg (which later divides) is fertilized by a single sperm; these twins are **monozygotic** (like many scientific terms, this comes from Greek: *monos*, meaning "single" and *zygotos*, meaning "yoked," as occurs when a sperm and egg are joined). Monozygotic twins have identical genes. In contrast, fraternal twins grow from two separate eggs that are fertilized by two different sperm; these twins are **dizygotic.** Fraternal twins share only as many genes as any other pair of brothers or sisters—on average, half. By comparing identical twins and fraternal twins, we get a good idea of the contribution of the genes, if we assume that the environment is the same for members of both sets of twins.

An even better way to gather evidence for the relative contributions of genes and environment is to study either related children who were separated at birth and raised in different households or unrelated children who were raised in the same versus different households. Called an **adoption study,** this type of investigation is particularly powerful when twins who have been separated at birth, or shortly thereafter, grow up in different environments. Even in these cases, however, it is difficult to separate genetic from environmental influences. If the twins are cute, for instance, caregivers in both households will treat them differently than if they look like little trolls; if they are smart and curious, both sets of parents may be inclined to buy books and read to them. So findings from studies of twins separated at birth are fascinating, but even they don't allow us to separate genes from environment with confidence. The best we can say is that genes contribute a certain amount to differences among people in particular environments, and that environments contribute a certain amount to such differences when people have particular genes.

Evolution and the Brain: The Best of All Possible Brains?

The loss of consciousness and brain damage suffered by the young soldier occurred because he breathed toxic fumes and was deprived of oxygen. Not all species would react the way this member of our human species did, though, if faced with this situation. Sperm whales, for instance, do just fine if they take a breath every 75 minutes or so. Why don't our brains give us this extra protection? This question leads to thoughts about **evolution,** the gene-based changes in the characteristics of members of a species over successive generations.

NATURAL SELECTION: REPRODUCTION OF THE FITTEST. A major driving force of evolution is **natural selection,** which was first described in detail in 1858 by Charles Darwin and, independently, Alfred Russel Wallace. Inherited characteristics that contribute to survival in an environment are the ones that will come to be widespread in a population because the individuals with those characteristics are the ones that live long enough to have many offspring. In turn, those offspring, equipped with the favorable characteristics inherited from their parents, will survive to have more offspring. In this way, the "selection" of the survivors is made by "nature." An inherited characteristic that contributes to such selection is called an **adaptation.** The term "survival of the fittest," coined by Darwin, is perhaps unfortunate; the key point is that some characteristics lead some organisms to have more offspring, who in turn have more offspring, and so on—until their inheritable characteristics are spread throughout the population. Plomin and colleagues (1997) point out that the principle might better have been termed "reproduction of the fittest."

Darwin saw this pattern in a brilliant insight; but where are the genes in the story? Nowhere. Genes were not discovered until the early part of the twentieth century, and not discovered to correspond to DNA until 1953. Darwin never knew

Twin study: Study that compares identical and fraternal twins to determine the relative contribution of genes to variability in a behavior or characteristic.

Monozygotic: From the same egg and having identical genes.

Dizygotic: From different eggs and sharing only as many genes as any pair of brothers or sisters—on average, half.

Adoption study: Study in which characterisitics of children adopted at birth are compared to those of their adoptive parents or siblings versus their biological parents or siblings (often twins). These studies often focus on comparisons of twins who were raised in the same versus different households.

Evolution: Gene-based changes in the characteristics of members of a species over successive generations.

Natural selection: Changes in the frequency of genes in a population that arise because genes allow an organism to have more offspring that survive.

Adaptation: A characteristic that increases "fitness" for an environment.

that the mechanism for the transmission of traits from one generation to the next is the gene. Today, we would say that natural selection depends on the fact that there is variation in the genes carried by members of a population, and if a gene allows an organism to have more offspring that survive (and they have more offspring, and so on), eventually more of that particular gene will be present in the population.

Evolution via natural selection tends to mold the characteristics of a group of organisms to the requirements of its environment. If a certain animal lives at the North Pole, those individuals with warm fur will tend to have more babies that survive, and those individuals that are white (and thus harder for predators to spot in the snow) will tend to have more babies that survive. If these characteristics are useful enough in that environment, eventually the species as a whole will have warm white fur.

Here's a contemporary analogy of the way natural selection works. There were two Chinese brothers; one settled in Louisiana and the other in Ohio. They both opened Chinese restaurants and began with identical menus. After the first month, the brother in Louisiana noticed that his blander dishes were not selling well, so he dropped them from the menu; in Ohio, they were doing fine, so they remained. In Louisiana, the chef one day accidentally knocked a jar of chili powder into a pot of chicken he was simmering. He found he liked the taste, so this new dish became the special of the day. It sold so well that it became a standard on the menu. Hearing the tale, the brother up north in Ohio tried the chili dish, but it didn't sell well. This chef bought a lot of corn, which was on sale. He tried adding it to a traditional dish and called it the special of the day. The Ohio chef wasn't trying to achieve a particular taste, he was just experimenting. That corn dish did not sell well, and so was dropped. But when he added corn to another recipe, the result was an instant hit. Both chefs continued with new elements in their cooking, with varying degrees of success on different occasions. After two years, the brothers' menus had little in common.

Two important principles of evolution are illustrated here. First, the "environment"—the hungry restaurant patrons—"selected" different aspects of the menus: The southerners, for example, apparently liked spicy food better than did the patrons in Ohio. Second, variation is at the heart of the process. Without the accidents and substitutions, the process would not have worked—the menus would not have evolved over time. Natural selection in the evolution of the two menus depended on random variation, which provided the "options" that proved more or less adaptive.

The same is true in the evolution of species, but in this case the "menu" is the set of genes different organisms possess. Genes that lead an organism to have offspring who have still more offspring stay on the menu, and ones that do not lead to this result eventually get dropped.

So, back to the question of the sperm whale and breathing. If our ancestors had had to go for long periods without breathing in order to survive, then only those who could do so would have survived and had offspring—and we lucky descendants would have inherited this ability. And the story of our young soldier might have had a happier ending.

NOT JUST NATURAL SELECTION: ACCIDENTS DO HAPPEN. A word of warning: Always exercise caution when trying to use the idea of natural selection to explain our present-day characteristics. Just because a characteristic exists doesn't mean that it is an adaptation to the environment or that it is the result of natural selection. Natural selection may or may not be the reason, for example, why some people are more prone than others to alcoholism; it may or may not explain certain students' violent rampages in high schools, or the frequency of heart disease in certain groups. For one thing, as human brains and bodies evolved, the environment also changed: People created not only furniture, houses, and cities but also automobiles, guns, computers, and candy. Our brains may not be ideally suited for what they are doing now.

Furthermore, natural selection is not the only way that evolution works. Accidents, sometimes very happy ones, occur. Sometimes characteristics piggyback on other characteristics. For example, sickle-cell anemia, a blood problem that is common among American blacks, is an unfortunate side-effect of protection from malaria. (The gene that causes the problem codes for a protein that destroys cells infected with the malaria-causing parasite, which is useful in the parts of Africa where malaria is common.) And sometimes characteristics appear because the original adaptation can be put to good use in a new role that has nothing to do with the original adaptation (Gould & Lewontin, 1979). For example, once we have the brain machinery to see lines and edges, abilities that probably helped our ancestors to discern prey, the brain can allow us to learn to read.

In short, some of our abilities, personality types, social styles, and so forth may have arisen from natural selection because they are useful, and others may have been accidental. It is not easy to sort out which is which, and we should not assume that there is a sound evolutionary reason for everything people do.

LOOKING AT LEVELS

Alcoholism, Muslims, and Mormons

As we've seen from our discussion of the interaction between genes and the environment, only rarely do genes determine completely whether you will have a specific characteristic. For example, men with a particular gene (for which they can be tested) are likely to become alcoholics if they drink at all (Goedde & Agarwal, 1987). Having this gene presents no downside, however, for men who obey the norms of a strict Muslim or Mormon culture, in which alcohol is forbidden. The ultimate effect of the gene depends on the person and the culture. And why do people adhere to certain rules and norms? At least in part, because of their beliefs. Thus, the adherence to group norms leads to behavior that regulates the genes. If a man knows he has this gene, this knowledge might even serve to support his beliefs and his group affiliation. Genes are merely one element in a larger system, which necessarily includes interactions among events at the different levels of analysis.

CONSOLIDATE!

▶ *1. Can "bad genes" make you more vulnerable to the environment? How do genes and the environment interact as the brain develops and functions?* When the brain is developing, there are more neurons and neural connections than are later used; the process of pruning eliminates connections that are not useful or effective. In addition, neurons grow more connections with use. The genes govern not only how neurons grow, but also how they function internally. Many genes are constantly being turned on and off, and the brain functions more or less efficiently depending on which genes are turned on and hence which proteins are expressed.

▶ *2. What does* heritability *mean?* Heritability refers to how much of the *variability* in a characteristic in a

population is due to genetics. Even if there is virtually no variability—and hence virtually zero heritability—in a characteristic, it can still be heavily under genetic influence (as is true not only for arms, but also for the components of the nervous system).

▶ *3. How has evolution shaped the functions of the brain?* Evolution has shaped the functions of the brain both through the process of natural selection (of characteristics that are adaptive) and accidents (including when one characteristic piggybacks on another).

A DEEPER LEVEL

Recap and Thought Questions

▶ Brain Circuits: Making Connections

The key building block of the brain is the neuron. The cell body receives inputs from the dendrites (or, sometimes, directly from axons of other neurons) and sends output via its axon. The axon is covered with myelin, a fatty insulating material that makes neural transmission more efficient. The terminal buttons at the end of the axon contain chemical substances that are released by an action potential. These substances are either neurotransmitters or neuromodulators. Neurotransmitters cross the synaptic cleft (the gap between the end of the sending axon and the receiving neuron) to affect another neuron. Both neurotransmitters and neuromodulators affect receptors, which are like locks that are opened by the right key. Once opened, the receptor causes a chain of events inside the neuron. Glial cells not only support neurons but also help to regulate neurotransmitters and can affect neurons directly. When the total input to a neuron is sufficiently excitatory, the neuron "fires"—that is, chemical reactions work their way down the axon. These reactions require energy (which requires, among other things, oxygen). After a neuron has fired, surplus neurotransmitter is reabsorbed back into the cells. Some drugs block this reuptake mechanism, so that enough neurotransmitter becomes available to affect other neurons.

How did the fumes the soldier inhaled affect his brain? We can narrow our explanation for his problems to the following three aspects of brain function: First, many—but not all—neurons in the occipital lobes died because of a lack of oxygen. This damage caused his fuzzy vision. Second, the parietal lobes, thalamus, or some other area that is used in attention was also damaged, so that he had a narrow range of attention and thus could not perceive the context in which shapes appeared. Hence, he only saw small details. Third, he saw small details because of damage to the temporal lobe in his right hemisphere, an area that typically registers overall shapes; or, possibly, the connections to the right temporal lobe from the occipital lobes were damaged. But his left hemisphere, particularly his left frontal lobe, apparently was intact enough to allow him to make up a story based on what he saw, allowing him to try to make sense of the stimulus. Thus, the soldier saw details in isolation and tried to think what they might be.

> **Think It Through.** Say you are a health-care provider who specializes in helping patients who have suffered brain damage. What would you try to do to help the young soldier? Are there any special strategies you could teach him that might help him? What jobs might he be trained to do in spite of the damage?
>
> Imagine that you have invented a new drug that protects one particular cognitive ability from being disrupted by brain damage. If you could choose, which ability would your drug protect? Why?

▶ Structure and Function: An Orchestra With Many Members

The nervous system has two major parts, the central nervous system (CNS) and the peripheral nervous system (PNS). The central nervous system (CNS) consists of the spinal cord and the brain itself. The peripheral nervous system consists of the autonomic nervous system (ANS) and the skeletal system.

First, the central nervous system. In addition to sending commands from the brain to the body and passing along sensory input to the brain, the spinal cord also underlies some reflexes. Reflexes depend on the action of interneurons, neurons that hook up to other neurons. The brain itself is organized into lobes and is covered by the cortex, a thin layer of neurons. The cortex contains many bulges (gyri) and creases (sulci), allowing a lot of cortex to be crammed into a relatively small space. The four major lobes in each hemisphere are the occipital, temporal, parietal, and frontal. The occipital lobe processes visual input; the temporal lobe is the seat of visual memories and is also involved in language comprehension, hearing, storing new memories, arithmetic, and some aspects of consciousness. The parietal lobe registers size, three-dimensionality, and location in space, and is also involved in attention, motor control, and consciousness; it includes the somatosensory strip, which registers sensation from parts of the body. The frontal lobe is involved in speech production, searching for memories, reasoning (and using memory to help in reasoning), fine motor control (governed by the motor strip), and making decisions. Each lobe is duplicated, one on the left and one on the right. The left hemisphere plays a larger role in language, and the right hemisphere plays a larger role in spatial attention and nonverbal functions; moreover, the left hemisphere may play a selective role in "approach" emotions and the right in "withdrawal" emotions. One apparent function of the left brain, particularly the frontal lobe, is to invent stories to make sense of the world.

Under the cortex, many subcortical areas are crucial to the brain's mission. The thalamus manages connections to and from distinct parts of the brain; the hypothalamus regulates hormones, which is important as it operates to control bodily functions such as eating, drinking, and sex; the hippocampus is involved in the storage of new memories; and the amygdala plays a role in fear and other emotions. The basal ganglia are used in planning and producing movements, as well as in learning new habits. The brainstem contains structures involved in alertness, sleep, and arousal; and the cerebellum is involved in motor control, timing, and attention.

The peripheral nervous system (PNS), which is engaged in part via the amygdala and hypothalamus, consists of two parts: the autonomic nervous system (ANS) and the skeletal system. The ANS is in turn divided into the sympathetic and parasympathetic nervous systems, which are critically involved in the "fight or flight" response. The neuroendocrine system produces hormones, which affect not only the body but also the brain itself (as in, for example, altering moods). Finally, the immune system is also affected by the brain.

How would his brain damage have affected his ability to be a soldier? The brain damage disrupted his ability to recognize and identify objects. Thus, not only would he have difficulty distinguishing friend from foe, he would also have trouble identifying his weapons, places of shelter, vehicles, and everything else used by the army. In addition, because recognition is the first step to reaction, he would not have the appropriate "fight or flight" emotional response. Indeed, he probably did not have the physical energy or stamina to perform on the parade field, let alone on the battlefield. In short, his damage would have devastating effects on the young man's ability to be a soldier.

> **Think It Through.** Clearly, the organization of the brain has a lot to do with why brain damage produces one disorder and not another. It is possible that some parts of the brain receive information that is not available to the parts that control language. If so, can you think of types of behaviors that might reveal that the information was "in there"?
>
> Can you think of a way to find out whether the soldier had a problem with attention, or whether his paying attention to a small area was just a strategy? That is, perhaps he believed that by focusing on details he would see better, and did so even though he was in fact able to pay attention to overall shapes. What difference, if any, would it make whether his problem stemmed from a faulty strategy or a problem beyond his control?
>
> More careful examination of the soldier might have suggested that his problem was not confined to visual processing. What would you think if it could be shown that his personality was particularly unemotional? What if he had shown little interest in eating or sex?

▶ Probing the Brain

The earliest method used to discover what the various parts of the brain do was to observe the effects of brain damage on behavior. Such so-called natural experiments led scientists to investigate the effects of lesioning, or damaging, parts of animal brains. Scientists can record electrical activity produced by neural firings while people and animals perform specific tasks, either from the scalp or from tiny electrodes placed in neurons, they find more vigorous activity in brain areas involved in the task than in those that are not being used. In addition, neurons can be electrically or magnetically stimulated to fire and the effects on behavior observed. Various neuroimaging techniques include the following: computer-assisted tomogra-

phy (CT), which uses X rays to obtain images of the structure of the brain; magnetic resonance imaging (MRI), which makes use of magnetic fields to produce very sharp pictures of the brain; magnetoencephalography (MEG), which detects faint magnetic fields that can be used as an index of neural activity; positron emission tomography (PET), which relies on small amounts of radioactivity to track blood flow or energy consumption in the brain; and functional magnetic resonance imaging (fMRI), which uses changes in the magnetic properties of blood when oxygen is bound to red blood cells to track blood in different brain areas.

Which techniques would be most useful for diagnosing the effects of the soldier's accident? If the soldier had his accident today, he would first receive either a CT or an MRI scan (depending on the facilities available at the local hospital) to discover the location and extent of the injury. To discover the functional consequences of the injury, he would receive either a PET or an fMRI scan. In addition, he would be given behavioral tests (like those described at the beginning of this chapter) to discover whether he had deficits in his vision, memory, reasoning, and other cognitive abilities.

> **Think It Through.** Dr. Scannering has invented a new form of brain scan, which shines very low-power lasers safely through the head and projects an image of brain activity as it is happening. This machine will be sold for less than the price of a personal computer. What uses can you think of for such a machine? What sort of education would you need to make the best use of this technological breakthrough?

▶ Genes, Brain, and Environment: The Brain in the World

The genes lay down the basic structure of the brain, but the environment molds both its structure and its function. During brain development, the environment affects brain structure and function by pruning connections that are not working well or frequently, and causes the brain to form new connections in response to increased activity. The genes place limits on what is possible, however (for example, people can't grow wings), and even small genetic changes can significantly affect cognition and behavior. Many of your genes are under the control of the environment and are turned on and off depending on what you are doing; specific genes can cause the manufacture of new neurotransmitters or neuromodulators at the terminal buttons, and can even cause neurons to hook up in new ways.

Behavioral genetics attempts to discover how much of the variability in a trait or ability is due to the genes versus the environment, but such estimates apply only to the environments in which the trait or ability is measured.

We have our present sets of genes because of evolution, which is partly a consequence of natural selection and partly of accidents.

How did the soldier's genes make him vulnerable to the fumes? Two ways: First, as a member of our species, he inherited a brain that requires certain amounts of oxygen. Thus, like any of us, his brain suffered when not enough oxygen reached it. Second, every one of us is unique, partly because of variations in our genes and partly because of effects those variations have had in response to our individual environments. Thus, depending on his genes and environment, the soldier could have been a bit more or a bit less vulnerable than the average person.

Think It Through. Did natural selection design the brain so that it is vulnerable to damage such as the soldier's brain sustained? Is there reason to think that natural selection formed the brain so that vision is carried out by separate areas from hearing and language? Which parts of the human brain would you expect to be shared by other animals, and why?

Can you think of any human abilities that you would bet are "adaptations"? How about ones that could be accidents? How could you tell whether a characteristic has prevailed because of natural selection?

3 SENSATION AND PERCEPTION

How the World Enters the Mind

Sue hated going to art museums. To her, some paintings just looked like scribblings or drips of paint, something a three-year-old would make. Others looked like bad photographs taken through a lens left out in the rain. The sculptures were even worse: Some of them looked to Sue like huge cardboard boxes that had been through a giant food processor operating at slow speed. But Sue's friend Tai liked to look at things like this and wanted Sue to come along while she did. It puzzled Sue, who was bored and annoyed in a museum or a sculpture garden, that Tai didn't feel the same way. And Tai couldn't understand why Sue took no pleasure in art, or why she didn't come away feeling refreshed and invigorated, as Tai did, after an afternoon at the museum.

Curiously, the friends had exactly opposite reactions when they went together to a rock concert. (They had agreed on "equal time" for their favorite adventures.) Sue would become completely absorbed, moving her body with the music, while Tai would become almost physically uncomfortable. Sue couldn't understand why Tai wasn't energized. Tai's reaction was that the groups were primitive and crude; she didn't understand how Sue could enjoy such loud and violent music.

At first glance, these reactions might seem mere "personality differences" between the two friends. But from the levels perspective, so-called personality differences can arise from differences in how our brains work, in what we believe and desire, in how we respond to the surrounding group.

How, when faced with the same stimuli—the same painting, the same music—can people's reactions be so different? Do Sue's and Tai's different perceptions reflect differences in their abilities to register different kinds of sensations? Or are they the products of differing degrees of exposure and learning? Or both? Could it be that the eyes and ears of the two friends, and the visual and auditory parts of their brains, are different, and thus produce different responses?

Despite their disagreement—the possible reasons for which we explore in this chapter—Sue and Tai share the fundamental ability to register and process (that is, to receive and interpret) the dizzying array of colors, shapes, sounds, and other sensations that whirl around them. How do our brains register that something is "out there"? And what of the other senses through which we register this amazing world—how do we smell, and hear, and taste; how are we able to be aware of our bodies? And is there a perception beyond these—a perception that is literally "extrasensory"—that some, if not all, of us possess? To a psychologist, the investigation of these questions provides fruitful clues in our discovery of ourselves.

SENSING AND SELECTING: OPENING UP TO THE WORLD

Electric guitars grated on Tai's ears and made her feel edgy, but they made Sue feel alive. Color and form delighted Tai and made her thirst for more; the same color and form gave Sue a headache. The act of sensing and perceiving stimuli of any kind, whether a song, a color-soaked canvas, or a soft caress, encompasses a remarkable series of events at the levels of the brain, the person, and the social group, all happening within the context of the physical world. The processes of sensation and perception lie at the root of our experience of being alive, serving as the foundation for most of what we know and do. If we cannot sense the world, then for all practical purposes it does not exist for us; if we sense it incorrectly, our world will be bent and distorted. To understand mental processes and behavior, then, we must understand how our senses allow us to make contact with the world.

▶ 1. What is "sensation," and how does it differ from "perception"?

▶ 2. People may vary in how they direct their attention; just what is "attention"?

Sensation and Perception: Being in the World

The Greek philosopher Plato, who some 2,500 years ago theorized about many aspects of existence, psychological and otherwise, offered an interesting explanation of how humans see. Plato believed that the eyes produce rays that illuminate objects and that these rays are the basis of sight. Recent surveys of college students reveal that a surprisingly high proportion of them—fully one third—believe the same thing! The percentage of students accepting this explanation actually doubled (to 67%) when participants were shown a computer-graphic illustration of the concept (Winer et al., 1996; see Winer & Cottrell, 1996). Furthermore, two thirds of the college students who believe in such rays also believe that a person whose rays fail will go blind (Winer et al., 1996).

To set the record straight, there are no rays that shine from your eyes; in fact, essentially the process works the other way. Rather than producing rays, the eye registers light that is reflected from, or is produced by, objects in the line of sight. Similarly, the ear registers vibrations of air, and the skin responds to an object when pressure from it stimulates nerves. Psychologists define **sensation** as the immediate experience of basic properties of an object or event that occurs when a type of receptor (such as those at the back of the eye, in the ear, on the skin) is stimulated. When enough physical energy strikes a receptor, the cell sends neural impulses to the brain. As discussed in Chapter 2, receptors in general are like locks, which are opened by the appropriate key; for these sensory receptors, the appropriate physical energy serves as the key. The entire cell that responds to physical stimulation is called a receptor, not just the key parts that register the input. It is the signals sent by these receptors that cause us to become aware of the outside world.

Psychologists call the registering of sensation when a physical event excites the appropriate receptors *early processing*, but this is not yet **perception**, which occurs when you organize and interpret the sensory input as signaling a particular object or event. Perception includes two major phases. In the first, called *intermediate processing*, the input is organized into coherent units. In vision, for example, you don't see isolated blobs and lines, you see surfaces and objects. In the second, termed *late processing*, your perceptual system interprets the meaning of these units. When Tai and Sue stand before the same abstract painting, Tai may discern a distinct pattern, whereas Sue perceives only a jumble of random markings. This is because Tai's visual system has had previous exposure to such paintings and has learned how to see them. But this window on the world is not permanently closed to Sue: She, like the rest of us, can learn to perceive things in new ways, and to enjoy the art she previously found unpleasant.

As with a painting or a piece of music, in which form and color, harmony and rhythm, are at work simultaneously, so too with processing. "Early," "intermediate," and "late" seem to indicate a simple sequential process, but more is happening. Processing may be **bottom up,** initiated by the stimulus, or **top down,** guided by knowledge, expectation, or belief. And the two sorts of processes may be in play at the same time (Humphreys et al., 1997; Kosslyn & Koenig, 1995). Here's how it works.

If you turn on the TV to a random channel, you will be able to understand what appears on the screen even if it's a complete surprise: the processing is bottom up, from the stimulus alone, unaided by any expectation you might have. Your eyes and ears register what's there, and your brain processes the resulting signals. Bottom-up processing operates like a row of standing dominoes: When the neural equivalent of the first domino is tripped by the light impulses reaching your eye and the sound vibrations reaching your ear, other neural signals are successively tripped, like falling dominoes, until you've understood what you're seeing and hearing.

Figure 3.1 illustrates a classic example of bottom-up processing. Bottom-up processes lead you to read the meaning of the word. Such processes also lead you to see the color the word is written in—and if the meaning of the word is different from the color of the ink, you experience interference when you try to name the color of the ink.

Back to the couch, watching TV. After the first few moments of watching this randomly selected channel, even if you are the very picture of a vegetating couch potato, you are in fact actively anticipating what will appear next and using this information to help you see. Now you are engaging in top-down processing, which occurs when you use your knowledge of what to expect to help you look for specific characteristics and fill in missing parts of the stimulus. You can watch top-down processing at work if the TV image is really blurry and you use the sound track to provide clues to what's in the picture. For example, if the sound track makes it clear that two people are about to kiss, you will be able to make out the outlines of the faces more easily.

Sensation: The immediate experience of basic properties of an object or event that occurs when a receptor is stimulated.

Perception: The act of organizing and interpreting sensory input as signaling a particular object or event.

Bottom-up processing: Processing that is initiated by stimulus input.

Top-down processing: Processing that is initiated by knowledge, expectation, or belief.

FIGURE 3.1
The Stroop Effect

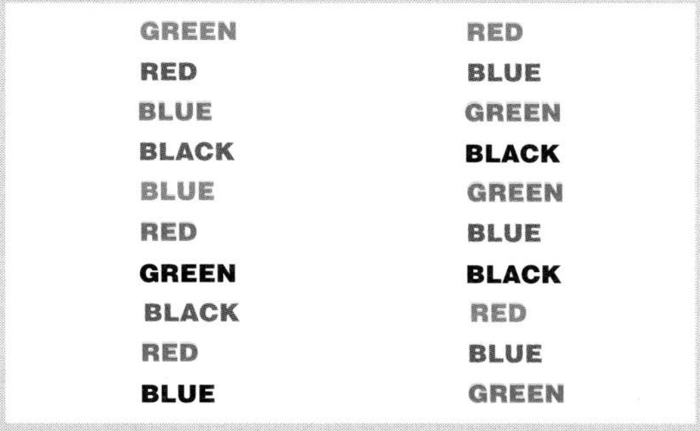

GREEN	RED
RED	BLUE
BLUE	GREEN
BLACK	BLACK
BLUE	GREEN
RED	BLUE
GREEN	BLACK
BLACK	RED
RED	BLUE
BLUE	GREEN

In 1935 John Ridley Stroop published a classic paper describing what is now known as the Stroop effect. Name the color of the ink used to print each word in the left column (not the color named by the word); then do the same for the words in the right column. Which is easier? You cannot help both seeing the color and reading the word, and when the meaning of the word is different from the color of the ink, you experience interference.

Psychophysics: A World of Experience

You may think that you have direct contact with the world—but you don't. You know the world only as it is filtered through your senses, and your senses are not always accurate. Your senses are your windows on the world, but sometimes the glass is not entirely transparent. The examples in Figure 3.2 show how far off base your perception can be.

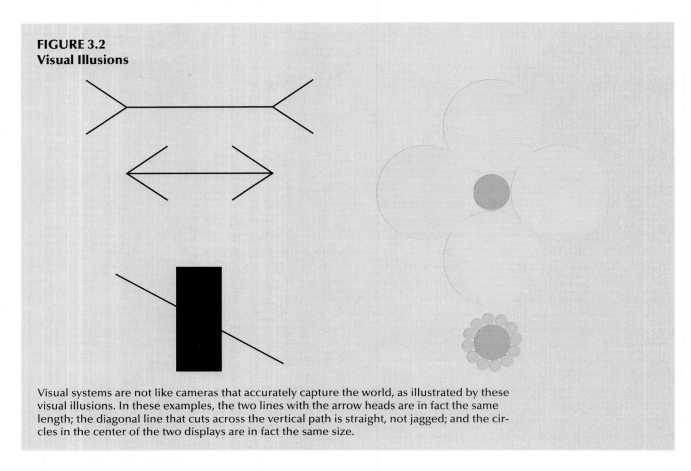

FIGURE 3.2
Visual Illusions

Visual systems are not like cameras that accurately capture the world, as illustrated by these visual illusions. In these examples, the two lines with the arrow heads are in fact the same length; the diagonal line that cuts across the vertical path is straight, not jagged; and the circles in the center of the two displays are in fact the same size.

Well over a hundred years ago, scientists began trying to discover the relation between the properties of events in the world and people's sensations and perceptions of them. German scientist Gustav Theodor Fechner (1801–1887) founded the field of **psychophysics,** which studies the relation between physical events and the corresponding experience of those events. Researchers in psychophysics made a series of discoveries, which apply to all the senses.

THRESHOLDS: "OVER THE TOP." Much as you cross a doorway when going from one room to the next, you cross a **threshold** when a physical event becomes strong enough to be noticed. For example, sometimes Tai feels that there is not quite enough light for her to appreciate a painting and wishes she could ask the museum guard to brighten the lighting. She knows that the guard can't change the lighting, and even if he could, how much should he turn it up? Just a tiny bit, just until Tai can tell that the lighting is in fact brighter? This sort of fine-tuning would result in a **just-noticeable difference (JND),** which is the size of the difference in a stimulus property (such as the brightness of light) needed for the observer to notice a difference. A JND is a kind of threshold. The change in light level might be so slight that sometimes you notice it, and sometimes you don't. This change would be defined as a **difference threshold** if you noticed the difference half the time.

Psychophysics: The study of the relation between physical events and the corresponding experience of those events.

Threshold: The point at which stimulation is strong enough to be noticed.

Just-noticeable difference (JND): The size of the difference in a stimulus property needed for the observer to notice a change has occurred.

Difference threshold: The difference needed to notice a stimulus change half the time.

The size of a difference threshold depends on the overall magnitude of the stimulus. If you are a thin person, a weight gain of 5 pounds is often noticeable at a glance, but if you are on the hefty side, a 5-pound gain might not be detected by anyone but you. Similarly, turning up the light the same amount is much more noticeable when the dimmer starts at a low setting than when it starts at a high setting. Why is this? Psychophysicists have an answer. **Weber's law** (named after another German researcher, Ernst Weber) states that a constant percentage of a magnitude change is necessary to detect a difference. So, the greater the magnitude of the light (or the thickness of the waist, or the volume of the sound), the greater the extra amount must be to be noticed. Weber's law is remarkably accurate except for very large or very small stimuli.

Have you ever wondered how far away something can be and still be seen, or how low you can turn down the sound before it becomes inaudible? An **absolute threshold** is the smallest amount of a stimulus needed in order to notice that the stimulus is present at all. But in spite of its label, there is nothing "absolute" about an absolute threshold. Like the difference threshold, the absolute threshold is defined as the magnitude of the stimulus needed to make it noticeable to the observer half the time. In establishing absolute thresholds, you are distinguishing between the background and the stimulus, and the stimulus must have enough of its defining quality that you are in fact able to notice it. If a warning light isn't bright enough, you won't notice that it's on—which could be a serious deficiency if the light is meant to indicate that your car's radiator is about to boil over.

DETECTING SIGNALS: NOTICING NEEDLES IN HAYSTACKS. Acting on the "equal time" principle, Sue and Tai are at a rock concert. Because of a bomb scare the previous day, the audience was warned at the outset to listen for a fire alarm that would be a signal to evacuate the arena. For Tai, who isn't enjoying the concert, the possibility that an alarm might call a halt to the event is almost appealing. Sue, on the other hand, devoutly hopes the concert will continue without interruption. Which of the friends do you think is more likely to hear a fire alarm? Tai might even "hear" an alarm bell that does not exist. This sort of error proved very important in World War II, when radar operators sometimes "saw" airplanes that did not exist and sometimes missed airplanes that did.

The simple fact that people make these kinds of errors led to a new way of thinking about thresholds. **Signal detection theory** seeks to explain why people detect signals in some situations but miss them in others. The key idea is that signals are always embedded in noise, and thus the challenge is to distinguish signal from noise. Noise, in this case, refers to other events that could be mistaken for the stimulus. Two key concepts explain how signals are detected or missed: sensitivity and bias. Greater **sensitivity** means a lower threshold for distinguishing between a stimulus (the "signal") and the background (the "noise"). For example, on a radar screen, the signal dots indicating enemy aircraft would not need to be very large or bright compared with the noise composed of random-appearing specks. **Bias** is the willingness to report noticing a stimulus (such as the willingness of a radar operator to risk identifying random specks as aircraft). At the concert, Tai and Sue have different biases to hear the alarm because Tai would be happy to leave and Sue longs to stay. And so Tai is continually nudging Sue to confirm whether an alarm really has sounded. Sensitivity and bias can be assessed by comparing the occasions when people *say* a stimulus is or is not present with the occasions when the stimulus is *in fact* present or not (Green & Swets, 1966; McNicol, 1972).

Attention: The Gateway to Awareness

Do you think you would be more sensitive to a slight change in lighting conditions if you were on the lookout for such a change? Research has shown that paying atten-

Weber's law: The rule that a constant percentage of a magnitude change is necessary to detect a difference.

Absolute threshold: The smallest amount of a stimulus needed in order to detect that the stimulus is present.

Signal detection theory: A theory explaining why people detect signals, which are always embedded in noise, in some situations but not in others.

Sensitivity: In signal detection theory, the threshold level for distinguishing between a stimulus and noise; the lower the threshold, the greater the sensitivity.

Bias: In signal detection theory, a person's willingness to report noticing a stimulus.

Attention: The act of focusing on particular information, which allows it to be processed more fully than what is not attended to.

tion increases sensitivity to the attended events (Nakayama & Mackeben, 1989; Yeshurun & Carrasco, 1998, 1999). **Attention** is the act of focusing on particular information, which allows that information to be processed more fully than information that is not attended to. One form of attention, *vigilance*, occurs when you are anticipating a particular event, for example, waiting to see whether a softball is going to be whacked your way when you are standing in the outfield. We are aware only of what we pay attention to. Attention operates in virtually all domains of human thought and feeling, not only in perception. We can pay attention to a nuance of a word, a feeling, a taste, a particular place, or a characteristic sound.

We pay attention for one of two reasons: either something about an event grabs us (such as a sudden change in illumination or movement), or we are actively searching for a particular characteristic, object, or event. One reason we know that these two types of attention are distinct is that they are accomplished by different parts of the brain. In the case of a sudden change in the environment, say a bright light or quick movement, the superior colliculus (a small subcortical structure) acts like a reflex, shifting attention automatically to that event. In contrast, during the voluntary shifts of attention that occur while you are searching for something or someone, the frontal eye fields (in the frontal lobes) are active (Kosslyn & Koenig, 1995; Paus, 1996). This second type of attention is useful in perception. Have you ever wondered whether you have actually glimpsed a friend in a crowd, or heard a familiar voice in an unexpected context? In many situations, your initial perception of an event may not be very clear, and you need a "second look" or "second hear." In these cases, your first suspicions of what you might have perceived guide top-down processes to collect more information in a very efficient way: You search for distinctive characteristics, such as the shape of a particular haircut, or the pitch of a certain voice.

Attention is not a product of the brain alone, but—like all other psychological events—it arises from the joint action of events at the different levels of analysis. What determines whether or not you will take that second look? That decision is influenced by what you believe (level of the person), which in part depends on your previous interactions with other people and your knowledge of the surrounding culture (level of the group). If you thought you saw a good friend, your attention would be engaged more fully than if you thought you saw a casual acquaintance. Similarly, if you are walking down the street and catch a glimpse of a dollar bill on the sidewalk, it will engage your attention differently from a scrap of paper; but a young child, who doesn't know about the value of money, may react to the two stimuli the same way. When Tai walks through a museum, her attention is grabbed when she thinks she glimpses a Monet or a Van Gogh, but Sue is oblivious; prior cultural experiences are governing how attention works.

Certain qualities or features of displays, such as advertisements, automatically leap out—a phenomenon psychologists refer to as **pop-out.** For example, look at the left panel of Figure 3.3. Is a red dot present? The red dot appears to pop out; it is immediately evident without your having to search for it. Attention is immediately drawn to this "odd man out." In general, pop-out occurs when objects differ in their fundamental qualities, such as size or frequency (you immediately hear a high-pitched flute in a band if all the other instruments are playing low notes). Conversely, when you try to find an object that is not distinct from the others around it, you aren't automatically drawn to it but must search for it, looking at each possible candidate one at a time. Treisman and her colleagues (Treisman & Gormican, 1988; Treisman & Souther, 1985) demonstrated how this works in an experiment like the one illustrated in Figure 3.3. The more letters there are in a display like the one in the right panel, the longer it takes to find a target. With enough letters, people end up searching the display one item at a time. Pop-out and searching are distinct activities that arise from distinct areas of the brain. Using magnetic pulses to disrupt the parietal lobe, researchers found that while the ability to search for arrangements of features was impaired, the ability to experience pop-out was not (Ashbridge et al., 1997).

Pop-out: Occurs when a stimulus is sufficiently different from the ones around it that it is immediately evident.

FIGURE 3.3
Pop-Out Versus Search

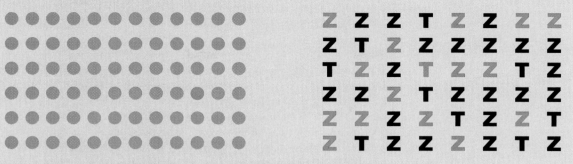

As shown in the left panel, basic features, such as color, are registered without the need for an item-by-item search. Is there a red *T* in the right panel? To find a conjunction, such as the arrangements of segments or a shape with a particular color, you must search the items one at a time.

LOOKING AT LEVELS

Romantic Interludes

The pupils of the eye expand, admitting more light when you are paying attention to something; this is a function of the sympathetic nervous system. So one way you can tell if someone is paying attention to you is to watch his or her pupils. Indeed, Hess (1975) showed that people judge faces with larger pupils as more attractive, which may reflect the knowledge (perhaps unconscious) that larger pupils indicate interest. During the Middle Ages, women used the juice of the poisonous plant belladonna to dilate their pupils and, they believed, make themselves more attractive. And they were right—about the effect, if not the safety, of the practice.

The pupils also enlarge in dim light. Say you are in a romantic situation, the lights are low, and you want to make use of some psychological principles by using pupil size as a cue that your companion is fascinated by what you are saying. To distinguish between pupil expansion due to dim light and pupil expansion due to rapt attention,

Which version of the picture do you find more attractive? If you are male, you probably find the one with the larger pupils (left) "more feminine," "soft," or "pretty," whereas the one with the small pupils (right) may appear "hard," "selfish," or "cold" (Hess, 1975).

you need both increased perceptual sensitivity (to notice a small difference in pupil expansion) and an absence of bias (either hoping for the best or fearing the worst). Fortunately, research has shown that the ability to distinguish one feature from another actually increases in situations in which discrimination is difficult. For example, Spitzer and colleagues (1988) located neurons in part of a monkey's brain that fired more vigorously when a closer discrimination had to be made (this study measured discrimination among colors or tints). This increase in firing rate is important because it allows the animals to perform the discriminations more accurately. These findings show that, as expected, selective attention causes more brain activity in the relevant perceptual areas of the human brain (Corbetta et al., 1990, 1991, 1993; Gauthier et al., 1997; Wojciulik et al., 1998).

Thus, you can see how a social event—one person's trying to assess another's interest—can be understood in part by analysis at the level of the brain. Not only do events in the brain make the pupils larger, but other events in the brain allow you to notice when someone else's pupils are in fact larger than they otherwise would be. And, of course, the desire to monitor a particular person's pupils in the first place depends on your beliefs and previous social interactions. Moreover, depending on what you think you see, you may respond differently, and that response will in turn have social consequences.

CONSOLIDATE!

▶ 1. *What is "sensation," and how does it differ from "perception"?* Sensations occur when a physical event in the world stimulates receptors (such as those at the back of the eye, in the ear, and on the skin), which then send signals to the brain. We detect events that are over threshold (a difference threshold to notice them against a background; an absolute threshold to see that they are present at all), but our sensitivity to stimuli must be distinguished from our bias to classify input as signal versus noise. Perception occurs when input is organized and interpreted as indicating that a particular object or event is present. Bottom-up processing is initiated by the stimulus, whereas top-down processing is guided by knowledge, expectation, or belief.

▶ 2. *People may vary in how they direct their attention; just what is "attention"?* Attention is the act of focusing on particular information, which allows it to be processed more fully than information to which you are not attending. Selective attention leads us to pick out a particular object or event, and we are aware only of what is captured by our attention. Some types of basic stimulus qualities pop out when they differ from surrounding ones, but other qualities must be searched for one at a time.

⌐ VISION

As Sue and Tai stood in front of a painting that seemed to Sue to be no more than blurry, smudged, and indistinct shapes, Tai spoke admiringly of the way the impressionists tried to present the changing effects of light and color in nature. Rather than competing with the realism of the camera, they sought to evoke the visual sensations leading to perception. To accomplish this, the artists used qualities inherent in color itself and took advantage of the way the human visual system works. The 19th century French impressionist Claude Monet produced a series of paintings of haystacks in a field as day wore on to evening, and from season to season. The shadows he painted on the stacks were in colors complementary to the haystacks themselves; his large green fields were accented with small strokes of complementary red. His brush strokes were broken, so there are no sharp edges in the forms he depicted. By this use of color, and the merging of subject (the "figure") and background (the "ground"), the impressionists—as their name suggests—tried to paint in a way that would replicate the process by which people actually see.

Visual perception is not accomplished in one fell swoop but, like other sensory processes, occurs in the three broad phases noted earlier (Marr, 1982; Nakayama et al., 1995): early, intermediate, and late. The registering of visual sensation relies on *early visual processes.* These occur in the eye and in the first parts of the brain to register visual input. An example of early visual processing is registering the colors in a painting. Patches of color are then, in *intermediate visual processing,* organized into coherent units, which usually correspond to objects, such as the haystacks in a Monet painting. These intermediate processes can operate on the initial input even if you don't know in advance "the whole picture" of what you will be seeing. They are a bridge between the early processes and *late visual processes,* which involve stored information. It is only in late visual processing that what you see becomes meaningful, that you realize you are seeing a haystack and not a honeycomb.

► 1. What is the nature of light, and how do we see color, shape, and motion?

► 2. How are we able to separate figure from ground and see the world as a stable collection of objects?

► 3. How do we make sense of what we see?

Early Vision: It's Sensational!

Early visual processing is the crucial first step of our ability to see the world around us. Without early vision, we could have no bottom-up processing—no visual stimulus could reach us—and our only visual experience would be hallucinations.

LET THERE BE LIGHT. You know, as Plato did not, that rays don't come from your eyes; rather, in order to see, you need light that either bounces off an object or is produced by the object. Light is a form of electromagnetic radiation. All of us swim in a sea of electromagnetic radiation. This sea has waves: some large, some small, some that come in rapid succession, some spaced far apart. The height of a wave is its **amplitude,** and the rate at which the wave peaks move past a given point is its **frequency.** The greater the frequency (the more often the peaks arrive), the shorter the **wavelength.** In the electromagnetic spectrum, which ranges from the terrifically long radio waves to the very short X rays and gamma rays, there is a narrow band of radiation perceived as visible light. An almost uncountable number of colors are conveyed in this light; the traditional seven we readily distinguish are red, orange, yellow, green, blue, indigo, and violet. The lower frequencies (and longer wavelengths) are toward the red end of the spectrum; the higher frequencies (and shorter wavelengths) are toward the violet end, as illustrated in Figure 3.4.

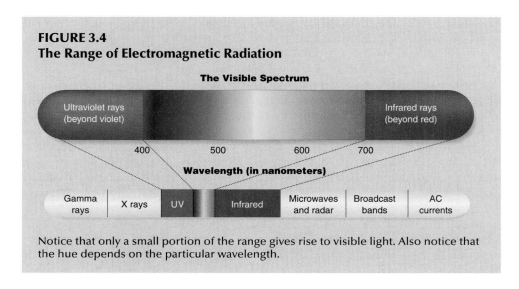

FIGURE 3.4
The Range of Electromagnetic Radiation

The Visible Spectrum

Ultraviolet rays (beyond violet)

Infrared rays (beyond red)

400   500   600   700

Wavelength (in nanometers)

| Gamma rays | X rays | UV | Infrared | Microwaves and radar | Broadcast bands | AC currents |

Notice that only a small portion of the range gives rise to visible light. Also notice that the hue depends on the particular wavelength.

FIGURE 3.5
Anatomy of the Eye

Cornea

Pupil

Iris

Lens

Retina

Fovea

Optic nerve

Blood vessels

The many parts of the eye either focus an image on the retina or convert light into neural impulses that are sent to the brain.

THE BRAIN'S EYE: MORE THAN A CAMERA.

The eye converts the electromagnetic energy that is light into nerve impulses; this conversion process is called **transduction.** As illustrated in Figure 3.5, light enters the eye through an opening called the **pupil.** Surrounding the pupil is a circular muscle called the **iris.** The iris changes the size of the pupil to let in more or less light. The light is focused partly by the **cornea,** the transparent covering over the eye, and then focused even more by the **lens.** Unlike a camera lens, the lens in a human eye flexes. In fact, muscles can adjust the lens into a more or less round shape to focus light from objects that are different distances away. **Accommodation,** the automatic adjustment of the eye for seeing at different distances, occurs when muscles change the shape of the lens so that it focuses light on the retina from near and far away objects. The world appears sharp and clear because we are constantly moving our eyes, and what we choose to look at can quickly be moved into focus. With age, the lens thickens and becomes less flexible (Fatt & Weissman, 1992), often causing older people to have trouble seeing nearer objects, for example, reading material.

The critical step in the transduction process occurs at the **retina,** a sheet of tissue at the back of the eye that is about as thick as a piece of paper. The central part of the retina contains densely packed cells that transform light to nerve impulses, and this region—called the **fovea**—gives us the sharpest images. We are not usually aware of how fuzzy our world looks. Most of the time we pay attention only to the images that strike the fovea, which are sharp and clear, but much of what we see is in fact not very sharply focused. Take a moment to look up and focus on a single spot on the other side of the room; notice how blurry things look even a short distance to the side of that spot.

When it comes to foveas, some animals have it all over us humans; some types of birds, for example, have two foveas. Next time you are annoyed at a noisy pigeon, appreciate the fact that it can focus to the side and ahead at the same time.

Two kinds of cells in the retina convert light to nerve impulses: rods and cones (see Figure 3.6). **Rods** (which actually look like little rods) are extraordinarily sensitive to light, but they register only shades of gray. Each eye contains between 100 million and 120 million rods. The **cones** (which look like, yes, cones) are not as sensitive to light as are the rods, but they respond most vigorously to particular wavelengths of light, allowing us to see color. Each eye contains between 5 million and 6 million cones (Beatty, 1995; Dowling, 1992). The cones are densest near the fovea, and the rods are everywhere within the retina except in the fovea. At night, there isn't enough light for the less-light-sensitive cones to work, so night vision is based on the firing of the rods alone. That is why an apple looks black and an orange cat looks gray under a moonlit night sky.

When you first enter a darkened theater, you can't see a thing. You may have noticed, though, that the risk of tripping or bumping into someone is a lot less if you wait even a brief time because you soon can see much better. In fact, after about 30 minutes in the dark, you are about 100,000 times more sensitive to light than you are during full daylight. In ideal conditions, the rods can respond when they receive a single photon, the smallest unit of light. This process of acclimatization is called **dark adaptation.** Part of the increased sensitivity to what light there is arises because your pupil enlarges when you are in darkness; in fact, it can expand to let in about 16 times as much light as enters in full daylight. In addition, the rods actually become more

Transduction: The process whereby physical energy is converted by a sensory neuron into neural impulses.

Pupil: The opening in the eye through which light passes.

Iris: The circular muscle that adjusts the size of the pupil.

Cornea: The transparent covering over the eye, which serves partly to focus the light onto the back of the eye.

Lens: The flexible disk under the cornea that focuses light onto the back of the eye.

Accommodation: Occurs when muscles adjust the shape of the lens so that it focuses light on the retina from objects at different distances.

sensitive as your eyes remain in the dark because your genes cause the production of a crucial chemical, called *rhodopsin*, that responds to light. Here's a hint: Because of the way the rods are arranged on the retina, if you want to see best at night, look slightly to the side of what you want to examine.

The axons from retinal cells in each eye are gathered into a single large cord called the **optic nerve,** which is about as thick as your little finger. There are no rods or cones at the place where the optic nerve exits the retina, which causes a "blind spot" in what you can see laid out in front of you. Because the brain completes patterns that fall across this blind spot, you are not aware of it as you look around every day. Look at Figure 3.7, though, and you can "see" where your blind spot is.

Researchers have known about rods and cones for well over 100 years, but only recently have they discovered evidence for a third kind of receptor in the eye that also registers light. Freedman and her colleagues (1999) observed that even mice whose eyes had no rods or cones still shifted their "circadian" behavior when light was shined on them. Circadian behavior is behavior that follows the daily pattern of light, such as waking and sleeping; in this case, the behavior was running, which in these mice varies depending on the time of day. But when the eyes were removed, the mice no longer made the adjustment in their "running schedule." Thus, the third kind of light-sensitive receptor must be in the eyes. In another study, Lucas and his colleagues (1999) investigated the decrease in production of a hormone called melatonin in the presence of light (melatonin is the hormone that some people use to overcome jet lag). Even mice without rods or cones showed a normal decrease in melatonin production when placed in light. Clearly, light affects the brain even when there are no rod or cone sensory cells. This work opens an exciting new frontier in the investigation of how we see.

FIGURE 3.6
Rods and Cones

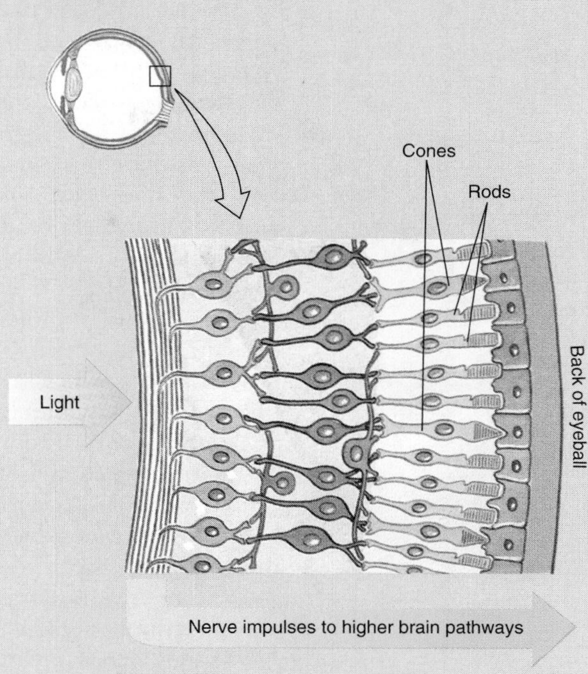

Two types of cells in the retina convert light into neural responses. The rods allow us to see with less light, but not in color; the cones allow us to see in color but are not as light-sensitive as the rods.

FIGURE 3.7
Finding Your Blind Spot

Cover your left eye and stare at the X with the other. Now slowly bring the book closer to you, continuing to focus on the X. When the picture on the right disappears, you have found your right eye's blind spot.

Retina: A sheet of tissue at the back of the eye containing cells that convert light to neural impulses.

Fovea: The small, central region of the retina with the highest density of cones and the highest resolution.

Rods: Retinal cells that are very sensitive to light but register only shades of gray.

Cones: Retinal cells that respond most strongly to one of three wavelengths and that play a key role in producing color vision.

Dark adaptation: The process whereby exposure to darkness causes the eyes to become more sensitive, allowing for better vision in the dark.

Optic nerve: The large bundle of nerve fibers carrying impulses from the retina into the brain.

COLOR VISION: MIXING AND MATCHING. How can you tell whether an apple is ripe? One way is to look at its color. Color also plays a key role in our appreciation of beauty in art, nature, and people. One of the remarkable aspects of human vision, which makes painting and appreciation of painting such rich experiences, is the huge range of colors that people can use and see.

At one point in the study of color vision, there was a debate about how humans can see such a large range of colors. One camp took its lead from observations reported by Thomas Young and Hermann von Helmholz in the 19th century. This approach focused on phenomena such as the mixing of colors to produce new colors (as mixing yellow and blue paint produces green). These researchers, arguing by analogy, believed that the brain registers color by combining responses to separate wavelengths. In particular, they argued that the eye contains three kinds of color sensors, each most sensitive to a particular range of wavelength: long, medium, and short. This view was therefore called the **trichromatic theory.**

The other camp followed the lead of German physician Ewald Hering, who worked at the end of the 19th century and the beginning of the 20th. Hering noticed that some colors cannot be mixed—you can't make reddish-green or yellowish-blue. (As any preschooler would be happy to demonstrate, you can of course mix the colors—but yellow and blue produce green, not yellowish blue, and red and green produce the color of mud.) This and similar observations led him to develop the **opponent process theory,** which states that the presence of one color of a pair (red/green, yellow/blue, and black/white) inhibits the perception of the other color.

Happily, it turns out that *both* theories are correct, but they describe processing at different places in the eye and brain. Consistent with trichromatic theory, our perception of colors arises because we possess three different types of cones. One type of cone is most responsive to light in the wavelength seen as yellow, another to light in the wavelength seen as green, and another in the wavelength seen as violet (Reid, 1999). The trick is that at least two of the three types of cones usually respond to *any* wavelength of visible light, but to different degrees (De Valois & De Valois, 1975, 1993). And here's the important part: The *mixture* of the three types of response signals is different for each of a huge range of wavelengths, and it is this mixture that is the crucial signal to the brain. The brain responds to the mixture, not the outputs from individual cones. Color television operates on this principle. Stare very closely at a color TV screen, and you will see little bubbles of three colors (red, green, and blue). Stand back, and a wide range of colors appears. Why? Because your eyes and your brain respond differently, depending on the mixture of wavelengths produced by clusters of these bubbles.

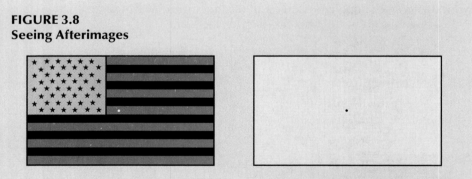

FIGURE 3.8
Seeing Afterimages

Does this flag look strange to you? Stare at the dot in the center for about 60 seconds in a bright light, and then look at the blank space. You should see a brilliant afterimage of Old Glory, with red and white stripes and a blue field.

Trichromatic theory of color vision: The theory that color vision arises from the combinations of neural impulses from three different kinds of sensors, each of which responds maximally to a different wavelength.

Opponent process theory of color vision: The theory that if a color is present, it causes cells that register it to inhibit the perception of the complementary color (such as red versus green).

Afterimage: The image left behind by a previous perception.

The mixtures of responses of the cones is not the whole story of color vision. If this were all there were to it, we should be able to see all mixtures of colors—but, as Hering originally observed, we can't. As the opponent process theory predicts, there's another factor, too, which will become apparent when you take a look at the strange colored flag in Figure 3.8. Stare at the flag, and then look at the space to its right; you should see an **afterimage,** an image left behind by a previous perception.

Furthermore, the flag should look normal in the afterimage, not strangely colored as it is actually printed. Why are the colors of afterimages different from those of the object? You need to understand more about color vision to answer that question. A key fact is that the cones feed into special types of cells in the retina and the lateral geniculate nucleus of the brain (part of the thalamus): red/green, yellow/blue, and black/white **opponent cells**. These cells are set up to pit the colors in each pair against each other, with exactly the effect Hering predicted. For example, when wavelengths that produce blue are registered by these cells, they inhibit the perception of wavelengths that produce yellow, and vice versa (Hurvich & Jameson, 1957). This process helps you to distinguish among colors that have similar wavelengths, such as green and yellow (Reid, 1999, discusses the role of the cortex in such processing, as do Livingstone & Hubel, 1984). This is why you can't see greenish red or yellowish blue: Seeing one member of a pair inhibits seeing the other. It also explains why you see afterimages like the one illustrated by staring at Figure 3.8. An afterimage occurs when one member of a pair of opponent cells inhibits the other (for example, green inhibits red), and then releases it. In the process, the previously inhibited one (red) temporarily overshoots the mark, creating an afterimage.

Color is thus the result of a complicated process that mixes and inhibits. And making matters more complex is the fact that colors vary in three separate ways. First, different wavelengths of light produce the sensation of different colors. This aspect of color—whether it looks red, blue, and so on—is called *hue*. Second, the purity of the input (the amount of white that's mixed in with the color) produces the perception of *saturation*, that is, how deep the color appears. And third, the amplitude of the light waves produces the perception of *lightness* or *brightness* (if the object, such as a television screen, produces light)—how sharp the color appears. An area of the brain called visual area 4 (or V4) in monkeys plays a major role in processing color (Zeki, 1993); a corresponding area lights up in human brains when color is perceived. If this area is damaged, the ability to see hue is lost. This acquired color blindness is called *acquired achromotopsia* (Damasio, 1985). In Oliver Sacks's book *An Anthropologist on Mars* (1995), a color-blind artist describes how hard it is for him to eat food, particularly red food (such as apples and tomatoes), which appears to him to be a repulsive deep black.

People who have **color blindness** are either unable to distinguish one hue from another or, in more serious cases, are unable to see hue at all. Most color blindness is present from birth. Depending on the specific group, as many as 8% of European men but less than 0.5% of European women are born color-blind (Reid, 1999). Rather than being completely insensitive to hue, most color-blind people are unable to distinguish red from green. Researchers have found that people with the most common type of color blindness possess genes that produce similar pigments in their cones (Neitz et al., 1996), and thus the cones do not respond to wavelengths as they should. A small number of people (roughly 2% of males, and a very small number of females) are actually missing a type of cone. Even more severe deficits occur when more than one type of cone is affected (Reid, 1999).

Opponent cells: Cells that pit the colors in a pair, notably blue/yellow or red/green, against each other.

Color blindness: An inability, either acquired (by brain damage) or inherited, to perceive hue.

People with normal color vision would see the crayons as shown on the left. People with the most common form of color blindness—inability to distinguish red from green—would see the crayons as shown on the right. Before traffic lights were arranged with red always on the top, not being able to see colors made driving hazardous for people with red/green color blindness. In what other ways would such a disorder affect your life?

FIGURE 3.9
Outputs from Different Channels

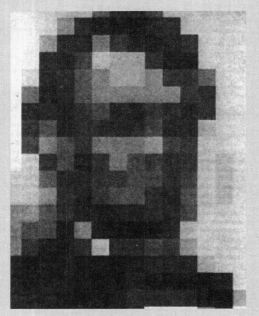

If you wear glasses, take them off and look at this picture. If you don't, prop up the book and move back. Can you see who is in the picture more clearly when the image becomes blurrier?

CHANNELS: BIG PICTURE, LITTLE PICTURE. Painting is about shape as well as color, and painters often instinctively take advantage of basic facts about how people see shapes. Look at Figure 3.9, and then prop the book up, stand back about 10 feet, and look again. Better yet, if you wear glasses, look at the picture from about a yard away with and without your glasses. Do you find that when the picture is blurred, it is easier to see Abraham Lincoln? What's going on here? Unlike a camera with a single lens, your visual system operates as if it has a series of lenses. When you look at an assortment of objects from the same distance, say 5 feet, one of these "lenses" picks up fine details, such as individual hairs; another picks up slightly larger details, such as the shape of a head; another, even larger shapes, such as a body; and another, shapes as big as a car. Each of these lens systems, called **channels,** registers a different sharpness of detail. Researchers suspect that the channels are processed in the brain by neurons that have different sized receptive fields (De Valois & De Valois, 1975, 1993; Wandell, 1995); the receptive field of a neuron is in a sense the "territory" in the outside world covered by that neuron—the particular region of space from which a stimulus will trigger it.

How do these channels explain what happens when you look at the picture of Lincoln? The edges of the blocks are picked up by the channels that register very sharp changes. By blurring the picture, these irrelevant edges are eliminated, and what you see is the output from the channels that pick up larger variations in shape. This information was there all along, but it became available to you only when the distracting information was eliminated.

VISUAL PROBLEMS: DISTORTED WINDOWS ON THE WORLD. Precisely because the visual system is so complicated, it does not always work perfectly. It is estimated that fewer than a third of the world's population have perfect vision (Seuling, 1986). People with *myopia,* or nearsightedness, have difficulty focusing on distant objects. As shown in Figure 3.10, myopia is usually caused by an eyeball that is too long to focus the image on the retina properly. This problem, which in the United States affects about one in five people, can be corrected by external lenses, either eyeglasses or contact lenses, that focus the image correctly on the retina. Moreover, laser surgery often can correct the lens of the eye itself. Time spent reading is correlated with myopia (see Young, 1981), but remember, correlation does not imply causation!

In contrast to nearsightedness, which involves problems with distance vision, people with *hypermetropia* have difficulty focusing on near objects. Such farsightedness usually results from an eyeball that is too short, or a lens that is too thin, to allow the image on the retina to focus properly. By the way, it is possible to be nearsighted in one eye and farsighted in the other, as was the case with President James Buchanan. This condition purportedly led him to tilt his head so he could see better when he was talking to someone (Seuling, 1978).

Astigmatism is a defect in the curvature of the cornea or lens, causing blurriness. Astigmatism, like nearsightedness and farsightedness, can be corrected with eyeglasses (and sometimes with contact lenses).

Of more serious concern, a *cataract* is a cloudy part of the lens of the eye, which can cause blurred vision, distorted images, and sensitivity to light and glare. About 70% of Americans over age 75 have (or have had) a cataract. Cataracts are responsible for at least half of all incidents of blindness (Riordan-Eva, 1992). Surgery can correct cataracts by removing the lens and replacing it with a substitute lens.

Channels: Sets of neurons in the visual system that pick up shape variations at different levels of resolution.

Figure: In perception, a set of characteristics (such as shape, color, texture) that corresponds to an object.

Ground: In perception, the background, which must be distinguished in order to pick out figures.

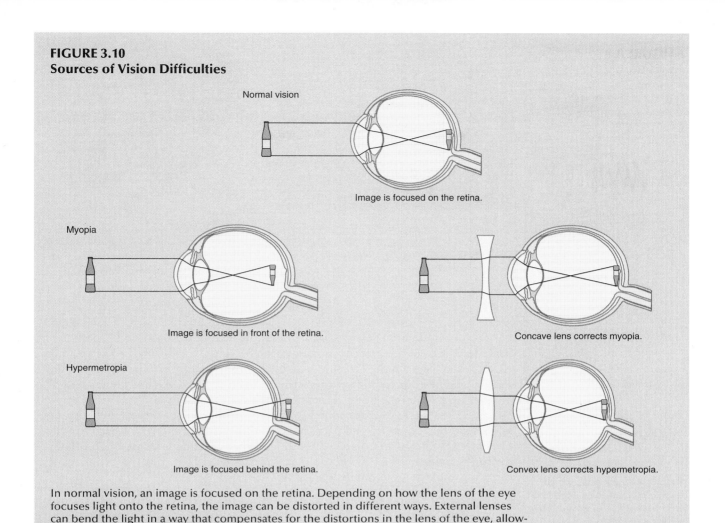

FIGURE 3.10
Sources of Vision Difficulties

Normal vision

Image is focused on the retina.

Myopia

Image is focused in front of the retina.

Concave lens corrects myopia.

Hypermetropia

Image is focused behind the retina.

Convex lens corrects hypermetropia.

In normal vision, an image is focused on the retina. Depending on how the lens of the eye focuses light onto the retina, the image can be distorted in different ways. External lenses can bend the light in a way that compensates for the distortions in the lens of the eye, allowing light to be focused properly on the retina.

Intermediate Vision: Organizing the World

Although it seems that we perceive what we see in, literally, the blink of an eye, a large number of mental steps actually occurs between the moment a pattern of light strikes our eyes and the time we become aware of seeing an object. At each step, different areas of the brain are crucial (Grill-Spector et al., 1998). The second, intermediate phase of vision is necessary before the input can become meaningful. The intermediate processes organize the input into shapes that correspond to surfaces and objects (Marr, 1982; Nakayama et al., 1995). Key features of intermediate-level vision include organizing the input into units that correspond to objects and registering the basic properties of objects, such as their actual sizes and shapes.

PERCEPTUAL ORGANIZATION: SEEING THE FOREST THROUGH THE TREES. On its own, the eye cannot organize visual input into shapes that correspond to objects: It is the brain that does this. To recognize the **figure** (the object of interest), the viewer must first distinguish it from the **ground** (the background). When figure and ground are similar, the figure is said to be *camouflaged*. Armies the world over have long taken advantage of this property of the perceptual system.

Can you see which animals are present? The coloring of the horses blends nicely with the background. Why might animals look like their surroundings?

Gestalt laws of organization:
A set of rules describing the circumstances under which marks will be grouped into perceptual units, such as proximity, good continuation, similarity, closure, and good form.

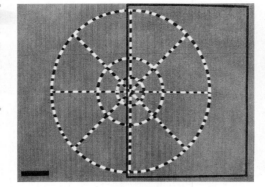 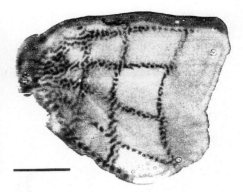

Tootell and colleagues (1982) produced this remarkable illustration of retinotopic mapping in the monkey brain. The animal looked at the figure on the left while radioactive sugar was being ingested by the brain cells. The dark lines on the right show which brain cells in the primary visual cortex were working hardest when the animal viewed the figure. The spatial structure of the figure is evident on the surface of the brain.

Separating figure from ground involves organizing regions into shapes that are likely to correspond to objects or their parts. A critical part of this process is finding edges. Visual areas in the occipital lobe of the brain are *topographically organized*—that is, the pattern falling on the retina is spatially laid out on the cortex. This arrangement helps the brain to delineate the edges of objects. Because of the way intermediate visual processes operate, however, people do not see isolated lines, dots, and so on, but rather overall patterns. Gestalt psychologists, who were introduced briefly in Chapter 1, discovered a set of laws that describe how the brain organizes the input from the eyes (Koffka, 1935; Wertheimer, 1923). The most important of these **Gestalt laws of organization** follow:

Proximity: Marks that are near one another tend to be grouped together. So, for example, we see **XXX XXX** as two groups, and **XX XX XX** as three groups, even though they have the same total number of **X** marks.

Good Continuation: Marks that tend to fall along a smooth curve or a straight line tend to be grouped together. So, for example, we see _ _ _ _ as a single line, not four separate dashes; and we see – – – – _ _ _ _ as two separate lines because all eight of the dashes do not fall on the same plane.

You can see the middle part of this picture as a set of birds or a set of fish, which illustrates how the figure can serve as the ground or vice versa. Such artwork demonstrates the roles of figure and ground, and your participation in interpreting which is which.

Similarity: Marks that look alike tend to be grouped together. So, for example, we see **XXXxxx** as two groups. Whether the elements are the same or different colors also affects similarity, another reason color vision is so important.

Closure: We tend to close any gaps in a figure, so a circle with a small section missing will still be seen as a circle.

Good Form: Marks that form a single shape tend to be grouped together. So, for example, we see [ ] as a single shape, but not [_.

Additional laws have been added since the time of the Gestalt psychologists (who began work in 1912). For example, Palmer (1992b) has shown that marks occurring in a common region tend to be grouped together. The details of how the brain actually works to organize the world in these ways are just now being discovered (Grossberg et al., 1997; Kovacs, 1996; Kovacs & Julesz, 1993; von der Heydt & Peterhans, 1989; von der Heydt et al., 1984).

FIGURE 3.11
Ambiguous Figures

In the left panel, you can see either two silhouetted faces or a vase, depending on what you pay attention to as the figure; in the right panel, you can see an old or a young woman, again depending on how you organize the figure.

Sometimes a figure can be organized and perceived in more than one way. Figure 3.11 shows some of the classic *ambiguous figure-ground relationships.* Certain artists—for instance, Dutch illustrator Maurits Escher and Belgian surrealist René Magritte—were intrigued by how the mind actively organizes the visual world, partly by what we pay attention to and partly by automatic processes that group visual information into units of perception.

KNOWING THE DISTANCE. Intermediate-level visual processing also specifies the layout of surfaces. Because the world is three-dimensional, we need to register distances (for example, to be able to reach and navigate properly). This poses an interesting problem: Our eyes project images onto the two-dimensional surface of our retinas, but we need to see objects in three dimensions. Given that our eyes capture images in only two dimensions, how is it that we see in three? Once again, the answer lies with the brain, which uses different types of cues to derive three dimensions from the two-dimensional images on the retinas of the eyes.

Binocular cues, those that arise from both eyes working together, help you assess how far away an object is. Your brain uses slight differences in the images striking your eyes to assess the distance of an object. Because your eyes are separated, you need to cross them in order to focus on an object (so that the same image appears on the central, high-resolution fovea in each eye). When you do this, however, the images of *other* objects—ones in front of or behind the one you are focused on—appear slightly differently on the retinas of the two eyes. This difference between the images on the two eyes is called **binocular disparity,** and the brain uses the amount of binocular disparity to determine which objects are in front of and which are behind others (Pinker, 1997, pp. 220–233). The process of figuring out depth from binocular disparity is called **stereopsis** (Anderson & Nakayama, 1994). Some neurons in the visual areas of the brain have been found to respond best with relatively little binocular disparity, whereas others fire more vigorously when lots of binocular disparity is present (Ohzawa et al.,

Magic Eye® drawings like this produce the experience of depth after you stare at them for a while because there are two versions of the same object, slightly displaced. If you focus your gaze just right, your brain will figure out the distance the object would have been to produce this disparity. And voilà! You'll see depth! (© 2000 Magic Eye Inc., www.magiceye.com)

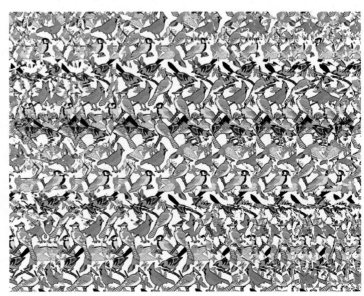

1990; Patterson & Martin, 1992). Thus, neurons register the information the brain needs to figure out distance from the objects in view.

Stereopsis works only for objects up to about 10 feet away—at distances greater than that, the eyes don't need to cross in order to focus, and thus there is no binocular disparity. **Motion cues,** on the other hand, can operate at any distance, and they are effective even with one eye. In fact, these cues work so well that Wesley Walker, blind in one eye from birth, could catch a football well enough to be the star wide receiver for the New York Jets football team (in fact, he played for them for 13 years). To notice a motion cue, try this: Hold up this book and move your head back and forth as you look at it. Note how the images of objects behind the book seem to shift. As you shift your head to the left, the distant objects seem to move to the left; as you shift to the right, they shift to the right. Now focus on the background, still holding the book, and move your head back and forth; note how the image of the book seems to shift. This time the object you aren't focusing on, the book, seems to shift in the opposite direction to the way you move your head! Objects closer than the one you are fixated on seem to move in the opposite direction to your movements, whereas ones farther away than the fixation point seem to move in the same direction. And depending on the distance, the objects will seem to shift at different speeds. This difference in shifting provides information about relative distance, a cue called *motion parallax.*

You use several types of cues to perceive motion. For example, if you are moving directly toward an object, it seems to expand symmetrically around its center and thus loom closer. Likewise, if you are moving toward its right side, that side will loom closer than the other. When silent movies were first shown to the public, the movement of an on-screen train rushing toward viewers was so startling that many moviegoers panicked and fled the theaters (Seuling, 1976). Only after they had experienced watching moving objects on a screen could they distinguish between the usual motion cues and the bogus ones in films (which are a kind of illusion), and relax and enjoy the show. Such learning was necessary because these cues are ordinarily so important. In fact, neuroimaging research with humans has revealed that special areas in the brain detect this kind of motion (Tootell et al., 1997; Zeki, 1978, 1993). Also, studies of brain-damaged patients have documented the role of particular brain areas for processing motion. For example, one patient could not pour tea into a cup; she would see the tea suddenly appear, not continuously flow. Instead of motion, she saw a series of static images (Zihl et al., 1983).

Notice the relative sizes and spacing of the bricks in this example of a texture gradient, one cue that the street is receding into the distance.

Not all cues for distance involve motion. **Monocular static cues** for distance can be picked up with one eye even without movement. Such monocular ("one-eyed") and static ("unmoving") cues are used effectively by artists to create the illusion of distance. One of these is the **texture gradient,** a progressive change in the texture of an object. Gibson (1966) described the way texture gradients signal distance. Look at the brick street in the photograph (or, for that matter, in life). The bricks that are closer to you, the observer, are larger in the photograph and appear so in life; you use this cue to determine distance.

In drawing pictures, artists also use *linear perspective,* or *foreshortening,* making the parts of objects that are farther away from the viewer actually smaller on the page. You also infer distance if one object partially covers another, indicating that the obscured object is behind the other and thus farther away; this relation is called an *occlusion cue.* And if the base of an object appears higher on the horizon than the base of another object, you take that as a cue that the higher one is farther away. Figure 3.12 provides good examples of the power of these monocular cues, and Figure 3.13 summarizes monocular and *binocular* depth cues.

PERCEPTUAL CONSTANCIES: STABILIZING THE WORLD. Information about distance is important for more than separating figure from ground; it also helps to specify the three-dimensional shape of an object seen from different vantage points. Imagine strapping a camera onto your head and making a videotape as you walk. What do you think the pictures would look like? The images striking your eyes change wildly depending on your viewpoint, but the objective world you relate to seems stable. Objects in the world appear to keep their shapes, their sizes, their colors, and so on, even when you view them in very different positions or circumstances. **Perceptual constancy** is the perception of the characteristics of objects (such as their shapes and colors) as the same even though the sensory information striking the eyes changes. For example, **size constancy** occurs when you see an object (such as a car) as the same size even when it is at different distances, so that its image (as in a photograph) is at different sizes. **Shape constancy** occurs when you see an object as the same shape, even when you view it from different angles (again, so that its image in a photograph would be different). This stabilization occurs not in the eyes, but in the brain, and is fundamental to the ability to recognize objects and know how to interact with them.

The cues we use to preserve shape constancy are also used in drawings. Interestingly, such cues are not used in all cultures. For instance, in some rural parts of Africa, children's books are very rare. Thus, it is not surprising that these children have difficulty understanding the depth, shading, and perspective cues in drawings (Liddell, 1997). Cross-cultural studies have shown that people must learn how to interpret these cues in drawings (for

FIGURE 3.12
A Monocular Depth Cue

Even though you know that the two white bars on the rails are in fact the same size, the one that appears farther away also appears larger. Because you see the top one as farther away, the fact that it is the same size on the page signals that it is larger. Painters use depth cues like these to fool the eye.

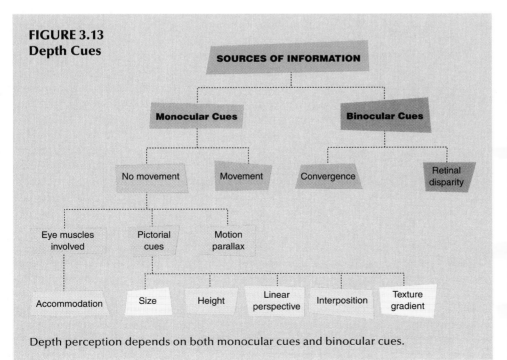

FIGURE 3.13
Depth Cues

Depth perception depends on both monocular cues and binocular cues.

Perceptual constancy: The perception of characteristics that occurs when an object or quality (such as shape or color) looks the same even though the sensory information striking the eyes changes.

Size constancy: Seeing an object as being the same size when viewed at different distances and visual angles.

Shape constancy: Seeing objects as having the same shape even when the image on the retina changes.

Brightness and color constancy: Seeing objects as having the same lightness, brightness, or color in different viewing situations.

example, Duncan et al., 1973). On the other hand, Western children appear to master these cues at earlier ages today than they did a century ago, possibly because children's books are more widely available (Peeck, 1987). In all cases, learning plays an important role in understanding how pictures portray depth (Leibowitz, 1971).

Finally, consider **brightness and color constancy.** Take a page from a notebook and look at it on a table indoors. Now take it outdoors on a day when the sun is out. It probably appears roughly as bright in the two conditions, but in fact there is much more light bouncing off the page when it is outside. Most researchers now believe that the key to understanding this phenomenon is that we do not see brightness as an absolute quality, but rather see *ratios* of brightness. We see the brightest thing as "bright" (regardless of the actual amount of light) and the brightness of everything else as proportional to it (Arend, 1994; Jacobsen & Gilchrist, 1988a, 1988b). Similarly, our ability to see colors as constant (green as green, red as red, and so on) even when the lighting changes (for example, in sunlight or in shadow) may arise because we see the lightest thing in a scene as white and everything else relative to that color (Land, 1959, 1977, 1983).

Late Vision: Recognition and Identification

Vision is more than organizing the world into shapes, of course. If that were all, how would you know if something was good to approach (such as a useful tool or a tasty sweet) or necessary to avoid (such as a dangerous animal or an angry boss). Late visual processes accomplish two major goals: They allow you to assign meaning to the shapes you see, and they allow you to map space so that you can guide your movements according to your goals (Goodale & Milner, 1992; Kosslyn, 1994b; Milner & Goodale, 1995; Ullman, 1996). These tasks are handled by separate mechanisms in the brain. From the results of experiments conducted with monkeys, Ungerleider and Mishkin (1982) described two major neural pathways, which they dubbed the *"what"* and *"where" pathways*. Further evidence for the existence of these distinct mechanisms comes from studies of humans who have had strokes. A stroke that affects the bottom parts of the temporal lobes impairs the patient's ability to recognize objects by sight, and a stroke that affects the back parts of the parietal lobes impairs the patient's ability to register locations (Levine, 1982). Moreover, these separate brain areas have been found to be activated during brain-scanning studies in which normal people are asked to distinguish shapes or locations (Bly & Kosslyn, 1997; Haxby et al., 1991, 1994; Kohler et al., 1995; Ungerleider & Haxby, 1994). The two pathways come together in the frontal lobes, where information about an object's identity and location is used to make decisions (Rao et al., 1997). Before reading on, take a moment to pick a card from Figure 3.14; we will return to these cards shortly.

FIGURE 3.14
Pick a Card, Any Card

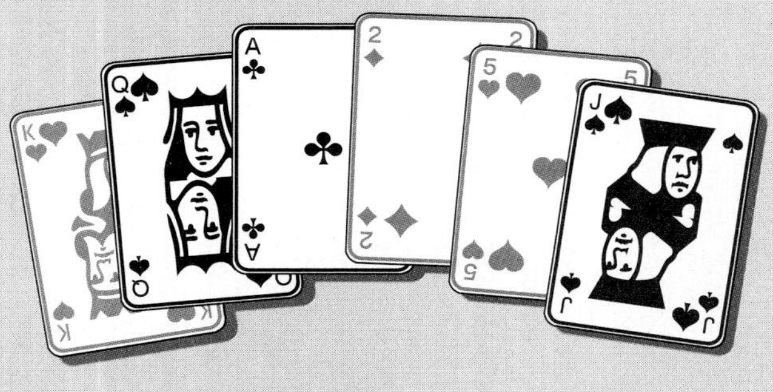

Before beginning, put your right hand over Figure 3.15, the set of cards on the page to the right. After you do that, look at this display and pick out a card. Then cover this display with your left hand, lift up your right hand from the display to the right, and read that caption.

Knowing More Than You Can See. When you see an apple, intermediate visual processes indicate a red, shiny object of a certain shape and size that is at a certain distance. But nothing in this information tells you that inside this object are seeds and, maybe, a worm. For you to know these things, the visual input somehow must activate information from your prior experience, which you have stored in your memory. To interpret what you see, you need to compare the input to stored information. If the input matches something you've stored, the information stored in memory can be applied to the present case (and that's how you know that an

Look at these faces, and then turn the book and look at them rightside up. One explanation for the peculiar lapse in noticing the parts is that when you view the entire face, you are attending to a single pattern picked up by a channel that focuses on large objects, and to see the parts in detail, you need to attend to the output from channels that register smaller things. Notice that if you focus on each part, you can see that some are upside down. But when you focus on the entire face, you see the overall pattern, not a collection of parts.

apple *may* have a worm inside, even if you can't see one *this time*). If the object is *recognized*, it seems familiar; if it is *identified*, you know additional facts about it.

Objects are sometimes recognized as collections of parts. Irving Biederman and his colleagues (Biederman, 1987; Hummel & Biederman, 1992) have suggested that objects are represented in the brain as collections of simple shapes, with each shape representing a part of the object, such as the head, neck, body, and legs of a dog. It is clear that we can see parts of objects individually (Hoffman & Richards, 1984). But take a look at the two photographs of Margaret Thatcher, and then turn the book around so you can see the figure rightside up. It should also be clear that we do not always recognize or identify objects in terms of their individual parts. If that were the case, we wouldn't need to turn the book over to see how weird one of the versions is. Rather, we usually use the outputs of channels that provide us with overall views of shapes, and look for details only if we need them (Cave & Kosslyn, 1993). When we do look at individual features, however, we need to pay attention to ensure that they are properly combined, as demonstrated in Figure 3.15.

FIGURE 3.15
Is Only Your Card Missing?

Look at this display only after you picked out a card in the display on the page on the left. After you picked out a card, look for it here. Did we remove the card you were thinking of? At first glance, it probably appears that we have removed only that card and left the others alone. Magic? No. Your brain coded the suits and values of the cards separately, and so you only see them combined properly when you pay attention to them (Arguin et al., 1994; Treisman & Schmidt, 1982). Thus, if you only paid attention to one particular card, you will notice its absence. As for the other cards, you will notice only the values and suits, not their combinations.

INFORMED PERCEPTION: THE ACTIVE VIEWER. Top-down processing can alter the mechanisms used in bottom-up processing (Humphreys et al., 1997; Kosslyn, 1994b). In a study by Delk and Fillenbaum (1965), for example, participants were shown stimuli that were all cut from the same orangish-red cardboard, including objects that are normally red (an apple and a valentine heart) and objects that are not normally red (a mushroom and a bell). The participants were to adjust the color of a display until they thought it matched the color of the cutouts. Apparently, the knowledge of the usual color of the objects affected how participants saw the actual color; when asked to match the color of the normally red objects, they consistently selected a redder color than the one they chose to match the color of the mushroom and the bell.

Depending on your beliefs and expectations, you will expect to see certain objects in certain contexts. When you walk into a restaurant, you will be surprised if there are no chairs (you may have had this experience the first time you visited an authentic Ethiopian or Japanese restaurant). People often use the context to form such *perceptual expectancies,* perceptions dependent on their previous experience. Loftus and his colleagues (1972) have shown that people require more time to identify an object when it is in an unusual context. When asked if an octopus is present in a picture display, for instance, people require more time to answer if the setting is unlikely—a barnyard, say—than if the setting is an underwater scene (Palmer, 1992a, reports similar findings).

SEEING WITHOUT AWARENESS. Some people who suffer strokes that leave them blind can nevertheless report accurately when spots of light are presented, and even know where they are. These people have no awareness of seeing the dots but rather simply "know" when they are present. Similarly, animals with damage to the visual cortex in the occipital lobe may appear to be blind at all other times, but when they are lowered onto a surface, they stick out their legs to support themselves at just the right point; some of these animals can avoid obstacles when walking, even though the primary visual cortex has been removed (Cowey & Stoerig, 1995). Such behavior has been called *blindsight* (Weiskrantz, 1986). Multiple pathways from the eye lead to many places in the brain (Felleman & Van Essen, 1991; Zeki, 1978, 1993). As noted, some of these pathways allow the brain to register movement, location, and other qualities—and some of these can function even though they do not pass through brain areas that give rise to conscious experience. Thus even when the areas crucial for consciousness, or connections from these areas, are damaged, some visual function nevertheless persists.

Our brains can respond when we see an object even if we are not aware of seeing it. Marcel (1983) took advantage of the finding that presenting a word makes it easier for people to read a subsequent word that has a related meaning; this kind of carry-over effect is one type of *priming*. Marcel and his collaborators found that priming occurs even when the first word is presented so quickly that people are not aware of having seen it (see Figure 3.16; Bar & Biederman, 1998, confirm these results). Perception of events outside awareness is called *subliminal perception*. Researchers have begun to track down the brain events responsible for this effect (Kolb & Braun, 1995; Luck et al., 1996).

But let's not overstate the case. More often than not, instead of perceiving more than you are aware of, you are actually perceiving less than you think. A classic real-world illustration of this situation occurred in 1878 when Eadweard Muybridge took a series of stop-action photographs of a running horse. These photos clearly showed that a running horse always has one foot on the ground, never all four in the air at once. So strong were people's beliefs about what they thought they saw when watching a horse gallop that they rejected Muybridge's first set of photographs, and he had to restage the event with witnesses from the press on hand to verify that the cameras were working properly (Sullivan, 1999). A large body of research shows that people can perceive with high accuracy only those stimuli to which they pay attention. Conversely, people are remarkably bad at noticing even large changes in stimuli if they are not paying attention to the relevant parts (O'Regan, 1992; Simons, 2000; Simons & Levin, 1997).

A bird in the hand is worth two in the the bush. Did you notice anything odd about the sentence you just read? Many people miss the repeated the, and in fact this

FIGURE 3.16
One Demonstration of Subliminal Perception

A word can be presented so briefly that the viewer has no awareness of having seen it.

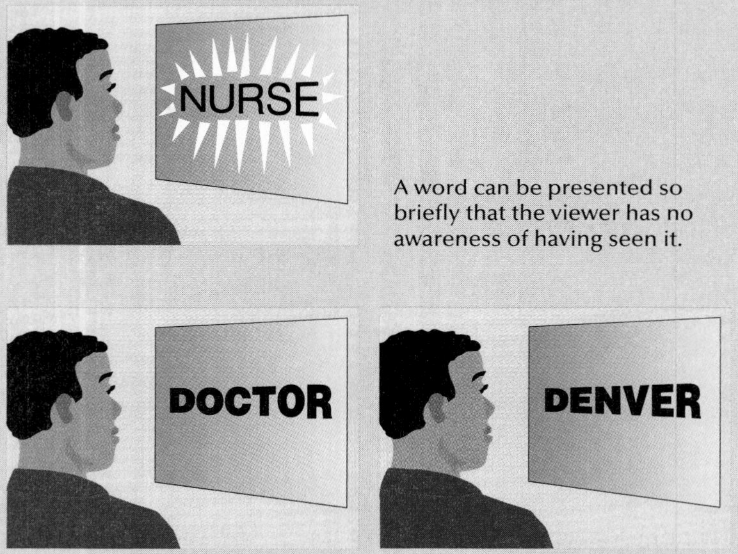

After the initial word, a second word is presented, long enough to be seen clearly. The word is either related to the first one, such as "Doctor," or unrelated, such as "Denver." If the two words are related, participants can read the second one more easily.

The two versions of these scenes were alternated every 640 milliseconds. In the pair of photos on the left, the railing changes, which is not of central interest. People had a difficult time noticing this change, requiring 16.2 alternations on average to spot it. In the pair of photos on the right, the location of the helicopter changes, which is of central interest. People noticed this change after only 4.0 alternations, on average (from Rensink et al., 1997).

is said to be the hardest error for a proofreader to catch. Kanwisher (1987, 1991) has dubbed this effect **repetition blindness** and has shown that people will fail to see a second example of an object if it occurs soon after the first instance. A related phenomenon is the **attentional blink,** in which attention is lost for a certain time immediately following a stimulus to which attention was paid. In contrast to repetition blindness, the attentional blink can occur for a different stimulus, not necessarily a second instance of the same or a closely related one, and the effect may actually be larger for stimuli that occur a few items after the one attended to (Arnell & Jolicoeur, 1999; Chun, 1997; Jolicoeur, 1998; Luck et al., 1996; Raymond et al., 1992). Proofreaders and copyeditors experience this unfortunate phenomenon all the time, missing obvious errors that happen to fall in the wake of a large error or string of errors. Repetition blindness appears to result because the stimuli are not registered as individual events, but simply as a "type" of event (Kanwisher, 1987), whereas the attentional blink may occur because the act of registering information in detail may "lock up" the system for a brief period, during which attention cannot easily be reengaged.

Repetition blindness: The inability to see the second occurrence of a stimulus that appears twice in succession.

Attentional blink: A rebound period in which a person cannot pay attention to one thing after having just paid attention to another.

LOOKING AT LEVELS

The Importance of Body Parts in Physical Beauty

Vision is used for more than identifying objects and registering their locations, as Tai surely knows from the pleasure she takes in looking at art. Through the visual system we also perceive what we call "beauty," including physical attractiveness. David Perrett and his collaborators (1998) asked Asian people (Japanese in Japan) and Caucasians (Scots in Scotland) to choose the most attractive faces from a set of photographs, some of which had been altered to emphasize features that reflect high levels of male or female hormones. The researchers found that both national groups preferred women's faces with a female "hormone enhanced" look to average faces. However, the effect was larger for faces within each participant's own population, a finding that was interpreted as indicating that this is a learned preference. In addition, both groups also found *male* faces more attractive if they showed effects of *female* hormones. Faces that showed effects of high levels of male hormones were rated as having high "perceived

Facial images of Caucasian and Japanese females and males were "feminized" and "masculinized" 50% in shape. Which face do you prefer? In general, faces that reveal effects of female sex hormones are seen as more attractive.

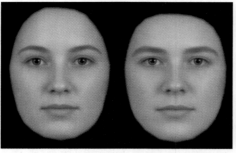

Caucasian female, feminized   Caucasian female, masculinized   Caucasian male, feminized   Caucasian male, masculinized

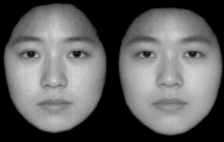
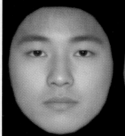
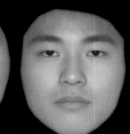

Japanese female, feminized   Japanese female, masculinized   Japanese male, feminized   Japanese male, masculinized

dominance," as being older, and as having less warmth, emotionality, honesty, and cooperativeness (as well as other attributes). Apparently, the effects of female hormones not only made faces look younger but also softened these negative perceptions.

However, when it comes to bodies, the story is not so consistent. For example, Ford and Beach (1951) considered what people in over 200 cultures looked at when evaluating attractiveness and found that different cultures focused on different parts and characteristics of the body (such as the size of the pelvis, pudginess, and height). How can there be such differences in what is thought of as "beautiful" if everyone has the same visual equipment? Several reasons become apparent when we use the levels of analysis approach. First, at the level of the group, values and tastes develop and are taught, either explicitly (via instruction) or implicitly (via example) to the individual members of the group. These standards may evolve for different reasons. For example, before the spread of AIDS, gay men were often very thin; after AIDS, having a little extra weight was perceived as a sign of health and thus became attractive. Second, at the level of the person, these standards produce values and beliefs. These values and beliefs in turn affect top-down processing, leading people to look for certain body parts or attributes. And of course, at the level of the brain, the mechanisms of attention are at work when people fixate on a salient part, registering it in detail. Once you evaluate someone as beautiful, various expectations and beliefs come to mind. Just as you know that once you've identified an object as an apple, you know it has seeds inside, you also believe that an attractive person is likely to be kind, nurturing, sensitive, and to have other positive attributes to boot (Dion et al., 1972).

CONSOLIDATE!

▶ *1. What is the nature of light, and how do we see color, shape, and motion?* Light is made up of electromagnetic waves. These waves enter the pupil of the eye, and the lens focuses the light on the retina. Special receptors and sensory cells in the retina transduce the light waves into neural signals, which continue along

(continued)

the optic nerve to the brain. There are two kinds of receptors in the retina: rods and cones. Rods are very sensitive to light but register only shades of gray. Cones are not as sensitive and respond to particular wavelengths of light, which is essential for color vision. There are three different types of cones, each most responsive to a particular color: yellow, green, and violet. Opponent cells, on the other hand, work in pairs—blue–yellow, red–green, and black–white. The activation of one color in the opponent cell pair inhibits the other. By changing the hue, saturation, and brightness of colors, artists can lead the viewer to have an almost infinite range of color experiences. Shape is registered by different channels, which represent form at different levels of resolution. Special parts of the brain register motion.

▶ *2. How are we able to separate figure from ground and see the world as a stable collection of objects?* We perceive figures as distinct from ground by using organizational principles, such as those described by the Gestalt laws of organization; these principles include proximity, similarity, good continuation, closure, and good form. Various cues, from both eyes or only one, from static images or moving images, help establish the perceptual constancies. Critical constancies include size constancy (objects appear the same size in spite of differences in the images that are projected on the retina), shape constancy (objects seem to have the same shape in spite of differences in the shape of their images on the retina), brightness constancy (the brightest object in a scene appears the same brightness in spite of large differences in the light reflected, and the brightness of other objects is seen relative to the brightest one), and color constancy (colors appear the same in different lighting conditions).

▶ *3. How do we make sense of what we see?* If we have seen an object before, information about it is stored in memory; when we see it again, we can match the input to the stored information and apply the information stored previously to the current example. We identify an object when associated information stored in memory is applied to the current stimulus. Once we have identified an object, information in memory can fill in information missing from the stimulus itself. In at least some situations, we can identify objects that we are not even aware of seeing, but in most situations attention is necessary to identify objects.

HEARING

Tai knew that loud noises could destroy her hearing, and this knowledge made blaring rock concerts even less appealing to her. When she went to a concert with Sue, she wore earplugs and took aspirin to ward off the inevitable headache she would otherwise suffer. But Sue reveled in the loud chords and jangling harmonies. How could the two friends have such different responses to the same music?

▶ 1. How do ears normally register sound?

▶ 2. What auditory cues allow us to organize sounds into coherent units and locate their sources?

▶ 3. How do we make meaning out of sound?

Early Audition: If a Tree Falls but Nobody Hears It, Is There a Sound?

We know that rays don't emanate from our eyes when we see. Now for a trick question: Do you think that sound waves emanate from our ears when we hear? In 1978, researchers found that when a click is presented to someone, the ear soon produces an echo (Kemp, 1978). Not long after this discovery, researchers (Kemp, 1979; Zurek, 1981, 1985; Zwicker & Schloth, 1984) found that even when a person isn't hearing a particular stimulus, the ear sometimes actually makes a sound. In fact, about 40% of normal people emit a detectable soft humming sound from their ears, of which they are unaware. In some cases, the humming is loud enough that other people can hear it. These sounds are not like the natural sonar used by whales, sound waves bouncing off objects and returning to the ear. These sounds play no role in hearing. They are probably caused by feedback from the brain to the ear; feedback (not the sounds produced by it) helps us hear slight differences in sounds (Pickles, 1988; Zurek, 1985). As in vision, there are many feedback connections between areas of the brain that process sound, and between these areas and the ear (Felleman & Van Essen, 1991). This is not the only similarity between hearing and seeing, as you will soon discover.

SOUND WAVES: BEING PRESSURED. Like vision, auditory processing occurs in three phases: early, intermediate, and late. Early auditory processing begins with the sensation of sound. Sound usually arises when something vibrates, creating waves of moving air that enter our ears. Sound can arise when any type of molecules—gas, liquid, or solid—move and create pressure waves. Thus we can hear when we are surrounded by either air or water or when we put an ear to the ground, to a wall, or to another solid object. An old (but true) cliché of Western movies is listening with an ear pressed to a rail to hear whether a train is approaching. But movies sometimes get it wrong. In outer space—where there are no molecules to be moved—we could not hear anything; the loud explosion of the demolished Death Star in the first *Star Wars* movie would in fact have been silent as the grave.

These pressure waves go up, and then down, repeatedly; each complete up-and-down movement is called a *cycle*. As with light waves for vision, sound waves have both frequency and amplitude. We usually hear variations in frequency as differences in **pitch**—how high or low the sound seems—and we hear variations in amplitude as differences in **volume**. (It probably is no coincidence that people are most sensitive to the frequencies of a baby's cry, around 2,000–5,000 Hertz; a Hertz, or Hz, is the number of cycles per second.) The same psychophysical concepts that apply to vision, such as thresholds, JNDs, and so on, also apply to hearing and are measured in comparable ways.

A question often asked in beginning philosophy classes is this: If a tree falls in the forest but nobody hears it, is there a sound? The answer is now clear: No. Sound is *caused* by waves of molecules (a physical event), but the waves themselves are not sound. Sound is a psychological event and hence depends on a nervous system to transduce the physical energy of the vibrations to nerve energy. Without a brain to register the physical energy, there can be no sound. The situation is exactly analogous to the relationships of wavelength to hue and of amplitude to lightness. Physical properties *lead to* psychological events, but they are not the events themselves. The discipline of psychophysics charts the relationship between physical events and our experience of them.

THE BRAIN'S EAR: MORE THAN A MICROPHONE. The anatomy of the ear is illustrated in Figure 3.17. The ear has three parts: the outer ear, middle ear, and inner ear. The eardrum (the *tympanic membrane*) stretches across the inside end of the auditory canal, and everything between the eardrum and the auditory nerve is designed to convert movements of the eardrum to nerve impulses that are sent to the brain. Specifically, waves move the eardrum, which in turn moves three bones in the middle ear (incidentally, these are the smallest bones in the human body). If you hear a loud sound, the muscles in the ear reflexively tighten, which protects against damage (Borg & Counter, 1989). These muscles also contract when you talk, which protects you from hurting your own ears. Such protection is necessary because the ear is amazingly sensitive: We can hear a sound when the eardrum is moved less than one billionth of an inch (Green, 1976). The three bones of the middle ear not only transfer but also amplify the vibration and cause the *basilar membrane* (which is inside the cochlea, as shown in Figure 3.17) to vibrate. The basilar membrane is where different frequencies of sound are coded into different nerve impulses. Hairs sticking up from cells lining the basilar membrane in turn trigger nerve impulses, which are then sent to the brain. These **hair cells** function in hearing the same way rods and cones do in vision; they produce the initial nerve impulses.

Pitch: How high or low a sound seems; higher frequencies of pressure waves produce the experience of higher pitches.

Volume: The strength of a sound; pressure waves with greater amplitude produce the experience of louder sound.

Hair cells: Cells with stiff hairs along the basilar membrane of the inner ear that, when moved, produce nerve impulses that are sent to the brain; these cells are the auditory equivalent of rods and cones.

Frequency theory: The theory that higher frequencies produce higher rates of neural firing.

Place theory: The theory that different frequencies activate different places along the basilar membrane.

FIGURE 3.17
Anatomy of the Ear

Outer Ear   **Middle Ear**   **Inner Ear**

Pinna

Hammer
Anvil
Stirrup
Semicircular canals
Cochlea
Auditory nerve
Bone

Sound waves

Auditory canal
Oval window
Eardrum (tympanic membrane)
Round window

Hair cells

Wave traveling along the basilar membrane

The major parts of the outer ear, middle ear, and inner ear. The semicircular canals have no role in hearing; they help us keep our balance.

If you unwound the cochlea and looked into it, you would see the basilar membrane with its hair cells.

There are two main theories about the way the basilar membrane converts pressure waves to perceived sound. **Frequency theory** holds that higher frequencies produce greater neural firing. This theory cannot explain the full extent of our ability to hear: Neurons can fire only about 1,000 times a second at most, so how is it that we can hear sounds produced by much higher frequencies (Gelfand, 1981)? According to **place theory**, different frequencies activate different places along the basilar membrane, as shown in Figure 3.18. This theory appears to be correct, at least for most frequencies; it is possible, however, that the rate of vibration does help us hear relatively low tones.

As in vision, a number of brain areas working together allow us to sense sound. The first part of the cortex to receive auditory information, the *primary auditory cortex*, is spatially organized. Researchers have shown that the lower the pitch, the farther activity shifts along this structure. Again, just as in vision, in which the pattern

FIGURE 3.18
Place Coding of Sound Frequency

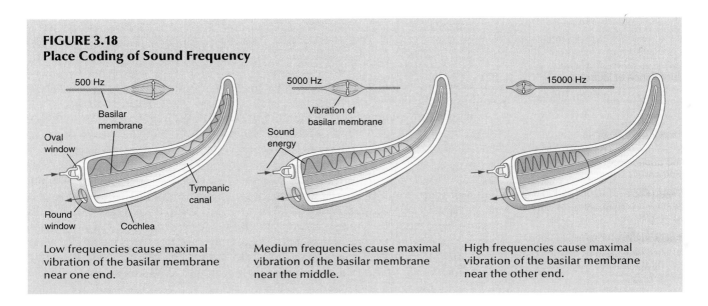

500 Hz
Basilar membrane
Oval window
Round window
Cochlea
Tympanic canal

5000 Hz
Vibration of basilar membrane
Sound energy

15000 Hz

Low frequencies cause maximal vibration of the basilar membrane near one end.

Medium frequencies cause maximal vibration of the basilar membrane near the middle.

High frequencies cause maximal vibration of the basilar membrane near the other end.

of activation on the eye is in turn laid out on the brain (see p. 104), the spatial arrangement of vibration on the basilar membrane is mimicked in the brain. This sort of spatial arrangement is called **tonotopic organization** (Clarey et al., 1992; Romani et al., 1982).

DEAFNESS: HEAR TODAY, GONE TOMORROW. Over 28 million Americans have some sort of difficulty in hearing (Soli, 1994). More than 30 genes have now been linked to deafness (Lynch et al., 1997), and thus we shouldn't be surprised to find that there are different forms of deafness and that some forms of deafness are inherited. Lynch and colleagues studied the deaf descendants of a deaf man who was born in 1713 and found that they inherited a gene involved in producing the protein actin. This protein apparently plays a crucial role in stiffening the hairs in the inner ear; if it is missing, the hair cells fail to function properly. Not all forms of deafness are genetic, however. One of the most serious is **nerve deafness,** which typically occurs when the hair cells are destroyed by loud sounds. A rock band heard at close range can produce sounds loud enough to cause this sort of damage; indeed, one study found that of a group of college students who went regularly to a dance club featuring loud music, almost a third exhibited permanent hearing loss for high-frequency sounds (Hartman, 1982). Nerve deafness may affect only certain frequencies; in those instances, a hearing aid can amplify the remaining frequencies, and hearing can be improved. Many researchers believe that surgery will soon allow doctors to make an end run around a damaged ear and allow auditory input to stimulate the auditory cortex directly (Ubell, 1995). Sue may have suffered some nerve deafness from the many concerts she attended and so wasn't bothered by the loud music that Tai experienced as painful.

Another form of hearing impairment, **tinnitus,** is signaled by a constant ringing or noise in the ears (McFadden, 1982). And some drugs, including aspirin, can dull a person's hearing (McFadden & Plattsmier, 1983). Could this effect explain why Tai didn't mind rock concerts so much if she took aspirin in advance? Fortunately, the dulling effects of aspirin are only temporary. **Conduction deafness** can result from any accident or other cause that impairs the functioning of the external ear or middle ear. A broken eardrum, for example, can cause conduction deafness.

It is worth noting that if someone becomes deaf as a child, other senses can eventually compensate. Catalan-Ahumeda and colleagues (1993), Neville and colleagues (1983), Wolf and Thatcher (1990), and others have found increased activation in the visual cortex of deaf people, and by adolescence the deaf can focus visual attention in many tasks better than can hearing people (particularly when they have to attend to something not currently being focused on; Loke & Song, 1991; Neville, 1988, 1990; Neville & Lawson, 1987).

Intermediate Hearing: Organizing the Auditory World

Watch people crossing a two-way street; how many of them look both ways before stepping off the curb? Many people apparently rely in part on their hearing when crossing a street, stepping forward before looking carefully. Intermediate auditory processing allows us to organize sounds as coming from distinct objects and to locate the sources of sounds.

SORTING OUT SOUNDS: FROM ONE, MANY. In daily life, a single complex jumble of many sounds usually assaults our ears, not individual sounds one at a time. To make sense of what we hear, we first need to sort out individual sounds. As in vision, we need to distinguish figure from ground. Bregman (1990, 1993) calls this process *auditory scene analysis,* which relies on organization very much like what occurs in vision. Indeed, the Gestalt laws help us here, too. For example, people organize sounds partly based on similarity (for example, grouping sounds with the same pitch) and good continuation (grouping the same pitch continued over time).

Tonotopic organization: The use of distance along a strip of cortex to represent differences in pitch.

Nerve deafness: A type of deafness that typically occurs when the hair cells are destroyed by loud sounds.

Tinnitus: A form of hearing impairment signaled by a constant ringing or noise in the ears.

Conduction deafness: Deafness caused by a physical impairment of the external or middle ear.

Recognizing and identifying speech is a good example of auditory scene analysis because the actual stimulus is continuous, with no indication of breaks to delineate the beginnings and ends of words, and yet to communicate, people must identify individual words. This problem is the **speech segmentation problem.** By analogy, *thisproblemisliketheoneyouarenowsolving* in vision.

In vision, we see continuous variations in the frequency of light not as continuous variations in hue, but rather as a set of distinct colors. Similarly, we hear speech sounds as distinct categories. This **categorical perception** produces categories with remarkably sharp boundaries. For example, if a computer is programmed to vary the time between the start of a syllable (the consonant being pronounced, such as *b*) and the "voiced" part of the syllable (the sound of the vowel being pronounced, such as *a*), we will hear "ba" if the voice starts from 0 to around 25 thousandths of a second after the consonant starts; but if the voice starts after a longer interval, we will hear "pa." There is very little intermediate ground; we hear one or the other (Eimas & Corbit, 1973). Monkeys, chinchillas, and various other animals also show categorical perception (Kuhl, 1989; Moody et al., 1990), which suggests that the perceptual system itself does this work—not the language systems of our various cultures. Indeed, the common ancestor of monkeys and humans may have evolved many of the "building blocks" that were later incorporated into speech.

Bats and barn owls are adept at using sound to localize objects (Konishi, 1993; Suga, 1990). The structure of the barn owl's face has developed to direct sound to its ears to maximize location cues. And bats produce sounds, and then listen for the echoes coming back. The echoes are precise enough for the bat to discern the shapes of even small objects (Simmons & Chen, 1989).

LOCATING SOUNDS: WHY TWO EARS ARE BETTER THAN ONE. In vision, our brains use slight differences in the images striking the two eyes to assess the distance of an object. Similarly, hearing makes use of differences in the stimuli reaching the two ears to assess the distance of a sound source; these differences are **binaural cues** (Yost & Dye, 1991). Three kinds of differences are particularly important. First, sound waves reach the two ears at slightly different phases, that is, at slightly different points in the wave cycle. The *difference in phase* reaching the two ears is particularly useful for detecting the source of relatively low-frequency sounds, which arise from longer waves (Gulick et al., 1989). Second, a *difference in volume* at the two ears is used as a cue. In addition to all their other functions, our heads are useful because they block sound, and thus the amplitude of sound waves is smaller when it reaches the ear on the side of the head away from the sound source. This cue is particularly effective for high-frequency sounds. Third, the sound wave will reach the two ears at slightly different times; this *onset difference* is tiny, but the brain uses it effectively.

As in vision, we use many different cues to assess where an object is. **Monaural cues** depend on only one ear, not two. Consider three such cues. First, the simple volume of a sound: Especially for familiar objects, we can use volume as an indicator of distance. If a motorcycle is approaching, we can get a good sense of how far away it is from its sound. Second, the way our external ears are crinkled bends sound waves in different ways; these variations help us detect the location of the sound source (Moore, 1982). Third, by moving our heads and bodies, we can compare the relative volume of a sound from different vantage points, which helps us locate its source.

Late Audition: Recognition and Identification

We use sound in many ways. In addition to interpreting speech and music, we also recognize that the snap of a green bean indicates freshness, that a knock on a door means someone wants to come in, that a cat's mewing may mean she wants to be fed. As in vision, sounds become meaningful when they are matched to information already stored in memory, which is the job of late auditory processing.

MORE THAN MEETS THE EAR. Just as in vision, top-down processing leads what you expect to hear to influence what you actually hear. If Tai tries to talk to Sue at the rock concert, Sue may be able to hear her friend, but a large part of what she hears is probably being supplied by her brain. A demonstration of such an effect was reported by Warren and Warren (1970), who asked people to listen to a tape-recorded

Speech segmentation problem: The problem of organizing a continuous stream of speech into separate parts that correspond to individual words.

Categorical perception: Identifying sounds as belonging to distinct categories that correspond to the basic units of speech.

Binaural cues: Differences in the stimuli reaching the two ears that are used to localize the sources of sounds.

Monaural cues: Cues to the location of the source of a sound (such as volume) that do not depend on two ears.

sentence after part of a word had been replaced with the sound of a cough. Although part of the word was actually missing, all the participants claimed that they actually heard the entire word and denied that the cough covered part of it. In fact, the listeners were not exactly sure at what point the cough occurred. This effect, more obvious for words in sentences than for words standing alone, is called the *phonemic restoration effect* (a phoneme is the smallest segment of spoken speech, such as "ba" or "da"). This filling-in effect occurs not only with speech sounds but also with musical instruments. In fact, if you see someone bowing the strings of a cello at the same time you hear the strings being plucked, the sight is enough to distort the sound you hear (Saldana & Rosenblum, 1993).

HEARING WITHOUT AWARENESS. As happens in vision, we pick up some auditory information without being aware of it. Perhaps the most common experience of perception without awareness is the **cocktail party phenomenon.** At an event like a party, you may not be aware of other people's conversation until someone mentions your name—which you hear immediately (Cherry, 1953). But in order to become aware of the sound of your name, you must have been tracking the conversation all along (using bottom-up processing); you simply were not aware of the conversation until that important word was spoken. In experiments she performed as an undergraduate, Treisman (1964a, 1964b) showed that when people listen to stimuli presented separately to the two ears (through headphones) and are instructed to listen to only one ear, they still register some information—such as whether the voice is male or female—from the ignored ear.

This discovery spawned an industry that proclaimed people can learn in their sleep, simply by playing tapes (purchased at low, low discount prices). Unfortunately, it turns out that unless a person is paying attention, not much gets through. And even when information does get through, it is retained very briefly; when tested hours later, people remember virtually none of the information presented outside awareness (Greenwald et al., 1991).

MUSIC: CULTURAL CREATIONS? Music is a part of virtually all cultures; in some, its importance is so great that governments have occasionally regulated what constitutes music itself. In the former Soviet Union, for example, some chords were labeled decadent and actually outlawed. Closer to home, in North Carolina, singing out of tune was at one time a prosecutable offense (Seuling, 1975). Aside from these cultural curiosities, however, the existence of music depends on the fact that the brain registers sounds relative to one another, not in isolation (Krumhansl, 2000). For example, when you double a frequency, you hear the same note but an *octave* higher (an octave in Western music is eight consecutive notes). The continuous variation in frequency between octaves is divided into distinct intervals, which form a *scale*. The nature of scales varies in different cultures. The Western scale relies on 12 half-steps for each octave, compared with more than 50 in Indian music. Nevertheless, all humans hear notes an octave apart as more similar than consecutive notes. This is another example of the way in which the physical nature of a stimulus differs from its psychological experience. Indeed, we can hear two different sequences of notes (which have different physical frequencies) as the same, provided that the notes are separated by the same intervals.

Within a given culture, the ease of identifying the notes in a scale depends partly on whether a person has **absolute pitch,** the striking ability to identify a particular note by itself, not simply in relation to other notes (Krumhansl, 1991, 2000). Studies have shown that Americans with absolute pitch identify the intervals between notes from a standard Western scale better if an instrument is "in tune" (that is, the notes are set to the correct absolute frequencies) than if it is a bit out of tune; people without absolute pitch do not show such a difference (Miyazaki, 1993). Many people with absolute pitch developed the ability during childhood (Krumhansl, 1991, 2000; Takeuchi & Hulse, 1993). People with absolute pitch have an unusually large planum temporale, a part of the auditory cortex that lies on the top part of the temporal lobe, near the back (Schlaug et al., 1995).

Cocktail party phenomenon: The effect of not being aware of other people's conversations until your name is mentioned, and then suddenly hearing it.

Absolute pitch: The ability to identify a particular note by itself, not simply in relation to other notes.

Beethoven, the Deaf Composer

Beethoven was stone deaf when he wrote much of his greatest music. How is this possible? The levels of analysis approach will help us understand his remarkable achievement. First, at the level of the brain, auditory mental imagery allowed him to hear music with his "mind's ear" as he was composing it. Auditory imagery arises when brain areas that are used in hearing are activated from stored memories (Halpern, 1988; Zatorre & Halpern, 1993). Right now, decide whether the first three notes of "Three Blind Mice" go up or down; to do this, you probably "heard" the tune in your head—you evoked auditory imagery. Imagery can occur even when the sense organs are damaged (for example, if the hair cells in the ear die). What Beethoven heard in his mind's ear would probably have been very similar to what he would have heard carried by sound waves had he not been deaf. Second, consider the level of the person. We can only speculate, but being forced to practice by his tyrannical father may have had at least two consequences for the young composer. Not only did he become a superb pianist and music theorist, but he also may have come to use his music as a refuge from his father (Freud would have called this reaction "sublimation," as you will see in Chapter 10). Third, at the level of the group, his playing may have been a way to appease his father and win his approval. Also, Beethoven lived in a society that appreciated music, and thus he was able to raise financial support for his work, despite the fact that he was deaf. (Beethoven was the first composer to "freelance" for a living.) Finally, music itself is a cultural invention, as are the various detailed systems of notation that different human societies use to write it down.

CONSOLIDATE!

▶ *1. How do ears normally register sound?* Normally, pressure waves move the eardrum, which in turn causes the bones of the middle ear to move, creating movement of the hair cells of the basilar membrane, which transduce the waves into neural impulses. The frequency of the waves determines the pitch of the sound, and the amplitude determines its volume. Frequency theory may explain the conversion of pressure waves to sound at low frequencies, and place theory explains it at most frequencies, especially high ones. Nerve deafness occurs when the hair cells do not function properly; conduction deafness occurs when the external or middle ear is impaired.

▶ *2. What auditory cues allow us to organize sounds into coherent units and locate their sources?* We use similarity of sounds and other Gestalt principles to organize sounds into units. In addition, categorical perception allows us to hear some types of sounds—particularly those from speech—as distinct units, not

as continuous variations. We use a variety of cues to localize the sources of sounds. Binaural cues depend on the two ears, and include differences in phase, volume, or arrival times at the two ears. Monaural cues do not depend on the two ears, and include volume, the way sound is bent by the external ear, and changes in volume as we move.

▶ *3. How do we make meaning out of sound?* As in vision, sounds become meaningful when they are matched to information already stored in memory. Both bottom-up and top-down processes are at work in audition. Top-down processes, which produce phenomena such as the phonemic restoration effect, can fill in fragmentary information. Some auditory recognition and identification takes place outside awareness and can guide attention. Our cultures have taught us how to interpret sounds as music. Moreover, some people have absolute pitch, which enhances the meaning of musical sounds.

SENSING IN OTHER WAYS

One of the reasons why Tai hates rock concerts is that they are so crowded, and Tai is particularly sensitive to body odor. Nor does she like the food that is available at the concession stands, which she finds greasy and unhealthy. Neither of these circumstances seem to bother Sue. On the other hand, unlike Tai, Sue finds that she sometimes becomes literally dizzy when she looks at art. Dizziness is not a novel feeling for her; she gets dizzy easily. Although she enjoys the sensation in other contexts, such as dancing spins, the dizziness makes her queasy in a gallery. Despite their differences, both friends agree strongly that they share another kind of sense. They believe they can sense other people's thoughts and are sometimes aware of future events.

► 1. How does the sense of smell work?

► 2. How does the sense of taste work?

► 3. How do we sense our bodies?

► 4. Does extrasensory perception (ESP) exist?

Smell: A Nose for News?

Smell and taste are often grouped together as the **chemical senses** because both, unlike the other senses, rely on registering the presence of specific chemicals. People differ widely in their sense of smell, or *olfaction*. Some people are 20 times more sensitive to odors than are other people (Rabin & Cain, 1986), a finding that might explain Tai's discomfort in a crowd. However, most people are remarkably poor at identifying odors, even though they often think they are good at it (de Wijk et al., 1995). Cain (1979) found that people could correctly identify only about half of 80 common scents; although we may know that an odor is familiar—that is, we recognize it—we may be unable to identify it. In general, women are better than men at detecting many types of odors (Cain, 1982), and younger adults are better than either children (up to 14 years old) or middle-aged adults (between 40 and 50 years old) (Cain & Gent, 1991; de Wijk & Cain, 1994; Murphy, 1986). So much the worse for Tai, who was probably at the peak of her olfactory sensitivity.

DISTINGUISHING ODORS: LOCK AND KEY. The best theory of odor detection can be described using the lock and key metaphor. Molecules have different shapes, and the olfactory receptors are built so that only molecules with particular shapes will fit in particular places. The molecules are like keys, and the receptors like locks. When the right-shaped molecule arrives at a particular receptor, it sends a signal to the brain and we sense the odor. Just as there is not a single type of cone for each color we can see, there is not a single receptor for each odor we can smell (see Figure 3.19); rather, the overall pattern of activity signals a particular odor (Freeman, 1991).

Two major neural tracks leave the olfactory bulb. One, passing through the thalamus, is particularly involved in memory; the other, connected to the limbic system, is particularly involved in emotions. These connections explain why odors often tap emotionally charged memories—remember the way you felt when you unexpectedly smelled an old girlfriend's perfume or boyfriend's aftershave?

OLFACTION GONE AWRY: IS IT SAFE TO COOK WITHOUT SMELL? Have you ever wished you could not smell? Maybe that would be a relief once in a while, but losing your sense of smell completely is not a good idea. Smell serves to signal the presence of

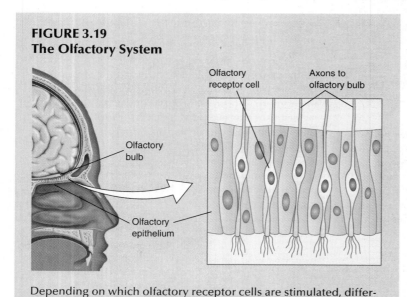

FIGURE 3.19
The Olfactory System

Olfactory bulb

Olfactory epithelium

Olfactory receptor cell

Axons to olfactory bulb

Depending on which olfactory receptor cells are stimulated, different messages are sent to the olfactory bulb, the first part of the brain to process such signals.

noxious substances; our brains are wired so that odors can quickly activate the "fight-or-flight" system. It would not be wise to ask a friend who has no sense of smell to cook dinner on a regular basis: Smell is often the only signal that meat or other food is spoiled. Relatively few people have no olfactory sense, a deficit that can arise from brain damage or a virus (Doty et al., 1991).

PHEROMONES: ANOTHER KIND OF SCENTS? Airborne chemicals released by female animals in heat arouse the male of the species. These are an example of **pheromones,** chemical substances that serve as a means of communication. Like hormones, they modulate the functions of various organs, including the brain. Unlike hormones, pheromones are released *outside* the body, in urine and sweat. The most famous example of effects of pheromones in humans was discovered by Martha McClintock (1971). She originally found that female roommates tend to synchronize their menstrual cycles and, along with Kathleen Stern (Stern & McClintock, 1998), has since found that this effect depends on certain pheromones' reaching the nose (Russell et al., 1980, report consistent results). The receptors that are triggered by pheromones are accessed via the nose, and odors may accompany these chemicals.

Taste: The Mouth Has It

When scientists discuss taste, they are talking about sensing via receptors located solely in the mouth. **Taste buds** (see Figure 3.20) are microscopic structures mounted on the sides of the little bumps you can see on your tongue in a mirror. You have taste buds in other places in your mouth as well, such as the back of the throat and cheeks (Smith & Frank, 1993). Your taste buds die and are replaced, on average, every 10 days (McLaughlin & Margolskee, 1994). Humans have more taste buds than some species, such as chickens, but fewer than others; some fish have taste buds spread all over their skin (Pfaffmann, 1978). Children have more sensitive taste buds than

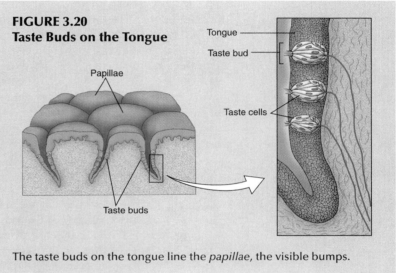

FIGURE 3.20
Taste Buds on the Tongue

Papillae

Tongue

Taste bud

Taste cells

Taste buds

The taste buds on the tongue line the *papillae*, the visible bumps.

adults, and thus flavors are presumably stronger for them than for adults—which may account for children's notoriously strong likes and dislikes of foods. Nevertheless, even adults can be remarkably sensitive to slight differences in taste. President Calvin Coolidge could tell that chickens raised in the White House yard didn't taste quite right. As it happened, they ate their feed on the ground that was once Teddy Roosevelt's mint garden, and the residual flavor of the mint made its way into their meat (Seuling, 1978). When wine tasters speak of wine as having a flavor of mushrooms or cloves, they may not be speaking metaphorically. Depending on the composition of the soil in which the vines grow, grapes acquire different tastes.

SWEET, SOUR, SALTY, BITTER. You've seen how a wide range of colors arises from three types of cones, and how patterns of odors arise from the combinations of receptors being activated. The brain uses this same mixing-and-matching trick for taste. The tastes of all foods are made up of combinations of four tastes: sweet, sour, salty, and bitter (Bartoshuk & Beauchamp, 1994; Scott & Plata-Salaman, 1991). In addition, however, free nerve endings in the mouth appear to be irritated by spicy foods (Lawless, 1984). These provide another source of information about taste, one that is not directly related to the taste buds. Different parts of the mouth and tongue are more or less sensitive to different tastes; you can detect bitter flavors best in the back of your mouth (Shallenberger, 1993). However, these different sensitivities are a

Pheromones: Chemicals that function like hormones but are released outside the body (in urine and sweat).

Taste buds: Microscopic structures on the bumps on the tongue surface, at the back of the throat, and inside the cheeks; the four types of taste buds are sensitive to sweet, sour, salty, and bitter tastes.

matter of degree: All kinds of taste buds are found in most locations on the tongue. Curiously, there is a "taste hole" in the middle of the tongue, an area where there are no taste buds at all. Moreover, you cannot taste something unless it can be at least partially dissolved by your saliva (Seuling, 1986); that is why you can't taste a marble.

TASTE AND SMELL. Most people think that the flavor of food arises from its taste (Rozin, 1982), but in fact much of what we think of as taste is actually smell, or a combination of smell and taste. In rats the two types of information converge on a region of the frontal lobes that is critical for the perception of flavor (Schul et al., 1996). Next time you have a stuffy nose, notice the flavor of your food, or lack thereof—particularly when you close your eyes and eliminate top-down processing to fill in your perception of the flavor. Researchers have found that people have a much harder time detecting most flavors when smell is blocked (Hyman et al., 1979). Tai might like the idea of not being able to smell the press of sweaty bodies, but not smelling at all would ruin the taste of everything from hot chocolate to pepperoni.

Somasthetic Senses: Not Just Skin Deep

The traditional five senses—sight, hearing, smell, taste, and touch—were listed and described by Aristotle more than 2,000 years ago. It would be a sad commentary on the value of science if we couldn't do better after all this time. Today, we are able to argue that there are nine senses, perhaps ten: sight, hearing, smell, taste, and then a collection of five senses that together are called **somasthetic senses.** These senses all have to do with perceiving the body and its position in space: kinesthetic (sense of where the limbs are and how they move), vestibular (sense of balance), touch, temperature sensitivity, and pain. There may be a sixth somasthetic sense, magnetic sense. And, finally, there is possibly one more sense: extrasensory perception, or ESP (also sometimes called *psi*).

KINESTHETIC SENSE: A MOVING SENSE. Read this, and then close your eyes and hold out your left arm in an odd position. Now, keeping your left arm in place, touch your left hand with your right hand. You shouldn't have any trouble doing this because you know where your hands are without having to see them. You know because of your **kinesthetic sense,** which registers the movement and position of the limbs. Two types of specialized cells sense this information: One type is in the tendons (the material that connects muscles to bones) and is triggered by tension; the other is in the muscles themselves and is triggered by the length of the muscle (Pinel, 1993).

VESTIBULAR SENSE: BEING ORIENTED. The inner ear is used not only for hearing, but also for balance. The **vestibular sense,** which provides information about how you are oriented relative to gravity, relies on an organ in the inner ear that contains three *semicircular canals* (illustrated in Figure 3.17). If these structures are disrupted, say by infection or injury (or spending too much time in weightlessness in outer space, as happens to astronauts), people have a difficult time keeping their balance.

TOUCH: FEELING WELL. Here's another trick question: What's your body's largest organ? The lungs? the intestines? The answer is the skin. As well as protecting our bodies from the environment (such as dirt, germs, flying objects, changes in temperature), making crucial vitamins, and triggering the release of various hormones, the skin is also a massive sensory organ. Millions of receptors in the skin produce impulses when stimulated in specific ways. Moreover, using the same mechanism as other senses, it is the particular combination of receptors being stimulated that produces a particular sensation. The mix-and-match principle is at work here, too: We can feel many more types of sensations than we have types of receptors. Receptors in the skin in different parts of the body send impulses to different parts of the somatosensory cortex (see Chapter 2); and in general the more cortex devoted to a particular area of the skin, the more sensitive we are there (Weinstein, 1968).

Somasthetic senses: Senses that have to do with perceiving the body and its position in space—specifically, kinesthetic sense, vestibular sense, touch, temperature sensitivity, pain sense, and possibly magnetic sense.

Kinesthetic sense: The sense that registers the movement and position of the limbs.

Vestibular sense: The sense that provides information about the body's orientation relative to gravity.

In general, women are more sensitive to touch than are men (Weinstein, 1968). Moreover, women are especially sensitive (relative to men) on some parts of their bodies, such as their backs and stomachs.

TEMPERATURE. The skin has separate systems for registering hot and cold; indeed, there are distinct spots on your skin that register *only* hot or *only* cold. These spots are about 1 mm across (Hensel, 1982). If a cold spot is stimulated, you will feel a sensation of cold even if the stimulus is something hot. This phenomenon is called **paradoxical cold.** People are not very good at telling exactly where a hot or cold stimulus is located, particularly if it is near the skin but not touching it (Cain, 1973).

PAIN. Despite the discomfort, even the agony, pain brings, the inability to feel pain is even worse in the long run than the inability to smell odors. Sternbach (1978) described children who could not feel pain normally and who picked off their nostrils and bit off their fingers because they didn't notice what they were doing. Pain serves to warn us of impending danger, and it is crucial to survival.

The sensation of pain arises when three different kinds of nerves are stimulated. These nerves differ in size and in the speed with which they transmit impulses. Thus, we can feel **double pain:** the first phase, of sharp pain, occurs at the time of the injury; it is followed by a dull pain. The two kinds of pain arise from different fibers sending their messages at different speeds (Rollman, 1991).

One of the ways we deal with pain is by producing substances in our brains, called **endorphins,** that have painkilling effects. Some drugs, such as morphine, bind to the same receptors that accept endorphins, which explains how those drugs can act as painkillers (Cailliet, 1993). However, pain involves more than simple bottom-up processing. Top-down processing can directly inhibit the interneurons that regulate the input of pain signals to the brain (Melzack & Wall, 1982). This **gate control** mechanism may explain how hypnosis can control pain (Kihlstrom, 1985); indeed, hypnosis can selectively alter our experience of the unpleasantness of pain without affecting how intense it feels. Hypnosis thus may alter processing in only some of the brain areas that register pain (Rainville et al., 1997). Inhibitory impulses from the brain to neurons that send signals from the body may also occur when pain is reduced by a *counter-irritant*—a painful stimulus elsewhere in the body (Willer et al., 1990). Such effects may explain how acupuncture, the placing of small needles to treat pain, works (Chapman & Nakamura, 1999).

People differ widely in the amount of pain they can stand; Rollman and Harris (1987) found that some people could put up with as much as eight times as much pain as others. However, women at certain phases of the menstrual cycle have a lower threshold for pain (Hapidou & De Catanzaro, 1988). MacGregor and colleagues (1997) found that the threshold for pressure-based pain was highly correlated among twins, but this correlation was equally high for both identical and fraternal twins. Because identical twins share all their genes, but fraternal twins share only half their genes, the finding of the same correlation suggests that there is no substantial genetic component to pain thresholds. Instead, this common correlation is more likely a result of common family environment.

Magnetic Sense: Only for the Birds?

Many birds migrate long distances each year, guided in part by the magnetic field of the earth. Tiny bits of iron found in crucial neurons of these birds apparently play a role in this sense. There is evidence that humans have a weak form of this sense (Baker, 1980), but the phenomenon has not yet been studied in enough detail to conclude with certainty that we all possess it. Magnetic fields have been shown to disrupt spatial learning in mice, at least for brief periods of time (Levine & Bluni, 1994). This is a sobering finding because the magnetic fields used in these studies were weaker than those commonly used in magnetic resonance imaging (MRI) machines.

Paradoxical cold: Occurs when stimulation of nerves by something hot produces the sensation of cold.

Double pain: The sensation that occurs when an injury first causes a sharp pain, and later a dull pain; the two kinds of pain arise from different fibers sending their messages at different speeds.

Endorphins: Painkilling chemicals produced naturally in the brain.

Gate control of pain: The top-down inhibition of interneurons that regulate the input of pain signals to the brain.

Extrasensory Perception (ESP)

The ability to perceive and know things without using the ordinary senses is described as **extrasensory perception (ESP).** Many forms of ESP have been asserted, including *telepathy,* the ability to send and transmit thoughts directly, mind to mind; *clairvoyance,* the ability to know about events directly, without using the ordinary senses or reading someone else's mind; and *precognition,* the ability to foretell future events. In addition, *psychokinesis (PK),* the ability to move objects directly, not by manipulating them physically, has also been reported (this ability does not derive from ESP proper, since it does not involve perception or knowing). Many experiments have been conducted in an effort to demonstrate the existence of the different forms of ESP (for example, Bem & Honorton, 1994; Haraldsson & Houtkooper, 1992). Louisa and Joseph Rhine are often credited with beginning the scientific study of ESP and PK (J. B. Rhine, 1934; L. E. Rhine, 1967). Many ESP experiments use the Ganzfeld procedure: Participants wear either half-pingpong balls over each eye or tight-fitting translucent glasses that allow only a blur to be seen; at the same time, they hear a dull hiss through headphones (Bem & Honorton, 1994; Haraldsson & Gissurarson, 1987). This procedure shuts off competing stimuli and thus supposedly increases the participant's sensitivity to ESP signals. Another person, sealed in another room, tries to project an image of a particular card or scene to the participant, who later is asked to pick out the image from a set of alternatives.

The results from some of these experiments suggest that the "recipient" can pick out the image "transmitted by the sender" more accurately than expected by chance (Bem & Honorton, 1994; Rosenthal, 1986). Nevertheless, most psychologists are skeptical about ESP and PK, for at least the three following reasons (Alcock, 1987, provides additional ones): First, the effects are difficult to repeat. For example, it wasn't long after Bem and Honorton (1994) claimed finally to have discovered how to produce reliable telepathy before Milton and Wiseman (1999a, 1999b) reported failures to replicate. To be fair, some ESP researchers have argued that such failures to replicate occur because the phenomena depend on personality, details of the setting, and other variables (Brugger, Landis, & Regard, 1990; Honorton, 1997; Watt & Morris, 1995). But as more such qualifications are added, the harder it becomes to disprove the claims, and the field is thus nudged further away from science. Second, it is not known how the brain could possibly produce or pick up ESP signals or produce PK signals. Third, it is not known what form these signals might take. For example, physical energy (such as magnetic or electrical waves) typically declines in strength with increasing distance from the source, but there is no hint that the same is true for ESP or PK signals.

In spite of many years of hard work by many dedicated scientists, this field remains highly controversial (Bem & Honorton, 1994; Child, 1985; Thalbourne, 1989).

LOOKING AT LEVELS

Is Body Odor a Problem?

Can culture affect senses as basic as smell? It can, and it does. Norwegians are less compulsive about eliminating all trace of natural human odors than are Americans (who, according to the *Los Angeles Times,* spent about $6 billion in 1997 on products to eliminate or mask body odor). Hence, the garments of Norwegians often retain more body odor than ours typically do. A young child, when his or her mother is gone, is sometimes given one of the mother's blouses to smell and is said to be comforted by this smell. To our knowledge, no rigorous studies of this phenomenon have been done, but observation alone is sufficient to make our point—that the interpretation of smell is in large part determined by cultural norms. In a pinch, one could probably hand the child a blouse from the mother's sister; Porter (1991) showed that people who share more genes also have more similar body odors. Body odor arises mostly from chemicals (specifically, steroids) produced by the sweat glands, and the genes determine the composition of these chemicals. Bacteria, which digest the chemicals, then produce the odor. Bartoshuk and Beauchamp (1994) have identified the genes that produce the distinguishing characteristics of body odor. Perhaps fortunately, simply living with someone will not make your body odor similar to his or hers, or vice versa (Porter et al., 1985).

So, consider the problem of body odor: It is only a problem if the culture defines it as such. If a person believes it is a problem, he or she will act accordingly—by buying deodorants (or feeling embarrassment). Consider the interactions among events at the different levels: If you feel threatened, the sympathetic branch of your autonomic nervous system is activated, producing sweat. The sweat contains chemicals that feed the ever-present bacteria, which produce more odor. The smell in turn, at least in the United States, may make others turn away from you.

CONSOLIDATE!

▶ *1. How does the sense of smell work?* We are able to smell when molecules are the right shape to fit into specific olfactory receptors, which in turn send impulses to the brain. As in vision, the range of possible smells arises from the combinations of outputs from different receptors; we do not have a different receptor for every possible odor we can distinguish.

▶ *2. How does the sense of taste work?* Taste arises from four types of taste buds (which produce the sensation of sweet, sour, salty, and bitter tastes) and from nerves that respond to irritation; combinations of outputs from these receptors produce taste. However, what we commonly think of as taste in fact relies in part on our sense of smell working in combination with taste.

▶ *3. How do we sense our bodies?* We sense the positioning of our bodies via the vestibular and kinesthetic senses. An impairment of the vestibular sense can cause the perception of imbalance and dizziness. The kinesthetic sense lets you know the positions of your limbs and whether your body has actually moved. We are also aware of our bodies if stimuli trigger receptors on the skin, which can produce the sensations of pressure, temperature, or pain. It is also possible that we are aware of our location in part by sensing changes in the magnetic field of the earth, but this has yet to be solidly established.

▶ *4. Does extrasensory perception (ESP) exist?* Although there is some evidence for some forms of ESP, these findings are difficult to replicate. It is not clear how the brain would register ESP signals or how ESP signal transmission would work. Thus, at this point, there is no convincing evidence for the existence of ESP, but the issue is still open.

A DEEPER LEVEL
Recap and Thought Questions

▶ **Sensing and Selecting: Opening Up to the World**

The brain relies on sensory organs that have particular kinds of receptors. When these receptors are stimulated appropriately (for example, by light for the rods and cones, vibration for the hair cells, and pressure for some receptors in the skin), these neurons transduce this physical energy into neural signals. These neural signals are sent into the brain and initiate the processes of sensation and perception. Sensation is the immediate experience of basic properties of an object or event, such as its color or volume, whereas perception is the organization and interpretation of the sensory input as signalling a particular object or event.

We detect signals when they cross a threshold, but the level of that threshold depends in part on how hard we try to detect the signals. In addition, we can adjust our criteria so that we are more or less willing to guess.

We can shift the focus of our attention, which usually allows us to detect signals more easily. For most types of stimuli, whatever is attended to is in focus and more easily detected than what is not attended. However, when simple features are embedded in other simple features (like a red light in a sea of green lights), the stimulus "pops out" and attention is not necessary for easy detection. Perception relies on a combination of bottom-up processes, which are initiated by stimulus properties striking receptors, and top-down processes, which are guided by knowledge, expectation, or belief.

Could Sue's and Tai's abilities to register sensations differ in basic ways, which might explain why they have such different reactions to the sensory delights of an art museum versus a rock concert? Because of perceptual learning, in which previous exposure teaches us to perceive things in particular ways, Tai may have been "tuned" to be more sensitive than Sue to noises during rock concerts, just as she is more aware of what to look for at art museums. This would explain the friends' differing sensitivities, or biases for registering certain kinds of stimuli. In their case, top-down processing, guided by knowledge, expectation, or belief, plays a prominent role.

> **Think It Through.** Do you think "boosted" or enhanced sensory sensitivities would be an advantage or a disadvantage? (Say you could hear a pin drop 50 feet away, or you could see the dirt in the pores on a friend's face across the room.) In what ways would such superabilities be a benefit? a drawback? What about being able to adjust your "sensitivity" and "bias" at will? In what kinds of situations would this power be desirable?

▶ Vision

Visual perception can be divided into three main phases. The first, early visual processing, begins with light, which consists of physical energy of certain wavelengths. The retina, a thin sheet of tissue at the back of the eye, contains two known types of cells that convert light to nerve impulses. Rods are sensitive to light but do not register color, whereas cones register color but are not as sensitive to light. The operation of the three kinds of cones (each tuned to be most sensitive to a different wavelength of light), in combination with the color-opponent cells, underlies our ability to see color. When we see shapes, different channels pick up shape variations at different degrees of resolution. Attention can be guided both by stimulus properties and by personal knowledge and expectations.

The second phase, intermediate visual processing, takes the outputs from early visual processing and organizes them into sets of perceptual units. These sets are figures, which are likely to correspond to objects (or sometimes to parts of objects). The Gestalt laws of organization (such as similarity, proximity, good continuation, good form, and closure) describe how the visual system organizes lines, dots, and other elements into units. The distance, size, and shape of figures are also specified in ways that do not vary when the object is seen from different viewpoints. Some of these processes are built in; some are learned.

Finally, late visual processing involves making the input meaningful. This is accomplished by matching the input to information already stored in memory, which allows you to know more about the stimulus than you can see at the time.

We do not simply wait for input, nor do we process only what is in the stimulus. Rather, the brain, guided by past learning (both personal and cultural), sends feedback via top-down processing to supplement the input. Finally, some information can be identified outside awareness.

Could Sue's and Tai's eyes, or visual parts of their brain, differ? Tai clearly sees more in a work of art than Sue does. It is possible that Tai's genetic makeup makes the cones in her eyes more sensitive to color differences. Beyond that, Sue is not color-blind and has no trouble seeing the paintings, but portions of her brain involved in interpreting what she sees may not be as well developed as Tai's, due to differences in the young women's exposure and experience.

> **Think It Through.** What do you think would happen if you had been born blind and suddenly had vision at age 50? Such cases have been studied in depth (see Gregory, 1974; Sacks, 1995), and even though light was being properly transduced in the eyes, these persons failed to realize they were viewing a human face (that of the person who took off their bandages) until the person spoke. Why? If you had to help such as person adjust after the sight-giving operation, what would you do? Why might part of your training involve attention?

▶ Hearing

Like vision, hearing can be understood in terms of three broad phases. Early auditory processing involves registering sound waves, pressure waves that move molecules (usually in air, but also in liquids and solids). Sounds differ in pitch (which reflects variations in frequency) and volume (which reflects variations in amplitude). For most frequencies, the ear uses the position of maximal activity on the basilar membrane to specify the frequency, but for low frequencies the rate of vibration of the basilar membrane may also indicate frequency. Hair cells along the basilar membrane, when stimulated, produce nerve impulses, which are sent to the brain. Hair cells that respond to specific frequencies can be impaired by exposure to loud sounds. The primary auditory area (the first cortical area to receive auditory input) is laid out as a strip, and the location of activation in this area depends on the frequency of the sound.

Intermediate auditory processing involves organizing sound into units and specifying the locations of those units in space. Sounds are organized using Gestalt principles (such as similarity in pitch) and are localized using a combination of binaural cues (differences in the phase, volume, and arrival times) and monaural cues (volume, distortions resulting from the shape of the outer ear, and changes in volume resulting from movement).

Late auditory processing involves using stored information to make sounds meaningful. Such processing can actually fill in missing sounds, as occurs in the phonemic restoration effect. Not only can we understand speech sounds by accessing the appropriate stored memories, we can also understand environmental sounds (such as the meaning of a fire alarm) and music.

Might Sue's and Tai's ears, or auditory cortex, differ in how they register auditory sensations? It is possible that Sue is deaf to certain frequencies (which is likely if she has been listening frequently to loud music), and thus is not bothered by loud sounds. The role of experience, however, should not be underestimated. As is evident in cultural differences in music, you learn to interpret what you hear. The friends also might differ in how they have learned to organize sound, in what they have learned to pay attention to, and in how they interpret what they hear. Moreover, depending on associations they have made to music, the music may give rise to different feelings. For Sue, rock music may remind her of the fun of a concert; for Tai, it may remind her of packed bodies and bad smells.

Think It Through. Will wearing a motorcycle helmet affect your ability to recognize sounds and localize them to the same extent? Why or why not? If one side of the helmet were made of thicker plastic than the other, which cues would be most affected?

Do you think that the way a musician looks or behaves when he or she is performing could influence the way the music sounds? How could this occur?

▶ Sensing in Other Ways

The senses of smell and taste are considered the "chemical senses" because they detect the presence of particular chemicals. Both involve a lock-and-key arrangement in which the right molecule triggers a specific receptor, which in turn sends neural signals to the brain. And both smell and taste rely on combinations of receptors being activated.

Instead of the traditional five senses, we have at least nine and possibly up to eleven: In addition to sight, hearing, smell, taste, and touch, we have a kinesthetic sense, vestibular sense, temperature sensitivity, pain sense, and possibly a magnetic sense. These additional senses all inform us about the state of our bodies (where limbs are located, how we are positioned or located, what is touching us or otherwise affecting our skin). Each part of the skin is mapped out on the somatosensory cortex, with the amount of brain surface reflecting our relative sensitivity in that region. Pain is registered by two different systems, which can produce the feeling of double pain. Top-down processing can affect interneurons involved in pain, allowing your beliefs and desires to affect the degree to which you feel pain.

Finally, some researchers have argued for extrasensory perception (ESP). However, the evidence for ESP is shaky, and there has yet to be a reliable demonstration that any form of ESP actually exists.

In what other ways could Sue and Tai differ when they are registering the world? Is it possible that Sue is better able to smell or taste things than Tai, but Tai has better extrasensory perception? Tai certainly seems to be more sensitive to odors and tastes than Sue is—just one more example of the wide range of individual differences in the most basic sensations. Her perception of odors and tastes as repugnant, however, probably involves previous experiences with unfamiliar foods and with strangers in crowded areas. Because the neural structures underlying various sensory systems are largely distinct, the two friends (and anyone else, for that matter) can vary in unique ways.

Think It Through. Say your uncle is a food fanatic, loving every morsel and seeking out only the best. Should you recommend that he blow his nose before each meal and not waste his money going to fancy restaurants when he has a bad cold? Why?

Should researchers spend time studying ESP instead of learning, perception, or other more ordinary senses? What are the potential pros and cons of studying ESP rather than abilities that clearly are used by everyone every day?

4 CONSCIOUSNESS

onsider Lewis Carroll's classic tale *Alice's Adventures in Wonderland* through a psychologist's looking glass, and you may see it in a new light—not as a charming children's story but as a reflection on different levels and states of consciousness. Let's take a look at the story. A young girl, Alice, tumbles down a rabbit's burrow and finds herself in a fantastic, topsy-turvy world. There, animals speak English, regularly become invisible (and reappear), and wear waistcoats with pocket watches. Alice finds things to eat and drink, but they make her grow and shrink. Although she understands the *words* that the strange inhabitants say to her, rarely do their *statements* make sense. And beyond all this, at times she feels not quite herself:

> "Dear, dear! How queer everything is to-day! And yesterday things went on just as usual. I wonder if I've been changed in the night? Let me think: was I the same when I got up this morning? I almost think I can remember feeling a little different. But if I'm not the same, the next question is, Who in the world am I? Ah, THAT'S the great puzzle!" (Carroll, 1992, p. 15)

Alice's situation immediately reveals one aspect of the nature of consciousness: It is a private, subjective experience, and one that can change so dramatically—from one moment to the next—that you may sometimes wonder, as Alice did, whether you are still the same person. Suppose you work intently for 10 solid hours in a windowless room, reading by the yellowish artificial light of a desk lamp. Finally finished with your research, you stumble out into the bright sunlight, dazed and disoriented. You feel distinctly different from the way you felt just hours before, when you were rested and full of vigor. This difference in feeling, like Alice's, is a difference in consciousness.

Why should psychologists care about consciousness? For one thing, our sense of the world and ourselves emerges from consciousness. **Consciousness** refers to our ongoing awareness of our own thoughts, sensations, feelings, our very existence. So a full understanding of what it is to be a person requires that we understand consciousness. Francis Crick, codiscoverer of DNA and subsequently a major theorist and researcher on the nature of consciousness, was asked by one of us what he meant by the term *consciousness*. He suggested the following exercise: "Hold both hands in front of you, but with one closer to you. Now look at the front one; now look at the back one. See how the front one seems different when you are focusing on the back one? That's what consciousness is all about." "Oh," his questioner remarked, "so consciousness is just attention!" "No," Crick replied with a tinge of amused annoyance, having no doubt heard similar responses before. "Consciousness is enriched by attention, but attention is not necessary for it." Crick and Koch (1998) develop this idea in detail and suggest that particular portions of the frontal lobes are crucial for consciousness.

Consciousness plays a key role in allowing us to put information together in novel ways. The first time you drive a new route, you are likely to be aware of every turn, every stoplight, every landmark. But after a dozen trips, chances are you no longer notice them. (It can be surprisingly difficult to describe a familiar route to someone who's never taken it before.) What has changed? On your initial journey, new experiences required you to coordinate input and output in novel ways. But as the experiences became habitual, the new connections you have established between input and output allow you to drive without the need to respond to stimuli that are no longer novel. Even after a hundred trips, however, if you unexpectedly find a tree lying in the road, your sudden consciousness of it will direct you to make the necessary response—and step on the brakes!

One way to regard consciousness, in some ways an intuitive view, is as a single, central, internal lightbulb illuminating the mind. Philosopher Daniel Dennett (1991), however, argues against such a single "consciousness center." His view is supported by recent studies indicating that different parts of the brain appear to be involved in the experience of consciousness. Depending on exactly what a person is aware of at a given time, different parts of the brain "light up" as they are activated (Alkire et al., 1998; Barbur et al., 1993; Bottini et al., 1995; Kosslyn, 1994b; Leopold & Logothetis, 1996; Vanni et al., 1996). But not all brain areas that are active when a person performs a task contribute directly to the experience of consciousness. In particular, consciousness apparently does not arise from activity in those parts of the brain that first register perceptual information, such as the primary visual cortex or primary auditory cortex (Crick & Koch, 1995, 1998). Instead, consciousness appears to rely on a number of areas in the brain (such as the right parietal lobe and frontal lobes) involved in the interpretation and integration of information (Bisiach & Luzzatti, 1978; Gazzaniga, 1995).

The fact that many different brain areas contribute to consciousness helps to explain why consciousness is multifaceted and fluid, and why, at times, you experience yourself or the world very differently from the way you do ordinarily, in **normal consciousness** (also called *waking consciousness*). These **altered states of consciousness (ASC)** may be natural states, such as sleeping, dreaming, hypnosis, and meditation, or may be induced by substances such as drugs and alcohol.

In many cultures, inducing an altered state of consciousness is a socially acceptable, and sometimes even mandated, ritual. The members of some cultures, for example, enter into altered states through apparent communication with spirits or souls of deceased people. Others, such as certain Native American tribes, use hallucinogenic mushrooms and other drugs as the route to altered consciousness. Such practices are often considered sacred (Bourguignon, 1973). In Bourguignon's study of 488 societies, 90% had at least one "institutionalized," or culturally approved, altered state. One such case is that of a group of religious women in Trinidad. For one week, the women enter a period of "mourning," spending much of the time lying down, often in darkness and isolation. They also engage in praying, chanting, and singing. During the week, the women experience lifelike hallucinations (mental images so vivid that they seem real) and revelations into their spiritual lives (Ward, 1994). These same practices (periods of isolation accompanied by praying and chanting) are used by members of many cultures seeking to attain such altered states.

Thus, although consciousness is a state we all experience, its definition can be tricky to pin down. The story of Alice and her experiences provides a springboard for an exploration of the nature of consciousness and its various facets. For example: Alice's adventures, we learn at the end of Carroll's book, have been only a dream. One of Alice's disconcerting experiences in Wonderland is the often-changing size of her body—an experience that can be obtained through hypnosis. Might odd experiences like Alice's be the result of a meditative state? Do our heroine's adventures parallel the experience of a drug- or alcohol-induced state? Following Alice's adventures may help describe this shifting awareness of ourselves and the world around us that makes us uniquely human.

TO SLEEP, PERCHANCE TO DREAM

Alice's story begins with an apparent change of consciousness on a hot afternoon:

> Alice was beginning to get very tired of sitting by her sister on the bank, and of having nothing to do, so she was considering in her own mind (as well as she could, for the hot day made her feel very sleepy and stupid), whether the pleasure of making a daisy-chain would be worth the trouble of getting up and picking the daisies, when suddenly a White Rabbit with pink eyes ran close by her. (p. 7)

It certainly appears that Alice is about to fall asleep, and perhaps by the end of the paragraph she has. As Alice's story closes, a crowd of the odd characters she met in Wonderland

> . . . rose up into the air, and came flying down upon her: she gave a little scream, half of fright and half of anger, and tried to beat them off, and found herself lying on the bank, with her head in the lap of her sister, who was gently brushing away some dead leaves that had fluttered down from the trees upon her face. . . .
>
> "Oh, I've had such a curious dream!" said Alice, and she told her sister, as well as she could remember them, all these strange Adventures of hers that you have just been reading about; and when she had finished, her sister kissed her, and said, "It WAS a curious dream, dear, certainly: but now run in to your tea; it's getting late." So Alice got up and ran off, thinking while she ran, as well she might, what a wonderful dream it had been. (pp. 97–98)

▶ 1. Brain and body function differently in sleeping and waking. What is the physiology of sleep?

▶ 2. Why do we dream? Do dreams have meaning?

▶ 3. What happens when we don't sleep enough? What are sleep disorders?

Consciousness: A person's awareness of his or her own existence, sensations, and cognitions.

Normal consciousness: State of awareness that occurs during the usual waking state; also called *waking consciousness*.

Altered state of consciousness (ASC): State of awareness that is other than the normal waking state.

Stages of Sleep: Working Through the Night

Sleep is perhaps the most obvious example of an altered state of consciousness. Some people think that sleep is like an electric light—either on (awake) or off (asleep). Until the invention of the electroencephalograph (EEG) (see Chapter 2) in 1928, that is what scientists used to think as well (Hobson, 1995). With the use of this new technology, they learned that **sleep,** a naturally recurrent experience during which normal consciousness is suspended, is not a single state. By using EEGs to record brain activity during sleep, researchers discovered several different types of sleep, which occur in five stages during the night. Everyone proceeds through these stages, but people differ in how much time they spend in each stage (Anch et al., 1988).

STAGE 1. This initial sleep stage, lasting approximately five minutes and sometimes described as **hypnogogic sleep,** marks the transition from relaxed wakefulness to sleep. In Stage 1 sleep, your breathing becomes deeper and more regular, and the EEG registers brain waves that are less regular and of lower amplitude than those that mark the waking state (see Figure 4.1). You can be awakened relatively easily from Stage 1 sleep, and if you are, you do not feel as if you have been asleep at all. In this stage you may "see" flashing lights and geometric patterns, experience a gentle falling or floating sensation, or feel your body jerk suddenly and rather violently in a movement called a hypnic jerk.

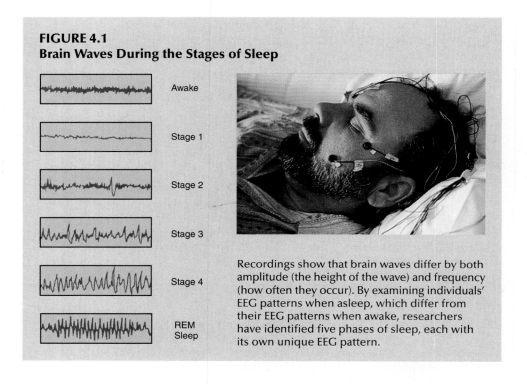

FIGURE 4.1
Brain Waves During the Stages of Sleep

Awake
Stage 1
Stage 2
Stage 3
Stage 4
REM Sleep

Recordings show that brain waves differ by both amplitude (the height of the wave) and frequency (how often they occur). By examining individuals' EEG patterns when asleep, which differ from their EEG patterns when awake, researchers have identified five phases of sleep, each with its own unique EEG pattern.

STAGE 2. Once you are clearly asleep, your EEG pattern begins to record *sleep spindles,* brief bursts of brain activity measuring 12 to 14 Hz, and occasional short bursts of high-amplitude brain waves (this pattern, known as the *K-complex,* is shown in Figure 4.1). You are now more relaxed and less responsive to your environment, although still relatively easy to awaken. But if you are awakened now, you will most likely report that you have been asleep. This phase lasts for approximately 20 minutes.

STAGES 3 AND 4. In Stages 3 and 4, your brain produces *delta waves*—slow, high-amplitude waves of 1 to 2 Hz on your EEG (see Figure 4.1). In Stage 3, 20 to

Sleep: The naturally recurrent experience during which normal consciousness is suspended.

Hypnogogic sleep: Characterized by the experience of gentle falling or floating, or "seeing" flashing lights and geometric patterns; describes Stage 1 sleep.

50% of EEG-recorded brain activity is in the form of delta waves; in Stage 4, the proportion is greater than 50%. In Stage 3, your heart rate and body temperature decrease, and you are no longer easily awakened. By the time you reach Stage 4, you are in a very deep sleep indeed, so deep that attempts by a friend (or an alarm clock) to wake you won't readily succeed. If you do wake up directly from this stage, you are likely to be briefly disoriented. During Stage 4 sleep, your heart rate, blood pressure, breathing, and body temperature slow down; all are now at their lowest ebb.

REM SLEEP. About an hour after going to sleep, you begin to reverse the sleep cycle, coming back from Stage 4 through Stages 3 and 2. Instead of going all the way back to Stage 1, though, you now enter a state of *rapid eye movement (REM)* under the lids and, as shown in Figure 4.1, your EEG registers marked brain activity—even more activity than when you are awake. It is in this stage of sleep that you are likely to have dreams vivid enough to remember. During **REM sleep,** your breathing and heart rate are fast and irregular, and your genitals may show signs of arousal (men may have an erection; women may have increased genital blood flow and vaginal lubrication). These events occur in REM sleep regardless of the content of your dreams, unless a dream is particularly anxiety-provoking, in which case genitals may not be aroused (Karacan et al., 1966). During REM sleep, your muscles are relaxed and unresponsive; in fact, except for the muscles needed for the respiratory and vascular systems, your muscles are so paralyzed that you could not physically enact the behaviors in your dreams. Nevertheless, your brain remains more active than usual; for this reason, REM sleep is sometimes called **paradoxical sleep.**

SLEEP CYCLES. After REM sleep, you descend again through at least some of the earlier stages, and then return, as shown in Figure 4.2. Each cycle takes about 90 minutes and occurs four or five times each night. However, the time you spend in each stage varies over the course of the night, and the course of a lifetime.

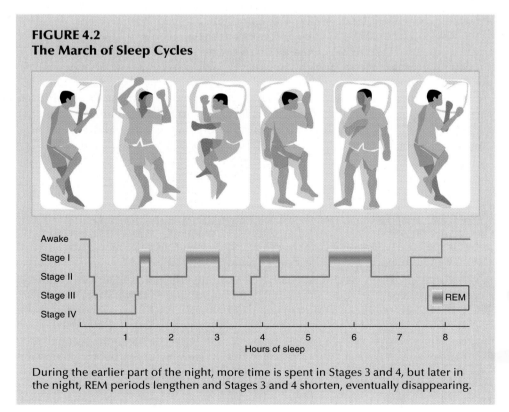

FIGURE 4.2
The March of Sleep Cycles

During the earlier part of the night, more time is spent in Stages 3 and 4, but later in the night, REM periods lengthen and Stages 3 and 4 shorten, eventually disappearing.

REM sleep: Stage of sleep characterized by rapid eye movements and marked brain activity.

Paradoxical sleep: Another name for REM sleep, used to emphasize the marked brain activity.

"WHEN I GROW UP I'D LIKE TO BE LIKE YOU, EXCEPT I DON'T KNOW IF I COULD SLEEP THAT MUCH."

Is this cartoon based on fact? How can we understand Dennis's comment if we know that children sleep more than adults, and much more than older adults?

FIGURE 4.3
Proportion of REM Sleep Over a Lifetime

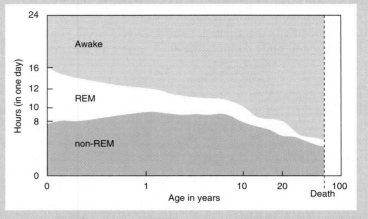

As we get older, we spend less time sleeping overall and less time in REM sleep.

The phrase "I slept like a baby" turns out to have more truth to it than most of us realize. Infants sleep longer than adults (13 to 16 hours per night in the first year; see Figure 4.3) and have a higher percentage of REM sleep. They often enter REM immediately after falling asleep and change stages often. With age, this percentage changes so that when you enter your forties, the amount of time spent in deep, slow-wave sleep begins to decrease. With less slow-wave activity, your sleep is shallower and more fragmented, you wake more easily, and the sleep you do get is less satisfying (Hobson, 1995). Stage 4 sleep is even less frequent as you move from middle age to older adulthood. With increasing age, the decreased production of hormones involved in the sleep process make deep sleep difficult (Center for the Advancement of Health, 1998; Klinkenborg, 1997). As the quality of your sleep declines, so does its restorative effect on the cardiovascular and endocrine systems.

Suppose you share a bed with someone. Do you affect each other's sleep cycles? Yes. Because most people who share a bed go to sleep at around the same time, they are likely to enter REM sleep at about the same time during the night. And if one partner is tossing and turning, the other is less likely to fall asleep until the first one does (Hobson, 1995). Thus, bed partners tend to dream together—although not necessarily about each other.

Dream On

In addition to the physiological changes that occur in sleep, there is a distinct change in consciousness—that of dreaming. It is *not* true that dreams take place only during REM sleep, but it *is* true that the dreams that take place during REM sleep are more memorable than those occurring during non-REM, or NREM, stages (Dement, 1974). If awakened during REM sleep, people recall dreams 78% of the time, compared with 14% recall during NREM sleep; moreover, NREM dreams are less vivid, less storylike, and less emotional (Farthing, 1992).

WHAT TRIGGERS PARTICULAR DREAMS? Although dreams may seem bizarre, disjointed, and nonsensical, their content is not necessarily totally random. President Gerald Ford once spoke the lines, "Thank you. Thank you. Thank you," in his sleep. He later told his wife, Betty, that he had dreamed he was in a receiving line (Seuling, 1978). By awakening dreamers at different stages of sleep and asking them about their dreams, or asking people to keep "dream diaries" at their bedsides, researchers have learned that certain types of dreams appear to be related to events occurring during the day (Hauri, 1970). Often these reflect the short-term lack of particular stimuli: Water-deprived people dream of drinking (Bokert, 1968), for example, and people socially isolated for a day dream of being with other people (Wood, 1963). Long-term deprivation seems to have a different effect, however: For individuals chronically deprived of an experience, over time there is a decrease in dreams related to the missing element (Newton, 1970).

Can someone interpret your dreams? Although dream interpretation can be interesting and fun, it is unclear that any meaning inferred from the content of dreams is accurate.

WHY DO WE DREAM? Dreams can offer us a pleasant respite from the daily grind, bring us terror in the form of a nightmare, or leave us puzzled about their confusing or curious content. In some societies, such as the Maya, telling dreams to others can provide a way to communicate feelings or solve problems (Degarrod, 1990; Tedlock, 1992).

Researchers and nonresearchers alike have long sought to know why we dream. The first modern dream theory was proposed by Sigmund Freud. Freud (1900), convinced that dream content originates in the unconscious—outside our conscious awareness—dubbed dreams the "royal road to the unconscious." Further, Freud believed that dreams allow us to fulfill unconscious desires. Such *wish fulfillment* may not always be apparent from the **manifest content** of a dream, that is, its obvious, memorable content. We have to dig to find the **latent content** of the dream, its symbolic content and meaning, which, according to Freud, might reflect sexual or aggressive themes associated with an inner conflict. In this view, the manifest content of Alice's dream includes her specific adventures in Wonderland; the latent content, according to Freud, might reflect her underlying anxiety about the integrity of her body in general, and her sexuality in particular (Schilder, 1938). Although Freud's theory of the unconscious origin of the content of dreams has yet to be supported by solid, objective evidence, the idea of dream interpretation has both ancient appeal and present fascination—witness the large number of dream interpretation books and Web sites on the Internet.

Freudians find dreams brimming over with meaningful, albeit disguised, content. The opposite view is at the heart of the **activation-synthesis hypothesis,** which contends that dreams arise from random bursts of nerve cell activity. These bursts may affect brain cells involved in hearing and seeing, and the brain's response is to try to make sense of the hodgepodge of stimuli (Hobson & McCarley, 1977), but the dreams do not disguise meaning, as Freud suggested (Goode, 1999a). The brain synthesizes the burst and other stored information to create the experience of a dream. This theory would explain why dreams sometimes seem so bizarre and unrelated. Stickgold and colleagues (1994) asked people to write down their dreams and then literally cut their reports in half. They asked other people to reassemble each dream, deciding which half came first. This proved a very difficult task, a result that is understandable if dreams are merely attempts to interpret random activity and have no cohesive story line.

As part of his effort to understand consciousness, Crick also investigated dreams, which he believes are used to edit out unnecessary or accidental brain connections formed during the day (Crick & Mitchison, 1983, 1986). Other theories of dreaming focus on the reverse notion: that dreams are used to *strengthen* such connections. This view is supported by a study by Karni and colleagues (1994). Participants learned to discriminate between two visual stimuli before falling asleep; those who slept normally

Manifest content: The obvious, memorable content of a dream.

Latent content: The symbolic content and meaning of a dream.

Activation-synthesis hypothesis: The theory that dreams arise from random bursts of nerve cell activity, which may affect brain cells involved in hearing and seeing; the brain attempts to make sense of this hodgepodge of stimuli, resulting in the experience of dreams.

improved their performance on the task when tested the following morning. But participants who were awakened when they entered REM sleep did not improve when tested in the morning. In contrast, participants who slept but were deprived of slow-wave, Stage 4 sleep did not show any learning impairment—which suggests that REM sleep is crucial for cementing in memory information gleaned during the day.

The largest and most systematic study of the neurological bases of dreaming was reported by Solms (1997), of the London Hospital Medical College. Solms interviewed more than 350 stroke patients about the changed nature of their dreams after their strokes. Consistent with the idea that consciousness arises from many parts of the brain, Solms found that dreaming was affected by damage to any number of areas. Perhaps Solms's most intriguing discovery was that dreaming stopped completely if a patient had damage that disconnected parts of the frontal cortex from the brainstem and the limbic system. These connections coordinate brain areas involved in curiosity, interest, and alert involvement with goals in the world (Pankseep, 1985, cited in Solms, 1997). This finding suggests that dreaming is not simply the brain giving itself a neurological tune-up, but is connected with our needs, goals, and desires. Solms speculates that dreaming may occur in response to any type of arousal that activates brain structures involved in motivation (Goode, 1999a). However, the inhibiting mechanisms of sleep prevent us from acting on these thoughts or desires, thus converting them into a symbolic hallucination.

So, although we cannot yet definitively answer *why* we dream, we do know something about *how* we dream. We know that dreaming is a neurological process, involving brain activity. We don't know whether dreams represent deep desires and conflicts, random bursts of nerve cell activity, the editing of unneeded neural connections, or the strengthening of neural connections. But it is interesting that all these theories, despite their differences, agree that in some way the day's events, or the neural connections they instigate, affect dreams.

The Brain Asleep

We spend about one third of our lives asleep. During that time our brains and bodies are working away, responding to outside stimuli such as light and dark, and sending out fluctuating levels of neurotransmitters and hormones. These chemical changes are crucial to our daily functioning.

THE CHEMISTRY OF SLEEP: UPS AND DOWNS. When you are awake, the genes in the system that produces the neurotransmitter acetylcholine are inhibited, but when you are in REM sleep, they are activated (Hobson et al., 2000; McCarley & Hobson, 1975). Your dreams of walking, flying, or falling may occur because of the increased acetylcholine during REM, which activates the motor and visual areas of your brain and may cause you to dream of a wild roller-coaster ride or other types of motion (Hobson, 1995). Perhaps it is because of motor system activation that dreams, according to sleep researcher Hobson, rarely portray sedentary activities such as computing, reading, or writing (Kelley, 1998). Moreover, the genes in parts of your brainstem that produce other neurotransmitters, specifically serotonin and norepinephrine, are most active when you are awake. Sleeping pills work in part by blocking production of these two "wake-up" neurotransmitters (Garcia-Arraras & Pappenheimer, 1983).

The hormone melatonin, which is secreted by the pineal gland, plays a role in promoting sleep. The body normally begins secreting melatonin around dusk, tapering off production at dawn. A person who takes melatonin in pill form soon feels drowsy and, if undisturbed, falls asleep within a half an hour. Unlike other sleep aids, melatonin appears to induce a natural sleep, with the appropriate amount and time of REM and NREM sleep (Zhdanova & Wurtman, 1996). Some have argued that taking melatonin at the right times can help a traveler overcome jet lag, but this effect has not yet been proven scientifically.

CIRCADIAN RHYTHMS. Our brain activity and internal chemistry dance in time to the daily rhythm of light and dark in a pattern called **circadian rhythms** (*circadian* means "about a day"). Daily physiological fluctuations governed by circadian rhythms include blood pressure, pulse rate, body temperature, blood sugar level, hormone levels, and metabolism. Every one of us has an internal clock that coordinates these fluctuations; this clock is regulated by a small part of the hypothalamus just above the optic chiasm, called the **suprachiasmatic nucleus (SCN)**, which is illustrated in Figure 4.4. The suprachiasmatic nucleus registers changes in light, which lead it to produce hormones that regulate various bodily functions. Researchers have found a gene in mice that is responsible for the regulation of their daily clocks; tissues in the eyes and the suprachiasmatic nucleus of the hypothalamus generate the signals that let the mice know, among other bodily functions, when to sleep and when to awaken (Antoch et al., 1997). The rudiments of circadian rhythms appear in human infants as early as one week after birth (McGraw et al., 1999).

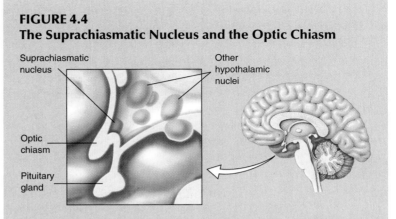

FIGURE 4.4
The Suprachiasmatic Nucleus and the Optic Chiasm

Suprachiasmatic nucleus

Other hypothalamic nuclei

Optic chiasm

Pituitary gland

This illustration of a human brain shows the proximity of the SCN to the optic chiasm. Given the SCN's role in regulating circadian rhythms, it is not surprising that it is so close to the optic chiasm, which relays visual input about light and dark to the brain.

What happens to the human sleep–wake cycle in the absence of external cues of dark and light (except for electric light, which can be turned on and off at will) and cultural cues such as clocks? Volunteers who have lived this way as part of a research project ended up living a 24.9-hour day. In a variant of this study, in which only subdued lighting was provided, with no opportunity for stronger reading light, participants were more likely to have a 24.2-hour day (Czeisler et al., 1999).

But what about people who are completely blind and cannot detect light at all? They too show evidence of a 24.9-hour day, with 76% of the blind people studied reporting difficulty falling asleep at their usual bedtimes, based on a 24-hour day (Coren, 1996; Miles et al., 1977). Thus the 24-hour schedule, so ingrained in us by the daily rotation of the earth, is not necessarily "natural" but instead is maintained by exposure to light–dark cycles, whether natural or artificial, and by cues from mechanical instruments such as clocks and radios.

Even within a 24-hour day, however, not everyone prefers to wake up or go to sleep at the same time. As you have no doubt noticed, some people are energetic and alert early in the morning, whereas others do not perk up until late morning or afternoon. People differ in the timing of their circadian rhythms: Morning people, or "larks," experience peak body temperature, alertness, and efficiency in the morning; evening people, or "owls," peak at night (Luce, 1971). Normally you are not aware of your circadian rhythms until you try to function well at your nonpeak time. If you're a night owl, for example, how do you feel when faced with a 9:00 A.M. class? Flying across time zones is bound to make you aware of your own circadian rhythms, especially if the trip is a long one. Regardless of the time of day that finds you most alert, however, most people have a late-afternoon dip in energy level. More industrial and traffic accidents occur between 1:00 and 4:00 P.M. than at any other time of day (Klinkenborg, 1997). Perhaps it is not a coincidence that many societies have a siesta or tea break during this period.

Are you grouchy on a Monday morning? If so, it might be more than simply "waking up on the wrong side of the bed." Boivin and colleagues (1997), who studied mood and circadian rhythms, found that bad moods occurred during times of day when the participants' circadian clocks said they should be asleep. These results suggest that even minor alterations in a sleep schedule, relative to individual circadian rhythms, can have a noticeable effect on mood after awakening. Thus, if you go to

Circadian rhythms: The body's daily physiological fluctuations in response to the dark and light cycle, which affects blood pressure, pulse rate, body temperature, blood sugar level, hormone levels, and metabolism.

Suprachiasmatic nucleus (SCN): A small part of the hypothalamus just above the optic chiasm that registers changes in light, which lead to production of hormones that regulate various bodily functions.

bed later and sleep later on weekends, you may be adversely altering your circadian rhythms. You are, in a sense, putting yourself in another time zone for the weekend, so when Monday morning rolls around, you are hit with jet lag. Even fifth-grade children are affected by having to wake up earlier to go to school. Regardless of how much sleep they had, those children who had to be in school by 7:10 A.M. reported more daytime fatigue and poorer attention and concentration at school than those whose school day started at 8:00 A.M. (Epstein et al., 1998).

What can you do if your schedule conflicts with your natural circadian tendencies? One remedy is to sleep on a disciplined schedule seven days a week. If, as in the case of jet lag, that isn't possible, try exposing yourself to plenty of light on Monday mornings; this may help reset your internal clock.

Sleep Deprivation: Is Less Just as Good?

In today's world of overscheduled lives and 10-hour workdays, can anyone claim to be getting a natural amount of sleep? A 1998 survey by the National Sleep Foundation found that two out of three people are not getting enough sleep (defined as approximately 8 hours), and one of those three gets less than 6 hours each night. Although falling asleep in a dull class *may* signal sleep deprivation, "boredom doesn't cause sleepiness, it merely unmasks it" (Dement, as cited in Brody, 1998). What else happens when you don't get enough sleep, or miss a night's sleep entirely?

REM REBOUND. When you don't get enough REM sleep on a given night, a higher percentage of the next night's sleep will be REM sleep (Brunner et al., 1990); this phenomenon is called **REM rebound.** You can become REM deprived by not getting enough sleep at either end (going to bed late or waking up early) or by using depressants of the central nervous system such as alcohol or sleep medications, which suppress REM sleep. If these substances are used habitually and then discontinued, REM rebound dreams can be so vivid, bizarre, and generally unpleasant that people resume their use to fall asleep, and to suppress dreaming as well. Some people with posttraumatic stress disorder (victims of rape or assault, for example) cite disturbing dreams or nightmares (Inman et al., 1990) as a reason for using alcohol or drugs before sleep.

SLEEP DEPRIVATION. If you have ever stayed up late, say, studying or partying, and then awakened early the next morning, you have probably experienced sleep deprivation. In fact, you may be sleep deprived right now. If so, you have company: 37% of adults claim to be so sleepy during the day that daily activities are affected (National Sleep Foundation, 1998). What happens as a result of sleep deprivation? Young adults who volunteered for a sleep deprivation study were allowed to sleep for only five hours each night, for a total of seven nights. After three nights of restricted sleep, volunteers complained of cognitive, emotional, and physical difficulties. Moreover, their performance on a visual motor task declined after only two nights of restricted sleep. Visual motor tasks usually require participants to concentrate on detecting a change in a particular stimulus, and then to respond as quickly as they can after they perceive the change by pressing a button (Dinges et al., 1997). Thus, you may be able to perform short mental tasks normally when sleep deprived, but if a task requires sustained attention and a motor response, your performance will suffer; driving a car is an example of such a task. In a survey by the National Sleep Foundation (1998), 25% of the respondents reported that they had at some time fallen asleep at the wheel; sleepy drivers account for at least 100,000 car crashes each year.

Moods are also affected by sleep deprivation (Dinges et al., 1997; Monk et al., 1997). The loss of even one night's sleep can lead to increases in the next day's level of cortisol (Leproult, Copinschi et al., 1997). As mentioned in Chapter 2 (and discussed in more detail in Chapter 12), cortisol helps the body meet the increased demands imposed by stress. However, sleep deprivation can lead to a change in cor-

REM rebound: The higher percentage of REM sleep following a night's sleep deprived of REM.

tisol level that, in turn, alters other physiological functions, creating an increased risk for diabetes. Chronically increased cortisol levels can cause memory deficits (Sapolsky, 1996) and decreased immune system functioning (Kiecolt-Glaser et al., 1995).

And what about a series of all-nighters, when you get no sleep at all, as might occur during finals period? Results from volunteers who have gone without sleep for long stretches (finally sleeping after staying awake anywhere from 4 to 11 days) show profound psychological changes, such as hallucinations, feelings of losing control or going crazy, anxiety, and paranoia (Coren, 1996). Physiologically, going without sleep alters the normal circadian rhythms of changes in temperature, metabolism, and hormone secretions (Leproult, Van Reeths et al., 1997). These findings are also seen in adult rats who are forced to stay awake. Within two weeks, they show major negative physiological changes; despite eating two and a half times their usual amount, they begin to lose weight. Moreover, their temperature does not stay in the normal range, and they die within 21 days (Rechtschaffen et al., 1983). Even rats deprived only of REM sleep (they are awakened each time they enter the REM stage) experience temperature regulation changes, but these changes are less extreme (Shaw et al., 1998). Results of a PET study on sleep-deprived humans found a different pattern of brain activation when learning verbal material, compared to the pattern of activation when not sleep deprived, suggesting an attempt to compensate for the brain changes induced by sleep deprivation (Drummond et al., 2000).

Thus, sleep deprivation affects us in at least three important psychological areas: attention, performance, and mood.

Troubled Sleep

When a young girl like Alice falls asleep in the middle of the day, the reason is often simply drowsiness. In some instances, however, the cause may be a sleep disorder. Too much sleep, too little sleep, and odd variations in between can disturb our needed rest and therefore our physiological and psychological functioning (see Table 4.1). Sleep disorders stem from a number of causes, in particular, hereditary, environmental, and physical problems.

TABLE 4.1

Sleep Disorders

DISORDER	MAIN SYMPTOM(S)
Night terrors	Vivid, frightening dreams; the dreamer cannot be woken and does not remember the dreams.
Nightmares	Dreams with negative emotion; they may be remembered the next day.
Narcolepsy	Sudden attacks of extreme drowsiness and possibly sleep.
Insomnia	Difficulty getting to sleep, difficulty staying asleep, or awakening too early.
Sleep apnea	Brief, temporary cessation of breathing during sleep for up to 70 seconds, following a period of difficult breathing accompanied by snoring; the sleeper then startles into a lighter state of sleep and may have no memory of these events and may not feel rested after sleeping.

NIGHT TERRORS: NOT YOUR USUAL NIGHTMARE. Most common among boys three to seven years old, **night terrors** are vivid and frightening dreams. Night terrors occur in Stages 3 and 4, usually in the first third of a night's sleep. During a

Night terrors: Vivid and frightening dreams; the sleeper may appear to be awake during the experience but has no memory of it the following day.

night terror, the child may sit bolt upright, screaming and sweating, and be impossible to wake. In the morning, the child usually has no memory of the terrors, not even that they happened. For parents, however, the memory of their terrified child, eyes open and wild with fear, unresponsive to their attempts to comfort and help, is apt to linger.

Fortunately, night terrors usually subside as the child grows older. No one knows why they occur, although genetics plays a part: Night terrors can run in families. Night terrors are qualitatively different from **nightmares,** which are essentially dreams with strong negative emotion. Nightmares often take place during morning REM sleep; the dreamer can be roused during the nightmare and generally retains at least some memory of it.

NARCOLEPSY: ASLEEP AT THE DROP OF A HAT.
At the March Hare's tea party in Wonderland, Alice meets a Dormouse who is always falling asleep; occasionally he wakes, says something, then drifts off again.

> "Wake up, Dormouse!" And they pinched it on both sides at once.
> The Dormouse slowly opened his eyes. "I wasn't asleep," he said in a hoarse, feeble voice: "I heard every word you fellows were saying."
> "Tell us a story!" said the March Hare.
> "Yes, please do!" pleaded Alice.
> "And be quick about it," added the Hatter, "or you'll be asleep again before it's done." (p. 58)

The Dormouse could be suffering from **narcolepsy.** This sleep disorder causes sudden attacks of extreme drowsiness so powerful that the person with narcolepsy finds it almost impossible *not* to fall asleep, typically for 10–20 minute spells (American Psychiatric Association, 1994). Once asleep, people with narcolepsy often enter REM sleep almost immediately. The overwhelming drowsiness sufferers experience may be triggered by a large meal or intense emotions, but it can occur at any time—even during such inopportune moments as while driving. Behavioral treatment is often recommended, and stimulant medication may also be prescribed (Guilleminault et al., 1976). Like some other sleep disorders, narcolepsy tends to run in families, a sign that the disorder has a genetic component.

INSOMNIA.
At the opposite end of the sleep spectrum from narcolepsy is a sleep disorder that may be more familiar to you, especially if you find it hard to get a good night's sleep. The symptoms of **insomnia** include repeated difficulty falling asleep or staying asleep, or waking too early. If you suffer from this disorder, you are certainly not alone. Half the adults in the United States experience occasional insomnia. Temporary insomnia may be related to environmental factors such as stress, which can cause increased sympathetic nervous system activity and make sleep difficult. When sleep does not occur rapidly, the stressed person becomes frustrated. The frustration serves to increase physiological arousal, compounding the problem.

For many Americans insomnia is a way of life. Chronic insomnia may stem from other disorders, such as anxiety and depression, as you will see in Chapter 13. Sleeping pills are the most common, but not necessarily the most effective, treatment for insomnia. They not only suppress needed REM sleep but also are addictive. Moreover, people develop tolerance to sleeping pills, requiring larger and larger dosages to get the same effect.

Nightmare: A dream with strong negative emotion.

Narcolepsy: Sudden attacks of extreme drowsiness.

Insomnia: Repeated difficulty falling asleep, difficulty staying asleep, or waking up too early.

What can you do if you have trouble sleeping? The following nonmedicinal techniques may help (Hobson, 1995; Lacks & Morin, 1992; Maas, 1998):

Restrict your sleeping hours to the same nightly pattern. When living in the White House, both Martha and George Washington went to bed promptly at 9:00 P.M. each evening (Seuling, 1978). The Washingtons were on to something: Keep regular sleeping hours. Avoid sleeping late in the morning, napping longer than an hour, or going to bed earlier than usual, all of which will throw you off schedule, creating even more sleep difficulties later. And try to get up at the same time every day, even on weekends or days off.

Control bedtime stimuli so that things normally associated with sleep are associated only with sleep, not with the frustration of insomnia. Use your bed only for sleep or sex (don't read or watch TV in bed). If you can't fall asleep within 10 minutes, get out of bed and do something else.

Avoid ingesting substances with stimulant properties. Don't smoke cigarettes or drink beverages with alcohol or caffeine in the evening. Alcohol may cause initial drowsiness, but it has a "rebound effect" that leaves many people wide awake in the middle of the night. Don't drink water close to bedtime; getting up to use the bathroom can lead to poor sleep.

Consider meditation or progressive muscle relaxation. Either technique can be helpful (see Chapter 14). Regular aerobic exercise four times a week may be a long-term solution, but it can take up to 16 weeks for the effect on insomnia to kick in (King et al., 1997).

SLEEP APNEA. Snoring can be a nuisance to those sharing a room with a snorer, but it can also be a sign of a more troublesome problem. **Sleep apnea** is a disorder characterized by a temporary cessation of breathing during sleep, usually preceded by a period of difficult breathing accompanied by loud snoring. Breathing may stop for up to 70 seconds, startling the sleeper into a lighter state of sleep. This ailment, which affects 1 to 4% of American adults, can produce many such events each hour, preventing restful sleep (Klinkenborg, 1997). Perhaps this explains the results of a research study of medical students who snore versus those who do not: 13% of nonsnorers failed their exams, compared with 42% of frequent snorers (Ficker et al., 1999). If the snorers had sleep apnea, they would not function as well because of their troubled sleep.

Sleep apnea results when muscles at the base of the throat relax and consequently block the airway. In obese patients, weight loss can help reduce the obstruction, although normal-weight people also can have sleep apnea. Sleep apnea can be fatal, so treatment is imperative. A device called Continuous Positive Airway Pressure (CPAP) can assist a person's breathing while asleep; alternatively, surgery is sometimes recommended. Those with undiagnosed sleep apnea may take barbiturates to get a good night's sleep—this is unfortunate because barbiturates seriously compound the problem by depressing the central nervous system, interfering with the normal reflex to begin breathing again.

SHIFT WORK: WORK AT NIGHT, SLEEP ALL DAY. Can work schedules affect sleep? Just ask people who have worked the swing shift (4:00 P.M. to midnight) or the graveyard shift (midnight to 8:00 A.M.)—a group that includes up to 20% of American workers (Klinkenborg, 1997). Some jobs even involve daily changes in the shift worked. Working during hours when you would normally be asleep can cause an increase in accidents, insomnia, and medical and psychological difficulties. The near-meltdown at the Three Mile Island nuclear power facility occurred after workers were placed on the night shift following six weeks of constant rotation; during their disastrous shift, they did not notice several warning indicators (Moore-Ede, 1982).

Researchers studying the effects of shift work have found that it is easier to switch to progressively later shifts (from the night to the day shift, and from the day to the evening shift) than to move in the opposite direction. In general, people differ

Sleep apnea: Difficulty breathing accompanied by loud snoring during sleep.

Zeitgebers: Environmental cues for sleeping and waking.

in their ability to adjust to such schedule changes; those with a greater range of body temperatures in their circadian cycles have an easier time (Reinberg et al., 1983). If your work involves swing or graveyard shifts, one way to minimize the negative effects on your circadian rhythms (as well as on your social life) is to try not to stay on these shifts for more than three days (Knauth, 1997). This way, your sleep won't be disrupted by being on the night shift for extended periods of time, and you can still socialize with family and friends regularly.

Recovery From Jet Lag

If you ever doubted that sleep, or its disruption, has an effect on consciousness, one good case of jet lag will convince you otherwise. *Jet lag* is that tired, grouchy, disoriented feeling you get after flying across different time zones. If you leave California on a 2:00 P.M. nonstop flight, after about six hours in the air (assuming the plane is on schedule) you will arrive in Boston, where it is about 11:00 P.M. local time—time for bed. But your body ignores the three-hour difference between the Pacific and Eastern time zones and experiences the time as 8:00 P.M. You are nowhere near ready to go to sleep. And come morning in Boston, your body will want to continue sleeping when the alarm says it is time to get up. The physiological changes, including altered hormonal and neurotransmitter activity, occur when the body's circadian rhythms are out of synch with the new time zone's physical and social cues. For example, your cortisol levels, which usually decrease before bedtime, are still high, and even if you do manage to get to sleep at what your body considers an early hour, the high level of cortisol is likely to lead to shallow and fragmented sleep (Center for the Advancement of Health, 1998).

How can you make a speedy recovery from jet lag? At the level of the brain, exposing yourself to light in the new time zone is thought to help reset the SCN in the hypothalamus, changing the levels of sleep- and wake-related hormones to suit the new time zone (Cassone et al., 1993). At the level of the person, motivation affects how easily you can adjust to jet lag (Bloom & Lazerson, 1988). Your willingness to get up in the morning when your alarm rings will help. In addition, exercise or activity can help shift circadian rhythms (Van Cauter & Turek, in press). At the level of the group, adjusting to the new time zone's environmental and social cues for meal times and bedtimes, called **zeitgebers** (literally, "time givers" in German) facilitates the resetting of your biological clock (Van Cauter & Turek, in press). Events at the different levels interact. Suppose you have flown east all night, leaving New York at 8:00 P.M. and arriving in London six hours later (7:00 A.M., U.K. time); further, you are meeting an old friend as soon as you arrive (which is the middle of the night to your body). You may be reasonably motivated to stay awake so you can enjoy your reunion over breakfast. But if no one is meeting you and you have no particular plans for the day, it may not seem worth the effort to ignore the activity of your neurotransmitters and hormones and try to stay awake.

CONSOLIDATE!

▶ *1. Brain and body function differently in sleeping and waking. What is the physiology of sleep?* From EEG recordings made during sleep, researchers know that sleep is normally divided into five stages. Stage 1 is the hypnogogic state of transition from wakefulness

to sleep. Stage 2 is characterized by sleep spindles and K-complexes. Stages 3 and 4 are both marked by delta waves, with Stage 4 representing very deep sleep. These four stages are sometimes referred to as non-REM (rapid-eye-movement) sleep and are distin-

(continued)

guished from REM sleep, which is characterized by marked brain activity and unresponsive voluntary muscles. When awake, the systems producing serotonin and norepinephrine are most active, while those that produce acetylcholine are inhibited. This is the reverse of what occurs during REM sleep.

▶ *2. Why do we dream? Do dreams have meaning?* Freud believed that dreams contain two levels of meaning: manifest content (the obvious, memorable content of a dream) and latent content (the symbolic content and underlying meaning of the dream). He theorized that dreams allow individuals to fulfill unconscious wishes. Contemporary researchers have offered a variety of theories about why we dream. Some view dreams as attempts to make sense out of random bursts of nerve cell activity (the activation-synthesis hypothesis, Hobson and McCarley); to edit out unwanted neural connections (Crick); to strengthen neural connections (Karni); or as representing a complex interplay of goals and desires,

arousal and inhibition, during sleep (Solms). There is some evidence that daytime deprivation of physical or social needs may influence the content of dreams. To date, no single, agreed-upon theory explains why we dream, nor does any body of scientific evidence lead to the accurate analysis of dream content.

▶ *3. What happens when we don't sleep enough? What are sleep disorders?* When people are sleep deprived, attention and concentration suffer, and the level of cortisol increases. Sleep disorders are chronic disruptions of normal sleep rhythms. Narcolepsy causes powerful and recurrent sleepiness during the day. Night terrors occur in childhood, usually affecting males. In sleep apnea, physiological problems related to breathing prevent restful sleep. Problems such as nightmares, worry, and anxiety may cause either temporary or chronic insomnia. Other kinds of interference with normal sleep, such as those associated with jet lag and shift work, are environmentally induced.

HYPNOSIS

When Alice fell down the rabbit hole, her descent seemed endless; she kept tumbling so long she thought she might be nearing the center of the earth. While this feeling could have been a result of Stage 1 sleep at the beginning of Alice's nap, it's also somewhat similar to the sensations associated with one method of entering a hypnotic trance. In this technique, participants are asked to imagine gradually descending an elevator or staircase, becoming more deeply relaxed (and hypnotized) as they go lower and lower.

▶ 1. What is hypnosis?

▶ 2. Can anyone be hypnotized? Is hypnosis a true brain state?

▶ 3. Hypnosis can be used to alter sensory perception. What are some other applications of hypnosis?

What Is Hypnosis?

When you think of hypnosis, you probably imagine a stage hypnotist speaking in a soft monotone, instructing a volunteer from the audience to look at a shiny pocket watch as it swings back and forth. The volunteer's eyelids grow heavier and heavier, he feels sleepier and sleepier. . . . Then, presto, he is hypnotized. At the hypnotist's suggestion, he will happily strut like a chicken, lie rigid between two chairs, or do the hula. Hypnosis as theatrical entertainment is rare. In fact, those whom the savvy hypnotist picks from the audience are highly hypnotizable, unlike some 90% of the U.S. population (Hilgard, 1965).

Hypnosis is characterized by a focused awareness on vivid, imagined experiences and a decreased awareness of the external environment. The state is brought on by **hypnotic induction,** a process in which the participant is encouraged to relax and focus his or her awareness in a particular way, often with closed eyes. For example, say you sought out a hypnotist to help you overcome the aftermath of trauma brought on

Hypnosis: A state of mind characterized by a focused awareness on vivid, imagined experiences and decreased awareness of the external environment.

Hypnotic induction: The procedure used to attain a hypnotic trance state.

FIGURE 4.5
Hypnotic Alterations in Perception, Mood, Memory, and Behavior

The hypnotist says, "Imagine water splashing on your skin. Notice the sensation on your skin, the coolness of the water."

The hypnotist says, "While lying by the waterfall, you will feel very relaxed and peaceful."

The hypnotist says, "You will still remember the experience of the fire, but the fear and anxiety about it will become less and less over time."

The hypnotist says, "Imagine magnets in the palms of your hands, pulling the hands toward each other."

by being trapped briefly in a burning building. The hypnotist might begin by asking you to close your eyes and imagine waves of relaxation gently washing over your body, the effect of which makes you increasingly relaxed.

Once you enter a **trance state,** an altered state of consciousness in which your awareness of the external environment is diminished, the hypnotist suggests that you focus your attention or alter your perception or behavior in some particular way, as illustrated in Figure 4.5.

There are at least two hallmarks of a trance state. One is called **generalized reality orientation fading,** a term used to describe a tuning out of external reality. As this occurs, you have a heightened awareness of "inner reality," your own imaginings and perceptions, and you experience this reality more vividly than in a daydream. Another hallmark of the trance state is the operation of **trance logic,** an uncritical acceptance of incongruous, illogical events, without being distracted by their impossibility. For instance, if you were instructed to imagine a place where you can feel safe and extremely relaxed, you might imagine a gazebo under a waterfall, or a beach colony on the moon. These images would come to you without your thinking twice about how such a place could exist or how safe it would really be.

Although these and other changes in awareness can occur because the hypnotist suggests them, they can also occur, with or without the hypnotist's suggestion, because of your expectations of the hypnotic situation (Kirsch & Lynn, 1999). People who expect their limbs to feel heavier during a trance have that experience, whereas people who don't expect their bodies to feel different do not, unless specifically directed to do so by the hypnotist. The hypnotist may also give you a **posthypnotic**

Trance state: A hypnotically induced altered state of consciousness in which awareness of the external environment is diminished.

Generalized reality orientation fading: A tuning out of external reality during hypnosis.

Trance logic: An uncritical acceptance of incongruous, illogical events during a hypnotic trance.

suggestion, a suggestion for specific changes in perception, mood, or behavior that will occur *after* you leave the hypnotic state (see Figure 4.5, lower left).

People who are highly hypnotizable do not even have to be in the same room with the hypnotist to become hypnotized. A hypnotist on television once suggested to a volunteer in the studio that the volunteer's arm would become numb; a highly hypnotizable television viewer also became hypnotized. She lost feeling in her hand and did not come out of the trance state until she smelled the burning flesh of her own hand, which had been resting on the stove near an open flame (Kennedy, 1979).

Individual Differences: Who Is Hypnotizable?

Some people are more hypnotizable than others (see Figure 4.6), and some people are more skilled at particular aspects of hypnosis than others. For example, some people can create extremely vivid visual images, whereas others are better at creating auditory, olfactory, or kinesthetic effects. Even those who are not very hypnotizable can go into a trance state if motivated strongly enough (Rossi & Cheek, 1988). In Western cultures, hypnotic ability appears to peak before adolescence and decline during the middle adulthood years. In contrast, in non-Western cultures, the ability to go into a trance state is often valued and encouraged throughout the lifespan and thus does not diminish (Ward, 1994).

Hypnotizability is not highly correlated with physiological indicators such as heart rate (Ray et al., 2000) nor with personality characteristics, such as shyness, emotionality, or thrill seeking. **Absorption,** or the capacity to concentrate totally on material outside oneself, is moderately correlated (Council et al., 1996; Kirsch & Council, 1992; Tellegen & Atkinson, 1974). Some people seem better able to lose their awareness of themselves than others; these people become deeply engrossed when watching a movie or reading a book. In highly hypnotizable individuals, absorption may account for brief hypnotic experiences that may occur when driving on a highway for a long time or when watching a fire in a fireplace. Hypnosis also appears to be modestly related to "openness to experience," a willingness to experience new things. People with posttraumatic stress disorder also appear to be more hypnotizable than the average (Spiegel & Cardeña, 1991); this finding may reflect a greater use of **dissociation,** the sense of being split off from a normal level of awareness, as a result of the traumatic experience.

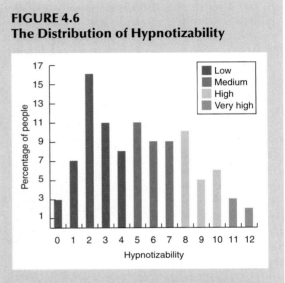

FIGURE 4.6
The Distribution of Hypnotizability

Not everyone is equally hypnotizable, and only a small percentage of people are *very* hypnotizable.

Hypnosis: Role Play or Brain State?

Do people really enter an altered state of consciousness during a trance? Or are they merely behaving the way they think people should behave when hypnotized? Three major theories address the way hypnosis works, and recent brain-scanning results help sort out these theories.

TRANCE THEORY. One view, **trance theory,** focuses on the cognitive changes that occur during a trance (Conn & Conn, 1967; Hilgard, 1992). According to trance theory, someone in a trance in fact experiences an altered state of consciousness, one characterized by increased susceptibility and responsiveness to suggestions. As a result, the person is dissociated, or separated, from his or her normal level of awareness (that is, consciousness). When, for instance, people are successfully hypnotized for relief of pain, while in the trance they report that they feel no pain. If, however, they are asked to write about their experience while in the trance, some people *do* report experiencing

Posthypnotic suggestion: A suggestion regarding a change in perception, mood, or behavior that will occur *after* leaving the hypnotic state.

Absorption: The capacity to concentrate totally on external material.

Dissociation: The sense of being split off from the normal level of awareness.

Trance theory: The view that a person in a trance experiences an altered, dissociated state of consciousness characterized by increasing susceptibility and responsiveness to suggestions.

pain. This "inner" experience has been attributed to the **hidden observer,** a part of the self that experiences (and can record) what the entranced part of the self does not consciously experience (Hilgard, 1992; Hilgard et al., 1978).

SOCIOLOGICAL ROLE THEORY. Whereas trance theory suggests that hypnosis occurs because the trance state does in fact induce an altered state of consciousness, **sociological role theory** (Coe, 1978; Sarbin & Coe, 1972) focuses on the social context in which hypnosis takes place. In this view, the behavioral and experiential changes associated with a trance result from the hypnotized person's expectations of the hypnotized state rather than from a true trance. According to this view, the person in a trance enacts the role of a hypnotized person as he or she understands it, which leads to behaviors believed to be produced by hypnosis.

TASK-MOTIVATION THEORY. Like sociological role theory, **task-motivation theory** does not regard hypnosis (and the changes that go with it) as a true altered state of consciousness (Barber, 1969; Barber et al., 1974). According to task-motivation theory, some people are predisposed to attend and respond to suggestions made by the hypnotist and are more motivated to perform the suggested tasks. Thus, volunteers who are appropriately motivated can perform hypnotic feats even if they are not hypnotized. Task-motivation theory differs from sociological role theory in seeing hypnosis as a set of positive attitudes, motivations, and expectancies directed toward the hypnosis-related tasks, rather than the acting out of a preconceived role.

EVIDENCE FROM BRAIN SCANNING. Both sociological role theory and task-motivation theory stress that hypnosis alters people's performance, not necessarily their consciousness. Neither theory presumes a special cognitive state, with distinctive changes in brain activity. Such a distinct internal state would be more in keeping with trance theory than the other two theories. Thus, important information about the nature of hypnosis can come from studies of the brain.

Studies done in the 1980s that recorded electrical current on the scalp found that hypnosis does alter brain events (Barabasz & Lonsdale, 1983; Spiegel et al., 1985, 1989), and more recent PET studies indicate that hypnosis changes specific brain states (Baer et al., 1990; Crawford et al., 1993; Sabourin et al., 1990–1991). However, most of the neurological changes observed during a hypnotic trance can be explained as arising from the *actions*, either actual or imagined, that people perform in hypnosis. To isolate the source of neurological changes more precisely, Kosslyn and colleagues (2000) showed that when highly hypnotizable people in a trance are told to view a pattern in color, an area that processes color in the brain is activated even if the pattern shown to them is actually in shades of gray. Similarly, if these people are told to see a pattern as shades of gray, a color area is deactivated, even if the pattern is brightly colored. Hypnosis could not only turn on or off this color area in accordance with what a person was experiencing (regardless of what was actually presented), but could also override the actual perceptual input. Clearly, hypnosis is not simply role playing or motivated behavior; people cannot intentionally alter brain processing in these particular ways.

Hypnosis as a Tool: Practical Applications

Hypnosis is much more than a stage trick. It is a different brain state with many therapeutic applications, including the treatment of anxiety, compulsive habit behaviors (such as smoking, hair pulling), certain medical conditions (such as asthma and warts), and stress-related problems (such as high blood pressure). Hypnosis has even been used to treat a particular complication during pregnancy. A study examined the use of hypnosis with 100 women pregnant with babies in the breech (feet first) position. One group was hypnotized and given the suggestion to relax bodily tensions and let nature takes its course; another group did not receive hypnosis. The babies of 81% of the hypnotized women changed position to head first, compared with only 48% of the control group (Mehl, 1994).

Hidden observer: A part of the self that experiences (and can record) what the part of the self responding to hypnotic trance does not "consciously" experience.

Sociological role theory: The view that a person in a trance enacts the role of a hypnotized person as he or she understands it, which leads to behaviors believed to be produced by hypnosis.

Task-motivation theory: The view that some people are predisposed to attend and respond to suggestions made by a hypnotist and are more motivated to perform the requested task.

Glove anesthesia: Hypnotically induced anesthesia of the hand.

Before the widespread availability of chemical anesthetics, hypnosis was used for the relief of pain (Winter, 1998). Pain can be controlled by top-down processing that directly inhibits the interneurons that regulate the input of pain signals to the brain (see Chapter 3); hypnosis is a particularly good way to affect this processing. Hypnosis is still used for pain control in many circumstances today—in the dentist's chair, the operating room, during childbirth, and at home and work (for a review, see Chaves, 1989; Hilgard & Hilgard, 1994). Hypnosis is used to induce relaxation before surgery, to lessen pain, and to speed healing (Forgione, 1988), as well as to alleviate tension and the fear of pain, both of which can worsen the *experience* of pain.

Hypnosis works to reduce pain by changing the way the sensation of pain is interpreted. Under hypnosis, a surgical patient might be led to experience an icy-cold numbness in the area where an incision will be made (Rossi & Cheek, 1988). Another use of hypnosis is to create imagined analgesia, or insensitivity to pain (Hilgard & Hilgard, 1994). For instance, one method used to treat headaches calls for the person in a trance first to create **glove anesthesia** (Barber & Adrian, 1982)—that is, to anesthetize the hand hypnotically. Once this is accomplished, the patient touches the painful part of the head with the anesthetized hand, transferring, by suggestion, the anesthetic effect to the head.

Hypnosis has also been used to enhance performance through hypnotic and posthypnotic suggestions; many athletes work with hypnosis consultants. Will a basketball player make more baskets or block more shots because of a hypnotic suggestion? Research findings suggest that hypnosis does not improve athletic performance per se but that it can help decrease anxiety, and thereby increase the athlete's focus; hypnosis also provides an opportunity for mental practice of athletic skills, a known benefit (Druckman & Bjork, 1994).

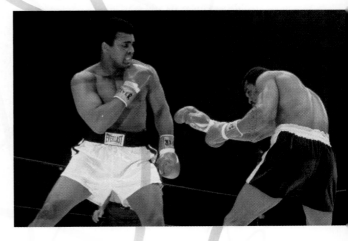

As part of his boxing training, Ken Norton used hypnosis before his match against Muhammed Ali (Spiegel, 1999). During that match, he broke Ali's jaw. Can hypnosis help athletes perform feats they would otherwise be unable to accomplish? No, but it can help them feel less anxious and free of distractions during competition, and it can help alleviate pain.

LOOKING AT LEVELS

Hypnosis as Possession Trance

Hypnosis appears in different guises in different cultures. In a study by Bourguignon (1973), for example, over half of the 488 societies surveyed practiced possession trance. In this form of hypnosis, the body of the person in a trance is said to be "taken over" by a spirit. Upon emerging from possession trance, the possessed person may be unable to recall the experience.

In societies in which possession trance is practiced, trance behaviors are learned and are bound by implicit cultural rules (Boddy, 1992). In the Comoros, off Madagascar, for instance, a wife is normally subservient to her husband. She may be regularly possessed by a male spirit, however, who speaks "man to man" with her husband about her. This spirit dispenses advice and information that would not otherwise be shared because of the tightly defined cultural roles that constrain husbands and wives (Boddy, 1992).

Let's look at possession trance in the Comoros from the levels of brain, person, and group, and the interactions of events at these three levels. We know that hypnosis causes changes in the brain that are only now beginning to be understood; we have no reason to think that possession trance would not reflect such changes (level of the brain). After experiencing possession trance, people report feelings of well-being and rejuvenation, along with a decrease in distressing physical or psychological symptoms (level of the person; Ward, 1994). Possession trance provides an opportunity for spouses to engage in new behaviors not normally allowed, and as a culturally sanctioned activity, the possession trance binds the couple to the traditions of their society (level of the group). Events at these levels interact: To the extent that possession trance enables a wife to communicate with her husband, it helps the couple's relationship, leading to a sense of well-being. The sense of well-being creates changes (and is created by changes) in both brain chemistry and the nervous system.

CONSOLIDATE!

▶ *1. What is hypnosis?* Hypnosis is characterized by a focused awareness on vivid imaginings that seem real and by a diminished awareness of the external environment. The components of hypnosis include generalized reality orientation fading, trance logic, and openness to suggestion.

▶ *2. Can anyone be hypnotized? Is hypnosis a true brain state?* Hypnotizability is a trait that has a normal distribution. Although moderately correlated with absorption, it is a distinct trait. Even those with low hypnotizability can go into a trance if sufficiently motivated. According to trance theory, hypnosis is a truly different, dissociated state of consciousness. Sociological role theory views the trance experience

as a role, defined by a person's expectations concerning the trance experience. Task-motivation theory argues that hypnosis is a set of positive responses to the hypnotist; hypnotic feats are attributable to motivation, not hypnosis per se. Recent brain-scanning studies tend to support the trance theory of hypnosis.

▶ *3. Hypnosis can be used to alter sensory perception. What are some other applications of hypnosis?* Hypnosis can be used to alter mood, memories, and behavior, either during the trance itself or afterward via posthypnotic suggestion. By facilitating relaxation, hypnosis can also help with anxiety, stress, compulsive behaviors, certain medical conditions, pain control, and performance enhancement.

MEDITATION

In the last pages of *Alice's Adventures in Wonderland*, after Alice awakens from her dream and goes home for her tea, her sister remains behind under the tree. As she watches the setting sun and thinks about Alice's adventures, she too begins to dream, after a fashion, of the characters in Wonderland:

> So she sat on, with closed eyes, and half believed herself in Wonderland, though she knew she had but to open them again, and all would change to dull reality—the grass would be only rustling in the wind, and the pool rippling to the waving of the reeds—the rattling teacups would change to tinkling sheep-bells, and the Queen's shrill cries to the voice of the shepherd boy—and the sneeze of the baby, the shriek of the Gryphon, and all the other queer noises, would change (she knew) to the confused clamor of the busy farm-yard—while the lowing of the cattle in the distance would take the place of the Mock Turtle's heavy sobs. (pp. 98–99)

Might Alice's sister be in a meditative state? or simply a relaxed state of mind?

▶ 1. What is meditation? What are the different types of meditation?

▶ 2. What is the difference between meditation and relaxation? What, if any, unique physiological state accompanies meditation?

Types of Meditation

Meditation is an altered state of consciousness characterized by a sense of deep relaxation and *loss* of self-awareness, in contrast to hypnosis, which is characterized by ongoing self-awareness. Nevertheless, meditation and hypnosis do share similar elements. Both forms of altered consciousness involve increased, focused awareness of a particular signal. In hypnosis, this signal may be the hypnotist's voice. In meditation, the signal can be an object in the environment (such as a flower or a geometric pattern called a *mandala*), a rhythmic physical motion of the body (such as breath-

Meditation: An altered state of consciousness characterized by a sense of deep relaxation and loss of self-awareness.

ing), or a *mantra* (a chant or phrase that the meditator repeats). Whereas the person in a hypnotic trance often uses focused attention imaginatively and creatively, the meditator focuses attention on a single stimulus during the meditation period with the goal of clearing his or her awareness of other thoughts and sensations. Meditators experience a "relaxed, blissful, and wakeful state" (Jevning et al., 1992, p. 415).

Prayer can be a form of meditation, as seen in the Buddhist and Hindu traditions. Other religions also incorporate meditative elements. For instance, Christians might focus attention on the cross, a verse of Scripture, or a mental image of Christ in a meditative manner. Rosary beads can be thought of as a meditative aid, helping to maintain the focus on prayer. In Judaism, the Torah may serve as the object of meditation, and many Orthodox Jews sway rhythmically while praying.

There are a number of other forms of meditation (Ornstein, 1986), all of which involve focused attention on an unchanging or repetitive stimulus. If you wanted to explore **concentrative meditation,** you would try to concentrate on one stimulus alone, disregarding everything else around you. Yoga and transcendental meditation (TM) are examples of this type of meditation. In **opening-up meditation,** a more advanced form of concentrative attention, you would focus narrowly on a stimulus and then try to broaden your focus to encompass your entire surroundings, almost as if you were merging with your environment. Both types of meditation bring about an altered sense of awareness or consciousness. **Mindfulness meditation** (also known as awareness meditation) is a combination of the two. Using this technique, you would try to maintain a "floating" state of consciousness, one that allows you to focus on whatever is most prominent at the moment. Whatever comes into your awareness—a physical sensation, sound, or thought—is what you focus on in a meditative way, fully aware of the stimulus but not judging it. In this way, everything around you can become part of your meditation.

For a sense of what a beginning meditator may experience, try the following exercise: Set a timer or alarm clock for 5 minutes and focus your attention on the word *one*. Close your eyes and try to clear your mind of distracting thoughts, sounds, smells, and sensations in your body; just focus on *one*. At the end of the five minutes, you may find that you have experienced a type of concentrative meditation. Another way to induce a meditative experience is to look at and focus on a crack in the ceiling or some other spot or object. As you do, try to maintain your focus on the object, letting distracting thoughts or sensations pass, and continually refocusing on your awareness of the crack. These suggested exercises may show you why meditation can be challenging for beginners; many people find themselves distracted by other thoughts or sensations and find it difficult to maintain their focus on the meditation. With practice, however, this type of focused attention becomes easier, and increasingly the meditator experiences the positive benefits of meditation.

What are those benefits? Regular meditation reduces tension and anxiety (Carrington, 1977) and decreases physiological levels of stress (MacLean et al., 1997). Indeed, meditation has been shown to lower anxiety in patients preparing for surgery (Domar et al., 1987; Leserman et al., 1989) and to help facilitate treatment for the skin condition psoriasis (Kabat-Zinn et al., 1998). Like hypnosis, meditation can improve performance by reducing stress and focusing attention.

Meditation and the Body: More Than a Pause That Refreshes

One of the documented benefits of meditation is that it quickly induces a state of deep restfulness. Merely by meditating for 20 to 30 minutes, a meditator can decrease his or

A mandala is a complex circular geometric design used to facilitate meditation.

Concentrative meditation: A form of meditation in which the meditator restricts attention and concentrates on one stimulus while disregarding everything else.

Opening-up meditation: A form of meditation in which the meditator focuses on a stimulus but also broadens that focus to encompass the whole of his or her surroundings.

Mindfulness meditation: A combination of concentrative and opening-up meditation in which the meditator focuses on whatever is most prominent at the moment; also known as *awareness meditation.*

her oxygen consumption to a level usually achieved only after six to seven hours of sleep (Wallace et al., 1971); meditation also decreases heart and respiration rates (Allison, 1970; Wallace, 1970). A meta-analysis of studies comparing regular meditators with people who do not meditate revealed lower baseline levels of respiration, heart rate, and other physiological measures in the meditators (Dillbeck & Orme-Johnson, 1987). But recall from Chapter 1 that correlation does not imply causation. The two groups may have differed in other ways. Why might some people begin to meditate and others not? Why might some who began meditation stick with it and others not?

MEDITATION VERSUS RELAXATION. Can you achieve the benefits of meditation simply by relaxing? Research has yielded contradictory findings. Relaxation training uses a number of techniques to alleviate muscle and emotional tension and achieve a relaxed physical and mental state. Some researchers find that the benefits of meditation can be obtained through relaxation training or even simply by resting (Holmes, 1984). But another study, which examined the differences between meditation and relaxation training in college students, found that meditation was more effective than relaxation training in achieving a sense of relaxation (Janowiak, 1994). Other studies, some of them done by researchers at the Maharishi School of Management (Alexander, Robinson et al., 1994), found that transcendental meditation was more effective than relaxation or other forms of meditation in reducing physiological arousal. However, other researchers (Morse et al., 1977; see Shapiro, 1982 for a review) have found no differences in skin conductance (which increases with anxiety-produced sweat), pulse, or respiration among meditators, those using self-hypnosis for relaxation, and those using a muscle relaxation technique. In sum, most, though not all, studies have shown that meditation alters heart rate, respiration rate, and physiological arousal more effectively than does relaxation training. Studies also show that, compared with other forms of relaxation, meditation appears to provide an enhanced experience of relaxation.

THE PHYSIOLOGY OF MEDITATION. Some EEG recordings taken during a meditative state resemble those found during sleep, with shifts between different levels of brain activity (Pagano et al., 1976). Deep physiological relaxation appears to occur during at least some phases of meditation, which differs both from resting with closed eyes and from the hypnotic state (Wallace, 1970; Wallace et al., 1971; see Jevning et al., 1992, for a review). Deep relaxation appears to be similar to non-REM sleep except that it occurs when the meditator is awake. Meditation is generally considered to be a distinct state of consciousness, although not all researchers agree with this view (Pagano et al., 1976).

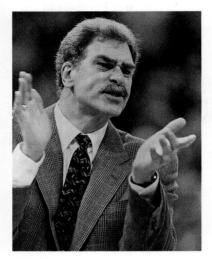

Does this man regularly meditate? Absolutely. Former basketball player and Chicago Bulls coach Phil Jackson says this about meditation and his basketball playing: "The more skilled I became at watching my thought in [meditation] practice, the more focused I became as a player. . . . The key is seeing and doing. If you're focusing on anything other than reading the court and doing what needs to be done, the moment will pass you by" (Jackson & Delehanty, 1995, pp. 50–51).

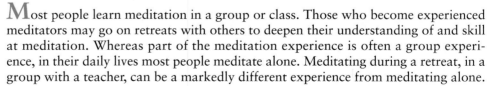

LOOKING AT LEVELS

Meditation on Retreat

Most people learn meditation in a group or class. Those who become experienced meditators may go on retreats with others to deepen their understanding of and skill at meditation. Whereas part of the meditation experience is often a group experience, in their daily lives most people meditate alone. Meditating during a retreat, in a group with a teacher, can be a markedly different experience from meditating alone.

Take Jonathan as an example. He has been meditating for about a year and recently attended a more advanced weeklong retreat. He came away from the week feeling relaxed and content, surprised at how different it was to meditate in a room full of people. After his initial class in meditation a year ago, he had always meditated alone. At the retreat, he at first had difficulty focusing during meditation, distracted by the presence of others; however, because members were not supposed to speak or have eye contact with one another, refocusing on the meditation was fairly easy. Over the course of the retreat, Jonathan came to enjoy the communal silence, and he found the leader of the retreat inspiring, giving appropriate guidance at the right time (Howell & Frost, 1989) and giving meaning to the purpose of the retreat (Conger, 1991).

Jonathan's retreat experience can be understood at the various levels of analysis. At the level of the brain, the meditation engaged his autonomic nervous system, particularly the parasympathetic branch. His endocrine and immune systems may also have been led to function differently. These physiological changes were associated with his deep relaxation. At the level of the person, Jonathan's increased energy and peaceful mood from sustained meditation contributed to his positive experience during the week. At the level of the group, both Jonathan's initial difficulty focusing and his later heightened experience in the presence of others demonstrate the impact of the group influence. The teacher, a strong leader, also played an integral part in the experience. Events at these three levels interacted: As Jonathan continued to meditate, he became more relaxed and emerged with a different perspective of himself and his place in the world. This new self-knowledge affected how he felt about and listened to the teacher, which in turn affected his meditation experience and physiological state.

CONSOLIDATE!

▶ 1. *What is meditation? What are the different types of meditation?* Meditation is a state of consciousness in which attention is focused on an object in the environment, a physical motion of the body, or a mantra (a repeated chant or phrase). There are three main types of meditation: concentrative, opening-up, and mindfulness meditation.

▶ 2. *What is the difference between meditation and relaxation? What, if any, unique physiological state accompanies meditation?* Most studies have shown

that meditation alters heart rate, respiration rate, and physiological arousal more effectively than relaxation training. Experienced meditators have a diminished need for sleep, and some studies show distinct EEG patterns. Such evidence has led some researchers to conclude that meditation may be a unique physiological state.

DRUGS AND ALCOHOL

Midway through Alice's adventures in Wonderland, she shrinks to a height of about three inches and longs to be taller. She meets a talking caterpillar, who suggests that she eat some of a nearby mushroom, remarking that one side of the mushroom would make her larger, the other side smaller.

> "And now which is which?" she said to herself, and nibbled a little of the right-hand bit to try the effect. The next moment she felt a violent blow underneath her chin: it had struck her foot!
>
> She was a good deal frightened by this very sudden change, but she felt that there was no time to be lost, as she was shrinking rapidly; so she set to work at once to eat some of the other bit. Her chin was pressed so closely against her foot, that there was hardly room to open her mouth; but she did it at last, and managed to swallow a morsel of the left-hand bit.
>
> "Come, my head's free at last!" said Alice in a tone of delight, which changed into alarm in another moment, when she found that her shoulders were nowhere to be found: all she could see, when she looked down, was an immense length of neck, which seemed to rise like a stalk out of a sea of green leaves that lay far below her. (pp. 41–42)

Many of the odd things that happen to Alice on her travels in Wonderland occur after she has eaten or drunk something. She drank from a bottle labeled "DRINK ME" and shrank; she ate cakes labeled "EAT ME" and grew. And, of course, there's the famous mushroom. Could changes such as those experienced by Alice be produced by the use of stimulants, depressants, or other chemical substances?

Although neither drugs nor alcohol can actually cause our bodies to change shape the way Alice's did, they can alter our perceptions, mood, thoughts, and behavior. So far, we've discussed natural ways of altering consciousness such as hypnosis and meditation, methods that rely solely on the abilities and skills that reside within a person. But it's also possible to alter consciousness through external means, with the use of psychoactive substances. These substances, which can be ingested, injected, or inhaled, affect the user's thoughts, feelings, and behaviors. Some substances—marijuana, tobacco, cocaine, and alcohol, certain types of mushrooms, and caffeine—can be found in nature and have long been used to alter consciousness, often in the context of religious ceremonies (Bourguignon, 1973). More recently, synthetically produced substances such as amphetamines, LSD, PCP, and barbiturates have also been used as consciousness-altering agents.

▶ 1. What is substance abuse, as defined in our society?

▶ 2. What are depressants? How do they work?

▶ 3. What are stimulants? What are their effects?

▶ 4. What are the effects of narcotic analgesics?

▶ 5. What are hallucinogens? What do they do?

Substance Use and Abuse

A woman drinks heavily, but only over the weekend, and she never misses work because of it. Is she an alcoholic? How about the man who smokes marijuana at the end of the day to feel relaxed, or the student who downs four cups of caffeinated coffee each evening while studying? Have these people crossed some physiological or psychological line between use and abuse? The American Psychiatric Association (1994) has developed three main criteria for **substance abuse**: (1) a pattern of substance use that leads to significant distress or difficulty functioning in major areas of life (for instance, at home, work, or school or in relationships); (2) substance use that occurs in dangerous situations (for instance, while or before driving a car); and (3) substance use that leads to legal difficulties.

Substance dependence results from chronic abuse. It is characterized by seven symptoms (see Table 4.2), the two most important of which are tolerance and with-

---

Substance abuse: Drug or alcohol use that leads to legal difficulties, causes distress or difficulty functioning in major areas of life, or occurs in dangerous situations.

Substance dependence: Chronic substance abuse that is characterized by seven symptoms, the two most important being tolerance and withdrawal.

TABLE 4.2

The Seven Symptoms of Substance Dependence

Source: *American Psychiatric Association (1994).*

1. Tolerance.

2. Withdrawal.

3. Larger amounts of substance taken over a longer period of time than intended.

4. Unsuccessful efforts or a persistent desire to decrease or control the substance use.

5. A lot of time spent in obtaining the substance, using it, or recovering from its effects.

6. Important work, social, or recreational activities are given up as a result of the substance.

7. Despite knowledge of recurrent or ongoing physical or psychological problems caused or exacerbated by the substance, substance use continues.

drawal (American Psychiatric Association, 1994). **Tolerance** is the condition, resulting from repeated use, in which the same amount of a substance produces a diminished effect (thus, more of the substance is required to achieve the same effect). Tolerance typically occurs with the use of alcohol, barbiturates, amphetamines, and opiates such as morphine and heroin. Withdrawal is the cessation of the use of a substance; **withdrawal symptoms** are the uncomfortable or life-threatening effects that may be experienced during withdrawal. Substance abuse presents costs to society as a whole as well as to the individual: In 1994 in New York City, for example, the cost of substance abuse and addiction was estimated to be over $20 billion, including treatment, prevention, the criminal justice and social service systems, and business-related costs (National Center on Addiction and Substance Abuse at Columbia University, 1994).

The various types of psychoactive drugs and their key properties are listed in Table 4.3.

Tolerance: The condition of requiring more of a substance to achieve the same effect (or the usual amount providing a diminished response).

Withdrawal symptoms: The onset of uncomfortable or life-threatening effects when the use of a substance is stopped.

TABLE 4.3

Psychoactive Substances: Their Physiological Actions and Effects

TYPE OF DRUG	EXAMPLE	PHYSIOLOGICAL ACTION	MAIN EFFECTS	TOLERANCE/ WITHDRAWAL SYMPTOMS
Depressants	Alcohol Barbiturates	Depresses the central nervous system.	Decreases behavioral activity, anxiety, and awareness; impairs cognition and judgment.	Yes / Yes
Stimulants	Amphetamines Cocaine	Stimulates the central nervous system.	Increases behavioral activity and arousal; creates a perception of heightened physical and mental abilities.	Yes / Yes
Narcotic-analgesics	Heroin	Depresses the central nervous system.	Dulls pain and creates an experience of euphoria and relaxation; with chronic use, the body stops producing endorphins	Yes / Yes
Hallucinogens	LSD	Alters serotonergic functioning.	Hallucinations and perceptual alterations; the user's expectations shape the drug experience.	Yes / No
	Marijuana	Affects neurons in the hippocampus involved in learning, memory, and integrating sensory experiences.		For heavy users only: Yes / Yes

Depressants: Focus on Alcohol

The **depressants**, also called *sedative-hypnotic drugs*, include barbiturates, alcohol, opiates, and antianxiety drugs such as Valium. Drugs in this category tend to slow a person down, decreasing the user's behavioral activity and level of awareness.

Approximately 9% of adults in the United States (14 million people) are considered to have either alcohol abuse or dependence (Leary, 1997), and more than 5% are considered to be heavy drinkers. The younger people are when they start drinking, the more likely they are to develop an alcohol disorder (Grant & Dawson, 1997). Binge drinking, defined as four or more drinks per episode, occurs on some college

Depressant: Class of substances, including barbiturates, alcohol, opiates, and antianxiety drugs, that depress the central nervous system, decreasing the user's behavioral activity and level of awareness; also called *sedative-hypnotic drugs*.

Blood Alcohol Levels and Their Effects

TABLE 4.4

BLOOD ALCOHOL LEVEL*	BEHAVIORAL EFFECTS
0.05	Lowered alertness, impaired judgment, release of inhibitions, feelings of well-being or sociability.
0.10	Slowed reaction time and impaired motor function, less caution.
0.15	Large, consistent increases in reaction time.
0.20	Marked depression in sensory and motor capability, decidedly intoxicated behavior.
0.25	Severe motor disturbance and impairment of sensory perceptions.
0.30	In a stupor but still conscious—no comprehension of events in the environment.
0.35	Surgical anesthesia; lethal dose for about 1% of adults.
0.40	Lethal dose for about 50% of adults.

In milligrams of alcohol per 100 milliliters of blood.

campuses, in some states more than others. College students in California are less likely to be binge drinkers than their counterparts across the nation, perhaps because California students are older on average and more likely to be married (Wechsler et al., 1997), and thus presumably more mature. Men are more likely than women to be binge drinkers (Schulenberg et al., 1996); women at women's colleges tend to binge drink less than do their female counterparts at coeducational colleges (Dowdall et al., 1998). Binge drinking is likely to occur in contexts in which the object is to get drunk (Schulenberg et al., 1996). People who engage in binge drinking are also at risk for other alcohol-related behaviors, such as driving while their functioning is impaired (Wechsler et al., 1998).

A blood alcohol content of 0.1% (well over the legal limit for driving in most states) is usually produced by having one drink for every 40 pounds of body weight in one hour (see Table 4.4); one drink is equivalent to 12 ounces of beer, 5 ounces of wine, or 1.5 ounces of 80 proof liquor (Grilly, 1994). The same amount of alcohol will have a slightly greater effect on a woman of the same size and weight as a man because men and women metabolize the drug differently (Frezza et al., 1990). Although the numbers in Table 4.4 are based on blood alcohol level, not everyone responds to the same dose of alcohol in the same way—some people have a more intense response than others. This response variability appears to be mediated in part by genes (Schuckit, 1999). People's expectations of what will happen to them as a result of drinking can also affect their behavior (see Kirsch & Lynn, 1999).

PHYSIOLOGICAL EFFECTS OF ALCOHOL. Alcohol is classified as a depressant because it depresses the nervous system through its inhibiting effect on excitatory transmitters. Although the exact mechanisms are not yet known, alcohol changes the structure of the membrane of the neuron, altering neural transmission (Goldstein, 1994; Grilly, 1994). But depressants such as alcohol can also inhibit the action of inhibitory neurotransmitters, so some neurons fire that otherwise would be inhibited. Thus, in addition to depressing some neural activity, depressants also activate neurons that otherwise would not fire. This phenomenon is called **disinhibition**.

Although it takes about an hour for alcohol to be absorbed into the blood, drinkers can feel an effect within a few minutes. The effects of alcohol depend on the

Disinhibition: Occurs when depressants cause the inhibition of inhibitory neurons, which make other neurons (the ones that are usually inhibited) more likely to fire.

dosage. At low doses, alcohol can cause a sense of decreased awareness and increased relaxation, and the drinker may become talkative or outgoing. At moderate doses, the drinker experiences slowed reaction time and impaired judgment (which is why drinking and driving don't mix). At higher doses, cognition, self-control, and self-restraint are impaired, and the drinker may become emotionally unstable or overly aggressive. "Barroom brawls" often occur because a drunk patron misconstrues a casual remark that otherwise might have passed unnoticed. As the effects of the alcohol take hold, the drinker's responses are more likely to be out of proportion to the situation. At very high doses, the drinker can have a diminished sense of cold, pain, and discomfort (which is why some people drink when in pain). At these high doses, the drinker may *feel* warm because the alcohol increases the amount of blood circulating through the skin. In reality, however, the body is losing heat because alcohol also causes dilation of the peripheral blood vessels. Thus, heavy drinking in the cold increases the chance of hypothermia (that is, decreased body temperature) and frostbite. Such high doses can bring on respiratory arrest, coma, or death.

PSYCHOLOGICAL EFFECTS OF ALCOHOL. Steele and Southwick (1985) conducted a meta-analysis of the effects of alcohol on social behavior, specifically in "high-conflict" and "low-conflict" situations. The type of conflict considered here is within the person, between two opposing desires. Specifically, Steele and Southwick wanted to see whether the use of alcohol changes the way people behave when they experience such internal conflict. They found a pattern of what they called **inhibitory conflict:** If a person in a high-conflict situation was sober, his or her response was "both strongly instigated and inhibited"; that is, the person would both want to act and not want to act. A person might very much want to engage in a particular behavior, but the consequences (moral, legal, social, personal) were great enough to inhibit it. After drinking, however, the same person would not restrain his or her behavior. And the more alcohol consumed, the greater the likelihood of engaging in the act despite societal or other sanctions. When the conflict level was low, it was still possible to inhibit the behavior; only in high-conflict situations was inhibition overcome by alcohol. This finding explains how date rape can happen: When sober, a man might want to have sexual relations but be inhibited from using force. But under the influence of alcohol, he might be more likely to act—in a high-conflict, sexually charged situation, he might have difficulty attending to the consequences that would otherwise cause him to inhibit such aggressive behavior.

Steele and his colleagues also looked at the effect of alcohol on conflict in helping situations (Steele et al., 1985). After doing tedious and boring paperwork for 30 minutes, participants in the study were asked if they would agree to do more of the same, without additional pay, while waiting for the investigator to arrange for their payment. Some participants were given an alcoholic drink before the request for additional help, and some were given water. Some participants received more pressure to help (high-conflict), and some were asked simply if they would mind helping but were not pressured by personal appeal (low-conflict). In the low-conflict situation, alcohol had no effect, and participants were able to inhibit themselves from continuing the boring task. In the high-conflict situation, alcohol affected participants' ability to inhibit their response, and they were more likely to agree to help. This result is consistent with the earlier findings: Alcohol made it more difficult for participants to inhibit their responses in the high-conflict situation. This set of findings may explain why, after drinking some alcohol, people may have a harder time saying no to a sexual proposition in high-conflict circumstances, such as the conflict between the desire for sexual intimacy and the simultaneous wish (for either moral or personal reasons) to delay a sexual encounter. One solution is to abstain from alcohol if a high-conflict situation is likely to occur.

The results of many studies have shown that the use of alcohol facilitates aggressive behavior (Bushman & Cooper, 1990). You have already seen one path for increased aggression with alcohol use: Alcohol can make it difficult to inhibit behavior in a high-conflict situation. Aggression can also result from misreading a situation, as

Inhibitory conflict: A response that is both strongly instigated and inhibited.

Alcohol myopia: Impaired ability, when drinking, to process information and perceive situational cues.

in the barroom brawl example. Alcohol impairs the ability to abstract and conceptualize information (Tarter et al., 1971) and to notice many situational cues (Washburne, 1956). This impairment results in **alcohol myopia,** "a state of shortsightedness in which superficially understood, immediate aspects of experience have a disproportionate influence on behavior and emotion" (Steele & Josephs, 1990, p. 923). Thus, stimuli that elicit aggression (such as someone's clenched fists or a date's refusal to have sexual intercourse) loom larger than stimuli that must be abstracted or require more thought (such as considerations that the aggressive behavior may be immoral, illegal, or unnecessary). Drinking also makes it more difficult to process ambiguous social situations, such as occasions when someone's words and body language are contradictory. For example, suppose friends have gone out drinking and all are now quite drunk. One of them might announce he is sick, but laugh about it. The others might not understand that their friend really *is* sick and needs medical care.

Given the fact that more than 50% of on-campus date rapes occur when men are under the influence of alcohol (Muehlenhard & Linton, 1987), some researchers (Johnson et al., in press) set out to determine exactly how drinking might be involved. They asked male volunteers to drink different levels of alcohol, then watch one of two videos of a woman on a blind date. In one video, she exhibited friendly, cordial behavior; in the other, she was unresponsive. The men were then asked how acceptable it would be for a man to be sexually aggressive toward his date (see Figure 4.7). Among the men who viewed the video with the unresponsive woman, alcohol intake made no difference in the men's answers. However, alcohol intake did make a difference for the men who viewed the video of the friendly woman: Those men who had more to drink thought that sexual aggression toward a friendly date was acceptable. The alcohol impaired the men's ability to understand that the friendliness the woman

FIGURE 4.7
Alcohol and Sexual Aggression

Male participants were assigned to one of four alcohol consumption groups: moderate alcohol intake, low alcohol intake, placebo alcohol intake (alcohol rubbed on the rim of glasses holding nonalcoholic drinks), and control group (drank ice water). The three alcohol groups did not know the strength of their drinks.

One group of men watched a video about a blind date in which the woman was very friendly; the other group watched a video about a blind date in which the woman was unresponsive and cold.

Regardless of alcohol intake, the participants who watched the unresponsive date were not very accepting of the idea of sexual aggression by the man and attributed any responsibility for aggression to *him*. In contrast, there was clear alcohol myopia in those who watched the friendly date: The more alcohol they drank, the more the men accepted the idea of sexual aggression toward the woman and the more they attributed any aggression by the man as being the *woman's* responsibility (Johnson et al., in press).

showed did not mean that it was all right for a man to force her to have sex. This type of reasoning, which involves conceptualization and abstraction, was compromised.

CHRONIC ABUSE: A BAD HABIT. Alcoholics come from all socioeconomic classes. Historically, more males than females have become alcoholics, and this pattern continues today, although the gap is narrowing (Nelson et al., 1998). Chronic alcohol abuse can cause severe memory deficits, even **blackouts,** periods of time for which the alcoholic has no memory of events that occurred while he or she was intoxicated. The chronic alcoholic often experiences difficulty with abstract reasoning, problem solving, and perceptual motor functions. It has been difficult for researchers to sort out to what degree these memory deficits are caused by the action of the alcohol itself or by the malnutrition that often accompanies alcoholism. Alcohol is highly caloric but contains very little in the way of nutrients; consequently, many heavy drinkers are inadequately nourished. Severe alcoholics may develop **Korsakoff's syndrome,** a disorder in which the brain's mammillary bodies are destroyed; these small structures receive input from the hippocampus that is critical for learning new information. Thus, these patients have profound learning and memory problems. They may be unable to learn the names of the nurses on the ward, and sometimes they cannot even remember why they are in the hospital; in general, they have grave difficulty learning new facts and the meanings of new words.

Almost all cultures recognize that drinking can create both tolerance and withdrawal symptoms, although problematic alcohol use is defined differently in different cultures (Gureje et al., 1997). What does a hangover indicate? That the body is experiencing alcohol withdrawal (Cicero, 1978). This explains why having "the hair of the dog that bit you"—more alcohol—will make hangover symptoms recede: After taking in large quantities of alcohol, your body needs more of it; otherwise, uncomfortable symptoms develop. Withdrawal symptoms for a heavy drinker include weakness, tremor, anxiety, and increased blood pressure, pulse rate, and respiration rate. Extremely heavy drinkers can experience convulsions and delirium tremens (the DTs), irritability, headaches, fever, agitation, confusion, and visual hallucinations; these typically begin within four days of stopping drinking (Romach & Sellers, 1991).

If you drink alcohol, answer these questions to see whether your drinking is problematic:

▶ Do you have a hangover the morning after drinking?

▶ Do you need to drink more now than you did 6 months ago to get the same feeling?

▶ Have you tried unsuccessfully to cut back on your alcohol intake?

▶ Have you ever had an accident during or after drinking?

▶ Do you spend a fair amount of money on alcohol?

▶ Have you missed work, class, or social obligations because of drinking or its aftereffects?

▶ Do you find yourself thinking about drinking, or counting the time until it's a "decent hour" to have a drink?

▶ Have you had blackouts while drunk—periods of time when you can't remember what occurred?

If you answered yes to any of these questions (particularly the first two, concerning tolerance and withdrawal), then you may have a problem with alcohol. You should seek more information from your doctor, counselor, or Alcoholics Anonymous.

OTHER DEPRESSANTS. Barbiturates, including Amytal, Nembutal, and Seconal, mimic the effects of alcohol in that they depress the central nervous system. Usually prescribed to aid sleep or to reduce anxiety, they can be lethal when combined with alcohol. Users will develop both tolerance and withdrawal symptoms: Withdrawal may be accompanied by agitation and restlessness, hallucinations, and delirium tremens.

Blackout: Loss of memory for events that transpired while intoxicated.

Korsakoff's syndrome: A disorder, related to alcoholism, in which the brain's mammillary bodies are destroyed, damaging learning and memory abilities.

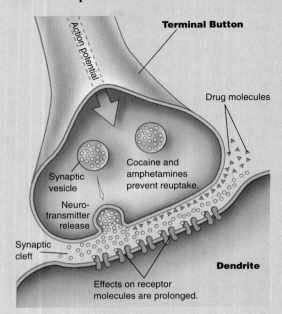

FIGURE 4.8
Action of Amphetamines on Neurotransmitters

Terminal Button

Action potential

Drug molecules

Synaptic vesicle

Cocaine and amphetamines prevent reuptake.

Neurotransmitter release

Synaptic cleft

Effects on receptor molecules are prolonged.

Dendrite

Cocaine and other amphetamines create their stimulant effects by blocking reuptake—preventing the normal reabsorption into the terminal button—of some norepinephrine and dopamine at the synaptic cleft. The net effect is more of these neurotransmitters in the synaptic cleft.

Stimulants: Focus on Cocaine

In contrast to depressants, **stimulants** excite the central nervous system, stimulating behavioral activity and heightened arousal. Low doses of amphetamines and cocaine can lead to a perception of increased physical and mental energy, diminished hunger, and a sense of invulnerability. Because "coming down" from this state is a disappointment, stimulant users often want to repeat the experience and so are at risk for continued drug use. Of all drugs, stimulants are the most likely to induce dependence.

In 1997 an estimated 1.5 million people in the United States used cocaine (Department of Health and Human Services, 1998). Cocaine is commonly inhaled in its powdered form, and it has a local anesthetic effect. The user has an enhanced sense of physical and mental capacity and a simultaneous loss of appetite. Chronic users develop paranoia, teeth grinding, and repetitive behaviors and may also experience disturbances in the visual field, such as seeing snow, or feeling that insects ("cocaine bugs") are crawling on the skin. This latter sensation is actually the spontaneous firing of sensory neurons caused by the cocaine.

Cocaine exerts its effects by inhibiting the reuptake of dopamine and norepinephrine (Figure 4.8). This increased presence of neurotransmitter in the synaptic cleft leads to a pleasurable, even euphoric, feeling. With continued use of cocaine, the drug becomes the main trigger for activation of the reward system, leading other sources of pleasure, such as food or sex, to have no effect (National Institute on Drug Abuse, 1998).

CRACK. Cocaine in crystalline form, or **crack,** is usually smoked in a pipe ("freebasing") or rolled into a cigarette. Crack is faster acting and more intense in its effect than cocaine powder inhaled through the nostrils; however, because its effects last for only a few minutes, the user tends to take greater amounts of crack than of powdered cocaine. Crack cocaine has more potential for abuse and dependence (Cone, 1995). The user experiences a feeling of euphoria, perceived clarity of thought, and increased energy. Crack increases heart rate and blood pressure and constricts blood vessels—a potentially lethal combination. After the drug wears off, the user experiences a massive "crash," with an intense depression and intense craving for more crack. Both cocaine and crack can create strong dependence, particularly if injected or smoked. The user can develop tolerance; with crack, the development of tolerance is particularly swift. Sudden death can occur even in healthy people who use the drug occasionally.

OTHER STIMULANTS. **Amphetamines** are synthetic stimulants such as Benzedrine and dextroamphetamine (Dexedrine); they are usually taken in pill form or injected. With high doses, the user can suffer amphetamine psychosis, which is similar to paranoid schizophrenia (discussed in Chapter 13); symptoms include delusions, hallucinations, and paranoia. Chronic use of amphetamines stimulates violent behaviors (Leccese, 1991). MDMA (also known as ecstasy, or "e") is a neurotoxic amphetamine—it destroys certain neurons. Research on animals indicates that MDMA, used even once, can permanently damage serotonin neurotransmitters, affecting memory, learning, sleep, and appetite (Fischer et al., 1995). Many of the side effects that occur with other stimulants also occur with MDMA.

Stimulant: A class of substances that excite the central nervous system, leading to increases in behavioral activity and heightened arousal.

Crack: Cocaine in crystalline form, usually smoked in a pipe (free-basing) or rolled into a cigarette.

Amphetamines: Synthetic stimulants.

Caffeine is present in coffee, tea, chocolate, and colas, among other foods. It causes increased alertness, raises pulse and heart rate, and produces insomnia, restlessness, and ringing in the ears. There is some degree of tolerance, and chronic users will experience withdrawal headaches if they miss their customary morning coffee. *Nicotine*, present in cigarettes and tobacco in any form, can cause increased alertness and relaxation, as well as irritability, increased blood pressure, stomach pains, cancer, dizziness, emphysema, and heart disease. Nicotine works by triggering the release of several neurotransmitters that lead to a pleasurable sensation. Nicotine is addictive, causing some level of tolerance and withdrawal symptoms when its use is stopped.

Narcotic analgesic: A class of strongly addictive drugs, such as heroin, that relieves pain.

Opiate: A narcotic, such as morphine, derived from the opium poppy.

Hallucinogen: A substance that induces hallucinations.

Narcotic Analgesics: Focus on Heroin

Certain drugs, including heroin, morphine, codeine, Percodan, and Demerol, are called **narcotic analgesics** because they are strongly addictive drugs that dull the senses and provide analgesia; that is, they relieve pain. These drugs affect certain endorphin receptors (see Chapter 3). Generally, drugs of this type are prescribed to relieve pain, severe diarrhea, protracted coughing, and troubled sleep. Heroin, an illegal drug, is one of the stronger narcotic analgesics. Like morphine, from which it is derived, heroin is an **opiate**, produced from the opium poppy.

Heroin can bring about a feeling of relaxation and euphoria, but these effects are very short-term and are followed by negative changes in mood and behavior. Like other opiates, heroin is a central nervous system depressant, causing a slowing of neural activity in brainstem areas responsible for respiration and coughing, as well as in other areas of the brain. When heroin is in the body, the user may experience pupil constriction, slower breathing, and lethargy. Tolerance and withdrawal symptoms occur, usually with periods of yawning, chills, hot flashes, restlessness, diarrhea, and goose bumps on the skin, followed by up to 12 hours of sleep.

As well as activating the dopamine-based reward pathway in the brain, heroin and other opiates work by binding to the brain's opiate receptors, where the body's own opiates such as endorphins usually bind. This creates a negative feedback loop, leading the body to decrease its production of endorphins and leaving the heroin user without natural means to relieve pain. Thus, more heroin is needed to achieve the analgesic effect. When the user tries to quit, endorphins do not kick in to alleviate the withdrawal symptoms, thus heightening the discomfort—and making it difficult to quit.

Alice wanted to be smaller and hoped to find a "book of rules for shutting people up like telescopes" (p. 31). Instead, she found a bottle (labeled DRINK ME) and, after drinking it, said, "What a curious feeling! . . . I must be shutting up like a telescope." (p. 31) This scene illustrates the effect of a user's expectations on his or her experience. Alice was hoping to find a way to shut herself up like a telescope, and that is just what she experienced after drinking the liquid. User expectations play a large role in the emotional tone of the LSD experience.

Hallucinogens: Focus on LSD

A **hallucinogen** is a substance that induces the perceptual experiences known as hallucinations. Although Alice's imaginings of Wonderland were a dream, other people, such as the sixties rock group Jefferson Airplane in their song *White Rabbit*, inferred that Alice's experiences stemmed from a hallucinogenic drug. Hallucinogens include mescaline, peyote, psilocybin, lysergic acid diethylamide (LSD), phencyclidine (PCP), ketamine ("Special K"), and marijuana. In general, all but marijuana can cause visual hallucinations at moderate dosages; much higher dosages are needed before marijuana will do so.

LSD is a synthetic substance that produces perceptual alterations. Exactly how LSD works is not well understood, but it is known to alter serotonergic functioning. Users commonly experience visual hallucinations, which often include geometric shapes, vivid colors, and violent movement. At higher doses, geometric shapes give way to quickly changing meaningful objects. Users may feel as if they are becoming part of whatever they observe. Auditory hallucinations include hearing invented foreign languages or symphonies. These symptoms may last several hours, and the user's expectations can shape the experience induced by LSD.

A CREATIVITY BOOST? Although some people report that they feel more creative as a result of taking LSD, research does not support the subjective experience of increased creativity after use (Dusek & Girdano, 1980). On the contrary, LSD can produce frightening experiences ("bad trips"), which could be caused by a change in dose, mood, expectations, and environment. A user may panic during a bad trip and need to be "talked down," repeatedly reminded that the frightening experience is in fact a drug-induced state that will wear off. Occasionally, suicide or murder takes place in the course of a user's hallucination. Hallucinations can recur without use of the drug; these spontaneous, perhaps alarming **flashbacks,** a not uncommon side effect, can happen weeks, even years, afterward, and can be triggered by entering a dark environment (Abraham, 1983).

OTHER HALLUCINOGENS. The most common hallucinogen in America is marijuana, whose active ingredient is tetrahydrocannabinol (THC). Although marijuana is less powerful than most other hallucinogens, every year approximately 100,000 Americans attend treatment centers in an effort to stop using it (Blakeslee, 1997). The effects of marijuana are dependent on the user's mood, expectations, and environment: If alone, the user may experience drowsiness and go to sleep; if with others, the user may feel euphoric. The effects of the drug can be subtle, including perceptual alterations in which sights and sounds seem more vivid. Distortions of space and time are also common, and perceptual motor skills may be impaired, making driving unsafe (Petersen, 1977, 1979; Sterling-Smith, 1976).

The substance ketamine, similar to phencyclidine, is legally used as an anesthetic for animals. Use by humans can induce hallucinations, anesthesia, and stimulation of the cardiovascular and respiratory systems. Ketamine use is also associated with violence, a loss of contact with reality, and impairment in thinking (White & Ryan, 1996). Users are likely to develop tolerance and dependence.

LOOKING AT LEVELS

Princess Diana's Death

Whatever the full circumstances of the automobile accident that killed Lady Diana, former Princess of Wales, along with her boyfriend and the driver of the car, it is known that chemically altered states of consciousness played a role. The driver, Henri Paul, had a blood alcohol level of 1.75 grams per liter (more than three times the legal limit in France of 0.5 gram per liter); the antidepressant Prozac was detected in his blood, as well as tiapride, a medication commonly prescribed in France for alcoholics to ameliorate aggression and anxiety. Paul had been off duty for several hours but was called back to work at the last minute. With what you know about drugs and consciousness, you can see how events at the three levels of brain, person, and group might interact in this situation.

At the level of the brain, a high dosage of alcohol causes disinhibition, which creates slower reaction time and impaired cognition and judgment. At the level of the person, intoxicated people may have difficulty assessing their own abilities, feel euphoric and invulnerable, yet also be more aggressive or emotionally volatile. Paul would no doubt have been a poor judge of his driving ability. Thus impaired, chased by a horde of motorcycling *paparazzi* (level of the group), he would be more likely to fall prey to aggressive or impulsive behavior. Events at these levels would interact: For example, with inhibitory mechanisms impaired and in a tense situation, the decision of how fast was safe to drive through a narrow, curving tunnel would not be grounded in a realistic assessment.

CONSOLIDATE!

▶ **1. What is substance abuse, as defined in our society?** Substance abuse is use that produces significant distress or dysfunction in major areas of life, use that occurs in dangerous situations, or use that leads to legal troubles.

▶ **2. What are depressants? How do they work?** Depressants, such as alcohol and barbiturates, are substances that decrease the user's behavioral activity and level of awareness. They can cause disinhibition and, at moderate doses, slowed reaction time and impaired judgment. Higher doses bring diminished sensation, possible respiratory arrest, coma, or death; and chronic use can lead to blackouts and Korsakoff's syndrome. Tolerance and withdrawal symptoms occur with repeated alcohol use.

▶ **3. What are stimulants? What are their effects?** Stimulant drugs, such as amphetamines, cocaine, and crack, cause increased behavioral activity and heightened arousal. Low doses of amphetamines and co-

caine can lead to perception of increased physical and mental energy, diminished hunger, and a sense of invulnerability, but users may experience a "crash" when the drug wears off. High doses can cause paranoia and violent behavior.

▶ **4. What are the effects of narcotic analgesics?** Narcotic analgesics, which include heroin, morphine, codeine, Percodan, and Demerol, produce a short-lived sense of relaxation and euphoria. Narcotics can relieve pain, but they are also central nervous system depressants, and their use can lead to tolerance and painful and difficult withdrawal.

▶ **5. What are hallucinogens? What do they do?** Hallucinogens are substances that cause perceptual alterations (including distorted body images) and visual hallucinations at even moderate dosages (except for marijuana). The user's experience depends on his or her expectations, mood, and other factors; users can experience "bad trips" and, later, flashbacks.

A DEEPER LEVEL ■ ▶ ▶
Recap and Thought Questions

▶ To Sleep, Perchance to Dream

There are five stages of sleep: Stages 1 through 4 (NREM sleep), and REM sleep, or paradoxical sleep, in which memorable, vivid dreams occur. REM rebound—a higher proportion of REM sleep—occurs on the night following deprivation of sufficient REM sleep.

Although researchers do not yet know with certainty why we dream, various theorists have proposed that dreams represent unconscious desires (Freud), random bursts of nerve cell activity (Hobson and McCarley), the elimination of unneeded connections in the brain (Crick), the strengthening of needed brain connections (Karni), or an interplay of goals and desires, and arousal and inhibition (Solms). The content of dreams can be affected by certain types of events before sleep, such as thirst and the lack of social interaction.

Lack of adequate sleep impairs performance on tasks that require vigilance and attention. Sleep deprivation also adversely affects mood and cortisol functioning (which, in turn, can affect learning and memory). Some sleep disorders, such as night terrors and narcolepsy, have a genetic basis; others, such as insomnia and sleep apnea, may have physical causes; still other types of insomnia are environ-

mentally caused, such as those related to jet lag and shift work.

Could Alice's adventures have been only a dream? Yes, Alice's adventures could very well have been a dream. The description includes many important elements of dreaming: Alice was bored and sleepy prior to seeing the talking rabbit, and the fall down the rabbit hole could have been Stage 1 sleep (a hypnogogic state), perhaps ending in a hypnic jerk when she reached the bottom. Many elements of Carroll's description contain the surreal, nonsensical elements that occur in dreams.

> ▶▶
> **Think It Through.** While trying to finish two papers, Antonio pulled two all-nighters in a row during finals week. On the morning after the second sleepless night, he has a final exam. What is his mental and physical state likely to be when he walks into the examination room? Which areas of functioning are likely to be impaired, and which are likely to remain undisturbed? What can you predict about the length and type of sleep Antonio will have when he finally sleeps?

▶ Hypnosis

Hypnosis involves a tuning out of the external environment and increased attention and openness to suggestion. Aspects of consciousness that change with hypnosis are generalized reality orientation fading and trance logic. Hypnotizability varies from person to person; the most closely correlated personality characteristic is absorption. Three theories of hypnosis—trance theory, sociological role theory, and task-motivation theory—attempt to explain the phenomenon. Recent brain-scanning results indicate that hypnosis is not simply role playing, but in fact leads to a distinct brain state. Hypnosis has been used to treat a variety of psychological and medical disorders, including pain.

Might Alice's experience of her body changing shape have occurred in a hypnotic trance? Hypnosis can bring about the perceptual alterations that Alice experienced in her body. Hypnosis can also alleviate the experience of pain. However, it is unlikely that hypnosis induced Alice's bodily experience; she had so many other odd adventures that other methods of altering consciousness better explain her escapades.

> **Think It Through.** Anna disliked her smoking habit and had been trying to quit for a year. Because her own efforts had failed, she decided to see a hypnotist. Can she be certain that the hypnotist will be able to hypnotize her successfully? How might the hypnotist use hypnosis to help her quit? If hypnosis helps her to quit smoking, how might sociological role theory account for Anna's experience?

▶ Meditation

Meditation, which focuses awareness on a single stimulus, generally brings a subjective sense of well-being and relaxation, along with such physiological changes as decreased heart and respiratory rates and shifting EEG patterns of brain activity. There are three main types of meditation: concentrative, in which the meditator focuses on one chosen image or word (such as a mandala or mantra); opening-up, in which the meditator's surroundings become part of the meditation; and mindfulness, in which the meditator focuses on whatever is most prominent at the moment.

Could Alice have been meditating to bring about her strange experiences? Theoretically, Alice could have been meditating to bring about her altered state of consciousness. However, concentrative meditation, with its emphasis on the repetition of one stimulus, is unlikely to have produced her adventures. Although "opening-up" and mindfulness meditation have a broader focus of awareness, including the environment surrounding the meditator, they, too, are unlikely to have inspired the creative, nonsensical elements of Alice's adventures.

> **Think It Through.** Simon was under considerable stress and knew that he should do something about it. He was thinking of either taking a relaxation class or learning meditation because he'd heard that both might help him cope with stress. But first he wanted to find out if *meditation* and *relaxation* were different names for the same activity, and whether one technique worked better than the other. What would you tell him?
>
> Simon decides to learn meditation, but he has heard that there are different types of meditation. What can you tell him about them, specifically with regard to how the meditator focuses awareness and handles intrusions (such as a barking dog) in different types of meditation?

▶ Drugs and Alcohol

Depressants such as alcohol depress the central nervous system and can create an altered state of consciousness through disinhibition, decreased awareness, and an increased sense of relaxation. Disinhibition may make it difficult for the user to inhibit (or stop) behaviors he or she would otherwise be able to prevent in high-conflict situations, and alcohol can promote aggressive behavior. Chronic alcohol abuse can lead to blackouts, and even Korsakoff's syndrome, as well as tolerance and withdrawal symptoms. In contrast, stimulants excite the central nervous system, leading to increases in behavioral activity, heightened arousal, and perceptions of increased physical and mental energy. However, the user will "crash" after the drug wears off, become depressed and irritable, and crave more of the drug. Chronic use of some stimulants (such as amphetamines and cocaine) can cause paranoia and violence.

Even moderate doses of hallucinogens (except marijuana) can cause visual hallucinations and perceptual alterations of other senses. The altered state of consciousness produced by a hallucinogen is influenced by the user's mood and expectations. Marijuana users may experience euphoria and relaxation. Flashbacks can occur after LSD use.

Narcotics such as heroin provide an analgesic effect, as well as a sense of euphoria and relaxation; they are depressants of the central nervous system. Tolerance and extremely uncomfortable withdrawal symptoms occur. Chronic use can suppress the body's production of endorphins.

Could Alice's adventures have been a drug- or alcohol-induced state of consciousness and, if so, due to what kind of substance? Alice's adventures could have been substance-induced. Her experience of her body's changes could have been produced by hallucinogenic drugs. However, depressants, stimulants, and narcotics would not be likely to induce her adventures.

Think It Through. A male, approximately 20 years old, was brought into the emergency room. He had been found in a local park, threatening passersby and muttering about bugs crawling on his skin. After waiting in the emergency room for an hour, he became extremely depressed and agitated. Assuming that he had no medical disorder other than drug use, what class of drug and what specific substance had he most likely taken? Suppose he hadn't complained of bugs but had trouble walking in a straight line and was slow to understand questions asked of him. What class of substance might be responsible for his actions? What specific substance?

5 LEARNING

It's a Friday night, and two couples in their late twenties are having dinner together at a restaurant. Each couple has been together for a few years. Isabel and Tony have a solid relationship and plan to marry; Paula and Chris's relationship has been more up and down, and although they are still together, they have no plans to marry. Isabel and Tony treat each other courteously, even when one of them privately thinks the other is being a little thick, and each tries to listen to what the other is saying. In contrast, Paula and Chris have been snapping at each other and not getting along too well recently, although they were both very happy the first year they were together. Now they fight a great deal, often over trivial matters.

Over coffee and dessert, the conversation turns to plans for the weekend. "Why don't we go to the beach?" asks Paula.

"Paula!" Chris responds in a tone of voice Paula has heard before and now dreads. "I already told you I don't want to go to the beach. I'm really tired, and I'm not up for all that driving and hassle with sand in my car. How can you be so selfish? Don't you listen when I talk to you?" Paula sits mute. Chris goes on, "You never listen to me. . . . What's the point?"

Now Paula reacts angrily. "Wait just a minute, Chris, don't lay all this on me! It's not just the beach—you never want to go anywhere fun. And you always call me selfish if I don't do exactly what you want! Well, I'm not going to play that game this time." In the silence that follows, Paula and Chris see that Isabel and Tony are looking at them, dumbstruck. Only then do they realize how much their relationship has deteriorated and how quick they've become to berate and hurt each other.

Sadly, scenes like this are far from uncommon, although not necessarily in public. Conflict, and specifically how to resolve it, is one of the many situations in life that spur our interest in learning. To learn is to discover, and the need to discover compels us from birth to the end of our days. Learning helps us both to survive and to realize our deepest dreams. It underlies virtually all our behavior: what we eat and the way we eat it, the way we dress ourselves, how we acquire the knowledge contained in books like this one, how we live in a society with other people. And not all learning is positive in its results: As Paula and Chris demonstrate, learning is a double-edged sword. We can learn to do things that hurt as well as help.

Whereas many fields focus on the content of what people learn (historians add to their knowledge by finding out more facts about history), psychologists interested in the field of learning focus on the *process* of learning: How does learning occur? To discover this, researchers have investigated both humans and animals, and in this chapter we look at some of the principles their research has uncovered. How did Paula "learn" to be alarmed when Chris spoke her name in a certain way? How did they learn to accept rude behavior from each other? Could Paula and Chris learn to behave differently toward each other by watching Isabel and Tony?

Psychologists define **learning** as a relatively long-term change in behavior that results from experience. When, for example, you have mastered tying your shoelaces, you will likely be able to secure your shoes properly for the rest of your life. This durability is true of all learned behavior, in virtually every domain of life, from riding a bicycle to participating in a conversation.

But what about this case: Suppose you watch someone write your name in Japanese characters. Having seen it done, can you claim that you have *learned* how to do it? What if you are able to duplicate the characters successfully? Can you legitimately say that you have learned to write your name in Japanese?

In the first instance, unless you have a photographic memory and excellent drawing ability, the answer is probably no. Merely watching someone do something complex and unfamiliar on a single occasion is usually not enough to allow you to learn it. In the second instance, even if you copy the characters correctly, the answer is still likely to be no. Just performing an action once is not enough; unless you can do it repeatedly and without assistance, you cannot claim that you have really learned to do it. You may have learned some elements of the task, but not the entire pattern, and so you cannot claim to have mastered it.

Learning can take place in a variety of ways. We often learn by association—relating one object or event with another object or event. This general phenomenon is what psychologists call *associative learning*. For instance, most people associate going to the dentist with pain. Specifically, with classical conditioning, learning occurs when a stimulus becomes associated with a reflexive behavior. At the dentist's office, this might occur when your palms get sweaty on seeing the dentist's drill. Learning also occurs when we link acts to their consequences; this process is known as *operant conditioning*. Operant conditioning is at work when children make the connection between asking for something politely and the increased likelihood of getting it. Another kind of learning occurs by watching other people, a process called *observational learning*. And, finally, we also learn by mentally storing material to be used at some later time; this is called *cognitive learning*. Regardless of which mode is in effect, the criterion for learning—that we demonstrate a relatively long-term change brought about by experience—remains the same.

Let's begin by exploring the model of associative learning investigated not quite a hundred years ago: classical conditioning.

CLASSICAL CONDITIONING

W hen Chris said "Paula!" in a certain tone of voice, her reaction—fear—was an automatic response. Chris had never done anything to Paula to make her physically afraid; he had never been violent or even threatened violence. But they had been verbally abusive to each other in the past. Paula developed a fear response to Chris's tone of voice because early in their relationship, he had used this tone whenever he had wanted to make the painful point that he thought their relationship wasn't going to work.

Paula's emotional response to the tone of Chris's voice is a complex example of classical conditioning. In its simplest form, **classical conditioning** is a type of learning in which a neutral stimulus becomes associated, or paired, with a stimulus that causes a reflexive behavior and, in time, becomes sufficient to produce that behavior. In this case, the tone of Chris's voice is the stimulus paired with an unhappy memory that elicits the physiological response of fear in Paula.

The simplest example of the way classical conditioning works is found in the famous experiments that established the principle: the work of Pavlov and his dogs.

▶ 1. What is classical conditioning? How was it discovered?

▶ 2. How are conditioned responses eliminated?

▶ 3. What are common examples of classical conditioning in daily life?

Learning: A relatively permanent change in behavior that results from experience.

Classical conditioning: A type of learning that occurs when a neutral stimulus becomes paired (associated) with a stimulus that causes a reflexive behavior and, in time, is sufficient to produce that behavior.

Unconditioned stimulus (UCS): A stimulus that elicits an automatic response (UCR), without requiring prior learning.

Unconditioned response (UCR): The reflexive response elicited by a particular stimulus.

Conditioned stimulus (CS): An originally neutral stimulus that acquires significance through the "conditioning" of repeated pairings with an unconditioned stimulus (UCS).

Pavlov's Experiments

Classical conditioning is also sometimes called Pavlovian conditioning because it was discovered, accidentally, by Ivan Pavlov (1849–1936), a Russian physiologist. As part of his work on the digestive processes, which won him a Nobel Prize, Pavlov studied salivation in dogs. To measure the amount of saliva that dogs produced when given meat powder (food for the dog), Pavlov collected the saliva in tubes attached to the dogs' salivary glands (see Figure 5.1). Pavlov and his colleagues noticed that even though salivation usually occurs *while* rather than *before* eating, his dogs were salivating *before* they were fed: They would salivate simply on seeing their food bowls or hearing the feeder's footsteps.

Intrigued, Pavlov pursued the issue with more experiments. His basic method is still in use today (see Figure 5.2 on page 168). Pavlov would sound a tone on a tuning fork just before the food was brought into the dogs' room. After several times of pairing the tone with the food, the dogs would salivate on hearing the tone alone. Because food by itself elicits salivation, Pavlov considered the food the **unconditioned stimulus (UCS)**—that is, a stimulus that elicits an automatic response and is not conditional on prior learning. The dogs' salivation is termed the **unconditioned response (UCR)**, the reflexive or automatic response elicited by a UCS. The UCR does not require learning, but it does depend on certain circumstances. For example, if an animal has just eaten and is full, it will not salivate when presented with food. In Pavlov's experiment, the tone is the **conditioned stimulus (CS)**—that is, an originally neutral stimulus that acquires significance through the "conditioning" of repeated pair-

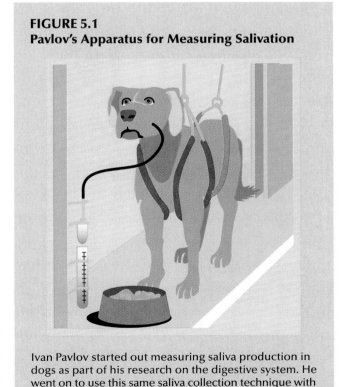

FIGURE 5.1
Pavlov's Apparatus for Measuring Salivation

Ivan Pavlov started out measuring saliva production in dogs as part of his research on the digestive system. He went on to use this same saliva collection technique with his investigations into classical conditioning.

FIGURE 5.2
The Three Phases of Classical Conditioning

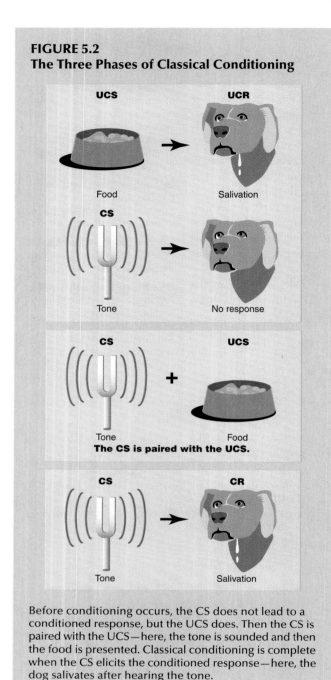

UCS → UCR
Food → Salivation

CS
Tone → No response

CS + UCS
Tone + Food
The CS is paired with the UCS.

CS → CR
Tone → Salivation

Before conditioning occurs, the CS does not lead to a conditioned response, but the UCS does. Then the CS is paired with the UCS—here, the tone is sounded and then the food is presented. Classical conditioning is complete when the CS elicits the conditioned response—here, the dog salivates after hearing the tone.

Conditioned response (CR): A response that depends, or is conditional, on pairings of the conditioned stimulus with an unconditioned stimulus; the conditioned response occurs in response to the CS alone.

Acquisition: The technical name given to the initial learning of the conditioned response (CR).

ings with a UCS. After hearing the tuning fork a number of times before they were fed, the dogs began to associate the tone with food. Now, whenever the dogs heard the tone, even when presented by itself, they salivated. From these observations, Pavlov theorized that when a CS (in this case, the tone) is paired with a UCS (in this case, food), it will, on its own, elicit the same or similar response as would the UCS alone (in this case, salivation). Salivation in response to the tone alone is thus a **conditioned response (CR)**, a response that depends (is conditional) on pairings of the CS with a UCS (Pavlov, 1927). Not surprisingly, psychologists call the initial learning of the conditioned response **acquisition**.

Classical Conditioning: How It Works

Researchers studying classical conditioning have discovered a good deal about how organisms (human or otherwise) respond to this form of learning. Some conditioned responses remain with us all our lives; others fade and even disappear altogether.

In an attempt to see what factors might affect the process of conditioning, Pavlov and researchers after him altered the variables involved in creating a conditioned response. Initially, researchers thought that to create a conditioned response, the UCS (the food) must immediately follow the CS (the tone). Now they wanted to see whether varying the timing of the presentations could still lead to a conditioned response. Pavlov tried the reverse order: He fed the dogs first and presented the tone 10, 5, or 1 second later. He found no conditioning; the dogs did not salivate when hearing the tone after eating the food. Even presenting the UCS and CS simultaneously did not lead to a conditioned response (Hall, 1984). Generally, in order for conditioning to occur, the UCS (food) should follow the CS (tone) immediately; however, there are exceptions, as is the case with certain food aversions, in which there may be a longer interval between the presentation of conditioned and unconditioned stimuli.

Another Russian researcher, Vladimir Bechterev (1857–1927), also conducted conditioning experiments. Here the UCS was a shock, and the UCR was the dog's withdrawal of its foot. When a neutral stimulus such as a bell (CS) was paired with the shock, the dog learned to withdraw its foot (CR) after the bell but before the shock, thus successfully learning to avoid pain. Bechterev's findings were an important expansion of Pavlov's work in that he extended the conditioned response to motor reflexes. Bechterev also established the basis for **avoidance learning** (Viney, 1993)—classical conditioning with a CS and an unpleasant UCS that leads the organism to try to avoid the CS. Does avoidance learning explain why some people put off going to the dentist for many years?

CONDITIONED EMOTIONS: GETTING A GUT RESPONSE. Paula came to dread hearing Chris speak to her in a certain tone of voice, even though this tone was not particularly offensive in itself and did not alarm her when she first heard it. But in one of their first fights, Chris had sounded this way when he said that their relationship was doomed from the start. This created a specific type of conditioned response

FIGURE 5.3
Classical Conditioning of a Phobia: Little Albert

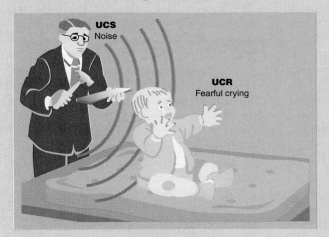

Initially, Little Albert did not show a fear of animals, but he *did* exhibit fear if a loud noise was made behind his back (a hammer striking a steel bar).

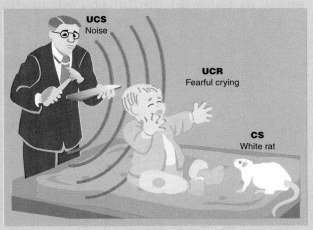

Then the researchers presented a white rat (CS) and made the loud noise (UCS).

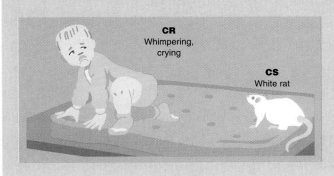

After five presentations of the CS and UCS, Albert developed a phobia of rats—he began whimpering and withdrawing (the conditioned emotional response) and trying to avoid the rat. After two more presentations of CS and UCS, he immediately began crying on seeing the rat. "He . . . fell over on his left side, raised himself . . . and began to crawl away so rapidly that he was caught with difficulty before reaching the edge of the table" (Watson and Raynor, 1920, p. 5).

called a **conditioned emotional response (CER)**—an emotionally charged conditioned response elicited by a previously neutral stimulus. Only after Chris made the painful remark did Paula pair his tone of voice with his dismal pronouncement, and the association produced a conditioned emotional response.

A landmark study by John B. Watson, the founder of behaviorism (see Chapter 1), and his assistant Rosalie Raynor (Watson & Raynor, 1920) illustrates how classical conditioning can produce a straightforward conditioned emotional response of fear, and how fear can lead to a **phobia,** an irrational fear of a specific object or situation. Watson and Raynor classically conditioned fear and then a phobia in an 11-month-old infant—Albert B.—whom they called "Little Albert" (see Figure 5.3). Through the use of classical conditioning, Watson and Raynor created in Albert a fear of rats; on seeing a white rat, Albert would cry and exhibit signs of fearfulness. This study could not be done today because of the rigorous ethical principles that govern psychological research (see Chapter 1), which did not exist at the time the study was undertaken. Although Watson and Raynor did have some concerns about the nature of the experiment and the possible effect on the child, their rationale was that this type of conditioning occurs not infrequently in life, and studying it experimentally would help people understand this phenomenon (Viney, 1994). Neither Watson nor Raynor ever mentioned what became of Albert after the study, and they did nothing to help the child overcome the fear of white furry objects that they had induced (Benjafield, 1996).

Avoidance learning: In classical conditioning, learning that occurs when a CS is paired with an unpleasant UCS that leads the organism to try to avoid the CS.

Conditioned emotional response (CER): An emotional response elicited by a previously neutral stimulus.

Phobia: An irrational fear of a specific object or situation.

Although it was initially thought that any response could be conditioned by any stimulus (Kimble, 1981), this supposition is not entirely true. Organisms seem to have a **biological preparedness,** a built-in readiness for certain conditioned stimuli to elicit particular conditioned responses, so that less learning is necessary to produce such conditioning. Research has shown that it is easier to condition a fear response to some objects than to others. Ohman and colleagues (1976) used pictures as the CS and shock as the UCS. They found that the fear-related response of sweaty hands is more easily conditioned, and less easily lost, if the CS is a picture of a snake or spider than if it shows flowers or mushrooms. Snakes, rats, and the dark are typical objects of a phobia. Some have argued that this makes sense from an evolutionary perspective—sensitivity to the presence of such possibly dangerous elements could help an organism survive (Seligman, 1971).

Contrapreparedness is a built-in disinclination (or even an inability) for certain conditioned stimuli to elicit particular conditioned responses. For example, Marks (1969) described a patient he was treating as an adult. When this woman was 10 years old, she was on a car trip and had to go to the bathroom. Her father pulled off the road so she could go in a ditch. As she stepped out of the car, she saw a snake in the ditch—and at that moment her brother accidentally slammed the door on her hand. At 43, she was still deathly afraid of snakes, but she was not afraid of car doors, which had actually done the damage. Similarly, Bregman (1934) failed—with 15 different infants—to replicate Watson and Raynor's experiment when, instead of a rat as the CS, she used various inanimate objects, such as wooden blocks and pieces of cloth. There was no evidence of conditioning when the UCS was a loud noise and the CS was an inanimate object. These two examples highlight the point that certain stimuli, such as a car door and a wooden block, do not make successful conditioned stimuli.

EXTINCTION AND SPONTANEOUS RECOVERY IN CLASSICAL CONDITIONING: GONE TODAY, HERE TOMORROW.

It is indeed tragic that Watson never followed the history of Little Albert because even after a conditioned response (such as Albert's fear of white rats) is acquired, it is possible to stop the response from occurring in the presence of the CS. This process is called **extinction** because the CR is gradually eliminated, or "extinguished," by repeated presentations of the CS without the UCS. How would this work with Pavlov's dogs? If the tone continues to be presented, but is not followed by the presentation of food, after a while the dogs will no longer salivate at the tone: The CR will be extinguished. This process is graphed in Figure 5.4.

However, when a conditioned response has been extinguished, the organism allowed to rest, and the CS presented again after the rest period, the CS will again elicit the CR, although sometimes not as strongly as before extinction. This event is called **spontaneous recovery** (see Figure 5.4). Look again at the case of the dogs: After the tone has been presented several times without any food forthcoming, the dogs' salivation response will extinguish, and they will stop salivating to the tone alone. However, if the tone is not presented for a period of time and then is presented, the previously learned conditioned response of salivation on hearing the tone alone will return. The dogs have spontaneous recovery of the response, but they may not salivate as much as they did when they were first classically conditioned to the tone.

Once classical conditioning has occurred, the stimulus–response connection apparently never completely vanishes. Once extinction occurs and the organism is then retrained so that the CS again elicits the conditioned response, learning

FIGURE 5.4
Extinction and Spontaneous Recovery in Classical Conditioning

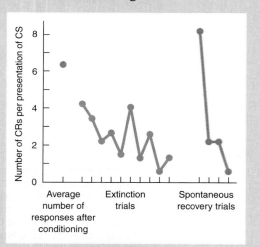

Using a tone (CS) and food pellets (UCS), rats were initially conditioned to respond to the tone alone (left), the response was extinguished (center), and then, after a rest period of 6 days, the rats exhibited spontaneous recovery (right).

takes place more quickly than it did during the original training period. It is much easier to condition again, after extinction, than it was in the first place.

In his work on extinction and spontaneous recovery, Bouton (1993, 1994) showed that what occurs during extinction is not the forgetting of old learning, but rather the overlayering of old learning by new learning. The new learning that occurs during extinction is that the CS (say, the tone) does *not* signal that the UCS (say, the food) will occur. This new learning interferes with the previous classically conditioned response. Thus, according to Bouton's work, if Little Albert's fear of rats had been extinguished (that is, if the rat had been presented without the loud noise), it is not that Albert's association between the rat and the noise would have disappeared, but rather that new learning would have occurred "on top of" his previous learning.

GENERALIZATION AND DISCRIMINATION IN CLASSICAL CONDITIONING: SEEN ONE, SEEN 'EM ALL?

Watson and Raynor wrote that, five days after the conditioning of Little Albert, a rabbit, a dog, a fur coat, cotton, and a Santa Claus mask all elicited the conditioned response of fear. This is an example of **stimulus generalization**, a tendency for the conditioned response to be elicited by neutral stimuli that are like, but not identical to, the conditioned stimulus; in other words, the response *generalizes* to similar stimuli. Moreover, because of a *generalization gradient*, the more closely the new stimulus resembles the original CS, the stronger the response. Stimulus generalization can be helpful for survival because often a dangerous stimulus may not occur in exactly the same form the next time. Without stimulus generalization, we might not know to be afraid of lions as well as tigers.

In addition to stimulus generalization, organisms are also able to distinguish, or discriminate, among stimuli similar to the CS and to respond only to actual conditioned stimuli; this ability is called **stimulus discrimination**. Stimulus discrimination can be extremely helpful for survival; consider that one type of mushroom may be poisonous, but another type is food. Should Albert have been shown a pile of cotton balls without a loud noise occurring (but continued to be presented with a rat paired with the loud noise), only the rat would elicit fear. Albert would have been able to discriminate between the two similar stimuli.

COGNITION AND THE CONDITIONED STIMULUS.

Although strict behaviorists might not agree that thoughts play a role in classical conditioning, research suggests otherwise (see Chapter 1 for an explanation of behaviorism). The context in which classical conditioning occurs and the expectations that arise following classical conditioning influence the learning (Hollis, 1997). For example, Rescorla (1967) presented rats with a tone (CS) immediately before delivering a shock (UCS); these rats quickly learned a fear response to the tone. However, another group of rats heard the tone and were shocked, but sometimes the tone was presented *after* the shock. As Pavlov had found years before, presenting the CS after the UCS does not produce conditioning: This group did not come to fear the tone. Apparently, the CS provides information by signaling the upcoming UCS (and therefore UCR), and conditioning occurs because the animal is learning that relationship: The CS is a signal that the UCS will occur.

Kamin (1969) provided more evidence that mental processes lie between stimulus and response during conditioning. He conditioned rats by pairing a tone with a brief shock; the rats developed a conditioned fear response to the tone. But when he added a second CS by turning on a light with the tone, the rats did not develop a conditioned fear response to the light alone. Kamin hypothesized that the original pairing of tone and shock was blocking new learning. The light did not add new information and was therefore of no consequence and not worth their attention. The noise was enough of a signal, and the rats didn't seem to view the light as a signal. Thus, Kamin concluded that classical conditioning takes place only if the pairing of CS and UCS provides useful information about the likelihood of occurrence of the UCS.

In addition, a mental image of an object—what you see in your "mind's eye" when you imagine something—can play a role in classical conditioning, either as a CS or a

Stimulus generalization: A tendency for the CR to be elicited by neutral stimuli that are like, but not identical to, the CS; in other words, the response *generalizes* to similar stimuli.

Stimulus discrimination: The ability to distinguish among similar conditioned stimuli and to respond only to actual conditioned stimuli.

UCS. For instance, imagining food can lead to salivation in humans (see Dadds et al., 1997 for a review).

DISSECTING CONDITIONING: BRAIN MECHANISMS. Classical conditioning has at least three distinct components; we know this because it has been shown that three different brain processes are involved. LeDoux (1995, 1996; also Beggs et al., 1999) and his colleagues have studied conditioned fear in detail and established that registration of the stimulus, the production of the response, and the connection between the two rely on distinct parts of the brain. Consider the case of a driver who has been honked at by a huge truck as it roars by and has barely missed being crushed; the driver experienced fear. When later hearing the sound of a horn and seeing a truck drive by, the images and sounds are registered in the visual and the auditory cortex. A specific part of the amygdala (see Figure 5.5) processes the sound and sight that triggers the conditioned fear. In experimental studies with animals, it has been shown that if this particular structure is removed, animals cannot learn that a shock will soon follow a tone.

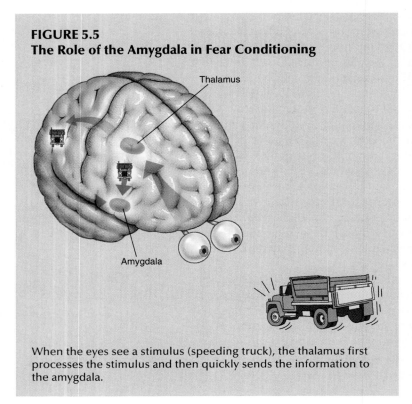

FIGURE 5.5
The Role of the Amygdala in Fear Conditioning

Thalamus

Amygdala

When the eyes see a stimulus (speeding truck), the thalamus first processes the stimulus and then quickly sends the information to the amygdala.

Another part of the amygdala, the central nucleus, leads to the behaviors that express conditioned fear, for example, wincing when an eighteen-wheeler blasts its horn. When this part of the amygdala is removed, the movements, autonomic responses, and other signs of fear are not produced.

Conditioning causes brain cells that register the stimulus (in the case of the honking truck, cells in the auditory cortex in the temporal lobe) to fire in tandem with cells in the amygdala that produce the fear response. Activity in the two sets of neurons becomes hooked together, so that whenever the stimulus occurs, the response is automatic. A crucial finding is that this linked activity never disappears entirely: Even after conditioning has been extinguished, linked activity remains, making it very easy for an animal to relearn a conditioned response. Indeed, extinction depends on the active suppression of the response, which is accomplished in part by the frontal lobe's inhibition of the amygdala (LeDoux, 1995, 1996).

Classical Conditioning Applied

If the investigation of classical conditioning had ended with the study of dogs' salivation, the great psychological importance of this kind of learning might not have been recognized. But classical conditioning showed that emotional responses, such as the fear response, can be conditioned, and emotional responses exert a powerful effect on people's lives. If a friend slaps you hard on the back every time you meet him, you are likely to wince even as he lifts his arm to begin his greeting, and in time classical conditioning affects how you feel about him. Classical conditioning can play a role in the effectiveness of medicines, affect your immune system, and influence other aspects of health and illness (as you will see in Chapter 12). It silently, even without our awareness, contributes to our feelings about events and objects (Bunce et al., 1999), even our sexual interests (Lalumiere & Quinsey, 1998).

Classical conditioning plays a role in deaths caused by drug overdoses. A user who generally takes a drug in a particular setting—the bathroom, say—develops a conditioned response to that place (Siegel, 1988). Here's what happens. Because of classical conditioning, as soon as the user walks into the bathroom, his or her body begins to compensate for the influx of drug that is soon to come. This conditioned response is the body's attempt to counteract, or dampen, the effect of the drug. When the user takes the drug in a new setting, perhaps a friend's living room, this conditioned response does not occur. Because there is no conditioned response to the new setting, the user's body does not try to counteract the effect of the drug. The net result is a higher effective dose of the drug than the user can tolerate, leading to an overdose. Similarly, classical conditioning also helps explain why people addicted to cocaine get drug cravings merely from handling money (Hamilton et al., 1998). Part of the experience of using cocaine is buying it, often just before using it. Thus, handling money becomes a CS. In the same way, among cigarette smokers certain environmental stimuli can elicit a desire for a cigarette (Lazev et al., 1999). So, classical conditioning explains why some smokers automatically reach for a cigarette when they get a phone call or have a cup of coffee, often without realizing what is happening.

Classical conditioning also serves as the basis for a number of therapy techniques based on learning principles, including *systematic desensitization,* which is used to treat phobias (this therapeutic technique and others are discussed in more detail in Chapter 14). Systematic desensitization is the structured and repeated presentation of a feared conditioned stimulus in circumstances designed to reduce anxiety. Systematic desensitization works to extinguish this response by teaching people to be relaxed in the presence of the feared object or situation, such as an elevator for those with an elevator phobia. With systematic desensitization, the CS no longer elicits the CR of fear; extinction has occurred.

Watson formalized the use of behavioral principles when he took a job in advertising. The use of "sex appeal" to sell products stems from Watson's ideas. Sex isn't the only unconditioned stimulus that can work to produce a desired response; Razran (1940) did a study showing that political slogans (CS) paired with the eating of food (UCS) led people to view those slogans favorably. Classical conditioning continues to be used in advertising to promote consumers' positive attitudes about a product (Grossman & Till, 1998; Kim et al., 1998; Till & Priluck, 2000). And, as shown in Figure 5.6, classical conditioning can be used to train animals. Two special cases of the application of classical conditioning are taste aversion and the conditioning of the immune system.

FIGURE 5.6
Classically Conditioned Animal Training

Dogs learn not to go beyond the boundary of an "invisible fence" because the fence delivers a mild shock through their collars. The boundary marker (shown to them by their owners) is the CS, the shock (when they attempt to cross the boundary) is the UCS, and fear is the conditioned emotional response.

TASTE AVERSION. When animals or people find a particular food or taste extremely unpleasant (and try to avoid it), they may have a **food** or **taste aversion.** This type of classical conditioning usually involves learning after only a single experience of the CS–UCS pairing. The UCS is the nausea- or vomiting-inducing agent, and the CS is a previously neutral stimulus that was paired with it, such as the sight or smell of food. The UCR is nausea or vomiting, and so is the CR.

If you have ever had food poisoning, you may have developed a classically conditioned food aversion. A likely scenario is that the food that made you sick had some unhealthy and unwanted ingredient, such as *salmonella* bacteria. The bacteria are the UCS, and the ensuing nausea and vomiting are the UCR. If the *salmonella* was in your dinner of broiled trout, trout might become a CS for you; whenever you eat it (or perhaps another fish similarly prepared), you become nauseated (the CR). Rather than put yourself through this experience, you are likely to avoid eating broiled trout, and a food aversion is born.

Food aversion (taste aversion): A classically conditioned avoidance of a certain food or taste.

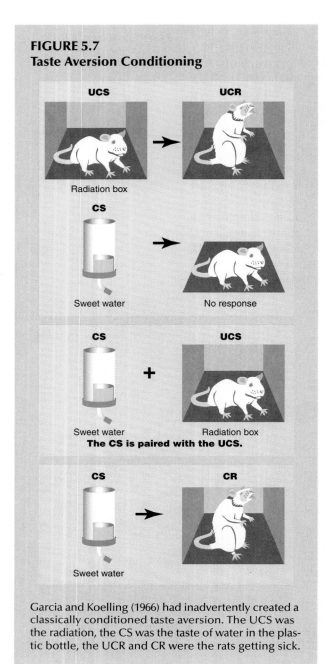

FIGURE 5.7
Taste Aversion Conditioning

UCS — Radiation box → UCR

CS — Sweet water → No response

CS — Sweet water + UCS — Radiation box
The CS is paired with the UCS.

CS — Sweet water → CR

Garcia and Koelling (1966) had inadvertently created a classically conditioned taste aversion. The UCS was the radiation, the CS was the taste of water in the plastic bottle, the UCR and CR were the rats getting sick.

Garcia and Koelling (1966) accidentally discovered the occurrence of taste aversion when looking at the effects of radiation on rats. The rats were exposed to high enough doses of radiation that they became sick. The researchers noticed that the rats drank less water from the plastic water bottle in the radiation chamber than from the glass water bottle in their "home" cage. Although this preference could have been due to many factors, it turned out that the water in the plastic bottle had a slightly different taste, thanks to the plastic, than the water in the glass bottle.

After uncovering this first finding, the researchers shifted their focus to discover *why* the rats drank less from the plastic than the glass bottle. Was it because the taste of the water in the plastic bottle had become associated, and thus conditioned, to the radiation that made the rats sick? If so, then the radiation was the UCS, the taste of the water from the plastic bottle the CS, and getting sick both the UCR and the CR. They tested this hypothesis and found that it was correct: The taste of water in the plastic bottle was a CS, causing the CR of the rats getting sick (see Figure 5.7). But this wasn't the surprise. The surprise was that the rats avoided the water even if the nausea didn't occur until several hours after the plastic-tainted water was presented. Garcia's research showed that, at least in this case, the UCS doesn't need to come immediately after the CS.

The Garcia research uncovered another important fact. Previously, researchers believed that conditioning could be created using just about any stimulus. As it happened, however, while the rats became sickened by different flavors of water that were presented in subsequent trials, they did not get sick from repeated pairings of other types of stimuli, such as lights, buzzers, or shocks, with the radiation (or sickness-inducing drugs). No matter how the researchers manipulated these visual and auditory stimuli, they could not elicit a conditioned response of nausea. Thus, not all stimuli can be conditioned to elicit a given response.

Garcia's findings stirred considerable controversy because they described exceptions to the "rules" of classical conditioning. Taste aversion can lead to a more generalized response; just the sight of the food can elicit a conditioned response. President Ulysses S. Grant, a soldier who had seen the carnage of the Civil War, became nauseated at just the sight of rare meat (Seuling, 1978). Classically conditioned taste aversion is the mechanism behind the use of Antabuse to treat alcoholism. Antabuse is a medicine that causes violent nausea and vomiting when mixed with alcohol. If an alcoholic took Antabuse and then drank, he or she would throw up and, if the drug was successful in its larger purpose, develop a taste aversion to alcohol. Unfortunately, Antabuse has not been as successful as was originally hoped; those who were having difficulty refraining from drinking tended to stop taking their Antabuse so that they could drink without getting sick. If Antabuse is used consistently, it does decrease how often alcoholics drink, but it does not increase the likelihood of total abstinence (Fuller et al., 1986; Sereny et al., 1986). It is the rare person who is willing to take Antabuse as recommended (Brubaker et al., 1987); married alcoholics whose spouses help ensure that Antabuse is taken at regular intervals have the best success with it (Azrin et al., 1982).

Classical conditioning is adaptive, whether it involves an animal's (including a human's) ability to learn which foods are poisonous, or which animals or objects in the environment (such as predators or guns) to fear and avoid. The more readily an organism learns these associations, the more likely that organism (or that species) will survive. Learned food aversions based on one exposure can be particularly adaptive: Animals who readily learn what not to eat will probably live longer and have more young.

CONDITIONING THE IMMUNE SYSTEM. Let's suppose you once worked day and night for a week, hardly taking the time to sleep or eat, and so severely weakened your immune system that you became very sick. During that exhausting work-filled week, you spent all your waking hours with a laptop computer on your bed, which has a bright red bedspread. Do you think that, after your recovery, simply sitting on the bedspread could cause your immune system to weaken? Ader and his colleagues (Ader, 1976; Ader & Cohen, 1975) have shown that this kind of conditioning does in fact happen in rats. Ader and Cohen paired saccharin-flavored water with injections of cyclophosphamide, a drug given to organ transplant donors that suppresses the immune system and has a side effect of nausea. Ader had intended to use this drug not for its immune-suppressing qualities, but as a way to induce nausea in a study of taste aversion. He wanted to see how long the taste aversion would last once injections of cyclophosphamide stopped. But a few rats died on day 45 of the experiment, and more died over the next several days. Ader was confused; he had done similar experiments before with a different nausea-inducing drug and none of his animals had died. He eventually showed that the taste of the sweetened water was triggering not just the nausea, but a suppression of the immune system (as the actual drug would do), causing the eventual death of the rodents. Each time the rats drank the sweetened water, their immune systems were weakened—even without the immune-suppressing drug! The taste of the saccharine-sweetened water was acting as a CS and was in essence a **placebo,** an inert substance that nevertheless seems to have medicinal effects. The rats' bodies responded to the CS as if it were cyclophosphamide.

Ader's accidental discovery and his follow-up studies were noteworthy for two reasons: First, they showed that the placebo effect could be induced in animals, not just humans; second, they showed that the organism doesn't have to believe that the placebo has medicinal properties in order to produce a placebo response. Although Ader and Cohen could not ask the rats what they believed would happen when drinking sweet water, we have no reason to think that they "believed" it would impair their immune systems (Dienstfrey, 1991). Ader and Cohen have reported a number of follow-up studies, all trying to rule out other explanations of their results, and their hypothesis about the conditioning of the immune system has stood up well. Indeed, another study with rats showed that the immune response could actually be boosted by conditioning (Gorcynski, cited in Dienstfrey, 1991). There is evidence that the placebo response may be a conditioned immune response that occurs in humans (Voudouris et al., 1985).

LOOKING AT LEVELS

Sick at the Thought of Chemotherapy

Like most psychological phenomena, classical conditioning provides an opportunity to understand how many events at the different levels of analysis affect one another in various organisms, including Pavlov's dogs and Ader's rats. The interplay of events at the levels of the brain, individual, and group are easy to understand even in humans.

Cancer patients undergoing chemotherapy often experience intense nausea and vomiting as side effects of the treatment. But some patients develop anticipatory nausea, a classically conditioned response to chemotherapy triggered by a previously neutral CS (Burish & Carey, 1986; Carey & Burish, 1988; Davey, 1992). Such a stimulus might be as innocuous as a florist's shop seen en route to the hospital. For others

undergoing chemotherapy, just thinking about the hospital where the treatment is received can produce nausea (Redd et al., 1993).

What is happening? At the level of the brain, the activity of neurons that feed into the patient's immune and autonomic nervous systems, stimulated by the UCS of the chemotherapeutic drugs that induce the UCR and CR of nausea, becomes paired with the activity of neurons that register certain sights and sounds, for example the CS of the florist shop. After enough such pairings, the two groups of neurons become functionally connected, and activity in one group triggers activity in the other.

In addition, some patients are more likely than others to develop anticipatory nausea. Some people are generally more autonomically reactive than others; that is, they have a tendency toward a stronger autonomic response to given levels of stimulation. Such autonomically reactive people are more likely to develop anticipatory nausea (Kvale & Hugdahl, 1994). At the level of the person, such adverse effects can lead to a sense of helplessness and can cause some chemotherapy patients to stop the treatment altogether (Siegel & Longo, 1981). Fortunately, behavioral interventions such as relaxation training can be helpful in controlling anticipatory nausea, as can newer antinausea medications (Vasterling et al., 1993).

At the level of the group, chemotherapy involves a social component. It is administered by medical staff, in the social setting of a hospital or clinic, and the patient may be escorted to treatment by a friend or family member. Those involved in the chemotherapy treatment can become the CS, leading a patient to become nauseated at the sight of a particular nurse who always administers the treatment (Montgomery & Bovbjerg, 1997). Events at these levels interact. Autonomic reactivity influences the likelihood of developing anticipatory nausea, which can create yet another challenge for chemotherapy patients, affecting how they see the illness and their ability to fight it, and how they deal with medical staff, family, and friends. Moreover, the social interaction of being taught behavioral interventions for the anticipatory nausea (such as relaxation techniques) can influence events at the level of the brain and the person by giving the patient some sense of control over the nausea.

CONSOLIDATE!

▶ **1. What is classical conditioning? How was it discovered?** Ivan Pavlov discovered classical conditioning through his studies of dogs' salivation. This phenomenon involves the pairing of a conditioned stimulus (CS, such as a tone) with an unconditioned stimulus (UCS, such as food). The UCS reflexively elicits an unconditioned response (UCR, such as salivation), and with repeated UCS–CS pairings, the CS will come to elicit a conditioned response (CR, salivation).

▶ **2. How are conditioned responses eliminated?** Extinction, the "unpairing" of the CS and UCS, is achieved by repeatedly presenting the CS without the UCS. If extinction is followed by a rest period, the CS may again elicit the classically conditioned response; this is known as spontaneous recovery. In stimulus generalization, a similar but nonidentical stimulus elicits the CR. In stimulus discrimination, the organism learns to distinguish among similar stimuli so that only a particular stimulus will elicit the CR.

▶ **3. What are common examples of classical conditioning in daily life?** Classical conditioning is used in advertising, behavior therapy, and animal training, and is the mechanism underlying food and taste aversion and conditioned immune responses (such as can occur with a placebo effect).

OPERANT CONDITIONING

Paula came to have an emotionally painful response to Chris's tone of voice through the effects of classical conditioning. However, the destructive pattern of interaction between these two people doesn't end there. Paula becomes tense and angry. She yells; he yells. But they want to improve their relationship, so Chris agrees to try not to use that tone of voice or to yell at her, and Paula also agrees to try not to yell. This sounds great in theory, but the reality is not that easy. Yelling is a habit Paula and Chris have learned, and changing habits is hard. If they are not to yell at each other when they are angry or annoyed, they must learn new behaviors, new ways of communicating with each other.

Operant conditioning: The process by which a behavior becomes associated with its consequences.

In contrast to Paula and Chris's explosive style, Isabel and Tony's interactions with each other are calmer and more constructive. When they are angry or annoyed, they try to verbalize their anger constructively, talking it through until they reach some understanding or compromise. While they hash out a disagreement, each tries not to say something rash or critical that might be hurtful or regretted later. How can Paula and Chris learn to interact more as Isabel and Tony do? The answer might lie with another kind of learning, **operant conditioning,** the process whereby a behavior becomes associated with its consequences.

► 1. What is operant conditioning? How does it occur?

► 2. What is the difference between reinforcement and punishment?

► 3. How are complex behaviors learned? How are these new behaviors maintained?

► 4. What changes occur in the brain during operant conditioning?

The Roots of Operant Conditioning: Its Discovery and How It Works

If your behavior is followed by a positive consequence, you are more likely to repeat the act in the future; if it is followed by a negative consequence, you are less likely to repeat it. This observation underlies the mechanism of operant conditioning. Unlike classical conditioning, in which the organism is largely passive, operant conditioning requires the organism to "operate" in the world, to *do* something. Whereas classical conditioning usually involves involuntary reflexes, operant conditioning usually involves voluntary, nonreflexive behavior.

Isabel and Tony have apparently learned to talk about their differences relatively calmly and without anger, rather than yelling at each other at the first sign of tension. They learned this more peaceful behavior because when they calmly talked about their disagreements, the conversations had satisfying conclusions: no fights, no tears, no sulks. Because of this positive outcome, they are more likely to express their concerns calmly when they disagree.

THORNDIKE'S PUZZLE BOX. At about the same time that Pavlov was working with his dogs, American psychologist Edward L. Thorndike (1874–1949) was investigating a different kind of learning with cats. Thorndike created a puzzle box, a cage with a latched door that a cat could open by pressing on a pedal inside the cage (see Figure 5.8); food was placed outside the cage door. Although the cat took a while to get around to pressing the pedal, once it did (and the door opened), the cat was quicker to press the pedal in its subsequent

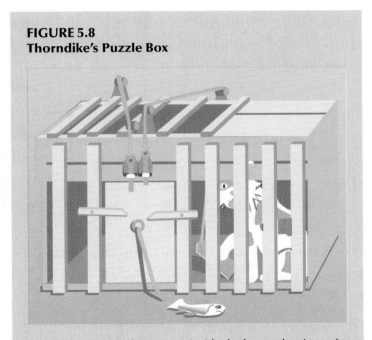

**FIGURE 5.8
Thorndike's Puzzle Box**

Thorndike placed a hungry cat inside the box and a piece of fish just outside the door in the cat's sight. The cat tried to get out of the box to the fish by emitting many behaviors, but only pressing the pedal would open the door. Eventually the cat pressed the pedal and the door opened. When the cat was put back inside the box, it pressed the pedal more quickly, improving each time.

FIGURE 5.9
The Phases of Operant Conditioning

Stimulus	Response	Consequence
Pedal	Pushing pedal	Food

Unlike classical conditioning, operant conditioning requires the organism to emit the desired behavior (the response). That behavior is then followed by positive or negative consequences.

sessions in the box: It had learned that pressing the pedal opened the door and enabled it to get the food (see Figure 5.9). Thorndike called this type of learning "trial-and-error learning." His finding led to his famous formulation of the **Law of Effect** (Thorndike, 1927), which lies at the heart of operant conditioning: Actions that subsequently lead to a "satisfying state of affairs" are more likely to be repeated (1933/1949, p. 14).

THE SKINNER BOX. B. F. Skinner (1904–1990), the twentieth century's foremost proponent of behaviorism, is important in the history of psychology not only because he most fully developed the concept of operant conditioning, but also because he showed how conditioning could explain much of our daily behavior. Working mostly with pigeons, he developed an apparatus to minimize his handling of the birds, which is now often referred to as a Skinner box. The box (see Figure 5.10) could both feed the animals and record the frequency of their responses, making it easy to quantify the responses (this enormously helpful feature was in fact an unintended bonus of the box's design; Skinner, 1956). If a rat is put in a Skinner box, it learns to associate pressing the lever or bar with the likelihood of a food pellet's appearing. Here, the lever is the stimulus, pressing the lever is the response, or behavior, and receiving the food pellet is the consequence.

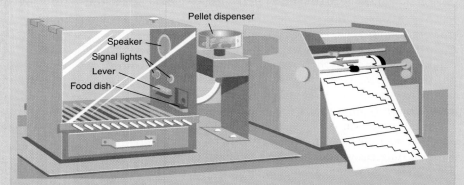

FIGURE 5.10
Skinner Box and Cumulative Recorder

Pellet dispenser
Speaker
Signal lights
Lever
Food dish

In a Skinner box, a hungry rat presses a lever (or pigeons peck a key). As with Thorndike's cat, the rat will emit random behaviors, eventually pressing the lever, causing a food pellet (reinforcement) to come down the chute into the food dish, increasing the likelihood of the response in the future. She presses the lever again, and another food pellet appears. She presses the lever (and eats) more frequently—she has learned that pressing the lever will be followed by the appearance of a food pellet. On the outside of the box is a device that records each lever press and the time interval between presses.

Law of Effect: Actions that subsequently lead to a "satisfying state of affairs" are more likely to be repeated.

Reinforcement: The process by which consequences lead to an increase in the likelihood that the response will occur again.

Principles of Operant Conditioning

Operant conditioning involves an association between a stimulus, the response to the stimulus (a behavior), and its consequence. (In classical conditioning, the association is between a neutral stimulus and a reflexive behavior.) With the rat, the bar or lever is the stimulus, pressing the bar is the behavior (or response to the stimulus), and the delivery of the food pellet is the consequence. Operant conditioning relies on **reinforcement,** the process by which consequences lead to an increase in the likelihood that the response will occur again. To be most effective, the reinforcement should be contingent on a desired response. Not surprisingly, this relationship between the response and the consequence is called **response contingency**; it occurs when a consequence is dependent on the organism's emitting the desired behavior.

A **reinforcer** is any object or event that comes after the desired response and strengthens the likelihood of its recurrence. In Thorndike's puzzle box and in the Skinner box, the reinforcer, or consequence, is food. Which reinforcer works best? The answer to this question is tricky: What one person considers a "reward" might leave another person cold. Reinforcement therefore is in the eyes of the recipient. For instance, for one person, a night at the ballet might be a wonderful reinforcer for doing well on a test. To another, a night at the ballet might seem like punishment. Parents who give stickers to their child for good behavior might conclude that behavioral programs don't work if that child makes no effort to win them. They'd be wrong: The problem is that their child doesn't view stickers as a reward. The parents simply need to find a reinforcer that *will* work for their child. For instance, when we were toilet training our children, we used reinforcers whenever they tried to use the potty. We had asked each child to name a reinforcer, and one of our children requested black olives. This is a reminder that the proof is in the pudding—the degree to which an object or event is a reinforcer is determined by its effect on the individual organism. Just calling something a reinforcer doesn't make it so.

What's the connection with Paula and Chris? Each responded to the other's negative behavior with negative behavior of his or her own, as can happen in couples (Weiss & Heyman, 1990). Learning to communicate without yelling will take some work, but if they reinforce each other for calmer, lowered voices, they will increase the likelihood of success. Of course, this assumes that the "reward" each of them receives is in fact a reinforcer. Paula may or may not want to ask Chris what reinforcement he wants. If she tries to guess, she might use affection as a reinforcer, perhaps smiling warmly, giving him a kiss, or saying something like, "Thanks, Chris, for not speaking to me in that tone of voice I dislike. I appreciate that you're making the effort, and it makes it much easier for me to hear what you're trying to say." However, she shouldn't assume that she is using the right reinforcer for him—Chris might find such a speech patronizing. To find out, she will need to see whether the desired behavior increases.

REINFORCEMENT: GETTING YOUR JUST DESSERTS.
There are two types of reinforcement, positive and negative. In **positive reinforcement**, a desired reinforcer is presented after a response, thereby increasing the likelihood of a recurrence of that response. The food for Thorndike's cat and black olives for our toddler are examples of positive reinforcement. Food is the usual positive reinforcer for animals; for humans, toys, money, and intangibles such as praise and attention can also be positive reinforcers. Sometimes even "bad attention," such as a scolding, can be a positive reinforcer if the only time a child receives any attention at all is when he or she misbehaves. Again, reinforcement is particular to the individual.

In contrast, **negative reinforcement** is the *removal* of an unpleasant event or circumstance following a desired behavior, thereby increasing the probability of the behavior's occurring again. If a rat is being mildly shocked in its cage, and the shocks stop when it presses a bar, then bar pressing is negatively reinforced. A teacher who gives a "time out" to a continually disruptive child may inadvertently be negatively reinforcing the disruptive behavior if the child views the time out as relief from having to sit at a desk and do schoolwork (Piazza et al., 1998). Imagine this common scenario: A child whines to get his way, his father gives in to the whining, the child stops whining. What

Response contingency: The relationship that occurs when a consequence is dependent on the organism's emitting the desired behavior.

Reinforcer: Any object or event that follows the desired response and changes the likelihood of the recurrence of that response.

Positive reinforcement: Occurs when a desired reinforcer is presented after a response, thereby increasing the likelihood of a recurrence of that response.

Negative reinforcement: Occurs when an unpleasant event or circumstance is removed following a desired behavior, thereby increasing the probability of the behavior's occurring again.

On a very hot day, going to an air-conditioned restaurant for lunch is negative reinforcement: You escape the heat by going to that restaurant and are thus reinforced for doing so. After this experience, you will be more likely to go to an air-conditioned restaurant again on another very hot day.

has happened? The aversive stimulus—the whining—has been removed, and so the father has been negatively reinforced for his behavior of giving in to the child. Dad is then more likely to give in the next time his child whines. This principle is at work when people use substances, such as alcohol, to decrease their anxiety (Hohlstein et al., 1998; Samoluk & Stewart, 1998). Both positive and negative reinforcement are described as reinforcing because they *increase* the likelihood of a behavior's recurring.

PUNISHMENT. A **punishment** is an unpleasant event that occurs as a consequence of a behavior. Punishment *decreases* the probability of the recurrence of a behavior, in contrast to reinforcement (both positive and negative), which *increases* the likelihood of recurrence. Although punishment is commonly confused with negative reinforcement, they are not the same; whereas punishment decreases the probability of a recurrence of a behavior, negative reinforcement increases the probability by removing an unpleasant consequence of the behavior (see Table 5.1).

TABLE 5.1

The Effects of Reinforcement and Punishment

Operant conditioning can be implemented with positive reinforcement, negative reinforcement, and punishment. In the examples below, the targeted behavior is Ben's playing the computer game *Spelling Blizzard*. Notice the effect that both types of reinforcement and punishment are likely to have on his game playing.

CONSEQUENCE	DEFINITION	EXAMPLE
Positive Reinforcement	The presentation of a desired reinforcer after a response, *increasing* the likelihood of a recurrence of that response.	After Ben plays the computer game *Spelling Blizzard*, his mother gives him something that he likes (such as praise or a treat). This increases the probability that Ben will play *Spelling Blizzard* again.
Negative Reinforcement	The removal of an unpleasant event after a response, *increasing* the likelihood of a recurrence of that response.	Ben's mother nags him to play *Spelling Blizzard* until he actually does so, at which point she stops nagging. This increases the probability that Ben will play *Spelling Blizzard* again.
Punishment	The occurrence of an unpleasant event as a consequence of a response, *decreasing* the likelihood of a recurrence of that response. The disagreeable consequence can be either the addition of something noxious or the removal of something pleasant.	After Ben refuses to play *Spelling Blizzard*, his mother punishes him by either doing something unpleasant (such as making him clean the bathroom) or taking away something he likes (such as denying TV privileges). Both of her actions decrease the probability that Ben will refuse again.

Punishment is most effective if it has three characteristics. First, punishment should be swift, occurring immediately after the undesired behavior. The old threat "Wait till you get home!" undermines the effectiveness of the punishment. Second, punishment must be consistent. The undesired behavior must be punished each and every time it occurs. If the behavior is punished only sporadically, the person or animal doesn't effectively learn that the behavior will be followed by punishment, and so doesn't decrease frequency of the behavior as consistently. Finally, the punishment should be sufficiently aversive without being overly aversive. If a child doesn't mind being alone in her room, then being sent there for pushing her brother won't be a very effective punishment; as with reinforcement, punishment is in the eye of the receiver.

We must make several cautionary points about the use of punishment. First, although punishment may decrease the frequency of a behavior, it doesn't eliminate

Punishment: An unpleasant event that occurs as a consequence of a behavior, thereby decreasing the probability of the recurrence of the behavior.

the capacity to engage in that behavior. Your little sister may learn not to push you because your mother will punish her, but she may continue to push her classmates at school because the behavior has not been punished in that context. She has learned not to push when she will be punished for it. Moreover, sometimes people are able to avoid punishment, but continue to exhibit the response. Suppose your little sister figured out that if she hit you, but then apologized, she would not get punished. This kind of learning is called **avoidance learning;** an organism learns to avoid an unpleasant consequence by emitting a particular response—in this case, apologizing. Whereas classically conditioned avoidance learning is based on previous experience with an unpleasant stimulus (US), operantly conditioned avoidance learning is based on previous experience with an unpleasant consequence.

Second, physical punishment, such as a spanking, may actually increase aggressive behavior in the person on the receiving end. Although punishment provides an opportunity for operant learning, seeing others use physical violence also creates an opportunity for observational learning—learning acquired by watching the behavior of others. Observational learning would account for the finding that abusive parents (and physically aggressive juvenile delinquents) tend to come from abusive families (Straus & Gelles, 1980; Straus & McCord, 1998).

A third problem created by punishment is that, through classical conditioning, the one being punished may come to fear the one doing the punishing. This may happen even if the punishment is infrequent. If the punishment is severe, a single instance may be enough for the person being punished to learn to live in fear of the punisher. Constantly living in fear can make people and animals chronically stressed, lead to depression, and contribute to the development of other mental and physical disorders.

Punishment alone hasn't been found to be as effective as punishment used in combination with reinforcement. This is because punishment doesn't convey information about what behavior should be exhibited in place of the undesired, punished behavior. Consider a preschool-age boy who draws on the wall. You don't want him to ruin the wallpaper so you punish him, and he learns not draw on the wall. But now when he's feeling creative, he draws on the floor or the door instead. However, if you punish him for wall- or floor-drawing *and then* provide him with paper and reinforce him for drawing on the paper, he is more likely to be artistically creative without inviting punishment. Because of the disadvantages of punishment, many training programs for parents emphasize positive reinforcement for good behavior; if children don't feel their parents are noticing and appreciating their efforts at good behavior, the incentive to keep it up may diminish.

PRIMARY AND SECONDARY REINFORCERS.
There are different levels of reinforcers: **Primary reinforcers** are events or objects that are inherently reinforcing (such as food, water, or relief from pain). **Secondary reinforcers,** such as attention, praise, money, good grades, or a promotion, are learned reinforcers and do not inherently satisfy a physical need. The theme park Sea World uses food as a primary reinforcer for its dolphins. It also uses secondary reinforcers such as touching and squirting the dolphins' faces with water. Secondary reinforcers are generally not instinctually satisfying.

Behavior modification is a technique that brings about therapeutic change in behavior through the use of secondary reinforcers. Programs involving mentally retarded children and adults, psychiatric patients, and prisoners have made use of secondary reinforcement. Participants in such programs earn tokens that can be

Simply punishing someone does not provide that person with appropriate alternative behaviors. This mother clearly stated an appropriate alternative to biting someone when angry—using words to express the feeling.

Avoidance learning: In operant conditioning, the process by which an organism learns to avoid an unpleasant consequence by emitting a particular response.

Primary reinforcer: An event or object that is inherently reinforcing, such as food, water, or relief from pain.

Secondary reinforcer: An event or object that does not inherently satisfy a physical need, such as attention, praise, money, good grades, or a promotion.

Behavior modification: A technique that brings about therapeutic change in behavior through the use of secondary reinforcers.

traded for candy or for privileges such as going out for a walk or watching a particular television show. Behavior modification techniques using secondary reinforcement have also been used in the workplace; when employees received bonus vouchers for arriving at work on time, management found a significant reduction in tardiness (Hermann et al., 1973).

An unusual use of behavior modification with secondary reinforcers was undertaken by researchers in the rural Philippines who wanted to improve nutrition among poor children (Guthrie et al., 1982). The study was designed to discover whether reinforcement would be more beneficial than simply providing mothers with information about health and nutritional care for children. All the mothers were given appropriate information. Then the health clinic provided reinforcement in various forms for increases in the children's heights and weights. Three different villages participated in the study. In one, the reinforcement was a ticket in a clinic lottery in which the prize was food; the reinforcer used in the second village was a photograph of the child. The third village was a control group, and these people received no reinforcement for height or weight gains. One year later, children in the two villages that received reinforcement had more growth and less malnutrition than those in the third village; no differences were observed between the first and second village.

IMMEDIATE VERSUS DELAYED REINFORCEMENT. The interval of time between behavior and its consequence can affect operant conditioning. In the Skinner box, for instance, if the rat receives a food pellet immediately after pressing the bar, it is receiving **immediate reinforcement,** reinforcement given immediately after the desired behavior. If the food pellet doesn't appear immediately but comes, say, 30 seconds later, the rat is receiving **delayed reinforcement.** With delayed reinforcement, the rat has some difficulty learning that bar pressing is followed by food. After pressing the bar but before receiving reinforcement, the rat may have sniffed some other section of the cage, scratched its ear, or done any number of things. It would be hard for the rat to "figure out" which behavior had produced the pellet.

One of the ways humans are different from rats is that we can learn effectively even if we receive delayed reinforcement. We work hard to get a promotion or raise, we practice kicking the soccer ball into the goal so that we'll be able to score at the next game, we study hard in college to get into graduate school or land a good job. Walter Mischel and his colleagues (1989) found that among the four-year-olds they studied, those who would forgo a small reward now for a big one tomorrow became more socially competent and were more likely to be high achievers during adolescence.

Choosing a delayed reinforcement over an immediate one has its advantages, but the choice is not necessarily easy. A dieter trying to obtain the delayed reinforcement of looking and feeling better sacrifices immediate reinforcement (ice cream, *now!*) for future personal benefits. But immediate reinforcement can be very powerful, and often difficult to reject in favor of some future good. At some point, the dieter may yield to the satisfaction of eating the ice cream, or even just a normal-size portion of dinner, instead of making yet another sacrifice for the sake of eventual slimness.

Beyond Basic Reinforcement

Operant conditioning can play a powerful role in people's lives. To see how, let's look at ways in which conditioning can be more than simply learning to respond when reinforcement is likely to result.

GENERALIZATION AND DISCRIMINATION IN OPERANT CONDITIONING. Just as in classical conditioning, the abilities to generalize and discriminate occur during operant conditioning, but in relation to responses as well as stimuli. Thus, in operant conditioning, **generalization** is the ability to generalize from the desired response to a similar response. When a child has a runny nose, most parents teach her to wipe her nose on a tissue. She may then generalize the response of wiping her nose and begin to

Immediate reinforcement: Reinforcement given immediately after the desired behavior is exhibited.

Delayed reinforcement: Reinforcement given some period of time after the desired behavior is exhibited.

Generalization: The ability to generalize both to similar stimuli and from the desired response to a similar response.

wipe it on any available soft surface—her sleeve, her parent's shirt, her pillow. Similarly, if Paula or Chris begin to speak calmly to each other all the time, they will have generalized the response of speaking calmly (or at least not yelling) when angry to speaking calmly in all situations.

Discrimination is the ability to distinguish between the desired response (wiping a runny nose on a tissue or handkerchief) and a similar but undesirable one (wiping a runny nose on a shirt sleeve). The child's parents could help her make this discrimination by reinforcing her every time she wipes her nose with tissues or handkerchiefs (making sure they are readily available), and not reinforcing her when she wipes her nose on her sleeve or theirs.

Discrimination depends on the ability to distinguish among the different situations in which a stimulus may occur. Animals can be trained to press a bar to get food only if a tone is sounding, or only if they hear a high tone (not a low or medium tone). A **discriminative stimulus** is the cue that tells the organism whether a specific response will lead to the expected reinforcement. Experienced drivers react to a red light without thinking, automatically putting a foot on the brake pedal. In this situation, the red light is the stimulus, stopping the car is the response, and the reinforcement (negative, in this case) is escaping a dangerous situation. But drivers don't stomp their right feet down if they encounter a red light while walking on the sidewalk. Driving a car is the discriminative stimulus that cues the response to stomp the right foot.

EXTINCTION AND SPONTANEOUS RECOVERY IN OPERANT CONDITIONING: GONE TODAY, BACK TOMORROW.

Have you ever lost money in a vending machine? If so, does this sequence of behaviors sound familiar? You deposit coins in the machine and press the button for your selection because you have learned that the reinforcement (the food) will come down the chute. When you press the button and no food appears, you press the button again. You then have a burst of pressing the button several times (and maybe a few other buttons for good measure), and only after these responses fail to make the machine deliver the goods do you give up. As this example shows, when someone has learned a behavior through operant conditioning (putting money in a vending machine), and the reinforcement stops (the food doesn't appear), initially there is an increase in responding. After this initial burst of behavior, the response fades. This is how **extinction** works in operant conditioning.

As with classical conditioning, the original response isn't lost through extinction; what happens is that new, opposing learning takes place. In the vending machine example, the opposing learning is that dropping coins in the slot does *not* lead to the appearance of food. As with classical conditioning, **spontaneous recovery** occurs: If a break follows extinction, the old behavior will reappear. So if you don't use that vending machine for a month, you might very well put money in it again, expecting it to dispense your bag of chips.

BUILDING COMPLICATED BEHAVIORS: SHAPING UP.

Many complex behaviors are not learned all at one time, but rather are acquired gradually. Moreover, complex behaviors may often be built on previously learned behaviors. How do the animal trainers at Sea World train the dolphins to do a high jump? The dolphins don't naturally do it, so they can't be reinforced for that behavior. Similarly, the tone of voice that Paula finds so upsetting in Chris might be so automatic for him that he isn't even aware of using it. **Shaping** is the gradual process of reinforcing an organism for behavior that gets closer and closer to the behavior you ultimately wish to condition. It is the method that helps train dolphins to do high jumps (see Figure 5.11 on page 184), and it could also train Chris to speak quietly to Paula even when he's angry. It is used when the desired response is not one that the organism would emit in the normal course of events. Shaping must be done in phases, nudging the organism closer and closer to the desired response. In shaping, the final behavior is considered as a series of smaller behaviors, which become increasingly similar to the desired behavior; these smaller behaviors are called **successive approximations.**

Discrimination: The ability to distinguish between the desired response and a similar but undesirable one.

Discriminative stimulus: The cue that tells the organism whether a specific response will lead to the expected reinforcement.

Extinction: In operant conditioning, the fading out of a response following an initial burst of a behavior after the withdrawal of reinforcement.

Spontaneous recovery: In operant conditioning, the process by which an old response reappears if there is a break after extinction.

Shaping: The gradual process of reinforcing an organism for behavior that gets closer to the desired behavior.

Successive approximations: The series of smaller behaviors involved in shaping a complex behavior.

FIGURE 5.11
Shaping Dolphins at Sea World

Training dolphins at Sea World to jump requires a number of phases, each getting closer to the final goal.

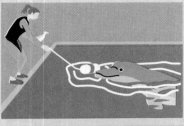

First the dolphin receives reinforcement (a food treat) after touching a target on the surface of the water.

The target is raised slightly out of the water. When the dolphin touches the target, it receives food.

The target continues to be raised until eventually the dolphin's body must come out of the water for it to touch the target. The dolphin receives a treat for doing so.

If Paula were to use shaping to help Chris change his tone of voice, she might start out reinforcing Chris for apologizing when he does use "that tone." With time and effort, Chris will probably catch himself whenever he uses the disturbing tone of voice and repeat Paula's name in a more pleasant way. Paula would then shift the response that she reinforces from his apology after the fact to his catching himself as he's doing it. Finally, she reinforces him only for using her name in the new, calmer way. To shape this new behavior, they might have "practice sessions" in which Chris pretends to be angry. Thus, the two of them would begin shaping the desired behavior—a more pleasant tone of voice—in successive approximations, with each approximation more closely resembling the desired behavior.

REINFORCEMENT SCHEDULES: AN HOURLY OR A PIECE-RATE WAGE? A critical element that can change the frequency of an organism's response is the schedule on which the reinforcement is delivered. Reinforcement can be given every time a desired response occurs, or it can be given less frequently. When an organism is reinforced for each desired response, it is receiving **continuous reinforcement.** When reinforcement does not occur after every response, but only intermittently, the organism is receiving **partial reinforcement.** Initial learning is slower with partial reinforcement than with continuous reinforcement. For this reason, when trying to shape a new behavior, continuous reinforcement is the best method until the desired behavior is stable. Thus, Sea World trainers reward a dolphin every time it touches the target on the surface of the water. An advantage of a partial reinforcement schedule, however, is that it is more resistant to extinction: The organism learns that it won't receive reinforcement after each response so it doesn't stop doing the behavior right away when no reinforcement is forthcoming. Some partial reinforcement schedules, called **interval schedules,** are based on time; reinforcement is given for responses after a specified interval of time. Other schedules, called **ratio schedules,** are based on a specified number of the desired responses; reinforcement is given after that number of responses is emitted.

Continuous reinforcement: Reinforcement given for each desired response.

Partial reinforcement: Reinforcement given only intermittently.

Interval schedule: Partial reinforcement schedule based on time.

Ratio schedule: Partial reinforcement schedule based on a specified number of emitted responses.

On a **fixed interval schedule,** the organism receives reinforcement for a response emitted after a fixed interval of time. In a Skinner box, a rat on a fixed interval schedule of 10 minutes would receive reinforcement for the first bar press that occurs 10 minutes after the previous reinforcement was given, but not during that 10 minutes, regardless of how many times it pressed the bar. The same applies for the next 10-minute interval: The rat would receive a food pellet only for the first bar press after 10 minutes since the last reinforcement. A study break after every hour of studying is reinforcement on a fixed interval schedule. So is a weekly paycheck: No matter how hard you work, you will not get an additional paycheck that week. With animals on a fixed interval schedule, the frequency of desired behavior tends to slow down right after reinforcement and pick up again right before reinforcement. As shown in Figure 5.12, this pattern has a scallop shape on the graph of cumulative responses.

In **variable interval schedules,** the interval is an average over time. If a rat were reinforced for its first response after 8 minutes, then after 12 minutes, then 13 minutes, then 7 minutes, it would be on a variable interval schedule of 10 minutes. If you took a study break after approximately an hour of studying, but sometimes after 45 minutes, sometimes after an hour and 15 minutes, sometimes after half an hour, sometimes after an hour and a half, the average would be every hour, and so you would be on a variable interval 60-minute schedule. In animals, this schedule creates consistent although somewhat slow responding (see Figure 5.12).

Fixed ratio schedules provide reinforcement after a fixed number of responses. If a rat is on a "fixed ratio 10," it receives a food pellet after its tenth bar press, then again after another 10, and so on. Factory piecework is paid on a fixed ratio schedule; for example, in the garment industry, workers may be paid a certain amount for every 10 completed articles of clothing. When responses on this schedule are graphed, they assume a steplike pattern (see Figure 5.12): a high rate of response until reinforcement is delivered, then a lull, followed by a high rate of response until the next reinforcement, and so on. This schedule has a high rate of responding when compared with fixed interval responding. For this reason, piecework can be exhausting, whether the work is inputting data (being paid for every 100 lines of data entered), sewing garments, or assembling machinery. On this schedule, workers have a good reason not to take breaks (they will not be paid for that time), but as people work long hours without breaks, efficiency and accuracy decline (Proctor & Van Zandt, 1994).

Variable ratio schedules present reinforcement at a variable rate. If reinforcement occurs on average after every tenth response, reinforcement could be presented after 5, 18, 4, and 13 responses, or it could presented after 24, 1, 10, and 5 responses. You never really know when the reinforcement will come. This is often called the "gambling reinforcement schedule" because most gambling relies on this type of unpredictable reinforcement. Slot machines hit the jackpot on a variable ratio reinforcement schedule. If you play long enough (and spend enough money), eventually you will win; unfortunately, you might spend years, and tens of thousands of dollars, trying

FIGURE 5.12
Schedules of Reinforcement

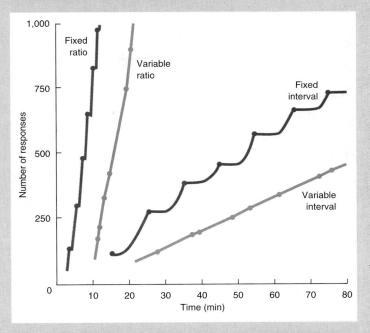

Research findings are mixed with regard to how well rodents' and humans' cumulative frequencies on four schedules of reinforcement correspond. Some studies with humans have found similar patterns of responding (Higgens and Morris, 1984); others have not (Lowe, 1979; Matthews et al., 1977). For both humans and rodents, however, variable reinforcement schedules get a more consistent rate of responding than their fixed reinforcement schedule counterparts.

Fixed interval schedule: Reinforcement schedule in which reinforcement is given for a response emitted after a fixed interval of time.

Variable interval schedule: Reinforcement schedule in which reinforcement is given for a response emitted after a variable interval of time.

Fixed ratio schedule: Reinforcement schedule in which reinforcement is given after a fixed ratio of responses.

Variable ratio schedule: Reinforcement schedule in which reinforcement is given after a variable ratio of responses.

The variable ratio reinforcement schedule, often referred to as the gambling reinforcement schedule, is the most resistant to extinction. If you were playing a slot machine and didn't hit the jackpot, how long would you need to play before you might think there was a problem with the machine?

to hit the jackpot. The variable ratio schedule is the most resistant to extinction (which is part of the reason why some people get hooked on gambling). Because you don't know exactly when you will be reinforced (but expect that eventually reinforcement will come), you keep responding. Animals on this schedule tend to respond frequently, consistently, and without long pauses, and this schedule tends to get the highest response rate; for example, Skinner (1953) found that when he shifted to reinforcing a pigeon on a variable, infrequent schedule, the pigeon continued to peck at a disk 150,000 times without reinforcement, as if still expecting reinforcement! Commission sales jobs are based on the same principle: The hope of an eventual sale (and therefore reinforcement in the form of an eventual commission) keeps salespeople pushing their wares. Returning to our couple, Paula and Chris each held their ground during a disagreement because each had been occasionally reinforced (by "winning" an argument) for doing so. Each had been reinforced on a variable ratio schedule, except that neither knew what the ratio was! This partly explains why their behavior had become so entrenched. In trying to change it, they should probably start out on a continuous reinforcement schedule, then switch to some type of partial reinforcement schedule; realistically, they could probably manage only a variable interval or variable ratio schedule. Of course, a variable ratio schedule would make their new behaviors the most resistant to extinction.

SUPERSTITIOUS BEHAVIOR: ACCIDENTS CAN HAPPEN. Do you ever walk around ladders rather than under them? Do you knock on wood when talking about a positive event? If so, like many people, you occasionally engage in superstitious behaviors. A **superstitious behavior** is a behavior that depends on an accidental association between two things; one isn't a consequence of the other—folks just think it is. It is possible that something bad once happened after a black cat crossed someone's path, but that doesn't mean that the bad thing was a consequence of the black cat's route. The two events might have been correlated, but one did not necessarily cause the other. When one event does not in fact cause another, the increased frequency of response following the first event is considered superstitious behavior.

However, most superstitious behaviors don't arise this way. You probably never had something bad happen after you walked under a ladder—rather, somebody warned you to expect trouble. Traditional behaviorists have a problem explaining how this sort of verbal report can produce new responses to stimuli that were not present when the association took place. Observational learning and cognitive learning, discussed shortly, may both play a role.

The Learning Brain

Until recently, learning theorists ignored the role of the brain in learning, focusing instead on overt behaviors. We now know, however, that an understanding of how the brain works can shed considerable light on this fundamental process (as shown by Beggs et al., 1999, among others). Recent research suggests, for example, that two neurotransmitters, acetylcholine and dopamine, play critical roles in several different aspects of learning.

DIFFERENT PARTS FOR DIFFERENT JOBS. Learning isn't a single process. As discussed earlier, when you walk down a street you don't stomp your right foot every

Superstitious behavior: A behavior that depends on an accidental association between two things, even though one is not a consequence of the other.

time you see a red light. From this we can infer that learning involves at least two major phases. First, we learn to discriminate the proper situation in which to make a response. Here the hippocampus plays an important role. The neurotransmitter acetylcholine (ACh) is key to the functioning of the hippocampus, and scopolamine is an antagonist for this chemical—in other words, it blocks it. Animals that are given scopolamine can't learn which stimuli should be grouped together as a signal for an appropriate response (Mishkin & Appenzeller, 1987).

Second, we learn the stimulus–response association itself. The key to operant conditioning is that specific consequences follow a response. Various parts of the brain produce the neurotransmitter dopamine, but one part—the nucleus accumbens, located behind the amygdala—appears particularly important for reward to be effective. When researchers block dopamine receptors, animals fail to respond to reinforcement, either positive (Spyraki et al., 1982) or negative (Beninger et al., 1980). Studies show, for example, that animals trained to press a lever to get a squirt of a dopamine agonist (which causes the production of dopamine) into their veins will work hard to obtain such reinforcement (Koob & Bloom, 1988). Similarly, amphetamines and cocaine, as well as nicotine and caffeine, are dopamine agonists; addicts will work hard to acquire these substances.

Thus, at the level of the brain, the fact that different neurotransmitters are crucial for different aspects of learning again shows us that learning is not a single activity.

CLASSICAL VERSUS OPERANT CONDITIONING: ARE THEY REALLY DIFFERENT?
Table 5.2 presents a comparison of classical and operant conditioning. Both types of conditioning depend on an association, either between a stimulus and response or between a response and reinforcement. Both classical and operant conditioning involve extinction and spontaneous recovery, generalization, and discrimination. Both types of learning are subject to moderating factors that affect response acquisition, such as time (in classical conditioning, the length of time between CS and UCS; in operant conditioning, immediate versus delayed reinforcement), and for both types of learning biological factors influence what can be learned easily.

Noting these similarities, some researchers have debated whether these two types of conditioning are really so distinct after all. Perhaps they are just different procedures

TABLE 5.2

Classical and Operant Conditioning Compared

	CLASSICAL CONDITIONING	OPERANT CONDITIONING
Similarities	• Learning is based on an association between stimulus and response.	• Learning is based on an association between response and reinforcement.
	• Avoidance learning.	• Avoidance learning.
	• Extinction.	• Extinction.
	• Spontaneous recovery.	• Spontaneous recovery.
	• Stimulus generalization.	• Generalization.
	• Stimulus discrimination.	• Discrimination.
	• External factors can affect learning.	• External factors can affect learning.
Differences	• The organism is passive.	• The organism is active, "operating" on the world.
	• Responses are reflexes (limited number of possible responses).	• Responses are voluntary behaviors (limitless possible responses).
	• Responses are elicited.	• Responses are emitted.
	• Responses are not followed by a reinforcer.	• Responses are followed by a reinforcer.

toward a similar end. Indeed, the differences are not so clear cut. Some studies, for example, show that voluntary movements can be shaped via classical conditioning (Brown & Jenkins, 1968). Similarly, involuntary responses, such as learning to control tense jaw muscles to decrease facial pain, can be operantly conditioned (Dohrmann & Laskin, 1978). However, the fact that the same ends can be reached with either type of conditioning does not imply that the means to those ends are the same. After all, bats, birds, and helicopters fly, but they do so in different ways.

Perhaps the best evidence that the two kinds of conditioning are truly different is that different neural systems are used in each. Although the debate over making neat distinctions between classical and operant conditioning continues, recent research on the brain appears to discount the position that they are variations of the same process. Not only do classical and operant conditioning clearly draw on different mechanisms, but different forms of classical conditioning also rely on different brain structures, depending on the response to be conditioned. For example, whereas classical conditioning of fear draws on the amygdala (LeDoux, 1996), classical conditioning of eye blinks relies heavily on the cerebellum (Thompson & Krupa, 1994). In contrast, operant conditioning involves neither structure, using instead the dopamine-based "reward system" centered in the nucleus accumbens (Robbins & Everitt, 1998). By providing evidence that different neural systems are used in the different types of learning, studies of the brain establish that the two types of conditioning are essentially different.

LOOKING AT LEVELS

Cornering the Professor

When one of the authors was an undergraduate, the teaching assistant in a course on learning coached the class to alter the behavior of the professor. As instructed, the class looked down and shuffled papers whenever the professor was in the center of the stage. But as soon as he moved, even a little, toward the back left corner of the stage, we students looked up attentively. After a while, we went back to shuffling, and then looked up only when the professor had moved a bit farther toward the corner. As the period wore on, we found that we actually were able to maneuver the professor into the corner! We had apparently shaped the professor's behavior, using our attention as the reinforcer, a powerful reinforcer for most teachers.

Consider this scenario from the levels perspective. Based on what we know about reward systems in the brain, it is reasonable to suppose that the way we oriented ourselves toward the professor (a social variable) literally manipulated his brain. When he drifted toward the corner, our bright and eager faces probably caused dopamine to squirt in his brain, making this behavior more likely in the future. Our professor later claimed that he didn't notice what was going on. If he had been more observant (level of the person), he might have seen what we were up to and been able to extinguish the response or not find attentive students reinforcing. Our ability to maneuver the professor depended on events at all three levels of analysis: The brain allowed his behavior to be shaped; his personality led him to be susceptible to this process; and the group provided the reinforcement. If we hadn't liked him as much as we did, and felt that he liked us, we might not have dared to try this experiment, and thus aspects of his personality affected the social reinforcement, which in turn affected his brain. And of course we were delighted as he gradually began to hang around in the corner (courtesy, ultimately, of brain mechanisms), so we were all the more engaged in the process and willing to play our group role as social reinforcer.

CONSOLIDATE!

▶ **1. What is operant conditioning? How does it occur?** Operant conditioning is a process whereby a behavior becomes associated with the consequences of performing that behavior; in contrast to classical conditioning, these behaviors are usually voluntary. Thorndike's work with cats in a puzzle box led him to develop the Law of Effect. Skinner's work with pigeons (and later, with rats in a Skinner box) showed that operant conditioning could explain much of everyday human behavior.

▶ **2. What is the difference between reinforcement and punishment?** Reinforcement *increases* the likelihood that a behavior will recur; punishment *decreases* that likelihood. Positive reinforcement is the *presentation* of a desired reinforcer after a particular response; negative reinforcement is the *removal* of an unpleasant stimuli after a particular response. Punishment by itself is not particularly effective. Reinforcement can be given via primary or secondary reinforcers (examples of the latter are money, praise, good grades); behavior modification programs make use of secondary reinforcers.

▶ **3. How are complex behaviors learned? How are these new behaviors maintained?** Complex behaviors are learned through shaping, which involves reinforcing behaviors that are successive approximations toward the desired, complex behavior. Generalization, discrimination, extinction, and spontaneous recovery all occur with operant conditioning. Reinforcement schedules help maintain learned behaviors, with the variable ratio schedule producing behaviors most resistant to extinction.

▶ **4. What changes occur in the brain during operant conditioning?** Learning has different aspects, each with its own brain changes. We learn to discriminate the proper situation in which to make a response; the hippocampus, through the functioning of the neurotransmitter acetylcholine, is involved in this phase. In addition, we learn the stimulus–response association itself. The neurotransmitter dopamine is involved here, as is the nucleus accumbens, a structure behind the amygdala. Research shows that although operant and classical conditioning share some similarities, they are also distinct from each other, relying on different brain systems.

COGNITIVE AND SOCIAL LEARNING

At a friend's suggestion, Paula and Chris took a couples' communication class, which met once a week for 6 weeks. Two coleaders (one male, one female) led the group. Each class began with the leaders role-playing a couple who were unsuccessful in resolving their differences. They then repeated the role play, this time incorporating techniques the couple might use to resolve their differences. Afterward, the leaders asked volunteers to act out the same scene, this time attempting to come to a resolution.

As part of the class, each couple received a manual and video on conflict resolution to read and view at home. The video included additional problem scenarios and demonstrated both maladaptive and adaptive ways that couples can react to such situations. In essence, both the manual and the video encouraged users to find new ways of interacting with their partners, and of thinking about conflict and its resolution in general. These aids relied on **cognitive learning,** the acquisition of information that is often not immediately acted on but is stored for later use.

▶ 1. What is cognitive learning? How does it differ from classical and operant conditioning?

▶ 2. What is insight learning?

▶ 3. How can watching others help people learn?

▶ 4. What makes some models better than others?

Cognitive learning: The acquisition of information that often is not immediately acted on but is stored for later use.

Cognitive Learning

The learning we have discussed so far focuses on behavior. In classical conditioning, the learned behavior is the conditioned response (CR); in operant conditioning, the learned behavior is the reinforced response. But even these types of learning involve the storing of new information, which guides the behavior. Information acquired through cognitive learning, on the other hand, may be used in planning, evaluating, and other forms of thinking, without producing any behavior—only, perhaps, more information to be stored. Learning how to add is an example of cognitive learning, as is learning the names of the 50 states or the meaning of a new word. You are engaged in cognitive learning right now.

FIGURE 5.13
Tolman and Honzik's Discovery of Latent Learning

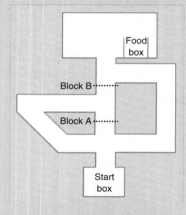

Three routes of differing lengths wind from start to finish. If two points along the most direct route are blocked, it is still possible to get to the end.

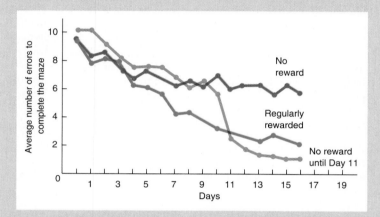

Rats who were rewarded for getting to the end of the maze made fewer "navigation" errors than rats who were not rewarded. Once rewarded (on day 11), the previously unrewarded rats made fewer mistakes than regularly reinforced rats, illustrating that the unrewarded rats had learned the spatial arrangement of the maze but did not apply that knowledge until reinforced.

Illustrating the fact that cognitive learning is more than simply associations between stimuli and responses, Tolman and Honzik (1930b, 1930c) conducted a series of classic studies of learning with rats. One group of rats was put in a maze that led to a food box, thus receiving a food reward for completing the maze (Figure 5.13, left panel). The other group was also put in the maze but received no reinforcement; the rats were simply removed from the maze after a certain amount of time. Sometimes routes were blocked, and the rats had to find a different way to the end. The first group of rats, those that were rewarded with food, quickly increased their speed in the maze and decreased the number of mistakes; the speed and accuracy of the unrewarded second group did not particularly improve. This finding was consistent with what behaviorists would predict. However, when rats in the second group received a food reward on the 11th day, their speed increased and their errors decreased, both dramatically (Figure 5.13, right panel). It appears that these rats had learned how to run the maze quickly and correctly before the 11th day, but had no reason to do so. Such learning that occurs without obvious evidence is called **latent learning**. Tolman reasoned that the unreinforced rats, in their wanderings around the maze, had developed a *cognitive map* of the maze, storing information about its spatial layout. However, they did not use the map until they were motivated to do so by the reinforcement. This study, and the concept of latent learning, also reminds us of the important distinction between learning something and performing it. Piaget (1962) described a situation

Latent learning: Learning that occurs without obvious evidence.

in which one of his daughters watched another child have a dramatic temper tantrum, complete with writhing on the floor and howling. His daughter also saw the other child's parents react with concern. Days later, his daughter tried out this behavior, presumably to see whether she would be given the attention she thought a tantrum deserved. She did not have to engage in the behavior at the time in order to learn it. Researchers now know that latent learning depends on the hippocampus (Myers et al., 2000), which is generally used when new facts are stored (Schacter, 1996).

The study of learning focuses on the *acquisition* of information; in contrast, the study of memory focuses on the *retention* of information. By its very nature, cognitive learning relies crucially on how information is stored in memory, and most of the recent research on this topic (explored in the next chapter) focuses on the way information is stored in memory.

Insight Learning: Seeing the Connection

Insight learning consists of suddenly grasping what something means and incorporating that new knowledge into old knowledge. It is based on the phenomenon known as the "aha experience," the triumphal moment when an idea becomes crystal clear. By its very nature, insight learning, unlike other types of learning, is accompanied by a sudden flash of awareness that one has learned.

The most famous psychological experiments regarding insight learning were done by Wolfgang Köhler (1887–1967), a German Gestalt psychologist. Köhler (1925) put a chimpanzee named Sultan in a cage; outside the cage, and out of reach, Köhler put fruit. Also outside the cage and out of reach, but closer than the fruit, he placed a long stick. Inside the cage, Köhler put a short stick. Initially, Sultan showed signs of frustration as he tried to reach the food. Then he stopped. He seemed suddenly to have an insight into how to snag the fruit: He used the short stick to get the long one, and then capture the fruit. In another study, Köhler put bananas in the cage but high, out of Sultan's reach. Also in the cage were stacks of boxes. At first, Sultan tried to jump up to grab the bananas. Eventually, he looked around at the objects in the cage and again appeared to have a flash of insight; he saw that stacking the boxes and climbing on them would enable him to reach the bananas.

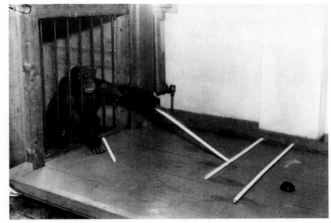

In another instance of opportunity for insight learning, Sultan is faced with a variant of the two-stick solution to help him retrieve food that is out of reach. Here, there are four sticks.

Observational Learning: To See Is to Know

Everyone, like Piaget's daughter, has had the experience of watching someone else's behavior and then being able to reproduce it. The behavior is probably voluntary (and thus not the result of classical conditioning) and may not have been reinforced (and thus not the result of operant conditioning), but it was learned nonetheless. A group of psychologists, led by Albert Bandura, developed *social learning theory*, which emphasizes the fact that much learning occurs in a social context. This kind of learning, which results simply from watching others and does not depend on reinforcement, is called **observational learning**. Observational learning helps people learn how to behave in their families (Thorn & Gilbert, 1998) and in their cultures: By watching others, we learn how to greet people, eat, laugh, tell jokes. Observational learning has helped you figure out how to behave in your class and on campus. Do you remember your first few days at college? By watching others, you learned how people talked to each other, what clothes were "fashionable," and how to interact with instructors.

Observational learning influenced Paula and Chris's behavior: Chris learned to yell by watching his father yell at his mother. In fact, most people in his family yelled at one another, and he grew up thinking that all families acted that way. In contrast,

Insight learning: Learning that occurs when a person suddenly grasps what something means and incorporates that new knowledge into old knowledge.

Observational learning: Learning that occurs through watching others, not through reinforcement.

Paula's parents didn't yell very often, and when they did, the episode was over quickly and everyone apologized. Thus, through observational learning, Paula and Chris had learned dramatically different ways of resolving disagreements and expressing anger.

FIGURE 5.14
Bandura's Study on Observational Learning

Three groups of children were tested; the groups differed only in the first part of the study. Children in one group watched an adult abuse a Bobo doll, for example, by slamming it with a mallet, kicking it, and yelling at it.

Children in a second group watched adults play with Tinkertoys and ignore the Bobo doll.

Children in a third group never saw a model (an adult) in the playroom.

In the second part of the study, all the children played in a room with a variety of toys, including Bobo. Children in the first group tended to imitate what they had seen, mistreating the doll (and inventing new ways to abuse it) and being more aggressive with the other toys in the room.

Children who observed the adult ignoring the Bobo doll were even less aggressive toward it than the control group!

Bandura focused much of his work on *modeling,* a process in which someone learns new behaviors through observing other people. These other people function as models, presenting a behavior to be imitated. With modeling, you observe others' behaviors, and then none, some, or all of these behaviors may be learned and repeated, or modified. In one of Bandura's famous studies involving a Bobo doll, an inflated vinyl doll that pops back up when punched (Figure 5.14; Bandura et al., 1961), children were divided into three groups: One group watched an adult beating up a Bobo doll, one group watched an adult ignoring the Bobo doll, and the third didn't see an adult at all. After being mildly frustrated by being placed in a room with toys, but not being allowed to play with some of them, all the children were then placed in another room with many toys, including a Bobo doll. Children who had observed the adult

behaving aggressively with Bobo were themsel
have found similar results, including the observ
live person has more of an impact than watchin
same behaviors. In turn, a realistic video has m
sion of the same behaviors (Bandura et al., 196

When Paula and Chris observed the leader
adaptive ways of interacting, they were preser
observation. These sorts of opportunities o
apprentice spends large amounts of time obser
thing more than handing over a tool. How-to
repair may be more effective than how-to bo
see the desired behavior. Observational learnii
form standards of judgment, and even discove:
(Bandura, 1986).

Learning From Models

Learning from models has many advantages
from models, you can avoid going through al
and go directly to the end product.

"Do as I Do." Observational learnii
sired learning. Models may say one thing a
both, saying what the model said and doin
1975; Rushton, 1975). If you are surrour

others, and powerful, high-st
likely to be more influent

Many television sh
children contain
is often imitat
Moreover,
often sh
tim a
qu

opportunity to learn a lot of positive behaviors; but if you don't have that opportunity, you may find it difficult to learn certain "skills." If adults in a family have trouble holding jobs, become explosively angry, exhibit little patience, and treat others
rudely, it can be harder for the children to learn the skills involved in maintaining a
job, effectively controlling anger, managing impatience and frustration, and treating
others kindly. On a more positive note, Bandura and colleagues (1967) did a study in
which preschool children who were afraid of dogs observed another child who had
no fear dogs. Over eight sessions, as prearranged, the model on each occasion played
more closely with a dog and for a longer time. Fearful children who watched the
other child with the dog had significantly more "approach" behaviors (those oriented toward a dog) than a control group of fearful children who did not observe the
model.

Both modeling and operant conditioning are involved in learning about culture
and gender. You may learn how to behave by observing others, but whether you'll
actually perform those behaviors depends, in part, on the consequences that occur
when you try. Imagine the following family interaction in a culture that has different
expectations of what constitutes appropriate play for girls and boys. A boy observes
his older sister asking her parents for a new doll and sees that they buy it for her. He
then asks his parents for a doll for himself and is severely punished. His request was
prompted by modeling; but because it resulted in punishment, he is unlikely to make
that request again. Similarly, ninth and tenth graders were more likely to get involved
in community activity if their parents were involved, or if parents reinforced them for
minor involvement (Fletcher et al., 2000).

Researchers have discovered that several characteristics of models can make
learning through observation more effective (Bandura, 1977a, 1986). Not surprisingly,
the more you pay attention to the model, the more you learn. You are more likely to
pay attention if the model is an expert, is good looking, has high status, or is socially
powerful (Brewer & Wann, 1998). Perhaps intuitively realizing the importance of
models for children's learning through observation, and recognizing the high-status
position of his office, cigar enthusiast President William McKinley refused to be pho-
tographed with a cigar (Seuling, 1978). We know that children learn by observing

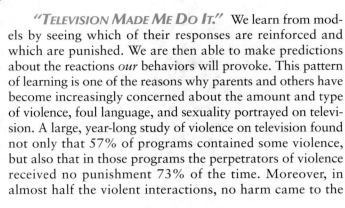

"TELEVISION MADE ME DO IT." We learn from models by seeing which of their responses are reinforced and which are punished. We are then able to make predictions about the reactions *our* behaviors will provoke. This pattern of learning is one of the reasons why parents and others have become increasingly concerned about the amount and type of violence, foul language, and sexuality portrayed on television. A large, year-long study of violence on television found not only that 57% of programs contained some violence, but also that in those programs the perpetrators of violence received no punishment 73% of the time. Moreover, in almost half the violent interactions, no harm came to the

...ows geared to ...violence, which ...ed by viewers. ...television violence ...ows no harm to the vic-...d no negative conse-...nces for the perpetrator.

TABLE 5.3

Modeling Aggressive Behavior

Aggressive behavior subsequent to viewing aggression on television is related to the following factors.

AGE

Children in middle childhood (8–12 years old) appear to exhibit a stronger relationship between watching violence on television and later behaving aggressively. Young adults who watched more violent television in their middle childhood years have been found to be more aggressive, regardless of the amount of violent television they watch as young adults.

TIME SPENT WATCHING TELEVISION

The number of hours spent watching television is related to aggressive behavior, regardless of program content. One theory is that the hectic, frenzied pace of programming may create a high level of arousal in young viewers. Boys who watched the most television at age 8 were most likely to have had a criminal conviction by age 30 (Huesmann & Eron, 1986).

IDENTIFICATION WITH TELEVISION CHARACTER

Particularly for boys, there is a positive correlation between identification with a character and the probability that the child will model the aggressive behavior of that character (Huesmann & Eron, 1986). These results were also found in a cross-cultural study of television violence and aggression in Australia, Finland, the Netherlands, Poland, Israel, and the United States (Huesmann & Miller, 1994).

PORTRAYAL OF VIOLENCE

The ways in which violence is portrayed on television can heighten its influence (Comstock & Paik, 1991). Viewers are more likely to act aggressively in the following cases.

- The television perpetrator is rewarded (or at least not punished) for the violent behavior.
- The violence is portrayed as justified.
- Aspects of the violent situation could possibly occur in real life.
- The perpetrator is seen as similar to the viewer.
- The violence does not appear disgusting.
- No critical commentary occurs during or after the portrayals of violence.
- The violence appears real.
- The violence is not interrupted by humor (as it is in parody films).

victim, and 58% of the victims showed no pain. Only 4% of violent programs included any emphasis on alternative, nonviolent solutions to problems (Farhi, 1996). From an observational learning perspective, this is disconcerting because children watching TV learn from the bulk of shows portraying violence that there are no negative consequences for the violent person.

Since Bandura's work on modeling, his findings have been replicated many times over, with many variations, and the findings have largely been consistent (Clapp, 1988; Huesmann & Eron, 1986). The establishment of a rating system for television programs grew out of this body of psychological research. Many studies have been designed to identify which aspects of violence on television lead observers to behave violently later. As shown in Table 5.3 on page 194, their results suggest that age, time spent watching television, identification with the television character, and the portrayal of violence all influence behavior (Clapp, 1988; Smith, 1993). At the same time, positive, nonviolent programs (such as *Sesame Street* or *Mr. Rogers' Neighborhood*) promote nonviolent observational learning: Preschool children who watched these programs were more likely to exhibit positive, helpful behaviors than children who did not watch these shows (Forge & Phemister, 1987).

LOOKING AT LEVELS

Mom and Dad on Drugs

In the 1980s, a long-running TV public service advertisement showed a father confronting his son with what is obviously the boy's drug paraphernalia. The father asks his son incredulously, "Where did you learn to do this?" The son, half in tears, replies, "From you, okay? I learned it from watching you!" Observational learning clearly appears to be a factor in an adolescent's willingness to experiment with drugs and alcohol. Andrews and her colleagues (1997) found that adolescents' relationships with their parents influence whether they will model the substance use patterns of the parents. Specifically, they found that adolescents who had a positive relationship with their mothers modeled her use (or nonuse) of cigarettes, and those who had a close relationship with their fathers modeled the father's marijuana use (or nonuse). Similarly, those who had a negative relationship with their parents were less likely to model their parents' use of drugs or alcohol. Although some of the more complex results of this study depended on the age and sex of the adolescent, the general findings can be understood by thinking about them from the three levels of analysis and their interactions.

At the level of the brain, observing someone engage in a behavior causes you to store new memories, which involves the hippocampus and related brain systems. These memories later can guide behavior, as they do in all types of imitation. At the level of the person, if you are motivated to observe someone, you are likely to be paying more attention to them (and therefore increasing the likelihood of your learning from them and remembering what you learn). At the level of the group, you are more likely to be captivated by models who have certain attractive characteristics. In this case, adolescents who had a positive relationship with their parents were more likely to do what their parents did; if their parents didn't smoke, the adolescents were less likely to do so. The events at these levels interact: Children who enjoy a positive relationship with their parents may accord their parents higher status than children who have a negative relationship with their parents. Thus, the former group of children probably increase the amount of attention they give to their parents' behavior. And, as you will see in the following chapter, paying attention engages the frontal lobes and other brain areas that are crucial for acquiring new information effectively.

▶ **1. What is cognitive learning? How does it differ from classical and operant conditioning?** Cognitive learning is the acquisition of information that often is not acted on immediately, but rather is stored for later use. This process contrasts with classical and operant conditioning, which focus on learning behaviors. Latent learning (such as creating a cognitive map) is an example of cognitive learning.

▶ **2. What is insight learning?** Learning can occur following an insight, by suddenly grasping what something means and incorporating that new knowledge into old knowledge. Insight learning is based on the "aha experience" and is marked by a cognitive "leap."

▶ **3. How can watching others help people learn?** Observational learning allows you to acquire knowledge "second hand," without having to perform a behavior yourself. This sort of learning helps explain how children (and adults) learn their family's and their culture's rules, and the different rules that sometimes exist for men and women, boys and girls.

▶ **4. What makes some models better than others?** Modeling is the process of learning a new behavior through observing others, and the more attention paid to the model, the more effective the learning will be. You are more likely to pay attention to a model who is an expert, is good looking, or has high status. Modeling has been the link in understanding how viewing television violence may lead to higher levels of aggressive behavior in children.

A DEEPER LEVEL
Recap and Thought Questions

▶ Classical Conditioning

Classical conditioning, which was discovered by Ivan Pavlov, has four basic elements:

1. The unconditioned stimulus (UCS), such as food, reflexively elicits an unconditioned response.
2. The unconditioned response (UCR), such as salivation, is automatically elicited by a UCS.
3. The pairing of a conditioned stimulus (CS), such as a tone, with a UCS, such as food, elicits a conditioned response (CR), such as salivation. (Note that salivation can be either a conditioned or an unconditioned response, depending on the stimulus that elicits it.)
4. The presentation of the CS alone then elicits the UCR (the tone presented alone elicits the response of salivation now as a CR).

A conditioned emotional response is involved in the development of phobias, as shown by Watson and Raynor in the case of Little Albert. Extinction is the unpairing of the CS and UCS; spontaneous recovery is the return of a classically conditioned response after a rest period following extinction. In stimulus generalization, a similar, but not identical, stimulus elicits the CR; in stimulus discrimination, the organism learns to distinguish among similar stimuli so that only a particular stimulus elicits the CR.

Why was Paula initially fearful when Chris said her name in a certain tone of voice? She was fearful because she had developed a conditioned emotional response to it: That tone of voice (CS) had become paired with his telling her he had doubts about the relationship (UCS), causing a fear response in Paula (UCR and CR).

> **Think It Through.** Dog obedience classes suggest that the following procedure will train a dog to stop barking. When the dog starts to bark, squirt water (from a water bottle) in its face. Right before you squirt, say, "Don't bark!" The dog startles because of the water and stops barking. Is this classical conditioning? If so, identify the UCS, CS, UCR, and CR. What would be happening if the dog stops barking as soon as you say, "Don't bark"? What learning process has occurred if the dog stops barking only when you give the command in a particular tone of voice?

▶ Operant Conditioning

Operant conditioning is the process whereby a behavior (usually a voluntary one) becomes associated with the consequences of performing that behavior. Operant conditioning has three basic elements:

1. The existence of a stimulus, such as a pedal
2. The response, such as pressing the pedal
3. The consequence, such as a cage door opening

Shaping makes it possible to learn, by successive approximations, behaviors that would otherwise not be emitted.

Both negative and positive reinforcement *increase* the behavior that precedes it; punishment *decreases* the behavior that precedes it. Extinction, spontaneous recovery, generalization, and discrimination all occur in operant conditioning. Reinforcers can be primary or secondary; the latter can be tokens that are exchanged for a primary reinforcer. Reinforcement schedules can be continuous or partial; if partial, reinforcement may be given for responses after an interval of time (interval schedule), or after a set number of responses (ratio schedule).

How did Paula and Chris learn to behave disrespectfully to each other? Paula and Chris would keep yelling at each other and saying hurtful things in an effort to "win" a fight. Sometimes one would win, sometimes the other, in the fashion of a variable reinforcement schedule. These hollow victories reinforced hurtful behavior and persistent arguing, making this harmful interaction pattern difficult to extinguish.

Think It Through. You are babysitting, and the child's parents have explicitly instructed you not to give her any more food. She whines for dessert, you say no, and she has a temper tantrum. What can you conclude about how her parents have handled her requests for snacks in the past? If you want her to stop carrying on, what would be two different types of operant conditioning you could use to increase the likelihood of changing her behavior? (Physical or emotional violence, threats of cruelty, and yelling are not options.) Which technique do you think will be the most effective? Why?

▶ Cognitive and Social Learning

Cognitive learning involves the acquisition of information that may be used in planning, evaluating, and other forms of thinking, but is not necessarily acted on immediately; latent learning and insight learning are examples. Observational learning is learning by watching the behavior of others. The more you pay attention to the model, the more you are likely to learn. Through observational learning, children may learn to behave aggressively from watching violent television shows.

Could Paula and Chris learn to behave differently toward each other by reading a manual and watching other couples? Reading a manual about conflict resolution for couples could help Paula and Chris to acquire new ways of resolving conflict, although they might not use those new methods immediately. Rather, such methods would likely be stored for later use. Watching other couples engage in more positive methods of conflict resolution would provide them with an opportunity for observational learning. Both modes of learning could help them behave differently with each other.

Think It Through. Curare is a drug that so totally paralyzes an animal, a heart–lung machine is necessary to keep it alive. Although the animal can't move, it can perceive and remember normally. Imagine showing a person in that situation how to open a simple combination lock on a box to obtain the $1,000 inside. When the effect of the curare has worn off and the person is able to move normally, will he know how to open the lock to get the reward? Why or why not?

---

6 MEMORY
Living With Yesterday

Juan and Fiona would never have met under ordinary circumstances. Juan works as a paralegal, spending much of his time sorting through papers and tracking down obscure references to laws and cases. Fiona is a high school basketball coach who spends most of her waking hours working with young would-be stars or thinking about sports. But, by coincidence, both happened to be on the corner of Elm and River Streets one day at about 5:00 in the afternoon when an accident took place. A young man, late to meet his fiancée at the airport, sped through the intersection, not seeing a bicycle in his path. He ran straight into it, knocking bike and rider high into the air. The rider's head struck the pavement with a sickening thud. He lay flat on his stomach, his bike twisted like a pretzel nearby.

Afterward, Juan told the police that the driver had ignored the stop sign at the intersection and run right into the bike. Fiona, however, claimed that the driver had stopped, but very briefly, before racing ahead. Both agreed that the driver had been going too fast. Juan and Fiona also agreed that, after a single whole-body twitch, the downed rider lay ominously still. The driver, they both said, had pulled over immediately, rushed to the victim's side, and then gently cradled the bike rider's head.

Fortunately, the cyclist soon started to mumble softly and then to move about. Fiona, who knew first aid from her coaching duties, ran over and cautioned the driver not to move the injured rider. Looking up, Fiona saw Juan standing a few feet away and asked him to call an ambulance. The driver glanced at his watch and let out a groan of despair. He dashed off a note, handed it to Fiona, and rushed to his car. It was later discovered that the driver had written his phone number incorrectly on the note.

The ambulance arrived; the police weren't far behind. They interviewed everyone on the scene. The cyclist regained consciousness, but he had no memory at all of what had happened; in fact, he couldn't remember anything about the last day or so. Fiona said that the car's license plate number was similar to the score of a game she had just coached and claimed to have no trouble recalling it. Juan recalled that the driver had spoken with a slight Southern accent and seemed to be well educated. He also was confident that he had remembered the license plate number, but the number he recalled was different from Fiona's version. Juan didn't remember exactly when the driver had left the scene, or what had been happening then.

As eyewitnesses to the same occurrence but with different stories to report, Juan and Fiona illustrate the complicated nature of memory, a multifaceted and fascinating psychological terrain. One theme we will revisit throughout this chapter is that memory is not a single ability and that, as Juan and Fiona demonstrate, people differ in their abilities to use certain types of memory. Another theme is that memory is constructive; that is, we assemble memories from bits and pieces that we've stored, and sometimes we fill in what's missing on the basis of our beliefs and expectations. We will also consider the subjective nature of memory: We remember what we experience, not necessarily what actually occurred. The levels perspective lends particular insight into the nature of memory because so much is now known about how memories are stored in the brain, and how events at the levels of the person and group affect them.

MEMORY: A MANY-SPLENDORED THING

Because she could usually remember complicated game plays very well, Fiona believed that she had an excellent memory, but in fact she had a hard time remembering names. And Juan, equally confident of his memory, couldn't remember dance moves to save his life, although he could recall facts flawlessly.

Both Juan and Fiona assumed that people have either "good" memories or "poor" ones—that memory is a single ability that either works well or doesn't. In fact, several kinds of memory operate within us simultaneously; we know this in part because different brain systems underlie these different forms. Even in the time it takes you to read this page, several kinds of memory are at work. Thus, rather than having a good memory or a poor one, people have different abilities to remember different kinds of information.

> ▶ 1. What is a memory store? How do memory stores differ?

> ▶ 2. How are different types of information stored over a long period of time?

> ▶ 3. How do neurons store memories, and what role do genes play in memory?

Storing Information: Time and Space Are of the Essence

Until someone asks for your address, chances are you aren't consciously aware of it—or even that you have one. But once you are asked, the information is at your mental fingertips. This difference, between memories we are aware of holding and those we are not, is one sign that different types of "memory stores" are at work. A **memory store** is a set of neurons that serves to retain information over time.

THREE TYPES OF MEMORY STORES. Although to Fiona it seems that her "hands remember" how to shoot baskets and that her "fingers remember" how to play the guitar, all memories are stored in the brain. We can distinguish among three types of memory stores, which differ in the time span over which they operate and in the amount of information they can hold. These three are known as sensory, short-term, and long-term memory stores.

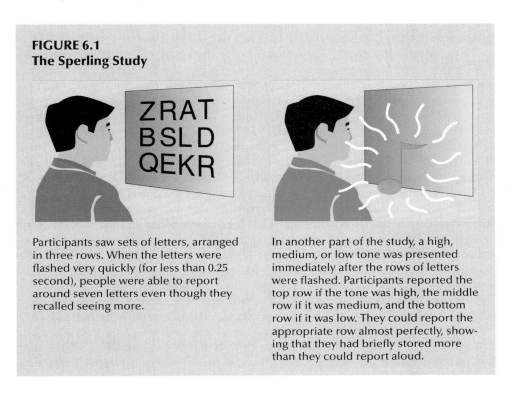

FIGURE 6.1
The Sperling Study

ZRAT
BSLD
QEKR

Participants saw sets of letters, arranged in three rows. When the letters were flashed very quickly (for less than 0.25 second), people were able to report around seven letters even though they recalled seeing more.

In another part of the study, a high, medium, or low tone was presented immediately after the rows of letters were flashed. Participants reported the top row if the tone was high, the middle row if it was medium, and the bottom row if it was low. They could report the appropriate row almost perfectly, showing that they had briefly stored more than they could report aloud.

Have you ever looked at scenery rushing past the window of a moving car and noticed that although you see literally miles and miles of landscape slipping by, you need to make an effort to remember more than fleeting images, which last about as long as the instant it takes for the image to flash by? **Sensory memory (SM)** holds a large amount of perceptual input for a very brief time, typically less than one second. Sensory memory happens automatically, without effort (via bottom-up processes; see Chapter 3); sensory memory arises because the activation of perceptual areas of your brain by the stimulus persists for a few brief moments. George Sperling (1960) reported an experiment, presented in Figure 6.1 and now regarded as a classic, that demonstrated this lingering sensory memory in vision (the visual form of sensory memory is called *iconic memory*). When shown sets of many letters or digits very briefly, people can report only a handful afterward. However, they claim that they can remember all the items for an instant or two, but then the memory fades too quickly to "read off" all of them during recall. Sperling was able to demonstrate that this claim was in fact correct. He briefly showed participants displays of items, more than they could report, and then presented a tone that cued which row to report. The participants were able to report the cued row virtually perfectly. Because the cue was presented *after* the display was removed, the participants had to have retained some memory of all of the rows in order

In iconic memory, sensory input lingers only briefly.

to perform so well. This finding shows that iconic memory stores a large amount of information but that it fades very quickly. The sense of a fleeting memory after the stimulus has ceased holds true for hearing as well. For example, you can continue to hear the sound of a voice after it finishes speaking for the brief time it is still in auditory SM (Cherry, 1953; the auditory form of sensory memory is called *echoic memory*).

Whereas sensory memory retains information for the briefest of time, **short-term memory (STM)** holds information for several seconds, perhaps as long as 30. Also in contrast to SM, which can hold a large amount of information, STM holds only a handful of separate pieces of information. You are conscious only of the information you have currently stored in STM. The very fact that you are aware of information, such as a telephone number you've just looked up and are rushing to the telephone to dial, is a sure sign that the information is in STM.

How much remembered information can we be aware of at one time—in other words, how much information can STM hold? Miller (1956) argued that STM can hold only about seven "chunks" at once, but more recent research suggests that the number is more like four (Cowan, in press). A **chunk** is a unit of information, such as a digit, letter, or word. The definition of a chunk is not precise, however, and research has shown that the amount of information STM can hold depends on the type of materials and the individual's experience with them (see, for example, Baddeley, 1994; Broadbent, 1971; Mandler, 1967). For instance, a word is usually treated as a chunk, but you can store more one-syllable words than five-syllable ones. Generally speaking, STM can handle somewhere between five and nine items; this is why telephone and license plate numbers are fairly easy to remember. Can you intentionally retain information such as telephone numbers in STM? Yes indeed. When you see something you want to remember (such as the numbers on a license plate of a car involved in an accident), you can hold this information in STM by **rehearsal**, repeating the information over and over. When you dash from telephone book to telephone, repeating like a mantra the number you've just looked up, you are rehearsing.

Rehearsal is important in part because it provides us with an opportunity to move information into a third type of memory store, **long-term memory (LTM)**. LTM holds a huge amount of information for a long time, from hours to years. You are not directly aware of the information in LTM—it has to move into STM before you are conscious of it. As an analogy, think of the difference between storing a file on your hard drive versus having it only in RAM, or random-access memory, the active memory in a computer. Once information is saved on the hard drive, it can be stored indefinitely; it cannot be disrupted if the power fails. If information faded rapidly from RAM (instead of being lost instantly when you close without "saving"), the difference between storing words simply by typing them into RAM and saving them on the hard drive would be much like the difference between memories storied in STM versus LTM.

LTM stores the information that underlies the meanings of pictures, words, and objects, as well as your memories of everything you've ever done or learned. Unlike the single general-purpose hard drive on a computer, LTM is divided into specialized parts, as if (to continue the analogy) it had different drives for different sensory modalities (such as vision and audition), verbal information, and motor memories. The storage capability of LTM is so large that some researchers question whether it has a limit. Shepard (1967), for example, investigated the capacity of LTM by showing people more than 600 pictures (photographs, colored prints, illustrations), mostly from magazines, and then testing for recognition. Pairing pictures seen in the first round with new, previously unseen ones, Shepard asked his participants to pick out the ones they had been shown in the first part of the study. He found that the participants could recognize over 99% of the images correctly two hours after seeing them, and 87% a week later. This remarkable degree of retention was found even though the participants had spent an average of only 5.9 seconds looking at each picture.

IS STM REALLY DIFFERENT FROM LTM? The distinction between STM and LTM matters in everyday life, sometimes a great deal. If you see the license number of

Short-term memory (STM): A memory store that holds relatively little information (typically 5 to 9 items) for a few seconds (but perhaps as long as 30 seconds); people are conscious only of the current contents of STM.

Chunk: A unit of information, such as a digit, letter, or word.

Rehearsal: The process of repeating information over and over to retain it in STM.

Long-term memory (LTM): A memory store that holds a huge amount of information for a long time (from hours to years).

a car that has just hit a cyclist but lose that information from STM, it is gone forever unless it has moved into LTM. But if the information has been stored in LTM, you should be able to retrieve it.

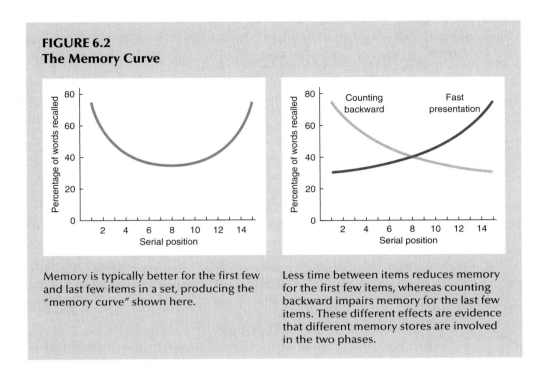

FIGURE 6.2
The Memory Curve

Memory is typically better for the first few and last few items in a set, producing the "memory curve" shown here.

Less time between items reduces memory for the first few items, whereas counting backward impairs memory for the last few items. These different effects are evidence that different memory stores are involved in the two phases.

Evidence for distinct short-term and long-term memory stores has been shown in many studies. The earliest of these took place over 100 years ago, when German philosopher and pioneering memory researcher Hermann Ebbinghaus (1850–1909) undertook a series of experiments to discover the factors that affect memory. To see how well he could memorize letters, digits, and nonsense syllables (such as *cac*, *rit*, and the like, which are not words but can be pronounced), Ebbinghaus (1885) wrote out a set of these stimuli, each on its own card; he then studied them, one at a time, seeing how many he later could recall. Ebbinghaus found—as many researchers have since confirmed—that the first and last ones studied were more easily remembered than the ones in the middle. The left panel of Figure 6.2 illustrates this *memory curve*. The increased memory for the first few stimuli is called the **primacy effect**; the increased memory for the last few stimuli is the **recency effect**.

Primacy and recency effects are evidence that short-term and long-term memories rely on distinct stores. To see how, we need to look at additional studies. First, it has been found that presenting items to be learned in rapid succession reduces the primacy—but, crucially, not the recency—effect; as the right panel of Figure 6.2 shows, memory is still enhanced for the later items, but not for the ones learned early. The simple fact that the time between items affects only one part of the memory curve is evidence that both parts cannot arise from the same mental processes. Why does reducing the presentation time affect only the primacy effect? The primacy effect occurs because we have more time to think about the earlier items than the later ones, and thus the earlier ones are more likely to be stored in LTM. By rehearsing information in STM for those early items, we stretch out the time we have available for storing it in LTM, and in general, the more time we have to rehearse information, the more likely we are to store it effectively in LTM. If a list is presented quickly, the retention advantage of moving material into LTM is lost for the early items; but because STM is not affected, the items learned last are still available.

There is also a reverse effect. Counting backward out loud immediately after the last item of a list is presented disrupts the recency effect (see Figure 6.2) but not the

Primacy effect: Increased memory for the first few stimuli in a set.

Recency effect: Increased memory for the last few stimuli in a set.

During working memory tasks, both the frontal lobes and perceptual areas of the brain are often activated. Working memory involves a system of areas operating together, not a single area. Depending on the nature of the task (for example, tasks that require holding locations in mind, indicated by blue, versus tasks that require holding shapes in mind, indicated by red), different portions of the frontal lobes and other brain regions are used (Smith, 2000).

primacy effect. Why? The recency effect occurs because the last few items are still in STM and thus can be recalled immediately (when told to recall a list, people typically start with the last few items, as if they are retrieving these items before the information stored temporarily in STM is lost). Counting backward disrupts information in STM, thus disrupting the recency effect. But counting backward does not affect the information in LTM any more than unplugging a computer affects what is stored on the hard drive. The different effects of presentation rate and the interference of backward counting indicate that different memory stores are used.

WORKING MEMORY: THE THINKING PERSON'S MEMORY.

When Fiona was asked how fast the motorist was driving, she thought about the amount of time it took him to move across the intersection. What kind of memory was she using? She was doing more than retrieving items from STM or LTM; she was *using* that information to draw inferences. Whenever you reason something out, whether determining the best route to a destination, buying a comforter that matches your sheets, or deciding which candidate to vote for, you remember relevant facts and use them to help you evaluate the options. In these kinds of situations, you have moved specific information into STM because you are using it or preparing to use it in some way.

Sagittal

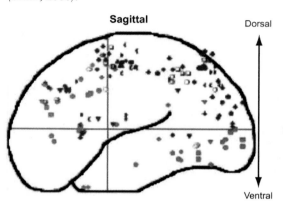

Dorsal

Ventral

Using information relies on yet another form of memory. **Working memory** comprises the components of the whole system that includes STM and the processes that interpret and transform information in STM as required by a given task (Baddeley, 1986, 1992). In some ways, the concept of working memory is an updated view of STM; instead of regarding STM as a passive receptacle, we think of it as part of a system that uses information retained "on line" for brief periods of time (Cohen et al., 1997; D'Esposito et al., 1995; Smith, 2000; Smith & Jonides, 1999).

The idea of working memory extends the original view of STM in two ways, as illustrated in Figure 6.3. First, we now know that there is more than one type of STM and that they differ in the kinds of information stored. Second, there is a **central executive** function that operates on information in one or another of these STMs to plan, reason, or solve a problem. Baddeley (1986, 1992) distinguishes between an STM that holds verbally produced sounds, which he calls the *articulatory loop*, and another STM that holds visual and spatial information, which he calls the *visuospatial sketchpad*. The articulatory loop is like a continuous-play loop on a tape recorder, on which the sound impulses fade when the tape isn't being played; you need to rehearse repeatedly to continue to store sounds. In contrast, the visuospatial sketchpad is like a pad with patterns drawn in fading ink, which briefly retains mental images of the locations of objects (Logie, 1986; Logie & Baddeley, 1990; Logie & Marchetti, 1991; Quinn, 1991). Both STMs are temporary stores of the information you are working on; depending on what you are doing, you add and delete sounds from the taped loop or you sketch and revise diagrams on the pad. In this analogy, you are the central executive, using the two STMs, tape recorder and pad, to help you do different sorts of reasoning. The central executive in your brain is at work when you plan what you will say on a first date or when you think about what you would like to do tomorrow. A crucial part of planning is the ability to use the fruits of past experiences, stored in long-term memory, to anticipate what would happen in a new situation. Working memory is used when you consider how to adapt previous experience to present or future circumstances.

FIGURE 6.3
Working Memory

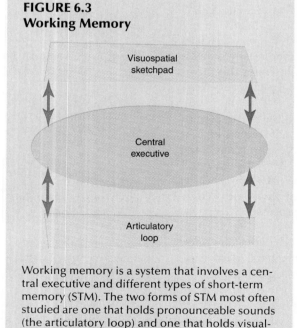

Working memory is a system that involves a central executive and different types of short-term memory (STM). The two forms of STM most often studied are one that holds pronounceable sounds (the articulatory loop) and one that holds visual-spatial patterns (visuospatial sketchpad).

Just as there are different types of STMs, there are different types of long-term memory (LTM). You can draw on these when you recall even the simplest event.

Types of Long-Term Memories: The Multimedia Brain

The fact that memory is not a single capacity becomes especially clear when we look closely at how different kinds of information are stored in LTM. Unlike computers, the brain has multiple "hard drives," if you will.

MODALITY-SPECIFIC MEMORIES. Which is the darker green, a pine tree or a frozen pea? Or, as we asked in Chapter 3, do the first three notes of "Three Blind Mice" go up or down? When answering such questions, most people report recalling visual or auditory memories, "seeing" a tree and a pea, "hearing" the nursery song. Fiona was apparently very good at this type of memory. As we saw in the discussion of perception in Chapter 3, our brains store visual memories so that we may recognize previously seen objects, auditory memories to recognize environmental sounds and melodies, olfactory memories to recognize previously encountered smells, and so on. These **modality-specific memory stores** retain input from a single sense or processing system. In addition to visual, auditory, and olfactory memory stores, we have separate memory stores for touch, movement, and language. Interestingly, nearly everyone finds visual memories easier to recall than verbal memories. If you have a vivid mental image of an event, your chances of accurately remembering the event increase (Brewer, 1988; Dewhurst & Conway, 1994). Thus, Fiona's excellent visual recall suggests that we can be more confident of the accuracy of her memory for the accident.

Many of the brain structures that register input during perception also store that input (Fuster, 1997; Karni & Sagi, 1993; Squire, 1987; Ungerleider, 1995). Damage to particular parts of the brain can disrupt each of these types of LTM (visual, auditory, and so forth) separately while leaving the others intact, which indicates that the information is stored separately (Gardner, 1975; Schacter, 1996; Squire, 1987). Furthermore, researchers have found that when people recall visual versus auditory information into STM (as you did when you answered the questions about the tree and the pea and the tune), different perceptual areas are activated (Halpern & Zatorre, 1999; Mellet, Petit et al., 1998; Thompson & Kosslyn, 2000). The fact that different brain areas are used for the different memories is solid evidence that distinct memory stores are at work.

SEMANTIC VERSUS EPISODIC MEMORY. In each modality-specific LTM store, you can retain two types of information. **Semantic memories** are memories of the meanings of words (a pine is an evergreen tree with long needles), concepts (heat moves from a warmer object to a cooler one), and general facts about the world (the original 13 colonies were established by the British). For the most part, you don't remember when, where, or how you learned this kind of information. In contrast, **episodic memories** are memories of events that are associated with a particular time, place, and circumstance (when, where, and how); in other words, episodic memories provide a *context*. The meaning of the word *memory* is no doubt firmly implanted in your semantic memory, whereas the time and place you first began to read this book are probably in your episodic memory. At first, a new word may be entered in both ways, but after you use it for a while you probably don't remember when, where, or how you learned its meaning. But even though the episodic memory may be gone, the word's meaning is nevertheless retained in semantic memory. Episodic memory for events of your own life are called *autobiographical memories* (Conway & Rubin, 1993).

Brain-scanning studies have provided evidence that semantic and episodic memories are distinct. The frontal lobe, for instance, plays a key role in looking up stored information. However, when we recall semantic memories, the left frontal lobe tends

Working memory (WM): The system that includes specialized STMs and the "central executive" processes that operate on them.

Central executive: The set of processes that operates on information in one or another STM; part of working memory.

Modality-specific memory stores: Memory stores that retain input from a single sense, such as vision or audition, or from a specific processing system, such as language.

Semantic memories: Memories of the meanings of words, concepts, and general facts about the world.

Episodic memories: Memories of events that are associated with a particular context—a time, place, and circumstance.

to be activated more than the right, but vice versa when we recall episodic memories. If the two types of memories were the same, the same parts of the brain would access both (Cabeza & Nyberg, 1997; Nyberg et al., 1996; Shallice et al., 1994).

IMPLICIT MEMORIES: NOT JUST THE FACTS, MA'AM. When you consciously think about a previous experience, you are recalling an **explicit** (also called a **declarative**) memory. Explicit memories can be "looked up" at will and represented in STM; verbal and visual memories are explicit if you can call them to mind in words or images (as you did with the pine tree and the pea). Episodic and semantic memories are explicit memories. Explicit memories are what is stored after cognitive learning occurs (see Chapter 5). When explicit memories are activated, they can be operated on in working memory: You can think about the recalled information in different ways and for different purposes, and build on them with new ideas.

But think of how exhausting it would be if every time you met a friend, you had to try consciously to recall everything you knew about him or her before you could have a conversation. The reason you don't have to go through such a tedious process is that you are guided through the world by **implicit memories,** memories you are unaware of having that nonetheless predispose you to behave in certain ways in the presence of specific stimuli or that make it easier to repeat an action you performed previously (Roediger & McDermott, 1993; Schacter, 1987, 1996). Unlike explicit memories, implicit memories cannot be voluntarily called to mind—that is, brought into STM and thus into awareness.

The first hint that memory can be either explicit or implicit arose from a dreadful accident. H.M., whom you met in Chapter 2, suffered after his surgery from such a severe case of epilepsy that nothing could control his body-wracking convulsions. Finally, in 1953, at age 27, he underwent surgery to remove his hippocampus (and related parts of the brain in the front, inside part of the temporal lobe). His doctors, whom H.M. had met many times, were pleased that the operation lessened his epileptic symptoms, but they were bewildered when he seemed not to recognize them. He could not remember ever having met them, and every time he saw them, he introduced himself and shook hands. To discover just how thorough this memory loss was, one day one of the doctors concealed a pin in his hand and gave H.M. a jab at the handshake. The next day, H.M. again behaved as if he had never seen the doctor before, but as he reached out to shake hands, he hesitated and pulled his hand back. Even though he had no conscious memory of the doctor, his actions indicated that he had learned something about him. He had acquired a type of implicit memory (Hugdahl, 1995a).

Implicit memories are of three major types. The first type is classically conditioned responses of the sort H.M. developed after the pin prick (see Chapter 5; Hugdahl, 1995). The second type of implicit memory is habits. A **habit,** as the term is defined by memory researchers, is a well-learned response that is carried out automatically (without conscious thought) when the appropriate stimulus is present. Habits include the entire gamut of automatic behaviors we engage in every day. When you see a red light, you automatically lift your foot from the accelerator, shift it left, and press it on the brake (we hope!); if you think something is automatic, that's a give-away that the action is being guided by implicit memory. Most of Fiona's memories about how to shoot baskets, for example, are stored as implicit memories. Some of H.M.'s implicit memory was revealed by the working of habit. When one of us examined him some years ago, H.M. was using a walker because he had injured himself slipping on ice. The walker was made of aluminum tubes, and several operations were needed to fold it properly for storage. H.M. did not remember falling on the ice (which would have been an explicit memory), but he could fold and unfold the walker more quickly than the examiner could—thanks to the habit learned through using the device. He clearly had acquired a new implicit memory, even though he had no idea how he had come to need the walker in the first place. The intact ability to learn new habits, but not new episodic memories, demonstrates the difference between implicit and explicit memory.

We know that habits are stored differently from explicit memories because different brain systems underlie the two types of memory. First, consider the neural bases of

Explicit (or declarative) memories: Memories that can be retrieved at will and represented in STM; verbal and visual memories are explicit if the words or images can be called to mind.

Implicit memories: Memories that cannot be voluntarily called to mind, but nevertheless influence behavior or thinking in certain ways.

Habit: A well-learned response that is carried out automatically (without conscious thought) when the appropriate stimulus is present.

explicit memories. Explicit memories cannot form unless the hippocampus and the nearby areas that feed into the hippocampus and receive information from it are functional. The removal of the hippocampus disrupts memory for facts (Mishkin, 1982; Squire, 1987, 1992), and brain-scanning studies have shown that the hippocampus and nearby parts of the cortex are activated when people learn and remember information (Dolan & Fletcher, 1997; Schacter, 1996; Schacter & Wagner, 1999; Squire et al., 1992). Differences in how effectively these brain areas operate could in part explain Juan's and Fiona's different memories of the accident: Nyberg and colleagues (1996) found that people who had more active hippocampi when they studied words later recognized more of the words (Brewer et al., 1998 and Wagner et al., 1998, report similar findings). Second, in contrast to explicit memories, habits can be acquired by animals and humans (remember H.M.) even when the hippocampus and nearby cortex are not functional (Squire, 1987, 1992). In fact, another circuit that bypasses the hippocampus allows us to learn habits (Mishkin & Appenzeller, 1987).

The third major type of implicit memory is **priming,** the result of having just performed a task that makes it easier to perform the same or an associated task more easily in the future (Schacter, 1987, 1996). If you just saw an ant on the floor, you would be primed to see other ants, and thus primed you would now notice them in places where you might previously have missed them (such as on dark surfaces). Priming occurs when a preexisting memory or combination of memories is activated and the activation lingers. Priming that makes the *same* information more easily accessed in the future is called **repetition priming** (this is the kind of priming that enables you to see more ants). Many studies have shown that you can recognize a word or picture more quickly if you have seen it before than if it is novel. Such priming can be very long-lasting; for example, Cave (1997) found that people could name previously seen pictures faster when shown them again 48 weeks after the initial, single viewing. Your first exposure to the stimulus "greases the wheels" for your later reaction to it; in fact, after priming with a familiar object, the brain areas that perform the task work less hard when repeating it than they did initially (Gabrieli et al., 1995, 1996; Henson et al., 2000; Squire et al., 1992). Priming that makes *related* information more easily accessed in the future is called **associative priming.** After discussing the condition of the apples and pears at the local market, you might be more inclined than usual to refer to something weird as "fruity." As with other implicit memories, we are not aware of this sort of priming.

Priming is clearly different from explicit memory. For one thing, Tulving and colleagues (1982) found that although priming was as strong a week after participants had seen a set of words as it was an hour after, explicit memory (as indicated by the ability to recall) had greatly diminished. In fact, priming was just as strong for words that the participants could *not* recall explicitly as it was for words they *could* recall. Indeed, priming occurs even in brain-damaged patients who cannot store new explicit memories (Cave & Squire, 1992; Schacter, 1987; Squire, 1987). Moreover, Jacoby and Dallas (1981) found that methods for improving explicit memory do not affect priming.

Priming is also different from habits. Some brain-damaged patients can learn motor tasks but don't show priming; other patients show the opposite pattern (Butters et al., 1990; Salmon & Butters, 1995). These results demonstrate that more than one type of implicit memory exists. The fact that Fiona acquires skills with ease does not necessarily imply that she will excel at being primed by perceptual information. The major different types of memory are summarized in Figure 6.4.

Priming: The result of having just performed a task that facilitates repeating the same or an associated task.

Repetition priming: Priming that makes the same information more easily accessed in the future.

Associative priming: Priming that makes related information more easily accessed in the future.

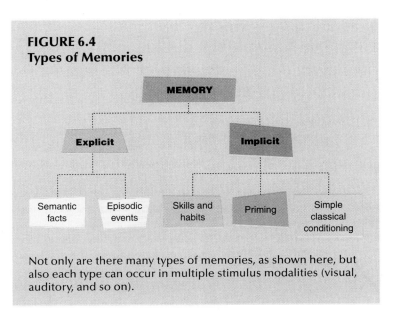

FIGURE 6.4
Types of Memories

Not only are there many types of memories, as shown here, but also each type can occur in multiple stimulus modalities (visual, auditory, and so on).

Foundations of Memory: Neurons and Genes

The next time someone complains that they have a bad memory, you now know to wonder, What sort of memory? Short-term or long-term? Which modalities? Explicit or implicit? In most cases, the different types of memory operate surprisingly independently of one another. Evidence is emerging that different genes underlie different types of memory, serving to demonstrate further that the different types of memory are in fact distinct. To see how genes affect memory, we need to look more closely at the brain.

LONG-TERM POTENTIATION: NEURONS THAT PLAY TOGETHER STAY TOGETHER. All forms of LTM rely on enduring changes in the strength of neural connections. How and why do these changes occur? One key method depends on two events happening at the same time: A sending neuron must release a particular neurotransmitter (glutamate) at the same time that the receiving neuron reaches a specific voltage level. When these two events co-occur, the neurotransmitter activates a special receptor, called the NMDA receptor (for N-methyl-D-aspartate). NMDA activation causes the receiving neuron to change so that the sending neuron needs to send less neurotransmitter to get the same effect in the future. This change essentially strengthens the connection between the sending and receiving neurons. This effect is called **long-term potentiation (LTP)**. Depending on which connections among neurons are altered, different types of memories are stored.

GENES AND MEMORY: TALES OF KNOCK-OUT MICE. Researchers have studied the genes that create the receptors that allow LTP to occur; without these receptors, the connections between neurons cannot be strengthened. How could we tell whether different genes affect different aspects of memory? One answer comes from the study of *knock-out mice*, so named because a particular gene has been "knocked out." Genes are knocked out when a part of the genetic code has been snipped away, deleting all (or crucial parts) of the gene so that it is disabled. The basic idea is that if a gene is used in a particular function, then knocking out the gene should create a deficit in that function. But tracing that connection is easier said than done. For example, early investigators thought they had found that knocking out particular genes disrupted a mouse's ability to remember the location of a concealed platform in a pool of water (the mice wanted to swim to the platform so that they could rest and hence were motivated to remember where it was; Morris, 1984). However, in one such study, Heurta and colleagues (1996) observed that the mice without the "remembering" gene weren't lost; they just didn't swim. When the researchers tickled the mice's hind feet, the animals swam and learned where the platform was located as quickly as normal mice. Their inability to find the platform wasn't caused by poor memory but by a lessened motivation to swim. (We have to wonder whether the researchers may have stumbled on a laziness gene!) One moral of this story is that removing a given gene can have multiple effects, which can cause the animal to do poorly on a test for a number of reasons (Gerlai, 1996).

In spite of these confounded results in early experiments, recent research with knock-out mice has revealed that certain genes do influence LTP, but their effects are limited to specific types of memory. Working together, groups led by Susumu Tonegawa of MIT and Eric Kandel of Columbia University were able to modify a certain gene that is necessary for the receptors used in LTP (McHugh et al., 1996; Tsien et al., 1996). In these studies, a *control sequence*, which turns specific genes on and off, was inserted into the DNA. This control sequence turned off the gene of interest only after the mouse had grown up, and thus the gene would stop working in an otherwise normal adult mouse. Researchers were able to eliminate the functioning of a gene that affects a single part of the hippocampus. Therefore, these animals did not show general problems, such as a lack of enthusiasm for swimming, but they did exhibit difficulty

Long-term potentiation (LTP): A receiving neuron's increased sensitivity to input from a sending neuron, resulting from previous activation.

remembering locations. This more precise study shows that LTP in the hippocampus plays a role in this sort of memory for location. Without the gene, the environmental event—trying to remember the location of a submerged platform—could not turn on the machinery that allows memories to be stored in the brain. However, the knock-out mice were not totally clueless in memory tasks. They did retain some information, and hence LTP in this part of the hippocampus alone cannot be responsible for all memory. Again we see evidence that memory is not a single ability.

Finally, strong evidence for the role of LTP in memory has come from researchers who succeeded in altering genes of mice so that LTP is *enhanced* in the hippocampus and other areas of the brain used in memory. The mutation made the adult mice's neurons respond more like the neurons of young mice, who generally learn better than older ones. These mutated mice could remember more effectively than normal mice. For example, when presented with two objects, mice will explore them. When later shown one of these objects paired with a novel object, the mice will spend more time exploring the new one—provided they can remember which one was shown before. The mutated mice were able to remember such information over longer periods of time than normal mice, in spite of having spent no more time "studying" the objects when they were first presented. Similarly, the mutated mice learned to find the concealed platform in a pool of water more quickly than normal mice (Tang et al., 1999; see also Manabe et al., 1998). No question about it: Forming stronger connections among neurons is key to memory.

LOOKING AT LEVELS

Stressed Memories

When you are stressed, your brain sends signals to your body to prepare it for a fight-or-flight response. One of these signals increases the production of the hormone cortisol (see Chapter 2), which converts protein and fat into sugar, readying the body for rapid action. However, cortisol is a two-edged sword. Sapolsky and his colleagues have shown that in rats and monkeys long-term exposure to cortisol actually kills neurons in the hippocampus (McEwen, 1997; Sapolsky, 1992). And the loss of hippocampal neurons disrupts memory.

Sapolsky studied a troop of monkeys in Africa. The monkeys had a well-defined social order, with some members of the troop being "on top" (getting the first choice of food, mates, and shelter), and others "on the bottom." The monkeys on the bottom were found to have higher levels of cortisol in their blood; their social circumstances put them in a state of near-constant stress. When Sapolsky examined the brains of some of the monkeys who died, he found that those near the bottom of the social order had smaller hippocampi than those who were not continually stressed.

Think about this from the levels perspective: The social situation caused the monkeys to be stressed; the stress caused them to produce high levels of cortisol; the cortisol degraded their hippocampi; the impaired hippocampi caused them to have poorer memories. Now shift to the monkeys' evolutionary cousins—ourselves. MRI studies of the brains of people who have undergone prolonged stress during combat have shown that they have smaller hippocampi than people who were spared these experiences (Bremner et al., 1993). These and similar findings suggest that the results from monkeys may apply to humans. People may become irritated with others who forget tasks, putting stress on the forgetful person. The irritation and implied or stated criticism would probably affect the forgetter's view of him- or herself, and that lowered self-esteem would likely affect whether the forgetter could rise in the social order. So social circumstances (the level of the group) cause stress, which triggers events in the brain that disrupt memory; bad memory can lead to more stress and lowered self-esteem and beliefs about abilities (the level of the person)—which in turn affect behavior in social settings (the level of the group). Fortunately, in humans the effects of stress on the hippocampus may be reversed if the environment changes (McEwen, 1997), a circumstance that introduces yet another set of possible interactions among events at the different levels of analysis.

CONSOLIDATE!

▶ **1. What is a memory store? How do memory stores differ?** A memory store is a set of neurons that serves to retain information. Three types of memory stores have been identified: sensory memory (SM), which briefly stores a large amount of perceptual information; short-term memory (STM), which stores relatively little information for a few seconds (but for perhaps as long as 30 seconds); and long-term memory (LTM), which stores a large amount of information for a long time (hours to years). Only information in STM is in immediate awareness, and such information can be recalled faster than information only in LTM. Working memory is a system that includes specialized STM stores plus a central executive that operates on information stored in STM.

▶ **2. How are different types of information stored over a long period of time?** Each sensory modality (such as vision, audition, and touch) has a separate LTM store; separate memories also exist for motor and verbal information. In addition, each of these types of LTM can be divided into semantic memory—which is memory for meaning, concepts, and facts about the world—and episodic memory—which is memory for events that occur in the context of a spe-

cific time, place, and circumstance. Finally, in addition to explicit memories, which can be voluntarily brought to mind, implicit memories in each modality are evident only in a single context and guide our actions outside our awareness.

▶ **3. How do neurons store memoriees, and what role do genes play in memory?** Neurons store memories by changing the strength of their connections. Long-term potentiation (LTP), which depends on the sending neuron being active at the same time that the receiving neuron has a certain level of voltage, is one method by which connection strengths are changed. Genes encode the production of proteins used to strengthen the connections between neurons during learning, as occurs in LTP. Mice have been created with defects in the genes underlying LTP in the hippocampus. Although they had difficulties, these mice did eventually learn; these findings indicate that memory relies in part on LTP in the hippocampus, but involves other brain areas as well. Findings from studies of mice with enhanced LTP in the hippocampus also provide strong evidence for the role of LTP in the hippocampus for the storage of new explicit memories.

ENCODING AND RETRIEVING INFORMATION FROM MEMORY

The statements Juan and Fiona each gave to the police after witnessing the accident presented certain difficulties. For one thing, they reported seeing different license plate numbers. To make matters worse, Juan was absolutely positive that the driver was of medium height and had dark brown hair, while Fiona insisted that he was rather small and had mousy brown hair. Both witnesses might have stored accurate information in memory but later had trouble digging it out. As you will see, some ways of retrieving information from memory are more effective than others.

▶ 1. What factors affect whether we retain information in memory?

▶ 2. How are memories reconstructed?

Making Memories

Encoding: The process of organizing and transforming incoming information so that it can be entered into memory, to be either stored or compared to previously stored information.

Encoding is the process of organizing and transforming incoming information so that it can be entered into memory, either to be stored or to be compared with previously stored information. Look at Figure 6.5; do you remember which way Abraham Lincoln faces on a penny? Most people don't. Unless you've had reason to pay attention to this feature and encode it, you probably didn't store this information explicitly. In this section we will examine what it means to "store" information in memory and then look at several factors that determine whether this storage will occur.

Information not only goes into STM and then LTM, but often moves in the other direction, from LTM to STM. Indeed, in order for a stimulus to be meaningful, information in LTM must have been activated because this is where meaning is stored. And most information in STM is *meaningful*: that is, you don't see the squiggle "6" as a curved line but as a recognizable number that conveys meaning; similarly, without conscious thought you see the letter pattern WORD as a recognizable word. (Remember the Stroop effect, described in Chapter 3: You can't ignore the meaning of color words when you try to report the color of the ink used to print them.) So when you look up a telephone number, you must first access LTM in order to know how to pronounce the numbers and then keep them in STM as you prepare to make the call. Nevertheless, STM is important in storing information in LTM because working memory relies on STM, and working memory plays a crucial role in helping you organize information in a memorable way.

FIGURE 6.5
Which Coin Is Correct?

Nickerson and Adams (1979) found that people perform remarkably poorly when asked to choose the correct coin. Because we need only to identify pennies versus other coins, not to notice which way Abe faces, we do not encode the profile information very well.

CODING: PACKAGED TO STORE. How convenient it would be if every time you scanned a picture into a computer, the computer automatically named it and stored a brief description. With such a feature, you could easily search for the picture (and its characteristics). As it happens, humans have this capacity and then some. In fact, we often register information using more than one memory system. Paivio and his collaborators (Paivio, 1971) have made a convincing case that the reason pictures are remembered better than words is that pictures can be stored using *dual codes*. A **code** is a mental representation, an internal "re-presentation" of a stimulus or event. Just as you can print letters, draw pictures, or write the dots and dashes of Morse code on a blackboard (all these forms are different representations), your brain can use many types of representations. Pictures can be stored with both a visual and a verbal code; that is, you can describe what you see in words as well as store it visually, so you can later recall it in your mind's eye. Research shows that illustrations improve memory for text (Levie & Lentz, 1982; Levin et al., 1987), particularly if the picture appears before the text (which is why in this book we have tried to place the pictures as close to the relevant text as possible).

As part of the encoding process, you can create new codes for storing material. For example, you can verbally describe visually perceived objects, creating a verbal code, or you can visualize verbally described information, creating a visual code. By creating and storing a verbal code when you perceive information, you don't need to use visual parts of the brain when later recalling the information. Thus when people were asked to name from memory the colors of objects shown to them in black and white drawings, such as fire trucks and tractors, the "color areas" of the brain were not activated (Chao & Martin, 1999). In this study, participants claimed not to use visual mental imagery; the associations apparently were stored verbally, and thus it was not necessary to access modality-specific memories themselves, which would be stored in the perceptual areas that originally registered the information.

Portions of the frontal lobes are often active when people encode new information, an indication that organizational processing is at work (Buckner et al., 1999; Kelley et al., 1998). Indeed, the degree of activation of the frontal lobes when infor-

Code: A mental representation; an internal "re-presentation" of a stimulus or event.

mation is studied predicts how well it will be remembered later (Brewer et al., 1998; Wagner et al., 1998).

CONSOLIDATION. If you were ever in a play, you probably found that although you knew your lines well for the performances, a week or two later you had almost forgotten them. What happened? Consider the following metaphor: Say you want to remember a path you are supposed to take in a few days. Someone shows it to you on a lawn, and to remember it you walk the path over and over, repeatedly tracing its shape. This is a metaphor for *dynamic memory*; if it is not continually active, it is lost. But if you stick with your chosen route long enough, the path you're tracing becomes worn, and grass no longer covers it; this kind of memory is called *structural memory*, and like the path, it no longer depends on continuing activity. When memories are stored in a dynamic form, they depend on continuing neural activity; when they are stored in a structural form, they no longer require ongoing activity to be maintained. The process of wearing a dirt path, of storing the memory as a new structure, is called **consolidation.** One goal of our *Consolidate!* sections is to help you accomplish just this process.

Many studies have shown that memories are initially stored in LTM in a dynamic form and are consolidated only after considerable amounts of time. For example, patients receiving electroshock therapy—powerful jolts of electricity to the head (see Chapter 14)—experience disruption of memory for recent events, even those that are no longer in STM, but memory for older information is unaffected (McGaugh & Herz, 1972). For some kinds of information, such as memories of current events, politics, and television shows, consolidation occurs after a couple of years; but consolidation of memories about your own life may take much longer (Nadel & Moscovitch, 1997).

The plight of H.M. is another piece of evidence that very-long-term explicit memories are stored in a structural form, but more recent memories are stored dynamically. After his operation, H.M. recalled events that occurred two years or more before the surgery well, but he couldn't recall more recent information—and could not, of course, store new explicit memories. The hippocampus and related brain areas are crucial to the consolidation process, but afterward they are no longer necessary. Consolidation also occurs for implicit memories, but in that process a different set of brain areas is involved (Brashers-Krug et al., 1996).

DEPTH AND BREADTH OF PROCESSING. If you want to remember the material in each of the sections of this book, we recommend you do the *Think It Through* exercises at the end of each chapter. We have designed these exercises to take advantage of a fundamental fact about memory: The more you think through information, the better you will remember its meaning. Craik and Lockhart (1972) account for this effect in terms of **depth of processing,** the number and complexity of the operations used when you process information. They argue that the greater the depth of processing, the greater the likelihood of remembering what you have processed. Craik and Tulving (1975) reported a particularly effective demonstration of this effect. They asked participants to read a list of 60 words, telling them that the experiment was a study of perception and "speed of reaction." On seeing each word, the participants were asked a question about it. Three types of questions were posed (but only one for any particular word, randomly interspersed): One question required participants simply to look at the appearance of the word (to decide whether it was printed in capital letters), which did not require accessing detailed information stored in memory; the second led them to access stored information about the sound (for example, to decide whether it

This man is likely to remember later whatever he's thinking about so intently.

rhymes with *train*), requiring a bit more processing; and the third, to access complex semantic information (for example, to decide whether the word would fit into the sentence "The girl placed the _____ on the table"), requiring the most processing. Following this exercise, the participants were unexpectedly asked to recognize as many words from the list as they could in a new list of 180 words (containing the 60 original words and 120 new words). Craik and Tulving found that the greater the depth of processing required to answer the question, the more likely participants were to recognize the word.

What you pay attention to plays a key role in what is encoded into memory. However, the effect is not simply one of "depth," of a matter of degree: If you are shown words and asked which ones rhyme with *train* (which forces you to pay attention to the sounds of the words), you later will recall the *sounds* of the words better than if you were initially asked to decide which words name living versus nonliving objects. But the reverse effect occurs if you are shown words and asked later to recall their meanings; in this case, you will later recall better if you initially judge whether the words named living versus nonliving objects than if you initially evaluated their sounds. The most effective processing is tailored to the reasons the material is being learned (Fisher & Craik, 1977; Morris et al., 1977; Moscovitch & Craik, 1976). Practice on one task will help you perform another to the extent that the two tasks require similar processing; this is the principle of **transfer appropriate processing** (Morris et al., 1977).

If your goal is to understand the material presented in this book, you would do best to think of examples that demonstrate statements made in the text (or, conversely, to think of examples that seem to refute these statements). As to success on tests, you should try to find out what kind of test the instructor will give: If it is an essay test, you would be better off figuring out the connections between the various facts you have read and asking yourself "why" questions about them (Pressley et al., 1995); this sort of studying will be much more helpful than simple memorization, both for success on the test and for lasting understanding. For a multiple-choice or true–false test, however, simple memorization might do as well as more complicated strategies designed to integrate and organize the material, but even here you probably will retain more of the relevant information if you understand the material better.

Information is encoded more effectively if it is *organized* and *integrated* into what you already know, thus engaging greater **breadth of processing.** Encoding that involves great breadth of processing is called **elaborative encoding** (Bradshaw & Anderson, 1982; Craik & Tulving, 1975). Perhaps the most dramatic demonstration of the benefits of elaborative encoding involved an undergraduate, S.F., who after a few month's practice could repeat lists of over 80 random digits (Chase & Ericsson, 1981). This is many, many more digits than can be held in STM, so how could he do it? S.F. was on the track team and was familiar with the times for various segments of races; thus, he was able to convert the numbers on the list into times, data with which he had associations. The digits 2145, for example, might be the times (with two digits each) needed to run two segments of a particular course. But in spite of his spectacular memory for numbers, S.F. was no better than average with letters. His memory in general had not improved over the months of practice with lists of numbers, only his tricks for organizing and integrating information about numbers.

The ability to organize and integrate explains why people in non-Western cultures recall stories better if the contents are familiar than if they are novel (Harris et al., 1992), and why Japanese abacus experts can remember 15 digits forward or backward, but have only average memory for letters or fruit names (Hatano & Osawa, 1983). This ability also explains another of Ebbinghaus's discoveries, that you can remember better if you study in small chunks of time, spread out over time. This kind of **distributed practice** is more effective than **massed practice,** studying all in one session—that is, cramming. For example, Bahrick and Phelps (1987) showed that distributed practice helps people recall new words in Spanish much better than massed practice. Each time you study, you have an opportunity to think of different things that are associated with the new material; these associations provide more hooks into your previously stored knowledge. And the more hooks, the better able you are to store the new material effectively.

Transfer appropriate processing: Processing that transfers to a task that requires similar processing.

Breadth of processing: Processing that organizes and integrates information into previously stored information, often by making associations.

Elaborative encoding: Encoding that involves great breadth of processing.

Distributed practice: Studying in small chunks of time, spread out over time.

Massed practice: Studying all in one session, or cramming.

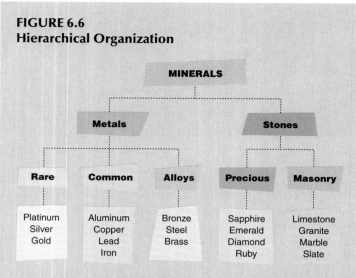

FIGURE 6.6
Hierarchical Organization

Bower and colleagues (1969) asked participants to learn lists of words that named objects in different categories. For some of the people, the words were presented in random order; for others, they were arranged hierarchically, as shown here. The participants who had the diagram to help them organize the list remembered over three times as many words.

The power of effective organization is illustrated in Figure 6.6. Indeed, people in Western cultures spontaneously organize words into categories, and later recall words in the same category before moving on to words from another category (Bousfield, 1953). However, in order to do this, the categories must be noticed; thus, it's a big help if the categories are presented explicitly.

One of the most remarkable discoveries in the study of memory is that it barely matters how much or how hard you *try* to learn something; what matters is how well you integrate and organize the material. Bower (1972) describes experiments in which participants were asked to form a mental image connecting each pair of words in a list (for example, pairing *car* and *desk*, perhaps by imagining a desk strapped to the roof of a car). In one part of the study, the participants were told to use the image to memorize the pairs of words; this kind of learning, in which you *try* to learn something, is called **intentional learning.** In another part, the participants were told simply to rate the vividness of the image and did not try to learn the pairs of words; learning that occurs without intention is called **incidental learning.** The interesting finding was that participants in the incidental learning part did as well as those who were told to memorize the words. The effort that went into organizing the objects into an image appears to have helped the participants learn, even without a specific instruction. This effect has been found repeatedly, with different kinds of learning tasks (Anderson, 2000; Hyde & Jenkins, 1973).

EMOTIONALLY CHARGED MEMORIES. Because Juan had previously lost a close relative in a car crash, the accident he witnessed with Fiona was an especially emotional event for him. This is an important factor in memory: People store emotionally charged information better in episodic memory than they do neutral information. Bradley and colleagues (1992) showed people slides with positive, negative, and neutral images, for example, an attractive nude young man hugging an attractive nude young woman, a burned body, a table lamp. The participants later remembered the arousing stimuli, both positive and negative, better than the neutral ones.

Why does emotion boost memory? Cahill, McGaugh, and colleagues (1994) have begun to answer this question in detail. They showed people pictures that illustrated a story. For some participants, the pictures were all described in a neutral way ("While walking along, the boy sees some wrecked cars in a junk yard, which he finds interesting."); for others, the pictures at the beginning and end were described in a neutral way, but the ones in the middle were described as depicting a bloody accident ("While crossing the road, the boy is caught in a terrible accident which critically injures him."). An hour before seeing the slides, half of each set of participants was given a medically inactive sugar pill; the other half was given a drug that interferes with noradrenaline, a neurotransmitter essential for the operation of the hippocampus (which, in turn, plays a crucial role in encoding new information into memory). A week later, all the participants were given surprise memory tests. As expected, the group that received the sugar pill showed better memory for the pictures that had an emotional context, but the group that received the noradrenaline blocker failed to show this memory boost for emotional material.

But why does emotion result in more noradrenaline's being produced, which in turn causes enhanced memory encoding? Cahill and McGaugh thought that the boost

Intentional learning: Learning that occurs as a result of trying to learn.

Incidental learning: Learning that occurs without intention.

in memory for emotional material reflects the activity of the amygdala, which is known to play a key role in emotion. To test this idea, Cahill and his colleagues (1996) used PET scanning to examine the relation between activity in the amygdala and the degree to which people could recall emotionally arousing or neutral film clips. The amount of activity in the right amygdala when the participants had seen the clips later predicted remarkably well how many clips they could recall. Thus, the enhanced memory for emotional material relies on the activation of the amygdala, which in turn influences the hippocampus.

A special case of emotionally charged memory is **flashbulb memory,** an unusually vivid and accurate memory of a dramatic event. It is as if a flashbulb in the mind goes off at key moments, creating instant records of the

Many people remember where they were and what they were doing when they first heard about the death of Princess Diana. Do you?

events. Perhaps you have such a memory for the moment you heard about the death of Princess Diana in 1997. Brown and Kulik (1977) coined the term "flashbulb memory" and conducted the first studies of the phenomena. They polled people about a number of events, counting the recollections as flashbulb memories if respondents claimed to remember details about where they were when they learned of the event, from whom they heard about it, and how they or others felt at the time. Most of the people they polled at the time had flashbulb memories of President John F. Kennedy's assassination. In contrast, although three quarters of the African Americans interviewed had flashbulb memories for the assassination of Martin Luther King, fewer than one third of the whites had such memories. Brown and Kulik suggested that only events that have important consequences for a person are stored as flashbulb memories. Neisser and Harsch (1992) studied college students' memory of the *Challenger* disaster, interviewing them within a day of the accident and again two and a half years later. They found that although people may be very confident of their flashbulb memories, these memories often become distorted over time. Moreover, this distortion becomes progressively worse with the passage of time (Schmolck et al., 2000). Nevertheless, in general, flashbulb memories are more accurate than other types of memories (Schacter, 1996, pp. 197–201), perhaps because of their emotional content.

Would it have been a good idea if we had written the opening story to be more memorable by making it more emotionally charged, perhaps adding that the bike rider split open his scalp and then convulsed in a pool of blood, his face contorted and splattered with gore? We considered doing this, but we realized that making the accident more memorable in this way could have distracted you from remembering the other content of the incident—and perhaps even of the chapter itself! When people are shown a set of neutral stimuli and then a highly emotionally charged one, not only do they recall the emotional one best, but they also tend to forget the stimuli that came immediately before and after this arousing one. This disruptive effect, called the *von Restorf effect,* occurs with any attention-grabbing stimulus, not just emotionally charged ones. People apparently are so busy thinking about the key stimulus that earlier and later ones are not encoded into LTM.

The Act of Remembering: Reconstructing Buried Cities

It is tempting to think of memory as a collection of file drawers that contain assorted documents, books, tapes, and disks, and that to recall something we simply open a drawer and fetch the sought contents, all neat and complete in labeled folders. But memory doesn't work this way. When we open that file drawer, we don't find, say, a book, but instead a bunch of partially torn pages that are not necessarily in order. Remembering is in many ways similar to the work archaeologists do when they find

Flashbulb memory: An unusually vivid and accurate memory of a dramatic event.

fragments of buildings, walls, furniture, and pottery, and reconstruct from them a long-buried city; they fit the pieces together in a way that makes sense and fill in the missing parts (Neisser, 1967). We store in episodic memory only bits and pieces of a given event and use information from episodic memories of similar situations and from semantic memories of general facts about the world to fit the pieces together and fill in the gaps.

The most famous demonstration that memory involves reconstruction was reported by British psychologist Frederic C. Bartlett in 1932. Bartlett had college students read a version of a Native American legend, previously unfamiliar to them, called *The War of the Ghosts* (these Cambridge University students knew little about Native American culture). According to the legend, a young Indian was hunting seals when he was recruited into a war party. He was wounded during a battle and thought he was being taken home by ghosts, but in fact he was rescued by others in his war party. Although he did not feel himself to be injured, he soon died; then something black came out of his mouth.

At different intervals after their first readings, the students were asked to recall the story. Bartlett found that as time went on, the students' memories of the story changed. Sometimes they added new events; for example, one student misremembered hearing that someone cried out that the enemies were ghosts. Sometimes they reorganized the events in the story, scrambling the order. Bartlett concluded that we store key facts and later use them to reconstruct a memory by filling in the missing information. This conclusion has been borne out by many subsequent studies (Alba & Hasher, 1983).

The fragmentary nature of memory is also revealed in the *tip-of-the-tongue phenomenon*. Have you ever had the feeling that you know a word but just can't remember it? Brown and McNeill (1966) studied this phenomenon by reading definitions of relatively rare words and asking the participants to recall the words being defined. As expected, people often "knew they knew it" but couldn't quite summon up the entire word. Instead, they recalled only some of the aspects of a word, such as its relative length and perhaps even its first syllable. We don't store words as unitary wholes but as collections of different specifications—which we can sometimes recall individually.

RECOGNITION VERSUS RECALL. All remembering involves tapping into the right fragments of information stored in long-term memory. We remember information in two ways. **Recall** is the intentional bringing to mind of explicit information or, put more technically, the transfer of explicit information from LTM to STM. Once information is in STM, you are aware of it and can communicate it. **Recognition** is the matching of an encoded input to a stored representation, which allows you to know that it is familiar and that it occurred in a particular context, such as on a list (as used by memory researchers, the term *recognition* also implies identification; see Chapter 3). Essay tests demand recall; the essay writer must retrieve facts from memory. Multiple-choice tests call for recognition; the test-taker must recognize the correct answer among the options.

All else being equal, tests that require you to recognize information are easier than tests that demand recall. But recognition can become difficult if you must discriminate between similar choices, as shown in Figure 6.7. The more similar the choices, the harder it is to recognize the correct one. Similar objects or concepts have more characteristics in common than do dissimilar ones. If the choices are dissimilar, you can pick out the correct one on the basis of just a few stored features. But if the choices are similar, you must have encoded the object or concept in great detail in order to recognize the correct answer. Professors who want to make devilishly hard multiple-choice tests put this principle to work. If the alternative answers on the test have very similar meanings, the test-taker must know more details than if the choices are very different. In general, the more distinctive properties of a stimulus you have stored in memory, the better you can recognize it.

Recall: The act of intentionally bringing explicit information to awareness, which requires transferring the information from LTM to STM.

Recognition: The act of encoding an input and matching it to a stored representation.

FIGURE 6.7
Discriminating Among Choices

In which lineup would it be easier to pick out the culprit? In which lineup would you be more likely to identify falsely?

Of course, you do not always know in advance which details you will need to remember. Suppose Juan and Fiona are asked to pick the driver who hit the cyclist from a police lineup. In the lineup both the driver and another man in the group of six are tall, a bit overweight, and brown haired. The major difference between them is that the driver has a scar on his left cheek. If neither Fiona nor Juan noticed the driver's cheek, they will be hard pressed to identify him. Both recognition and recall rely on activating collections of fragments stored in LTM. If the appropriate fragments are not present, you cannot distinguish among similar alternatives and will have difficulty recalling information.

THE ROLE OF CUES: HINTS ON WHERE TO DIG. How does an archaeologist know where to dig to find the right bits of pottery to reconstruct a water jug? A logical place to start might be in the ruins of a kitchen. The archaeologist digs, finds bits of a typical kitchen floor from the period, and then is encouraged to continue digging in the same area. Similarly, a good cue directs you to key stored fragments, which then allow you to remember. **Cues** are stimuli that help you remember; they are reminders of an event.

Imagine running into an acquaintance in a bookstore and trying to remember his name. You might recall that when you met him, he reminded you of someone else with

If you have seen both the original Frankenstein *movie and the 1974 Mel Brooks film* Young Frankenstein, *you may have noticed how "authentic" Dr. Frankenstein's laboratory looked in the newer movie. This authenticity is not accidental; Brooks bought the original laboratory set from the 1931 Boris Karloff version of* Frankenstein *and used it in his movie (Seuling, 1976). This set and its furnishings were retrieval cues, which Brooks hoped would help you experience the movie in the way he intended.*

FIGURE 6.8
What Makes a Good Cue?

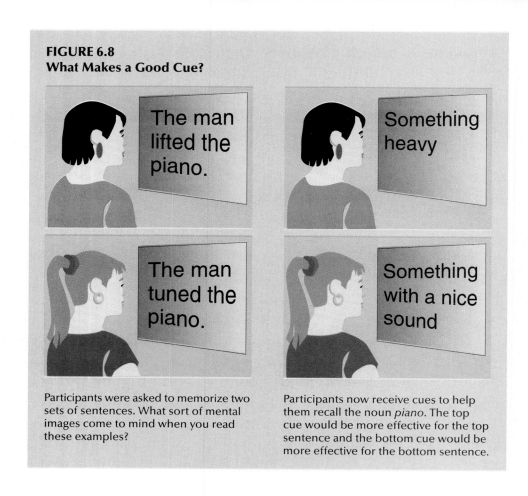

The man lifted the piano.

Something heavy

The man tuned the piano.

Something with a nice sound

Participants were asked to memorize two sets of sentences. What sort of mental images come to mind when you read these examples?

Participants now receive cues to help them recall the noun *piano*. The top cue would be more effective for the top sentence and the bottom cue would be more effective for the bottom sentence.

the same name who had a similar hairline. Here the hairline is a cue, reminding you of your friend Sam and allowing you to greet this new Sam by name. Would it help Fiona and Juan to remember details if they later saw a photograph of the crumpled bike and the injured cyclist at the scene of the accident? What makes something a good cue? As illustrated in Figure 6.8 (Barclay et al., 1974), a helpful cue matches fragments of information stored in LTM.

Godden and Baddeley (1975) dramatically illustrated the role of cues in an ingenious experiment. They asked scuba divers to learn a list of words either when they were underwater or when they were on land. They then tested half the divers in the same setting where they learned the list, and the other half in the other setting. The results showed that the participants remembered more words if they were tested in the environment in which they had originally learned the words. The significance of this finding is that when we learn, we are learning not only the material, but also the general setting and other incidental events that occur at the same time; and these events can later help cue us to recall the information (Flexser & Tulving, 1978; Koutstaal & Schacter, 1997; Parker & Gellatly, 1997). So, if at all possible, study as much as you can in circumstances similar to those of the testing room—if there won't be music playing during the test, don't study while listening to music.

SUPPLYING YOUR OWN CUES. Some cues are internally generated. We remember information better if we are in the same mood or psychological state (such as being hungry or sleepy) when we try to remember it as when we first learned it. If you were hungry when you studied material, you will remember it better if you are hungry at the time of recall than if you are stuffed. This can be a sobering thought if you are preparing for an exam: If you drink alcohol while studying, you will recall the information better if you are drinking later when you try to remember it. This effect is called **state-dependent retrieval** (Eich, 1989): Information is better remembered if recall is attempted in the same psychological state as when the information was first encoded. A closely related effect occurs with mood: If you are in a happy mood at the time you learn something, you later may remember it better when you are feeling happy than when you are feeling sad (Bower, 1981, 1992). The effects of mood are not always very strong, however, and they can be overshadowed by other factors, such as how well the information is organized (Eich, 1995). Neither your psychological state nor your mood appears to be a very powerful retrieval cue.

As shown in Godden and Baddeley's study of divers, the properties of the environment in which you learn something become associated with that information in memory and can also serve as retrieval cues. If you are not in the original environment when you want to remember particular information, try to "supply the environment yourself" by visualizing it; memory is improved when you can mentally supply cues from the original setting in which the material was learned (Smith, 1988). If you lose your keys or wallet, retrace your steps in your mind's eye, if not in reality. This retracing puts you in the same environment as when you last saw the missing item, so that you are more likely to remember where you left it.

Cues can also arise when you remember information associated with a sought memory. Psychologists were surprised to discover that, if they showed people pictures and then asked them to recall the names of the pictures over and over, after a while recall improved, even though the participants were not given feedback or other additional cues. If at first you don't remember, try, try again. Improved memory over time, without feedback, is called **hypermnesia** (Erdelyi, 1984; Payne, 1987). Hypermnesia probably occurs because you remember different aspects of the information each time you try to recall it, and the bit that is remembered is then used as a retrieval cue. Some of these self-supplied cues will be effective, and thus you remember pictures better as you keep trying to remember them. So if at first you cannot recall someone's name, don't give up. Eventually you may hit on the memory of a retrieval cue, such as the shape of a hairline, which in turn will allow you finally to remember the name. Fiona and Juan would be well advised to keep trying to remember the scene of the accident, over and over.

State-dependent retrieval: Recall that is better if it occurs in the same psychological state as when the information was first encoded.

Hypermnesia: Memory that improves over time without feedback, particularly with repeated attempts to recall.

LOOKING AT LEVELS

Memory in Tribal Africa

Michael Cole and his colleagues (Cole et al., 1971, p. 120) tested members of the Kpelle tribe in rural western Africa by giving them names of objects in different categories and then asking them to recall these words. What would you do if you were asked to remember the words *shirt, apple, pear, sock, pants, banana, grapes,* and *hat.* We've seen that Westerners tend to organize the words into categories (in this case, clothing and fruit). But the tribal members did not. They could use this strategy when it was pointed out to them, but they did not do so on their own. Why not? Their culture stresses the importance of each object, animal, and person as an individual being. Organizing according to categories is not important in their society and in fact might impede them in going about their daily lives.

At the level of the group, learning the words was affected by the fact that categorization is not important to this culture. At the level of the person, the culture led tribe members to hold beliefs about the worth and uniqueness of each object and event in the world. At the level of the brain, it is known that parts of the frontal lobes are critically involved in categorization. Indeed, patients with brain damage to these regions often fail to group objects normally when recalling them (Gershberg & Shimamura, 1995; Stuss et al., 1994).

Think about how events at these levels interact: The training that the members of the tribe receive when growing up, during which time they absorb their culture's worldview, affects how their brains work. At the level of the person, according to their values categorizing is not particularly useful, and categorizing words is not useful at all. It was also clear that when asked by the investigators to categorize (which is a social interaction), the members of the tribe could perform the task—which is another example of the influence of events at the level of the group on the operation of the brain. All normal adults can categorize; whether they choose to do so is another question.

CONSOLIDATE!

▶ *1. What factors affect whether we retain information in memory?* One key to storing memories effectively is to organize the information well. In addition, using two codes, verbal and visual, is more effective than using only a single code. Material must be consolidated, that is, stored structurally, which can take years to complete. In general, thinking deeply about material, which requires retrieving information from memory at the time, results in more effective storage, as does breadth of encoding, that is, thinking about how the new material relates to previously stored material. However, the effectiveness of encoding depends on its purposes; for example, encoding sound ("superficial" encoding) at the time of study is more effective than encoding the meaning of a word ("deep" encoding) if the memory test requires recalling sound. Finally, emotionally charged material is generally stored more effectively than emotionally neutral material.

▶ *2. How are memories reconstructed?* Recognition is the determination that presented information is familiar or that it occurred in a particular context; recall is the retrieval of required information from long-term memory. Both recognition and recall rely on activating collections of fragments stored in LTM. If the appropriate fragments are not present, you cannot distinguish among similar alternatives and will have difficulty recalling information. Cues, or reminders, are effective to the extent that they match material stored in LTM. To aid memory, you can supply your own cues by thinking about the context in which the information was encoded, such as the time of day or the physical environment.

FACT, FICTION, AND FORGETTING: WHEN MEMORY GOES WRONG

A few months after the accident, Fiona was still convinced that her memory was accurate, even though it was now conclusively proved that the car did not stop at the stop sign. Moreover, both Juan and Fiona had forgotten what they had said was the car's license plate number. They could, however, still remember other things they'd noticed about the accident. But the injured bike rider could not remember anything he had seen or done for many hours before the accident, or the accident itself. What causes losses and failures of memory such as these?

▶ 1. How can actual memories be distinguished from false ones?

▶ 2. Is a forgotten memory necessarily gone forever, or is it still stored but difficult to retrieve?

▶ 3. What is amnesia?

▶ 4. Are memories ever repressed?

False Memories

Not everything we remember actually happened. **False memories** are memories of events or situations that did not in fact occur.

IMPLANTING MEMORIES. Deese (1959) and Roediger and McDermott (1995) showed that people regularly make errors of the sort illustrated by Figures 6.9 and 6.10. (If you weren't fooled, read the list of words to a friend and wait 5 minutes before testing; this will increase the likelihood of an error.) We associate the idea of "sweet" with all the words, so its representation in LTM becomes activated and associated with the context of the list, and we misremember having seen it. Here is the critical point: In general, we do not necessarily remember what actually happened but rather what we *experience* as having happened.

Lest you think that misremembering only occurs when associated material is stored, consider this disturbing study reported by psychologist Elizabeth Loftus (1993). She asked one member of a pair of siblings to tell his younger, 14-year-old brother about the time the younger brother had been lost in a shopping mall when he was five years old. This story was told as if it were fact, but it was entirely fiction. No special effort was made to encourage the younger brother to remember the story. However, after merely hearing about being lost, the youngster later gave every indication of having genuine memories of the event, adding rich detail to the story he had been told. For example, the boy claimed to remember the flannel shirt worn by the old man who found him, his feelings at the time, and the scolding he later received from his mother. When this study was repeated with many participants, about one quarter of them fell victim to the implanting of such false memories (Loftus & Pickrell, 1995). Moreover, these participants clung steadfastly to their false memories, refusing even on debriefing to believe that they had been artificially created. Similar results have been reported by Hyman and his collaborators (Hyman & Billings, 1998; Hyman & Pentland, 1996).

However, some false memories are easier to create than others. Pezdek and colleagues (1997) found that whereas some participants did acquire false memories of being lost in a shopping mall, none acquired false memories of having been given a rectal enema during childhood. People may have an intuitive grasp of the role of emotion in memory, which leads us to know that we would be sure to remember such an incident if it had actually happened. (The ethics of carrying out such studies might be an interesting topic for discussion.)

Distortions of memory can be implanted in very simple ways. In a now-classic experiment, Loftus and colleagues (1978), asked people to watch a series of slides that showed a red Datsun stopping at a stop sign and then proceeding into an accident. The participants were then asked either "Did another car pass the red Datsun while it was stopped at the stop sign?" or "Did another car pass the red Datsun while it was stopped at the yield sign?" The questions differed only by a single word, *stop* or *yield*. Loftus and her colleagues found that many more people who had been asked the yield-sign version of the question later mistakenly recalled that a yield sign had been present. In this case, the question itself interfered with memory. Loftus initially speculated that the misleading question erased the accurate memory, but later evidence suggests that the original memory was still present but difficult to access after the misleading question was presented (McCloskey & Zaragoza, 1985).

These kinds of memory errors have direct practical—and often quite serious—implications. After a crime is committed, for instance, witnesses are interviewed by the police, read newspaper stories about the crime, perhaps see television reports. All this

**FIGURE 6.9
False Memory**

candy	caramel
soda pop	chocolate
honey	cake
pie	icing
fudge	cookie
cotton candy	

Please read this list of words. Now go to Figure 6.10 on page 222.

False memory: Memory for an event that did not actually occur.

FIGURE 6.10
True or False?

candy	chocolate
soda pop	cake
honey	sweet
pie	icing
fudge	cookie
cotton candy	

Did the words *candy, chocolate,* or *sweet* appear on the list you read on page 221? Are you sure? In fact, the word *sweet* does not appear. If you think it did, you are not alone; most people do. This exercise is an example of a false memory that was easily implanted in your head.

Reality monitoring: An ongoing awareness of perceptual and other properties that distinguish real from imagined stimuli.

Source amnesia: A failure to remember the source of information.

information can interfere with actual memories. Moreover, during a trial, the way a question is asked can influence a witness's faith in his or her recollection, or even change the testimony altogether.

DISTINGUISHING FACT FROM FICTION. Does any aspect of false memories distinguish them from real memories? Daniel Schacter and his colleagues (1996) performed the "sweet" experiment, using similar key terms, while the participants' brains were being scanned. The participants were then asked which words were on the list and which words were merely implied by the listed ones. The hippocampus, which plays a key role in encoding new information into memory, was activated both when participants recognized actual words listed *and* when they identified associated words not on the original list. Crucially, when words actually on the list were correctly recognized, brain areas in the temporal and parietal lobes that register the sound and meaning of spoken words also were activated. In contrast, these areas were *not* active when people encountered words not on the list. Apparently, the construction of memory activates the representations of the perceptual qualities of stored words. Because the false words were not actually heard when the original list was read, this information was not activated. This cue of a "missing perception" may not be used all the time, but it is clearly operative in many situations (Johnson et al., 1997).

The same principle applies to remembering a real versus an imagined event. Johnson and her colleagues (Johnson & Raye, 1981; Johnson et al., 1993) found that people often confuse actually having seen something with merely having imagined seeing it (which may be the basis of some false memories; Garry & Polaschek, 2000). Indeed, Dobson and Markham (1993) found that people who experience vivid mental images are more likely to confuse having read a description of an event with having seen it. **Reality monitoring** is the ongoing awareness of the perceptual and other properties that distinguish real from imagined stimuli. Reality monitoring can be improved greatly if people are led to pay attention to the context in which stimuli occur (Lindsay & Johnson, 1989). Mather and colleagues (1997) and Norman and Schacter (1997) found that when people are asked to pay attention to the amount of perceptual detail in their memories (as would occur if they tried to notice the texture of objects, other nearby objects, and shadows), they are better able to distinguish actual memories from false memories. However, there is a limit to how well people can use such cues to distinguish real from false memories; false memories produced in the "sweet" task, for example, are remarkably persistent even when people are warned in advance about the possibility of such memories (McDermott & Roediger, 1998).

A related problem was illustrated by Juan's comment to one of the detectives who was continuing to investigate the accident. He remarked that the cyclist must have been very near the side of the road when the accident occurred, given the position of the ruined bike. He was embarrassed when the detective pointed out that he himself had made this observation to Juan a couple of weeks earlier. Juan was suffering from **source amnesia,** a failure to remember the source of information. Patients who have suffered frontal lobe damage sometimes have an extreme version of this impairment; they generally cannot remember who said what, or when and where they heard it. But even people without brain damage, like Juan or you, can experience source amnesia; all it requires is forgetting the source of information in episodic memory (Schacter, 1996). Such problems are surprisingly common; indeed, some cases of unintentional plagiarism may be a result of source amnesia (Marsh et al., 1997; Schacter, 1999). In general, false memories are not always easy to distinguish from actual ones.

Forgetting: Many Ways to Lose It

It was unfortunate that the police took as long as they did to arrive at the scene of the accident. As first shown in 1885 by Hermann Ebbinghaus, people recall recent events better than more distant ones, and most forgetting occurs soon after learning. However, as time goes on, people lose less and less additional information from memory (Wixted & Ebbesen, 1991, 1997). Ebbinghaus discovered the **forgetting curve**, illustrated in Figure 6.11, which shows the rate at which information is forgotten over time.

Why do people lose information from memory? Sometimes the information was not well encoded in the first place. Remember the path traced over and over again into the grass? If the walker abandons the path before it is completely worn through to bare dirt, the pattern of the path is not stored structurally. Similarly, you must not "abandon" information—you must actively think about it if it is to be encoded effectively in LTM. An **encoding failure** results if you do not process information well enough to begin consolidation (Schacter, 1999).

Encoding failure produces huge losses of information shortly after learning, which may be one reason for the sharp drop at the beginning of the forgetting curve. But even if information is properly encoded, it can be lost later. Why? For many years memory researchers hotly debated the fate of information that was once stored but then forgotten. One camp argued that once memories are gone, they are gone forever. The memory decays and disappears, just as invisible ink fades until nothing is left. The other camp claimed that the memories themselves are intact but cannot be "found." The ink hasn't faded, but the message has been misfiled. Both camps were partly right.

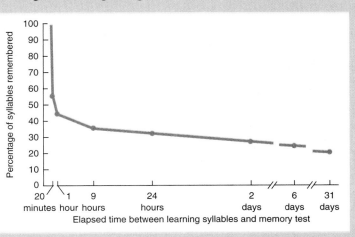

FIGURE 6.11
Ebbinghaus's Forgetting Curve

The forgetting curve shows that information becomes harder to recall over time but that most forgetting occurs relatively soon after learning.

DECAY: FADE AWAY. The invisible ink theory proposes that memories **decay**; that is, they degrade with time. The relevant connections between neurons are lost. What evidence supports this theory? In the sea slug Aplysia, which has a relatively simple nervous system, it has been possible to document that the strength of the connections between neurons established by learning fades away over time (Baily & Chen, 1989). If human neurons are similar, as seems likely, memories may in fact decay over time. Indeed, researchers have produced evidence not only that certain genes promote stronger connections among neurons, but also that other genes prevent such connections and hence block memory (Abel et al., 1998). When these "memory suppressor genes" are turned on, they could cause the decay of connections that store memories.

Evidence refuting the decay theory seemed to come from dramatic findings described by Penfield (1955). Before performing brain surgery, neurosurgeons such as Penfield sometimes put small electrodes on the exposed cortex of awake patients and stimulated neurons electrically. A few patients reported vivid images and memories of long-forgotten events. For example, on having a particular area of the brain stimulated, one patient said, "Yes, sir, I think I heard a mother calling her little boy somewhere. It seemed something that happened years ago." However, at least some of these reports may not have been memories but images created on the spot (Squire, 1987). There is no strong evidence that all memories stay stored forever. In fact, these oft-cited results occurred for only a minority of patients, and later work failed to reveal compelling evidence that memories are stored forever.

Forgetting curve: A graphic representation of the rate at which information is forgotten over time: Recent events are recalled better than more distant ones, but most forgetting occurs soon after learning.

Encoding failure: A failure to process to-be-remembered information well enough to begin consolidation.

Decay: The fading away of memories with time because the relevant connections between neurons are lost.

INTERFERENCE: TANGLED UP IN MEMORY. The view that a mix-up in memory often explains forgetting has long been supported by strong direct evidence. If every summer you work with a group of kids as a camp counselor, you will find that learning the names of the current crop impairs your memory of the names of last year's campers. This is an example of interference. **Interference** is the disruption of the ability to remember one piece of information by the presence of other information. Two types of interference can plague your memories: retroactive and proactive.

Retroactive interference is interference that disrupts memory for something learned earlier. Learning the names of the new campers can interfere with your memory of the names of the previous group. **Proactive interference** is interference by something already learned that makes it difficult to learn something new. Your having learned the names of previous groups of kids may interfere with your learning the names on this summer's roster, particularly if some of the new names are similar to old ones.

Why does interference occur? The capacity of LTM is not the problem. You are not overloading a "memory-for-people" box in your brain; some politicians, after all, can remember the names of thousands of people with little or no difficulty. Interference probably occurs because the retrieval cues for various memories are similar, and thus a given cue may call up the wrong memory. The more similar the already-known and to-be-remembered information, the more interference you get (Adams, 1967).

The first president of Stanford University, David Starr Jordan, apparently worried that he might eventually fill up his memory if he learned too much. (He was wrong, of course; remember the paradox of the expert discussed in *Using Psychology to Learn Psychology*.) President Jordan was an ichthyologist, an expert on fish who knew the names and habits of thousands of underwater species. At the beginning of each year he met the new students and politely smiled as they were introduced, but ignored their names. One bold student asked President Jordan if he had heard his name clearly, and repeated it. Jordan listened and realized he had now learned the student's name. He slapped himself on the forehead and exclaimed, "Drat, there goes another fish!"

Amnesia: Not Just Forgetting to Remember

When the bike rider regained consciousness, he could not recall anything that had happened to him since the previous evening. Why? Neither normal decay nor interference accounts for such unusual losses of memory. Instead, the cyclist's memory failure is an example of **amnesia**, a loss of memory over an entire time span, typically resulting from brain damage caused by accident, infection, or stroke. Amnesia is not like normal forgetting, which affects only some of the material learned during a given period.

Amnesia produced by brain damage usually affects episodic memories while leaving semantic memories intact (Warrington & McCarthy, 1988). Most people who

A gunshot wound to the head, as happened to Harrison Ford's character in the movie Regarding Henry, *is only one way that amnesia can occur.*

have an accident such as the cyclist's have no idea what they were doing immediately before the accident, but they can remember semantic information such as their names and birth dates. Sometimes, however, amnesia impairs only semantic memory. For example, De Renzi and colleagues (1987) report a patient who forgot the meanings of words and most characteristics of common objects. Nevertheless, she remembered details about key events in her life, such as her wedding and her father's illness.

Amnesia may be retrograde or anterograde (Mayes & Downes, 1997; Parkin, 1987). **Retrograde amnesia** disrupts previous memories. This is the sort of amnesia often popularized in soap operas and movies. In the movie *Regarding Henry*, the title character played by Harrison Ford is shot during a convenience store robbery and loses his memories about his family, his job, and other aspects of his life history. But he can still speak fluently and seems to know everyday facts about the world and even facts about the nature of his job as a lawyer. Most of us suffer from a special form of retrograde amnesia called *infantile amnesia* or *childhood amnesia* (Newcombe et al., 2000): We don't remember our early childhood experiences. **Anterograde amnesia** leaves already consolidated memories intact but prevents the learning of new facts. It affects all explicit memories—that is, memories of facts that can be brought to consciousness voluntarily—and produces massive encoding failure. H.M. had a form of anterograde amnesia. Its manifestation is well presented in an old joke. A man runs into a doctor's office, screaming, "Doc! I've lost my memory!" The doctor asks him, "When did this happen?" The man looks at him, puzzled, and says, "When did what happen?" It is no joke for people with anterograde amnesia, who live as if frozen in the present moment of time.

What happens in the brain to produce amnesia? Often, as in the case of H.M., the cause involves damage to the hippocampus or its connections to or from other parts of the brain. Indeed, Zola-Morgan and colleagues (1986) studied the brain of an unfortunate man who suffered a bizarre fencing injury in which a long narrow foil slipped up his nostril and damaged part of his brain. This accident produced anterograde amnesia. The researchers studied his brain after his death and found only a tiny amount of damage to one part of the hippocampus. This seemingly slight damage, in just the wrong spot, had a major impact on the fencer's memory, and thus on his life.

Sometimes amnesia can result when areas of the cortex that serve as memory stores become degraded. As noted earlier, all memories are a result of changes in the interactions of individual neurons, and most neurons involved in memory are in the cortex. *Alzheimer's disease*, for example, typically begins with small memory deficits, which become progressively worse. In the later stages of the disease, people with Alzheimer's cannot remember who they are, where they are, who their family and friends are. Alzheimer's disease not only affects the hippocampus but also degrades other parts of the brain that serve as memory stores. Depending on which other parts of the brain are affected, these patients can have greater amnesia for one form of information or another; for example, some patients have worse spatial memory than verbal memory, and vice versa for others (Albert et al., 1990).

Repressed Memories: Real or Imagined?

Recent years have witnessed many dramatic reports of suddenly recollected memories. Some people claim to have suddenly remembered that they were sexually molested by their parents decades before, when they were no more than 3 years old. One person claimed that as a child he had been strapped to the back of a dolphin as part of a bizarre devil worship ritual. Are these false memories, or are they **repressed memories**, real memories that have been pushed out of consciousness because they are emotionally threatening, as Freud believed? Whether or not repressed memories exist is perhaps the most controversial issue in memory research today (Benedict & Donaldson, 1996; Golding et al., 1996; Knapp & VandeCreek, 1996; Melchert, 1996; Pope, 1996; Rubin, 1996).

Evidence for repressed memories comes from studies reported by Williams (1994). She interviewed 129 women 17 years after each had been admitted to a hospital emergency room for treatment of sexual abuse in childhood. Thirty-eight percent of the women had no memory of an event of sexual abuse; in fact, 12% claimed that they had never been abused. These results suggest that some people may forget traumatic memories. Could this finding simply reflect infantile amnesia, the forgetting of events that occurred in early childhood? Not likely, for two reasons: First, whereas 55% of the women who had been 3 years old or younger at the time of abuse had no recall, fully 62% of those who were between 4 and 6 years old at the time had no recall; if forgetting were simply a reflection of age, the women abused at a younger age should have had poorer memory. Second, more of the women who were abused by someone they knew, as was determined from independent evidence, claimed to have forgotten the incident than women who were abused by a stranger.

Anterograde amnesia: Amnesia that leaves consolidated memories intact but prevents new learning.

Repressed memories: Real memories that have been pushed out of consciousness because they are emotionally threatening.

Again, this difference should not have occurred if the forgetting simply reflected infantile amnesia. Indeed, a review of 28 studies of memory for childhood sexual abuse found robust evidence that such memories can be forgotten and later recalled (Scheflin & Brown, 1996). In some cases, people who suddenly remembered being abused as children then proceeded to track down the evidence for the event (Schacter, 1996).

There is a mystery here. As noted earlier, highly charged, emotional information is typically remembered *better* than neutral information. So why should this particular kind of emotionally charged information be recalled poorly, or forgotten for decades? Schacter (1996) suggests that, in these cases of forgetting, the person has not really unconsciously pushed the memories out of awareness. Instead, it is as if the individual were "someone else" during the abuse and thus has few retrieval cues later for accessing the memories. Nevertheless, the memories may be stored and may under some circumstances, with appropriate cues, filter into awareness. If so, then people sometimes would seem to forget emotionally charged events, but after long periods of time could come to remember them. Clancy, McNally, and Schacter (1999) have found that people who experience recovered memories of childhood abuse are more likely to mistakenly remember words such as "sweet" when asked to remember a previously presented list of sweet things in experiments along the lines of the Deese-Roediger-McDermott technique discussed earlier. This finding might suggest that these people are unusually sensitive to stored fragments of information. Leavitt (1997) has shown that people who recover memories are not especially prone to making up information when given suggestions, which indicates that they are not simply prone to forming false memories. That said, not all claims of recovered memories can be taken at face value; you've already seen how false memories (perhaps including being strapped to the back of a dolphin) can be implanted.

LOOKING AT LEVELS

False Truths

Social psychologist Daniel Gilbert (1991) reports experiments in which people are given statements about nonsense objects, such as "A bilicar is a spear." For each statement, participants are told that it is true or false. Later, memory for the truth of the statements is tested. When people forget whether a statement was true or false, they are biased to say it was true. Thus the participants end up with unwarranted beliefs about objects. The same principle probably operates regarding facts about people. For example, if you hear that a beloved high school teacher does not seduce students, you may later misremember that he does seduce them. It's fascinating, but disturbing, that a person's reputation could easily be ruined because of a simple psychological principle.

According to Gilbert, it requires extra effort to realize that a statement is false than to accept it as true; to determine that it is false, you must search for stored information that is inconsistent with the statement, which requires using working memory. Thus, because of properties of the brain, specifically the increased processing in the frontal lobes to look up and process stored information, events at the level of the person are affected: The person's beliefs are distorted. And the influences work the other way, too: Depending on your beliefs, you will be inclined to work more or less hard to search memory to verify a statement. If you are not strongly motivated to put in the extra work, you will be more inclined to fall prey to the bias to believe an assertion is true. This distortion in turn affects social interactions. And of course, social interactions lead us to hear about characteristics of people, "So-and-so is this or that," statements that may lead to false beliefs.

CONSOLIDATE!

▶ **1. How can actual memories be distinguished from false ones?** At least under some circumstances, real memories include perceptual information from the modality in which a fact was learned—perhaps by seeing it, hearing it, reading it—whereas false memories do not include this sort of information. In many circumstances, however, it is difficult to distinguish between actual and false memories.

▶ **2. Is a forgotten memory necessarily gone forever, or is it still stored but difficult to retrieve?** Memories may be lost by decay, probably because the relevant connections between neurons are lost. However, many "forgotten" memories are in fact still present, just difficult to retrieve. Memories become difficult to retrieve because of retroactive interference, in which current learning disrupts previously acquired knowledge, or because of proactive interference, in which earlier learning impairs the ability to learn something new.

▶ **3. What is amnesia?** Amnesia is a loss of explicit memory, typically (but not always) only episodic mem-

ory. Retrograde amnesia disrupts previous memories; anterograde amnesia disrupts the ability to acquire new memories. These sorts of amnesia usually involve damage to the hippocampus or related brain structures or damage to the areas of the cortex that store particular types of LTM. Infantile amnesia, the forgetting of early childhood events, is very common, as is source amnesia, the forgetting of the context in which a fact was learned.

▶ **4. Are memories ever repressed?** Memories have been thought to be repressed as a defense against trauma—threatening information is forced into the unconscious. But little evidence backs such a mechanism. Nevertheless, at least in some situations, encoding failure or a failure to encode information that can later be used as retrieval cues could result in poorer memory for traumatic events. In general, however, strong emotion enhances, not reduces, memory.

IMPROVING MEMORY: TRICKS AND TOOLS

If, like Juan's and Fiona's, your memory is not as good in some areas as in others and you want to improve the accuracy of your memory overall, what should you do? In many bookstores you can find at least a dozen books on the topic, all containing similar messages. Ways of improving your odds of retaining information in memory include linking visual images with text (dual coding); thinking through information (depth and breadth of processing); and studying in small chunks while trying to integrate and organize material (distributed practice). Let's now look at techniques that take advantage of such principles to improve memory.

▶ 1. How should you try to organize and integrate new information in order to remember it?

▶ 2. What tricks will help you dig out information you want to retrieve?

You can improve the accuracy of your memory at both ends: when information goes in and when it is taken out. The fact that memory is so dependent on the strategies people use explains why it has among the lowest heritabilities (see Chapter 2) of all specific cognitive abilities. Even if a number of people in your family have fabulous memories, their gifts won't help you a bit. Memory ability is made, not inherited (Nichols, 1978). For memory, the crucial differences between "good" and "bad" memories appear to be the strategies and tricks used when storing and retrieving information.

Storing Information Effectively: A Bag of Mnemonic Tricks

Tricks for improving memory typically require elaborative encoding and often involve either visualizing objects interacting with other objects or forming organized units where none previously existed. The essential element is that you *organize* the material so that you *integrate* it, making connections between what you want to remember and what you already know. Here are some **mnemonic devices,** or strategies that improve memory (*mnemonic* is derived from the Greek word for "memory"). Such memory tricks rely on organization and integration. Mnemonics can easily double your recall and are well worth the effort of learning and using. Using mnemonic devices not only helps you learn something in the first place, but should you forget it, you will be able to relearn it more effectively.

Probably the single most effective mnemonic device is the use of *interactive images.* As discussed earlier, forming images of objects interacting will improve memory even without any effort to learn the material (Bower, 1972; Paivio, 1971). For example, if you want to learn someone's first name, visualize someone else you already know who has the same name, and imagine that person interacting with your new acquaintance in some way. You might envision them hugging, or fighting, or shaking hands. Later, when you see the new person, you can recall this image, and thus the name.

A related method was discovered by the ancient Greek orator Simonides. He was attending a banquet one evening when he was called out of the room to receive a message. Shortly after he left, the ceiling collapsed, mangling the guests' bodies so badly that they were difficult to identify. When asked who had been at the feast, Simonides realized that he could remember easily if he visualized each person sitting at the table. This led him to develop a technique now called the *method of loci* (*loci,* the plural of *locus,* means "places" in Latin). To use this method, first memorize a set of locations. For example, you could walk through your house and memorize 12 distinct places, such as the front door, the computer desk, the potted plant, and so on. Later, when you want to memorize a list of objects, such as those on a shopping list, you can imagine walking along this path and placing an image of one object in each location. For instance, you might visualize a lightbulb leaning against the front door, a box of tissues on the computer desk, a can of coffee beside the plant, and so on. When you want to recall the list, all you need to do is visualize the scene and walk through it, "looking" to see what object is at each place.

To use the method of loci, pick out a set of locations in your house and visualize each to-be-remembered object in a different location as you mentally walk through the house. To recall, later repeat this mental walk and "see" what's in each location.

The *pegword system* is similar to the method of loci, except that instead of places, you first memorize a set of objects in order. For example, you might memorize a list of rhymes, such as "One is a bun, two is a shoe, three is a tree, four is a door," and so on. Then you can treat the memorized objects (bun, shoe, tree, door) in the same way as the locations in the method of loci. You could associate the first item on your grocery list, for example, with a bun, the second with a shoe, and so on. In this case, when you want to remember the list, you remember each of the pegwords (such as bun and shoe) in order and "see" what is associated with it.

When Henry Roediger (1980) asked people to use different mnemonic devices to remember sets of words, he found that these three methods—interactive imagery, the method of loci, and the pegword system—were the most effective. However, as you know, there are many types of memory, and people differ in how well they can use various techniques. You might find these other mnemonic devices more useful:

Rhyming words provide a simple method for keeping concepts straight. For example, learning the rhyme "rhyming priming rhyming" might help you remember that priming makes the same processing (like the same word repeated) easier to repeat in the future.

Hierarchical organization, as in the experiment by Bower and colleagues (1969; summarized on p. 214), can improve learning and memory. You might memorize the errands you need to do by organizing your tasks in the same way you organize your trip: Break the trip down into separate segments, and organize the events in each of those separately. Think about which tasks need to be done at one end of

Mnemonic devices: Strategies that improve memory, typically by using effective organization and integration.

town, or in one part of the store, which need to be done at another specific location, and so on. The key is to think of ways to organize the material hierarchically, so that the big task breaks down into smaller ones, which themselves may break down into yet smaller ones; the goal is to group together relatively small sets of material.

Acronyms are pronounceable words made from the first letters of the important words in a phrase, such as NOW for National Organization for Women; *initialisms* are simply the initial letters, pronounceable or not, such as DNA for deoxyribonucleic acid. Initialisms may be easier to make up for most situations; the idea in both cases is to create a single unit that can be unpacked as a set of cues for something more complicated.

In short, the key to mnemonics is figuring out a way to organize information so that you can link something new with something you already know. For example,

MNEMONIC. A memory aid. Think of trying to remember something by putting a name on it: putting a NEM-ON-IC.

You can use mnemonics throughout this book, setting up mental connections or associations from one thing to another, perhaps with the use of imagery. For example, to remember that the word *suppression* means "voluntarily forcing unwanted thoughts back into the unconscious," you might visualize SUPerman PRESSing down demons that are bursting out of someone's head, shoving them back inside. When you form the image, you need to remember that the first part of Superman's name and what he's doing (pressing) are critical, so make sure the S on his cape is very vivid and visible, and that he is clearly pressing with his hands. Showing you a drawing of the scene would work almost as well; but challenging you to make up your own image has the added advantage of forcing you to "process" the information more thoroughly, which in and of itself improves memory.

In addition, you can remember information by stringing it into a story. For example, if you wanted to remember that Freud came before the cognitivists, you can make up a story in which Freud wishes he had a computer to help him bill his patients but gets depressed when he realizes it hasn't been invented yet. Making the story a bit silly or whimsical may actually help memory (McDaniel & Einstein, 1986; McDaniel et al., 1995)—and certainly makes it more fun to think about!

One of the fundamental facts about learning is that you will learn better if you are actively involved. Instead of just reading, try to find connections across areas, try to think of your own mnemonics. You won't go wrong if you simply form a visual image, make up an association, invent a rhyme or joke. You will be better off if you try to be an active learner.

Improving Memory Retrieval

As Juan and Fiona discovered when asked to give statements to the police, sometimes you need to remember things that you didn't expect to need or didn't have the opportunity to store effectively. Police officers are regularly faced with the effect of this unexpected demand on witnesses' memories. The need for accurate witness statements has been one impetus for developing methods to help people remember after the fact. Fisher and colleagues (1989) used the results of laboratory studies to develop a method to help witnesses and victims of crimes recall what actually happened (see also Fisher & Geiselman, 1992). Detectives trained with their methods were able to lead witnesses to recall 63% more information than was obtained with the standard police interview then in use. Their methods made use of the following memory principles and techniques:

1. Recall is better when you mentally reinstate the environment in which information was learned. If you want to remember something, try to think of where you were when you learned it, what the weather was like, how you felt at the time, and so on.

2. Focus. Searching for information in LTM requires effort and is easily disrupted by other stimuli. To remember well, focus on the task, shutting out distractions.

3. Keep trying. The more times you try to remember something, the more likely you are eventually to retrieve it (Roediger & Thorpe, 1978).

4. If you cannot recall something immediately, try to think of characteristics of the information sought. Fisher and colleagues, in their 1989 study, advised detectives that if a witness could not remember a criminal's name, they should try to remember its length, first syllable, ethnic origin, and so on. This information can serve as retrieval cues.

5. For certain kinds of memory retrieval, you can arrange the world in such a way that you are reminded what to remember. In other words, use *external cues* as mnemonic devices. If you are prone to forgetting your backpack, leave it by the door; if you forget to check the weather forecast before you leave home in the morning, put an umbrella on the door handle. A clever use of external cues was developed by historian Alistair Cooke, who hit on a novel way to remember where he shelved his books. He had a large number of books on the United States and its regions, but he couldn't always recall the author of a particular book. Arranging the books alphabetically by state didn't work because he couldn't decide where to put books about regions, such as the Rocky Mountains. The system that finally worked was simple: He arranged the books about western regions on the left, eastern regions at the right, northern regions at the top, and southern regions at the bottom. The location in the bookcase mirrored the location in the country, and his problem was solved—all he had to do was look in the right place on his bookcase "map" (Morris, 1979).

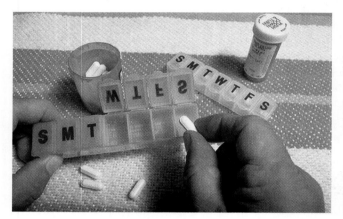

Arranging your world properly can aid memory. In this case, the pill holder makes it easy to recall whether or not you've taken your medication each day.

If you can find a method that is fun and easy, and that works for you, you are more likely to use it, and benefit by it. As in the case of mnemonic devices, our advice is to try each of the methods we have noted and see which suit you.

LOOKING AT LEVELS

Hypnosis and Memory

Would hypnotizing Juan and Fiona help the police clear up the disparities between their memories of the accident? Possibly; hypnosis sometimes improves memory of prior events. In 1976 in Chowchilla, California, a school bus was hijacked, all of the children within kidnapped. The bus and all those inside were buried and held for ransom. When freed, the bus driver remembered the car driven by his assailants but no other details. In a hypnotic trance, he was able to recall the car's license plate, which ultimately led to the arrest of the kidnappers.

In many cases, however, hypnosis increases people's confidence in their recollections but not their accuracy (Sheehan, 1988; Worthington, 1979). Indeed, studies have found no overall differences in accuracy of memory between witnesses who were hypnotized and those who were interviewed using techniques based on cognitive strategies such as those summarized above (Geiselman et al., 1985). In addition, hypnosis may actually lead people to believe that suggested events happened, rather than simply help them to recall actual events (e.g., Barber, 1997; Bryant & Barnier, 1999; Green et al., 1998). Thus, after hypnosis Fiona and Juan might still have different memories, but each would be even more convinced that he or she was right.

As discussed in Chapter 4, hypnosis affects the brain, in part by focusing attention. But attention can be focused on material suggested by an interviewer (a social interaction), and such suggestions can change the interviewee's beliefs. Thus, the social interaction between the hypnotist and the person hypnotized need not alter the ability to access memories, but instead can implant false memories. And false memories, if taken at face value, can have a devastating impact on how other people are treated.

CONSOLIDATE!

▶ **1. How should you try to organize and integrate new information in order to remember it?** Tricks for improving memory typically require elaborative encoding: they often involve either visualizing the objects interacting with other objects or forming organized units where none previously existed. How can you decide which methods are best for you? The imagery-based techniques have been shown to be generally the most successful, and given Fiona's strong visual memory, we would definitely recommend them for her. Juan is more verbally oriented, and rhyming or a similar technique may be better for him. For you, the best course of action is to try the different techniques and see which ones are most effective.

▶ **2. What tricks will help you dig out information you want to retrieve?** Mentally recreating the situation in which learning occurred, focusing attention on retrieving the information, repeatedly trying to recall, generating new cues based on partial recall, and paying attention to the source of remembered information are all techniques that can improve retrieval. It is also possible to arrange the world—your immediate circumstances—in such a way that you are reminded of what to do.

A DEEPER LEVEL
Recap and Thought Questions

▶ **Memory: A Many-Splendored Thing**

The three types of memory stores—sensory memory (SM), short-term memory (STM), and long-term memory (LTM)—differ in the amount of information they can retain and how long they can retain it. Working memory (WM) is the use of STM to reason or to solve problems; working memory involves not only specialized STMs (such as the articulatory loop and visuospatial sketchpad) but also a central executive, which is a set of processes that manipulates information in these temporary storage structures. In addition, there are multiple types of LTMs. We store information in different sensory modalities, such as the visual and auditory. Some of the information stored in LTM is episodic, pertaining to events that occurred at a specific time, place, and circumstance, and some is semantic, pertaining to meaning, concepts, and facts about the world. Some memories in LTM are explicit (stored so information can voluntarily be retrieved) and others are implicit (stored as tendencies to process information in specific ways). Implicit memories in LTM include classical conditioning, habits (automatic responses to appropriate stimuli), and priming; repetition priming makes it easier

to repeat a process in the future. All memories arise when neurons change their patterns of interaction, so that new connections become strengthened. Long-term potentiation (LTP) is one mechanism whereby new memories are stored. The process of storing new memories depends on the actions of specific genes.

Might Fiona and Juan differ in what sorts of memories they can store effectively? Because different systems are used for different types of memories, people can be good at one type of memory but poor at another. Fiona stores habits well in memory, but she may not generally store explicit memories exceptionally well; the opposite situation applies to Juan—he stores explicit memories well, but not habits.

> **Think It Through.** If you were Fiona or Juan, how could you try to discover which aspects of your memory are good and which are not? Would it help to test yourself on a set of tasks that assess the different forms of memory? In what ways could you use the results of such testing?

▶ Encoding and Retrieving Information From Memory

Encoding is the act of organizing and transforming incoming information so that it can be entered into memory. The effectiveness of encoding depends in part on what is perceived to be important. Memory is improved as more time is spent thinking about the material to be stored and how it relates to your current knowledge, and memory is most effective if the learner focuses on the properties that will be relevant later. Depth of processing involves thinking about the more complex properties of objects; elaborative encoding involves thinking of relations and associations of material to be stored. In addition, the information already in LTM makes it more or less easy to encode new information. It takes time to consolidate information to be stored, converting it from a dynamic form to a structural form.

Memory retrieval depends on a constructive process; you must retrieve the right pottery fragments to build the right jug. Recognition is often easier than recall, but the ease of recognition depends on the choices you must distinguish among; the more attributes the choices have in common, the harder it is to distinguish among them. Effective retrieval depends on having cues, or reminders, that match part of what is in memory, allowing you to reconstruct the rest.

What factors could lead Juan and Fiona to have different memories of the accident? If Juan and Fiona thought about different aspects of the accident, their resulting memories would be different because of differences in elaborative encoding. In addition, as a sports coach, Fiona may be familiar with different postural cues and body positions, making it easier for her to remember that kind of information. It is also possible that if Fiona has a better visual memory than Juan, she is better able to take advantage of dual coding. On the other hand, if Juan was more emotionally aroused by the accident because of his previous association with a car crash, he may have encoded it better. In addition, Juan and Fiona's memories might differ because of the retrieval cues they use—which lead them to summon up different information.

> **Think It Through.** Would you study the same way for a multiple-choice test and an essay exam? What would be different about your methods?
>
> If you were setting up a new business to teach executives how to improve their memories, what would you need to know about your clients' daily activities? What would you include in your curriculum?
>
> If you were advising detectives, how could you help them determine which witness was remembering more accurately? What new retrieval cues could you produce that might be effective?

▶ Fact, Fiction, and Forgetting: When Memory Goes Wrong

False memories occur when a person stores information about an event that did not happen, or that did not happen in the way that is "remembered." False memories may not include information about the perceptual features of the stimuli, and thus it may be possible to distinguish them from actual memories. Reality monitoring can be used to check for such features in memory.

Forgetting occurs in various ways. Decay results when neural connections are weakened to the point where they are no longer functional, whereas interference (either retroactive or proactive) prevents the digging out of stored information. In contrast to ordinary forgetting, amnesia wipes out explicit memory for a span of time, not just isolated aspects of memories. Finally, strong emotion seems to amplify memory, not diminish it. However, memories may be difficult to recall because the stored information may not match later retrieval cues, and thus the information is difficult to summon up from memory.

What factors could have led Juan and Fiona to forget key features of the accident? Fiona's and Juan's memories could have suffered from either decay or interference (from movies, books, or similar experiences in the past). In addition, they may have failed to remember key facts because of encoding failure, which prevents information from being entered into LTM in the first place. However, it is unlikely that either had amnesia, or that Fiona or Juan experienced repressed memories that were unconsciously pushed out of awareness.

> **Think It Through.** If methods for implanting false memories effectively are demonstrated conclusively, should they be outlawed? In general, or only in certain circumstances (such as their being used by advertisers who want you to "remember" how much you like their products)? Can you think of any circumstances under which implanting a false memory might be a good idea? Explain.
>
> From a practical point of view, what difference does it make whether Fiona had experienced decay, encoding failure, or interference? What would you do differently in each case? In what circumstances would her forgetting some information actually improve her memory for other information? In what circumstances would such forgetting be a good idea? Why?
>
> Passionate controversy surrounds the topic of repressed memories. Why do you think it is so important to some people to believe in them, and so important to others to debunk them?

▶ Improving Memory: Tricks and Tools

Many methods are proven memory boosters. Some techniques help you store information effectively by organizing it and integrating it into other information in memory; these include interactive images, including the method of loci; the pegword system; rhyming words; hierarchical organization; and acronyms and initialisms. Mental imagery is generally the most effective of these techniques when it is used to organize information in a meaningful way.

Other techniques have also been shown to help dig out information previously stored in long-term memory. One trick is to provide effective retrieval cues by thinking about where you were and how you felt at the time. Another major factor is effort: Focus and keep trying, and if you cannot recall the information, then try to recall its characteristics or associated information (which in turn can serve as retrieval cues). Finally, sometimes just arranging for external cues to remind you can be enormously helpful.

What could Fiona and Juan do to help improve their memories of the accident? After the fact, they can only try to enhance retrieval. They could try visualizing the scene of the accident, and keep trying to "see" different aspects of the situation in their images. Better yet, they could return to the scene of the accident. In any case, they should keep trying to recall key features of the situation that could serve as retrieval cues.

Think It Through. In his work as a paralegal, Juan had learned to describe and organize hundreds of situations that led to judicial rulings, which helped him memorize abstract material. Fiona, in contrast, rarely had to consider abstract material in her work, and so had little practice in such processing. In what ways do you think this difference may have affected their memories of the accident?

Can you think of additional ways to improve memory, either at the time of learning or at the time of recall? If a technique works for you, can you think of a way to remind yourself to use it? It isn't enough simply to be *able* to use a technique effectively—you must *remember* to use it!

7 LANGUAGE AND THINKING

In the year 2180, a cop's best friend was his android, or droid for short. Droids had been perfected some 30 years before, and now it was hard to imagine a time when they didn't exist. Frank was thinking about this as he and his droid partner, Hans, cruised a few feet above the ancient road surfaces of New York City. Droids were decent companions, but they were sometimes a little peculiar. Just today Frank had joked with Hans about a weird hat he'd seen a woman wearing, a hat that looked like a cross between an umbrella and a water lily. He'd said to Hans, "Boy, is that supposed to be the latest fashion from Mars?" He knew perfectly well that Mars had neither rain nor exposure to the sun, but thought it wasn't a bad joke. Hans's response was dry and literal: The hat, he said, was "not fully functional for that planet in the solar system."

Frank realized that he could have felt threatened by Hans's machine-like accuracy, but he didn't: Even though Hans was more advanced than humans in many ways, in others he fell woefully short. For one thing, although Hans spoke perfect English (as well as 13 other languages), never making an error in pronunciation or grammar, he almost never got a joke. And Frank's fluent and frequent use of metaphor and slang was beyond him; Hans could neither make word play nor understand it, unless he'd heard and stored the meaning of a particular expression before. And although Hans could read very obvious nonverbal cues, recognizing that a smile reflects pleasure and a frown displeasure, he often missed nonverbal subtleties—an ironic glance or a subtle shrug was lost on him.

But overall, Hans's mind was sharp as a laser scalpel, making him a valuable companion to a policeman. When faced with a difficult problem, Hans could start from the known facts and make deductions that would have put Sherlock Holmes to shame; his logic was flawless. Nevertheless, unlike Frank, he was utterly incapable of making leaps of intuition or of approaching a problem from a different angle. This wasn't a drawback when the partners were dealing with cases in which the facts were firmly established and the solution was in sight if not yet achieved, but Hans's literal-mindedness could be an obstacle in cases that were not so clear-cut.

These differences between the human Frank and and his droid partner Hans are differences in language and cognition, the subject of this chapter. As you explore the nature of language and cognition, you'll find out what Hans is missing cognitively—that is, what keeps him from being able to think as we understand thinking—and consider what it would take to make him function in a fully human fashion. As for Frank, how does his human brain enable him to use language and to think in ways that would be a mystery to Hans (if indeed he could conceive of them at all)? And on the other hand, what limitations in solving problems and reasoning does Frank face because he is a human? Let's begin by considering first the nature of language and then its role in thought. Next, we'll look at other forms of thought and, finally, at the different ways in which people can solve problems and use reasoning.

LANGUAGE: MORE THAN MEETS THE EAR

When Frank first began to work with Hans, he was startled when Hans failed to understand, for instance, that being a "rigid thinker" had nothing to do with the solidity of one's gray matter. After a while, Frank learned that Hans could hear an expression and store it for future use, but only in an identical context. Even though he looked like an adult, Hans was only about 5 years old, and some aspects of language cannot be preprogrammed. For example, slang and expressions are constantly changing and thus can only be acquired by encountering them.

▶ 1. What are the essential characteristics of all languages?

▶ 2. How do we acquire language?

▶ 3. Which sorts of nonspeech communication are language, and which are not? Can animals be taught to use language?

▶ 4. Are first and second languages used in different ways?

The Essentials: What Makes Language Language?

Language is a two-pronged process of sending and receiving. **Language production** is our ability to speak or otherwise use language to *send* information. Perhaps the most remarkable thing about language production is that it is *generative*. We create, or "generate," new sentences all the time; we don't simply retrieve and repeat stored sentences. The number of new sentences we can produce is astounding. Psychologist Pinker (1994, p. 86) estimates that we would need at least 100 trillion years to

Language production: The ability to speak or otherwise use language to send information.

memorize all the sentences any one of us can possibly produce. **Language comprehension** is the ability to understand language. Unlike the droid Hans, who can be programmed to decode literal references but not much more, we humans are endowed with the extraordinary ability to comprehend even fragments of speech, mispronounced or "speech badly with grammar." We can understand the speech of the very young, speech flavored with foreign or regional accents, and lisping speech, even though in each case the actual sounds made are very different. To put things in perspective, even today's most sophisticated speech recognition devices can decode only a fraction of what a competent 5-year-old can do effortlessly.

So, if language is a process of sending and receiving information, what about a dog that whines when it is hungry, barks to go for a walk, and sits when told to? This pet is sending and receiving all right, but is it using language? The intuitive answer is no, and the intuitive answer is right—there's more to language than that. Language units are built from simple building blocks that can be combined in many ways, but only according to specific rules. Four types of units, and the rules for combining them, distinguish language from other communicative sounds such as whines. These units and rules are described by the phonology, syntax, semantics, and pragmatics of a language. Let's look at each of these aspects of language in turn.

PHONOLOGY: SOME SAY "TOMATO." **Phonology** is the structure of the sounds that can be used to produce words in a language. Linguists Roman Jakobson and Morris Halle (1956) provided evidence that the sounds of any language are built up from sets of **phonemes,** which are the basic building blocks of speech sounds (Halle, 1990). The difference between *boy* and *toy* is one phoneme.

Humans can produce about 100 phonemes, but no single language uses all 100; English, for instance, uses about 45. Back-of-the-throat, soft French *r*'s do not exist in the world of hard American *r*'s, and Japanese has no *r*'s at all. One of the reasons why French is difficult for people who learned English as their native tongue, in fact, is that the two languages use different phonemes (such as those for *r* and *u*).

In English, some sounds in each word are accented, given extra emphasis. Some say *toMAYto* and some say *toMAHto,* but in both cases the second syllable is stressed. Some other languages do not usually stress one of the syllables in a word. In French, for example, each sound typically is given equal emphasis. Linguist Lisa Selkirk (personal communication) suggests that this difference explains why French rock and roll often sounds bland: French rock artists can't synchronize the "beats" in the language with the rhythm of the music.

Curiously, the left cerebral hemisphere is primarily activated when males process phonemes, but both hemispheres are strongly activated when females process phonemes (Shaywitz et al., 1995); perhaps this is one reason females tend to be better with language than males (Halpern, 1997).

Although it may seem that we prepare to say a word the instant before uttering it, in fact we mentally compose the sounds, the phonemes, of an entire phrase before we actually begin to talk. One piece of evidence for such advance preparation is that sounds from a word later in a phrase can sometimes be mistakenly assigned to a word earlier in the phrase. For example, when asked about his new apartment, someone we know replied, "It seats my nudes"; after only a moment's puzzlement, we knew he meant to say, "It suits my needs." The word *seats* could not have picked up the sounds intended for *needs* unless the sounds for the later word were already accessed when the sentence began to be produced. Such transpositions are called **spoonerisms** after William Archibald Spooner (1844–1930), an English clergyman and educator who was famous for making such errors. Freud believed that such slips of the tongue provide glimpses into the unconscious. What would he have said about our friend's slip? He probably would have claimed that this error reveals deep conflict about sexuality. However, modern researchers have found that slips of the tongue are best explained not in terms of the unconscious, but rather in terms of how speech sounds are programmed in the brain (Dell, 1990; Dell et al., 1997).

Language comprehension: The ability to understand language.

Phonology: The structure of the sounds that can be used to produce words in a language.

Phoneme: The basic building block of speech sounds.

Spoonerisms: Transpositions of speech sounds, as in "tons of soil" instead of "sons of toil."

Syntax: The internal grammatical structure of a sentence, determined by how words that belong to different parts of speech are organized into acceptable arrangements.

Grammar: The rules that determine how words that belong to different parts of speech can be organized into acceptable sentences.

Empiricism (approach to language): The approach that views language as entirely the result of learning.

Nativism (approach to language): The approach that views crucial aspects of language as innate.

Language acquisition device (LAD): An innate mechanism, hypothesized by Chomsky, that contains the grammatical rules common to all languages and allows language acquisition.

Aphasia: A disruption of language caused by brain damage.

Broca's aphasia: Problems with producing language following brain damage (typically to the left frontal lobe).

Wernicke's aphasia: Problems with comprehending language following brain damage (typically to the left posterior temporal lobe).

SYNTAX: ARE THE RULES OF THE ROAD LEARNED OR INNATE? Every language has building blocks of sound and rules for cementing them together into words. Similarly, all languages include rules for how words can be organized into sentences. Sentences in any language contain an internal structure, an acceptable arrangement of words called **syntax**. The syntax of a sentence is determined by the **grammar** of a language, a set of rules for combining different categories of words, such as nouns, verbs, and adjectives. For example, in English you cannot say, "Kicked girl ball the blue." The basic units of a grammar are parts of speech, not the individual words that fall into each category. A sentence in English needs a noun phrase (which must at a minimum have a noun—a word that names a person, place, or thing) and a verb phrase (at a minimum a single verb—a word that describes an action or a state of being). Thus, the shortest possible sentence in English has only three letters: "I am."

Ask a friend to help you perform this experiment. Turn on the lights and shut all the blinds in your room at night. Read aloud from any book. Ask your friend to turn off the lights at some random point. You should find that you can keep saying the words leading up to the next major syntactic boundary (usually indicated by a verb, a conjunction, or a comma, period, or other punctuation). Fluent readers take in entire parts of the syntactic structure, one part at a time.

As a philosophy, **empiricism** takes the view that all knowledge derives from experience, and Skinner believed that language is entirely the result of learning. In contrast, **nativism** centers on the idea that the crucial aspects of language are innate. Linguist Noam Chomsky (1972) championed this view, theorizing that we are all born with an internal **language acquisition device (LAD)**, which contains a set of grammatical rules common to all languages. According to Chomsky, we don't actually learn the grammar of a language. Rather, we *discover* which particular human language is being spoken around us, and our LAD "tunes" our built-in set of rules so that we can speak that language. Others, including Elman, Bates, and their colleagues (Elman et al., 1996), have argued that language emerges from more general cognitive abilities, such as ones used in motor control and perception; but even these theorists assume that at least some of these abilities are built in, part of our genetic heritage. The fact that virtually all normal humans come to speak a language, even without formal instruction, is evidence that there is something special about the way our brains are constructed to acquire and use language.

The effects of brain damage on language reveal that it involves a system of mechanisms, not simply stored associations among words (Shelton & Caramazza, 1999). Patients with brain damage that disrupts language are said to have **aphasia**. In 1861 French anthropologist and neuroanatomist Paul Broca described how damage to the left frontal lobe—in an area later named *Broca's area*—disrupts speech much more than comprehension; this disorder is now called **Broca's aphasia**. These patients often have large pauses between words and leave out function words, such as *and*, *if*, and *but*. For example, Goodglass (1976, p. 278) describes such a patient who said, "And, er Wednesday . . . nine o'clock. And er Thursday, ten o'clock . . . doctors. Two doctors . . . and ah . . . teeth . . . ." A little more than a decade after Broca's discovery, Carl Wernicke, a German neurologist, reported that damage to the back parts of the left temporal lobe has the reverse effect, disrupting comprehension more than production; this area was later named *Wernicke's area* (see Figure 7.1), and this disorder is now called **Wernicke's aphasia**. These patients not only have difficulty comprehending, but also produce "empty speech," which doesn't make sense. For example, when asked about the kind of work he did before being hospitalized, one such patient said, "Never, now mista oyge I wanna tell you this happened when

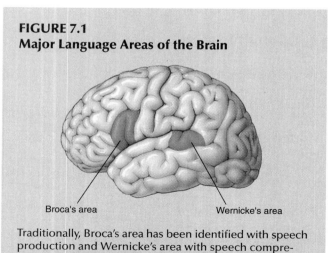

FIGURE 7.1
Major Language Areas of the Brain

Broca's area

Wernicke's area

Traditionally, Broca's area has been identified with speech production and Wernicke's area with speech comprehension, but we now know that Broca's area is involved in the use of grammar to understand sentences.

happened when he rent" (Kertesz, 1981, p. 73, as cited in Carlson, 1994, p. 517). Part of the problem may have been that the patient didn't understand the request, but this man clearly had trouble producing coherent speech.

However, even though production and comprehension rely on largely different mechanisms, the effects of brain damage demonstrate that both processes rely on accessing the rules of grammar. Damage to Broca's area can produce difficulties not only in forming grammatical sentences but also in understanding grammar (Caramazza & Zurif, 1976; Zurif et al., 1972). Moreover, PET studies have shown that Broca's area is activated when people must comprehend sentences with increasingly complex syntax (Stromswold et al., 1996). Thus, Broca's area is involved in the use of grammar in both production and comprehension. Comprehension, however, being tied to the meanings of words, may be less disrupted than production when grammar is impaired.

SEMANTICS: THE MEANING IS THE MESSAGE.

Language is, of course, more than sounds and sentence structures. To do its job, language must convey meaning. The **semantics** of a word or sentence is its meaning. Just as the sounds of words are represented by smaller elements (phonemes) and the syntactic aspects of a sentence are represented by grammatical elements (parts of speech), semantics is represented by **morphemes,** the smallest units of *meaning* in a language. The word *wet* includes but a single morpheme, but the meanings of many words are determined by more than one morpheme. Prefixes and suffixes are obvious examples of such morphemes used in combination with other morphemes. For example, adding the morpheme *-ing* to a verb, as in *walking, talking, flirting,* creates a word expressing a continuing state, whereas adding the morpheme *-ed* indicates a completed state. Just as the other elements of language are combined according to rules, so, too, with morphemes. We cannot add *-ing* at the front of a word, or *mis-* (another morpheme) to the end. Different sets of morphemes underlie the different meanings of ambiguous words, words with more than one meaning; thus *park* as in "park the car" has different morphemes than *park* as in "place with benches and pigeons."

Meanings are often assigned arbitrarily to different sounds or written words; the sound *dog* could easily have been assigned to refer to that feline we keep as a pet, and *cat* to the animal that likes to gnaw on bones and slippers. Specific events in the past have a lot to do with how specific words have come to have their meanings. For example, early medieval Scandinavian warriors wore bearskin shirts, for which the Old Norwegian word is *berserkr;* from the ferocity of the Vikings' frenzied attacks in battle we inherit the expression "going berserk." Of more recent vintage is the word *bedlam,* which since the 16th century has meant "chaos and confusion"; its origins are in the name of the Hospital of St. Mary of Bethlehem in London, where "lunatics" were confined. Sometimes the meanings of words seem to reveal deeper aspects of a culture: The Chinese character for *crisis* is composed of two other characters, one signifying "risk" and the other "opportunity."

The meaning of a sentence and its syntax are to a large extent distinct. For example, Chomsky (1957) pointed out that the sentence "Colorless green ideas sleep furiously" is grammatically correct—it has an acceptable English syntax—but entirely meaningless. On the other hand, "Fastly dinner eat, ballgame soon start" has the opposite properties: It is grammatically incorrect but completely understandable. The wise alien Yoda of the *Star Wars* movies often uttered grammatically incorrect but comprehensible sentences, probably in part to remind the audience that he was not an ordinary person.

That semantics, understanding what words and sentences mean, is distinct from phonology, understanding sounds as signaling certain words, was demonstrated convincingly by Damasio and her collaborators (1996), who used PET scanning to show that different brain areas are involved in processing the sounds of words versus their meanings. These researchers also found that a third brain area literally bridged the meaning and sound regions; this third area may serve to cross-reference representations of sounds and meanings.

Semantics: The meaning of a word or sentence.

Morpheme: The smallest unit of meaning in a language.

Just as morphemes are combined into representations of the meanings of words, the representations of words in turn are combined into *propositions*. **Propositional representations** are mental sentences that express the meaning of statements. The same sets of words can express different propositions, depending on how they are organized. For example, consider this anecdote:

> An English professor wrote the words "Woman without her man is a savage" on the blackboard and directed his students to punctuate the sentence. The men wrote, "Woman, without her man, is a savage." The women wrote, "Woman: Without her, man is a savage."

As you see, the punctuation has organized the words in different ways to express different propositions. Propositional representations are not ambiguous; they specify the meanings that underlie the particular sense of a statement. Many studies have shown that people store not the literal words used in sentences, but rather the propositions that specify the meaning. For example, Sachs (1967) had participants in a study listen to paragraphs and then tested their memories for specific sentences. The participants had to indicate whether each test sentence had been presented in a paragraph or was changed from one that had been presented. The participants remembered the meanings well, but not the particular wordings (Bransford & Franks, 1971, report comparable results).

PRAGMATICS: BEING INDIRECT. The droid Hans was perfectly able to understand the semantics of words (he understood morphemes and how they are combined into words) and sentences (he understood how the meanings of words are combined into phrases and sentences and their underlying propositional representations); but he often failed at a third aspect of meaning. Utterances have not only a literal meaning but also an *implied* meaning. The **pragmatics** of a language are concerned with the way language implies meaning. Have you ever asked a 13-year-old, "Do you know where the restroom is?" and got back the response "Yes"? This question can be interpreted literally as an inquiry about your knowledge of, say, the layout of a large building or indirectly as a request for directions. In some contexts, such as kids being addressed by a parent who is dropping them off at an auditorium by themselves, the question might really be meant literally. But in most instances you would understand that the questioner has a need for the facilities. This understanding depends on your grasp of pragmatics, which often involves knowledge of the world as well as of language and its specific conventions about how to communicate (Grice, 1975).

Although some aspects of pragmatics depend on being able to understand the meaning of rising or falling pitch in a sentence, as in spoken questions, pragmatics are pervasive in linguistic communication—even in reading (Kintsch, 1998). Pragmatics depend critically on our ability to draw correct inferences. The fact that we humans can draw the correct inferences quickly and seemingly without effort obscures how difficult these processes really are. Indeed, the use of pragmatics has stymied attempts to create computer programs that can truly understand language, which is one of the reasons why droids probably won't be on patrol for a couple of hundred years. And when they do arrive, they may often seem a bit dense, even denser than Hans.

Pragmatics play a key role in understanding metaphor, a direct comparison of two things in which one is described as being the other. "The road snaked down the mountain" cannot be understood literally; one must understand that *snaked* implies "following a long, twisted path." The fact that pragmatics involve different mechanisms than the rest of language is attested to by the role of the right cerebral hemisphere. Other language abilities depend primarily (in right-handed people) on the left hemisphere, but pragmatics as well as the ability to understand humor, depend crucially on the brain's right hemisphere. Patients who have suffered damage to the right hemisphere might understand a metaphorical statement such as "Can you lend me a hand" as asking literally for a hand on a platter. Indeed, in normal people, the right hemisphere is particularly active (as measured in PET) when they are interpreting metaphors (Bottini et al., 1994).

Propositional representation: A mental sentence that asserts the unambiguous meaning of a statement.

Pragmatics: The way that language conveys meaning indirectly, by implying rather than asserting.

Brownell and his colleagues (1990; Bihrle et al., 1986; Brownell et al., 1983, 1995) told jokes to brain-damaged patients and asked them to select the appropriate punch line from a few choices. For example: "A woman is taking a shower. All of a sudden, her doorbell rings. She yells, 'Who's there?' and a man answers, 'Blind man.' Well, she's a charitable lady, so she runs out of the shower naked and opens the door." At this point, the patient is asked to select the appropriate punch line from five choices:

1. The man says, "Can you spare a little change for a blind man?"
2. The man says, "My seeing eye dog is 10 years old."
3. The man says, "I really enjoy going to the symphony."
4. The blind man throws a pie in the woman's face.
5. The man says, "Where should I put these blinds, lady?"

The patients with damage to the right hemisphere preferred the surprising but non sequitur endings, such as choice 4.

Language Development: Out of the Mouths of Babes

All normal humans learn language without needing to be taught it explicitly, an accomplishment no computer has even come close to mastering. It is clear that we humans are innately gifted with the ability to acquire language. But this doesn't mean that we acquire language all at once; many genetically influenced characteristics do not manifest themselves in their entirety at birth. Language ability develops in an orderly progression.

FOUNDATIONS OF LANGUAGE: ORGANIZING THE LINGUISTIC WORLD. To help the child learn language, caregivers (typically, in Western culture, mothers) intuitively adjust their speech so that the baby receives clear messages. The language that caregivers use to talk to babies, once called "motherese" and now dubbed **child-directed speech (CDS)**, relies on short sentences with clear pauses between phrases, careful enunciation, and exaggerated intonation that is spoken in a high-pitched voice (Bornstein et al., 1992; Cooper et al., 1997; Fernald et al., 1989). A similar pattern has been observed in the sign language caregivers use to communicate with deaf infants: They make signs more slowly, often repeat a sign, and use exaggerated movements (Masataka, 1996); babies attend more closely to such signing than to the more rapid, fluent signing used between adults. People often make similar adjustments when they talk to foreigners who do not speak their language well. In all cases, the adjustments are intended to make it easier for the one being addressed to understand what is being communicated.

Infants are surprisingly sophisticated in their abilities to encode spoken sounds. Although adults have difficulty hearing distinctions in spoken sounds that are not used in their language (for instance, English speakers often have trouble distinguishing between two "wah" sounds used in French), babies have no such difficulty (Jusczyk, 1995). Infants 2 to 3 months old can register in less than half a second that a syllable has been changed ("ga" to "ba"; Dehaene-Lambertz & Dehaene, 1994). However, after about 6 months of age, they start to ignore distinctions among sounds that are not used in the language spoken around them (Kuhl et al., 1992). Moreover, by 14 months, infants pay attention to different sound distinctions in different tasks: When they are required to distinguish between speech sounds, they are sensitive to differences in the sounds that they ignore when they are learning to pair words with particular objects (Stager & Werker, 1997).

The ability of infants to discriminate and organize sounds outstrips their ability to produce them. All babies, even deaf ones, begin by babbling at around 6 months of age (Stoel-Gammon & Otomo, 1986). Initial babbling includes the sounds made in all human languages. However, as the child is exposed to speaking adults, the range of sounds narrows; at about 1 year, the child's babbling begins to have adultlike

Child-directed speech (CDS): Speech to babies that relies on short sentences with clear pauses, careful enunciation, exaggerated intonation, and a high-pitched voice; also known as *motherese*.

intonation patterns (Levitt & Wang, 1991). Deaf children do not develop the more advanced types of babbling, but if they are exposed to sign language, their hand and arm motions develop in corresponding ways—beginning with a wide range of motions and eventually narrowing down to the ones used in the sign language they see around them (Petitto & Marentette, 1991). The first words children in all languages say grow directly out of their babbles, such as "ma-ma" and "da-da."

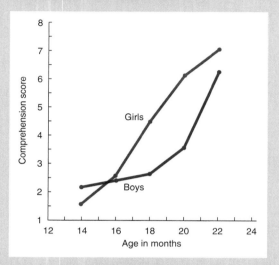

FIGURE 7.2
The Number of New Words Understood During the First Two Years of Life

Notice the difference in comprehension rates for boys and girls.

THE YOUNG LINGUIST. Most children begin to speak when they are about a year old. Two-year-olds can learn words even when the object or action being named is not present (Akhtar & Tomasello, 1996). By the time they are 6 years old, children know approximately 10,000 words (Anglin, 1993). This learning is not constant over age, however, as shown in Figure 7.2. Children begin by understanding words far in advance of their ability to say them. Indeed, they can understand about 50 words at about 13 months but cannot say this many words until about 18 months (Menyuk et al., 1995). Studies of brain activity in children, as measured by electrical activity on the scalp, have shown that when they are just beginning to learn words (at about 13 to 17 months), brain activity is widely distributed over both cerebral hemispheres. In contrast, at 20 months, adultlike patterns of activation are found in the temporal and parietal areas of the left cerebral hemisphere (Mills et al., 1997). Such findings suggest that the brain is changing as language is learned, that maturational changes in the brain facilitate language learning, or—as seems most likely (Mills et al., 1997)—that both events occur.

Even 3-year-olds can often learn words, or facts about objects, after hearing them only a single time (Carey, 1978; Markson & Bloom, 1997). Which words children learn first depends partly on their cultures; in Vietnam, children learn the respectful pronouns used to refer to elders before learning the words for many objects (Nelson, 1981). However, rather than learning the entire meaning of words in one fell swoop, children sometimes make **overextensions,** using words overbroadly when referring to new objects or situations. They might call a dog a dog, and a cat a dog, and a horse a dog, and even a sawhorse a dog. This makes sense if their initial idea of "dog" is anything with four legs. With learning, they discover which features—in the case of a dog, more than just four-leggedness—restrict the appropriate use of the word (Clark, 1983, 1993). Overextensions may sometimes occur simply because the child has trouble recalling the appropriate word and uses the apparently next best one instead. Children also make up new uses for words, such as *cutter* for someone who is teaching them how to cut out shapes from paper; when they learn and can recall a conventional name, such as *teacher*, they abandon the invented one (Clark, 1995). Moreover, children often can look at the appropriate object when given its name, even when they cannot produce the name (Naigles & Gelman, 1995); the act of recall, as discussed in Chapter 6, is generally a harder task than recognition.

The heart of any language is its grammar, which by its rules allows words to be combined into an infinite number of sentences. By looking at the patterns of sounds to which babies became habituated, Marcus and colleagues (1999) showed that even 7-month-old babies can already abstract grammarlike rules. However, it is only around 2 years of age that children start putting words together into the simplest sentences, two-word utterances such as "Go dog." These utterances are often called **telegraphic speech** because, like the telegrams of days gone by, they pack a lot of information into a few choice words. Within the next year, children who speak English start to use sentences that follow the sequence subject–verb–object ("Dog chase cat"). Words such as *the, a,* and *of* are left out. The particular order of the words depends on the language

Overextension: An overly broad use of a word to refer to a new object or situation.

Telegraphic speech: Speech that packs much information into few words.

being learned, but in all cases the child at this stage makes sentences with words in the appropriate order (de Villiers & de Villiers, 1992).

Adults do not teach grammatical rules to children, or even systematically correct grammatical errors (de Villiers & de Villiers, 1992; Pinker, 1994), but even 4-year-olds acquire such rules. Berko (1958) showed that most children this age generalize grammatical rules. This is true even when sentences contain nonsense words. For example, a child is given this problem:

This is a wug.

Now there is another one. Now there are two _____.

When asked to say the missing word, most 4-year-olds have no trouble saying "wugs."

Most verbs in a language are *regular*, following an easily derived rule for changes in tense—*play* becomes *played*, *work* becomes *worked*. But typically the most frequently used verbs in a language are *irregular*—for example, *eat* becomes *ate*. Children may start off using irregular verbs properly, but then begin to make mistakes such as *runned* instead of *ran*. These **overregularization errors,** mistakes caused by the misapplication of the rule for regular verb formation, occur because the child has now learned the rule and begins to apply it systematically, even when it is inappropriate (Pinker, 1999). The same thing happens with plurals; a child who could use *feet* correctly last week may suddenly start saying, "Mommy, my feets are tired."

The 5-year-old's language is in most ways like that of the adults in the community. Indeed, subtle testing is required to observe ways in which the language ability of 7-year-olds is less than complete. By such testing Carol Chomsky (1969) has shown that even 7-year-olds may confuse the meanings of statements such as "Please *tell* Sally" and "Please *ask* Sally"; but remarkably, even 3-year-olds understand that "I need a pencil" is a request, not a statement, and respond appropriately (Garvey, 1974). Subtle pragmatics and conversational skills emerge between the ages of 5 and 9—for example, learning to change topics by gradually, not suddenly, altering the direction of the conversation (Wanska & Bedrosian, 1985, 1986).

One of the great milestones in language development in childhood is learning to read and write. But not all children learn to read easily. Does difficulty learning to read mean that a person won't go very far in life? Not if you take President Woodrow Wilson as an example; before the age of 9, he used to read words backward (Seuling, 1978). There now is evidence that reading problems arise, at least in part, because the child's brain has not developed in such a way as to divide speech sounds into words properly. With extensive training in listening to speech and dividing the continuous stream into separate words, many reading-impaired children have dramatically improved their reading abilities, presumably because they have learned to store separate representations of words in memory (Merzenich et al., 1996; Tallal et al., 1996).

IS THERE A CRITICAL PERIOD FOR LEARNING LANGUAGE? Throughout history, there have been reports of children who grew up in the wild, never exposed to human language. Reports of such "feral," that is, wild, children include the story of Romulus and Remus, the legendary founders of Rome, who supposedly were abandoned as children and raised by a wolf; Edgar Rice Burroughs's novels about Tarzan of the Apes; and the true account of Victor, the Wild Boy of Aveyron. This boy was found naked and filthy in the woods near Paris, France in 1799; he bit and scratched those who annoyed him and generally acted more like a wild animal than a human. He was incapable of speech, making only animal-like sounds (Ball, 1971; Lane, 1976; Pinker, 1994). When cases like these occur in real life, they provide a critical test of the theory that language can only be learned during a narrow window of time called the **critical period.** This theory holds that the brain is "set" for the development of language (or other attributes) at a particular point and trying to acquire it either earlier or later is fruitless. Critical periods are different from **sensitive periods,** which define time windows when learning is *easiest*, but are not the only times when such

Overregularization error: A speaking error that occurs because the child applies a rule even to cases that are exceptions to the rule.

Critical period: A narrow window of time when certain types of learning are possible.

Sensitive period: A window of time when a particular type of learning is *easiest*, but not the only time it can occur.

learning can occur. Lennenberg (1967) claimed that language had to be learned prior to puberty, during the period when the two halves of the brain were becoming fully specialized; if language was not learned before this, he believed, it would never be learned well (see also Grimshaw et al., 1998).

Although the Wild Boy of Aveyron and other such children did have language difficulties, it is impossible to know whether they were mentally deficient to begin with; that may even be why they were abandoned. However, more recently scientists have been able to study similar children in detail. Consider, for example, the dreadful case of a girl called Genie, whose deranged parents locked her up, nearly immobilized, in a back room from the age of 20 months until she was slightly over 13 years old (Curtiss, 1977, 1989; Rymer, 1993). Genie was not allowed any contact with other people, was not talked to, and was punished if she made any sounds. She was not intellectually slow, nor had she had difficulty beginning to speak as a toddler. After she was discovered, she received intensive training in language, with mixed success. Genie was able to learn many words and eventually had reasonably good language comprehension, so there doesn't seem to be a critical period for acquiring all aspects of language. But she was never able to grasp the rules of grammar fully, and thus there does seem to be a critical period for acquiring grammar (Grimshaw et al., 1998; Pinker, 1994).

The existence of a critical period for grammar explains why brain damage has much greater long-term effects on language in adults than in children. Bates and her colleagues (1997) studied language acquisition in 53 infants and preschoolers with brain damage and concluded that although there are in fact innate biases for certain parts of the brain to take on language functions, if those parts are damaged in children's brains, other parts can take over these functions. Indeed, if the entire left half of a young child's cortex, including the areas normally used in language, has to be removed because of disease or injury, the child will nevertheless learn language. In fact, such children can sometimes learn language so well that careful testing is necessary to detect deficits (for example, Aram et al., 1992; Bishop, 1983; Vargha-Khadem et al., 1991). In contrast, it is very difficult for an adult to recover language abilities following brain damage that produces aphasia.

Other Ways to Communicate: Are They Language?

True language must have phonology, syntax, semantics, and pragmatics. Think about that as you read the following sections. Which of these examples of communication do you think truly qualify as language?

All but the best actors "leak" nonverbal information when they lie. Some people have an almost uncanny ability to detect lies on the basis of subtle changes in facial expression, but the cues they use have yet to be fully understood.

NONVERBAL COMMUNICATION. In ancient Egypt, law courts met in the dark so that the judges could not see the accused, the accuser, or the witnesses (Seuling, 1988), so as not to be swayed by their demeanors. People are remarkably good at **nonverbal communication,** such as interpretation of facial expressions and body language (Ambady & Rosenthal, 1992, 1993). Indeed, we can detect whether someone is lying by registering *microexpressions*, flickers of expressions—such as frequent eyeblinks, sideways glances, or downcast eyes that last as little as a tenth of a second (Ekman, 1985; Ekman & Friesen, 1975). We recognize different types of nonverbal information and can detect lies when inconsistent information arises from different sources, such as a stiff body posture combined with trusting, direct eye contact. We are also sensitive to the fact that the pitch of the voice tends to go up when someone is lying (Zuckerman et al., 1981), as well as that liars often speak more slowly and less fluently, and may exaggerate their facial expressions.

Pretty impressive, we agree. But is such nonverbal communication language? Consider again the four criteria: phonology, syntax, semantics, and pragmatics. Nonverbal communication does not have a set of perceptual units like phonemes that are combined according to rules to form new units. Instead, it consists of a set of specific physical signs and gestures. In addition, these specific signs cannot be combined in novel ways to create brand new, meaningful expressions. For instance, if you arch your eyebrows, open your mouth, and scrunch up your nose, people may think you're weird but won't read a distinct message. Nonverbal communication lacks the generative power that comes from having a true grammar; whereas language can convey an infinite number of messages, nonverbal communication lends itself to a relatively small set of messages. Finally, no clear distinction separates the literal from the implied meaning of nonverbal cues. Although nonverbal communication *is* communication, it is not truly language. Still, we shouldn't underestimate its importance.

SIGN LANGUAGE. One of the most remarkable things about language is that any normal person will develop it without being formally taught (Pinker, 1994). This is true for people in all cultures, including the culture of the deaf. Deaf children who are raised by speaking parents who do not sign will spontaneously invent sign languages (Goldin-Meadow & Mylander, 1998). Sign languages are not like the motions you might make when playing charades. Rather, the gestures specify the manual equivalent of phonemes, small units that are combined to make appropriate perceptual signals. Symbols for individual words are combined according to syntactic, semantic, and pragmatic rules (Emmorey, 1993; Klima & Bellugi, 1979). Just as there are different spoken languages, there are different sign languages: American Sign Language (ASL), for example, is not understandable to someone who uses British Sign Language (BSL), and vice versa.

One indication that sign language is a true language is that brain damage can disrupt it in ways that parallel the impairments of spoken language of hearing people (Bellugi et al., 1993; Poizner et al., 1987; Poizner & Kegl, 1992). Damage in the same brain areas results in corresponding effects in hearing speakers and deaf signers. For example, damage to Broca's area, in the left frontal lobe, can cause signers to have trouble using grammar when producing and comprehending sentences (Poizner et al., 1987), just as with people who use oral languages.

APING LANGUAGE? In evolutionary terms, chimpanzees are very close to humans: We have at least 98% of our genes in common. Nevertheless, no one has succeeded in teaching a chimpanzee or other nonhuman primate to talk. Some heroic researchers have gone so far as to raise a chimp alongside their own child, but even then the animal did not learn to speak (Kellogg & Kellogg, 1933). More recent studies have told much the same story (Terrace et al., 1976; Terrace, 1979). Because part of the problem seems to be that the animal's throat cannot make the sounds of speech, some researchers have tried to teach chimps sign language (Gardner & Gardner, 1969; Terrace, 1979) or to use arbitrary symbols such as cut-out plastic shapes or computer icons to communicate (Greenfield & Savage-Rumbaugh, 1990; Savage-Rumbaugh et al., 1986). With both sign language and arbitrary shapes, animals can in fact be taught to string symbols together to make "sentences." However, Terrace (1979) found that the chimps usually were simply imitating sequences they had previously seen and could not learn rules for re-ordering the signs to produce novel sentences. Nevertheless, members of one species of chimp, the pygmy chimpanzee, have spontaneously created new statements using the symbols (Greenfield & Savage-Rumbaugh, 1990), and at least some researchers believe that certain nonhuman primates are capable of using true language (Fouts & Mills, 1997). However, only humans spontaneously invent language (Pinker, 1994).

Some nonhuman primates can be trained to understand the meaning of symbols, such as these pieces of plastic, and to arrange them to form simple sentences. But is this true language?

Bilingualism: A Window of Opportunity?

All normal people learn a language, but only some learn a second language at some point in life. Is learning a second language the same as learning a first one? Using functional magnetic resonance imaging (fMRI), Kim and his colleagues (1997) scanned the brains of two groups of bilingual people while they thought about what they had done the previous day, using each of their two languages in turn. One group had learned their second languages as young children, the other as adults. Wernicke's area, involved in comprehension, was activated the same way in both languages and in both groups. But Broca's area told a different story: If the participants had learned the second language as young children, the same part of Broca's area displayed activity for both the first and the second languages. If they learned the second language after childhood, however, activity for that language appeared in a different part of the left frontal lobe—in a part used in working memory.

In spite of the fact that languages learned as an adult are not as well learned as those acquired during childhood, it is remarkably easy to learn some aspects of second languages. Dupuy and Krashen (1993) asked third-semester college students who were taking French to read five scenes from a script from a French movie, after having seen the first five scenes to get the story line. The scenes that were read contained many highly colloquial words that the students were unlikely to have seen or heard before. A surprise vocabulary test after reading showed that participants were learning almost five words per hour, without trying! This rate is remarkably close to the learning rates of children who are reading in their native languages.

Unfortunately, as you would expect from knowing that there is a critical period in childhood for learning grammar, it is not so easy to learn the grammar of a second language as an adult. In addition, it is not easy to learn the sound pattern of a second language after childhood. Indeed, the vast majority of people who learn a second language after puberty will make grammatical errors and speak with an accent. But even for these difficult tasks, some people can learn to pronounce words in another language almost flawlessly (Snow, in press). People differ greatly (perhaps even genetically?) in their abilities to acquire second languages.

LOOKING AT LEVELS

Specific language impairment: A specific problem in understanding grammar and complex words that is not related to more general cognitive deficits.

Is There a Language Gene?

If you think about what makes people special, different from other animals, language probably comes to mind immediately. We are the talking animal. Some researchers have claimed that we humans have special genes for language. The best evidence for this claim involves two steps. First, researchers (Gopnik 1990, 1997; Gopnik & Crago, 1991) found families in which many members have a disorder called **specific language impairment**. These people have trouble understanding grammar and even complex words, those made up of many morphemes, such as *predisposing*. Basing their conclusions on results from many types of tests, Pinker (1994) and others have argued that this disorder is not caused by general cognitive difficulties or an overall lack of intelligence—hence the name *specific* language impairment. This disorder has been identified in speakers of English, Greek, French, and Japanese, even though these languages convey information very differently.

Second, having established a very specific disorder of language, the next step is to link it to the genes. There is evidence for a genetic contribution to specific language impairment. In particular, the disorder is more likely to occur in both identical twins (who have the same genes) than in both fraternal twins (who share only half their genes). Moreover, language difficulties in general often run in families. Both siblings and parents of children with reading problems also display difficulties in reading

(DeFries et al., 1986; DeFries et al., 1987). Communication disorders in general—that is, impairments in the ability to express ideas in words and understand others when they do—are about 80% heritable (that is, about 80% of the variability in these disorders can be explained by variation in the genes; Bishop et al., 1995; Lewis & Thompson, 1992); stuttering, for example, is in part genetic (Ambrose et al., 1993; Kidd, 1983).

Does this mean that there is a single gene for language? Probably not (Gilger, 1995). As you are discovering, language is a complex phenomenon, and it is as unlikely that it is controlled by one gene as it is that a bakery would rely on a single ingredient for a cake. To bake a cake, you need not only the multiple ingredients, but also the oven and the means to make it hot and to time the baking process. An intricate system of events is involved in baking cakes and in using language. In either case, knocking out a link in the process disrupts the end result: No flour or liquid, no source of heat, no timing—any one of these failures means no cake. Similarly, language involves many key factors, any one of which may be affected by a different gene or genes. Indeed, many cases of language disorder involve many facets of language (Vargha-Khadem et al., 1995).

At the level of the group, language is clearly a social phenomenon. In fact, it is doubtful that language would have developed if not for the group. Being exposed to a community of speakers appears to turn on certain genes (see Chapter 2) that allow language learning to operate. If those genes don't work quite right, not only are our abilities to interact with other people affected but also the way we feel about ourselves is changed. Pinker (1994) describes in vivid detail the anxiety that people with specific language impairment experience, even in common social interactions, because they worry about their difficulties using language. Again, we see events at all three levels interacting: To understand the effects of this disorder, we need to consider events in the brain, the person, and the group.

CONSOLIDATE!

▶ *1. What are the essential characteristics of all languages?* All languages have four key characteristics: First, they have phonology. Phonemes are the basic units of speech, and they are arranged in sequences to form words. Before you begin to speak, you set up the sequence of phonemes you are about to say. Second, languages have grammar. Grammar is a set of rules for combining words that is based on the relationships among parts of speech. Every sentence has a syntax, which is its grammatical organization. We use grammar for both producing and understanding language. Third, languages have semantics, which specifies meaning. The semantics of a word arises from its morphemes, small elements of meaning. Propositional representations are sentencelike mental representations that express the unambiguous meaning of a set of words. Fourth, languages have pragmatics, the indirect or implied aspects of meaning. Pragmatics play a key role in understanding whether a question is actually a request, and whether a statement ending with a rising pitch is actually a question. Pragmatics are also involved in understanding metaphor and humor.

▶ *2. How do we acquire language?* Very young children learn to ignore the distinctions in sounds that are not used in their languages, and also to distinguish sounds that correspond to words and to memorize the words. However, they may overextend the words, using them for inappropriately broad categories, and they may overregularize rules of grammar (for example, for creating the past tense). Children begin by combining words "telegraphically," and with age come to use more complete and complex organizations. Older children learn to use indirect meaning (pragmatics) effectively. Research findings suggest that to master the grammar of a language, we must learn it during a critical (or sensitive) period, prior to puberty.

▶ *3. Which sorts of nonspeech communication are language, and which are not? Can animals be taught to use language?* Sign language is a true language, having language's four defining features (phonology, syntax, semantics, and pragmatics). However, nonverbal communication is not truly language, and it is debatable whether nonhuman animals can learn true language. Although animals can learn to use signs and symbols to communicate, they do not use grammar to produce large numbers of novel utterances; nevertheless, there are hints that some nonhuman

(continued)

primates may be capable of being taught a simple grammar. Unlike humans, however, no other animal invents language spontaneously.

▶ *4. Are first and second languages used in different ways?* Depending on your age when you learn it, a second language functions in the brain either in the same way as the first language or in a different way. Using a language learned later in life appears to rely,

at least in part, on working memory (whereas using a language learned early does not require working memory to the same degree). At least for people of college age, acquiring vocabulary in a second language is remarkably easy. However, mastering the grammar and sound patterns (phonology) of a second language learned after puberty is extraordinarily difficult.

MEANS OF THOUGHT: WORDS, IMAGES, CONCEPTS

One day it hit Frank that some of his difficulties in communicating with his droid might stem from the fact that Hans didn't think the same way he did—if Hans thought at all. Frank gently tried to find out just how Hans "thought." Frank usually thought in words, but he supposed that someone could also think in pictures. So he asked Hans if he often pictured things in his mind's eye. Hans's first response was, "How should I know?" This stumped Frank. Then he asked Hans if he talked to himself. This query merely earned him a cold stare. Hans did offer that he was not experiencing any mental instabilities, if that was the point, and how was Frank feeling today?

Thinking involves manipulating information in your head. Sometimes it involves solving problems; sometimes it involves simply determining what is implied by or associated with information at hand. Frank wasn't alone in assuming that we think partly by using language, but this isn't always the case. As you will see, language is a tool that may be used in thinking, but it is not the sole basis of thought.

▶ 1. Does language mold our thoughts?

▶ 2. Can we think with mental images? How might the brain give rise to these images?

▶ 3. What is a concept?

We are usually aware of what we are thinking about, but our awareness appears to be limited to language and mental images. Inner speech—talking to ourselves—and images are manipulated in working memory, and thus they play a key role in thinking; as discussed in Chapter 6, working memory operates on stored information to allow us to perform a task. Language and images help us to think but cannot themselves be the only means by which we think. To see why, let's consider each in turn, and then look at another way in which information is specified in the mind.

Words: Inner Speech and Spoken Thoughts

Many people, if asked, would say they think with words. And at first glance, that seems plausible: After all, to communicate with someone we usually have to express ourselves in words, so why not use words when thinking?

PUTTING THOUGHTS INTO WORDS. There are at least three problems with the idea that thinking is just talking to yourself, as was claimed by the founder of behaviorism, John B. Watson (1913). First, if this were true, why would you ever have trouble "putting a thought into words"? If thoughts were already formed in language, expressing them in language should be child's play. Second, words are often ambiguous, but thoughts are not. If you are thinking about "the port," you don't wonder whether you are thinking about a wine or a harbor. Third, anyone who has owned a dog or cat probably has sensed that at least some animals can think, and yet they don't use language. In fact, there is ample evidence that many animals can not only think but can also solve problems—remember Kohler's work with the chimpanzee Sultan, discussed in Chapter 5.

DOES LANGUAGE SHAPE THOUGHT? Even if thought is not the silent equivalent of talking to yourself, many people have been fascinated by the possibility that our perceptions and thoughts are shaped by the particular language we speak. This idea, known as the **linguistic relativity hypothesis**, was championed by Benjamin Lee Whorf (1956). For example, some have suggested that because the Inuit of northern Canada have many words for the different types of snow they recognize, they can see and think about subtle differences in snow better than speakers of English can with their paltry single word for the white stuff. If this idea is correct, then people who speak languages with lots of color words should be able to perceive more distinctions among colors than people who speak languages with few such words. Rosch (1973, 1975) tested this idea by studying the Dani, a remote tribe living in Papua New Guinea. The Dani use only two words for color, corresponding to *light*

Even though the Dani have only two words for color, light *and* dark, *they can perceive and learn shades of color as easily as people who speak languages with many terms for color.*

and *dark*. However, they perceive variations in color and are able to learn shades of color as readily as people who speak languages with words that label many colors.

Nevertheless, even if language does not entirely determine how we can think, it does influence some aspects of thought and memory. In some cases, we do appear to use words as a crutch to help us think, particularly when working memory is involved. In such circumstances, we often perform relatively slow, step-by-step reasoning—for example, memorizing a series of directions and recalling them one at a time, holding them in working memory long enough to turn the right way and continue to the next landmark. In addition, language can enhance memory. For example, if you look at clouds, you can remember their shapes better if you come up with a distinctive characterization for each (such as "a rabbit sticking out of a tube" or "a face without a chin") than if you use a single label for them all (Ellis, 1973). If the label really does help to identify the object, then remembering both the label and the visual form of the cloud gives you two ways to recall it later (see Chapter 6). However, this relationship between language and perception is not the same thing as language's actually shaping the nature of our thoughts.

Mental Imagery: Perception Without Sensation

If language is not the basis of thinking, what might be? Virtually all the great thinkers who applied themselves to this question in the past, including Plato and Aristotle, and later John Locke and other British philosophers, identified thought with a stream of mental images (Kosslyn, 1980). **Mental images** are representations like those that arise during perception, but they arise from stored information rather than from immediate sensory input. Visual mental images give rise to the experience of "seeing with the mind's eye," an experience you will have if someone asks you, for example, whether the Statue of Liberty holds the torch in her left or right hand. Auditory mental images

Linguistic relativity hypothesis: The idea that perceptions and thoughts are shaped by language, and thus people who speak different languages think differently.

Mental images: Internal representations like those that arise during perception, but based on stored information rather than immediate sensory input.

give rise to the experience of "hearing with the mind's ear," as likely happened when you were deciding whether the first three notes of "Three Blind Mice" rise or fall in pitch. Because visual imagery is the most common form of imagery (Kosslyn et al., 1990; McKellar, 1965), we will focus on it here.

MENTAL SPACE. There are many types of mental images (Kosslyn, 1994b); the most common seems to occur in a kind of "mental space." This space has three properties: spatial extent, limited size, and grain (grain is the equivalent of resolution on a television screen or computer monitor). Let's investigate these properties in turn.

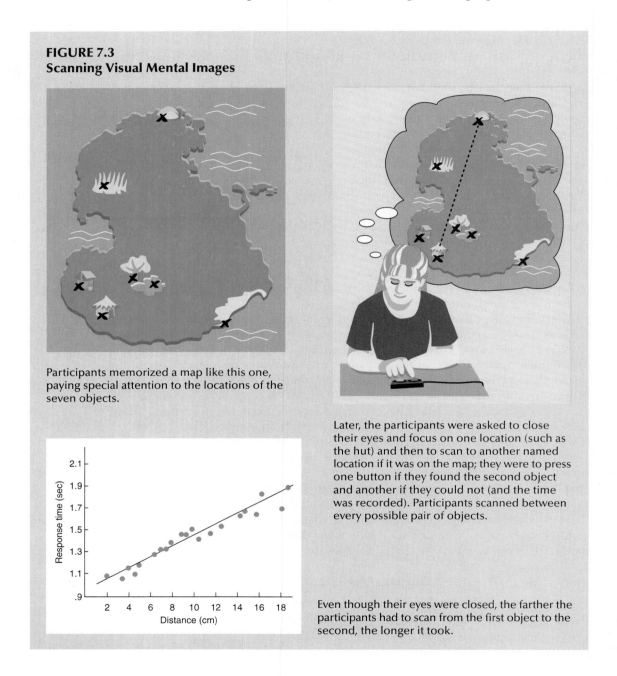

FIGURE 7.3
Scanning Visual Mental Images

Participants memorized a map like this one, paying special attention to the locations of the seven objects.

Later, the participants were asked to close their eyes and focus on one location (such as the hut) and then to scan to another named location if it was on the map; they were to press one button if they found the second object and another if they could not (and the time was recorded). Participants scanned between every possible pair of objects.

Even though their eyes were closed, the farther the participants had to scan from the first object to the second, the longer it took.

First, visualize your living room, and count the number of windows. Does it feel as if you are scanning the walls? As illustrated in Figure 7.3, the greater the extent of your scan, the longer it takes to do the job; these results show that when you visualize something, its mental representation has a definite *spatial extent* (Denis & Kosslyn, 1999).

Second, how large can an object in a mental image be? When you mentally counted the windows in your living room, you scanned across each wall one by one because you couldn't "see" the whole extent at once; you have only a limited field of view in a mental image. Now imagine you are walking toward an elephant, mentally staring at the center of its body. Imagine walking closer and closer to it, keeping your mental gaze fixed on its center. Most people doing this exercise report that when they are at a certain distance from the elephant, its edges seem to blur, to "overflow" their field of vision—that is, their mental space. Note the distance at which the edges of the elephant seem to blur. Now try the same exercise with a rabbit. Fixate on its center, and imagine seeing it loom up as you get closer and closer to it. When you imagine walking toward the rabbit, can you get closer to it than you could to the elephant before the edges seem to blur? When this study was done carefully, the larger the object, the farther away it seemed to be in the mental image when it began to overflow (Kosslyn, 1978). This result is as expected if mental space has a *limited size:* Bigger objects must be "seen" from farther away to fit within it.

Third, try this: Imagine stretching out your arm and looking at a butterfly perched on your fingertip. Can you see the color of its head? Many people find that they have to "zoom in" mentally to answer that question. Now move the butterfly to your palm and gently bring it to within 10 inches from your eyes; this time, zooming probably isn't necessary to "see" its head. Studies have shown that people require more time to "see" properties of objects that are visualized at small sizes than large ones (Kosslyn, 1975, 1976). It is as if the imagery space has a *grain.* If you look at a television screen close up, you will see that the picture is made up of lots of small dots. The dots are the grain of the screen; if an object is too small, there will not be enough dots to define the details, and thus the details will be blurred.

In short, objects in images have many of the properties of actual objects, and thus images can "stand in" for objects. You can think about an object in its absence by visualizing it.

THE VISUALIZING BRAIN. Visual images rely on many—about two-thirds—of the same parts of the brain that are used in visual perception (Kosslyn et al., 1997). This overlap may explain some of the key facts about imagery. First, *spatial extent.* Many of the areas of the brain that process visual input are organized so that images on the retina are laid out on the cortex in what are called "topographically organized areas" (from the Greek *topos,* "place"). As shown in Chapter 3, there are literally "pictures in the brain" in these areas. Many researchers have found that when people visualize with their eyes closed, these areas are active (Chen et al., 1999; Kosslyn, Alpert et al., 1993, 1995, 1999; LeBihan et al., 1993). Moreover, if these areas are temporarily impaired by the effect of strong magnetic pulses, visual mental imagery is disrupted (Kosslyn et al., 1999).

Second, *limits* on spatial extent. The brain needed to evolve only to process input from the eyes, and we don't see behind our heads. Objects in images overflow at about the same size that actual objects seem to become blurred in perception (Kosslyn, 1978). Like screens, topographically organized areas have definite boundaries, and images cannot extend beyond them. Of course, these areas are not literally screens, functioning like movie or television screens: No hidden observer in the brain looks at them—rather, the areas organize and process signals, which are sent to other areas in the brain.

Third, *grain.* Topographically organized visual areas of the brain have a property called *spatial summation:* If a neuron is excited by a point of light in a particular place in space, another point of light close to it typically will add to the effects of the first. If the spots are far enough apart, they are registered by different neurons. Spatial summation produces a kind of grain: If objects are small enough, points on their surfaces are too close together to be discriminated, and hence details are lost.

In short, we can understand the properties of this sort of mental imagery, which clearly depicts the surfaces of objects, because images arise in brain areas used in vision. Other types of images, such as the sense you have of where things are around you at any given moment, do not depict surfaces but rather specify locations; such spatial images, which even blind people can have, do not activate topographically organized areas (Mellet, Petit et al., 1998). In addition, in at least some tasks for some people, it is possible that images arise on the basis of memories formed by topographically organized areas, but may no longer rely on such memories (Behrmann, 2000).

But images take us only so far. Their limitations prevent them from being the only tools of the mind, even in combination with words. For one thing, images cannot represent abstract concepts. Take justice, for example. How would you represent "justice" with an image? You might choose a blindfolded woman holding a pair of scales. But how would you know if that image represented the familiar statue or was supposed to stand for the abstract concept of justice? Another problem is that images are often ambiguous. An image of a box seen from the side could just as easily be an image of that side alone, detached from the box. Furthermore, not everybody can produce good images; perhaps 2% of the population have poor visual imagery (McKellar, 1965). Yet another problem is, how do you "decide" which images to form? Some other process must pick out which images will be useful. Like language, imagery can contribute to our thought processes, and like language, it cannot be the only means by which we think.

Concepts: Neither Images nor Words

A **concept** is a grouping of a set of objects (which may include living things) or events (which can specify relations between things, such as "falling" or "on"). A concept is an unambiguous internal representation that may be abstract (such as the concept of truth or justice). Concepts may be *expressed* by images and words, but they are not the same as either (Kosslyn, 1980; Pinker, 1994). Thought arises from the manipulation of concepts, but words and images are used to express thoughts and further expand on them in working memory. Words and images play much the same role that a notepad does when you are planning a shopping trip; they not only help you work through and organize your thoughts, but also provide a way to store them.

The oldest idea of the nature of concepts was proposed by Aristotle in the fourth century B.C. According to this view, a concept corresponds to a set of features. For example, for the concept "bird" the features might be "wings, feathers, a beak, and the ability to fly." The features not only describe perceivable characteristics (such as wings and beak), but also specify appropriate activities (such as flight). The morphemes that underlie the meaning of the word *bird* would capture each of these properties. Some concepts are captured by the meanings of words, but others require a phrase or two to be fully expressed. Like the meanings of words, concepts are unambiguous.

PROTOTYPES: AN OSTRICH IS A BAD BIRD. According to Aristotle, the features of a concept must be both necessary and sufficient. A *necessary* feature is one that all members of the group must have; a *sufficient* condition is one that is enough—that "suffices"—to put an entity into a given category (so feathers would be a sufficient condition for "birdness"; if it has feathers, it's a bird). But Aristotle's formula doesn't always work: Although "the ability to fly" is a feature of birds, it is also a feature of insects and bats, but they're not birds; so flying is not a sufficient condition for birds. And an ostrich is a bird, but it can't fly, so flying is not a necessary condition for birds.

In addition, Aristotle's notion leads us to make wrong predictions. For example, according to his theory of how concepts are specified, if an object has the required properties, it is a member of the concept, period; all members of concepts have equally good standing. But Rosch (1978) showed that some objects are actually "better" members of their concept category than others. How good an example of its category an object is depends on its **typicality**—that is, how representative it is of that type of thing. As illustrated in Figure 7.4, people name objects that are typical members of a concept category faster than objects that are not typical members. If asked whether the headgear Frank saw (the one that looked like a cross between an umbrella and a water lily) was a hat, most people might say yes but take a long time to make the decision and still

Concept: An unambiguous, sometimes abstract, internal representation that defines a grouping of a set of objects (including living things) or events (including relationships).

Typicality: The degree to which an entity is representative of its category.

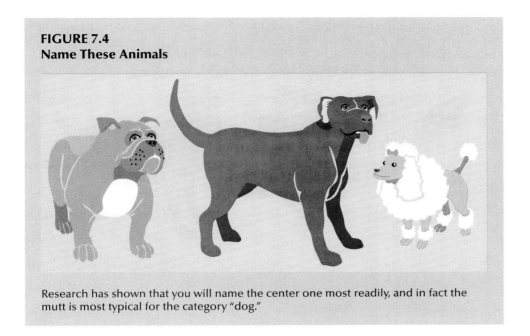

FIGURE 7.4
Name These Animals

Research has shown that you will name the center one most readily, and in fact the mutt is most typical for the category "dog."

be a little uncertain. The droid's thought processes apparently did not operate the same way as the human's; for a droid, a hat is a hat if it's worn on the head, and that's all there is to it. Typicality affects not only the time it takes you to identify an object, but also your confidence in naming the object as an example of a specific concept (Smith & Medin, 1981).

Most such effects can be explained if a concept corresponds to a set of features that describe the **prototype** of the category—that is, its most typical member—but only a *percentage* of those features need to be present in any particular member. In this case, the more features that apply, the faster you can name the object—and more prototypical members of a concept have more such distinguishing features (Rips et al., 1973). Thus, people take longer to name ostriches as birds because fewer bird features apply to them (they cannot fly; they are not the size of the standard bird); on the other hand, robins are named faster because more of the features of birds in general apply to them.

If you want to impress your friends, ask them to participate in a "mind reading" exercise. Pick a category that has a well-defined prototype, for example "vegetables." And then say, "Quick, think of a vegetable!" Predict that they have selected "carrot"—because in most cases, "carrot" (the prototype) is the vegetable they will have chosen.

However, some researchers have argued that at least some concepts may be stored as prototypes that are not collections of features, such as the prototype of an odd number between 1 and 10 (Armstrong et al., 1983). Quick, think of an odd number between 1 and 10. Most people select 3, and on that basis 3 can be considered as the most typical member of this category. But such concepts are unusual in that, by definition, they require selecting a single example, so these special cases may be represented by a single example stored individually. Other researchers have made the case that not all concepts are stored as prototypes, but rather some concepts rely on storing sets of examples of the category (Medin & Schaffer, 1978; Smith & Medin, 1981). For example, your concept of a chair might correspond to representations of a collection of chairs (rocking, desk, easy chair, and so on), not a single prototype. At least some concepts may be stored in multiple ways, and the different representations are used in different situations (Medin et al., 2000; Smith et al., 1998).

HOW ARE CONCEPTS ORGANIZED? Many concepts can be applied to any given object. We can name an object with words that correspond to concepts at different levels of specificity: "Granny Smith apple" is very specific, "apple" is more general, and "fruit" more general still. How are different concepts organized?

Prototype: A representation of the most typical example of a category.

FIGURE 7.5
Basic-Level Names

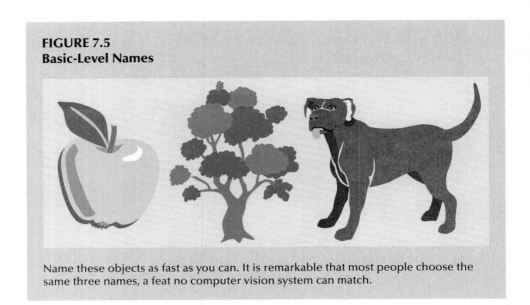

Name these objects as fast as you can. It is remarkable that most people choose the same three names, a feat no computer vision system can match.

Look at the objects in Figure 7.5 and name them as fast as you can. We bet that you named them "apple," "tree," and "dog." We strongly suspect that you didn't name the apple a "fruit" or a "Granny Smith," or call the tree an "oak" or the dog a "mammal" or an "animal." People consistently name objects at what Rosch and her colleagues (1976) have called the **basic level**. The basic level is like the middle rung of a ladder, with more general concepts above it and more specific concepts below it. So "apple" is the basic level; "fruit" is on a rung above it, and "Granny Smith" on a rung below. Each more general concept includes a number of more specific concepts; for example, "apple" includes "Granny Smith," "Delicious," "McIntosh," and many more.

At each level there are prototypes for the concept. For example, "apple" might be the prototypical fruit, and McIntosh might be the prototypical "apple." The basic level indicates the level of specificity with which we are likely to apply a concept to an object. Rosch offered several ways to identify the basic level. For example, one way is based on shape: At the most specific level, if we compare individual Delicious apples with other Delicious apples, their shapes are pretty similar. Moving up a rung of generality, if we compare Delicious apples with McIntosh apples, Cortland apples, and so on, their shapes are pretty similar. But, moving up another rung, if we compare apples with other fruits, such as bananas, watermelons, or grapes, their shapes are not similar at all. The basic-level category is the one that is as general as possible while still limited to objects having similar shapes.

Some researchers theorize that sets of concepts are organized not only according to levels that vary in specificity, but also into schemas (Rumelhart, 1975; Schank & Abelson, 1977). If the basic level is like a rung on ladder that organizes concepts in terms of specificity, a schema is like a basket that contains things that usually go together. A **schema** is a collection of concepts that specify necessary and "optional" aspects of a particular situation. For example, the schema for "room" indicates that it must have walls, a floor, a ceiling, and at least one door. In addition, this schema indicates that a room can also have windows, carpeting, and various types of furniture. If you know that something is a room, the "room" schema is activated, the necessary concepts apply to this case, and the schema guides you to look to see which other, optional features also apply.

CONCEPTS IN THE BRAIN. Studies of how concepts are stored in the brain have shown that they are organized not only in terms of specificity and their interrelations in schemas, but also according to how they are used. For example, brain damage can cause impairment to the ability to name living things but not manufactured objects

Basic level: A level of specificity, which is usually the most likely to be applied to an object.

Schema: A collection of concepts that specify necessary and optional aspects of a particular situation.

(Warrington & Shallice, 1984), or vice versa (Warrington & McCarthy, 1987). This finding suggests that the brain organizes concepts according to these two general classes. In addition, Martin and colleagues (1996) found that when the participants in their study named tools, one of the areas of the brain that was activated (as measured by PET) is used to direct movements. In contrast, this area was not activated when the participants named animals, although in this case visual areas were activated. Characteristic actions are important for specifying the concept "tool," whereas visual properties are particularly important for specifying the concept "animal."

Prototypes That Lead to Heavy Drinking

Prototypes not only play a key role in thinking, they also affect how we behave. Gibbons and Gerrard (1995) theorized that whether someone will engage in a health-risk behavior, such as excessive drinking of alcohol, depends on how similar they think they are to a prototype of the typical person who engages in that behavior. Blanton and colleagues (1997) tested this theory by studying 463 adolescents (roughly half male, half female) who lived in rural Iowa. To assess prototypes for drinking, the participants were told, "We would like you to think for a minute about the *type of person your age who drinks (alcohol)* frequently." They stressed that they were not interested in anyone in particular, just "the typical teenage drinker." Following this introduction, the participants were given a set of adjectives and rated the degree to which those adjectives described their prototype. On the basis of these ratings, Blanton and colleagues inferred the degree to which the typical teenage drinker was generally viewed by the participant as "self-assured–together (such as self-confident and independent), unattractive (unattractive and dull), or immature (immature and careless)." To the extent that an individual participant rated people who drink high on the first factor and low on the other two, he or she was said to have a "positive prototype" of drinkers.

Three results are of particular interest. First, participants who had more positive prototypes of drinkers reported drinking more. This was exactly as predicted, if feeling that you are similar to the prototype shapes your behavior. Second, the positive prototype itself was apparently a consequence of the participant's peer group; the more their peers tended to drink, the more the participants tended to drink. Third, adolescents who had poor relationships with their parents were more likely to associate with a drinking peer group. Thus, the parents had an indirect influence on drinking by affecting the choice of peer group, which in turn affected the prototype.

Consider these findings from the levels perspective: The brain is set up to store representations of prototypes. In this case the prototypes arose from social experience, particularly with the peer group. In addition, social interactions with the parents led teens to favor particular peer groups, which in turn helped mold a positive prototype for drinking. And the prototype in turn affects behavior. The events interact: By becoming a heavier drinker, a person will tend to spend more time with a peer group of drinkers, which in turn will further mold his or her prototypes.

CONSOLIDATE!

▶ **1. Does language mold our thoughts?** Although some researchers have claimed that language shapes thought, the evidence does not support this view. Thinking cannot rely entirely on words; for example, words are ambiguous but thoughts are not, and people sometimes have difficulty putting thoughts into words. Nevertheless, some thought does make use of language, and it is clear that being able to name something makes that object or idea easier to remember.

(continued)

▶ *2. Can we think with mental images? How might the brain give rise to these images?* Objects in images can "stand in" for the actual objects, as evidenced by the facts that they have spatial extent, they occur in a mental space with a limited size, and they have grain. Many studies have found that the visual parts of the brain in the occipital lobe are activated when people visualize shapes, and the properties of these brain areas may explain the characteristics of images. Nevertheless, thinking cannot rely entirely on mental images, which are difficult to use to represent abstract ideas and, like words, can be ambiguous.

▶ *3. What is a concept?* A concept is a grouping of a set of objects or events (including relations, such as the concept of an object being "on" another). This grouping is often accomplished by sets of features that unambiguously specify key characteristics of the concept, but only a percentage of the features must apply in any given instance. Members of concepts that have more of the key features are "better" (more typical) examples of the concept. An example that has the most specifying features is a prototype. Some concepts may be specified by prototypes that are not collections of features; others may be specified by sets of examples of the concept. Concepts are organized both according to levels of specificity and according to their relevance to particular situations (schemas). Although words and images are not themselves concepts, they can be used to express concepts.

PROBLEM SOLVING

Forming concepts is only a small part of what we do while thinking. Once we form concepts, we use them in various ways, such as in solving problems. Hans was particularly good at solving problems that were clearly stated. One day an old woman's life savings, stored in bags under her bed, were stolen. The perpetrator had pried open a window and crawled through into the bedroom. The window was high, and only one set of (very large) footprints (but no ladder marks) sank into the ground below it. So Hans reasoned that the thief must have been tall. Using his enhanced eyes and perfect memory, he was able to see microscopic threads on the window sill and to identify them immediately as a type of Australian wool used in only one brand of coat. He was also able to determine that this particular coat was dark blue and had been recently purchased. Hans then spotted a long blond hair on the floor of the bedroom. Searching his infallible memory to recall known tall, blond burglars, he came up with three suspects. Their photographs were printed, and one of them was immediately identified by the saleswoman at the one store in town that carried those coats. In 2 hours, the case was closed.

Clearly, many different skills feed into our ability to solve problems. But problems are not simply the sum of those abilities. Solving a problem depends crucially on how you set it up. You can use language, images, or word–picture combinations to specify the problem, but first you must conceptualize it—otherwise you won't know which words and images to use. Once you set up a problem in a particular way, you can manipulate your verbal descriptions and mental images to try to solve it. In this section we explore the differences among various kinds of problem solving.

▶ 1. What methods can we use to solve problems?

▶ 2. Do experts solve problems differently from the rest of us? How so?

▶ 3. What is artificial intelligence?

▶ 4. How can you improve your problem-solving abilities?

How to Solve Problems: More Than Inspiration

A **problem** is an obstacle that must be overcome to reach a goal. Problems come in many types and can often be solved in many ways. In this section, we consider the tools at your disposal for solving a diverse range of puzzles and predicaments.

Problem: An obstacle that must be overcome to reach a goal.

Representation problem: The challenge of how best to formulate the nature of a problem.

Functional fixedness: When solving a problem, getting stuck on one interpretation of an object or one part of the situation.

Strategy: An approach to solving a problem, determined by the type of representation used and the processing steps to be tried.

SOLVING THE REPRESENTATION PROBLEM: IT'S ALL IN HOW YOU LOOK AT IT. The first step to solving any problem is figuring out how to look at it. This fundamental challenge is called the **representation problem.** If you hit on the right way to represent a specific problem, the solution can be amazingly simple. Consider the example of the hiking monk in Figure 7.6 (based on Duncker, 1945). You have to decide whether at any one time of day the monk would be at precisely the same spot on the path going up and coming down. At first glance, this problem may seem difficult. If the precise specifications of departure times, speed, and so on lure you into trying to use algebra, you may work on it for hours. But if you hit on the right representation, it's easy: Imagine a mountain with a monk leaving from the top at the same time that another monk leaves from the bottom. It is clear that the two monks must pass each other at a particular point on the path, so the answer is simply yes.

Finding the right representation for a problem can be tricky because once you think of a problem in a certain way, you may find it hard to drop this view and try out others (Smith & Blankenship, 1989, 1991). For example, consider the problem in Figure 7.7 (adapted from Duncker, 1945). At first, you probably thought of the box simply as a container, and not as a potential part of the solution. Becoming stuck on one interpretation of an object or aspect of the situation is called **functional fixedness.**

ALGORITHMS AND HEURISTICS: GETTING FROM HERE TO THERE. To solve a problem, you need a **strategy,** an approach to solving a problem determined by

FIGURE 7.6
The Hiking Monk Problem

A monk leaves the bottom of a mountain every Monday at 5:00 A.M. and walks up a twisty path, climbing at a rate of 1.5 miles an hour, until he reaches the top at 4:00 P.M., having taken off a half-hour for lunch. He meditates on the mountain until sundown. At 5:00 the next morning he departs and walks down the path, going 3.5 miles an hour, until he reaches the bottom. Is there *any* point in the two journeys when he is at precisely the same location at precisely the same time of day? You don't need to say what that time is, just whether there would be such a time.

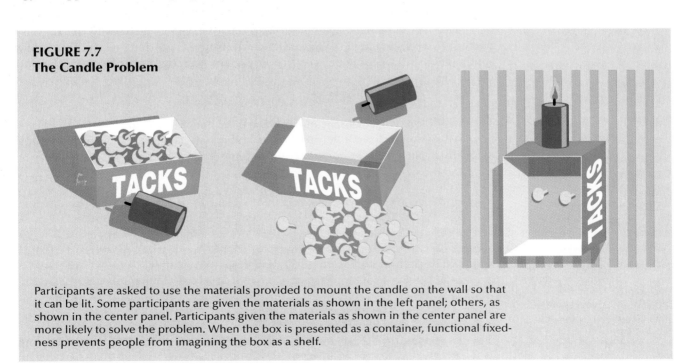

FIGURE 7.7
The Candle Problem

Participants are asked to use the materials provided to mount the candle on the wall so that it can be lit. Some participants are given the materials as shown in the left panel; others, as shown in the center panel. Participants given the materials as shown in the center panel are more likely to solve the problem. When the box is presented as a container, functional fixedness prevents people from imagining the box as a shelf.

the type of representation used and the processing steps to be tried. There are two types of strategies: algorithms and heuristics. Let's say you heard about a fantastic price being offered on a hit alternative music CD by an independent record store, but you don't know the name of the store. You could try to find it by calling every relevant listing in the yellow pages. This process involves using an **algorithm,** a set of steps that if followed methodically will guarantee the right answer. But you may not have time to call every store. Instead, you might guess that the record store is in a part of town where many students live. In this case, having reduced the list of candidates to those located near the campus, you might find the store after calling only a few. This process reflects use of a **heuristic,** a rule of thumb that does not guarantee the correct answer but offers a likely shortcut to it. One common heuristic is to divide a big problem into parts and solve them one at a time.

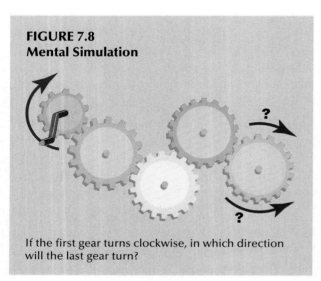

FIGURE 7.8
Mental Simulation

If the first gear turns clockwise, in which direction will the last gear turn?

MENTAL SIMULATION. Another way to solve problems relies on mental images more than on language. **Mental simulation** is the technique of operating on a represented object as if it were real, "seeing" what would happen in the corresponding actual situation (for example, Schwartz & Black, 1999). In many situations, objects in images behave as would the corresponding actual objects. You might visualize how best to cram luggage into the trunk of your car before deciding which bags to pack for a weekend trip. You would have an image of the trunk and visualize moving various bags around, "seeing" how to fit them in (Kaufmann, 1990). Figure 7.8 illustrates an example of mental simulation.

Mental simulations depend on your prior experience and the concepts you have derived from that experience (Schwartz & Black, 1999); if you haven't noticed how things work, your mental simulations of their behavior will be faulty. For example, visualize a penny and a bowling ball being dropped from a second-floor balcony at the same time. Which will hit the ground first? Many people report that the bowling ball hits first. But in fact, both objects will hit the ground at the same time. Faulty knowledge will guide the images incorrectly. However, you can use imagery to correct your knowledge: Repeat the experiment, but now imagine dropping three bricks from the same initial height. They should all hit the ground at the same time, right? Now imagine that two of the bricks are next to each other when dropped. All three still hit the ground simultaneously. Now imagine the two bricks not only right next to each other but glued together. The pair will still hit the ground at the same time as the single brick. Clearly, the weight of the object does not affect how quickly it will fall, as shown in your imagery experiment.

In addition, your mental simulations will be limited by your imagery abilities—how easily you can form, interpret, retain, and manipulate images. People differ dramatically in each of these abilities (Kosslyn, 1994b).

SOLVING PROBLEMS BY ANALOGY: COMPARING FEATURES. Another way to solve problems requires you to compare the features of two situations (Hummel & Holyoak, 1997). Let's begin with the following problem (based on Duncker, 1945): A surgeon has to remove a cancerous tumor from deep within a patient's brain. The use of a scalpel would cause permanent brain damage. An alternative is to use a beam of X rays to demolish the cancerous cells. However, the beam will also kill healthy cells in its path. Is there a way to reach only the cancerous cells and spare the healthy ones?

The solution is to split the beam into several minibeams, each aimed from a different angle. Each minibeam is so weak that it will not hurt the healthy tissue, but their combined impact will destroy the tumor. Gick and Holyoak (1980, 1983) found that most people do not realize this solution. However, if they are first presented with

Algorithm: A set of steps that, if followed methodically, will guarantee the solution to a problem.

Heuristic: A rule of thumb that does not guarantee the correct answer to a problem but offers a likely shortcut to it.

Mental simulation: The technique of operating on a represented object as if it were real, "seeing" what would happen in the corresponding actual situation.

an analogous problem and are told to think about how it relates to the second problem, success rates skyrocket. In this case, they first read about a problem faced by a general who wants to attack a fortress. If he advances all of his troops along a single road, mines would blow them to pieces. But smaller groups could travel on various approach roads without exploding the mines. The solution is to divide the army into smaller parties and have each take a separate road to the fortress. Once people see this solution and know it is relevant, the solution to the tumor problem becomes much easier (in fact, close to 80% get the problem right). If the participants are not told that the army problem is relevant to the tumor one, however, thinking about it does not help them much. At first glance, the two problems are unrelated. One involves soldiers and a fortress; the other, beams of radiation and a tumor. But beneath these surface differences, the problems have the same structure: Something too big is broken into parts, the parts are delivered separately, and then they are recombined. To see how a previous experience can be applied to a present case, you must recognize the similarities in the structure of the problems. Solving problems this way can involve both words and images.

Analogical thinking relies on having solutions to previous problems stored in memory, spotting similarities between a new and a previous problem, and seeing how the structure of the previous problem allows its solution to be applied to the new problem. This process is guided by your goals, which lead you to seek a particular kind of solution to the present problem (Holyoak & Thagard, 1997; Hummel & Holyoak, 1997).

SUDDEN SOLUTIONS. People do not always have to work consciously through a problem, step by step. In some cases, they can "see" the solution right away; in others, the solution dawns on them after they have set the problem aside for a while.

Many researchers have suggested that people sometimes can see a solution to a problem in a flash, full-blown and complete (Guilford, 1979; Olton, 1979; Torrance, 1980). This phenomenon results from an **insight,** a new way to look at a problem that implies the solution. Insights can arise following a trial-and-error exploration in which the problem is represented in different ways. Once the problem is represented in the right way, the answer is obvious. A good example of insight is the *Wheel of Fortune* experience; once you solve the word puzzle yourself, the solution becomes so obvious that you can't imagine how the stumped television contestants can be so dense.

Insights may occur after a period of **incubation.** Olton (1979, p. 10) defines incubation as "a facilitation of thinking that is evident after a period during which no conscious work was done on the task (assuming an earlier period of substantial conscious work)." To study incubation, Goldman and colleagues (1992) asked participants to solve difficult anagrams—words or phrases created by rearranging the letters of other words or phrases ("dormitory" is an anagram of "dirty room"). Those who did not solve the anagrams within the allotted time were given the same problems again, either immediately, 20 minutes later, or 24 hours later. New anagrams were presented along with those previously seen but not solved. Goldman and colleagues found that the participants solved more old anagrams than new ones if they had a break, and performed even better after a longer break. They point out at least five ways to explain this result: First, the participants could have kept working on some of the problems during the break. Second, they could have come across cues that helped them figure out the anagrams during the break, with more cues being likely with more time. Third, they could have forgotten strategies that were not useful but that had kept them fixated during the initial session (Smith & Blankenship, 1989, 1991, have shown such effects). Fourth, they could simply have been better rested after the break. Finally, it is possible that the unconscious does work on problems even when you are not thinking about them. Various scientists have reported experiences like this (Shepard & Cooper, 1982). For example, Friedrich Kekule, one of the founders of organic chemistry, reported that he realized that the molecule for benzene has a ring shape only after he began to nod off to sleep and visualized snakes biting their own tails (Koestler, 1964).

Insight: A new way to look at a problem that implies the solution.

Incubation: Improved thinking following a period of not consciously working on solving a problem or performing a task.

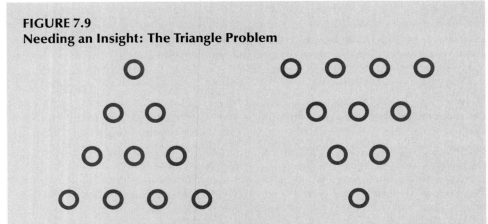

FIGURE 7.9
Needing an Insight: The Triangle Problem

Can the pattern on the left be transformed into the pattern on the right by moving only three dots? Solving this problem depends on having a specific insight. (See Figure 7.10 for the solution.)

Metcalfe (1986) tested the idea that insight involves unconscious restructuring by asking people to predict in advance whether they could solve specific problems. If people solve all problems by remembering relevant information, then they should be good at predicting their performance. In contrast, if problems can be solved by insight, a sudden shift in the way you look at a problem, success should be difficult to predict. Metcalfe found that people could accurately predict their ability to answer questions about real-world trivia, but not their performance on insight problems such as the one in Figure 7.9.

The mechanisms underlying insight and incubation are not well understood, but it would be surprising if they turned out to be much different from the mechanisms used in problem solving discussed earlier in this chapter. Many insights may emerge after we try out a new way to represent a problem, or after we spot an analogy. The fact that processes may occur unconsciously does not make them any more mysterious than the implicit memory mechanisms discussed in Chapter 6 (Kihlstrom, 1987).

Expertise: Why Hard Work Pays Off

The droid detective Hans was anything but humble, and his human companion Frank sometimes had to remind him that he was only 5 years old. "So what?" Hans would grumble. "What difference does that make?" Not only was Hans young, but he didn't know as much as he apparently thought he did. At least for humans, expertise in any given field typically takes about 10 years to achieve, in part because it comes from encountering many examples of the types of problems in a particular area (Ericsson et al., 1993; Simon & Chase, 1973). For example, why do you have to play chess for years to become a master? Chase and Simon (1973) tried to find out what made chess masters different from novices and very good chess players. Basing their study on the pioneering work of DeGroot (1965, 1966), Chase and Simon asked their participants to study chessboards with pieces on them for 5 seconds, and then to place the pieces properly on another board. The masters proved far superior to the novices and very good players, but only when the positions to be remembered were ones that could occur in an actual game. When the pieces were placed randomly on the board, the masters performed no better than the novices and very good players.

Chase and Simon inferred that the experts had seen so many games that they could recognize familiar positions in new games and so were able to group the pieces into single units (chunks); the novices and the very good players did not possess this information from experience. Chase and Ericsson (1981) subsequently showed that a key to enhancing problem-solving abilities is not storing larger chunks in short-term memory, but rather learning strategies for storing relevant information quickly and effectively in long-term memory, thus making an end run around the limitations of short-term memory (Ericsson & Charness, 1994, elaborate on this idea). Note that becoming an expert at chess is not merely a matter of developing a better memory for actual chess positions: Charness (1981) tested players who ranged in age from 16 to 64 and found that even the older players who had relatively poor memories could still make good decisions about which pieces to move.

Deliberate practice: Practice that is motivated by the goal of improving performance, usually by targeting specific areas of weakness and working to improve them.

Many researchers have shown that expertise involves numerous attributes (Chi et al., 1982; Chi & Glaser, 1985). Mayer (1997) reviews four types of knowledge that distinguish experts from nonexperts: (1) Experts organize their knowledge around fundamental principles, whereas nonexperts have more fragmented organizations; (2) experts use specific concepts, such as "momentum" in physics, whereas novices rely on vaguer ideas; (3) experts categorize problems based on the relevant underlying principles, whereas novices categorize them on the basis of the literal objects or other directly observable features; and (4) experts develop strategies more carefully in advance, whereas novices try to solve parts of the problem without an overall scheme in mind. Some aspects of these strategies involve knowing what to pay attention to, and how to use attention effectively (Posner et al., 1997). In addition, experts are more flexible when solving problems and, if necessary, can reorganize their strategies.

An interesting aspect of expertise is that it is limited to a specific field. Being an expert in one area does not generalize to another: Chess masters are no better than anyone else at solving different sorts of problems. The skills that are acquired by experience apply only to the specific area in which they were originally developed.

Ericsson and Charness (1994) and Ericsson and colleagues (1993) review much literature on expertise and reach a surprising conclusion: Talent plays little, if any, role in determining who becomes an expert. Rather, the crucial variable is simply how much deliberate practice is invested in performing a task. **Deliberate practice** is practice motivated by the goal of improving performance. When you engage in deliberate practice, you aren't necessarily having fun, and you aren't necessarily getting any kind of immediate reward (Ericsson & Charness, 1993). Deliberate practice involves spotting a weakness in a given domain (such as having a poor backhand in tennis, weak breath control in singing, or difficulty integrating functions in math), and specifically targeting that weakness for practice. Ericsson and colleagues (1993) found that the sheer amount of time spent in deliberate practice is the primary mechanism for achieving expert levels of performance (Bloom, 1985).

What leads one person to put in lots of practice and someone else to shy away? According to Ericsson and colleagues (1993), motivational factors such as temperament and preferences are crucial. However, for some skills, such as learning languages, the age at which you begin to learn is also significant, as you saw earlier in this chapter.

Artificial Intelligence

In 1997, our species seemed to suffer a minor setback: A computer (with special hardware and custom software) called Deep Blue beat the world's best human chess player, Garry Kasparov. Does this mean that computers will soon be able to solve all sorts of problems better than we can? Will Frank someday be replaced by a new, improved model of Hans? Not to worry. Deep Blue relied, basically, on a boring program. Because Deep Blue was so fast, it could work out and evaluate every possible move, one at a time. Deep Blue, unlike its human challengers, used a "brute force" algorithm, similar to calling every music store in the phone book alphabetically to find a CD. Deep Blue was an advance over earlier computer programs partly because

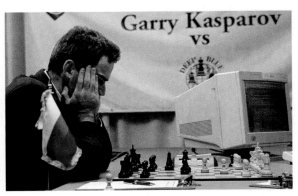

Computers—specialized hardware plus customized software—can now beat the human world chess champion. What's next?

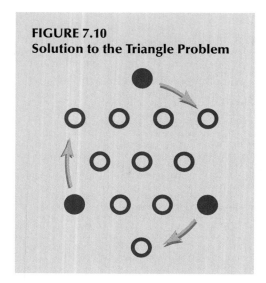

**FIGURE 7.10
Solution to the Triangle Problem**

it could "anticipate" more possible consequences of any given move, and partly because it was better at noting which moves eventually led to disaster and which put the opponent in a bad position. Moreover, it had access to information on hundreds of thousands of important previous games (including every one of its opponent's games), and thus could detect whether Kasparov was doing anything that ever had been done before. Deep Blue could play a mean game of chess, to be sure, but it couldn't figure out how to open a tin can or buy a bottle of milk. In contrast, chess-playing humans use analogical thinking, knowledge of principles, and various heuristic strategies in pursuing a checkmate. A surprisingly complex network of brain areas is involved in playing chess, tapping areas used in recognizing objects, registering spatial relations, and formulating plans (Nichelli et al., 1994).

Artificial intelligence (AI) is the name of the field devoted to building smart machines, machines that can "think." The existence of the human brain is the only proof that a mechanism can think, and thus many AI researchers believe that the best way to make computers truly intelligent is to make them in our image. AI research has led to the creation of *expert systems,* computer programs that can solve problems in ways that human experts would pursue. Although these programs sometimes are impressive, so far they have lacked the flexibility and creative flair of human thought.

An innovation in AI has been the programming of **neural networks** to imitate (roughly) the way the brain works. These computer programs have many small units that interact via connections, akin to the networks of neurons in the brain. Unlike most computer programs, these programs depend on having many processes operating at the same time (McClelland & Rumelhart, 1986; Rumelhart & McClelland, 1986). Neural networks can recognize objects remarkably well and can generalize to novel examples of a familiar category. Furthermore, when parts are disrupted, the networks often mimic the effects of human brain damage (Kosslyn & Koenig, 1995).

Combined research in AI and cognition has spawned a field called **cognitive engineering** (Norman, 1988). Cognitive engineering designs products and devices on the basis of theories of how humans process information. For example, look at car radios. Are the more important controls, those for power and volume, more easily spotted than the less important ones, such as those for tone or balance? Do you move logically from left to right to adjust the controls, in the same order used when reading, or do you have to search? Are the controls labeled with terms you can easily read and understand? Cognitive engineering would build a radio with those questions in mind.

Cognitive engineering sometimes involves forms of AI, as in the design of machines that are made to be intelligent, for example, by anticipating repeated requests of the same type. A good spell checker does this, immediately offering the correct word the second time a misspelling occurs, having learned the word that should be substituted.

Artificial intelligence (AI): The field devoted to building smart machines.

Neural network: A computer program whose units interact via connections that imitate (roughly) the way the brain works.

Cognitive engineering: The field devoted to using theories of human information processing to guide the design of products and devices.

Overcoming Obstacles to Problem Solving

You can improve your ability to overcome obstacles to solving problems if you keep the following points in mind (Ellis & Hunt, 1993).

1. A major challenge is to represent the problem effectively. One way to meet this challenge is to make sure you really understand the problem. Explain the problem to somebody else; sometimes, the simple act of explaining leads to a representation that immediately implies a solution.

2. Keep your eye on the ball: Don't lose sight of what actually constitutes the problem. People sometimes tend to transform the problem—resist this. If the problem is "how to get to Hawaii," don't redefine the problem as "how to talk your parents into subsidizing the trip." This advice also applies to de-

bates and arguments. You'd be surprised at how much more effective you'll be if you keep the issue in mind and don't allow yourself to be drawn off on tangents.

3. Don't get locked into viewing your resources in only one way, which is a form of functional fixedness. See whether you can come up with more than one strategy for approaching the problem.

4. Don't get stuck with a certain mental set, a fixed way of viewing the kind of solution you seek. It's okay to begin by focusing on one possible solution, but recognize that there may be more than one happy outcome. Be willing to consider alternatives. (Southern California is a great spring break destination, too.)

5. If you do get stuck, walk away from the problem for a while. A fresh look can lead to new ways of representing it or devising new strategies for solving it.

LOOKING AT LEVELS

Groupthink

Not only can you be stymied by your own personal obstacles to clear and effective problem solving, but the dilemma can become worse when other people are involved. At the level of the group, we enter *groupthink*, the realm first described by George Orwell in the futuristic novel *1984* and later discussed by social psychologist Irving Janis (1972). Groupthink refers to the tendency of people who try to solve problems together to accept one another's information and ideas without subjecting them to critical analysis. According to Janis, people are most likely to fall into groupthink when the group members are especially close. In such instances, rather than realistically thinking through a problem, members are more concerned with agreeing with one another. This concept has been used to explain many real-life disasters, such as why NASA launched the space shuttle *Challenger* despite widespread concerns about its booster rockets. Although the evidence that groupthink leads to bad decisions is mixed (Aldag & Fuller, 1993), a meta-analysis revealed that cohesive groups tend to make poorer decisions if the cohesiveness grew out of "interpersonal attraction"—the members' feelings about one another (Mullen et al., 1994).

Groupthink is not goodthink for many reasons (Aldag & Fuller, 1993), but let's consider just one: If a group is cohesive because of interpersonal attraction (level of the group), the members may not want to look stupid or uncooperative and therefore tend to go along with the crowd. This explanation implies that the group leads its members to define one of their individual goals (at the level of the person) as gaining the approval of the other members. That desire for approval would inhibit members from making comments that would rock the boat. Such inhibition arises from the operation of the frontal lobes (Damasio et al., 1996) and may often involve working memory (which would be required to think about the possible effects of comments before making them). Thus, the motivation induced by the group leads the frontal lobes to operate in ways that gauge the possible impact of comments, and inhibit remarks that might disrupt group harmony. Unfortunately, some of these comments are potentially constructive. As usual, events at the three levels interact. For example, a person's goals, needs, beliefs, and tastes must lead him or her to find the other members attractive, or the group will not lead each individual to engage in groupthink. In addition, the very act of inhibiting certain thoughts or comments requires effort (probably involving working memory), and that effort in turn interferes with additional critical thinking—and makes members more susceptible to following the herd.

▶ *1. What methods can we use to solve problems?* The first step is to discover how best to specify the problem, how to represent it to yourself. If you find the proper representation, the solution is sometimes obvious. To solve a problem, you can use an algorithm or heuristic. One common heuristic is to divide a problem into a set of smaller problems and to tackle them one at a time. For some types of problems you can visualize the situation and imagine various scenarios. The usefulness of such mental simulations is limited by how effectively you can visualize. In addition, you can search for correspondences with other situations and use analogical thinking to solve a problem. Finally, after working on a problem but failing to find a solution, sometimes stopping conscious work and letting the problem incubate will produce an insight.

▶ *2. Do experts solve problems differently from the rest of us? How so?* In short, yes. Experts have a vast body of knowledge of their field, which typically requires about 10 years of hard work to acquire. This database in long-term memory allows experts to avoid the limitations of short-term memory. In addition, experts have learned to organize their knowledge in long-term memory around fundamental principles, use specific concepts for their area of expertise, cate-gorize problems in terms of basic principles, develop strategies more carefully before beginning a problem-solving task, and use strategies flexibly.

▶ *3. What is artificial intelligence?* Artificial intelligence (AI) is the field devoted to constructing machines that behave in ways that mimic human intelligence. So far, such machines have limited applications, usually in a very narrow domain. AI has joined cognitive psychology to produce the field of cognitive engineering, which makes use of theories of human information processing to design products and devices. Some aspects of cognitive engineering focus on producing intelligent devices that work well with humans.

▶ *4. How can you improve your problem-solving abilities?* Make sure you really understand the problem so that you can make an effective representation of it. Keep in mind what the fundamental problem is; don't be distracted by tangential issues. Try to develop more than one strategy for approaching the problem. Don't get stuck on seeking a single solution; consider alternative happy outcomes. Finally, sometimes it's best to let go of the problem for a while, and see whether incubation works to spark an insight or if a fresh approach later produces a solution.

LOGIC, REASONING, AND DECISION MAKING

Frank was proud to be a human being instead of a machine, even a machine with superhuman sensory abilities and a flawless memory. Frank firmly believed that he had something no machine would ever have: intuition. When Frank spoke of acting on a hunch, or using his intuition, the droid Hans had no idea what Frank was talking about. Hans made decisions not on the basis of some vague feeling, but rather on the firm foundation of the laws of logic.

▶ 1. Do people reason logically?

▶ 2. Why do we commit reasoning errors?

▶ 3. Can emotion aid reasoning?

Are People Logical?

Logic: The process of applying the principles of correct reasoning to reach a decision or evaluate the truth of a claim.

Deductive reasoning: Reasoning that applies the rules of logic to a set of assumptions (stated as premises) to discover whether certain conclusions follow from those assumptions; deduction goes from the general to the particular.

Not all thinking consists of figuring out how to overcome obstacles; sometimes thinking is considering what follows from what, evaluating alternatives, and deciding what to do next. Decision making requires us to evaluate possible outcomes and choose one over the other. **Logic** is the process of applying the principles of correct reasoning to reach a decision or evaluate the truth of a claim. "Hector is a man; all men are human; therefore Hector is a human" is correct logic. But note that "Hector is a man; all men are Martians; therefore Hector is a Martian" is *also* correct logic. The first two statements in each case are the *premises*, and the only question in logic is whether the final statement, the *conclusion*, follows from the premises. The *content*—the actual meaning of the premises—is irrelevant to logic; only the *form*, the sequence of what-implies-what, counts in logic. If you accept the premises, logic dictates the conclusions you must also accept. In this process of **deductive reasoning**—that is, reasoning from the general to the particular—the rules of logic are applied to a set of assumptions stated as premises to discover what conclusions inevitably follow from those assumptions.

Much research has shown that, unlike the Vulcan Mr. Spock and the droid Hans, humans are not entirely logical. For example, people often make the error of **affirming the consequent;** that is, we assume that a specific cause is present because a particular result has occurred. Here is a cause–effect relation: "If it is sunny out, Hector wears a hat." Does it follow that this statement is true: "Hector is wearing a hat; therefore, it is sunny out"? Not necessarily. Maybe Hector's on his way to a ballgame and has put on a hat with his team's logo. Maybe after checking The Weather Channel, he has put on a rain hat. Maybe he simply thinks a particular hat looks good with his outfit. Maybe—well, there might be any number of reasons, including that it is in fact sunny out. Affirming the consequent occurs because we incorrectly work backward, from result to cause.

Wason and Johnson-Laird (1972) devised a task that laid bare more of our reasoning frailties. Look at Figure 7.11: What would you do? The answer is that both *A* and 7 must be flipped. People tend to flip *A*, to see whether an odd number is on the other side; if not, the rule would be wrong. If there is an even number on the reverse of *A*, most people assume the rule is confirmed. Very few think to turn over the 7: If there is a vowel on the other side, then the rule is wrong no matter what's on the reverse of *A*. Most people do not think about what it would take to *disconfirm* the rule. A **confirmation bias** occurs when people seek information that will confirm a rule but do not seek information that might refute it.

Now consider a variation of this task. Instead of *A*, *D*, 4, and 7, the cards say *beer, coke*, 22, and 16, and the rule relates to drinking age: If a person is drinking beer, then he or she must be over 21 years old. Griggs and Cox (1982) found that participants in this version of the task had little problem realizing that they had to turn over both the *beer* and the 16 cards. Instead of using the rules of logic, they used their knowledge of state drinking laws.

Much deductive reasoning appears to rely on setting up **mental models** (Johnson-Laird, 1995), images or descriptions of a specific situation used as an aid in reasoning about abstract entities. Try this: Sam is hungrier than Susan, but Susan is less hungry than George; is Susan the least hungry? Problems like this are very easy to solve if you imagine a line with a dot for each entity and place the dots standing for entities with more of the value (here, hunger) farther to the right (Huttenlocher, 1968; Huttenlocher et al., 1970). If you do this, when asked about the relative positions of the entities, you can simply "look" at your image and "read" the position of the dot of interest (Demarais & Cohen, 1998). Neuroimaging of people performing such reasoning shows activity in the spatial processing structures in the parietal lobes (Baker et al., 1996; Osherson et al., 1998), as expected if people are mentally manipulating spatial relations.

Reasoning can be inductive as well as deductive. The opposite of deductive reasoning, **inductive reasoning** works toward a conclusion by moving from the particular case to a generalization. Induction uses individual examples to figure out a rule that governs them. If you ate two green apples and each was sour, you might induce that green apples in general are sour. However, your conclusion would be faulty: You ignored the evidence of Granny Smiths (which are sweet). Here's another example. What number comes next: 2, 4, 6, _? You probably said 8, but what if the underlying

FIGURE 7.11
Wason and Johnson-Laird's Card Task

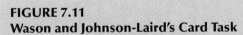

Here is a rule: If a card has a vowel on one side, then it will have an even number on the other side. How many and which of these cards must be flipped over to decide whether this rule is true?

Affirming the consequent: A reasoning error that occurs because of the assumption that if a result is present, a specific cause must also be present.

Confirmation bias: A tendency to seek information that will confirm a rule, and not to seek information that is inconsistent with the rule.

Mental model: An image or description of a specific situation used to reason about abstract entities.

Inductive reasoning: Reasoning that uses examples to figure out a rule; induction goes from the particular (examples) to the general (a rule).

rule were simply "larger numbers"? Then 21, or 101, would also work. Or the rule might be "even numbers," and 2 would satisfy the condition, or "one-digit numbers," in which case 7 would work, and so on. The point is that every one of these additional generalizations is just as consistent with the set 2, 4, 6 as is the number 8 (Goodman, 1983). That inductive reasoning works at all is something of a miracle—nevertheless, it often does (Prasada, 2000), and much of scientific discovery relies on just this kind of reasoning. To remember the difference between deductive and inductive reasoning, try these mnemonics: To DEduce is to move DOWN FROM something larger; to INduce is to move INTO something larger.

Much reasoning involves a combination of deductive and inductive processes. Although evolutionary theories have been used to explain why our reasoning abilities work as well as they do and have the quirks they have (Cosmides, 1989; Gigerenzer & Hug, 1992; Oaksford & Chater, 1994), other, more general explanations also apply (Almor & Sloman, 1996; Fodor, 2000). Sperber and colleagues (1995) provide evidence that people try to minimize cognitive effort when reasoning, and Kirby (1994) showed that people assess the relative cost and benefit of each decision. It has proved very difficult to provide evidence for evolutionary theories of reasoning that cannot be explained equally easily and satisfactorily by other types of theories.

Heuristics and Biases: Cognitive Illusions?

If the laws of logic lead to inescapable conclusions, why do people make errors in reasoning? The answer is implied in the question: because people do not always use the laws of logic, but rely instead on sets of heuristics. While often useful, these heuristics, or rule-of-thumb strategies, sometimes steer us to the wrong conclusions.

REPRESENTATIVENESS. The **representativeness heuristic** assumes that the more similar something is to a prototype stored in memory, the more likely the entity belongs to the category of the prototype. Tversky and Kahneman (1974) asked participants to read this passage:

> Jack is a 45-year-old man. He is married and has four children. He is generally conservative, careful, and ambitious. He shows no interest in political and social issues and spends most of his free time on his many hobbies, including home carpentry, sailing, and mathematical puzzles.

The participants were told that Jack was selected at random from a group of 100 people, all of whom were either lawyers or engineers. Here's the trick: Half the participants were told that 70 members of the group were lawyers and 30 were engineers; the other participants were told that 30 members of the group were lawyers and 70 engineers. Pause for a moment and imagine that there are 100 balls in a jug, 70 red and 30 black, randomly mixed up. Imagine shutting your eyes and drawing out one ball. Do you think you would be more likely to pluck out a red one than a black one? Sure. Now reverse the colors, so that 70 are black and 30 red. Now you would be more likely to pull out a black one. However, when asked to decide whether Jack, who was selected at random from the group, was a lawyer or an engineer, the great majority of all participants, no matter what they had been told about the constitution of the group, said he was an engineer. The description of Jack, especially his interest in mathematical puzzles, fit the participants' ideas about the characteristics of engineers better than it fit their ideas about lawyers, and thus they labeled Jack "engineer" because he matched the prototype. The participants used their knowledge—or assumptions—about typical properties of people in different professions to make their decision, ignoring the **base-rate rule**. This rule states that if something is sampled at random, the chances of obtaining a particular type are directly proportional to its percentage in the set from which the sample is taken. Our failure to appreciate the working of this rule can be thought of as a *cognitive illusion*.

Gigerenzer, however, argues that people do not often have true cognitive illusions, but instead simply have trouble understanding descriptions of probabilities. Gigerenzer

Representativeness heuristic: The heuristic that the more similar something is to a prototype stored in memory, the more likely it is to belong to the prototype's category.

Base-rate rule: The rule stating that if something is sampled at random, the chances of obtaining a particular type are directly proportional to its percentage in the set from which the sample is taken.

and his colleagues (1988) performed an experiment that ensured that the participants understood the information about the proportions of different professions in the group. They took 10 slips of paper and on each one wrote a description of a person and the person's profession. Seven slips had one profession written on it, and three another; the slips were folded and put in an urn. Each participant drew out a single slip and read the description (but not the profession), and then guessed the profession. In this situation, the participants did well, proving themselves able to keep in mind the relative proportions of the two professions. According to Gigerenzer and colleagues, in earlier experiments, such as the one with Jack, participants did not understand the proportions of the two professions well enough to override their prior knowledge about types of people; they categorized Jack based on prior knowledge, not probability (additional support for this conclusion is provided by Goodie & Fantino, 1996).

Gigerenzer (1994) claims that people judge probabilities by thinking about frequencies, how often events occur (Estes, 1976); people are very good at remembering frequencies (Hasher & Zacks, 1979, 1984). So if they have trouble understanding probabilities, they may rely on their knowledge of relative frequencies of the different choices. However, the results suggest that when people cannot use prior knowledge about how often events occur (for example, in thinking about events that only happen once, such as the *Challenger* disaster), people use reasoning heuristics. The bottom line is that people use different strategies in different situations—sometimes heuristics, sometimes relative frequencies, and sometimes other kinds of information (Ayton & Wright, 1994; Gigerenzer, 1996; Gigerenzer & Goldstein, 1996; Kahneman & Tversky, 1996; Teigen, 1994).

AVAILABILITY. Another shortcut is the **availability heuristic,** which states that we tend to judge objects or events as more likely or frequent if they are easier to bring to mind. For example, Tversky and Kahneman (1974) asked people to judge the relative proportions of words that begin with the letter *k* and words with *k* in the third position. What do you think? Most of the participants in the study thought that *k* occurred more often as a first letter than a third letter, but in fact almost three times as many words have *k* in the third position as in the first one. Why this error? Because it is much easier to bring to mind words starting with *k* than words that have *k* in the third position. The availability heuristic may also explain why people tend to think that infrequent but highly memorable events, such as murders and plane crashes, are more common than they really are, and that more frequent but mundane killers, such as stomach cancer and stroke, are less common.

If you have ever budgeted time to work on a paper, and then run out of hours way too soon, you may have fallen victim to the **planning fallacy,** the tendency to underestimate the time it takes to accomplish a task. This error may arise because the *completion* of similar tasks is more available in your memory than is their *duration*. The good news is that the planning fallacy can be reduced by thinking carefully about how long past projects actually took to complete (Buehler et al., 1994). If you are doing a group project, it may be helpful to tell the other members of the group about the planning fallacy and how to counter it.

IMPROVING REASONING: COLLEGE HELPS. Every once in a while a study is published that we professors find particularly gratifying. One by Lehman and Nisbett (1990) definitely falls into this category. (It should also please you.) Lehman and Nisbett examined the reasoning abilities of University of Michigan undergraduates during the first term of their freshman years and then again during the second term of their senior years. They focused on assessing two types of reasoning skills: statistical reasoning, such as the ability to use base rates, and conditional reasoning, of the form "if *X* is true, then *Y* is true," as used in the Wason card selection task described on page 265. Lehman and Nisbett separately examined students who had different majors. Although there was no difference in scores among the freshmen in the different majors, by the fourth year students who majored in psychology and the social sciences showed large increases in the ability to reason statistically, increases far

Availability heuristic: The heuristic that the easier events or objects are to bring to mind, the more likely, common, or frequent they are judged to be.

Planning fallacy: The tendency to underestimate the time it takes to accomplish a task.

larger than the improvement shown by natural sciences or humanities majors. In fact, the average gain was over 60% for psychology and social science students. In contrast, the opposite result was found for conditional reasoning: Here, the natural sciences and humanities students were far better than the psychology and social science students. It is heartening to see that the kind of reasoning used in course work generalizes to novel problems that rely on such reasoning. Going to college really *can* help you learn to think better.

Emotions and Decision Making: Having a Hunch

Star Trek's Mr. Spock and the droid Hans agree: Emotion clouds reason and distorts our ability to be objective. Doesn't it? Well, not exactly. Researchers have found that sometimes emotion can actually help reasoning. Bechara and colleagues (1997) found that people played a gambling game better once they had "hunches," even though they were not aware of the basis of the hunch. Evidence of a hunch was detected by the researchers as a skin-conductance response. Such responses occurred when the brain signaled the body that certain choices were risky before the participants consciously realized it. But perhaps the most interesting results concern the contrast between the normal participants and patients who had damage to the ventral medial frontal lobes, parts of the brain known to play a crucial role in using emotional information to guide behavior (Damasio, 1996). These patients never showed skin-conductance responses prior to making a choice and never expressed having a hunch. By the end of the experiment, even the normal people who never consciously figured out the situation still tended to choose properly, whereas the brain-damaged patients never did.

Such emotional responses may underlie what we mean by *intuition,* having an idea that is not easy to express. These responses appear to be based on implicit memories (see Chapter 6) and nudge the conscious decision-making system. Without such nudges, people do not choose wisely. In real life, patients with damage to the ventral medial frontal lobes squander their money, have erratic personal lives, and may fight with coworkers.

But Mr. Spock and Hans weren't all wrong: It is true that negative emotion can sometimes disrupt reasoning (Gray, 1999). For example, in his second game against the chess-playing computer Deep Blue, the world champion Garry Kasparov became shaken by the unexpectedly strong performance of the computer and resigned when he still could have managed a draw (Chabris, personal communication, 1999). Research has shown that seeing upsetting movies can disrupt subsequent deductive reasoning about material having nothing to do with the movie (Kosslyn & Hugdahl, 1999). Schwartz and Bless (1992) summarize much evidence showing that emotions, both positive and negative, play a key role in many forms of reasoning.

LOOKING AT LEVELS

Reasoning Rhythms

Are you more clear-headed in the morning or the evening? There is good evidence that people differ in this regard, a finding that has obvious implications for timing your major decisions. Bodenhausen (1990) asked people to fill in a questionnaire that assessed whether they were "morning people" or "evening people." Both groups were tested in the morning and in the evening with two stories and asked to make judgments about them. For example, participants were asked whether the woman in one story was more likely to be a feminist, a bank teller, or a feminist bank teller. Logically, the combination should always be less likely than either feature alone, but if someone is described as a prototype of the category of "feminist bank teller," people will say that the combined categories are more likely than either alone (Tversky & Kahneman,

1974). The morning people made fewer errors when tested in the morning than in the evening, and vice versa for evening people.

Mental effort is required to avoid making such errors in reasoning, and people don't expend this energy when their circadian rhythms (which produce fluctuations in blood pressure, pulse rate, body temperature, blood sugar level, and metabolism) are at a low point. Bodenhausen's findings show that to understand a person's reasoning ability, we need to know about events in the brain, such as individual circadian rhythm fluctuations. In addition, we expect events at the group and brain levels to be modulated by events at the level of the person. For example, perhaps if someone believed that it was really crucial to reason properly in a given situation (for instance, to support a good friend), the strength of the motivation could overcome the effects of being at a low point in the daily cycle. To our knowledge, this possibility has yet to be investigated. The levels perspective not only allows us to see how events at the different levels interact, but also directs our attention to novel questions—which clearly can be answered by new studies.

CONSOLIDATE!

▶ **1. Do people reason logically?** In deductive reasoning, logic involves following rules to determine what specific conclusions must follow from a set of general premises. People often make errors in this kind of reasoning, for example, by affirming the consequent and by having a confirmation bias. Inductive reasoning goes in the other direction, from particulars to a generalization. Inductive reasoning is also prone to errors because it is not always obvious what general principle is suggested by a set of examples.

▶ **2. Why do we commit reasoning errors?** We often use heuristics in reasoning, which can lead to specific types of errors. The representativeness heuristic, for example, can lead us to ignore the base-rate rule. The availability heuristic can lead to the planning fallacy, which arises because different aspects of an event are more or less easy to recall. The courses you take in college can help you learn to reason more effectively in general.

▶ **3. Can emotion aid reasoning?** Yes. Emotion plays a key role in the intuitions that underlie hunches. Such emotions can nudge your decisions in the right direction. However, strong negative emotion can cloud reasoning.

A DEEPER LEVEL
Recap and Thought Questions

▶ Language: More Than Meets the Ear

Language relies on phonology (proper speech sounds), syntax (sentences that are formed according to the rules of grammar), semantics (words, phrases, and sentences that convey meaning), and pragmatics (indirect or implied meaning). Animals that are taught to use sign language (which is a true language) may not grasp key aspects of grammar. However, some animals have exhibited remarkable abilities to form novel utterances, which reveal the use of simple grammar. But such abilities do not have the expressive power of human language, and—unlike humans—no nonhuman animal has ever spontaneously invented language. Although it is unlikely that a single gene is involved in the uniquely human ability to use language, it seems likely that our genes do, directly or indirectly, bless us with this capacity.

Could Hans really use language? Hans has perfect phonology, syntax, and semantics, but his pragmatics are faulty. He is unamused by humor and befuddled by novel metaphors. He would probably understand metaphors better as he memorized more of them, but might always be humor-challenged. The fact that Hans hasn't mastered pragmatics perfectly does not mean that he fails to have language—he has the ability to use all four of the key characteristics, just not perfectly. Similarly, someone who speaks a language with an accent still speaks it, just not perfectly.

Think It Through. If it had been your job to teach Hans English, where would you have started? Is one aspect of language—phonology, syntax, semantics, or pragmatics—more important than the others? Which of them, if partially lacking, would be least missed?

Hans apparently has difficulty using the pragmatic aspects of language. How would this affect him socially? Do you think Hans's difficulties with pragmatics have anything to do with his inability to make inferences from nonverbal cues? What is the relation between pragmatics and such cues?

▶ Means of Thought: Words, Images, Concepts

Thought cannot rely solely on words or images: For one thing, both types of representations are ambiguous, and thoughts are not. Moreover, if thought were based only on words, we would never have difficulty figuring out how to put our thoughts into words; and if thought were based only on images, we would have trouble thinking about abstractions (such as truth and justice). Thoughts arise from manipulations of concepts, which specify groupings of objects or events (including relations among objects or events); these representations are unambiguous and can be concrete (such as the concept of a bird) or abstract (such as the concept of justice). Concepts have an internal structure, with some examples being "better" (more typical) than others. In addition, concepts are organized, according to how specific or general they are and according to how they are grouped to apply to a particular situation (via a schema). We use words and images in thinking as a way of keeping track of thoughts and storing them effectively, akin to making notations on a pad of paper while devising a plan.

Could Hans have been built to use only language when thinking? Even if a language could be designed that directly expressed Hans's concepts, that language would not be one spoken by human beings. If Hans is to work effectively with Frank and other humans, he needs to speak English or another natural language—and such languages cannot be the sole vehicle of thought.

Think It Through. Is it better to use words or images when thinking? in general or for certain purposes? If only for certain purposes, which kinds of thinking would best be accomplished with words? with images?

Some forms of representation play critical roles in pragmatics. Consider this joke: A man showed up for work one day with a huge bandage over each ear. A coworker asked him what happened. He replied, "I was ironing and was lost in thought. The phone rang, and without thinking I lifted my hand to answer it." The coworker was aghast, but then asked, "But what about the other ear?" "Oh," he replied, "then I had to call the doctor." This is a visual joke, and people who

do not form images well don't seem to get it. Can you think of other such jokes? If Hans did in fact lack the ability to use mental imagery, such jokes would be lost on him. What other sorts of things would you avoid asking him? How would such a limitation affect his social life?

▶ Problem Solving

If the problem is not specified appropriately from the outset, it will be difficult to solve. People can solve problems by using heuristics (rules of thumb) and algorithms (sets of steps that are guaranteed to produce the answer). Humans can use both algorithms and heuristics with mental simulations and analogies. Both images and words can play important roles in helping you keep track of where you are in a problem and in providing insights into how to proceed. Sometimes it pays to put a problem aside and let it incubate, but the emergence of insight depends on first having thought hard about the problem. Experts develop skills in a particular area, which do not generalize beyond that area. Deliberate practice is essential as the would-be expert learns the relevant information and strategies. Artificial intelligence (AI) is based on the idea that human abilities can be duplicated in a machine. Present-day efforts are impressive, but still a far cry from human abilities. Finally, knowing about the pitfalls of problem solving can help you to overcome them.

How would Hans be affected if he could not use heuristics? Not only would he sometimes require a long time to solve problems, he would be unable to solve a problem at all if he didn't have an appropriate algorithm. Unlike humans, Hans would be stumped unless the problem were stated in a way that invited the use of a specific algorithm; he would be unable to use trial-and-error strategies or other vague approaches that humans use in the hope of hitting on a solution.

Think It Through. What is the most important unsolved problem you can think of (for example, poverty, crime, AIDS, the greenhouse effect)? Which approach to problem solving is most likely to be useful? In what ways might different methods of problem solving be combined to approach such a megaproblem?

▶ Logic, Reasoning, and Decision Making

Reasoning involves seeing what follows from a given set of circumstances and making decisions at pivotal points. Decisions require you to evaluate possible outcomes and choose one over the others. We often rely on heuristics, such as availability, when reaching decisions. These shortcuts often lead us to draw the correct conclusion faster than we could with a step-by-step algorithm; however, they also sometimes lead to errors. Although many people may consider emotion a weakness when reasoning, in fact emotion often helps us to develop hunches and good intuitions.

In what ways is Frank's reasoning superior to Hans's? Hans is literally a logic machine, but Frank's heuristic shortcuts often lead him to draw the correct conclusion faster than Hans, in spite of Hans's superfast circuits. Indeed, Frank's use of heuristics is often aided by emotion, which not only helps him select which heuristic to use in a given situation, but also guides him in using heuristics effectively.

Think It Through. Who do you think would be more likely to win at gambling, Frank or Hans? Would your answer depend on what sort of game they were playing? Do you think our universal human weakness in using logic adversely affects world politics? Why or why not?

8 TYPES OF INTELLIGENCE

What Does It Mean to Be Smart?

Janet never seemed able to do anything right. When she was little, her mother constantly yelled at her and called her "stupid" whenever she made a mistake. In time Janet realized that her mother was unreasonable, but she still couldn't shake the idea that she was dumb. It didn't help that she did poorly in school, that she dressed more shabbily and talked more slowly than her classmates. In fourth grade, a classmate had called her "Retard"; now, 4 years later, she still feared that someone might resurrect that dreaded label. Janet sometimes wondered whether something had gone wrong when she was born. She knew her mother wasn't stupid. Janet had seen her bargain at the flea market and had heard her analyze political speeches they had watched on television. And although she didn't remember her father, she knew he hadn't been stupid either. Although her mother resented his leaving their family a few days after Janet was born, she still paid grudging respect to his business skill.

Janet tried to talk to her mother about her feelings, but her mother just brushed her aside every time, sending her to do her chores or homework. Fortunately, Janet had a hobby: She kept a diary and wrote poetry—good poetry. One of her teachers had called her gifted and creative, and even said that her poems were good enough to be published.

Anyone who didn't know Janet well might conclude that she wasn't very intelligent. After all, her grades never climbed above Cs and Ds, and she often seemed slow and confused. But what does it mean to say that someone is "not very intelligent"? *Intelligence* is certainly not a concrete entity that can be quantified, like the amount of water in a jug; rather, it is a concept. Psychologists have offered many definitions of intelligence, and there is considerable disagreement about what intelligence is and whether it can be accurately measured (Gardner et al., 1996; Sternberg, 1986b, 1990; Sternberg & Detterman, 1986). What most researchers mean by **intelligence** is pretty close to the standard dictionary definition: the ability to solve problems well and to understand and learn complex material. In this chapter we discuss the nature of intelligence, intelligence testing, kinds of intelligence, how nature and nurture affect intelligence, mental retardation, giftedness, and, lastly, creativity—which may be the highest form of intelligence.

Is There More Than One Way to Be Smart?

Despite all her problems in school, Janet was interested in most of her classes. One day she mustered up enough courage to stay after class and talk with her English teacher about a book they were reading. How, she asked, could the author have written such a lighthearted story when he was so poor? The teacher stared at her. Thinking she had said something stupid again, Janet turned to leave. The teacher leapt up and insisted that she stay. The two ended up talking for over an hour. Janet couldn't help noticing the dawning respect on her teacher's face and left feeling elated. Janet wondered whether she might not be so stupid after all; perhaps she should ask to have an IQ test to find out once and for all if she was smart.

▶ 1. What is IQ?

▶ 2. Is intelligence a single characteristic, or a complex set of characteristics?

What Is IQ?

If Janet finds out that she has a "low IQ," should she decide not to apply to college? We think this would be a bad idea. To see why, let's look at exactly what "IQ" is.

What Is an IQ Test? IQ is short for **intelligence quotient**, a test score used in Western countries as a general measure of intelligence. To understand the IQ test, and the meaning of IQ scores, it will be helpful to see how this test has evolved over time. The original test from which modern IQ tests derive had a more specific and different purpose than the modern test. Responding to a call from the French government, which had recently enacted universal elementary education, a French physician named Alfred Binet (1857–1911) and his collaborator, Theodore Simon (1873–1961), devised the first intelligence test between 1904 and 1911 (Matarazzo, 1972). Their aim was to develop an objective way to identify children in the public schools who needed extra classroom help. They started with the idea that intelligence shows itself in a wide variety of things people do, a perspective that led them to construct a test consisting of many sorts of tasks. Among other things, children were asked to copy a drawing, repeat a string of digits, recognize coins and make change, and explain why a particular statement did not make sense. Binet and Simon assumed that the children's performance on the tests reflected educational experience, and thus that special classes could help those who did poorly.

Intelligence: The ability to solve problems well and to understand and learn complex material.

Intelligence quotient (IQ): A score on an intelligence test, originally based on comparing mental age to chronological age but later based on norms.

Wechsler Adult Intelligence Scale (WAIS): The most widely used intelligence test; consists of both verbal and performance subtests.

To assess performance, Binet and Simon first gave the test to a group of normal children of various ages. They noted which problems were solved by most of the 6-year-olds, most of the 10-year-olds, and so forth; then they compared the performance of other children of the same age with those "normal" scores. So if a child could solve all the problems solved by most 9-year-olds, but failed those passed by most 10-year-olds, the child's *mental age (MA)* was said to be 9. Children with a mental age lower than their *chronological age (CA)* were considered relatively slow.

Binet and Simon's test was quickly adopted and adapted to suit new purposes. In 1916 Lewis Terman and his colleagues at Stanford University developed the Stanford-Binet Revision of the Binet-Simon test, which is still used to test people ages 2 to adult. David Wechsler (1958) developed another set of intelligence tests, the **Wechsler Adult Intelligence Scale (WAIS)** and the *Wechsler Intelligence Scale for Children (WISC)*. Today, the WAIS-III and the WISC-III ("III" denoting the third major version) are the most widely used IQ tests in the United States.

Believing that Binet's test relied too much on verbal skills, Wechsler divided his test into two major parts, summarized in Table 8.1. The *verbal subtests* assess the test-taker's ability to understand and use language by assessing vocabulary, comprehension, and other aspects of verbal ability. The *performance subtests* consist of nonverbal tasks such as arranging pictures in an order that tells a story and spotting the missing element in a picture. Because the performance subtests do not focus on the ability to use and manipulate

The WISC-III is administered to children individually by a trained examiner.

TABLE 8.1

WAIS-III Subtests With "Simulated" Examples of Questions

Actual test items cannot be published; part of this table was adapted from Gardner et al., 1996, pp. 80–81. This version is intended for people aged 16 to 89. Three additional tests are included as "spares," to be used if there are problems in administering the basic set summarized here.

I. VERBAL SUBTESTS

- *Vocabulary:* Written and spoken words, which must be defined; the words are ordered in terms of increasing difficulty. *Example:* "What does 'trek' mean?"

- *Similarities:* Questions that require explaining how the concepts named by two words are similar. *Example:* "How are an airplane and a car alike?"

- *Arithmetic:* Problems, all but one presented orally (one involves using blocks); the test is timed. *Example:* "If two men need four days to paint a house, how long would four men need?"

- *Digit Span:* Lists of digits, 2–9 numbers long, are presented. The test-taker repeats the digits, either in the same or reverse order. *Example:* "6, 1, 7, 5, 3."

- *Information:* Questions that draw on literature, history, general science, and common knowledge. *Example:* "Who was Martin Luther King, Jr.?"

- *Comprehension:* Questions that require understanding of social mores and conventions. *Example:* "Why are there taxes?"

II. PERFORMANCE SUBTESTS

- *Picture Completion:* Drawings of common objects or scenes, each of which is missing a feature. The test-taker must point out what's missing. *Example:* A beach umbrella that isn't casting a shadow, even though the sun is high in a cloudless sky.

- *Digit Symbol-Coding:* The test-taker learns a symbol for each of the numbers 1–9 and then sees numbers and must write their appropriate symbols; the test is timed. *Example:* The digit 1 is paired with +, 2 with X, and so forth.

- *Block Design:* Problems that require the test-taker to arrange blocks colored on each side—white, red, or half white and half red—to reproduce a white-and-red pattern in a fixed amount of time. *Example:* A white arrow on a red background.

- *Matrix Reasoning:* Items that require the test-taker to study a progression of stimuli in a sequence from which a section is missing. The test-taker must choose which of five given possibilities completes the sequence.

- *Picture Arrangement:* Sets of cards that must be arranged to tell a story. *Example:* Pictures of a bird sitting on the ground, a bird taking off from the ground, a cat sitting licking its lips.

words, they probably rely less heavily than do the verbal subtests on the test-taker's education or cultural experiences.

SCORING IQ TESTS: MEASURING THE MIND. Modern IQ tests have been modified from earlier versions both in the nature of the tasks and in the way they are scored. Binet and Simon were satisfied with simply knowing whether a child was below or at par for his or her age, but later researchers wanted a more precise measure of the degree of intelligence. Early in the 20th century, William Stern, a German psychologist, developed the idea of an *intelligence quotient,* computed by dividing mental age (MA) by chronological age (CA) and multiplying by 100 to avoid fractional scores. Thus, a score of 100 meant that a child's mental age exactly matched the child's actual age. Computing IQ scores using the MA/CA ratio presents a major disadvantage, however: Because mental age does not keep developing forever, whereas chronological age marches on, older test-takers cannot help but appear to become less intelligent with age. For example, if your mental age is 25 and you are 25 years old, you would be average; but if your mental age is the same in 5 years, your IQ would drop from 100 to 83, even though you are just as smart at 30 as you were at 25. And at 40, your IQ would be about 62. But people do not automatically become stupider with age. Therefore, today's IQ tests are scored not by the MA/CA ratio but by specifying how a test-taker stands relative to the performance of other people of the same age. A score of 100 is set as the average score.

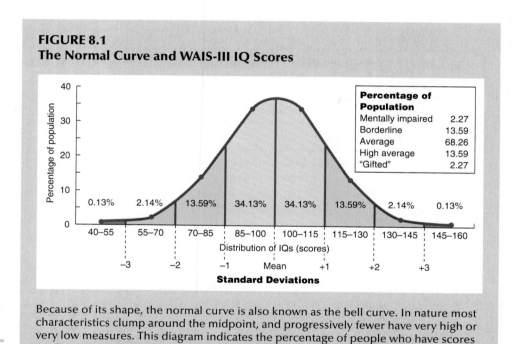

FIGURE 8.1
The Normal Curve and WAIS-III IQ Scores

Percentage of Population	
Mentally impaired	2.27
Borderline	13.59
Average	68.26
High average	13.59
"Gifted"	2.27

Because of its shape, the normal curve is also known as the bell curve. In nature most characteristics clump around the midpoint, and progressively fewer have very high or very low measures. This diagram indicates the percentage of people who have scores on the WAIS-III IQ test that fall within different regions of the distribution.

Standardized sample: A random selection of people, drawn from a carefully defined population.

Population: A group of people who share certain characteristics, such as age, sex, or other relevant variables.

Normal curve: A particular distribution of scores, in which most fall in the middle, and symmetrically fewer toward the extremes; also known as a *bell curve.*

Although the average IQ score is set as 100, most people do not achieve this precise score. How can we interpret the meaning of scores above or below this benchmark? IQ test scores are based on a large **standardized sample,** a random selection of people from the appropriate population. In this sense, a **population** is defined as a group of people who share certain characteristics such as age, sex, or any other relevant variables. Almost always, scores are spread along a **normal curve,** illustrated in Figure 8.1. When the distribution of scores follows a normal curve, most scores fall near the middle, with gradually fewer scores toward either extreme (see Appendix A for a further discussion of normal curves).

After the test has been given to a standardized sample, the developers "norm" the test to make it easy to interpret the meaning of any one test-taker's score relative to the others in the standardized sample. **Norming** a test involves setting two measures: The first is the mean, or average; the mean of an IQ test is set at 100. The second is the **standard deviation,** which indicates the degree to which the individual scores deviate from the mean. The greater the number of standard deviations from the mean, the farther above or below the score is from the mean (see Appendix A for details). If the scores fall into a normal distribution, a certain percentage of them occur at each standard deviation from the mean, as shown in Figure 8.1 (each marked unit on the bottom corresponds to one standard deviation).

For the WAIS-III IQ test, scores are adjusted so that a standard deviation is 15 points. As shown in Figure 8.1, about two thirds of all people have IQs from 85 to 115 points (that is, within one standard deviation above or below the mean), but only a bit more than a quarter have IQs between 70 and 85 or between 115 and 130 (within the second standard deviation above or below the mean). Only 4.54% are above or below those scores.

For IQ scores to be meaningful or useful, the test must be *reliable*. A reliable test produces consistent results; that is, if you test the same group of people on two occasions, the two scores will be highly positively correlated. The WAIS-III has been shown to be highly reliable. In addition, a useful test must be *valid*. A valid test measures what it is supposed to measure. Do IQ tests really measure intelligence; do they measure the ability to solve problems well and to understand and learn complex material? One way to find out whether IQ tests in fact measure intelligence is to see whether scores on these tests are related to measures of performance in other tasks that seem to require intelligence, an investigation we will pursue in the next section.

The issue of validity has become more complex recently with the realization that more than one type of intelligence may exist. Many of today's tests, such as the WAIS-III, provide both an overall score and scores for various subtests, such as those that measure arithmetic and vocabulary. Thus "intelligence" is broken down into abilities of different types, and we can ask whether each measure is valid for a particular type of intelligence. This is a crucial idea, to which we will return repeatedly: The single-number "IQ score" can signify very different things depending on the relative scores on the subtests that contribute to it.

IQ AND ACHIEVEMENT: IQ IN THE REAL WORLD. More than likely, IQ scores would have ceased to interest us long ago if they did not somehow relate to performance in the real world. In the United States, people with higher IQ scores, particularly in the verbal component, overall earn higher grade point averages in high school and college (Cronbach, 1990; Jensen, 1980; Snow & Yalow, 1982). IQ also predicts job success to some extent (Cronbach, 1990; Wagner, 1997). People with higher IQs tend to land higher-prestige jobs and make more money; they are also more likely to enjoy stable marriages and stay out of jail (Herrnstein & Murray, 1994).

The IQ scores of college students typically fall between 112 and 120, considerably above the population average of 100 (Gottfredson, 1997). But before you get too giddy over this news, note that not everybody who is successful has a high IQ, nor are all people with high IQs necessarily successful. Correlations between IQ and job performance show that, at most, only about a quarter of the variation in levels of job success can be predicted by IQ (Hunter, 1983; Jensen, 1980; Streufert & Swezey, 1986; Wagner & Sternberg, 1986; see Chapter 1 and Appendix A for discussions of the concept of correlation). This means that the lion's share of the variation reflects motivation, education, and other factors. Culture clearly plays a role. For example, Asian cultures, with their strong family bonds and emphasis on hard work, foster achievement (Stevenson et al., 1986), and IQ actually underpredicts job success among Japanese and Chinese Americans (Flynn, 1991, 1999). Furthermore, the correlations between IQ and achievement decrease for people who have had more experience on the job. As workers become experienced, they develop expertise, which has little to do with IQ (Hunt, 1995).

Norming: The process of setting the mean score and standard deviation of a test, based on results from a standardized sample.

Standard deviation: A measure of the degree to which individual scores deviate from the mean.

Even when IQ and achievement are highly correlated, the relationship may be difficult to interpret: The positive correlation between IQ and success may occur because another variable is separately affecting them both, not because IQ itself leads to success. For example, healthy people, or people who had healthy parents, would be expected both to score higher on IQ tests and to be more successful than people who are not healthy or who had chronically sick parents. Similarly, people who were raised to have high self-esteem might not be flustered in test-taking circumstances or in real-world job situations, and thus would tend to do well in both (indeed, this idea is consistent with findings reported by Steele, 1997). Janet did not score well on her IQ test, which may reflect the high level of anxiety she experienced while taking the test.

IQ tests do produce useful information. Janet's teachers could use the results of her IQ test to identify some of her cognitive strengths and weaknesses. They might use her scores to try to predict how well she could do in college or in certain types of jobs. But like other standardized tests, such as those that assess academic achievement, they are in part measures of how well a person performs in a test-taking situation. Performance under test conditions is influenced by many factors: anxiety, skills (or lack of them) in the mechanics of taking a test, and earlier experiences with tests. IQ is a test score that reflects many variables.

Intelligence: One Ability or Many?

As noted above, in the United States a high IQ score predicts, to some degree, success in school and in life. To interpret these findings, we need to know more about what, precisely, IQ tests measure. Is there some general ability, some basic intelligence, that determines IQ score? And do IQ tests tap everything meant by "intelligence"? There are different ways to solve problems, and so it seems reasonable that there should be different forms of intelligence. There is ample evidence that this is true.

IQ, g, AND SPECIALIZED ABILITIES. How do researchers determine whether IQ scores reflect some basic, overall type of intelligence or a collection of various cognitive abilities such as the ability to solve puzzles or identify patterns? Psychologists who have investigated this question have used correlations and other statistical measures as key tools in their attempts to find an answer. As discussed, IQ tests include a variety of subtests, such as the picture completion, vocabulary, block design, and arithmetic subtests included in the WAIS-III. It turns out that people who do well on one subtest tend to do well on others; that is, scores on different types of tests are positively correlated.

This finding has led researchers to infer that there is a single form of intelligence that cuts across the different subtests. Early in this century, British psychologist Charles Spearman (1927) argued that the positive correlations among scores on different types of mental tests indicate the existence of a single underlying intellectual capacity, which he labeled *g*, for "general factor." But if intelligence is simply *g*, then all of the scores from the different subtests should be correlated to the same degree. This is not the case: Spearman also noted a wide variation in the sizes of the correlations, which he took to reflect the influence of "specific factors," or *s*. When you perform a task, according to Spearman, you are drawing on *g* as well as on a particular type of ability, *s*, specific to that task. For example, spelling draws on a specialized ability, which is largely independent of other abilities. The very first First Lady of the United States, Martha Washington, is a case in point: She was generally very intelligent (that is, she probably had a high *g*) but was such a poor speller, misspelling words such as *cat* with two *t*s, that her husband, George, frequently wrote her letters for her (Seuling, 1978). Some tasks, such as being able to analyze Shakespeare, rely more on *g* than on *s*; others, such as discriminating musical tones, rely more on a particular *s* than on *g*. But in Spearman's view, IQ scores depend mostly

g: "General factor," a single intelligence that underlies the positive correlations among different tests of intelligence.

s: "Specific factors," or aspects of performance that are particular to a given kind of processing—and distinct from *g*.

on *g*; how smart you are overall depends on how much of this general intellectual capacity you have.

A second perspective on what IQ scores reflect comes from Louis L. Thurstone (1938). Thurstone devised a battery of 56 tests and then analyzed the correlations of scores on these tests using a method, worked out by Spearman, called factor analysis. **Factor analysis** is a statistical method that uncovers the particular attributes ("factors") that make scores more or less similar. A factor analysis of the correlations among different measures of performance would show, for example, that speed of processing is one important factor in many tasks, and the amount of information that can be held in short-term memory is another.

When Thurstone analyzed his test results, he found that how well you can do arithmetic has little if anything to do with how well you can notice whether a scene has changed or how well you can figure out the best way to get home when traffic is heavy (Thurstone & Thurstone, 1941). Instead of believing in a single general capacity, such as *g*, Thurstone found evidence that intelligence consists of seven separate **primary mental abilities,** fundamental abilities that are the components of intelligence and that are not outgrowths of other abilities. Verbal comprehension and spatial visualization are two of Thurstone's primary mental abilities; the others are listed in Table 8.2 on page 280. According to this view, Janet's low IQ score might reflect deficiencies in one or two specific abilities dragging down her overall score.

In the decades since Thurstone proposed his list of primary abilities, other researchers seeking to discover the facets of intelligence have analyzed and reanalyzed similar data with varying results. Carroll (1993) infers over 70 separate abilities, and some (such as J. P. Guilford, 1967) have reported finding more than a hundred distinct factors that underlie intelligence. One especially influential alternative, however, was proposed by Raymond B. Cattell (1971), and then developed further by his student and collaborator John Horn (1985, 1986, 1989, 1994; Horn & Cattell, 1966). These researchers suggested that instead of possessing one general capacity, *g*, people possess two types of intelligence: crystallized and fluid. **Crystallized intelligence** relies on knowing facts and having the ability to use and combine them. This is the sort of intelligence that develops as you become an expert in an area. If you make good use of your college experience, you should boost your crystallized intelligence. In contrast, **fluid intelligence** is the more free-form ability to figure out novel solutions, such as how to catch fish without a hook. As we grow older, crystallized intelligence does not suffer much, if at all; we are still able to maintain our expertise in areas of strength. But the ability to shift gears quickly to solve new problems tends to decrease (Horn, 1985, 1986, 1994; Horn & Noll, 1994; Salthouse, 1996). That age affects the two types of intelligence differently is evidence that they are in fact different; if there were only a single form of intelligence, aging should have the same effects on it. After the discovery of crystallized and fluid intelligence, Cattell and Horn provided evidence for a number of other "broad" factors (to use Jensen's term [Jensen, 1998]), as listed in Table 8.2.

Table 8.2 summarizes five prominent views about the makeup of intelligence. Today, psychologists generally agree with Spearman's theory that people have a collection of special mental abilities (*s*), and most agree that something like *g* exists. However, there is considerable disagreement over exactly what *g* is. Researchers have found that the higher people score on IQ tests overall, the more often there are sharp disparities in the scores on different subtests: In other words, the relative strengths and weaknesses of people with high IQs are likely to differ greatly from individual to individual (Deary & Pagliari, 1991; Detterman & Daniel, 1989; Hunt, 1995; Spearman, 1927). For example, some high scorers may be particularly good at vocabulary and digit span; others at digit span, matrix reasoning, and block design; and still others at yet additional combinations of abilities. In contrast, people who score low on IQ tests tend to perform consistently and generally poorly on all of the tasks. As Hunt (1995) observed, "It appears that general intelligence may not be an accurate statement, but general lack of intelligence is!" (p. 362).

Factor analysis: A statistical method that uncovers the particular attributes (factors) that make scores more or less similar; the more similar the scores, the more attributes they should have in common.

Primary mental abilities: According to Thurstone, seven fundamental abilities that are not outgrowths of other abilities.

Crystallized intelligence: According to Cattell and Horn, the kind of intelligence that relies on knowing facts and having the ability to use and combine them.

Fluid intelligence: According to Cattell and Horn, the kind of intelligence that underlies the creation of novel solutions to problems.

TABLE 8.2

The Nature of Intelligence: Seven Views

Spearman (1927)	• *g* (generalized ability) • *s* (specialized abilities) • IQ mostly reflects *g*
Thurstone and Thurstone (1941)	7 primary mental abilities: • Verbal comprehension • Word fluency (how well one can produce words) • Number facility (how well one can do arithmetic) • Associative memory • Perceptual speed (for recognizing stimuli) • Reasoning • Spatial visualization
Carroll (1993)	• *g* plus 8 special abilities similar to those identified by Thurstone • Special abilities broken down into even more specialized aspects of intelligence • More than 70 separate abilities
Guilford (1967)	150 distinct abilities underlie intelligence, each with three facets: • Contents (such as visual, auditory, or semantic) • Products (such as some type of unit or transformation) • Operations (such as memory or evaluation)
Cattell (1971) and Horn (1985, 1986, 1989)	Cattell's original theory: • Crystallized intelligence • Fluid intelligence Later versions added: • Speed of inspecting visualized patterns • Visual-spatial reasoning • Auditory thinking • Quantitative reasoning • Fluency of recall (for example, how quickly one can recall names of common objects) • No *g*
Gardner (1993b, 1999)	• Linguistic • Spatial • Musical • Logical-mathematical • Bodily-kinesthetic • Interpersonal • Naturalistic
Sternberg (1985, 1988b)	• Analytic • Practical • Creative

Theory of multiple intelligences: Gardner's theory of eight distinct types of intelligence, which can vary separately for a given individual.

MULTIPLE INTELLIGENCES: MORE THAN ONE WAY TO SHINE. Howard Gardner (1993b, 1995, 1999) developed a very influential view of intelligence, the **theory of multiple intelligences,** which holds that there are eight basic forms of intelligence:

Linguistic intelligence is the ability to use language well, as relied on by journalists and lawyers.

Spatial intelligence is the ability to reason well about spatial relations, as relied on by architects and surgeons.

1. *Linguistic intelligence.* The ability to use language well, as relied on by journalists and lawyers.
2. *Spatial intelligence.* The ability to reason well about spatial relations, as relied on by architects and surgeons.
3. *Musical intelligence.* The ability to compose and understand music, as relied on by audio engineers and musicians.
4. *Logical-mathematical intelligence.* The ability to manipulate abstract symbols, as used by scientists and computer programmers.
5. *Bodily-kinesthetic intelligence.* The ability to plan and understand sequences of movements, as drawn on by dancers and athletes.
6. *Intrapersonal intelligence.* The ability to understand oneself, as used by clergy.
7. *Interpersonal intelligence.* The ability to understand other people and social interactions, as used by politicians and teachers.
8. *Naturalist intelligence.* The ability to observe carefully, as used by forest rangers. (Gardner, 1995)

Musical intelligence is the ability to compose and understand music, relied on by audio engineers and musicians.

Finally, in more recent formulations of the theory, Gardner (1999) has tentatively suggested a ninth form of intelligence: *existential intelligence,* which is the ability to address "the big questions" about existence. Gardner's classifications are not isolated "special abilities" that allow a person to become skilled at a narrow range of particular tasks. Rather, these are separate *types* of intelligence, which involve a collection of abilities working together. Each type of intelligence allows you to solve a range of problems well and to understand and learn complex material of the appropriate type.

We have shown repeatedly that different parts of the brain perform different functions; the brain is like an orchestra with separate sections playing different parts of the improvisational symphony of thinking, feeling, and behaving. Gardner's theory is unique in that it grew not out of correlations among test scores, but rather from a variety of distinct types of neurological and behavioral observations. Gardner worked for many years at the Boston Veterans Administration Medical Center, where he studied people who had suffered brain damage. He noticed that brain damage often resulted in the loss of a certain ability while leaving others relatively intact. For example, language would be disrupted but patients could still sing, and vice versa; mathematical ability would be disrupted but patients could still speak, and vice versa; social skills would be disrupted while ordinary reasoning was unimpaired, and vice versa. In developing his theory, Gardner also considered other kinds of data. He noted, for example, that although everybody learns language in a few years, very few people master complex mathematics so easily. If two abilities develop at different rates during childhood, he reasoned, they must rely on different underlying processes. In addition, he observed that some abilities, such as music and mathematics, can be extraordinarily well developed in child prodigies, whereas these same children perform at average levels in other areas. This coexistence of the extraordinary and the ordinary, Gardner believes, suggests that some capacities, such as those related to music and mathematics, may be psychologically distinct from other capacities.

According to Gardner, most professions require combinations of different types of intelligence; to be a good novelist, for example, you need linguistic, intrapersonal, and interpersonal intelligence. Each person can be characterized by a *profile of intelligences*, with some types of intelligence being relatively strong and others relatively weak (Walters & Gardner, 1985). Part of being successful in life is matching your particular profile to your career goals. President Richard Nixon is reported to have said, "I never made the [football] team. . . . I was not heavy enough to play the line, not fast enough to play halfback, and not smart enough to be a quarterback" (Collier, 2000). What do you think he meant by "smart" when he lamented his inadequacy?

As appealing as Gardner's theory of multiple intelligences is to many, it has not been embraced by all researchers. One problem is that the theory is difficult to test rigorously because some of the types of intelligence (such as bodily-kinesthetic, intrapersonal, and interpersonal) are difficult to measure reliably. Another problem is more fundamental: Some question whether the word *intelligence* should be applied so liberally; many of the abilities Gardner identifies, they say, have more to do with talents and skills than with intelligence per se.

Robert Sternberg (1985, 1988b) has also developed a theory of multiple intelligences, but he proposes only three types: analytic, practical, and creative. *Analytic intelligence,* the ability to learn to write clearly, do math, and understand literature, is critical for academic performance. *Practical intelligence* involves knowing how to do such things as fix a car or sew on a button, and sometimes relies on implicit memories, the unconscious biases and tendencies that guide our actions (see Chapter 6); "street smarts" are a form of practical intelligence. *Creative intelligence,* which seems closely related to fluid intelligence, is the ability to formulate novel solutions to problems.

How do these three types of intelligence relate to IQ? Analytic intelligence is what IQ tests measure. According to Sternberg and his colleagues (Sternberg & Wagner, 1993; Sternberg et al., 1993), however, measures of practical intelligence are better predictors of how well someone will do on the job than are standard measures of IQ, and practical intelligence is largely distinct from analytic intelligence. One study found that some Brazilians who as children failed math in school nevertheless could do the math required in their business lives (Carraher et al., 1985). Creative intelligence is also distinct from IQ, but people do need a certain level of IQ to be able to find creative solutions to problems or create novel products that have specific uses (Guilford, 1967; Runco & Albert, 1986; Sternberg, 1985).

People unquestionably differ in their relative strengths and weaknesses of various aspects of intelligence. Sternberg and his colleagues (summarized in Sternberg, 1997) found that if you are taught in a way that is compatible with your strongest type of intelligence, you will learn better. Thus, if you tend toward the practical, you would more easily learn how to construct something by observing a hands-on demonstration than by reading a set of directions. This is exciting research, which may eventually allow the detailed characterization of learning styles, permitting the development of teaching methods that play to the strengths of different students.

Children learn more easily if the teaching technique is compatible with their particular cognitive strengths.

EMOTIONAL INTELLIGENCE: KNOWING FEELINGS. In everyday life, whether you act intelligently or not often depends in large part on how well you understand both your own emotions and how your actions will affect others. Have you ever seen someone you *know* is smart do something incredibly dumb—for instance, unintentionally or uncontrollably make a remark that infuriates a spouse or boss? Salovey and Mayer (1990) refer to the ability to understand and regulate emotions effectively as **emotional intelligence (EI).**

Emotional intelligence comprises five key abilities (Goleman, 1995; Mayer & Salovey, 1997, p. 5):

1. *Knowing your emotions*, which involves the ability to recognize emotions as they occur. For example, if you have high EI, you notice when you are becoming angry or depressed; by recognizing emotions as they arise, you are in a position to manage them rather than be managed by them.

2. *Managing your feelings*, which is essential for controlling impulses and bouncing back from failures. For example, when you feel yourself getting angry, you know that you should take a deep breath, count to 10, and bite back the reflexive nasty response on the tip of your tongue. Similarly, if you have high EI, you can put your disappointment at not reaching a goal in perspective and not let that emotion cloud your judgment.

3. *Self-motivation*, which is essential for persistence and self-control. For example, if you have high EI, you are able to decide that you want a good grade in a particular course (perhaps this one?) and be disciplined enough to study hard in spite of the tempting social distractions of college life.

4. *Recognizing others' emotions*, which is crucial for empathy. If you have high EI, you are able to infer how someone else feels, and to respond to them accordingly. People with high EI can easily learn to become good negotiators.

5. *Handling relationships*, which involves knowing how others will react emotionally to you. If you have high EI, you not only can recognize and understand your own emotions and those of others, but you also can anticipate what emotions your actions will trigger in others.

Emotional intelligence would seem to underlie at least part of what Sternberg means by practical intelligence, but it extends beyond that (Fox & Spector, 2000). Emotional intelligence can help you reason analytically by not allowing emotion to distract you or cloud your judgment; it can also inspire creative acts. Emotional intelligence can play a role in each of Gardner's multiple intelligences. Clearly, there is more than one type of intelligence, and IQ tests assess only some of them.

LOOKING AT LEVELS

A Threat in the Air

Taking IQ tests isn't simply a matter of flexing your intellectual muscles. As you no doubt know from experience, test-taking of any kind, whether an achievement test such as the SAT, or an IQ test, can be anxiety provoking. Test stress may manifest itself in distinct physical symptoms, such as a speeded-up heart rate and sweaty palms. And as you feel literally "put to the test," your thinking may become clouded by a variety of distracting thoughts. Thus, factors unrelated to intelligence may affect IQ scores and other test scores.

Researchers Steele and Aronson (1995) conducted a study to investigate the possible effects of negative racial stereotypes on the test-taking performance of African Americans. They asked African American and white college students to take a test that

included the most difficult items from the verbal portion of the Graduate Record Examination (GRE), an SAT-like test for graduate school. Some students, both African Americans and whites, were told that the test assessed intellectual ability; another mixed group was told that it was a study conducted by the laboratory. African Americans and whites did equally well when they were told that the test was simply a laboratory experiment, but African American students did much worse than whites when they thought the test measured intelligence. In another study, Steele and Aronson (1995) asked half the participants of each race to list their race immediately before taking the test. The test was always described as a laboratory study, not a test of intelligence. African Americans and whites performed the same when they did not list their races, but the simple act of being asked to list race drastically reduced the African American students' scores (such effects have since been reported by others, such as Croizet & Claire, 1998).

These studies dramatically illustrate the interactions of events at the levels of the brain, the person, and the group. According to Steele (1997), asking African Americans about race activates information in long-term memory about negative stereotypes, such as that African Americans are not smart. If you believe that a negative stereotype addresses issues that are important to you, then the mere possibility that others will see you as conforming to the image is threatening, even if you do not believe that you have the properties of the stereotype. Steele terms this phenomenon *stereotype threat*. When you are threatened, the autonomic nervous system is aroused (see Chapter 2) and leads you to become highly focused. In this case, the African American students may have focused on the threat presented by the stereotype. If so, then they would not focus as well on the task at hand. Kosslyn and Hugdahl (1999) have shown that reasoning is disrupted when a person has just witnessed an upsetting event, and a similar mechanism may be at work here.

Thus, a social invention—stereotypes about groups—can become part of an individual's knowledge (level of the person). And that knowledge in turn can be activated by social situations. When activated, the knowledge produces events in the brain (as well as in the body—pounding heart, sweaty palms, and so on; see Chapter 12 for a discussion of the stress response), which in turn disrupt performance. And the disrupted performance can then reinforce the stereotypes.

CONSOLIDATE!

▶ **1. What is IQ?**   IQ (intelligence quotient) is a score on an intelligence test. IQ originally was a comparison of mental age to chronological age, but now IQ scores relate performance to a norm. The most common tests, the Wechsler Adult Intelligence Scale (WAIS) and the Wechsler Intelligence Scale for Children (WISC), consist of two main parts, one that assesses verbal performance and one that assesses nonverbal performance. The scores are normed so that 100 is the mean, and each standard deviation is 15 points. Scores on IQ tests predict, to some extent, many aspects of performance, ranging from grades in school to success on the job.

▶ **2. Is intelligence a single characteristic, or a complex set of characteristics?**   Intelligence has many facets. Although intelligence probably involves, as Charles Spearman theorized, a single general intellectual ability (symbolized as *g*), virtually all theorists agree that it also includes many specialized abilities. These abilities may be strong or weak, independently of *g*. Thurstone, for example, proposed that intelligence consists of seven primary mental abilities. Cattell and Horn initially theorized that instead of one general capacity, *g*, people possess two types of intelligence—crystallized and fluid—and then later expanded this list to include abilities like those identified by Thurstone. Gardner, in his theory of multiple intelligences, suggests eight basic forms of intelligence ranging from linguistic, to logical, to interpersonal. According to Sternberg, the different types of intelligence boil down to three: analytic, practical, and creative. Finally, emotional intelligence may affect the operation of all other types.

WHAT MAKES US SMART? NATURE AND NURTURE

Janet was brought up by her mother alone in a home with few financial resources. Janet's mother was harsh and sometimes even abusive toward her, and the girl had few companions her own age. Her schoolbooks were the only books in her house, and, in any event, Janet rarely bothered to read because it took her so long to finish anything. She often wondered whether this slowness was caused by something wrong with her brain. Janet spent a great deal of time watching television, but she was not a passive viewer. Often she tried to guess what would come next in the story, and sometimes she thought about other ways the plots could have unfolded.

How might the circumstances of Janet's life have molded her intellectual strengths and weaknesses? It's difficult to know, in part because the vast bulk of research on intellectual development has focused on IQ alone. However, psychologists have learned a great deal about the forces that shape those aspects of intelligence that are indexed by IQ scores.

▶ 1. What aspects of brain function underlie intelligence?

▶ 2. How do environment and genetics contribute to intelligence?

▶ 3. How can we interpret group differences in IQ?

▶ 4. Can "exercising the mind" raise IQ?

The Machinery of Intelligence

Intelligence is the ability to solve problems well and to understand and learn complex material. Thus, it seems reasonable to expect that smart people would be good at the information processing required to solve problems, such as retrieving information from long-term memory or using information in short-term memory. Many theorists have examined the information processing that underlies intelligence (Anderson, 1992; Ceci, 1990; Sternberg, 1985, 1988b). But pinpointing just how the intellectual "machinery" of smart people differs from that of others has not been easy. Are some people smarter than others because they have bigger, faster, or more efficient brains?

BRAIN SIZE AND INTELLIGENCE: IS BIGGER ALWAYS BETTER? Many studies have shown that the larger a person's brain, the greater his or her intelligence as measured by IQ tests (Neisser et al., 1996; Rushton & Ankney, 1996). Larger brains do tend to contain more neurons (Haug, 1987, as cited in Rushton & Ankney, 1996). But it isn't clear whether larger brain size causes greater intelligence or whether acting intelligently causes larger brain size. As discussed earlier, interacting with the environment can change your brain, even causing it to grow. For example, as discussed in Chapter 2, rats raised in stimulating environments developed larger brains.

In addition, the key variable may not be overall brain size, but the size of crucial areas. For instance, the part of the brain that controls the left hand is larger in professional musicians who play string instruments than in other musicians, or in other people in general (Elber et al., 1995). Consider also the brain of Albert Einstein, whose name has become nearly synonymous with genius. Shortly after Einstein died, his brain was removed and preserved. When it was initially examined, researchers found that his brain had an usually large number of glial cells (which help to support neurons; Chapter 2), particularly in the bottom portions of the left parietal lobe (Gardner et al., 1996); this part of the brain is involved in mathematical thinking (Dehaene, 1997) and spatial visualization (Kosslyn, 1994b). These cells may have helped that part of his brain function more efficiently than normal. A more recent analysis of Einstein's brain showed that he actually had more neurons in this key area in both hemispheres (Witelson et al., 1999). Indeed, Einstein's parietal lobes were about 15% wider than normal. In addition, the Sylvian fissure, the major horizontal crease in the brain (above the temporal lobe) was largely missing, perhaps because extra neurons were squeezed in. However, other areas of Einstein's brain were relatively small, making the overall size of his brain only average.

From such research findings, can we conclude that the larger your brain, or the larger certain key parts, the smarter you are? No, the relation between brain size and intelligence is not so simple. First, females have about the same average intelligence as males, but generally have smaller brains (Ankney, 1992; Rushton & Ankney, 1996). Second, the Neanderthals had larger brains than we do, but there is no evidence that they were smarter. Third, the correlation between brain size and IQ is typically small and does not apply to particular individuals. Fourth, correlation does not imply causation—as usual, some third variable (perhaps related to maternal nutrition or stress) might separately affect brain size and intelligence. At present, the meaning of correlations between brain size and intelligence is not clear. Moreover, skull size and brain size are weakly correlated, so resist the temptation to measure your friends' heads before forming a study group!

SPEED: OF THE ESSENCE?

Janet is generally slow; is she therefore stupid? President John F. Kennedy could read 2,000 words per minute, understanding almost all of it (Seuling, 1978); does this mean he was smart? The answers depend in part on what you mean by "stupid" and "smart." Intelligence is a complicated beast, and most research on it has focused only on what is measured by IQ. IQ does correlate with the time taken to respond to a stimulus such as a light in a laboratory experiment—the higher the IQ, the faster the response (Jensen, 1980, 1987, 1991). At first glance, this correlation does not seem surprising: Many of the subtests in the WAIS-III are timed, and thus faster test-takers will tend to complete more of the questions and therefore have a chance at higher scores. However, people with higher IQs also require less exposure time to a stimulus in order to judge accurately which of two lines is longer (Anderson, 1992; Bates & Eysenck, 1993; Kranzler & Jensen, 1989; Nettelbeck, 1987). From such evidence, many researchers conclude that IQ reflects, at least in part, the speed of mental processes (Anderson, 1992; Ceci, 1990; Deary, 1995). Indeed, there may be a relation between the size of the brain areas used in a task and how quickly it can be performed: If more neurons are working on a task, the task may be processed more quickly than if fewer neurons are available.

Close examination, however, shows that just as the relationship between brain size and intelligence is complicated, so is the relation between speed and intelligence. Sternberg has devised ingenious ways to measure the speed of specific aspects of information processing. He finds that people who score high on IQ tests are faster only at certain steps in processing information. For example, people with higher IQs tend to spend *more* time digesting a problem and figuring out what kind of reasoning will be needed; as a result, they can then produce responses more quickly. So it's not that people with high IQs are necessary faster; rather, they process information more effectively. In some cultures the importance of deliberation is recognized and considered to be a sign of intelligence (Gardner et al., 1996). Speed alone cannot determine intelligence.

WORKING MEMORY: JUGGLING MORE BALLS.

Some researchers have reported that the correlation between IQ and speed is best for tasks that are neither too easy nor too difficult (Jensen, 1993; Lindley et al., 1995). The highest correlation between IQ and speed is found when the task exercises working memory as much as possible without exceeding its capacity. This correlation reflects, in part, how efficiently working memory operates (for a further discussion, see Chapter 6). If Janet's mother quickly read her a list of 5 things to buy at the market, Janet could use working memory to organize the list so that she could remember it. But if her mother quickly read a list of 20 unrelated items, the task would tax working memory beyond the capacity of most people. IQ may index, at least in part, how well the central executive of working memory can manage information when the going gets tough, but not so tough as to be impossible (Carpenter et al., 1990; Lehrl & Fischer, 1990).

Studies of the brain have also supported the relationship between working memory and intelligence. Prabhakaran and colleagues (1997) used functional magnetic resonance imaging (fMRI) to study which brain areas are activated while participants perform a test called the **Raven's Progressive Matrices** (Figure 8.2). This test requires you to discover how a series of patterns is progressively changing, and then to select from a set of possible choices which comes next in the sequence (Raven, 1965, 1976). The rule governing the change in the patterns can be very subtle and difficult to discern. Scores on the Raven's Progressive Matrices index fluid intelligence and *g*. Prabhakaran and colleagues found that items requiring visual-spatial reasoning activated parts of the frontal lobes used in holding information about objects and spatial relations in working memory (see Chapter 6), and items requiring analytical reasoning (that is, items that require finding an abstract rule) activated these structures *and* parts of the frontal lobes used in verbal working memory.

Studies of the brain also show that not all aspects of intelligence are related to the functioning of the frontal lobes. Remember, it was Einstein's parietal lobes that were remarkable, not his frontal lobes. Prabhakaran and colleagues (1997) found activation in the parietal lobes in both types of reasoning, visual-spatial and analytical; in fact, items requiring visual-spatial reasoning evoked more activation in the back parts of the brain (where the parietal lobes are) than in the front parts. All the problems used by Prabhakaran and colleagues (1997) tapped fluid intelligence; Prabhakaran and colleagues point out that other areas of the brain, those involved specifically in the storage of memories (in the temporal lobes), are activated when we draw on crystallized intelligence. This finding allows us to understand why damage to the frontal lobes does not always disrupt IQ (Hebb & Penfield, 1940). Patients with frontal lobe damage are typically older adults, with many years of living behind them; this experience builds crystallized intelligence, which does not rely on working memory. Many of the tasks in standard IQ tests can be performed by relying on long-term memory or well-learned strategies that do not depend on working memory. Damage to the frontal lobes does, however, disrupt fluid intelligence (Duncan, 1995; Duncan et al., 1995, 1996).

In response to research on the nature of intelligence, the WAIS-III, which was released in 1997, can be scored to assess four general aspects of intellectual ability: verbal comprehension, perceptual organization, working memory, and processing speed.

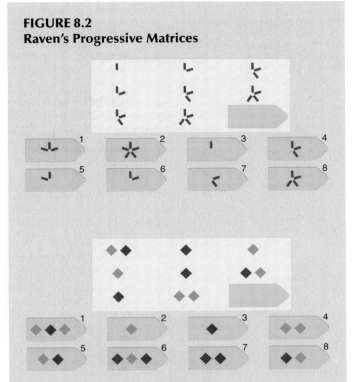

FIGURE 8.2
Raven's Progressive Matrices

Two examples from Raven's Progressive Matrices test, which is often taken to measure fluid intelligence and *g*. Which of the numbered selections fits in the empty shape in each rectangle? The top example relies on visual-spatial ability, the bottom on analytic ability.

Smart Genes, Smart Environment: A Single System

Intelligence is related to the way the brain functions; to what extent are differences in such functioning linked to genes? Could Janet be bright in some ways and less bright in others, because of the genetic deck of cards she was dealt by her parents?

To understand the genetic contributions to intelligence, we first need to examine a bit more about genes themselves. In 1866 Gregor Mendel, an Augustinian monk living in what is now the Czech Republic, wrote one of the fundamental papers in all science. In it he formulated the core ideas of what is now known as **Mendelian inheritance,** the

Raven's Progressive Matrices: A nonverbal test that assesses fluid intelligence and *g*.

Mendelian inheritance: The transmission of characteristics by individual dominant and recessive elements acting separately.

transmission of characteristics by individual elements of inheritance, each acting separately. Two ideas are key: (1) for each trait, an offspring inherits an "element" from each parent; and (2) in some cases, one of the elements dominates the other, and that is the one whose effect is apparent. If an element is not *dominant,* it is *recessive:* The effect of a recessive element is evident only when the offspring receives two copies of it, one from each parent. Mendel, through careful experimentation and record-keeping, traced these patterns of inheritance for a number of organisms (such as pea plants), but he never knew their mechanism. That great biochemical discovery, that the mysterious "elements" are genes, was not made until the early part of the 20th century.

In his pea plants, Mendel studied *traits,* such as skin texture and color; each trait, he observed, could appear in different "flavors," such as smooth or wrinkled, yellow or green. Thus a gene for a trait can have different forms, called *alleles,* one for each flavor. To inherit attached ear lobes or flat feet, for example, you need to receive the appropriate recessive allele from each of your parents. The sum total of your particular set of genes is your *genotype.*

Many genes express their effects only in combination with other genes. When this occurs, we see *quantitative* variations in characteristics, such as differences in height, size, or intelligence, not *qualitative* variations such as attached versus unattached ear lobes. In general, when a characteristic varies continuously, it reflects **complex inheritance,** the joint action of combinations of genes working together, rather than Mendelian inheritance, which describes the effects of individual elements of inheritance (Plomin & DeFries, 1998).

The genetic basis of intelligence is so complex that researchers initially had trouble identifying genes that are related to general intelligence as measured by IQ (Ball et al., 1998; Hill et al., 1999; Petrill et al., 1997a, 1997b; Skuder et al., 1995), and it took years to locate genes involved with intelligence (Chorney et al., 1998; Fisher et al., 1999; Miller, 1997). However, because intelligence is not unitary, we would not expect it to be determined by a single gene, or even a small number of genes. Studies have shown that multiple genes contribute to intelligence (for instance, Fisher et al., 1999), and it is now possible to use genetic data to help identify the different types of intelligence. For example, a portion of DNA has been found to be associated with one type of spatial ability (Berman & Noble, 1995) and not with general cognitive ability (Petrill et al., 1997b).

HOW IMPORTANT ARE GENES FOR INTELLIGENCE? Since genes contribute to intelligence in complex ways, how can we begin to sort out the relative contributions to intelligence of the genetic component and of other factors? How strong is the genetic influence?

The most common method of assessing the contribution of genes to a characteristic is to observe correlations among relatives who share different proportions of their genes versus unrelated people (see Chapter 2). Virtually all the research on the genetics of intelligence has focused on IQ scores, and this research is worth considering; however, we must always keep in mind the limited implications of such scores.

One way that researchers have tried to sort out the effects of genes versus environment is through *adoption studies.* In these studies the scores of adopted children are compared to those of their adopted versus biological relatives. In some of these studies, tests are given to twins who were separated soon after birth and adopted into different families (for example, Bouchard et al., 1990). Because these twins were reared in different homes, any similarities between them are thought to reflect their common genetics. What do adoption studies find? The correlations of IQs of adult identical twins who were raised apart is higher than that both for fraternal twins and for nontwin siblings raised together (Bouchard & McGue, 1981; Bouchard et al., 1990; Plomin, 1990). In addition, an adopted child's IQ correlates higher with the biological mother's IQ than with the adopted mother's IQ. Moreover, although the IQs of an adopted child and the biological children in a family are positively correlated, by the time the children grow up, virtually no correlation remains (Plomin, 1990; Scarr & Weinberg, 1983). These findings provide clear evidence that genes affect IQ.

Complex inheritance: The transmission of characteristics that depends on joint actions of genes working together; in general, when a characteristic varies continuously, it reflects complex inheritance.

Other studies have tried to find out exactly how large a role genes play in determining IQ by comparing IQs of people with different numbers of genes in common. The results clearly show that the more genes in common, the higher the correlations (Figure 8.3). The usual estimate is that the heritability of IQ is around .50, which means that about half the variation in IQ can be attributed to inherited characteristics (Chipuer et al., 1990; Loehlin, 1989). (Heritability scores indicate what proportion of observed variability in a characteristic is caused by inherited factors [Bell, 1977; Lush, 1937]; see Chapter 2 for a further discussion of heritability.) Keep in mind that heritability estimates have no bearing on how much of *your* personal intelligence is the result of your genes versus environmental factors. The number that denotes heritability refers to the proportion of causes of variation within a population, not to the proportion of the characteristic that is inherited; and because it is an average, it does not apply to individuals.

EFFECTS OF THE ENVIRONMENT: MORE REAL THAN APPARENT? Take another look at Figure 8.3, and compare the correlations between fraternal twins and those between other siblings. These pairs have the identical amount of common genes, 50%, and thus their IQ scores should be the same if intelligence is wholly determined by genes. But as you can see in the figure, the IQs of nontwin siblings are less correlated than those of fraternal twins (.45 versus .60), even though they have the same percentage of genes in common. What can account for this difference? Researchers assume that if scores are not related to genes, they must reflect effects of the environment.

It is clear that the environment affects intelligence as assessed by IQ. The observed relationship between IQ and achievement, noted earlier, can also run in the opposite direction: People who achieve more can develop higher scores (for example, see Kohn & Schooler, 1973; Neisser et al., 1996). Perhaps the best evidence for this comes from studies of the effects of formal schooling. For example, when poor black children moved from the rural South to Philadelphia in the 1940s, their IQs increased by a bit more than half a point for each year they spent in their new schools (Cahan & Cohen, 1989; Ceci, 1991; Ceci & Williams, 1997; Lee, 1951).

The correlations on which heritability scores are based may overestimate the role of genes and underestimate the role of the environment, even when the correlations are drawn from adoption studies. Consider some factors that make it difficult to interpret heritability scores based on studies of twins and relatives.

First, twins share much the same environment in the womb before birth and are subject to most of the same pluses and minuses of that residence. The fetus suffers when the mother has a bad diet, takes drugs or alcohol, smokes, or experiences a great deal of stress; the fetus profits when the mother eats well, takes vitamins, and doesn't drink, smoke, or take drugs. In addition, about two thirds of identical twins even share the same placenta and amniotic sac in the uterus (see Figure 8.4 on page 290), which increases the similarity of the prenatal environment compared with that of fraternal twins, who are almost always in separate sacs (Phelps et al., 1997). Twins in the same sac share blood, which contains chemicals that affect brain development. Aspects of this common environment affect later IQ (Devlin et al., 1997) and are shared even by twins separated at birth and raised apart (Phelps et al., 1997). Thus, the high correlations between identical twins separated at birth may reflect their early shared environment as well as their shared genes.

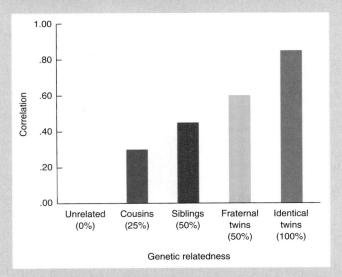

FIGURE 8.3
Genetic Relatedness and IQ

The correlations between people who are unrelated, cousins, siblings (nontwin brothers and sisters), and twins are graphed, along with their shared amounts of genes (in parentheses).

FIGURE 8.4
Fraternal and Identical Twins

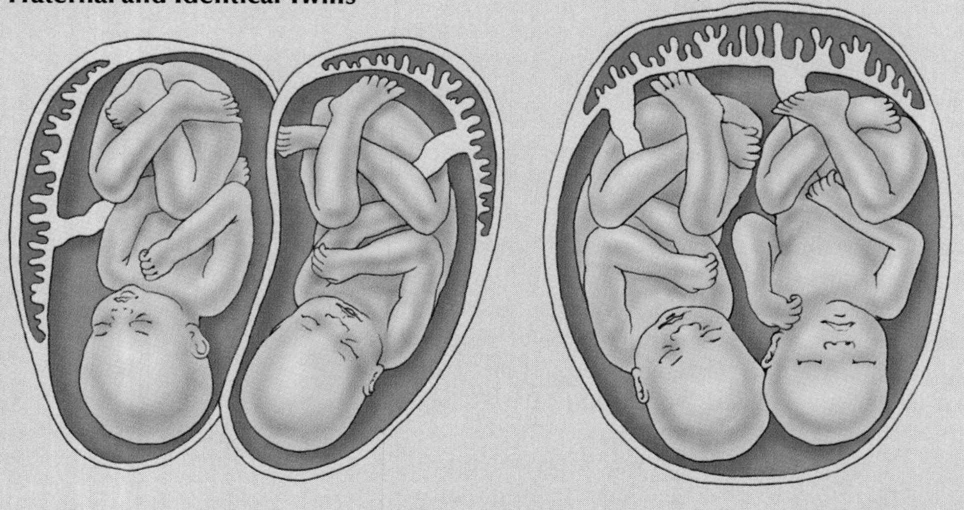

Twins can have separate placentas and separate amniotic sacs or share a single placenta and sac; sharing results in greater similarity prior to birth. Virtually all fraternal twins are in separate sacs (left), whereas about two thirds of identical twins are in the same sac (right).

Second, after birth, it is not clear just how different the environmental influences on twins raised in different homes really are. Families that seek to adopt a child share many characteristics, and these similarities are further enhanced by the fact that adoption agencies frown on placing children in deprived conditions. The households in which twins are placed often are more similar than not. When Stoolmiller (1999) mathematically corrected for the small variations among adopting families, he estimated the effects of environment on IQ to be 57%. It is not clear, however, whether this estimate applies only to this special situation of twins raised apart or can be taken as a general estimate.

Third, aspects of the genes can help shape the environment itself. The **microenvironment** is the environment you create by your very presence. For one thing, identical twins may have more aspects of their environments in common than fraternal twins because much of our environment is social, and people respond to us in part because of the way we look and behave. So if both twins are physically appealing, they will be treated very differently than if both are homely; ditto for twins who are sluggish and overweight or are athletic and trim. Also, to the extent that children have similar inborn tendencies, their behavior may shape their environments in similar ways. For example, children who enjoy being read to will reinforce adults for this activity, leading the adults to buy or borrow more books and thus providing more opportunity for stimulating interactions. In addition, depending on their personalities, people select aspects of the environment that appeal to them (perhaps, initially, for genetic reasons), and thus what appear to be different environments may in fact function as very much the same environment for two people with similar inclinations. For example, two homes may differ in the number of books they contain, but a child who likes to read may seize on whatever is available and end up reading as much in a home with few books as a child who lives in a home with many books. In short, identical twins share many characteristics that define the microenvironment, and so they live in more similar microenvironments than do other siblings. Even twins separated at birth may create similar microenvironments, and so it is not clear exactly how different the environmental influences on the twins are in the different homes.

Finally, researchers have typically observed that only about a quarter or a third of the variability in *g* can be explained by shared environment, aspects of the family

Microenvironment: The environment created by a person's own presence, which depends partly on appearance and behavior.

setting that are present for all siblings in a household, such as the number of books in the house (Plomin et al., 1997, p. 142). If genes account for about half the variability, and shared environment for less than half of what remains, what accounts for the rest? Some aspects of the environment don't have the same effect on all children growing up in the household; the same event can be a very different experience for different people. Watching television can be the mindless pastime of a couch potato, but Janet made watching TV into a stimulating experience. Even if the environment of two children appears to be identical, its influence depends in part on each child's predispositions and inclinations, which may be partly innate (Kagan, 1994a; Turkheimer & Waldron, 2000). A shy child, for example, will be pleased to be left alone to find solitary amusements; but the same treatment would be a punishment for an outgoing, gregarious child. The *perceived* environment, not the objective environment, is the important one.

In general, any effects of a shared family environment on children's IQs, which produce positive correlations among the scores of all children who grow up in the same house, wear off by adulthood, and genetic influences become increasingly evident with age (McCartney et al., 1990; McGue et al., 1993; Plomin, 1990). Why? One theory is that, as people age, they are increasingly able to select their environments, and genetically determined properties, such as temperament, lead people to select some environments over others. For example, if you are temperamentally shy, you will not take a job in sales; if you are outgoing, you might enjoy managing a hotel. Thus, as you grow older and have more choices about how to live, the effects of your early environment are increasingly dependent on the effects of genes (Neisser et al., 1996). This does not mean, however, that the environment is not playing a crucial role in helping you function well.

Within this context, the concept of a "reaction range" (Scarr, 1976; Scarr & McCartney, 1983) offers a framework for understanding the significance of heritability. The **reaction range** (also sometimes called the *range of reaction*) is the range of possible reactions to environmental events that is established by the genes; but the environment sets your position within that range (Weinberg, 1989). For example, consider height. Genes set limits on how tall Janet can be, but her actual height depends on nutrition and other particular environmental influences that regulate her genes. Depending on their environments, two people with different genetic potentials could have the same height, and two people with the same genetic potential could have different heights (Hirsch, 1971, 1997). In general, the greater the reaction range, the more evident the effects of the environment. Conversely, the narrower the reaction range, the more deterministic the effects of the genes. For some genes, notably those associated with certain diseases (such as Huntington's disease; De Marchi & Mennella, 2000; Gontkovsky, 1998), simply having the gene is enough to produce an effect—these genes have very narrow reaction ranges. But most genes that affect our psychologies do not seem to be like these; rather, the operation of these genes is regulated by our interactions with the environment.

Group Differences in Intelligence

How would you feel if you were told that you are a member of a group that is genetically stupid? Many groups have faced such charges, often with far-reaching consequences. The Immigration Act of 1924 aimed to minimize immigration to the United States of "biologically weak stocks," a term that was defined to include Italians and Jews of southern and eastern Europe. During congressional testimony, supporters of the bill pointed to the results of intelligence tests, on which recent immigrants scored less well than established Americans with northern European roots. There is debate about the extent to which this testimony mattered (Snyderman & Herrnstein, 1983), but no debate over the catastrophic effects of this bill less than 20 years later, during World War II, when Jews attempting to escape Nazi Germany were severely restricted from immigrating to the United States.

Reaction range: The range of possible reactions to environmental events that is set by the genes.

Contemporary studies comparing IQ scores find that some groups score lower than others on IQ tests; for example, Jews of European descent in Israel score about 15 points higher than Jews of North African descent. What do such findings mean?

WITHIN-GROUP VERSUS BETWEEN-GROUP DIFFERENCES. If, as most experts have concluded, about 50% of the differences in IQ can be accounted for by differences in genes, is it reasonable to say that differences in IQs between groups are largely genetic? Absolutely not. The genetic contribution to intelligence *within* a given group cannot say anything about possible genetic differences *between* groups (Block, 1995; Lewontin, 1976a, 1976b; Plomin, 1988). To see why not, imagine that you have two orchards with the same kind of apple trees. You make sure that each orchard receives exactly the same amounts of sunlight, fertilizer, water, and so on. If you succeed in making the environments identical, then any differences in the sizes of apples from the two orchards should reflect genetic differences among the trees. However, say the two orchards have overall different conditions, that one gets more sunshine and water than the other. *Within* each orchard, differences in the sizes of the apples would reflect genetic differences. But those differences say nothing about the differences *between* the orchards. The disadvantaged environment puts the trees in one orchard in a generally lower part of the reaction range than those benefiting from the advantaged environment. It is even possible that the differences within the "advantaged" orchard reflect the operation of one set of genes, whereas the differences within the "disadvantaged" orchard reflect the operation of another set that allows the trees to make the most of skimpy amounts of sunshine or water. No question about it: Differences within one group cannot be used to explain differences between groups or within another group.

When you see an apple, all you have to go on is its present size; you have no way of knowing the range of possible sizes. Similarly, when you meet Janet, you have no way of knowing the range of her possible intelligence. Further, heritability only tells you about the effects of a *certain environment* on the genes; it says nothing about the possible effects of *other environments* (Hirsch, 1971, 1997). There is no way to know how tall, or smart, Janet would have been if she (or her mother, while pregnant) had had a different diet, experienced less stress at certain periods of their lives, and so on.

RACE DIFFERENCES: BIAS IN TESTING? Asian Americans tend to score higher on IQ tests than white Americans, who in turn tend to score higher than African Americans (Neisser et al., 1996; Rushton, 1995; Suzuki & Valencia, 1997); Hispanics tend to score between whites and African Americans. For decades, the relatively low IQ scores of African Americans have attracted attention, and controversy has flared over arguments that their scores, and their poorer achievement, are rooted in their genes. A firestorm of debate raged when Richard Herrnstein and Charles Murray (1994) published *The Bell Curve*, in which they argued that IQ not only predicts many aspects of life and performance, but also that differences in IQ are largely genetic. However, as discussed earlier, it's not easy to disentangle effects of the environment (particularly the microenvironment) and genes. Although we focus on whites and African Americans in the following discussion, as has most of the research literature, keep in mind that the same issues also apply to all groups that generally score relatively poorly on IQ tests.

What do we make of the finding that white Americans have an average IQ that is 10 to 15 points higher than the average among African Americans? Block (1995) and Nisbett (1996), among others, discuss this issue at length. The following observations are worth some thought. First, some have argued that the disparity in test scores simply reflects the fact that the tests were designed for a white middle-class culture and thus are biased against African Americans, who have a different set of common experiences. This sort of **test bias** is relevant for the verbal and general information parts of the IQ test, but what about the performance parts? The race difference in IQ is present even here. So a simple "biased testing" explanation is probably not correct (Neisser et al., 1996). However, it is possible that people with different backgrounds are more or less comfortable taking these sorts of tests at all. Indeed, Serpell (1979)

Test bias: Test design features that lead a particular group to perform well or poorly and that thus invalidate the test.

found that Zambian children could reproduce patterns better using wire models (which they often used to make their own toys) than using pencil and paper, but vice versa for English children from the same social class (who were used to paper and pencil but not to wire models).

Second, others have argued that the IQ difference is caused by environmental differences. The people who are best off in U.S. society tend to score higher on IQ tests, and so do their children. (Some children from better-off families even receive expensive tutoring in how to take SAT tests, which are in many ways similar to IQ tests; Schwartz, 1999.) African Americans typically make less money than do whites, and this factor could cause environmental differences that lead them to score lower than whites. Some orchards get less sun and water than others, and thus the trees tend to bear smaller fruit. If this is the crucial cause of the IQ difference, then we would expect IQ to rise among African Americans as their economic circumstances improve. And in fact researchers have noted that recently the gap between African American and white IQ scores is shrinking. For older children the difference between the IQs of African Americans and whites is now only two thirds of what it had been (Thorndike et al., 1986); some researchers have found even smaller differences (Vincent, 1991; see also Flynn, in press). Flynn (1999) points out that IQ differences between whites and African Americans can be accounted for if "the average environment for African Americans of 1995 matches the quality of the average environment for whites in 1945" (p. 15). The increased scores may reflect more than the rising economy. Grissmer and colleagues (1994) report that the education level of the parents of African American children has risen faster than that of other groups, and this factor appears to affect the children's achievement. In addition, children from smaller families tend to have higher IQ scores, and African Americans showed the largest shift of any racial or ethnic group toward smaller family sizes in the years 1970 to 1990. The fact that such environmental factors can contribute to changing IQ scores suggests that these factors may have had something to do with the scores in the first place. However, these data are only correlations, which cannot tell us about causes and effects.

Third, some have argued that the microenvironment plays a key role in race differences. African American people have darker skin, which is part of their microenvironment; in the United States, this cue may elicit certain negative treatment from the white majority. What would happen in a society in which the majority did not respond this way? Consider this example: Eyferth (1961) studied the IQs of German children who were fathered by white or African American U.S. servicemen right after World War II. If the African American fathers had lower IQs than the white fathers, which is not known but is likely given the group averages, then the notion that genes are responsible for this difference would lead us to expect that their children should also have had lower IQs. But they didn't. Both groups of children had the same average IQs. At that time, there were very few African Americans in Germany and the majority whites may not have had negative stereotypes about them. Thus, the children may not have experienced negative environmental influences because of their racial background.

Finally, it is crucial to realize that the distributions in IQ between races overlap; plenty of African Americans have higher IQs than plenty of whites. Group differences do not necessarily apply to any particular individual.

African children who are accustomed to making their own playthings, like this toy car made of wire, are more adept at using wire models in pattern reproduction tests.

SEX DIFFERENCES. Group differences in intelligence are often cast as race differences, but consider another possible group difference that would affect fully half the population. Are there sex differences in IQ scores? Although some findings may suggest very small sex differences in IQ (Dai, 1994; Held et al., 1993), these effects are not always found (Aluja-Fabregat et al., 2000; Jensen, 1998). Instead, researchers typically find that males are better at some tasks than are females, and vice versa. In general, males tend to be better than females at tasks that require spatial reasoning, whereas females tend to be better than males at tasks that require verbal reasoning. Such differences have been found in at least 30 countries (Beller & Gafni, 1996; Halpern, 1992; Vogel, 1996).

Some theorists have tried to explain sex differences in spatial ability by the role differences of our primitive ancestors (Buss, D. M., 1995; Eals & Silverman, 1994; Geary, 1996a). The men, in this view, were out hunting, which required the ability to navigate and recall where the home cave was, whereas the women stayed home, picking berries, weaving baskets, and tending children. But we really don't know much about what our male and female ancestors actually did, and even in this scenario it isn't clear that women engaged in fewer spatial tasks. Gathering food requires remembering where the food is likely to grow and remembering how to return home, and weaving baskets and cloth certainly requires spatial processing (Halpern, 1997).

At least some of the sex differences arise from the effects of sex hormones (Kimura, 1994). One study examined women who were about to have sex-change operations to become men. As part of the procedure, the women received massive doses of male hormones, specifically testosterone. Within three months of treatment, spatial abilities increased and verbal abilities decreased (Van Goozen et al., 1995). Researchers have even found that a woman's spatial abilities shift during the course of her monthly cycle, as the balance of hormones changes (Hampson, 1990; Hampson & Kimura, 1988). By the same token, the level of male hormones shifts during the course of the day and over the seasons, and researchers have found that American males are worse at spatial abilities in the fall, when their levels of male hormones are highest, than in the spring. The effects of these hormones are not more-is-better, but rather are like an upside-down U: Too little or too much is worse than intermediate amounts (Kimura, 1994). Elderly men have low levels of male hormones, and thus it is interesting that testosterone supplements boost their scores on spatial tests (Janowsky et al., 1994).

Researchers are also now discovering differences in the structure and function of the brains of men and women. For example, it has long been known that the cerebral hemispheres are not as sharply specialized in women as in men (Jancke & Steinmetz, 1994; Springer & Deutsch, 1998), and such anatomical differences may underlie some functional differences (Gur et al., 1999; Mansour et al., 1996; Shaywitz et al., 1995).

In addition, at least part of the sex differences may arise from how boys and girls are treated in our society. Boys and girls are encouraged to take part in "sex appropriate" activities (Lytton & Romney, 1991). This is important in part because if you do not perform spatial activities, spatial abilities do not develop (Baenninger & Newcombe, 1989). And traditionally, girls have not been encouraged to participate in as many spatial activities, such as climbing trees and playing ball, as boys. In terms of genes, it's analogous to your muscles getting bigger only if you lift heavy things, causing genes to turn on to produce more proteins. Lack of participation in spatial activities means that the neural systems that underlie spatial activities are not exercised. Subrahmanyam and Greenfield (1994) showed that spatial abilities could be improved by having children play certain video games, and that boys and girls in their studies improved the same amount. However, sex differences can be measured even in early childhood, and so are unlikely to be totally the result of learning (Reinisch & Sanders, 1992; Robinson et al., 1996).

Finally, keep in mind that many females are better at spatial reasoning than many males, and many males are better at verbal abilities than many females. Here, too, differences in the means of groups say nothing about differences among particular individuals.

Boosting IQ: Pumping Up the Mind's Muscle

As you have seen, genetics and the environment must be considered as a single system; "genetic" effects may in part reflect the environment. So it is not surprising that varying the environment can boost general intelligence as measured by IQ.

THE FLYNN EFFECT: ANOTHER REASON TO LIVE LONG AND PROSPER. One of the most potent ways to improve your IQ apparently is simply to keep on living!

Many researchers had noted informally a trend that was documented by Flynn (1984, 1999a) and is now called the **Flynn effect**: In the Western world, IQ scores have generally risen about 3 points every 10 years. This means that the average IQ today would be 115 if the tests were scored the same way they were 50 years ago. (The way tests are scored is periodically adjusted, to keep the mean at 100.) Flynn (1999a) reports that the largest gains are on tests that are probably the most free of cultural influence, such as the Raven's Progressive Matrices. There is even evidence that the Flynn effect is accelerating: Between 1972 and 1982, IQ increased by an average of 8 points.

Neisser and colleagues (1996) offer three possible explanations for the Flynn effect. First, daily life today is more challenging than life in previous years, and the very act of coping with life's complexities may have increased IQ (Kohn & Schooler, 1973). Second, nutrition is better. Lynn (1990) noted that height has increased along with IQ, and characteristics that improve brain functioning might also have increased along with height. Third, perhaps intelligence itself has not risen, but only the kind of reasoning ability that is useful in taking tests (Flynn, 1999a); technology may have led people to become more comfortable with abstract thinking. Indeed, television shows such as *Sesame Street* and interactive computers help children and adults alike learn to pay attention and to think more quickly, as well as expose them to tasks similar to those on IQ tests. Flynn (1999a) and Williams (1998) offer other possible accounts, but at present the definitive explanation for this rising curve is not known.

INTELLIGENCE ENHANCEMENT PROGRAMS: MENTAL WORKOUTS. Many educational and social programs have been developed with the aim of raising intelligence. Probably the most famous is Project Head Start, which was a grand initiative of the 1960s designed to provide additional intellectual stimulation for disadvantaged children and prepare them to succeed in school. Unfortunately, most such programs show only short-term gains in IQ, and the gains evaporate with time (Consortium for Longitudinal Studies, 1983; Neisser et al., 1996). However, a few studies have shown that IQs can be raised if children are given hours of daily supplemental schooling, beginning at a young age and continuing for years (Brody, 1997). Perhaps the best known is the Abecedarian Project (Campbell & Ramey, 1994), which was started at the University of North Carolina in 1972. It provided intensive intellectual enrichment (as well as pediatric care, nutritional supplements, and help from social workers) for children at risk of failing in school. Entering the program as young as 6 weeks of age, children were placed in a specially designed daycare setting between 6 and 8 hours a day, 5 days a week. After 5 years, they entered a public kindergarten. By age 15, children who had been in the program still had higher IQ scores (by about 5 points) than those in a control group. Although a 5-point boost is not very large (a third of a standard deviation), the enhanced intellectual skills and abilities that underlie it may help participants succeed at school and at work.

What determines whether enrichment programs succeed in raising intelligence? The key may be whether they help the participants reorganize how they think (Perkins & Grotzer, 1997). In particular, successful programs teach people new strategies for making decisions, organizing problems, and remembering information. People are also taught how to plan and monitor progress as they try to solve problems, and how to know when to stop and change strategies. They are also taught to learn to detect situations that require particular patterns of thinking. (For example, remember problems that began like this: "A box of candy has twice as many chocolates as . . ."? The trick is often being able to figure out how to translate the situation into a specific kind of problem that you already know how to solve.) Wagner (1997) reviews ways in which people develop cognitively, many of which rely on "cognitive apprenticeship." Cognitive apprenticeship involves, among other things, intellectual coaching—having a mentor who can show you how to think.

Finally, we should note that various activities have been reported to raise intelligence. For example, Rauscher and colleagues (1993) reported that listening to Mozart could briefly improve spatial reasoning. However, before changing your musical tastes

Flynn effect: Increases in IQ in the population with the passage of time.

or investing in a new set of CDs, note that efforts to repeat this effect have produced spotty results (Carstens et al., 1995; Chabris, 1999; Newman et al., 1995; Steele et al., 1997, 1999; Wilson & Brown, 1997), and researchers disagree about when the effect is likely to occur (for example, Chabris, 1999, versus Rauscher, 1999). In any event, at best the effect is short-lived.

LOOKING AT LEVELS

Accidentally Making Kids Smarter

For Janet, and for the rest of us, genes and the environment have interacted to create a complex mix of strengths and weaknesses. Neither theories about information processing in the brain nor data about group differences in IQ can predict what Janet will be able to accomplish. The right conditions might help her perform better, but their effects would depend on the interaction of events at three levels: the brain, the person, and the group.

The importance of these interactions is highlighted in a study by Rosenthal and Jacobson (1968; Rosenthal, 1993, 1994). They showed that if teachers thought the children in their classes were going to become smarter, those expectations led the teachers to behave in such a way that those children actually *did* become smarter. Rosenthal and Jacobson performed a large-scale study in a public elementary school in the San Francisco area (in grades 1–6). The students first were given a nonverbal intelligence test, which was disguised as a "test of intellectual potential" (and called, nonsensically, the "Harvard Test of Inflected Acquisition"). Rosenthal and Jacobson chose at random about 20% of the children in each of three classrooms at each of six grade levels; they then told the teachers that these children had scored exceptionally well on the test and that they should expect to see these children bloom intellectually over the next 8 months. The teachers did not know that the children had been assigned randomly to this group, and there was no difference in intelligence between them and the remaining students. At the end of the year, the children were tested again, and lo and behold, those whom the teachers thought were smarter actually showed larger gains in intelligence scores than their classmates, especially in grades 1 and 2.

How could this have happened? Rosenthal and his colleagues observed the teachers interacting with the kids and found that the teachers treated the students they thought were smarter differently. Most important, the teachers not only behaved more warmly to the supposedly brighter students, but also put more effort into teaching them more information and more difficult material. In addition, the teachers called on these children more often and gave them more time to answer questions; they also gave them more informative feedback about their performance, providing correct answers after wrong ones were offered. These findings have since been repeated (Babad, 1993; Eden, 1990; Raudenbush, 1984; Rosenthal, 1993), and the effects are especially pronounced if the teachers don't know the children very well (Raudenbush, 1984).

Think about this effect: At the level of the group, the teachers were given information about students, information that changed their beliefs. These beliefs in turn led them to treat the children differently, which in turn actually affected how well the children's brains worked! This is a *self-fulfilling prophecy*. The favored children may also have developed different views about themselves (at the level of the person), which affected how they treated other people (at the level of the group), and so on. Similar effects—positive and negative—may occur if expectations are invoked because the students have personal characteristics, such as skin color, way of talking, gender, and other characteristics that define a microenvironment; teachers make inferences, and the self-fulfilling prophecy rolls on.

▶ *1. What aspects of brain function underlie intelligence?* People with larger brains tend to have higher IQs, but size per se cannot be all that is important— not even the relative size of particular parts of the brain. Nor is simple speed crucial. Instead, the speed of the central executive aspect of working memory may be key, at least for some forms of intelligence.

▶ *2. How do environment and genetics contribute to intelligence?* In general, about 50% of the variability in IQ scores can be attributed to variations in genes. However, at least some of these effects may in fact reflect the way the environment is regulating the genes, or the way genes in turn affect the environment (including by influencing appearance and temperament, which affect the microenvironment). Genes define a reaction range, and the environment sets each individual within that range.

▶ *3. How can we interpret group differences in IQ?* Although group differences definitely exist, it is im-

possible to sort out the relative contributions of genes and the environment to such differences. Findings about the genetic contribution to within-group differences do not apply to between-group differences. In addition, all distributions of abilities within any group overlap those of other groups, and hence group differences cannot be applied to particular individuals.

▶ *4. Can "exercising the mind" raise IQ?* The Flynn effect indicates that IQs are steadily rising with time, which may reflect the increased intellectual demands of modern times. In addition, successful programs for boosting IQ generally teach people new strategies for making decisions, organizing problems, and remembering information, as well as for recognizing when to use a particular kind of thinking in a given situation. Although even the most successful programs raise IQ only a relatively small amount, the underlying skills and abilities developed by these programs may be valuable in their own rights.

RARE INTELLIGENCE

By the time Janet became a teenager, she was showing a talent for writing in general and for writing poetry in particular. But she was no better than average at other things, and in some school subjects she did poorly. Her writing gave her a sense of confidence in her intellectual abilities, but this confidence could be quickly offset by failures or disappointments in other areas. As a result, her fears of being intellectually deficient, or even mentally retarded, persisted. The fourth grade label "Retard" stayed in her mind, sowing doubts. But rather than being mentally impaired, in some ways Janet was gifted. In this section we consider the extreme forms of intelligence, high and low.

▶ 1. What is mental retardation? What causes it?

▶ 2. What does it mean to be "gifted"?

Mental Retardation: People With Special Needs

How could Janet, seriously worried about her mental abilities, settle her concerns once and for all? For want of a better definition, people with an IQ score of 70 or lower (that is, who fall more than two standard deviations below the mean) are traditionally considered to be **mentally retarded.** The American Association for Mental Retardation (1992) specifies two additional criteria: "significant limitations" in two or more everyday abilities, such as communication, self-care, and self-direction; and the presence of the condition since childhood.

About 7 million Americans are considered mentally retarded (Fryers, 1993). Mental retardation affects about 100 times more people than does total blindness (Batshaw & Perret, 1992). One out of every 10 families in the United States is directly affected by mental retardation (American Association for Mental Retardation, 1992).

Mentally retarded: Having an IQ of 70 or less and significant limitations in at least two aspects of everyday life since childhood.

Retardation does not imply an inability to learn. Mildly retarded people can learn to function well as adults, and behavioral techniques that involve explicit shaping and reinforcement (see Chapter 5) can allow even severely retarded people to master many tasks.

Furthermore, many otherwise retarded children display **islands of excellence,** areas in which they perform remarkably well. *Savants* (previously called *idiot savants),* such as the main character, Raymond, in the movie *Rain Man,* have dramatic disparities in their abilities. For example, a savant may be able to determine the day of the week for any calendar date, including dates centuries from now or in the past (Horwitz et al., 1965), or to draw outstandingly vivid, detailed pictures. But these same people may be incapable of doing simple addition.

One type of retardation that includes islands of excellence occurs in *Williams syndrome* (Bellugi et al., 1993, 1999a, 1999b; Udwin & Yule, 1990, 1991). Although people with Williams syndrome are in general retarded, they have large vocabularies and often detailed knowledge of facts. Frequently, however, they fail to understand the facts they apparently have at their command. For example, consider this interview of S.K., a 21-year-old woman with Williams syndrome, who liked novels about vampires:

> When asked what a vampire is, she replied, "Oooh, a vampire is a man who climbs into ladies' bedrooms in the middle of the night and sinks his teeth into their necks." When asked why vampires do this, she was visibly taken aback—she hesitated and said, "I've never thought about that." She then thought for a long time before finally answering, "Vampires must have an inordinate fondness for necks." (Johnson & Carey, 1998)

S.K. apparently had absorbed facts about vampires from the books she had read, but had never put them together. She did not understand that vampires sucked blood, that they were dead and killed people to create new vampires, and so on. But note her use of the word *inordinate*—she had an impressive vocabulary and could use it appropriately. Again, we see that intelligence is not a single capacity and that various aspects of intelligence can be affected separately from the rest.

Mental retardation results when the brain fails to develop properly, which can happen in the womb or during childhood. Although hundreds of causes have now been identified, the causes of about one third of all cases are still mysteries. However, it is clear that both genetic and environmental factors can lead to retardation (see Table 8.3).

GENETIC INFLUENCES: WHEN GOOD GENES GO BAD. The most common type of mental retardation (occurring in about 1 in 1,000 births) is known as **Down syndrome,** first described by British physician J. Langdon Down in 1866. Down children have an average IQ of 55, and as teenagers they have the linguistic abilities of 3-year-olds. The most common form of Down syndrome is not inherited, but it is caused by a genetic problem—the creation of an extra chromosome (number 21) during conception. This problem is more likely to occur in older mothers, whose eggs have been dormant for many years.

The second most common cause of mental retardation is also genetic, but in this case the child inherits a quirk: a small bit of DNA on the X chromosome repeats itself many times. Because this defect makes the chromosome prone to breaking up when observed in the laboratory, the disorder is called **fragile X syndrome** (Madison et al., 1986; Murray et al., 1996). About twice as many males as females suffer from this disorder because males have only one X chromosome, and females have two. It is rare that both of a female's X chromosomes carry the disorder; only one of her two X chromosomes is actually functional, and about half the time the functioning one does not have the disorder. The repetition of the bit of DNA is compounded over generations, and the more repeats, the more severe the symptoms (Levitas, 2000; Siomi et al., 1996). Thus, with each succeeding generation, the syndrome becomes worse.

Mental retardation also typically accompanies **autism,** a condition of intense self-involvement to the exclusion of external reality. Only about 25% of autistic people

Islands of excellence: Areas in which retarded people perform remarkably well.

Down syndrome: A type of retardation that results from the creation of an extra chromosome during conception; it is genetic but not inherited.

Fragile X syndrome: A type of retardation that affects the X chromosome; it is both genetic and inherited.

Autism: A condition of intense self-involvement to the exclusion of external reality; about three quarters of autistic people are mentally retarded.

TABLE 8.3

Causes of Retardation: Common Examples

Source: *From http://thearc.org/faqs/mrqa.html*

Genetic conditions
- Down syndrome
- Fragile *X* syndrome
- Phenylketonuria (PKU)

Problems during pregnancy
- Use of alcohol or drugs
- Malnutrition
- Rubella
- Glandular disorders and diabetes
- Illnesses of the mother during pregnancy
- Physical malformations of the brain and HIV infection in the fetus

Problems at birth
- Prematurity
- Low birth weight

Problems after birth
- Childhood diseases such as whooping cough, chicken pox, and measles, which may lead to meningitis and encephalitis, which can in turn damage the brain
- Accidents such as a blow to the head or near drowning
- Lead and mercury poisoning

Poverty and cultural deprivation
- Malnutrition
- Disease-producing conditions
- Inadequate medical care
- Environmental health hazards

have IQs higher than 70, and thus most people with this disorder are also mentally retarded (Volkmar et al., 1994). Depending on the severity of the disease, people with autism are socially bizarre, disoriented, sometimes engage in repetitive body movements such as rocking or hand flapping, and have severe attentional difficulties; they may also be self-destructive. Although the disorder is rare (estimates range from as low as 3 out of 10,000 live births to as high as 1 out of 500), it is highly heritable: If one identical twin has it, the chances are around 60% that the other does, too. In contrast, if one fraternal twin is autistic, the chances are only 10% that the other is. Four times as many boys as girls are afflicted with autism.

Although normal intelligence relies on complex inheritance—that is, the contribution of many genes—abnormal intelligence can result when even one gene is awry. In this sense, mental retardation can obey the laws of Mendelian inheritance. **Phenylketonuria (PKU)**, which arises from a recessive gene, is a classic example of such a disorder. A child must inherit two copies of the gene, one from each parent, in order to develop the disorder. If one of the children in a family has PKU, the chances are about one in four that a sibling will also have it. Phenylketonuria results when failure of the genes to produce a particular enzyme causes toxic substances to build up in the blood and damage the baby's developing brain. At one time, 1% of all people institutionalized for mental retardation had PKU. However, if diagnosed early, the disease is easily treated with dietary supplements and retardation is prevented. If the correct diagnosis is delayed, there is a good chance the child will be retarded.

Phenylketonuria (PKU): A genetic form of retardation that can be treated with dietary supplements if detected early in life.

Lidsky and colleagues (1985) located the gene that causes PKU, leading to the development of better tests to determine whether parents are carriers.

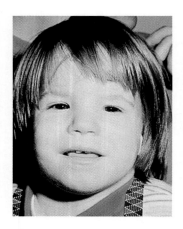

If a mother drinks alcohol heavily during pregnancy, her child can be born with fetal alcohol syndrome—one aspect of which is mental retardation.

ENVIRONMENTAL INFLUENCES: BAD LUCK, BAD BEHAVIOR. Drinking and driving don't mix; neither do drinking and pregnancy. If the mother drinks heavily during pregnancy, her child can be born with **fetal alcohol syndrome.** Part of this syndrome is mental retardation (Streissguth et al., 1989, 1999). Indeed, many environmental factors can lead to mental retardation. If the pregnant mother experiences malnutrition, rubella, diabetes, HIV infection, high doses of X rays, or any of a number of infections, her child may be born with mental retardation. Streissguth and colleagues (1989) found that taking antibiotics and even aspirin during pregnancy also can adversely affect the developing baby's brain. Because in their cases the condition is environmentally induced, people whose retardation is due to such circumstances tend not to have retarded children themselves.

Mental retardation can also arise if the birth is unusually difficult and the infant's brain is injured. Premature birth and low birth weight put the child at risk for retardation. In addition, some childhood diseases, such as chicken pox and measles, can sometimes cause brain damage, as can ingesting lead, mercury, or poisons. Vaccines and other treatments have greatly reduced the incidence of mental retardation over the past several decades (Alexander, 1991).

The Gifted

There is no hard and fast way to determine whether a person is **gifted;** the term is sometimes used to refer to people who have IQs of at least 135, but more commonly *gifted* denotes the 150–180 range (Winner, 1997). Much of the research on the gifted has focused on people with very high IQs, greater than 150, and that is the criterion we will adopt here. It is not known how genes and the environment, including the environment in the womb, contribute to the condition.

As expected from the idea of multiple intelligences, children can be gifted in some domains while not being gifted in others. **Prodigies,** children with immense talent in a particular area, may be perfectly normal in other domains; for example, mathematically gifted children often are not gifted in other domains (Benbow & Minor, 1990). Achter and colleagues (1996) found that over 95% of the gifted children they tested had sharply differing mathematical and verbal abilities.

According to some researchers (such as Jackson & Butterfield, 1986) gifted children do the same kinds of processing as average children but simply do it more effectively. As Winner (1997) notes, however, some children "as young as three or four years of age have induced rules of algebra on their own (Winner, 1996), have memorized almost instantly entire musical scores (Feldman & Goldsmith, 1991), and have figured out on their own how to identify all prime numbers (Winner, 1996)" (p. 1071). Such intellectual feats suggest that the cognition of gifted children may be qualitatively different from that of the rest of us. Specifically, Winner suggests that gifted children may be exceptionally able to intuit solutions to problems and may be driven by an extraordinary passion to master tasks.

The gifts are sometimes bestowed with a price. Gifted children are often socially awkward and are sometimes treated as "geeks" and "nerds" (Silverman, 1993a, 1993b; Winner, 2000). In addition, they are often solitary and introverted (Silverman, 1993b). They have twice the rate of emotional and social problems as nongifted children (Winner, 1997).

If you aren't gifted as a child, does this mean you have no hope of becoming a gifted adult? Not at all. Many distinguished adults—Charles Darwin, for example— showed no signs of being gifted as children (Simonton, 1994); and, vice versa, most gifted children grow up to be rather ordinary adults (Richert, 1997; Winner, 2000).

Many eminent adults had the help of able mentors at critical phases of their lives (Bloom, 1985; Gardner, 1993a). Having an apprentice relationship with an appropri-

Fetal alcohol syndrome: A type of retardation caused by excessive drinking of alcohol by the mother during pregnancy.

Gifted: People who have IQs of at least 135, but more commonly between 150 and 180.

Prodigies: People who early in life demonstrate immense talent in a particular domain, such as music or mathematics, but who are normal in other domains.

ate role model can make a huge difference. That is one reason why graduate education in the sciences in the United States is based on apprenticeship: Students in Ph.D. programs in the sciences learn at the elbows of their supervisors, not simply from reading books or listening to lectures.

Which Termites Were Successful?

The quality of being gifted in adulthood depends on a complex interplay between genes and various life experiences, as was well illustrated by the work of Lewis Terman and his colleagues at Stanford University (Terman & Oden, 1959). They selected 1,470 children who had IQs between 135 and 196 (and hence scored in the top 1% of the population) from over a quarter million students in the California public schools. These children (along with 58 of their siblings who were added to the study later) were tested and interviewed every 7 years or so as they grew up; they came to be known as "Termites." Many of them did remarkably well in life (Ceci, 1996; Minton, 1988). Oden (1968) found that by about age 50 the 759 men she studied had published over 200 books, 2,500 papers, 400 short stories, poems, and musical compositions, as well as television and movie scripts. They had also filed more than 350 patents.

However, Ceci (1990, 1996) observed that success could not be predicted from IQ scores alone. Motivation apparently played a big role. Termites from modest backgrounds did much worse than those from more upper-income families, and people raised during the Great Depression did less well than those raised later. Researchers have suggested that for groups who performed less well, economic circumstances affected the Termites' perceptions of what was possible, and thus what was worth striving to achieve. Some Termites were notorious underachievers who never did very well. Few of these underachievers came from families that were as successful as those of the high-achieving Termites. The underachievers apparently were not highly motivated to succeed, in large part because their families did not instill in them the value of success.

Thus, events at all three levels of analysis must be considered to understand why one high-IQ child becomes a successful adult and another does not. The ability to score well on an IQ test is not enough; as you've seen, there are multiple types of intelligence, many of which are not tapped by an IQ score. At the level of the brain, you must have the ability to solve problems and to understand and learn complex material in the context in which you work, and different abilities are relevant for different jobs. At the level of the person, you must also be motivated to succeed. And the origins of such values and beliefs depend on factors at the level of the group: Motivation comes in part from the way you are raised and in part from your perceptions of what is possible. If you grow up during a time when there are few opportunities, you may not see the point in straining to succeed. As usual, events at the different levels interact: If you don't have the mental machinery, the opportunity to succeed may not be enough; if you don't have the motivation, the mental machinery is not enough.

CONSOLIDATE!

▶ *1. What is mental retardation? What causes it?* Mental retardation is usually defined as having since childhood an IQ that is more than two standard deviations below the mean IQ and having significant limitations in two or more everyday abilities. There are hundreds of causes of mental retardation. Some types are caused by genetic abnormalities, which may or may not be inherited, and others are caused by environmental events, such as childhood infections.

(continued)

CONSOLIDATE! *continued*

► *2. What does it mean to be "gifted"?* Gifted people are defined as those having high IQs, typically well over two standard deviations above the mean, and often over three or more. It is not clear how the genes and environment interact to produce such high IQs. Not all gifted children go on to become accomplished adults. In fact, most gifted children grow up to be undistinguished adults, and most distinguished adults were not obviously gifted as children. Motivation, experience, and opportunity have a lot to do with who ultimately is most successful.

CREATIVE FORCES

Sometimes Janet writes several poems in a rush, hardly thinking about the flow of words. Images and feelings seem to swirl around in her head, out of control, and she thinks she might be a little crazy. At other times, she struggles to write and wonders whether she'll ever produce a good poem she can be proud of again. She wishes she could find some technique that would help her be creative when she wants to be.

► 1. What is creativity?

► 2. What makes some people more creative than others?

► 3. Is there any way to enhance creativity?

What Is Creativity?

Creativity is the ability to produce something original of high quality or to devise effective new ways of solving a problem. Creativity necessarily involves the ability to recognize and develop a novel approach; the ability to consider a problem from multiple angles and to change points of view repeatedly; and the ability to develop a simple idea in different ways. Creative thought can be applied to practical problems (such as raising money), intellectual tasks (making new connections in a term paper), or artistic work (writing a poem).

FIGURE 8.5
Stages of Creative Thought

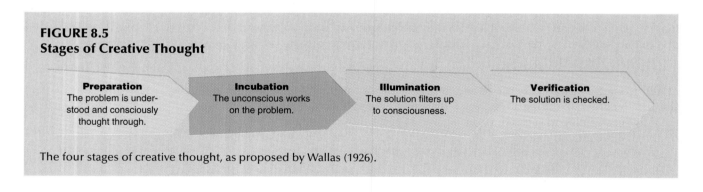

The four stages of creative thought, as proposed by Wallas (1926).

Creativity: The ability to produce something original of high quality or to devise effective new ways of solving a problem.

Many theorists have suggested that creativity involves multiple stages. Wallas (1926) described a four-stage theory of creativity, illustrated in Figure 8.5. Many variants of this idea have since been proposed (Sapp, 1992); support is strongest for a simpler, two-stage process. In the first stage, you generate a variety of possible solutions to a problem; in the second stage, you interpret and select among them (Campbell, 1960; Martindale, 1990; Simonton, 1995, 1997).

The two-stage technique is a key aspect of an approach called *creative cognition*, in which the processes of normal cognition, such as memory and imagery, function to produce novel solutions to problems (Finke, 1996; Finke et al., 1992). Much research on creative cognition has grown out of the task illustrated in Figure 8.6. Finke and Slayton (1988) gave participants a set of simple shapes and asked them to combine the shapes mentally to create a recognizable form or object. In these studies, the first stage involved "mental play" with images of the forms, by rotation, size adjustment, and repositioning; the second stage involved recognizing what a combination of the forms could represent. Finke and colleagues (1992) found that participants were more creative if they combined shapes without a particular goal in mind at the outset, attempting an interpretation only after producing novel combinations.

It is possible that either stage of creativity can occur unconsciously (as can aspects of problem solving; see Chapter 7). Consciously, each stage can be approached with different forms of thinking, and optimal creativity probably involves a mixture of them. Guilford (1967) distinguishes between convergent thinking and divergent thinking. In **convergent thinking,** you stay focused on one particular approach to a problem and work through a series of steps to arrive at a solution; all lines of thought converge on a single correct solution. Routine problems with straightforward solutions, such as those amenable to logical reasoning, often rely on convergent thinking. In **divergent thinking,** you come at a problem from a number of different angles, exploring a variety of approaches to a solution before settling on one (Mednick, 1962). For example, imagine that you are moving and trying to decide whether to take with you some bricks stored in the basement. Given their weight, you decide that you will pack them only if you can think of a very good use for them. Divergent thinking might lead you to consider them as doorstops, supports for bookshelves, or as bookends. After generating such possibilities in the first stage, you move to the second stage. In the second stage, you might decide that using the bricks for bookshelves is a good idea and so lug the bricks with you when you move. Creativity appears to be enhanced if you begin by using divergent thinking in either stage, to produce possibilities (in the first stage) or to consider alternative interpretations of the possibilities (in the second stage).

Convergent thinking also has an important role in creativity—in setting up a problem in the first place, or in cutting back the lush jungle of ideas created by divergent thinking. If all you ever used was divergent thinking, you would probably have a hard time drawing any firm conclusions.

What Makes a Person Creative?

Some people are undoubtedly more creative than others. Why? Eysenck (1995) claims that very creative people tend to make loose associations and engage in divergent thinking. However, studies of creative people suggest that they have special abilities that affect both stages of the creative process: Not only can they generate more possible solutions, but they are also able to select among them more effectively. Amabile

FIGURE 8.6
Creative Cognition

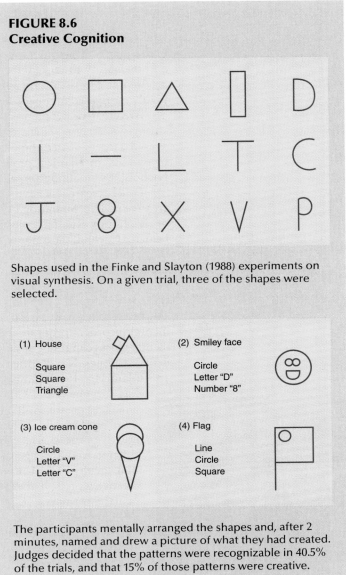

Shapes used in the Finke and Slayton (1988) experiments on visual synthesis. On a given trial, three of the shapes were selected.

(1) House

Square
Square
Triangle

(2) Smiley face

Circle
Letter "D"
Number "8"

(3) Ice cream cone

Circle
Letter "V"
Letter "C"

(4) Flag

Line
Circle
Square

The participants mentally arranged the shapes and, after 2 minutes, named and drew a picture of what they had created. Judges decided that the patterns were recognizable in 40.5% of the trials, and that 15% of those patterns were creative.

Convergent thinking: Thinking that involves focusing on a particular approach and following a series of steps to converge on a solution.

Divergent thinking: Thinking that involves taking different perspectives on a problem and exploring different approaches to a solution.

(1983, 1998) found that creative people keep options open, do not make snap decisions about the likely outcome of an effort, and are good at seeing a problem from a new vantage point. Similarly, when Guilford used factor analysis to discover which underlying abilities are tapped by various tests of creativity, he found that flexibility and the ability to reorganize information were key (similar conclusions were drawn by Aguilar-Alonso, 1996, and Eysenck, 1995). In addition, creative people are often highly motivated and persistent, driven to create (Sulloway, 1996).

Are creative people born that way? Unlike IQ, differences in creativity are not strongly related to genetic differences, if at all. Moreover, and also in contrast to IQ, shared aspects of the home (such as exposure to cultural resources, home libraries, or parents' mechanical or artistic hobbies) strongly affect creativity (Canter, 1973; Nichols, 1978; Simonton, 1988).

Other researchers have looked for the roots of creativity by examining the lives of creative people. Simonton (1984, 1988, 1990) found that in spite of romantic images of the moody Russian composer, the drunken Irish poet, and the poor Southerner beaten as a child, the amount of stress people experience is not related to how creative they are, and social recognition of a person's accomplishments neither increases nor decreases creativity. In addition, the most creative people had intermediate amounts of formal education; either too much or too little formal education apparently stifles creativity (Simonton, 1988).

Are highly creative people mentally unstable? It has long been believed that certain mental disorders promote creativity (Kraepelin, 1921). Manic-depressive (bipolar) mental illness can result in shifts between very "high" energetic moods and very "low" depressed ones. Kay Redfield Jamison and her collaborators (Goodwin & Jamison, 1990; Jamison, 1989; Jamison et al., 1980; see also Hershman & Lieb, 1988, 1998) have argued that a "loosening" of thought that occurs during the manic phase enhances creativity. If so, the manic phase may spur creativity by increasing the number of possible solutions a person can formulate during the first phase of the creative process. Isaac Newton, Charles Dickens, and Kurt Cobain apparently suffered from this disorder, and Andreasen (1987) found that almost half the visiting faculty in the University of Iowa Writers' Workshop, an intensive course for creative writers, had experienced it. Jamison (1989) reports similar findings, particularly for poets.

Others have claimed, however, that mental illness is independent of creativity; these claims are consistent with analyses of Dennis (1966) and Simonton (1984, 1997), who showed that the quality of a creative person's work tends to be constant over their productive years; in years when a large number of particularly good works are produced, a correspondingly large number of inferior works are also produced.

In short, many different factors underlie creativity. Although creative people may share certain general strategies, they have little else in common.

In some ways creativity is like pitching in baseball. Cy Young was the pitcher with the greatest number of wins in baseball history. The pitcher with the most losses? Cy Young. People who produce increased numbers of creative works are also likely to produce increased numbers of mundane works.

Enhancing Creativity

Many techniques, focusing on ways to find novel effective solutions to problems, have been developed in an effort to enhance creativity. When designing an object, for example, Crawford (1954) suggests listing its attributes, and then considering how to modify each attribute to improve the object. Say you are developing a beach chair; you would first list the essential attributes—it must support weight, recline at different angles, and so on. Then you think about how to design different systems for supporting weight (webbing fabric, air cushions) and for adjusting the angle (ropes, gears, air pressure), and so forth. Another useful technique is to consider how to combine attributes in new ways (Davis, 1973). For example, consider how the properties of knives, spoons, and forks could be combined to create new multipurpose eating tools.

Destination Imagination (DI) is an international organization that encourages team brainstorming and creativity in the context of preparing the most creative possible "solution" to the team's choice of a challenging problem. This group performed a commercial for a nutritional product that they created.

Some techniques for enhancing creativity rely on interactions among people. Probably the most well known of these is *brainstorming* (Osborn, 1953), in which members of a group say the first thing that comes to mind, volunteering ideas almost at random, thus triggering new ideas from one another. For this technique to be productive, the members of the group must suspend judgment and agree not to criticize one another's ideas at this stage. However, research findings suggest that relying on a group discussion to find creative solutions may be a bad idea. People actually produce fewer ideas in groups than when they work alone, perhaps because they are more inhibited with others than they are in the private recesses of their own minds (Dennehy et al. 1991, as cited in Finke et al., 1992; Diehl & Stroebe, 1987).

Many people believe that true creative thought requires freedom, but others have argued that creativity thrives when there is a great deal of structure; in this view, the more precisely a problem is specified, and the clearer the approach, the easier it is to be creative. A particularly powerful demonstration of this was provided by Goldenberg and colleagues (1999), who programmed a computer to engage in the most extreme form of structured thinking: following an algorithm, a step-by-step set of rules. The researchers first studied effective advertisements and noticed that they seemed to rely on a few simple ideas (which are involved in creativity in general; Boden, 2000). For instance, many involved replacing properties of one thing with those of another: An ad for Bally shoes, for example, suggested that their shoes gave wearers a sense of freedom by showing clouds or an inviting island in the shape of a shoe; the sense of freedom conveyed by clouds and the island were intended to transfer to the shoes. After being armed with such rules, the computer was asked to describe ads for specific products in order to convey certain messages; its suggestions were then compared to those from humans (who were not in the ad business). Here are some examples of what the computer and humans produced (as reported by Angier, 1999):

Goal: Convey that Apple computers are user-friendly.

Computer idea: An Apple computer offers flowers.

Human idea: An Apple computer next to a PC, with the claim: "This is the friendliest computer."

Goal: Convey that Jeeps have very quiet engines.

Computer idea: Two Jeeps communicating in sign language.

Human idea: A car alone in the country.

Goal: Convey that an airline has on-time performance.

Computer idea: A cuckoo in the shape of a jumbo jet popping out of a cuckoo clock.

Human idea: A family running to an airplane, with one of the parents screaming, "Let's run, I know this airline's planes are always right on time."

Which do you like better? When the ads were judged by both advertising professionals and others, the computer's ideas came out on top: The judges rated its suggestions as more creative and original than those of the humans. In fact, the computer's suggestions were often judged virtually as good as actual award-winning ads. But don't give up on the power of human creativity: When humans were taught the rules programmed into the computer, they did as well as, and sometimes better than, the computer. Although such training is highly limited to a particular type of problem, such as writing advertisements, it is important to recognize that, in at least some situations, structure helps creativity rather than hindering it.

LOOKING AT LEVELS

Undermining Creativity

Given that structure can boost creativity, can creativity be enhanced by reinforcing it, thereby "building in" well-structured approaches? The principles of reinforcement state that if an action is rewarded, the organism is more likely to repeat that action in the future. But not all types of reward have the same effects, and creativity can be impaired by the "wrong" types of rewards. Amabile (1985) asked 72 participants, all of them writers, to write brief poems in the laboratory. After writing the first poem, which served as a baseline, the participants were divided into three groups. In one group, they filled in a questionnaire asking them to focus on reasons for the enjoyment of writing "for its own sake." In another group, participants filled in a questionnaire asking them to focus on external reasons for writing, such as financial rewards or approval from others. The third group, which did not fill in any sort of questionnaire, was the control. Then all the participants wrote a second poem. Judges who were unaware of the conditions then rated the creativity of the poems. They found no differences among the first poems from all three groups; but they found that the second poems written by those who were asked to focus on external reasons for writing were less creative than those written by people in the other two groups. Simply thinking about different motivations disrupted creativity. (These results are supported by the findings of Amabile et al., 1986; Lepper et al., 1973.)

Apparently, even the mere suggestion of external rewards, which in this case were social (the level of the group), undermines how well the brain functions during the two stages of the creative process. For example, if you focus on external reasons for being creative, you may become distracted or tense, and thus not allow the generative stage to operate loosely, or you may focus on the wrong kinds of characteristics in the second stage and thus select poorly among the possible choices. And if you write badly, others' reactions (level of the group) will provide discouraging feedback, which in turn will affect your beliefs about yourself (level of the person). Such beliefs in turn can affect what you choose to do in the future.

Does this mean that creative acts should never be rewarded? Fortunately, no. If the reward is given for novel performance per se, without focusing on specific aspects of the performance, rewards need not undermine later creativity (Eisenberger & Armeli, 1997; Eisenberger et al., 1999). Thus, the precise nature of the reward interacts with all the other factors.

CONSOLIDATE!

▶ **1. What is creativity?** Creativity is the ability to produce something original of high quality or to devise effective new ways of solving a problem. Creativity is not simply devising new products or solutions to problems, but rather making new works or finding new solutions of high quality.

▶ **2. What makes some people more creative than others?** Creative people may make loose associations, engage in an interplay between divergent and convergent thinking, are flexible, keep options open, don't make snap decisions about the likely result of an effort, and have the ability to reorganize information. At least some forms of creativity depend on spe-

cific knowledge and skills, but there may also be a general creative ability. Although creative people are typically highly motivated, driven to create, their creativity is not a by-product of mental instability.

▶ **3. Is there any way to enhance creativity?** Various techniques have been developed to enhance creativity, ranging from methods for mentally rearranging properties to brainstorming. However, groups generally do not produce as creative solutions as those produced by individuals working alone. Defining the problem in detail and working within a clear framework for solving a problem can, at least sometimes, enhance creativity.

A DEEPER LEVEL
Recap and Thought Questions

▶ Is There More Than One Way to Be Smart?

The most common measure of intelligence is the score on an intelligence test, IQ. This measure is a composite of many different underlying abilities, and the same IQ score can arise from different mixtures of relative strengths and weaknesses. Today, scores are based on norms, which are updated periodically so that the mean score on the WAIS and WISC is always 100 and a standard deviation is 15. Scores on IQ tests are positively correlated with achievement in school and on the job, at least during the initial phases of performance; they are also correlated with many aspects of success in life, such as staying out of prison or having an enduring marriage.

There are many forms of intelligence; you can be smart in some ways, not so smart in others.

Is Janet smart? This question has built into it an unwarranted assumption; namely, that anyone could be described simply as "smart" in general. Janet's English teacher arranged for her anxious student poet to be tested; it turns out that Janet is average at most things, not so good on timed tasks, and above average at language-related skills, provided that she has enough time. Thus, Janet is neither "smart" nor "stupid." Like the rest of us, she has an intelligence profile that includes areas of relative strength and weakness.

Think It Through. For what purposes does it make sense to have only a single overall IQ score? For what purposes might it be better to have separate scores for the subtests? Can you think of ways in which making

all high school students take an IQ test would be potentially harmful? helpful?

If you were designing the ideal school, how would you organize it so that different types of intelligence were properly nurtured? Can you think of ways of disguising tests to minimize test-taker anxiety and to eliminate stereotype threat?

▶ What Makes Us Smart: Nature and Nurture

How can we explain differences in intelligence among individuals? One possible factor is that key parts of people's brains vary in size or efficiency. The additional neurons in a larger brain area could allow it to process more complex information, and to do so faster. Crucially for some forms of intelligence, parts of the frontal lobes involved in working memory may allow a person to hold more information "on-line" simultaneously. The variations probably reflect an intimate dance between genes and the environment. Genes set the reaction range, the extreme upper and lower limits, of different aspects of an individual's intelligence; the environment positions an individual within this range. Although about 50% of the variability in scores on IQ tests can be explained in terms of inheritance, this number is an average and does not apply to individuals.

Group differences in IQ have been well documented, but their interpretation is not clear. Some group differences in some abilities, such as sex differences in spatial abilities, may reflect biological differences, for example, in hormone levels. However, other group differences, in IQ, for example, may arise in part from the ways in which the environment affects individuals, and the ways individuals' characteristics, which create their microenvironments, influence the reactions of others to them. Environmental effects can also occur at the time an IQ test is administered; when this happens, test scores are not valid indicators of ability. Intensive early training can raise IQ, which is as we would expect because many genes can be turned on and off by environmental events. However, training intelligence generally does not raise IQ very much. IQs in general have been rising with the passage of time, perhaps because the environment has become more complex and our brains have risen to the challenge.

Are Janet's intellectual weaknesses genetic? All we have to go on is Janet's present intelligence profile. Thus, it is impossible to know what her reaction range is, or was; all we know is where her environment has set her within that range. Her present levels of intelligence arose from a combination of the reaction ranges established by her genes and the way her genes and environment interacted.

Think It Through. Say that you could measure someone's reaction ranges for given types of intelligence (some abilities for a given person could have larger reaction ranges than others). What could you do with this information?

Do you think tests should be designed so that they do not distinguish between men and women or between other groups? What are the pros and cons of such an approach?

If someone came to you feeling intellectually doomed because he thought his parents were stupid, what would you say? What concrete advice could you offer for raising intelligence?

What implications, if any, would group differences in IQ have for the way schools should be organized? How would you explain the fact that group differences in IQ are actually shrinking with time?

▶ Rare Intelligence

Retardation is traditionally defined on the basis of overall IQ score and significant difficulty with everyday tasks, both conditions existing since childhood. By this definition, someone who is retarded cannot be gifted; giftedness is defined by a very high IQ score. Nevertheless, even people who perform much worse than the average in many tasks can have "islands of excellence" and perform superbly in one or two areas. Mental retardation can arise for many reasons, some genetic and some environmental. Not all the genetic reasons reflect inherited defects, but rather some reflect accidents during conception or environmental damage to genes.

Today's definitions of both retardation and genius are based in large part on IQ scores. Most children who are identified as unusually intelligent do not go on to have remarkable careers as adults, and many distinguished adults were not exceptional as children. The environment may have a major effect in shaping motivation, which can overshadow differences in the kinds of reasoning abilities assessed by IQ tests.

Is it possible that Janet is retarded? Her isolated exceptional ability to write poetry might tempt you to consider this possibility, but Janet clearly is not retarded; if she were, she could not function as well as she does in normal classrooms without intensive additional help. Moreover, she has no difficulties with the normal activities of everyday life.

Think It Through. The eugenics movement seeks to improve the human species by encouraging those with extremely low IQs not to have children. What do you think about this idea? What counts as "smart" depends on the problems that need to be solved. Can you think of ways in which the problems of everyday life have changed since prehistoric times, since the Middle Ages, since the 19th century, or even since the 1920s? How has this affected what counts as "being smart"? What kinds of abilities do you think "being smart" will require in the future?

Do you think it is useful to define people as mentally retarded or gifted? Why or why not?

▶ Creative Forces

Creativity leads to the production of original works or to innovative effective solutions to problems. True creativity involves producing something of value, not just something novel. It is not always clear when a "new" product or solution is different enough from old ones to be considered creative. The usual method of resolving this issue is to have impartial judges decide whether a product is creative. In addition, various tests of aspects of creative thinking (such as divergent thought) have been devised, and creativity can be assessed in the laboratory by observing whether people generate novel products or solutions.

Creative people tend to make loose associations, engage in divergent thinking, keep options open, avoid snap decisions, and see problems from many points of view. They are flexible and able to reorganize information well. However, creative people are not any more likely than anyone else to be mentally ill or unstable. Many techniques have been developed to enhance creativity, such as thinking of ways to vary attributes of an object to or combine them in new ways. Sometimes brainstorming is used, but in general individuals are more creative than groups. At least sometimes, making sure that the problem is clearly specified and working within a well-structured framework can enhance creativity.

Can Janet's creative writing be improved? Creativity thrives when a task is appropriately structured. If Janet is taught conventions of poetry, she will be free to work within them or violate them, as she sees fit. By mastering the structures, she will have more tools at her disposal as well as better-defined "problems" to solve. In addition, she might profit from learning about attributes and practices of creative people, such as the use of imagery in mental play and the value of not making snap decisions. Finally, creativity has a very low heritability and is strongly influenced by shared environment. Thus, her mother and teachers can have an effect on this ability.

Think It Through. Does it make sense to insist that true creativity results in a valued product or an effective solution to a problem? Why not just treat creativity quantitatively, measuring it purely in terms of the number of new products or solutions?

Is creativity always desirable? What would the world be like if everyone were supercreative, always trying to change things? In what circumstances might creativity be more of a drawback than a benefit?

9 EMOTION AND MOTIVATION

Feeling and Striving

John had been looking forward all day to his evening's date. Dinner with his girlfriend, Barbara, would mark the first anniversary of their meeting. But he had become absorbed working on his computer. With a start he noticed the time and realized that he might be late. Agitated at the thought of beginning a romantic evening on the wrong foot, he dashed out of the building and rushed down the street. He decided to take a shortcut down an alley. In the last of the daylight, the narrow alley was in deep shadow, but he could see the other end and felt sure he could get through quickly. But there was so little light between the old warehouses that he had to look carefully to avoid bumping into trash cans and dumpsters. As he hurried along, he thought he heard a noise behind him, and he became edgy. He walked faster. The noise seemed to be coming closer. He walked even faster. He tried to convince himself that what he heard was only a cat, but in his heart he knew better.

Suddenly he felt a strong hand grab his shoulder and then an arm snake around his neck, while something sharp dug into his ribs. His entire body froze; he felt literally paralyzed by fear. He handed over his wallet as he was told, although his heart was pounding so hard that he could barely hear the mugger's demand. Without another word, the mugger ran away, leaving John shaken but not really hurt. John ran ahead and gasped with relief when he emerged into the main street.

John hurried on to the restaurant, now far more interested in the comfort of talking to Barbara than in his romantic fantasies. Although he had been hungry when he left work, he was no longer thinking about food. He just wanted to be away from that alley, safe in his girlfriend's company.

In that harrowing experience John was driven by emotion and motivation. What these two forces have in common is their power to "move" us. (The root of both these English words comes from the Latin *movere*, "to move.") Our motivations and emotions are intimately interwoven: We are often motivated to do something because we are feeling an emotion, as happens when love leads us to hug someone; or we are motivated because we look forward to changing our emotions, as happens when we work on a project in the expectation of replacing guilt with pride. Our emotions and motivations are not always obvious; they may confuse us, or compel us to do things that surprise us. In this chapter we consider first the nature of emotion and how it affects our behavior. This leads us to consider motivation—what makes us act. Finally, we focus on two of the most important motivations: hunger and sex.

EMOTION: I FEEL, THEREFORE I AM

John felt an odd mixture of emotions as he continued to the restaurant after his encounter with the mugger. He had no thought of what might happen later in the evening; his romantic after-dinner plans were no longer on his mind. Instead, he was trembling with fear. Now he felt nervous when he passed an alley, even though the mugger who had assaulted him was surely far away. Also, he was surprised at the strength of his feelings both when he was grabbed by the mugger and after the terrifying episode was over. When he saw Barbara, he was overwhelmed with intense feelings of warmth and relief.

An **emotion** is a positive or negative reaction to a perceived or remembered object, event, or circumstance; emotions are accompanied by subjective feelings (Damasio, 1999). Emotions not only help guide us to approach some things and withdraw from others, but they also provide visible cues that help other people know key aspects of our thoughts and desires.

▶ 1. What are the different emotions?

▶ 2. What causes emotion?

▶ 3. How does culture affect our emotional lives?

Types of Emotion: What Can You Feel?

Think of the emotions you have experienced in your life. Fear? Guilt? Guilt tinged with fear? Love? Love tinged with joy? The range of human emotions is huge. In the realm of emotion the brain apparently uses the trick of producing many gradations and types of experienced reactions by combining sets of simple signals. Just as all colors can be produced by mixtures of three primary colors, researchers have argued that all emotions, even the most complex, arise from combinations of a simple set we all possess, which, like primary colors on an artist's palette, lie ready for us to blend, experience, and present to the world.

BASIC EMOTIONS. Charles Darwin (1872), for one, believed that many emotional behaviors—the outward acts that arise from our emotions—are inborn. He noticed that people of many races and cultures appear to have very similar facial expressions to signal similar emotional states. Moreover, blind people show those same expressions, even if they have never had the chance to observe the way others look

Emotion: A positive or negative reaction to a perceived or remembered object, event, or circumstance, accompanied by a subjective feeling.

when they have particular emotional reactions. Are we all born with a built-in set of emotions? If so, these emotions would be an essential part of what we call "human nature," constituting a defining characteristic of what it means to be human in every time and culture.

Ekman and Friesen (1971) described the results of experiments that were designed to investigate this possibility (see Figure 9.1). They wanted to know whether people

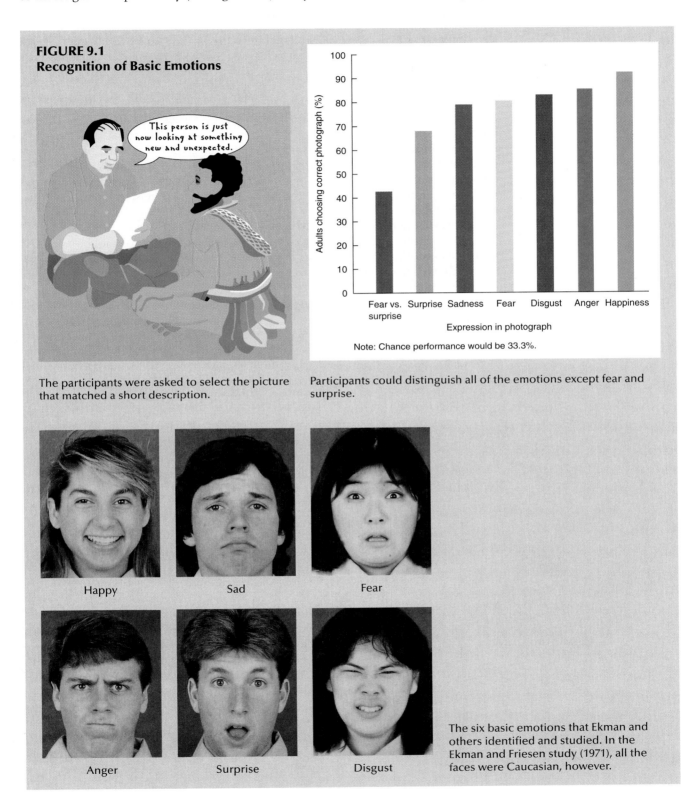

FIGURE 9.1
Recognition of Basic Emotions

This person is just now looking at something new and unexpected.

Note: Chance performance would be 33.3%.

The participants were asked to select the picture that matched a short description.

Participants could distinguish all of the emotions except fear and surprise.

Happy

Sad

Fear

Anger

Surprise

Disgust

The six basic emotions that Ekman and others identified and studied. In the Ekman and Friesen study (1971), all the faces were Caucasian, however.

Basic emotion: An innate emotion that is shared by all humans, such as surprise, happiness, anger, fear, disgust, and sadness.

who had never seen Caucasian faces could nevertheless identify the emotions underlying their facial expressions. They visited a New Guinea tribe, the Fore, who had rarely if ever seen white people in person, in movies, or on television. Nonetheless, the Fore were able to identify expressions of happiness, anger, sadness, disgust, fear, and surprise. The one difficulty they had was in distinguishing the expression of fear from that of surprise, probably because the two are very similar emotions. Also, it is possible that in Fore culture the two often go together: Most surprises in the jungle, such as the unexpected wild boar, are life-threatening, fear-inducing ones. In an interesting twist on their original study, Ekman and Friesen also videotaped the faces of members of the Fore as they displayed these same six emotions and showed the tapes to American college students. The students, too, could identify which emotions were being displayed, even though they had never seen before people like the ones displaying them.

Ekman (1984) concludes that surprise, happiness, anger, fear, disgust, and sadness are **basic emotions,** emotions that are innate and shared by all humans. Other theorists have proposed slightly different lists of basic emotions. Tomkins (1962) proposes surprise, interest, joy, rage, fear, disgust, shame, and anguish, for example. Some of the apparent disagreements may just be simply a matter of word choice; *joy* and *happiness*, for example, probably label the same emotion (LeDoux, 1996). Although the precise number of basic emotions is debated (LeDoux, 1996), there is widespread agreement that humans do have a set of built-in emotions that express the most basic types of reactions. Evidence about the way the brain gives rise to emotion also supports the existence of distinct basic emotions; for example, damage to the brain can selectively disrupt the ability to detect fear and sadness without disrupting the ability to discern other emotions (Adolphs et al., 1996).

But even when there is agreement that a particular emotion is "basic," that does not mean it is "simple." Basic emotions may be complex. For example, Rozin and colleagues (1994) distinguish among three types of disgust, each of which is signaled by a different facial expression. A nose-wrinkling expression of disgust is associated with bad smells (and, sometimes, bad tastes); an open mouth with the tongue hanging down is associated with foods perceived as disgusting (the "yech" reaction); and a raised upper lip accompanies feelings of disgust such as those associated with death and filth.

FIGURE 9.2
Plutchik's "Emotional Palette"

Plutchik proposed a set of emotions that can be combined to form other emotions, much as primary colors can be mixed to create other colors.

COMBINATIONS OF EMOTIONS. Not only do we experience shades of some emotions, but we also can experience many more emotions than those on anybody's list of "basics." How do feelings such as guilt, jealousy, and love arise? Plutchik and his collaborators (Plutchik & Kellerman, 1980) proposed that basic emotions combine to produce more complex and subtle ones. The key to Plutchik's theory is that each basic emotion is independent of the others. For example, you can feel "joy" whether or not you feel "acceptance" (which he includes as a basic emotion), and vice versa. According to Plutchik, the closer together two basic emotions are on the circle illustrated in Figure 9.2, the more easily they can be combined. Just as blue and yellow paint can be mixed to produce green, joy and acceptance can be mixed to produce love. In contrast, if two distant emotions mix, you will feel conflict: The mixture of joy and fear produces guilt, an unsettling emotion indeed. Whenever something provokes such positive and negative emotions at the same time, you are bound to feel torn. Further, each emotion can have a different intensity, which can affect the mixture in much the same way that mixing paints of different brightnesses affects the end result. If you feel really joyful but only a little fearful, the emotion you experience is different from what you feel if the proportions are reversed or if both emotions are of comparable intensity.

SEPARATE BUT EQUAL EMOTIONS. Have you ever watched a movie that was a certified four-star tear-jerker and found yourself racked with sobs *and* rolling with laughter? There is good evidence that positive and negative emotions are not really opposite sides of the same coin. If they were, how could we have complex emotions that arise from combinations of positive and negative basic emotions, as Plutchik claims? Rather, positive and negative emotions can occur separately, in any combination (Bradburn, 1969; Cacioppo et al., 1997; Diener & Emmons, 1984; Goldstein & Strube, 1994). For example, Cacioppo and his colleagues (1997) asked students to rate how positively they felt about their roommates on one scale, and how negatively they felt about their roommates on another scale. The researchers found that the degree of negative feelings students had toward their roommates was not related to the degree of positive feelings they had toward them. Moreover, the amount of time the roommates spent together was correlated with the amount of positive feeling—more time was associated with more positive feeling—but time together was not related to negative feelings. The two types of feelings clearly governed different types of behavior and were not linked to each other. In short, positive and negative emotions can coexist, and we are not necessarily limited to the experience of only one or the other at any given time.

The notion that positive and negative emotions are independent is also supported by what happens in the brain when people experience emotions. Davidson and his colleagues have provided several types of evidence that there are separate systems in the brain for two general types of human emotions: *approach* emotions (such as love and happiness) and *withdrawal* emotions (such as fear and disgust; Davidson, 1992a, 1992b, 1993, 1998; see also Lang, 1995; Solomon & Corbit, 1974a). In general, approach emotions are positive, and withdrawal emotions are negative. EEG recordings show that the left frontal lobe tends to be more active when people have approach emotions, whereas the right frontal lobe tends to be active when people have withdrawal emotions. Moreover, people who normally have more activation in the left frontal lobe tend to have a rosier outlook on life than people who have more activation in the right frontal lobe. And positron emission tomography (PET) scanning has shown that clinically depressed patients have relatively diminished metabolic activity in the left frontal lobe (Davidson, 1993, 1994a, 1998; Davidson et al., 1999).

What Causes Emotions?

Distinguishing among and characterizing different emotions is interesting, but it doesn't tell us what emotion is for, or why particular emotions arise as they do, any more than a theory of how color arises can explain how Leonardo painted the *Mona Lisa*. Why did John feel fear *after* the mugger had left? What possible good would that do him? The three major theories of emotion, and the ideas arising from them, provide the impetus for much of the research into these questions.

THEORIES OF EMOTION: BRAIN, BODY, AND WORLD. It seems both obvious and logical that emotion would work like this: You are in a particular situation; that situation induces a specific emotion; that emotion leads you to behave in a certain way. John is mugged, becomes afraid, and runs. Over 100 years ago, William James (1884) argued that this intuitively plausible relation between emotion and behavior is exactly backward. James believed that you feel emotions *after* your body reacts (see Figure 9.3 on page 316). For example, if you come across someone who begins acting like a mugger, James would say that you would first run and *then* feel afraid, not the other way round. The emotion of fear, according to James, arises because you sense your bodily state as you are fleeing. You are aroused, and you sense your heart speeding up, your breathing increasing, and the other signs of your sympathetic nervous system's becoming active (see Chapter 2). According to his theory, different emotions arise from different sets of bodily reactions, and that's why emotions feel

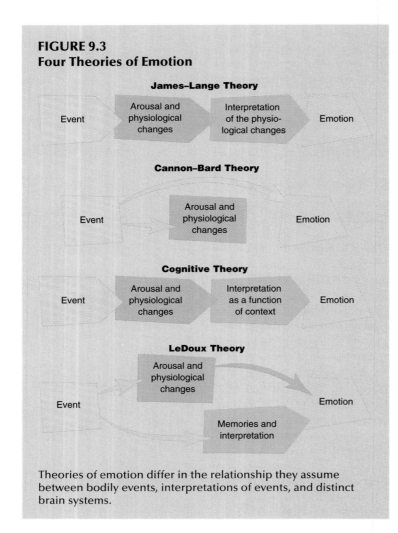

FIGURE 9.3
Four Theories of Emotion

James–Lange Theory

Event → Arousal and physiological changes → Interpretation of the physiological changes → Emotion

Cannon–Bard Theory

Event → Arousal and physiological changes → Emotion

Cognitive Theory

Event → Arousal and physiological changes → Interpretation as a function of context → Emotion

LeDoux Theory

Event → Arousal and physiological changes → Emotion
Memories and interpretation

Theories of emotion differ in the relationship they assume between bodily events, interpretations of events, and distinct brain systems.

different. Carl Lange (1887), a Danish physiologist, independently developed a similar theory, and thus the theory has come to be called the *James–Lange theory* (Lang, 1994).

Walter Cannon (1927) claimed that the James–Lange theory focused too much on noticing bodily signals, such as heart and breathing rates. He raised a telling criticism of the James–Lange theory—that it takes many seconds for the body to become aroused and yet emotions are usually present well before this happens. Instead, he claimed, the brain itself is all that matters. You perceive the potential mugger, and the results of that perception marshal the body's resources for fleeing or fighting *at the same time* that they generate an emotion. According to the *Cannon–Bard theory* (see Figure 9.3), formulated by Cannon and Philip Bard, another physiologist, physiological arousal and the experience of emotion arise in tandem.

The third theory, *cognitive theory,* holds that an emotion arises when you interpret the situation as a whole—your bodily state in the context of everything that surrounds it. According to this theory, unlike James–Lange, you don't react to a stimulus and then feel an emotion after the reaction; and unlike Cannon–Bard, you don't have separate bodily and emotional reactions. Rather, your reactions and the general situation are all of a piece. For example, the act of running and the accompanying arousal have equal chances of accompanying the emotions of joy (as you rush to embrace someone you love), fear (as you flee a pursuing mugger), or excitement (as you join the crowd on the field to celebrate a football victory). The difference is not in the bodily state, but in how you interpret it at the time it occurs. Richard Lazarus, Stanley Schachter, and Magda Arnold were pioneers in developing this view. In general, cognitive theories of emotion rest on the idea that, as Lazarus puts it, emotion "cannot be understood solely in terms of what happens in the person or in the brain, but grows out of ongoing transactions with the environment that are evaluated" (Lazarus, 1984, p. 124). This statement of course embodies our by-now familiar approach of looking at events at the levels of brain, person, and group.

Joseph LeDoux (1996) has modified the cognitive theory in an important way. He claims that there are different brain systems for different emotions. Some of these systems operate as reflex systems do, *independent* of thought or interpretation, whereas others *depend* on thought and interpretation. Fear, for example, is experienced through the activation of the amygdala, without need for cognitive interpretation. But other emotions, such as guilt, rely on cognitive interpretation and memories of previous similar situations. Thus, the emotions we feel at any moment arise from (1) a mixture of brain and body reactions and (2) interpretations and memories pertaining to the situation.

Which theory comes closest to the mark? To find out, let's take a closer look at the nature of emotion.

PHYSIOLOGICAL PROFILES: ARE EMOTIONS JUST BODILY RESPONSES? Suppose John had been so anxious about his anniversary date that he took a powerful tranquilizer beforehand. If this drug kept his heart from pounding and otherwise prevented his sympathetic nervous system from becoming fully activated, would he still have felt fear after the mugging? Yes, he probably would have. Let's see why.

Perhaps the strongest evidence against James's idea that emotions arise when people interpret their own bodily states is the finding that even people with spinal cord injuries so severe that they receive no sensations from their bodies still report having emotions (Bermond et al., 1991). However, it is possible that these patients experience emotions differently than do people with intact spinal cords. For example, one such patient described in this way what it felt like when a lit cigarette fell onto his bed: "I could have burned up right there, but the funny thing is, I didn't get all shook up about it. I just didn't feel afraid at all, like you would suppose." Speaking about another common emotion, he said, "Sometimes I act angry when I see some injustice. I yell and cuss and raise hell, because if you don't do it sometimes, I've learned people will take advantage of you, but it doesn't have the heat to it that it used to. It's a mental kind of anger" (Hohman, 1966, pp. 150–151). These quotations suggest that this man's emotions were largely rational evaluations, not reactions to events that were accompanied by feelings.

The James–Lange theory implies that we feel different emotions because each emotion corresponds to a different physiological state. John's heart was pounding and his palms began to sweat when he felt a sharp object jabbing into his ribs, and these bodily events may have played a key role in the emotions he felt. The lag in time for these bodily events to arise after the mugging could explain why John continued to feel fear after he had fled the alley. In contrast, the Cannon–Bard theory implies that our bodies are aroused similarly in different arousing situations. According to this view, arousal is arousal; it occurs not only if you are mugged but also if you win the lottery. But physiological evidence leads us to question the Cannon–Bard theory. Many emotions are accompanied by *distinct patterns* of heart rate, temperature, sweat, and other reactions. For example, when you feel anger, your heart rate increases and so does the temperature of your skin; and when you feel fear, your heart rate increases but your skin temperature actually decreases (Levenson et al., 1990). Even if some of these distinct bodily responses arise because of the different levels of effort required to respond to various emotion-causing situations (Boiten, 1998), distinguishing bodily events do accompany at least some different emotions.

It is possible that emotion also corresponds to another bodily state, one that is not defined in terms of autonomic reactions. There are 44 separate muscles in your face, only 4 of which are used for chewing—the rest are involved in forming facial expressions (Rinn, 1984). When you move these muscles, your brain receives feedback from them. According to the **facial feedback hypothesis,** you feel emotions in part because of the way your muscles are positioned in your face (Izard, 1971; Tomkins, 1962).

There is evidence that "putting on a happy face" is not just a good lyric; it can actually make you feel happier. Following up on other studies (Duclos et al., 1989; Laird, 1974, 1984), Ekman and colleagues (Ekman, 1992; Ekman et al., 1990) tested this idea by leading participants to shift parts of their faces until they held specific expressions—for example, lifting the corners of the mouth until a smile and other signs of happiness were formed. The participants maintained these configurations while they rated their mood. If their faces were posed in a positive expression, they tended to rate their mood more positively than if their faces were posed in a negative expression.

Strack and colleagues (1988) developed an interesting way to improve mood: Stick a pencil sideways (not point first) in your mouth, so that as you bite down on it, the corners of your lips turn up. Simply making this motion will actually make you feel happier. For more dramatic results, try to make a big smile, raising your cheeks.

However, putting on a happy face does not lead our brains to be in exactly the same state as when we are genuinely happy (Ekman & Davidson, 1993). Thus, although facial feedback may affect emotions, smiles, frowns, and glowers are not the only causes of our emotional experiences.

Facial feedback hypothesis:
The idea that emotions arise partly as a result of the position of facial muscles.

FIGURE 9.4
The Schacter–Singer Experiment

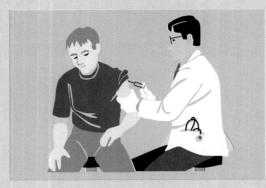

Participants received an epinephrine injection.

Stooges acted very differently while the participants waited.

And the participants reacted very differently to the drug, depending on what the stooge was doing.

COGNITIVE INTERPRETATION. Bodily factors are not enough to explain the range of feelings we have. What's missing? Our own interpretation of objects and events, and the context in which they occur, both of which affect our feelings.

The classic experiment in this area was reported by Stanley Schacter and Jerome Singer in 1962; it is illustrated in Figure 9.4. The participants, who believed that they would be taking part in a test of vision, received an injection of what they were told was a vitamin supplement. The injection was really a shot of epinephrine, which causes general arousal. Each participant then waited in a room before beginning the "vision test." Also waiting in the room was a "stooge"—that is, someone posing as a participant who in fact cooperates with the investigators in establishing the conditions of the experiment. The experiment consisted of having the stooge act in different ways during the "waiting period" and recording the effects of his behavior on the participant. In one condition, the stooge was manic, playing with a hula hoop, tossing paper airplanes, and generally acting silly. In another condition, the stooge was sullen and irritable; he tried to make the participant angry, and eventually stormed out of the room. The participants who had waited with the manic stooge reported that they felt happy, whereas the participants who had waited with the angry stooge reported that they felt angry.

Although the participants had the same physiological arousal induced by the drug, they experienced this arousal very differently depending on the context in which it occurred; and this difference apparently led them to attribute different causes to the arousal. In contrast, when participants were told in advance about the drug and its effects, they did *not* feel differently in the different contexts; it was only when they interpreted the arousal as arising from the context that their feelings differed. In addition, participants in a control group, who did not receive an injection, experienced no effects of context. It is worth noting that this study took place more than 35 years ago; today, giving participants drugs without their knowledge is considered unethical and would not be done.

If you interpret signs of bodily arousal incorrectly, making a cognitive error called the **misattribution of arousal,** you may experience emotions that ordinarily would not arise in that situation. For example, in one study male participants were given false feedback about their own internal responses (Valins, 1966). They had been asked, while looking at slides of partially nude women, to listen to what they were told was their own heartbeat. The heartbeats they heard were in fact not their own; they were sometimes faster and sometimes slower than their actual heart rates. When the participants later were asked to rate the attractiveness of each woman, their ratings were based not just on what they saw but also on what they heard: If they had associated a rapid heartbeat with a picture, they rated the woman as more attractive. It is clear that our interpretation of bodily feedback depends on the situation—and how we interpret the situation depends at least in part on bodily feedback (Palace, 1999). Emotion is a complex mixture that arises from the "whispers and shouts" of the body as filtered through the expectations and interpretations of the mind.

The fact that cognitive interpretations affect how we feel does not imply that the interpretations must be conscious. You have seen that unconscious associations between stimuli and their value can lead to hunches, which can in turn guide reasoning (Chapter 7).

FEAR: THE AMYGDALA AND YOU. Because it is one of the emotions scientists understand best, fear has become a testing ground for theories of emotion. Fear causes changes in the brain, in the autonomic nervous system, in hormones, and in behavior. When people are afraid, they tend to freeze (to be "paralyzed by fear"), and they have an increased tendency to be startled, a tendency called *fear-potentiated startle* (Davis, 1992; Lang, 1995; Vrana et al., 1988). As John walked down the alley, the noises he heard made him afraid, which made him even more susceptible to being startled, so that he was particularly thrown off balance when the mugger grabbed him.

Researchers have discovered four important facts about fear from studying the brain systems that produce it. First, after you have learned to fear an object, fear can well up later as a kind of "emotional reflex," with no thought or interpretation at all (LeDoux, 1996). The amygdala, a small structure located at the front inside part of the temporal lobes (see Chapter 2), plays a crucial role in producing the reactions you have when you are afraid. It sends signals to other brain areas, such as the hypothalamus, that cause your heart to speed up, your muscles to freeze (as John did when he was grabbed), and all the other autonomic reactions associated with fear. In fact, conscious awareness is not needed for a stimulus to trigger the amygdala into producing a fear response. For example, in an fMRI brain-scanning study, the amygdala responded when participants were briefly shown faces with fearful expressions—so briefly that they were not even aware of having seen the expressions (Whalen et al., 1998). Moreover, in this study the amygdala actually decreased activation when happy faces were presented, even when the participants were not aware of the expressions.

Second, there is evidence that once you learn to associate fear with an object or situation, you will always do so. To this day, whenever John sees that alley, his palms sweat and his heart beats a little faster. Even after he thought he was finally over the experience, he found himself avoiding that block. Fear is a classically conditioned response, and even after extinction, the sets of neurons that were created by an association still fire together (see Chapter 5). This is one reason why it is so easy to reinstate conditioned fear. Even though you are not aware of the association, it is never fully lost (LeDoux, 1996).

Third, in spite of its reflexive nature, fear interacts with mental processes. For example, if you merely visualize yourself in a scary situation, you become susceptible to being startled (Cook et al., 1991; Lang et al., 1990; Vrana & Lang, 1990). The parts of the brain involved in cognition play a key role in "setting you up" to be easily startled.

Finally, the amygdala plays a role in producing the emotional "feel" of fear. People with damaged amygdalas sound a lot like the patient described earlier, who knew he should be afraid when his lighted cigarette fell, and angry at injustice, but really couldn't get riled up about anything. In addition, people with damage to the amygdala (but with little other brain impairment) cannot recognize fear or anger in the tone of other people's voices (Scott et al., 1997); the emotional response produced by the amygdala apparently plays a role in the recognition of other people's emotions (Adolphs et al., 1996; Calder et al., 1996; Hamann et al., 1996; Young et al., 1996).

What does all this tell us about emotion in general? First, there are distinct events that underlie fear, a finding that is consistent with the James–Lange theory. However, these states are not just bodily reactions; they also involve the brain. Second, the events underlying fear appear to produce both the experience and the bodily reaction at the same time, which fits the Cannon–Bard theory. However, the experience and reaction are not entirely separate; rather, your interpretation of the event can affect both. Third, although interpretation is not always necessary, it is clear that mental events do interact with emotion. Thus, aspects of cognitive theory are supported.

In short, the three oldest theories capture important aspects of fear; all contain a grain of truth. However, the sum total of the findings is most consistent with

LeDoux's revision of cognitive theory, which includes roles for both brain-based, re-flexive reactions and for the interpretation of bodily states in particular contexts.

HAPPINESS: MORE THAN A FEELING. Lest you think that psychologists have a morbid fascination with the dark side, we must note that much has also been learned about happiness (Diener, 2000; Myers, 2000; Peterson, 2000; Ryan & Deci, 2000). What kinds of events make us happy? Self-reported measures of happiness depend on many variables, which affect events at the different levels of analysis. Many of these factors reflect events at the level of the group. Not surprisingly, a survey of happiness in 40 countries found that money *can* buy happiness, at least to some extent: People tend to be happier when they are living in better economic conditions (Schyns, 1998). In addition, happiness was correlated with the number of opportunities for cultural enrichment only in rich countries, which may suggest that basic needs (such as ade-quate shelter and nutrition) take precedence and, until they are satisfied, other events or opportunities cannot substitute for them in producing happiness. This notion might explain the results of surveys, taken over the period 1972–1993, showing that in the United States whites tend to be happier than blacks (Aldous & Ganey, 1999). How-ever, other factors must be at work; although white women generally make less money than white men, they were generally happier than white men. One possible additional contributor is social support, the degree to which you feel that other people are willing and able to listen and help (Myers, 2000). In China, the strongest predictor of happi-ness was a measure of social support (Lu, 1999; Lu et al., 1997).

But we must be cautious about generalizing from one culture to another. When asked about the sources of happiness, Chinese people focused on interpersonal inter-actions and external evaluation, whereas Westerners focused on the achievement of personal goals and internal evaluation (Lu & Shih, 1997a). Culture also mitigates the effects of other variables. For example, many overweight people are troubled by their weight, but this concern is particularly acute for those who live in a culture in which thinness is the norm. In addition, ethnic group plays a role. Pinhey and colleagues (1997) found that Asians and Filipinos in Guam who were overweight reported being less happy than did Chamorros and Micronesians, who generally have larger average body mass. These results suggest that people gauge themselves relative to a reference group, and the same personal characteristics can be viewed as acceptable or unaccept-able, depending on the results of comparison with that group.

Researchers have also found that in 16 of 17 countries they examined (the excep-tion was Northern Ireland), marriage is linked to greater happiness than is either being single or living with someone to whom you aren't married. This increase in hap-piness was comparable for both men and women (Ross, 1995; Stack & Eshleman, 1998; Weerasinghe & Tepperman, 1994). Apparently, most of the effects of marriage on happiness are indirect: increasing satisfaction with household finances and improv-ing perceived health. However, this is not all there is to it; the simple fact of being married, all by itself, contributed to happiness.

It is also clear that events at the level of the person affect happiness. For example, at least in Western countries, assertive people tend to be happier than nonassertive people (Argyle & Lu, 1990). At the level of the brain, at least some of the factors that affect whether you are happy are biological. We have already noted that people with more activation in the left frontal lobe (not only during a particular task, but in gen-eral) tend to be happier than people with more activation in the right frontal lobe (Davidson, 1992a, 1992b, 1993, 1994a, 1998). Other specific brain areas, including the ventral medial frontal cortex, were activated when participants in a study watched or recalled films that induced happiness, but not other emotions (Lane et al., 1997a).

Expressing Emotions: Letting It All Hang Out?

Emotions occur in the social context of family, friends, and culture. As in John's story, many of our emotions arise from social interactions, both positive (the comforting dinner with Barbara) and negative (his fear during and in the wake of the mugging). Not only do social stimuli trigger emotions, but emotions in turn serve social roles; these roles range from communicating to providing connections among people.

CULTURE AND EMOTIONAL EXPRESSION: RULES OF THE MODE.

In many ways emotional experience is a private affair, inaccessible to others. But emotional expression is crucial for our daily interactions with other people. According to Ekman (1980), each of us learns a set of **display rules** for our culture that indicate when, to whom, and how strongly certain emotions can be shown. For example, he notes that in the United States people will find it suspicious if at a man's funeral his secretary seems more upset than his wife. In the display rules of U.S. culture, the closer the relation to the deceased, the more emotion may be displayed. Display rules are partly a function of habit (individuals do differ in their styles), but they largely reflect "the way things are done" in a particular region, class, or ethnic culture.

Ekman (1984) describes a fascinating test of his theory that all people share the same basic emotions but that emotional expression may be different because of different display rules. He challenged head on the stereotype that Asians are less emotional than Westerners. Americans in Berkeley and Japanese in Tokyo were shown the same films, one positive (scenery) and one negative (a surgical procedure). Participants viewed the films either alone or in the company of a white-coated scientist. Both national groups showed the same range of emotional expression when they viewed the films in individual screenings, one person at a time, but the Japanese participants were notably more restrained when they were in company. Ekman analyzed slow-motion videotapes of the participants as they watched. The tapes revealed that a Japanese participant watching alone reacted in the same way as the Americans. But a Japanese watching in company would begin showing that reaction, then quickly squelch it. According to Ekman, the initial Japanese reaction reflected the basic, innate emotions; then display rules came to the fore, and the participants regulated their show of emotions accordingly.

Culture affects not only how willing you are to express emotion in specific situations, but also how sensitive you are to the emotional expressions of others (Stephan et al., 1996). It is almost as if when a culture makes emotions harder to detect, its members develop better abilities to detect them. For example, although China has more restrained display rules than Australia, Chinese children can detect basic emotions more accurately than Australian children (Markham & Wang, 1996).

BODY LANGUAGE: BROADCASTING FEELINGS.

Nonverbal communication isn't really language (see Chapter 7), but it is a form of communication that is particularly effective at conveying emotion. We are remarkably good at reading cues about emotion, acquiring information from even minimal cues. Dittrich and colleagues (1996) attached 13 small lights to the bodies of each of two professional dancers and had them perform dances that conveyed fear, anger, grief, joy, surprise, and disgust. Undergraduate students who later watched videotapes of the dances were able to recognize the intended emotions, even in the dark when only the lights were visible. Similarly, Bassili (1978) showed that people can recognize facial expressions of emotion in the dark from only the movement of lights attached to faces; the specific locations of the lights did not seem to matter.

Animals also express emotion with body language. If you see a gorilla sticking out its tongue, avoid getting too close—this signal means the animal is angry.

Men and women differ in their characteristic nonverbal behavior. Hall (1978) performed a meta-analysis of studies of nonverbal behavior and found that men tend to be more restless (for instance, they had more frequent leg movements) and expansive (such as by leaving their legs open) than women, but women tend to be more expressive, as evidenced by their gestures (Gallaher, 1992). These conclusions are consistent with the finding that women are more expressive than men when watching emotional films (Kring & Gordon, 1998). There are also gender differences in the ability to decode nonverbal cues. Apparently women can register nonverbal signs of happiness better than men, but men can register unspoken signs of anger better than women (Coats & Feldman, 1996).

As these differences may suggest, at least some of our nonverbal behaviors may result from innate factors. Although there has yet to be a good rigorous study of this, one anecdote is highly suggestive. In reviewing 30 studies of identical twins who were separated and raised apart, Faber (1981) wrote: "As with voice, the way the twins held themselves, walked, turned their heads, or flicked their wrists was more alike than any quantifiable trait the observers were able to measure. . . . If one twin had a limp, moist handshake, so did the other. If one had a spirited prance, so did the partner" (pp. 86–87). However, the ability to *read* nonverbal communications is at least partly determined by experience. For example, children who watch more television tend to be better at judging emotional expressions (Feldman et al., 1996).

Body language plays an important role in conveying sexual interest. For example, studies have shown that men and women hold their bodies differently with someone of the opposite sex if they are interested in that person than if they are not interested. However, interest is not conveyed in exactly the same way by men and women. Grammer (1990) found that interested men had "open postures" (with the legs relaxed and open) and watched the women, whereas interested women avoided eye contact, presented their body rotated slightly to the side (so that their breasts were seen in profile), and uncrossed their arms and legs. For both males and females, a closed posture conveyed lack of interest.

Body language also plays a role in unwanted sexual encounters. This is important for students to recognize because college women experience sexual victimization three to four times more frequently than women in general (Cummings, 1992; Hanson & Gidycz, 1993). Researchers asked observers to view videotapes of ordinary people walking down the street and to rate how vulnerable they were to physical assault (Grayson & Stein, 1981). Those viewed as victims tended to move awkwardly and disjointedly, whereas "nonvictims" moved smoothly, in a coordinated, confident way. Murzynski and Degelman (1996) conducted an experiment to discover exactly which aspects of body language lead women to be perceived as vulnerable to sexual assault. They defined two victim profiles. In one, potential victims tend to walk with a long, exaggerated stride and lift their feet up rather than smoothly swinging them; in the other, they may walk with short, mincing steps. Both police officers and college students rated the women who walked in the manner of the victim profiles as more likely to be sexually assaulted than the women who walked in the style of the nonvictim profile.

LOOKING AT LEVELS

Lie Detection

John reported the mugging to the police but was frustrated when they failed to identify a suspect. And even if they did make an arrest, would they be able to prove anything? Lie detector tests may not be admissible evidence in court, but they are used in various investigations nonetheless. What do they really "detect"?

If different brain states and bodily states accompany different emotions, researchers have reasoned, then there might be distinct biological "footprints" of the feeling of guilt. This idea underlies a long history of attempts to detect deception objectively. One result has been machines called **polygraphs**, known misleadingly as lie detectors. These machines don't "detect lies" directly; they monitor the activity of the sympathetic and parasympathetic nervous systems—in particular, changes in skin conductance, breathing, and heart rate.

The most basic technique used with a polygraph is the *relevant/irrelevant technique* (*RIT*; Larson, 1932). Suppose you are trying to determine whether the suspect in a crime is telling the truth. When the RIT technique is used, the suspect is asked crime-related questions ("Did you break into Mr. Johnson's house last night?") and neutral questions ("Do you live at 43 Pleasant Street?"). The responses to the two types of questions are then compared. However, there is clearly a large difference in the emotional weight of the two types of questions. Thus, a greater physiological response to a crime-related question may reflect not guilt but simply the fact that the idea posed by the question is more arousing. To avoid this possibility, the *control question technique* (*CQT*; Reid, 1947) includes comparison questions that should have an emotional

Polygraphs are used to detect changes in autonomic nervous system activity, which may signal that the person being interviewed is lying.

weight roughly equivalent to that of the crime-related questions. For example, in addition to the two questions above, the suspect might be asked, "Did you ever do anything you were ashamed of?"

A more recent technique is the *guilty knowledge test* (*GKT*; sometimes called the "concealed information test"), developed by Lykken (1959, 1960). In contrast to the RIT and CQT, the GKT does not rely on asking direct questions about the crime. Instead, this test uses indirect questions that presumably only the guilty person would be in a position to answer correctly. In addition, the GKT relies on multiple-choice questions. So the suspect might be asked, "Was the color of the walls in Mr. Johnson's bedroom white? yellow? blue?" Someone who has never been in the room should have comparable responses to each of the choices, whereas someone who has guilty knowledge should respond selectively to the actual color. A modification of this approach is the *guilty actions test* (Bradley & Warfield, 1984; Bradley et al., 1996), which observes responses when people are given statements about actions they may have committed.

Do these techniques work? Ben-Shakhar and Furedy (1990) report that in the laboratory the CQT on average correctly classifies 80% of the guilty and 63% of the innocent (p. 44). Thus, this technique unfortunately leads too often to the classification of honest responses as lies. The GKT has a better track record; the guilty were detected 84% of the time, and the innocent 94%. However, the range of accuracy in the reviewed studies was from 64% to 100% for detecting the guilty, and 81% to 100% for detecting the innocent. More recent techniques that measure electrical activity in the brain can sometimes be as high as 95% accurate, but there is still enough variability to cast doubt on the test's ability to classify individual answers or reports from individual people as untruthful (Allen & Iacono, 1997).

Are these tests any better than simply asking observers to detect lies and taking seriously only those cases in which they are very confident? DePaulo and her collaborators (1997) reported a meta-analysis of research on the relation between an individual's confidence that he or she has spotted a lie and the level of accuracy, and found essentially no relation between the two (a correlation of essentially zero). However, more recent evidence suggests that *some* people can distinguish truth from lies extraordinarily accurately, particularly some (but not all) of those who have been trained in law enforcement or clinical psychology with an interest in deception (Ekman et al., 1999). Rarely, some people are intuitively able to pick up tell-tale cues of deception, but scientists have yet to isolate those cues.

How can we best understand lie detection? The goal of lie detection is to assess a particular social interaction in which one person is misleading another person. However, the technique depends on interactions among events at the three levels of analysis. Perhaps the greatest problem with all the traditional techniques is that they are methods of detecting guilt (the level of the person). If the person being tested lies but does not *feel* guilty, the palms won't become sweaty, heart rate won't increase, and so

Polygraph: A machine that monitors the activity of the sympathetic and parasympathetic nervous systems, particularly changes in skin conductance, breathing, and heart rate. These machines are used in attempts to detect lying.

forth; the brain will not produce the autonomic responses associated with guilt. And the interviewer will not have any basis for detecting the lie, which in turn may alter how the person is being treated during the interview (a social interaction), and that treatment in turn affects the person's reactions to the questions. Thus, in order to understand lie detection, we need to consider all three levels of analysis: The activity in the brain that produces the autonomic results; the personality differences that could lead a person to feel guilty; and the rules of the society, together with the person's understanding of them, which would lead the person to feel guilty under certain circumstances.

CONSOLIDATE!

► **1. What are the different emotions?** Ekman and his collaborators offer much evidence that six emotions are "basic"—happiness, anger, sadness, disgust, surprise, and fear—but the last two are more easily confused with each other than are any of the others. Each of these emotions can be categorized as "approach" or "withdrawal," and each can be further differentiated into subtypes (for example, Rozin and his collaborators have identified three different types of disgust). In addition, Plutchik has noted that emotions can be combined to form new emotions, much as primary colors can be combined to form new colors.

► **2. What causes emotion?** The James–Lange theory states that emotion follows bodily reactions; the Cannon–Bard theory holds that emotions and bodily reactions occur at the same time, not in the order claimed by James and Lange; cognitive theory holds that emotions arise when bodily states are interpreted in the context of the specific situation; and, most recently, LeDoux's revision of cognitive theory maintains that some emotions arise reflexively from specific brain activity whereas others rely on cognitive interpretation and memory. All the theories have captured a facet of how emotions work. As James–Lange predicts, emotions may be caused in part by differences in internal bodily state (such as heart rate and breathing rate) and in facial expression. As Cannon–Bard predicts, some emotions are reflexes that simultaneously produce both the experience and the bodily reaction. As cognitive theory predicts, how you interpret the causes of your bodily states influences which emotion you will feel. But as LeDoux predicts, some emotions (in some circumstances) rely more on cognitive interpretation than others. Environmental events also play a key role in emotion; a person's happiness, for example, depends in part on his or her economic and cultural context.

► **3. How does culture affect our emotional lives?** Culture affects the display rules we use, which determine the circumstances in which emotions are shown. Culture also shapes our emotional reactions to moral violations. In addition, culture affects how well we read body language to discern other people's emotions (but the specific strengths are different for men and women).

MOTIVATION AND REWARD: FEELING GOOD

John enjoyed his work so much that on the afternoon of his first anniversary celebration he completely forgot his plans for dinner and thereafter—until he looked at the clock. When he saw the time, all thoughts of work flew from his head and he focused entirely on getting to the restaurant. Because of the pleasures that he believed lay in store for him—and because he didn't want to risk spoiling the evening by being late—John was highly *motivated* to get to the restaurant from the moment he left work, and even more so after the mugging. We often take a particular action because we expect to feel good afterward; in this sense, emotions motivate us. To motivate is to set in motion, and in psychology the term **motivation** is used to refer to the requirements and desires that lead animals (including humans) to behave in a particular way at a particular time and place.

Motivation: The requirements and desires that lead animals (including humans) to behave in a particular way at a particular time and place.

► 1. What are the sources of motivation?

► 2. What is the difference between "needs" and "wants," and how does culture affect them?

Getting Motivated: Sources and Theories of Motivation

There is no single, widely accepted, grand theory that can explain all of human motivation. There are motives based on biological needs (such as the need to keep warm) and motives based on learning (such as the desire for money); motives rooted in the internal state of a person (such as hunger) and motives sparked by the external world (such as exploration); motives based on a current situation and motives based on an expected future situation. Psychologists have analyzed, classified, and identified human motives in numerous ways, developing a variety of theories of motivation. Let's look at the key concepts in these theories and find out what each has to offer as an explanation of human behavior.

INSTINCTS: MY GENES MADE ME DO IT. Why do birds fly south for the winter and spiders make certain kinds of webs? Instinct. For many animals, instincts provide the main motivation for behaviors. An **instinct** is an inherited tendency to produce organized and unalterable responses to particular stimuli. For several decades at the beginning of the twentieth century, some psychologists tried to explain human motivation in terms of instincts (for example, McDougall, 1908/1960); their approach is termed *instinct theory*. Much of Freud's theory, for example, hinges on ideas about how we grapple with our sexual urges, which he considered to be instinctive (these ideas are discussed in Chapter 10). But unlike many other animals, we humans are remarkably flexible in the way we can respond to any stimulus, so it is difficult to assign an important role to instincts in human motivation.

Evolutionary psychology has offered an alternative to instinct theory. Instead of proposing that a behavior itself is "hard-wired," these theorists believe that goals that motivate us (such as finding attractive mates) and general cognitive strategies for achieving goals (such as deception) are inborn (Barkow et al., 1992; Buss, 1998; Cosmides & Tooby, 1996; Pinker, 1997; Plotkin, 1997). However, evolutionary theories of motivation are notoriously difficult to test because we can never know for sure what our ancestors were like and how they evolved. Nevertheless, evolutionary thinking can be a source of inspiration and can lead to novel hypotheses that can be tested in their own right (Pinker, 1997).

DRIVES AND HOMEOSTASIS: STAYING IN BALANCE. Instinct theory and evolutionary theory focus on specifying particular innate behaviors or cognitive tendencies. In contrast, *drive theory* focuses on the mechanisms that underlie such tendencies, whether or not they are innate. A **drive** is a motivation that pushes you to reach a particular goal. Drives differ in terms of the goals to which they direct you, but all are aimed at satisfying a requirement (decreasing a tension). For example, hunger is a drive that orients you toward food; thirst is a drive that impels you toward drink; being cold is a drive that nudges you toward a source of warmth. Some drive theories link drives and reinforcement: Something is reinforcing only if it reduces tension: If you are hungry, food is reinforcing because it reduces the tension experienced when you have the hunger drive; if you are not hungry, food is not reinforcing.

What is the nature of the tension that is quelled by reinforcement? In 1920 Walter B. Cannon wrote a groundbreaking book titled *The Wisdom of the Body*, in which he pointed out that for life to be sustained, certain characteristics and substances of the body must be kept within a certain range, neither rising too high nor falling too low. These characteristics and substances include body temperature and the amounts of oxygen, minerals, water, and food taken in. Bodily processes such as digestion and

Instinct: An inherited tendency to produce organized and unalterable responses to particular stimuli.

Drive: A motivation that pushes an animal to reach toward a particular goal.

respiration work toward keeping the levels steady. The process of maintaining a steady state is called **homeostasis.** Homeostasis works not simply to keep the system in balance, but to keep it in balance in the range in which the body functions best. The usual analogy to homeostasis is a thermostat and furnace: the thermostat turns the furnace on when the temperature drops too low and turns it off when the temperature reaches the desired level. But Cannon pointed out that in living creatures, homeostasis often involves active behavior, not simply the passive registering of the state of the environment. To stay alive, you must nourish yourself by obtaining and taking in food and water, and you must maintain body temperature by finding shelter and wearing clothing. So now we can see how "tension" arises: If the homeostatic balance goes awry, tension results—and behavior is initiated to correct the imbalance.

The power of homeostasis in motivation was dramatically illustrated by the classic case of a boy, referred to as D.W., who developed a craving for salt when he was a year old (Wilkins & Richter, 1940). He loved potato chips, salted crackers, pretzels, olives, and pickles. He would also eat salt directly, upending salt shakers and pouring their contents directly into his mouth. When his parents took away his salt, he would cry and carry on until they relented. When he began to talk, one of his first words was "salt." At 3½ years old, he was hospitalized and forced to eat standard hospital fare. Deprived of his usual salt intake, D.W. died within a few days. An autopsy revealed that he died because his adrenal glands were deficient and could not produce a hormone that is essential for the body to retain salt, which is crucial to the maintenance of homeostasis. Because D.W. needed an abnormal supply, his strong drive for salt led to behavior that caused his parents to give it to him.

ARROUSAL THEORY: AVOIDING BOREDOM, AVOIDING OVERLOAD. People are also motivated to maintain another kind of balance, one that has nothing to do with physiological homeostasis: Simply put, we don't like stimuli that are either too boring or too arousing and instead seek to maintain an intermediate level of stimulation. Berlyne (1960, 1974) showed that people like random patterns, paintings, or music best when they are neither too simple nor too complex, but rather somewhere in the middle. What counts as "simple" or "complex" depends partly on the person as well as the nature of the stimulus. For example, children find patterns complex that adults find less so.

These findings conform to the *Yerkes–Dodson law* (Figure 9.5), named after the researchers who first described it. This law states that we perform best when we are at an intermediate level of arousal. If we are underaroused, we are sluggish; if we are overaroused, we can't focus and sustain attention. Intermediate levels of arousal may occur when we are challenged not too much and not too little. For example, if you have to speak before a large group, you may become tongue-tied because of overarousal; if you are rehearsing the speech alone in your room, you may be understimulated and give a lackluster presentation. Indeed, people adapt to a constant set of stimuli, become bored, and then seek additional stimulation (Helson, 1964). We are apparently drawn to moderate stimulation. As intuitive as this idea may seem, not all studies have supported it (for example, Messinger, 1998), perhaps because it is difficult to define precisely levels of stimulation and how they vary.

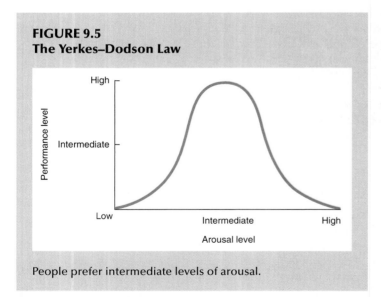

FIGURE 9.5
The Yerkes–Dodson Law

People prefer intermediate levels of arousal.

INCENTIVES AND REWARD: HAPPY EXPECTATIONS. Homeostasis is a useful concept for understanding thirst, hunger, and certain other drives (such as those for salt, oxygen, and temperature control), and arousal theory helps explain why people select certain activities and situations and reject others. However, neither principle helps to explain other motivations, such as sex (Beach, 1956). Your body doesn't actually need sex in the way you need food and oxygen; you can't die from celibacy. Moreover, sex is an example of seeking high arousal, not the intermediate levels we apparently prefer in other areas of stimulation. Like sex, much of what motivates us is best understood in terms of **incentives,** which are stimuli or events that draw us to achieve a particular goal in anticipation of a reward. Drives push, incentives pull. Sex is a good example of incentive-related motivation; so, too, is any money-making activity.

The notion that much of motivation can best be understood in terms of incentives has led theorists to think about some aspects of motivation in terms of *expectations* of reinforcement. We tend to behave in ways that experience has shown us produce a desirable outcome (see Chapter 5), either a positive consequence of the behavior (positive reinforcement) or the removal of a negative condition (negative reinforcement). If working 20 hours a week in a store has led to a regular paycheck, you will likely want to keep working (assuming that the check is large enough!). Classical conditioning may play a role in determining what is an incentive by making a previously neutral stimulus desirable (Bindra, 1968; see Chapter 5).

We can further distinguish between two types of incentives—those that are intrinsic to performing a task and those that are not. Some research has shown that rewarding children for activities they already enjoy can make them less likely to engage in the activity when they are no longer reinforced for doing so. When an activity is inherently rewarding, it is said to provide **intrinsic motivation:** The activity is desirable for its own sake. An activity that is attractive for other reasons, such as a favorable response from other people or satisfactory payment, is said to provide **extrinsic motivation.**

A classic study on the relation between intrinsic and extrinsic motivation for an activity was reported by Mark Lepper and his colleagues (1973). Children participating in the study who expected to be rewarded for drawing later spent less time drawing when not rewarded for doing so compared to children who never expected a reward and never received one. The investigators concluded that drawing is intrinsically motivating for children, and by leading them to expect a reward for drawing (thus providing extrinsic motivation for the behavior), they were decreasing the children's desire to draw for its own sake. (Most of the investigations in this area have been conducted with children, partly because of the relevance to schooling and partly because children are not likely to figure out the point of the studies.)

Does this mean that you should never reward children for an activity they enjoy? Not at all. Cameron and her colleagues (Cameron & Pierce 1994; Eisenberger & Cameron, 1996) report a meta-analytic study that revealed circumstances in which reward does not reduce intrinsic motivation (see also Deci et al., 1999a, 1999b; Kohn, 1996; Lepper et al., 1999; Ryan & Deci, 1996; Sansone & Harackiewicz, 1998; Tang & Hall, 1995). For example, when children were praised rather than given a tangible reward such as a gold star, they spent *more* free time doing that activity than when they were not rewarded at all—the opposite of what occurred with the children in the original study (Lepper et al., 1973), who were given tangible rewards versus nothing. Praising a child for a picture led her to do more drawing than when praise was not offered. Similarly, Cialdini and colleagues (1998) found that if the reward is attributed to an enduring trait (for example, "I knew you'd share, Timmy, because you're a good boy, and good boys share"), and thus serves to reinforce a child's belief that he or she possesses the trait, the reward can in fact *increase* the likelihood of the behavior in the future.

In addition, when a reward was given merely for performing an activity (not for the quality of the performance), children were in fact subsequently less likely to engage in that activity (Deci et al., 1999b). This is consistent with the original study results of Lepper and colleagues (1973), and is the classic *undermining intrinsic motivation* result. However, in sharp contrast, being rewarded for the *quality* of the performance need not have a negative impact on intrinsic motivation (Eisenberger & Cameron, 1996). Thus,

What motivated medieval architects to design castles so that the staircases spiral upward in the clockwise direction? This design gave the defenders (if they were right-handed, and they usually were) an advantage over the invaders because it allowed more room for the defenders' fighting hand to move freely in the tight confines of the staircase. Thinking along the same lines, a Scottish clan of left-handers built their castles so that the stairs spiraled in the opposite direction. How can you understand the motivation for such designs in terms of incentives?

Incentive: A stimulus that draws a person toward a particular goal, in anticipation of a reward.

Intrinsic motivation: Motivation that leads a person to want to engage in an activity for its own sake.

Extrinsic motivation: Motivation that leads a person to want to engage in an activity for external reasons.

the key is what you are rewarded for: If children are given a tangible reward for a particular activity, independent of how well they performed it, intrinsic interest is likely to decline, but if they are rewarded by praise for having a certain trait or for producing something of high quality, they will be encouraged to produce more such behavior.

For example, suppose you are taking a Spanish class and you enjoy the language lab part of the class, listening to tapes in Spanish and translating them into English. In fact, you like the work so much that you do even more translations than are required. Based on the research findings, we expect that if you were reinforced for just showing up at the language lab, not for the accuracy of your translations, you would become less intrinsically motivated to listen to the tapes. However, if you were reinforced for the quality of your work, you would continue to be intrinsically motivated.

Needs and Wants: The Stick and the Carrot

Different things motivate different people: A monk is not motivated to make money; an entrepreneur is not motivated to give away all earthly possessions and seek enlightenment on a mountaintop. Moreover, you are not motivated by the same forces day in and day out; rather, motivations may shift over the course of the day (or year, or life span). A particular motivation comes to the fore when you have a *need* or *want*. A **need** is a condition that arises from the lack of a requirement. Needs give rise to drives, which push you to reach a particular goal that will reduce the need. Lacking nutrients is a need; being hungry is a drive. In contrast, a **want** is a condition that arises when you have an unmet goal that will not fill a requirement. A want causes the goal to act as an incentive. You might *need* to eat, but you don't *need* a fancier wristwatch, although you might desperately *want* one—and the promise of a Rolex as a reward for getting good grades would be an incentive for you to work hard. You are not necessarily aware of your needs or wants; **implicit motives** are needs and wants that direct your behavior unconsciously. After the mugging John wasn't aware of his need to eat, but he was only too well aware of his wanting to be with Barbara.

IS THERE MORE THAN ONE TYPE OF REWARD? For all needs and wants, we think of the goal as reinforcing the behaviors that lead to it. But what makes the goal rewarding? What is "reward"? Even the strongest regulatory needs, creating drives such as hunger and thirst, arise from the brain—and those needs are satisfied not by what we do directly, but rather by the effects of our actions on the brain. To understand why something is rewarding, we must look more closely at the brain's response to events in the world. By looking at the brain mechanisms underlying reward, we find support for the distinction between needs and wants.

In Chapter 2 we discussed the idea of a "pleasure center." Olds and Milner (1954) found that rats who received electrical stimulation in certain brain areas acted as if they desired more of it. Later research showed that Olds and Milner had stumbled on a brain system that underlies reward when an animal has been deprived of the reinforcer. **Deprived reward** is reward that occurs when you have filled a biological need. Such reward arises from the brain pathway that runs from certain parts of the brain stem, through the (lateral) hypothalamus, on up to specific parts of the limbic system and the frontal lobes (Kalivas & Nakamura, 1999; Rolls & Cooper, 1974; Wise, 1996). Many of these neurons use the neurotransmitter *dopamine*. Drugs that block the action of dopamine also block the rewarding effect of brain stimulation (Nader et al., 1997) and of normal reinforcers such as food or water. When given these dopamine-blockers, experimental animals (usually rats) begin to respond normally, but then lose interest. Because the drugs are blocking the rewarding effect of the reinforcer, the animals' response undergoes extinction (Geary & Smith, 1985; Schneider et al., 1990). Blocking dopamine can disrupt both unconditioned and conditioned positive reinforcement (Beninger, 1983, 1989; Wise, 1982). At least in some situations, the dopamine may actually signal that a reward is expected, not simply that a reward has

Need: A condition that arises from the lack of a requirement; needs give rise to drives.

Want: A condition that arises when you have an unmet goal that will not fill a requirement; wants turn goals into incentives.

Implicit motive: A need or want that unconsciously directs behavior.

Deprived reward: Reward that occurs when a biological need is filled.

been obtained (Garris et al. 1999; Hollerman & Schultz, 1998; Hollerman et al., 1998; Schultz, 1997; Schultz et al., 1997).

There is strong evidence that the brain has a second system, which operates for **nondeprived reward,** reward that occurs when you haven't actually required the rewarding stimulus or activity—in other words, when you had a want but not a need. John hadn't eaten since noon on the day of the mugging. After the fear and excitement of that experience, and the calming effect of Barbara's company, he realized how hungry he was. The pleasure he then found in eating was mediated by brain circuits used in deprived reward, which rely on dopamine. In contrast, at the end of the meal, even though he was no longer hungry, he ordered a sinful ice-cream-drenched-in-hot-chocolate-sauce dessert simply for the pleasure of eating. In this case, he was nondeprived. Although dopamine plays a crucial role in producing the rewarding effects of a stimulus or activity that fills a deprivation, it does not play a role when you are not deprived. The part of the brain involved in nondeprived reward is in the brain stem. Lesions in this area knock out the system that registers reward when an animal is not deprived, but leave intact the system for deprived reward (Bechara & Van der Kooy, 1992; Berridge, 1996; Nader et al., 1997).

The existence of two different brain systems for reward is grounds for drawing a psychological distinction between needs and wants, between motivation that arises when a requirement must be filled and motivation that arises when a goal that is not a requirement is desired. Figure 9.6 summarizes the relation between these different facets of motivation.

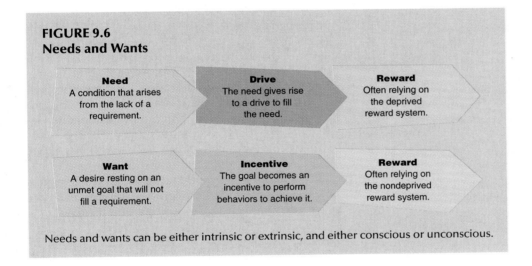

FIGURE 9.6
Needs and Wants

| Need | Drive | Reward |
| A condition that arises from the lack of a requirement. | The need gives rise to a drive to fill the need. | Often relying on the deprived reward system. |

| Want | Incentive | Reward |
| A desire resting on an unmet goal that will not fill a requirement. | The goal becomes an incentive to perform behaviors to achieve it. | Often relying on the nondeprived reward system. |

Needs and wants can be either intrinsic or extrinsic, and either conscious or unconscious.

TYPES OF NEEDS: NO SHORTAGE OF SHORTAGES. There are psychological as well as bodily needs. Researchers have proposed that these include a need to be competent, to be autonomous (Sheldon et al., 1996), to have social approval, to be dominant or in control (Kim & Kim, 1997), to be affiliated with others, to be powerful (McClelland et al., 1989), to reach closure (Kruglanski & Webster, 1996; Taris, 2000), to understand, to maintain self-esteem, and even to find the world benevolent (Stevens & Fiske, 1995). Most of the pertinent studies examine individual differences in various needs. These individual differences probably arise from differences in personal inherited temperament (Kagan, 1994a) and differences in personal experiences, such as interactions with peers (Harris, 1998) and family (Sulloway, 1996).

A classic example of a psychological need is the *need for achievement* (*nAch*; McClelland & Atkinson, 1953), and there is a large body of research assessing the consequences of differences in this need (for example, Neel et al., 1986; Spangler, 1992).

Nondeprived reward: Reward that occurs even when a requirement is not being met.

People who have a high need for achievement tend to assume that their successes are due to their personal characteristics, whereas their failures are due to environmental circumstances (Nathawat et al., 1997; Weiner & Kukla, 1970). In a meta-analysis, Spangler (1992) found that measures of "implicit" (that is, not conscious) need for achievement predict actual success better than "explicit" (or conscious) need, as measured by questionnaires filled in by participants.

Another need that has attracted considerable research is the *need for cognition (NC)*, which is the need to engage in and enjoy thinking (Cacciopo & Petty, 1982; Cacciopo et al., 1996). To assess whether an individual is motivated by the need for cognition, John Cacciopo and his collaborators developed a test that includes true–false items such as "I really enjoy a task that involves coming up with new solutions to problems." People whose test scores indicate that they have high NC share key characteristics. They tend to draw more inferences when they evaluate an advertisement (Stayman & Kardes, 1992), think more about a persuasive communication and subsequently remember more of it (Cacciopo, Petty, Kao et al., 1986), think more about attitudes they have just expressed (Lassiter et al., 1996; Leone & Ensley, 1986), are less affected by the way a problem is stated when they reason (Chatterjee et al., 2000; Smith & Levin, 1996), and tend to get better grades (Sadowski & Guelgoez, 1996).

Abraham Maslow (1970) created a hierarchy of physical and emotional needs, illustrated in Figure 9.7. Lower-level needs are considered more essential to life, and must be met before needs further up the hierarchy can be addressed and satisfied. Ascending the hierarchy, the needs are considered less basic because they arise less frequently and, if not met, do not seriously impair the quality of life. You can live without understanding the world, but not without air or food. According to Maslow's theory, once a need is met, it becomes less important, and unmet, higher-level needs become more important. During crises (such as loss of a home by fire), needs regress to a lower level and higher-level needs are put on hold. This theory allows us to understand Albert Einstein's remark, "An empty stomach is not a good political advisor."

FIGURE 9.7
Maslow's Hierarchy of Needs

Self-Actualization Needs
To be all that you are capable of becoming

Aesthetic Needs
Need for harmony and order

Cognitive Needs
Need to understand the world, creating curiosity

Esteem Needs
Desire for mastery and feeling appreciated by others

Belongingness Needs
Desire for a sense of belonging and love

Safety Needs
Shelter, protection

Physiological Needs
Water, food, air

According to Maslow's theory, needs lower in the pyramid must be met before needs higher in the pyramid become the focus of concerns.

Maslow's hierarchy of needs has had an enormous impact on how people think about motivation, particularly in the business world (Soper et al., 1995). But is it right? There are three major difficulties with Maslow's theory. First, research has produced mixed evidence, at best, for the idea that needs are organized into a hierarchy. Results of questionnaire studies generally show that the levels are not clearly distinct from one another, as revealed by factor analysis (Wahba & Bridwell, 1976). In addition, there is no clear-cut ordering of needs (Soper et al., 1995; Wahba & Bridwell, 1976). Beer (1966), for example, found that female clerks reported strong social needs and a strong need for self-actualization but not a strong need for self-esteem. Second, there is no good evidence that unmet needs become more important and that met needs become less important. In fact, Hall and Nougaim (1968) found that the longer a need was satisfied, the more important it became. Third, it fails to explain various phenomena—for example, why people voluntarily go to war and put themselves in the line of fire (Fox, 1982).

WANTING MORE: IT'S ALL RELATIVE. Much of our motivation is not based on needs, but on wants. People evaluate the worth of something relative to what they have now, constantly looking up to the next rung of the ladder, striving to have a little more than what they have now; but once they achieve this goal, they quickly adapt and then have to repeat the process, striving for yet another increase (Myers, 1993). In one study, participants evaluated their present lives more positively immediately after writing down a major low point in their lives than after writing down a major high point (Strack et al., 1988). As in other kinds of perception (see Chapter 3), people judge differences in value relative to baselines. And because the baseline changes shortly after we climb another rung, we are always left wanting at least a little bit more. People differ in the strength of this orientation, however; some people focus more on preserving what they have, others on achieving more than they currently have (Higgins, 1997; Shah et al., 1998).

ACHIEVEMENT IN INDIVIDUALIST VERSUS COLLECTIVIST CULTURES. Many of the goals that motivate us are provided by groups, and the structure of the society determines what sorts of activities will be reinforced. Cultures can be divided into two general types that affect achievement motivation differently. **Individualist cultures,** such as that of the United States, emphasize the rights and responsibilities of the individual over those of the group. **Collectivist cultures,** such as those of Asia, emphasize the rights and responsibilities of the group over those of the individual. Such cultural differences have been shown to affect achievement goals. For example, Anglo-Australians (from an individualist culture) have been found to be focused more on personal success than on family or groups, whereas Sri Lankans (from a collectivist culture) are oriented more toward their families and groups (Niles, 1998). Similarly, Sagie, Elizur, and Hirotsugu (1996) found that Americans had higher achievement motivation (as measured by scales that emphasize individual achievement) than Japanese or Hungarians, members of collectivist cultures.

Thus, growing up in one or the other type of culture influences a person's needs and wants. Some of these effects may occur because people have different ideas about their important characteristics; for example, Americans have been found to have higher feelings of self-competence than Chinese. But the effects of growing up in an individualist culture are not without a cost: Tafarodi and Swann (1996) found that Americans like themselves less than do Chinese. Why? Tafarodi and Swann believe that members of collectivist cultures are raised in a way that leads others to like them, in part by de-emphasizing competition among individuals. This may lead to greater self-liking if we assume that our self-liking is increased if other people like us. In individualist cultures, on the other hand, members are raised to strive for freedom and independence, which tends to produce competition and conflict. In such cultures, there are more feelings of self-competence, but fewer of self-liking.

What sorts of needs do you suppose motivated President Franklin Delano Roosevelt? During all the days of FDR's presidency (1933–1945), he could not walk without the use of metal braces or crutches (he contracted polio in 1921 and was paralyzed thereafter). However, this did not stop him from getting around the White House on his own by using his hands to crawl from one room to another.

Individualist culture: A culture that emphasizes the rights and responsibilities of the individual over those of the group.

Collectivist culture: A culture that emphasizes the rights and responsibilities of the group over those of the individual.

LOOKING AT LEVELS

Learned Helplessness

People not only can learn new strategies for coping with problems, but they also can learn to give up trying. Martin Seligman and his colleagues first described **learned helplessness,** which occurs when an animal has an aversive experience in which nothing it does can affect what happens to it, and so it simply gives up and stops trying to change the situation or to escape (Mikulincer, 1994). As shown in Figure 9.8 on page 332 (Overmeier & Seligman, 1967), when dogs were put in a cage in which they could not escape shocks, they eventually gave up responding and just huddled on the floor and endured—and they continued to do so even when they were moved to a new cage in which it was easy to escape the shocks. This condition can also afflict humans who experience a lack of control over negative events: If nothing you do

FIGURE 9.8
The Classic Experiment of Overmeier and Seligman

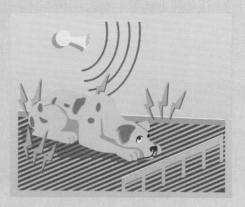

An animal is placed in a cage and shocked. Initially, the animal tries to escape, but it can do nothing to avoid or prevent the shocks.

The animal eventually gives up.

When the animal is moved into a new cage in which only a small barrier separates the side where shocks are delivered from the side where no shocks occur, it does not try to escape the shock, even when the shock is signaled by a tone.

seems to make an abusive spouse stop tormenting you, you may eventually just give up and stop trying. Learned helplessness can lead to depression and a range of stress-related problems.

It is clear that learned helplessness depends on events at the different levels of analysis. At the level of the group, others may create the situation from which you cannot escape. For example, a child trapped in an abusive family, who has no control over the situation, may eventually exhibit learned helplessness. Events at the level of the group can directly interact with an individual's experience, which then affects the tendency toward learned helplessness. This connection has been clearly demonstrated with rats, which were given inescapable shock either alone or in pairs. When in pairs, the rats fought with each other when they were being shocked. When tested individually 2 days later, the rats who were stressed in pairs displayed less learned helplessness than those stressed alone (Zhukov & Vinogradova, 1998). The fighting may simply have distracted them from the shock, or this effect may reflect neural events that occurred when the rats fought, which in turn protected them against learned helplessness.

In addition, many studies have examined what happens in the brain when an animal has received uncontrollable shock and descends into learned helplessness. The findings indicate that learned helplessness has a wide range of complex effects throughout the brain. For example, there is evidence that learned helplessness can lower the levels of the neurotransmitter serotonin, or decrease the numbers of receptors that are affected by it, in various parts of the brain (Amat et al., 1998; Papolos et al., 1996). Although some of these effects may be caused by stress per se (Wu et al., 1999), at least some are caused by the effects of the impossibility of escaping shock, not solely the shock itself (Edwards et al., 1992; Petty et al., 1994). It is possible to breed rats that are particularly susceptible to this syndrome (Lachman et al., 1993). Thus, some people could conceivably be prone to this problem. Clearly, events at the different levels interact, and all must be taken into account if we are to understand when and why animals and humans come to behave as if they were helpless—even when they're not.

Learned helplessness: The condition that occurs after an animal has an aversive experience in which nothing it does can affect what happens to it, and so it simply gives up and stops trying to change the situation or to escape.

HUNGER AND EATING: NOT JUST ABOUT FUELING THE BODY

When he sat down to dinner the evening of the mugging, John ate mechanically, paying little attention to what was in front of him. Food was now the last thing on John's mind, and he didn't have much of an appetite, even after joining Barbara in the safety and warmth of the restaurant. But after the first few bites, he realized that he was terrifically hungry and had no trouble polishing off a large dinner. He particularly liked Italian food, partly because it was one of his mother's specialties. Now, just smelling the richness and flavor of the homemade ravioli and fresh tomato sauce relaxed him and made his mouth water.

One of the drives that is best understood—and that motivates each of us every day—is hunger. Hunger is the classic drive that relies on the deprived reward system; by definition, to be hungry is to be deprived of food. However, not all eating occurs because we are hungry. Sometimes we eat because it's fun, in which case the pleasure ultimately relies on the operation of the nondeprived reward system. Hunger, and its satisfaction, affects many aspects of our lives, social and experiential as well as physiological.

▶ 1. What makes us hungry and leads us to eat particular foods at particular times?

▶ 2. How is our weight kept relatively constant? And why do some people become obese?

Eating Behavior: The Hungry Mind in the Hungry Body

Hunger arises from a particular state of the body, but eating is not always a result of hunger (Woods et al., 2000). What factors determine what and when we eat?

Is Being Hungry the Opposite of Being Full? Although you might think of hunger as a continuum from starvation to satiety, hunger in fact arises from the action of two distinct brain systems. One system leads you to feel a need to eat; another leads you to feel satiated (Davis & Levine, 1977; Yeomans & Gray, 1997).

The feeling of a need to eat arises when your brain senses that the level of food molecules in your blood is too low. The brain registers the quantities of two major types of food molecules: *glucose* (a type of sugar) and *fatty acids* (Friedman, Tordoff, & Kare, 1991; Friedman, Tordoff, & Ramirez, 1986). In contrast, "feeling full" does not depend on the level of food molecules in the blood: You feel full well before food is digested and food molecules enter the bloodstream. If you suspect that feeling full has something to do with the state of your stomach, you're on the right track. If food is removed with a flexible tube from the stomach of a rat that has just eaten to satisfaction, the rat will eat just enough to replace the loss (Davis & Campell, 1973). But a full stomach is not enough to tell an animal to stop eating. Filling an animal's stomach with saltwater does not diminish appetite as much as filling it with milk, even if the fluids are placed directly into the stomach so that the animals cannot taste them (Deutsch et al., 1978). The stomach contains detectors that register the food value of its contents, and this information is transmitted to the brain. People know when to stop eating largely because of signals sent by sensory neurons in the stomach to the brain. Similar signals are also sent by other organs, including the upper part of the small intestine and the liver.

What part of the brain detects these signals? Some 50 years ago researchers thought they had found "start" and "stop" eating centers in the brain. They had discovered that even small lesions (holes) in the lateral (side) part of the hypothalamus caused an animal to lose interest in food, even to the point of death by starvation. When this structure was electrically stimulated, the animal ate more and worked harder for food (Anand & Brobeck, 1952; Teitelbaum & Stellar, 1954). In contrast, the ventromedial (bottom, central) part of the hypothalamus was thought to be the center in the brain that told an animal it was full and should stop eating.

Other research, however, soon highlighted the difficulties in interpreting these findings. Lesions to the lateral hypothalamus suppressed the animals' interest not only in eating but also in drinking, sex, and even caring for their young; the result was often a general sluggishness. Researchers found that the lesions were disrupting not only the neurons in the lateral hypothalamus, but also connections between other areas. Similarly, when the ventromedial hypothalamus is damaged, animals don't just fail to stop eating, they become picky eaters (Ferguson & Keesey, 1975); indeed, they initially overeat carbohydrates (Sclafani & Aravich, 1983; Sclafani et al., 1983).

The brain system that regulates eating is surprisingly complex, as is revealed when it is disrupted by a stroke. For example, a person can develop what is known as gourmand syndrome, *a neurological disorder in which people become obsessed with fine food. Such people do not report being hungry all of the time, and may not overeat—but their entire lives become centered on food.*

Improved methods allowed researchers to clear these muddy waters. When chemicals are used to destroy only the lateral hypothalamus and none of the connections that pass through it, hunger *is* reduced more than most other drives (Dunnett et al., 1985; Stricker et al., 1978). The ventromedial hypothalamus appears to affect other brain regions that allow stored food molecules to be released; thus, when it is damaged, the animal has no choice but to keep eating (Weingarten et al., 1985). Rather than having centers in the hypothalamus that say "eat" or "don't eat," we, and other animals, have some neurons that signal when nutrient levels are low, and others that signal when stored food molecules should be released. These neurons act not so much like buttons or switches as like sensors that provide information that guides attention and behavior.

APPETITE: A MOVING TARGET. The early phases of eating depend on the taste of food. When you take the first bites of a meal or snack, you probably experience the *appetizer effect*; if those first bites taste good, your appetite is stimulated. This effect is driven in part by *opioids* in the brain; as you might suspect from their name, opioids are chemicals that behave like opium-derived drugs and cause you to experience pleasure. The opioids are released when you first eat food that tastes good (Yeomans & Gray, 1997).

As you continue to eat, your responses to food-related stimuli change. After eating some fresh-baked cookies, the smell of them doesn't seem quite as heavenly as it did while they were cooling. If people have had their fill of a certain food, they rate its odor as less pleasant than they did before eating it (Duclaux et al., 1973). However, when the flavor, texture, color, or shape of a food is changed, people will eat more of the same food (Rolls, Rowe et al., 1981). After you've eaten a few chocolate chip cookies, you might find yourself not interested in more cookies, but happy to have some fresh-baked bread.

Tarantulas can go for 2 years without eating. Humans, on the other hand, can last for about a month without eating, provided that they can drink.

Not surprisingly, these changes in your appetite are linked to events in the hypothalamus. Neurons in the lateral hypothalamus initially fire to the sight or taste of a food, and then reduce their firing after an animal has eaten its fill of that food (Burton et al., 1976). These neurons are selective: After they stop responding to one food, they can still be stimulated by another (Rolls, Rowe et al., 1981; Critchley & Rolls, 1996, report similar findings in regions of the frontal lobe that are involved in emotional responses).

To understand why you eat the amount you do, you need to consider events at the different levels of analysis. Eating is not simply about events in the brain. The presence of other people influences how much you eat (De Castro, 1990). People report eating a greater amount when more people are present for a meal. Part of this effect may simply reflect the fact that when more people are present, the meal takes longer to complete. But this can't be all there is to it: When people eat in groups, they do not vary the size of their meals to reflect their degree of hunger—for example, by eating less for dinner if they had a late lunch—but they do make such adjustments when eating alone.

Anything that reminds you of good food you've eaten on a previous occasion—an event at the level of the person—can increase hunger. This effect occurs in part because your body responds not only to perceptions of food but also to thoughts of food by secreting **insulin**. Insulin is a hormone that stimulates the storage of food molecules in the form of fat. Thus, insulin reduces the level of food in the blood, which may increase hunger.

WHY DOES IT TASTE GOOD? What about preferences for specific foods? Some of our tastes clearly are a consequence of beliefs that develop with experience. Some people develop disgust reactions to certain foods (Rozin & Fallon, 1986), and the very idea of that food then keeps them away from it. Such *cognitive taste aversion* is apparently long-lasting and can be formed without classical conditioning (for instance, without being nauseated after eating the food; see Batsell & Brown, 1998). Rozin and his colleagues have shown that people apparently believe that "once in contact, always in contact." If a neutral food was in contact with an aversive food, the aversive properties seem to transfer. Suppose someone dunked a sterilized, dead cockroach briefly in your glass of water. Would you want to take a sip? The answer is probably a resounding no. Similarly, if a morsel of premium chocolate fudge were molded into the shape of feces, the shape alone would make it unappealing. Rozin and his colleagues have also shown that Americans harbor exaggerated beliefs about the harmful effects of some foods; in fact, many believe that salt and fat are harmful even at trace levels (Rozin et al., 1996).

Beliefs also play another role in determining what we want to eat: Perhaps unconsciously, people believe that "you are what you eat." Nemeroff and Rozin (1989) asked people to rate qualities of people who "ate boar" and those who "ate turtle." The boar eaters were believed to be more likely to have boarlike qualities, such as being bearded and heavy-set.

Culture plays a key role in shaping our tastes in food: Koreans find pickled snakes delicious; Filipinos enjoy unhatched chicks in the shell; the French would never give up their beloved snails or rabbit; the Germans savor stuffed pig intestines; and Chileans eat a kind of sea anemone whose looks would qualify it to star in a science-fiction

Insulin: A hormone that stimulates the storage of food molecules in the form of fat.

Set point: The particular body weight that is easiest for an animal (including a human) to maintain.

Metabolism: The sum of the chemical events in each of the body's cells, events that convert food molecules to the energy needed for the cells to function.

movie. Cultures even differ in what they consider food: Every time you lick a stamp, you're consuming ¹⁄₁₀ of a calorie, so in Israel the glue on postage stamps has to be certified kosher.

Overeating: When Enough Is Not Enough

We humans like the taste of fatty foods, which is bad news because eating too much fat can lead to a variety of diseases, such as diabetes, cardiovascular disease, cancer, high blood pressure, and gallbladder disease (Schiffman et al., 1999). Diet books and cookbooks are best-sellers. Does this seem ironic to you? Do we want to lose weight so that we can eat more? Or does our love of eating make us need to diet? Our culture places a premium on being thin. Nonetheless, some of us overeat, and some of us are obese.

SET POINT: YOUR NORMAL WEIGHT.
Animals, including humans, settle at a particular body weight that is easiest to maintain; this weight is called the **set point.** The set point is relatively constant, and homeostatic mechanisms keep it that way (Nisbett, 1972; Stunkard, 1982). Your life is sustained by your body's **metabolism,** the sum of the chemical events in each of your cells, events that convert food molecules to the energy needed for the cells to function. Between meals, food molecules enter the bloodstream from fat cells and supply most of the energy your body needs to keep going. If your weight falls below the set point, fat cells become less likely to give up their stored fat. Receptors in your brain that are sensitive to low levels of fat then become active and make you hungry. Thus you end up gaining weight and getting back to your set point.

The set point is relatively constant, but it can be changed. If you overeat at a party, your body will still be able to keep your weight near its set point; the extra pound or two will come off easily within the week. But if you overeat for a prolonged time, the number of fat cells in your body increases, and your body has difficulty maintaining the set point weight. Thus, you gain weight. Moreover, the set point itself may change, becoming higher. In contrast, when you lose weight, each fat cell becomes thinner, but you don't lose fat cells. This may explain why the set point goes up as a result of chronic overeating—but then does not go down easily. Regular, moderately vigorous exercise can speed up your metabolism, leading your cells to need more energy even when you are not exercising. This is the best method of adjusting your set point.

OBESITY.
An obese person is defined as one who is more than 20% heavier than the medically ideal weight for that person's sex, height, and bone structure. By this standard, almost one third of Americans are obese. Do these people have weak characters that make them slaves to food? No. The personality characteristics of obese and nonobese people are similar (Nilsson et al., 1998; Poston et al., 1999). Indeed, President William Howard Taft (1909–1913) was a grossly obese man, weighing over 300 pounds. He was so overweight that, after getting stuck in a White House bathtub, he had a new tub constructed that would hold four average-sized men. However, his size did not deter him from achieving the highest office in the land.

So why are some people obese? Some explanations have grown out of psychodynamic theory. According to one such theory, people become obese because they are threatened by their own sexuality. This *defense mechanism theory* holds that such people are afraid of being attractive and overeat in order to make themselves unattractive to others. However, as Bess (1997) points out, there is no scientific support for this theory. Another psychodynamically inspired theory maintains that obese people eat when they feel stress, again as a kind of defense. In this case, the evidence is mixed: Obese people do not always overeat when they feel stress and may instead tend to overeat when aroused, positively or negatively (Andrews & Jones, 1990; McKenna, 1972).

There is good reason to believe that at least some forms of obesity have a genetic basis. In fact, Bouchard, a researcher in this area, estimates that several dozen genes may affect weight in one way or another: "Some affect appetite, some affect satiety. Some affect metabolic rate" (quoted in Gladwell, 1998, p. 53). Thus, the genetics of obesity will not be a simple story, but the story is beginning to be told. First, the neu-

Obese people have the same "will power" to resist eating junk food as nonobese people.

rons involved in brain regions that register satiety appear to rely in part on the neurotransmitter serotonin (Blundell, 1977, 1984, 1986; Blundell & Halford, 1998), and mutant mice that lack specific receptors for this neurotransmitter will keep eating until they become obese (Tecott et al., 1995). The notion that humans may act the same way is supported by the finding that people gain weight if they take medication that happens to block these receptors (Fitton & Heel, 1990); in addition, people who take drugs that activate these receptors report being less hungry, and actually lose weight while on the medication (Sargent et al., 1997).

A gene that plays a role in governing eating and weight is known as *ob* (short for *obese*). This gene governs the release of a hormone called *leptin* (*leptos* is Greek for "thin"), which is released by fat cells. The more fat, the more leptin is in the blood. Leptin decreases food intake and increases energy expenditure (in part by increasing heat production; Wang et al., 1999). Leptin affects eating in part by interfering with a neurotransmitter called Neuropeptide Y (NPY), which induces eating (Inui, 1999). This interference occurs in the hypothalamus, by activating or inhibiting specific neurons (Yokosuka et al., 1998); indeed, hungry rats will work hard to receive electrical stimulation of key parts of the hypothalamus, but giving them leptin decreases the rate of such responding (Fulton et al., 2000). Rosenbaum and Leibel (1999) suggest that leptin may serve to maintain a constant level of body fat by acting as a signal to the brain that the amounts of stored fat and food intake are adequate.

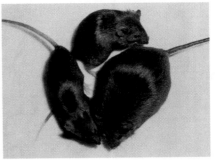

Genes can make a big difference. Researchers in a Seattle genetics laboratory found that by altering a single gene, they could increase a rat's metabolism so the animal burns more fat.

However, only extremely obese people have a deficit in the ob gene, and this problem is unlikely to underlie most obesity (Mantzoros, 1999). Another gene has been discovered that determines whether the excess fat in food is converted to body fat or is turned into surplus body heat (Fleury et al., 1977). Animals that do not have this gene become fat when they eat amounts that normally do not increase weight. How does such a gene work? One mechanism could be the "fidget factor"; that is, the gene could affect the overall level of physical activity (Bouchard, as quoted in Gladwell, 1998, p. 53). Consider the findings reported by Levine, Eberhardt, and Jensen (1999), who asked a group of normal people to overeat a large amount each day for 8 weeks. At the end of this period there were large differences in how much fat the volunteers gained—some people gained literally 10 times as much as others. Levine and his colleagues found that the single biggest factor that determined whether people gained fat was the number of physical movements unrelated to sports or fitness regimens—"activities of daily living, fidgeting, spontaneous muscle contraction" and the effort of maintaining posture when not reclining. Each movement burned up extra energy in the extra food so that it was not stored as fat. We know that temperament is partly innate (Kagan, 1994), and it is possible that differences in temperament lead to differences in such activity levels, which in turn affect whether extra calories are burned or stored.

As we have seen, genes determine a reaction range, and the environment sets individuals within that range (Chapters 2 and 8). Some people have a propensity to become fat, but do so only in certain environments. Overeating is encouraged by many aspects of our environment: Food is relatively cheap, fast foods are high in fat, and portions have grown larger in the United States (but not in many parts of Europe). At the same time, people exercise less not only because most of us drive or ride to work, but also because our amusements, such as watching television and surfing the Web, are sedentary. Hill and Peters (1998) suggest approaches to "curing the environment," which is supporting a virtual epidemic in obesity: (1) educating people to eat smaller portions; (2) making foods that are low in fat and calories more available; and (3) encouraging more physical activity.

Some obese people are capable of losing large amounts of weight, and keeping the weight off (Tinker & Tucker, 1997). These people are able to adopt healthier eating and exercise habits. Note, however, that changes in the environment will be effective only if the reaction range for weight is relatively large (that is, if the genes define a wide range of possibilities). If the reaction range of certain genes that result in obesity is small, then people who have those genes may not have much choice in determining how heavy they are.

The Starvation Diet

In our culture most of us are at some point concerned about our weight and thus may go on a diet. The most commonly recommended diet for obese people requires them to cut their normal food intake in half (Stallone & Stunkard, 1994). Keys and his colleagues (1950) studied the effects of such a diet on a group of 36 healthy young men. After 6 months, these men weighed on average 25% less than they had at the outset. In addition, they experienced many dramatic psychological changes, resulting from events at all three levels of analysis. At the level of the brain, their perceptual processes and sleep patterns changed. They slept less, became more sensitive to light and noise, had less tolerance for cold, and showed various other physical symptoms.

At the level of the person, the content of their thoughts changed. They became obsessed with food. Many began to hoard not only food, but also random junk. (This also happens with rats who are put on such diets [Fantino & Cabanac, 1980] and with people who have eating disorders and put themselves on similar diets [Crisp et al., 1980].) At the level of the group, they lost interest in sex and in interacting with other people. They also became irritable, anxious, depressed, and argumentative. Many of these symptoms persisted for months after the men began to eat normally again.

Of course, the effects at the three levels also interacted. Because the men were more irritable, others were less likely to seek their company and thus provide distraction from thoughts of food. Because their senses had become more acute, they were likely to avoid social situations. The most sobering point about this study is the realization that many people today voluntarily put themselves on stringent diets, without realizing the consequences.

CONSOLIDATE!

▶ **1. What makes us hungry and leads us to eat particular foods at particular times?** Hunger occurs when the brain determines that the level of glucose and fatty acids in the bloodstream is too low. Hunger is not the opposite of being full; different mechanisms determine whether you are hungry or full. Being sated depends in large part on having nutrients in your stomach. At the beginning of a meal, taste plays an especially important role in determining whether you eat. As a meal progresses, changes in the type of food will keep your appetite up, and taste (as well as thoughts) that cause insulin to be released will increase hunger. Beliefs about the history of a food item (such as whether it was ever in contact with something repulsive), and even associations to the shape of a food affect how appealing it is. You eat not only when you are hungry, but also when certain environmental and social cues are present.

▶ **2. How is our weight kept relatively constant? And why do some people become obese?** The set point operates to keep your weight constant. However, chronic overeating can lead the set point of your body weight to move up, and once moved up, set points are difficult to move down again. At least some obese people are genetically predisposed to becoming obese.

SEX: NOT JUST ABOUT HAVING BABIES

John had planned his anniversary dinner with Barbara carefully. He picked a restaurant that was a sentimental favorite of theirs, with fabulous food, soft lighting, and relaxing music. He suggested that they eat early so that there would be time for a romantic evening at his apartment. Unfortunately, after the mugging, he wasn't in the mood. But when they arrived at his apartment, he found that romantic thoughts returned and he enjoyed Barbara's company more than ever.

► 1. What is the nature of sexual response? What factors lead to it?

► 2. What determines whether we are attracted to the same or to the opposite sex?

► 3. What is "normal sexual behavior"? How does culture affect our standards of normality?

Sexual Behavior: A Many-Splendored Thing

People engage in sexual relations for two general reasons: to have babies (*reproductive sex*) and for pleasure (*recreational sex*). The vast majority of sexual acts, on the order of 98% (Linner, 1972), are for pleasure, as opposed to procreation. Sex leads to some of the most intense of all positive emotions, and hence it is valued highly by members of our species. The earliest known attempts at contraception were developed 4,000 years ago by the Egyptians; they thought dried crocodile dung would do the job.

Alfred Kinsey began the first systematic surveys about human sexual behavior in the late 1940s. He and his colleagues interviewed thousands of Americans about their sex lives. Kinsey found that people frequently reported sexual practices then considered rare or even abnormal. However, attempts to study sexual behavior ran into some unique problems. As Freud wrote (1910, p. 41), "People in general are not candid over sexual matters, they do not show their sexuality freely, but to conceal it wear a heavy overcoat of a tissue of lies, as though the weather were bad in the world of sexuality." Psychologists have had difficulty getting beyond this "tissue of lies," and even today there is debate about whether we have reliable information about many facets of human sexuality.

Most studies of sexual behavior rely on surveys. But would you volunteer to be in a study of sexual behavior? How about filling in a questionnaire about your most intimate moments? Researchers have found that not everybody is equally willing to participate in studies of sexual behavior, and thus the data are likely to come from a biased sample. Bogaert (1996), for example, found that the undergraduate males who volunteered for a study on human sexuality differed in many ways from males who volunteered for a study on personality: The former group had more sexual experience, were more interested in sexual variety, were more inclined to seek out sensation and excitement, and were less socially conforming and likely to follow rules (Trivedi & Sabini, 1998, report similar findings). In addition, people from different cultures may respond differently when asked about their sexual and reproductive behavior: Researchers found that Hispanic women reported less sexual activity when their interviewers were older, but African American women did not display this bias as strongly (Ford & Norris, 1997). The researchers suspected that this bias arose because the Hispanic culture has traditionally frowned on premarital sex for women, leading Hispanic women to underreport their sexual activity to older women who might disapprove.

In short, interview data about sex are suspect. Sampling bias as well as response bias can distort the results.

SEXUAL RESPONSES: STEP BY STEP. William Masters and Virginia Johnson (1966) were the first researchers to study systematically actual sexual behavior, not just reports of descriptions of it, with a large sample of participants. Their effort was the first that provided a look behind the "tissue of lies" about sex. Over the course of many years, Masters and Johnson brought thousands of men and women into their laboratory and devised ways to measure what the body does during sex. The outcome was a comprehensive description of the **sexual response cycle** (**SRC**), the stages the body passes through during sexual activity. They discovered that both men and women pass through four such stages: (1) *excitement* (during the initial phases, when the person becomes aroused); (2) *plateau* (a full level of arousal); (3) *orgasm* (accompanied by muscle contractions, and in men ejaculation); and (4) *resolution* (the release of sexual tension). These stages meld into one another, with no sharp divisions separating them (Levin, 1980, 1994).

Sexual response cycle (SRC): The stages the body passes through during sexual activity, now characterized as including sexual attraction, desire, excitement, and performance (which includes plateau, orgasm, and resolution).

The mountain of research they conducted led Masters and Johnson to reach four general conclusions: (1) Men and women are similar in their bodily reactions to sex; (2) women tend to respond more slowly than men, but stay aroused longer; (3) many women can have multiple orgasms, whereas men typically have a *refractory period*, a period of time following orgasm when they cannot become aroused again; and (4) women reported that penis size is not related to sexual performance, unless the man is worried about it.

Others have built on Masters and Johnson's research, sometimes focusing on the very first stages of sexual activity, triggered by *sexual desire* (Kaplan, 1979). Our current understanding is that *sexual attraction* leads to *sexual desire*, *sexual excitement* (arousal), and possibly *sexual performance* (which involves becoming fully aroused, reaching orgasm, and then experiencing resolution followed by a refractory period).

Why do we have sexual responses at the times, and with the partners, we do? Not unexpectedly, events at all three levels of analysis play crucial roles in our sexual behavior.

THE ROLE OF HORMONES: DO CHEMICALS DICTATE BEHAVIOR? In 1849, German scientist Arnold Berthold wondered why castrated roosters acted like hens. They stopped crowing, mating with hens, fighting, and engaging in other typical rooster behaviors. So he castrated roosters and then put the testes into their abdominal cavities. Shortly thereafter, the roosters started behaving like roosters again. Berthold reasoned that the testes produced their effects not because of nerves or other physical connections, but because they released something into the bloodstream. We now know that what the testes release is the male hormone *testosterone*.

Hormones are chemicals that are secreted into the bloodstream primarily by endocrine glands and that trigger receptors on neurons and other types of cells (see Chapter 2). Hormones are controlled in large part by the pituitary gland, the brain's "master gland." The pituitary gland in turn is controlled by the hypothalamus, which plays a major role in emotion and motivation and is affected by hormones produced in the body. When you are sexually aroused, hormones from the gonads (the testes and ovaries) act on the brain and genital tissue. **Androgens** are male hormones (such as testosterone), which cause many male characteristics such as beard growth and a low voice. **Estrogens,** female hormones, cause many female characteristics such as breast development and the bone structure of the female pelvis. The presence of the different hormones is not all-or-none between the sexes. Both types of hormones are present in both males and females, but to different degrees. Unlike their direct effects on physical characteristics, hormones don't directly dictate behavior. Rather, they lead to a tendency to *want* to behave in certain ways in the presence of particular stimuli. That is, they modify motivation.

For example, changes in the level of sex hormones over the course of a woman's menstrual cycle affect the degree to which she is inclined to become sexually aroused. Slob and colleagues (1996) found that erotic videos increased the temperature of the female genital area more during the days just before ovulation than during the days following ovulation, and the women who were about to ovulate generally had increased sexual desire and sexual fantasies for the next 24 hours. In fact, researchers have found that women who were about to ovulate tended to classify very briefly presented pictures as sexual stimuli, both when the stimuli were in fact in this category (pictures of nude men) and when they were not (pictures of babies or objects related to body care; Krug et al., 1994). However, the effects of shifting hormone levels are only tendencies, affecting different people to different degrees (Regan, 1996). For example, Van Goozen and colleagues (1997) found that only those women who had premenstrual complaints had peak sexual interest during the ovulatory phase.

The relationship between hormones and motivation runs in both directions. In a famous study, a researcher who signed his paper only as "Anonymous" (1970) reported the effects of his building anticipation of female companionship after sustained periods of enforced celibacy. This man was a scientist who worked on a small island and only occasionally visited the mainland, where he would have brief periods of con-

Androgens: Male hormones, which cause many male characteristics such as beard growth and a low voice.

Estrogens: Female hormones, which cause many female characteristics such as breast development and the bone structure of the female pelvis.

tact with the opposite sex. He apparently had time on his hands when he was alone, and decided to measure his beard growth every day by weighing his beard clippings after shaving. He found that his beard grew thicker as his visits to the mainland approached. Just thinking about the visit apparently caused increases in male hormones, which in turn caused increased beard growth.

But we are not simply creatures of our hormones. To study the role of testosterone on sexual behavior and mood, Schiavi and colleagues (1997) injected men who had difficulty having erections with the hormone twice a week for 6 weeks; this course was followed by injections of a placebo for 4 weeks (the change was not known to the participants). Although the participants did ejaculate more often when they were receiving the testosterone than when they were receiving the placebo, little else changed. Testosterone did not affect the amount of sexual satisfaction, the rigidity of the penis during sex, or mood. Clearly, sex is about much more than just hormones. What are some of the other factors that contribute to sexual behavior?

PHEROMONES: SEXUAL FEELINGS IN THE AIR? Some animals secrete **phero-mones,** chemicals that function in some ways like hormones but are released outside the body and serve as a means of communication. In some species, pheromones signal that the female is fertile, serving as an unconditioned stimulus for males, leading them to want to mate with the female. Research by Stern and McClintock (1998) has shown that humans are sensitive to some pheromones. These researchers asked women to wear pads in their armpits during different phases of their menstrual cycles. When the secretions produced by women in the early part of the cycle were rubbed on the upper lips of other women, those women had shorter menstrual cycles; when secretions produced by women in the late phase of their cycles were rubbed on the upper lips of other women, their cycles were lengthened. Both groups of women found their own menstrual cycles shifting to synchronize with the phase of the menstrual cycle of the person who wore the armpit pads. Because such pheromones can become airborne, they can cause female roommates to have their menstrual periods at the same time (Russell et al., 1980, report consistent results).

SEXUAL STIMULI. Even if sexual pheromones operate in certain circumstances for humans, they do not play as important a role as they do for nonhuman animals. Why not? First, we humans are visual creatures—probably about half the cortex is concerned with vision. Visual stimuli play a major role in sexual attraction, particularly for men (Przybyla & Byrne, 1984). Second, even the tendency for visual stimuli to be less important for women is modified by culture. Effa-Heap (1996) reports that Nigerian 15- to 20-year-olds of both sexes preferred adult videos over other forms of pornography. Third, the precise nature of the video material matters. Pearson and Pollack (1997) assessed women's level of sexual arousal when they watched sexually explicit films. The researchers compared two types of films, those designed for men and those designed specifically for women or male–female couples. The women who viewed the latter films reported greater arousal.

Fourth, people use sex to satisfy different psychological needs. Cooper and colleagues (1998) showed that motivations for having sex can be thought of in terms of the two dimensions illustrated in Figure 9.9, which range from avoidance to approach (the horizontal dimension) and from social connection to independence (the vertical dimension). The importance of these dimensions is different for different people and in different contexts—for instance, for people in stable relationships, exclusive relationships, or relationships that are both stable and exclusive.

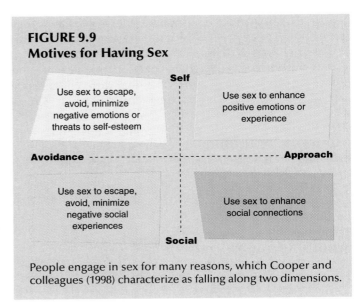

FIGURE 9.9
Motives for Having Sex

People engage in sex for many reasons, which Cooper and colleagues (1998) characterize as falling along two dimensions.

Fifth, there are clear sex differences in the importance of some types of stimuli. Notably, women reported that body odor was the most important sensory quality that could turn them off sexually, whereas men were neutral regarding body odor (Herz & Cahill, 1997).

Finally, sexual responses can be triggered in many ways, affecting events at the different levels of analysis. For example, adolescents apparently model their behavior after that of their friends, and hence are more likely to have sexual relations early if their friends are having sexual relations early (DiBlasio & Benda, 1990). Such social interactions can be mediated by biological events. Indeed, there is evidence that people who have certain genes that affect the brain receptors for the neurotransmitter dopamine have sexual intercourse at an earlier age than do people who do not have those genes. This finding applies to both sexes, but the relation is especially strong for males (Miller et al., 1999).

Sexual Orientation: More Than a Choice

People who are sexually attracted to the opposite sex are termed **heterosexual;** people attracted to the same sex are termed **homosexual;** people attracted to both sexes are termed **bisexual.** Sexuality might best be regarded as a continuum, with most people being primarily heterosexual and somewhere between 4% and 10% of the U.S. population being primarily homosexual in their behavior (Fay et al., 1989). Studies of bisexual men have shown that many of them tend to become more homosexually oriented over time (Stokes et al., 1997). For many years, homosexuality was considered either a personal choice or the result of being raised a certain way (for instance, with a weak father and an overly strict mother). However, programs to train homosexuals to prefer the opposite sex have failed, even those that relied on extreme techniques such as electric shock to punish homosexual thoughts or behavior (Brown, 1989, offers a personal account).

There is now evidence that people do not simply choose to be homosexual or heterosexual, nor are homosexuals or heterosexuals created by the ways their parents treat them as young children. Rather, biological events appear to play a major role in determining sexual orientation. LeVay (1991) studied the brains of homosexual men and found that a small part of the hypothalamus, about as large as an average-sized grain of sand, was about twice as small in them as in the brains of heterosexual men (Allen & Gorski, 1992, report related evidence). This is interesting in part because others had previously found that this same structure typically is smaller in women than in men. However, all of the brains LeVay studied came from men who had died of AIDS, and it is possible that the disease had something to do with the structural abnormality. Thus, it is an important finding that when this same structure was surgically disrupted in monkeys, they displayed atypical sexual behavior (Slimp et al., 1978). These and similar data suggest that there is a biological predisposition for some people to become homosexual (for a review, see LeVay & Hamer, 1994).

Other differences between heterosexual and homosexual people point toward biological differences. Consider, for example, the sound that is emitted from the ears of some people in some circumstances (see the discussion in Chapter 3). In some cases the sound is a response to a heard click, and the ears of some people actually emit sound even without such a trigger event. It turns out that this response to a click is less frequent and weaker for homosexual and bisexual women than for heterosexual women—in fact, men in general have less frequent and weaker ear responses than heterosexual women (McFadden & Pasanen, 1999). Apparently, parts of the ear are different in these women. However, no such difference appears among heterosexual, bisexual, and homosexual men. Thus, these results not only show a biological difference for homosexual and bisexual women, but may also hint at different biological bases for male and female homosexuality.

The findings of biological differences between homosexual and heterosexual people do not indicate whether the causes are hereditary (that is, genetic), the result of ex-

Heterosexual: A person who is sexually attracted to members of the opposite sex.

Homosexual: A person who is sexually attracted to members of the same sex.

Bisexual: A person who is sexually attracted to members of both sexes.

periences in the womb, or the result of experiences during early childhood. Hamer and his colleagues (1993) studied 114 families that included a homosexual man and found that inheritance of homosexuality seemed to be passed from the mother. This result led them to examine the *X* chromosome, which is the sex chromosome from the mother (females have two *X* chromosomes, one from the mother and one from the father; males have only one *X* chromosome, from the mother, and a *Y* chromosome from the father). And in fact a small portion of the *X* chromosome appears to be related to homosexual preference and behavior. Although Bailey and Pillard (1991) conducted a study with twins that supported the idea that homosexuality is at least partly inherited, a more recent study failed to find this effect (Rice et al., 1999). Thus, the evidence for the claim that homosexuality is determined in part by genes is mixed, and we must await further research before reaching strong conclusions.

To say that homosexuality has biological roots is not to rule out a role for the environment. Bem (1996, 1998) has argued that young boys who are not typical of their sex, in that they are not physically strong and have gentle temperaments, prefer to play with girls—and it is this socialization experience that later leads them to become homosexual. In Bem's view, "exotic becomes erotic": If young boys identify with girls and engage in girl-like behavior, it is boys who become "dissimilar, unfamiliar and exotic" and thus "erotic." For girls, the reverse would hold true, with "tomboy" girls choosing to associate with boys and engage in boy-like activities, and thus later finding girls exotic and hence erotic. According to this theory, biology would affect the body and temperament, and only indirectly affect sexual orientation. However, in order to explain why it has proved so difficult to alter sexual orientation in adulthood, we would need to assume that at a certain age sexual orientation is set and thereafter difficult to modify.

What's Normal?

For many years the manual of the American Psychiatric Association classified homosexuality as a psychological disorder, but (after conducting a poll of its members) in 1973 this classification was deleted. What is normal sexual behavior?

CULTURAL VARIATIONS: EXPERIENCE COUNTS. Sexual behavior is partly instinctive, but like eating, it is also molded by personal tastes and by culture (see Figure 9.10). For example, among the people of the Grand Valley Dani in Indonesia the men apparently have extraordinarily little interest in sex (Heider, 1976). They reportedly do not have intercourse with their wives for 5 years after a child is born; nor do they seem to have other sexual outlets. Nonetheless, these people do not seem unhappy. At the opposite extreme, the Mangaians, who live on an island in the South Pacific, may have sex up to the time when a woman goes into labor and may resume sex within a few days after the birth of a child, although they typically wait a few months (Marshall, 1971).

Cultural variations occur over time, even within a single group. In the 20 years that followed the decade of the 1950s, attitudes about sex changed dramatically in the United States, in large part because of the development of effective birth control. "Free sex," a motto of the '60s generation, encouraged sexual liberation; people should be free, proponents said, to have sex when and where they choose (in those days, young women sometimes brought a condom and toothbrush with them on the first date). Today, with the spread of

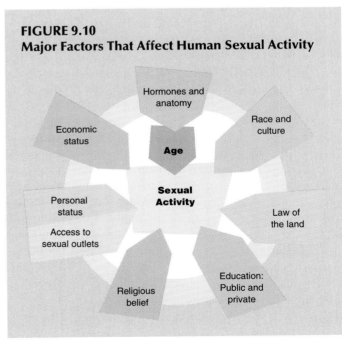

**FIGURE 9.10
Major Factors That Affect Human Sexual Activity**

AIDS and the resurgence of fundamentalist and evangelical religions, sexual behavior may be changing again, becoming less casual. Culture clearly affects how, when, and where sexual behavior occurs.

The male praying mantis can copulate only after its head has been ripped off, a service readily provided by the receptive female. Some lions copulate over 50 times a day. Human sexual behavior is also shaped by our biologies, but it is much more variable than that of other animals.

SEXUAL DYSFUNCTION: WHEN GOOD THINGS GO WRONG. Despite the many variations in human sexual behavior in different times and places, psychologists do consider some sexual behaviors to be dysfunctional. Categorizing a behavior as "dysfunctional" depends in part on the individual, in part on the relationship, and in part on the standards of the surrounding culture. *Sexual dysfunctions*, according to the fourth edition of the *Diagnostic and Statistical Manual of Mental Disorders* (American Psychiatric Association, 1994), "are characterized by disturbance in sexual desire and the psychophysiological changes that characterize the sexual response cycle and cause marked distress and interpersonal difficulty" (p. 493). Included in this description are disorders of sexual desire, arousal, orgasmic disorders, and sexual pain. Many, if not most, problems in the sexual response cycle have psychological causes; they are not caused by physical problems with the sex organs. An example is the inability to reach orgasm. In men, the disorder is called *male erectile dysfunction* (or *impotence*); in women, it is known as *female arousal dysfunction* (previously called *frigidity*). Masters and Johnson found that such sexual disorders often arise because of a preoccupation with personal problems, fears about the possible consequences of sexual activity, or anxiety about sexual performance.

However, at least some sexual dysfunction may have a biological cause. The drug Viagra caused quite a stir when it was first released in the late 1990s because it provided a safe and effective medical treatment for impotence. Viagra doesn't cause an erection. Rather, the drug operates only when a man is sexually excited, by increasing the flow of blood to the penis. Thus Viagra is not a cure but a treatment for impotence, and it is effective only if it continues to be taken. The user of this drug who would derive the most benefit would be a middle-aged man who has difficulty keeping an erection and wants to be sexually active. Some women also use this drug now that it has proved to have a similar effect on the clitoris. However, Viagra commonly has side effects, which range from headache and stomachache to changes in color vision (such as difficulty discriminating between green and blue). Furthermore, in some cases impotence is an early warning sign of something more serious: the veins carrying blood to the penis can become narrowed by buildup of plaque in the blood vessels, which can also lead to heart attacks and stroke. Thus, purchasing Viagra over the Web without seeing a physician is not medically sound.

Another sort of sexual dysfunction can arise when certain stimuli become necessary for sexual arousal. Objects can sometimes become conditioned stimuli for sexual arousal; a common example is a shoe, or even a picture of a shoe. When an object that has no inherent sexual meaning comes to be sexually arousing, it is called a *fetish*. Mental health professionals consider fetishes a problem only if they are necessary for arousal or if they are objectionable to the partner.

Sexual dysfunction is not the same thing as sexual abnormality, which may or may not be dysfunctional. For example, people afflicted with *androgen insensitivity syndrome* have a genetic mutation that does not allow androgen receptors to develop. Thus, the lock is missing for the hormonal key, and the hormone has no effects either during development or afterward. These people, who should have been boys, grow into girls, but with testes tucked up in the belly and no uterus or ovaries. In some cases, the vagina is too shallow and must be surgically altered later in life. In spite of their genetic identities as males, the failure of male hormones to have an effect does not allow the genes to influence their sexuality. In fact, although they sometimes require appropriate female hormone supplements, these people look like women, often marry, and have normal female sex lives (which include normal orgasms during intercourse).

Such cases must be distinguished from *transvestites,* men who dress as women. Docter and Prince (1997) asked more than 1,000 men who sometimes dressed as women to complete a survey about their lives, sexual identities, and behavior. One finding of interest is that the vast majority (87%) claimed to be heterosexual, not homosexual. Eighty-three percent had been married at one time, and 60% were married when they filled in the survey. These men apparently enjoyed their male and female modes of interaction equally.

Homophobia

To study one possible basis of strong negative views of homosexuals, Adams and colleagues (1996) asked two groups of male heterosexuals to watch videotapes that showed heterosexuals, lesbians, or gay men engaging in explicit sex acts. One group of men had scored high on a test of *homophobia,* which is a strong aversion to homosexuality; the other group scored low. While both groups watched the tapes, the researchers recorded changes in penile circumference as an indication of sexual arousal. All the participants became aroused when they saw the heterosexual and lesbian videos, but only the homophobic males were aroused by the homosexual male videos. The investigators note that psychoanalytic theory might explain these results by claiming that the homophobic men had repressed homosexual impulses. Alternatively, they note that another theory would explain the results in terms of anxiety (Barlow, 1986). In this view, the homosexual stimuli produce negative emotions, which in turn lead to anxiety, which in turn enhances arousal, which leads to erection.

Consider this result from the levels perspective. First, it is clear that visual stimuli can trigger the brain mechanisms that lead to arousal. Second, which stimuli are arousing depends on personal characteristics: Men who disliked homosexuals had stronger penile responses to the homosexual videos than did men who were not homophobic. Third, we are led to ask the question, Why did the men who were most aroused by the homosexual video express the greatest dislike of homosexuals? It is easy to speculate that they would not have felt this way in a different culture, such as that of ancient Greece, in which homosexuality was accepted. If the arousal was in fact sexual, these men may actually have been denying their own homosexual tendencies because cultural norms stigmatized such behavior. On the other hand, if the arousal was a consequence of a negative reaction to the films, this response too may have been mitigated had they grown up in a different culture. And of course, such a reaction affects how these people behave and think. For example, they may avoid certain bars or have negative reactions to gays or embrace socially restrictive policies regarding homosexuals.

CONSOLIDATE!

▶ **1. What is the nature of sexual response? What factors lead to it?** According to the most accepted descriptions of sexual activity, people first experience sexual attraction, next desire, and then excitement (arousal), which may be followed by sexual performance; sexual performance involves becoming fully aroused (plateau), orgasm, and finally resolution (followed by a refractory period for men). Hormones play a role in sexual behavior by biasing people to behave in certain ways. Although pheromones play a key role in sexual attraction in some lower animals, they probably play a minor role in humans; humans are more affected by visual stimuli and—for women—odor cues.

▶ **2. What determines whether we are attracted to the same or the opposite sex?** Biological events, caused by either the genes or events in the womb or childhood, appear to play a key role in determining sexual orientation. It is possible that biological events may only indirectly affect sexual orientation, by leading the child to select environments and have experiences that in turn shape sexual orientation.

▶ **3. What is "normal sexual behavior"? How does culture affect our standards of normality?** Sexual variations are considered disorders only if they "cause marked distress and interpersonal difficulty." Although some such variations may have biological roots, they are considered disorders only if they lead to personal and interpersonal unhappiness. Standards of normality are established by culture and can vary over time.

A DEEPER LEVEL
Recap and Thought Questions

► Emotion: I Feel, Therefore I Am

It is useful to distinguish between basic emotions and emotions that arise from combinations of these key building blocks. Ekman and his collaborators have identified six basic emotions: happiness, anger, sadness, disgust, surprise, and fear. Research results have shown that surprise and fear are more easily confused with each other than are any of the others. Plutchik has argued that, like primary colors that can be mixed to form new colors, basic emotions can be combined to form other ones, such as guilt. Emotions can be organized into two broad categories, approach and withdrawal, which rely on different parts of the brain.

Although theories of emotion are often considered alternative views, each in fact has captured a grain of the truth. The James–Lange theory holds that you feel emotion after your body reacts to a situation; the Cannon–Bard theory holds that emotions and bodily reactions occur at the same time; cognitive theory claims that emotions arise when you interpret your bodily reactions in the context of the specific situation; and LeDoux's revision of cognitive theory rests on the idea that some emotions arise from brain responses that do not involve interpretation whereas others arise from cognitive interpretation. As James–Lange predicts, emotions may be caused in part by differences in bodily reactions, such as heart rate, breathing rate, and facial expression. As Cannon–Bard predicts, some emotions, such as fear, are reflexes that produce the experience and the bodily reaction simultaneously. As cognitive theory predicts, how you interpret the causes of your bodily reactions does in fact influence which emotion you feel. Finally, as claimed by LeDoux, some emotions, such as fear, arise via brain mechanisms (particularly those involving the amygdala) that do not rely on interpretation, whereas others do rely on interpretation. Environmental events influence emotion; our happiness, for example, depends in part on our economic and cultural context. Emotions also arise in response to other people's emotional signals, which vary depending on their cultures. Culture affects the display rules we use, the rules that determine when and how we express emotion. Culture also shapes the emotional reaction we will have to moral violations. In addition, culture affects how effectively we can read body language to determine another person's emotion.

Can basic emotions allow us to understand Barbara's emotional state during her dinner with John? Probably not. Emotions are communicated both verbally and nonverbally, and women are particularly good at such nonverbal communication. When John first arrived, Barbara no doubt perceived his emotional state and was probably alarmed, sympathetic, and supportive. None of these emotions are simple "primary colors," but rather are examples of the complex mixtures of emotion that nuance our lives.

Think It Through. Would the world necessarily be a better place if people could control their emotions perfectly? Do you think children have the same emotions as adults? If interpretation plays a key role, in what ways would this limit the emotions very young children feel? How might this change with increasing development?

What would be the advantages and disadvantages of a machine that always detected lies and never mistook the truth for lies? If your school offered a course in reading body language, would you take it? Why or why not?

► Motivation and Reward: Feeling Good

Motivation arises for many reasons. Some of our motivations arise from evolutionarily shaped instincts, sex being an obvious example; others are drives, such as thirst; some drives are designed to maintain homeostasis, such as occurs when we are cold and seek warmth; other motivations center on a preference for an intermediate level of arousal, as happens when we withdraw from even a pleasurable sensation such as music when we've "had enough." We are often motivated by incentives, such as the potential rewards (including money) for engaging in a behavior. Intrinsic motivations propel us to do something for its own sake, and extrinsic motivations propel us to do something for external reasons, such as for a reward you may receive.

A need is a condition that arises when you lack a requirement, which in turn gives rise to a drive to acquire specific rewards to fulfill the requirement; a want is a condition that arises when you have an unmet goal that will not fulfill a requirement, which in turn causes the goal to act as an incentive. The distinction between needs and wants lines up with a distinction between two different brain systems involved in motivation. Needs may be related to a brain system that provides an internal reward when a deprivation is satisfied, such as by eating when you are hungry. In contrast, many wants may be related to a system that provides a reward when you achieve a desired goal but are not deprived. Although our physiological needs can be satisfied, we quickly adapt to our present circumstances and thus our wants can never be fully satisfied. There are many types of needs; the importance of a given need depends partly on your culture, particularly on whether the culture is individualist or collectivist.

Which theory of emotion best explains John's reactions during the mugging? You could make a case for instinct theory, but this theory would not explain why John was particularly prone to being startled as he rushed down the alley. Probably the best account would stem from LeDoux's revision of cognitive theory: John's cognitive interpretation of the situation "potentiated" the brain circuitry (which relies on the amygdala) that is responsible for startle and for freezing. After the mugging, his interpretation of his bodily state, in that context, probably produced his continued fear and left him emotionally unsettled. And when he finally met Barbara, the same mechanisms shifted him to a more positive emotional state.

> **Think It Through.** If you could design a school for young children, how would you organize it so that the children were motivated as strongly as possible? How can you find out what motivates a particular person?
>
> If wants can never be satisfied for very long, does it make sense to try to fulfill them at all? How could you tell if a motivation is a need or a want?
>
> Do you think it might be useful to develop a drug that blocks the deprived reward system? the nondeprived system? Why might such a drug be dangerous? beneficial?

▶ Hunger and Eating: Not Just About Fueling the Body

We eat for many reasons: pleasure, nutrition, as a social activity. The brain senses when the quantity of nutrients in the blood is too low and causes us to feel hungry. We usually eat until signals from the stomach (and other digestive organs) indicate that we've consumed enough food. At the beginning of a meal, taste plays an especially important role in determining whether you want to eat. As a meal progresses, changes in the type of food will keep your appetite up, and tastes (as well as thoughts) that cause insulin to be released will increase hunger. Beliefs about the history of a food item (for example, whether it was ever in contact with something repulsive), and even associations with the shape of the food affect how appealing it is. Overeating can lead the set point of your body weight to move up, and once moved up, set points are difficult to move down again. Obese people do not have "weak characters" but rather often may be genetically predisposed to becoming obese.

During their anniversary dinner, could John and Barbara have been eating for different reasons? John was not hungry initially, and only after beginning to eat did he become hungry. In spite of her sympathy for John's plight, Barbara would not have experienced the same hunger-dampening trauma and thus would probably have begun eating because she was sensitive to signals that her blood sugar level was low. Toward the end of the meal, John may have decided to "reward himself for surviving" and thus indulged in a large dessert, whereas Barbara may have had no such desire.

> **Think It Through.** In the 1930s, Coke bottles held 6.5 ounces; today, they hold a liter—more than five times the original amount. We tend to think of a bottle as a single serving or perhaps two servings. What effects do you think this sort of change has on consumption? Does it make a difference that a lot of Coke is consumed on social occasions with a lot of people? If so, how could such a difference be minimized?

▶ Sex: Not Just About Having Babies

Sexual attraction leads to sexual desire, sexual excitement (arousal), and possibly sexual performance (which involves becoming fully aroused, reaching orgasm, and then experiencing resolution followed, for men, by a refractory period). Hormones play a key role in sexual development and modify motivation toward sexual behavior. Sexual desire and arousal can be triggered by various cues, with visual stimuli often playing a critical role (and odor playing a particularly important role for women).

There is evidence that male homosexuals have differences in certain brain structures, and that female homosexuals have differences in the operation of certain neural systems (involved in hearing), from heterosexuals. Such biological differences are caused either by genes or by events in the womb or during childhood. There is evidence that at least some forms of homosexuality are genetic. Sexual behaviors differ in different cultures, and what constitutes normal sexual behaviors varies widely. Sexual variations are considered disorders only if they cause "marked distress and interpersonal difficulty."

Could John have been sexually aroused because of his traumatic experience? Sexual arousal depends partly on the context; when John was in fight-or-flight mode, he was not likely to be thinking of sex. However, in another context, he might misattribute the beating of his heart, heavy breathing, and so on as indicators of sexual arousal. In this case, he probably correctly attributed his emotional upheaval and during dinner may even have misattributed bodily signs of arousal as additional results of his mugging—leading him to be less sexually aroused than he would otherwise have been.

> **Think It Through.** Could someone feel sexual desire for a partner but have a hard time becoming sexually aroused? Why or why not? Would it be ethical to use a perfume or aftershave lotion that contained pheromones that made you sexually attractive when you were going out on a date?
>
> Do you think researchers should be trying to find a gene (or genes) for homosexuality? What positive uses could such knowledge have? what negative uses? Would it be ethical to try to alter such genes either before conception or in the womb?

10 PERSONALITY

Vive la Difference!

Tina and Gabe met in their introductory psychology class. They were immediately attracted to each other and started studying together. After a few conversations they were pleased to discover they had similar values and political views. Predictably, they began going out together. On their fourth date, though, Tina began to realize that she and Gabe weren't as much alike as she had thought; she was surprised by this because their views on so many issues were so similar. Tina sometimes had trouble "reading" Gabe because he was shy and emotionally steady, without many highs or lows; his manner was "mellow." She wondered why he wasn't more enthusiastic when she proposed activities she thought would be fun to do together, such as in-line skating, bungee-jumping, or biking. "Well, opposites attract, I guess," she thought. And although Gabe enjoyed Tina's spirit, her outgoingness and emotional vibrancy, her interest in trying new things, now and then he asked her why she was so emotional and always in such a hurry. Tina began to worry that, even though they were strongly attracted to each other, a long-term relationship might reveal persistent problems between them that would be difficult to overcome.

Do these differences reveal something fundamental about Tina and Gabe as people? Do they reflect their personalities? And if so, are personalities set in stone? This chapter explores the idea of personality, how psychologists measure it, and the perspectives of a number of different theorists who have sought to describe and explain it. We'll consider issues such as the genetic influence on personality development; the relation of inner motives, thoughts, and feelings to personality; and the effects of the social environment on personality.

WHAT IS PERSONALITY?

As Tina got to know Gabe, she began to make certain assumptions about him, about who he was as a person. He studied hard and did well on psychology exams and quizzes, so Tina figured he was smart, hard-working, and conscientious. (Tina did well on her psychology exams and quizzes, too, but she didn't study much. She considered herself smart, but not particularly hard-working.) So she was surprised to discover that Gabe's apartment was a disaster area—she had assumed he would be as orderly and neat in his personal space as he was in his approach to schoolwork, and so she wondered whether his "personality," as she thought of it, was altogether consistent. Tina also noticed that, on dates, Gabe preferred to get together for dinner and a movie, not for lunch or an afternoon break ("Too much studying," he said). If she suggested going to a party together, Gabe invariably declined; he didn't like parties. Tina attributed this reluctance to his shyness.

The concept of personality infuses daily life. When you describe a co-worker as "intense," wonder how a friend will handle a piece of bad news, or think about the type of partner you would like to have in life, personality is exerting its influence. What exactly is this quality, which is part and parcel of each of us? **Personality** has been described as the "consistent patterns of thoughts, feelings, and actions that people demonstrate" (Maddi, 1989, p. 4) that distinguish individuals from each other. Thus the very concept of personality implies that people have enduring, stable qualities such as, say, talkativeness or curiosity. These qualities are called **personality traits,** relatively consistent characteristics exhibited across a range of situations. But notice the "relatively" in the preceding sentence. Let's see just what that means.

▶ 1. Does such a thing as a consistent personality really exist, or do our behaviors, thoughts, and feelings depend primarily on the situation?

▶ 2. How do psychologists group personality traits into sets of personality types?

▶ 3. What methods do psychologists use to measure personality?

Personality: Traits or Situations?

Traits exist on a continuum (for example, from extremely quiet to extremely talkative). Gabe's shyness and Tina's adventurousness can be considered traits. Many trait theorists—personality psychologists who study traits and believe that personality is built on traits—assume that everyone has the same set of traits, but that for each person each trait falls at a different point on its continuum. Some trait theorists propose that our traits lead us to behave in certain ways; this view would suggest that Gabe avoided parties because of his trait of shyness. Not all trait theorists share the belief in this cause-and-effect relationship, however; some trait theorists regard traits simply as labels for collections of behaviors rather than as causes of them (Buss & Craik, 1984).

Traits by definition imply consistency. But are our personality traits always consistent? Bem and Allen (1974) found that people are not equally consistent on *all* traits. When they asked participants to rate how *consistently* friendly and conscientious they were, they found large variability in consistency; not all participants felt that they were

Personality: A consistent set of characteristics that people display over time and across situations, and that distinguish individuals from each other.

Personality trait: A relatively consistent characteristic exhibited in different situations.

consistent on these traits. People who rated themselves as consistent on the trait of friendliness were more likely to have their behaviors reflect that trait than people who viewed themselves as inconsistent on the trait of friendliness. For instance, those consistent on the trait of friendliness were more likely to strike up a conversation with a sales clerk. Similar results were found for the trait of conscientiousness: People who rated themselves as consistent on this trait were more likely to exhibit relevant behaviors, such as carefully double-checking term papers for typing and spelling errors. Kenrick and Stringfield (1980) further refined Bem and Allen's research by showing that everyone is consistent on some traits, but that the particular traits on which people differ vary across individuals. Thus, everyone does not have some level of each trait; some traits are just irrelevant for some of us—they aren't important in our lives (Britt & Shepperd, 1999). For example, Gabe may be inconsistent on the general dimension of conscientiousness, which would explain the coexistence of his conscientious attention to schoolwork and his careless housekeeping at home. Whether or not traits are viewed as causing behavior, they certainly aren't always accurate in *predicting* behavior (witness Gabe's domestic messiness). The situations in which we find ourselves can exert powerful influences on behavior, thoughts, and feelings.

The names of Snow White's seven dwarves fit their personalities. Imagine the personalities of dwarves named Dirty, Hungry, Shifty, Flabby, Puffy, Crabby, Awful, Doleful, all of which were on Disney Studios' list of possible names (Seuling, 1976). The final choices work so well because we view their personalities as consistent with their names; but what if Grumpy were, in fact, upbeat and easy-going!

SITUATIONISM: DIFFERENT TRAITS FOR DIFFERENT CONTEXTS.
Does the following paragraph represent an accurate description of your personality?

> You have a strong need for other people to like you and for them to admire you. You have a tendency to be critical of yourself. You have a great deal of unused capacity which you have not turned to your advantage. While you have some personality weaknesses, you are generally able to compensate for them. Your sexual adjustment has presented some problems for you. Disciplined and controlled on the outside, you tend to be worrisome and insecure inside. At times you have serious doubts as to whether you have made the right decision or done the right thing. You prefer a certain amount of change and variety and become dissatisfied when hemmed in by restrictions and limitations. You pride yourself as being an independent thinker and do not accept others' opinions without satisfactory proof. You have found it unwise to be too frank in revealing yourself to others. At times you are extroverted, affable, sociable, while at other times you are introverted, wary, and reserved. Some of your aspirations tend to be pretty unrealistic. (Ulrich et al., 1963, p. 832)

Does this sound like you? If you had taken a personality test and this paragraph was given to you as a summary of your test results, you probably would have agreed with it. That is exactly what happened in a study in which undergraduate participants were asked to take a personality test and then *all the participants* were given this same paragraph as a summary of their results, *regardless of their responses on the test*. The students rated the summary interpretation as good or excellent (Snyder & Larson, 1972; Ulrich et al., 1963). But how could "one size fit all"—how can we make sense of these results? Because most people experience some of the traits described in the summary *in some situations* and at *some points in their lives*. Hence, the statements were true—some of the time. Reread the paragraph, and note how many of the statements present descriptions of two opposing characteristics, such as being extroverted at times, introverted at other times. This kind of dual presentation is what makes horoscopes so often seem to be on the mark.

A larger question arises, then, about the consistency of personality traits: If much of our behavior depends on the situation in which we find ourselves, is there such a thing as a consistent personality trait at all? To investigate this question, Hartshorne and May (1928) gave grade-school children the opportunity for undetected deceit: to lie about how many push-ups they were able to do, to lie to their parents about how much work they did at home, to cheat on a school test, and to keep money they were given for other purposes. The researchers found that children who were dishonest in one situation were not necessarily dishonest in another; a child who cheated on a test would not necessarily lie to his or her parents. Although the children showed some consistency across situations, less than 10% of the variation of behaviors across situations could be explained by a single, common, underlying trait of honesty. Not surprisingly, though, the less similar the situations, the lower were the correlations of honesty between situations; lying and stealing were not highly correlated. Remember that a correlation (see Chapter 1) is an index of how closely related two sets of measured variables are, in this case lying and stealing.

Similarly, Mischel and Peake (1982) observed college students and recorded 19 different behaviors reflecting conscientiousness, as defined by how regularly they attended class, how promptly they completed assignments, how neatly they made their beds, and how neatly they recorded class notes. They found that the students were likely to be consistent in similar situations, but not across different types of situations. The researchers did not find a single "conscientiousness trait" that governed behavior in all situations.

In later research, Mischel (1984) found that inconsistency across situations is pervasive; he found this not only with the traits of honesty and conscientiousness, but also with other traits, such as aggression and dependency. Furthermore, different measures of what should be the same trait often were only weakly correlated, or not related at all. Such findings led to the theory of **situationism,** which holds that a person's behavior is mostly a function of a given situation, not of internal traits. Situationism recognizes that, in part, we create our own situations, not necessarily by our actions but simply by who we are. In other words, characteristics such as age, sex, race, religion, ethnicity, and socioeconomic status can influence other people's behavior toward us, often in culturally determined ways, creating a different "situation," which can in turn lead to differences in people's behavior (see the discussion of microenvironments in Chapter 8). Nineteen-year-old Tina behaves very differently with Gabe—drinking from his cup, calling him past midnight—than with her 52-year-old female economics professor. In each case, Tina's age, sex, and status relative to the other person might be said to change her behavior. If you knew Tina only from economics lectures, you might be surprised by how different her "personality" seemed when she was with Gabe.

Most Americans do not view Hillary Rodham Clinton as having a light-hearted, fun-loving personality. Situationism would say that people have a certain view of her personality because we usually only see photos or video clips of her in a particular kind of situation (political), but don't see her in other types of situations (relaxed and having fun). If we did, her personality would not appear so consistent. This is what makes the photo on the right striking; it suggests a different personality than the one we usually see.

Taken to its extreme, situationism views traits as mere illusions. People we know seem to have stable personalities because we tend to see them in the same kinds of situations. Thus, when we label someone's behavior as part of a personality trait, we are imposing order on his or her behavior, much as the Gestalt laws of organization (see Chapter 3) impose an order on what is before our eyes. It makes us more comfortable to think that we can "peg" someone, that we can predict how he or she will behave. For example, at one time, the state of Iowa required people wanting to buy liquor to have liquor cards, which were punched with every purchase. Parents learned to ask to see their daughter's date's liquor card in an attempt to infer his personality from the number of holes in his card (Seuling, 1988). If the date had a card that looked like Swiss cheese, the trait "heavy drinker" (or, even more broadly, "irresponsible lout") became the lens through which his subsequent behaviors were filtered. If his car had a flat, that was seen as another example of his irresponsible behavior. Of course, it was possible that his card was practically see-through because the previous week he threw a surprise anniversary party for his

Situationism: A view of personality that regards behavior as mostly a function of the situation, not of internal traits.

parents and purchased champagne for many guests. Nonetheless, viewing the number of holes on a date's card was, for a girl's parents, a way of attempting to impose order and make predictions about his probable future behavior.

INTERACTIONISM: WHO, WHERE, AND WHEN. Not surprisingly, situationism has had strong critics who point out that, over long periods of time and over many situations, people are fairly consistent, and that the more precisely a trait is defined, the more accurate it is in predicting behavior (Wiggins, 1992). Thus, saying that someone is sociable will not predict his or her behavior at a party nearly as well as saying the person appears at ease in interactions with new people. This is the tradeoff: The more narrowly a trait is defined, the better it is a predictor of behavior, but the fewer circumstances there are to which it can be applied.

Nevertheless, the power of the situation cannot be denied: People do behave differently in different contexts. Thus, a synthesis of the traditional trait view and situationism evolved, called **interactionism**, which suggests that traits, situations, and their interactions affect behavior, thoughts, and feelings. As proof, the interactionists point to studies such as the one by Endler and Hunt (1969), in which participants were asked to describe their reaction to various threats. Some of the threats involved a loss of self-esteem, such as might accompany failing an exam; others involved physical harm, such as being on a high ledge of a mountain; and still others involved an ambiguous threat, such as getting a summons from the police. The results showed that *both* individual differences in traits *and* differences in the situation affected people's reactions. Some people appeared to be generally more fearful than others (a trait), and some situations (such as being approached by cars racing abreast) were more fear-provoking than others (such as sitting in a favorite restaurant). Moreover, people differed with regard to which situations were particularly fear-provoking, and how they responded to those situations. Similarly, on personality tests, Asian Americans tend to show lower levels of assertiveness than do whites. However, Zane and colleagues (1991) found that this is true only when the people involved are strangers. Thus, the interactionists say, it isn't really accurate to describe Asian Americans as "high on the anxiety trait" in general; a better characterization would be the more specific "anxiety when among strangers."

Thus, people's personalities can affect their situations in two major ways. First, people often can choose their situations—their jobs, their friends, their leisure activities. And, insofar as they are able, people tend to choose environments that fit their personalities. It's up to you, for instance, to decide whether to go bungee-jumping or sunbathing at the beach for the day. Second, people also find opportunities to create their environments. An aggressive person, for instance, will create a tense situation by words or deeds (A. Buss, 1995), and others will react accordingly.

Factors of Personality: The Big Five? Three? More?

How many personality traits are there? The answer depends on how specific you want to be about a given trait. You could be very specific, narrowing down behavior all the way to a "shy-so-only-goes-on-dates-to-dinner-and-a-movie-but-not-to-parties" trait. Narrowing traits to this level of precision, however, poses certain problems. Each trait explains only particular patterns of behaviors and thoughts in very specific instances. For example, you could consider sociability (which personality psychologists call "extraversion") a trait. Or you could say that extraversion is really a combination of the more specific traits of warmth, gregariousness, and assertiveness. In this case, you could say that sociability is a *personality dimension*, a set of related personality traits. Using the statistical technique of factor analysis (see Chapter 8), some researchers have sought to discover whether specific traits are in fact associated and, together, constitute a more general trait; such a personality dimension is sometimes called a *superfactor*.

Interactionism: A view of personality in which both traits and situations are believed to affect behavior, thoughts, and feelings.

TABLE 10.1

The Big Five Superfactors and Their Traits

Source: *Adapted from Costa, McCrae, & Dye (1991).*

SUPERFACTOR	TRAITS
Extraversion	Warmth, gregariousness, assertiveness, activity, excitement seeking, positive emotions.
Neuroticism (also called *Emotionality*)	Anxiety, hostility, depression, self-consciousness, impulsiveness, vulnerability.
Agreeableness	Trust, straightforwardness, altruism, compliance, modesty, tender-mindedness.
Conscientiousness (also called *Dependability*)	Competence, order, dutifulness, achievement striving, deliberation, self-discipline.
Openness	Fantasy, aesthetics, feelings, actions, ideas, values.

Many factor analytic studies have revealed that traits can be reduced to five super-factors, which are listed along with their included traits in Table 10.1 (Digman, 1990; McCrae & Costa, 1987). These superfactors are sometimes referred to as the Five Factor Model, or the **"Big Five"** (Goldberg, 1981): extraversion (also called *sociability*), neuroticism (also called *emotionality*), agreeableness, conscientiousness (also called *dependability*), and openness to experience (Costa et al., 1991). However, depending on the personality inventory used, different individual traits may make up each of the five superfactors, and hence some of the superfactors are given different names by different researchers. Some versions of extraversion and neuroticism, however, are found in almost all lists, perhaps reflecting how fundamental these two dimensions are to personality.

Psychologist Hans Eysenck identified not five but three superfactors or, as he labeled them, personality dimensions: extraversion, neuroticism, and psychoticism. While Eysenck's first two dimensions resemble the Big Five's superfactors of the same names, the third—psychoticism—was originally thought to measure a propensity toward becoming psychotic, that is, toward loss of touch with reality, as occurs in schizophrenia (Eysenck, 1992). It is true that people with schizophrenia score high on this dimension; however, psychoticism as defined by Eysenck also contains traits related to social deviance, such as criminality and substance addiction, and to a lack of conventional socialization, such as respect for rules and the feelings of others (Costa & McCrae, 1995). For this reason, Eysenck's psychoticism includes some of the traits listed under the Big Five's superfactors of agreeableness and conscientiousness (or lack thereof) (Draycott & Kline, 1995; Saggino, 2000).

Instead of using the term psychoticism, others have suggested using a broader term such as *nonconformity* or *social deviance* in order to highlight the traits of creativity and nonconformity that are also a part of this dimension. Artists, for example, tend to score higher on this personality dimension than people who are truly psychotic (Zuckerman et al., 1988). The Big Five's openness superfactor has no direct counterpart in Eysenck's model.

Although personality dimensions may be a useful way of conceptualizing personality, they are less predictive of behavior than the traits on which they are built (Paunonen, 1998). And although the identification and description of traits and personality dimensions were and continue to be important contributions to the process of understanding personality, this sort of cataloging work doesn't take the crucial next step: attempting to explain and thereby predict human behavior. For this explo-

"Big Five": Five superfactors of personality—extraversion, neuroticism, agreeableness, conscientiousness, and openness—determined by factor analysis.

ration we must turn to theories of personality that focus on explaining and predicting behavior. An essential tool in all such theories is reliable measurement.

Measuring Personality: Is Grumpy Really Grumpy?

Let's assume for the moment, despite the view taken by situationism, that personality does exist. If so, psychologists, employers, teachers, and parents—indeed, all of us—might be able to understand and predict the behavior of others by discovering as much as possible about their personalitities. Various instruments for assessing personality attempt to do just that. Most personality assessments focus on measuring overt behaviors that psychologists believe to be manifestations of a given trait, inferring the strength of a trait from an individual's behavior. The use of behavior to infer personality traits is at the heart of all the methods of personality assessment discussed here.

INTERVIEWS. Interviews to assess personality are usually *structured*; that is, the interviewer asks all interviewees questions from predetermined sets, adding or omitting specific questions spontaneously based on the subjects' responses. The questions often focus on specific behaviors or beliefs and do not require the person being interviewed to reflect on his or her personality. An advantage of the structured interview is that the interviewer comes away with a sense of knowing the interviewee and is able to infer different aspects of his or her personality.

The interview also has disadvantages: Unless the interviewee answers the questions honestly and accurately, the personality assessment is not valid. In addition, from a research perspective, it is difficult to generalize about personality characteristics beyond one interviewee. An interviewer might discover that Gabe has many conscientious behaviors and beliefs, yet he confesses to keeping a messy apartment. It does not follow that all people who have many conscientious behaviors and beliefs are terrible housekeepers.

OBSERVATION. Whether we are aware of it or not, we all use observation to learn about other people's personalities; that's what Tina did to get a sense of Gabe's personality. When psychologists use observation to assess personality, they assign observers, known as "judges," to rate participants' behaviors. Each participant's personality is then inferred from the ratings.

How accurate are observations? The better the judge knows the person about whom ratings are being made, the more accurate the ratings (Paulhus & Bruce, 1992; Wiggins & Pincus, 1992). But strangers can also provide accurate ratings as long as their judgments are based on observations of the appropriate behaviors related to the personality trait being assessed (Ozer & Reise, 1994). If you attempt to assess assertiveness by counting how often someone raises a hand in class, your conclusion may not be very accurate: Reluctance to volunteer may reflect reading assignments that were never read!

INVENTORIES: CHECK THIS. Perhaps the most common method of personality assessment is a **personality inventory,** a paper-and-pencil test that requires those being assessed to read statements and indicate whether each is true or false about themselves (only two choices) or how much they agree or disagree with each statement along a multipoint rating scale (three or more choices). Personality inventories usually assess many different traits and contain a great number of statements, often more than 300. This comprehensiveness, including statements on different aspects of each trait, ensures the validity of the inventory.

Rather than producing a single indicator of personality (such as "friendly" or "seeks excitement"), the results of a personality inventory provide information about a number of traits in the form of a *personality profile*, a summary of the different

Personality inventory: A pencil-and-paper method for assessing personality that requires the test-taker to read statements and indicate whether each is true or false about themselves.

FIGURE 10.1
Personality Profiles and Employment

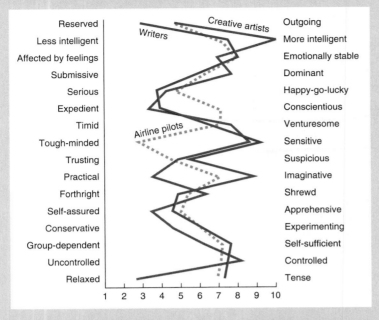

Completed personality inventories provide personality profiles of different traits. According to Cattell's personality inventory (the 16PF for 16 personality factors), writers, creative artists, and airline pilots show different profiles.

traits that constitute someone's personality (see Figure 10.1). Personality inventories are used in a variety of settings and for a variety of purposes: by mental health professionals to assess psychopathology; by research psychologists to assess personality traits as they relate to other variables; by employers to assess personality characteristics related to aspects of the job (Borman et al., 1997). For example, many employers use scores on the trait of conscientiousness to predict employee theft, absenteeism, termination, and "good citizenship" at work (Organ & Ryan, 1995; Sackett, 1994). But not all jobs are well served by very conscientious people; work that requires artistic ability appears to fare better in the hands of those low on conscientiousness (Hogan & Hogan, 1993).

The advantage of personality inventories is that they are easy to administer; the drawback is that responses can be biased in several ways. Some people are more likely to check off "agree" than "disagree," regardless of the content of the statement. This response style, called *acquiescence*, can be reduced by wording half the items negatively. Thus an item such as "I often feel shy when meeting new people" would be reworded as "I don't usually feel shy when meeting new people." Another bias is **social desirability:** answering questions in a way that you think makes you look "good," even if the answer is not true. For instance, some people might not agree with the statement "It is better to be honest, even if others don't like you for it" but think that they should, and respond accordingly. To compensate for this bias, many personality inventories have a scale that assesses the respondent's propensity to answer in a socially desirable manner. This scale is then used to adjust or, in the language of testing, to "correct" the scores on the part of the inventory that measures traits. Some researchers have found relatively high correlations between personality assessment by inventory and judges' ratings of personality (Johnson, J. A., 2000; McCrae & Costa, 1989b), lending support for the idea that the easier-to-administer personality inventories yield information similar to personality assessment by judges. One personality inventory is Raymond Cattell's 16PF (Cattell et al., 1970; see Figure 10.1). Another, the **Minnesota Multiphasic Personality Inventory-2 (MMPI-2)**, is commonly used to assess psychopathology (Butcher & Rouse, 1996).

PROJECTIVE TESTS: FACES IN THE CLOUDS.

A **projective test** presents the respondent with an ambiguous stimulus, such as a shapeless blot of ink or a drawing of people, and asks the respondent to make sense of the stimulus. The respondent is then asked to provide the story behind the stimulus: What does the inkblot look like? What are the people in the drawing doing? The theory behind projective tests is that people's personalities can be revealed by what they project onto an ambiguous stimulus as their minds impose structure on it. This is the reasoning behind the

People are shown a drawing like this one from the Thematic Apperception Test (TAT) and asked to explain what is happening in the picture, what led up to it, what will happen later, and what the characters are thinking and feeling.

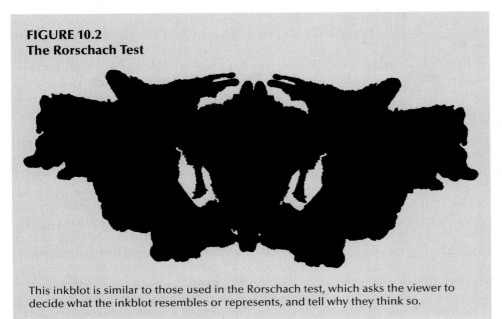

FIGURE 10.2
The Rorschach Test

This inkblot is similar to those used in the Rorschach test, which asks the viewer to decide what the inkblot resembles or represents, and tell why they think so.

Rorschach test (see Figure 10.2). Developed by Herman Rorschach (1884–1922), this commonly used projective technique has 10 cards, each with a different inkblot. The ambiguous shapes of the inkblots allow people to use their imaginations as they decide what the shapes might represent or resemble (for example, a bat or a butterfly) and what features of the inkblot made them think so.

The *Thematic Apperception Test (TAT)*, developed in the 1930s by Henry Murray, relies on the same concept as the Rorschach but uses detailed black-and-white drawings, often with people in them. The reliability and validity of the Rorschach test and the TAT have been the targets of criticism. One person taking the test on two occasions, for example, may give dramatically different answers each time, leading to different personality assessments (Anastasi, 1988; Entwisle, 1972).

LOOKING AT LEVELS

Genes and Personality Dimensions

As you have seen, psychologists have categorized personality traits by clustering them into personality dimensions, or superfactors. Is this the best way to categorize traits, or is there perhaps a better way? Cloninger and his colleagues (1993) suggest organizing personality traits so that they correspond to distinct biological systems. These researchers believe that people differ on four basic personality dimensions: novelty seeking (an "exhilaration or excitement in response to novel stimuli"); harm avoidance; dependence on rewards; and persistence. Cloninger further proposes that there are distinct biological systems that correspond to these four traits, each of which cuts across the Big Five. For example, novelty seeking corresponds to a combination of a high score on extraversion and a low score on conscientiousness in the Big Five (as cited in Benjamin et al., 1996). Cloninger and his colleagues hypothesized that the novelty-seeking dimension arises directly from the functioning brain systems that use dopamine. Earlier studies with animals had shown that dopamine is involved in exploratory behavior, and a lack of dopamine in people with Parkinson's disease leads to low novelty seeking (Cloninger et al., 1993). In normal people, according to Cloninger, differences in novelty seeking are caused by genetically determined differences in the effects of dopamine.

To test this hypothesis, Ebstein and colleagues (1996) examined people who have a particular gene that produces a type of dopamine receptor. They found that people who have this gene score higher on novelty seeking than do people without it. This result held true for men and women, for different age groups, and for different ethnic backgrounds. Although the effects of this gene were evident (in opposite ways) on extraversion and conscientiousness when the Big Five scales were used, these effects were captured more simply by the single trait of novelty seeking.

Consider in more detail what this novelty-seeking scale measures, and the implications of genetic influence. Ebstein and colleagues note that people who score higher than average on this measure are "impulsive, exploratory, fickle, excitable, quick-tempered and extravagant, whereas those who score lower than average tend to be reflective, rigid, loyal, stoic, slow-tempered, and frugal" (p. 78). Take loyalty, for example. This is a key aspect of most intimate human relationships. Is it possible that genes affect whether a person is likely to be loyal? If so, we would then have startling interactions among the levels of analysis, with genes affecting events in the brain, which affect personality, which in turn affects relationships and the social activities to which people are drawn. According to this theory, genes can produce consistent impulsive, extravagant behavior; what sort of person would be attracted to someone with that personality? If in this instance "opposites attract" and someone at the other end of the range becomes the partner, how are things likely to go for this couple in which one member is not particularly loyal and loves novelty and excitement?

It is important to emphasize, however, that although genes do bias people in certain ways, these influences are biases only and do not inevitably and unvaryingly lead to those behaviors (see Chapters 2 and 8). The average difference in novelty-seeking scores between people who did and did not have the dopamine receptor gene were about half a standard deviation (this is a difference similar to that between an IQ of 110 and an IQ of 118, which is not a huge difference). Nevertheless, it is clear that, to understand personality, we need to look at all three levels of analysis: events at the level of the brain (in this case dopamine), the person, and the group (including the situation and physical environment).

CONSOLIDATE!

▶ **1. Does such a thing as a consistent personality really exist, or do our behaviors, thoughts, and feelings depend primarily on the situation?** Trait theorists argue that personality is composed of enduring traits that lead people to behave in specific ways. Situationism argues that there are no enduring personality traits; rather, behavior depends on the situation. Interactionism proposes that some enduring personality traits do exist, and the interaction of traits with the situation determines behavior, thoughts, and feelings.

▶ **2. How do psychologists group personality traits into sets of personality types?** The Big Five superfactors refer to the Five Factor Model of personality, which was derived through the statistical technique of factor analysis of personality inventories. The five superfactors are extraversion, neuroticism, agreeableness, conscientiousness, and openness to experience. Each superfactor is composed of a number of specific traits. Eysenck proposes three rather than five personality dimensions (his term for superfactors): extraversion, neuroticism, and psychoticism. Cloninger proposes a different set of four dimensions, based on biological systems.

▶ **3. What methods do psychologists use to measure personality?** There are four major ways to assess personality: interviews; observation; inventories, such as Cattell's 16PF, which yields a personality profile; and projective tests, such as the Rorschach test and the Thematic Apperception Test (TAT). Psychologists most commonly use inventories to assess personality.

THE BRAIN: THE PERSONALITY ORGAN

As their relationship progressed, Tina began to notice a host of ways in which she and Gabe were different: She loved in-line skating, biking, dancing, and skiing;

he liked to read outdoors (weather permitting), go on long walks, and watch movies. She liked to meet new people or hang out with her friends and generally didn't enjoy being alone; Gabe had a few close friends but was happy spending time by himself. Tina was fairly straightforward and, up to a point, flexible; Gabe seemed less direct and more rigid. Tina was spontaneous and a bit anxious; Gabe was not spontaneous and never seemed anxious, depressed, or worried. Tina could be impatient, sometimes even snappish; Gabe was always kind and gentle. When Tina was finally able to drag Gabe to a party (he kept forgetting he had agreed to go), she was surprised by his reaction: He stayed in a corner talking to one person for half an hour, then announced that he'd had enough and was ready to leave. Tina, on the other hand, felt like the party was just beginning. Taken together, the differences between them left Tina increasingly puzzled and wondering why they were attracted to each other.

As described in Cloninger's classification of personality, some aspects of personality are biologically based, so personalities are partly born, not made. Is Gabe shy and mellow because of his physiology? Is Tina outgoing and a bit anxious because of her genes or hormones? And given that there is a biological factor to personality, are our personalities set in stone before we are even born, or does the environment play a role in forming our personalities? Let's explore the biological basis of personality.

▶ 1. What are "introverts" and "extraverts"? How does Eysenck's theory explain the origin of personality?

▶ 2. What, exactly, is temperament?

▶ 3. What does the field of behavioral genetics say about the genes' effects on personality?

Eysenck's Theory

Hans Eysenck viewed each of his three personality dimensions—extraversion, neuroticism, and psychoticism—as the top point of a pyramid, built on a most basic level of associations between stimulus and response (see Figure 10.3), which form habit responses, which then form traits. However, Eysenck went beyond simply describing personality dimensions and attempted to discover the origins of their variations. Eysenck viewed these three dimensions and their associated traits as hereditary and universal among humans, and even among some other animals, such as

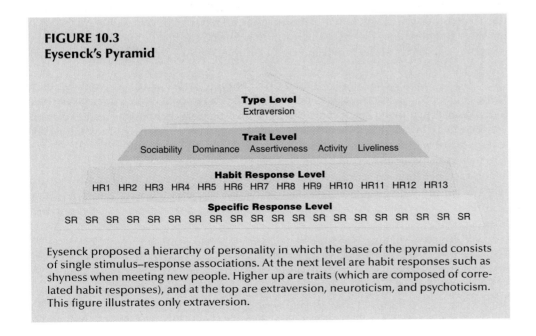

FIGURE 10.3
Eysenck's Pyramid

Type Level
Extraversion

Trait Level
Sociability   Dominance   Assertiveness   Activity   Liveliness

Habit Response Level
HR1 HR2 HR3 HR4 HR5 HR6 HR7 HR8 HR9 HR10 HR11 HR12 HR13

Specific Response Level
SR SR SR SR SR SR SR SR SR SR SR SR SR SR SR SR SR SR SR SR

Eysenck proposed a hierarchy of personality in which the base of the pyramid consists of single stimulus–response associations. At the next level are habit responses such as shyness when meeting new people. Higher up are traits (which are composed of correlated habit responses), and at the top are extraversion, neuroticism, and psychoticism. This figure illustrates only extraversion.

rhesus monkeys. From his own research and that of other investigators, he came to view personality differences as arising in large part from physiological differences, not differences in environment or social surroundings. Eysenck argued that these physiological differences affect everyday behaviors and thus personality (Eysenck, 1967). As you will see, there is support for Eysenck's idea of a biological basis of personality (Matthews & Gilliland, 1999).

THE EXTRAVERTED NERVOUS SYSTEM. Think about someone (a real or fictitious person) whom you'd describe as subdued, quiet, perhaps shy and solitary; now think of someone who enjoys people and social stimulation. The first person would probably score low on Eysenck's extraversion dimension and would be termed an *introvert;* the second, scoring high, would be an *extravert.* Researchers have identified differences at the level of the brain between introverts and extraverts. The nature of these differences seems at first surprising, but less so after a little thought.

In contrast to introverts, extraverts are less "arousable" (Haier et al., 1984); it takes more stimulation to arouse or overstimulate them (Eysenck & Eysenck, 1967). This at first seems an unlikely finding, but consider what it means: Because of this greater need, extraverts seek out activities that are more stimulating and arousing (recreational activities such as hang gliding, or occupations such as espionage). Introverts and extraverts also have different physiological responses to caffeine, nicotine, and sedatives (Corr & Kumari, 1997; Corr et al., 1995; Stelmack, 1990). Differences are also found in skin conductance and EEG recordings (Eysenck, 1990a; Matthews & Amelang, 1993). The biological influence of this dimension has been further refined by Gray (1987), who suggests a mechanism based on activation or "reward," and a mechanism based on inhibition or "punishment." Extraverts are more sensitive to, and more easily conditioned by, reward, whereas introverts are more sensitive to, and more easily conditioned by, punishment. Gray views these differences as attributable to specific brain structures, neurotransmitters, and neuromodulators, and research has shown differences in EEG activation in introverts and extraverts during a card game in which money is lost (punishment) or won (reward; Bartussek et al., 1993). However, more recent research has shown that it may be the trait of anxiety, not introversion per se, that moderates the effect of punishment (Corr et al., 1997).

THE NEUROTIC NERVOUS SYSTEM. Those who score high on the dimension of neuroticism are easily and intensely emotionally aroused and so are more likely to experience conditioned emotional responses—that is, emotional responses elicited by previously neutral stimuli (see Chapter 5; Eysenck, 1979). Thus, someone high on this dimension who is stuck in an elevator is more likely to develop an elevator phobia than someone low on this dimension. Zuckerman (1991) hypothesizes that an increased sensitivity of the amygdala is responsible for this ease of emotional arousal (see Chapter 9).

Canli and colleagues (in press) used fMRI to monitor brain activity while women looked at positive pictures (such as puppies playing, a happy couple) and negative pictures (such as people crying, a cemetery). The investigators then looked at the relation between the women's extraversion and neuroticism scores and their brain activity in several regions. Extraversion scores were correlated with activation in one set of brain areas when the women looked at the positive pictures (compared with negative ones); in contrast, neuroticism scores were correlated with activation in another set of brain areas when the women looked at negative pictures (compared with positive ones). This result is convincing evidence that these dimensions are measuring different types of processing.

THE HIGH-PSYCHOTICISM NERVOUS SYSTEM. Eysenck views those high on psychoticism as having less control over their emotions and therefore as more likely to be aggressive or impulsive. Zuckerman suggests that those high on psychoticism have difficulty learning not to engage in particular behaviors. Eysenck theorized that tendencies toward criminal behavior among males are genetically determined. In fact, he claimed that 50–60% of the variability in such tendencies is inherited (Eysenck, 1990b). This does not mean that some people are born crooks, but rather that some are born with autonomic and central nervous system underarousal that indirectly leads them to seek risks—and some of these risks, given exposure to certain environmental influences, may be associated with criminal behavior (Eysenck, 1977). Low arousal may occur in part because of low levels of activity of the neurotransmitter serotonin in the central nervous system, a condition that has been associated with impulsive behavior (Klinteberg et al., 1993; Linnoila et al., 1983). Indeed, Raine and colleagues (1990) showed that underarousal at age 15 (as assessed by three different measures of autonomic and central nervous system activity) predicted criminality at age 24 in 75% of cases.

Although showing an impressive link between physiology and criminality, these findings do not prove that biology is destiny, in this or many other areas. By analogy, our biology leads us all to need to eat, but how, what, and when we eat are determined in large part by the way we are raised. Environmental factors play a strong role in the development of criminality (Eysenck & Gudjonsson, 1989; Henry et al., 1996). Support for the influence of environmental factors in criminality is found from twin studies: If one identical twin is a juvenile delinquent, 87% of the time the other will be too, which may at first glance lead you to think that genes play a major role. But if one fraternal twin is a juvenile delinquent, 72% of the time the other will be too (McGuffin & Gottesman, 1985). Because identical twins share all of their genes and fraternal twins share only half their genes, the small difference between the two types of twins cannot reflect only genetic influences. Plomin and colleagues (1997) note that juvenile delinquency provides the strongest evidence of shared environmental influence of any such characteristic studied to date.

Temperament: Waxing Hot or Cold

Psychologists use the term **temperament** to refer to innate inclinations to engage in a certain style of behavior. Arnold Buss (1995) views temperament as having more influence on behavior than personality traits or factors, affecting not just *what* people do, think, and feel, but *how* they act, think, and feel. Such inborn tendencies can appear at an early age and persist through adulthood. Longitudinal studies have found that children's temperaments at age 3 are correlated with their personalities, as assessed by a personality inventory, at age 18 (Caspi, 2000; Chess & Thomas, 1996). A study of 21-year-olds also linked temperament with health-risk behaviors such as unsafe sex, alcohol dependence, violent crime, and dangerous driving (Caspi et al., 1997). One such temperament is *sensation seeking*: the pursuit of novelty, often in high-stimulation situations, such as sky diving, fast driving, or drug and alcohol use, or occupations, such as working in a hospital emergency room (Zuckerman, 1979). A study of personality predictors of driving accidents found that those drivers who had car accidents or traffic violations were more likely to be thrill seekers and risk takers compared with drivers who had neither (Trimpop & Kirkcaldy, 1997). Tina appears to have a sensation-seeking temperament, and Gabe, who actively shies away from adventurous activities, doesn't. Sensation seeking is associated with lower levels of the chemical monoamine oxidase (MAO) in the blood, at least in males (Shekim et al., 1989).

Buss and Plomin (1984; A. Buss, 1995) propose four dimensions of temperament: activity, sociability, emotionality, and impulsivity. **Activity** is the general expenditure of energy; it has two components: *vigor* (intensity of activity) and *tempo* (speed of activity). People can differ in the intensity of vigorous activity they prefer (for example, preferring skiing to bowling), and the pace of the activities (for instance, preferring fast-paced activities and performing activities more quickly). Tina seems to have a temperament that is vigorous *and* has a fast tempo, as evidenced by her enjoyment of in-line skating, biking, and skiing, and by the impression she gives of perpetually being in a hurry.

Temperament: Innate inclinations to engage in a certain style of behavior.

Activity: A temperament characterized by the general expenditure of energy; activity has two components—vigor (intensity of the activities) and tempo (speed of the activities).

Arctic explorer Matthew Henson, the first person to reach the North Pole, spent years patiently navigating the Arctic cold, wind, and ice. He endured months of minimal, if any, companionship, and physical hardships such as starvation, isolation, and freezing weather. Do polar explorers have to have a certain kind of temperament?

Other dimensions of temperament are **sociability**, the preference to be in the company of other people rather than alone, and **emotionality**, the inclination to become physiologically aroused in emotional situations, but only when the emotions of distress, fear, and anger are involved. Emotionality is similar to the Big Five superfactor of neuroticism, also known as "emotional instability." Studies of identical versus fraternal twins have shown that a person's degree of emotionality is partly inherited. In these studies, twins answered questionnaires about their own temperaments (Eaves et al., 1989; Saudino et al., 1999) and about their cotwins' temperaments (Heath, Neale, et al., 1992); parents were asked about the temperaments of their twin children (these questionnaires also included ratings of activity and sociability, with results that also indicated genetic influence) (Buss & Plomin, 1975; Plomin & Foch, 1980). Research on twins who are raised apart has also produced evidence that activity level and sociability are partly inherited (Loehlin et al., 1985; emotionality was not assessed).

The fourth temperament, **impulsivity**, is the propensity to respond to stimuli immediately, without reflection or concern for consequences. Impulsivity refers to the time lag from stimulus to response, as opposed to tempo, which refers to the rate of a response once it is initiated.

Genes and Personality

We pointed out earlier that the personality dimension of novelty seeking can be influenced by a single gene, which in turn influences physiology. Since physiology can influence personality, the question arises, are all physiological differences genetically determined? If so, would this imply that all aspects of our personalities are genetically determined? Behavioral geneticists seek to ascertain the influence of heredity on behavior, and in so doing investigate a wide range of psychological phenomena, including personality. One way these researchers try to tease apart the effects of heredity from those of the environment is to compare twins separated at birth and raised apart with twins raised together (see Chapter 8). Also compared are identical and fraternal twins who share an environment but have exactly the same genes (identical twins) or on average only half their genes in common (fraternal twins). If the identical twins are more similar than the fraternal twins, that difference is usually attributed to effects of the genes.

These identical twins were separated in infancy and adopted by different working-class families. In school, neither liked spelling, but both liked math; as adults, both worked as part-time deputy sheriffs, vacationed in Florida, had first wives named Linda, second wives named Betty, and gave their sons the same names (although with different spellings: James Alan and James Allan). They both drove Chevys, had dogs named Toy, liked carpentry (Holden, 1980), and built nearly identical benches around trees in their backyards (Rosen, 1987). Moreover, their medical histories were remarkably similar, including the onset of migraine headaches at age 18. However, they wore their hair differently and preferred different ways of expressing themselves: one preferred writing, the other talking (Holden, 1980). Are these similarities a result of coincidence, or of their shared genetics? How many similarities would any two random people have if they compared such detailed information?

TABLE 10.2

Correlations of Twin, Family, and Adoption Studies for Extraversion and Neuroticism

Source: *Adapted from Loehlin (1992).*

Note that low numbers indicate little if any correlation, and higher numbers indicate a stronger correlation. Notice that identical twins' levels of extraversion and neuroticism are more similar to each other than those of fraternal twins, and that twins reared together are generally more similar than twins reared apart.

TYPE OF RELATIVE	CORRELATION	
	Extraversion	Neuroticism
Identical twins reared together	.51	.46
Fraternal twins reared together	.18	.20
Identical twins reared apart	.38	.38
Fraternal twins reared apart	.05	.23
Nonadoptive parents and offspring	.16	.13
Adoptive parents and offspring	.01	.05
Nonadoptive siblings	.20	.09
Adoptive siblings	–.07	.11

Sociability: A temperament characterized by a preference to be in other people's company rather than alone.

Emotionality: A temperament characterized by an inclination to become physiologically aroused in situations in which the predominant emotions are distress, fear, and anger.

Impulsivity: A temperament characterized by the propensity to respond to stimuli immediately, without reflection or concern for consequences.

The largest study of twins reared apart, the Minnesota Study of Twins Reared Apart (MISTRA), was undertaken at the University of Minnesota. In this study, the researchers located 59 pairs of identical twins and 47 pairs of fraternal twins adopted into different families at some point after birth (Bouchard, 1994). Once enrolled in the program, adult twins spent 6 days taking personality, intelligence, psychophysiological, and medical tests, and answering 15,000 written questions (Rosen, 1987; Segal, 1999). In addition, about 24,000 pairs of twins raised together were studied to produce the correlations in Table 10.2 (Loehlin, 1992). As the results indicate, both extraversion and neuroticism have substantial heritability—the fraction of observed variability of a characteristic that arises from inherited factors (see Chapter 8). Similar results have been found when twins rate themselves and when others rate them (Angleitner et al., 1995). However, longitudinal studies of adoptive families have not found such high correlations (Loehlin et al., 1981). In sum, although most twin research finds evidence of substantial heritability of some personality dimensions, not all nontwin research supports this finding. In addition, although personality traits may have some heritability, even in research among twins not all traits are equally heritable, as shown in Figure 10.4 (Heath & Martin, 1990; Loehlin, 1992; Pederson et al., 1988).

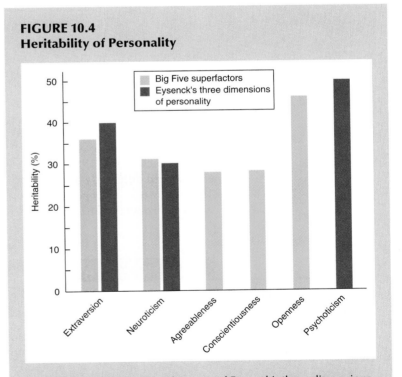

**FIGURE 10.4
Heritability of Personality**

Heritability of the five superfactors and Eysenck's three dimensions of personality based on research with twins. (Data for Big Five superfactors from Loehlin 1992. Data for Eysenck's three dimensions of personality—extraversion and neuroticism from Pederson et al., 1988; psychoticism from Heath & Martin, 1990.)

Despite these conflicting results, some researchers propose that very specific behaviors have a genetic origin (Bergeman et al., 1990; Kendler et al., 1992; Lyons et al., 1993), from the amount of time spent watching television (Prescott et al., 1991) and childhood accidents (Phillips & Matheny, 1995) to divorce (McGue & Lykken, 1992) and religious attitudes (Waller et al., 1990). Similarly, Lykken and colleagues (1993) found a heritability of 50% in work and leisure interests in a twin study and estimate that a subjective sense of well-being (what some might call happiness) has a heritability of between 44% and 80% (Lykken & Tellegen, 1996)!

Of course, nobody claims that the amount of time you spend watching television is explicitly coded in your genes. What some researchers do claim, however, is that certain aspects of temperament and personality dimensions, which may have a genetic component, will produce specific behaviors such as watching television. If, for instance, your activity level is both "low vigor" and "low tempo" and you tend to be shy, you are more likely to spend time alone in sedentary pursuits (such as watching television) than if you are a gregarious person who likes vigorous, fast-paced activity. It is also important to note that simply because some aspects of personality have a genetic component does not mean that personality is fixed from birth to death. All researchers agree that other factors, such as environment and experience, also shape personality. Even Eysenck (1993), who argues that much of behavior is biologically determined, concedes that the environment makes a difference in whether someone high in psychoticism will become a creative, productive researcher or an artist, or be disabled by schizophrenia.

Personality psychologists generally consider two aspects of the environment to play roles in forging personality. One is the common family environment; the other is the individual's unique experiences (such as winning a spelling bee or single-handedly causing the team to lose the soccer finals). Interestingly, the MISTRA group has generally not found the family environment to be a large contributor to personality traits. The exceptions are "social closeness," that is, the desire for intimacy with others (Tellegen et al., 1988), and "positive emotionality," a trait "characterized by an active engagement in one's environment" (p. 1037). The relatively small contribution of a common family environment to other personality traits may simply reflect the fact that many important aspects of the family environment are not in fact shared. Parents do not treat each of their children exactly the same. Children create their own micro-environments based on their own temperaments and personalities at birth, leading parents to develop different patterns of interaction with each of their children and different expectations of each child (Graziano et al., 1998; Plomin & Bergeman, 1991; Scarr & McCartney, 1983). Similarly, the same family event, such as a divorce, will be experienced differently by children of different ages and cognitive abilities (Hoffman, 1991). Moreover, it is possible that there are individual differences in their susceptibility to environmental forces in personality development (Holden, 1980).

LOOKING AT LEVELS

The Wallflower Personality

Are you shy, or do you know someone who is? Have you ever wondered what causes one person to be shy and another outgoing? Is shyness innate? To understand the origins of shyness, it is necessary to look at shy people from the vantage points of events at all three levels—the brain, the person, and the group.

At the level of the brain, Kagan and his colleagues (1988) have found that some babies are more reactive, or sensitive, to environmental stimuli and thus are more fussy than other babies. These "high-reactive" infants are more likely than "low-reactive" babies to respond to a recording of a woman's voice or to a colored toy with crying, general distress, and increased motor activity. Such infants tend to have a reactive nervous system, as indicated by faster heart rates and higher levels of the stress hormone cortisol. Kagan and his colleagues have shown that babies with a fast heart rate in the womb are more likely later to become inhibited, fearful children who startle more easily; in fact, the heart activity of even 2-week-old infants can predict later inhibition (Snidman et al., 1995). These children's sympathetic nervous systems are more easily aroused, leading to a preference for situations less likely to create high arousal. As these inhibited children get older, they are usually the ones who hide behind their parents in a room full of adults.

At the level of the person, shy people are extremely self-conscious, so much so that they may painfully and ruthlessly analyze their behavior after a social interaction, an unhappy process that leads them to avoid interaction with others in the future. They become preoccupied with their shyness and its effects ("I can't stop imagining what they're thinking about me"). These preoccupying thoughts can occur in response to physiological reactions (a pounding heart), to behavior (what to do with the hands), and to thoughts ("No one wants to talk to me"). Fear and distress in social situations are common feelings for inhibited people.

But not all inhibited toddlers are still inhibited at age 7, and not all inhibited children become shy adults (Kagan, 1989a). Events at the level of the group can play a role either in diminishing the effects of shyness or in maintaining shyness into adulthood. Fox (cited in Azar, 1995) found that the home environment, specifically parents, can help inhibited children by recognizing and supporting the children's temperaments. As one previously inhibited 7-year-old explained, "My parents introduced me to new things slowly" (Azar, 1995).

Events at the three levels all interact: Physiological reactivity may produce a bias toward shyness, but the view taken by the environment of family and culture toward such behavior will determine how a person thinks and feels about him- or herself. American culture tends to favor outgoing people, a social bias that puts shy people at a disadvantage. Their self-image as social beings is more likely to be negative, and this negative self-concept increases the likelihood of an autonomic reaction in social situations, thereby perpetuating the cycle. Moreover, Kagan (1989a) has found that a larger proportion of inhibited children are later-borns, whereas a larger proportion of uninhibited children are firstborns. He hypothesizes that those with an inhibited temperament who have older siblings live in a more stressful environment, which exaggerates their physiological responses. Those who are firstborn or only children grow up in a less stressful environment and are less likely to become shy children or adults.

CONSOLIDATE!

▶ 1. *What are "introverts" and "extraverts"? How does Eysenck's theory explain the origin of personality?* Eysenck proposed that personality varies along three dimensions, each with distinct physiological underpinnings: extraversion, neuroticism, and psychoticism. Extraverts are less "arousable" than introverts and are more sensitive to reward; introverts are more easily overstimulated and are more sensitive to punishment. Neuroticism, or emotionality, is hypothesized to be related to the functioning of the amygdala.

▶ 2. *What, exactly, is temperament?* Temperament refers to an innate style of behavior. Examples of temperaments are shyness, activity (which has two components, vigor and tempo), sociability, emotionality, and impulsivity.

▶ 3. *What does the field of behavioral genetics say about the genes' effects on personality?* Based on twin studies, behavioral geneticists propose that personality is between 28% and 50% heritable, but this value depends in part on the trait or factor being assessed and whether the studies were conducted with twins or nonbiological family members. Despite this high percentage, environmental factors still play an important role in personality development.

THE PERSON: BELIEFS AND BEHAVIORS

Tina wanted to understand why Gabe was the way he was—or, put another way, why he had the personality he did. Lately when they studied together, he'd have a big bag of pistachio nuts and sit there cracking and eating nuts while they read. It was driving Tina, well, nuts. She couldn't understand how he could just sit there hour after hour, cracking and crunching nuts. She wanted to ask him about it—why didn't he just buy shelled nuts—but she didn't feel comfortable asking him. Why were they so different? How do our personalities develop, and why do they develop differently? Does experience build on the genetic and physiological framework of our personalities, affecting our beliefs, motivations, and views of ourselves? Among the notable theories that attempt to answer these questions are the psychodynamic theory of Sigmund Freud, humanistic theory, and the cognitive view of personality.

▶ 1. What is the Freudian view of personality?

▶ 2. What is the main emphasis of humanistic theories?

▶ 3. What is the cognitive approach to personality theory?

Freud's Theory: The Dynamic Personality

Sigmund Freud viewed personality as a bubbling cauldron, rocked by unconscious, irrational forces at war with one another, competing for expression and preventing the individual's exercise of free will. He believed in **psychological determinism,** the view that all behavior, even something as mundane as forgetting someone's name or being late for an appointment, has an underlying psychological cause. Freud proposed that two major drives, sex and aggression, are the primary motivating forces of human behavior. Tension occurs when these drives are not given opportunity for expression.

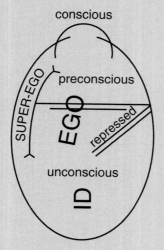

FIGURE 10.5
Freud's Drawing of Personality Structure

In Freud's view, only part of the mind is available for inspection and provides normal awareness (conscious); some of it is occasionally conscious (preconscious), and some is hidden, not available for observation (unconscious). Repressed thoughts, feelings, and wishes are hidden from awareness. Freud's drawing also illustrates the relationship among the id, ego, and superego.

THE STRUCTURE OF PERSONALITY. In order to understand Freud's view of the structure of personality, it is necessary first to understand his view of consciousness. Freud proposed that consciousness is not one thing, but rather can be thought of as divided into three layers (see Figure 10.5). The topmost layer is normal awareness, or the *conscious*, which includes thoughts, feelings, and motivations of which you are aware. The second layer, the *preconscious*, holds subjective material that can easily be brought into conscious awareness but of which you are not aware most of the time. For example, your telephone number is in your preconscious until someone asks you what it is, at which point it moves into your conscious awareness. The final layer is the *unconscious*, which houses the thoughts, feelings, and motivations that you cannot bring into consciousness but which nevertheless influence you. A much greater proportion of your thoughts, feelings, and motivations are in the unconscious than are in the conscious.

As part of the dynamic nature of personality, Freud proposed three personality structures—the id, superego, and ego (see Figure 10.5). These are not physical structures, but abstract mental entities. The **id,** which exists from birth, houses the sexual and aggressive drives, physical needs such as the need to sleep or eat, and simple psychological needs such as the need for comfort; these needs and drives constantly vie for expression. The id lives by the *pleasure principle*, wanting immediate gratification of its needs by a reduction in pain, discomfort, or tension, regardless of the consequences. Because of this insistent urge for immediate gratification, the id is sometimes compared with a demanding infant. Freud proposed that when the id's instincts threaten to erupt, anxiety can develop. When that anxiety reaches a sufficiently high level, abnormal behavior and mental illness can result.

A second structure, the **superego,** forms during early childhood; this entity houses the child's (and later the adult's) sense of right and wrong. The child learns morality by internalizing—that is, taking in—the values of the parents and of the immediate culture. The superego tries to prevent the expression of the id's sexual and aggressive impulses. The superego thus isn't a Jiminy Cricket whispering in your ear, but the internalized voice of society. The superego's morality, however, because it was internalized during early childhood, remains childlike in nature.

The superego is the home of the conscience, and depending on the parents' way of teaching right and wrong, it can be more or less punishing. If your superego is very harsh, you experience much anxiety and strive for perfection. The superego can cause feelings of *guilt,* an uncomfortable sensation of having done something wrong, which results in feelings of inadequacy. The superego's morality is responsible for the *ego ideal,* which provides the ultimate standard of what a person should be (Nye, 1992).

A third structure, the **ego,** also develops in childhood, before the superego, and works very hard to balance the demands of the id and superego. The ego tries to give the id enough gratification to prevent it from making too much trouble, while at the same time making sure that no major moral lapses lead the superego to become too punishing. The ego must also make sure that the actions of the id and superego, as well as its own actions, don't create problems in the real world. The ego is guided by the *reality principle,* which leads it to assess what is realistically possible in the world. Although he believed that the ego develops out of the id, in his later life Freud (1937) wrote that the ego's characteristics may be determined by heredity (Nye, 1992). The ego is also responsible for cognitive functions such as problem solving and reasoning.

PERSONALITY DEVELOPMENT: AVOIDING ARREST. Freud viewed childhood as central in determining the formation of personality. He proposed five distinct phases, or stages, of development, each having an important task requiring successful resolution for healthy personality development. Four of Freud's five stages involve specific erogenous zones, areas of the body (mouth, anus, and genitals) that can provide satisfaction of instinctual drives. Freud believed that each zone demanded some form of sexual gratification, with a different zone prominent during each stage. For this reason, Freud's stages are called **psychosexual stages** (see Table 10.3).

Superego: A Freudian psychic structure that is formed during early childhood and houses the sense of right and wrong, based on the internalization of parental and cultural morality.

Ego: A Freudian psychic structure, developed in childhood, that tries to balance the competing demands of the id, superego, and reality.

Psychosexual stages: Freud's developmental stages based on erogenous zones; the specific needs of each stage must be met for its successful resolution.

TABLE 10.3

Freud's Psychosexual Stages

Note: Ages are approximations.

PSYCHOSEXUAL STAGE	EROGENOUS ZONE	AGE	DEVELOPMENTAL TASK
Oral stage	Mouth	0–1½ years	Successful weaning
Anal stage	Anus	1½–3 years	Successful toilet training
Phallic stage	Genitals (clitoris/penis)	3–6 years	Identification with same-sex parent
Latency period	None	6–puberty	Transformation of sexual urges into socially acceptable activities
Genital stage	Genitals (vagina/penis)	Puberty–adulthood	Formation of sexual love relationships and development of a capacity for productive work

If a child does not satisfy the needs of a given stage, he or she will develop a *fixation*, a state in which energy is still focused on an earlier stage of development even as the child moves on to the next stage. A fixation results from incomplete resolution of an earlier stage. In times of stress, Freud argued, the person will regress to the behaviors, thoughts, and feelings of the fixated stage. Such arrested development could create a **neurosis:** an abnormal behavior pattern relating to a conflict between the ego and either the id or the superego. According to Freud (1938), conflict between the ego and reality results in *psychosis*.

The *oral stage* extends from birth until approximately age of 1½. In this stage, the child's pleasures come from the mouth, primarily via sucking and biting; the developmental task in the oral stage is successful weaning from mother's breast or the bottle. If oral needs are frustrated at this stage, the child will develop a fixation, developing one of two kinds of personality. One is the *oral–receptive*, which is characterized by oral pleasure seeking, such as putting food or cigarettes into the mouth. According to Freud, people with oral–receptive personalities tend to become dependent on others and expect others to take care of them. The other personality style, the *oral–aggressive*, is characterized by a predilection for oral pleasures that emphasize biting, such as chewing ice or smoking pipes. Freudian theory proposes that oral–aggressive people are often verbally hostile in relationships. Would Freud have interpreted Gabe's preference for pistachio nuts as a sign of an oral–aggressive personality? Possibly, although Gabe doesn't exhibit other signs of the oral–aggressive personality; maybe he just likes pistachios.

The developing child leaves the oral stage for the *anal stage,* which lasts from about age 1½ to age 3. The primary zone of pleasure shifts from the mouth to the anus. Retaining and expelling feces are the primary pleasures in this stage, and the developmental task is successful toilet training. Freud believed that parents who are rigid about toilet training, requiring their children to "go" on demand, can create a battle of wills, resulting in a fixation in adulthood. One type of fixation, the *anal–retentive,* can be thought of as producing a constipated personality that waits until the last moment to "go." Such people are more likely to delay gratification and, according to Freudian theory, are neat, methodical, miserly, and stubborn. In contrast, the *anal–expulsive* personality is characterized by cruelty, destructive acts, emotional outbursts, and a disregard for conventional rules. Although a Freudian might see in Gabe's personality some traits akin to the anal–retentive type (his methodical manner, his organized schoolwork, his fairly inflexible nature), he does not entirely fit the bill because he isn't neat in other aspects of his life and is not miserly, but in fact quite generous.

The third stage, the *phallic stage,* occurs from around 3 to 6 years old. The locus of pleasure is now the clitoris or penis, gratification occurring primarily through masturbation. The developmental task is successful identification with the same-sex parent. Freud proposed that children of this age are preoccupied with the discovery that girls don't have penises, a discovery that in girls creates jealousy of the male's penis, and in boys fear of castration. Freud took inspiration from the ancient Greek story of Oedipus, who unknowingly killed his father and married his mother. Freud believed that boys in this stage jealously love their mothers and view their fathers as competitors for their mothers' love, so they both fear and hate their fathers. Freud called this dynamic the *Oedipus complex*. A boy fears that, as punishment for loving his mother and hating his father, his father will cut off his penis, the primary zone of pleasure; this concern leads to the boy's **castration anxiety.** For successful resolution, a boy must renounce his passionate love for his mother and make peace with his father, choosing to identify with him and accept his position instead of viewing him as a competitor. In doing so, the boy "introjects," or internalizes, his father's morality as part of his superego. According to Freud, fixations at this stage can create either a Don Juan personality, obsessed with attaining sexual gratification, or, following poor identification with the father, a less masculine, more feminine personality, possibly although not necessarily homosexual.

Neurosis: An abnormal behavior pattern relating to a conflict between the ego and either the id or the superego.

Castration anxiety: A boy's anxiety-laden fear that, as punishment for loving mother and hating father, his father will cut off his penis (the primary zone of pleasure).

Girls' personality development at this stage, according to Freud, is different from that of boys; girls' version of the Oedipal complex has been labeled the *Electra complex*, after a Greek myth about a girl who avenges her father's murder, committed by her mother and her mother's lover, by persuading her brother to kill their mother. Girls at this stage experience *penis envy*, a sense of being ineffectual owing to the lack of a penis and the ensuing desire to have a penis. Girls also struggle with feelings of anger and jealousy toward the mother: anger for neither providing a penis for her daughter nor having one herself, and jealousy because of the mother's relationship with the father. Girls ambivalently identify with their mothers. As a product of the Victorian era, Freud justified women's inferiority to men by explaining that they only partially resolved this stage. Because they do not experience castration anxiety, they are not motivated to resolve fully this ambivalent identification with their mothers. They remain fixated at this stage, and as a result have a less-well-developed superego, less ego strength, and less ability to negotiate reality and the id.

After the phallic stage, the sexual impulse in both boys and girls becomes subdued for a time during the *latency period*, which lasts from approximately age 6 until puberty. In this stage sexual urges are repressed, and the developmental task is transforming these repressed urges into socially acceptable activities. Stimulation of an erogenous zone is not the focus of this stage; rather, sexual urges are transformed into more culturally acceptable, nonsexual behaviors. For example, competitive games with peers may take the place of the Oedipal drama for a boy fixated at the phallic stage.

Freud's final psychosexual stage is the *genital stage*, which begins at puberty; the erogenous zones now are the vagina for girls and the penis for boys. Gratification occurs in sexual intimacy, and one of the two developmental tasks of this stage, the ability to form a sexual love relationship, marks the beginning of mature sexual relationships. The other task of this stage is to develop interests and talents related to productive work. Freud believed that individuals with fixations at earlier developmental stages would have problems in the genital stage. According to Freud, girls' erogenous zones now shift from the "immature" clitoris to the "mature" vagina, and the "vaginal orgasm" is evidence of successful resolution of this stage. There is no evidence, however, that women experience two different kinds of orgasm; rather, the female orgasm involves both clitoris and vagina, not "either/or" (Harris, 1976; Kaplan, 1981; Masters & Johnson, 1966).

DEFENSE MECHANISMS: PROTECTING THE SELF. The ego's job of handling threatening material is made easier by the use of **defense mechanisms,** unconscious psychological means by which we try to prevent unacceptable thoughts or urges from reaching conscious awareness, thereby decreasing anxiety (see Table 10.4 on page 370). Freud proposed a number of defense mechanisms; these were further developed by his daughter, Anna Freud (1895–1982), herself a noted psychoanalyst. The most important defense mechanism is **repression,** a process that occurs when the unconscious prevents threatening thoughts, impulses, and memories from entering consciousness. An example of repression might be "forgetting" to go to a dreaded dentist appointment. According to Freud, overreliance on particular defense mechanisms may lead to the development of neuroses.

FREUD'S FOLLOWERS. Freud attracted many followers, a number of whom modified his theory of personality or added ideas of their own. Among those who expanded on Freud's work, termed *neo-Freudians*, were Carl Jung, Alfred Adler, and Karen Horney.

Carl Jung (1875–1961) was a Swiss psychiatrist whom Freud befriended but with whom he later severed communication over disagreements about theory. Jung agreed with Freud's concepts of the unconscious, ego, and id but diverged from Freud over his emphasis on the centrality of sexuality in personality development. Jung developed his own theory of personality that added to Freud's concepts of the unconscious,

Defense mechanism: An unconscious psychological means by which a person tries to prevent unacceptable, id-based thoughts or urges from reaching conscious awareness.

Repression: A defense mechanism that occurs when the unconscious prevents threatening thoughts, impulses, and memories from entering consciousness.

TABLE 10.4

Common Defense Mechanisms

Source: *From Freud (1933/1965), p. 70.*

Note: Defense mechanisms are used by the ego to prevent threatening thoughts from entering awareness.

DENIAL

Threatening thoughts are denied outright. *Example:* You have a drinking problem but deny that it is a problem (and truly believe this).

INTELLECTUALIZATION

Threatening thoughts or emotions are kept at arm's length by thinking about them rationally and logically. *Example:* While watching a frightening part of a horror movie, you focus on the special effects, make-up, camera angles, and other emotionally nonthreatening details.

PROJECTION

Threatening thoughts are projected onto (attributed to) others. *Example:* You accuse your partner of wanting to have an affair rather than recognizing your own conscious or unconscious wish to have one yourself.

RATIONALIZATION

Creating explanations to justify threatening thoughts or actions. *Example:* In response to watching a football game instead of studying, and subsequently doing poorly on an exam, you say, "Oh, I can make up for it on the final and the research paper."

REACTION FORMATION

Unconsciously changing an unacceptable feeling into its opposite. *Example:* You harbor aggressive impulses toward your boss, but instead you experience warm, positive feelings toward him, transforming your anger about his obnoxious behavior into an appreciation of "his fairness as a manager."

REPRESSION

Anxiety-provoking thoughts, impulses, and memories are prevented from entering consciousness. *Example:* After failing an exam, you keep forgetting to tell your parents about it.

SUBLIMATION

Threatening impulses are directed into more socially acceptable activities. *Example:* You sublimate your unacceptable aggressive urges to engage in physical fights by playing ice hockey.

UNDOING

Your actions try to "undo" a threatening wish or thought. *Example:* After having the thought of eating several slices of chocolate cake, you go to the gym and work out for an hour.

---

ego, and id an entity Jung termed the *collective unconscious.* According to Jung, the collective unconscious contains a rich storehouse of ideas and memories common to all humankind, which we all share on an unconscious level. The common themes in myths and stories around the world and throughout the ages, Jung claimed, spring forth from the collective unconscious in each generation. Stored in the collective unconscious are many **archetypes,** symbols that represent "aspects of the world that people have an inherited tendency to notice" (Carver & Scheier, 1996, p. 268). Among these archetypes are God, the shadow (that is, the dark side of personality), and Mother Earth.

Jung saw personality as composed of polarities, or opposites, such as sensing versus thinking, and introversion versus extraversion. The Myers-Briggs Type Indicator, a personality inventory, is loosely based on Jungian polarities and includes four dimensions of personality: Thinking–Feeling; Sensation–Intuition (how one perceives infor-

Archetype: A Jungian concept of symbols that represent basic aspects of the world.

mation); Judging–Perceiving; and Introversion–Extraversion. Although the Myers-Briggs Type Indicator is commonly used in research, business, counseling, and education, some researchers question whether it is a valid application of Jung's theory (McCrae & Costa, 1989a).

Whereas Freud viewed sexual and aggressive impulses as integral to personality development, Alfred Adler (1870–1937) viewed feelings of inferiority and helplessness as important in forming personality (1956). Feelings of inferiority fuel a *striving for superiority*, which Adler viewed as the source of all motivation. When severe, such inferiority feelings can hamper strivings for superiority and lead to strong feelings of inferiority—an **inferiority complex**. This can arise from parents' neglect or hatred. Adler viewed the Oedipus complex not as universal, but as experienced only by children who are overindulged by the opposite-sex parent (Adler, 1964).

Karen Horney (1885–1952) agreed with Freud that anxiety-inducing childhood experiences are central to later psychological problems. She disagreed, however, about the role and primacy of sexual and aggressive drives. Horney emphasized the importance of parent–child interactions in early childhood. If parents do not provide their children with consistent and real interest, warmth, and respect, Horney claimed, the children are likely to grow up with *basic anxiety*, an "all-pervading feeling of being lonely and helpless in a hostile world" (Horney, 1937, p. 89). Horney offered an alternate explanation for penis envy, which she called *privilege envy*. Rather than wanting a penis per se, Horney theorized, girls desire the privileges that go along with having a penis. Even privilege envy, however, is not a cultural universal; in some cultures, Horney noted, men are envious of women's reproductive ability. Horney felt that Freud had disregarded the cultural and social factors that influence personality development.

CRITIQUING FREUDIAN THEORY: IS IT SCIENCE?

Psychosexual theory remains fascinating a century after Freud first conceived it, and legions of people worldwide—psychologists, writers, filmmakers, and others—have seen truth in its insights into personality. But as fascinating as Freud's theory may be, is it grounded in good science? First, as you saw in Chapter 1, a scientific theory must be testable, but many aspects of Freud's theory are difficult to test. Some key concepts were not concretely defined, some changed over time, and often the interpretation of these concepts was left open. For example, as you also saw in Chapter 1, when Freud was asked about the meaning of his sucking on a cigar, he replied, "Sometimes a cigar is only a cigar." Maybe so, but a good theory would tell us when it is and when it isn't "only a cigar."

A second criticism of Freud's theory is that it is so complicated, it can explain, or explain away, almost anything. When there is an apparent contradiction within someone's personality, it is almost always possible to appeal to a defense mechanism to explain that contradiction. If Gabe had had a difficult time with toilet training, resulting in frequent constipation, we could predict that he would have an anal–retentive personality. But how do we then explain that he is often generous and, at home, downright sloppy? Psychodynamic theory could say that his generosity and sloppiness are an undoing of his desire to be selfish and orderly.

Third, Freud developed his theory by analyzing patients, mostly women, and by analyzing himself. And Freud's views of women, of proper parenting, and of appropriate development were all biased by his sensibilities and surroundings, as we are biased by ours. He and his patients were upper-middle-class or upper-class products of late 19th-century Vienna; their sensibility was not necessarily representative of other classes, times, or cultures. Applying a theory based on a particular group of people at a particular time to other people at another time raises issues of validity.

However, some aspects of Freud's theory have received support from contemporary research (see Westen, 1998, 1999). For example, the type of attachment we have to our parents predicts the type of attachment we will have to a partner and to our own children (see Shaver & Hazan, 1994, for a review). Although not supporting Freud's specific psychosexual stages, such findings support the general idea that relationships with parents can affect aspects of later development. Moreover, research on defensive styles has supported some aspects of Sigmund and Anna Freud's views on

Inferiority complex: The experience that occurs when inferiority feelings are so strong that they hamper striving for superiority.

defense mechanisms (Bond et al., 1983; Mikulincer & Horesh, 1999; Newman, Duff et al., 1997; Silverman, 1976). More generally, research on conditioned emotional responses (see Chapter 5), implicit memory (see Chapter 6), and aspects of thinking (see Chapter 7) support the broad idea that some mental processes can be unconscious—that is, without awareness. Despite the difficulty in evaluating most of Freud's theory, many aspects of it remain with us because it offers a truly comprehensive, and sometimes insightful, view of people and of personality.

Humanistic Psychology

Partly as a reaction to Freud's theory, which in many ways draws a pessimistic picture of human nature and personality formation, the humanist psychologists focused on the positive aspects of the individual—on people's innate goodness, creativity, and free will. Rather than being driven by forces outside of their control, as the Freudians claimed, the humanists believe that people can create solutions to their problems. A cornerstone of their theories is that we all have a drive toward **self-actualization,** an innate motivation to attain our highest emotional and intellectual potential. The work of two psychologists, Abraham Maslow and Carl Rogers, represents the humanistic perspective on personality.

MASLOW. The personality theory developed by Abraham Maslow (1908–1970) is really a theory of motivation based on a hierarchy of physical and emotional needs (see Chapter 9). Lower-level needs, said Maslow, must be met before needs further up the hierarchy can be satisfied; the highest level need is that for self-actualization. During crises, needs regress to a lower level, and higher-level needs are put on hold.

TABLE 10.5	**Characteristics of Self-Actualizing People**

Source: *Based on Maslow (1968).*

- Perceive reality accurately and efficiently
- Accept themselves, others, and nature
- Appreciate ordinary events
- Try to solve cultural rather than personal problems
- Form deep relationships, but only with a few people
- Often experience "oceanic feelings" (a sense of oneness with nature that transcends time and space)

Maslow studied the lives and characteristics of historical figures he considered to be at the self-actualizing level, including Albert Einstein, Mahatma Gandhi, Abraham Lincoln, and Eleanor Roosevelt. His investigation led him to propose that people who are self-actualizing have these qualities: a true perception of reality, an acceptance of themselves and their environments, an appreciation of the ordinary, a focus on cultural rather than social problems, few but deep personal relationships, and what Maslow called "oceanic feelings" (see Table 10.5). Maslow regarded oceanic feelings as *peak experiences,* moments of intense clarity of perception (Privette & Landsman, 1983), a suspended sense of time, and wonderment at the experience. Oceanic feelings are similar to the idea of **flow,** the feeling of complete absorption with and merging smoothly into an activity and losing track of time (Csikszentmihalyi & Csikszentmihalyi, 1988). You may have had such an experience, becoming totally engrossed in, say, sketching, listening to music, or playing a musical instrument. Various researchers have studied

Self-actualization: An innate motivation to attain the highest possible emotional and intellectual potential.

Flow: The experience of complete absorption in and merging smoothly into an activity and losing track of time.

Maslow's theory, particularly as it relates to motivation on the job. In the end, many of Maslow's concepts are difficult to test, and the validity of his theory remains questionable (Fox, 1982; Soper et al., 1995; Wahba & Bridwell, 1976).

ROGERS. Carl Rogers (1902–1987) is noted for his formulation of client-centered therapy and his notions of personality and its development. In **client-centered therapy,** the therapist provides not interpretation but an unconditionally supportive and positive environment for the client. Like Maslow, Rogers viewed humans as possessing a need for self-actualization. But rather than viewing the satisfaction of lower- to higher-order needs as the driving force behind personality, he believed that *self-concept*—our sense of ourselves and of how others see us—is central to personality development. Rogers proposed that our feelings about ourselves are in part a function of how others see us. Thus we have a basic need for **unconditional positive regard,** acceptance without any conditions. Receiving unconditional positive regard, according to Rogers, is crucial for the development of a healthy self-concept. Of course, it is impossible to receive or provide unconditional positive regard all the time, and the socialization process praises children for behaving in accordance with societal rules. This praise for specific behaviors leads us to learn *conditions of worth*, or "what it takes" to be treated as worthwhile. According to Rogers, people whose lives revolve around meeting such conditions of worth will not achieve their full human potentials.

In order to prevent such obstruction of potential, yet meet society's need for children to learn what it considers appropriate behavior, Rogers advised parents to make the distinction between a child's inappropriate *behavior* and his or her *worth* as a human being.

Humanistic theories appeal to many because of their emphasis on the uniqueness of each person and on free will. According to this view, how you live your life is determined not by unconscious forces but with your conscious awareness and the freedom to choose your experiences. Critics of humanistic theory point out that, as with psychodynamic theory, many of its concepts are difficult to test and have received little research support. Moreover, the uplifting, positive view of human nature has struck a discordant note for many in light of the amount of violence and evil in the world.

Good or bad child? Rogers argues that a child may at times behave unsuitably, but that does not mean he or she is a bad child. Labeling children as "bad" may affect their developing self-concepts.

The Cognitive View of Personality: You Are What You Expect

The cognitive approach to personality emphasizes that the development of personality is affected by people's thoughts: Thoughts influence feelings and behavior, and consistent thoughts (consistent at least in a given situation) create personality. One aspect of the cognitive view of personality development is the idea of **expectancies:** What you *expect* to happen has a powerful influence on your behavior, thoughts, feelings, and in turn personality. Expectancies about the outcomes of behavior, often based on past experiences, can explain why operant conditioning works. You learn that a certain stimulus signals a likely outcome if you behave in a certain way, so you come to expect certain outcomes from particular behaviors in certain situations. Perhaps Gabe

Client-centered therapy: Therapy developed by Rogers that focuses on the client's potential for growth and the therapist's role as provider of unconditional support.

Unconditional positive regard: Acceptance without any conditions.

Expectancies: Expectations that have a powerful influence on behavior, thoughts, feelings, and in turn personality.

Our expectancies can shape our behavior in consistent ways. Is Peter Seller's character, Inspector Clouseau (The Pink Panther movies), paranoid because he expects to be attacked when he walks into his apartment? No. He has been attacked often enough when entering his apartment that he expects to be attacked—his expectancies shape his thoughts, feelings, and behaviors: He is prepared.

Locus of control: The source perceived to be the center of control over life's events.

Efficacy expectancy: The sense of being able to follow through and produce the behaviors one would like to perform.

Reciprocal determinism: The interactive relationship between the environment, cognitive/personal factors, and behavior.

doesn't like parties because, from his previous experience of them, he expects that he will have a miserable time and feel socially isolated (in the language of conditioning, this would be "punishment" for attending the party; see Chapter 5). Such expectancies have a powerful influence on behavior even without our awareness. Killen and his colleagues (1996) found that among ninth-grade non-drinkers, both male and female, those who had the expectancy that drinking would enhance social behavior (that is, the outcome of drinking would be more or better social behavior) were more likely to begin drinking within a year.

One type of personality difference related to expectancy focuses on **locus of control,** the source we perceive as exerting control over our life events (Rotter, 1966). People who have an internal locus of control, called *internals,* are more likely to see control over events as coming from within themselves when the situation is ambiguous; that is, they feel personally responsible for what happens to them. Gabe's responsible approach to studying would indicate that he has an internal locus of control. In contrast, *externals* are people with an external locus of control; these people are more likely to see control as coming from outside forces, and they feel less personal responsibility. Because Tina does well in her classes without studying much, she chalks up her grades to easy tests. She feels less personally responsible for her success than does Gabe. In this way, she seems to have more of an external locus of control.

Internals and externals have different responses to success and failure. Internals are more likely to increase their expectancies in response to success and to lower their expectancies in response to failure. Externals are likely to do the opposite, lowering their expectancies after success and raising them after failure. Thus, what you believe about a situation depends on whether you attribute the consequences to your own behavior or to outside forces. As an internal, Gabe has lowered expectations about future parties because of what he sees as his failures at past ones. Tina, as an external, doesn't fully expect to maintain her high grades because she doesn't feel completely responsible for them in the first place.

People also differ with respect to **efficacy expectancy,** the sense that we have the ability to follow through and produce the behaviors we would like to perform (Bandura, 1977b). Efficacy expectancy is distinct from locus of control, which focuses on whether consequences arise from internal or external causes when the situation is unclear. Albert Bandura hypothesized that efficacy expectancy helps people believe in themselves and in their ability to change or perform behaviors previously viewed as difficult or impossible. Those with high efficacy expectancy persist more than others when working on difficult problems (Brown & Inouye, 1978). Both Gabe and Tina have high efficacy expectancies, a correspondence that partly accounts for the initial sense they had of being a lot alike.

Another aspect of the cognitive view of personality stems from the idea of self-reinforcement (Bandura, 1976, 1977a)—that is, the reinforcement we give ourselves for our behavior. Tina might reward herself for studying all day by going skating the next day. Self-reinforcement can occur by just thinking about your actions. When you like the way you behaved in a given situation, you praise yourself (providing reinforcement), and when you disapprove of your behavior, you blame yourself (providing punishment). Self-reinforcement is a powerful tool in determining behavior and feelings, which in turn contribute to personality.

Bandura (1978) regarded human behavior as part of an interactive process involving psychological and social forces: Thoughts, expectancies, feelings, and other personal factors influence both the environment (including the social world) and behavior; in turn, the environment and personal factors influence, and are influenced by, behavior (see Figure 10.6). Bandura called this interactive relationship **reciprocal determinism.** In essence, Bandura was calling attention to the interaction among events at different levels of analysis, as we do in our Looking at Levels sections, except he did not include biologically based factors. Reciprocal determinism might explain Tina's desire for highly stimulating activities (such as bungee-jumping) by pointing out that because of certain aspects of her environment, such as moving a lot as a child, Tina came to *expect* a certain level of newness, excitement, even danger, from her experiences (cognitive/personal). These expectations influence her thrill-seeking behavior (bungee-jumping), but all the factors influence one another. Because Tina has a great time bungee-jumping, she expects to enjoy doing something similarly thrilling next time, and she seeks out such stimuli in her environment.

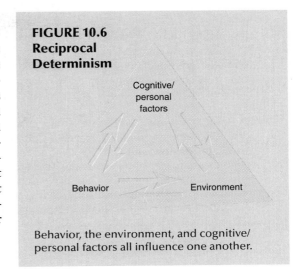

**FIGURE 10.6
Reciprocal Determinism**

Behavior, the environment, and cognitive/personal factors all influence one another.

LOOKING AT LEVELS

Rose-Colored Glasses Can Make a Rosy World

Expectancies do not operate only at the level of the person. That expectancies affect, and are in turn affected by, the other levels of the brain and the group is evidenced in a study by Snyder and colleagues (1977). Participants were asked to talk on the telephone with a member of the opposite sex. Some of the men were led to believe that the woman to whom they were speaking was physically attractive; others were told that their telephone partner was not physically attractive. The women on the receiving end knew nothing of this manipulation. The two sides of the conversations were recorded separately, and tape recordings of the women's parts of the conversations were given to judges to rate how friendly, attractive, and sociable each seemed. Like the women themselves, the judges knew nothing about the manipulation; nevertheless, they could pick out those women who had been identified to the men as attractive simply from the women's style of conversation; these women spoke in a friendly, warm manner.

The men apparently behaved differently depending on their expectations, which in turn induced different behavior on the part of the women. When judges heard only the men's part of the conversations, they rated the men who thought they were talking to attractive women as more sociable, interesting, outgoing, and humorous than the others.

Here we see how beliefs (at the level of the person) can affect how we interpret and organize information (at the level of the brain), which can give rise to pleasure if, in this instance, a man thinks he is charming an attractive woman. This pleasure in turn makes the man more relaxed, sociable, and so on, which in turn makes the woman respond more positively, and thus fuels a social interaction (level of the group). It is clear that events at all three levels operate at the same time, and unless we appreciate how those events interact, we cannot understand what is happening in this situation.

CONSOLIDATE!

▶ *1. What is the Freudian view of personality?* There are three different levels of consciousness (unconscious, preconscious, and conscious), and three structures of personality (id, ego, superego) in a dynamic relationship with each other. Freud proposed five psy-

chosexual stages (oral, anal, phallic, latency, and genital) and theorized that when resolution of a psychosexual stage is incomplete, people's development is arrested, creating a neurosis. Moreover, sexual and aggressive impulses can create anxiety, prompting the

(continued)

use of defense mechanisms. Neo-Freudians—Carl Jung, Alfred Adler, and Karen Horney—have added to or altered aspects of Freud's theory. Although a comprehensive and intriguing theory, many aspects of Freud's theory are difficult to test scientifically.

► 2. *What is the main emphasis of humanistic theories?* Humanistic theories (for example, those of Abraham Maslow and Carl Rogers) celebrate each person's uniqueness and stress positive qualities of human nature and free will. They also emphasize self-actualization. Although uplifting, many aspects of humanistic theories are difficult to test scientifically.

► 3. *What is the cognitive approach to personality theory?* The cognitive approach stresses the roles of expectancies on people's thoughts, feelings, and behaviors: What you expect to happen will influence personality development. Expectancies include people's locus of control, the source we perceive as exerting control over our life events, and efficacy expectancy, the sense that we have the ability to follow through and produce the behaviors we would like to perform. Albert Bandura proposed the notion of reciprocal determinism to explain the interactive influence of behavior, environment, and cognitive/personal factors on one another.

THE WORLD: SOCIAL INFLUENCES ON PERSONALITY

Tina wondered whether some of the differences between Gabe and herself might reflect the different environments in which they had grown up. Gabe was an only child; Tina was the youngest of three, with two older brothers. Gabe grew up in a rural part of the United States and, before college, had lived in the same town his whole life. Tina, an Air Force "brat," had lived in half a dozen countries before she was 12.

Although some percentage of personality may have genetic or biological components, the environment also plays a role. Our family environments and the ways in which we are raised contribute substantially toward personality traits of social closeness and positive emotionality. Other environmental influences on personality that psychologists have investigated include birth order, peer relationships, gender differences, and culture.

► 1. To what extent does birth order shape personality?

► 2. Can friends affect the way personality develops?

► 3. Do social factors produce gender differences in personality?

► 4. Do different cultures produce different types of personalities?

Birth Order: Are You Number One?

Have you ever noticed that people who are firstborns seem more responsible and better organized, and that last-borns seem more agreeable and accommodating? If you have, you're not the first person to make a connection between personality and birth order. Alfred Adler (1964), himself a younger sibling raised in the shadow of a high-achieving brother, was one of the early personality theorists who proposed that birth order affects personality. In the past, research has not shown clear-cut evidence for the impact of birth order on personality development (see Ernst & Angst, 1983, for a review), but more recent reviews of birth order research, using meta-analytic procedures, have found consistent and interesting results.

Science historian Frank Sulloway (1997) used meta-analyses to support his proposal that at least one aspect of personality, openness to experience (one of the Big Five superfactors), is shaped by birth order. But, Sulloway was careful to point out, birth order acts along with other factors, such as the number of children in a family and the level of conflict between each child and his or her parents. Moreover, a person's sex (and that of his or her siblings), the number of years between siblings, temperament, social class, and loss of a parent can also affect this aspect of personality.

Sulloway developed his theory in an attempt to understand why, throughout history, some people have supported scientific and political revolutions whereas others have insisted on maintaining the status quo, especially why such opposite views occur within the same family. From available information about the lives of historical figures, Sulloway proposed that, in general, firstborns, by virtue of their place in the birth order, are more likely to support parental authority, see things as their parents do, and be less open to new ideas and experiences. Younger siblings, because they must find a different niche in the family and in the world around them, are more likely to be open to new ideas. In their personalities, "only" children are similar to firstborn children.

TABLE 10.6

The Effects of Birth Order on Personality

FIRSTBORNS AND ONLY CHILDREN
- More responsible, ambitious, organized, academically successful, energetic, self-disciplined (*Conscientious*)
- More temperamental, more anxious about their status (*Neurotic*)
- More assertive, dominant (*Extraverted*) (Sulloway, 1997)

MIDDLE-BORNS
- Less closely identified with family
- Less likely to ask for parental help in an emergency
- Less likely to report having been loved as child
- Compared with siblings, more likely to live farther from parents and less likely to visit parents (Salmon, 1999; Salmon & Daley, 1998)

LATER-BORNS
- More tender-minded, easy-going, trusting, accommodating, altruistic (*Agreeable*)
- More adventurous, prone to fantasy, attracted by novelty, untraditional (*Open to experience*)
- More sociable, affectionate, excitement seeking, fun-loving (*Extraversion*)
- More self-conscious (*Neuroticism*) (Sulloway, 1997)

Although not all psychologists agree with his meta-analytic conclusions about birth order and personality development (Modell, 1996), and not all subsequent research has supported his theory (Freese et al., 1999), Sulloway (1999) has extended and replicated his results with over 5,000 adults; the results are summarized in Table 10.6. Salmon's work (1998, 1999; Salmon & Daly, 1998) has focused on middle-born children. She found that middle-borns were less close to their families than were their elder or younger siblings. For instance, when hearing political speeches, middle-borns responded most positively to the speeches when the speaker used the term *friend* than when the terms *brothers* and *sisters* were used. In contrast, first- and last-borns responded most positively to speeches in which family terms were used (Salmon, 1998). Further, when asked to define themselves, middle-borns were least likely to define themselves by their last names, that is, their family names (Salmon & Daly, 1998).

Findings about the importance of birth order come from more than self-reported measures. When spouses were asked to complete a personality inventory about their partners, partners who were firstborns were described as having different personality characteristics than later-born partners (Sulloway, 1999). As rated by their partners, later-born spouses were less conscientious and more extraverted, agreeable, and open to experience than the firstborn spouses. A similar correlation between personality and birth order was found among college roommates: Firstborn roommates were perceived differently than were later-born roommates.

Peer Relationships: Personality Development by Peer Pressure

In 1995, Judith Harris wrote an article (and later a book, *The Nurture Assumption*) proposing that, beyond the genes they give their children, parents do not really affect their children's personality and social behavior. She claimed that it is children's peers, not their families, who shape how they behave and determine the nongenetic elements of their personalities. For example, she pointed out that immigrant children learn their new country's language fluently, even though they may speak their native language at home with their parents. She proposed that both contact with their peers and the desire to fit in lead children quickly to learn how to speak the new language without an accent.

According to Harris (1998), there are only two main ways that parents' behaviors can have enduring effects on their child's personality and social behavior. These are severe abuse and choice of where to live and where to send their children to school (and the latter is significant only because it gives parents some small control over their children's peer group). Beyond this, she theorizes, parents have little lasting influence on their children's personality and social behavior.

Harris's view of minimal parental influence on childhood development rests on the assumption that all children in the same family experience the same environment, but there are several flaws with this assumption. First, as we have noted, people create their own microenvironments based on their temperaments, past experiences, and appearances. Thus, there is no single "family environment" that is the same for each child, and any measure of an aspect of family environment, such as the number of books in the house, does not necessarily reflect the actual environment for a particular child. Second, if families had no effect on children's personalities, then birth order effects would not exist (Sulloway, 1998). The fact that firstborns have been shown to have consistently different personalities than their younger brothers and sisters speaks to the fact that interactions within the family—including the manner in which parents treat their children—*does* affect personality.

Third, the same event in a family has different meaning for each of its members, based on age and cognitive ability (Hoffman, 1991). This can be clearly seen in studies of the effects of parents' divorce on their children. Children who are 5 years old when parents divorce respond in predictable ways that are *different* from the predictable ways that 11-year-olds respond. Five-year-olds assume the divorce is a result of something they did, whereas 11-year-olds can reason and understand that the divorce may be caused by other factors. Thus, siblings of different ages may have the same stimulus, in this case the divorce, but the effects on their personalities are very different (Hoffman, 1991).

Another flaw in Harris's general theory is that she ignores the role that parents, and the family in general, can have in the way people feel about themselves, and how these feelings, in turn, lead to the particular thoughts, feelings, and behaviors that constitute personality. For example, if the youngest child in a family is always belittled, that consistent experience, in tandem with his or her temperament, can create a child who longs to grow up and prove his or her worth (Dunn & Plomin, 1990).

Finally, Harris does not address the literature showing that parents influence their children's values, which in turn influence how they think, feel, and behave. Although peer relationships can affect personality development, these relationships are not the only environmental factor to affect personality.

Research designed to test elements of Harris's hypothesis directly has thus far provided mixed results at best (Loehlin, 1997; Vernon et al., 1997). For example, twins who have more friends in common have more similar personalities than do twins who have fewer friends in common; however, the statistics indicate this relationship is weak.

Gender Differences in Personality: Nature and Nurture

In general, personality differences between females and males are not very great, especially when compared with the large differences among people within each sex. In fact, some have proposed that it is counterproductive to look for sex differences in personality, arguing that the context in which behavior takes place has a larger role in personality development (Lott, 1996). For example, there are no notable sex differences in social anxiety, locus of control, impulsiveness, or reflectiveness (Feingold, 1994).

Nonetheless, some consistent differences have been found (Feingold, 1994). Women tend to score higher on traits reflecting *social connectedness*, which is a focus on the importance of relationships (Gilligan, 1982). In contrast, men tend to score higher on traits reflecting *individuality* and *autonomy*, with a focus on separateness from others, achievement, and self-sufficiency. Women tend to be more empathic than men (Lennon & Eisenberg, 1987) and report more nurturing tendencies (Feingold, 1994). In addition, as noted in Chapter 9, women do better on tasks assessing emotion in other people (Hall, 1978, 1987). For example, women are better than men at spotting when their partners are deceiving them (McCornack & Parks, 1990).

While some studies have found a sex difference in individuality, others have not (Archer & Waterman, 1988). The observed sex differences in individuality and social connectedness show themselves in part in the way males and females try to resolve moral dilemmas. Gilligan (1982) and others have argued that females think through moral dilemmas differently from, not less well than, males. Females are more likely to pay attention to the interpersonal context of a moral decision, to whether and how others will be hurt by the decision; males are more likely to make a moral decision based on laws or abstract principles. We will discuss this in more detail in Chapter 11.

Males and females also differ in their amounts of neuroticism, with men scoring lower (Lynn & Martin, 1997; Zuckerman et al., 1988). However, women generally score lower on anger and aggression (Shields, 1987) and on assertiveness (Feingold, 1994).

These findings are consistent with stereotypes about men and women, but the fact that a difference exists doesn't tell us *why* it exists—what might be the role of biological or cultural factors (sex differences caused by cultural factors are sometimes referred to as *gender differences*)? Biological explanations for sex differences include the effects of testosterone (see Chapters 2 and 9), as well as the premise that men and women have evolved differently because of differences in mate selection and parenting strategies (D. Buss, 1995). According to this view, women have a greater investment in their offspring because physiologically they cannot have as many children as can men. This greater investment, and their caretaker role, caused women to develop more of an attachment to their children, an attachment with an evolutionary advantage: These women were more likely to have children who survived into adulthood and had children themselves.

Several cultural and social theories attempt to explain personality differences between men and women. Social role theory proposes that boys and girls learn different skills and beliefs. For example, some computer games pitched to girls emphasize social interactions and a concern for others, and portray getting along as more important than winning. This emphasis is in contrast to the more typical genre, which involves killing the enemy, capturing others' territory, and defending against capture or death. These two types of computer games let the user cultivate different skills and lead to different moral lessons. Expectancy effects can also play a role in sex differences in personality; through direct interaction with their environments, boys and girls come to have different expectancies about likely responses when gender-role appropriate or inappropriate behavior is exhibited (Henley, 1977).

Another cultural explanation for personality differences between men and women rests on the fact that women are most often the primary caretakers of children. Choderow (1978) proposes that between the ages of 3 and 5, boys realize they are a different sex from their mothers, a realization that leads them to feel a loss of identification and connection with their mothers and to experience themselves as autonomous individuals. In contrast, girls do not experience this loss because they and their mothers are the same sex, and girls maintain a sense of connection to others. An additional cultural explanation for gender differences in assessing others' emotions is the difference in power between men and women. Traditionally, women have been less likely to hold positions of power. In such circumstances, being able to read the emotions of others provides some degree of safety by being able to make rapid assessments of a situation (Snodgrass, 1985; Tavris, 1991).

The importance of context, or situation, has raised the question of whether examining sex differences in personality is valid; after all, different situations can yield contradictory findings (Eagly, 1987, 1995; Lott, 1996). For example, a study on empathy found that, although women scored higher on self-reported measures of empathy, among both sexes, those scoring higher in empathy were more likely to report that their parents were affectionate, spent time with them, and discussed feelings with them (Barnett et al., 1980). In addition, Moskowitz (1993) found differences between men and women when participants interacted with same-sex friends (males were more dominant, females were more friendly), but those differences disappeared when the interactions were between opposite-sex strangers. Thus, although differences between men's and women's personalities have been observed, they do not necessarily hold in all situations.

From what we know of Tina and Gabe, we cannot say with certainty that the personality differences between them are explained by sex or gender differences. Although he prefers to be alone more than she, he does have friends, and we can't say if their contrasting preferences reflect a gender difference, a difference in social connectedness and individuality, temperament, or their learning histories.

Culture and Personality: Are There National Personalities?

It is more difficult to compare personalities across cultures than you might think. Although it is possible to translate personality measures into other languages, some concepts don't translate very well, even if the words themselves can be rendered in different languages. For example, it is possible to translate the phrase *self-esteem* into French, but the concept of self-esteem as we understand it is not generally familiar in France, and so a simple translation of words from English to French doesn't convey the meaning of the idea.

Yet personality measures that have been carefully translated to compensate for such problems reveal the same Big Five personality factors in many, although not all, cultures (Katigbak et al., 1996; McCrae & Costa, 1997; McCrae et al., 1998; Paunonen & Ashton, 1998; Paunonen et al., 2000). Personality measures developed in the native language of a culture, rather than translated into it, may be more accurate for that culture. For example, Chinese college students were asked to rate other people on qualities described by Chinese adjectives (not English adjectives translated into Chinese); five factors were identified, but they were not the same as the Big Five found in English-language tests (Yang & Bond, 1990).

People in collectivist cultures tend to define themselves as part of a group, are very attached to the group, and see their personal goals are secondary to the group's goals. People from individualist cultures define themselves as individuals, are less attached to the group, and see their personal goals as more important than the group's goals (Triandis et al., 1988).

In general, personality differences have been found between collectivist and individualist cultures (see Chapter 9). Collectivist cultures often find the needs of the group more important than those of the individual: Chinese, African, Latin American, and Arab cultures tend to have this orientation (Buda & Elsayed-Elkhouly, 1998). In contrast, individualist countries such as the United States, Great Britain, Canada, and Australia emphasize the individual, even at the expense of others. Collectivist countries tend to value humility, honoring the family, and efforts to maintain the social order (Triandis et al., 1990), and are more likely to have a populace that cares about others, even strangers (Hui & Triandis, 1986). Individualist countries value personal freedom, equality, and enjoyment. This distinction between cultures has been used to explain differences in crime rates, which are higher in individualist cultures: Collectivist cultures exert more social control over the individual, and criminals' actions reflect not only on themselves but also on their families. And, in fact, as the global economy leads collectivist cultures to shift their work habits and values to those of individualist countries, crime rates and other social ills increase (Strom, 2000).

Consider that, using the five-factor approach, bilingual Hong Kong university students were given a personality inventory in both English and its Chinese-translation equivalent. Results showed that, compared with North American university students, Hong Kong students were low in extraversion in general, and in the particular traits of excitement seeking, competence, and altruism. Moreover, they were high in vulnerability, straightforwardness, and compliance (McCrae et al., 1998). As proof of the impact of culture on personality, after Chinese immigrants move to North America, their personality profiles begin to resemble those of native-born North Americans; the longer they have lived in North America, the more similar the profiles (McCrae et al., 1998).

Although the United States is an individualist country, individualism varies by region (Vandello & Cohen, 1999; see Figure 10.7 on page 382). The Deep South (perhaps because of its strong self-identification as a cultural region, its history of collective farming, and the prominence of religion) is the most collectivist. The states of the Southwest are also collectivist; these states have a distinct history and an influx of immigrants from Mexico, a collectivist country. In contrast, the Great Plains and western mountain states are particularly individualistic, in part because of the "vast distances, sparse population, and harsh, unpredictable weather" in this part of the country (Shortridge, 1993, p. 1011), as well as the frontier values of individuality. Thus, although people may live in a country that falls on a particular location on the collectivist–individualist continuum, there are regional, as well as individual,

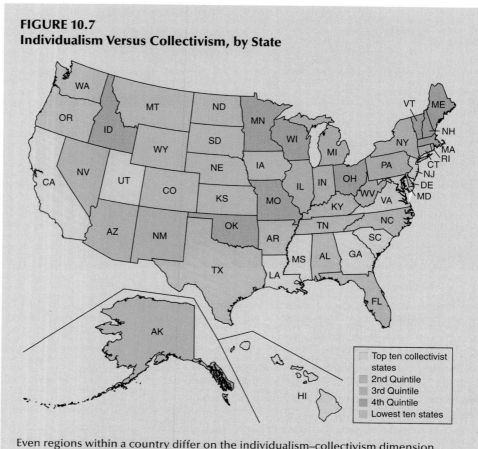

FIGURE 10.7
Individualism Versus Collectivism, by State

Top ten collectivist states
2nd Quintile
3rd Quintile
4th Quintile
Lowest ten states

Even regions within a country differ on the individualism–collectivism dimension. Utah, with its strong collectivist orientation, ranks as one of the top 10 states in collectivism, along with some states in the Deep South and the Southeast. Some of the Great Plains and western mountain states are the most individualist, perhaps because of the individualist "frontier" mentality and rugged geographic features. (Data from Vandello & Cohen, 1999.)

differences. So, to the extent that experience shapes personality, the very different experiences of Tina's and Gabe's childhood years may well have contributed to their different approaches to life.

LOOKING AT LEVELS

Two's Company

How can we explain cultural differences in personality? Perhaps people from different cultures have different genes, or the environment leads different genes to be expressed in certain cultures and not others. Let's look again at a study by Ekman (1980) described in Chapter 9. Japanese and Americans watched emotional films, either alone or with a white-coated investigator in the room. When alone, the Japanese and the Americans reacted to various events in the film in very similar ways. But in company, the Japanese tended to respond more politely and with a narrower range of emotions, whereas the Americans responded much as they did when alone. Thus, it isn't the case that the Japanese actually had different emotional responses than the Americans, that they had lower levels of emotionality. Rather, their learned behaviors (politeness and less expression of emotion) masked their true emotional responsiveness.

When in the company of authoritative strangers (such as the white-coated investigator), the Japanese do not display the same range of emotions that is permissible when alone. The collectivist Japanese culture leads to a change in behavior (changing facial expressions), and the Japanese have learned to make this change very well, extremely quickly, and apparently automatically. Both their initial response to the film and their subsequent learned responses can be considered elements of personality, although they are influenced by different factors. The initial response may be influenced more by temperament (emotionality, at the level of the brain), whereas the subsequent response is influenced more by the social environment (in this case, culture). The cultural differences in personality between the Americans and the Japanese trace back to learning during childhood (level of the person), learning that not only shapes the individual's personality, but also regulates the expression of biological responses.

CONSOLIDATE!

▶ *1. To what extent does birth order shape personality?* From studying historical figures, Sulloway suggests that birth order, along with other moderating variables such as the number of children in a family and the level of conflict between parents and children, can influence openness to experience. Further research has found additional differences between first-, middle-, and later-borns. Specifically, firstborns are less open to new experiences and are more conscientious, middle-borns identify less closely with family, and later-borns are more agreeable and more open to new experiences.

▶ *2. Can friends affect the way personality develops?* Research suggests that peer relationships *can* affect personality. However, findings to date are mixed at best that peer relationships are the main environmental element that influences personality development.

▶ *3. Do social factors produce gender differences in personality?* Although men and women exhibit few broad personality differences, there are noteworthy differences in social connectedness (versus individuality) and in emotionality (high versus low). Social explanations for these differences range from social role theory, identification with the primary caretaker, and differences in power. Given the importance of context, gender may not be predictive of behavior in a given situation.

▶ *4. Do different cultures produce different types of personalities?* There are cultural differences in personality: The native-born citizens of countries that emphasize the needs of the group tend to have personalities that reflect the collectivist orientation. In contrast, the native-born citizens of countries that emphasize individualism tend to have personalities that reflect the individualist orientation.

A DEEPER LEVEL ■ ➡ ➡
Recap and Thought Questions

▶ **What Is Personality?**

Personality is a consistent set of characteristics that people display over time and across situations, and that distinguish individuals from each other. People do not behave in the same manner in all situations: The context, or situation, influences the way people behave, and people can influence the situation. Some researchers have found that personality traits can be statistically grouped under five superfactors (extraversion, neuroticism, agreeableness, conscientiousness, and openness) or, according to Eysenck, three personality dimensions (extraversion, neuroticism, and psychoticism). Personality can be measured by interviews, observation, inventories (such as Cattell's 16PF), and projective tests (such as the Rorschach test and the Thematic Apperception Test, or TAT), with inventories being the most common method.

Do the differences between Tina and Gabe reflect their different personalities? Some of the differences probably do reflect personality differences, but the situation also exerts its own influence, evidenced by Tina's different behavior when with her economics professor and with Gabe.

> **Think It Through.** Suppose you are interested in dating someone and wanted to assess his or her personality before getting too involved. Why would you choose a particular type of assessment method? If you could assess a prospective employer's personality, why might you use the same method or a different one? Would you be able to predict your future employer's behavior if you knew his or her Big Five characteristics? Why or why not? Why might it change the accuracy of your predictions if you knew more about the scores on the specific traits that make up the five superfactors?

▶ The Brain: The Personality Organ

Eysenck proposed that each of his three personality dimensions (extraversion, neuroticism, and psychoticism) has a corresponding biologically distinct system. Aspects of this theory have been supported by brain-scanning and other physiological research. Some psychologists and behavioral geneticists estimate that approximately 50% of the variations in personality is inherited, although some traits appear more heritable than others. These innate inclinations, often referred to as temperaments, include activity, sociability, emotionality, and impulsivity. Differences in physiology, such as emotional arousability, can affect thoughts, feelings, motivation, and behavior, and can make people more or less prone to conditioned emotional responses and shyness.

Were Tina and Gabe born with their personalities? Based on behavioral genetics research, it is likely that Tina and Gabe were born with some elements of their personalities, particularly their temperaments. However, other elements have likely been forged by their cultural experiences, family events, and learning histories.

> **Think It Through.** Imagine that you know a family in which both parents are highly extraverted, emotionally stable, not particularly creative, and very conscientious. Would you predict that their child would have the same personality features? Why or why not? If their child was very shy (one of Kagan's "inhibited" children), would that mean that the child will always be shy, or might he or she become like the parents? (Hint: Think about what you have learned about temperament.)

▶ The Person: Behaviors and Beliefs

Questions of motives, thoughts, and feelings are at the heart of Freud's psychodynamic theory, which focuses on the three structures of personality (id, ego, and superego, and their dynamic relationships), three levels of awareness (unconscious, preconscious, and conscious), as well as sexual and aggressive drives, defense mechanisms, and psychosexual stages (oral, anal, phallic, latency, and genital). According to Freud, when resolution of a psychosexual stage is incomplete, people's development is arrested, creating a neurosis. Moreover, sexual and aggressive impulses can create anxiety, causing the use of defense mechanisms. Neo-Freudians (such as Jung, Adler, and Horney) have added to or altered aspects of Freud's theory. Maslow's and Rogers's humanistic theories also address motives, feelings, and the self, but celebrate each person's uniqueness, stress positive qualities of human nature and free will, and emphasize self-actualization. The cognitive view of personality focuses on the roles of expectancies on people's thoughts, feelings, and behaviors: What we expect to happen will influence our personality development. Personality differences in expectancies include locus of control, the source we perceive as exerting control over life events, and efficacy expectancy, the sense that we have the ability to follow through and produce the behaviors we would like to perform.

How might Tina's and Gabe's inner motives, thoughts, and feelings reflect their personalities? We don't know enough about Tina and Gabe or their childhood experiences to be able to understand how each one's personality may reflect their motives, thoughts, and feelings. We could infer such attributes based on Freudian, humanistic, and cognitive theories of personality, but based on our limited knowledge of Tina and Gabe, these would be mere speculations.

> **Think It Through.** If you used Freudian theory to understand a historical figure's personality and motivations, do you think you could be sure of your analysis? Why or why not? Could you use a humanist theory to understand this person? What would you need to know about him or her? Which aspects of this person's life would you need to know about in order to apply a cognitive theory of personality?

▶ The World: Social Influences on Personality

Birth order, along with other moderating factors, such as the number of children in a family and the level of conflict between parents and children, can influence openness to experience and other aspects of personality. Moreover, although there are a few broad personality differences between women and men (social connectedness versus individuality, and high versus low emotionality), in general differences between the sexes tend to be small, and it is not clear whether they are due to biological or social factors. Social explanations for these differences range from social role theory, identification with the primary caretaker, and differences in power. Context may be more predictive of personality than sex. Personality differences have also been found between citizens of cultures that are collectivist as opposed to individualist, with people in each culture tending to have personality traits that are more valued in their culture.

Could Tina's and Gabe's different childhood environments have affected how their personalities developed? It is possible that aspects of Tina's and Gabe's different childhood environments could have influenced their personalities. Their differences could reflect their birth order positions (perhaps Gabe is conscientious because he is a firstborn?), sex differences (perhaps Tina is more emotionally responsive because she is female), or cultural differences. Moreover, family events, such as divorce, would have affected their personalities.

Think It Through. What are two possible explanations for regional personality differences between "mellow" Californians and "fast-paced" northeasterners? (Hint: Genetic? environmental?) How might you go about trying to determine whether your explanation is supported by research data? What type of study could you design, and what kinds of participants would you need? What is your hypothesis—that is, what kind of results would you expect to find?

11 PSYCHOLOGY OVER THE LIFE SPAN

Growing Up, Growing Older, Growing Wiser

"Spielbug," some of his classmates called him. Girls thought he was nerdy and unattractive. His father, Arnold, a pioneer in the use of computers in engineering, was hardly ever around and, to make matters worse, frequently uprooted his family, moving from Ohio to New Jersey, to Arizona, and finally to Northern California. Steven was a perpetual new kid on the block. He was also, by all accounts, an unusual child, both in his appearance (he had a large head and protruding ears) and in his fearful and awkward behavior (McBride, 1999). Spielberg himself has said that he "felt like an alien" throughout his childhood. He desperately wanted to be accepted, but didn't fit in. So at age 12 he began making films, "little 8mm things. I did it to find something that, for me, could be permanent" (quoted in Sullivan, 1999, p. 66). Spielberg continued to make movies as a teenager, often casting his three sisters in roles. He discovered that making movies was one way to win his peers' acceptance, as well as some small measure of power—for he sometimes induced his worst enemies to appear in his films.

When he was 16, Spielberg's parents divorced, and Spielberg blamed his father's constant traveling for the breakup. His unhappiness only deepened when his father remarried, taking for his second wife a woman Spielberg couldn't stand. At the same time that he withdrew from his father, Spielberg continued to have a close relationship with his mother, Leah, a concert pianist and artist. The split with his father lasted some 15 years.

In many ways, Spielberg's films, like the rest of his life, are shaped by his childhood. Spielberg himself has said about *E.T., The Extra-Terrestrial*, "The whole movie is really about divorce. . . . Henry's [the main character's] ambition to find a father by bringing E.T. into his life to fill some black hole—that was my struggle to find somebody to replace the dad who I felt had abandoned me" (Sullivan, 1999, p. 68). Many of Spielberg's other films include children who are separated from their parents (such as the girl in *Poltergeist* and the boy in *Close Encounters of the Third Kind*). And *Back to the Future* might represent his longings to change the past, if only he could. Only when he turned 40 did he turn to adult contexts. As he matured, Spielberg's identification with oppressed people in general (not just oppressed children) led him to make movies such as *The Color Purple*, *Schindler's List*, and *Amistad*.

Steven Spielberg married and had a child, but eventually divorced his wife, actress Amy Irving. His own experiences made him extremely sensitive to the effect of the divorce on his son, and he made every attempt to ensure that his son, Max, did not feel abandoned. When he married again, he became deeply involved with his family (which includes seven children, some of them adopted). There was a happy development in the previous generation's father–son relationship as well: Arnold became a well-loved grandfather who is now a regular presence in the Spielberg household.

Spielberg's journey is one version of the universal story of human development: A skinny kid beset by fears and with few friends becomes one of the most powerful figures in the global entertainment industry; from a family with little family life develops a man's resolve to make the best possible life for his own family; across generations, a father and a son come to like each other, now as father and grandfather, after 15 years of estrangement. *Developmental psychologists* study exactly these sorts of events in our lives: the fascinating and varied process of human development over the life span. In this chapter, we begin by considering prenatal development and the newborn, and we see that even here genes and environment are intimately intertwined. We next turn to infancy and childhood and observe the interplay between maturation and experience in the shaping of the child's physical, mental, emotional, and social development. Then we consider adolescence, a crucial time in development. And finally, we discuss adulthood and aging, and gain insights that help us understand how Arnold could develop from a less-than-optimal father into a terrific grandfather.

IN THE BEGINNING: FROM CONCEPTION TO BIRTH

Steven Spielberg has been celebrated as one of the most successful moviemakers of all time. He just seemed to have a natural bent for making movies (he never attended film school). Where did his talent come from? In this section we begin at the beginning and think about the foundations of our skills and abilities.

▶ 1. How does development progress in the womb?

▶ 2. What are the capabilities of newborns?

Prenatal Development: Nature and Nurture From the Start

For each of us, life began with the meeting of two cells, a sperm and an egg (or *ovum*, which in Latin means "egg"). These specialized cells are sex cells, or *gametes*. The sperm penetrated the egg, and the genetic material of the sperm melded with that of the ovum. The ovum is not a passive partner in this dance of life; the sperm is drawn to the egg by chemical reactions on the surface of the egg. And when a sperm has been accepted within the egg, other reactions prevent additional sperm from penetrating. The ovum is a supercell, the largest in the human body. Even so, it is barely the size of a pin prick, and sperm are much smaller (about 1/500 of an inch). But despite their small sizes, within the ovum and sperm reside all the machinery necessary to create a new life. And, even at this earliest stage of development, *genes* (*nature*) and the *environment* (*nurture*) are intimately intertwined.

GETTING A START IN LIFE. The genetic heritage of every normal human being is 23 pairs of chromosomes, one member of each pair coming from an egg and the other from a sperm. A *chromosome* is a strand of *DNA* (*deoxyribonucleic acid*) in the nucleus of the cell. A molecule of DNA is shaped like a twisted ladder—the famous "double helix"—in which the rungs are formed by the bonds between pairs of chemicals. Each *gene* on the chromosome is a series of particular "rungs" (see Chapter 2). All cells in the body except the gametes (eggs and sperm) contain all 23 pairs of chromosomes; each gamete contains only a single member of each chromosome pair. In an egg, one of these 23 is a chromosome known as *X*; in a sperm, the corresponding chromosome is either an *X* chromosome or a shorter version called a *Y* chromosome.

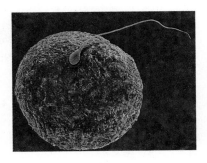

At the moment of conception, a sperm penetrates an ovum. The egg, however, is not a passive recipient; by changing its surface properties, it actively regulates the behavior of the sperm.

The fertilization of the egg by the sperm creates a cell called a **zygote,** in which the chromosomes from the egg and from the sperm pair up so that the zygote contains the full complement of 23 pairs. If the sperm contributes an *X* chromosome, the offspring will be female (*XX*); if *Y*, male (*XY*). The *Y* chromosome contains a gene (the SRY gene, for "sex-determining region of the *Y* chromosome") that produces a chemical substance that ultimately causes the zygote to develop into a male; if this substance is not present, genes on the *X* chromosome will produce other substances that cause the baby to be female (Goodfellow & Lowell-Badge, 1993; Hawkins, 1994).

Much of early development is determined by **maturation,** the process that produces genetically programmed changes with age. But from the very start, genes and the environment interact. Although the genes of the sperm that fertilizes the egg will have a major impact on what kind of person develops, the environment plays a crucial role in whether the sperm ever reaches the egg. Sperm actually "surf" on subtle muscle contractions in the uterus; these waves usually move in the correct direction in fertile women, but they either move in the wrong direction or are weak in infertile women (Kunz et al., 1997; Lyons & Levi, 1994). In addition, the fluid in the uterus must be the right consistency and have the right chemical composition for the sperm to complete their journey (Mori et al., 1998; Shibahara et al., 1995; Singh, 1995).

The members of each pair of chromosomes are similar—but they are not identical. For example, the gene for the shape of your earlobes is on the same spot on both chromosomes, but because of its particular chemical composition, the gene on one chromosome may code for an attached earlobe and the gene on the other for an unattached earlobe. (These variant forms of genes, which produce different forms of the same trait, are called *alleles*, and in this case the one for unattached earlobes is *dominant*—given even one copy, you will inherit the trait; see Chapter 8.) The gametes are formed from specialized cells that, while themselves containing the full 23 pairs, in the course of division produce cells with half that number, with only one member of each pair. So, because the members of each pair are not identical, the genetic contents of the resulting gametes are not all the same. And there's another wrinkle, which further contributes to our wonderful human variety: In the course of

Zygote: A fertilized ovum (egg).

Maturation: The developmental process that produces genetically programmed changes with increased age.

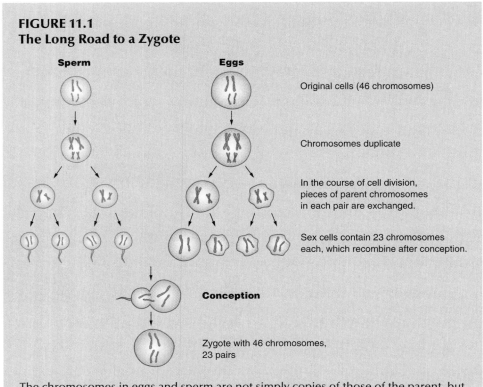

FIGURE 11.1
The Long Road to a Zygote

Sperm   Eggs

Original cells (46 chromosomes)

Chromosomes duplicate

In the course of cell division,
pieces of parent chromosomes
in each pair are exchanged.

Sex cells contain 23 chromosomes
each, which recombine after conception.

Conception

Zygote with 46 chromosomes,
23 pairs

The chromosomes in eggs and sperm are not simply copies of those of the parent, but rather unique combinations of the material in the two chromosomes in each pair of the parent's chromosomes. The sperm and egg combine to form the basis of a unique individual (or individuals, in the case of identical twins).

cell division, the chromosomal decks of cards are shuffled so that pieces of the parent chromosomes in each pair are exchanged, as shown in Figure 11.1, to form new combinations of genes.

Each zygote thus consists of a unique combination of genes. In fact, in theory, each human couple can produce some 70 trillion genetically different children! Moreover, the same genetic material can produce different results, depending on whether it is inherited from the mother or the father. This effect is called *genomic imprinting* (or *gametic imprinting;* Keverne, 1997; Kirkness & Durcan, 1992). For example, a deletion of part of chromosome 15 leads to Angelman's syndrome if it is inherited from the mother; this syndrome includes an awkward way of walking, inappropriate laughter, and severe mental retardation. When the same deletion comes by way of the father, it leads to Prader-Willi syndrome, which involves depression, overeating, and "having a temper" (Barlow, 1995; Clarke et al., 1995; Dykens & Cassidy, 1999). Researchers have yet to discover how such genomic imprinting works.

Once formed, the zygote begins to divide. The production of certain hormones causes genes to turn on and off in a specific sequence, guiding the zygote's development (Brown, 1999; as discussed in Chapter 2, genes produce specific proteins only when they are "turned on"). Soon a cluster of cells has developed. After 3 days, about 60 to 70 cells have formed and organized themselves into a sphere called a *blastocyst*. This cluster proceeds through an orderly progression, first rolling up into a tube, then developing features that in early stages look much like those of relatively simple animals, then more complex ones. When you first see how similar the human fetus is to those of other animals at different stages of development, it is hard not to imagine that you are witnessing a fast-forward version of the evolution of our species. (This notion is captured by the phrase "ontogeny recapitulates [repeats] phylogeny"; *ontogeny* is the development of the individual, *phylogeny* the evolutionary development of species.)

Human development in the womb is divided into *trimesters*, three equal periods of 3 months each. The first trimester is divided into three stages: the zygote, the embryo, and the fetus (and the developing baby is called a fetus thereafter, until he or she is born). At the end of the second trimester, the great bulk of the neurons each individual possesses are in place (Nowakowski, 1987; Rakic, 1975; Rodier, 1980), but they are not completely fixed; researchers have recently found that new neurons can be produced in adult brains (Gould et al., 1999).

The path from zygote to birth is not always smooth. Perhaps surprisingly, about half of all fertilized eggs contain some kind of abnormality in their chromosomes. Most of these eggs are spontaneously aborted (in fact, about 30% of zygotes don't even make it to the embryo phase), but even so, about 1 in 250 babies is born with an abnormality that is obvious, and probably more have abnormalities that are not obvious (Plomin et al., 1997, p. 54; Sadler, 1995).

IN THE WOMB. A popular—and misleading—image shows the fetus floating peacefully asleep in the womb. But in truth the fetus is active nearly from the start, at first with automatic movements, such as the heart beating, and then with large-scale coordinated behaviors. As the fetus develops, the heart rate slows down (but becomes more variable), the fetus moves less often but more vigorously when it does stir, and the heart rate and movement patterns become coordinated. Some researchers have even reported sex differences in behavior in the womb, with male fetuses more active than females (DiPietro et al., 1996). After 20 to 25 weeks of gestation, the fetus is sensitive to both sound and light (Nilsson & Hamberger, 1990; Pujol et al., 1990). How do we know this? Because if a fetus is examined, as is sometimes medically necessary, by a special light-emitting instrument called a *fetoscope*, it will actually move its hands to shield its eyes. As the fetus develops, its movements become increasingly coordinated, and by 28 weeks, it responds to external stimulation. A bit later its heart rate can change if the mother is startled (DiPietro et al., 1996; Kisilevsky & Low, 1998), and between 25 and 34 weeks, a fetus can detect human speech (Cheour-Luhtanen et al., 1996; Zimmer et al., 1993).

In addition, there is evidence that fetuses can learn. Sandman and colleagues (1997) measured the heart rate of fetuses between 30 and 32 weeks after conception while a buzzing vibrator was placed on the mother's belly, positioned right over the fetus's head. The fetus's heart would speed up when it first received a series of stimuli, but this response decreased as more stimuli were presented in the series. This is a classic case of habituation—that is, diminishing response with repeated exposure to the same stimulus. The researchers then presented a new stimulus, which differed in both frequency and intensity, and the fetus's heart speeded up again. This finding shows not only that a fetus can discriminate between the two stimuli, but also that the diminishing response was not the result of the fetus's becoming fatigued or failing to sense the stimuli. In a third round, a series of the original stimuli was presented again. This time the fetus consistently responded to these stimuli, not habituating as it had done previously. What does this mean? The different response to the second presentation of the original stimuli shows that the fetus learned their properties from the first time they were presented—if it hadn't, it would have responded to the second presentation the same way that it did originally.

TERATOGENS: WHEN THE ENVIRONMENT HURTS. A **teratogen** is a chemical, virus, or type of radiation that can cause damage to the zygote, embryo, or fetus. Because of events at different stages in the course of development, different organs are vulnerable to teratogens at different times. Unfortunately, the central nervous system is vulnerable at virtually every phase. For example, the development of the brain can be disrupted if the mother catches a virus, such as chicken pox or rubella (3-day German measles); more than half the babies born to mothers who contract rubella will be mentally retarded if the developing child is in the embryonic period at the onset of the disease. In addition, a mother who is HIV-positive can pass the virus on to the baby during gestation or birth (but only about one third of these babies contract the virus).

Teratogen: Any chemical, virus, or type of radiation that can cause damage to the zygote, embryo, or fetus.

The HIV virus causes brain damage, leading to problems in concentration, attention, memory, movement control, and the ability to reason (Clifford, 2000; Grant et al., 1999). Another potential teratogen is alcohol, which can damage the eggs before fertilization (Kaufman, 1997) as well as affect the developing baby throughout pregnancy, starting with the embryo phase. Using heroin or cocaine during pregnancy can cause a host of problems: physical defects, irritability, and sleep and attentional problems in the newborn (Fox, 1994; Miller et al., 1995; Vogel, 1997). Moreover, various environmental pollutants and ionizing radiation can have effects ranging from birth defects and cancer to behavioral difficulties, such as in paying attention. It is known that, in other animals at least, these effects can be passed on to the third generation, to the offspring of the offspring (Friedler, 1996). In fact, even the father's health habits can affect the fetus and subsequently the child. Certain drugs (both prescription and illegal, such as cocaine) can affect the sperm and thereby affect the growing fetus and child (Yazigi et al., 1991).

Major diseases and strong drugs are not the only threats to healthy prenatal development. Excessive amounts of caffeine (three cups of coffee a day, according to one study) can lead to miscarriage or low birth weight, irritability, and other symptoms (Eskenazi, 1993; Eskenazi et al., 1999). Another study found that children of mothers who drink four or more cups of coffee per day had increased risk of *sudden infant death syndrome (SIDS)* (Ford et al., 1998). Smoking during pregnancy affects both mother and fetus; it is correlated with higher rates of miscarriage, lower birth weights, stillbirth, and infant mortality, and can cause attentional difficulties in the infant (Floyd et al., 1993; Fried & Makin, 1987; Fried & Watkinson, 2000). A mother's poor diet can lead her infant to have fewer brain cells than normal (Morgane et al., 1993), and the lack of even a single important vitamin or mineral can have significant effects. For example, insufficient folic acid (vitamin B) can disrupt the early development of the nervous system (Nevid et al., 1998).

Stressors in the mother's life can also endanger the developing fetus, and when the stress is severe enough, infants may experience attentional difficulties, be unusually anxious, and exhibit unusual social behavior (Weinstock, 1997). In fact, fetuses of mothers of lower socioeconomic status, who are often more stressed than those of higher socioeconomic status, move less often and less vigorously, and show other differences from fetuses of better-off mothers (Pressman et al., 1998). There are several physiological reasons for these effects. When the mother is stressed, more of her blood flows to parts of the body affected by the fight-or-flight response (such as the limbs and heart), and less to the uterus. She produces hormones such as cortisol, which slows down the operation of genes that guide prenatal development of the brain, suppressing brain growth (Brown, 1999). There is evidence that the babies of stressed mothers are born with smaller heads than those of unstressed mothers, which may be related to the poorer behavioral functioning scores seen for such babies (Lou et al., 1994).

POSITIVE ENVIRONMENTAL EVENTS: THE EARLIEST HEAD START. The previous paragraphs might seem to suggest that our species would be better off if maturation alone controlled development. But environmental effects are not all bad, and some prenatal experiences help the fetus. Consider a study by Lafuente and colleagues (1997). Each of 172 pregnant women was assigned to an experimental or a control group. The participants in the experimental group were given a waistband with a tape recorder and small speakers, on which they played tapes of violin music for an average of 70 hours, starting at about 28 weeks after conception and continuing until the birth of the baby. The researchers then tracked the development of the babies during their first 6 months of life and found that the children of mothers in the experimental group were more advanced than those in the control group; for example, they had better motor control and better vocal abilities of the sort that precede language. (Note that this study in its design and conclusions is very different from the "Mozart effect" discussed in Chapter 8, in which music is played for very brief periods to adults who are then tested on aspects of IQ.) Steven Spielberg's mother played piano frequently while she was pregnant; could these prenatal concerts have had long-term positive effects on him?

A particularly good illustration of the importance of interactions among events at different levels of analysis is the finding that social support during pregnancy combats the possible effects of maternal stress on the developing infant. Having friends and family available can lead to healthier babies being born to stressed mothers (McLean et al., 1993). Social support presumably helps to reduce the mother's stress, which in turn keeps her from the fight-or-flight state and its accompanying unfortunate consequences for the developing baby.

The Newborn: A Work in Progress

In many ways, the human infant compares unfavorably with the infants of some other species. A baby kitten is much more competent, able to walk on its own and explore its environment at only 6 weeks, an age when the human infant has no hope of even crawling. The human brain is not fully developed at birth, perhaps because if it were, the baby's head would not fit through the birth canal. Much human brain development continues after birth.

Nevertheless, although the typical infant may seem thoroughly incompetent, capable of eating, sleeping, cooing, crying, drooling, and not much else, such an assessment would be off the mark. The baby is not a blank slate, waiting for learning or maturity to descend. On the contrary, babies come equipped with a surprising range of abilities and capacities.

SENSORY CAPACITIES. Even at the earliest phases of development, babies have the beginnings of sophisticated sensory capabilities. They are born sensitive to the range of frequencies of women's voices (see Hauser, 1996) and have a relatively sensitive sense of smell. Even babies who are fed by bottle prefer the odor of a woman who is breast-feeding another infant to that of a woman who is not breast-feeding (Porter et al., 1992).

Two-day-old infants can learn to pair information coming from different sensory modalities, as is necessary to learn that a particular voice is associated with a particular face. Slater and colleagues (1997) showed infants two visual stimuli, which differed in both color and orientation; at the same time that they presented one of the stimuli, they also presented a distinctive sound. They then switched the pairings and found that the infants paid more attention to the new combinations. These results showed that even 2-day-old infants can put visual and auditory stimuli together; if they couldn't, they wouldn't have noticed the changed pairings.

REFLEXES. Infants also come equipped with a wide range of reflexes, the most important of which are summarized in Table 11.1 on page 394. A *reflex* is an automatic response to an event, an action that does not require thought. Some of these reflexes have obvious survival value, such as sucking, and some may have had survival value for our ancestors, such as the Moro reflex, in which the startled baby throws its arms wide, as if to grab hold of someone. Other reflexes, such as the Babinski reflex, in which the baby's big toe flexes while the other toes fan out when the sole of his or her foot is stroked, are less obviously useful.

Curiously, many of the reflexes that babies have at birth disappear after a while. Some of the reflexes appear to be simpler versions of later behaviors, such as walking or swimming. Should we try to preserve these reflexes? It has been shown, for example, that the stepping reflex can be retained longer if the baby's leg muscles are exercised and become stronger (the reflex appears to disappear in part because the baby gains weight and the legs can no longer support the body; Thelen, 1983, 1995). However, infants who walk earlier do not walk *better* than infants who walk later.

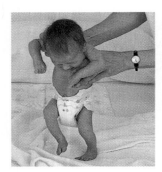

Stepping

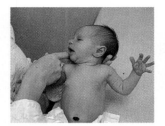

Rooting

Moro (startle)

TABLE 11.1

Major Reflexes Present at Birth

REFLEX	STIMULUS	RESPONSE	DURATION (approx.)
Withdrawal	Sharp stimulus to sole of foot	Leg flexes	Weakens after 10 days of age
Stepping	Held upright over flat surface	Stepping movements	Until about 2 months of age
Sucking	Finger in mouth	Sucking	Until about 3 months of age
Rooting	Stroking cheek lightly	Turns head toward stimulus, starts trying to suck	Until about 3 or 4 months of age
Palmar grasp	Pressing the palm	Grasps object pressing the palm	Until about 4 months of age
Moro (startle)	Sudden loud sound	Throws apart arms and extends legs, then brings arms together, cries	Until 5 months of age
Swimming	Face-down in water	Kicks and paddles in water	Until about 6 months of age
Tonic neck	Head turned to one side	One arm straightens while other bends, and one knee bends (resembling a "fencing" position)	Until 7 months of age
Plantar	Pressing the ball of the foot	All toes curl under	Until about 1 year of age
Babinski	Stroking sole of the foot	Big toe flexes, other toes fan out	Until about 1 year of age
Eye blink	Bright light in eyes	Eyes close	Life

TEMPERAMENT: INSTANT PERSONALITY. A friend describing the birth of his second son expressed amazement as he realized, when handed the child immediately after birth, that the infant was already *different* from his first son, calmer and steadier. Our friend should not have been surprised. From their earliest hours, babies show the makings of individual personalities. They demonstrate differences in *temperament*, in their innate inclinations to engage in a certain style of behavior (see Chapter 10). Some babies may be inclined toward "approach," others toward "withdrawal" (Thomas & Chess, 1996). Infants characterized by an approach response generally react positively to new situations or stimuli, such as a new food, toy, person, or place. Infants characterized by a withdrawal response typically react negatively to new situations or stimuli, either by crying, fussing, or otherwise indicating their discomfort (Chess & Thomas, 1987). Some babies are considered "easy" in that they do not cry often and are not demanding, whereas others are "difficult" in that they are fussy and demanding.

That such differences are present virtually from birth suggests, at least in part, biological factors. As we saw in Chapter 10, babies who had a fast heart rate in the womb are more likely to become inhibited, fearful children (Kagan, 1994b). Indeed, heart rate differences between inhibited, fearful babies and uninhibited, relaxed babies have been found at 2 weeks of age (Snidman et al., 1995). Further, at 14 and 21 months of age, inhibited babies often have narrow facial structures, whereas uninhibited babies often have broader faces. These differences may reflect the fact that facial growth at these ages can be affected by high amounts of cortisol (Kagan, 1994a). Babies who had greater EEG activation in the right frontal lobe at 9 months of age tend to be inhibited at 14 months (Calkins et al., 1996); this is interesting because greater EEG activation over the right frontal lobe in adults has been identified with a relatively depressed mood (see Chapter 9). The importance of biological variables in temperament is also evident in the fact that 24-month-old identical twins have more similar temperaments than do fraternal twins (DiLalla et al., 1994). Indeed, this study of twins showed that the tendency to be inhibited has a high heritability (that is, the variability in this tendency among people is largely accounted for by genetic differences).

For temperament, like other characteristics, the story of development over the life span reveals themes of both stability and change. As you saw in Chapter 10, not all inhibited infants became shy children and adults. In fact, only children who are extremely inhibited or uninhibited are likely to stay that way; the majority of children, who fall in the middle ranges, can change dramatically (Kerr et al., 1994; Robinson et al., 1992; see also Kagan et al., 1998; Schwartz et al., 1996). Nevertheless, for those infants who exhibit marked inhibited or uninhibited behavior, these early temperaments are likely to be enduring core characteristics of later personality.

Some of the stability of temperament may arise not from inherited predispositions, but from early nurturing experiences. Probably the most compelling evidence of this comes from research with nonhuman animals. Meaney and his colleagues (Anisman et al., 1998; Liu et al., 1997; Meaney et al., 1991; Zaharia et al., 1996) have shown that simply handling rat pups during the first 10 days after birth has enormous effects on the way the animals later respond to stressful events. As adults, these animals don't become as nervous as other rats when put in a large open field (as reflected by fewer feces, less "freezing" responses, and more exploration), and have lower cortisol responses (and thus are less vulnerable to the negative effects of prolonged exposure to cortisol, as discussed in Chapter 6). They are also less prone to learned helplessness (discussed in Chapter 9; Costela et al., 1995). The effects of handling occur naturally when the mother rat licks her pups and engages in nursing with an arched back (so the pups are directly under her); offspring of mothers that behaved this way later had lower amounts of the type of RNA that produces cortisol (Liu et al., 1997). We have good reason to believe that similar effects extend to humans: Touching infants not only can enhance growth and development, but also can reduce the right frontal lobe EEG activation that is associated with depression (even in 1-month-old infants!) and can boost immune function (Field, 1998; Field et al., 1986; Jones et al., 1998).

LOOKING AT LEVELS

Social Support for Premature Infants

Social support has been shown to help combat the effects of stress on a mother's developing fetus. Social support can also help babies who are born prematurely. These infants used to be kept in incubators and were rarely touched. However, work by Field and her colleagues (1986) changed that; she found that 15-minute sessions of touching (moving the babies' limbs, stroking their bodies), three times a day, made a difference in their development: A group of "touched" premature infants grew 50% faster, developed more quickly behaviorally, were more alert and active, and were discharged from the hospital sooner than those premature infants who were not touched three times a day. And the "touched" babies were still doing better months after release from the hospital.

Touching is clearly a social interaction, and the extent to which it occurs depends partly on beliefs: When nurses and caregivers felt that touching premature infants was unwarranted, they didn't do so—and now that they know its benefits, touching is routine. The reason these beliefs changed is that this social act affected the brains of the developing infants, triggering the release of hormones and probably enhancing neural growth (see Chapter 2). And of course, by becoming more alert, the babies interacted more actively with the caregivers, which in turn resulted in additional stimulation from them. This happy feedback cycle is a good illustration of how events at the different levels interact.

CONSOLIDATE!

► *1. How does development progress in the womb?* The genes and environment interact even in the womb. Your mother's and father's genes recombined when their gametes (eggs and sperm) were formed, leading you to have a unique combination of alleles. Development unfolds in an orderly progression through a series of stages, or trimesters, as the zygote becomes first an embryo, then a fetus. The developing fetus is active and becomes increasingly coordinated over time. Moreover, the fetus is capable of some forms of learning and can detect human speech, preferring the mother's voice. These maturational processes can be disrupted by teratogens or enhanced by certain environmental events, such as those that reduce the level of stress experienced by the mother.

► *2. What are the capabilities of newborns?* Newborns have a good sense of smell and can learn that different stimuli tend to occur together. They are equipped with a host of inborn reflexes, such as sucking and the Moro reflex. These reflexes often disappear as the child grows and develops. However, in some infants aspects of temperament that are present at birth may persist for many years.

INFANCY AND CHILDHOOD: TAKING OFF

Spielberg has repeatedly noted that his ability to make movies that appeal to children and to "the child inside adults" stems from the fact that he's never grown up himself. But although he may retain many childlike characteristics, the filmmaker has indeed matured. That is, his motor, perceptual, cognitive, and even social abilities have long outstripped those of even a preadolescent child. In this section we will see how this development occurs.

> ► 1. How does the ability to control the body develop with age?
>
> ► 2. What perceptual and cognitive abilities emerge during the course of development?
>
> ► 3. How do social and emotional development occur?

Physical and Motor Development: Getting Control

If we continued to grow throughout childhood at the same rate as during infancy, we would all be giants. A newborn can look forward to being 50% longer on his or her first birthday and 75% longer on his or her second. But growth does not continue at this rate; rather, it usually occurs in a series of small spurts. Similarly, control over various parts of the body does not occur simultaneously and smoothly, but in phases. Good motor control (that is, control of the muscles) is a necessary first step for normal interaction with the world.

Developmental psychologists have spent many years studying the precise ways in which babies' movements change as they grow. Two of the early pioneers, Arnold Gesell (Gesell & Thompson, 1938) and Myrtle McGraw (1943), described a series of milestones that all babies, from all races and cultures, pass in an orderly progression. In general, control progresses from the head down the trunk to the arms, and finally to the legs; at the same time, control extends out from the center of the body to the periphery (hands, fingers, toes). By the age of 2, the child has good control over all the limbs.

The early theorists believed that the consistent and universal order of motor development implied that it was entirely maturational. However, later studies of motor control showed that this view cannot be correct. Consider that if a baby is held so that its feet are on a treadmill, he or she will make stepping movements very much like those involved in true walking (Thelen & Ulrich, 1991). This behavior was found well after the infants no longer had the stepping reflex, but before they could walk. The brain was directing the legs and feet in response to environmental cues, and without those cues it performed very differently. Clearly, motor control involves a number of factors: specifying the goal of a movement correctly in the current situation (which requires a tight link with perception); coordinating the muscles given the current goal and starting position (depending on its position at the start of a movement, a limb will be moved by different muscles); making good use of natural spring-like properties of muscles; and both taking advantage of and compensating for gravity (Turvey, 1990). Thus, developing motor control involves more than maturation; it also involves learning about the body and the world (Thelen, 1995). Some of us do this better than others; Steven Spielberg, for example, was notoriously clumsy and uncoordinated throughout his childhood.

Perceptual and Cognitive Development: Extended Horizons

A parent probably would not tell as elaborate a story to a 3-year-old as to a 10-year-old. The reason is obvious: The younger child not only has a shorter attention span and understands fewer concepts about objects and events, but also can grasp only concepts of simple relations (such as that one object can physically cause another to move). Where do these concepts come from? In part from perception, the organization and identification of information received through our senses; in part from cognition, our mental processes; and in part from our social environment.

PERCEPTUAL DEVELOPMENT: OPENING WINDOWS ON THE WORLD. Along with the rest of the body, the sensory organs develop with age. Visual acuity, for example, increases in part because of developments in the eye, particularly in the lens and the retina (Banks & Bennett, 1988).

You obviously can't ask them, so how might you determine what babies are capable of seeing? Psychologists working in this area have developed a number of clever

Babies are placed on the sheet of glass over a floor that appears to be directly under the glass. A short distance ahead, the floor drops down (although the glass remains level). If the baby can perceive depth, he or she will be reluctant to crawl on the glass that is over the "deep end." This is the famous "visual cliff" invented by Gibson and Walk (1960).

techniques. For example, to determine depth perception, infants are placed on a level sheet of glass that at first lies directly on the floor, but then extends over a part of the floor that has been stepped down. In this *visual cliff* experiment, researchers have found that even 6-month-old infants don't want to crawl over the "deep end"—even when coaxed by their mothers—thus demonstrating that they can perceive depth before they can talk (Gibson & Walk, 1960).

But the visual cliff task is of no use with babies who are not yet able to crawl, so it is possible that even younger babies can see depth. How can we tell? Other techniques for examining infants' visual

FIGURE 11.2
The Habituation Technique

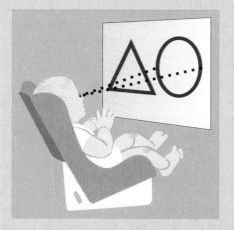

In the habituation task, the baby is first shown one stimulus and allowed to look at it until he or she is bored with it (has habituated to it).

After habituation, the baby is shown the original stimulus along with another stimulus. The baby prefers to look at something new. This technique can be used to determine what shape differences babies see and whether they see depth or other physical properties.

perception measure the amount of time they look at stimuli. For example, the *habituation technique* (also sometimes called the *looking time technique*), illustrated in Figure 11.2, is based on the fact that animals *habituate* to a stimulus: if a baby looks at a particular shape long enough, he or she will no longer find it interesting—and thus will prefer to look at something new. This technique can be used to discover what babies can see, hear, or feel as "different." If you simply added a copy of the habituated stimulus, it would be no more interesting than the original. The infant has to perceive it as different to find it interesting. By varying how two stimuli differ (in shape, distance, color, pattern of movement, and so on), and seeing in what circumstances babies will prefer a new stimulus after habituating to a previous one, it is possible to discover what differences they can detect. Habituation techniques have shown that babies can detect depth between 2 and 3 months of age.

Newborns aren't very attentive companions; they don't even look at your face when you talk. This state of affairs soon changes as visual perception develops during infancy and early childhood. At first, infants notice only isolated portions of objects, but within 2 or 3 months, they can perceive overall shapes (Spelke et al., 1993). As they get older, they become increasingly adept at making finer differentiations in what they see (Gibson, 1969), partly because of developments in the lens and retina of the eye (Banks & Bennett, 1988). This ability allows them to distinguish among increasingly similar objects (such as distinguishing among different toys, a prerequisite to having a single favorite toy). As they grow older, babies need less stimulus information to recognize patterns. It is tempting to speculate that their enjoyment of playing "peek-a-boo" may reflect this developing ability, in which they can use top-down processing (see Chapter 3), using their knowledge about objects to infer a whole from a part.

When you look at a picture, you immediately see not the two-dimensional form but the object or scene it depicts; if this were not true, movies would have none of their power. Steven Spielberg is counting on the fact that you will relate emotionally to his images on film in the same way you would relate to the events and characters if you met them in reality. Nonetheless, you are in no doubt that you are seeing a picture, not the thing itself. Apparently, however, 9-month-old infants aren't quite sure about which properties of objects are captured by pictures. DeLoache and her colleagues (1998) showed infants high-quality color photographs and observed the babies' reactions. The babies reached for and touched the pictures as if they were seeing the actual objects, and sometimes actually tried to pick them off the page! It wasn't as if the babies thought that the pictures *were* objects; they weren't surprised or upset when they couldn't pluck them off the page. Rather, they apparently *did not know* what pictures were and so were exploring their properties in the way that seemed most sensible. But 10 months later, at 19 months of age, the babies pointed toward the objects in the pictures and no longer tried to manipulate them. Babies apparently have to learn what pictures are, and this learning takes time. This learning transcends culture: Babies from the Ivory Coast of Africa and babies from the United States acted the same way in this experimental situation.

Compared with visual perception, auditory perception appears to be more fully developed at an earlier age. Even 6-month-old infants seem to hear well enough to detect different musical intervals. Schellenberg and Trehub (1996) showed that when infants hear pairs of tones, one after the other, they notice a change (as is evidenced by their turning their heads toward the appropriate audio speaker) from the first to the second only when the second is different according to a simple frequency ratio, such as a perfect fifth. In another study, researchers played to 4-month-old infants consonant or dissonant versions of two sequences of tones. When the sequence was consonant, the infants looked longer at the speakers than when it was dissonant. Not only did they look away when the stimulus was dissonant, but they were more physically active. The authors suggest that infants are innately tuned to find consonance more pleasing than dissonance (Zentner & Kagan, 1998). Apparently, to appreciate dissonant music, you must learn to overcome preferences that may be innate.

Perceptual development continues beyond the first year of life. When, for instance, toddlers (2- and 3-year-olds) are shown an array of objects and asked whether it includes a specific object, they look haphazardly from place to place (Vurpillot, 1968). But 6- to 9-year-olds will search the array systematically, left to right, then top to bottom, as if they were reading a page. In general, by about age 11, children have perceptual abilities that are similar to (although often slower than) those of adults (Lobaugh et al., 1998; Piaget, 1969; Semenov et al., 2000), but some aspects of perceptual processing (used in organizing complex patterns) probably continue to develop until late adolescence (Sireteanu, 2000).

Piaget was an extraordinarily sensitive observer of children's behavior.

STAGES OF COGNITIVE DEVELOPMENT: PIAGET'S THEORY.

The great Swiss psychologist Jean Piaget (1896–1980) developed a far-reaching and comprehensive theory of cognitive development. Interest in Piaget's theory helped generate other lines of research that have focused on how changes in information processing, the maturation of the brain, and the social environment contribute to cognitive development.

Early in his career, Piaget worked in Paris with Alfred Binet's collaborator, Theodore Simon, helping to standardize Binet's newly developed intelligence tests for children (see Chapter 8). Piaget was curious about the types of reasoning mistakes children were likely to make. This new interest connected with his long-term interests in biology and the nature of the mind, and led him to a general investigation of the reasoning processes of children at various ages. Piaget believed that babies begin with very simple, innate **schemas,** mental structures that organize perceptual input and connect it to the appropriate responses. For the youngest infant, such schemas trigger grasping and sucking at the nipple when the infant is hungry and in the presence of a bottle or breast. According to Piaget, the process

Schema: A mental structure that organizes perceptual input and connects it with the appropriate responses.

Assimilation: In Piaget's theory, the process that allows use of existing schemas to take in new sets of stimuli and respond accordingly.

Accommodation: In Piaget's theory, the process that results in schemas' changing as necessary to cope with a broader range of situations.

Object permanence: The understanding that objects (including people) continue to exist even when they cannot be immediately perceived.

of **assimilation** allows the infant to use existing schemas to take in new stimuli and respond accordingly. For example, the schema for sucking a breast can also be used for sucking a bottle or thumb. In contrast, the process of **accommodation** results in schemas changing as necessary to cope with a broader range of situations. As the child develops, the schemas develop in two ways. First, they become more fully *articulated*; for example, more precise motions are used to locate the nipple and suck. Second, they become *differentiated*; an original schema may give rise to two separate schemas, one for bottles and one for thumbs, which in turn may give rise to schemas for drinking with a straw, drinking from a cup, and eating solid food.

TABLE 11.2

Piaget's Periods of Cognitive Development

PERIOD	AGE	ESSENTIAL CHARACTERISTICS
Sensorimotor	0–2 years	The child acts on the world as perceived and is not capable of thinking about objects in their absence.
Preoperational	2–7 years	Words, images, and actions are used to represent information mentally. Language and symbolic play develop, but thought is still tied to perceived events.
Concrete Operations	7–11 years	Reasoning is based on a logic that is tied to what can be perceived. The child is capable of organizing information systematically into categories, and can reverse mental manipulations.
Formal Operations	11 years (at the earliest)	Reasoning is based on a logic that includes abstractions, which leads to systematic thinking about hypothetical events.

Only after a baby has object permanence does he or she understand that objects continue to exist even after they are no longer being perceived.

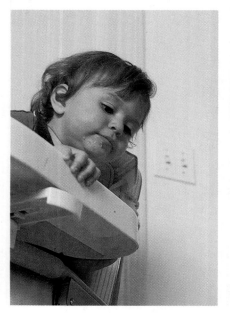

These two processes—assimilation and accommodation—are the engine that powers cognitive development. Piaget's theory of development hinges on the results of assimilation and accommodation working in tandem, which he claimed produce a system of rules—in Piaget's terms, a "logic"—that guides the child's thought. Depending on the available schemas, different kinds of logical operations are possible. Thus, according to Piaget, the child's thinking changes systematically over time as new schemas develop.

Piaget described four major stages, or *periods*, of cognitive development, as shown in Table 11.2; each period is governed by a different type of logic and includes many substages, with key characteristics. The periods overlap slightly, and they may occur at different ages for different children; thus, the ages given in the table are only approximate.

The infant's experience begins in the *sensorimotor period,* which extends from approximately birth to 2 years of age. According to Piaget's theory, infants initially conceive of the world solely in terms of their perceptions and actions. In this period infants lack the ability to form mental representations that can be used to think about an object in its absence (see Chapter 7). In the early stages of the sensorimotor period, the infant does not yet have the concept of **object permanence,** the understanding that objects (including people) continue to exist even when they cannot be immediately perceived. For example, a rattle dropped by an infant over the side of the high chair is quickly forgotten—and more than forgotten: Out of sight means not just out of mind but out of existence! Piaget claimed that by the end of the sensorimotor period, by about age 2, the toddler understands that objects exist even when they are no longer perceived.

Imitation is a second key achievement of the sensorimotor period. Piaget observed that before about 4 months, infants imitate someone only if that person performs an action that the baby has just performed; this act is called **pseudoimitation.** For example, if the mother repeats a babbling noise the baby has made, the baby may make the sound again. In contrast, genuine **imitation** consists of mimicking another person's actions purely from having seen or heard them. Piaget's observations led him to conclude that the infant cannot imitate well until about 9 months of age.

Once out of the sensorimotor period, the toddler enters the *preoperational period*, from roughly age 2 until age 7. Armed with the ability to form mental representations, children in the preoperational period are able to think about objects and events that are not immediately present. As a result, they can imitate actions that occurred in the past. This newfound capacity for mental representation allows the child to engage in fantasy play. Whereas the infant might play with a bar of soap in the bath by squeezing it and watching it pop out, the preoperational child, performing the same actions, might think of the soap as a submerged submarine that is breaking the surface.

FIGURE 11.3
Conservation of Liquids

In the classic conservation of liquids test, the child is first shown two identical glasses with water at the same level.

The water is poured from one of the short, wide glasses into the tall, thin one.

When asked whether the two glasses have the same amount, or if one has more, the preoperational child replies that the tall, thin glass has more. This is a failure to conserve liquids.

A cook asks two boys who have just ordered a large pizza, "How many slices do you want me to cut your pizza into, 8 or 12?" One boy immediately answers, "Please cut it into 12 pieces, because I'm very hungry!" This is a joke for older children and grown-ups, but not for preoperational children, whose thoughts are limited in part because they do not yet have a "logic" for manipulating, or *operating* on, mental representations. Therefore, they often reason on the basis of appearances. One important result is that they do not understand **conservation,** the principle that properties of an object, such as its amount or mass, remain the same even when the appearance changes, provided that nothing is added or removed. Many studies have documented that preoperational children do not conserve, and so they would not realize that cutting a pizza into 12 pieces instead of 8 does not increase the total amount of pizza. A classic example, illustrated in Figure 11.3, is that preoperational children do not understand that pouring liquid from a short wide glass into a tall thin glass does not alter the amount of liquid. Similarly, they typically think that flattening a ball of clay decreases

Pseudoimitation: Mimicking another person's actions only when those actions are ones the mimicker (baby) has just performed.

Imitation: Mimicking another person's actions based purely on observing them.

Conservation: The principle that certain properties of objects remain the same even when their appearance changes, provided that nothing is added or removed.

the amount of clay and that spreading the objects in a row farther apart changes the number of objects in the row.

Both sensorimotor and preoperational children show **egocentrism,** which does not mean "selfishness" in the ordinary sense of the word, but instead the inability to take another's point of view. For example, children in this period will hold a picture they've drawn up to the telephone, to "show" it to Grandma. They mistakenly assume that others see the same things they do.

By the end of the preoperational period, about age 7, children develop the ability to take another person's perspective. This ability is linked to the fact that they can now perform **concrete operations,** manipulating mental representations in much the same way they could manipulate the corresponding objects. So the child is now able to begin to classify objects and their properties, to grasp concepts such as length, width, volume, and time, and to understand various mental operations such as those involved in simple arithmetic. This *period of concrete operations* is Piaget's third period of cognitive development, which takes place roughly between the ages of 7 and 11. Concrete operations allow the child to reason logically, partly because this mode of conceptualizing is *reversible*; that is, it can be used to make or undo a transformation. For example, having seen the liquid being poured into a tall thin glass, the child can mentally reverse the process and imagine the liquid being poured back into the original container. Seeing that no liquid has been added or subtracted in the process, the child realizes that the amount in both glasses must be the same. The cognitive advances of the child who has entered the period of concrete operations are so striking that many researchers refer to the transition from the preoperational to the concrete operational period as the *5–7 shift* (Sameroff & Haith, 1996; White, 1965).

By definition, concrete operations cannot be used for reasoning about abstract concepts; children in the period of concrete operations cannot figure out, for example, that whenever 1 is added to an even number, the result will always be an odd number. To be able to reason abstractly, Piaget said, requires that the child be capable of **formal operations,** reversible mental acts that can be performed even with abstract concepts. This ability emerges roughly during the ages of 11 or 12, at the onset of what Piaget termed the *period of formal operations.* Rather than simply understanding the logic of "what is," as occurs with concrete operations, the emerging adolescent is now able to imagine the possibilities of "what could be." Formal operations allow children to engage in abstract thinking, to think about "what-would-happen-if" situations, and to think systematically about the possible outcomes of an act by being able to list alternatives in advance and consider each in turn. For example, formal operations would permit a child to think about how best to spend his or her money and to weigh the benefits and drawbacks of each possible budget decision.

THE CHILD'S CONCEPTS: BEYOND PIAGET. Do children follow the stages Piaget described? When researchers use techniques different from Piaget's in order to see what children do or do not understand, they often come up with results that differ from his. Although Piaget conducted very clever tasks (such as those used to assess conservation), they typically assessed only easily observable aspects of behavior. When more subtle measurements are taken, evidence sometimes emerges that children can show competence well before they have reached the appropriate Piagetian stage.

Very young infants can imitate some facial expressions, as shown in these photos from Meltzoff and Moore's study.

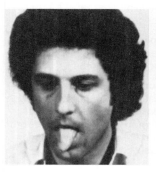

Andrew Meltzoff and his colleagues (notably, Meltzoff & Moore, 1977) have found that 2- to 3-week-old infants can show true imitation, and others have found that even 2-day-old infants can imitate happy and sad facial expressions (Field et al., 1982). Other researchers have shown that babies as young as 3 months old know that previously seen objects continue to exist after they are removed from sight, thus refuting the idea that object permanence does not establish itself until the child is a toddler (Baillargeon, 1993; Spelke et al., 1992). Indeed, even 3-month-old infants can remember faces after a 24-hour interval (Pascalis et al.,

1998). Moreover, when appropriately tested, children as young as 3 years show that they understand the conservation of amount or mass (Gelman, 1972).

Piaget's theory seems to underestimate the sophistication of young children's conceptions of the world. Infants demonstrate an understanding of some physical laws even before they have developed the kinds of perceptual–motor schemas that Piaget claimed are the foundations of such knowledge. By applying looking time techniques, which take advantage of infants' preference for novel stimuli (see Figure 11.2), researchers have concluded that even young infants realize that objects need to be physically supported to remain stable (Figure 11.4), that objects can't move *through* other objects, and that objects don't flit from place to place but shift along connected paths (Spelke, 1991; Spelke et al., 1992).

In contrast to Piaget's idea that formal operations are necessary to formulate and test theories, recent research suggests that in many ways the young child relates to the world as a young scientist. Faced with a bewildering set of phenomena, children try, as scientists do, to organize stimuli and events into categories and develop theories of how those categories interact (Carey, 1985, 1988, 1995b; Keil & Silberstein, 1996; Spelke et al., 1992; Wellman, 1990). Even 1-year-old babies begin to organize categories (Waxman, 1992), and preschoolers develop sophisticated ways to determine whether an object belongs in a particular category. For example, they begin to understand that animals beget animals of the same type and that the internal biology—not the external appearance—defines the type (Keil, 1989a, 1989b).

Current thinking suggests that children develop a **theory of mind,** a theory of other people's mental states—their beliefs, desires, and feelings. This theory allows them to predict what other people can understand and how they will react in a given situation (Flavell, 1999; Frye et al., 1998; Johnson, S., 2000; Lillard, 1999; Wellman, 1990). One way to assess children's theory of mind is to tell a story and see whether the children draw the proper inferences about the protagonist's mental state. In one story used for this purpose, a boy hides his candy in a drawer, but after he leaves the room, his mother moves the candy to a cupboard. Children are then told that the boy returns and is asked where he thinks his candy is hidden. By age 4, children believe that the boy thinks the candy is still where he put it originally, but children under 4 do not—they often think that the boy believes the candy is in the cupboard. In order to get this right, the child must understand that belief does not necessarily reflect reality.

How does a theory of mind develop? It is possible that children learn to "put themselves in another person's place," seeing things through another's eyes (Harris, J. R., 1995). It is also possible that children build a theory of the situations that give rise to other people's feelings (for example, seeing a child scream after being stung by a bee leads to the theory that bee stings hurt; Wellman, 1990); this approach has been called the *theory theory* (see Gopnik, 1996).

The particular theory of mind a child develops depends in part on the surrounding culture. Among many African tribes, calamities such as AIDS or fires are believed to have supernatural causes (Lillard, 1999). Even within a culture, different subgroups can develop different types of theories. Lillard and colleagues (1998, as cited in Lillard, 1999) asked children to explain the behavior of a character in a story and found that children growing up in cities tended to use psychological explanations—for example, referring to the character's likes and dislikes—even at 7 years of age. In contrast, children growing up in the country rarely used such explanations (20% of the time, compared with 60% for children growing up in the city). Instead, rural children usually relied on aspects of the situation to explain behavior. It is not clear why this difference exists.

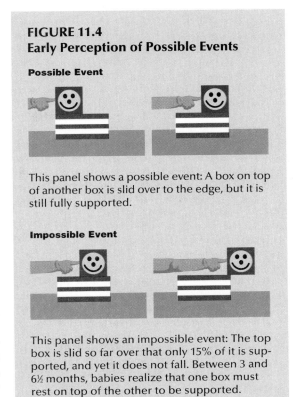

FIGURE 11.4
Early Perception of Possible Events

Possible Event

This panel shows a possible event: A box on top of another box is slid over to the edge, but it is still fully supported.

Impossible Event

This panel shows an impossible event: The top box is slid so far over that only 15% of it is supported, and yet it does not fall. Between 3 and 6½ months, babies realize that one box must rest on top of the other to be supported.

Theory of mind: A theory of other people's mental states (their beliefs, desires, and feelings) that allows prediction of what other people can understand and how they will react in a given situation.

Although researchers agree that culture plays a role in the development of a theory of mind, how do we explain the evidence that children as young as 6 months begin to develop a theory of mind? For example, after being habituated by watching someone reach for the same toy repeatedly, these infants looked longer when a person reached for a new toy than when the person used a new movement to reach for a familiar toy (Woodward, 1998). Apparently the infant inferred that the person had the goal of reaching for the first toy and was surprised when the goal changed—but not when the motion changed. Such effects were not found when inanimate objects were used to do the reaching (see also Baldwin, 2000; Johnson, S., 2000).

In short, the finding that many abilities are evident much earlier than Piaget expected challenges his idea that all of a given child's thought reflects a single underlying logic, a logic that changes with increasing age and development. Moreover, later research showed that many children do not enter the period of formal operations until high school, and some never enter it at all (Hooper et al., 1984; Lunzer, 1978). Nevertheless, Piaget has been proven correct in his seminal observation that there are qualitative shifts in children's performance as they age. He must also be credited with discovering many counterintuitive phenomena, such as a failure to conserve and egocentrism, that all theories of cognitive development must now be able to explain.

INFORMATION PROCESSING AND NEURAL DEVELOPMENT. Efforts to explain the findings sparked by Piaget's theory have looked at specific changes in the way children process information and how their brains mature. The *information processing approach* is based on the idea that perception and cognition rely on a host of distinct processes, and not all necessarily develop at the same rate. Researchers have thus studied very specific aspects of development and have found that some mental processes do indeed develop more quickly than others. For example, even very young children are adept at using *sensory memory* (the very brief memory of perceptual stimulation) and at accessing *long-term memory* (the relatively permanent store of information). However, anyone who has spent time with children knows that young children often perform more poorly than older children in many tasks. There are many reasons for this: Young children are not able to focus attention effectively; they are not able to formulate and follow plans effectively (Scholnick, 1995); they have fewer strategies to select from (Lautrey & Caroff, 1996; Siegler, 1989); and they do not have stored information that can be used in organizing and remembering input (Chi, 1978). Moreover, young children are simply slower than older children and adults (Kail, 1988, 1991).

One common reason young children may perform more poorly than older children is that their *working memory*—their ability to use information held in an active state—does not stack up well against that of older children or adults. Working memory involves different types of short-term memory and a central executive that operates on information in those short-term memories (see Chapter 6). Thus, working memory deficits can arise either because of problems in effectively using the central executive or in holding information in short-term memory (Brown & Campione, 1972). Such deficits are important because a certain amount of information must be held in working memory to carry out many tasks—especially novel tasks that require reasoning through a step-by-step process. And, many tasks are "novel" for the young child, who is relatively new to the world. Thus, children will be able to perform such tasks only when they have the necessary working memory capacity (Case, 1985, 1992a). It has been shown that measures of working memory capacity increase with age throughout childhood (Case, 1977, 1978). When the child has enough working memory capacity, he or she can perform tasks that were previously beyond reach.

The finding that working memory increases with age allows us to explain many of the phenomena documented by Piaget. In this case, a *quantitative* change (simple increase in size) in capacity can lead to *qualitative* changes in performance (the transition to new stages; see Case, 1992b; Pascual-Leone, 1970). By analogy, if you have a relatively small amount of RAM memory in your computer, then only relatively simple programs will run (such as basic word processing or e-mail), but not more complicated ones (such as a spreadsheet). If you increase the amount of memory, you not only can run more complex programs, but also multiple programs at the same time. A quantitative change in the amount of memory underlies a qualitative change in performance.

What accounts for the child's improvements in working memory with age? The initial immaturity of the brain may be key. The brain undergoes rapid growth spurts (Epstein, 1980) around the times of transitions to new periods in Piaget's scheme. Some of the increase in brain weight with age may be due to myelinization (the laying down of myelin, a fatty substance that serves as an insulator, on the axons), which increases the speed and efficiency of neural transmission, and some to larger numbers of synapses and long-distance connections (Case, 1992c; Thatcher, 1994; Thompson et al., 2000). These changes might allow more information to be activated at the same time, which in turn would increase working memory capacity.

VYGOTSKY'S SOCIOCULTURAL THEORY: OUTSIDE/INSIDE. Appreciating the importance of events at different levels of analysis leads us to look beyond any single source to explain psychological events. Thus, it isn't surprising that at least some aspects of cognitive development reflect not brain events, but social interactions. Russian psychologist Lev S. Vygotsky (1896–1934) emphasized the role of social interaction during development (Vygotsky, 1978, 1934/1986). Whereas Piaget believed that the child constructs representations of the world in the course of experiencing it firsthand, Vygotsky believed that the child constructs representations of the world by absorbing his or her culture, and the culture, as represented in the child's mind, then serves to guide behavior (Beilin, 1996; Kitchener, 1996). According to Vygotsky, adults promote cognitive development by guiding and explicitly instructing the child, and cultural creations, particularly language, play a crucial role in development (Cole & Wertsch, 1996; Karpov & Haywood, 1998).

One of Vygotsky's key ideas is that once children learn language, they begin to use "private speech" to direct themselves (Berk, 1994a; Smolucha, 1992; Vygotsky, 1962, 1988). **Private speech** (also sometimes called *inner speech*) is language used by the child in planning or prompting him- or herself to behave in specific ways. Children initially begin to use language in this way by actually speaking aloud to themselves, but then language becomes internalized and silent. As Vygotsky predicted, researchers have found that young children use private speech more when trying to solve a difficult task (such as folding paper in a particular way or arranging events into a story; Duncan & Pratt, 1997; see also Berk, 1992a, 1994b) than when working on an easy task. They also use private speech more after they have made an error (Berk, 1992a, 1994b). Preschoolers (ages 3 to 5) also use private speech more frequently when they have to decide what to do in a free play situation than when they are put in a highly structured play situation (Krafft & Berk, 1998).

Vygotsky theorized that, rather than proceeding through a series of lockstep Piagetian stages, once they have acquired language, children develop in a variety of different ways, depending on the particular instruction they receive and the social environment in which they live (for comparisons of the theories of Piaget and Vygotsky, see Beilin, 1996; Kitchener, 1996; Tomasello, 1996; Tryphon & Vonèche, 1996; van der Veer, 1996). Thus, children in different cultures become adept at different kinds of activities.

It is clear that children in different cultures master different skills; for example, middle-class North Americans often master the visual–motor skills needed to play computer games, whereas street children in Brazil may master the kinds of arithmetic needed to bargain over the prices of goods with tourists (Saxe, 1988). However, it is not clear that private speech plays a major role in the processes whereby culture imbues children with different skills. Nor is it clear that the ability to engage in complex thinking can emerge only via the effects of culture (Geary, 1996b). Nevertheless, Vygotsky's theory has proved invaluable by alerting psychologists to possible roles of culture in shaping the child's mental processes.

Private speech: The use of language in planning or in prompting oneself to behave in specific ways.

Social and Emotional Development: The Child in the World

The psychological development of a child includes more than improvements in mental processing and the acquisition of knowledge and beliefs. Equally impressive development occurs in the child's social interactions, such as the ability to form relationships.

ATTACHMENT: MORE THAN DEPENDENCY. In our closest relationships we develop deep attachments to other people. **Attachment** is an emotional bond that leads us to want to be with someone and to miss him or her when we are separated. The tendency to form such an emotional bond begins during infancy, when normal infants become attached to their primary caregivers.

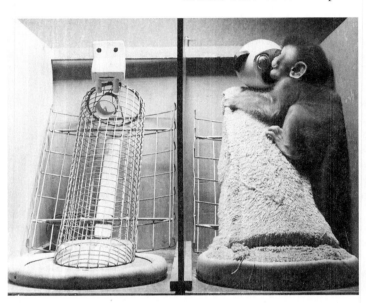

Baby monkeys were separated from their mothers shortly after birth and were raised with two substitute "moms." One was wire and held the baby bottle, and each young monkey needed to climb on this one to be fed. The other was covered with terry cloth and did not provide food. Baby monkeys preferred to cling to the warm and fuzzy models, even though those models never provided food.

What is the origin of the infant's attachment? Decades ago, a prominent theory—sometimes called the "cupboard theory" because it centered on food—held that infants become attached because their caregivers feed them and thus become associated with positive feelings (Sears et al., 1957). However, classic experiments by Harry Harlow and his collaborators disproved this and similar theories. These researchers found that baby monkeys became much more attached to a model "mother" that had a pleasing, warm texture than to one without these characteristics, even though it fed them. The impulse to seek comfort from something warm and soft is an innate rather than a learned characteristic of mammals.

British psychoanalyst John Bowlby (1969) developed a theory of attachment that has become widely accepted among developmental psychologists. According to Bowlby, children go through phases during the development of attachment. Just as in Piaget's stages, the order of the phases is thought to be determined biologically, but the precise ages depend on experience. A major shift, usually occurring between 6 months and 2 years, is characterized by **separation anxiety,** which is fear of being away from the primary caregiver. This shift may arise on the heels of cognitive development, specifically because infants can now think about and remember objects (including the primary caregiver) when they are no longer present.

Not all babies become attached to their caregivers in the same way. Ainsworth and her colleagues (1978) developed a way to assess attachment using a scenario they called the *Strange Situation.* The setup involves a staged sequence of events designed to discover how a child reacts when left with a stranger or alone in an unfamiliar situation. If the child has developed strong attachment, he or she should show separation anxiety, becoming upset when the mother leaves, and should not be soothed equally well by a stranger or by the mother. Studies using the Strange Situation revealed four types of attachment:

Secure attachment (about 60–70% of American babies) is evident if babies venture away from the mother, are upset when she leaves and not well comforted by a stranger, but calm down quickly when the mother returns.

Avoidant attachment (about 15–20% of American babies) is evident if babies don't seem to care very much whether the mother is present or absent, and are equally comfortable with her and a stranger; when she returns, they do not immediately gravitate to her.

Resistant attachment (about 10–15% of American babies) is evident if babies do not use the mother as a base of operations but rather stay close to her and become

Attachment: An emotional bond that leads us to want to be with someone and to miss him or her when we are separated.

Separation anxiety: Fear of being away from the primary caregiver.

angry when she leaves; some of these babies may go so far as to hit the mother when she returns and do not calm down easily thereafter.

Disorganized/disoriented attachment (5–10% of American babies) is evident if the babies become depressed and have periods of unresponsiveness along with spurts of sudden emotion at the end of the procedure.

The type of early attachment can have long-lasting effects. Infants with secure attachment who were later studied at age 11 were found to have closer friendships and better social skills than children who had not been securely attached as infants (Shulman et al., 1994). Moreover, secure attachment can lead the child to be more comfortable exploring, which leads to better learning and can lead to more intimate love relationships later in life (Sroufe & Fleeson, 1986; Weiss, 1986).

IS DAYCARE BAD FOR CHILDREN?

Obviously, a child will not have an opportunity to become attached to a parent who is never around. This was a major concern of Steven Spielberg's, whose own father was often absent. However, according to Scarr (1998), "Exclusive maternal care of infants and young children is a cultural myth of an idealized 1950's, not a reality anywhere in the world, either now or in earlier times" (p. 95). Since 1940 less than half of all persons in the United States have lived in a "traditional" family with a full-time working father and a mother who works only in the home, and the percentage has been declining since 1950. In the United States today, over half of the mothers of babies younger than 1 year old work outside the home (Behrman, 1996). Most of these children are in some form of daycare.

Is daycare bad for children? This question has been the subject of a long and sometimes intense debate; parents have felt trapped between guilt about leaving their children and the necessity to support their families. Research examining the strength of attachment of children raised at home versus those raised partly in daycare centers has found that children who entered daycare relatively early in life were as strongly attached to their mothers as those who entered relatively late (Scarr, 1998; see also NICHD Early Child Care Research Network, 1997; Roggman et al., 1994). However, other research has shown that slightly more of the home-raised children are "securely attached" in the Strange Situation (Scarr, 1998, p. 103). Also, the effect of the daycare is overshadowed by the effects of the mother's education and income, with higher levels of both predicting better mother–child interactions (NICHD Early Child Care Research Network, 1999).

Other studies have shown long-term benefits for poor children in the United States who are put in "high-quality" daycare—that is, daycare with supportive and well-trained caregivers. The Centers for Disease Control and Prevention estimate that as many as 300,000 people who are now considered mentally retarded might have avoided this fate if they had had proper early and continuing special education instead of being kept at home (Boyle et al., 1994; Ramey & Ramey, 1998). Careful studies in a number of countries, including Sweden, Holland, Bermuda, and the United States, have come to the same conclusion: Putting children in high-quality daycare does not harm their long-term social or cognitive development.

SELF-CONCEPT AND IDENTITY: THE GROWING SELF.

A critical aspect of social development is the emerging sense of who you are and how you stand relative to other people. Psychologists use the term **self-concept** to refer to the beliefs, desires, values, and attributes that define a person to him- or herself. A key aspect of Steven Spielberg's self-concept as a child was his many fears, both large and small; part of his gift for making movies today is his ability to engage other people in sharing his own fears and fantasies (McBride, 1999).

We know that at least some aspects of attachment are learned because infants in different cultures become attached differently. For example, American infants show less resistant attachment than do Japanese infants. In Japan, many more women are full-time mothers than in the United States, and their children are not used to being left with other adults (Takahashi, 1990).

Self-concept: The beliefs, desires, values, and attributes that define a person to himself or herself.

Knowledge of your appearance is part of your self-concept.

For young children, the self-concept is necessarily grounded in their level of cognitive development. Thus, preschoolers think of themselves in very concrete terms, in terms of behaviors and physical appearance (Keller et al., 1978). At what age do children begin to conceive of themselves as having specific characteristics? To find out, a dab of red paint was placed on babies' noses without their knowledge, and the babies then looked in a mirror. Some babies of about 15 months of age notice the smudge and rub it off. By age 2, virtually all children have this response (Amsterdam, 1972; Lewis & Brooks-Gunn, 1979). However, this test may in fact assess understanding of temporary changes in appearance, not self-concept (Asendorpf et al., 1996). Other researchers have argued that the roots of the self-concept are present much earlier than toddler age. Bahrick and her collaborators (1996) found that even 3-month-olds prefer to look at the face of another child of the same age rather than at their own faces, which suggests that they are already familiar with the appearance of their own face. Even newborns distinguish between touching themselves and being touched by someone else, a distinction that may mark the beginning of a self-concept (Rochat & Hespos, 1997).

By 3 years of age, children begin to appreciate that they have distinct psychological characteristics, such as being happy in certain situations and not in others (Eder, 1989). Children of about 8 to 11 begin to describe themselves in terms of personality traits, perhaps as "energetic" or "musical." The oldest children also describe themselves in terms of social relations (Rosenberg, 1979), such as the relationships they have with their siblings and friends. This ability to self-label depends on reasoning abilities that develop during the period of formal operations.

Culture clearly affects a person's self-concept. In the collectivist cultures of Japan, China, and other Asian countries, children's self-concepts typically revolve around their relations to the group (Markus & Kitayama, 1991). In contrast, in the individualist cultures of most Western countries, children's self-concepts typically revolve around defining themselves as distinct entities that must negotiate with, and navigate through, the group.

GENDER IDENTITY: NOT JUST BEING RAISED WITH PINK OR BLUE.

A crucial aspect of the self-concept is **gender identity,** which is the belief that you are male or female. There is evidence that biological factors strongly predispose us to view ourselves as male or female. Consider the following case history (Colapinto, 2000): At 8 months of age, a boy's penis was accidentally sliced off as a split foreskin was being surgically repaired. The family and surgeons decided that it would be best to raise the boy as a girl, and so his testicles were removed and a vagina was surgically formed. The boy, previously known as "John," was now called "Joan," and her past was never discussed. Joan was treated in every way like a girl, and her friends and classmates had no reason to suspect that she was in any way extraordinary. When Joan was 9 years old, John Money (1975) wrote a famous paper in which he reported that Joan had a female gender identity, in sharp contrast to her identical twin brother, who had a strong male gender identity. This report, and others like it, led researchers to believe that gender identity was essentially neutral at birth and was formed by culture and upbringing.

However, Diamond and Sigmundson (1997) revisited John/Joan some 20 years later and recount a very different story. They found that as a young child she sometimes ripped off her dresses and tried to urinate standing up. At 14, she refused to have any more vaginal surgery or to live as a girl. She was not attracted to boys and

Gender identity: A person's belief that he or she is male or is female.

considered suicide. Even though she had been treated as a girl and even received female hormones that caused breasts to develop, she was deeply unhappy and confused. Her father finally broke down and told her about the accident. Instead of being upset on learning that she had been born a boy, she was greatly relieved. She renounced her female identity, underwent surgery to remove her breasts and reconstruct a penis, and was determined to establish a relationship with a woman. Joan became John once again. He eventually married and adopted his wife's children from a previous marriage.

What was going on here? The crucial event probably was that John's brain had been exposed to high levels of male sex hormones in the womb, which let him "know" that he was male. This gender identity was not something that could be arbitrarily changed simply by treating him as a female. Indeed, certain disorders result in a fetus's being exposed to high levels of male hormones in the womb, even if the fetus is genetically female. Studies of such children have shown that the hormones can affect gender identity. These girls later preferred to play with boys' toys and participate in boys' games (Berenbaum, 1999; Berenbaum & Hines, 1992). Boys can also be affected by the hormonal environment; boys who receive relatively little male sex hormone in the womb engage in less rough-and-tumble play than do boys who are exposed to the usual amount (Hines & Kaufman, 1994).

MORAL DEVELOPMENT: THE RIGHT STUFF. A key aspect of social development is the emergence of more complex ideas of morality, which center on the ability to tell right from wrong. As children grow older, their developing cognitive abilities allow them to draw more subtle inferences. The young child may feel that a girl who knocks over a lamp and breaks it is equally to blame if she smashed it intentionally, bumped it by accident while horsing around, or fell against it accidentally when the dog jumped on her. The older child would make clear distinctions among the three cases, seeing decreasing blame for each in turn. Piaget was a pioneer in the study of moral as well as cognitive development. His studies often involved telling children stories in which he varied the intentions of the characters and the results of their actions, then asking the children to evaluate the characters' morality. Lawrence Kohlberg extended Piaget's approach and developed an influential theory of moral development. He presented boys with **moral dilemmas,** situations in which there are moral pros and cons for each of a set of possible actions. Kohlberg asked participants to decide what the character should do, and why. This is the famous dilemma that confronted Heinz (Puka, 1994):

> In Europe, a woman was near death from a special kind of cancer. There was one drug that the doctors thought might save her. It was a form of radium that a druggist in the same town had recently discovered. The drug was expensive to make, but the druggist was charging 5 times what it cost him to make the drug. He paid $400 for the radium, and charged $2,000 for a small dose of the drug. The sick woman's husband, Heinz, went to everyone he knew to borrow the money, but he could only get together about $1,000, half of what it cost. He told the druggist that his wife was dying, and asked him to sell it cheaper or let him pay later. But the druggist said, "No, I discovered the drug and I'm going to make money from it, so I won't let you have it unless you give me $2,000 now." So Heinz got desperate and broke into the man's store to steal the drug for his wife.
> Should Heinz have done that? Why?

Kohlberg was not so much interested in what the children decided as in the way that they reached their decisions. What kinds of factors did they consider? Which conflicts did they identify (such as the conflict between the value of human life and the value of private property), and how did they try to resolve these conflicts? Kohlberg interviewed boys and men at length, and from their responses he identified three general levels of moral development, each of which has two stages (Kohlberg, 1969; Rest, 1979). The *preconventional level* rests on the idea that good behaviors are rewarded and bad ones are punished. Correct action is what an authority figure says it is. In *Stage 1: Punishment and obedience orientation,* the child tries to avoid

Moral dilemmas: Situations in which there are moral pros and cons for each of a set of possible actions.

punishment and obey authorities to the letter of the law; a Stage 1 response to the Heinz dilemma might be, "If you let your wife die, you will get in trouble" (this and the following examples are adapted from Kohlberg, 1969, and Rest, 1979). In *Stage 2: Instrumental purpose orientation*, the child thinks of what gives someone a personal advantage, what is best for the individual, while trying to avoid punishment ("If Heinz decides to risk jail to save his wife, it's his life he's risking").

The *conventional level* rests on the role of rules that maintain social order and allow people to get along. The focus is no longer simply on the personal consequences of a behavior. In *Stage 3: The good boy–good girl orientation*, the child wants to be viewed as a "good person" by friends and family and tries to follow the Golden Rule ("Do unto others as you would have them do unto you"). Morality is still closely tied to individual relationships ("If he lets his wife die, people would think he was some kind of heartless lizard"). In *Stage 4: Social-order-maintaining orientation*, laws are seen as the glue that allows people to get along, and thus they must be respected by everyone. Morality is no longer tied closely to individual personal relationships ("A man must protect his wife, but would also have to pay the druggist or go to jail because he broke the law").

The *postconventional level* (also called the *principled level*) rests on the development of abstract principles that govern the decision to accept or reject specific rules. In *Stage 5: Social-contract orientation*, laws are seen as intended to allow people to get along, and they must be viewed flexibly and interpreted within the special conditions of each situation. People follow the rules because they are seen to be for the common good, but the rules must be adapted to ensure that they remain so ("People have a natural right to live, which is more important than the right of the druggist to make money. The law needs to take this into account"). Finally, in *Stage 6: Universal-ethical-principle orientation*, principles are adopted that are believed to apply to everyone. The principles are abstract and are held above all specific rules and laws ("Human life is the highest principle, and everything else must be secondary. People have a duty to help one another to live").

Some researchers have questioned the generality of Kohlberg's stages. For example, some have found that the stages don't apply well to people in non-Western cultures. Okonkwo (1997) studied Igbo students in Africa with Kohlberg's methods, and found that in some cases the responses did not fit into any stage. Although the responses clearly relied on moral reasoning, the reasoning sometimes involved factors such as family interdependence and the supreme authority of a divine being. Perhaps the strongest objection to Kohlberg's theory came from Carol Gilligan (1982), who argued that because it was based on studies of boys and men, it applies only to males. She believed that females tend to focus on an *ethic of care*, a concern and responsibility for the well-being of others. In contrast, Kohlberg's higher stages of moral development focus on abstract rights and justice, which Gilligan saw as a male-oriented perspective.

However, later studies have shown that the differences between the moral reasoning of males and females do not reflect fundamental differences in the way their minds work. Although there is evidence that males and females do emphasize different principles in their moral reasoning (Wark & Krebs, 1996), this seems more a reflection of their daily activities (and the assumptions and general orientations that result from such activities) than an enduring gender difference. For example, if people are presented with dilemmas that feature concerns about raising children, men and women reason in the same ways (Clopton & Sorell, 1993). In addition, males and females score comparably on Kohlberg's tests, and both sexes reveal concerns with both caring and justice (Jadack et al., 1995; Walker, 1995).

Finally, moral development is not rapid; in fact, a majority of people move into Stage 4 only at about age 32 (Colby et al., 1983). Very few people move into the postconventional level, and there is little evidence that people actually pass through Stage 5 to attain Stage 6. Moreover, it is not clear that the stages are like traits, which characterize a person in all situations. Rather, people may use different types of moral reasoning, depending on the details of the dilemma (Trevethan & Walker, 1989). Thus, to the extent that we pass through stages, the stages may only define general tendencies to reason in a certain way, which can be affected by the situation.

Gender roles: The culturally determined appropriate behaviors of males versus females.

LOOKING AT LEVELS

Gender Role Development

Gender roles are the culturally determined appropriate behaviors of males versus females. It is one thing to identify yourself as male or female, but something else again to understand what behaviors are appropriate for your gender. Gender roles vary in different cultures, social classes, and time periods; for example, a proper woman in Victorian England (or, perhaps, 19th-century America) would probably be very surprised to learn that a woman can be a senator or the president of a major corporation today. Conceptions about gender roles develop early. President Theodore Roosevelt's wife, Ethel, was particularly good at sports—so good that her son Quentin commented, "I'll bet Mother was a boy when she was little" (Seuling, 1978, p. 49). Even preschool boys apparently believe that if they played with cross-gender toys (say, dishes instead of tools), their fathers would think that was "bad" (Raag & Rackliff, 1998). Indeed, by age 2 children have apparently learned about gender role differences (Caldera & Sciaraffa, 1998; Witt, 1997).

Freud argued that children identify with the same-sex parent, and that this is the main way in which gender roles develop (see Chapter 10). But Eleanor Maccoby believes that identification with the same-sex parent may be the *result* of sex-role development, not the cause. Her account rests on events at all three levels. At the level of the group, in Maccoby's view, peer-group interactions are key to learning gender roles. It is in the peer group, she argues, that boys first learn about how to gain and maintain status in the hierarchy, and that girls develop their styles of interaction (Maccoby, 1990, 1991). Maccoby and Jacklin (1987) found that by age 4 children spent about three times as much time playing with same-sex peers as with opposite-sex peers, and this ratio shot up to 11 times more when the children were 6 years old. According to Maccoby (1990, p. 514), "Gender segregation . . . is found in all the cultural settings in which children are in social groups large enough to permit choice."

Why does gender segregation occur? Maccoby (1988) suggests that part of the answer many harken back to biological, particularly hormonal, differences. Boys play more aggressively than do girls, and their orientation toward competition and dominance may be aversive to many girls. However, shifting to the level of the person, Maccoby (1990) also notes that girls may not like playing with boys because they believe that boys are too difficult to influence; the polite manner in which girls tend to make suggestions apparently doesn't carry much weight with boys. Girls find this response (or lack of response) frustrating and retreat to the company of other girls.

In short, even for something as clearly influenced by culture as gender role development, we must consider events at all three levels of analysis. As usual, these events interact: If not for hormonal differences between the sexes, girls probably would not come to believe that boys are difficult to influence, and if not for that belief, they would have different interactions with boys.

Boys and girls play in characteristic ways, partly because of biological differences.

CONSOLIDATE!

▶ *1. How does the ability to control the body develop with age?* In general, control progresses from the head down the trunk to the arms and, finally, to the legs; at the same time, control extends out from the center of the body to the periphery (hands, fingers, toes). Motor control involves not only attaining more control over muscles but also learning how muscles interact with one another and with properties of the world (such as gravity).

▶ *2. What perceptual and cognitive abilities emerge during the course of development?* Perception develops so that the child can make finer discriminations, needs less stimulus information to recognize objects, and can search more systematically. Piaget proposed that during cognitive development the child moves through a series of major periods, each subdivided into stages, but researchers have since found that children have at least the rudiments of many abilities far earlier than Piaget's theory would predict. In addition, the child develops a theory of mind at a very early age, which becomes increasingly sophisticated with development. Cognitive development arises in part from improved information processing, particularly more efficient working memory, which to some degree probably reflects increased neural development. Finally, as Vygotsky pointed out, culture and instruction also play a role in cognitive development.

▶ *3. How do social and emotional development occur?* Children become attached to their caregivers, going through a series of stages, but may end up being attached in different ways. Attending daycare does not necessarily lead to poorer attachment to the mother or father. The self-concept begins to develop during very early infancy, which in turn probably affects many social interactions, including gender roles. Gender identity is part of the self-concept, which is determined in part by biological factors present since conception; these biological factors may persist in spite of a child's being raised as a member of the opposite sex. People may move through a series of stages in the way they tend to reason about moral issues, and males and females may tend to reason slightly differently at the later stages—but this divergence is mostly a function of their different concerns in daily life, and is not intrinsic to their genders per se.

ADOLESCENCE: BETWEEN TWO WORLDS

Steven Spielberg's adolescence was different from that of many of his peers in many ways; nonetheless, the challenges he faced in those years—forming friendships, testing limits, coming to terms with a new and unfamiliar body—are essentially universals. Because his family had moved so often, in high school none of his friends from early childhood were still with him; most of his classmates, on the other hand, were firmly established in cliques. Spielberg craved their acceptance and used his newfound love of moviemaking and storytelling as a way of gaining it. Nevertheless, his obsession with movies and his lack of interest in most of the usual teenage pursuits of dating, sports, and schoolwork continued to set him apart.

Not surprisingly, Spielberg's adolescence was not an easy time for him or, sometimes, for those around him. On one occasion he and some friends spent 3 hours throwing rocks through plateglass windows at a shopping mall, causing about $30,000 worth of damage (McBride, 1999, p. 88). He later said that *Poltergeist* was "all about the terrible things I did to my younger sisters" (McBride, 1999, p. 89). He fought his father's wishes for him to study math and science, declaring that someday he was going to be a famous movie director and didn't need to know those kinds of things (McBride, 1999). Extreme behavior, yes. Adolescent behavior, yes.

▶ 1. How does puberty affect the body?

▶ 2. How do thought processes change in adolescence?

▶ 3. Does adolescence always lead to emotional upheaval?

Physical Development: In Puberty's Wake

Adolescence begins with **puberty,** the time when hormones cause the sex organs to mature and secondary sexual characteristics to appear, such as breasts for women and a beard for men. These changes typically begin between ages 8–14 for girls and between ages 9–15 for boys. **Adolescence** is the period between the appearance of these sexual characteristics and, roughly, the end of the teenage years. McClintock and Herdt (1996) have argued that puberty actually starts with hormonal changes that begin at age 6, and it is clear that crucial changes often occur at about age 8. For example, 8-year-old girls begin to store more fat on their bodies than do boys, a trend that continues through puberty. Although both sexes develop more muscle during puberty, this is especially the case for boys. Moreover, boys develop greater lung capacity and larger hearts than do girls, as well as more red blood cells, which allow more oxygen to be carried to the larger muscles (Katchadourian, 1977).

During infancy and childhood, the body grows from the trunk outward; the upper arms grow before the lower arms, which in turn grow before the hands. At puberty, the trend is reversed: Rapid growth of the hands, feet, and legs is followed by growth of the torso (Wheeler, 1991). Do you remember when you stopped needing larger shoes but still needed larger coats? That's why. The uneven growth during adolescence can lead to an awkward, gawky look, which doesn't do wonders for a teen's sense of self-confidence.

Girls tend to mature faster than boys.

Once the sex hormones start operating in earnest, the shoulders of young boys grow large relative to their hips, and vice versa for girls. At age 11, girls typically are taller and heavier than boys because their major growth spurt starts about 2 years before that of boys. By age 14, however, boys' heights and weights have taken off, whereas girls have stopped growing or begun to grow more slowly. American girls typically stop growing at around age 13 (some may continue to grow until about age 16), but American boys usually continue to grow until about their 16th birthdays (some may continue growing until they are almost 18 years old; Malina & Bouchard, 1991; Tanner, 1990).

Cognitive Development: Getting It All Together

The major cognitive development of adolescence, achieved by some but not all adolescents, is the ability to reason abstractly. Piaget's period of formal operations describes the adolescent's cognitive achievements. According to Piaget, formal operational thinking allows a person not only to think abstractly, but also to think systematically about abstract concepts and possible scenarios. In one of his experiments, now regarded as a classic, Piaget gave a child a set of weights, string that could be attached to the weights, and a bar to which the string could be attached, allowing the weight to swing like a pendulum. The child was asked to vary both the weight and the length of the string in order to discover what factors would make the weight swing most quickly. Adolescents in the formal operational period are not only able to figure out the possibly relevant factors (size of weight, length of string, how high the weight is raised before being dropped, force with which it is pushed), but also to understand that to discover the role of each variable, they must alter only one thing at a time. These adolescents have grasped the very essence of scientific experimentation: holding everything else constant while systematically varying one factor at a time. In short, all the cognitive machinery

Puberty: The time when hormones cause the sex organs to mature and secondary sexual characteristics appear, such as breasts for women and a beard for men.

Adolescence: The period between the onset of puberty and, roughly, the end of the teenage years.

necessary to think scientifically can be present by about 11 or 12 years of age. But not all adolescents develop these abilities this early, and some never do.

Most adolescents in Western societies are able to grasp the rules that underlie algebra and geometry. The ability to think systematically about abstractions also allows them to think about concepts such as justice and politics, as well as relationships and the causes of human behavior.

How does the ability to think abstractly and logically emerge? It might be tempting to conclude that it is a result of the final stages of brain maturation (and the brain does in fact continue to develop well into adolescence—see Sowell et al., 1999), but the assumption that events at any one level alone could account for such a sweeping change would be rash indeed. Cole (1990) has found that, in many traditional African societies, even the adults cannot use the kinds of abilities described by "formal operations," but there is no indication that their brains have failed to develop fully. Culture must play a role, perhaps shaping the developing child's thought, as Vygotsky theorized.

Adolescents have sometimes been portrayed as prone to distortions in their thinking. In particular, they have been seen as unable to make well-reasoned judgments about themselves. This assumption contains a grain of truth, but bear in mind that adults aren't so good at making such judgments either. The authors of one study asked adults and adolescents to assess the probability of various misfortunes happening either to them or to someone else. Adolescents and adults made remarkably similar estimates (Quadrel et al., 1993). It is sobering to note that both age groups tended to *underestimate* the amount of risk they would face in various circumstances (such as having a car accident or being mugged). Both groups exhibited signs that they thought they were, to some extent, invulnerable. Such findings are consistent with a review of the literature, which concluded that there are few differences in how adolescents and adults make decisions about health care (U.S. Office of Technology Assessment, 1991).

Social and Emotional Development: New Rules, New Roles

A bridge between childhood and adulthood, adolescence is a time of transition. This transition involves not only changing roles in the larger society, which requires obeying new sets of rules, but also learning to live with cognitive and biological changes that affect interactions with others in many ways.

"STORM AND STRESS": RAGING HORMONES? The picture of adolescents as moody and troubled is nothing new. In the 18th century, German authors developed an entire genre of stories (the best known is Wilhelm von Goethe's *The Sorrows of Young Werther*) about passionate, troubled young people so immersed in anguish and heartache that they committed impetuous acts of self-destruction. This body of literature came to be called *Sturm und Drang*, which translates roughly as "storm and stress." G. Stanley Hall (1904) popularized this term among psychologists when he wrote his now-classic two-volume work on adolescence.

The notion that adolescents experience a period of "storm and stress" has waxed and waned in popularity. Anna Freud (1958) not only believed that adolescent "angst" was inevitable but also that "normal" behavior during adolescence was in itself evidence of deep *abnormalities* in the individual. A strong reaction to this view soon followed, and only a few years ago, many psychologists were dismissing the idea as another popular misconception. However, recent studies have shown that there is in fact a normal tendency for adolescents to have three sorts of problems.

First, adolescents tend to have conflicts with their parents (Laursen et al., 1998). The *frequency* of the conflicts is greatest in early adolescence, whereas the *intensity of the conflicts* is greatest in midadolescence (Laursen et al., 1998). Adolescent–parent conflicts occur most often between mothers and daughters on the brink of adolescence (Collins, 1990). These conflicts can be even worse if the parents are not getting along or become divorced. Steven Spielberg claims that *E.T.* is really about the trauma he suffered during the divorce of his parents (McBride, 1999, p. 72); he broke down sobbing at the end of its first screening (p. 333).

Second, adolescents experience extreme mood swings (Buchanan et al., 1992; Larson & Richards, 1994; Petersen et al., 1993), and by the middle of the teen years about one third of adolescents are seriously depressed (Petersen et al., 1993). Adolescents also often report feeling lonely and nervous.

Third, adolescents are prone to taking risks. Anticipating Anna Freud's view, Hall (1904) went so far as to say that "a period of semicriminality is normal for all boys" (Vol. 1, p. 404, referring to adolescent boys). Steven Spielberg's rock-throwing episode at the shopping mall is a perfect example of what Hall had in mind. Adolescents are relatively likely to commit crimes, drive recklessly, and have high-risk sex (Arnett, 1992; Gottfredson & Hirschi, 1990; Johnston et al., 1994). Such behaviors tend to peak in late adolescence.

Not all adolescents have these problems; rather, as Arnett (1999) documents, these problems are simply more likely to occur during adolescence than at other times. But why do they occur at all? Many people assume that they are an unavoidable result of the hormonal changes that follow puberty. The notion that the emotional turmoil of adolescence is rooted in biology was neatly captured by Greek philosopher Aristotle's remark that adolescents "are heated by Nature as drunken men by wine."

In fact, the hormonal changes that follow puberty do make the adolescent prone to emotional swings (Brooks-Gunn et al., 1994; Buchanan et al., 1992). But hormones only predispose, they do not cause; environmental events trigger these emotional reactions. Moreover, the biological effects can be indirect. For example, such changes can lead adolescents to want to stay up late at night and sleep late in the morning (Carskadon et al., 1993). If they are forced to wake up early to go to school, their mood and general emotional tenor will no doubt be affected.

Anthropologist Margaret Mead (1901–1978) appeared to have solid evidence against the view that biology caused the "storm and stress" of adolescence when she returned from fieldwork on the tropical island of Samoa. In 1928 she reported that the adolescents in Samoan culture had a very smooth transition to adulthood. She attributed this to cultural variables such as relaxed attitudes toward sexuality and open social relationships. However, Freeman (1983) found a very different picture when he studied this same culture. It seems that bored Samoan teenagers had enjoyed pulling Mead's leg, filling her with stories of the way they *wished* things were rather than how they actually were. In fact, even in this far-off, seemingly idyllic isle, being an adolescent is not easy, and Samoans have reported experiences much like those of adolescents in Western society.

In sum, adolescents do tend to experience "storm and stress," which arises in part from the workings of hormones. However, this is only a tendency, and the degree to which an adolescent will experience such turmoil depends on personal and cultural circumstances.

Who is the "imaginary audience"?

ADOLESCENT EGOCENTRISM: IT'S ALL IN YOUR POINT OF VIEW.

The enhanced cognitive abilities of adolescents allow them to take other points of view easily—in particular, to see themselves as they imagine others see them. Theorists have claimed that these new abilities can lead to two kinds of distortions in their conception of how others view them.

First, the *imaginary audience* is a belief sometimes held by adolescents, in which they view themselves as actors and everyone else as an audience (Elkind, 1967; Elkind & Bowen, 1979). This leads teenagers to be extremely self-conscious and easily embarrassed; a pimple feels like a beacon, not unlike Rudolph's nose. Second, some teenagers have a

personal fable, which is a story in which they are the star, and as the star they have extraordinary abilities and privileges. Teenagers may have unprotected sex and drive recklessly because they believe that they are immune to the possible consequences (Lapsley, 1990; Lapsley et al., 1988). Adolescents often report feeling that their experiences are so unique that no one could possibly understand what they are going through; this feeling too is part of the personal fable.

One possible consequence of the imaginary audience is that teenagers are especially vulnerable to peer pressure, especially regarding their appearance (Brown, Clasen et al., 1986). Because they are so self-conscious, they are particularly vulnerable to being made to feel different. This tendency can work in combination with a personal fable of invulnerability ("bad things happen to other people, not me") to lead teenagers into dangerous activities such as illegal drug use. In spite of these tendencies, adolescents are mostly influenced by peers in domains of social behavior, and remain influenced primarily by their families with regard to basic values and goals (Brown, Clasen et al., 1986).

LOOKING AT LEVELS

Sex and the Teenager

In 1990 approximately 1,040,000 American teenage girls became pregnant, and slightly over half delivered their babies (Alan Guttmacher Institute, 1994). In general, U.S. teenage girls engage in amounts of sexual activity comparable to those of girls in other industrialized societies, but U.S. teens do not use contraception as effectively. In fact, somewhere between one third and one half of sexually active U.S. teenagers do not use condoms regularly (or at all; Braverman & Strasburger, 1993). In 1995, 75% of the births to American teenagers were to unmarried mothers.

Which teenagers are likely to become pregnant? Those at greatest risk are poor students who do not have clear career plans. Maynard (1996) reports that a third of the teenagers who become pregnant drop out of school even before they become pregnant. Further, over half of teenage mothers were living in poverty when they had their children. For many of these young women, particularly African Americans, having a baby is part of "coming of age," and is in many ways equivalent to a career choice (Merrick, 1995).

Consider these events from the different levels of analysis. First, sex is a biological drive, but your brain is constructed so that you can regulate your urges. The frontal lobes allow us to inhibit impulses, if we so choose. Second, why would someone choose to forgo immediate pleasure? Only if there were a good reason—so good that it overshadowed the passions of the moment. If you don't believe that staying in school will give you a future, and if you believe that having a child is the easiest way to create meaning in your life, why worry about becoming pregnant? Third, cultures create norms about when and in what circumstances—married, not married, financially secure, financially insecure—people should have babies. And of course, events at the different levels interact. Your belief structure leads you to either heed societal norms or ignore them in favor of your own goals. Moreover, the specific consequences of having a child depend on your behavior and social group: If teenage mothers do not drop out of school, they are about as likely to graduate as other girls who did not give birth, and African Americans appear to suffer the fewest economic consequences of having given birth as a teenager. Apparently, African American girls tend to live at home, continue school, and benefit from the assistance of other members of their families (Rosenheim & Testa, 1992). Thus, the consequences of having a baby for changing the mother's brain via education are very different for members of different social groups. Events at the different levels of analysis clearly interact, even when we consider a decision as personal as whether to have a baby.

► **1. How does puberty affect the body?** Sex hormones affect muscle mass and lung and heart capacities as boys and girls develop. They are also responsible for the fact that the extremities (arms and legs) grow rapidly, with the trunk lagging behind, a pattern that can produce a gawky appearance. During this period the body grows pubic hair and acquires other sex characteristics.

► **2. How do thought processes change in adolescence?** Adolescents can become capable of reasoning logically. In addition, if the adolescent reaches the period of formal operations, he or she can reason about abstract concepts systematically—and thus becomes capable of scientific thought. The enhanced reasoning abilities that appear during adolescence affect all aspects of thinking, including conceptions of self and society.

► **3. Does adolescence always lead to emotional upheaval?** The adolescent is prone to experiencing "storm and stress," but this turmoil is not inevitable. Although hormones do prime the adolescent to experience more conflicts with parents as well as to have major mood swings and be prone to taking risks, these tendencies are neither certain nor necessarily severe. Some of the changes during adolescence arise from enhanced cognitive capacity, which allows the teen to think about relationships in more sophisticated ways and can lead to the distorting formulations of an imaginary audience and a personal fable.

ADULTHOOD AND AGING: THE CONTINUOUSLY CHANGING SELF

Steven Spielberg was an unhappy teenager and—in some aspects of life—a spectacularly successful young adult. But being successful in his chosen career did not mean that he was successful in all aspects of life. His first marriage ended; his relationship with his father was strained; and he was concerned that he himself would not measure up as a father (several of his movies deal with difficult relationships between fathers and sons). When he had children of his own, he realized that he needed to be an adult for them; he, and his relationships, had to change, and they did.

Famous moviemaker or not, the grown-up Steven Spielberg is in a very different phase of life than his children; he is also in a very different phase of life than his father. This is the human condition, and we now turn to an exploration of the stages of adult development.

► 1. How do changes in bodily organs affect us as we age?

► 2. How does aging affect perception, memory, and intelligence?

► 3. What is the course of social and emotional development during adulthood?

► 4. How do people cope with the knowledge of their own impending deaths, and with the deaths of friends and family members?

The Changing Body: What's Inevitable, What's Not

By your early 20s, it is unlikely that you will grow taller, and your weight has typically stabilized for many years to come. For the next several decades, changes in your body should be relatively minor. True, you may come to need bifocals, and your hair may begin to gray or to thin. But the basic systems continue to function well. However, after age 50 or so, noticeable changes in the body begin to occur (Lemme, 1995).

Aging has two aspects: changes that are programmed into the genes and changes that arise from environmental events (Busse, 1969; Rowe & Kahn, 1998). Many

If women do not get enough calcium, through diet or supplements, their bones are liable to become weak as they age. This condition can be avoided with proper nutrition at critical periods in the life span.

aspects of aging may in fact arise not from inevitable processes, but rather from lack of adequate nutrition (such as the hunched posture that results from osteoporosis-related calcium deficiency; Hendricks & Hendricks, 1986), lack of exercise (resulting in obesity in some elderly people and frailty in others), or lack of meaningful activities (which can lead to feelings of helplessness or apathy; Avorn & Langer, 1982; Langer & Rodin, 1976; Rodin & Langer, 1977; Rowe & Kahn, 1998).

A major challenge of aging is to accommodate to those changes that are inevitable and to forestall undesirable changes when you can. Many older people develop diseases or conditions that are uncomfortable or even painful, such as arthritis or collapsed vertebrae. However, in most cases, older people can cope with pain effectively, particularly if they adopt a "can-do" attitude (Melding, 1995; Rowe & Kahn, 1998). One of the inevitable age-related changes in women is *menopause*, the gradual ending of menstruation that typically occurs between the ages of 45 and 55; following menopause, eggs are no longer released and pregnancy is not possible (Wise et al., 1996). Hormone changes that accompany menopause can lead to various bodily sensations (such as "hot flashes"); the knowledge that childbearing is no longer possible, along with the decline in youthful appearance, can adversely affect a woman's self-concept and self-esteem. On the other hand, for many women the physical discomforts are slight, if present at all, and the idea of sexual intercourse without the threat of an unwanted pregnancy provides new pleasure. Some women discover "post-menopausal zest" and are reinvigorated by this change and the freedom it represents. Men have no known corresponding physiological event, but do experience declining vigor (strength and energy) with age that can affect sexual performance.

Why do all of us inevitably become less vigorous as we age? The combined effects of changes in the body have been likened to the effect of hitting a table with a hammer over and over (Birren, 1988). Eventually, the table will break, not because of the final blow, but because of the cumulative effects of all the blows. Some researchers believe that aging and death are programmed into the genes. An oft-cited piece of evidence for this idea was reported by Hayflick (1965), who found that human cells grown in the lab will divide on average only about 50 times, and then simply stop. However, all the findings that suggest programmed death can also be interpreted in other ways. Instead of accepting that the genes have been programmed for death, we might assume that over time errors accumulate, and finally there are so many errors that the genes no longer function properly. If you photocopy a drawing or page of text, and then copy the copy, and so on, you'll see how errors in reproduction multiply over repeated copying. In the case of the body, the damage may not be caused by the copying process itself, but rather by the repeated effects of bodily chemicals on each copy (Arking, 1991; Harman, 1956; Levine & Stadtman, 1992).

Perception and Cognition in Adulthood: Taking the Good With the Bad

Cognitive abilities remain relatively stable through most of adulthood, but by age 50 signs of decline begin to appear in some abilities. Is mental decline an inevitable result of aging? Yes and no. The bad news is that you are constantly losing brain cells, even if you don't drink too much alcohol or take drugs, destructive behaviors that only hasten the process. The good news is that through most of adulthood these changes are not noticeable because your brain has built-in redundancy and apparently becomes more efficient at processing as you age. However, unlike pruning during infancy, which eliminates nonfunctional neurons and connections, this cell loss continues as you age (Matsumae et al., 1996). Aging most severely affects the white matter of the brain—the connections among neurons (Guttmann et al., 1998). These changes in the brain will eventually catch up with you and lead you to perform more slowly and be more prone to making errors. Indeed, by age 60 people perform most cognitive tasks more slowly than do younger people (Birren et al., 1962; Cerella, 1990; Salthouse, 1991b). The harder the task, the larger the difference in time taken by young adults and the elderly.

But how large is a "large" difference in time? Although even healthy elderly people require more time to carry out most tasks, the elderly are usually only a second or so slower than young people (Cerella et al., 1980), a difference that is often barely noticeable in daily life. The slowing with age is probably not responsible for the more important declines in cognition and memory.

Shortly before death, however, many people exhibit *terminal decline* (Kleemeier, 1962). Their performance on a wide range of cognitive tasks takes a dramatic turn for the worse (Berg, 1996). This decline appears most dramatically in those who will die from cerebrovascular diseases, such as strokes and heart attacks, and may be related to such disease states (Small & Bäckman, 2000). Thus, terminal decline is probably not an inevitable final chapter of the book of life.

A flood of herbs, vitamins, and other medicinal remedies promise to reverse the negative cognitive effects of aging. For example, the herb Ginkgo biloba and the drug acetyl-L-carnitine have been reported to improve blood flow to the brain (Dean et al., 1993). However, much more research is necessary before we will know for sure whether such treatments work as advertised for everyone.

PERCEPTION: THROUGH A GLASS DARKLY? During early and middle adulthood, worsening vision can usually be corrected with eyeglasses. Later in life, however, more severe visual difficulties emerge. Over half the population 65 and up has *cataracts*, a clouding of the lens of the eye, and in older people, the pupil, the opening of the eye through which light enters, becomes smaller. Surgery can remove cataracts and result in greatly improved vision. Until that point, even moderate optical difficulties cause older people to need greater contrast to see differences in light (Fozard, 1990). Contrasts between lit and unlit surfaces, such as shadows caused by steps, can define differences in depth, and if older people cannot perceive such definition, they are more likely to stumble over a step. Simply providing more light will not necessarily help older people to see well; because of the clouding of the lens, more light causes more glare. Thus, the best level of illumination is a compromise between what produces the best contrast and the least glare.

Hearing is also affected by age. After age 50 or so, people have increased difficulty hearing high-frequency sounds (Botwinick, 1984; Lemme, 1995). Because consonants (such as *k*, *c*, *p*, and *t*) are produced with higher frequency sounds than are vowels, older people will have trouble distinguishing between words that differ by a single consonant, such as *kill* and *pill*. Older people also have more difficulty shutting out background noise, a problem that may actually be worsened by hearing aids, which boost the loudness of irrelevant background sounds as well as of relevant sounds.

Unlike vision and hearing, taste per se does not decline with age (Bartoshuk et al., 1986; Ivy et al., 1992). Even in 80-year-olds, the taste buds are replaced frequently. But much of what we think of as the sensation of taste actually comes in part from smell, and the sense of smell does decline after the middle 50s (Doty et al., 1984; Ivy et al., 1992; Schiffman, 1992). As a result, as people move beyond middle age, they may prefer spicier foods; they may also have difficulty noticing if food has gone bad (Lemme, 1995).

MEMORY: DIFFICULTIES IN DIGGING IT OUT. Parts of the brain that produce the neurotransmitter acetylcholine become impaired with age (Albert & Moss, 1996); this neurotransmitter is crucial for the proper functioning of the hippocampus, which plays a key role in memory. The loss of efficient processing in this part of the brain is probably one reason why older people often have trouble with some kinds of memory (Schacter, 1996).

Even so, aging affects some aspects of memory more than others. *Semantic memory* (memory for facts, words, meanings, and other information that is not associated with a particular time and place) remains relatively intact into very old age (Light, 1991), and the storing of new *episodic memories* (memory for specific events) is often relatively intact. People in their 70s and 80s do relatively well if they are given a list of words and then asked to pick out these words from a longer list that also contains other words (Craik & McDowd, 1987). Moreover, they can recall the gist of a description and its implications at least as well as younger people (Radvansky, 1999).

However, the elderly have difficulty when they must actively recall specific episodic memories: For example, they do poorly if they are given a list of common words to remember and later asked to recall them (Craik & McDowd, 1987). Tasks that require the *recall* of specific information appear to rely on the frontal lobes to dig the information out of memory, and these processes are not as efficient in the elderly as they are in younger people. Indeed, the frontal lobes lose proportionally more brain cells in old age than do other brain areas (Ivy et al., 1992). There are about 17% fewer neurons at age 80 than at age 20 in key parts of the frontal lobes (Haug et al., 1983). In fact, even healthy people over age 67 or so have trouble with the same tasks that are difficult for patients with frontal lobe damage (such as sorting cards first by one rule, then switching to another rule; Schacter, 1996). Moreover, just as patients with frontal lobe damage sometimes show "source amnesia," forgetting the source of a learned fact, so do elderly people (Craik et al., 1990; Glisky et al., 1995; Schacter et al., 1991, 1997; Spencer & Raz, 1995). For example, Schacter and colleagues (1991) asked people to listen to novel facts (such as "Bob Hope's father was a fireman"), which were read aloud by either a man or a woman. When later asked to recall which voice read the facts, 70-year-olds were much less accurate than young people, even when they could recall the facts themselves (see also Schacter et al., 1994).

Frontal lobe impairment probably also is responsible for difficulties the elderly have with tasks involving working memory. Such deficits are particularly evident when the elderly must hold information in mind while doing something else at the same time (Craik et al., 1995). If strategies are needed to perform a task (such as figuring out the most efficient way to move through a store to collect different items), the frontal lobe impairments of the elderly can affect their performance (Gabrieli, 1996). As Salthouse (1985) suggests, slowed cognitive processes may also lead the elderly to use inefficient strategies, strategies composed of many steps, each relatively simple.

INTELLIGENCE AND SPECIFIC ABILITIES: DIFFERENT STROKES FOR DIFFERENT FOLKS. It might seem likely that as you age, your accumulated life experience adds up to an increasingly important determinant of your intelligence. But this is not so. Researchers were surprised to discover that genetic influences on general intelligence actually *increase* with age (Finkel et al., 1995; Plomin et al., 1994). Investigators have asked whether aging affects all types of intelligence in the same way. In particular, they have examined the effects of age on *fluid intelligence,* which involves flexibility in reasoning and the ability to figure out novel solutions, and *crystallized intelligence,* which involves using knowledge as a basis of reasoning (see Chapter 8). It might seem that crystallized intelligence, which by definition relies on effects of experience, would be less influenced by age than fluid intelligence would. How could we tell? These two types of intelligence have been assessed in **longitudinal studies,** which test the same group repeatedly, at different ages. These findings suggest that *both* types of intelligence are stable until somewhere between the mid-50s and early 70s, at which point both decline (Hertzog & Schaie, 1988). However, the very strength of longitudinal studies, the continuing use of the same group, also leads to a weakness: The participants become familiar with the type of testing, and this familiarity can influence their performance on later assessments. **Cross-sectional studies** involve testing different groups of people, with each group at a different age. The key here is to ensure that the groups are equated on all possible measures other than age (such as sex, educational level, and health status). Such studies have led most researchers to believe that fluid intelligence begins to decline as early as the late 20s

Longitudinal study: A study in which the same people are tested repeatedly, at different ages.

Cross-sectional study: A study in which different groups of people are tested, with each group at a different age.

(Salthouse, 1991a), whereas crystallized intelligence may actually grow with age and decline only at the very end of life (Baltes, 1987).

Crystallized intelligence, rooted in experience, may be thought of as underlying much of what we mean by "wisdom." The ability to draw on such intelligence may explain why researchers found that older adults were rated as telling more interesting, higher quality, and more informative stories than younger adults (James et al., 1998). This should be cheering news for Steven Spielberg, who plans to keep telling stories as long as he can.

General intelligence is distinct from special abilities, such as the ability to do arithmetic or imagine objects rotating. Genetics has a smaller influence on special abilities than on general intelligence (Petrill et al., 1998; Plomin et al., 1994). However, as people age, general intelligence is increasingly related to individual differences in special abilities, such as processing speed and spatial abilities (Petrill et al., 1998). Even so, there is evidence that not all the special abilities of a given person are affected by aging to the same degree. For example, a longitudinal study by Schaie (1983, 1989, 1990b) examined the effects of aging on five measures of special abilities, including the ability to recognize and understand words and the ability to rotate shapes mentally. When performances 7 years apart were compared, two results were particularly noteworthy: First, virtually no one had decrements on *all* the tasks; in fact, by age 60 about three fourths of the participants maintained their level of performance from the previous 7 years on at least four of the five abilities tested, and by age 81 more than half the participants maintained this level of performance. Second, the pattern of decline varied enormously from person to person, not only in which combinations of abilities were affected, but also in the rate and severity of decline. Indeed, even though performance at age 53 was generally better on all tasks than performance at age 81, between these ages many participants showed "little or no decrement" on the specific abilities that were assessed.

In general, only about 25% of the variation in cognitive abilities among people is related to their ages (Salthouse, 1991b). Furthermore, aging has varying effects on different people and on different cognitive abilities. In short, depending on genetics and personal experiences, some aspects of intelligence will be affected by aging more than others (Schaie & Willis, 1993).

The Flynn effect (see Chapter 8) is the finding that average IQ has risen steadily through the years throughout the industrialized world. Additional research has shown that during the 20th century, one of the best ways to preserve cognitive ability into old age was simply to have been born later. Although nobody knows for sure why this is true, obvious possibilities are improved nutrition and more enriching intellectual experiences (for example, as provided by experience operating technology). People who were born at about the same time form a **cohort,** which means that they move through life at the same time and go through many of the same experiences. Figure 11.5 shows the results of a study examining different cohorts, which found that age alone does not predict performance. If you look at the results when the participants were 57 years old, for example, you can see that people who were born later in the century do better on spatial orientation tests than the other cohorts. The people who began to be tested at this age did much worse than did

Cohort: A group of people who were born at about the same time and thus move through life together and share many experiences.

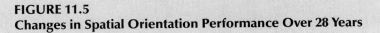

FIGURE 11.5
Changes in Spatial Orientation Performance Over 28 Years

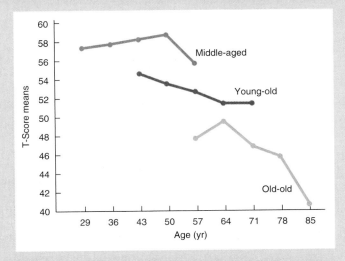

This graph shows scores on a spatial abilities test for middle-aged (mean 57 years old), young-old (mean 71 years old), and old-old (mean 85 years old) people, who were tested repeatedly over time but began to be tested at different ages. People who reached age 57 at a later year in the century apparently had experiences that led them to perform better when they were older.

others who began to be tested at age 43, and people who began to be tested at age 43 did worse than people who began to be tested at age 29. (Examination of the shapes of the lines graphed in Figure 11.5 suggests that the results do not simply reflect how often the participants had been tested previously, which, as noted earlier, is a problem with longitudinal studies.)

Practice can improve some abilities in the elderly (Baltes, 1987; Salthouse & Somberg, 1982; Verhaeghen et al., 1992), such as the ability to perform calculations (Campbell & Charness, 1990). However, practice is not equally effective for all cognitive abilities. In contrast to the ability to do calculations, the ability of the elderly to use working memory was only slightly improved by practice (Campbell & Charness, 1990).

People can often compensate for declining abilities by using abilities that are still intact (Baltes, 1987; Baltes et al., 1984). Some typists can retain their speed as they age by looking farther ahead on the page, thus taking in more as they go (Salthouse, 1984). Similarly, tennis players may compensate for reduced speed and vigor by developing better strategies (Perlmutter, 1988; see Lemme, 1995).

Social and Emotional Development During Adulthood

The term "grow up" might seem to imply that psychological development is like height: After a certain age, you reach a plateau, and that's where you stay. Not so. At least in mentally healthy people, development continues through the life span. In discussing Steven Spielberg's 15-year split with his father, an expert on father–son relationships, James Levine, commented: "In such a split, you don't recognize that under the anger is sadness. There's denial: pretending it's not important to heal the rift. But a split in the father–child relationship always has an effect" (quoted in Sullivan, 1999, p. 67). Still, as in Spielberg's case, relationships change and evolve over time.

After a 15-year split, Steven Spielberg developed a new relationship with his dad.

THEORIES OF PSYCHOSOCIAL STAGES IN ADULTHOOD. Some theorists, Freud included, believed that personality stops developing in childhood. But Erik Erikson (1921–1994) believed there are three stages of adult **psychosocial development,** or effects of maturation and learning on personality and relationships, in addition to five stages of psychosocial development through childhood and adolescence (see Table 11.3). The adult stages were defined by issues that adults are most likely to confront and need to resolve. The first, *intimacy versus isolation,* occurs in young adulthood. To navigate this phase successfully, the young adult must develop deep and intimate relations with others and avoid becoming socially isolated. Steven Spielberg had serious difficulty being intimate with people, which may be one reason why his first marriage dissolved (McBride, 1999, p. 295). The second stage, characterized by *generativity versus self-absorption,* occurs during the middle adult years. The challenge now is for men and women to think about the future and decide what their contributions will be for their children or for society at large. People in this stage who fail to accomplish these goals will be faced with a sense of meaninglessness in life. Steven Spielberg not only cares for his own children but also makes it a point to help young directors who are just starting out; such altruism is another type of generativity. The third stage, characterized by *integrity versus despair,* occurs during old age. The task here is to be able to reflect back on life and feel that it was worthwhile, thereby avoiding feelings of despair and fear of death.

Many theorists have picked up where Erikson left off, modifying his theory or replacing it altogether (Gould, 1978; Havinghurst, 1953; Vaillant, 1977; for a review, see Lemme, 1995). Levinson (Levinson, 1977, 1978, 1986, 1990; Levinson et al., 1978), basing his work on interviews with 40 men, developed an influential theory of developmental transitions in men's lives. Following Erikson, he too proposed a series

Psychosocial development: The effects of maturation and learning on personality and relationships.

TABLE 11.3

Erikson's (1950) Psychosocial Stages

ISSUE TO BE RESOLVED	AVERAGE AGE	SUMMARY
Basic trust vs. mistrust	0–1 year	Depending on how well they are treated by caregivers, infants either develop a basic trust that the world is good or fail to develop such a basic trust.
Autonomy vs. doubt	1–3 years	The child either is allowed to choose and make independent decisions or is made to feel ashamed and full of self-doubt for wanting to do so.
Initiative vs. guilt	3–6 years	The child either develops a sense of purpose and direction or is overly controlled by the parents and made to feel constrained or guilty.
Industry vs. inferiority	6–11 years	The child either develops a sense of competence and ability to work with others or becomes beset with feelings of incompetence and inferiority.
Identity vs. role confusion	Adolescence	The adolescent either successfully grapples with questions of identity and future roles as an adult or becomes confused about possible adult roles.
Intimacy vs. isolation	Young adulthood	The young adult either develops deep and intimate relations with others or is socially isolated.
Generativity vs. self-absorption	Middle adulthood	The adult in the "prime of life" must look to the future and determine what to leave behind for future generations; failing this task leads to a sense of meaninglessness in life.
Integrity vs. despair	Old age	In reflecting back on life, a person either feels that life was worthwhile as it was lived or feels despair and fears death.

of stages. These stages charted the changes in the *life structure*, the "underlying pattern or design of a person's life at a given time," of a man's life as he aged (Levinson, 1990, p. 41). Levinson claimed that periods of relative stability alternate with periods of transition. As shown in Table 11.4, the stages are organized into general "eras," with

TABLE 11.4

Levinson's Periods in Early and Middle Adulthood

The Early Adult Transition (17–22)	A bridge from Preadulthood to Early Adulthood.
The Entry Life Structure for Early Adulthood (22–28)	Constructing and maintaining a style of adult living.
The Age-30 Transition (28–33)	A time of reappraisal of oneself and modification of the Entry Life Structure.
The Culminating Life Structure for Early Adulthood (33–40)	The completion of the Early Adulthood Era; coping with the realization of youthful aspirations.
The Mid-Life Transition (40–45)	A great cross-era shift that ends Early Adulthood and begins Middle Adulthood.
The Entry Life Structure for Middle Adulthood (45–50)	The initial basis for life in the Middle Adulthood Era.
The Age-50 Transition (50–55)	A mid-era chance to attempt to improve the life structure developed in the previous period.
The Culminating Life Structure for Middle Adulthood (55–60)	Developing a framework to conclude the Middle Adulthood era.
The Late Adult Transition (60–65)	A period that separates and links the previous era and the era of Late Adulthood.

cross-era transitions between them (Levinson, 1990). Levinson focused on the eras between the Early Adulthood Transition and Late Adulthood Transition.

Perhaps the most important and interesting aspect of Levinson's theory is the *midlife transition*, which occurs when a man begins to shift from thinking of his life as marked by the time that's passed since birth to thinking of his life as marked by the time left until death. This transition typically occurs somewhere between the ages of 40 and 45. This change in perspective can have profound consequences, often leading a man to question the path he has chosen. According to Levinson, many men have *midlife crises*, which can lead them to end marriages and begin others, change jobs, or make other major life changes. In Steven Spielberg's case, this crisis seems to have caused him to deal with conflicting emotions about being Jewish; one result was his movie *Schindler's List*, in which he confronted his fears and ambivalence about his Jewish identity (which were particularly severe because of his strong need for acceptance; McBride, 1999).

One difficulty with Levinson's approach is that it relies on interviews, which in turn depend on: (1) the participants' accurate recall; (2) their willingness not to censure or gloss over the rough spots of their lives; (3) the interviewer's accuracy in recording the testaments without injecting his or her own interpretations at the time; and (4) the intuitive analysis of the interviews as the means for developing or supporting the theory. Given all these potential problems, it is not surprising that research by others (for example, McCrae & Costa, 1984) has cast doubt on whether most men in fact undergo a midlife crisis.

Levinson's original study focused only on men; it was not long before others undertook similar studies of women. The initial reports of such studies sometimes concluded that women went through similar stages, at similar ages, but their overall goals were different from those of men. For example, Levinson believed that people are motivated by a "Dream." According to Levinson and colleagues (1978), "the Dream is a vague sense of self-in-adult-world. It has the quality of a vision, an imagined possibility that generates excitement and vitality" (p. 91). Roberts and Newton (1987) reported that women had more complex Dreams than men, which often revolved around their roles in a community as well as their goals of marriage, children, and a career; men's Dreams, in contrast, often focused on a very concrete image of themselves in a particular occupation or playing a particular role. Interestingly, women's Dreams were not as motivating to them as were men's. Roberts and Newton emphasized, however, not the differences between men and women, but the similarities—particularly the importance of the Age-30 Transition, which occurs between 28 and 33, a time when women are reconsidering marriage and careers.

Even so, Roberts and Newton noted that women's lives were often "conflicted and unstable throughout much of early adulthood and into middle age. This appears to differ from Levinson's sequence of alternating stable and transitional periods" (p. 162). Levinson himself was finishing a book on women when he died in 1994; the book was published in 1997, with the help of his wife and collaborator, Judy Levinson. The Levinsons' conclusions, based on interviews of 45 women, were similar to those of Roberts and Newton, although they emphasize the similarities to the findings for men. In contrast, others who have studied women (such as Mercer, 1989) report that women do not follow a regular stagelike progression through life.

The findings that do support the existence of stages in adulthood can be interpreted as evidence that our society poses different challenges to people of different ages or as evidence that personality develops with age. Research findings suggest that this second interpretation is probably incorrect. Costa and McCrae (1988) tested more than a thousand people, both men and women, using standardized measures (not interviews) of the Big Five personality dimensions: openness to experience, conscientiousness, extraversion, agreeableness, and neuroticism (see Chapter 10). The participants ranged in age from 21 to 96 years. In addition to asking the participants to complete the measures, they also asked 167 spouses to fill in the measures about the participants. Eighty-nine men and 78 women were tested twice, 6 years apart; thus, both cross-sectional and longitudinal data were collected. The results were clear: There

Average age of the Rolling Stones in 1994: 50.6 years.

Average age of top GM executives in 1994: 49.8 years.

Many roles are open to us as we age, despite stereotypes to the contrary!

were very few differences in any of the dimensions of personality over the years, and when such differences were found, they were very small. Moreover, Costa and McCrae found that personality was equally stable over time for men and women. They concluded that "aging itself has little effect on personality. This is true despite the fact that the normal course of aging includes disease, bereavement, divorce, unemployment, and many other significant events for substantial portions of the population" (p. 862). Thus, any apparent changes in personality over time probably reflect not so much changes in the person as changes in the life challenges being confronted at the time.

A later meta-analysis showed, however, that adult personality does continue to develop in one respect: Until around age 50, people become increasingly consistent in the degree to which they can be described by particular traits, and thereafter are stable (Roberts & DelVecchio, 2000). Consistency, in this sense, refers to the relative ordering of people according to a trait—with increasing age, your ranking relative to other people will become more stable. This stability could reflect, in part, your settling into a niche in life, and thus restricting the range and variety of situations you encounter.

At one point, approximately 2,500 people well over 100 years old were reported to be living in countries comprising the former Soviet Union. One purportedly 168-year-old gentleman, who was still walking half a mile daily and gardening, attributed his longevity to the fact that he didn't marry until he was 65 (Seuling, 1986). Many elderly people, such as this Belgian couple—he's 98 and she's 74!—enter second marriages.

ADULT RELATIONSHIPS: STABLE CHANGES.

In general, as people age they interact with fewer people, but these interactions tend to be more intimate (Carstensen, 1991, 1992). Relationships earlier in life tend to include more friends than relatives, but with age the mix reverses, with more time spent with relatives than with friends. This pattern is even more pronounced among Latinos than Anglos (Levitt et al., 1993). In later life, a relationship long dormant can be picked up and reestablished with minimal effort (Carstensen, 1992); after young adulthood, temperament and personality variables are relatively stable, which makes it easy to "know" someone again even after a long lapse.

During young adulthood, people are concerned that their relationships with friends and relatives are equitable—that neither party gives more than he or she receives (Lemme, 1995; Walster et al., 1978). As people age, such concerns recede into the background. In successful marriages, the members of the couple think of themselves as a team, not separate people who are in constant negotiations (Keith & Schafer, 1991). Because they are in it for the long haul, people trust that the balance of favors and repayment will even out over time.

Death and Dying

We began this chapter with the very earliest phase of development, and we close it with the last of life's experiences. The psychology of death has two faces: The effects on the person who is dying and the effects on friends and family. Perhaps the most influential theorist of the psychology of death is Elisabeth Kübler-Ross (1969), who studied the psychological events that accompany the knowledge of impending death. After extensive interviews with people dying of cancer (usually in middle age), she developed a theory that there are five stages people pass through in dealing with their own impending deaths:

> ▶ Stage 1: Shock, disbelief, and denial
> ▶ Stage 2: Anger and a sense of injustice
> ▶ Stage 3: Bargaining, with God and others, for continued life
> ▶ Stage 4: Depression and withdrawal
> ▶ Stage 5: Acceptance

However, these stages probably apply only to people who are dying at a relatively early age, and even then, not everyone follows the stages in order or experiences every stage (Retsinas, 1988). Kübler-Ross's theory also suffers from the usual problems of theories based on interviews (such as those noted in connection with Levinson's theory), and there is little empirical evidence to back it up.

Concern about our own deaths apparently does not increase with age: Death anxiety either stays the same over the course of life, or may actually decrease near the end (Lemme, 1995). Women report fearing death more than do men (Lonetto & Templer, 1986). However, this finding could simply mean that women are more honest or self-aware, or that men are consciously or unconsciously avoiding confronting the topic. In addition, because women tend to live longer than men, they may have had more opportunity to witness and become concerned about death than men.

Cultural differences clearly influence the ways people view death (Kalish & Reynolds, 1977; Platt & Persico, 1992). Researchers who studied the Mayan people of South America found that they did not try to fight death. Elderly people announce that their time has come and then retire to a mat or hammock and wait to die. They refuse food or water, ignore attempts by others to talk to them, and soon die. Their attitude toward death is fostered by their strong belief in an afterlife in paradise (Steele, 1992). In contrast, the Kaliai, a tribe in Papua New Guinea, almost never die of old age, instead meeting death in battle or as a result of an accident. Thus, they do not view death as a natural occurrence; they look for someone to blame, usually a sorcerer (Counts & Counts, 1992).

Grief is the emotion of distress that follows the loss of a loved one, and **bereavement** is the experience of missing a loved one and longing for his or her company. People in the United States tend to go through the grieving process in three phases (Lindemann, 1991; for a good summary, see Lemme, 1995). First, until about 3 weeks after the death, the bereaved person is in a state of shock. He or she feels empty, disoriented, and, sometimes, in a state of denial and disbelief; these feelings eventually settle into a state of deep sorrow. (This shock may be buffered by having to make funeral arrangements, deal with lawyers, and so on, but nevertheless apparently develops during this period.) Second, from 3 weeks to about a year following the death, the bereaved person experiences emotional upheavals, from anger to loneliness and guilt. During this time, people often review their relations with the deceased, wondering whether they should have done things differently, whether the death was inevitable. During this phase, people may think that they catch glimpses of the deceased in crowds or hear the person talk to them. Third, by the beginning of the second year, grief lessens. The bereaved person may largely stop thinking of the deceased and, in the case of a spouse's death, be ready to become committed to a new intimate relationship. However, bereavement may continue indefinitely, particularly when a person is reminded of the deceased by special places or events, such as anniversaries or birthdays.

Grief: The emotion of distress that follows the loss of a loved one.

Bereavement: The experience of missing a loved one and longing for his or her company.

The effects of the death of a friend or loved one depend in part on the age of the deceased. Most deaths in the United States and Canada tend to occur at a relatively old age; the average age of death in some Latin American countries is much younger. The grief for someone who has had a full life is different from the grief for someone who has been cut down in his or her prime.

LOOKING AT LEVELS

Keeping the Aging Brain Sharp

In old age, particularly the years just before death, many people do not function as well mentally as they did earlier in life, even if they are physically healthy (Small & Bäckman, 1999). Is this deterioration inevitable? As people age, the brain receives less blood, which means that it is sustained by fewer nutrients and oxygen (Ivy et al., 1992). The blood supply to the brain decreases with age because the vessels themselves become smaller. Why does this happen? One reason may be that the brain cells are not working as hard, so they need less blood—which in turn leads the vessels to adjust (Ivy et al., 1992). This is a catch-22: The neurons don't work as effectively because they receive fewer blood-borne nutrients and less oxygen, but the reason they don't receive as much is that they haven't been functioning as effectively as they did before. Thus, if your otherwise healthy grandparents are understimulated by their surroundings (as occurs in some nursing homes as well as in many home environments), this could affect their brains. The lack of mental challenge and engagement can lead to a change in their self-concepts and levels of self-esteem. These changes then may lead them to become lethargic and not to try to challenge themselves (including with other people), which could lead to even less effective neural functioning, and so on. Events at all three levels clearly interact.

Although the appropriate research has yet to be conducted, it is tempting to hypothesize that if you managed to engage your elderly parents, grandparents, or other family members in more challenging tasks, you could literally increase the blood supply to their brains and improve their thinking abilities. This result is plausible because "mental workouts" appear to enhance cognitive function in the elderly (Rowe & Kahn, 1998). Moreover, dendrites continue to grow normally even into old age (Coleman & Flood, 1986), and as neurons die, new connections may be formed to compensate for losses (Cotman, 1990). In one study, when elderly rats were moved from their standard cages into a rat playpen full of toys and other rats, they developed heavier brains with more extensive connections among neurons. Very likely the same would be true for humans who were moved to more stimulating environments (see Avorn & Langer, 1982; Langer & Rodin, 1976; Rodin & Langer, 1977; Rowe & Kahn, 1998).

However, it is unlikely that *all* the functions that are impaired with age can be helped simply by getting your grandparents to use their brains more. MRI scans of over 3,600 apparently normal elderly people (aged 65 to 97) revealed that slightly over one third had brain lesions. These were often small and usually affected subcortical structures, but some of the lesions may have been large enough to affect a specific cognitive function (Bryan et al., 1997). Thus, possible effects of changing beliefs and social interactions must be considered within the context of the state of the brain. As always, events at the three levels interact.

CONSOLIDATE!

▶ *1. How do changes in bodily organs affect us as we age?* The adult body remains relatively stable until around age 50. At about this point, women experience menopause, and both men and women may become less vigorous. Many of the changes in the body can be treated, however, either by dietary supplements (such

(continued)

as calcium for bone weakness) or changes in activities (which can reduce obesity).

▶ *2. How does aging affect perception, memory, and intelligence?* With age the lens clouds and the pupils dilate less, leading to difficulty in seeing light–dark contrasts; the elderly also have difficulty hearing high-frequency sounds such as consonants; and the sense of smell declines. With advancing old age, working memory operates less effectively, and people sometimes experience source amnesia. Although intelligence declines with advanced age, fluid intelligence may be more affected than crystallized intelligence, and special abilities need not be affected much if at all (but in different people different abilities tend to be affected). As they approach death, many, but not all, people experience terminal decline—a dramatic degradation of cognitive abilities.

▶ *3. What is the course of social and emotional development during adulthood?* Many theorists, includ-

ing Erik Erikson and Daniel Levinson, have proposed that people pass through psychosocial stages as they age. These stages may be a result of challenges posed by a particular culture; little evidence points to personality changing after age 30. Adult relationships focus on fewer people (often relatives) and tend to be stable over long periods of time.

▶ *4. How do people cope with the knowledge of their own impending deaths and with the deaths of friends and family members?* People may go through a series of stages in coming to terms with their own impending deaths (at least if they are middle-aged). Grief for another's death may also pass through stages, which may extend over 2 years following the death; the sense of bereavement may never entirely disappear. Concern about our own deaths does not increase, and may in some cases decrease, with age.

A DEEPER LEVEL
Recap and Thought Questions

▶ **In the Beginning: From Conception to Birth**

The development of both the brain and the body relies on the activation of specific genes, which are regulated in part by environmental events. If those events disrupt gene function, the brain and body may develop abnormally. The newborn comes into the world equipped with a variety of reflexes, many of which disappear in short order. In addition, a newborn has sophisticated sensory capacities, including those necessary to begin organizing sounds into words and recognizing objects. Individual newborns differ in their temperaments, and may retain their temperaments indefinitely.

Was Steven Spielberg born with his abilities to make movies? Probably not. Like all of us, his abilities were affected by a combination of innate factors, effects of teratogens, nutrition, and appropriate stimulation (perhaps even the sounds of his mother's piano playing) during his prenatal development.

Think It Through. If you were going to design a program to teach newly pregnant women how best to care for their unborn children, what would you emphasize?

▶ **Infancy and Childhood: Taking Off**

As they grow, children are increasingly able to control their bodies. They learn to coordinate muscles in the context of perception and knowledge of specific properties of the world. Perceptual development involves increasingly finer discriminations and the use of more and more complex sources of information. As characterized by Jean Piaget, cognitive development involves a series of stages, which research has shown in part to reflect brain growth, increased capacity of working memory, and the results of explicit instruction. However, these stages may not be fixed, and many abilities are evident at earlier ages than originally believed. Culture plays a role in cognitive development, if only because language is acquired through immersion in a culture.

Social and emotional development are reflected by changes in attachment, self-concept, gender identity, moral reasoning, and gender roles. Even young babies have the beginnings of a self-concept and develop social relationships from the start, including attachment (of one type or another) to a caregiver. Further, babies apparently are born with a biological bias to be male or female, a bias that probably results from the effects of hormones in the womb. Simply raising babies as boys or girls is not likely to make them comfortable or happy with that gender if their experiences in the womb inclined them toward the other gender.

According to Lawrence Kohlberg, moral reasoning also develops through a series of stages. However, it isn't clear whether all these stages actually exist, or whether they depend at least in part on culture and the tasks of daily life (which may include having to take care of children or elderly parents). Moral reasoning appears to depend on the cognitive capacity to engage in certain types of thinking.

Has Steven Spielberg exhibited full perceptual and cognitive development? His movies give every evidence of his having developed a sophisticated ability to reason, not only about physical events, but also about psychological and even moral dilemmas (as illustrated in *Amistad, The Color Purple,* and *Schindler's List*).

Think It Through. Why would you expect variations in the age at which stages of cognitive development are reached?

Do you think schools should focus on speeding up cognitive development, so that children pass through the stages more quickly? Why or why not?

What would you do if you had a child who was born with sexual organs that were partly male and partly female, as sometimes happens?

Can a child experience normal emotional development if he or she spends much of the day watching television? Which aspects of emotional development do you think would be affected by television?

▶ Adolescence: Between Two Worlds

The hormonal changes that herald the onset of puberty not only affect the body in dramatic ways, but also alter the child's emotional and social interactions. Adolescence is usually accompanied by cognitive changes that allow the adolescent to conceive of events in the world in more abstract and complex ways. Emotional, social, and cognitive changes can lead to a period of "storm and stress," although not every adolescent experiences such a period and those who do may experience it to different extents.

Was adolescence a particularly important period for Steven Spielberg? Apparently so, given the themes that recur in his films. Not only was his parents' divorce a key event in his life, but so was his striving to be accepted by his teenage peers.

Think It Through. If you were going to design a school program that takes into account the biological changes that occur during adolescence, how would it differ from your own middle school or high school experience? What kinds of classes, activities, or schedule might make the transition to adulthood easier?

▶ Adulthood and Aging: The Continuously Changing Self

Some of the bodily effects of aging are programmed into the genes, but some are not. Proper diet and exercise can help the body function effectively well into old age. Although most perceptual abilities (such as vision and hearing) decline with advanced age, they need not impair the ability to get around or communicate with others. Similarly, although it may become more difficult to retrieve information from long-term memory in old age, and source memory may be lost more often than previously, many aspects of memory continue to function effectively. The brain functions well until close to death, and intelligence, particularly crystallized intelligence, may remain virtually normal until shortly before death. Similarly, special abilities (such as spatial ability) can be remarkably intact until very late in life. Although many people experience terminal decline, this does not appear to be an inevitable final phase of life.

As people age, they face different social and emotional challenges. If these challenges are not resolved satisfactorily, they will be unhappy and not well adjusted to the realities of growing old. During middle age, people must learn to cope with the deaths of those they love, and at the end of life, they must come to terms with their own death.

Have Steven Spielberg's relationships changed as he has gotten older? Yes. Like most people, his relatives seem to have become more important. If he is like other people, the size of his circle of friends may shrink. Nevertheless, it will be easy for him to retain old friendships.

Think It Through. If you could choose several of your own abilities to protect from decaying with age, which would they be? Why? As you age, what factors do you think will influence whether you stay close to friends you made earlier in life?

12 STRESS, HEALTH, AND COPING

Lisa, a college sophomore, was becoming worried about her father, Al. Only 54 years old, he always seemed exhausted, regardless of the time of day or the amount of work he'd been doing. Whenever Lisa asked him why he was so tired, he answered in generalities: "Oh, work's crazy. That's all, honey." He'd also been coughing a lot, and when Lisa asked about this, he'd reply, "I've been sick more than usual—it's just been a bad winter."

Lisa used to look forward to her visits home and her telephone conversations with her father, but now she dreaded talking to him because he always sounded so tired and dejected. Lisa suggested that he see his doctor, exercise, maybe learn some type of relaxation technique. Al finally told her the real reason he was so tense and tired: His company had laid off several of his colleagues, and he was afraid he'd be next. It also meant that now Al's department was responsible for more work with less staff. In addition, as part of the downsizing, the company had moved to smaller premises. His new office was cramped, noisy, and generally unpleasant. He had trouble concentrating, and he knew his work was suffering, which made him even more concerned that he'd be fired. There was a possibility of a job offer from another company, but at a substantially lower salary. Lisa, listening to his story, understood that he

431

had tried to protect her by not telling her. If he was fired, or took the other job, he wouldn't be able to help with her college expenses, and she was already working 25 hours a week. If Al's fears materialized, she would probably have to leave school, at least for a while, or take out very large loans. He was worried himself, and worried about his daughter; Lisa understood the burden of those worries, which she now shared. She worried, too, about his persistent cough—was it just from lots of winter colds, or was it something more?

This situation produced stress in both father and daughter. Just what is "stress"? Can it affect our health? How can we deal with it?

WHAT IS STRESS?

Al began to hate going to work. Often as he worked at his desk, he felt as if he'd just finished a race—heart beating, palms sweating, breath coming hard—but without any accompanying sense of relief or accomplishment. He was simply exhausted all the time and felt as if his heart wasn't pumping his blood fast enough for his body's needs. He began to be seriously worried about his health, as well as his job.

But Maya, a colleague who so far had survived at the company, didn't seem disturbed by the changes happening around them. Maya had two children and, like Al, needed her job, but she seemed to be taking this difficult situation in stride. Al didn't understand how Maya was able to stay so calm—didn't she understand what was going on?

And what about Lisa's response to pressures? She had been managing the demands of college and job well; but after her father explained his situation at work and the possible repercussions for both of them, she noticed physical symptoms in herself— sweaty palms, racing heart—even while studying or taking class notes. Al and Lisa are responding to stress.

▶ 1. What exactly is stress?

▶ 2. What is the physiology of stress?

▶ 3. What are common sources of stress?

Stress: The Big Picture

Today even third graders complain of feeling "stressed out," and adults take evening courses in "stress management." But what exactly *is* stress? **Stress** is the general term describing the psychological and bodily response to a stimulus that alters your equilibrium (Lazarus & Folkman, 1984). The stimulus that throws the body's equilibrium out of balance is called a **stressor**; a piece of glass that you step on while walking barefoot is a stressor. For Al, the threat of losing his job is a stressor, and the resulting combination of physical reactions (heart racing and so on) and psychological reactions (difficulty concentrating at work) is the stress. More specifically, the body's response to a stressor is the **stress response**, also called the *fight-or-flight* response, the physiological changes that occur to help you cope with the stressor. If you step on a piece of glass, your body may produce chemicals called endorphins and enkephalins, its own version of painkillers, and cause white blood cells to congregate at the site of the injury to fight off any infectious agents. These responses work to bring the body back to normal, to restore homeostasis.

The list of potential stressors is long, and categorized according to a number of criteria (Table 12.1). Stressors can be short-term (**acute stressor**) or long-term (**chronic stressor**); they can be physical, "psychological" (which affect events at the level of the person), or social (or, of course, some combination). Physical stressors, such as not eat-

Stress: The general term describing the psychological and bodily response to a stimulus that alters a person's state of equilibrium.

Stressor: A stimulus that throws the body's equilibrium out of balance.

Stress response: The physiological changes that occur to help people cope with a stressor; also called the *fight-or-flight response.*

Acute stressor: A stressor of short-term duration.

Chronic stressor: A stressor of long-term duration.

TABLE 12.1

Examples of Types of Stressors

| TYPE OF STRESSOR | TYPE OF STRESSOR | |
	Acute	Chronic
Physical	Being injured in a car crash	Being underfed; having cancer
Psychological (level of the person)	Working against a deadline	Chronically feeling pressured by work
Social	Getting fired	Chronic isolation; overcrowding

ing for 2 days, generally apply to most people; psychological and social stressors, on the other hand, can be much more subjective. Going to a dance club for hours can be a party animal's idea of a great time or a shy person's nightmare. In general, it is our *perception* of a stimulus that determines whether it will elicit the stress response, not necessarily the objective nature of the stimulus itself.

The Physiology of Stress: The General Adaptation Syndrome

Austrian-born researcher Hans Selye (1907–1982), who pioneered the study of stress, established that the body responds to stressors in generally predictable ways (Selye, 1976). He called the overall stress response the **general adaptation syndrome (GAS)** and suggested that it has three distinct phases: alarm, resistance, and exhaustion (Figure 12.1).

THE ALARM PHASE: FIGHT OR FLIGHT. Perception of a stressor triggers the **alarm phase,** which is characterized by the fight-or-flight response. In this response, the body mobilizes itself to fight or to flee from a threatening stimulus, which can be a physical threat, such as a knife at the throat, or a psychological one, such as an emotional rejection.

When you perceive a threat, your brain responds to it by activating the sympathetic nervous system and inhibiting the parasympathetic nervous system (see Chapter 2 and Figure 2.10). Neurotransmitters and hormonal secretions such as epinephrine and norepinephrine cause breathing, heart rate, and blood pressure to increase. (Norepinephrine is considered a neurotransmitter when it is found in the brain, but a hormone when dispersed in other parts of the body.) This serves to bring more oxygen to the muscles as you prepare to "fight" or "flee." In addition, these sympathetic nervous system changes cause the pupils to dilate (allowing more light to enter for greater visual acuity) and the palms to sweat (for better gripping).

When the stress response is triggered, the hypothalamus secretes a substance that causes the release of **glucocorticoids,** another group of hormones. *Cortisol*, a glucocorticoid, not only increases the production of energy from glucose, but also has an anti-inflammatory effect, which makes it effective in helping restore the body's equilibrium after physical injury. In the short run, all these changes sharpen the senses, improve some qualities of memory (Sapolsky, 1997), and make it easier to fight or flee.

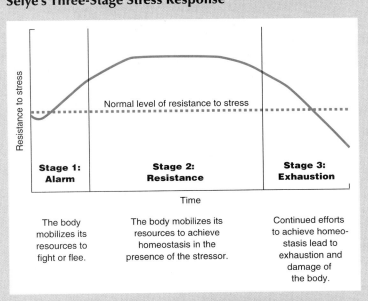

FIGURE 12.1
Selye's Three-Stage Stress Response

Hans Selye proposed that the body's response to prolonged stress is comprised of three stages: alarm, resistance, and exhaustion.

General adaptation syndrome (GAS): The technical name for the three phases of the body's response to stress.

Alarm phase: The first phase of the GAS, in which a stressor is perceived and a fight-or-flight response is activated.

Glucocorticoids: A type of hormone that is released when the stress response is triggered. Glucocorticoids have anti-inflammatory properties.

Resistance phase: The second phase of the GAS, in which the body mobilizes its resources to attain equilibrium, despite the continued presence of the stressor; also called the *adaptation phase*.

Exhaustion phase: The final stage of the GAS, in which the continued stress response itself becomes damaging to the body.

Although this general stress response occurs with all stressors, the speed of action and amount of each hormone produced may differ, depending on the particular stressor (Henry, 1977; Romero & Sapolsky, 1996).

For most of us, however, the threats we experience do not require the kind of *physical* response required of our distant ancestors. Taking a final exam requires sitting in a chair, not running or climbing away from an enemy. Nonetheless, your body still reacts with the fight-or-flight response; it gets all revved up with nowhere to go.

RESISTANCE AND EXHAUSTION. Once your body is primed to fight or flee, you enter the **resistance phase** (also known as the *adaptation phase*), in which the body mobilizes its resources to achieve equilibrium despite the continued presence of the stressor. In other words, it *adapts* to the stressor.

Both the initial stress response and the resistance phase require energy, which comes from fat cells, muscles, and the liver. The increased blood flow (which results from increased heart and respiration rates) helps deliver the energy quickly and efficiently to the parts of the body that need it most. Digestion, growth, sex drive, and reproduction are slowed during times of stress. In women, menstruation may stop, or occur irregularly; in men, sperm and testosterone levels may decrease. As a matter of survival, why waste energy on these processes when it is needed elsewhere? In addition to these changes, no new energy is stored during stress; this means that with chronic stress, no reserve of energy is available to repair bodily damage, leaving a sense of fatigue.

During the resistance phase, cortisol serves to help the body return to a more normal state in the presence of continued stressors (McEwen & Schmeck, 1994). The more extreme the stressors, the more glucocorticoids are produced in an attempt to restore equilibrium, and this process decreases the functioning of the immune system. If the stressor continues, the **exhaustion phase** sets in; the continued stress response begins to damage the body, producing a risk of stress-related diseases. In addition, cortisol can damage hippocampal cells (see Chapter 6), adversely affecting learning and memory (Newcomer et al., 1999; Sapolsky, 1992).

Sources of Stress

Is a new relationship stressful? writing a term paper? hearing a baby cry? being stuck in a traffic jam? The answer to all these is maybe, maybe not. Many psychological, social, and even physical stimuli are stressors only if you *perceive* them as stressful. Some people are more likely to perceive many stimuli as stressful, and some situations are more likely than others to be perceived as stressful.

Even among college students, what is considered stressful differs, depending on whether the student is traditional (went to college straight from high school) or nontraditional (took some time off between high school and college, or has multiple roles such as student and parent or employee). Social activities have a larger impact on traditional students, whereas nontraditional students are more likely to enjoy doing homework and going to classes and worry less about how they are doing academically (Dill & Henley, 1998).

STRESSORS IN THE EYES OF THE BEHOLDER. Physical stressors, such as a piece of glass stuck in your bare foot, are generally easy to identify, but the definition of a psychological or social stressor is more subjective. Maya is not bothered about the recent firings because she wants to spend more time with her children. Part of her wouldn't mind being out of work (and collecting unemployment) so that she could stay home for a while; between savings and her husband's paycheck, the family could get by for a few months. So for Maya, the threat of being fired is not a stressor. It is the *perception* of whether or not a stimulus is a stressor that is crucial for determining whether the stress response will occur (Lazarus & Folkman, 1984).

The importance of perceptions in determining whether something is a stressor was demonstrated in a classic study by Speisman and colleagues (1964). Participants were asked to watch a film of a primitive ritual involving a crude genital operation called "subincision." Participants in one group heard a "trauma" soundtrack for the film that emphasized the pain experienced by those undergoing the rite. Another group heard a "denial" soundtrack, which emphasized the positive aspects of the ritual and minimized the experience of pain. A third group heard an "intellectualization" soundtrack, which described the ceremony in a detached, clinical manner. Those in either the denial or the intellectualization group showed less of a physiological response to the film and reported being less upset than those in the trauma group. This study demonstrated that the content of the narration about the ritual (the context, and therefore how the stimulus is perceived) affected the stress response of the participants in the study.

This process of appraising a stimulus occurs in two phases. First, the stimulus is assessed for the likelihood of danger; this is the *primary appraisal*. This assessment is followed by *secondary appraisal*, the determination of the resources available to deal with the stressor. In other words, the question "Am I in danger?" is followed by the question "What can I do about it?" (Bishop, 1994). After secondary appraisal comes **coping**; that is, the person experiencing stress takes some course of action regarding the stressor, its effects, or his or her reaction to it.

PERCEIVED CONTROL. It is clear that certain stimuli, such as illness or injury, are associated with physical stress; similar associations apply to certain types of psychological and social stressors. One such stimulus is the lack of a sense of control. Actual control is not important; what is important is whether you *perceive* a sense of control (Shapiro et al., 1996). The perception of control can affect your performance.

Not everyone is equally eager to feel in control; in fact, some people experience more stress when they perceive themselves as having more control, such as some cancer patients who find that taking responsibility for and control of their medical treatment is overwhelming and stressful. Such patients prefer not to learn about and weigh the statistics and other facts about their illness, and want their doctors to make all the decisions about chemotherapy, radiation, and other treatments. On the other hand, some people want very much to feel that they can control a situation but may, at least after a certain point, not have much real opportunity to do so. Once graduate school or job applications are written and interviews past, for example, there's not much you can do to get yourself accepted or hired; nothing is left but to wait for the answer. Thus, there can be a mismatch between perceived control and the preferred level of control (Shapiro et al., 1996).

Cultural factors also affect people's perception of control. Western, particularly U.S., culture emphasizes active control of yourself and mastery of your environment. Some other cultures emphasize adaptation—accepting yourself and circumstances (Shapiro et al., 1996).

Even for those who prefer to have more control, perceiving a lack of control doesn't always produce stress. This apparent contradiction is resolved by another factor: Many things that are beyond our control are at least predictable. You have no control over whether or not you take math quizzes (at least, not if you want to pass the course), but announced quizzes are likely to be less stressful than surprise quizzes. If quizzes are announced, you can relax on the days none are scheduled, but the custom of surprise quizzes means that the beginning of every class can be stressful as you wait to learn your fate. However, if the surprise quizzes are a frequent feature of the course, you would habituate to them and not view them to be as great a stressor—the quizzes, unpleasant as they might be, would no longer be so unpredictable.

On a larger stage, the effects of unpredictable events were illustrated during the bombing of London during World War II. In the early stages of the Luftwaffe campaign, bombs were dropped on London nightly (a predictable pattern). In contrast, the suburbs were bombed only periodically (an unpredictable pattern). Although you might think that getting bombed nightly would lead to a greater stress response, the

Coping: Taking a course of action regarding the stressor, its effects, or the person's reaction to it.

In England during World War II, the predictability of the Luftwaffe's bombings had an effect on the ulcer rates of the residents: Suburban dwellers who were bombed unpredictably but less frequently had more ulcers than Londoners who were bombed nightly.

suburban residents developed more ulcers than did the Londoners. Their periodic bombings were unpredictable, and therefore produced greater stress. However, after three months of bombing (nightly or sporadic), ulcer rates in both regions returned to normal as habituation occurred (Stewart & Winser, 1942). Similarly, there was an increase in reported gastric ulcers after the unexpected and devastating Kobe earthquake in Japan (Aoyama et al., 1998), and during the negotiations over Hong Kong's sovereignty prior to the end of British rule in 1997 (Lam et al., 1995), a time when the future was particularly uncertain.

Perceived lack of control in the face of a stressor can lead to the onset of *learned helplessness* (see Chapter 9). When animals cannot escape being shocked, they may respond with learned helplessness and depression. This is also true for humans who feel they have no control in an aversive situation. Another example of the importance of control and unpredictability is seen in the administration of pain medication. When postsurgery patients are allowed to determine when and how much pain medication they receive (through a pump connected to an IV by their beds), they give themselves less medication than when it is administered by a nurse they have called. Why is this? Because a patient who must ring for a nurse has little control of the situation *and* cannot predict what will happen—what the dosage will be, when the nurse will come, even if the nurse has heard the call. So the uncertainty and unpredictability of when the pain medication will come can heighten the experience of pain. When medication is self-regulated, predictability and control are restored, and the pain becomes more manageable (Chapman, 1989).

Although warning of an upcoming stressor can reduce the sensations of stress, vague information can make the stress worse. When Al heard that there were going to be unspecified changes at work, this vague information only served to increase his general level of stress response. This is the feeling Shakespeare's Macbeth had when, trying to unravel the three witches' mysterious prophecies, he remarked, "Present fears are less than horrible imaginings." But even specific warnings are not helpful if they come either too far in advance of or immediately before an event. When too far in advance, the information serves only to increase anticipation; when immediately before, there may be no time to put coping strategies to use (Sapolsky, 1997).

In general, perceived control is helpful only when you can see how much worse things could have been; then you can feel positive about what you have controlled. In the face of a catastrophic stressor, such as the diagnosis of a terminal illness, perceived control actually *increases* the stress: Things can't be much worse, and with perceived control the person diagnosed may feel responsible for the catastrophic stressor (Pitman et al., 1995; Sapolsky, 1997).

Researchers looking at the role of social class in the perception of control and health found that, not surprisingly, people with lower incomes perceived less control in their lives *and* were in poorer health. Those who did have a greater sense of control, regardless of income, had better health (Lachman & Weaver, 1998).

Conflict: The emotional predicament experienced when making difficult choices.

Approach–approach conflict: The internal predicament that occurs when competing alternatives are equally positive.

INTERNAL CONFLICT. Stress can be caused by internal **conflict**, the emotional predicament people experience when they make difficult choices. The choices may involve competing goals, actions, impulses, or situations. Miller (1959) categorized three types of conflict. **Approach–approach conflict** results when competing alternatives are equally positive. Although this kind of conflict can be stressful, it is not necessarily experienced as unpleasant because both options are pleasing. For instance, if you have to choose between two very good job offers and want both jobs about equally, you would be facing an approach–approach conflict. The contrary case is **avoidance–avoidance conflict,** which results when competing alternatives are equally unpleasant. In such circumstances, making a choice can be very stressful. Faced with the choices of either taking a job you really don't want or being unemployed (and needing to pay back college loans), you would experience an avoidance–avoidance conflict. The third type, **approach–avoidance conflict,** occurs when a possible course of action has both positive and negative aspects and thus encourages *both* approach *and* avoidance. When offered a job that you want, but that requires you to move to a city in which you don't want to live, you would experience approach–avoidance conflict.

LIFE'S HASSLES. In the 1960s, researchers began to explore the stressfulness of various life experiences. These investigations led to the idea that certain events, such as divorce or job loss, were stressful for almost everyone (Holmes & Rahe, 1967). What was perhaps more surprising was the finding that positive events, such as vacations and job promotions, could also be stressors. Subsequent research, however, has not shown these events, positive or negative, to be reliable predictors of stress-related illness. Because this line of research focused on the events themselves and not the *perception* of the events, it was not in fact a valid way to measure life's stressors. More recent work has focused on life's daily hassles, rather than major changes in life circumstances, as more predictive of distress and stress-related illnesses (Chamberlain & Zika, 1990; Tein et al., 2000).

All the daily hassles—the "little things" (and sometimes not so little but ongoing), such as concern about the health of someone in your family, having too many things to do, misplacing or losing things, trying to lose weight, and so on—add up to create stress. Those who report more daily hassles also report more psychological (Kanner et al., 1981) and physical symptoms (DeLongis et al., 1982), are more likely to have suppressed immune systems (Bosch et al., 1998; Martin & Dobbin, 1988), and have higher cholesterol levels (Twisk et al., 1999). Consider this study: Participants were asked to solve a three-dimensional puzzle within 8 minutes; the participants did not know that a full solution was impossible. They were then asked to explain to another person how to solve the puzzle. To increase the stressful nature of the task, the explanations had to be verbal only; they could not demonstrate with the puzzle pieces themselves or use gestures. Those participants who had experienced a high number of daily hassles over the previous 2 months were more likely to have suppression of their immune systems after the puzzle task than those who did not report a high number of daily stressors (Brosschot et al., 1994). Thus, experiencing frequent daily stressors can cause an encounter with a mild stressor, as represented by the puzzle task, to be experienced as more distressful and more apt to provoke a change in the immune system. Think what this means for the stress levels of the many people caring for an ill relative or friend, as occurs in nearly a quarter of American households (National Alliance for Caregiving and American Association of Retired Persons, 1997). The stress of such daily, long-term caretaking creates a risk of illness for the caregiver.

Interruptions are another feature of daily life that can be a stressor. Think how you feel when you're trying to study or write a paper and are repeatedly interrupted by phone calls or visitors. If your reaction is to feel more "stressed out," you're not alone. Interruptions during a mentally challenging task can be stressful enough to cause large increases in cortisol levels (Earle et al., 1999; Suarez et al., 1998).

Thus, what you perceive as a stressor depends on the amount and nature of stress you are already experiencing. If you have four tests, quizzes, essays, or papers due each week, a week with only two of these will seem less stressful. But if you've been lucky enough to take courses with only modest homework assignments, a week with two tests or quizzes can feel overwhelming. If you perceive the situation as an improvement, you will perceive the stimulus as less stressful than if you perceive things as getting worse (Sapolsky, 1997).

Avoidance–avoidance conflict: The internal predicament that occurs when competing alternatives are equally unpleasant.

Approach–avoidance conflict: The internal predicament that occurs when a course of action has both positive and negative aspects.

WORK-RELATED FACTORS. Work, like any other task or combination of tasks, can be a source of stress. Some work-related stressors are environmental: bad lighting, noise, crowding, and the demands of shift work (see Chapter 4). Other stressors relate to the job itself: the physical and mental workload, level of control of the job, and time pressure. Still other work-related stressors involve personality: People bring their personal characteristics to work with them, and some of these can create stress not just for the individuals, but for those who must interact with them.

Density is the number of people in a given space; *crowding* is the subjective experience created by density. As with many other potential stressors, crowding is perceived only if density is experienced in a particular way. You would not find crowding stressful if you have chosen to be in a crowded situation, such as a concert or a sporting event, and can easily leave it (Baron & Rodin, 1978). And if you grew up in the higher density of a city, you are less likely to feel crowded in a work setting whose density would cause a rural dweller to feel trapped like a sardine in a can (Zhou et al., 1998).

FIGURE 12.2
Closed and Open Office Plans

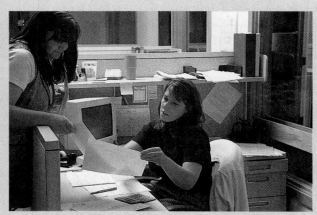

How office space is arranged can affect stress level. Traditional office layouts like the one on the left have the advantage of some privacy and less noise, but they use space inefficiently and can make communications within the organization difficult. The more modern layout on the right provides efficiency of space and communication, but neither privacy nor quiet.

The arrangement of work spaces can also cause stress. In a traditional "closed plan" office, the walls extend from floor to ceiling and employees work alone or in small groups in enclosed offices entered by a door (Figure 12.2, left). In an attempt to maximize available space and increase communication efficiency, a number of other work space configurations have been tried, many of which are "open plan" designs (see Figure 12.2, right). Open plans do not provide auditory or visual privacy, and noise made by the activities of other people cannot be avoided (Proctor & Van Zandt, 1994). Al's office changed from a closed plan to an open one. He now has no door, no window, no privacy. Those exposed to environmental noise for prolonged periods of time tend to perform more poorly, have higher blood pressure, and exhibit a lower tolerance for frustration (Cohen et al., 1986; Evans et al., 1998; Repetti, 1993); the inability to control exposure to noise is the most important predictor of negative effects of noise (Glass & Singer, 1972).

The job itself, of course, can be another source of stress. It isn't surprising that jobs entailing unrealistic deadlines, time pressure, responsibility for the safety of other workers, or a demanding workload can lead to stress, insomnia, and illness (Kalimo et al., 2000). In general, stressful jobs are ones that both are very demanding and allow the employee little control over how the demands of the job are met, such as a job on an assembly line. A study of English workers found that employees who feel they do not have much control over their jobs have a 50% higher risk of developing coronary heart disease than those who do have such a sense of control (Marmot, 1998). And those who feel that they work hard at their job but receive little in the way of recognition or promotion are twice as likely to develop coronary heart disease as those who feel they receive recognition or job advancement (Bosma et al., 1998). And of course being unemployed (not by choice) is a significant stressor, affecting health and well-being (Hamilton et al., 1993).

Air traffic controllers have an extremely stressful job. They are literally controlling the lives of millions of air travelers.

Jobs that require more work than you can do in the allotted time (*quantitative overload*) or work that you find too difficult because of a lack of training or ability (*qualitative overload*) can be stressors. Perhaps surprisingly, jobs that are too easy can also be stressors. This occurs when the work is not challenging enough, either because there is too little to do (*quantitative underload*) or because the work is understimulating (*qualitative underload*). Women whose jobs were characterized by quantitative overload and qualitative underload reported more anxiety, depression, and hostility than did women who had a more reasonable workload and who felt they had more control over their jobs (Williams et al., 1997).

Particularly stressful are jobs in which workers must make decisions that affect others, must keep others busy and happy, and, most notably, are responsible for others' lives (McLean, 1980). Air traffic controllers are a good example. A study of Canadian, New Zealander, and Singaporean air traffic controllers found some similarity about which elements of the job they found most stressful: working at peak traffic conditions; a fear of causing accidents; and equipment limitations. However, they did not always find the same aspects of the job equally stressful. Those in Western cultures were similar in viewing the general work environment as stressful, but those from a collectivist country (Singapore) reported stress from their fear of slowing down as a controller and from their relationships with local management (Shouksmith & Taylor, 1997). These cross-cultural differences highlight the interplay between the universality of the stress of being responsible for others' lives and the role that culture can play on what specific aspects of a job are perceived as stressors.

Chronic stressors on the job, physical and mental exhaustion, and a sense of little accomplishment add up to **burnout**. Employees with burnout feel tired all the time, often show symptoms of depression, and frequently feel trapped in the job and cynical about it. The likelihood of burnout is increased if the work role is ambiguous; the demands of the job lead to quantitative overload; social support is chronically lacking; a sense of ineffectiveness or lack of appreciation prevails; promotions are unlikely; and the job entails rigid rules that seem unfair. People who work for inconsiderate supervisors tend to have higher rates of burnout (Green et al., 1991; Seltzer & Numeroff, 1988). Jobs that require involvement and commitment to others (such as nursing or teaching) have a higher risk for employee burnout than jobs without those elements.

Personal characteristics as well as working conditions can contribute to burnout. Those who take their work more seriously than necessary, for example, and those in jobs requiring involvement with others who do not obtain satisfaction from this involvement are more likely to experience burnout. Although vacations help temporarily, burnout returns quickly when the person goes back to the same job with the same stressors (Westman & Eden, 1997). The remedy for burnout can be drastic—changing jobs or beginning a new career (Bernier, 1998)—but social support (Sand & Miyazaki, 2000) and outside interests can also help.

Burnout: A work-related state characterized by chronic stress, accompanied by physical and mental exhaustion and a sense of low accomplishment.

The workplace can be the battleground for several types of stress-inducing conflict:

▶ *Interdependence.* In order for most employees to get their jobs done, they must depend on others. But such interdependence means that if others don't do their jobs (or do them to your standards), you are affected. You have less control, and your own work is compromised.

▶ *Limited resources.* Because budgets impose limits, employees or departments may compete with one another to receive more of limited resources.

▶ *Personal conflicts.* Perhaps because you don't like another employee or another employee doesn't like you, or because of miscommunication or misunderstanding, tension can build up. Such conflict can be reduced by bargaining, by having a third party mediate the disagreement, and by creating goals that both parties must cooperate on to achieve (Paulus et al., 1996).

Employees rate poor communication, interdependence, a feeling of being treated unfairly, ambiguity of responsibility, and the poor use of criticism as the top five potential causes of workplace conflict (Baron, 1993).

Sometimes conflict at work can lead to violence, as seen in far too many news reports. When workplace violence erupts, typically an employee feels that a supervisor has been unfair in assigning raises, jobs, or promotions. Moreover, a dictatorial supervisor and very stressful working conditions also contribute to the likelihood of violence (Neuman & Baron, 1998). The likelihood of violence can be decreased by teaching and rewarding cooperative behavior, dealing with the causes of anger (Deffenbacher et al., 1996), and training supervisors to be sensitive to employees' experiences on the job (Baron, 1977).

HOSTILITY. Although some jobs and work (or home) environments may be more stressful than others, some people seem to experience stress more than others, regardless of their circumstances. Cardiologists Meyer Friedman and Ray Rosenman (1974) studied men who had coronary heart disease and discovered a common set of traits, including a sense of urgency, competitiveness, and interpersonal hostility. Friedman and Rosenman called this constellation of traits *Type A* personality. Subsequent research was unable to obtain the same clear-cut findings relating Type A personality and the incidence of coronary heart disease, but investigators were able to refine the concept of a stressed, heart disease–prone personality (Hecker et al., 1988). The most important component of the Type A personality in predicting heart disease was **hostility,** a trait characterized by mistrust, an expectation of harm and provocation by others, and a cynical attitude (Miller et al., 1996; Williams et al., 2000). For instance, Barefoot and his colleagues (1983) found that medical students who scored in the top 20% on a hostility scale were more than four times as likely to develop heart disease 25 years later than their low-hostility colleagues. Those same high-hostility doctors were seven times more likely to die of any cause by age 50 than their low-hostility colleagues. Further research (Barefoot et al., 1989) found that, among lawyers, increased mortality was associated with an untrusting and cynical view of people, repeated negative emotions in personal interactions, and recurrent expressions of overt anger and aggression in the face of difficulties or frustrations.

Men are generally more hostile than women (Miller et al., 1999; Räikkönen et al., 1999), and researchers found that even at the same level of hostility, men's blood pressure is more affected by their hostility than women's (Räikkönen et al., 1999). When interrupted while concentrating on a task, highly hostile men had elevated heart rates, blood pressure, and cortisol production, as well as other physiological changes associated with a negative mood such as anger (Suarez et al., 1998). Regardless of sex, people high in hostility are more likely to have a higher heart rate and blood pressure throughout the day, no matter what their mood. In contrast, people low in hostility had cardiac changes only when they were in a negative mood (Davis et al., 2000; Räikkönen et al., 1999).

Hostility: The personality trait associated with heart disease, characterized by mistrust, an expectation of harm and provocation by others, and a cynical attitude.

Hostility need not be a lifelong trait. Cognitive and behavioral programs designed to help reduce anger levels (see Chapter 14) can reduce not only the trait of hostility (Beck & Fernandez, 1998) but also anger-related physiological arousal and blood pressure increases (Gidron et al., 1999); these changes were generally maintained 1 year after the end of a 5-week program (Deffenbacher et al., 1996).

The once-popular idea that it is better, or healthier, to "vent" your anger so that it "drains away" is not only false, but the opposite is true: Venting your anger is more likely to keep you angry and make your behavior toward others more aggressive. A study by Bushman and his colleagues (1999) illustrates how the expression of anger begets more anger. Participants were divided into two groups. One group, called the *procatharsis* group (*catharsis* comes from a Greek word that means "a cleansing") read about a study that found that venting anger *decreased* anger. The second group, the *anticatharsis* group, read about a study that showed the opposite, that venting anger *increased* anger. All participants were then asked to write a one-paragraph essay about abortion, taking whatever position they wanted, and were told that each essay would be read by a participant. Although the essays were not in fact read, the participants received written negative comments about their essays that were designed to make them angry.

Some participants in each group were then asked, among other things, to hit a punching bag while the others were asked just to sit for 2 minutes. Bushman and colleagues then asked participants to compete in pairs on a reaction time test, each participant trying to press a button as fast as possible after hearing a signal. The winning participants could select how loud and for how long an obnoxious noise would sound when their opponents lost.

Researchers found that those participants exposed to the message that venting anger is good were more likely to be aggressive toward another person, as measured by the loudness and duration of the obnoxious sound they imposed on their partners, compared with those who received either the anticatharsis message or no message (control group). Moreover, those who were in the group that hit a punching bag were more likely to be aggressive against their opponents in the reaction time test than those who simply sat still for 2 minutes. This part of the study demonstrated that venting anger leads to more anger and aggression. The study also showed the influence of culture: In an environment that encourages the venting of anger, people are more likely to be aggressive against others. But even if people believe that venting anger will lower their anger levels, that doesn't happen; the expression of anger makes them more likely to act aggressively and maintain their anger.

Road rage is a way of expressing anger and frustration. However, research shows that directly venting anger in this way may actually heighten people's anger, not reduce it.

LOOKING AT LEVELS

The Hostile Heart

Hostile people, as measured in many studies by a self-report paper-and-pencil test or by a structured interview, are more likely than nonhostile people to experience stress in social situations—that is, they perceive stressors in situations in which those who are not hostile do not perceive stressors (level of the person). Hostile and nonhostile people do not have different levels of stress hormones or blood pressure when experiencing a nonsocial stressor such as figuring out a math problem (Sallis et al., 1987). Yet when they are asked to play a role that involves confrontation with another person, such as asking an acquaintance to repay a small loan (level of the group), those who were more hostile had a greater sympathetic nervous system response (level of the brain), as evidenced by higher levels of epinephrine and norepinephrine and

higher blood pressure (Hardy & Smith, 1988). Similar physiological results were found when participants were interrupted while trying to solve a puzzle (Suarez & Williams, 1989). Social stressors such as these did not elevate the stress response in nonhostile people.

The way life's little social stressors become large stressors for hostile people can be seen as an interaction of events at the levels of the group, person, and brain. Social stressors, which by definition are events at the level of the group, are influenced by hostility, a characteristic at the level of the person. Specifically, the way hostile people perceive of and think about other people affects their physiological responses to social stimuli (level of the brain). Moreover, changing events at one level of analysis (decreasing behaviors associated with hostility—level of the person) can affect events at other levels. In this case, the changed behaviors result in a decreased risk of a subsequent heart attack (which in turn affects the functioning of the brain; Friedman et al., 1986) and a different pattern of interaction with people (level of the group).

CONSOLIDATE!

▶ *1. What exactly is stress?* Stress is the general term describing the psychological and bodily response to a stimulus that alters equilibrium. A stressor is a stimulus that throws the body's equilibrium out of balance. Stressors can be acute or chronic in duration, and physical, "psychological," or social in nature.

▶ *2. What is the physiology of stress?* The stress response consists of physiological changes in the sympathetic and parasympathetic nervous systems that prepare the body for physical effort and repair of injury. These include changes in heart and respiration rates and the release of epinephrine, norepinephrine, and glucocorticoids. These changes occur during the alarm phase of the general adaptation syndrome. If the stressor continues, the body tries to return to homeostasis in the adaptation (resistance) phase. During the exhaustion phase, the stress response itself begins to cause damage, leading to stress-related diseases.

▶ *3. What are common sources of stress?* The perception of whether a stimulus is a stressor is critical in determining if a given stimulus will lead to a stress response; this is often called primary appraisal. Certain factors likely to lead to a stress response include a lack of perceived control, unpredictability, internal conflict, and daily hassles. Environmental factors of crowding and noise can cause work-related stress. Work that is too challenging or not challenging enough can cause stress, as can having too much or too little to do at work. Jobs that do not allow a worker a sense of control over how the work is done, and jobs that include responsibility for the welfare of others can be particularly stressful. Work-related conflict can also cause stress. Some people are more stress-prone than others: Hostile people are more likely than others to view social situations as stressors.

STRESS, DISEASE, AND HEALTH

Al was clearly experiencing a great deal of stress, and his being sick so often made matters worse. He'd had to miss work some days, which didn't help his sense of control in his difficult situation at work. Sometimes he'd cough so much he would have trouble sleeping, and then he'd lie awake worrying that he had lung cancer. He had started smoking again, after having quit 5 years before, so it was hard to know whether the more frequent colds and coughs were from the cigarettes or from the stress of work. He'd been having a few more drinks than usual, and he wasn't getting any exercise; he worried that if he started exercising, he'd bring on a heart attack. In short, Al wasn't doing very well, and he knew it.

The stress response is a good thing, very useful when the stressor is acute, such as the physical danger of a piece of glass in the foot; but there can be too much of a good thing. Too strong a stress response for too long a time can lead to stress-related illnesses.

1. Can stress affect the immune system and make illness more likely?
2. Are stress and cancer related?
3. Can stress cause a heart attack or heart disease?
4. Can problematic health-related behaviors be changed?

The Immune System: Catching Cold

It is now established that stress can affect the immune system, which functions to defend the body against infection. Critical to the immune system are two classes of white blood cells: **B cells,** which mature in the bone marrow, and **T cells,** which mature in the thymus, an organ located in the chest. One type of T cell is the **natural killer (NK) cell,** which detects and destroys damaged or altered cells, such as precancerous cells, before they become tumors. Glucocorticoids, which are released when the stress response is triggered, hinder the formation of some white blood cells (including NK cells) or kill white blood cells (Cohen & Herbert, 1996; McEwen et al., 1997), making the body more vulnerable to infection and tumor growth. For this reason, many studies investigating the relationship between stress and the immune system look at the number of circulating white blood cells, such as NK cells. People who exhibit greater sympathetic nervous system responses to stress also show the most changes in immune system functioning (Bachen et al., 1995; Manuck et al., 1991), indicating that changes in the immune system are moderated by changes in the sympathetic nervous system.

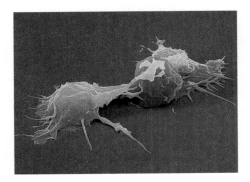

The immune system's job is to fend off infectious agents such as viruses, tumors, and precancerous cells. The release of glucocorticoids (as occurs during stress) suppresses the functioning of the immune system, making it more difficult to fight the invader and leaving the body more vulnerable to infection. This photo shows two natural killer (NK) cells (yellow) attacking a leukemia cell (red). The NK cells have made contact and are beginning to engulf and destroy the leukemia cell.

Even day-to-day events and stresses, such as taking exams (Kiecolt-Glaser et al., 1986), can affect functioning of the immune system (Stone et al., 1994). As noted in Chapter 1, a study looking at the relationship between stress and catching a cold found that the more stress a participant reported before exposure to a cold virus, the more likely he or she was to catch a cold (Cohen et al., 1991). The aspects of stress that best predicted whether participants would get a cold were how uncontrollable and unpredictable they rated their lives to be and how likely they were to experience negative feelings (such as guilt, anger, and being upset) (Cohen et al., 1993). How do we reconcile such findings with preventative measures such as those shown in Figure 12.3?

Because stress can impair the functioning of the white blood cells, it can play a role in the length of time it takes a wound to heal: The wounds of women who experienced a high level of stress by caring for a relative with Alzheimer's disease took 9 days longer to heal than those of women of similar age and economic status who were not engaged in such caretaking (Kiecolt-Glaser et al., 1995). In another study, dental student participants received slight mouth wounds on two different occasions (3 days before a major test and during summer vacation). The wounds given before exams when, presumably, the students were experiencing more stressors, took 40% longer to heal (Marucha et al., 1998).

FIGURE 12.3
Old Wives' Tales and Colds

Misguided or not, every morning, Thomas Jefferson soaked his feet in cold water in an effort to ward off colds (Seuling, 1978). Could such a regimen work? On what factors would it depend?

Traumatic events, such as experiencing the devastation of a hurricane, can affect the immune system, as well as produce psychological symptoms such as anxiety and depression.

Major stressors such as natural disasters (devastating earthquakes and hurricanes) or victimization (being robbed or raped) can affect the immune system. Among people living in Florida neighborhoods damaged by Hurricane Andrew in 1992, the victims who perceived their losses to be most severe experienced the most changes in NK cells (Ironson et al., 1997). But not everyone who is exposed to trauma responds the same way physiologically. Some survivors later (sometimes considerably later) experience *posttraumatic stress disorder (PTSD)*, a psychological disorder characterized by an involuntary reexperiencing of the trauma through unwanted thoughts, sensations, and dreams, heightened physiological arousal, and an avoidance of anything associated with the trauma. (A further discussion of PTSD appears in Chapter 13.)

In general, trauma survivors who had higher heart rates immediately after the trauma were the ones more likely to develop posttraumatic stress disorder (Yehuda et al., 1998). Moreover, those who did develop posttraumatic stress disorder often had a physiological hyperresponsivity or hyperarousal to stimuli similar to those present during the trauma (Casada et al., 1998; Keane et al., 1998). Thus, for example, survivors of Hurricane Andrew who have posttraumatic stress disorder are more likely to experience a large stress response on a windy day compared with people who have never experienced a severe hurricane. Even when not in the presence of such stimuli, those who go on to develop posttraumatic stress disorder are generally more physiologically reactive (Cohen, Kotler et al., 1998).

Cancer

Although stress can't cause cancer, there is evidence that it can affect the growth of some cancerous tumors. How can this happen? First, if the immune system is suppressed, NK cells do not work as well to prevent the spread of tumor cells. Levy and her colleagues (Levy et al., 1985, 1987, 1988) found a relationship among the perception of inadequate social support, feelings of distress and fatigue with little joy, and lower NK cell activity levels. Such negative psychological experiences, by weakening the immune system, left people more vulnerable to the growth of cancerous tumors. Locke and colleagues (1984) found similar results.

A second way that stress can affect tumor growth is by facilitating the growth of capillaries feeding into the tumor. If the stressor is an injury or infection (such as would be caused by glass in the foot), capillary growth is beneficial because the vessels would carry more blood, and hence more white blood cells, to the part of the body that needs it. However, if a tumor is already present in the body, the stress response will cause more blood to be supplied to the tumor, literally feeding it and supporting its growth. Stress does not appear to *cause* a tumor to develop, only to assist in its growth.

The perception of control can also play a role in the progression of some types of cancer. Among cancer patients, those who did not perceive much control and felt helpless about their cancer were likely to have a recurrence sooner and die earlier from the cancer (Andersen et al., 1994; Watson et al., 1991).

Although psychological factors can affect the immune system, these findings should be interpreted with caution. The type of cancer, and biological factors related to cancer progression, can outweigh psychological factors in tumor growth (Compas et al., 1998; Grossarth-Maticek et al., 2000), especially in the final stages of the disease (Cohen & Herbert, 1996). Moreover, some people may be genetically endowed with an immune system more likely to ward off illness. Data on twins reared together and apart suggest that, on average, identical twins have more key antibodies in common (seven out of a possible nine) than fraternal twins (four out of a possible nine) (Kohler et al., 1985).

Heart Disease

The increased blood pressure created by stress, in combination with the hormonally induced narrowing of the arteries, promotes plaque buildup, or **atherosclerosis,** in the arteries (Figure 12.4). As plaque, or fatty deposits on the insides of the artery walls, accumulates, the arteries narrow so the heart has to work even harder to meet the body's need for blood and oxygen. Working harder means pumping the blood with more power, creating more damage to the arteries, and a vicious cycle is created. This chronic wear and tear on the cardiovascular system can lead to heart damage, which can lead to sudden death from inadequate blood supply to the heart muscle or from irregular electrical firing of the muscle, preventing coordinated heartbeats. For someone who already has heart disease, even extremely positive states of stress, such as joy or orgasm, can precipitate these demands on the heart and cause sudden death.

The course of heart disease can be affected by a change in lifestyle. A study of people with severe coronary heart disease found that intensive changes in diet, exercise, stress management (such as meditation), and social support made a difference not only in halting the narrowing of the arteries, but also in reversing the atherosclerosis, as well as in minimizing further damage to the heart (Ornish et al., 1998).

Depression appears to be a stressor that increases the likelihood of heart disease. People with depression have a faster heartbeat even when at rest (Moser et al., 1998) and tend to have high blood pressure (Carney et al., 1999). It isn't surprising, then, that those who have had an episode of depression have a higher risk of developing heart problems, and once having had a heart attack, those who are depressed are more likely to have further health problems (Frasure-Smith et al., 1999). When the depression is treated, however, these stress-related responses subside, and heart rate and blood pressure decrease (Kolata, 1997).

FIGURE 12.4
Stress on the Arteries

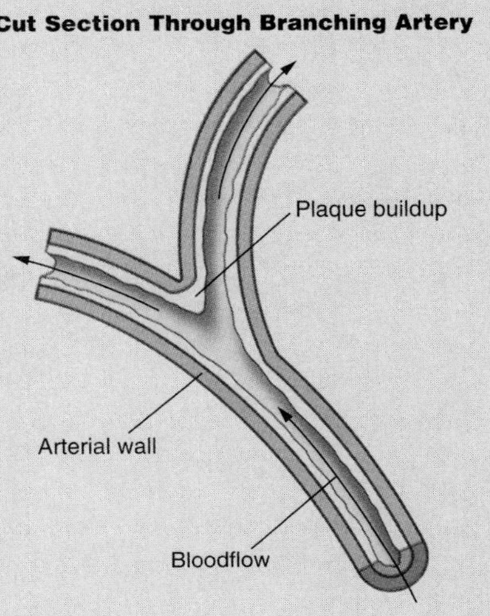

Cut Section Through Branching Artery

Plaque buildup

Arterial wall

Bloodflow

Each time a stressor causes an increase in blood pressure, the branching points of arteries are at risk for damage. The hormones released during the fight-or-flight response also cause blood vessels to constrict, which has the net effect of making blood pressure increase even more. Thus, if someone experiences frequent stressors, his or her blood vessels take a pounding. With each stressed heartbeat, blood pounds against the same spot, wearing away some of the lining, creating a place for plaque to attach itself to the artery wall. Once this occurs, the artery gets narrower and narrower (as plaque builds and builds). This atherosclerosis makes the work of pumping blood through the body even harder for the heart.

Changing Health-Impairing Behaviors

Stress can also have an indirect, though no less serious, effect on health. In attempting to cope with stressors, people may engage in self-destructive behaviors such as overeating, smoking, or having one drink too many (Steptoe et al., 1998). Often, our estimations of long-term risks are not very accurate, at least not in relation to ourselves (see Chapters 7 and 11). We may see ourselves as "invulnerable" and underestimate the risks of such behaviors (Weinstein, 1984, 1993). Thus, although people may know the statistics of health problems for a variety of unhealthy behaviors, often they don't think it could happen to them.

Many Americans regularly engage in some sort of self-destructive behavior, such as smoking, drug use, overeating, and unsafe sex. Changing the problematic behavior

Atherosclerosis: A medical condition characterized by plaque buildup in the arteries.

pattern can be difficult, as most smokers have learned when they try to quit and have to make several attempts at quitting before they are successful.

Some programs that target unhealthy behaviors such as smoking, drinking, and overeating look at progress as either–or: Participants either change their behavior or they continue it; they either quit or they don't quit. Based on extensive research, Prochaska and his colleagues (Prochaska, Norcross et al., 1994) have proposed a different model of change, with five stages:

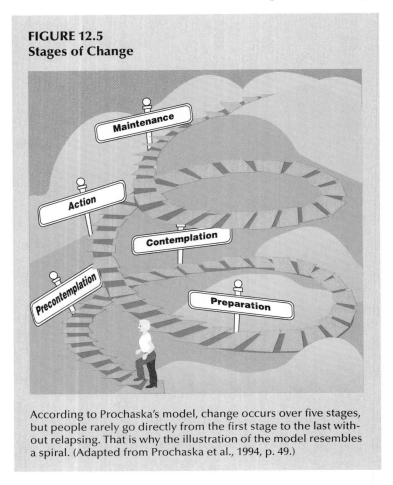

FIGURE 12.5
Stages of Change

According to Prochaska's model, change occurs over five stages, but people rarely go directly from the first stage to the last without relapsing. That is why the illustration of the model resembles a spiral. (Adapted from Prochaska et al., 1994, p. 49.)

Precontemplation: The person has no intention of changing the problematic behavior and will often deny that there is a problem. He or she may change temporarily if a lot of pressure is applied by others but will relapse once that pressure is removed.

Contemplation: The person acknowledges that there is a problem and may even begin to think about doing something about it. Real action, though, is seen as far in the future, not in the present. It is easy for people to get stuck in this phase.

Preparation: The person has a plan of action to change, makes adjustments to the plan, and intends to begin changing within a month, making a specific commitment to change. However, some people in this stage still have mixed feelings about change and may not begin to change when they intended, leading to a relapse to an earlier stage. People in this stage are very aware of the problem, its causes, and possible solutions.

Action: This is the stage most obvious to others because people in this stage change their behaviors and their environments. People in this stage also receive the most support.

Maintenance: The person in this stage is consolidating the gains made and has an eye on relapse prevention. Without a strong commitment to maintenance, relapse to the first or second stage is likely. Friends and family may be less supportive because action has already been taken, but because people in this stage are still vulnerable to relapsing, support is still important.

Prochaska's model proposes that, in reality, most people go through stages of change, each stage having its own tasks people must complete in order to progress to the next. Moreover, progress is not necessarily constant, and people may relapse to an earlier stage before resuming forward movement (see Figure 12.5). This model of change has been applied to a variety of problematic behaviors: stopping harmful behaviors such as smoking, drinking, drug use, or overeating, and starting healthful behaviors such as condom use, sunscreen use, exercise, or mammography screening (Prochaska, Velicer, et al., 1994).

If you have a behavior you'd like to change, take this test to find out which stage of change you are in:

	YES	NO
1. I solved my problem more than 6 months ago.	☐	☐
2. I have taken action on my problem within the past 6 months.	☐	☐
3. I intend to take action in the next month.	☐	☐
4. I intend to take action in the next 6 months.	☐	☐

If you answered no to all four questions, you are in the precontemplation stage. If you answered yes only to question 4, you are in the contemplation stage. If you answered yes to questions 3 and 4, you are in the preparation stage. If you answered yes to question 2, but not to question 1, you are in the action stage. If you answered yes to question 1—honestly—then you are in the maintenance phase (from Prochaska, Norcross et al., 1994, p. 68).

A number of different processes or interventions may help people move from one stage of change to another. For those in the earliest stages, one important process is *consciousness raising*, or developing an awareness of both the problem and the way the person avoids addressing it. Al's view of his smoking and drinking was that they would take care of themselves when his work problems were resolved, so he didn't feel that he had to *do* anything about them. Another helpful process in moving people along from an early stage of change to the next is *social liberation*: external forces that help create more alternatives to the behavior and provide both information about the problematic behavior and support. This process addresses the level of the group. Social liberation is imposed on Al at work, where he can't smoke because the office is smoke-free. The hours he can smoke each day are limited because he has to leave the building to have a cigarette. This also makes the act of smoking less convenient, less comfortable, and less pleasurable.

In the move from contemplation through preparation toward action, two other processes are helpful: emotional arousal and self-reevaluation. *Emotional arousal* is focused awareness and emotion directed toward change. Al experienced emotional arousal when he realized that his body was a wreck and he couldn't go on this way. *Self-reevaluation* is taking stock, both emotionally and intellectually, and addressing the question of whether engaging in the problematic behavior is what you really want to be doing—whether it really reflects the person you want to be. Often, part of this reevaluation is weighing the pros and cons of changing or maintaining the behavior.

These lists of pros and cons can be useful for identifying stages of change. The pros of changing the problematic behavior usually increase between the precontemplation and the contemplation stages, and the cons of changing the behavior usually decrease between the contemplation and the action stages. From precontemplation to preparation, the pros often go up twice as much as the cons go down; what's happening is that as you get ready to act, you realize there are more reasons to change the behavior. Thus, interventions for people in the precontemplation stage should focus on the pros of changing the behavior (for Al, focusing on the advantages of quitting smoking). For those in the contemplation stage, interventions should focus on decreasing the cons of changing the problematic behavior (Herzog et al., 1999; Prochaska, Velicer et al., 1994). For Al, this would mean questioning the reasons to keep smoking—are those reasons still as appropriate as they had been? In the terms of internal conflict discussed earlier, the "approach" desires begin to clearly outweigh the "avoidance" desires, and the scale of conflict tips toward change.

Going from the action stage to the maintenance stage is facilitated by many operant conditioning techniques such as reward, stimulus control, and *countering*, the substitution of healthier behaviors for the problem behaviors. Thus, as Al becomes more motivated to change his smoking habit, he can reward himself for not buying cigarettes, or for days or hours spent without smoking, with a healthier indulgence such as buying an intriguing paperback or a music CD; he can substitute pulling out a cigarette, lighting up, and puffing away with taking a walk around the block. Relationships can also be helpful in providing physical, emotional, and moral support in the effort to change the behavior.

Most people who are actively trying to change a problematic behavior or maintain a healthier alternative behavior have an occasional lapse, once or twice engaging in the old behavior. This is distinct from a *relapse*, a regular pattern of engaging again in the problematic behavior. The hard reality is that for many harmful behaviors, relapse is common. For example, only 5% of smokers who contemplate quitting make it through the stages of change over 2 years without a relapse (Prochaska, Velicer, et al., 1994).

Breast Cancer Support Groups

Knowing that stress can affect the immune system and the progression of cancerous tumors, we can examine the results of a study of the effectiveness of breast cancer support groups from the different levels of analysis. Spiegel, Bloom and colleagues (1989) conducted a study of 86 women with breast cancer that had spread to other parts of their bodies. All the women received treatment for the cancer, and 50% were assigned to a yearlong weekly breast cancer support group. The goal of the group was to improve the women's quality of life—to help them live "as fully as possible," communicate better with others, control pain, and master concerns about death. They were taught self-hypnosis for pain management but were not encouraged to think that their participation in the group would make them live longer. An unanticipated finding was that women in the support group survived twice as long as those who were not in the support group. How can a support group make such a difference? Although the exact mechanisms are not yet known, we can understand this remarkable phenomenon by looking at events at the levels of brain, person, and group. At the level of the brain, social support lowers stress, which in turn boosts immune functioning, including NK cell activity levels. In fact, these women had higher NK cell activity than the women in the control group. At the level of the person, Spiegel and his colleagues propose that the skills learned in the support group, such as pain management, may have increased interest in eating and decreased pain-related depressive symptoms, thereby elevating the immune system. This, in turn, encouraged better self-care and helped to eliminate feelings of hopelessness and perceived lack of control. The support group also may have motivated the women to comply more rigorously with their treatments and provided a sense of community (level of the group), decreasing isolation.

More recent research on the role of the support group for breast cancer patients has found that women who were not in a support group (as compared with women who were) were more likely either to tolerate chemotherapy poorly or to refuse that treatment entirely. Moreover, those who were not in a support group had higher levels of cortisol 4 to 8 months after their surgery and were more depressed than those who were in a support group (Kass, 1999). Events at the three levels interact: The more the breast cancer patients could control their pain and side effects, alleviate their depression, and feel less isolated, the more likely their immune systems were to increase functioning. And the better they felt about the group, the more enthusiastically and faithfully they participated in it.

CONSOLIDATE!

▶ **1. Can stress affect the immune system and make illness more likely?** Yes. Stress increases the production of glucocorticoids, which can depress the immune system, including the formation and functioning of white blood cells such as natural killer (NK) cells. This makes the body more vulnerable to infection, tumor growth, and slowed healing.

▶ **2. Are stress and cancer related?** Although stress does not cause tumors to develop, increased glucocorticoid production (part of the stress response) can depress the level of tumor-fighting cells, such as natural killer cells, and can increase capillary growth that provides a blood supply to nourish a tumor. Conversely, decreasing the stress response leads to an increase in natural killer cells' ability to fight tumors. However, not all cancers are equally responsive to psychological stressors or their absence.

▶ **3. Can stress cause a heart attack or heart disease?** The stress response causes blood pressure to increase and the arteries to narrow. These two events can promote atherosclerosis, the buildup of plaque. This requires the heart to work even harder to supply blood to the body and can lead to coronary heart disease. The course of heart disease can be affected by psychological and social factors, such as stress management and social support.

(continued)

CONSOLIDATE! *continued*

▶ *4. Can problematic health-related behaviors be changed?* Although people do not necessarily stop health-impairing behaviors overnight, problematic behaviors that are associated with poor health, such as smoking, drinking, and overeating, can be changed.

Research shows that most people progress through stages of change, not uncommonly relapsing to earlier stages. Different processes or interventions can help people progress from one stage to the next.

STRATEGIES FOR COPING

Once the realization that he was truly in bad shape sank in, Al finally recognized that he needed to take action. He looked around the office to see how other people were doing, how they were handling the stress of the difficult situation at work. He paid particular attention to Maya, who didn't seem ruffled by the unsettled atmosphere and the layoffs. Al was puzzled by her reaction, or apparent lack thereof, and he talked with Lisa about it. Lisa suggested that perhaps Maya had particularly effective ways of dealing with stress. She pointed out that the perception of stress depends not only on your view of a situation, but also on the conscious actions you take in response to the stressors. *Coping* is the inclusive term for the multitude of techniques that people employ to handle stress. Some of these may "come naturally," resulting from temperament; others can be learned.

▶ 1. What are the different types of coping strategies?

▶ 2. Are some people better equipped than others to handle stress?

▶ 3. How do relationships affect stress and health?

▶ 4. What are mind–body interventions?

▶ 5. Do gender and culture play a role in coping?

Coping Strategies: Approaches and Tactics

Different people tend to use different coping strategies, and the use of a particular strategy may also depend on the situation. People may be born with a propensity to use certain strategies, and they can learn to use others.

PROBLEM-FOCUSED AND EMOTION-FOCUSED COPING. One way to classify coping strategies is by considering whether they address internal or external circumstances (Carver et al., 1989). **Problem-focused coping** strategies alter either the environment itself or the way in which the person and the environment interact (see Table 12.2 on page 450). This type of coping is more common when people believe that their actions can affect the stressor, and it tends to be used by people with a high score on the Big Five personality factor conscientiousness (see Chapter 10; Watson & Hubbard, 1996). In contrast, **emotion-focused coping** strategies change a person's emotional response to the stressor (see Table 12.2). This type of coping usually decreases arousal. People are more likely to adopt emotion-focused coping when they do not think their actions can affect the stressor itself and so they must alter their perception of, or response to, the stressor.

Typically, people use more than one strategy in response to a given stressor. Whether a particular strategy is effective depends in part on whether a person is correct in assessing whether the environment can in fact be changed. For example, suppose Lisa assumes that if she gets straight A's in the spring term, she can probably get a scholarship to cover next year's tuition. Here she is approaching the need to pay for

Problem-focused coping: Coping focused on changing the environment itself, or how the person interacts with the environment.

Emotion-focused coping: Coping focused on changing the person's emotional response to the stressor.

TABLE 12.2

Problem-Focused and Emotion-Focused Coping Strategies

Source: *Adapted from Carver et al. (1989).*

STRATEGY	DESCRIPTION
Problem-Focused Strategies	
Active coping	Actively tries to remove or work around stressor, or to ameliorate its effects.
Planning	Thinks about how to manage stressor.
Instrumental social support	Seeks advice, assistance, information.
Suppression of competing activities	Puts other activities on hold in order to cope with stressor.
Restraint coping	Waits to act until the appropriate time.
Emotion-Focused Strategies	
Emotional social support	Gets moral support, sympathy, understanding from others.
Venting emotions	Focuses on and talks about distressing feelings.
Positive reinterpretation/growth	Reinterprets the situation in a positive way.
Behavioral disengagement	Reduces efforts to deal with the stressor (as occurs with learned helplessness).
Mental disengagement	Turns to other activities to distract attention from the stressor.

her education with the problem-focused coping strategy of planning: She is coping with a stressor by thinking about how to manage it (see Table 12.2). She works hard all spring and carefully rations her social time. Lisa is using two problem-focused strategies: active coping and suppression of competing activities. What Lisa doesn't know, however, is that the financial aid office has already awarded all of next year's scholarships before the end of the spring term, so her efforts for top grades do not help her achieve her goal of a scholarship. As this example demonstrates, although it is adaptive to try to exert problem-focused coping in the face of stressors, such a strategy is effective only when applied to factors that are controllable. Accurate information and appraisal are important to determine if this is the case.

The coping strategies people use are affected by the level of stressors in their lives: The more stressors they face, the more people are likely to use avoidance coping strategies such as distraction, or behavioral or mental disengagement, which aim to decrease the focus on the stressor and increase the focus on other matters (Ingledew et al., 1997). In *behavioral disengagement*, people reduce their efforts to deal actively with the stressor (Table 12.2). In its extreme form, this disengagement can lead to a sense of helplessness. In *mental disengagement*, people turn to other activities to distract their attention from the stressor. So, the more stressors Al and Lisa have, the less likely they are to cope actively with them. Studies (with male participants) have indicated that those perceiving less control over events are less likely to use problem-focused coping strategies involving direct action and more likely to use emotion-focused strategies such as distraction and emotional support (David & Suls, 1999). If Al doesn't think anything he does at work ultimately affects whether he gets laid off, he is less likely to use active coping strategies.

Another type of emotion-focused coping is *venting* (see Table 12.2)—that is, focusing on and talking about the stressor. As noted earlier, venting anger does not help. But what about venting other emotions? Pennebaker (1989) asked a group of college students to write for 20 minutes a day for 4 consecutive days; they were told their writing samples would remain confidential. He gave half of them, referred to as the "emotional expressiveness" group, the following instructions:

During each of the 4 writing days, I want you to write about the most traumatic and upsetting experiences of your whole life. You can write on different topics each day or on the same topic for all 4 days. The important thing is that you write about your deepest thoughts and feelings. Ideally, whatever you write about should deal with an event or experience that you have not talked about with others in detail.

Another group, serving as a control, was asked to write each day about superficial topics. In this study and other variants of it, students who were asked to write about an emotional topic were more likely to report negative moods immediately after writing, although their overall moods were more positive by the end of the school year (Pennebaker et al., 1990). Perhaps paradoxically, those who wrote about traumatic events were less likely to get sick (as measured by visits to the student health center) in the months following the expressive writing. Other studies asking medical students and first-year college students to write either about traumatic experiences or about the transition from high school to college had similar results (Pennebaker & Francis, 1996; Pennebaker et al., 1990), with the additional finding of enhanced immune function (Petrie et al., 1995, 1998). Written emotional expression among university employees was associated with decreased absenteeism from work (Francis & Pennebaker, 1992). Studies using expressive writing with people with asthma and rheumatoid arthritis found comparable results: Four months after writing, patients underwent a positive change in their health, as compared with patients who wrote about superficial matters (Smyth et al., 1999). It appears, however, that writing only briefly, say just a 3-minute outline of a traumatic experience, isn't enough emotional expression to derive the benefits; the participants must actively process their experiences by writing about them in detail (Páez et al., 1999). These studies suggest that focusing on and venting feelings about a traumatic experience has positive effects, although it may take a while for these effects to appear. "Venting" need not mean that internal "pressure" is released, as Freud believed. Rather this process could simply help a person come to terms with an emotion—to make sense of and make peace with emotional events.

THOUGHT SUPPRESSION. Purposefully trying not to think about something emotionally arousing or distressing is **thought suppression** (Wegner et al., 1987). Suppose Al and Lisa used thought suppression. They would try not to think about Al's work situation and all that depended on it. However, research has shown that trying *not* to think about something can have the paradoxical effect of causing that "suppressed" thought to pop into consciousness more than not trying to suppress it. This phenomenon is referred to as a *rebound effect.* Research on the application of thought suppression to health and illness has shown that the act of suppressing emotional thoughts actually magnifies both the intensity of the thoughts and the physiological reactions to those thoughts (Clark et al., 1991; Wegner et al., 1987). Attempts at suppressing thoughts that are emotionally charged (either positive or negative) have also been associated with changes in the sympathetic nervous system (Gross & Levenson, 1997).

Pennebaker and colleagues (Petrie et al., 1998) examined the effects of both emotional expressiveness and thought suppression. Their study began in the usual way by dividing the participants, in this case medical students, into two groups: an "emotional expressiveness" group and a control group. They asked the emotional expressiveness group to write about a stressful event and the control group to write about something superficial. However, after spending 15 minutes writing, half the students in each group were then asked to try to put what they had written out of their minds. The other half of each group was asked to focus exclusively on what they had written. The study found that thought suppression led to decreases in some aspects of immune functioning. In addition, the investigators again found that emotional expression boosted aspects of immune functioning, even months after the experiment; moreover, those who had written about a stressful event viewed the study as having had more of a positive impact in their lives, and as more meaningful, than did the control group, regardless of whether they were asked to use thought

Thought suppression: The coping strategy that involves purposefully trying not to think about something emotionally arousing or distressing.

suppression. These results, along with those of similar studies, point to the positive effects of emotional expression on the immune system (Futterman et al., 1992; Pennebaker, 1993).

SHORT-TERM AND LONG-TERM STRATEGIES.

The effectiveness of a given coping strategy depends on whether you look at the short-term benefits or the long-term benefits (Suls & Fletcher, 1985). Avoidant strategies (those that attempt to avoid the stressor, such as mental disengagement) may work better in the short term, but nonavoidant strategies, which focus on the stressor, lead to better long-term results in handling a chronic stressor. This was clear from the results of a classic study of parents whose children were dying of cancer. Some of these parents had high levels of glucocorticoids, which are known to be a bodily response to stress, but other parents had hormone levels that were within the normal range. How could this be? Wolff and colleagues (1964) tried to find out what coping strategies were used by the parents with normal stress hormone levels. They found several factors that moderated the experience of stress. First, parents who brought their religious beliefs to bear on this difficult situation experienced less stress: Those who, for example, felt that they had been chosen by God to handle the task of having a sick child showed lower levels of stress. This type of coping strategy, in which events are recast in a more positive light, is called *positive reinterpretation*. Second, those parents who displaced their worry onto something less threatening than their child's impending death exhibited fewer signs of stress: For instance, those who worried about leaving their child's bedside for fear the child might be lonely had lower glucocorticoid levels than those who worried about leaving for fear their child would die while they were gone. When the cancer was in remission, those parents who denied the likelihood of their child's having a relapse and dying had lower stress hormone levels. But eventually all the children did relapse and die, and those parents who had earlier denied this possibility (and had lower levels of the stress response during remission) had the highest levels of glucocorticoids after their children's deaths (Hofer et al., 1972).

Is humor an effective coping strategy? Should we all try to be like Whoopie Goldberg? Thankfully for those who can't tell a joke, people who have the ability either to produce or appreciate humor benefit from its stress-buffering effects. Those who scored high on either of those dimensions showed fewer negative effects of life stress (Martin & Dobbin, 1988; Nezu et al., 1988).

HUMOR: IS LAUGHTER THE BEST MEDICINE?

Although humor may not work as well as an antibiotic in curing strep throat, it can be an effective form of emotion-focused coping. Humor provides an opportunity to vent emotions, mentally disengage, and make a positive reinterpretation of a stressor (Robinson, 1977a, 1977b). A study looking at the effects of humor on anxiety while participants waited for medical treatment found that those who watched a humorous silent film felt less anxiety than those who watched a nonhumorous silent film, or than a control group that did not watch any film (Nemeth, 1979). Berk (1989) found that participants in his study had higher levels of NK cells and other positive immune changes while watching an hourlong funny video than on another day, when they did not watch a funny tape. Moreover, after watching a humorous video (as compared with a nonhumorous one), participants had increased production of certain immune system secretions in saliva (Perera et al., 1998). In various ways, these studies illustrate the effect of humor on the immune system.

Generally, studies of the relationship between humor and stress indicate that people with a greater sense of humor appear to have a different appraisal of a situation. They are more likely to view a potentially stressful situation as challenging rather than threatening, and they are more likely to develop realistic expectations of their own performance (Martin, 1996).

AGGRESSION: COPING GONE AWRY. For good or ill, one way to cope with stressors is by **aggression,** which has been defined as "behavior directed toward the goal of harming another living being who is motivated to avoid such treatment" (Baron & Richardson, 1994, p. 5). Thus, couples who were more verbally and physically aggressive with each other were more likely to report a higher number of stressful events than couples who were not as abusive (Straus, 1980). However, this is of course only a correlation, and thus cause and effect are unclear: It is possible that stress leads to aggression, but it is also possible that people who are abusive *create* more stressful events in their lives by their aggressive manner (see Chapters 8 and 10 for detailed discussions of how people create their own microenvironments). However, using both correlational designs, which assess only whether two factors vary together, not whether one causes the other, and experimental ones, which can reveal causation, investigators have found a number of specific stressors that are associated with or lead to aggression.

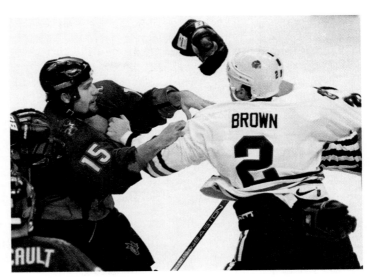

Some people are more aggressive than others. For example, the personality trait of aggressiveness (measured by a self-report paper-and-pencil test) predicts actual aggressive behavior. Hockey players who scored higher on aggressiveness before the hockey season spent more time in the penalty box for aggressive penalties, but not for nonaggressive penalties (Bushman & Wells, 1998).

External factors in the environment, such as noise and heat, can spark aggression in some people, and the target is usually innocent people who happen to be in the line of fire. Depression and pain are also associated with increased aggression (Berkowitz, 1998). These unpleasant experiences have in common the ability to predispose people to making a negative appraisal of a stimulus, particularly if the potential for threat is ambiguous. For instance, if Al has a headache, he may be more likely to assume that a colleague's comment ("Hey Al, quitting early?" on a day he's going to pick up Lisa for a weekend visit) has hostile intent than if he were pain-free. Rather than taking the remark as office kidding, he might worry that he was viewed as a slacker and thus a good candidate to be laid off next.

While external stressors such as noise and pain can clearly lead to inaccurate and negative appraisals of a stimulus, some people are more likely than others to make a negative appraisal of an ambiguous, or even neutral, stimulus, even without the presence of such stressors. The propensity to misread the intentions of others, interpreting them negatively, is referred to as the **hostile attribution bias** (Dodge & Newman, 1981; Nasby et al., 1979). Because Al doesn't have a hostile attribution bias, he would not normally interpret his colleague's statement as a threat.

Frustration, which results when an obstacle is placed in the way of achieving expected gratification, has long been thought to be a precursor to aggression (Dollard et al., 1939). An implication of this view is the prediction that when unemployment is high, frustration will also be high, as will aggression. And in fact, researchers have found increased rates of homicide and domestic abuse when unemployment is high (Berkowitz, 1998).

Most stressors lead to an unpleasant internal state and increased negative mood, which in turn leads to the fight-or-flight response. Whether a person responds to this internal state with aggression is determined in part by the person's biology (including his or her genes, hormones, arousal levels, and central nervous system traumas or abnormalities); in part by his or her thoughts, beliefs, feelings, and expectations; in part by his or her history of reinforcement and observational learning; and in part by the culture's expectations of appropriate behavior. And all these factors interact (Berkowitz, 1998).

Clearly, however, not everyone responds to an unpleasant emotional state and negative mood with aggression. Some people, whose initial response to a threat is fear, will try to "flee" by escaping or avoiding whatever instigated the negative mood. Others will respond initially with irritation, annoyance, or anger (see Figure 12.6).

Aggression: Behavior directed toward harming another living being who is motivated to avoid such treatment.

Hostile attribution bias: The propensity to misread the intentions of others as negative.

FIGURE 12.6
Factors Leading to Aggression

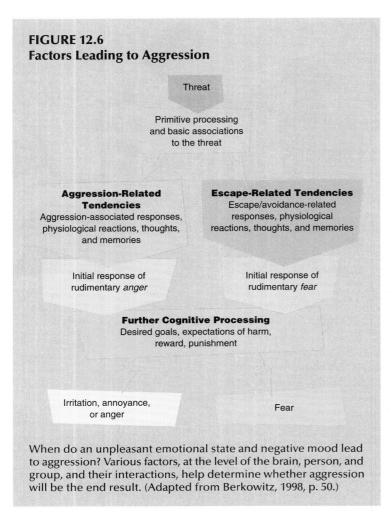

When do an unpleasant emotional state and negative mood lead to aggression? Various factors, at the level of the brain, person, and group, and their interactions, help determine whether aggression will be the end result. (Adapted from Berkowitz, 1998, p. 50.)

Berkowitz proposes that this initial response is then tempered by further cognitive processing about the desired goals and expectations of punishment, reward, or harm, allowing people to make a final determination of a feeling of anger or fear, although some people fight or flee without further appraisal.

If aggression is defined by physical acts, then as children and adults, males are more aggressive than females. The results of a meta-analysis by Eagly and Steffen (1986) found that females are less likely to be aggressive if they think the aggression will physically harm another person, backfire on themselves, or cause them to feel considerable guilt or shame. However, when considering acts of aggression that do not cause physical harm, such as hurting other people's relationships (or threatening to do so), males are not necessarily more aggressive than females. Nonphysical aggression includes threatened or actual social exclusion of a friend, gossiping, or withdrawing acceptance of another person. Because of her gender (that is, the social expectations for someone of her sex), Lisa may be less likely to shove someone when she feels aggressive; however, she might gossip about someone, or slight that person in some way. *Relational aggression* is the term for nonphysical aggression that damages relationships or uses relationships to injure others psychologically, for example, by socially excluding them (Crick & Grotpeter, 1995); relational aggression is instigated more by females than by males.

Males and females differ with regard to the types of situations likely to elicit aggression, whether physical or verbal. Results from a meta-analytic study show that males are more likely to be aggressive in response to criticism of their intellectual ability, and females are less likely to respond aggressively (Bettencourt & Miller, 1996).

Not surprisingly, hostile people are more likely than others to behave aggressively (Anderson & Bushman, 1997). However, determining why some people use aggression as a coping strategy is more difficult than you may think. Conventional wisdom, at least in the United States, has been that aggression is more likely to be perpetrated by people who feel badly about themselves—that is, who have low self-esteem—and that their aggression toward others is a way of bolstering their view of themselves. Is conventional wisdom right? Recent lines of research indicate that the answer is a resounding no (Baumeister et al., 1996; Bushman, 1998). On the contrary, most aggressors are people who think exceedingly well of themselves (that is, have high self-esteem) and experience an insult as a threat to their positive self-view. Their aggression is a response to a perceived threat (Bushman, 1998). Not *all* people with high self-esteem are likely to be more aggressive; the aggressors in this group are a subset of people whose positive view of themselves may be either overinflated (that is, it doesn't correspond to reality) or unstable (Baumeister et al., 1996). This subset may view a threat to their positive self-image as likely to lead to a drop in self-esteem and thus defend against this drop with aggressive behavior.

This subcategory of aggressive people high in self-esteem has been referred to as *narcissists:* people who think well of themselves but whose feelings of high self-esteem are not firmly grounded in reality (Bushman, 1998). That is, they have an overinflated, unjustified positive view of themselves. Other people who are high in self-esteem may have a well-founded self-assessment. The concept of narcissism (or exaggerated self-love, as originally conceived by Freud) takes its name from the Greek myth of Narcissus, who fell in love with his own reflection in the water, pined away, and died from unrequited love of his own image. Just as men are more likely to be physically aggressive, men also score higher on scales of narcissism (Bushman, 1998); they also have higher self-esteem in general.

Imagine that you agreed to participate in a psychological study and, as part of the study, wrote an essay on some topic. You get the essay back with the comment, "This is the worst essay I've ever read." Later, you are competing with the person who wrote this comment on a reaction time test (like the one described in this chapter, p. 441), in which the winner sets the loudness of a buzzer. How would you respond? How obnoxious would you let the sound be? Bushman (1998) hypothesized that people who score high on narcissism would be more likely to behave aggressively than those who score low, and indeed that is what he found. For high narcissists, a poor evaluation endangered their view of themselves, and was enough to elicit aggression toward the person doing the evaluating. Low narcissists were less likely to perceive negative evaluations of their essays as threats, and they were less aggressive. Not only was Bushman correct in his prediction, but he also found that high narcissists were more likely to be aggressive *even if their essays were positively received*; a negative evaluation simply increased their aggressive behavior. For narcissists, then, it appears that *any* evaluation is a stressor that threatens their view of themselves. If the criticism is negative, they are unable either to brush it off or to respond to it rationally, and they avenge themselves against the perpetrator of the threat.

Thus, to someone whose high self-esteem is unwarranted or unstable, accurate feedback (such as justified criticism) is unwelcome. It will be perceived as a threat and will elicit an aggressive response (Baumeister et al., 1990, 1996). The aggression serves to punish the evaluator (and thus discourage a repetition) and may even cause the evaluator to "undo" the negative evaluation by saying it was in error. The aggression also allows the narcissist to feel superior by establishing dominance over the evaluator and thus restoring some measure of positive self-esteem. In reviewing the literature on rape and murder, Baumeister and his colleagues (1996) find evidence supporting the theory

On April 20, 1999, Littleton, Colorado's Colombine High School students Dylan Klebold (left inset) and Eric Harris (right inset) killed 14 people (including themselves). It was reported that Eric Harris would get enraged at the smallest slight (Lowe, 1999), as would be predicted from the work on aggression and threats to self-esteem among narcissists. Before the rampage, Harris had received several rejections, including a rejection for entry into the Marine Corps 5 days before the killings.

that these forms of aggression are related to a threat to shaky or unstable high self-esteem. This work on aggression also helps explain some triggers to violence in the workplace (p. 440): Not getting an expected or hoped-for promotion or raise might be experienced as a threat by someone with unstable high self-esteem. Some have suggested that nationalism, the belief that one's own country is superior to others, is narcissism on a grand scale. Prejudice, oppression, and genocide may stem from the same root—threatened self-esteem—on a cultural level (Baumeister et al., 1996).

Other personality traits may lead people to seek out situations that are more likely to elicit aggression. People who are sensation seekers (see Chapter 10) or who have high energy levels may be more prone to be in situations that are likely to lead to violence (Gottesman et al., 1997). At least some of these personality variables have a moderate level of heritability (see Chapter 10).

We are all, at one time or another, confronted by stressors that can elicit aggression; Thornton Wilder has written, "We have all murdered, in thought." Why do only some of us act on our aggressive thoughts? Baumeister and Boden (1998) propose that the answer may lie in the difficulty aggressive people have in regulating, or controlling, themselves. In turn, the ability to control ourselves and our impulses toward aggression are related to a host of factors, including community standards, the likelihood of punishment, our ability to monitor our behavior, and a conscious decision *not* to control ourselves (as occurs when people, knowing the likely outcome will be physical aggression, still decide to drink or use drugs).

Personality and Coping

A person's coping style can be thought of as a personality trait, as much as, say, messiness or curiosity or talkativeness. In other words, different people typically use different coping strategies when experiencing a stressor.

Hardy people are less likely to have physical illnesses in response to stress. Such individuals have a strong sense of commitment, control, and challenge.

THE HEALTHY PERSONALITY: CONTROL, COMMITMENT, CHALLENGE.
Some personality characteristics are associated with health, even in the face of stress. Kobasa (1979; Kobasa et al., 1982) has found that people with what she defines as a **hardy personality,** the constellation of personality traits associated with health, have a strong sense of *commitment* to themselves and their work; a sense of *control* over what happens to them, similar to the concept of self-efficacy (see Chapter 10); and a view of life's ups and downs as challenges, as opportunities to learn, rather than as stressors. In a study of middle- and upper-level male managers, Kobasa found that those reporting high stress levels had more illnesses, while the hardy managers had lower rates of illness; not all subsequent studies, however, have found such results (Funk & Houston, 1987; Hull et al., 1987; Wiebe & McCallum, 1986). Hardy people are prepared to deal with life's stressors because they believe in themselves. Not surprisingly, those with a high sense of self-efficacy tend to be less ill when confronted by stressors than those with a low sense of self-efficacy (Holahan et al., 1984). Hardy people are less likely to be depressed, regardless of their stress level, compared with nonhardy people (Pengilly & Dowd, 1997).

Attempts to teach the development of hardiness have been somewhat successful. Ten-session hardiness training helped participants to develop new ways of appraising stimuli so that they were not always perceived as stressful, to expand their repertoire of coping strategies, and to increase their sense of control and commitment. Those managers who received hardiness training experienced more job satisfaction and social support and less illness than managers who learned relaxation techniques or who were in a support group (Maddi, 1998).

OPTIMISM AND PESSIMISM: LOOK ON THE BRIGHT SIDE. A personality trait that serves as a buffer against stress is *optimism*. Optimists generally have positive expectancies (see Chapter 10 for a more detailed discussion of expectancies) about the future and work hard to attain them even when the going is rough. Optimists tend to disagree with statements such as "I hardly ever expect things to go my way" (Scheier & Carver, 1985). This personality trait is relatively stable over time. Studies have shown that optimists have a much lower likelihood of reporting illness during very stressful times (such as final exams); recover more quickly after surgery (Scheier et al., 1989; Scheier & Carver, 1993); are less likely to be rehospitalized following heart bypass surgery (Scheier et al., 1999); and are less likely to develop symptoms of depression (Vickers & Vogeltanz, 2000). During stressful periods, optimists generally report a higher level of psychological well-being (Scheier & Carver, 1993). First-year law students who were optimists had better moods, coping skills, responses to stress, and immune functioning during examination time (Segerstrom et al., 1998).

The other side of the coin is *pessimism*, which is associated with anxiety, stress, depression, and poor health (Robinson-Whelen et al., 1998). Pessimism can be further divided into two types: *true pessimism*, in which negative expectations are anchored in past experiences of failure, and *defensive pessimism*, in which a more negative outcome is expected than is warranted by the facts. Defensive pessimism may protect against possible failure, and so may be adaptive. But even defensive pessimists report more psychological symptoms and a lower quality of life than do optimists (Cantor & Norem, 1989).

How does optimism confer its physical and psychological benefits? It appears that optimists (as compared with pessimists) are more likely to use problem-oriented coping strategies that involve direct action, and are more focused on coping. They are also more likely to accept the reality of a stressful situation and try to make the best of it, to learn and grow from the experience. This response contrasts with that of pessimists who, when faced with a stressor, rely on denial and attempt to avoid dealing with the stressor, or give up when the stressor seems too difficult to manage (Scheier & Carver, 1993). Thus, the way optimists cope with stressors makes them more effective in managing difficult situations.

Are optimists born or made? As with many personality traits, the answer is a little of both. Studies of Swedish twins reared together and apart found a heritability of 25% (Plomin et al., 1992). Possible environmental factors include learning from prior experiences, observational learning from parents and others, and direct instruction in coping skills (Scheier & Carver, 1993).

AVOIDERS VERSUS NONAVOIDERS. Another personality factor related to health is the extent to which a person habitually uses avoidant coping strategies or takes the opposite approach and focuses on the stressor. "Avoiders" are often referred to as *repressors*, and nonavoiders as *sensitizers*. Repressors habitually use an avoidant strategy such as thought suppression, trying *not* to think about emotionally arousing, distressing matters, whereas sensitizers habitually think about these things. Research has found that repressors, who reported fewer problems or less stress, are more likely to have higher blood pressure (Nyklicek et al., 1998) and compromised immune function. Thus, the use of avoidant strategies has possible negative effects on health (Jamner et al., 1988; Jamner & Leigh, 1999; Levy et al., 1985; Shea et al., 1993).

GENES AND COPING. If your personality helps determine the way you cope—such as whether you are an optimist or pessimist—then a question integral to personality research comes to the fore: Is the choice of coping strategies genetically based, learned, or an interaction of the two? Recent research suggests that the answer may depend on the specific strategy. Busjahn and colleagues (1999) found evidence that genetics influence 14 out of 19 coping strategies they examined. In contrast, although nonshared environment (individual personal life experience) affected

TABLE 12.3

Coping Strategies, Genes, and Environment

The coping strategies indicated by responses to the statement "When I have been upset by somebody, disturbed by anything, or somehow thrown off balance . . ." can be divided into three categories. All strategies were influenced by nonshared environmental factors.

Strategies With Significant Heritability	Strategies With No Significant Heritability but Influenced by Shared Environment
• I tell myself, "It isn't that bad."	• I concentrate on something else.
• I compare myself with others.	• I get enraged.
• I tell myself, "I am not to blame."	
• I try to concentrate on something else.	**Strategies With Heritability and Influenced by Shared Environment**
• I treat myself to something nice.	
• I think about success in other areas.	• I plan how to solve the problem.
• I try to keep my behavior under control.	• I start to avoid this kind of situation.
• I tell myself not to give up.	• I ask myself, "Why me?"
• I talk with someone about the problem.	
• I try to leave the situation.	
• I think about the situation over and over.	
• I give up.	
• I blame myself.	
• I use medication/alcohol (have a few beers).	

all coping strategies, shared environment (common influences of the family) affected only 2 strategies, and both genetic and shared environment affected 3 strategies (Table 12.3).

This research on the genetic aspects of coping (and by extension, on health), and much of the research on personality and its relation to coping, are not necessarily as straightforward as you might think. Investigations often involve asking participants how they have coped or would cope in certain situations, and then assessing different measures of stress, well-being, immune system functioning, or other variables. But people's behavior often differs from one situation to another (see Chapter 10), and in fact, recent research shows that how people cope differs across situations (Schwartz et al., 1999). Furthermore, simply *asking* people how they coped in stressful situations does not necessarily lead to an accurate picture of their coping behavior (Schwartz et al., 1999; Smith et al., 1999). So the idea that people have a *typical* way of coping may not be as accurate as researchers have assumed. However, this does not mean that the results of studies showing a personality difference in coping and health are invalid: There could be a third, moderating variable that accounts for the results. For example, people who are optimists may report coping more effectively or positively than they actually do, but because they view the glass as half full rather than half empty, they selectively remember using certain strategies more than others (Schwartz et al., 1999; Smith et al., 1999). This very distortion of fact—how they *remember* themselves coping, the third variable—may be an important link between their experiences of stress and their health.

Coping and Social Support

Social support, the help and support gained through interacting with others, buffers the adverse effects of stress. Certain types of positive relationships, such as a good marriage, positive contact with friends and family, participation in group activities, and involvement in a religious organization, can lengthen life expectancy. Just having such connections can have as much influence on mortality as being a nonsmoker or being physically active (House et al., 1988). In a study of over 4,000 men and women in Alameda County, California, death rates for socially isolated people were twice that of people with strong social ties (Berkman & Syme, 1979). Deaths were due not only to coronary heart disease, but also to cancer, infectious disease, and other causes. The benefits of social support can also be gained simply by holding hands or making some other kind of physical contact (Sapolsky, 1997); and for those undergoing a painful and frightening surgical procedure, just talking with their doctors the night before surgery can affect recovery (Egbert et al., 1964). In a study of people with severe coronary heart disease, half the group without social support died within 5 years, three times the rate of those who had a close friend or spouse (Williams et al., 1992). Social support may also provide a buffer against depression: Among college students experiencing high levels of stress, those reporting high levels of social support were less likely to be depressed than those reporting lower levels of social support (Pengilly & Dowd, 1997).

Social support is also related to immune system functioning (Seeman et al., 1994). Consider that participants who reported more loneliness had lower immune functioning (Kiecolt-Glaser et al., 1984). Looking at the relation between social support and catching a cold, researchers found that participants who had a wide range of acquaintances (friends, neighbors, relatives, work colleagues, people from social or religious groups, and so forth) were half as likely to catch a cold as those who were socially isolated (Cohen et al., 1997). You might think that exposure to more people would bring a higher likelihood of exposure to cold germs, but in fact, social isolation is as strong a risk factor for colds as smoking, stress, and not getting enough vitamin C (see Chapter 1). The key is not the total number of supportive relationships, rather their variety. Not just any relationship will do the trick: Bad marriages are associated with suppressed immune function, at least in men (Kiecolt-Glaser et al., 1988), and relationships filled with conflict and criticism can increase stress.

Given the positive effects of social support, it is not surprising that attempts have been made to help isolated people develop such support. Unfortunately, this has proved surprisingly difficult (Lakey & Lutz, 1996), perhaps in part because isolated people lack the motivation or social skills to develop more supportive relationships.

Perceived social support, the subjective sense that support is available should it be needed, is distinct from the actual size and variety of your social network, and from **enacted social support,** specific support that is provided to you, such as when a friend brings you a meal when he or she knows you aren't feeling well. Research has shown that it is perceived support, not enacted support, that provides the buffer

Social support: The help and support gained through interacting with others.

Perceived social support: The subjective sense that support is available should it be needed.

Enacted social support: The specific supportive behaviors provided by others.

The person (dressed in yellow) in the photo is receiving enacted social support. However, she may not necessarily have the sense that support is available when she needs it (perceived social support) because these two aspects of social support are not necessarily correlated. Also, what constitutes support may differ from person to person.

against stress (Cohen & Wills, 1985). It has also been shown that the perception of support is unrelated to actual support. For instance, a study of college students, some of whom perceived a high degree of social support in their lives and some of whom perceived much less, were observed responding to stressors in the presence of their friends. All participants' perceptions of their friends' support was unrelated to the actual support offered (Lakey & Heller, 1988). People who perceive low support tend to view a given social interaction more negatively (Lakey & Dickenson, 1994); if Al is such a person, that would explain both his reluctance to tell his friends about what is happening to him at work and his feeling that his interactions with his colleagues during this crisis are more negative than positive.

Memory also is involved in the perception of social support. Consider the finding that people who perceive that they have a great deal of social support have better memories for supportive behaviors (Lakey et al., 1992). Al's coworker Maya is managing her stress well not only because she perceives other people in her life as being supportive, but also because she remembers past support during her current situation. Like the perception of stress, the perception of support is important (Lakey & Lutz, 1996).

People's styles of attachment in their relationships influence their styles of coping. For instance, during the Gulf War of 1991, Israelis were warned that Iraq might use chemical warheads in the missiles they launched on Israel, and the ensuing days were fraught with stress. Researchers found that participants with different attachment styles reported different ways of coping with the crisis. These adult attachment styles are similar to the children's attachment styles discussed in Chapter 11. Among those adults with an *anxious/ambivalent attachment style* (characterized by a desire for but also a fear of relationships) reported the highest level of distress; these participants used emotion-focused coping strategies to reduce their sense of being overwhelmed. Participants with an *avoidant attachment style* (characterized by discomfort with intimacy) tended to report physical symptoms of stress; they coped by mental disengagement, attempting to distance themselves from what was happening. Participants with a *secure attachment style* (characterized by a desire for closeness without anxiety about losing the relationship) experienced the lowest stress levels; they employed coping strategies that involved social support. These differences in coping strategies were more prominent among those closer to the danger sites (Mikulincer et al., 1993).

Mind–Body Interventions

The focus of mind–body interventions is not on changing a stressful stimulus, but on adapting to the stimulus. Mind–body interventions often address changes in awareness and consciousness. Natural methods of altering consciousness, such as relaxation techniques, meditation, and hypnosis (Wickramasekera et al., 1996), all involve a mind–body interaction and can lead to alterations in heart and breathing rates, hormone secretion, and brain activation (see Chapter 4 for a further discussion). Research examining the effectiveness of several stress management techniques in decreasing physiological reactivity to stress found that progressive muscle relaxation and hypnosis were both effective, and deep abdominal breathing was somewhat effective. Even sitting quietly with your eyes closed for a few minutes causes a decrease in pulse rate (Forbes & Pekala, 1993). Moderate physical exercise also helps buffer the effects of stress (Brown, 1991).

Many mind–body interventions for people who are physically ill provide specific cognitive and behavioral coping strategies, relaxation training (to decrease arousal and increase perceived control), social support (Andersen, 1997), disease-related information, and a supportive environment in which to address fears about the illness. These interventions can lead to improvement in mood and immune system functioning (Fawzy et al., 1990; Zakowski et al., 1992), pain control (NIH Technology Assessment Panel, 1996), and decreases in emotional distress and poor coping strategies (Timmerman et al., 1998). Kiecolt-Glaser and colleagues (1986) examined different stress reduction techniques to determine whether they could help medical students' immune systems during examinations. Half the participants were taught hypnosis and other relaxation techniques and encouraged to practice at home; the other half were taught nothing. The students in the relaxation group had better immune functioning during the exams than those who did not use relaxation techniques.

Recent research has shown the benefits of exercise for alleviating the symptoms of some major psychological disorders, such as depression, and for pain (Tkachuk, 1999). Mind–body interventions are used by people from many walks of life, including medical patients, athletes (Ryska, 1998), managers, and teachers (Anderson et al., 1999).

The effectiveness of placebos also illustrates the link between mind and body. Simply believing that you are receiving a remedy (even if it has no medicinal effects) can affect your immune system's functioning. Certain properties of the placebo itself and the way it is dispensed can make it more effective. If the person dispensing the treatment is friendly, sympathetic, and shows an interest in the patient's problems, the placebo is more likely to be effective (Shapiro & Morris, 1978). Even the practitioner's own view of a placebo's effectiveness can make a difference: If the treatment provider has high expectations for the treatment, it is more likely to be effective (Shapiro, 1964). To avoid this effect, research with placebos often has a double-blind design, in which the provider doesn't know whether he or she is dispensing a placebo or active medication. In a review of research that reported successful results from five treatments (for three diseases) that were later proved worthless, Roberts and colleagues (1993) found that when presented enthusiastically, in these cases placebos were 70% effective.

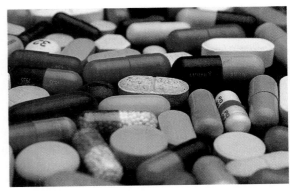

The effectiveness of placebo medications is an illustration of the power of the mind–body interaction. Research shows that certain properties of a placebo medication can make it more or less effective. For example, placebo injections can be more effective than oral medication, capsules are more effective than pills, and more (placebo) pills work better than fewer (placebo) pills. Finally, the color of the capsule can make a difference: Blue capsules work best as tranquilizers; yellow, pink, and red ones work best as stimulants (Buckalew & Ross, 1981).

Gender, Culture, and Coping

Do men and women experience the same amounts of stress? Do people in different cultures experience different amounts of stress? Do they cope with stress to different degrees of effectiveness? Psychologists have begun to pose questions such as these in an effort to learn if stressors affect different groups of people differently.

There is some evidence that women in Western cultures experience more stress than men. A survey of 2,500 Swedes found that women, particularly younger women, reported feeling more hassled, depressed, anxious, and hostile (Scott & Melin, 1998). As women have entered the workforce, a number of studies have focused on the effects of their multiple roles: employee, wife, mother, daughter. The effects of having multiple roles can be both positive and negative; when women are also parents, they tend to have more to do than men, experience more conflict among their different roles, and be less able than men to unwind at home (Clay, 1995). Women generally report more stress with multiple roles than do men, and women employed outside the home generally do more work than men in their "second shift" at home: cooking, cleaning, and shopping (Hochschild, 1989; Phillips & Imhoff, 1997). However, these multiple roles can also confer advantages: increased feelings of self-esteem and control (Pietromonaco et al., 1986), financial gain, social support from colleagues (Brannon, 1996), and decreased psychological stress (Abrams & Jones, 1994). Thus, although employment outside the home can be more stressful (particularly if there are children), it is not necessarily more stressful for women than men. Having financial and familial resources and control over the job (Taylor et al., 1997; Tingey et al., 1996), as well as a sense of mastery at work (Christensen et al., 1998), can reduce the stress of multiple roles.

Culture can help determine what constitutes a stressor, as well as when and how to ask for assistance in coping with stressors. Moreover, culture plays a role in helping people experience a sense of control over stressors. Different cultures bring different understandings to various stressors, creating meaning and defining how much control a person believes he or she has over the stressor. For example, cultures that view certain kinds of illness as a result of sin or as caused by enemies require different types of actions and different coping strategies.

Crowding is an example of a culturally defined stressor. In different cultures, different levels of density produce the perception of crowding. Members of Asian cultures experience less stress than Westerners would in the high-density living conditions that prevail; Asians have also developed ways of creating a sense of privacy in the midst of density, thus providing a sense of control (Werner et al., 1997).

Culture also plays a role in defining the choices of coping strategies, as well as in the use of social support (Aranda & Knight, 1997; Patterson et al., 1998). For instance, although family caregivers of patients with Alzheimer's disease in San Diego, California, and Shanghai, China, all reported more physical health problems and depression compared with noncaregivers in those cities, the Chinese caregivers reported less access to social support (Patterson et al., 1998).

In examining the effects of culture on heart disease, Marmot and Syme (1976) studied more than 3,000 Japanese American men in the San Francisco area. Men whose upbringing was more traditionally Japanese and who still maintained strong ties with the Japanese culture had two and a half times less coronary heart disease than those Japanese American men whose upbringing was more assimilated. The difference held even when the researchers controlled for diet, smoking, and other risk factors. Those most closely tied to the Japanese culture were five times less likely to have heart disease than those least involved in Japanese culture. The researchers proposed that this difference arose because of the cultural and social cohesiveness found in Japanese culture, and that this cohesiveness protected against heart disease.

In the United States, people with lower socioeconomic status (SES) have consistently been found to have poorer health than those with higher SES. Those whose jobs have less status and who are paid less tend to live in poorer neighborhoods, which tend to have fewer shops, recreational facilities, health care facilities, and higher crime—all factors that make life more difficult and stressful. The residents have poorer health and higher mortality rates (Taylor et al., 1997). Familial and community environments can affect health in a variety of ways. Stressful living situations such as abuse or lack of emotional or financial resources can create a chronic stress response and inhibit the development of effective coping strategies. In addition, children tend to imitate the health behaviors of their family members and peers, so if those people have bad health habits, the children are more likely to acquire those habits by adulthood (Taylor et al., 1997).

LOOKING AT LEVELS

Voodoo Death

In some cultures, it has been reported that when a shaman (religious leader) puts a curse on someone, death sometimes ensues; this phenomenon is known as voodoo death (Cannon, 1942). Although there is some debate as to whether voodoo death actually exists (see Hahn, 1997), research has shown that expectations of sickness can in fact cause sickness. This is the **nocebo effect,** a variation of the placebo effect, but with the expectation of a negative outcome rather than a positive outcome. (*Placebo* in Latin means "I will please"; *nocebo* means "I will harm.") Voodoo death represents an extreme example of the nocebo effect.

Among presurgery patients who consulted a psychiatrist before their surgeries about their fears of the procedure, expectations about the surgery affected its outcome. Weisman and Hackett (1961) report that all five patients who were convinced of their impending death did die during surgery, whereas most of those who were unusually apprehensive about the surgery, but not convinced of death, did not die. Moreover, research with people with asthma has found a powerful nocebo effect: One group of sufferers was asked to inhale what they were told was an irritant or allergen, but that was in fact a harmless saline solution. Almost half of this group experienced an asthmatic reaction. Another group of people with asthma received the same saline solution but without any such information and had no reaction (Luparello et al., 1968).

How can we understand the nocebo response? At the level of the brain, the expectation of a negative outcome appears to trigger a physiological response consistent with the expected outcome. At the level of the person, the *expectation* of a negative outcome leads the person to be hypervigilant for any bodily changes and to attribute any changes to the nocebo instead of to some other stimulus. At the level of the group, the culture promotes certain ideas and expectations about sickness and health. Events at these levels interact: For the people with asthma who were told they were inhaling a noxious stimulus, their culture provided the context (level of the group), which led them to be hypervigilant (level of the person) to their physical response (level of the brain), which in turn led them to interpret the bodily changes in a particular way (level of the person).

Nocebo effect: A variation of the placebo effect in which the subject expects a negative outcome instead of a positive outcome.

CONSOLIDATE!

▶ *1. What are the different types of coping strategies?* Coping strategies are the ways in which people handle stress. They can be classified into two general categories: problem-focused and emotion-focused. Problem-focused coping attempts to alter either the environment itself or the way in which the person and the environment interact, and is helpful when the person can affect the stressor. Emotion-focused coping attempts to change the emotional response to a stressor and can be particularly helpful when the stressor itself cannot be changed. Whether a given strategy will be effective depends on an accurate assessment of the possibility of changing the environment; a strategy designed for the short term may not be effective in the long term.

▶ *2. Are some people better equipped than others to handle stress?* "Hardy" individuals, those who are more stress-resistant, have a sense of commitment to themselves and their work, feel a sense of control, and view life's hardships as a challenge to be met. Optimists have better health than pessimists.

▶ *3. How do relationships affect stress and health?* Positive relationships can provide social support, which can buffer the negative effects of stress and boost the immune system. There are different types of social support, including perceived support and enacted support. Perceived support is more effective in buffering stress, even though it can be unrelated to actual support provided by others.

▶ *4. What are mind–body interventions?* Some coping strategies (such as relaxation, meditation, and hypnosis) take advantage of the mind–body interaction, using psychological tools to change psychological and physiological states.

▶ *5. Do gender and culture play a role in coping?* Although a woman may experience more stress because of multiple roles (particularly if one of the roles is mother), these multiple roles can provide a buffer against stress and depression; the financial, self-esteem, and collegial benefits of the employee role can outweigh the increased daily stress. Culture helps determine what is perceived to be stressful and provides ways to increase a sense of control in the face of a stressor. Crowding is an example: The perception of crowding can vary from culture to culture as a function of density. In cultures with high density, such as parts of Japan, ways have been found to create a sense of privacy to help people feel some control over the stressor of crowding.

A DEEPER LEVEL
Recap and Thought Questions

▶ What Is Stress?

Stress is the general term describing the psychological and bodily response to a stimulus that alters your equilibrium. The stress response of the autonomic nervous system increases heart rate and blood pressure and suppresses the immune system. Continued stressors lead to a shift within the general adaptation syndrome (GAS) from the alarm phase to the adaptation phase to the exhaustion phase. The *perception* of stress helps determine what constitutes a stressor. Common sources of stress include a sense of a lack of control and predictability, internal conflict, and the irritations of daily life. The workplace can also cause stress, through environmental factors such as noise or crowding, work-related conflict, or work overload or underload (quantitative or qualitative). Work can also be a stressor because of a perceived lack of control over how the job is done or because the job entails responsibility for other people's lives or welfare.

How do we know that Al is experiencing stress? Al has many of the signs of the sympathetic nervous system's response to stressors, including a racing heart and sweaty palms. Moreover, his work situation is a stressor because of his perceived lack of control over the uncertain upcoming layoffs and because of the noise and crowding in his new, smaller office environment.

> **Think It Through.** Suppose you wanted a job that wasn't very stressful. What job-related factors would you look for as being least stressful—the nature of the job itself, deadlines, the physical work environment, or other factors? What stressful employment-related factors would you want to avoid? Once you start work, what physiological indicators might suggest that your new job was, in fact, fairly stressful? Why do those physiological changes occur?

▶ Stress, Disease, and Health

Frequent activation of the stress response can lead to changes in the immune system, such as increased vulnerability to contracting a cold or the growth of existing tumors, and cardiovascular changes and heart disease. Stress can also increase the likelihood of engaging in unhealthy behaviors such as smoking, substance abuse, poor eating habits. People often go through stages of change, and relapse, when trying to change a problematic behavior.

Al has been sick and coughing a lot lately. Could stress be affecting his health? Stress could be affecting Al's health in a number of ways, direct and indirect. His immune system's functioning is affected by his general level of stress, which would explain his frequent illnesses. Al has also responded to stress by overindulging in alcohol and starting to smoke again—both self-destructive behaviors—which means that stress is indirectly hurting his health. His realization of the need to act, however, puts him at the precontemplation stage of making some changes that would lower his stress level and improve his health.

> **Think It Through.** Suppose you were caught in a thunderstorm and were soaking wet by the time you got home. Would you now be more likely to catch a cold? Why or why not? What factors might make you more or less likely to catch a cold? What if you had been out very late, or if you had had a lot of sleep? Why might these factors matter, or would they not matter?

▶ Strategies for Coping

A realistic appraisal of whether your actions can affect a stressor will help you to determine what coping strategies will be effective. Emotion-focused coping strategies are best when the situation can't be changed, and problem-focused strategies work best when it can. There are a variety of problem-focused and emotion-focused coping strategies, including humor and venting feelings. Stress-management techniques—relaxation training, meditation, hypnosis—can decrease the physical effects of stress. Some people are more stress-resistant, or hardy, than others; such people tend to have a sense of commitment, control, and challenge, and tend to be optimists. Social support (particularly perceived social support) can be helpful in decreasing the experience of stress. And culture can affect both the appraisal of a stimulus as a stressor and the choice of coping strategies for managing the stressor.

Given Al's particular stressors, what are the best coping strategies for him? Al's stressors include a lack of perceived control; a crowded, noisy workplace; and an uncertain future. It will be important for Al to assess carefully and realistically whether his actions can affect the stressors; this will help determine which coping strategies will be effective: emotion-focused coping when he can't change the situation, and problem-focused coping when he can. Right now, Al is employing such emotion-focused strategies as disengaging (by overindulging in cigarettes and alcohol) and thought suppression. Al might benefit from learning some stress-management techniques to decrease the physical effects of stress.

Think It Through. If your next-door neighbor plays music very loud every night when you are trying to go to sleep, and you find this to be a stressor, what could you do to lower your stress response? What type of coping strategies would work best in this situation? What personality characteristics would make you less likely to feel stressed by a noisy neighbor? If you were in a non-Western culture, would the nightly serenade be as stressful? Why or why not?

13 PSYCHOLOGICAL DISORDERS

In 1998–1999, record numbers of people came to the National Gallery of Art in Washington, D.C., to see an exhibit of the works of Vincent van Gogh. Born in Holland in 1853, van Gogh created extraordinary art and took much joy in painting, but his life is a tale of misery. The son and grandson of Protestant ministers, van Gogh was the second of six children. A memoir by his sister-in-law records, "As a child he was of difficult temper, often troublesome and self-willed" (Roskill, 1963, p. 37). According to his parents, when punished, Vincent became more "difficult." As a child he showed no particular awareness of his great gifts; but on two occasions, when he modeled a clay elephant and drew a cat, he destroyed what he had made when he felt a "fuss" was being made about them (Roskill, 1963).

When he was 16, he worked as a clerk in an art gallery, but his long, moody silences and irritability isolated him from his coworkers. After 4 years, he was transferred to the gallery's London office, where he fell in love with his landlady's daughter, Ursula. They spent many months together until she revealed her engagement to a previous tenant and rejected van Gogh. Feeling utterly defeated, he found it difficult to concentrate at work. He frequently argued with his coworkers and was soon fired.

Van Gogh next decided on a career in the ministry but could not master the Greek and Latin necessary for the entrance exams. Instead, he became a lay pastor, preaching to miners in the Borinage, a coal-mining area in Belgium. He went without bathing and slept in a hut on bare planks as the miners did. But the miners feared this unkempt, wild-looking man, and the church elders dismissed him. Increasingly, van Gogh found comfort in painting and drawing.

His life continued to be marked by instability. After he left the Borinage, he lived in and out of his parents' home and wandered around the country. Whereas once his interest in religion had been intense, if not obsessional, he now turned his back on religion. He developed a relationship with a pregnant prostitute, Sien, but their liaison ended after about a year and a half. Van Gogh reported that he had "attacks" during which he would hear voices; at times he believed he was being poisoned.

When he was 35, van Gogh convinced fellow painter Paul Gauguin to share a house with him in Arles, France. As was true for all of van Gogh's relationships, he and Gauguin frequently quarreled. According to Gauguin, after one particularly violent argument, van Gogh approached him threateningly with an open razor, but Gauguin stared him down. Van Gogh then ran to their house, where he cut off his earlobe, which he then sent to a local prostitute (not Sien). The next day he was found at home, bleeding and unconscious, and was taken to a hospital, where he remained for 2 weeks. His brother Theo spent time with him in the hospital and found Vincent in great spiritual anguish.

After his release from the hospital in January 1889, van Gogh's behavior became increasingly bizarre, so much so that within 2 months the residents of Arles petitioned for him to be confined, and he again stayed for a time in the hospital. In May, van Gogh moved to the asylum at Saint-Remy, not far from Arles, where he lived on and off for the next year and a half, and where he produced many paintings. Shortly after his last release, less than 2 years after the incident with Gauguin, he purposefully ended his anguish and his life by going out into a field with a gun and shooting himself in the stomach. Yet, a few weeks before his death, he could say, "I still love art and life very much indeed" (Roskill, 1963).

Questions of art aside, van Gogh's experiences focus our attention on psychological disorders: What defines a psychological disorder? Who establishes criteria for determining what is abnormal behavior? What are the symptoms and origins of some specific disorders?

IDENTIFYING PSYCHOLOGICAL DISORDERS: WHAT'S ABNORMAL?

What distinguishes unusual behaviors from behaviors that are symptoms of a psychological disorder? Before he rejected religion, van Gogh was tormented by religious ideas and believed in ghosts. Are these signs of psychological disturbance? What about his self-mutilation? What would you want to know about him before drawing any conclusions?

Mental health professionals face questions such as these every day. In this section you will see how formulations of and findings about psychological disorders suggest answers to those questions.

▶ 1. How is abnormality defined?

► 2. How are psychological disorders explained?

► 3. How are psychological disorders classified and diagnosed?

Defining Abnormality

What is psychological abnormality? What are psychological disorders? It is probably easier to begin to answer these questions by saying what "abnormalities" and "disorders" are not. Psychological disorders are *not* synonymous with insanity, which is a legal term, not a psychological or medical one. *Insanity* describes the mental state of people who cannot be held legally responsible for their actions. If this definition seems less than definitive, in a sense it is: Legal systems at different times and in different cultures have set different standards for defining insanity. And psychological disorders are *not* synonymous with unusual behaviors, such as body piercing, dressing only in black, laughing at odd moments, or crying at a compliment.

In the psychological, not the legal, realm, how can we decide whether a particular behavior, feeling, or thought is normal or abnormal? How are lines drawn between normal functioning and abnormal functioning—and who draws them? Let's take a look at some different levels of analysis.

We can begin by noting that abnormal physiology, such as imbalances in particular neurotransmitters or hormones, or abnormalities in brain structure, can affect mental or emotional functioning. But what if those abnormalities are not accompanied by behavioral symptoms? An important aspect of a definition of psychological disorders rests on objective symptoms that are manifested in behavior. By this standard, people with psychological disorders exhibit objectively unusual behavior, such as spending an hour washing their hands or feeling too sad to get out of bed.

But sometimes people who neither exhibit unusual behavior nor have abnormal brain states nevertheless have the subjective experience of psychological distress or discomfort. They may feel they are not "normal," even though other people might not notice anything amiss. This sense, too, must be taken into account in defining abnormality. But if there are no behavioral or physiological indicators of a disorder, could someone who feels this way be said to have a psychological disorder?

Context and culture also play a role in defining abnormality. Picture someone hopping on one leg, thumb in mouth, trying to sing the French national anthem during a hockey game. You would probably think this was abnormal; but what if the behavior was part of a fraternity initiation ritual, or a new kind of performance art? A behavior that is bizarre or inappropriate in one context may be entirely appropriate in another. Furthermore, a culture's definition of abnormality may shift over time. For example, in 1851, Dr. Samuel Cartwright of Louisiana wrote an essay in which he declared that slaves' running away was evidence of a serious mental disorder, which he called "drapetomania" (Eakin, 2000). More recently, homosexuality was officially considered a psychological disorder in the United States until 1973, when it was removed from the *Diagnostic and Statistical Manual of Mental Disorders,* the manual used by mental health clinicians to classify psychological disorders. And in the last decade, the determination of abnormality has taken a new turn in the United States; as health maintenance organizations (HMOs) and other types of managed care organizations try to keep costs down, they have developed their own criteria for the symptoms and disorders they will pay to have treated, as well as for the frequency and duration of the treatment.

Van Gogh's painting of the church at Auvers is unusual because of its unconventional perspective, use of color, and brushstrokes. Do these differences reflect a psychological disorder, or just a different way of seeing or conveying the structure and its surroundings?

Thus, when deciding what should be considered a psychological disorder, it can be helpful to be aware of all these factors: differences in physiology, objective behaviors and subjective experiences, and the surrounding culture. The line between normal and abnormal behavior is perhaps easiest to draw in the case of **psychosis,** which is an obvious impairment in the ability to perceive and comprehend events accurately, combined with a gross disorganization of behavior. People with psychoses may have **hallucinations,** mental images so vivid that they seem real, or **delusions,** which are entrenched false beliefs (such as that their thoughts are being controlled by aliens). However, such beliefs, even if false (or at least not susceptible to rational proof), should not be considered abnormal if they are an accepted part of the culture. For instance, in some religious groups, such as Pentecostals, it is not considered abnormal to hear voices, especially the voice of God (Cox, 2000). Another example is *zar,* or spirit possession, experienced in some North African and Middle Eastern cultures. Those affected may shout, laugh, hit their heads against a wall, or exhibit other behavior that otherwise would be considered inappropriate; an experience of *zar* is not considered abnormal in the cultures in which it occurs (American Psychiatric Association, 1994). Because of such cultural differences, even psychosis can be difficult to identify: The Comoros Islands woman in a possession trance discussed in Chapter 4 would likely have been diagnosed as psychotic in an American hospital, but would have been regarded as normal (although possessed) in her own culture.

It is difficult to give an exact definition of psychological disorders—also referred to as psychiatric disorders, mental disorders or, less systematically, mental illnesses—because they can encompass many aspects of behavioral, experiential, and physiological functioning. However, a good working definition is that a **psychological disorder** is a constellation of symptoms that create significant distress or impairment in work, school, family, relationships, or daily living. This definition takes into account three factors: distress, disability, and danger. People with psychological disorders may display or experience *distress,* perhaps repeatedly bursting into tears and expressing hopelessness about the future, for no apparent reason. People with psychological disorders may experience a *disability,* or inability to function in some aspect of life (examples might be a police officer subject to panic attacks on duty, or someone whose emotional outbursts drive others away). *Danger* can occur when symptoms of a psychological disorder cause an individual to put life (his or her own, or another's) at risk, either purposefully or accidentally. For instance, a hallucination may obscure the sight of an oncoming car, depression may lead to a suicide attempt, or extreme paranoia may provoke an attack on other people.

Psychological disorders can be very debilitating, and worldwide they rank second among diseases that lead to death and disability, a higher ranking than cancer (Murray & Lopez, 1996). According to some estimates, up to 48% of Americans have experienced 1 of 30 common psychological disorders at some point in their lives (Kessler et al., 1994), and 20% of Americans have a diagnosable mental disorder in any given year (Regier et al., 1993; Satcher, 1999). Psychological disorders can affect people's relationships, their ability to care for themselves, and their functioning on the job. For every 100 workers, an average of 37 work days per month are lost either because of reduced workloads or absences necessitated by psychological disorders (Kessler & Frank, 1997).

Explaining Abnormality

Explanations for abnormal behavior have changed with the times and reflect the thinking of the culture. In ancient Greece, abnormal behaviors, as well as medical problems, were thought to arise from imbalances of the body's four fluids, or "humors": yellow bile, phlegm, blood, and black bile. Too much phlegm, for instance, made you sluggish and "phlegmatic"; too much black bile made you melancholic. In 17th century New England, abnormality was thought to be the work of the

Psychosis: An obvious impairment in the ability to perceive and comprehend events accurately, and a gross disorganization of behavior.

Hallucinations: Mental images so vivid that they seem real.

Delusions: Entrenched false beliefs that are often bizarre.

Psychological disorder: A constellation of symptoms marked by an individual's significant distress or impairment in work, school, family, relationships, or daily living.

devil. In the middle of the 20th century, Sigmund Freud's work was influential, and psychodynamic theory was the instrument used to understand abnormality. Currently, in order to understand psychological disorders, many psychologists and others in the field have used the *biopsychosocial model*. This model focuses on factors at the levels of the brain, the person, and the group. In this discussion, we go one step further and show how events at those three levels are not discrete but affect one another in various interactions.

Diathesis–stress model: A predisposition to a given disorder (diathesis) and specific factors (stress) that combine with the diathesis to trigger the onset of the disorder.

THE BRAIN. Van Gogh's family history points to a possible cause of his psychological disorders. Van Gogh's brother Theo was often depressed and anxious, and he committed suicide within a year after Vincent's suicide; his sister Wilhelmina exhibited a long-standing psychosis; his youngest brother Cor is thought to have committed suicide. Does this history indicate that van Gogh inherited some vulnerability to a psychological disorder? Not necessarily; but researchers are finding increasing evidence that genetic factors frequently contribute to the development of some disorders.

Biological factors, including, for example, neurotransmitters (such as serotonin), hormones (such as adrenaline), and abnormalities in the structure of the brain, appear to play a role in the development of some psychological disorders. From this point of view, depression can be seen as a manifestation of an abnormal serotonin level. Similarly, the cause of an irrational fear of spiders could be the outcome of an overreactive amygdala. While these explanations may be valid, they are only a part of the picture. *Why* are someone's serotonin levels abnormal? *Why* is someone else's amygdala overreactive to the sight of a spider? As previously noted in many contexts, our own thoughts, feelings, and behaviors, as well as our interactions with others and our environment, can affect the workings of our brains.

Thus, abnormality cannot be considered solely as a function of brain chemistry or structure. Many researchers and clinicians today believe that psychological disorders can best be explained by a **diathesis–stress model** (*diathesis* means a predisposition to a state or condition). This model, illustrated in Figure 13.1, states that "for a given disorder, there is both a predisposition to the disorder (a *diathesis*) and specific factors (*stress*) that combine with the diathesis to trigger the onset of the disorder" (Rende & Plomin, 1992, p. 177). According to the diathesis–stress model, because of certain biological factors (such as their genes, abnormality of brain structures, or neurotransmitters), some people may be more vulnerable to developing a particular disorder, but without certain environmental stressors, the disorder is not triggered. By the same token, when experiencing a stressor, people without a biological vulnerability for a disorder may not develop that disorder. From this perspective, neither factor alone can cause illness, and as noted in Chapter 12, not everyone perceives a particular event or stimulus to be a stressor. Whether because of learning or genetics, or an interaction of the two, some people are more likely to perceive more stressors (and therefore to experience more stress) than others. For instance, although schizophrenia appears to have a genetic component, even if an identical twin has schizophrenia, the co-twin will not necessarily develop the disorder. The diathesis–stress model proposes that it is the *combination* of physiological vulnerability and specific other factors, such as a trauma or the death of a loved one, that elicits the disorder.

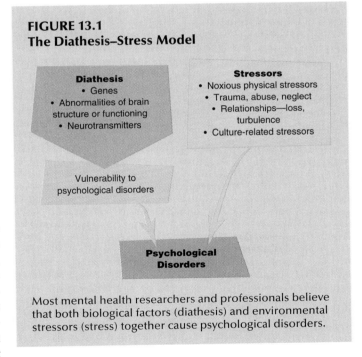

FIGURE 13.1
The Diathesis–Stress Model

Diathesis
• Genes
• Abnormalities of brain structure or functioning
• Neurotransmitters

Stressors
• Noxious physical stressors
• Trauma, abuse, neglect
• Relationships—loss, turbulence
• Culture-related stressors

Vulnerability to psychological disorders

Psychological Disorders

Most mental health researchers and professionals believe that both biological factors (diathesis) and environmental stressors (stress) together cause psychological disorders.

THE PERSON. Several factors at the level of the person also play a role in psychological disorders. One factor is classical conditioning, as in the case of Little Albert

(Chapter 5), who developed a phobia of white furry things based on his classical conditioning experiences with a white rat and a loud noise. Operant conditioning and observational learning can also help explain some psychological disorders, as can the pattern of a person's thoughts. For instance, chronic negative thought patterns ("I'm incompetent; I can't do anything right") can lead to depressing feelings and contribute to the development or maintenance of depression. Learning, thoughts, and feelings may help explain why certain psychological disorders develop in some people.

THE GROUP. For a period during the 1960s, a number of mental health professionals proposed the idea that mental illness is a myth, merely a label applied to culturally undesirable behavior (Szasz, 1961). In this view, the label determines how people are treated and, in a self-fulfilling prophecy, may even play a role in how the "mentally ill" person behaves, once labeled.

FIGURE 13.2
On Being Sane in Insane Places

David Rosenhan and six colleagues (pseudopatients) each went to the admissions office of a different hospital, complaining of hearing voices, although behaving normally. Each was admitted: six were diagnosed as *schizophrenic* and one as *manic depressive.*

Once hospitalized, the pseudopatients acted normally, and they said that they felt fine and that the voices had stopped. Even so, they were kept in the hospital for an average of 19 days. Not a single staff member questioned whether the diagnoses were correct, but some of the other patients did.

As soon as the pseudopatients were labeled schizophrenic, the doctors and nurses interpreted normal behaviors in a different way. For example, the pseudopatients kept notes on their experiences, and one of the nurses wrote in the case record "Patient engages in writing behavior."

David Rosenhan (1973) tested an aspect of this idea. In his study, people without a psychological disorder gained admittance to psychiatric hospitals by claiming that they heard voices. Once in the hospital they behaved normally (see Figure 13.2). But because they were given a psychiatric diagnosis, their normal behavior was interpreted as pathological, and they were treated accordingly. For example, when these "pseudopatients" asked about eligibility for grounds privileges, the psychiatrists responded to such questions only 6% of the time; in 71% of the encounters, the doctors just moved on.

Rosenhan's experiment illustrates the power of labels. But does it tell us anything about the reality of mental disorders? The pseudopatients originally reported auditory hallucinations that were troubling enough to drive them to request admission to a mental hospital; people do not normally have such symptoms. How was the staff to know that the pseudopatients were lying when they described their "symptoms"? Kety (1974, p. 959) notes:

If I were to drink a quart of blood and, concealing what I had done, came to the emergency room of any hospital vomiting blood, the behavior of the staff would be quite predictable. If they labeled and treated me as having a bleeding peptic ulcer, I doubt that I could argue convincingly that medical science does not know how to diagnose that condition.

Similarly, the fact that the staff in Rosenhan's experiment labeled and treated the pseudopatients as if their symptoms were genuine does not indicate that psychological disorders with these symptoms do not exist.

Certain disorders—schizophrenia being one—are recognized worldwide. But cultures differ in which behaviors they consider abnormal, and the symptoms, course, and prognosis of disorders may vary from culture to culture (Basic Behavioral Science Task Force, 1996), and even within a country such as the United States, cultural differences influence how people are diagnosed with and treated for psychological disorders. Moreover, diagnosing individuals involves making judgments that, like all judgments, are subject to error. A systematic type of error in diagnosis is called a *diagnostic bias* (Meehl, 1960), often with the result that some people receive certain diagnoses based on nonmedical factors, such as race. For instance, studies of racial bias show that African American patients in the United States have an increased likelihood of being evaluated more negatively than white patients (Garb, 1997; Jenkins-Hall & Sacco, 1991; Strakowski et al., 1995) and are prescribed higher doses of medication (Strakowski et al., 1993).

The film Girl, Interrupted *tells the disturbing true story of Susanna Kaysen, a troubled young woman who was institutionalized after an aspirin overdose. After being labeled with a diagnosis during her hospitalization, she soon began to live up to the role it described. One underlying message of the film was that, during the late sixties, women were routinely institutionalized for socially unacceptable behavior.*

Factors at the level of the group play a role in triggering psychological disorders, as well as in increasing the risk of a disorder's recurrence. For example, the "stress" part of posttraumatic stress disorder is usually caused by other people (such as a terrorist or a rapist) or the environment (natural disasters such as floods and earthquakes).

Events at all three levels and the interactions among them must be examined to understand the various psychological disorders discussed in this chapter. Biological factors; learning principles and thought patterns; familial, cultural, and environmental factors; and the relationships among them all play a role in explaining psychological disorders.

Categorizing Disorders: Is a Rose Still a Rose by Any Other Name?

Suppose a man comes to a clinical psychologist's office complaining that he feels he is going crazy and that he has a strong sense of impending doom. How would the clinical psychologist determine the nature of this man's difficulties and figure out how best to help him? What questions should the psychologist ask? One guide to help the psychologist and other mental health clinicians is the *Diagnostic and Statistical Manual of Mental Disorders,* known to its users simply as the *DSM.*

In 1952 the American Psychiatric Association published the inaugural edition of the *DSM,* the first manual of mental disorders designed primarily to help clinicians diagnose and treat patients. This edition was based on psychodynamic theory. In later editions of the manual, its developers tried to avoid relying on any one theory of the causes of disorders and to base the identification of disorders on a growing body of empirical research. The fourth edition, the *DSM-IV,* published in 1994, was an attempt to refine the diagnostic criteria and make the diagnostic categories more useful to mental health researchers and practitioners.

TABLE 13.1

The Five *DSM-IV* Axes

Source: *Adapted from American Psychiatric Association (1994).*

AXIS I. CLINICAL DISORDERS

This axis addresses the diagnosis of clinical disorders, such as mood disorders and anxiety disorders, and represents the majority of *DSM-IV* diagnoses.

AXIS II. PERSONALITY DISORDERS AND MENTAL RETARDATION

This axis assesses whether the patient has mental retardation or a personality disorder (ingrained, inflexible traits that are maladaptive). Such disorders include narcissistic personality disorder and antisocial personality disorder.

AXIS III. GENERAL MEDICAL CONDITIONS

The third axis assesses whether the patient might have physical disorders or handicaps that could be relevant to a mental or behavioral problem. For instance, a problem walking might lead to panic attacks about leaving the house.

AXIS IV. PSYCHOSOCIAL AND ENVIRONMENTAL PROBLEMS

This axis focuses on psychosocial and environmental problems that could affect the diagnosis, treatment, and prognosis of an Axis I or II disorder. For example, if diagnosing someone with depression, it would be important to know that a parent has recently died.

AXIS V. GLOBAL ASSESSMENT OF FUNCTIONING

The last axis focuses on the highest level of functioning the patient achieved in work, relationships, and leisure activities within the past year. This information can be useful in planning and predicting the outcome of treatment, since treatment is unlikely to lead to a higher level of functioning than the person had before the development of his or her illness.

Since the third edition, the *DSM* has described five *axes*, or types of information, that should be considered in the assessment of a patient (see Table 13.1). Clinical disorders are noted on Axis I, and personality disorders and mental retardation on Axis II. Axis III notes any general medical conditions that might be relevant to a diagnosis on Axis I or II. Psychosocial and environmental problems are identified on Axis IV, and Axis V records the patient's highest level of functioning in major areas of life within the past year. An appendix to the manual outlines aspects of the patient's cultural context that clinicians should take into account when making a diagnosis. Most of the manual, however, is devoted to describing disorders. It defines 17 major categories of psychological problems. All told, almost 300 mental disorders are specified.

The sheer number of disorders included in the *DSM-IV* has provoked criticism of the manual; the breadth of the major diagnostic categories is shown in Table 13.2. As the *DSM* has evolved, it has introduced categories that define medical problems as psychological disorders, leading to a pathologizing of people's mental health. For example, a new diagnosis in the *DSM-IV* is "Breathing-Related Sleep Disorder" (one cause of which is sleep apnea; see Chapter 4). Thus, the *DSM-IV* created a *psychological* or *psychiatric* disorder for a medical problem. Moreover, the *DSM-IV* does not provide a discrete boundary separating abnormality from normality (Frances, 1998); a clinician's judgment determines whether an impairment is "clinically significant." Another criticism leveled at the *DSM-IV* is that some of the disorders are not clearly distinct from one another (Blais et al., 1997), although they are often presented as if they were (Tucker, 1998).

Despite these criticisms, the *DSM-IV* is the predominant means of categorizing psychological disorders in the United States. The discussion of disorders in this chapter uses the *DSM-IV* system of categorization.

TABLE 13.2

DSM-IV's 17 Major Categories of Disorders

Source: *Adapted from American Psychiatric Association (1994).*

MAJOR CATEGORY OF DISORDERS	EXPLANATION
Disorders usually first diagnosed in infancy, childhood, or adolescence	Although describing disorders usually first evident early in life, some adults are newly diagnosed with disorders in this category, such as attention-deficit/hyperactivity disorder.
Delirium, dementia, and amnestic and other cognitive disorders	Disorders of consciousness and cognition.
Mental disorders due to a general medical condition not elsewhere classified	Disorders in which mental and psychological symptoms are judged to be due to a medical condition (coded on Axis III).
Substance-related disorders	Disorders of substance dependence and abuse, as well as disorders induced by a substance, such as a substance-induced psychotic disorder.
Schizophrenia and other psychotic disorders	Disorders related to psychoses.
Mood disorders	Disorders of affect/feelings.
Anxiety disorders	Disorders of anxiety.
Somatoform disorders	Disorders in which physical/medical complaints have no known medical origin (or the symptoms are not proportional to a medical condition) and so are thought to be psychological in nature.
Factitious disorders	Disorders in which the person intentionally fabricates symptoms of a medical or psychological disorder, but not for external gain (such as disability claims).
Dissociative disorders	Disorders in which there is a disruption in the usually integrated functions of consciousness, memory, or identity.
Sexual and gender identity disorders	Disorders of sexual function, the object of sexual desire, and/or of gender identity.
Eating disorders	Disorders related to eating.
Sleep disorders	Disorders related to sleep.
Impulse-control disorders not elsewhere classified	Disorders related to the ability to contain impulses (such as kleptomania).
Adjustment disorders	Disorders related to the development of distressing emotional or behavioral symptoms in response to an identifiable stressor.
Personality disorders	Disorders related to personality traits that are inflexible and maladaptive, and that cause distress or difficulty with daily functioning.
Other conditions that may be a focus of clinical attention	A problem receiving treatment for which there is no psychological disorder, or the symptoms do not meet criteria for a disorder.

LOOKING AT LEVELS

Did Charles Whitman Have a Psychological Disorder?

If a person is violent, does this automatically mean that he or she has a psychological disorder? No; there is no simple, single criterion. Psychological disorders can most clearly be identified by looking at events at all three levels of analysis. Consider the case of Charles Whitman. On August 1, 1966, long before anyone imagined today's far more common occasions of violence in schools and workplaces, Whitman, a 25-year-old student at the University of Texas in Austin, climbed to the top of a tower on the campus and opened fire on students casually walking below. After an hour and a half, 16 were dead and another 30 wounded. As Gary Lavergne, author of *A Sniper in the Tower: The Charles Whitman Murders* (1997) wrote, Whitman "introduced America to public mass murder" (p. xi). At the time, a local reporter described Whitman as "a good son, top Boy Scout, an excellent Marine, an honor student, a hard worker, a loving husband, a fine scout master, a handsome man, a wonderful friend to all who knew him—and an expert sniper" (Lavergne, 1997, p. xi).

What drove Whitman to murder? Was he unhappy at school? Yes; he was extremely frustrated by his heavy course load (an explanation at the level of the person). What about his relationship with his family? His parents were about to divorce, a circumstance that upset him greatly. He had a long history of bad blood with his abusive father. In fact, the night before his rampage, he killed his mother and his wife, and then wrote an angry letter about his father. In this same note, Whitman asked that his brain be examined after his death, to see if "there is any mental disorder."

Charles Whitman's hunch was correct—something *was* wrong with his brain. An autopsy uncovered a pecan-sized tumor near his hypothalamus, a part of the brain involved in emotion. Whitman had complained of massive headaches for weeks before the shooting and was seen regularly gobbling huge doses of aspirin.

Can we conclude that with the discovery of the tumor the case is closed—that Whitman had a medical disorder, not a psychological one? Probably not. It's unlikely that the brain tumor was the sole cause of his behavior. After all, most people with similar brain tumors don't become mass murderers. Perhaps the tumor intensified Whitman's violent feelings, but this still doesn't tell us how and why those feelings led to violent acts. Whitman was clearly deeply unhappy (level of the person), but again, this by itself was probably not enough to trigger his violent rampage.

Whitman's killing spree can best be understood by looking for interactions among events at all three levels. He may have interpreted the discomfort and feelings produced by the tumor in terms of his frustration over his school work and his unhappiness (level of the person), and his rage toward his parents and others (level of the group). Such thoughts may have caused severe stress, which amplified the headaches caused by the tumor (level of the brain), thereby ratcheting up his misery and rage. This in turn may have led him to finally revert to his training as a Marine and lash out at a world of innocent people on the ground below.

CONSOLIDATE!

▶ **1. How is abnormality defined?** Abnormality, as distinct from insanity, can be defined by events at the levels of the brain, by biological or structural abnormalities; of the person, by objective behaviors and subjective distress; and of the group, in which abnormality is defined by the culture and context of the behaviors.

▶ **2. How are psychological disorders explained?** The diathesis–stress model explains psychological disorders, specifically that certain biological factors make some individuals more vulnerable to developing particular disorders, which are then triggered by stressors.

▶ **3. How are psychological disorders classified and diagnosed?** Psychiatric disorders are classified in the *DSM-IV* along two axes: clinical and personality disorders. Three other axes address factors affecting the disorders, the nature of the problem, and the highest level of functioning attained. Impairment in functioning at work, in school, in relationships, or in daily living are necessary to merit a diagnosis of a disorder.

ANXIETY AND MOOD DISORDERS

We cannot diagnose from a distance, but we know enough about van Gogh's life and behavior to make some educated guesses about the nature of his moods and turmoil. We know, for example, that he had what he called "attacks." He frequently spoke of feeling sad; still, he clung to the commonality of human feeling, saying "I prefer feeling my sorrow to forgetting it or becoming indifferent" (Lubin, 1972,

p. 22). Painting was the one thing that drove away his sadness, and sometimes he painted in a frenzy. He would have bouts of irritability, had difficulty concentrating, was often miserable, and frequently quarrelsome. People described him as odd, argumentative, very sensitive, nervous, and unpredictable. He described himself as an alcoholic. He had frequent thoughts of suicide, and in the end, at the age of 37, he died after he intentionally shot himself (Lubin, 1972).

Can we recognize a pattern in these symptoms? How would today's methods of identifying psychological disorders explain them? What might be their causes?

▶ 1. What are the main types of anxiety disorders? What are their symptoms and causes?

▶ 2. What are mood disorders? What causes them?

Anxiety Disorders

Many people are nervous when they have to speak in public. But suppose you become *so* nervous before an in-class presentation that your mouth is dry, you feel lightheaded, your heart begins to race, and you think you're having a heart attack and going crazy at the same time. These reactions are not normal "stage jitters." They are typical signs of an **anxiety disorder**, a state characterized by extreme fear (a response to an external stimulus, such as a snake) and extreme anxiety (a vague but persistent sense of foreboding or dread when not in the presence of the stimulus). Fear and anxiety are part of life, but people who have anxiety disorders experience *intense* or *pervasive* anxiety or fear, or *extreme* attempts to avoid these feelings. These experiences create exceptional distress that can interfere with the ability to function normally. Four major types of anxiety disorders are panic disorder, phobias, posttraumatic stress disorder, and obsessive-compulsive disorder.

PANIC DISORDER. The hallmark of **panic disorder** is the experience of **panic attacks,** episodes of intense fear or discomfort accompanied by symptoms such as palpitations, breathing difficulties, chest pain, nausea, sweating, dizziness, fear of going crazy or doing something uncontrollable, fear of impending doom, and a sense of unreality. Symptoms reach their peak within a few minutes of the beginning of an attack, which can last from minutes to hours. Often these attacks are not associated with a specific situation or object and may even seem to occur randomly. One study of college students found that 12% of the participants experienced spontaneous panic attacks in college or in the years leading up to college (Telch et al., 1989). Internationally, approximately 3% of all people will experience panic disorder during their lifetimes (Rouillon, 1997). Some people may have episodic outbreaks of panic disorder, with years of remission; others may have more persistent symptoms.

Anxiety disorder: A disorder whose hallmark is intense and pervasive anxiety and fear, or extreme attempts to avoid these feelings.

Panic disorder: A disorder whose hallmark is panic attacks.

Panic attack: An episode of intense fear or discomfort accompanied by physical and psychological symptoms such as palpitations, breathing difficulties, chest pain, fear of impending doom or doing something uncontrollable, and a sense of unreality.

Although Indiana Jones was able to divert a panic attack when confronted by snakes, not everyone is so lucky.

Panic Disorder From the Inside

Here is one person's description of a panic attack:

> My breathing starts getting very shallow. I feel I'm going to stop breathing. The air feels like it gets thinner. I feel the air is not coming up through my nose. I take short rapid breaths. Then I see an image of myself gasping for air and remember what happened in the hospital. I think that I will start gasping. I get very dizzy and disoriented. I cannot sit or stand still. I start pacing. Then I start shaking and sweating. I feel I'm losing my mind and I will flip out and hurt myself or someone else. My heart starts beating fast and I start getting pains in my chest. My chest tightens up. I become very frightened. I get afraid that these feelings will not go away. Then I get really upset. I feel no one will be able to help me. I get very frightened I will die. I want to run to some place safe but I don't know where. (Beck et al., 1985, p. 107)

People with panic disorder worry constantly about having more attacks, and in their attempts to avoid or minimize panic attacks, they may change their behavior. Some people fear or avoid places that might be difficult to leave should a panic attack occur—for example, a plane or car. Such fear and avoidance can lead to **agoraphobia** (literally, "fear of the marketplace"), a condition in which the avoidance of places or activities restricts daily life. In severe cases, people with agoraphobia might not leave home at all, or do so only with a close friend or relative. In some cases, people have agoraphobia without panic attacks, avoiding many places because they fear either losing control of themselves in some way (such as losing bladder control) or they fear the occurrence of less severe but still distressing panic symptoms.

What causes panic attacks? A biological vulnerability for panic, an event at the level of the brain, is apparently inherited (Crowe et al., 1983; Torgersen, 1983). Evidence of one possible route to such a vulnerability comes from animal studies, which suggest that panic attacks may arise from a hypersensitivity involving the locus coeruleus, a small group of cells deep in the brainstem (Gorman et al., 1989). The locus coeruleus is the seat of an "alarm system" that triggers an increased heart rate, faster breathing, sweating, and other components of the fight-or-flight response (see Chapters 2, 9, and 12), and can lead to the experience of panic. Recent EEG studies (Wiedemann et al., 1999) have also found unusually strong activation in the right frontal lobe relative to the left when people with panic attacks see potentially panic-inducing stimuli. This suggests that the "withdrawal" system (as characterized by Davidson, 1992b) is relatively easily activated in people with panic attacks, further evidence of brain involvement in the development of panic symptoms. People with panic disorder may be more physiologically sensitive than others to changes in carbon dioxide inhalation (Beck et al., 1999; Papp et al., 1993, 1997), which can come about through hyperventilation. Changes in carbon dioxide levels can elicit panic, perhaps through a "suffocation alarm" in the brain (Klein, 1993).

How a person interprets and responds to these signals from the body—that is, events at the level of the person—may be critical to the development of panic disorder. For instance, people who have *anxiety sensitivity,* defined as the "belief that autonomic arousal can have harmful consequences" (Schmidt et al., 1997, p. 355), are at higher risk of experiencing spontaneous panic attacks (Schmidt et al., 1999). Those high in anxiety sensitivity believe that their experiences of shortness of breath necessarily indicate suffocation or that their heart palpitations must be signaling a heart attack. Studies have found that people with panic disorder are more accurate than other people at detecting changes in their heart rates when their breathing is restricted (Richards et al., 1996).

The misinterpretation of the cause of physiological events may itself increase sympathetic nervous system activity (Wilkinson et al., 1998) and lead to panic. For instance, changes in breathing can lead to changes in carbon dioxide levels, which are then misinterpreted and can lead to panic (Coplan et al., 1998). Thus, changes in the body act like a *false alarm* (Beck, 1976), and after several false alarms, the sensations associated with them become *learned alarms,* which themselves trigger panic (Barlow, 1988). People can also become hypervigilant for the signals that have led to panic in the past. Thus, in a vicious cycle, these people are more likely to experience anticipatory anxiety, which increases sympathetic nervous system activity (including increased heart rate and breathing changes), which in turn triggers panic.

At the level of the group, although 80% of people with panic disorder reported a stressful life event before the development of the panic disorder, the presence of such stress did not predict how severe the disorder would be, nor whether the symptoms would become chronic (Manfro et al., 1996; Rouillon, 1997). This is in contrast to other disorders, such as depression, in which the particular life stressor before the development of an illness is associated with the severity or course of the disorder. However, other studies have found that people with panic disorder tend to have a higher total number of stressful life events during childhood and adolescence, not the year before the development of the disorder. In addition, there is evidence that specific types of stressors, such as those occurring in love and family relationships in

Agoraphobia: A condition in which people fear or avoid places that might be difficult to leave should a panic attack occur.

adulthood, are related to the onset of panic disorder (Horesh et al., 1997). Longitudinal studies of children who go on to develop, or not develop, panic disorder may help sort out the role of stressful events in the development of panic disorder.

For people with agoraphobia, group-level events can play an important role. When a person with agoraphobia feels anxious, the presence of a close relative or friend (referred to as a "safe person") can help decrease negative, panicky thinking. The presence of a safe person can also lower the amount of physiological arousal experienced (Carter et al., 1995).

Although van Gogh was anxious and irritable, we do not know enough about what happened during one of his so-called attacks to know whether these episodes were panic attacks or something else. In any event, panic disorder alone would not account for his symptoms of depression, irritability, impulsiveness, and bizarre behavior.

PHOBIAS: SOCIAL AND SPECIFIC. A **phobia** is an exaggerated fear of an object, class of objects, or situations, accompanied by avoidance that is extreme enough to interfere with everyday life. Phobias can be sorted into types, based on the object or situation that is feared. **Social phobia,** the fear of public embarrassment or humiliation and the ensuing avoidance of social situations likely to arouse this fear, is one of the most common psychiatric diagnoses (major depression is *the* most common; American Psychiatric Association, 1994). Estimates are that approximately 13% of Americans currently experience social phobia (Fones et al., 1998). People with social phobia fear what they perceive to be occasions of great embarrassment or public humiliation, and so avoid social situations in which they think this might occur (Kessler, Stein et al., 1998). They might try to avoid eating, speaking, or performing in public, or using public restrooms or dressing rooms. When unable to avoid these situations, they invariably experience anxiety or panic.

A **specific phobia** is focused on a specific object or situation. Most people with phobias about blood, for example, faint if they see blood and may, because of their phobia, avoid getting appropriate treatment for medical problems (Kleinknecht & Lenz, 1989).

<table>
<tr><td rowspan="8" style="writing-mode:vertical-rl">TABLE 13.3</td><td colspan="2">**Five Subtypes of Specific Phobias**
Source: *American Psychiatric Association (1994).*</td></tr>
<tr><td>**PHOBIA SUBTYPE**</td><td>**EXAMPLES (Fear of . . .)**</td></tr>
<tr><td>Animal fears</td><td>Snakes, rats, insects</td></tr>
<tr><td>Blood–injection–injury fears</td><td>Seeing blood or receiving an injection</td></tr>
<tr><td>Natural environment fears</td><td>Storms, heights, the ocean</td></tr>
<tr><td>Situation fears</td><td>Public transportation, tunnels, bridges, elevators, dental work, flying</td></tr>
<tr><td>Miscellaneous fears cued by stimuli not already mentioned</td><td>Choking, vomiting, contracting an illness, falling down</td></tr>
</table>

Phobia: A fear and avoidance of an object or situation extreme enough to interfere with everyday life.

Social phobia: A type of phobia involving fear of public humiliation or embarrassment and the ensuing avoidance of situations likely to arouse this fear.

Specific phobia: A type of phobia involving persistent and excessive or unreasonable fear triggered by a specific object or situation, along with attempts to avoid the feared stimulus.

People may have phobias about flying or of heights, spiders, or dental work (see Table 13.3). The fear may occur in the presence of the stimulus or in anticipation of it, despite an intellectual recognition that the fear is excessive or unreasonable. By avoiding the object or situation, the sufferer avoids the fear, anxiety, or panic that it might elicit.

Studies with twins suggest that phobias have a genetic component that affects events at the level of the brain (Kendler et al., 1992). The genetic vulnerability may rest on hyperreactivity of the amygdala and other fear-related brain structures (see Chapter 8) in certain situations (LeDoux, 1996). However, not all identical co-twins are phobic if their twins are phobic, so nongenetic factors must play a role. Humans seem biologically *prepared* to develop phobias about certain stimuli and not others (see Chapter 5).

Some people who have social phobias may have been extremely shy as children (see Chapters 10 and 11; Kagan, 1989). Thus, they do not *develop* a phobia; rather, they never lost their discomfort in certain social situations (level of the group). Once a social phobia has developed, the sufferer's thoughts about how other people might be evaluating him or her can become distorted and constant. This distorted thinking about social situations maintains the social phobia (Rapee & Heimberg, 1997).

Learning may play a role in the development of a specific phobia. Classical and operant conditioning in particular could be involved in producing some phobias (Mowrer, 1939; see Chapter 5). If a stimulus such as a thunderstorm (the *conditioned stimulus*) is paired with a traumatic event (the *unconditioned stimulus*), anxiety and fear may become *conditioned responses* to thunderstorms. Furthermore, because fear and anxiety are lessened by avoiding the feared stimulus, the avoidant behavior is operantly reinforced. According to this theory, the phobic person need not experience classical conditioning directly: Observational learning from the behavior of other people who fear particular objects or situations can lead to the development of a phobia, by indicating what should be feared (Mineka et al., 1984). However, more recent work in this area questions the importance of classical conditioning because studies of people with phobias of spiders, heights, and water have not found evidence that such conditioning played the predicted role in the majority of cases (Jones & Menzies, 1995; Menzies & Clarke, 1993, 1995a, 1995b; Poulton et al., 1999). Nevertheless, operant conditioning principles are still involved in maintaining a phobia because avoidance of the feared stimuli decreases any fear and anxiety that would be experienced in the presence of the feared object or situation.

Some soldiers develop posttraumatic stress disorder.

POSTTRAUMATIC STRESS DISORDER (PTSD). An anxiety disorder can occur as a consequence of a traumatic event such as war, physical or sexual abuse, terrorism, or natural disasters. Victims of rape, for example, may be afraid to be alone, especially shortly after the attack. Women who have been raped may become afraid of and angry at all men, or they may experience more general feelings of anger, helplessness, guilt, pain, embarrassment, or anxiety. They may have sexual difficulties because the sexual act has been linked with such negative experiences and feelings. They may also develop physical symptoms of stress, such as stomachaches, headaches, back problems, inability to sleep, or diminished appetite. Depression may come and go over a long period. Long after the rape, they may remain afraid to trust anyone.

Posttraumatic Stress Disorder From the Inside

Mr. E, age 65, complained that ever since World War II he experienced extreme nervousness that was somewhat alleviated by chewing tobacco. He also complained of amnestic periods lasting from seconds to minutes that he called blackout spells. . . . Mr. E stated that others would not tell him what happened during the blackout episodes, but family members reported that sometimes he would take his clothes off, pull at his hair, and scream. He was amnestic for a six-week period of his military service, during which he had been told that he was "crazy" and unfit for duty. After this wartime nervousness—consisting of subjective feelings of anxiety, itching, and shaking—developed [it got to the point where he experienced] eight such episodes in the month before he came to the hospital.

> During the war Mr. E manned a landing craft that transported soldiers to the beaches. He was particularly distraught about an experience in which he felt something underfoot on a sandy beach and discovered that he was stepping on the face of a dead GI. He also described an incident in which his ship had been torpedoed and several crewmen killed. He experienced intense survivor guilt about this incident, and it was the precipitant for his six-week amnestic episode. (Hierholzer et al., 1992, p. 819)

The diagnosis of **posttraumatic stress disorder (PTSD)** is made when three conditions are met. First, the person experiences or witnesses an event that involves actual or threatened serious injury or death. Second, the traumatized person responds to the situation with fear and helplessness. Third, the traumatized individual then experiences three sets of symptoms. One set is the persistent reexperiencing of the traumatic event, which may take the form of intrusive, unwanted, and distressing recollections, dreams, or nightmares of the event, or may involve flashbacks that can include illusions, hallucinations, and a sense of reliving the experience. The second set of PTSD symptoms is a persistent avoidance of anything associated with the trauma and a general emotional numbing. The third set of symptoms is a heightened arousal, which can cause people with PTSD to startle easily (Shalev et al., 2000), have difficulty sleeping, or be in a constant state of hypervigilance. These symptoms do not always appear immediately after the traumatic event, and they can persist for months or even for years.

The majority of people who experience trauma do not go on to experience PTSD (Breslau et al., 1998; Resnick et al., 1993; Shalev et al., 1998), and the type of trauma makes a difference in the outcome. For example, one study found that women were more likely to develop posttraumatic stress disorder when their traumas resulted from crimes rather than from natural disasters (Resnick et al., 1993), and other studies corroborate this finding (Breslau et al., 1998). Among Vietnam veterans, those who were wounded or spent more time in combat were more likely to develop the disorder (Gallers et al., 1988; King et al., 1999). People with severe mental illnesses, such as schizophrenia or bipolar disorder, are *also* likely to have PTSD based on traumatic experiences, including childhood sexual abuse, but in this population PTSD may go unrecognized (Mueser et al., 1998). Other factors that affect whether PTSD will occur can be found in the interactions of events at each level of analysis: the brain, the person, and the group.

Some people may be biologically at risk for developing symptoms of posttraumatic stress disorder, perhaps because of a genetic predisposition (Shalev et al., 1998; True et al., 1993). One possible way such a predisposition could manifest itself is in a hypersensitivity of the locus coeruleus, as occurs with panic disorder. In addition, the limbic system (including the amygdala) of people with this disorder appears to be more easily activated by mental imagery of traumatic events versus nontraumatic events (Rauch et al., 1996; Shin et al., 1997). Macklin and his colleagues (1998) found that combat veterans who had lower IQ scores were more likely to develop PTSD in response to war traumas. This work suggests that people with fewer cognitive and intellectual resources, as defined by lower intelligence scores, are at risk for developing PTSD in response to a trauma.

Factors at the level of the person include the traumatized person's psychological characteristics before, during, and after a trauma (Ehlers et al., 1998). A history of social withdrawal, depression, or a sense of not being able to control stressors all increase the risk of developing PTSD after a trauma (Joseph et al., 1995). The perception that your life is at risk during the traumatic event or that you have no control over it can also facilitate development of PTSD, regardless of the actual threat (Foa et al., 1989). Risk of suffering the disorder rises, too, if you begin to believe the world is a dangerous place (Keane et al., 1985; Kushner et al., 1992). Among individuals who experienced a common type of trauma—a car accident—those who coped during the accident by experiencing dissociation (disruptions in the normal processes of perception, awareness, and memory) were more likely to go on to develop PTSD than those

Posttraumatic stress disorder (PTSD): A disorder experienced by some people after a traumatic event, whose symptoms include an unwanted re-experiencing of the trauma, avoidance of anything associated with the trauma, and heightened arousal.

who did not experience dissociation. Other factors that influenced the likelihood of the development of PTSD in this situation were particular ways of coping with the aftermath of the trauma: Ruminating about it, thought suppression (see Chapter 12), and the intrusion of unwanted thoughts and memories about the accident all made PTSD more likely (Ehlers et al., 1998).

As in the case of phobias, classical and operant conditioning may help explain the avoidance symptoms of PTSD. Operant conditioning also helps us understand why people with PTSD are at a higher risk of developing drug abuse or dependence than those who experienced trauma that did not lead to PTSD (Chilcoat & Breslau, 1998). The substance abuse can be seen as leading to negative reinforcement: When the substances are taken, the symptoms of PTSD temporarily subside.

Whether trauma will lead to PTSD also depends, in part, on events at the level of the group. Support from friends, family, or counselors immediately after a trauma may help decrease the likelihood that PTSD will develop (Kaniasty & Norris, 1992; Kaniasty et al., 1990). In the case of those exposed to trauma as part of military service, social support on arrival home plays an important role in reducing the risk of PTSD (King et al., 1998). Group factors play an integral role in creating the "trauma" part of the disorder, since these traumas almost always involve other people or environmental causes, and certain types of traumatic events (crimes versus natural disasters) are more likely to lead to PTSD.

These factors interact. Because of differences in physiological and psychological characteristics, different people are likely to experience and make sense of the traumatic event differently (Bowman, 1999) and to have different experiences with social support. Consider that among male Vietnam veterans who are identical or fraternal twins, a willingness to volunteer for combat, or to accept more risky assignments, is partly heritable (Lyons et al., 1993). This heritability may be reflected in certain temperaments such as sensation seeking (see Chapter 10): High sensation seekers may be more likely to volunteer for combat and thus be more at risk for certain kinds of trauma. People's personality traits and ways of viewing the world may also influence the level of available social support to them: Extraverts are likely to have more social support available to them than are introverts. Such traits and ways of thinking also influence how people use, or don't use, social support. In turn, the use of social support moderates the effects of the trauma.

OBSESSIVE-COMPULSIVE DISORDER (OCD).

Approximately 2 to 3% of Americans suffer from obsessive-compulsive disorder at some point in their lives (Robins & Regier, 1991), and although the same percentage of people experience this disorder in different countries, culture plays a role in the particular symptoms displayed (Weissman et al., 1994). **Obsessive-compulsive disorder** (OCD) is marked by the presence of *obsessions*, either alone or in combination with *compulsions*.

Obsessive-compulsive disorder can be disabling, affecting every aspect of daily living.

Obsessive-compulsive disorder (OCD): A disorder marked by the presence of obsessions, and sometimes compulsions.

Obsessive-Compulsive Disorder From the Inside

One woman with OCD describes the ordeal of grocery shopping:

> Once I have attained control of the car, I have the burden of getting into it and getting it going. This can be a big project some days, locking and unlocking the doors, rolling up and down the power windows, putting on and off the seat belts, sometimes countlessly. . . . Sometimes while driving I must do overtly good deeds, like letting cars out of streets in front of me, or stopping to let people cross. These are things everyone probably should do, but things I *must* do. . . . My trip in the car may take us to the grocery store. Inside I have certain rituals I must perform. I am relatively subtle about how I do them to avoid drawing attention to myself. Certain foods must have their packages read several times before I am allowed to purchase them. Some things need to be touched repetitively, certain tiles on the floor must

be stepped on by myself and my family. I'll find myself having to go from one end of an aisle to the other and back again, just to make everything all right. I fear being accused of shoplifting sometimes because of the way I behave and the way I am always looking around to see if people have noticed my actions. (Steketee & White, 1990, pp. 12–13)

Obsessions are recurrent and persistent thoughts, impulses, or images that feel intrusive and inappropriate, and that are difficult to suppress or ignore. These are more than excessive worries about real problems, and may cause significant anxiety and distress. Common obsessions involve thoughts of contamination ("Will I become contaminated by shaking her hand?"), repeated doubts ("Did I lock the door? Did I turn off the stove?"), the need to have things in a certain order (a perfect alignment of cans of food in a cupboard), or aggressive or horrific impulses (such as the urge to shout an obscenity in church).

Compulsions are repetitive behaviors or mental acts that some individuals feel driven to perform in response to an obsession. Examples of compulsive behaviors are *washing* in response to thoughts of contamination (washing the hands repeatedly until they are raw), *checking* (checking again and again that the stove is turned off or the windows closed so that it can take hours to leave the house), *ordering* (putting objects in a certain order or in precise symmetry, a task that may take hours until perfection is attained), and *counting* (counting to 100 after each obsessive thought, such as thinking about hitting one's child or shouting an obscenity). Some people with OCD believe that a dreaded event will occur if they do not perform their ritual of checking, ordering, and so on, but these compulsions are not realistically connected to what they are trying to ward off, at least not in the frequency and duration with which the compulsion occurs.

OCD can be understood by looking at events at the three levels and their interactions. At the level of the brain, studies of families have produced evidence for a genetic contribution, although not a straightforward link: If one member of a family has OCD, others are more likely to have an anxiety disorder, but not necessarily OCD itself (Black et al., 1992; Torgersen, 1983). Brain structures and neurotransmitters have been implicated: Obsessions and compulsions have been related to a loop of neural activity that occurs in the caudate nucleus of the basal ganglia (Breiter et al., 1996; Jenike, 1984; Rauch et al., 1994). Obsessions may occur when the caudate nucleus does not do its normal job of "turning off" recurrent thoughts before they become obsessions about an object or circumstance; carrying out a compulsion may temporarily end the obsessional thoughts (Insel, 1992; Jenike, 1984; Modell et al., 1989). The neurotransmitter serotonin appears to play a role in the presence of OCD symptomatology; serotonin-based medications such as Prozac reduce symptoms, although the exact mechanism is unknown (Greenberg et al., 1997).

As with other anxiety disorders, operant conditioning may be involved. Because compulsive behavior may momentarily relieve the anxiety created by the obsessions, the compulsion is reinforced and thus more likely to recur. Research has found that obsessions themselves are not all that uncommon (Weissman et al., 1994), and many people experience obsessive thoughts during their lives, including thoughts about a partner during the early stages of a relationship, without developing a disorder. Salkovskis (1985) proposes that such obsessions develop into a disorder when someone with obsessive thoughts determines that those thoughts are about an unacceptable action (such as killing a newborn child). Obsessive thoughts of this nature may imply danger to the person with the obsession or to someone else. As a result, extremely uncomfortable feelings arise, and mental rituals are created and invoked in an effort to reduce these feelings. Paradoxically, these attempts to alleviate the uncomfortable feelings associated with the obsession perpetuate its ability to induce uncomfortable feelings, and, through negative reinforcement, strengthen the mental rituals. Similarly, Rachman and his colleagues (Rachman, 1997; Shafran et al., 1996) propose that people with OCD view a disturbing thought as the moral equivalent of carrying

Obsession: A recurrent and persistent thought, impulse, or image that feels intrusive and inappropriate, and is difficult to suppress or ignore.

Compulsion: A repetitive behavior or mental act that an individual feels compelled to perform in response to an obsession.

out the thought, leading to higher levels of distress in response to the initial obsessional thought.

In research studies, people with more serious OCD tended to have families who were more rejecting of them and to have experienced more kinds of family stress (level of the group; Calvocoressi et al., 1995). However, the direction of causation is unclear: Were families more rejecting because their OCD relatives were more symptomatic, and therefore more difficult to live with? Or did the strong rejection by the families produce stronger symptoms of OCD in the affected relatives? Perhaps future research will be able to say more about causation.

Mood Disorders

By some estimates, about half of those who have suffered from anxiety disorders will also go on to suffer from depression (Kessler, Stang et al., 1998), which is a mood disorder. **Mood disorders** are conditions marked by persistent or episodic disturbances in affect that interfere with normal functioning in at least one realm of life. Among the most common mood disorders are major depressive disorder, dysthymia (a less intense but longer lasting form of depression), and bipolar disorder (also known as manic-depressive disorder).

MAJOR DEPRESSIVE DISORDER: NOT JUST FEELING BLUE. When people are feeling sad or blue, they may say they are "depressed," but generally they do not mean they are suffering from a psychological disorder. **Major depressive disorder (MDD)** is characterized by at least 2 weeks of depressed mood or loss of interest in nearly all activities, along with at least four of the other symptoms of depression listed in Table 13.4 (American Psychiatric Association, 1994). Thus, major depression affects a person's "ABC's": affect (mood), behavior (actions), and cognition (thoughts). It is estimated that up to one in five people in the United States will experience this disorder in their lifetimes (APA, 1994; Ross, 1991), and that by the year 2020, depression will probably be the second most disabling disease in the nation,

Mood disorder: A condition marked by persistent or episodic disturbances in affect that interfere with normal functioning in at least one realm of life.

Major depressive disorder (MDD): A disorder characterized by at least 2 weeks of depressed mood or loss of interest in nearly all activities, along with sleep or eating disturbances, loss of energy, and feelings of hopelessness.

TABLE 13.4

Diagnostic Criteria for Major Depressive Disorder
Source: *American Psychiatric Association (1994).*

During a period of at least 2 weeks, five or more of the following symptoms have occurred and represent a change in functioning.

- Depressed mood most of the day, almost daily (based on subjective report or observations of others).

- Markedly diminished interest or pleasure in nearly all daily activities (based on subjective or objective reports).

- Significant weight loss, not through dieting.

- Daily insomnia or hypersomnia (sleeping a lot).

- Daily psychomotor agitation (intense restlessness) or retardation (physical sluggishness).

- Daily fatigue, or loss of energy.

- Almost daily feelings of worthlessness, or inappropriate or excessive guilt.

- Almost daily diminished ability to think or concentrate, or indecisiveness (based on subjective or objective reports).

- Recurrent thoughts of death or suicide with or without a specific plan.

after heart disease (Schrof & Schultz, 1999). Some people with depression may experience only one episode; others experience recurrent episodes that may be frequent or separated by years; or the depression becomes more chronic (Judd et al., 1998). A recent 10-year study of over 300 people diagnosed with major depressive disorder found that more than one third of the participants did not have a recurrence of depression (Solomon et al., 2000).

Some people—approximately 6% of the American population—experience a less intense but longer lasting type of depression called **dysthymia** (American Psychiatric Association, 1994). People who are given this diagnosis do not suffer an episode of extreme depression but do have a depressed mood for most of the day for at least 2 years and experience two other symptoms of depression (see Table 13.4; APA, 1994).

Artist Kate Monson, who experienced depression, describes her painting as a reflection of her depression.

Major Depressive Disorder From the Inside

The experience of depression is captured in words by Elizabeth Wurtzel, author of *Prozac Nation*:

In my case, I was not frightened in the least bit at the thought that I might live because I was certain, quite certain, that I was already dead. The actual dying part, the withering away of my physical body, was a mere formality. My spirit, my emotional being, whatever you want to call all that inner turmoil that has nothing to do with physical existence, were long gone, dead and gone, and only a mass of the most . . . god-awful excruciating pain . . . was left in its wake.

That's the thing I want to make clear about depression: It's got nothing at all to do with life. In the course of life, there is sadness and pain and sorrow, all of which, in their right time and season, are normal—unpleasant, but normal. Depression is in an altogether different zone because it involves a complete absence: absence of affect, absence of feeling, absence of response, absence of interest. The pain you feel in the course of a major clinical depression is an attempt on nature's part (nature, after all, abhors a vacuum) to fill up the empty space. But for all intents and purposes, the deeply depressed are just the walking, waking dead. (Wurtzel, 1995, p. 22)

Elizabeth Wurtzel's description of her depression captures the essence of the painful, extremely disturbing quality of many of the symptoms. In some cases, severely depressed people also have delusions or hallucinations. Often these psychotic symptoms feature themes of guilt, deserved punishment, and personal inadequacy, such as voices asserting the individual's worthlessness.

However, not all cultures share exactly the same symptom list. In Latin and Mediterranean cultures, people with major depressive disorder tend to experience "nerves" or headaches, not necessarily sadness and guilt. In Asian cultures, people with major depression are likely to report weakness, tiredness, or a sense of "imbalance."

Major depressive disorder, the most common psychological disorder in the United States (Kessler et al., 1994), is found among all cultural and ethnic groups (Weissman et al., 1991), as well as across the economic spectrum. In developing countries, rates are estimated to be about the same for men and for women (Culbertson, 1997), but American women are diagnosed with depression two to three times more frequently than American men (APA, 1994; Culbertson, 1997; Gater et al., 1998). Further, the overall rate of depression is increasing in the United States (Lewinsohn et al., 1993).

Many, if not most, suicide attempts seem to be motivated by the sense of hopelessness that is often a part of depression. Approximately 30% of people with depression attempt suicide, and half of those succeed. One estimate is that 19,200 depressed people in the United States commit suicide every year (American Foundation for Suicide Prevention, 1996). Suicide prevention programs try, in part, to treat depression and alcohol use, factors leading to suicide (Reifman & Windle, 1995).

Dysthymia: A mood disorder similar to major depressive disorder, but less intense and longer lasting.

TABLE 13.5

Common Misconceptions of Suicide

Source: *Adapted from Suicide Awareness\Voices of Education (SA\VE), P.O. Box 24507, Minneapolis, MN 55424; Phone: (612) 946-7998; Internet: http://www.save.org; E-mail: save@winternet.com.*

- *If you talk about suicide, you won't really do it.* (False: Most people who commit suicide gave some clue or warning. Threats or statements about suicide should not be ignored.)

- *People who attempt suicide are "crazy."* (False: Suicidal people are not "crazy"; they *are* likely to be depressed, upset, or feel hopeless.)

- *Someone determined to commit suicide can't be stopped.* (False: Almost all suicidal people have mixed feelings about living and dying up until the last moment. Moreover, most suicidal people don't want to die; they want their pain to stop. And the suicidal impulse often passes.)

- *People who commit suicide weren't willing to seek help.* (False: Studies have shown that more than half of suicide victims sought medical help within the 6 months before death.)

- Talking about suicide could give someone the idea, so you shouldn't talk or ask about it. (False. Discussing suicide openly can be helpful to someone who is suicidal.)

Several common misconceptions about suicide are listed in Table 13.5. Test yourself to see if your views of suicide are accurate.

BIPOLAR DISORDER: GOING TO EXTREMES. In contrast to depression, **bipolar disorder** is a mood disorder marked by one or more manic episodes or the less intense hypomania; some people with this disorder also experience depression. Approximately 1% of Americans have this disorder (Regier & Kaelber, 1995). A **manic episode** is a period of at least a week during which an abnormally elevated, expansive, or irritable mood persists (see Table 13.6). Being manic is not just having an "up" day. During a manic episode, the sufferer may be euphoric and enthusiastic about everything, starting conversations with strangers and making grandiose plans.

TABLE 13.6

Diagnostic Criteria for a Manic Episode

Source: *American Psychiatric Association (1994).*

- Grandiosity or elevated sense of self-esteem.

- Less need for sleep.

- More talkative than usual, or feels pressure to keep talking, and may be difficult to interrupt.

- Racing thoughts (sometimes described as watching three different television programs simultaneously).

- Distractibility and difficulty screening out useful from extraneous material.

- Increase in goal-directed activity (this could be socially, at work, at school, or sexually) or psychomotor agitation.

- Excessive involvement in pleasurable activities that have a high potential for painful consequences (for example, unrestrained shopping sprees, sexual infidelity, unwise business investments).

Bipolar disorder: A mood disorder marked by one or more episodes of either mania or hypomania.

Manic episode: A period of at least 1 week during which an abnormally elevated, expansive, or irritable mood persists.

Bipolar Disorder From the Inside

Psychologist Kay Redfield Jamison describes her personal experience with mania:

There is a particular kind of pain, elation, loneliness, and terror involved in this kind of madness. When you're high, it's tremendous. The ideas and feelings are fast and frequent like shooting stars, and you follow them until you find better and brighter ones. Shyness goes, the right words and gestures are suddenly there, the power to captivate others a felt certainty. There are interests found in uninteresting people. Sensuality is pervasive and the desire to seduce and be seduced irresistible. Feelings of ease, intensity, power, well-being, financial omnipotence, and euphoria pervade one's marrow. But, somewhere, this changes. The fast ideas are far too fast, and there are far too many; overwhelming confusion replaces clarity. Memory goes. Humor and absorption on friends' faces are replaced by fear and concerns. Everything previously moving with the grain is now against—you are irritable, angry, frightened, uncontrollable, and enmeshed totally in the blackest caves of the mind. You never knew those caves were there. It will never end, for madness carves its own reality. (Jamison, 1995, p. 67)

Psychologist Kay Redfield Jamison, like many people with bipolar disorder, had difficulty recognizing that she had a psychological disorder and resisted attempts at treatment for a number of years. People experiencing **hypomania** have less severe symptoms of mania, and their symptoms are less likely to interfere with social functioning. Manic or hypomanic episodes are often preceded or followed by episodes of depression, and the cycling of the mood usually takes place over a number of years, although some people may experience rapid cycling, with four or more mood shifts in a year. If left untreated, mood swings often become more frequent over time, leading to a poorer prognosis. The early phase of an episode, before the symptoms become acute, is termed the *prodromal phase* (a *prodrome* is a warning symptom). Some people with bipolar disorder report prodromal indicators of manic or depressive symptoms that signal that an episode will occur (Keitner et al., 1996).

EXPLAINING MOOD DISORDERS. Although bipolar and major depressive disorders are distinct disorders, recent research has characterized these disorders, as well as dysthymia, as lying along a spectrum of mood disorders (Akiskal, 1996; Angst, 1998) that are related by biological and psychological factors. As with anxiety disorders, mood disorders can best be understood by considering events at three levels of analysis and their interactions: the brain, the person, and the group.

Twin studies show that if one identical twin has a major depression, the co-twin is four times more likely to experience a depression than the co-twin of an affected fraternal twin (Bowman & Nurnberger, 1993; Kendler et al., 1999). This appears to be good evidence for genetic influence. However, adoption studies have not shown the same clear-cut evidence for a genetic role (Eley et al., 1998; Wender et al., 1986). More definitive support for biological factors comes from research with depressed people with relatives who also suffer from depression: The depressed people studied had unusually low activity in one area of the frontal lobe that has direct connections to many brain areas involved in emotion, such as the amygdala. This part of the frontal lobe also has connections to the systems that produce serotonin, norepinephrine, and dopamine (Kennedy et al., 1997). In contrast, there is evidence that the amygala is enlarged in people with bipolar disorder (Altshuler et al., 1998). These abnormalities in or affecting the amygdala in people with mood disorders are consistent with the role of the amygdala in regulating mood and accessing emotional memories (LeDoux, 1996; see Chapters 8 and 9). Recent brain-scanning studies of people with bipolar disorder have found shifts in temporal lobe activity during manic episodes that are not present during other mood states (Gyulai et al., 1997), which may be related to activity in parts of the limbic system that are located in this structure.

There is clear evidence for an underlying genetic relationship between bipolar and depressive mood disorders. For example, if an identical twin has bipolar disorder, the

Hypomania: A mood state similar to mania, but less severe, with fewer and less intrusive symptoms.

co-twin has an 80% chance of developing some kind of mood disorder (such as depression), although not necessarily bipolar disorder (Karkowski & Kendler, 1997; Vehmanen et al., 1995).

Evidence that neurotransmitter or neuromodulator activity plays a role in depression was uncovered years ago. In fact, some researchers thought that the puzzle of depression was nearly solved with the discovery that medications that alter the serotonin or norepinephrine systems, discussed further in the next chapter, can diminish or remove symptoms of depression. Unfortunately, it is not yet clear which substances are most involved in depression; it is not even clear whether the problem is having too much or too little of those substances (Duman et al., 1997). What *is* clear, however, is that some change occurs in the activity of serotonin, norepinephrine, and possibly a more recently discovered neurotransmitter, *substance P* (Kramer et al., 1998), among people with depression.

Neurotransmitters are also implicated in bipolar disorder, although the exact mechanism is unknown. There is some support for the theory that bipolar disorder involves disturbances in the functioning of serotonin (Goodwin & Jamison, 1990). Moreover, it is known that lithium, the medication usually prescribed for bipolar disorder, lowers the activity level of norepinephrine in the brain (Bunney & Garland, 1983), but just how this happens is not yet known.

Events at the level of the person can be associated with a higher risk of depression. Compared with people who are not depressed, depressed people make more negative comments and less eye contact, are less responsive, and speak more softly and in shorter sentences (Gotlib & Robinson, 1982; Segrin & Abramson, 1994). Aaron Beck (1967) found evidence of a "negative triad of depression" in the thoughts of depressed people. This triad consists of (1) a negative view of the world, (2) a negative view of the self, and (3) a negative view of the future. Beck proposes that people with depression commit errors in their thinking, or "cognitive distortions," based on these three sets of beliefs, and that these errors in logic maintain an outlook on life that perpetuates depressing feelings and behaviors. These cognitive distortions may be based on early learning.

Of particular interest is evidence that people's views of themselves and the world can influence their risk of developing depression. A person's characteristic way of explaining life events—his or her **attributional style**—affects the risk of depression. For people who attribute blame to themselves (versus external factors), the risk of depression rises, especially after a stressful event (Monroe & Depue, 1991). Research on attributional styles and depression find that those people who tend to attribute unfortunate events to internal causes (their own thoughts, abilities, behaviors, and the like), and who believe that these causes are stable, are more likely to become depressed. Thus, depressing thoughts (such as "I deserved to be fired . . . I wasn't as good at my job as some other people") are more likely to lead to depressing feelings. In contrast, patterns of attributing blame to external causes ("I was laid off because I didn't have enough seniority"), even if inaccurate, are less likely to lead to depression (Abramson et al., 1978).

Research has found that at the beginning of a semester, college students whose attributional style led them to blame internal causes were more likely to become depressed when receiving a bad grade than those who blamed external causes. They were more likely to attribute a bad grade to their lack of ability rather than to the difficulty of the test, poor teaching, or other external factors. Similarly, prison inmates who showed this attributional style when they began to serve their sentences were more likely than other prisoners to become depressed after months of incarceration. And mothers with an internal attributional style during the second trimester of pregnancy were more likely to be depressed 3 months after childbirth (Peterson & Seligman, 1984). Generally speaking, when bad things happen, if you consistently blame yourself as opposed to some aspect of the situation, you are more likely to become depressed.

Occurrences at the level of the group have also been tied to depression. Life stresses that occur before the development of depression can influence the severity of the depression. Moreover, as would be expected according to the principles of operant

Attributional style: A person's characteristic way of explaining life events.

conditioning (see Chapter 5), the less opportunity there is for social reinforcement because of decreased activity and contact with other people, the more likely it is that depressive symptoms will occur (MacPhillamy & Lewinsohn, 1974). Similarly, environments that not only lack positive reinforcements but also provide many "punishing" experiences (such as being regularly criticized) put people at risk for depression. Programs designed to help those with depression increase the frequency and quality of positive interactions with others (as well as decreasing the frequency and quality of punishing interactions) to minimize depressive symptoms (Teri & Lewinsohn, 1985).

Although not necessarily associated with the *onset* of depression, the family environment can be influential in *recovery* from a depressive episode. Living with unsupportive and critical relatives can increase the risk of a relapse of depression (Hooley & Licht, 1997; Miller et al., 1992). Culture may also play a role in facilitating depression. Nolen-Hoeksema (1987) offered a cultural explanation for the finding that women in developed countries experience depression more often than men. She and others (Nolen-Hoeksema & Morrow, 1993; Vajk et al., 1997) have found that people in developed countries who ruminate about their depressed mood are more likely to have longer periods of depression. She proposes that as children, boys and girls are taught to respond differently to stressors, and they carry these response styles with them through adulthood. She contends that boys are encouraged to de-emphasize feelings and to use distraction and action-oriented coping strategies, whereas girls are encouraged to be introspective and not to take action. A ruminative response is known to promote depression; action and distraction can serve as protection. And in fact, research has shown that depressed mood improves when college students learn to increase strategies of distraction and decrease their ruminations (Nolen-Hoeksema & Morrow, 1993). Other psychologists propose that the substantially higher rate of depression in women may also be due to biases in how the diagnosis is made and how depression is measured (Hartung & Widiger, 1998; Sprock & Yoder, 1997).

Events at the level of the group can also affect the course of bipolar disorder. Social stressors that affect biological rhythms or schedules, such as frequent plane travel or repeated changes in work schedules, can adversely affect the course of the disease (Johnson & Roberts, 1995; Post, 1992), as can events that disrupt social rhythms, such as moving to a new residence (Malkoff-Schwartz et al., 1998). As with depression, there is evidence that more Americans are experiencing bipolar disorder than ever before, and at earlier ages (Goodwin & Jamison, 1990). One cause may be the unnaturally lengthened day in modern society brought about by electric lights. When a patient with rapid cycling bipolar disorder was put in an environment without electric lights (thereby experiencing 10–14 hours of darkness a night), the cycles lengthened, bringing more stability of mood (Wehr et al., 1998).

First episodes of bipolar disorder are invariably preceded by significant stressors (Goodwin & Ghaemi, 1998). And, as with depression, people with bipolar disorder are more likely to relapse if they live with critical families (Honig et al., 1997; Miklowitz et al., 1988). Life stressors can also impede recovery after a hospitalization for bipolar disorder (Johnson & Miller, 1997). On a positive note, programs designed to reduce the critical behavior of families appear to be effective in reducing relapses (Honig et al., 1997). Events at the three levels are not independent but interact in a number of ways. In particular, James Coyne (1976; Coyne & Downey, 1991) has proposed an interactional theory of depression. He theorized that the depressed person, who may be biologically vulnerable to depression, alienates others who might provide support through his or her verbal and nonverbal actions (Nolan & Mineka, 1997). Such actions include negative attitudes, dependent behavior, and an inclination to ignore or be unable to use help or advice from others. These actions eventually lead other people to reject or criticize the depressed person, confirming the depressed person's negative view of him- or herself, and increasing the likelihood of negative future events.

We know that van Gogh suffered from bouts of depression, at times had poor hygiene, narrowed his activities severely, and took pleasure only in painting. MDD seems like a possible diagnosis. Van Gogh's attempted assault on Gauguin, as well as the self-mutilation of his ear might be explained by MDD with psychotic features. Perhaps the auditory hallucination that told him to kill Gauguin was caused by his depression. Although MDD could explain the majority of these symptoms, it is not the only possibility. Bipolar disorder is another potential diagnosis. Perhaps van Gogh's episodes of frenzied painting were manic episodes, although they could also have been an intense restlessness that can occur with depression. His attacks, which became more frequent over time, might have been episodes of mania that became psychotic; untreated episodes of mania do become more frequent.

Depression Is as Depression Does

Have you ever noticed that it's no fun being with a depressed person? A depressed mood can be contagious, and family and friends of depressed people may find themselves being and acting somewhat depressed, further limiting their assistance to the depressed person (Coyne et al., 1987). Thomas Joiner (1994) found that people who spent time with depressed roommates over a period of 3 weeks themselves became more depressed. Indeed, anger, anxiety, depression, and sadness have also been found to be contagious (Coyne, 1976; Hsee et al., 1990; Joiner, 1994; Katz et al., 1999; Segrin & Dillard, 1992; Sullins, 1991).

One possible way that you "catch" emotions from others is by acting like them, which leads you to feel similarly. At the level of the brain, just as putting on a happy face can make you feel better, putting on a frown can make you feel worse (Ekman et al., 1990; see Chapter 9). This response could be unconscious. In fact, just seeing a happy or an angry face causes muscles in your own face to respond, and to respond very quickly—in less than a half a second (Dimberg & Thunberg, 1998). At the level of the person, when participants were asked to inhibit their facial movements when they watched happy films, they later reported enjoying the films less than when their facial muscles were allowed to move spontaneously as they watched; however, large differences were reported in the degree to which making an expression led to the experience of the corresponding emotion (Laird et al., 1994). Moreover, at the level of the group, someone's behavior may directly affect a close companion. For example, a depressed person is less responsive, which in and of itself may lead a companion to become depressed (Coyne, 1976). In addition, those who develop depression are more likely to behave in ways that create stress in their environments, which in turn can trigger the onset of depression in others (McGuffin et al., 1988; Rende & Plomin, 1992).

CONSOLIDATE!

▶ *1. What are the main types of anxiety disorders? What are their symptoms and causes?* The anxiety disorders include panic disorder (with or without agoraphobia), specific and social phobias, PTSD, and OCD. Panic symptoms include nausea, dizziness, palpitations, and a fear of doing something crazy or uncontrollable. Phobias involve avoiding a feared object or situation that would cause anxiety or panic if encountered. PTSD occurs in response to traumatic events; it involves some symptoms of panic, as well as a reliving of the trauma. OCD involves obsessions and often compulsions.

▶ *2. What are mood disorders? What causes them?* Mood disorders include major depressive disorder, dysthymia, and bipolar disorder (which may have psychotic features). Major depressive disorder is characterized by depressed mood, loss of pleasure, fatigue, weight loss, poor sleep, a sense of worthlessness or guilt, and poor attention and concentration. Dysthymia is a less intense but longer lasting type of depression. Bipolar disorder involves the presence of manic or hypomanic episodes. Although all of these disorders appear to have a genetic and biological component, events at the levels of the person and group can play a role in onset or relapse.

SCHIZOPHRENIA

In the last years of his life, van Gogh apparently had increasing difficulty distinguishing between his internal experiences and external reality. He would become disoriented and not know who he was. He had delusions of being poisoned and attacked. Gauguin claimed that van Gogh referred to himself as a ghost before cutting off part of his ear. During a period of mental clarity, when van Gogh was asked about the assault on Gauguin, he said that he was given to hearing voices, that he had heard voices telling him to kill Gauguin. Then he remembered the biblical injunction, "If thine own eye offend thee, pluck it out." His ear had offended him by "hearing" the voice that suggested he kill Gauguin, so he cut part of it off to do penance for his sin against Gauguin (Lubin, 1972).

These aspects of van Gogh's life and behavior suggest the possibility of schizophrenia. Books or movies sometimes portray schizophrenia as if it meant having a split personality, but schizophrenia is characterized by a split from reality, not a split from different aspects of oneself.

The word *schizophrenia* is derived from two Greek words, *schizo* meaning "to split" or "to cut," and *phren* meaning "mind" or "reason." **Schizophrenia** is a psychotic disorder that profoundly alters affect, behavior, and cognition, particularly the pattern or form of thought.

▶ 1. What are the symptoms of schizophrenia?

▶ 2. What are the subtypes of schizophrenia?

▶ 3. Why do some people develop schizophrenia?

Symptoms: What Schizophrenia Looks Like

The term *schizophrenia* actually embraces a number of subtypes of this disorder, each with distinct symptoms and prognoses (prospects of recovery). Symptoms of schizophrenia are usually divided into two groups (see Table 13.7). **Positive symptoms** involve an excess or distortion of normal functions, such as hallucinations. They are called positive not because they indicate something desirable, but because they mark the *presence* of certain unusual behaviors. **Negative symptoms**, on the other hand, involve a *diminution* or *loss* of normal functions, such as a restriction in speech or movement.

TABLE 13.7

Positive and Negative Symptoms of Schizophrenia

POSITIVE SYMPTOMS

Delusions of
- Persecution (beliefs that others are out to "get" you)
- Grandeur (beliefs that you are an important person)
- Reference (beliefs that normal events have special meaning directed toward you)
- Control (beliefs that your feelings, behaviors, or thoughts are controlled by others)

Hallucinations
- Disordered behavior
- Disorganized speech

NEGATIVE SYMPTOMS
- Flat affect
- Alogia (brief, slow, empty replies to questions)
- Avolition (inability to initiate goal-directed behavior)

Schizophrenia: A psychotic disorder in which the patient's affect, behavior, and thoughts are profoundly altered.

Positive symptom: An excess or distortion of normal functions, such as a hallucination.

Negative symptom: A diminution or loss of normal functions, such as a restriction in speech.

Positive symptoms include *delusions* (distortions of thought), and *hallucinations*. Positive symptoms are usually more responsive than negative symptoms to antipsychotic medication (discussed in the next chapter). Delusions can be complex, centering on a particular theme, such as the belief that someone, or some people, are out to "get" you (see Table 13.7). Hallucinations in schizophrenia are typically auditory; hearing voices is a common symptom. *Disorganized behavior* can include inappropriate, childlike silliness or unpredictable agitation. People with disorganized behavior may have difficulty with everyday tasks such as organizing meals, maintaining hygiene, and selecting their clothes (they might wear two overcoats in the summer). Another positive symptom is *disorganized speech*, as in the following example: "I may be a 'Blue Baby' but 'Social Baby' not, but yet a blue heart baby could be in the Blue Book published before the war" (Maher, 1966, p. 413).

Negative symptoms include flat affect, alogia, and avolition (see Table 13.7). *Flat affect* is a general failure to express or respond to emotion. There may be occasional smiles or warmth of manner, but usually the facial expression is constant; eye contact is rare and body language minimal. *Alogia*, or "poverty of speech," is characterized by brief, slow, empty replies to questions. Alogia is not an unwillingness to speak; rather, the thoughts behind the words seem slowed down. Someone with alogia speaks less than others and doesn't use words as freely. *Avolition* is an inability to initiate or persist in goal-directed activities. Someone exhibiting avolition may sit for long periods without engaging in any behavior or social interaction.

Not all these symptoms are present in everyone affected with schizophrenia. According to the *DSM-IV*, a diagnosis of schizophrenia requires that two or more symptoms are displayed for at least a week and that other signs of socially inappropriate behavior are exhibited for at least 6 months. The average age of onset of schizophrenia is the 20s, although in some people (particularly women) onset does not come until later in life. Symptoms often occur gradually, with a prodromal phase characterized by slow deterioration in functioning, including withdrawal from other people, poor hygiene, and outbursts of anger. Eventually the symptoms reach an active phase, in which full-blown positive and negative symptoms arise.

Did van Gogh appear to exhibit symptoms of schizophrenia? We know that he had auditory hallucinations and that he exhibited inappropriate social behavior (including poor hygiene and outbursts of anger), but he does not appear to have had negative symptoms of schizophrenia (at least not between his attacks). Not enough is known about his behavior during his attacks to determine whether additional symptoms accompanied them.

Types of Schizophrenia

People with schizophrenia, as mentioned earlier, tend to suffer from only some of the full range of possible symptoms. The symptoms of schizophrenia tend to cluster into

TABLE 13.8

Four Subtypes of Schizophrenia, According to *DSM-IV*
Source: *American Psychiatric Association (1994).*

PARANOID
Delusions of persecution are prominent; intellectual functioning and affect are relatively intact, but auditory hallucinations are common.

DISORGANIZED
Disorganized speech and behavior and flat or inappropriate affect are prominent.

CATATONIC
Catatonic (bizarre, immobile, or relentless) motor behaviors are prominent.

UNDIFFERENTIATED
Symptoms do not clearly fall into any of the above three subtypes.

groupings, and from these groupings mental health professionals and researchers have identified subtypes of schizophrenia. The *DSM-IV* specifies four subtypes of schizophrenia (see Table 13.8): paranoid, disorganized, catatonic, and undifferentiated.

> ### Paranoid Schizophrenia From the Inside
>
> Jeffrey DeMann describes his first hospitalization for schizophrenia at the age of 27:
>
> I recall vividly the delusion of believing my mother was to take my place in the shock treatments. Then I was to be quietly murdered and placed in an acid bath grave, which would dissolve any physical evidence of my existence. At this time, auditory hallucinations also were present. I could actually hear the slamming of my mother's body on the table while being administered the deadly shock. I truly believed my mother was now dead in my place. I also recall curling up on an old wooden bench and repeatedly chanting the words "Die quickly now." (DeMann, 1994, p. 580)

Paranoid schizophrenia is marked by delusions and auditory hallucinations that are limited to specific topics related to a coherent theme. Delusions may reflect an explicitly paranoid theme (of being hunted by the CIA) or a grandiose one (of being God). At the same time, those with paranoid schizophrenia have cognitive and affective functioning that is often relatively intact when not pertaining to the delusion; as a result, diagnosing people with this type of schizophrenia can be difficult. Unless they are talking about the topic of their delusions, they are likely to seem normal. Of people affected with schizophrenia, those with this subtype have the best prognosis for recovery, although they are more likely to exhibit aggressive behavior, toward either themselves or others, and have the highest suicide rate (13%; Fenton & McGlashan, 1991).

Disorganized schizophrenia is marked by disorganized behavior and speech and inappropriate affect, such as laughter at odd times or places. People with this type of schizophrenia may giggle, dress strangely, speak obscenely or babble, and urinate or defecate in public. This behavior contrasts with that of people who have OCD or panic disorder, who may *fear* behaving in some inappropriate or socially unacceptable way but do not actually *perform* the behaviors that preoccupy them. Disorganized schizophrenia has a poor prognosis, and individuals with this diagnosis may require constant care.

Catatonic schizophrenia features bizarre movements, including immobility—remaining in the same odd posture for hours—or facial grimacing. Someone with catatonic schizophrenia may not speak at all or may involuntarily and senselessly repeat words or phrases said by others or mimic other people's body movements. Like those with disorganized schizophrenia, people with catatonia may require constant care to prevent them from hurting themselves or others.

Undifferentiated schizophrenia is the diagnosis for those whose symptoms do not cluster together so as to meet the criteria for the other subtypes. Those diagnosed with a particular subtype of schizophrenia at one time may not have the same set of symptoms at a later time. Thus, for someone with schizophrenia, the subtype diagnosis may change over the course of the illness.

Were van Gogh schizophrenic, the paranoid subtype diagnosis would seem to fit him best because his intellectual functioning and affect remained relatively intact between attacks. But he apparently did not have extended periods of paranoid delusions, and schizophrenia would not account for his lengthy bouts of depression.

Why Does This Happen to Some People, But Not Others?

With few exceptions, schizophrenia occurs at about the same rate worldwide, about 1 in 100 (Gottesman, 1991). However, industrialized countries have lower recovery rates than do developing nations (American Psychiatric Association, 1994). Explanations why some people and not others suffer from schizophrenia, and why recovery rates are different in different places and circumstances, involve the three levels of analysis and the interaction of events at these levels.

THE BRAIN. Twin, family, and adoption studies point to the influence of genetic factors in the development of schizophrenia (Gottesman, 1991; Kendler & Diehl, 1993; Tiernari, 1991). Having relatives with schizophrenia increases the risk of developing schizophrenia; the closer the relative, the greater the risk. However, it is important to note that even for those who have a close relative with schizophrenia, the actual incidence is still quite low. More than 80% of people who have a parent or sibling diagnosed with schizophrenia do *not* have the disorder themselves (Gottesman & Moldin, 1998). Even in the case of the highest level of genetic resemblance, identical twins, the co-twin of a schizophrenic twin has only a 48% risk of developing schizophrenia. If the disease were entirely genetic, we would expect a 100% risk in this circumstance. And a fraternal co-twin has only a 17% likelihood of developing the disorder (Gottesman, 1991). Although genes may play a role in the etiology of schizophrenia, they are clearly not the only factor.

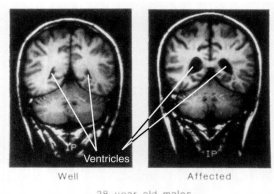

Well   Affected

28 year old males

Those with schizophrenia have larger ventricles, smaller amounts of frontal and temporal lobe cortex, and a smaller thalamus. This decreased cortical volume probably accounts for some of the cognitive deficits found in people with schizophrenia (Andreasen et al., 1986, 1992).

Evidence from autopsies and brain-scanning studies suggests that schizophrenia may involve abnormalities in brain structures. Someone with schizophrenia is more likely than others to have enlarged *ventricles*, cavities in the center of the brain filled with cerebrospinal fluid. Increased ventricle size means a reduction in the size of other brain areas, including the frontal cortex (Goldstein et al., 1999), which plays a central role in abstract thinking and planning. Impaired frontal lobe functioning has been the focus of a substantial amount of the research on schizophrenia. Results indicate that at least some deficits in functioning may occur because of excessive pruning of neural connections in the frontal lobe during adolescence (Keshavan et al., 1994). This finding is supported by brain-scanning studies that have revealed abnormally low numbers of dopamine receptors in the frontal lobes of people with schizophrenia (Okubo et al., 1997).

Enlarged ventricles are also associated with decreases in the size of the temporal lobe (which, among other things, processes auditory information, some aspects of language, and visual recognition) and of the thalamus, which transmits sensory information to other parts of the brain (Andreasen et al., 1994). There is evidence that these abnormalities already exist at the time of a first episode of psychosis and thus are not the consequences of either the disorder or medications given to treat the disorder (Velakoulis et al., 1999).

Researchers looking at different ways in which these brain abnormalities might arise have found several possible causes. One focus has been on the fetus's developing brain, and how normal brain development may go awry during gestation, the 9 months the fetus is developing in the mother's uterus. Possibilities include maternal malnourishment during pregnancy (Brown, van Os, et al., 1999), maternal illness (Buka et al., 1999; Gilmore et al., 1997; Mednick et al., 1998), and prenatal or birth-related medical complications that lead to oxygen deprivation (Cannon, 1997; Geddes & Lawrie, 1995; McNeil et al., 2000; Zornberg et al., 2000). Because research has found a higher incidence of prenatal and birth complications in babies born to mothers with schizophrenia, some have further argued that fetuses with a genetic predisposition to schizophrenia have an increased likelihood of abnormal development, which in turn leads to the higher rate of prenatal and birth complications (Goodman, 1988). However, some researchers suggest that complications in and of themselves do not create a risk for schizophrenia in the absence of genetic vulnerability (Buka et al., 1999). Rather, it is the combination of the genetic vulnerability and the physical complications during gestation and birth that together heighten the risk for the alteration in brain development and later schizophrenia.

Similarly, children who are at risk for schizophrenia—those who show an extreme discomfort with close relationships and exhibit relatively high levels of quirky or odd behavior—are more reactive to stress and have higher baseline levels of the stress-related hormone cortisol (Walker et al., 1999; see Chapter 12). Some suggest that the increased biological changes and stressors of adolescence lead to higher levels of stress hormones, which in turn are thought to affect dopamine activity. Prodromal symptoms of schizophrenia often begin to emerge during adolescence.

Neurotransmitters, particularly dopamine, have been implicated in schizophrenia (Walker & Diforio, 1997). It was once thought that an overproduction of dopamine, or an increased number or sensitivity of dopamine receptors, was responsible for schizophrenia. This *dopamine hypothesis* received support from research showing that medications that decrease the amount of dopamine reduce the positive symptoms of schizophrenia. Moreover, when people who do not have schizophrenia are given drugs that increase dopamine activity, they experience schizophrenia-like symptoms (Syvalathi, 1994). Perhaps, it was thought, excess dopamine triggers a flood of unrelated thoughts, feelings, and perceptions, and the delusions are attempts to organize these disconnected events into a coherent, understandable experience (Gottesman, 1991). However, research soon indicated that the dopamine hypothesis is too simple. Although dopamine clearly plays a role in schizophrenia, other neurotransmitters and neural processes are also involved (Laruelle et al., 1993; Nestler, 1997; Syvalathi, 1994; Walker & Diforio, 1997; Weinberger & Lipska, 1995).

Using careful analyses of home movies taken during the childhoods of people who were later diagnosed with schizophrenia, Walker and colleagues (Grimes & Walker, 1994; Walker et al., 1993) found that those who went on to develop schizophrenia were different from their siblings. They found that from infancy through adolescence these people exhibited more involuntary movements, such as writhing or excessive movements of the tongue, lip, or arm (Walker et al., 1994). The more severe the involuntary movements, the more severe the schizophrenic symptoms in adulthood (Neumann & Walker, 1996). Although the exact mechanisms responsible for this finding have not yet been discovered, these results are consistent with other findings of a biological vulnerability to schizophrenia that exists prior to adulthood.

Similar results were found in a group of Finnish people with schizophrenia. Looking back at their school performance, researchers found that the children who went on to develop schizophrenia did not do significantly worse academically than other children. But they did do significantly worse at sports and handicrafts, activities that require motor coordination (Cannon et al., 1999).

In sum, researchers now agree that prenatal and birth complications may play a role in the development of schizophrenia, and some individuals are genetically vulnerable to the disorder. These factors may create abnormalities in brain structure, particularly in the frontal lobe, and in the structure and function of neurotransmitter systems. The exact mechanism for the brain abnormalities in some people with schizophrenia, however, has yet to be found.

THE PERSON. The home movies study mentioned above also found that those children who went on to develop schizophrenia exhibited fewer expressions of joy than their unaffected siblings (Walker et al., 1993). This emotional dampening may also cause other people to respond less positively (because of emotional contagion, as described earlier).

THE GROUP. For someone who has had episodes of schizophrenia, a stressful life event may act as a trigger, leading to a recurrence of symptoms (Gottesman, 1991; Ventura et al., 1989).

Almost two thirds of people hospitalized with schizophrenia live with their families after leaving the hospital, and the way a family expresses emotion can affect the likelihood of a recurrence of acute schizophrenia symptoms, although it does not *cause* schizophrenia. Families that are critical, hostile, and overinvolved, termed **high expressed emotion** families, are more likely to include someone with schizophrenia

High expressed emotion: An emotional style in families that are critical, hostile, and over-involved.

who has had a recurrence; this higher rate is strongest for those with more chronic schizophrenia (Butzlaff & Hooley, 1998; Kavanagh, 1992; Vaughn & Leff, 1976). However, it is possible that high expressed emotion families may be responding to a relative with schizophrenia who is more bizarre or disruptive, and that low expressed emotion families include someone whose schizophrenic symptoms are less extreme. A longitudinal study of people with schizophrenia found that after their first psychotic episodes, those who had larger numbers of nonrelated people in their social support networks before their first episodes had the best recoveries 5 years later (Erikson et al., 1998).

Another environmental stressor that may facilitate the expression of the disorder is being brought up in an institution such as an orphanage; studies show that children born to a parent with schizophrenia are more likely to develop schizophrenia as adults if they were raised in an institution rather than by the parent with schizophrenia. Such children raised in foster families without schizophrenia had even less likelihood of developing the disorder (Mednick et al., 1998).

A higher rate of schizophrenia is found in urban areas and in lower socioeconomic classes (Freeman, 1994; Mortensen et al., 1999). Why might this be? Two factors appear to play a role: *social selection* and *social causation* (Dauncey et al., 1993). **Social selection,** also called *social drift,* refers to the "drifting" to lower socioeconomic classes of those who have become mentally disabled. This often happens to those who are no longer able to work and who lack family support or care (Dohrenwend et al., 1992). **Social causation** refers to the chronic psychological and social stresses of life in an urban environment, particularly for the poor. The stress of these living conditions may trigger the disorder in persons who are biologically vulnerable (Freeman, 1994).

Culture may influence the recovery rate of schizophrenia, although not all studies support this finding (Edgerton & Cohen, 1994; von Zerssen et al., 1990). Industrialized countries generally have lower recovery rates than do developing nations (American Psychiatric Association, 1994). Possible explanations include a more tolerant attitude and lower expressed emotion in extended families among people in developing countries (El-Islam, 1991). Moreover, developing countries also tend to have collectivist cultures, which place an emphasis on the community versus the individual (see Chapters 9 and 10). People in developing countries who have schizophrenia thus may have more support available to them.

Events at the three levels interact: As suggested by the finding that 48% of identical co-twins develop schizophrenia if the twin has schizophrenia, biological factors play a role in the development of the illness, leading to a vulnerability theory of the disorder. Such a biological vulnerability, in combination with environmental and social factors, and with the individual's learning history, help determine whether the disorder manifests itself. Walker and Diforio (1997) propose a specific diathesis–stress model to explain how stress can worsen schizophrenic symptoms. They note that although people who develop schizophrenia do not experience more life stressors than people who do not develop the disorder, individuals with schizophrenia who experience more stressful events are likely to have more severe schizophrenic symptoms and experience more relapses (Hultman et al., 1997). And, in fact, people with schizophrenia have higher baseline levels of cortisol, an indicator of the stress response. This relationship goes even further, since not only people with schizophrenia but also those at risk for the disorder (because of family history or evidence of some symptoms of schizophrenia) are more likely to have higher levels of cortisol. And antipsychotic medications decrease cortisol levels in people with schizophrenia.

Walker and Diforio further propose that this heightened susceptibility to stress comes about because of cortisol's effect on dopamine activity, namely an overactivation of dopamine pathways, which can worsen symptoms of schizophrenia. They propose that the negative symptoms of schizophrenia, such as social withdrawal, are attempts to reduce stress. Thus, genetic, prenatal, or birth factors increase a susceptibility to stress, and stress aggravates symptoms.

Social selection: The tendency of the mentally disabled to drift to the lower economic classes; also called *social drift.*

Social causation: The chronic psychological and social stresses of living in an urban environment that may lead to an increase in the rate of schizophrenia (especially among the poor).

Van Gogh had a family history of schizophrenia, implicating a possible genetic factor, and some biographical material suggests that van Gogh's extremely strict father could be regarded as a high expressed emotion parent. And before becoming an artist, van Gogh repeatedly returned to live with his parents after leaving his various jobs. Moreover, after becoming an artist, he generally lived off monies sent by his brother Theo. He was so poor he often had to choose between spending Theo's gift of money on painting supplies or on food, and often chose the former (Auden, 1989).

LOOKING AT LEVELS

The Genain Quadruplets

Now that you know more about schizophrenia and its causes, you can see how the factors at the different levels are involved, and how they interact. We can apply this knowledge to the Genain quadruplets, four girls born in the early 1930s in the Midwest into a family of limited financial means with an abusive, violent, alcoholic father and a strict mother. All four girls developed schizophrenia, although each presented different symptoms. Myra attained a substantially higher level of functioning than her sisters before the onset of the disorder and had fewer and briefer relapses than they did. The youngest and most sickly, Hester, fared the worst (Rosenthal, 1963).

The sisters' paternal grandmother had symptoms of paranoid schizophrenia, so they probably had a genetic vulnerability for the disorder (level of the brain). Still, from statistical probabilities, the odds of all four developing schizophrenia were one in a billion. However, the prenatal difficulties involved in carrying quadruplets, which may have led to impairment in brain development, would have increased the likelihood. CT scans of the quads when they were in their 50s showed similar brain abnormalities in all four sisters (Mirsky & Quinn, 1988). Although genetically identical quadruplets, they varied biologically: Nora and Hester showed more evidence of neurological difficulties and fared much worse when off medication.

At the level of the person, the quads, particularly Hester, exhibited odd behavior. Even as a child, Hester could not keep up mentally and physically with her sisters, and her bizarre behavior included putting on four new pairs of underwear over an old pair. In kindergarten, she appeared fearful and cried more than her sisters. The girls were forbidden to play with other children, had no outside social life, and were overprotected; they didn't mix well with other children at school and were teased. The sisters were seldom separated from one another and appeared unhappy to neighbors. Myra had the most social skills and social desire, even having a "boyfriend" at school, with whom she would exchange notes; she was not allowed to see him after school (Rosenthal, 1963). Nora and Myra made the most skilled pair, and Iris was often paired with Hester.

The Genain family would be considered a high expressed emotion family (level of the group). Psychologist David Rosenthal (1963) reported that the quads' father was particularly critical, angry, and extremely controlling—he forbade his daughters to close any doors, even the one to the bathroom. Although Nora was less physically abused by him than her sisters were, her doctors and medical team thought that he may have sexually abused her. Nora was the closest to her father and was able to appease him. Myra was their mother's favorite. Hester, who was difficult to control,

All four of these identical quadruplets—from oldest to youngest, Nora, Iris, Myra, and Hester—went on to develop schizophrenia. Their symptoms and the onset and course of their illness differed. Nora and Myra were paired off by the parents as the smartest. Hester and Iris were paired off as the least able, and their illness was more disabling.

received the most physical punishment, including being whipped and having her head dunked in water. Other social stressors included a long history of financial problems. On tests of attention taken when the quads were 20 years old, Myra was the only one to perform well enough to predict a possibility of a normal life; Iris's and Hester's attentional abilities indicated that they would not be able to live independently for long periods of time. In fact, their performance on these attentional tests fairly accurately predicted the course of their lives.

Events at the different levels interact: A family history of schizophrenia as well as prenatal and birth complications made the quads more vulnerable to developing schizophrenia. They were socially isolated, were teased by other children, and experienced physical and emotional abuse. Among the many familial stressors were high expressed emotion parents and financial hardship. Myra, the most socially motivated and skilled sister, was the one whose schizophrenia was least severe, and she was able to remain off medication and out of the hospital for long periods of time; she eventually married and had two sons (Mirsky & Quinn, 1988). Hester, the sickliest sister, was the one most physically abused and the most bizarre as a child. Had the quads grown up in a different home environment, with parents who treated them differently, it is possible that not all four would have developed schizophrenia, or if they had, they might have suffered fewer relapses.

CONSOLIDATE!

▶ 1. *What are the symptoms of schizophrenia?* Positive symptoms of schizophrenia include delusions, hallucinations, and disorders of behavior and speech. Negative symptoms include flat affect, alogia, and avolition.

▶ 2. *What are the subtypes of schizophrenia?* Subtypes of schizophrenia are paranoid, disorganized, catatonic, and undifferentiated. Subtype diagnosis is not permanent, and if symptoms shift over time, the subtype may also shift.

▶ 3. *Why do some people develop schizophrenia?* A biological vulnerability to schizophrenia is a prerequisite. This vulnerability can be genetic, related to prenatal maternal illness, or derived from prenatal or birth complications; all these factors may lead to brain abnormalities. The biological, psychological, and interpersonal stressors of adolescence can play a role in the onset of schizophrenia, and environmental factors, such as living with high expressed emotion families or financial stressors, can increase the risk of relapse.

OTHER AXIS I DISORDERS: DISSOCIATIVE AND EATING DISORDERS

Perhaps van Gogh, like many people, suffered from more than one psychological disorder. Consider that, at the age of 24, he spoke of an "evil self" that caused him to become a disgrace and bring misery to others. He sometimes had trouble with his memory. He wrote to Theo that his frail memory "also seems to me to prove that there is quite definitely something or other deranged in my brain, it is astounding to be afraid . . . , and to be unable to remember things" (Auden, 1989, p. 363).

At times van Gogh ate only breakfast and a dinner of coffee and bread. And while in the hospital during the last year of his life, he would eat only meager dinners of half-cooked chick-peas or alcohol or bread and a little soup (Auden, 1989). Not surprisingly, van Gogh had a history of stomach trouble, poor appetite, dizziness, and headaches.

▶ 1. What are dissociative disorders? What causes them?

► 2. What are the symptoms and causes of eating disorders?

In addition to the disorders in the major diagnostic categories already discussed are several less common Axis I disorders; some unfortunately are becoming more common. Two such categories of disorders are dissociative and eating disorders.

Dissociative Disorders

The hallmark of **dissociative disorders** is a disruption in the usually integrated functions of consciousness, memory, or identity, often caused by a traumatic or very stressful event. The disruptions may be fleeting or chronic; they may come on suddenly or gradually. They can lead to several symptoms (Steinberg, 1994): *identity confusion,* a state of uncertainty about one's identity, or *identity alteration,* the adoption of a new identity; *derealization,* the sense that familiar objects have changed or seem "unreal"; *depersonalization,* the experience of observing oneself as if from the outside; and amnesia, the loss of memory. These symptoms are not necessarily signs of pathology; people often have dissociative experiences in the course of ordinary life. For example, it is common to experience derealization on returning home after a long absence: The ceiling may seem lower, the furniture smaller, and so on. Even identity alteration need not signify abnormality. Possession trance (discussed in Chapter 4), which is not uncommon in some cultures, can lead to dissociation of identity, but in those cultures the dissociation is not considered pathological. In dissociative disorders, as defined by the *DSM-IV*, the dissociative experiences are severe enough to cause distress or to impair functioning. It is unclear how many people suffer from these disorders, although they are more frequently diagnosed now than in the past. In fact, some researchers and clinicians believe that several of these disorders are now overdiagnosed: One estimate is that 10% of Americans have been diagnosed with a dissociative disorder (Loewenstein, 1994).

One type of dissociative disorder is **dissociative amnesia,** marked by an inability to remember important personal information, usually about a traumatic or extremely stressful event; this inability to remember is often experienced as "gaps" in memory. A soldier who has seen several days of intense and brutal combat but then cannot remember much about the battlefield experience might be suffering from dissociative amnesia. In time, some people are able recall such terrible memories; others may never remember, developing instead a chronic form of amnesia.

Dissociative fugue is another dissociative disorder, marked by an inability to remember some or all of the past, combined with abrupt, unexpected disappearances from home or work. The disturbed state of consciousness may last hours, days, or months, and during it there are no obvious signs of a disorder, nor does the sufferer otherwise attract attention. People in a dissociative fugue may ultimately come to the attention of health care or law enforcement officials because of their loss of awareness of their identities. People suffering from this disorder do not usually create new identities for themselves. At any given point in time, only 0.2% of the American population experiences this disorder, but this rate may increase during times of war or large-scale natural disasters (American Psychiatric Association, 1994).

The most controversial dissociative disorder—because not everyone agrees that the disorder exists—estimated to affect 1% of the American population (Loewenstein, 1994) is **dissociative identity disorder (DID),** a condition in which two or more distinct personalities take control of the individual's behavior. This disorder was formerly known as *multiple personality disorder* and attracted immense interest after it was portrayed in the movies *The Three Faces of Eve* (1958) and *Sybil* (1976). Each personality, or *alter,* may be experienced as if it had a distinct personal history, self-image, and identity, including a separate name, mannerisms, and way of talking. Not all alters know of the existence of the other alters, a circumstance that can lead to amnesia. The gaps in memory are substantial enough that they cannot be considered ordinary forgetfulness. People with dissociative identity disorder have been reported

Dissociative disorder: A disorder marked by a disruption in the usually integrated functions of consciousness, memory, or identity.

Dissociative amnesia: An inability to remember important personal information, often experienced as memory "gaps."

Dissociative fugue: An abrupt, unexpected departure from home or work, combined with an inability to remember some or all of the past.

Dissociative identity disorder (DID): A disorder in which a person has two or more distinct personalities that take control of the individual's behavior.

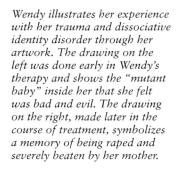

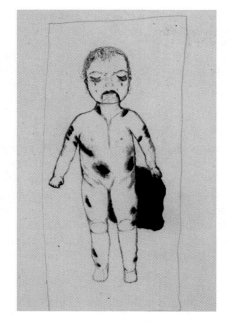

Wendy illustrates her experience with her trauma and dissociative identity disorder through her artwork. The drawing on the left was done early in Wendy's therapy and shows the "mutant baby" inside her that she felt was bad and evil. The drawing on the right, made later in the course of treatment, symbolizes a memory of being raped and severely beaten by her mother.

to have from 2 to 100 alters, although 10 or fewer are more commonly reported. Stress can trigger a transition to a different alter; this switch often occurs within seconds, although it can be more gradual.

Dissociative Identity Disorder From the Inside

Wendy's story captures the essence of DID:

> As a child, Wendy lived with her violent and abusive mother in a small urban area; her father had left the household when Wendy's mother was pregnant with her. . . . [She] had been physically and sexually abused as far back as she could remember . . . and there were hospital records of severe physical abuse . . . that occurred before Wendy was 2 years old. Wendy's mother was extremely sadistic and had tortured her regularly with extreme and violent means. For example, without any provocation, Wendy's mother would burn and cut her on various parts of her body. . . . Wendy had learned to rely on her hypnotic abilities to psychologically distance herself from her distressing memories and emotions. . . . Since childhood, Wendy had developed more than 20 distinct personalities! . . . Even subtle cues or reminders of abuse incidents could trigger a dissociative episode in which Wendy would switch to a different personality; once she had returned to her usual state, Wendy could not recall what had occurred during the episode. . . . Each of Wendy's personalities had its own distinct pattern of behaviors (e.g., speech, posture, mannerisms), perceived ages, sex, and appearance. Each personality had a unique store of information, memories, and access to feelings, . . . each of Wendy's personalities possessed different physical reactions or different physical abilities. . . . By dividing things up this way, Wendy was able to have parts of herself that could contain the feelings and knowledge about the tortures and abuse that were going on at home and thereby still be able to have other parts of herself that could handle going to . . . work. One personality handled being burned by her mother and was able to be insensitive to and tolerant of physical pain. Yet another personality was experienced as having no mouth, stemming from experiences where Wendy's mother burned her every time she screamed. (Brown & Barlow, 1997, pp. 102–108)

What might cause dissociative identity disorder? According to some researchers, most people who suffer this disorder share two characteristics: They experienced severe and usually repeated physical abuse as young children (Ross et al., 1991), and they have very high hypnotizability and dissociative capacity (Bliss, 1984; Frischholz, 1985). These two factors are related: Children who experience extreme abuse later recount a sense of their minds temporarily leaving their bodies in order that they might endure the abuse. In other words, because of the severity of the situation, they dissociate. With continued abuse, and continued use of dissociation, the dissociated state develops its own memories, feelings, and thoughts, and becomes an alter (Putnam, 1989). This view is supported by work by Perry and his colleagues (1995), who found that young children who have been severely traumatized have a tendency to dissociate or become hyperaroused in response to an aversive stimulus.

There are reports that different alters have different EEG patterns, visual acuity, pain tolerance, symptoms of asthma, sensitivity to allergens, and response to insulin (American Psychiatric Association, 1994). Some researchers and clinicians question whether dissociative identity disorder is a verifiably distinct diagnosis, since similar physiological differences occur when researchers ask participants who do *not* have symptoms of the disorder to role-play the condition (Coons et al., 1982). Just as role play induces physiologically different states, Sarbin (1995) proposes that DID is the product of the beliefs and expectations of the therapist, who, without realizing it, induces patients to behave in ways consistent with the condition known as dissociative identity disorder. However, researchers have found independent evidence of severe abuse histories in people diagnosed with DID (Lewis et al., 1997; Putnam, 1989; Swica et al., 1996). These same people had either amnesia or scant memories of the abuse (Lewis et al., 1997; Swica et al., 1996) and evidenced signs of dissociation in childhood (Lewis et al., 1997), as would be expected from the theory of how DID develops. Because symptoms of dissociative identity disorder overlap those of posttraumatic stress disorder, some researchers believe that dissociative identity disorder is a subtype of PTSD (Dell, 1998). Despite the debate about the existence of dissociative identity disorder, we do know that severe trauma can lead to disruptions in consciousness and to other dissociative disorders, and can have other adverse effects (Putnam, 1989; Putnam et al., 1995).

DID thus results from interacting events at the three levels: Severe trauma (level of the group) leads to changes in bodily reaction such as hyperarousal (level of the brain) and psychological changes such as the increased use of dissociation (level of the person). These various types of changes are likely to become chronic responses to stressors. Repeated and lengthy dissociations become the building blocks for DID.

Could van Gogh's "attacks" have been episodes of dissociation? He once referred to his "evil self," but there is no evidence that he had any alters; and although he may have suffered some memory loss during his attacks, he could very well have been psychotic, not dissociative, at those times. Amnesia alone is not an indication of a dissociative disorder.

Eating Disorders: You Are How You Eat?

Do you have a friend who's on a diet? If you do, the chances are that friend is a woman. Is her mood determined by the numbers on the scale? Does she want to lose more weight, even if she stops menstruating and others tell her she is too thin? If she eats more than she wants, does she feel that she must exercise, even if she's tired or sick? Is her view of herself dependent on whether she exercises today? Does she eat as little as possible during the day, and then find herself "losing control" with food in the afternoon or evening? A yes response, even to every question, does not necessarily indicate the presence of an eating disorder, but it does indicate a preoccupation with food, body image, and weight. These preoccupations are typical of people with **eating disorders**, disorders involving severe disturbances in eating behavior. And although more than 90% of those diagnosed with eating disorders are females, males are increasingly suffering from these disorders too.

Eating disorder: A disorder involving a severe disturbance in eating behavior.

An anorexic woman writes in her journal as part of her counseling at Radar Institute in Culver City, California.

ANOREXIA NERVOSA: YOU CAN BE TOO THIN. **Anorexia nervosa** is a potentially fatal disorder characterized by a refusal to maintain even a low normal weight. Someone with anorexia nervosa pursues thinness regardless of the physical consequences. Of those hospitalized with anorexia nervosa, 10% will eventually die of causes related to the disorder (American Psychiatric Association, 1994).

Eating Disorder From the Inside

People with anorexia nervosa develop irrational and unhealthy beliefs about food, as recounted by one woman's experience:

Yesterday . . . I had a grapefruit and black coffee for breakfast, and for dinner I had the . . . salad I eat every night. I always skip lunch. I had promised myself that I would only eat three-quarters of the salad since I've been feeling stuffed after it lately—but I think I ate more than the three-quarters. I know it was just lettuce and broccoli but I can't believe I did that. I was up all night worrying about getting fat. (Siegel et al., 1988, p. 17)

Included in the list of symptoms required for a diagnosis of anorexia nervosa (see Table 13.9) are distortions of how they see their bodies ("body image"), an intense fear of becoming fat, a refusal to maintain a healthy weight, and, among females, amenorrhea, or the cessation of menstruation. It is common for extremely anorexic women to "know" that they are underweight, yet when they look in the mirror, they "see" fat that is not there, or generally overestimate their body size (Smeets et al., 1997). They are often obsessed by thoughts of food, and these thoughts are usually based on irrational or illogical thinking (such as what are "good" and "bad" foods). They often deny that their low weight is a problem, or even that they have a problem. Some symptoms of anorexia nervosa differ from culture to culture. For example, half of young Chinese women with this disorder do not have the fear of being fat common among North Americans, but explain their restricted diet in terms of a distaste for food or bodily discomfort when eating (Lee, 1996).

TABLE 13.9

Diagnostic Criteria for Anorexia Nervosa

Source: *American Psychiatric Association (1994).*

- Refusal to maintain a healthy body weight; weighing less than 85% of what the individual should weigh for her height.
- Intense fear of becoming fat or gaining any weight, despite possible acknowledgment that she may be presently underweight.
- Disturbed body image; not seeing or experiencing her body as others see it.
- Amenorrhea—three consecutive missed menstrual periods in those who have begun menstruation, due to the loss of body fat.

Anorexia nervosa: An eating disorder characterized by the refusal to maintain even a low normal weight and an intense fear of gaining weight.

Bulimia nervosa: An eating disorder characterized by recurrent episodes of binge eating, followed by some attempt to prevent weight gain.

Some, but not all, people with anorexia nervosa periodically engage in *binge eating* (eating substantially more food within a certain time period than most people would eat in similar circumstances) or *purging* (getting rid of unwanted calories through vomiting or the misuse of laxatives, diuretics, or enemas), or both. Thus, there are two types of anorexia nervosa: the *binge-eating/purging type* and the classic *restricting type*, in which weight loss is achieved primarily by undereating, without purging.

BULIMIA NERVOSA. People with bulimia nervosa, like those with anorexia nervosa, are usually women, but they may be of normal weight or even overweight, and thus not usually amenorrheic. **Bulimia nervosa** is marked by recurrent episodes of

TABLE 13.10

Diagnostic Criteria for Bulimia Nervosa

Source: *American Psychiatric Association (1994).*

- Recurrent binge eating episodes (eating an amount of food that is larger than most people would eat under similar circumstances, within a discrete period of time, or not feeling in control while eating).

- Subsequent attempts to prevent weight gain (including purging methods, such as self-induced vomiting, misuse of laxatives, diuretics, enemas, or other medications, or nonpurging methods such as fasting or excessive exercise).

- Binge eating and purging an average of at least 2 times per week for 3 months.

- The person's view of herself is overly affected by her body shape and weight.

binge eating, followed by an attempt to prevent weight gain (see Table 13.10). When that attempt is made through purging (by vomiting or with the use of laxatives), the diagnosis of bulimia nervosa is further specified as *purging type*. Attempts to restrict weight gain may also occur through other methods such as fasting or excessive exercise, and in this case the disorder is the *nonpurging type*.

Some people with bulimia purge even when their eating does not constitute a binge: "If I had *one* bite of bread, just one, I felt as though I blew it! I'd stop listening to whomever was talking to me at the table. I'd start thinking, *How can I get rid of this?* I'd worry about how fat I'd look, how I couldn't fit into my clothes. My head would be flooded with thoughts of what to do now. . . . I had to undo what I'd done. The night was blown. I was a mess" (Siegel et al., 1988, p. 18). Although most people with bulimia do not realize it, in the long run, purging does not usually eliminate all the calories ingested and is, in fact, a poor method of weight loss (Garner, 1997).

EXPLAINING EATING DISORDERS. Why do people, most often women, develop eating disorders? There is evidence of a genetic predisposition for anorexia (level of the brain). In one study, 56% of identical co-twins were likely to have anorexia if their twins did, compared to 5% of co-twins of affected fraternal twins (Holland et al., 1988). Moreover, in a 1998 study, relatives of those with anorexia nervosa had a higher incidence of obsessive-compulsive symptoms than relatives of those with bulimia nervosa or control subjects. This finding suggests that obsessive personality traits in a family may increase the risk for anorexia nervosa (Lilenfeld et al., 1998). However, learning principles can also account for this finding: People with obsessional relatives may learn to be obsessional; those with eating disorders have focused the obsession on food and weight. The data for bulimia nervosa in twins shows a sharply different pattern: Twenty-three percent of identical co-twins were likely to have bulimia if their twins did, compared with 9% of co-twins of affected fraternal twins (Kendler et al., 1991). In bulimia, the environment, not genes, plays the larger role (Wade et al., 1998).

As was shown by the University of Minnesota starvation study (see Chapter 9), decreased caloric intake leads to pathological eating behaviors and other symptoms of eating disorders. The malnutrition and weight loss that occur with anorexia nervosa lead to changes in neurotransmitters, particularly serotonin. This neurotransmitter is also involved in obsessive-compulsive disorder, and the obsessional thinking about food and pathological eating in anorexia is hypothesized to be related to alterations in serotonergic functioning (Kaye, 1995). Lower levels of serotonin have been implicated as a predisposing factor for bulimia nervosa (Pirke, 1995) since one effect of serotonin is to create a feeling of satiety (Halmi, 1996). The physiological effects of dieting may also make women vulnerable to developing bulimia nervosa: Some, though not all, studies indicate that dieting sometimes precedes the onset of bulimia in some people (Garner, 1997). Although the research points to abnormalities or dysregulation of neurotransmitters, it is as yet unclear how the changes in different neurotransmitters are related; nor is it known whether these changes *precede* the development of an eating disorder and thus may create a susceptibility to it, or whether they are a *consequence* of an eating disorder (Halmi, 1995).

Numerous personal characteristics have been linked with eating disorders (level of the person). An increased risk of developing anorexia occurs among women who are perfectionists and have a negative evaluation of themselves (Fairburn et al., 1999). More generally, people with eating disorders often exhibit irrational beliefs and inappropriate expectations about their bodies, jobs, relationships, and themselves (Garfinkel et al., 1992; Striegel-Moore, 1993). They tend to engage in dichotomous, black-or-white thinking: Fruit is "good"; pizza is "bad."

Perhaps people with these characteristics are especially likely to find rewards in the behaviors associated with eating disorders. Preoccupations with food can provide distractions from work, family conflicts, or social problems. By restricting their eating, people may gain a sense of increased control—over food and over life in general—although such feelings of mastery are often short-lived as the disease takes over (Garner, 1997). By purging, they may relieve the anxiety created by overeating.

The family and the larger culture also play important roles in the development of eating disorders (level of the group). They may contribute to these disorders by encouraging a preoccupation with weight and appearance. Children have an increased risk of developing eating disorders if their families are overly concerned about appearance and weight (Strober, 1995). Symptoms of eating disorders increase among immigrants from less weight-conscious cultures (such as the Chinese and the Egyptian) as they assimilate to American culture (Dolan, 1991; Lee & Lee, 1996). Eating disorders are increasing among men who regularly take part in appearance- or weight-conscious activities such as modeling and wrestling (Brownell & Rodin, 1992). Among U.S. women, the focus on appearance and weight may derive from their desire to meet the culture's ideal of femininity (Striegel-Moore, 1993).

More specifically, cultural pressure on women to be thin and attain an "ideal" body shape is thought to be influential in the development of eating disorders; it also explains why there is a higher incidence of eating disorders now than 50 years ago, as the ideal figure has changed from the generous proportions of Marilyn Monroe to the rail-thin silhouettes of supermodels (Andersen & DiDomenico, 1992; Field et al., 1999; Nemeroff et al., 1994). Culture plays a role by simply promoting the idea that body shape *can* be changed and by determining the rationales people offer for their symptoms (Becker & Hamburg, 1996).

Van Gogh had bizarre eating habits; could he have had an eating disorder? It is unlikely; although van Gogh often purposefully ate sparingly and peculiarly, he did not appear to be preoccupied with weight gain or body image, and no information suggests that he purged in any way.

LOOKING AT LEVELS

Binge Eating

You have learned what eating disorders are and explanations of why they might occur. Let's consider in detail a core aspect of bulimia nervosa—binge eating. Why do some people chronically binge eat? At the level of the brain, food restriction is a contributor to binge eating (Polivy & Herman, 1993). In their efforts to be "in control" of food, people with bulimia generally consume fewer calories at nonbinge meals than do nonbulimics, thus setting the stage for later binge eating because they are hungry and have food cravings (Walsh, 1993), and the bingeing becomes reinforced. A binge/purge episode may be followed by an endorphin rush (and the ensuing positive feelings that it creates), further reinforcing the binge/purge cycle. As one woman with bulimia reported, "I go to never-never land. Once I starting bingeing, it's like being in a stupor, like being drunk . . . I'm like a different person. It's very humiliating—but not then, not while I'm eating. While I'm eating, nothing else matters" (Siegel et al., 1988, p. 20).

The dichotomous thinking typical of people with eating disorders leads them to view themselves as either "good" (when dieting or restricting food intake), or "bad" (eating "forbidden foods" or feeling out of control while eating). This thinking (level of the person) sets the stage for bingeing if any small amount of forbidden food is eaten; a bite of a candy bar is followed by the thought, Well, I shouldn't have eaten *any* of the candy bar, but since I did, I might as well eat the whole thing, especially since I really shouldn't have a candy bar again. This line of reasoning is part of the *abstinence violation effect* (Polivy & Herman, 1993), the sense of letting go of self-restraint after transgressing a self-imposed rule about food: Once you violate the rule, why not go all the way? In addition, purging is negatively reinforcing (remember, negative reinforcement is reinforcement, not punishment; see Chapter 5): Eating too much, or eating forbidden foods, can cause anxiety, which is then relieved by purging. This reinforcement then increases the likelihood of purging in the future.

Bingeing and purging are usually done alone, increasing the affected person's sense of isolation and decreasing his or her social interactions; if social interactions are stressful, then bingeing and purging are reinforced by the isolation they provide (level of the group). Events at the levels interact: Cultural pressures to be thin, or to eat small meals, lead vulnerable individuals to try to curb their food intake. The hunger caused by this undereating may trigger a binge. The binge may also be triggered by stress, social interactions, or negative affect (Polivy & Herman, 1993); bingeing can create positive changes (such as decreased hunger, distraction from an uncomfortable feeling or thought, and removal from difficult social interactions). This immediate reinforcement often outweighs the negative consequences that are experienced later. Moreover, the social isolation may be positive and therefore reinforcing.

CONSOLIDATE!

▶ *1. What are dissociative disorders? What causes them?* Dissociative disorders are characterized by identity confusion or alteration, derealization, depersonalization, and amnesia. The diagnosis of dissociative identity order is marked by the presence of one or more alters.

▶ *2. What are the symptoms and causes of eating disorders?* Symptoms of anorexia nervosa in American women include a fear of fat or weight gain, refusal to maintain a healthy weight, disturbed body image, and amenorrhea. Symptoms of bulimia nervosa include recurrent binge eating, purging, and self-esteem linked to an idealized weight and shape.

PERSONALITY DISORDERS

By now, it should come as no surprise to know that van Gogh was more than just unconventional; his difficulties in life went beyond his attacks, his hallucinations, and his periods of depression. Van Gogh's relationships with other people were troubled, and they often followed a pattern: Initial positive feelings and excitement about someone new in his life (such as happened with Gauguin and Sien) were invariably followed by a turbulent phase and an eventual falling out. Throughout his life, he had emotional outbursts that sooner or later caused others to withdraw their friendship. His relationship with his brother Theo is the only one that endured. Is such a pattern suggestive of a personality disorder?

▶ 1. What are personality disorders?

▶ 2. What is antisocial personality disorder?

Axis II Personality Disorders

Axis II of the *DSM-IV* allows for the possibility of an array of **personality disorders** (see Table 13.11), which are sets of relatively stable personality traits that are inflexible and maladaptive, causing distress or difficulty with daily functioning. A personality disorder may occur alone, or it may be accompanied by an Axis I disorder.

TABLE 13.11

Axis II Personality Disorders

Source: *American Psychiatric Association (1994).*

ANTISOCIAL PERSONALITY DISORDER
A pattern of disregard or violation of the rights of others.

AVOIDANT PERSONALITY DISORDER
A pattern of social discomfort, feelings of inadequacy, and hypersensitivity to negative evaluation.

BORDERLINE PERSONALITY DISORDER
A pattern of instability in relationships, self-image, and feelings, and pronounced impulsivity (such as in spending, substance abuse, sex, reckless driving, or binge eating). Relationships are often characterized by rapid swings from idealizing another person to devaluing him or her. Recurrent suicidal gestures, threats, or self-mutilation, such as nonlethal cuts on the arm are common, as are chronic feelings of emptiness.

DEPENDENT PERSONALITY DISORDER
A pattern of clingy, submissive behavior due to an extreme need to be taken care of.

HISTRIONIC PERSONALITY DISORDER
A pattern of excessive attention seeking and expression of emotion.

NARCISSISTIC PERSONALITY DISORDER
A pattern of an exaggerated sense of self-importance, need for admiration, and lack of empathy.

OBSESSIVE-COMPULSIVE PERSONALITY DISORDER
A pattern of preoccupation with perfectionism, orderliness, and control (but no obsessions or compulsions, as occur with obsessive-compulsive disorder).

PARANOID PERSONALITY DISORDER
A pattern of suspiciousness and distrust of others to the extent that other people's motives are interpreted as ill-intentioned. However, unlike the paranoid subtype of schizophrenia, there are no delusions or hallucinations.

SCHIZOID PERSONALITY DISORDER
A pattern of detachment from social relationships and a narrow range of displayed emotion.

SCHIZOTYPAL PERSONALITY DISORDER
A pattern of extreme discomfort in close relationships, odd or quirky behavior, and cognitive or perceptual distortions (such as sensing the presence of another person or spirit).

Personality disorder: Relatively stable personality traits that are inflexible and maladaptive, causing distress or difficulty with daily functioning.

Whereas Axis I symptoms feel as if they are inflicted from the outside, the maladaptive traits of Axis II are often experienced as parts of the person's personality.

The maladaptive traits of personality disorders cause distress or difficulty with daily functioning in school, work, social life, or relationships. They can be so subtle as to be unnoticeable in a brief encounter. It is only after getting to know someone over time that a personality disorder may become evident.

Some researchers argue that the combinations of traits now defined as personality disorders should not be called "disorders" at all. Doing so, they contend, either treats normal variations in personality as pathological or creates separate Axis II categories for conditions that could be part of an Axis I clinical disorder (Hyman, 1998; Livesley, 1998). For example, the clinging, submissive behavior that *DSM-IV* categorizes as Axis II "dependent personality disorder" might also characterize a personality that is within the normal range. And the symptoms of avoidant personality disorder overlap those of Axis I social phobia—only the greater severity of anxiety and depressive symptoms distinguishes avoidant personality disorder from social phobia (Johnson & Lydiard, 1995); the two disorders are quantitatively, not qualitatively, different.

Other researchers argue that each personality disorder is not a research-validated disorder distinct from all others (Atre-Vaidya & Hussain, 1999; Horowitz, 1998). Furthermore, the criteria for the various personality disorders do not all require the same level of dysfunction. Thus, a lesser—and in some cases quite mild—degree of impairment is required for a diagnosis of obsessive-compulsive, antisocial, and paranoid personality disorders (Funtowicz & Widiger, 1999).

From what is known about his life, it is not impossible that van Gogh had a personality disorder; but we have no way of knowing if he in fact met all of the criteria.

Antisocial Personality Disorder

The most studied personality disorder is **antisocial personality disorder (ASPD)**, evidenced by a long-standing pattern of disregard for others to the point of violating their rights (American Psychiatric Association, 1994). People with this disorder have been called *psychopaths, sociopaths,* and *social deviants,* and they may engage in unlawful behavior. Symptoms include a superficial charm; egocentrism; impulsive, reckless, and deceitful behavior without regard for others' safety; a tendency to blame others for any adversity that comes their way; and a lack of conscience, empathy, and remorse. People with this disorder talk a good line and know how to manipulate others, but they don't have the capacity to know or care how another person feels.

John Wayne Gacy, a psychopathic serial killer, tortured and murdered 33 young men and boys and buried their bodies in the basement of his house.

Antisocial Personality Disorder From the Inside

A common feature among psychopaths is that they see *themselves* as the real victims. While discussing the murders he committed, John Wayne Gacy portrayed himself as the 34th victim:

> I was made an asshole and a scapegoat . . . when I look back, I see myself more as a victim than a perpetrator. . . . I was the victim; I was cheated out of my childhood. . . . [He wondered whether] there would be someone, somewhere who would understand how badly it had hurt to be John Wayne Gacy. (Hare, 1993, p. 43)

Antisocial personality disorder occurs three times more frequently in men than in women, and although only 1 to 2% of Americans are diagnosed with this disorder, 60% of male prisoners are estimated to have it (Moran, 1999). Cross-cultural studies have found a similar pattern of symptoms in both Western and non-Western cultures (Zoccolillo et al., 1999). Many people diagnosed with antisocial personality disorder also abuse alcohol and drugs (Nigg & Goldsmith, 1994).

Antisocial personality disorder: A long-standing pattern of disregard for others to the point of violating other people's rights.

Understanding Antisocial Personality Disorder

What causes antisocial personality disorder? Evidence for a biological basis (level of the brain) arises from a number of sources. Some of the data on antisocial personality disorder come from studies of certain types of criminality, which are related to some of the symptoms of antisocial personality disorder. These data show that the disorder runs in families (Nigg & Goldsmith, 1994). Moreover, adoption studies show that environment matters only if a child's biological parents were criminals; if they were, there was a slight increase in criminal behavior for boys adopted into a family of law-abiding people, but there was a whopping increase in criminal behavior if they were adopted into a family of criminals. If the biological parents were not criminals, growing up with adoptive parents made no difference in the child's later criminal behavior (Mednick et al., 1984). Criminal behavior provides a clear example of how genes and environment can interact. The genes predispose; the environment triggers.

At the level of the person, research suggests that people with antisocial personality disorder have difficulty modulating their anger (Zlotnick, 1999). In addition, their difficulty in understanding how others feel and their lack of empathy may be related to a poor attachment to their primary caretaker (Gabbard, 1990; Pollock et al., 1990), perhaps because of emotional deprivation, abuse, and inconsistent or poor parenting (Patterson, 1986; Patterson et al., 1989).

As children, people with antisocial personality disorder often experienced or witnessed abuse, deviant behavior, or a lack of concern for the welfare of others by peers, parents, or others (level of the group). The behaviors of models who lack basic regard for others may later be imitated (Elliott et al., 1985).

How might events at these levels interact? To begin with, genes may lead to a relatively underresponsive central and autonomic nervous system (level of the brain). In turn, this might lead people with such genes to seek out highly arousing, thrilling activities (Quay, 1965). A depressed central and autonomic nervous system might also leave them relatively unaffected by social rejection or mild punishment. In other words, when people have an underresponsive nervous system, the normal social and legal consequences of inappropriate behavior might not make them feel anxious (level of the person). Conversely, a moderate level of arousal is optimal for performance (see Chapter 9). Together, these consequences of an underresponsive nervous system might produce another important result: difficulty in learning to control impulses. In fact, Schacter and Latané (1964) found that psychopaths have difficulty learning to avoid shocks. But when they are injected with adrenaline so that their level of arousal is increased, they learn to avoid shocks at the same rate as other people.

This physiological underresponsiveness may also be related to poor parental bonding, in that the normal stimulation provided by parents may not be enough to engage these infants. Moreover, as they grow up, learning antisocial behavior from others in the immediate environment may be arousing enough to hold their interest and increase their learning, which creates a vicious cycle. Their underresponsiveness may have *caused* their caregivers to treat them differently. Poor attachment (a group-related factor) can then make it difficult for them to identify with others, which leads to a lack of empathy (Kagan & Reid, 1986), the inability to understand how others feel (level of the person). Thus, violating the rights of others does not lead people with antisocial personality disorder to feel for people they have hurt or wronged.

A CAUTIONARY NOTE ABOUT DIAGNOSIS

The events of van Gogh's life present an opportunity to explore ways in which the human psyche can be troubled, and the ways in which the mental health field presently classifies disorders. But that is not the same as proposing a diagnosis of someone who, while in art is very close to us, is in his person very distant in time.

No mental health clinician can really know with certainty from what, if any, specific disorder van Gogh suffered. Major depressive disorder and schizophrenia are possibilities, as is bipolar disorder (Jamison, 1993). Alternatively, his attacks and hallucinations might have been due to *delirium tremens* (DTs), caused by withdrawal from alcohol (see Chapter 4); but such a diagnosis would not explain why van Gogh had attacks even during lengthy periods of sobriety (Lubin, 1972). Possibly he suffered from a form of epilepsy, and his "attacks" were seizures; before epileptic seizures, victims are sometimes overcome with religious feelings and delusions. The consideration of epilepsy, a neurological disorder not a psychological one, in our speculations points to the importance of ensuring that the patient does not have a medical disorder that can cause psychological symptoms. Only after ruling out medical illnesses can the mental health clinician or researcher have confidence in a diagnosis of a psychological disorder.

A DEEPER LEVEL

Recap and Thought Questions

▶ **Identifying Psychological Disorders: What's Abnormal?**

Significant impairment or distress interfering with work, school, relationships, or self-care is the hallmark of behaviors that constitute a psychological disorder, as compared with behaviors that are merely unusual in a given context. The catalog of psychiatric disorders in the *DSM-IV* distinguishes among disorders by the symptoms exhibited or re-

ported, and by the history of the symptoms. The *DSM-IV* includes both clinical and personality disorders.

Did van Gogh have psychological problems? Given our definition of psychological disorders, it appears that van Gogh may have suffered from one or more psychological disorders: He had significant emotional distress, difficulty keeping a job or even painting without interruption by his so-called attacks, and his suicidal feelings and actions made him a danger to himself. Both van Gogh's own reports of his depression, attacks, and hallucinations, as well as reports by friends, family, and neighbors, suggest the strong possibility of a psychological disorder—but again, without the opportunity to examine him closely, we cannot know for sure.

> **Think It Through.** If a classmate tells you in all seriousness that someone you both know is "weird" and a "basket case," how would you respond? What would you want to know about the behavior that led your friend to this conclusion? What other questions should you ask? Why?

▶ Anxiety and Mood Disorders

Anxiety disorders include panic disorder, specific and social phobias, posttraumatic stress disorder, and obsessive-compulsive disorder. These disorders involve a biological vulnerability (possibly genetic) to the overactivity of certain brain areas or neurotransmitters. Classical and operant conditioning and social learning may be important in the evolution of these disorders.

Major depressive disorder is characterized by depressed mood, loss of pleasure, fatigue, weight loss, poor sleep, a sense of worthlessness or guilt, and poor attention and concentration. Bipolar disorder involves episodes of mania or hypomania, which may or may not alternate with depression. These disorders also involve a biological vulnerability (possibly genetic); further, neurotransmitters and neuromodulators are implicated in both disorders, although the exact mechanisms are not yet understood. People's worldviews and attributional styles may also play a role in the development of major depressive disorder. Operant conditioning and the level of available reward or punishment in the environment also may be related to the development of depression.

Could extreme anxiety or profound disturbances in mood account for van Gogh's problems? Although van Gogh suffered from "attacks," we do not know enough about them to say if they were anxiety related, nor did he have the history or symptoms of someone with either PTSD or OCD. Van Gogh apparently suffered from depressive episodes, an indicator of some type of mood disorder. Although we have limited knowledge of the details of some of his symptoms, nothing we do know contradicts the possibility of MDD with psychotic features or bipolar disorder.

> **Think It Through.** Suppose someone you know, someone whose sharp style of dress and confident manner you admire, starts looking unkempt and acting tired, nervous, and fidgety. Would this change suggest a psychological disorder? Why or why not? If so, what type of disorder do you have in mind and why? Would psychological impairment be the only explanation?

▶ Schizophrenia

Schizophrenia involves a markedly restricted range of affect and odd or disorganized thoughts (delusions or hallucinations) and behaviors; it is characterized by positive and negative symptoms. The *DSM-IV* specifies four subtypes: paranoid, disorganized, catatonic, and undifferentiated. Research findings on schizophrenia point to genetic and biological abnormalities, as well as a heightened responsivity to stress as factors in the development of this disorder.

Would schizophrenia best explain van Gogh's symptoms? Van Gogh did not appear to have any prominent delusions when not experiencing a so-called attack, and if anything, his mood was apparently consistently depressed, not flat. When not having an attack, his behavior is not known to have been disorganized, but we do not know very much about his attacks. Paranoid schizophrenia might account for his hallucinations and, perhaps, his attacks; but this characterization leaves some symptoms unexplained, such as the predominance and lengthy history of his depressed mood.

> **Think It Through.** Would someone who has exhibited positive and negative symptoms of schizophrenia be able to function relatively normally again? Does having a parent with schizophrenia guarantee the development of the disorder? Can the environment of someone with schizophrenia affect the symptoms? If so, in what way?

▶ Other Axis I Disorders: Dissociative and Eating Disorders

Dissociative disorders are characterized by identity confusion, derealization, depersonalization, and amnesia. Trauma or severe stress influences the development of these disorders.

Eating disorders are characterized by preoccupations with weight and body image, as well as abnormal eating (restriction, binges, purges). Genetic factors are more influential in the development of anorexia than bulimia, and environmental factors, specifically the cultural emphasis on thinness, affect the development of both bulimia nervosa and anorexia. Biological factors related to food restriction and binge eating are also involved.

Could van Gogh have had a dissociative or eating disorder? Although van Gogh had some episodes that seem dissociative in nature, they did not appear to be beyond those normally experienced and so would not have been pathological. Despite the fact that he had bizarre eating habits and sometimes ate sparingly, an eating disorder is not indicated.

▶ Personality Disorders

Personality disorders are sets of maladaptive and inflexible personality traits that can create difficulty in work, school, or in other social spheres. In contrast to Axis I disorders, which seem to the sufferer to be inflicted from the outside, personality disorders, which are on Axis II, are experienced as part of the personality itself. Antisocial personality disorder is the most studied personality disorder; the key symptom is a long-standing pattern of disregard for others to the point of violating their rights.

Might van Gogh have had a personality disorder? Van Gogh's relationships were characterized by instability. It is possible that van Gogh had a personality disorder, but the information about his life does not provide enough necessary detail to say with certainty that he did.

14 TREATMENT

At 2 A.M., Beth sat hunched over her textbook and notes, studying for her midterm. Concentration was difficult; she had to struggle to make sense of the words before her eyes. She'd read the same page four times and still couldn't remember what it said. She tried to give herself a pep talk ("Okay, Beth, read it one more time, and then you'll understand it"), but her upbeat words would be drowned out by a different, negative internal monologue (*Well, Beth, you've really screwed yourself, and there's no way out of it now. You're going to fail, get kicked out of school, never be employed, end up destitute, homeless, hopeless, talking to yourself on the street*).

Beth was 21 years old, a junior in college. She'd already had to walk out of two exams because she couldn't answer most of the questions, although she had understood the material in class. Her thoughts had been jumbled, and she'd had a hard time organizing her answers to the questions. She'd always been nervous before a test or class presentation, but this year her anxiety had spun out of control. Taking the first quiz of the semester, she simply drew a blank when she tried to answer the questions.

Since then, she'd become more anxious, and depressed as well. With each quiz she couldn't finish, with each paper that required more concentration than she could summon, she felt herself spiraling downward, helpless. She had no hope that the situation would change by itself, and no amount of good intentions or resolutions or even effort made a difference. She began cutting classes and spent much of her time in bed; she had no interest in doing anything with her friends because she felt she didn't deserve to have fun. She'd put off saying anything to her professors; at first she figured things would get better, and then she was too embarrassed to face them. But she knew that eventually she'd have to talk to them or else she'd definitely fail her courses.

She finally did talk to her professors. Several of them suggested that she seek treatment, or at least go to the campus counseling center, but she didn't want to do that. Taking that step, she felt, would be admitting to herself and to the world not only that something was wrong with her, but also that she was too weak to deal with it herself.

Beth was reluctant to seek help partly because when she was growing up, her mother had experienced bouts of depression severe enough that she had been hospitalized several times. Beth recognized that she, too, was becoming depressed, and she was afraid that if she went to see a therapist, she'd end up in the hospital.

Finally, Beth confided in a family friend, Nina, who had been the school nurse at Beth's elementary school. Nina told Beth that people with problems like hers often felt much better after psychotherapy and that her problems were not severe enough to warrant hospitalization. She also pointed out that there were many forms of therapy available to Beth that were not as readily available to her mother 20 years ago. Modern treatments, Nina said, ranged from psychologically based therapies such as insight-oriented, cognitive, and behavioral therapies to biologically based treatments such as medication. Beth agreed to see a therapist, but didn't know where to begin. The campus counseling center could be useful, Nina said, but Beth might also explore other possibilities, such as the Internet and referral organizations, in finding a therapist who would be right for her needs.

Let's make a similar exploration in this chapter, examining the different schools of therapy, how they work, and what research has to say about the effectiveness of the therapies.

INSIGHT-ORIENTED THERAPIES

Beth didn't know much about psychotherapy, so she made an appointment with a psychotherapist whose name she had gotten from the counseling center. Beth didn't know it, but if the therapist she contacted was an insight-oriented therapist, chances are that the therapist would begin by asking Beth about her past, how she felt about her family and her relationships with the people in it, and about her feelings in general. This therapist might ask surprisingly little about Beth's current anxiety or her depression.

Therapies that aim to remove distressing symptoms by leading someone to understand their causes through deeply felt personal insights are called **insight-oriented therapies.** The key idea underlying this approach is that once someone truly understands the causes of distressing symptoms (which often arise from past relationships), the symptoms themselves will diminish. Psychoanalysis is the original insight-oriented therapy; other therapies, including client-centered and Gestalt therapies, are also considered insight-oriented therapies because they rest on the belief that therapeutic change follows from the experience of insight.

▶ 1. What is the focus of treatment in psychodynamic therapy? What are its main techniques?

Insight-oriented therapy: Therapy that aims to remove distressing symptoms by leading people to understand their causes through deeply felt personal insights.

▶ 2. How would client-centered and other humanistic therapists approach treatment? What techniques would they use?

Psychodynamic Therapy: Origins in Psychoanalysis

Developed by Sigmund Freud, **psychoanalysis** is a type of therapy directly connected to Freud's notion of personality, which holds that people's psychological difficulties are caused by conflicts among the three psychic structures of the mind: the id, ego, and superego. According to Freud, the id strives for immediate gratification of its needs, the superego tries to impose its version of morality, and the ego attempts to balance the demands of the id, superego, and external reality. These unconscious competing demands can create anxiety and other symptoms (see Chapter 10). The goal of psychoanalysis is to help patients understand the unconscious motivations that lead them to behave in specific ways; if the motivations and feelings remain unconscious, those forces are more likely to shape patients' behavior, without their awareness. According to this theory, only after true understanding—that is, insight—is attained can patients choose more adaptive, satisfying, and productive behaviors.

In psychoanalysis, patients talk about their problems, and the analyst tries to infer the root causes. Early on, this method was revolutionary because, before Freud, most European patients were treated medically for psychological problems. Freud started out using hypnosis but over time developed the method of **free association,** in which the patient says whatever comes into his or her mind. The resulting train of thought reveals the issues that concern the patient, as well as the way he or she is handling them. Because Freud (1900/1958) viewed dreams as the "royal road to the unconscious," another important feature of psychoanalysis is the use of **dream analysis,** the examination of the content of dreams to gain access to the unconscious. Freud did not believe that psychoanalysis was a cure, but rather that it could transform abject misery into ordinary unhappiness.

Psychoanalysis has declined in popularity over the last several decades, in part because of the cost and time required for the four to five sessions per week. The average

Psychoanalysis: An intensive form of therapy, originally developed by Freud, based on the idea that people's psychological difficulties are caused by conflicts among the id, ego, and superego.

Free association: A technique used in psychoanalysis and psychodynamic therapies in which the patient says whatever comes to mind and the train of thoughts reveals the patient's issues and ways of dealing with them.

Dream analysis: A technique used in psychoanalysis and psychodynamic therapies in which the therapist examines the content of dreams to gain access to the unconscious.

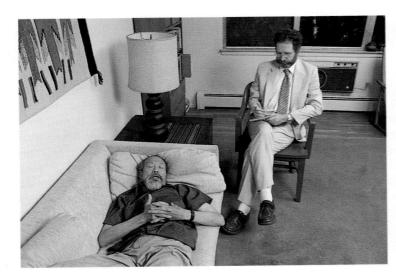

Psychoanalysis usually takes place 4 to 5 days a week for a number of years. Psychodynamic therapy can take place anywhere from several times a month to twice a week. The patient lies on a couch in psychoanalysis, and the analyst sits in a chair behind the couch, out of the patient's range of sight so that the patient can better free associate without having to see the analyst's reactions to his or her thoughts. In psychodynamic therapy, the client and therapist sit in chairs facing each other.

patient engages in 835 sessions before completing psychoanalysis (Voth & Orth, 1973), which usually lasts at least 4 years. Some patients who begin psychoanalysis never complete it.

A less intensive form of psychoanalytically oriented treatment, and one that is more common today, is **psychodynamic therapy.** Although based on psychoanalytic theory, its techniques differ in some important ways, including less frequent sessions, a decreased emphasis on sexual and aggressive drives, and an increased emphasis on current life rather than past experiences. However, both psychoanalysis and psychodynamic therapy try to link the patient's current difficulties with past life experiences, and both view the patient's relationship with the therapist as an integral part of treatment. Recent trends in psychodynamic therapy include the development of short-term versions of psychotherapy (Bloom, 1997; Malan, 1976; Sifneos, 1992), which might involve therapy lasting 12 to 20 sessions. At least one study found that psychiatrists referring patients for psychological treatment do not refer all prospective patients to psychodynamic therapy, only those who are healthier and who do not have a personality disorder (Svanborg et al., 1999). Such patients seeking help for relationship difficulties may find insight attained through short-term therapy useful in relieving symptoms (Kivlighan et al., 2000).

THEORY. The goal of psychodynamic therapy, like that of psychoanalysis, is to bring unconscious impulses and conflicts into awareness. Doing so leads to both intellectual and emotional insights, which are supposed to give the patient more control over these impulses. With this control, the patient can actively and consciously *choose* behaviors instead of acting on unconscious impulses. More recent psychoanalytic theorists have placed greater emphasis on people's current relationships (as opposed to an almost exclusive emphasis on childhood relationships) and their possible role in the evolution of emotional distress (Greenberg & Mitchell, 1983; Kohut, 1977; Sullivan, 1953). Psychodynamic therapy uses the relationship between therapist and patient itself as an agent of change. Given the importance of relationships, the therapy relationship can provide a "corrective emotional experience"—that is, a new, positive experience of relationships, which can lead to changes in symptoms, behavior, and personality (Alexander & French, 1946).

From a psychodynamic perspective, Beth's anxiety and depression might reflect two competing desires. On the one hand, Beth wants to be different from her mother. Doing well in school and going on to graduate school represent a path different from that taken by her mother who, although she did well in college, elected not to pursue a graduate degree. Although her plan was not necessarily logically thought out, Beth hoped that by making different choices in her own life, she could avoid the intermittent depressions that had plagued her mother. On the other hand, Beth loves her mother, and the idea of academically passing a parent by, in essence, abandoning her, causes Beth to feel guilty about her accomplishments. Although Beth's anxiety and depression are upsetting and debilitating, part of her may feel relief that those symptoms prevent her from leaving her mother behind. Psychodynamic theory would say that, by gaining insight about these issues, Beth will not have to "act out" these ambivalent feelings unconsciously and will have more control over her anxiety and depression.

TECHNIQUES. Along with dream analysis and free association, psychodynamic therapists rely on **interpretation,** deciphering the patient's words and behaviors and assigning unconscious motivations to them. Through the therapist's interpretations, the patient becomes aware of his or her motives and potential conflicts within the unconscious. The patient's own interpretations are not considered as accurate as those of the therapist because they are biased by the patient's own conflicts. Slips of the tongue—"Freudian slips"—are interpreted as having unconscious meanings. For example, should Beth tell her therapist that her mother recommended that she come to therapy (instead of her mother's friend, which was the case, and what she meant to say), her therapist might interpret this as Beth's wish that her mother would take care of her by suggesting that she seek therapy.

Psychodynamic therapy: A less intensive form of psychoanalysis.

Interpretation: A technique used in psychoanalysis and psychodynamic therapies in which the therapist deciphers the patient's words and behaviors, assigning unconscious motivations to them.

Through interpretation, patients also become aware of their defense mechanisms, unconscious mechanisms used to handle conflictual and distressing thoughts and feelings (see Chapter 10). At some point in the course of psychodynamic therapy, patients are likely to experience **resistance**, a reluctance or refusal to cooperate with the therapist. Resistance can range from unconscious forgetting to outright refusal to comply with a therapist's request. Resistance can occur as the patient explores or remembers painful feelings or experiences in the past. Therapists may attribute resistance to a difficult phase of treatment, or to the patient's desire to avoid exploration of the topic. Thus, if Beth comes late to a therapy session, a psychodynamic therapist might interpret this behavior as resistance: Perhaps Beth does not want to work on the issues currently being explored or is concerned about something that she doesn't want to share with her therapist.

Over the course of therapy, patients may come to relate to their therapist as they did to someone who was important in their lives, perhaps a parent. This phenomenon is called **transference**. If Beth began asking how the therapist is feeling, or if she began to talk less about her own distressing feelings because she worried that the therapist might become upset, Beth would be "transferring" onto her therapist her usual style of relating with her mother, in which she views her mother as fragile and needing protection. The therapeutic value of transference is that patients can talk about what they are experiencing (which they may very well have been unable to do with the parent) to heighten understanding. Moreover, the therapist's acceptance of uncomfortable or shameful feelings helps patients accept those feelings in order to *choose* whether to act on them. An insight-oriented therapist would likely interpret Beth's questions about the therapist's well-being as transference. Beth and her therapist would then talk about what it was like for Beth to feel so protective and careful with her mother. **Countertransference** is the therapist's response to the patient's transference; this phenomenon stems from the therapist's own transference-related issues. That is, the therapist responds to the patient's transference on the basis of the therapist's own unresolved conflicts. Historically, countertransference was viewed as a hindrance to treatment, but more recently, psychodynamic therapists are likely to be trained both to recognize these feelings toward a patient and to make therapeutic use of them (Khwaja, 1997).

Humanistic Therapy: The Self in a Mirror

Like the humanistic approach to personality (see Chapter 10), humanistic therapy emphasizes free will, personal growth, self-esteem, and mastery. This approach is in contrast to psychodynamic therapy, which emphasizes the past, psychic determinism, and the working through of conflictual impulses and feelings.

CLIENT-CENTERED THERAPY: THE HELPFUL MIRROR. One of the early proponents of humanistic psychology (see Chapter 10) was Carl Rogers, who developed a therapeutic approach that came to be called **client-centered therapy**, which focuses on people's potential for growth and the importance of an empathic therapist. It is revealing that instead of using the term *patient*, a medical term that suggests illness, Rogers substituted the term *client*.

Theory. Rogers viewed people's distressing symptoms as caused by a blocked potential for personal growth. The goal of client-centered therapy is to dismantle that block so that people can reach their full potential. According to Rogers, problems arise because of a lack of a coherent, unified sense of self. An example is a mismatch, or **incongruence**, between the *real self* (who you actually are) and the *ideal self* (who you would like to be). By allowing people to become more like their ideal selves, client-centered therapy lessens the incongruence and the client feels better. According to client-centered therapy, Beth's problems may stem from incongruence between her real self (a self that has to work hard for good grades and feels shame and guilt about the imperfections that remind her of her mother's depressions) and her ideal self (a self that

Resistance: A reluctance or refusal to cooperate with the therapist, which can range from unconscious forgetting to outright refusal to comply with a therapist's request.

Transference: The process by which patients may relate to their therapists as they did to some important person in their lives.

Countertransference: The therapist's own response to the patient, stemming from the therapist's own transference-related issues.

Client-centered therapy: A type of insight-oriented therapy that focuses on people's potential for growth and the importance of an empathic therapist.

Incongruence: According to client-centered therapy, a mismatch between a person's *real self* and his or her *ideal self*.

is without struggle—a good student who always does the "right thing" and who never experiences sadness, hopelessness, or anxiety). The tension between her real and ideal selves creates a fragmented sense of self, which drains Beth's time and energy; these different parts of herself are in conflict with each other and prevent her from reaching her full potential.

Techniques. The client-centered therapist should be warm, able to see the world as the client does, and able to empathize with the client. The therapist does not offer analyses to the client; instead the therapist reflects back the thrust of what the client has said. However, the therapist must not simply parrot the client's words or phrases but show *accurate* and *genuine* empathy. Such empathy lets the client know that he or she is really understood. If the therapist is inaccurate in reflecting what the client says, or if the empathy seems false, the intervention will fail. The therapist must also provide **unconditional positive regard;** that is, he or she must convey positive feelings for the client regardless of the client's thoughts, feelings, or actions. The therapist does this by continually showing the client that he or she is inherently worthy as a human being. Genuine empathy and unconditional positive regard allow the client to decrease the incongruence between the real and ideal selves. Although Beth was unable to take some of her exams (real self), a client-centered therapist's empathy and unconditional positive regard would allow Beth to see that she is still smart (ideal self) and that everyone sometimes has negative, uncomfortable feelings. This therapeutic approach could help Beth see her real and ideal selves in a different light and allow her to think of herself more positively.

The client-centered therapist provides both genuine empathy and unconditional positive regard by making a distinction between the client as a person and the client's behaviors. The therapist could dislike a client's *behavior* but still view the client as a good person. If Beth were seeing a client-centered therapist, the topic of a therapy session might be what it was like for Beth during her mother's bouts of depression. A session might include this exchange:

Being rejected by a partner can leave a person feeling badly about him- or herself. Client-centered therapy would make a distinction between the person's actions *in the relationship and the fact he or she is still a worthwhile, good person.*

BETH: I was so disappointed and ashamed when I'd come home from school and she'd still be in bed, wearing her bathrobe.

THERAPIST: Yes, it must have caused you to feel ashamed, anxious, and worried when you came home and found your mother still in bed.

BETH: And I felt that it was *my* fault, that I wasn't doing enough to make her feel better.

THERAPIST: Although you felt that it was your fault, you did all that you possibly could. You were concerned about her. You were, and still are, a good, worthwhile person.

BETH: And now I spend most of the day in bed and don't bother to get dressed . . . am I becoming like my mother?

THERAPIST: You and your mother are two separate individuals. Although you may have some things in common, and right now that may include depression, that doesn't mean that your path in life is identical to hers.

Unconditional positive regard: The stance taken by a client-centered therapist that conveys positive feelings for the client, regardless of the client's thoughts, feelings, or actions.

The therapist repeatedly emphasizes the worthiness of the client until the client comes to accept this valuation and is able to reach his or her potential, and make different, healthier choices and decisions. When successful, client-centered therapy can achieve its objective in a few months rather than years.

GESTALT THERAPY: THE WHOLE SELF. European-trained psychoanalyst Fritz Perls (1893–1970) believed that clients must be responsible for their lives in the "here and now" and that their therapy didn't need to focus on the past, as psychodynamic and to some extent client-centered therapy did. His form of insight therapy is called **Gestalt therapy** (Perls, 1969). Gestalt therapy focuses on helping clients experience their authentic, spontaneous needs and desires by expanding their moment-to-moment awareness of their bodies, feelings, and thoughts, an awareness that may have been long buried. Gestalt therapy recognizes the importance of the whole self, as Gestalt psychology emphasized the perception of a whole as more than the sum of its parts (see Chapter 3).

Theory. Gestalt therapy helps clients become more fully aware of their feelings in the moment, their sensations in their bodies, and the nature of present reality (that is, what is happening outside themselves) so that they can respond to current difficulties more appropriately. When people are unaware of their feelings, they are apt to develop *false lives* and continue to operate in ignorance of the tension and repression at the root of their problems. Even breathing and body postures reflect feelings that may be hidden from clients' awareness. Gestalt therapy aims to help people become fully aware of their experiences. For example, someone who was taught as a child not to show sadness ("Don't be sad . . . look on the brighter side") might as an adult strive to push sad feelings from awareness. Gestalt therapy would help that person regain awareness of the feelings of sadness that are a legitimate part of life. From a Gestalt perspective, Beth's problems might be seen as caused by her false life, which has no awareness of her sadness and anger about her mother's illness. Her anxiety and depression are then manifestations of her having pushed these feelings out of awareness. According to Gestalt therapy, as Beth develops full awareness of these feelings, her own symptoms of anxiety and depression will diminish.

Techniques. To increase awareness of feelings, Gestalt clients may be asked to relive a past event in their minds while the therapist asks about feelings *at the moment.* If the client is avoiding reality or an awareness of feelings, the Gestalt therapist may take a confrontational stance. Clients may be asked to try out new behaviors and see how they feel doing these things. Perls developed the **empty chair technique,** in which the client imagines talking to a particular person, perhaps a parent or friend, who is "sitting" in an empty chair in the room. This technique can be very powerful, allowing the client to express thoughts and feelings that might otherwise remain unarticulated, and can help the client understand how these feelings affect his or her behavior and current relationships. The client may be asked to pretend to talk to a different aspect of him- or herself as if that aspect were a separate person. The empty chair technique can be particularly helpful in resolving grief over the loss of an important relationship or person.

Had Beth contacted a Gestalt therapist, she might be asked to relive what it was like to come home after school to find her mother still in bed. The therapist might ask Beth to notice her feelings while she relived the experience or, using the empty chair technique, to imagine going into her mother's room and saying the things that she had thought but had never actually said to her mother. Or the therapist might ask Beth to imagine talking to different parts of herself, such as the part that was ashamed of her mother and the part that genuinely worried about her mother. Alternatively, a Gestalt therapist might ask Beth to focus her awareness in the "here and now" while attempting to study or when lying in bed in the morning unable to summon the energy to face the day. All these techniques have the goal of helping Beth gain awareness of her feelings and insight into her problems, so as to feel differently about herself and thus to behave differently.

Some psychotherapists have criticized Gestalt therapy for its emphasis on feelings and its minimization of thoughts; moreover, the "here and now" focus can discourage client interest in long-term goals. Not all clients are good candidates for this type of

Gestalt therapy: A type of insight-oriented therapy that helps clients experience their authentic, spontaneous needs and desires by expanding their moment-to-moment awareness of their bodies, feelings, and thoughts.

Empty chair technique: A Gestalt therapy technique in which the client imagines talking to a particular person (parent, friend) who is "sitting" in an empty chair in the room.

treatment; people with severe mental illness and difficulty in maintaining a sense of reality (such as those with psychotic disorders) may be overwhelmed by the emphasis on feelings and unable to balance them with reality.

TABLE 14.1

Differences Among Psychodynamic, Client-Centered, and Gestalt Therapies

Although psychodynamic, client-centered, and Gestalt therapies have in common their use of insight, the various treatments differ in some important ways, including the focus of treatment, its goals, and techniques.

TYPE OF THERAPY	FOCUS	GOAL	TECHNIQUES
Psychodynamic therapy	Unconscious conflict and sexual/aggressive drives	To make unconscious conflict conscious	Free association, dream analysis, use of transference, interpretation
Client-centered therapy	Each person's unique experiences and potential for growth	To unblock the person's potential for growth by decreasing incongruence	Empathy, unconditional positive regard, genuineness toward the client
Gestalt therapy	Ways that people create false lives and decreased awareness of their feelings	To develop full awareness of feelings, bodily experiences, and reality so that the person can respond to current situations more appropriately	Awareness exercises, reliving of past events, empty chair technique

In sum, although there are differences among the insight-oriented therapies (Table 14.1), the clients most likely to benefit from these treatments are similar in that they are relatively healthy, articulate individuals who are interested in knowing more about their own motivations.

LOOKING AT LEVELS

The Importance of Expressing Emotions

In all three types of insight-oriented therapy, clients spend time focusing on and talking about their feelings. Does the expression of emotion have a therapeutic effect? The answer appears to be yes. In studies where participants were asked to write about their feelings concerning a stressful event, participants in the writing group had fewer doctor visits, improved immune functioning, and a greater sense of well-being than those in the control group (these studies are discussed in greater detail in Chapter 12; see Esterling et al., 1999; Pennebaker et al., 1990). When participants were asked about their writing experiences, 76% described the benefits of writing as helping them attain insight: One said, "It made me think things out and really realize what my problem is" (Pennebaker et al., 1990). In fact, studies comparing the benefits of this particular form of expressive writing with the benefits of a few sessions of psychotherapy have found both interventions to have similarly positive effects (Murray et al., 1989), although those participants seeing a psychotherapist had more positive moods immediately after therapy sessions compared with those using expressive writing, who had more negative moods immediately after writing. It is as if the act of deliberately processing the emotional experience, whether in writing or with a therapist, transforms the experience into a less upsetting event.

The psychotherapy sessions focused on feelings surrounding a traumatic event that occurred in the past, often an event about which the participants had not told anyone. Thus, the therapy (and the writing group) provided an opportunity for participants to think about issues that they had not previously explored. The treatment focused on examining a deeper understanding about the traumatic event, similar to the task given the expressive writing group. It should be noted, however, that most studies on emotional expression through writing have used relatively healthy college undergraduates as participants. It remains to be seen whether the therapeutic results would be the same with participants who are diagnosed with psychological disorders.

Nonetheless, these results about the positive effects of expressing emotions and gaining insight support some of the basic tenets of psychodynamic therapy specifically and of insight-oriented therapy more generally. Moreover, the outcome can be understood from the levels approach. Expressing feelings by making what is unconscious conscious and deriving insight (level of the person) has an effect on the immune system (level of the brain; see Chapter 12). Further, participants in studies on emotional expressiveness who did express their feelings report feeling better in the long run and attribute this positive emotional state to the insights gained (level of the person). At the level of the group, those gaining insight through therapy had less negative moods immediately after sessions in which they expressed emotions than did those writing about their feelings, illustrating the importance of expressing the feelings *with another person*. In addition, cultural factors led the participants to have certain beliefs about what would occur in the therapy sessions and how they might feel about the sessions.

CONSOLIDATE!

▶ *1. What is the focus of treatment in psychodynamic therapy? What are its main techniques?*   Psychodynamic therapy seeks to help patients become aware of their unconscious motivations, which can cause psychological symptoms. Through insight, they can choose whether to respond to those impulses. According to this theory, at some point in the treatment, patients will experience transference to the therapist and resistance. Techniques include dream analysis, free association, and interpretation.

▶ *2. How would client-centered and other humanistic therapists approach treatment? What techniques would they use?*   Client-centered therapy focuses on helping clients experience congruence between their real and ideal selves, thereby reducing the clients' problems. The therapist should be warm, empathic, and genuine, and should show unconditional positive regard toward clients. According to this theory, these elements are enough to bring about therapeutic change. Gestalt therapy focuses on the "here and now" and helps clients become fully aware of current feelings and experiences so that they can respond more appropriately. Techniques focus on increasing awareness of feelings and reality by having clients relive past events to capture their feelings in the moment and by using the empty chair technique. If the client is avoiding reality, the Gestalt therapist may take a confrontational stance.

COGNITIVE AND BEHAVIOR THERAPY

A cognitive–behavior therapist would begin by asking Beth quite a different set of questions, questions that dealt with neither her family nor her feelings: What does she do before she sits down to study or take an exam? What does she think about when she starts to study or walks to a classroom to take an exam? What, in detail, does she do during the day? Has she ever tried any relaxation techniques? What does she believe about herself and her abilities? These are questions not about insight, but about thought patterns and behaviors.

▶ 1. What is the focus of behavior therapy? What are some of its techniques?

▶ 2. What are the goals of cognitive therapy? What techniques are used?

▶ 3. How does cognitive–behavior therapy differ from cognitive or behavior therapy alone?

Behavior Therapy

Even after patients had developed an awareness of the origins of their problems through insight-oriented therapies, behavioral change did not necessarily follow. **Behavior therapy,** which focuses on observable, measurable behavior, developed out of frustration with this lack of change. Joseph Wolpe (1915–1997) profoundly changed the practice of psychotherapy in 1958 when he published *Psychotherapy by Reciprocal Inhibition*. He was a psychiatrist, but his emphasis on behavior rather than on unconscious motivation created a new form of treatment that particularly appealed to psychologists because of its emphasis on quantifiable results. Moreover, behavior therapy rested on well-researched principles of learning (see Chapter 5; Wolpe, 1997).

THEORY. In behavior therapy, distressing symptoms are seen as the result of learning, not of unconscious forces. Through the use of social learning—that is, modeling—as well as by classical and operant conditioning, clients can change unwanted behaviors by learning new ones; it is easiest to change a behavior by replacing it with a new, more adaptive one. The behavior therapist is interested in the ABCs of the behavior: its *antecedents* (what is the stimulus that triggers the behavior?), the *behavior* (what is the exact nature of the behavior?), and its *consequences* (what is reinforcing the behavior?). Behavior therapy's lack of interest or belief in an unconscious "root cause" was revolutionary. Behaviors and performance are emphasized, the therapist takes a more active, directive role in treatment, and "homework"— between-session tasks on the part of the client—is an important component of the treatment. Therapists took a new look at treatment results: Did the client experience less frequent or less intense symptoms after therapy?

In Beth's case, a behavior therapist would be interested in the antecedent, or stimulus, of Beth's problematic behaviors. Consider her anxiety: The antecedent might be the act of sitting down to study for an exam, or waiting in class to receive her exam booklet. The behavior is the conditioned emotional response of fear and anxiety, evidenced by her sweating hands, racing heart rate, and other behaviors associated with anxiety (see Chapter 13). The consequences include negative reinforcement (the uncomfortable symptoms go away) when skipping an exam. Thus, related nonacademic avoidant behaviors such as sleeping through an exam are reinforced. In addition, her anxiety and subsequent social isolation led to a loss of pleasant activities and opportunities for social reinforcement, which in turn led to depression. Unlike cognitive therapy, which views depressive thoughts as producing depressive feelings and behaviors, behavior theory views depressive behaviors as leading to depressive thoughts (see Chapter 13; Emmelkamp, 1994).

TECHNIQUES. Behavioral techniques rest on classical conditioning, operant conditioning, and social learning principles. One classical conditioning technique is **systematic desensitization,** a procedure that teaches people to be relaxed in the presence of a feared object or situation. This technique, developed by Wolpe for treating phobias, grew out of the idea that someone cannot be fearful (and hence anxious) and relaxed at the same time. Systematic desensitization uses **progressive muscle relaxation,** a relaxation technique whereby the muscles are sequentially relaxed from one end of

Behavior therapy: A type of therapy, based on well-researched principles of learning, that focuses on observable, measurable behaviors.

Systematic desensitization: A behavior therapy technique that teaches people to be relaxed in the presence of a feared object or situation.

Progressive muscle relaxation: A relaxation technique whereby the person relaxes muscles sequentially from one end of the body to the other.

the body to the other, often from feet to head. Although progressive muscle relaxation is used in systematic desensitization, it can be used by itself to induce relaxation. You can try progressive muscle relaxation yourself by following the instructions below. Read them several times until you essentially know them and can say them to yourself with your eyes closed; or, have a friend read them to you; or tape record them for playback. The instructions should be recited slowly and clearly. If you're repeating the instructions to yourself from memory and you forget a group of muscles, the technique can still be effective. (If you have an injury in a particular part of your body, you may want to skip tensing the muscles in that area.) Like any new skill, relaxation induction becomes easier and more effective with practice.

> Sit in a comfortable position, take a deep breath, and close your eyes. Curl your toes, and hold that position for a few seconds . . . not so tightly that it hurts, just enough so that you can notice what the tension in your foot muscles feels like (5–10 seconds). . . . Relax. . . . Notice the difference between the tension and the relaxation, the pleasantness of the relaxation. . . . Now point your toes up toward the ceiling, keeping your heels on the floor. . . . Feel the tension, the pull . . . keep breathing. . . . Relax. . . . As before, notice the difference between the tension and the relaxation. . . . Press your knees toward each other . . . not so much that it hurts, just enough to notice the tension in those muscles. . . . Relax. . . . Tense your thighs and buttocks, and notice your body lift slightly. . . . Notice the tension in the muscles, remember to breathe. . . . Relax. . . . Notice how pleasant the relaxation feels. . . . Tense your abdominal muscles as if you were a prize fighter. . . . Feel the tension, keep breathing. . . . Relax. . . . Take a deep breath and hold it while counting to 5, then slowly exhale. . . . Notice the way the muscles in your chest feel as you hold the breath and then exhale, and how your sense of relaxation is enhanced. . . . Raise your shoulders up toward your ears and hold it. . . . Notice what the tension feels like in those muscles, breathe. . . . Relax. . . . Now push your shoulders down toward the floor, focusing your awareness on how this new tension feels. . . . Relax. . . . Notice a sense of relaxation spreading over your body. . . . Purse your lips together and notice the tension in the lower part of your face, your jaw, perhaps your neck. . . . Relax. . . . Notice the difference between the tension and the relaxation, and how much more pleasant relaxation is. . . . Close your eyes tightly, but not so tightly that it hurts. . . . Notice the tension. . . . Relax. . . . Notice the pleasantness of the relaxation. Take a moment and check your body for any residual tension; if you find any, tense and relax those muscles. . . . Enjoy the sensation of relaxation. In a few moments, open your eyes, and bring this sense of relaxation with you into the day. (Adapted from Jacobson, 1925)

Using systematic desensitization to overcome a phobia, the therapist and client construct a hierarchy of real or imagined activities related to the feared object or situation (such as a fear of elevators; see Figure 14.1 on page 524). This hierarchy begins with the least fearful activity, such as pressing an elevator call button, progressing to the most fearful, being stuck in a stopped elevator. Over the course of a number of sessions, clients work on becoming relaxed when imagining increasingly anxiety-provoking activities. At the outset, the client is asked to relax. After becoming fully relaxed, the client is then asked to imagine the activity or object at the bottom of the hierarchy—that is, the least feared scenario. If anxiety intrudes (which the client indicates by some prearranged signal), the therapist asks the client to abandon imagining the fearful scene and use the relaxation technique until he or she is relaxed again. After successfully mastering this first scene—that is, thinking about it without feeling anxious—the client imagines the next most fearful scene in the hierarchy, again alternating imagining with relaxation when the anxiety is uncomfortable. The procedure continues in this fashion until the client can imagine being fully immersed in the actual feared situation without an anxious response. After these mental exercises, the client will experience the situation in reality, now better able to control any anxiety.

A behavioral therapist would have asked Beth about her "learning history": When did she start to feel anxious about tests? What external conditions made it worse? The therapist might teach Beth relaxation techniques and instruct her to practice them

FIGURE 14.1
Systematic Desensitization of an Elevator Phobia

With systematic desensitization, a man with an elevator phobia would list a hierarchy of activities related to using an elevator. Next, he would successfully learn to make himself relax, using techniques such as progressive muscle relaxation.

He then starts out imagining items at the low end of the hierarchy, such as pressing an elevator button. When he becomes anxious, he stops imagining that scene and uses relaxation techniques to become fully relaxed again.

When he can imagine the elevator-related situations on the lower end of the hierarchy without anxiety, he progresses to situations that make him more anxious, stopping to do the relaxation technique when he becomes anxious.

Systematic desensitization continues in this fashion until the man can imagine being fully immersed in the most feared situation (a stuck elevator) without anxiety. He would then follow the same procedure in a real elevator, although his anxiety may no longer be troublesome, making this final phase unnecessary.

between sessions. Once Beth successfully learned to how to become relaxed, she and her therapist might begin systematic desensitization.

Another behavioral technique that relies on classical conditioning principles is **exposure with response prevention,** a planned, programmatic procedure that exposes the client to the anxiety-provoking object but prevents the usual maladaptive response. For instance, clients with an obsessive-compulsive disorder that compels them to wash their hands repeatedly would purposefully get their hands dirty during a therapy session and then be prevented from washing their hands immediately afterward. In this way, they would habituate to the anxiety. Exposure with response prevention has been found to be as effective as medication for OCD, and the behavioral treatment can have longer-lasting benefits (Marks, 1997). However, not all people who have OCD are

Exposure with response prevention: A behavior therapy technique that, in a planned, programmatic way, exposes the client to an anxiety-provoking object and prevents the usual maladaptive response.

willing to use this behavioral technique (Stanley & Turner, 1995). The technique is also used in treating bulimia nervosa: Clients would eat a food normally followed by forced vomiting, and then would not throw up (or would delay it as long as possible). Beforehand, client and therapist develop strategies that the client could use while trying *not* to engage in the maladaptive behavior. The technique of **stimulus control** involves controlling the exposure to a stimulus that elicits a conditioned response, so as to decrease or increase the frequency of the response. For example, if an alcoholic drank to excess only in a bar, limiting or eliminating the occasions of going to a bar would be using stimulus control.

Techniques based on operant conditioning make use of the principles of reinforcement, punishment, and extinction, with the goal of **behavior modification**—that is, changing the *behavior*, not focusing on thoughts or feelings. Setting the appropriate *response contingencies*, or behaviors that will earn reinforcement, is crucial. If Beth used behavior modification techniques, she would establish response contingencies for behaving in desired new ways: She might reward herself with a movie or a dinner out after taking an exam, or allow herself an hour's conversation with a friend after studying for 2 hours.

FIGURE 14.2
Daily Self-Monitoring Log

Name _____	Day _____	Date _____

Time of Day	Problematic Behavior	Where the Behavior Occurred	What happened before the behavior occurred (thoughts/feelings, interactions with others, etc.)?

This daily self-monitoring log helps clients develop an awareness of the antecedents, or "triggers," to their problematic behaviors. The column for time of day helps determine whether there is a daily or weekly pattern. Noting where the behavior occurred helps establish whether certain environments play a role in the behavior, perhaps serving as conditioned stimuli. Writing down thoughts, feelings, interactions with others, or other factors (such as level of hunger) that preceded the problematic behavior helps identify irrational thought patterns, distressing feelings, states, or situations that lead to the behavior. With knowledge of the factors, the client and therapist can develop appropriate targets of change for the therapy.

Extinction, eliminating a behavior by not reinforceing it, is another important tool of the behavioral therapist. **Self-monitoring techniques,** such as keeping a daily log of a problematic behavior, can help identify its antecedents (see Figure 14.2). Daily logs are used for a variety of problems including poor mood, anxiety, overeating, smoking, sleep problems, and compulsive gambling. Observational learning also plays a role in behavior therapy, particularly with children and in the treatment of some phobias, especially animal phobias (Goetestam & Berntzen, 1997).

Psychodynamic therapists predicted that some of clients' symptoms—that is, their maladaptive behaviors—might disappear with behavioral treatment, but that because the unresolved underlying conflicts remained, new symptoms would develop.

Stimulus control: A behavior therapy technique that involves controlling the exposure to a stimulus that elicits a conditioned response, so as to decrease or increase the frequency of the response.

Behavior modification: A category of therapeutic techniques for changing behavior based on operant conditioning principles.

Self-monitoring techniques: Behavioral techniques that help the client identify the antecedents, consequences, and patterns of a targeted behavior.

The psychoanalysts termed this process *symptom substitution*. According to this view, should Beth's anxiety symptoms respond well to behavior therapy, her unconscious conflicts would reemerge through some other symptom—perhaps being unable to get up for classes in the morning or staying out partying every night. The new symptoms, just like the old ones, would impede Beth's academic success, and according to psychodynamic theory, new symptoms would continue to arise until her unconscious conflict was resolved. However, research has not supported the concept of symptom substitution (Nurnberger & Hingtgen, 1973). Other criticisms of behavior therapy focus on its exclusive emphasis on observable behaviors, which ignores thoughts, feelings, and motivation.

Cognitive Therapy: It's the Thought That Counts

The ripples of the cognitive revolution in psychology (see Chapter 1) were felt in therapy as well as in research. Therapists began to examine the mental processes that contribute to behavior, not simply physical stimuli. It was clear that people's thoughts ("cognitions"), not just their learning histories or "unconscious forces," influence their feelings and behavior, and do so in myriad ways. Just thinking about a past positive experience with love can put you in a good mood, and thinking about an unhappy love experience can have the opposite effect (Clark & Collins, 1993). A cognitive therapist would focus on Beth's thoughts and the way in which one thought leads to another, contributing to her emotional experience of anxiety and depression.

THEORY. The way people perceive or interpret events can affect their well-being (Chapter 12). **Cognitive therapy** emphasizes the role of attempts to think rationally in the control of distressing feelings and behaviors. It is the perception of any experience that determines the response to that experience, and cognitive therapy highlights the importance of the way people perceive and think about events. Two particularly important contributors to cognitive therapy were Albert Ellis and Aaron Beck.

Albert Ellis (1902–1987) was a clinical psychologist who in the 1950s developed a treatment called *rational-emotive therapy (RET)*. RET emphasizes rational, logical thinking and assumes that distressing feelings or symptoms are caused by faulty or illogical thoughts:

> Thinking and emoting are so closely interrelated that they usually accompany each other, act in a circular cause-and-effect relationship, and in certain (though hardly all) respects are essentially the same thing, so that one's thinking becomes one's emotion and emotion becomes one's thought. (Ellis, 1958, pp. 35–36)

People may develop illogical or irrational thoughts as a result of their experiences and never assess whether these thoughts are valid. They elevate irrational thoughts to "godlike absolutist musts, shoulds, demands, and commands" (Ellis, 1994a, p. 103). According to RET, Beth's thought that she needs to do well in school is a dysfunctional, irrational belief that in order to be a lovable, deserving human being, she must earn good grades; if she does not, she believes she will be unlovable and worthless.

RET treatment thus focuses on creating more rational thoughts. In Beth's case, they might be, *I might be disappointed or disappoint others if I don't do well this semester, but I am still a worthwhile, lovable human being.* This more rational thought should then cause the problematic behavior to diminish, allowing her to choose other emotions and actions. Part of the goal of RET is educational, and clients should be able to use the techniques on their own once they have mastered them. Like behavior therapy, RET is oriented toward *solving* problems as opposed to psychologically exploring them.

Ellis (1994a) proposed three processes that interfere with healthy functioning: (1) *self-downing*—being critical of oneself for performing poorly or being rejected; (2) *hostility and rage*—being unkind to or critical of others for performing poorly; and (3) *low frustration tolerance*—blaming everyone and everything for "poor, dislikable conditions."

Cognitive therapy: Therapy that focuses on the client's thoughts rather than his or her feelings or behaviors.

Like a Gestalt therapist, a rational-emotive therapist challenges the client but focuses on thoughts rather than feelings. The RET therapist challenges the client's assumptions, which are based on thoughts and beliefs, and helps the client develop more realistic, appropriate thoughts. The RET therapist strives to have the client feel accepted and encourages self-acceptance and a new way of thinking; self-blame is viewed as counterproductive because it involves faulty beliefs. Shortcomings or failures are viewed as simply part of life, not as crimes or signs of moral weakness.

Five Common Cognitive Distortions

Source: *Adapted from Beck (1967).*

DICHOTOMOUS THINKING

Also known as black-and-white thinking, which allows for nothing in between the extremes; you are either perfect or a piece of garbage.

Example: Beth thinks that if she doesn't get an A on a test, she has failed.

THE MENTAL FILTER

Magnifying the negative aspects of something while filtering out the positive.

Example: Beth remembers only the things she did that were below her expectations but doesn't pay attention to (or remember) the things she did well.

MIND READING

Thinking you know exactly what other people are thinking, particularly as it relates to you.

Example: Beth believes that she *knows* her professors think less of her because of what happened on the exams (when in fact they don't think less of her, but are concerned about her).

CATASTROPHIC EXAGGERATION

Thinking that your worst nightmare will come true and that it will be intolerable.

Example: Beth's fear is that she'll be kicked out of school and end up homeless; a more likely reality is that she may have to take some courses over again.

CONTROL BELIEFS

Believing either that you are helpless and totally subject to forces beyond your control, or that you must tightly control your life for fear that, if you don't, you will never be able to regain control.

Example: Until talking to her family friend, Nina, Beth thought there was nothing she could do to change the downward spiral of events, and that she was either totally in control of her studying or else not in control at all.

Psychiatrist Aaron Beck developed a form of cognitive therapy that, like RET, rests on the premise that irrational thoughts are the root cause of psychological problems, and that recognition of irrationality and adoption of more realistic, rational thoughts cause psychological problems to improve. Irrational thoughts that arise from a systematic bias, such as the belief that if you tell your friend you are mad at her she will reject you, are considered **cognitive distortions** of reality; several common distortions are presented in Table 14.2. However, unlike RET, which relies on the therapist's attempts to persuade the client of the irrationality of his or her beliefs, Beck's version of cognitive therapy encourages the client to view beliefs as hypotheses to be tested. Thus, interactions with the world provide opportunities to perform "experiments" to ascertain the accuracy of the client's beliefs (Hollon & Beck, 1994). Beck and his colleagues have approached treatment empirically, developing measures to assess depression, anxiety, and other problems, and to evaluate the effectiveness of treatment.

Cognitive distortion: Irrational thoughts that arise from a systematic bias in the way a person thinks about reality.

TECHNIQUES. The RET therapist helps the client identify his or her irrational beliefs, relying on verbal persuasion (Hollon & Beck, 1994). The therapist works through a sequence of techniques with the client, which can be remembered by the alphabetical sequence ABCDEF. Distressing feelings exist because an *activating event* (A) along with the person's *beliefs* (B) lead to a *highly charged emotional consequence* (C). It is not the event per se that created the problem, but rather the beliefs attached to the event that led to a problematic consequence. Thus, changing the beliefs will lead to a different consequence. This is done by helping the client *dispute* (D) the irrational beliefs and perceive their illogical and self-defeating nature. Such disputes lead to an *effect* (E; also called *effective new philosophies*), a new way of feeling and acting. Finally, clients may have to take *further action* (F) to solidify the change in beliefs. Each session is devoted to a specific aspect of the client's problem. Often at the outset of a session, client and therapist will determine what effect the client wants from the intervention.

Beth and a RET therapist might agree on what the effect should be when studying—namely, less anxiety—and would discuss the activating events (sitting down to study), beliefs (that if Beth does not do well on a test, she will be a failure as a person), and consequences (anxiety). The bulk of their work together would focus on disputing the beliefs: Beth is still a worthwhile person even if she doesn't do well on a test, and even if she gets a B or C, her grade is not a failure, nor is she. The end result of this process is that Beth should feel less anxiety.

When working on a dispute, a RET therapist helps the client distinguish between a thought that is a "must" and one that is a "prefer." Beth's thought *I must get an A* is irrational and creates unpleasant feelings. Its more realistic counterpart is *I prefer to get an A*, which makes it clearer that she has some choice about the grade she sets as a goal. The therapist sometimes argues with the client to help him or her confront (and dispute) the faulty cognitions that contribute to the client's distress. The RET therapist may also use role playing to help the client practice new ways of thinking and behaving (Ellis, 1994b). RET can be helpful with anxiety, unassertiveness (Haaga & Davison, 1989), and unrealistic expectations. Like insight-oriented treatment, RET is generally not successful with psychotic disorders.

Beck's cognitive therapy often makes use of a daily record of dysfunctional thoughts (see Figure 14.3). Clients are asked to identify the situation in which their automatic thought (comparable to irrational beliefs) occurred, rate their emotional state (Emotions column), write down the automatic thought, their rational response to

FIGURE 14.3
Daily Record of Dysfunctional Beliefs

Situation	Emotion(s)	Automatic Thought(s)	Rational Response	Outcome
Actual event or stream of thoughts	Rate (1–100%)	ATs that preceded emotion Rate belief in ATs (1–100%)	Write rational response to ATs Rate belief in rational response (1–100%)	Rerate AT (1–100%)
1. Sit down to study	Anxious 70%	I won't be able to do as well on the test as I would like. —100% (Dichotomous thinking)	I might not be able to do as well as I want, but that doesn't mean that I will necessarily fail. —50%	Anxious 50%
2. In bed in the morning	Sad 80%	There's no point in getting out of bed—the day will be awful. I fail at everything I try. —90% (Mental filter)	Although I may not "succeed" in the goals I set for myself, it is possible that my expectations are too high, that I have too many expectations, or that I only notice the goals I don't attain, and don't notice the ones I do. —70%	Sad 6%

Keeping a written daily record like Beth's, shown here, can help identify triggers to dysfunctional, automatic thoughts and make them more rational. (Format adapted from Beck et al., 1979.)

the automatic thought (comparable to the RET "dispute"), and then rerate their emotional state (Outcome column). Clients should rate their emotional state as lower after going through this process. Although this technique appears straightforward, it can be hard to do because the client is so used to believing the "truth" of the automatic thought that it doesn't seem to be distorted or irrational. The process of helping clients shift their thinking away from automatic, dysfunctional thoughts to more realistic ones is called **cognitive restructuring.** The therapist helps clients examine and assess the accuracy of the automatic thoughts, and search for alternative interpretations or solutions to their automatic thoughts and habitual ways of viewing themselves and the world.

Cognitive therapy also makes use of **psychoeducation**—that is, educating clients about therapy and research findings pertaining to their disorder or problem. This knowledge is then used to help clients develop a more realistic, undistorted view of their problems. Beth was afraid to seek treatment because she was afraid she would be hospitalized; a cognitive therapist might explain to her the criteria for a hospital admission so this fear wouldn't become the basis for developing irrational automatic thoughts. Cognitive therapy has been found to be particularly helpful with panic and other anxiety disorders, depression, eating disorders, and anger management.

Cognitive–Behavior Therapy

In the last quarter of the 20th century, therapists began to use both cognitive and behavioral techniques within the same treatment. This merging of therapies grew out of the recognition that both cognitions and behaviors affect feelings and are a part of most psychological disorders. The two sets of techniques can work together to promote therapeutic change: Cognitive techniques change thoughts, which then affect feelings and behaviors; behavioral techniques change behaviors, which in turn lead to new experiences, feelings, ways of relating, and changes in how one thinks about oneself and the world. Two examples of cognitive–behavior therapy (CBT) that focus on providing specific skills are *assertiveness training* and *social skills training*.

ASSERTIVENESS TRAINING: LEARNING TO BE HEARD. Assertiveness training is taught to people who have difficulty clearly communicating their preferences, feelings, thoughts, and ideas. They may be afraid of being ridiculed or making others angry; or they may never have really asked themselves their preferences because they were not taught to be assertive (historically, this has been more of an issue for women than for men). Or, they may become explosively angry when trying to express their desires. Assertiveness training involves helping people identify their irrational beliefs about being assertive ("If I tell them what's really on my mind, they might be upset" or "If I don't yell, they won't pay attention"). Although such thoughts may sometimes be irrational, at other times they may be true. The behavioral component encourages people to try out assertive behaviors with the therapist (or other members of a therapy group) so that they can see how it feels to be assertive, discuss the reactions others might have, and learn how to respond to other people's reactions. If some of the people in the client's life really will be upset if some preferences or thoughts are articulated, part of the work in therapy will focus on how to handle that situation, identifying irrational thoughts about it, and developing appropriate ways to behave.

SOCIAL SKILLS TRAINING. The goal of social skills training is to help the client develop better skills when interacting with people. These may include learning to "read" other people's behaviors, to respond to others in a different way, or to know what is expected behavior in particular situations. Cognitive techniques focus on clients' irrational beliefs about themselves, their social abilities, interactions with other people, and others' thoughts; such beliefs often prevent clients from attempting to interact with others. The behavioral component of such treatment would focus on how to behave in troubling social situations or when meeting new people. The therapist and client might engage in role playing in therapy sessions, allowing the client to try out

Cognitive restructuring: The process of helping clients shift their thinking away from the focus on automatic, dysfunctional thoughts to more realistic ones.

Psychoeducation: The process of educating clients about therapy and research findings pertaining to their disorders or problems.

new behaviors and get feedback on them in the safety of the therapist's office. Homework assignments might involve arranging to meet new people, perhaps by taking an adult education class or joining an activity club, with the goal *not* necessarily of making new friends but simply trying out the new behaviors in a new context. The client and therapist would then talk over what happened in subsequent sessions.

TABLE 14.3 Differences Among Behavioral, Cognitive, and Cognitive–Behavior Therapies

Although behavioral, cognitive, and cognitive–behavior therapies all address a client's symptoms more than insight-oriented therapies do, focus on symptom relief as a goal in and of itself, and employ between-session homework, they also have differences.

TYPE OF THERAPY	FOCUS	GOAL	TECHNIQUE
Behavioral therapy	Maladaptive behaviors	Change the behavior, its antecedents, or its consequences	Relaxation techniques, systematic desensitization, exposure with response prevention, stimulus control, behavior modification, observational learning
Cognitive therapy	Automatic, irrational thoughts	Change dysfunctional, unrealistic thoughts to more realistic ones Recognize the relationship among thoughts, feelings, and behaviors	Cognitive restructuring (or Ellis's ABCDEF technique), help the client develop more realistic thoughts, psychoeducation, role playing
Cognitive–behavior therapy	Thoughts and behaviors	Goals of cognitive and behavioral therapies	Techniques of both cognitive and behavioral therapies

Despite differences between cognitive and behavioral therapies (see Table 14.3), both approaches and the combined CBT are appropriate for a wide range of clients and disorders. These treatments focus on clients' problems rather than on the client as a "whole" person, as insight-oriented treatments do. Cognitive therapy, behavior therapy, and CBT provide the client with the opportunity to learn new coping strategies and master new tasks. These therapies are appropriate for any disorder.

LOOKING AT LEVELS

Token Economies

As you have seen, behavioral techniques focus on changing maladaptive behaviors. They can also be used in inpatient psychiatric units. In these facilities, it is possible to change the response contingencies for an undesired behavior as well as for a desired behavior. Behavior modification can be used to change even severely maladaptive behaviors. Secondary reinforcers, those that are learned and don't inherently satisfy a physical need, are used in treatment programs not only with psychiatric patients but also with mentally retarded children and adults, and even in prisons. Patients and residents must earn "tokens" that can be traded for small items such as cigarettes or candy at a "token store," or for privileges such as going out for a walk or watching a particular television show.

These **token economies**—treatment programs that use secondary reinforcers to change behavior—can be used to mold social behavior (level of the group) directly by modifying what patients say to one another and to nonpatients. For instance, using a token economy, hospitalized schizophrenics can learn to talk to others, answer questions, or eat more normally. The token economy itself is a social creation, and it is only within the confines of the values of the culture that certain behaviors come to be reinforced and others extinguished. Operant conditioning also modifies how patients perceive specific stimuli, such as interpreting a question as something that requires an answer (level of the person). At the level of the brain, operant conditioning can affect the dopamine-based reward system in the nucleus accumbens (see Chapter 5), increasing the likelihood of a reinforced behaviors occurring again. Thus, behavior modification as a treatment for severely disturbed behavior can best be understood by regarding events at the three levels: how conditioning changes the brain and how it changes the meaning of stimuli, which in turn changes behavioral interactions with objects. Moreover, such conditioning affects and is affected by social interactions. Although token economies can be effective, their use is declining because of ethical and moral questions about depriving patients and clients of secondary reinforcers (such as television, cigarettes, walks on the grounds) if they do not earn them through behavior change (Glynn, 1990).

Token economy: A treatment program that uses secondary reinforcers (tokens) to bring about behavior modification.

CONSOLIDATE!

▶ *1. What is the focus of behavior therapy? What are some of its techniques?*   Behavior therapy assumes that maladaptive behavior is based on previous learning and focuses on changing distressing or abnormal behavior via learning principles. Behavioral therapists use techniques such as systematic desensitization, exposure with response prevention, stimulus control, behavior modification programs, and observational learning.

▶ *2. What are the goals of cognitive therapy? What techniques are used?*   Cognitive therapy rests on the assumption that thoughts influence feelings and behaviors. According to this approach, someone experiencing distressing symptoms such as depression has

irrational, automatic thoughts that affect feelings and behavior. The goal of cognitive therapy is to reduce these irrational cognitive distortions via cognitive restructuring, psychoeducation, and challenging irrational beliefs or, using Ellis's term, disputes.

▶ *3. How does cognitive–behavior therapy differ from cognitive or behavior therapy alone?*   Cognitive–behavior therapy (CBT) focuses both on changing problematic irrational thoughts and on providing new, more adaptive learning to replace old, maladaptive learning. This treatment makes use of techniques from both cognitive therapy and behavior therapy; assertiveness training and social skills training are examples of CBT.

OTHER FORMS OF THERAPY

During the course of her therapy, Beth talked about her vivid memories of her mother's episodes of depression, about the times when she would lie in bed most of the day. However, her mother had not had an episode of severe depression in the last 5 years. Beth was surprised when her therapist raised the possibility of having her mother come in for a few sessions; the idea had not occurred to her. Thinking about her mother's depression led Beth to wonder whether medication might help her anxiety and depression, since medication seemed to help her mother. After her last hospitalization 5 years ago, Beth's mother had participated in a research study in the hospital, where she was treated successfully with antidepressant medication and cognitive–behavior therapy.

Beth's questions continued. Cost-related forces were changing the way health care was delivered. How might these changes affect her mother and the course of her own therapy?

▶ 1.   What are some types of prevention against the onset of major mental illness?

> 2. What are other forms, or modalities, of therapy besides individual therapy?

> 3. What biomedical treatments are available?

> 4. What therapies use theories and techniques drawn from a number of different orientations?

> 5. What recent trends might affect the future of mental health care?

As health insurance companies and health care professionals seek ways to provide effective treatment in a time- and cost-efficient manner, some psychological therapies have changed; today, there is more of an emphasis on intervening early, and on considering a wider array of treatments that might be helpful.

Prevention: Sometimes Worth More Than a Pound of Cure

Programs intended to prevent mental illness aim to halt the development or progression of psychological disorders by using social or cultural interventions. **Primary prevention** programs focus on eliminating sociocultural causes of psychological disorders and are often offered to the public at large. For instance, experiencing child abuse increases the risk for many types of disorders, which may develop in childhood or adulthood. Some primary prevention programs aim to decrease the occurrence of child abuse, through educational programs for new parents on the prevention of child abuse and through hot-line services for parents who feel they might abuse their children.

Secondary prevention seeks to intervene to prevent the occurrence of a disorder in those who are at risk for developing it. For instance, research suggests that children with a depressed parent are at higher risk than those without a depressed parent for psychological disorders such as depression, anxiety disorders, and alcohol dependence (Weissman et al., 1997). People at risk might receive cognitive therapy to help modify any irrational automatic thoughts that could lead to depression. Another example involves an experimental treatment for adolescents at high risk to develop schizophrenia: Some of these young people are given a low dose of an antipsychotic medication and others are given a placebo; a form of cognitive therapy is also provided (Goode, 1999b). The hope is that such preventive treatment will minimize the frequency and duration of episodes of schizophrenia, and early results indicate that such secondary prevention efforts can be effective (McGorry & Edwards, 1998), although more research in this area is needed to reach a definitive conclusion. Programs in secondary prevention may be administered by a community mental health center, hospital, or other facility providing mental health services.

Tertiary prevention strives to decrease the severity, duration, and frequency of a psychological disorder once it has developed. Community mental health centers, which came into existence to treat those with psychological disorders who could not otherwise afford help, offer programs in tertiary prevention. Psychological therapies themselves are types of tertiary prevention.

Some prevention programs are available through publicly funded services such as community rape crisis centers or Head Start preschool programs. Others may be offered through private sources, such as health insurance companies or employers; stress management programs or support groups for relatives of those diagnosed with Alzheimer's disease, who experience significant amounts of stress and are at risk for developing disorders such as anxiety and depression (see Chapter 12), are examples of these programs.

Modalities: When Two or More Isn't a Crowd

Each therapy approach mentioned thus far can be implemented in a variety of **modalities**, or forms. **Individual therapy**—therapy in which one client is treated by one ther-

Primary prevention: A type of program that focuses on eliminating sociocultural causes of psychological disorders.

Secondary prevention: A type of program that seeks to intervene with those at risk for developing a disorder to prevent its occurrence.

Tertiary prevention: A type of program that tries to decrease the severity, duration, and frequency of a psychological disorder once it has developed.

Modality: A form of therapy.

Individual therapy: A therapy modality in which one client is treated by one therapist.

apist—is a modality. Other modalities have one or more therapists working with a family, or with a group of people who share some commonality, such as a particular diagnosis of agoraphobia. Each theoretical orientation discussed earlier can be used in these various modalities: individual, family, or group.

GROUP THERAPY. Clients with compatible needs who meet together with one or two therapists are engaging in **group therapy**. This modality became more frequently offered after World War II, when there were many more veterans seeking treatment than therapists available to treat them individually. The course of treatment can range from a single occasion (usually an educational session) to ongoing treatment lasting for years. Some groups are for members who have a particular problem or disorder, focusing on, for instance, recent divorce or posttraumatic stress disorder. These groups offer emotional support, psychoeducation, concrete strategies for managing the problem or disorder, or all these elements. Other groups have members who

Group therapy can help reduce shame and isolation and can provide support and an opportunity to interact differently with other people.

may not share such a specific problem or disorder, but rather want to learn more about maladaptive or inappropriate ways in which they are interacting with people; the therapy group provides an opportunity to change their patterns of behavior. Therapy groups can have theoretical orientations ranging from psychodynamic to client-centered, to Gestalt, to CBT, or other orientations.

In addition to offering information, support, and (if the group has a cognitive–behavioral orientation) between-session homework assignments, group therapy provides something that individual therapy cannot: interaction with other people who are experiencing similar difficulties. The group experience can decrease the sense of isolation and shame that clients sometimes feel. In revealing their own experiences and being moved by others', clients often come to see their own lives and difficulties in a new light. Also, because some clients' problems involve interpersonal interactions, the group provides a safe opportunity for clients to try out new behaviors.

FAMILY THERAPY. In **family therapy**, a family as a whole, or a subset of some of its members, such as a couple, are seen for treatment. "Family" is often defined as those who think of themselves or function as a family; thus, blended families created by marriage are seen in family therapy, as are other nontraditional families. The most common theoretical orientation among those providing family therapy is **systems therapy**, which starts from the premise that no client is an island: A client's symptoms occur in a larger context, or system (the family and subculture), and any change in one part of the system will affect the rest of the system. Thus, the client is referred to as the "identified patient," although the system (the couple, the family) is considered the "patient" that is to be treated. Systems therapy was originally used exclusively with families; in fact, some of the pioneers in systems therapy would refuse to see individuals without their families. For this reason, systems therapy is sometimes referred to as "family therapy," although this is a misnomer. Some therapists treat entire families, but not necessarily from a systems approach. They may use a psychodynamic or behavioral approach. Similarly, some systems therapists see individuals without their families, but the therapy makes use of systems theory. Systems therapy can also be the theoretical framework used to treat couples in therapy.

Systems therapy focuses on family communication, structure, and power relationships. The theory views the identified patient's symptoms as attempts to convey a message. Initially, a systems therapist takes a family history to discover which members of the family are close to one another or angry with one another, and to ascertain more generally how anger, sadness, and other feelings or issues are handled within the family. Systems therapists often illustrate these relationships graphically

Group therapy: A therapy modality in which a number of clients with similar needs meet together with one or two therapists.

Family therapy: A therapy modality in which a family (or certain members of a family) is seen for treatment.

Systems therapy: A type of therapy that views a client's symptoms as occurring in a larger context, or system (the family and subculture), in which a change in one part of the system affects the rest of the system.

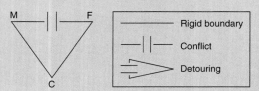

FIGURE 14.4
Systems Therapy: Family Interaction

This triangle graphically represents the following type of family interaction: The mother and father criticize each other and then reroute their conflict by both attacking their child. Systems therapy would focus on decreasing the conflict between the parents and strengthening their relationship. (From Minuchin, 1974, pp. 53, 61.)

(see Figure 14.4). In some cases, one parent may be underinvolved and the other overinvolved; treatment would be directed to encourage the underinvolved parent to be more involved, and the overinvolved parent to be less involved. Or, the parents' relationship with each other may need strengthening, with consequences to others in the family, because conflict between parents affects their children's behavior (Kitzmann, 2000). For instance, in a family in which the parents fight a lot, an adolescent boy's rebelliousness may serve to unite his parents in their anger and frustration at him. The systems therapist might explain to the family that their son was purposefully being rebellious to keep his parents united, for fear of what would happen to the parents' relationship if he weren't causing them problems. The family therapist might praise the son for his efforts at keeping his parents together, and even urge him not to stop being rebellious yet, because his parents hadn't yet practiced how to relate to each other more effectively. This type of intervention is sometimes referred to as **paradoxical intention,** which encourages a behavior that seems contradictory to the desired goal (Stanton, 1981). This technique has also been called "prescribing the symptom" and is useful in treating families who appear resistant or unable to change, or aren't able to implement suggestions from the therapist. Other techniques include **reframing,** in which the therapist offers a new way of conceptualizing, or "framing," the problem, and **validation,** in which the therapist conveys his or her understanding of clients' feelings and wishes (Minuchin, 1974; Minuchin & Fishman, 1981).

A therapist with a systems orientation treating Beth might, after taking a family history, reframe the problem. The therapist might propose that Beth is sacrificing herself: Beth's difficulties allow her mother to be a "good mother" to Beth in ways she had not been when Beth was younger. Thus, Beth's illness serves the function of allowing her mother to feel good about herself as a mother. The therapist might also validate Beth's offering of herself in this way—suggesting that her concern for her mother is so great that she would allow herself to sacrifice her own current opportunities in order to provide this opportunity for her mother. The therapist might even give Beth a paradoxical intention: Beth should not get better until her mother becomes a "nervous wreck" worrying about Beth. This paradoxical intention serves the purpose of indirectly pointing out how Beth's behavior may in fact have the opposite effect of the one she desires.

SELF-HELP THERAPIES. **Self-help groups** (sometimes referred to as *support groups*) can be used to supplement psychotherapy, or on their own, and are focused on a specific disorder or event. They do not usually have a clinically trained leader, although a mental health professional may be involved in some capacity (Shepherd et al., 1999). Alcoholics Anonymous (AA), the first self-help program, is based on 12 steps of recovery (Table 14.4). Most 12-step programs view a belief in a Higher Power (for most people, God) as crucial to recovery, and meta-analytic results show that weekly attendance in group meetings is associated with drug or alcohol abstinence, whereas less than weekly attendance is not (Fiorentine, 1999). People who are not religious can also benefit from attendance at AA meetings (Winzelberg & Humphreys, 1999). A self-help group that does not use the 12-step approach is the National Depressive and Manic Depressive Association, which helps those suffering from bipolar disorder or depression, and their families and friends. Self-help groups are not only valuable sources of information and support, they can also make referrals to therapists who are knowledgeable about the particular disorder or problem. Relatives of those with a psychological disorder report that such groups are helpful in providing support and self-understanding (Citron et al., 1999). As is true in group therapy, self-help groups can be invaluable in decreasing feelings of isolation and shame.

The last decade has witnessed a proliferation of self-help books and tapes dealing with a wide range of problems; the use of such materials is sometimes referred to as

Paradoxical intention: A family therapy technique that encourages a behavior that seems contradictory to the desired goal.

Reframing: A therapy technique in which the therapist offers a new way of conceptualizing, or "framing," the problem.

Validation: A therapy technique in which the therapist conveys his or her understanding of the client's feelings and wishes.

Self-help group: A group whose members focus on a specific disorder or event and do not usually have a clinically trained leader; also called a *support group.*

TABLE 14.4

The 12 Steps of Alcoholics Anonymous

Source: *Alcoholics Anonymous (1999); http://www.addictions.org/aa/steps.htm.*

1. We admitted that we were powerless over alcohol—that our lives had become unmanageable.

2. We came to believe that a Power greater than ourselves could restore us to sanity.

3. We made a decision to turn our will and our lives over to the care of God as we understood Him.

4. We made a searching and fearless moral inventory of ourselves.

5. We admitted to God, to ourselves, and to another human being the exact nature of our wrongs.

6. We were entirely ready to have God remove all these defects of character.

7. We humbly asked Him to remove our shortcomings.

8. We made a list of all persons we had harmed, and became willing to make amends to them all.

9. We made direct amends to such people wherever possible, except when to do so would injure them or others.

10. We continued to take a personal inventory and when we were wrong promptly admitted it.

11. We sought through prayer and meditation to improve our conscious contact with God as we understood Him, praying only for knowledge of His will for us and the power to carry that out.

12. Having had a spiritual awakening as the result of those steps, we tried to carry this message to alcoholics, and to practice these principles in all our affairs.

bibliotherapy. Many of these materials incorporate philosophies and techniques of the therapies discussed in this chapter, and therapists often suggest that clients read particular books (Starker, 1988). Meta-analyses of studies examining the effectiveness of such self-help materials found that they helped primarily people with depression (Cuijpers, 1997), headache, sleep disturbances, and fears (Gould & Clum, 1983); anxiety is also lessened through the use of self-help materials (Finch et al., 2000; Scogin et al., 1990). Those trying to eliminate habits such as smoking, drinking, and overeating were not helped as much. Not surprisingly, those who complied with the materials' recommendations fared better than those who did not (Gould & Clum, 1983). At least for many people, the self-administered treatment programs available through books and audiotapes appear to be more effective than no treatment at all (Scogin et al., 1990).

Biomedical Therapies

With recent advances in knowledge about the brain have come advances in biomedical treatments of many disorders.

PSYCHOPHARMACOLOGY. The use of medication to treat psychological disorders and problems is known as **psychopharmacology.** In the last two decades, the number and types of medications for the treatment of psychological disorders have multiplied. As scientists learn more about the brain and neurotransmitter systems, researchers are able to develop new medications to target symptoms more effectively and with fewer side effects. Thus, for any given disorder, there are more medication options.

Schizophrenia and Other Psychotic Disorders. The most common type of medication for the treatment of schizophrenia and other psychotic disorders is **antipsychotic medication** (also called *neuroleptic medication*), which generally reduces psychotic symptoms but does not cure the disorder. Antipsychotic drugs have long been known to have an effect on the positive symptoms of schizophrenia (see Chapter 13), such as hallucinations. Traditional antipsychotic medications include Thorazine and Haldol. However, long-term use of these medications can cause **tardive dyskinesia,** an irreversible movement disorder in which the affected person involuntarily smacks his or

Bibliotherapy: The use of self-help books and tapes for therapeutic purposes.

Psychopharmacology: The use of medication to treat psychological disorders and problems.

Antipsychotic medication: Medication that reduces psychotic symptoms.

Tardive dyskinesia: An irreversible movement disorder in which the person involuntarily smacks his or her lips, displays facial grimaces, and exhibits other symptoms, caused by traditional antipsychotic medication.

Tricyclic antidepressant (TCA): A common set of anti-depressant medications named for the three rings in the chemical compound.

Monoamine oxidase inhibitor (MAOI): A type of antidepressant medication that requires strict adherence to a diet free of tyramine-based foods.

Selective serotonergic reuptake inhibitor (SSRI): A type of antidepressant medication that affects only *selective* serotonin receptors, with fewer side effects.

Serotonergic/noradrenergic reuptake inhibitor (SNRI): A newer antidepressant that affects both serotonin and noradrenergic neurotransmitter systems.

St. John's wort: An herbal remedy for mild to moderate depression.

Studies so far show that the herbal remedy St. John's wort can be effective in treating mild to moderately severe depression. However, to date, no guidelines exist about the strength of each pill or the exact dosages for maximal effectiveness.

her lips, displays facial grimaces, and exhibits other symptoms. *Atypical antipsychotics* are a new group of antipsychotic drugs that affect the neurotransmitter dopamine (as does traditional antipsychotic medication) as well as other neurotransmitters. For instance, the atypical antipsychotic medication Risperdal cuts down on the amount of free serotonin and dopamine available in the brain, which affects the ease with which signals cross synapses. In addition to decreasing positive symptoms, such as hallucinations, these newer drugs also counteract negative symptoms such as apathy, lack of interest, and withdrawal, and are effective in improving cognitive functioning (Keefe et al., 1999), all of which allow psychological therapies to be more effective (Ballus, 1997). These drugs also appear to have fewer side effects than traditional antipsychotic medication. There are increasing amounts of data suggesting that pharmacological treatment administered soon after the first psychotic episode is associated with a better long-term prognosis, compared to treatment begun later (see Chapter 13; Wyatt et al., 1997).

Mood Disorders. Effective pharmacological treatment for depression began in earnest in the 1950s with the discovery of **tricyclic antidepressants (TCAs)**, named for the three rings in the chemical structure of these compounds. Elavil is an example of this class of drug. For decades, TCAs were the only effective antidepressant medication readily available, although common side effects include constipation, dry mouth, blurred vision, and low blood pressure. These medications affect serotonin levels, and they can take weeks to work. Although another type of medication, **monoamine oxidase inhibitors (MAOIs)**, was the first antidepressant medication discovered, it has never been as widely prescribed as TCAs, for two major reasons. First, MAOIs require users not to eat foods with tyramine (such as cheese and wine) because of potentially fatal changes in blood pressure. Second, they are particularly effective with atypical depression involving increased appetite and hypersomnia (increased need for sleep; Prien & Kocsis, 1995), and less effective with typical depressive episodes.

Then **selective serotonergic reuptake inhibitors (SSRIs)**, such as Prozac, Zoloft, and Paxil, were developed in the 1980s. Although they have fewer side effects (they only work on *selective* serotonin receptors), a common one is decreased sexual interest, and many people experience a "Prozac poop-out" after a while, no longer attaining the same benefit from what had previously been an effective dosage. A meta-analysis of the use of Prozac in treating depression found an effectiveness rate comparable to that of TCAs, but not greater (Agency for Health Care Policy and Research, 1999; Greenberg et al., 1997). Researchers continue to discover ways to alleviate symptoms of depression without as many side effects and to develop new physiological pathways of effectiveness so that those who do not respond to existing antidepressants can obtain relief from medication. Some newer antidepressants (such as Serzone, Effexor, and Remeron) don't fall into the existing categories; these drugs, which affect both the serotonin and norepinephrine systems, are sometimes referred to as **serotonergic/noradrenergic reuptake inhibitors (SNRIs)**. Antidepressant medications are also given to people experiencing dysthymia.

Studies of the effectiveness of an extract from the flowering plant **St. John's wort,** *Hypericum perforatum,* suggest that it may be effective as a short-term treatment of mild to moderately severe depression (Agency for Health Care Policy and Research, 1999; Gaster & Holroyd, 2000), although not without minor side effects. Further investigations about the exact dosages and long-term effects are under way. In addition, medications that block *substance P,* a neurotransmitter, show success in treating depression (Kramer et al., 1998), although further study will ultimately determine their effectiveness. Substance P–related medications do not derive their effectiveness by altering norepinephrine or serotonin, as do other antidepressants, but rather work by some other, as yet undetermined mechanism (Bender, 1998).

For bipolar disorder, mood stabilizers such as *lithium* can prevent a recurrence of both manic and depressive phases, although up to half of those with this disorder either will show no significant improvement or will be unable to tolerate the side effects. When this happens, a mood stabilizer such as Depakote or Tegretol is given to minimize the recurrence of manic episodes. During a manic episode, antipsychotic drugs or antianxiety drugs are often used. The usual medication regimen for schizophrenia and bipolar disorder may involve lifelong use of medication.

Anxiety Disorders. For most anxiety disorders, including panic disorder, the panic symptoms of specific phobias, and PTSD, **benzodiazepines** are often the medication prescribed. Xanax and Valium are types of benzodiazepines, which affect the target symptoms within 36 hours and do not need to be taken for 10 days or more to build up to an effective level, as is the case with antidepressants. However, they can cause drowsiness and are potentially lethal when taken with alcohol. In addition, a person using benzodiazepines can develop tolerance and dependence (see Chapter 4) and can experience withdrawal reactions. For these reasons, drugs of this class are often prescribed only for short periods of time, such as during a particularly stressful period. Antidepressants (TCAs, SSRIs, or SNRIs) may be prescribed for long-term treatment of anxiety disorders, although the dosage may be lower than that used in the treatment of depression (Gorman & Kent, 1999). Social phobia may be treated with antianxiety or antidepressant medication. Obsessive-compulsive disorder can be treated effectively with SSRI antidepressants such as clomiprimine, although at a higher dose than that prescribed for depression or other anxiety disorders.

ELECTROCONVULSIVE THERAPY. Essentially a controlled brain seizure, **electroconvulsive therapy (ECT)** was developed in the 1930s as a treatment for schizophrenia. It was based on the idea that schizophrenia and epilepsy were incompatible, and thus that ECT-induced epilepsy would relieve the symptoms of schizophrenia. Although it did not cure schizophrenia, it is still a recommended treatment when medication does not work (Lehman & Steinwachs, 1998). ECT has been particularly helpful in treating certain mood disorders, specifically psychotic depression and manic episodes of bipolar disorder. In fact, 80% of those receiving ECT suffer from depression (Sackheim et al., 1995).

People with severe depression who have not received much benefit from psychotherapy or medication (Lam et al., 1999), or those for whom drugs are medically contraindicated, may receive ECT. Although the treatment can be effective, the reasons are not well understood. The patient is given a muscle relaxant before each ECT treatment and is under anesthesia during the procedure; because of the anesthesia, ECT is administered in a hospital and generally requires a hospital stay. Patients may experience temporary memory loss for events right before, during, or after each treatment. After a course of 6 to 12 sessions over several weeks, usually twice a week (Shapira et al., 1998; Vieweg & Shawcross, 1998), depression often lifts; relief may come sooner for the depressed elderly (Tew et al., 1999).

ECT was considered a major biomedical treatment in the 1940s and 1950s, but the ready availability of medications in subsequent decades led to a decline in its use. Another reason for its decreased use was that some patients seemed to experience significant cognitive impairment, including memory loss. And, as it became known that it was sometimes used in understaffed institutions to produce a docile patient population, ECT became politically unpopular. However, improvements in the way ECT is administered have significantly reduced the cognitive deficits and undesirable side effects, and since the 1980s, the use of ECT has increased. This trend reflects a new appreciation of its usefulness, and a recognition that not all people with depression, mania, or schizophrenia can either take medication or find it helpful. In recent years, ECT is more frequently administered to affluent patients than to those in publicly funded hospitals (Sackheim et al., 1995).

TRANSCRANIAL MAGNETIC STIMULATION. A new treatment currently being researched is **transcranial magnetic stimulation (TMS)**, a procedure in which an electromagnetic coil on the scalp transmits pulses of high-intensity magnetism to the brain in short bursts lasting 100 to 200 microseconds. Although it is not yet known exactly how this magnetic field changes brain neurophysiology and neurochemistry, TMS has varying effects, depending on the exact location of the coil on the head. Studies of TMS

Benzodiazepine: A type of antianxiety medication that affects the target symptoms within 36 hours and does not need to be taken for more than a week to be effective.

Electroconvulsive therapy (ECT): A controlled brain seizure, used to treat people with certain psychological disorders such as psychotic depression or those for whom medication has not been effective or recommended.

Transcranial magnetic stimulation (TMS): An experimental treatment for psychological disorders involving the use of electromagnetic stimulation.

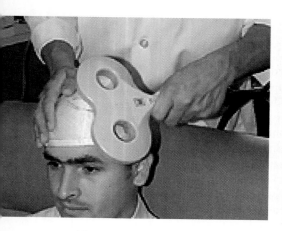

Unlike with ECT, the person receiving transcranial magnetic stimulation is awake and does not need anesthesia.

for people with psychological disorders have been experimental; early results suggest that it may provide a therapeutic benefit similar to that of ECT. Placebo studies of TMS (in which the procedure of TMS is administered, but at an angle that does not affect the brain) have found actual TMS to be more effective than the placebo (George et al., 1999; Klein et al., 1999). Studies of people with depression who have not responded to medication have yielded positive results: Approximately half of those receiving TMS have not needed to go on to receive ECT (Epstein et al., 1998; Figiel et al., 1998; Klein et al., 1999). Preliminary results also suggest that TMS works as well or better with nonpsychotically depressed people, but that ECT is superior for those with psychotic depressions, indicating the possibility that the two procedures act through different mechanisms (George et al., 1999). Should additional studies confirm these early results, TMS offers a number of advantages over ECT, including easier administration (it requires neither anesthesia nor hospitalization) and minimal side effects. The most common short-term side effect, experienced by 5 to 20% of patients, is a slight headache.

TMS has been tried with people with depression, bipolar disorder (Grisaru, Chudakov et al., 1998), schizophrenia (see George et al., 1999 for a review), and PTSD (Grisaru, Amir et al., 1998). But more research is necessary before TMS can definitively be declared a treatment of choice rather than an experimental one. Information about the precise optimum location of the coil and the frequency and intensity of the stimulation is needed.

Psychotherapy Integration: Mixing and Matching

In the last decade, many therapists have moved away from identifying their work as exclusively from one theoretical orientation, such as psychodynamic or behavioral. Surveys found between 68% (Jensen et al., 1990) and 98% (Smith, 1982) of mental health professionals identify themselves as eclectic in orientation. A therapist using **psychotherapy integration** uses techniques from different theoretical orientations, with an overarching understanding of how the different techniques will achieve the goals of treatment. This integrative approach includes incorporating new techniques based on research findings and the clinical needs of a particular client at a specific point in the treatment (Stricker, 1993). Such an approach provides the aspects of therapy that are common to all theoretical orientations (such as offering hope, a caring listener, and a new way of thinking about problems) and employs specific techniques for a given disorder (Weinberger et al., 1995), such as exposure with response prevention for people with OCD. A therapist's integrating of specific techniques *without regard for an overarching theory* is referred to as **technical eclecticism** (Beutler & Hodgson, 1993). With technical eclecticism, research findings—not the therapist's theoretical orientation—help determine which specific treatments are used. The therapist determines which techniques to use at any given point in treatment based on diagnosis, research findings, and consideration of the particular client; these create an individualized guide to treatment. Two clients with the same diagnosis may receive different integrative treatments from the same therapist, based on factors other than diagnosis—perhaps family issues, client preference for directive versus nondirective treatment, and other concerns.

Psychotherapies of the Future?

The end of the 20th century brought a number of changes to psychotherapy, in part because of financial factors and technological changes.

MANAGED CARE AND PSYCHOTHERAPY. The cost of health care became extremely expensive in the last two decades of the 20th century, and the system of health care administration known as *managed care* was developed as a way to contain costs. Managed care seeks to limit the expense of health care while providing services

Psychotherapy integration: The use of techniques from different theoretical orientations with an overarching understanding of how the different techniques will be used to achieve the goals of treatment.

Technical eclecticism: The use of specific techniques that may benefit a particular client, without regard for an overarching theory.

deemed medically necessary by health care administrators. In mental health, one way to reduce costs has been to limit the amount of inpatient and outpatient services. Thus, psychological therapies, regardless of theoretical orientation or modality, have tried to meet the challenge of attaining the same level of effectiveness in a reduced number of sessions. There is in fact some support for the idea that a time limit on psychotherapy can accelerate the rate of therapeutic change (Reynolds et al., 1996).

Although therapists have become effective at helping clients get better in fewer sessions, it is unclear whether brief therapy provides long-term positive change or protection against relapse. There is a dose–effect relationship between therapy and outcome: the more therapy, the greater its positive effect. The standard of what constitutes good care is being driven not by clinicians, but by the financial bottom line. Many of the studies examining the effectiveness of time-limited psychotherapy were based on treatments of approximately 20 sessions, more than is currently allowed by some insurance companies, except in the case of chronic mental illness such as schizophrenia.

Strupp (1997; Strupp & Hadley, 1977) suggests that three groups should determine how mental health is defined: society (of which managed care is a part), which determines the use of funds and defines mental health via stability, conformity, and predictability; the individual client, who often defines mental health subjectively; and the mental health professional, who may define mental health according to a theoretical approach.

TIME AND THERAPY: THERAPY PROTOCOLS AND BRIEF THERAPY.

The last 20 years has seen a rise in the use of *therapy protocols*, detailed session-by-session manuals of how therapy should proceed for a specific disorder from a certain theoretical orientation (such as behavioral treatment for panic disorder, or cognitive therapy for depression). These manual-based treatments were created, in part, to ensure that when a research study was testing the effectiveness of a given therapy (for example, CBT), all CBT therapists were actually using the same techniques in the same way. This meant, of course, that the results of the study were in fact relevant to the effectiveness of the treatment because all therapies of the same orientation were comparable. The drawback of research studies using manual-based treatment is that they often exclude people whose symptoms do not meet the exact criteria for a disorder, or who may simultaneously have more than one diagnosis (such as depression *and* panic disorder).

Some clinicians advocate the use of therapy performed without deviation from treatment manuals (Addis, 1997). Others point out that because research with treatment manuals excludes those who have more than one diagnosis, many of their clients would be excluded from consideration in the manuals (Seligman, 1995); therapy provided on the basis of treatment manuals may not be relevant for such clients.

Many of the protocols were developed for treatment lasting 15 to 20 sessions. Today, many managed care programs in different part of the United States will not pay for 20 sessions of treatment for many disorders, or at least not initially. Rather, they may approve 3 to 10 sessions, and the therapist must request additional sessions. Thus, although the course of treatment is becoming briefer, the total number of sessions cannot be used in a systematic way and may not fit into many of the existing protocols. Moreover, clients who have more than one problem may not reap the benefits of time-limited therapy. Research indicates that those with focused problems in one sphere of life (such as work) receive more benefit from brief psychotherapy than those who have difficulties in multiple spheres (Barkham & Shapiro, 1990; Klosko et al., 1990; Strupp & Binder, 1984).

In the future, computer technology may be commonly used to facilitate brief treatment. Research on the use of palmtop computers preprogrammed with cognitive–behavioral tasks found that 4 weeks of computer-assisted treatment (plus 8 weeks of practice with the palmtop) was, as determined at follow-up, as effective as 12 weeks of regular cognitive–behavior therapy (Newman, Kenardy et al., 1997). This study was conducted with a total of only 18 participants, and thus further research will be needed to clarify the potential role for this or similar technology.

High-tech gadgets such as this palmtop computer may be at the cutting edge of brief cognitive–behavior treatments. In one research study of cognitive–behavior treatment for people with panic disorder, palmtops were preprogrammed with cognitive–behavioral tasks to help participants self-monitor their thoughts. One group had 4 weeks of training with the palmtop (plus 8 weeks of practice). Another group had 12 weeks of standard cognitive–behavior therapy without a palmtop. Although the palmtop group did not fare quite as well as the standard group at the end of the 12 weeks, both groups were doing equally well at a 6-month follow-up (Newman et al., 1997).

CYBERTHERAPY: DOCTOR ONLINE. A new form of treatment is **cybertherapy,** or therapy over the Internet. This sort of therapy may be helpful for those who have no ready access to mental health services: rural residents, the severely medically ill, or people with agoraphobia. Several types of cybertherapeutic interactions are possible. One involves an Internet version of individual therapy, such as a "pay-for-each-response" e-mail exchange with a therapist. However, most therapists consider this type of cybertherapy to be less than an optimally desirable form of treatment. First, the anonymity offered via the Internet works two ways, and the "therapist" offering this service may not be professionally trained or licensed. Second, confidentiality and privacy cannot be guaranteed on the Internet. Third, the multitude of nonverbal cues (facial expressions, tone of voice) that pass between client and therapist are absent during cybertherapy (Bloom, 1998). On the plus side, it has been argued that simply having to put thoughts and feelings on paper (or rather, on screen) can be therapeutic, as can the ability to have a complete transcript of the treatment for later reading and reflection (Murphy & Mitchell, 1998). However, no studies have yet compared cybertherapy with live psychotherapy, and so it is much too early to say whether some form of cybertherapy is more or less effective for some people. E-mail has also been used in family therapy in cases when members of the family lived too far away to attend sessions (King et al., 1998). The effectiveness of this tool in the realm of family therapy has yet to be rigorously tested.

The Internet has also produced a proliferation of electronic support groups that focus on particular disorders or problems. A study examining the postings for an eating disorder electronic support group found that the most common types of message were self-disclosures, requests for information, and messages of emotional support to other members. The support group was most often used in the evening or late at night, times when other forms of support are often less available. The types of support used were the same as those used in support groups in which members are all physically present (Winzelberg, 1997). Thus, electronic support groups may, for some people, serve a very similar function to face-to-face support groups.

LOOKING AT LEVELS

Treating Obsessive-Compulsive Disorder

Medication can be effective in treating the symptoms of many disorders. Medication works by changing neurochemistry, which in turn affects thoughts, feelings, and behaviors. Does psychotherapy's beneficial effect work in a similar way? Until recently this question could not have been answered. But brain scanning has made it possible to begin to understand the positive effects of both medication and psychotherapy, at least in their effects on people with obsessive-compulsive disorder. We can understand their effects by looking at events at the three levels and their interactions.

Obsessive-compulsive disorder (OCD) is marked by intrusive, illogical thoughts and overpowering compulsions to repeat certain acts, such as hand washing to get rid of germs (see Chapter 13). In some cases, OCD can be disabling. The brain functioning of nine people with OCD was examined by PET scanning before and after behavior therapy (Baxter et al., 1992), as were the brains of nine people with OCD before and after they received fluoxetine (Prozac), a serotonergic medication that suppresses some of the symptoms of OCD. The scans revealed that behavior therapy and Prozac both change the way a certain part of the brain works. In both cases, the activity in the right caudate (part of the basal ganglia involved in automatic behaviors) decreased following the intervention. (The drug also affected the anterior cingulate and thalamus, both of which are involved in attention.) The effects of behavior therapy on the brain were replicated by Schwartz, Stoessel and colleagues (1996).

At the level of the person, trying new behaviors (such as not washing dirty hands or not rechecking a locked door) and experiencing the success of not *having* to perform the compulsions give the patient a sense of mastery and hope, which leads him or her to keep engaging in the new behavior. At the level of the group, it was interactions with another person—the therapist—that changed the brain. In addition, personal relationships change. For example, some of the time and energy that was devoted to OCD rituals can now be spent on relationships. Thus, the three levels of analysis inform us about different aspects of the disorder and how events at the three levels interact.

CONSOLIDATE!

▶ **1. What are some types of prevention against the onset of major mental illness?** There are three types of prevention: primary prevention is aimed at eliminating sociocultural causes of psychological disorders; secondary prevention is aimed at intervening with those at risk to develop a disorder; tertiary prevention aims to decrease the severity, duration, and frequency of a psychological disorder once it has developed.

▶ **2. What are other forms, or modalities, of therapy besides individual therapy?** As well as meeting with a therapist for individual therapy, a client and therapist can meet in a group (often a group of people with similar problems); the client can be a family (usually working with a therapist who has a systems approach) or a couple. Self-help groups and bibliotherapy may also be beneficial.

▶ **3. What biomedical treatments are available?** Biomedical treatments include medication and electroconvulsive therapy. Antipsychotic medication can help people with schizophrenia and other psychotic disorders; antidepressants may help those with depression and anxiety; lithium may help people with bipolar disorder; and antianxiety drugs can help with anxiety disorders. Electroconvulsive therapy, a controlled brain seizure, may be used for those who remain severely depressed despite the use of other therapies.

▶ **4. What therapies use theories and techniques drawn from a number of different orientations?** In integrative psychotherapy, the therapist systematically integrates two or more different theoretical approaches and their techniques into a treatment regimen based on research and clinical factors.

▶ **5. What recent trends might affect the future of mental health care?** Managed care has changed the delivery of psychotherapy by limiting the number of sessions (with some exceptions in the case of chronic mental illness), necessitating brief courses of treatments. Protocol-based treatment has also increased. Although there is no research yet on the effectiveness of cybertherapy (therapy over the Internet), it is possible to receive psychotherapy without ever talking directly to a therapist.

WHICH THERAPY WORKS BEST?

After a number of sessions, Beth began to feel better. She was going to class more often, and felt better able to handle studying and preparing for tests. She wanted to know what it was about the therapy that was helping her, and why her therapist used specific techniques at certain times. Her treatment had not included medication, and she still wondered whether she would be feeling better—or worse—if she had taken medication. She also wondered whether her therapy would be as effective for other people in her situation. If her best friend went to see Beth's therapist for anxiety and depression, would her friend fare as well as Beth, or perhaps even better?

▶ 1. What key issues should be kept in mind when reading research studies of psychotherapy?

▶ 2. What are good ways to find a therapist?

Issues in Psychotherapy Research

More than 400 types of psychotherapy are currently available (Garfield & Bergin, 1994), but many of them do not rest on well-constructed and replicated research.

Research on psychotherapy is crucial for determining the effectiveness of a new or old therapy in treating a particular problem. It is easy to claim that a new therapy is a wonder cure, but harder to prove it. There are many issues to consider when evaluating findings about psychotherapy.

RESEARCHING PSYCHOTHERAPY. Research that asks whether the client is feeling better, functioning better, living more independently, or has fewer symptoms after treatment is called **outcome research.** These questions are trickier to answer than it would seem because they depend on how you define "outcome"; in research lingo, the answers to the questions depend on what you designate as the therapy's dependent variable. For example, you could have clients rate their thoughts, feelings, or behaviors, which are not necessarily highly correlated and might yield different outcomes (Kazdin, 1994). You must also decide how long after the end of treatment to assess outcome: immediately afterward? a month later? a year later? Moreover, in their review of studies, Luborsky and colleagues (1999) noticed an "allegiance effect": Researchers of a particular orientation tend to find evidence supporting that orientation.

Initially, much outcome research focused on assessing the superiority of one treatment over another, not taking into account clients' diagnoses. Results revealed that therapy was more effective than no therapy. Most often, the no-therapy group was a wait-list control, people who were on a waiting list for therapy but had not yet received treatment (Lambert & Bergin, 1994). The findings also seemed to suggest that all therapies are equally effective, a position later described as the *dodo bird verdict* of psychotherapy (Luborsky et al., 1975), named for the Dodo bird in *Alice's Adventures in Wonderland*, who declared, "Everyone has won, and all must have prizes."

TABLE 14.5

Questions About Psychotherapy Research

Source: *Kazdin (1994).*

1. Are the participants randomly assigned?
2. Is a specific disorder being treated?
3. Are there exclusion criteria (must participants have only one diagnosis)?
4. Are the therapists' treatments representative of their stated approaches?
5. What types of outcome measures are selected, who is the evaluator, and how is success defined?
6. Are clients more likely to drop out of some types of therapy than others?
7. Is a follow-up assessment planned, and if so, at what interval of time after the end of treatment?

But is the dodo bird verdict all there is to it? Several questions, listed in Table 14.5, should be addressed when designing or evaluating studies of psychotherapy, and the answers to these questions determine what conclusions can be reached and how far those conclusions can generalize. Let's look at one well-known investigation in detail. Initiated in 1977, the National Institute of Mental Health sponsored a study called the Treatment of Depression Collaborative Research Program, or TDCRP, to assess the effectiveness of four different treatments for depression: cognitive–behavior therapy (CBT); interpersonal therapy (IPT); antidepressant medication with supportive visits with a psychiatrist; and a placebo medication with supportive visits with a psychiatrist. The medication group, which was taking the TCA imipramine (the study predated Prozac), was labeled IMI-CM (CM for "clinical management"), and the placebo group was labeled PLA-CM (see Figure 14.5).

Interpersonal therapy (IPT) focuses on the client's current relationships, issues that arise in those relationships, and attempts to link what happens in those relationships to mood. The goal of IPT is to help the client's relationships work better and become more satisfying. IPT rests on the assumption that if the relationships are functioning

Outcome research: Research that asks whether, after psychotherapy, the client is feeling better, functioning better, living more independently, has fewer symptoms.

better, the depression will lessen. Therapeutic techniques include helping clients explore the consequences of their actions in their relationships and facilitating better personal communication, perhaps by encouraging clients to tell others how they feel. This type of therapy was developed in the late 1970s; most IPT treatments are based on IPT therapy protocol manuals and can be considered insight-oriented. All treatments in all four TDCRP groups were brief, lasting 16 weeks.

Participants in the TDCRP were randomly assigned to one of the four treatment groups; the design of the study addressed Question 1 in Table 14.5. What would it mean if the assignments weren't random? Suppose those who were more depressed were put in the medication group, but the therapy groups were more effective; we couldn't then conclude that therapy was more effective than medication, because the participants in the medication group were in worse shape to begin with. Random assignment is crucial if we want to be able to infer anything about the effectiveness of one treatment over another.

In trying to determine whether certain types of treatment are more effective for certain disorders (Question 2), many studies exclude participants with more than one diagnosis (Question 3). Although this exclusion makes research findings more clear-cut, it limits their generalizability, because many clients going to a therapist's office have more than one type of diagnosis. For example, more than half of those diagnosed with an anxiety disorder or PTSD have at least one additional disorder, and 30 to 40% of those with a diagnosis of depression also have a diagnosis of a personality disorder (Sleek, 1997). The TDCRP study restricted inclusion to those who met the exact criteria for major depressive disorder, without any other disorder.

One difficulty in assessing research on a particular therapeutic orientation is that therapists who by their own statements would seem to have different orientations may in fact be remarkably similar in the way they actually provide therapy (Lambert & Bergin, 1994). This makes comparisons among therapies difficult (Question 4). Suppose that in the TDCRP study, a self-defined CBT therapist focused on relationship issues, and a self-defined IPT therapist gave concrete suggestions, such as those given in assertiveness training or social skills training, for improving relationships. If there were no differences in outcome between the two therapy groups, it could be because therapists in the two groups were doing much the same thing! In an effort to address this problem, the TDCRP developed therapist manuals for each of the four treatments, providing in each case a detailed guide and techniques to be used with clients for each session. These standardized forms of treatment ensured that all therapists categorized as using one approach (for example, CBT) were actually providing similar therapy.

Question 5 addresses the difficult issue of how to measure outcome. Measures can focus on behaviors, thoughts, or feelings in relation to specific symptoms, or on more general patterns of functioning. Different types of therapy might be differentially effective with each of these possible outcome measures. In the TDCRP, medication might be more effective with some symptoms of depression (tiredness, poor appetite), but not help with relationships or negative thinking as much as psychological treatment (Segal et al., 1999). The type of outcome measures used can bias the results in favor of one form of therapy over another. In order to avoid this pitfall, the TDCRP study looked at multiple types of outcome measures, but surprisingly, it found comparable results for the different measures of outcome (Imber et al., 1991).

In addition, there is the problem that 50% or more of those who begin treatment in a research study may drop out (Kazdin, 1994). And if more participants drop out of one group than another, the conclusions you can draw about the treatment are limited (Question 6). The TDCRP results showed that *of those completing the study*, all four groups improved, but CBT and IPT treatment were about as effective as antidepressant medication in decreasing depressive symptoms (Antonuccio & Danton, 1995; Elkin et al., 1995). However, more participants dropped out of the medication group before the completion of the program because of unpleasant side effects. So, if you consider all those *starting* the TDCRP study rather than only those *completing* it, both CBT and IPT were *more* effective than medication-and-support or placebo-and-support groups (Elkin, 1994). Knowing the attrition rates can make a difference in understanding the results.

Finally, it is important to determine what happens after treatment ends, and if the outcome results change with the passage of time (Question 7). In the TDCRP study, CBT had a more sustained effect at an 18-month follow-up, with fewer relapses, particularly when compared with the group given imipramine (Elkin, 1994; Shea et al., 1992). This result is consistent with other findings (Antonuccio et al., 1995). However, further analyses showed that, across all four treatment groups, both medication and IPT were slightly more effective than CBT for severely depressed clients (Elkin et al., 1995). Moreover, the quality of the collaborative bond between client and therapist (as measured by independent raters who watched videotapes of the sessions) affected outcome; this influence was stronger than that of the type of treatment (Krupnick et al., 1996). In both CBT and IPT, clients reported feeling supported and reassured and indicated that the therapy had given them new ways of relating to others and had encouraged their independent opinions (Ablon & Jones, 1999). But not all therapies are equally useful for all disorders, as you will see in the following section.

CURATIVE FACTORS: THE HEALING POWERS. Although therapy does not always reduce the frequency or intensity of the troublesome symptoms that bring people to treatment, it often works (Garfield & Bergin, 1994; Matt & Navarro, 1997). Despite the fact that people aren't necessarily "cured," as they might be cured of a bacterial sinus infection, psychologists refer to the therapy-related factors that help make clients better as **curative factors.** As psychologists have attempted to understand why psychotherapy works, they have isolated two types of factors—*common factors* and *specific factors.* **Common factors** are curative factors of therapy common to all types of treatment. For instance, just going to and being in therapy provides hope, a chance of emotional expression, support and advice, an explanation and understanding of one's difficulties, and an opportunity to experiment with new behaviors and thoughts (Garfield & Bergin, 1994). Carl Rogers appears to have been at least partly correct: A supportive and warm therapy relationship facilitates the success of the therapy (Beutler et al., 1994). In contrast, **specific factors** are those that relate to the particular type of therapy employed. For people with OCD, exposure with response prevention is a specific factor, and the most important factor in improvement (Abramowitz, 1997). Another example would be specific techniques of CBT that can be particularly helpful in treating panic disorder, leading to better outcomes than other types of therapy or medications (Gould et al., 1995).

Research on therapy also looks at broader outcome measures, such as quality of life—the client's psychological, social, and material well-being (Gladis et al., 1999). This new focus addresses complaints that looking at symptoms alone is too narrow a scope and takes the position that health is not simply the absence of disease (World Health Organization, 1948).

PSYCHOTHERAPY VERSUS MEDICATION. Is the TDCRP the only study to have found that psychotherapy can work as well as medication? And is depression the

Curative factor: A therapy-related factor that helps make clients better.

Common factor: A curative factor of therapy common to all types of treatment.

Specific factor: A curative factor related to the specific type of therapy being employed.

only disorder that can claim this general result? The answer to these questions is no (Gloaguen et al., 1998; Reynolds et al., 1999; Thase et al., 1997).

Medication does alleviate depression for many people; why, therefore, might someone choose psychotherapy over medication? According to research, the main drawback of medication becomes apparent when you look at how people fare over the long haul. When medication is discontinued, the relapse rate is high, a fact that has led some doctors to recommend continued use of medication for those at risk for additional depressive episodes (Hirschfeld, 1997). Cognitive–behavioral treatment appears to provide an equivalent benefit without the side effects of drugs (Antonuccio et al., 1995). CBT may also be helpful in treating residual symptoms of depression following treatment with antidepressant medication. This supplemental use of CBT lowers the relapse rate when medication is discontinued (Fava et al., 1998a). At 6-year follow-up, those who had supplemental CBT were less likely to have had another episode of depression than those without CBT (Fava et al., 1998b). Similarly, a number of studies have found that medication and cognitive therapy combined may be more helpful than medication alone, even with severely depressed people (Macaskill & Macaskill, 1996; Thase et al., 1997), although not all studies have found an added benefit to combined treatment (Oei & Yeoh, 1999). Further research will help clarify the role of CBT in preventing relapse after medication is discontinued.

For anxiety disorders, research on the question of medication versus psychotherapy yields results similar to those of the research on depression: That is, particular types of psychotherapy (CBT, IPT) provide as much, if not more, long-term relief of symptoms than does medication (Gould et al., 1995). In the treatment of panic disorder, for instance, although medication and CBT may work about equally well, CBT does a better job of preventing symptom relapse (Chambless & Gillis, 1993; Otto et al., 1994). And as with OCD, behavior therapy is as helpful as medication. Early results of a large-scale study of OCD, similar in design to the TDCRP study, confirm that behavior therapy (in this case, exposure with response prevention) is as helpful as medication, and possibly more so over the long term. However, as with other manual-based treatments that exclude participants with more than one diagnosis, there are questions as to whether these findings generalize to behavior therapy with clients diagnosed with more than one disorder (Kozak et al., 2000).

In the treatment of social phobias, research shows that MAOIs and group CBT are equally helpful (Heimberg et al., 1998). However, research does not support the conclusion that medication is superior to therapy, particularly because of the high relapse rate after medication is discontinued. Meta-analytic studies of medication versus CBT with participants with bulimia nervosa have found CBT to be more effective (Whittal et al., 1999). However, for other disorders, such as schizophrenia and bipolar disorder, medication is clearly superior to psychotherapy. For people with these disorders, psychotherapy can play a role in helping them accept the need to take medication on a lifelong or long-term basis (Colom et al., 1998; Tohen & Grundy, 1999) and can provide an opportunity to learn new relationship skills after the medication has helped them to be more stable. Moreover, psychological treatment in conjunction with medication can be helpful in identifying triggers of psychotic, manic, or depressive episodes, and can help prevent relapses (Buchkremer et al., 1997; Goldstein, 1992). Recent guidelines for the treatment of schizophrenia advocate behavioral and cognitive skills training to encourage compliance with the medication regimen and to help improve functioning by social skills training (Lehman & Steinwachs, 1998). CBT can also be effective in helping reduce positive symptoms in schizophrenic patients who are not helped by medication (Kuipers et al., 1997, 1998; Sensky et al., 2000; Tarrier et al., 1998). A recent meta-analysis of nonmedication treatments for schizophrenia found that those with more chronic schizophrenia were more responsive to psychotherapy than those whose symptoms were less chronic (Mojtabai et al., 1998).

However, like all research that has examined groups of people, the results do not necessarily apply to a particular individual. Thus, for any particular person, psycho-

Although medication can work in treating social phobia, such as a fear of public speaking, it is not necessarily superior to cognitive–behavior therapy because symptoms often return after medication is stopped. Cognitive–behavior therapy's benefits usually last after treatment ends.

therapy may be more effective than medication, and the opposite may be true for someone else with the exact same set of symptoms.

THE CONSUMER REPORTS STUDY. In 1994 *Consumer Reports* magazine asked its readers to evaluate not just their dishwashers but their mental health treatments as well. Approximately 180,000 subscribers received a detailed questionnaire about cars, appliances, and mental health. Those who had experienced stress or other emotional problems over the preceding 3 years and had sought help from friends, relatives, members of the clergy, mental health professionals (such as psychologists), family doctors, or support groups were asked to complete the mental health section. Seven thousand subscribers responded to the mental health questions, with 3,000 reporting that they talked only to friends, relatives, or clergy, and 4,100 reporting that they went to some combination of mental health professionals, family doctors, and support groups. Of these 4,100, 2,900 saw mental health professionals. In addition, 1,300 joined self-help groups, and about 1,000 saw family doctors. The respondents had a median age of 46, were highly educated, and mostly middle class; men and women were almost equally represented.

Results from the survey indicated that treatment by a mental health professional is effective: Most of those who responded said they felt much better after treatment (Seligman, 1995). These findings are consistent with meta-analyses of research studies on the efficacy of therapy (Lipsey & Wilson, 1993; Shapiro & Shapiro, 1982; Smith & Glass, 1977). Of those who reported doing very poorly before treatment, 54% said that treatment made things a lot better, and 33% said it made things somewhat better. Treatment by a mental health professional was superior to treatment by a family doctor; this result has also been found in subsequent studies (Meredith et al., 1996; Schulberg et al., 1996). Moreover, long-term therapy provided more improvement than short-term therapy, a result that is consistent with other findings about the length of treatment (the dose–effect relationship). A meta-analysis of 2,431 patients over a 30-year period showed that 50% improved measurably by the eighth session, and 75% improved after 26 sessions of weekly therapy (Howard et al., 1986). Those respondents who went to Alcoholics Anonymous (AA) reported themselves as doing well. In addition, those who actively sought out a therapist and at the outset discussed such matters as the therapists' qualifications and the frequency and duration of treatment were more likely to fare better than those who were more passive in their treatment. Those whose choice of therapist and duration of treatment were limited by their health insurance plan did worst overall. Generally, the dodo bird verdict seemed to hold true: No specific form of therapy generally had better results than any other.

Several caveats are in order when interpreting the results of the *Consumer Reports* survey. First, very few respondents had schizophrenia or bipolar disorder, so no specific conclusions could be made about treatment of those disorders. Second, the results were not based on controlled, methodologically rigorous studies (as was the TDCRP), and generalization is therefore difficult. Many other criticisms have been leveled against the *Consumer Reports* study on methodological grounds (for detailed criticism of the study, see Jacobson & Christensen, 1996), limiting confidence in the results. In its favor, the *Consumer Reports* study addressed the question of therapy as it is actually delivered for most people: not as part of a research study, and without the use of therapy manuals, in a prescribed number of sessions, or restricted to those with a single diagnosis.

Although controlled psychotherapy research studies can attempt to answer specific questions about outcome, or which treatment works best for which disorder, the *Consumer Reports* study chiefly addressed the question, "Do people have fewer symptoms and a better life after therapy than they did before?" The respondents generally answered yes. The survey also stimulated research about the generalizability of controlled psychotherapy studies ("research therapy") to therapy as it is actually done by most practitioners ("clinic therapy"). Another indication of the effectiveness of clinic therapy is found in a community study examining long-term mental health outcomes for some residents of Baltimore, Maryland. The study found that participants who had received individual or group therapy were less distressed at a 15-year follow-up than those who either received medication or did not seek out mental health treatment (Bovasso et al., 1999). Can research therapy tell us anything about clinic therapy? Recent analyses provide tentative evidence that the results of research therapy may generalize to clinic therapy (Shadish et al., 1997), although more research must be done before the evidence can be considered conclusive.

WHICH THERAPY WORKS BEST FOR WHICH DISORDER? For some disorders, the dodo bird verdict appears to be true, possibly because of common curative factors among all therapies; for other disorders, particular types of therapy are preferred. The results of thousands of research studies and meta-analyses show that some treatments are better than others for certain disorders: Cognitive therapy and interpersonal therapy provide relief from depression; exposure and response prevention provides long-term symptom relief for those with OCD; cognitive therapy is helpful for people with panic disorder (Clark et al., 1999; Wolfe & Maser, 1994) and agoraphobia (Hoffart, 1998); systematic desensitization works well for those with specific phobias (see Seligman, 1995, for a review).

In contrast, psychodynamic therapy appears to work best with patients who are able to articulate their feelings and want to understand their unconscious (and who have the time and money for lengthy treatment). Some meta-analyses find short-term psychodynamic therapy to be as effective as other short-term treatments (Crits-Christoph, 1992), but other studies contradict this result (Svartberg & Stiles, 1991), particularly studies with a 1-year follow-up (Barkham et al., 1999).

There are several difficulties in evaluating the effectiveness of psychodynamic therapies. One is that there isn't much actual research to evaluate. Consider that for every research article on transference, there are 500 on theory. Moreover, although psychodynamic therapists may believe in the accuracy of their interpretations, they may not be correct. For instance, research shows that interpretations of the transference relationship do not appear to be particularly helpful in psychodynamic treatment (Henry, Strupp, et al., 1994). Psychodynamic therapists have tended to view treatment failures as the patient's responsibility rather than the therapist's. It is possible that this view is correct—lack of behavioral change may result from insufficient insight—but insight is not objectively measurable, at least not yet.

Although Rogers did much to bring about the first real insight-oriented alternative to psychoanalysis and made the treatment amenable to research by tape recording therapy sessions, research has not been as supportive as he might have wished. Almost all forms of therapy agree with Rogers's view that the therapist's warmth, empathy, and positive regard for the client are fundamental for a working relationship between client and therapist (Lambert, 1983). However, not all agree that these factors are *enough* to bring about change. Moreover, although client-centered therapy was the first major school of therapy to focus on assessing the effectiveness of the treatment, it can be difficult to measure which clients have achieved their potentials.

Gestalt therapy may be useful with a limited number of problems and disorders: A 12-week Gestalt therapy that made use of the empty chair technique was found to be more effective than psychoeducation in helping to resolve persistent, previously unresolved negative feelings toward significant others (Paivio & Greenberg, 1995). These benefits were also found at a 1-year follow-up.

And although cognitive, behavioral, and CBT treatments have been found to be helpful for specific disorders, these classifications may be too broad, and it seems that specific techniques from each approach are the appropriate units of comparison. For example, in the treatment of OCD, although exposure with response prevention (a behavioral technique) has been the most well-documented technique to produce long-term symptom relief, there is evidence that cognitive therapy may be as effective. In contrast, progressive muscle relaxation, another behavioral technique, was not as beneficial (Abramowitz, 1997). However, not all studies agree (van Balkom et al., 1994). Two distinct types of treatment, CBT without exposure and exposure therapy only, *both* worked well for social phobia (Feske & Chambless, 1995), although later research has found that the combination can be effective (Gould et al., 1997; Taylor,

1996). In the treatment of PTSD, both exposure with response prevention and cognitive restructuring worked equally well, and those two treatments combined were no more effective than each treatment by itself. However, all were superior to relaxation training (Marks et al., 1998). Similar results were found in a meta-analysis of various therapies for PTSD (Sherman, 1998).

And although cognitive therapy in general has been found to be as helpful as medication or IPT, recent research has looked at whether just a subset of CBT techniques is equally as helpful. Jacobson and his colleagues (1996) found that techniques that increase a depressed person's activity level are as effective as CBT treatment, which also changes dysfunctional attitudes or attributional styles. These results were consistent at follow-up 2 years later (Gortner et al., 1998). Similar results were found in treatments for chronic posttraumatic stress disorder: Imaginal exposure (a behavioral technique that uses mental images of the distressing event or object) and cognitive therapy were equally helpful (Tarrier et al., 1999). Thus, asking about the effectiveness of behavioral, cognitive, or cognitive–behavior therapies appears to be too broad a question; further research will clarify which components of therapy are most helpful for particular disorders.

As well as attempting to match disorders and therapy, research has also attempted to match clients and therapy, asking "Which type of therapy works best with what type of client?" This question has been addressed by the National Institute on Alcohol Abuse and Alcoholism (NIAAA). This organization sought to discover whether certain types of treatment for alcohol abuse are more effective with certain types of clients. Some client characteristics thought to be potentially relevant were severity of the alcoholism, sex of the client, and presence of other psychiatric disorders. Treatment included CBT, a 12-step treatment program to prepare clients to join AA, and motivational enhancement therapy, which was directed toward increasing readiness to change drinking habits. Results found that all three treatments had good overall results, increasing the number of abstinent days from 20% before treatment to 80% after treatment, with only a slight dip after 1 year. However, none of the planned "matches" between client and assignment to a particular type of treatment enhanced treatment effectiveness (Project MATCH Research Group, 1997).

Research on matching a treatment to a given client has also looked at the possible effect of a patient's personality. For instance, among depressed clients in the TDCRP, those who also had an avoidant personality disorder (and thus didn't like to dwell on their experiences) were more likely to fare better with cognitive therapy, a result that was consistent with their externally oriented coping style. In contrast, depressed people who had an obsessive-compulsive personality did better in interpersonal therapy, consistent with their internally oriented coping style (Barber & Muenz, 1996). Similar results have been found for the superiority of CBT in helping depressed people who are externalizers versus internalizers (Beutler et al., 1991, 1993).

TREATMENT FOR AN ETHNICALLY DIVERSE POPULATION. According to the 1990 census, 25% of the population of the United States are members of an ethnic minority, and this number continues to grow. As the composition of America changes, so too does the composition of those seeking mental health services. At least until the early 1990s, most psychotherapy research did not include information about race, education, or economic status. However, it has been shown that these factors may influence the effectiveness of a given treatment for a particular client (Francis & Aronson, 1990). Psychotherapists are now more aware of the need to consider a client's background, cultural values, and view of seeking psychological assistance (McGoldrick et al., 1996; Ramirez, 1999). A client's immigrant or refugee experience creates a stressor that can affect mental health. And members of minority groups who are born and raised in the United States may experience prejudice and other hardships that can affect mental health.

An example of the importance of understanding a symptom's cultural context can be found in *ataques de nervios* (Spanish for "attack of nerves"), which some Puerto Rican women experience. This condition is a physical expression of strong emotions and includes trembling, heart palpitations, numbness, difficulty breathing, loss of consciousness, and a hyperkinetic state (Rivera-Arzola & Ramos-Grenier, 1997). The context for this illness is a culture in which women are likely to endure great hardships, have little real power, and are actively discouraged from expressing anger. *Ataque de nervios* provides a culturally sanctioned way for them to express an inability to cope with a current situation, and the community responds (Rivera-Arzola & Ramos-Grenier, 1997). It is clear that the most effective therapist is one who is aware of both the cultural and familiar contexts of a disorder.

It is part of a therapist's responsibility to be aware of cultural or racial issues that can affect all aspects of treatment—diagnosis, the process of the therapy, and its goals (Helms & Cook, 1999; Ramirez, 1999). The therapist should inquire about the client's understanding of the meaning of the problem, so that therapist and client can discuss and come to agreement on the nature of the problem, interventions to be used, and expected goals (Higgenbotham et al., 1988; Kleinman, 1978).

Although age, sex, and ethnicity do not appear to play a systematic role in therapy outcomes generally (Beutler et al., 1994), research suggests that some people (such as some Asian Americans) prefer a therapist from their ethnic group, and such matching leads to better outcomes for them (Sue et al., 1994). In general, however, there is no clear-cut evidence to date that matching by ethnicity for most ethnic groups results in better outcomes (Garfield, 1994). Some attempts have been made to develop particular therapies for different ethnic groups, with varying success; for example, *cuento therapy* (from the Spanish word for "fable"), which uses folktales or stories, has proved helpful with Latino American children (Sue et al., 1994).

Therapists try to be aware of unique ethnic and cultural factors that can play a role in treatment, such as immigrant, cultural, or racial stressors.

How to Pick a Psychotherapist

Suppose you decide to seek psychotherapy. How do you pick a therapist? Keep several factors in mind when trying to find someone who could most effectively help you. If your problem is identifiable (such as depression or anxiety), it can be helpful to see someone who has experience in treating people with that problem. Many state and national referral agencies or professional associations are available, such as the American Psychological Association, the National Association of Social Workers, and the American Psychiatric Association. Regional organizations can also provide referrals for specific problems, such as the Massachusetts Eating Disorders Association or the Manic-Depressive and Depressive Association of Boston (MDDA-Boston). These organizations all have national associations that can also supply the names of therapists with expertise in treating specific problems.

It may be helpful to get the names of more than one therapist because any one therapist may not have compatible office hours, location, and so on. You can also ask friends, family, teachers, and religious leaders for recommendations, as well as the counseling center at your college or university (Practice Directorate, 1998). Many insurance companies will reimburse or authorize psychotherapy only if the provider is on their list. If this is true for you, tell the therapists you are considering what insurance coverage you have and ask if their services are reimbursed by that company; if they don't know, call the company and check. Alternatively, call your insurance company and ask for referrals.

It is important that you feel comfortable with your therapist. If you don't, you may be less likely to talk about what's on your mind or share how you are really doing. And if you aren't able to talk about these things, the therapy can't be as helpful. It's also important to feel that the therapist is trustworthy—if the therapist doesn't have your trust, you will find it easy to discount what he or she says if it is something that you don't want to hear. If after one or two sessions, you realize you just don't feel comfortable, make an appointment with someone else and see whether the situation feels different.

How Do You Know Whether Psychotherapy Worked?

If you were designing a study to test the effectiveness of a particular therapy, how could you decide whether that treatment had been successful? The answer depends on what you measure, and the measures can be defined at each of the three levels of analysis. At the level of the group, you could ask members of the clients' families to report their impressions about their interactions with the client, or you could measure the frequency of certain social behaviors, such as the amount of time the client spends talking to other people. At the level of the person, you could have clients rate their thoughts, feelings, or behaviors, or fill in questionnaires about their psychological states. And at the level of the brain, you could take PET scans or other measures of brain activity, or you could obtain biochemical measures and examine the levels of key neuromodulators and neurotransmitters (although not all new learning that occurs at the level of the brain can be assessed in this way). What would you think if some measures showed changes, but not others? Would you be willing to say that someone had improved if only the brain-based measures showed a change after therapy? What if only other people's reports of clients' social interactions, or only the clients' own subjective reports, showed a change? Sure, if he or she feels better, that may be good enough for the client—but unless changes actually occur in the brain and in behavior, what grounds are there for thinking of the improvement as enduring? Any new learning, whether it is having insight into problems, changing maladaptive behavior patterns, or replacing irrational thoughts with rational ones, creates changes in the brain. Lasting changes following psychotherapy can be reflected at all three levels of analysis.

CONSOLIDATE!

▶ **1. What key issues should be kept in mind when reading research studies of psychotherapy?** Overall, therapy is more beneficial than no treatment. However, methodological issues have a bearing on what conclusions we can draw from a psychotherapy study, such as what has been measured and when it was measured. Curative factors include (a) common factors that apply across all types of treatment and (b) specific factors that relate to a particular intervention of an approach. Studies should note the ethnic composition of the participants, and treatment should consider ethnic and cultural factors that may affect the treatment.

▶ **2. What are good ways to find a therapist?** A therapist can be chosen by a referral from a counseling center, family and friends, self-help organizations, professional associations, and insurance companies. The therapist should be someone with whom the client feels comfortable; if trust is lacking, another therapist should be sought.

A DEEPER LEVEL
Recap and Thought Questions

▶ **Insight-Oriented Therapies**

Insight-oriented therapies focus on helping people gain insight into their problems and propose that such insight will lead to changes in thoughts, feelings, and behavior. Psychodynamic, client-centered, and Gestalt therapies are examples. These therapies rest on the belief that psychological problems are caused by emotional forces.

If Beth were seeing an insight-oriented therapist, what would be the focus of treatment? Beth's treatment would no doubt focus on her feelings (rather than her thoughts or behaviors) and on her relationships, with an emphasis on her relationships with people during her childhood, particularly her mother. This would be especially true if her therapist were psychodynamically oriented.

> **Think It Through.** Imagine two people, one of whom is the ideal candidate for insight-oriented therapy and one of whom is the worst possible candidate. How would you describe these two people? If a friend tells you that he is in insight-oriented therapy, what can you assume about his therapy? What can't you assume?

▶ Cognitive and Behavior Therapy

The foundation of cognitive and behavior therapies is the idea that psychological problems are caused by faulty perceptions or interpretations, or are a product of a client's learning histories; they therefore seek to help the client develop more realistic thoughts and adaptive behaviors. Therapy is generally active, focuses on current problems, and often assigns between-session homework.

If Beth were in treatment with a cognitive–behavior therapist, what would be the likely focus of her treatment? Beth's treatment would focus on her thoughts and behavior. Specifically, a cognitive–behavior therapist would probably use cognitive techniques to modify Beth's automatic thoughts about tests and studying, as well as about her depression and fear of becoming like her mother. This therapist might also use behavioral techniques such as systematic desensitization for her anxiety about tests, daily logs to monitor her mood and anxiety and to identify their ABCs, and set up a schedule of pleasurable activities. Such a schedule would ensure that Beth has an opportunity to do enjoyable things: People who are depressed often restrict their social outings and become isolated, depriving themselves of positive social contact and opportunities to have a good time.

> **Think It Through.** If you read about a study that claimed CBT treatment effectively reduces kleptomania (compulsive stealing done for pleasure, not for material need), what questions would you ask about how the study was done? Suppose each therapist in the study treated some clients with CBT and some with Gestalt therapy. What would you need to know before agreeing with their conclusions about the superiority of CBT? Why? Would CBT be effective if the client was not motivated or had a poor memory? Explain your answer.

▶ Other Forms of Therapy

Psychological treatment exists in a variety of forms, including prevention programs; individual, family, and group therapy; and self-help resources. Psychotherapy protocols and integrative psychotherapy have been more widely practiced in recent years, partly because of the demands of managed care. Biologically based treatments include medications (such as antipsychotics, antidepressants, and antianxiety drugs) and electroconvulsive therapy, which is used with severely depressed people when other treatments have failed. Still considered experimental is treatment by transcranial magnetic stimulation.

What are the different forms of therapy available to Beth? In addition to individual therapy, Beth could receive group or family therapy, make use of various self-help books, or attend a support group. Moreover, Beth could take medication, and if her depression were severe enough and had not been relieved by other treatments, Beth might be a candidate for electroconvulsive therapy or the experimental transcranial magnetic stimulation.

> **Think It Through.** Suppose your best friend's mother had bipolar disorder. What might be her likely treatment? Why? Suppose instead that your friend's father was schizophrenic; what treatment might he receive? Explain your answer. And if they were both depressed? If your friend showed no sign of any disorder, but was involved in a prevention program, what level of prevention would that be?

▶ Which Therapy Works Best?

Research on psychotherapy shows that, overall, those who receive psychotherapy fare better than those who don't receive treatment. This is generally true regardless of therapeutic approach. However, research also shows that certain types of therapy are more effective with certain disorders than others; for example, exposure with response prevention is a particularly good treatment for OCD. It is also important to understand the ethnic and cultural factors related to a client's problems and goals.

How is Beth's therapy likely to turn out, based on research on the effectiveness of psychotherapy? As indicated by the dodo bird verdict, Beth's therapy may be effective, regardless of the orientation of the therapist. If the treatment is specifically designed for anxiety and depression, the likelihood of a positive treatment outcome would likely increase. However, it is difficult to apply group results to a specific individual.

> **Think It Through.** Suppose you were designing a treatment program for depression for an ethnically diverse set of clients. What would you want to know about the clients? How would you use that information? How would you design a study to test the effectiveness of your new program? Why would you do it that way?

15 SOCIAL PSYCHOLOGY

Meeting of the Minds

In 1993 Sarah Delany, known as Sadie, and her younger sister Elizabeth, called Bessie, published their first book, *Having Our Say* (Delany, Delany, & Hearth, 1993). What's remarkable about these authors is that they were 104 and 102 at the time of publication. Their book recounts the story of their lives, their experiences as black children and then as black women during a century of American history. It was during their childhood that the South's Jim Crow laws came into effect, legalizing separate facilities—separate schools, separate water fountains, separate seats on the bus, separate toilets—for blacks and whites; it was during their adulthood that these laws were struck down.

Sadie and Bessie had eight brothers and sisters. Their father, Henry, had been born a slave but was freed by emancipation. He became vice principal of St. Augustine's School (now St. Augustine's College), a black college in Raleigh, North Carolina. Their mother, Nanny James, who had both black and white grandparents, was light-skinned. In addition to managing her ten children, she was the matron of the college, overseeing many of its daily functions. The Delany children were educated at "St. Aug's," where their father taught. All ten children became college-educated professional men and women—a remarkable feat for anyone of that era, regardless of race or sex. Sadie earned both a bachelor's and a master's degree from Columbia University and became a teacher. In 1926 she became the first black woman appointed to teach home economics at the high school level in New York City. Bessie went to dental school at Columbia in 1923, where she was the only black woman, and she was the second black woman licensed to practice dentistry in New York City.

The Delany family, well known in black society in North Carolina and in New York City's Harlem neighborhood, was considered to be part of an elite group of educated blacks. But the road was not easy for the sisters. People, black and white, developed attitudes and stereotypes about the sisters, and some discriminated against them—because they were black, because they were women, or simply because they were Delanys.

Like the Delanys, we are all targets of other people's attitudes and stereotypes, and we have attitudes and stereotypes of our own about other people. And like the Delanys, we all feel pressure from others to behave in certain ways and exert pressure on others to behave in certain ways. How we think about other people and interact in relationships and groups makes up the subfield of psychology called **social psychology.**

Many of the phenomena psychology seeks to understand—sensation, learning, and memory, to name just a few—take place primarily at the levels of the brain and the person, but are influenced, as shown in the Looking at Levels sections, by the environment and the social world. In this chapter, the central emphasis is the level of the group. By definition, social psychology is about our relationships with the world around us; it focuses on the way we think about other people and act toward them, individually and in groups. And these interactions affect our thoughts, feelings, behavior, even our brains. Are there psychological principles that underlie the ways we think about and behave toward other people? If so, what are they?

SOCIAL COGNITION: THINKING ABOUT PEOPLE

Sadie and Bessie's parents worked hard to protect their children as much as possible from prejudice, discrimination, and intimidation. They also tried to instill in their children a sense of dignity, self-respect, and respect for and support of others. They encouraged their children to think about the world and their places in it, in specific ways. For example, their parents called each other Mr. and Mrs. Delany in front of others, including their children. This was a conscious decision. It was common for whites to call blacks by their first names in instances in which they would use surnames for whites; therefore, Mr. and Mrs. Delany deliberately chose to use formal titles to convey respect for each other and the expectation of respect from others.

▶ 1. Do first impressions really make a difference?

▶ 2. What is the relationship between people's attitudes and their behaviors?

▶ 3. What are stereotypes? Why do people have them? What are the differences between stereotypes and prejudice?

▶ 4. How do we determine responsibility for positive and negative events, and what difference does it make?

In this chapter we focus largely on the ways people think about other people, in other words, on social cognition—*cognition* because it is about how we think, and *social* because the thoughts involve other people and the social world in general. **Social cognition** is concerned with the ways we attend to, store, remember, and use information about other people and the social world.

Social psychology: The field of psychology pertaining to how people think about other people and interact in relationships and groups.

Social cognition: The area of social psychology that focuses on how people attend to, store, remember, and use information about other people and the social world.

Making an Impression

The Delany children, like many other children, were always told to "make a good impression." Have you ever been told, even long after childhood, essentially the same thing—to comb your hair or dress up a bit before meeting someone for the first time? You may have wondered, "I know what kind of person I am. Why do I need to appear a particular way for other people?" An obvious answer is, of course, that other people *don't* know what kind of person you are, and they make inferences about you from things they notice at that initial meeting. Social psychologists have found that first impressions can make a difference (Schlenker, 1980); we tend to give earlier information more weight than later information. Even the position you assume when sitting shapes other people's impression of you: When females sit with their legs open and their arms held away from their upper bodies (more common among males), they are seen as less feminine; when males sit with their thighs against each other and their arms touching their upper bodies (more common among females), they are seen as less masculine (Vrugt & Luyerink, 2000).

The name psychologists use for the process by which we develop such impressions of others is **impression formation**. The creating and receiving of impressions is a two-way street, and the term **impression management** refers to our efforts to control the type of impression we create.

Do you remember what, specifically, you did the last time you wanted to make a good impression—perhaps on a date, on a job interview, when meeting with a professor? Chances are that you used one of these two general types of impression management strategies:

1. *Self-enhancement strategy.* You tried to make yourself look good, perhaps by appearing particularly well groomed or knowledgeable about particular topics. You should be aware that some self-enhancement strategies border on deception, for example, if you present yourself as someone you are not; this may be especially true in initial dating situations (Rowatt et al., 1998).
2. *Other-enhancement strategy.* You tried to elicit a positive mood or reaction from the other person. You might have asked for the other person's feedback or advice (Morrison & Bies, 1991), or you might have been particularly attentive to the other person in an effort to convey the impression that you liked him or her (Wayne & Ferris, 1990).

These photos show Marcia Clark—the prosecutor in O. J. Simpson's criminal trial—before (left) and after (right) her makeover. What differences do you notice? Does each photo give you a different impression of Ms. Clark? If so, what causes you to have different impressions?

Other-enhancement strategies work well on the job, at least for new employees; those who use this strategy increase the chances that their supervisors will view them as similar to themselves and that their supervisors will like them more. These reactions in turn shape the performance ratings given by supervisors (Wayne & Liden, 1995).

Attitudes and Behavior: Feeling and Doing

When you read or hear the news, your attitudes affect your interpretation of the events being reported. In a smaller arena, your attitudes about people from a particular ethnic group will determine how you feel about them. For instance, your attitude about African Americans will determine how you *feel* about African Americans, which will in turn affect how you feel when you read about the Delanys. And in your own circle, if your friend tells you she's had an abortion, your attitude toward abortion will help determine how you feel about your friend. An **attitude** is an overall evaluation—often considered a feeling—about some aspect of the world: people, issues, or objects (Petty

Impression formation: The process of developing impressions of others.

Impression management: A person's efforts to control the type of impression he or she creates.

Attitude: An overall evaluation about some aspect of the world.

& Wegener, 1998). Your beliefs and behavior can affect your attitudes, and your attitudes can affect your beliefs and behavior. The opportunity for the interplay of attitude and behavior can be seen in Sadie's father's comment to her: "Daughter, you are college material. You owe it to your nation, your race, and yourself to go. And if you don't go, then shame on you" (p. 91). His remarks reflected his attitude toward higher education for blacks: He was passionate about it (feeling); he had no doubt about the power of education to elevate the position of blacks in American society (belief); and this attitude was formed, in part, by his own experiences with education as well as those of his family (behavior).

Attitudes can be positive, such as being in favor of nuclear disarmament; negative, such as disliking speed limits on highways; or neutral, such as not being moved one way or the other by a political candidate. The same issue—for instance, whether American troops should intervene in a foreign war—can evoke equally strong negative (NO!) and positive (YES!) attitudes. These different evaluations are accompanied by different physiological changes in facial muscles (Cacioppo, Petty, Losch et al., 1986) and brain activation (Davidson, 1992a). We can also have ambivalent attitudes, with simultaneous negative and positive attitudes being equally strong.

Attention can play an important role in how we process and remember perceptual information in the physical world (see Chapters 3 and 6). Similarly, attitudes play an important role in how we process information and remember events in our social world (Eagly & Chaiken, 1998). Particularly in ambiguous social situations, our attitudes help organize events and thus determine what information is attended to, processed, encoded, and remembered. This is one reason why people in the same social situation can come away with different versions of what occurred. In one study, Princeton and Dartmouth students watched a motion picture of a controversial Princeton–Dartmouth football game. Although all students saw the same motion picture of the game, students from the different schools described different events (Hastorf & Cantril, 1954).

Our attitudes also affect the way we shape our goals and expectations, and how we interpret obstacles we encounter in trying to achieve our goals, perhaps inducing stress. (It is not an event itself, but how it is perceived that determines whether it induces stress; see Chapter 12.) Our attitudes guide us as we selectively evaluate information; generally, we find information that is contrary to our attitudes to be unconvincing, and we may even try to disprove it (Eagly & Chaiken, 1998). As an example, consider the effect of socioeconomic class in the workplace (Gerteis & Savage, 1998). If you think that someone from a lower socioeconomic class will make a bad colleague, you will look for any evidence of shoddy work. You may not notice your colleague's well-performed tasks, and if you do notice them, you make up reasons that discount or discredit your colleague's abilities—perhaps, you say, those are easy tasks.

Our attitudes also shape our view of the world because they are the basis for classifying things as "good" or "bad"—a classification that can be made immediately, without our awareness (Bargh, 1997). Research has shown that mere exposure to words related to a stereotype can affect behavior (Bargh et al., 1996). In one study, students were given scrambled groups of five words and asked to construct a grammatically correct four-word sentence from each group (Figure 15.1). Some students were given neutral words. Other participants were given words consistent with stereotypes of the elderly, such as *wrinkled, lonely, helpless, dependent, cautious, obedient,* and *selfish.* After finishing the task, participants walked down the corridor to leave the building, unobtrusively timed by researchers. Students who were given scrambled word groups that included stereotyped words about the elderly walked more slowly than those who were given neutral word groups. The participants reported that they hadn't been aware of the theme of the words, nor had they been aware that their behavior had been affected, but these words nonetheless caused a change in behavior, and one that was outside participants' awareness. Think about the implications of this research: If you see a commercial for a new product, meet a new person, hear about a new political organization, you will immediately make a judgment about what you've

FIGURE 15.1
Stereotypes Can Affect Behavior Without Our Awareness

Participants were asked to unscramble sentences with words related to the elderly or with neutral words, such as the ones shown here.

Those who unscrambled words pertaining to stereotypes about the elderly walked more slowly after completing the task than those who unscrambled neutral words. Participants reported that they did not realize the task had included stereotypic words about the elderly, nor did they think the unscrambling task had affected them in any way—the effects were outside their conscious awareness.

(Adapted from Bargh et al., 1996.)

seen or heard, *without necessarily being aware of having done so.* And this judgment will influence your willingness to buy the product, talk to the new person, or get more information about the new organization.

PREDICTING BEHAVIOR. If you know someone's attitudes, can you predict their behavior? Consider the experience of psychologist Richard La Piere (1934), who traveled the country in the 1930s with a young Chinese couple. They stayed in 67 paid lodgings and ate in 184 restaurants and cafés. Six months after each visit, La Piere sent a questionnaire to those establishments inquiring whether they would accept Chinese people as customers. More than 90% of the lodgings and restaurants said no. Yet on their trip La Piere and his colleagues were refused only once. Attitudes influence behavior, but do not always lead to behavior consistent with attitudes.

Several factors determine how likely an attitude toward a behavior will lead to the behavior's occurrence. An attitude is more likely to affect behavior when it is (1) strong, (2) relatively stable, (3) directly relevant to the behavior, (4) important, or (5) easily accessed from memory (Eagly & Chaiken, 1998). For instance, suppose you strongly dislike eating Moroccan food—an attitude. Against your better judgment, you went to a Moroccan restaurant recently and only picked at the food. If a friend invites you today to a meal at a Moroccan restaurant, you are likely to suggest another place to go: Your attitude about Moroccan food is strong, stable, directly relevant to your behavior, and easily accessed from memory. But if you haven't eaten this type of food in years, don't feel that strongly about it now, and have almost forgotten why you ever disliked it, you would be less likely to object to your friend's choice of a Moroccan restaurant (Sanbonmatsu & Fazio, 1990). Attitudes based on indirect experience, such as hearsay, have less influence on behavior than those based on direct experience (Regan & Fazio, 1977).

BEHAVIOR AFFECTS ATTITUDES. If a professor assigned an essay on a topic about which you didn't have very strong feelings (say, supporting curbside recycling versus recycling at a local center), do you think writing the essay would influence your subsequent views? Research has shown that it can: When people are asked to repeatedly assert an attitude on a given topic, thus priming that attitude, and making it easier to access, they are more likely to behave in ways consistent with that attitude, compared with those who did not repeatedly express the attitude (Fazio et al., 1982; Powell & Fazio, 1984). In fact, repeatedly asserting an attitude can make the attitude more extreme (Downing et al., 1992). Many self-help or self-improvement programs capitalize on this finding, encouraging participants to express frequent "affirmations," positive statements about themselves, their intentions, and their abilities. Such repeated affirmations can strengthen people's positive attitudes about themselves.

COGNITIVE DISSONANCE. Attitudes and behavior don't always go hand in hand, as dramatically demonstrated by La Piere's study. But most people prefer that their attitudes and behavior be consistent (Snyder & Ickes, 1985). When an attitude and behavior—or two attitudes—are inconsistent, an uncomfortable state that psychologists refer to as **cognitive dissonance** arises. Cognitive dissonance is accompanied by heightened arousal (Losch & Cacioppo, 1990).

FIGURE 15.2
Cognitive Dissonance

In Festinger and Carlsmith's classic 1959 study, participants were asked to perform a very boring, repetitive task: putting spools on a tray, then dumping them out, and starting all over again.

(From Festinger & Carlsmith, 1959.)

Participants were then offered either $1 or $20 (a lot of money in those days) to tell another person that the task was in fact quite interesting.

After telling the other person about the task, the participants were asked to rate how much they liked the task. Those who were paid $1 to tell the other person they liked the task reported actually liking the task more than those paid $20 to do so!

Cognitive dissonance: The uncomfortable state that arises because of a discrepancy between an attitude and behavior or between two attitudes.

Festinger and Carlsmith's (1959) classic study on cognitive dissonance found that, counterintuitively, participants who were paid less to tell someone that a boring task was really enjoyable reported afterward that they enjoyed the task more than those who were paid a greater amount (Figure 15.2). How can we understand this? By the effects of cognitive dissonance reduction. The participants who were paid less, only $1, could not have justified performing a boring task for that amount. In order to reduce dissonance, they appear to have convinced themselves, unconsciously, that they really *did* enjoy the task, so much that they were willing to do it for little reimbursement. The participants who were paid more felt no such compulsion; the money they received, they felt, adequately compensated for the boredom, so there was no dissonance to be resolved. In general, research has shown that the less reason there is to engage in a behavior that is counter to our attitudes, the stronger the dissonance. Cognitive dissonance does not occur with every inconsistency; it is experienced only by people who believe that they have a choice and that they are responsible for the course of action, and thus for any negative consequences (Cooper, 1998; Goethals et al., 1979).

Another explanation for cognitive dissonance findings comes from **self-perception theory,** which states that people understand themselves by making inferences from their behavior and the events surrounding their behavior—much as they would draw inferences from observing another person's behavior (Bem, 1972). The influence of such self-perception is especially clear when we do not have strong feelings or motivations that help us understand our behavior. This theory would say that participants in Festinger and Carlsmith's study tried to understand why they would tell someone they liked a boring task when they were paid only $1. They explained it to themselves the same way they would explain the behavior in someone else: They must have actually liked the task. However, this explanation doesn't rule out cognitive dissonance.

To get a sense of what cognitive dissonance feels like, before you read the next sentence, turn to page 273 and reread the story that opens Chapter 8. What race did you imagine Janet to be? Why? What assumptions had you made about her? What stereotypic ideas did you have that influenced your picture of her? Now imagine that Janet is of a different specific race from the one you first assumed. What new stereotypes now come to mind? You may feel uncomfortable after this exercise. If you had not previously thought you harbored prejudices, but found that you did, the resulting uncomfortable feeling arises from the contradiction—the dissonance between your actual, prejudicial attitudes and your view of yourself as not having prejudicial attitudes.

Because cognitive dissonance creates an uncomfortable state, we try to decrease it. How do we minimize cognitive dissonance once it has occurred? We can use indirect strategies, such as trying to feel good about ourselves in other areas of life, or direct strategies, which involve actually changing our attitudes or behavior. Direct strategies also include attempts to obtain additional information supporting our attitude or behavior. Or, we can trivialize an inconsistency between two conflicting attitudes (or between an attitude and a behavior) as being unimportant, and therefore less likely to cause cognitive dissonance (Simon et al., 1995). For example, suppose you really believe in, and talk about, a desire to help feed starving people. Then a friend points out that you talk about this desire repeatedly but don't do anything about it. This observation would probably induce cognitive dissonance in you. To lessen it, you could use an indirect strategy by telling yourself what a good person you are, or by finding information about how hard it is for one individual to do anything about world hunger, or simply by saying "Well, my heart's in the right place." Or, you could implement a direct strategy that has an impact on world hunger, such as volunteering to work in a food bank.

Some researchers have argued that it is not the inconsistency itself that leads to the dissonance, and thus to a change in an attitude or behavior, but rather the resulting threat to a person's self-view. A discrepancy between attitude and behavior (or between two attitudes) makes the person who becomes aware of it look foolish, and so it is a threat to his or her integrity (Aronson et al., 1995). This threat explains why African Americans may discount the importance of their performance on standardized tests, and why women taking tests in math or science may do the same: They are concerned that their performance is seen as a reflection on their race or sex. The risk of seeming to conform to a negative stereotype in the eyes of others or oneself is termed *stereotype threat* (Steele & Aronson, 1995). Regardless of their performance on the tests, by discounting the importance of their test performance, the test-takers allow themselves to construct a positive self-identity from abilities in other domains (Steele, 1997). Stereotype threat (see Chapter 8) occurs not only in women and people of color: White athletes who derived their self-worth from their athletic performance showed stereotype threat and decreased performance when their performance was framed as an indication of their natural ability (Stone et al., 1999).

Self-perception theory: The theory that people come to understand themselves by making inferences from their behavior and the events surrounding their behavior, much like those they would make about another person's behavior.

Using such cognitive dissonance to increase behaviors that promote health, Stone and his colleagues (1997) set up a situation in which participants were induced to feel that they were being hypocritical. Sexually active college students were asked to prepare and videotape a talk on AIDS prevention for to high school students. Students who were asked to write speeches based on reasons they *personally* had not always used condoms were then more likely to purchase offered condoms than students who were asked to include in their speech reasons why *other* people might not use condoms.

ATTITUDE CHANGE: PERSUASION. Walking to class, have you ever been approached by someone offering you a leaflet about an upcoming event, a political candidate, a new product? If so, someone (or some company) was trying to encourage you to do something: go to the event, vote for the candidate, buy the product. We are bombarded by attempts to change our attitudes about things, through advertisements, editorials, and conversations with friends. These efforts to change your attitudes are called **persuasion.**

Social psychologists have identified several factors that make attempts at persuasion more likely to be successful. You can probably guess some of them; others may surprise you. As you might expect, people are more likely to be persuaded by what they read, hear, or see when the person doing the persuading is an expert (Hovland & Weiss, 1951). If your doctor tells you to stop smoking, the instruction is more persuasive than when suggested by a friend. Similarly, an attractive persuader is more likely to change attitudes than an unattractive one; think about commercials and advertisements, and what the people in most of them look like (Kiesler & Kiesler, 1969). Fast speakers are generally more persuasive than slow speakers (Miller et al., 1976). And if the attempt at persuasion arouses strong emotions in you, particularly fear, it is more likely to work, especially if it includes specific advice about what you can do to bring about a more positive outcome (Leventhal et al., 1965). This technique is used in public service messages that try to scare people into behaving differently, such as ads that graphically describe how someone contracted AIDS by not using a condom and then strongly recommend condom use. Not surprisingly, people who are perceived as honest are more persuasive (Priester & Petty, 1995). People with low self-esteem are more susceptible to persuasion than people with high self-esteem (Janis, 1954).

Other methods of persuasion—and the audiences most easily persuaded—are less obvious. If you are not paying full attention to an attempt at persuasion, you are more likely to be persuaded, at least in part because you have less ability to develop a counterargument (Allyn & Festinger, 1961; Romero et al., 1996). So, if you are watching a television commercial while sorting the laundry, you are more likely to be persuaded by it than if you're focused on it. If you've ever heard a Republican speaking to a group of Democrats (or vice versa), you may have noticed a persuasion technique used to convince people who hold the opposite view, whatever that view is: The would-be persuader uses a two-sided approach. The speaker presents both sides of an argument rather than only one side, as is common if the audience already agrees with the speaker. And when a message does not appear to be *trying* to persuade you to change your attitude, it is often more effective than one that is obviously trying to move you. (These factors are summarized in Table 15.1.)

The ancient Egyptians recognized the power of some of these persuasion techniques. Their law courts met in the dark; the judges weren't able to see the accused, the accuser, or the witnesses, and were thus less likely to be persuaded by factors other than the merits of the case itself. Furthermore, the *mere exposure effect* (see Chapter 9)

In an effort to persuade smokers to quit, Canadian health officials proposed that packs of cigarettes feature graphic photographs of the consequences of smoking, such as the one shown here. What persuasion factors are at work in this campaign?

Persuasion: Attempts to change people's attitudes.

Factors That Make Persuasion More Effective

- Experts are more persuasive than nonexperts.

- Attractive people are more effective in changing attitudes than unattractive ones.

- People who speak quickly are more persuasive than people who speak slowly.

- Messages that arouse strong emotions (particularly fear) can enhance persuasion, particularly if the message provides concrete recommendations about how the change in attitude or behavior will prevent the proposed negative consequences.

- Those who are perceived to be honest are more likely to be persuasive.

- People can be more susceptible to persuasion when distracted than when they are paying full attention to what is being said because they have less ability to develop a counterargument.

- People with low self-esteem are more subject to persuasion than people with high self-esteem.

- If an audience already holds the opposite view, the would-be persuader is better off using a two-sided approach than presenting only one position.

- Messages that do not appear to be designed to change our attitudes are often more successful than those obviously designed to do so.

can change attitudes: Simply becoming familiar with something can change your attitude toward it—generally, favorably.

Attempts at persuasion are often foiled by four common obstacles:

1. *Strong attitude.* If we, as listeners, already have a strong attitude about an issue, as opposed to a weak one, we are less likely to be persuaded to change our current attitude (Petty & Krosnick, 1996). Indeed, among identical twins reared apart (see Chapter 10), certain attitudes appear to be heritable, strong, and resistant to change. For instance, the attitude toward the death penalty has a high heritability; whatever is responsible for this attitude is, at least in part, affected by the genes (Tesser, 1993).

2. *Reactance.* Reactance is the development of a negative reaction to someone who is seen as trying too hard or too often to change our opinion. In this case, we may very well change our minds in the *opposite* direction from that intended by the persuader, even if we would not otherwise take that position; this response is called *negative attitude change* (Brehm, 1966).

3. *Forewarning.* If we know in advance that someone is going to try to persuade us of something, we are less likely to be persuaded (Cialdini & Petty, 1979; Petty & Cacioppo, 1981), although this is not always the case (Niemeyere et al., 1991; Romero et al., 1996).

4. *Selective avoidance.* We may simply bypass someone's attempt to persuade us by deliberate selective avoidance, such as changing the channel during television commercials.

Stereotypes: Seen One, Seen 'Em All

In the social world around us, we could easily be overwhelmed by the torrent of information conveyed by other people—their words, postures, gestures, facial expressions—to say nothing of what we can infer about their attitudes and goals, and even further, what other people have said about them. The world is full of information and stimuli, and if we had no way of organizing this input flying at us from all directions, assaulting our senses, we would live in chaos. In the physical realm, we categorize all this information by principles such as Gestalt groupings of visual stimuli (see Chapter 3). To avoid drowning in this sea of social information, we create *stereotypes*, a type of schema (see Chapter 7) that helps provide a cognitive shortcut for processing all this information about the social world (Gilbert & Hixon, 1991; Macrae et al., 1994). A **stereotype** is a belief (or set of beliefs) about people in a particular social category; the category can be defined by race, sex, social class, religion, hair color, sport, hobby, and myriad other characteristics. A stereotype may be positive, such as "women are nurturing"; neutral, such as "Mexicans eat spicy food"; or negative, such as "Australians drink too much."

As with other types of classification, stereotypes can be useful shortcuts. But the nature of the stereotypes we use is not static. Just as mood can influence what we remember (see Chapter 6), mood can also influence our use of stereotypes, including our stereotyping of ethnic groups (Alexander et al., 1999; Esses & Zanna, 1995). In addition, stereotypes are caricatures, not reasoned formulations, and are to some extent outside conscious awareness; we may deny having them at all. Moreover, stereotypes are often incorrect. For example, when lawyers select a jury, they try to have certain potential jurors excluded because of stereotypes about how people of a certain race, sex, age, or profession are likely to view the case. But one study found that lawyers' stereotype-based expectations of whether jurors would be likely to convict were often incorrect (Olczak et al., 1991). Not only can stereotypes affect how we feel about other people, but our expectations of others based on our stereotypes can lead *them* to behave in certain ways. (See Chapter 10 for an example of how expectations of others can change their behavior.)

The effect of errors we make when using stereotypes is anything but trivial. Perhaps because of our desire for cognitive efficiency, we prefer to read information consistent with our stereotypes, and we process such information more quickly (Smith, 1998). As with attitudes, we are less likely to attend to, and therefore encode or remember, information inconsistent with our stereotypes (Johnston & Macrae, 1994), and in fact we may deny the truth of such information (O'Sullivan & Durso, 1984). And once a stereotype is activated, we respond to a person's membership in a social category, not to the characteristics of the individual person. The stereotype thus lives on and may shape the rest of our thinking. One way this occurs is that additional information relevant to the stereotype is recalled faster than unrelated information (Dovidio et al., 1986). However, if we are motivated to be accurate, and do *not* assume that a stereotype applies to a particular individual, we can minimize the impact of stereotypes (Wyer et al., 2000).

Here's how this works. Suppose that you have a positive stereotype of New Englanders, believing them to be hard-working, thrifty, and honest. When you meet a new colleague from Maine, your "New Englander" stereotype is activated. You will then be more likely to notice aspects of her behavior that are consistent with your stereotype, and in thinking about her, you will be more likely to remember those aspects. You may not notice when she comes in late, or you will come up with plausible excuses for her tardiness.

Sometimes the conflict between a stereotype and actual behavior is too great to be ignored—but rather than change a stereotype, we are more likely to create a new subtype within the stereotype (Anderson, 1983; Anderson et al., 1980). So in this case, when your New England colleague's chronic lateness and inefficiency are too great to ignore, you might create a subtype—"female New Englander on her first job." This allows you to preserve your stereotype of New Englanders as hard-working. Because of this psychological phenomenon—creating subtypes in order to preserve a stereotype—stereotypes can be extremely difficult to change or eliminate. However, under certain circumstances, stereotypes *can* change, when the exception is made to appear typical of its group and when we are encouraged to think that the person's behavior results from his or her characteristics, *not* the situation (Wilder et al., 1996).

COGNITION AND PREJUDICE. Stereotyping can lead to **prejudice**, which is an attitude, generally negative, toward members of a group. Prejudice includes not only

Stereotype: A belief (or set of beliefs) about people in a particular social category.

Prejudice: An attitude (generally negative) toward members of a group.

beliefs and expectations about the group but also an emotional component: Simply thinking about members of a disliked group can produce strong feelings about them (Bodenhausen et al., 1994). As is the case with attitudes and stereotypes, information inconsistent with a prejudice is less likely to be attended to and remembered accurately than is information consistent with a prejudice, making prejudice self-perpetuating.

Prejudice may be conscious and intentional; it may also be conscious and unintentional, or even unconscious and unintentional (Carter & Rice, 1997; Fazio et al., 1995; Greenwald & Banaji, 1995). Conscious but unintentional prejudice occurs among people who are confused about their beliefs. They know their prejudice is unjustified but retain it and, at times, unintentionally display it. Other people are unaware of their prejudice and even deny it, but it nonetheless manifests itself in actions or words.

Prejudice can stem from emotions in two ways. The presence of negative feelings may account for conscious prejudice, whether intentional or unintentional. But even if someone does not have negative feelings toward a group, prejudice can also arise from the *absence of positive feelings* (Pettigrew & Meertens, 1995), leading to unconscious prejudice. Thus, someone can be prejudiced against a group with whom he or she has no experience; for instance, someone from an Asian country might have a prejudice against people with red hair that is engendered by the absence of any positive feelings or experiences.

Some cognitive operations perpetuate unconscious prejudice. **Social categorization theory** proposes that people are driven to divide the world automatically into categories of "us" and "them." This sorting is done consciously as well as unconsciously. People usually think of their own group—the **ingroup**—favorably. The other group, the **outgroup,** is usually disliked, assumed to possess more undesirable traits, and generally believed to be more homogeneous (Brewer & Brown, 1998; Fiske, 1998; Judd et al., 1991; Lambert, 1995; Linville & Fischer, 1993; Rustemli et al., 2000; Vonk & van Knippenberg, 1995). When we identify with an ingroup, we are more inclined to like, trust, help, and cooperate with other ingroup members than we are to like, trust, help, and cooperate with outgroup members (Brewer & Brown, 1998). Our views of the ingroup and outgroup can lead to unconscious prejudice.

Another cognitive operation that can lead to unconscious prejudice is the *illusory correlation,* which is a tendency to overestimate the strength of a relationship between two things (Mullen & Johnson, 1990). This cognitive operation may explain why white people overestimate actual crime rates among African American men, and hence maintain their prejudice (Hamilton & Sherman, 1989). The *illusion of outgroup homogeneity* is an inclination to view an outgroup as more homogeneous (that is, it has members who are more similar to one another) than the ingroup. The corollary, *ingroup differentiation,* is the inclination to view members of an ingroup (that is, your own group) as more heterogeneous—members are more diverse than those of another group. Table 15.2 presents a summary of these unconscious cognitive operations that perpetuate prejudice.

TABLE 15.2

Cognitive Operations That Perpetuate Unconscious Prejudice

- *Social categorization:* Automatically classifying people as "us" or "them."
- *Illusory correlation:* Overestimating the strength of a relationship between two things.
- *Illusion of outgroup homogeneity:* Viewing other groups as more homogeneous, or as having members who are more similar to one another, than the ingroup.
- *Ingroup differentiation:* Viewing one's own group as more heterogeneous, or as having members who are more diverse, than an outgroup.

Social categorization theory: The theory that people are driven to divide the world automatically into categories of "us" versus "them."

Ingroup: An individual's own group.

Outgroup: A group different than a person's own.

For example, a research study found that non-Hispanic Americans were less likely to distinguish among different types of Latinos (a perceived outgroup from the point of view of the non-Hispanics) than were Latinos themselves. However, Latinos only differentiated their own subgroup from all other Latino groups; thus, Mexican Americans were more likely to categorize themselves as a particular group—the ingroup—and lump Cuban Americans and Puerto Ricans together as Latinos—the outgroup (Huddy & Virtanen, 1995).

When Bessie Delany was in dental school, a white professor failed her on some work that she knew was good. A white girlfriend, also a dental student, offered to hand in Bessie's work as her own to see what grade the work would be given this time. Bessie's friend passed with the same work that had earned Bessie a failing grade.

Bessie's experience was one of discrimination; specifically, she suffered the effect of prejudiced behavior. Her professor's behavior was influenced by his prejudice against Bessie because of her race, her membership in a particular social category. As with stereotypes, people discriminate on the basis of just about anything that distinguishes groups: gender, race, social class, hair color, religion, college attended, height, and on and on. As with prejudice, discrimination may be subtle, and sometimes even unconscious.

Most Americans believe discrimination is wrong; and when their own discriminatory behavior is pointed out to them, they are uncomfortable (Devine & Monteith, 1993), and they may subsequently reduce their discriminatory behaviors (Monteith, 1996). This phenomenon provides another example of the way we act to reduce cognitive dissonance: Becoming aware of the discrepancy between attitudes and behavior leads to the discomfort of cognitive dissonance, which can be reduced through changing future behaviors.

WHY PREJUDICE? The effects of prejudice are limiting, damaging, and painful. Why then does prejudice exist? The *realistic conflict theory* (Bobo, 1983) suggests a

FIGURE 15.3
The Creation of Prejudice: The Robber's Cave Study

Eleven-year-old boys at a special overnight summer camp (called the Robber's Cave) were the participants in this study. In the initial phase of the study, the boys were randomly divided into two groups and separated from each other for a week. During this time, activities fostered a sense of cohesion in each group.

During the 2-week-long second phase, the two groups competed for highly desired prizes such as pocket knives and medals. Conflict between the two groups quickly escalated from name calling to direct acts (destroying the other group's personal property). Negative attitudes as well as negative behavior developed, with each group labeling the other with pejorative terms such as "coward."

In the third phase, the two groups were brought together to work on a number of superordinate goals such as restoring the camp's water supply. Tensions between the groups dissolved by the 6th day of this phase.

reason: competition for scarce resources such as good housing, jobs, and schools. As groups compete for these resources, increasingly negative views of the other groups take form, eventually becoming prejudice.

A classic experiment, the Robber's Cave study, showed how easily prejudice can be created from competition (see Figure 15.3; Sherif et al., 1961). A set of 11-year-old boys was divided into two groups, Eagles and Rattlers, at a special overnight camp called the Robber's Cave. The two groups competed for valued prizes. Conflict between the two groups quickly escalated into prejudice and discrimination, with the groups calling each other names and destroying each other's property. However, such attitudes and behavior stopped when the two groups no longer competed for resources but cooperated for larger, mutually beneficial goals such as restoring the camp's water supply. Although the study has several limitations (it is unclear if the findings generalize to girls, nonwhite boys, or adults), it does illustrate how prejudice can both develop and dissipate (Sherif et al., 1961).

The Robber's Cave study supports the view of realistic conflict theory that competition between groups for scarce resources can produce prejudice. But are scarcity and competition necessary to produce prejudice, or can it arise without them? Social categorization theory provides one explanation for prejudice in the absence of scarcity or competition: In this view, the psychological forces leading to ingroup favoritism are so powerful that creating even an *arbitrary* "us" and "them" can lead to unconscious favoritism and discriminatory behavior (Feather, 1996; Perdue et al., 1990). This social categorization can lead to discrimination in two distinct ways: (1) The ingroup is actively favored; and (2) the outgroup is actively disfavored.

Although social categorization can perpetuate a skewed picture of other people, it is efficient because once we've made an "us" versus "them" distinction, we can then use our stereotypes about "us" and "them" to understand behavior, saving us the effort of paying close attention to other people and actively processing our observations of their behavior. Because we expect certain behaviors from outgroup members, just being in their presence can activate our stereotypes about them (Bargh et al., 1996). We may then behave in ways that elicit behavior from an outgroup member that is consistent with that stereotype, even if he or she wouldn't otherwise behave that way (Snyder, 1984, 1992). This process thus becomes a self-fulfilling prophecy: The elicited behavior confirms our stereotype, and we regard the outgroup member's behavior as "proof" of the validity of our prejudices (Fiske, 1998). However, our goals in a given situation or interaction can lessen the use of these cognitive shortcuts: If it is important to be accurate in our view of an outgroup member, we are more motivated to think actively, and perhaps accurately, about that person (Fiske, 1998).

Once a prejudicial attitude is in place, *social learning theory* (see Chapter 5) explains how it can be spread and passed through generations as a learned stereotype. Parents, peers, television, movies, and other aspects of the culture provide models of prejudice (Pettigrew, 1969). When prejudice is translated into words and actions, it may be reinforced. Scarce resources, competition, natural cognitive mechanisms, and learning may all contribute to the development and maintenance of prejudice.

What are children in Bosnia being taught about Gavrilo Princip, the man who started World War I by assassinating Archduke Franz Ferdinand D'Este of Austria-Hungary in 1914? Textbooks in the Serb-controlled part of Bosnia call the act heroic; a Croatian textbook refers to Princip as an "assassin trained and instructed by the Serbs to commit this act of terrorism"; and a Muslim textbook refers to him as a nationalist and says the resulting anti-Serbian rioting "was only stopped by police from all three ethnic groups" (Hedges, 1997). Social learning theory explains how these different perspectives can lead to prejudice toward other ethnic groups.

CHANGING PREJUDICE: EASIER SAID THAN DONE. Psychology has shown us how prejudice develops and deepens; equally important, can psychology show us how to arrest the development of prejudice? The answer is yes, but the task is not easily accomplished.

One method of decreasing prejudice is described by the *contact hypothesis,* which holds that increased contact between different groups will decrease prejudice between them (Pettigrew, 1981). Increased contact serves several purposes: (1) Both groups are more likely to become aware of similarities between the groups, which can enhance mutual attraction; (2) even though stereotypes resist change, when stereotypic views are met with enough inconsistent information or exceptions, those views *can* change (Kunda & Oleson, 1995); and (3) increased contact can shatter the illusion that the outgroup is homogeneous (Baron & Byrne, 1997).

TABLE 15.3

Conditions in Which Intergroup Contact Decreases Prejudice

Increased contact between two groups can decrease prejudice when

- The groups are cooperating toward a shared goal.
- The groups are similar in social, economic, or task-related status.
- Contact is informal and has the potential to create meaningful relationships.
- The interactions provide disconfirmation of each other's prejudicial views.
- Those in each group view members of the other as typical of their group.
- The setting assumes equality among participants.

Increased contact between two groups prejudiced against each other can decrease prejudice, but only if certain conditions are met (see Table 15.3). Did the increased contact between the Israelis and Palestinians at the Oslo peace conference fulfill all these conditions?

Recategorization: A means of reducing prejudice by shifting the categories of "us" and "them" so that the two groups are no longer distinct entities.

Increased contact works best under certain conditions, such as when working toward a shared goal and when all participants are deemed to be equal (see Table 15.3). For example, politically influential members of Israeli and Palestinian groups met informally and unofficially for sessions of intensive interactive problem solving. The increased contact that occurred while working on the larger goal of resolving obstacles to peace talks was partly successful in lowering the barriers between the two sides. After the Oslo Peace Accord in 1993, many of those involved viewed these informal group meetings as directly and indirectly laying the foundation for the beginning steps toward peace (Kelman, 1997). The meetings, although not designed to reduce prejudice, nonetheless fulfilled one of the steps in that direction: coming together to work toward a shared goal. Other conditions, however, were not met: The participants from the two sides were *not* equal (Brewer & Brown, 1978, 1998) nor did they view each other as typical of their respective populations. Although they were able to work together for this one overarching goal of beginning peace discussions, the larger task of hammering out an agreement and sticking to it did not progress as smoothly.

Another way to decrease prejudice is through **recategorization**—that is, shifting the categories of "us" and "them" so that the two groups are no longer distinct entities. Examples of recategorization are familiar in everyday life. An assembly-line worker who is promoted to management experiences recategorization: The identity of "us" and "them" changes. When distinctions between groups are minimized so that different groups can be thought of as a single entity, recategorization can decrease prejudice. Working together toward a common goal facilitates recategorization, such as occurred in the Robber's Cave study when, instead of being Eagles or Rattlers, all boys became simply campers who had no running water.

Many science fiction stories rely on recategorization to shift the animosity from country against country to a united Earth defending against a common enemy—aliens. Recategorization may decrease prejudice to the new members of the ingroup, but some outgroup is still likely to be thought of negatively (Tajfel, 1982). For example, in the movie Men in Black, *humans are allied with some aliens—a new definition of "us"—against a different type of alien.*

Attributions: Making Sense of Events

When you read about the Delany sisters' successes, how did you explain them? Did you say to yourself, *The sisters worked hard and persevered?* Or, *They were lucky?* Whatever your reaction, it reflects not only your attitudes, stereotypes, and prejudices, but the attributions you make. **Attributions** are our explanations for the causes of events or behaviors.

WHAT IS THE CAUSE? Usually, events and actions have many possible causes. An unreturned telephone call to a friend might be an indication that your friend is very busy, is annoyed at you, or simply is out of town. If a politician you admire changes position on an issue, do you explain the behavior as a sincere change of heart, a cave-in to heavy campaign contributors, or a calculated attempt to appeal to new supporters?

The particular attributions people make are of two broad types: internal and external. **Internal attributions** (also called *dispositional attributions*) explain a person's behavior in terms of that person's preferences, beliefs, goals, or other characteristics. For instance, if a friend leaves a math lecture really confused, you could attribute his confusion to internal factors: "I guess he's not very good at math." **External attributions** (also called *situational attributions*) explain a person's behavior in terms of the situation (Kelley, 1972; Kelley & Michela, 1980). If you make an external attribution for your friend's confusion, you might say, "The professor gave a really bad lecture today."

The attributions you make about events affect both you and other people (see Table 15.4): Blaming yourself for negative events (internal attribution) can suppress

Attribution: An explanation for the cause of an event or behavior.

Internal attribution: An explanation of someone's behavior that focuses on the person's beliefs, goals, or other dispositions; also called *dispositional attribution.*

External attribution: An explanation of behavior that focuses on the situation; also called *situational attribution.*

TABLE 15.4	**Types of Attributions**		
		INTERNAL ATTRIBUTIONS	**EXTERNAL ATTRIBUTIONS**
	Attributions about oneself	*Positive:* I did a good job because I'm smart.	*Positive:* I did a good job because the task was easy.
		Negative: I did a bad job because I'm inept.	*Negative:* I did a bad job because the time allotted for the task was too short.
	Attributions about others	*Positive:* She did a good job because she's smart.	*Postive:* She did a good job because the task was easy.
		Negative: She did a bad job because she's inept.	*Negative:* She did a bad job because the time allotted for the task was too short.

your immune system (Segerstrom et al., 1996; see Chapter 12). Blaming yourself or others affects behavior: Mothers who view their children's misbehavior as the children's fault are likely to discipline their children more harshly than mothers who attribute such misbehavior to other causes, such as their mothering (Slep & O'Leary, 1998).

People at times behave in ways that do not reflect enduring traits, goals, beliefs, feelings, and other internal characteristics. How can you tell the difference—how do you decide whether to attribute someone's behavior to internal or external causes? Take the following situation: When Sadie wanted a job teaching at a high school, there were no black high school teachers in New York. At Bessie's urging, Sadie applied for the job. After her application was received, school administrators asked Sadie to come in for a meeting; she simply didn't go. (She later apologized, explaining she had "forgotten.") She subsequently received a letter that offered her the job. When she appeared on the first day of school, the school administrators were very surprised to find out she was black but did not deny her the job. Did Sadie's decision to miss the face-to-face interview reflect an enduring "doesn't play by the rules" trait, or was it based on the realities of that particular situation? How do we decide? Harold Kelley's **theory of causal attribution** identifies rules for deciding whether to attribute a behavior to a person's enduring traits or to the situation. In this view, when people try to understand the behavior of others, they automatically, without conscious awareness, take into account three dimensions: consensus, consistency, and distinctiveness.

> *Consensus.* Would other people react similarly in the situation? If so, greater weight should be given to the situation than to personal traits. For example, would other black women applying for the high school teaching job that Sadie eventually obtained not show up for the face-to-face interview? If so, the behavior has high consensus.
>
> *Consistency.* Has the person responded in the same way in the same situations? If so, the cause of the behavior is likely to be stable (either internal or external). For example, if Sadie avoided personal interviews when applying for similar jobs, her behavior would have high consistency.
>
> *Distinctiveness.* Has the person responded differently in situations that are not similar? If so, the cause may be situational. For example, if Sadie didn't usually miss meetings or appointments on purpose, her behavior in this case has high distinctiveness.

According to Kelley's theory, you attribute someone's behavior to internal causes if consensus and distinctiveness are low and consistency is high. In contrast, if consensus, consistency, and distinctiveness are all high, you attribute the behavior to external causes. You attribute behavior to both internal and external causes if consensus is low and consistency and distinctiveness are high. If we knew that Sadie's behavior during the application process had high consensus, consistency, and distinctiveness, we would be able to attribute her behavior to external causes.

Do people really think this way? If you follow Kelley's rules, making causal attributions involves a lot of cognitive work. Nonetheless, people apparently do use all the factors proposed by Kelley if an event or behavior is either unexpected or has a negative outcome. In other cases, however, people usually take shortcuts, letting their general beliefs and biases guide their judgments.

TAKING SHORTCUTS: ATTRIBUTIONAL BIASES. Like stereotypes, **attributional biases** are cognitive shortcuts for determining attributions that generally occur outside our awareness. They help lessen the cognitive load required to make sense of the world, but they can lead to errors. These errors have implications for social relationships, the legal system, and social policy. Suppose, for example, you are a member of a jury and hear that the defendant confessed to the crime. It turns out that the

Theory of causal attribution: Rules for deciding whether to attribute a given behavior to a person's enduring traits or to the situation.

Attributional bias: A cognitive shortcut for determining attribution that generally occurs outside our awareness.

confession was extracted after many hours of tough, coercive questioning by police. The judge then throws out the confession, striking it from the record, and tells you, the jury, to ignore it. Would you? Could you? Researchers using mock juries found that jurors in this situation assume that the confession was heartfelt and vote guilty more often than jurors who do not hear about a confession (Kassin & Wrightsman, 1981). The "jurors" are demonstrating the **fundamental attribution error** (Ross et al., 1977), the strong tendency to interpret other people's behavior as caused by internal (dispositional) causes rather than external (situational) ones. In the courtroom example, jurors would thus be more likely to view the confession as evidence of guilt (an internal, dispositional attribute) than coercion (an external, situational attribute).

As its name suggests, the fundamental attribution error is one of the most common attributional biases and a frequent source of error. Like other aspects of social cognition, it is affected by mood: When we are in a bad mood, we use this bias less, and when we are in a good mood, we use it more (Forgas, 1998). The fundamental attribution error is at work, for example, when the sight of a homeless man on a bench leads us to assume his plight is due to an internal trait such as laziness rather than external factors such as a run of bad luck, a high unemployment rate, and a lack of affordable housing. The fundamental attribution error helps perpetuate discrimination because fault is attributed to the person, not to the circumstances. Once you make the fundamental attribution error, you are likely to ignore the context of future behavior (that is, the surrounding situation), and thus the effect of the initial error is multiplied.

Related to the fundamental attribution error is the **self-serving bias** (Brown & Rogers, 1991; Miller & Ross, 1975), the inclination to attribute your failures to external causes and your successes to internal ones. A result of the self-serving bias is the **actor–observer effect** (Jones & Nisbett, 1971), which is the inclination to attribute your own behavior to external factors but to attribute others' behavior to internal factors. Together these can be summarized as: "I can do no wrong, but you can do no right" (Baron & Byrne, 1997, p. 58). As a result, you consider the negative actions of others as arbitrary and unjustified, but perceive your own negative acts as understandable and justifiable (Baumeister et al., 1990). You are angry and slam things around because you've had a terrible day; your roommate throws tantrums because he or she has an awful temper. A society as a whole may engage in this type of bias, leading one culture, ethnic group, or nation to attribute positive values and traits to its own group, and negative values and traits to other cultures and ethnic groups, sustaining ethnic conflict (Rouhana & Bar-Tal, 1998).

Not all cultures use these various biases to the same degree. Just as different cultures promote different personality traits (see Chapter 10), they also use attributional biases somewhat differently. For example, accounts of crimes in Chinese-language newspapers are more likely to give external explanations, whereas for the same offense, English-language newspapers are more likely to emphasize internal factors (Morris & Peng, 1994).

Attributions can also be distorted by a **belief in a just world** (Lerner, 1980), the assumption that people get what they deserve. Because most Americans are richer than most Egyptians, Colombians, or Bulgarians, they must, according to this bias, also be smarter or work harder. According to the belief in a just world, if you get what you deserve, you must have done something to deserve what you get—notice the circular reasoning here! The belief in a just world can shape reactions to violent crime (particularly rape; Karuza & Carey, 1984) and contributes to the practice of *blaming the victim*. For example, those who strongly believe in a just world are more likely than others to view AIDS as a deserved punishment for homosexual behavior (Glennon & Joseph, 1993) and to view the plight of a disadvantaged group, such as immigrants, as deserved (Dalbert & Yamauchi, 1994). This belief maintains discriminatory behaviors (Lipkus & Siegler, 1993). Table 15.5 summarizes these attributional biases.

Fundamental attribution error: The strong tendency to interpret other people's behavior as due to internal (dispositional) causes rather than external (situational) ones.

Self-serving bias: A person's inclination to attribute his or her own failures to external causes and successes to internal causes, but to attribute other people's failures to internal causes and their successes to external causes.

Actor–observer effect: A person's inclination to attribute his or her own behavior to external factors but to attribute others' behavior to internal factors.

Belief in a just world: An attributional bias that assumes people get what they deserve.

TABLE 15.5

Attributional Biases

ATTRIBUTIONAL BIAS	DEFINITION
Fundamental attribution error	The strong inclination to explain someone's behavior in terms of internal causes rather than external ones.
Self-serving bias	The attribution of your failures to external causes and your successes to internal causes.
Actor–observer effect	The inclination to attribute your own behavior to external factors but to attribute others' behavior to internal factors.
Belief in a just world	The assumption that people get what they deserve, which contributes toward blaming the victim.

LOOKING AT LEVELS

Punishing Rapists

Think about how we can understand people's different beliefs about how severely rapists should be punished. The death penalty? At the level of the brain, we have seen that among identical twins reared apart, certain attitudes, such as the attitude toward the death penalty, are in part heritable; genetic factors indirectly affect this attitude, which can range from very much in favor to very much opposed. These attitudes will affect how we evaluate information about whether the death penalty is a successful deterrent in reducing crime. However, people's attitudes about the death penalty may not predict how they would vote on it unless their attitudes are strong, or based on direct experience with a capital crime.

At the level of the person, you have developed stereotypes about the kinds of people who are rapists or who are raped. Because of the nature of stereotypes, should you meet a convicted rapist who doesn't fit your stereotype, you are not likely to change your stereotype, but rather will create a separate subtype of rapist, leaving the larger category unchanged. If you like this person, you might attribute blame for the rape to the victim, not the rapist.

This analysis at the level of the person may conflict with analysis at the level of the group. If a member of your group, perhaps defined by class, race, or family, has been raped by someone not in your group, you may vilify all members of outgroups, particularly the ones to which the rapist belongs. Thus, events at the three levels need not be entirely consistent and will interact in complex ways. Depending on the precise situation, events at one level or another may win out; if so, the result may be cognitive dissonance, perhaps leading you to modify your behavior or attitudes.

CONSOLIDATE!

▶ *1. Do first impressions really make a difference?*
First impressions are often given more weight than later information. The process of forming an initial impression is referred to as impression formation. In their efforts at impression management, people can use self-enhancement and other-enhancement strategies; the latter works well in employment settings.

▶ *2. What is the relationship between people's attitudes and their behaviors?* Attitudes affect how we process, encode, store, and retrieve information about the social world. Attitudes that are strong, stable, relevant, and salient are likely to affect behavior. Moreover, direct experience, mere exposure, and how we think we will be judged for the behavior all relate to

(continued)

an attitude's impact on behavior. Attitudes and future behavior can change as a result of cognitive dissonance and persuasion. A persuader is more likely to facilitate attitude change if he or she is an expert, is attractive, speaks quickly, or is perceived as honest.

▶ *3. What are stereotypes? Why do people have them? What are the differences between stereotypes and prejudice?* Stereotypes are beliefs or sets of beliefs about people in a particular social category; these beliefs help us to organize efficiently, though perhaps incorrectly, the multitude of information presented by the social world. These cognitive shortcuts can be influenced by our moods, can be outside of our awareness, and are resistant to change. Prejudice is a stereotype that contains a generally negative view toward members of a group; prejudice can be either conscious or unconscious, intentional or unintentional. Prejudice can arise from negative feelings or from the absence of positive feelings. Social categorization theory, the illusory correlation, and other cognitive biases can account for the perpetuation of unconscious prejudice.

▶ *4. How do we determine responsibility for positive and negative events, and what difference does it make?* Attributions are ways we explain the cause of events or behaviors. There are two types of attributions: internal (dispositional) and external (situational). The theory of causal attribution helps explain how people make attributions when an event is unexpected or has a negative outcome. The fundamental attribution error, the actor–observer effect, and the self-serving bias can lead to incorrect attributions.

SOCIAL BEHAVIOR: INTERACTING WITH PEOPLE

The Delanys had very definite ideas about how they were supposed to behave with people. Based on their ideas about marriage, both Sadie and Bessie decided early on not to marry. They both definitely wanted careers, and women of that era often had to choose between a career and marriage. Moreover, their father instilled in them a sense of self-reliance, evidenced by his advice to Sadie about going to Columbia University: He advised her not to take a scholarship because she might then feel indebted to the people who offered it. He encouraged her to pay for her own education.

The Delanys also had definite ideas about how other people should be treated. They were taught to help others, regardless of skin color; the family motto was "Your job is to help someone." The Delanys stuck by their beliefs, even when others did not agree. Bessie recounts a time she vacationed in Jamaica with a darker-skinned Jamaican-born friend. There, Bessie learned that there were two official classes of Jamaican Negroes: "white Negroes," who had more privileges in society, and "black Negroes," who were considered to be in a lower social class. The young women stayed with the family of Bessie's friend, who was a "black Negro." "White Negroes" extended invitations to Bessie (a lighter-skinned African American) and ignored her friend and hostess. Bessie refused all invitations until her friend was invited as well.

▶ 1. What psychological principles explain why we like certain people and not others?

▶ 2. Why do all groups have rules for social behavior and organization?

▶ 3. Why do we sometimes "go along" with others even when we don't want to? What makes us able to refuse?

▶ 4. Does being part of a group change our behavior? How do groups make decisions?

▶ 5. Are some people more helpful than others? Why would we not help other people?

Relationships: Having a Date, Having a Partner

Sadie and Bessie's white maternal great-great-grandmother had a liaison with a slave while her husband was away fighting in the War of 1812. This relationship produced two daughters, half-sisters to the seven children she had already had with her husband. When her husband returned home, he adopted the two girls as his own. No one knew exactly what happened to her lover, although it was rumored that he ran away on the husband's return. The relationship between the Delanys' great-great-grandmother and biological great-great-grandfather would appear to have been based on more than a passing interest, given that the relationship spanned a number of years. Why were they attracted to each other? Why are we attracted to certain people? Why do we like particular people, and love others?

As the Delany children's ancestors undoubtedly experienced over a century ago, and you may be experiencing now, relationships are strong stuff. They can lead to our most positive emotions and, as you saw in Chapter 12, can help us regulate our emotions in response to events outside the relationship (Berscheid & Reis, 1998). They can also be the source of negative emotions: When asked about the "last bad thing that happened to you," almost half the respondents reported conflict in a significant relationship (Cupach & Spitzberg, 1994).

LIKING: TO LIKE OR NOT TO LIKE. Even though Sadie and Bessie decided not to marry, they still had boyfriends. Why were they attracted to certain men—why are you attracted to some people and not others? First impressions play an initial role, as does *repeated contact,* which usually leads to a more positive evaluation of someone (Moreland & Zajonc, 1982; Zajonc, 1968). The Delany sisters recount that a lot of "racial mixing, especially after slavery days, was just attraction between people, plain and simple, just like happened in our family, on Mama's side. You know, when people live in close proximity, they can't help but get attracted to each other" (p. 76). More recent research recognizes that physical distance itself may no longer be as important in defining "repeated contact": Internet chat rooms and interest groups make it possible for a couple to "meet" and have a relationship without any physical contact (Parks & Roberts, 1998).

Similarity is a second factor in the development of liking; the more similar a stranger's attitudes are to your own, the more likely you are to be attracted (Tesser, 1993). In this case, the adage "Opposites attract" has *not* been borne out by research. Similarity of preferred activities (Lydon, Jamieson et al., 1988), even similar ways of communicating, can lead to increased attraction and liking. For instance, we are more likely to be attracted to someone whose nonverbal cues are the same as those used in our own culture (Dew & Ward, 1993). In general, the greater the similarity, the more probable it is that our liking for another person will endure (Byrne, 1971).

A third, and major, factor is *physical attraction* (Collins & Zebrowitz, 1995; Hatfield & Sprecher, 1986). In part, the role of physical attraction in liking may be influenced by our stereotypes about attractive people—such as that they are smarter and happier. Although the stereotype that people who are physically more attractive possess more desirable attributes is found in different cultures, what constitutes "more desirable" differs across cultures. For instance, in Korea (a collectivist country; see Chapters 9 and 10), attractive people are thought to have greater integrity and concern for others—qualities more valued in that collectivist culture than in individualist Western ones (Wheeler & Kim, 1997).

Can all human beings agree on what makes someone attractive? Research that seeks to answer this question has generally focused on facial features. What makes a man attractive to women are large eyes, a large chin, prominent cheekbones, and a big smile (Cunningham et al., 1990); men prefer women with a small nose, prominent cheekbones, and a big smile (Cunningham, 1986). Findings of what constitutes attractiveness are consistent across cultures. For example, when shown photographs of faces of Hispanic, black, Asian, and white American women, ratings of attractiveness by recent Asian and Hispanic male immigrants were similar to those of American black and white men (Cunningham et al., 1995). There is some evidence that cultures rate as attractive faces that are "average" looking—that is, their proportions approximate the population average (Jones & Hill, 1993). One theory that explains this preference is that "average" faces are more likely to look familiar because they are more similar to the faces of the rest of the population, and familiarity, via the mere exposure effect, can lead to liking. We also prefer faces that are symmetrical (Grammer & Thornhill, 1994). Thus, one proposal is that people's preference for symmetry reflects a desire to choose a mate who "looks healthy" because facial asymmetries may reflect the presence of disease (Grammer & Thornhill, 1994; Thornhill & Gangestad, 1993). There is also evidence that people prefer men's and women's faces that are "feminized"—that is, faces that reflect higher levels of female hormones (Perrett et al., 1998; see Chapter 3).

LOVING: HOW DO I LOVE THEE? Despite all the poems and plays, novels and movies, that chronicle, celebrate, and analyze love, its mystery endures. Its variations, components, styles, and fate over time have all been examined by psychologists. Loving appears to be a qualitatively different feeling from liking, not simply very strong liking (Rubin, 1970). Moreover, attitudes about and experiences with love appear to be similar across cultures as diverse as Russia, Japan, and the United States (Sprecher, Aron, et al., 1994).

People talk about "loving" all sorts of things in all sorts of ways. You might say you love a pet, a friend, a parent, a mate, and pizza with anchovies; obviously you don't mean quite the same thing in each case. Sexual or **passionate love**—the intense, often sudden feeling of being "in love"—involves sexual attraction, a desire for mutual love and physical closeness, arousal, and a fear that the relationship will end. **Compassionate love** is marked by very close friendship, mutual caring, liking, respect, and attraction (Caspi & Herbener, 1990).

What do the various sorts of love have in common, and how can we understand their differences? Robert Sternberg has proposed a **triangular model of love** (1986a, 1988a). Love, he says, has three dimensions: (1) passion (including sexual desire); (2) intimacy (emotional closeness and sharing); and (3) commitment (the conscious decision to be in the relationship). Particular relationships reflect different proportions of each dimension, in amounts that are likely to vary over time (see Figure 15.4). According to Sternberg's theory, most types of love relationships involve two of the three components; only "consummate love" has passion, intimacy, *and* commitment.

Attachment style is another way of thinking about different kinds of love relationships. The attachment style with a partner stems from the interaction pattern developed between parent and child (Waller & Shaver, 1994). For instance, adults who seek closeness and interdependence in relationships and are not worried about the possibility of the loss of the relationship, about 59% of an American sample, are said to have a *secure* style of attachment (Mickelson et al., 1997). Those who are uncomfortable with intimacy and closeness, about 25% of an American sample, have an *avoidant* style and structure their daily lives so as to avoid closeness (Tidwell et al., 1996). Those who want but simultaneously fear a relationship

Passionate love: An intense feeling that involves sexual attraction, a desire for mutual love and physical closeness, arousal, and a fear that the relationship will end.

Compassionate love: A type of love marked by very close friendship, mutual caring, liking, respect, and attraction.

Triangular model of love: A theory of love marked by the dimensions of (1) passion (including sexual desire), (2) intimacy (closeness), and (3) commitment.

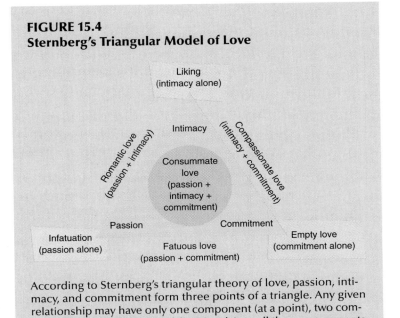

FIGURE 15.4
Sternberg's Triangular Model of Love

According to Sternberg's triangular theory of love, passion, intimacy, and commitment form three points of a triangle. Any given relationship may have only one component (at a point), two components (one of the sides of the triangle), or all three components (the center of the triangle).

have an *anxious–ambivalent* style (Hazan & Shaver, 1990); about 11% of Americans have this style. Although by extrapolation from these studies, a majority of Americans have a secure style (Hazan & Shaver, 1987), an anxious–ambivalent style is more common in Japan and Israel, and an avoidant style more common in Germany (Shaver & Hazan, 1994).

Are our love relationships in part genetically determined? Apparently not. When twins were tested on six scales that measured different aspects of romantic relationships, little evidence of heritability was found (Waller & Shaver, 1994). As Plomin and his colleagues (1997, p. 205) put it, "Perhaps love *is* blind, at least from the DNA point of view." If our relationship style isn't genetically influenced, are we doomed to repeat the style of our childhood interactions with our parents? Although these early interactions affect attachment style, the outcome is not set in stone at childhood's end. The relationships we have as adults can change our attachment style (Shaver & Hazan, 1994).

If you learned the psychology of love from soap operas and romantic comedies, you might expect that romantic love is a woman's domain. The young bachelor wants his freedom, but to get his girl he must bind himself to home and hearth in marriage. Contrary to these stereotypes, however, men are more romantic than women (Dion & Dion, 1988). Men report being in love earlier in their relationships than women, and the idea that love lasts forever is endorsed by men more frequently than women (Peplau & Gordon, 1985).

As you may have experienced in your relationships, a sense of intimacy usually progresses in stages (Honeycutt et al., 1998), and how we feel in the relationship influences the relationship itself. A growing feeling of intimacy comes from three factors: (1) feeling understood by your partner; (2) feeling "validated," that is, feeling that your emotions and point of view are respected; and (3) feeling that the other person cares for you (Reis & Shaver, 1988). As a relationship progresses, love seems to deepen over time (Sprecher, 1999). And just as mood can influence other aspects of our lives, such as memory and stereotyping, it influences us in this area as well: We are more likely to think our relationships are good when we're in a positive mood. Moreover, our attributions for serious conflicts in our relationships shift in response to our moods: In a bad mood, we are more likely to attribute relationship problems to vague, stable, internal factors; in a good mood, we are more likely to attribute the causes of conflict to specific, unstable, external factors (Forgas et al., 1994).

As noted, the way we think about people, things, and events can have a powerful effect on our feelings, behavior, and subsequent thoughts. This is also true of relationships. If you are asked to think about the external reasons and pressures to stay in a relationship (having something to do on Saturday nights, your parents' approval), you will view commitment to the relationship as less likely, and report less love for your partner, than if you think about the enjoyment you experience in the relationship and other intrinsic motivational factors (Seligman et al., 1980).

Research results indicate that sex is only one facet of lasting love. Myers (1993) summarizes four factors that determine whether love will be sustained. First, "similarity breeds content" (p. 170): You are more likely to stay involved with someone who is similar to you. Opposites may attract initially, but not for long (Byrne, 1971). Second, successful couples have sex more often than they argue, and people in successful marriages have sex more often than those in less successful marriages. Third, successful couples are intimate: They share their innermost thoughts and feelings. Fourth, people in successful marriages share in decision making and in the daily burdens of maintaining a house and home.

Reciprocity also has a part in close relationships: If you want to sustain close relationships, you should help people who help you, and not hurt them (Gouldner, 1960). If someone does you a favor, you have an obligation to return the favor in the future, although this debt will not necessarily concern you indefinitely (Burger et al., 1997). However, in successful long-term relationships members do not keep track of debts, assuming that they will average out over time.

MATING PREFERENCES: YOUR CAVE OR MINE? Is love the reason why people settle down and have children? According to evolutionary theory, among our ancestors those couples more closely bonded to each other and to their children were more likely to have offspring who survived. Thus, evolutionary theorists propose, humans today are genetically predisposed not only to search for sex but also to fall in love and to tend to their children (Trivers, 1972).

Finding someone to be attractive and liking, or even loving, that person is different from choosing him or her as a mate; we may date people we wouldn't necessarily want to marry. Why do we view certain people as potential mates, and not others? Evolutionary theorists propose that men look for certain physical attributes that signal fertility and health, such as a well-proportioned body and symmetrical features (Thornhill & Gangestad, 1993). This view is supported by research with identical female twins; the twin whose face was more symmetrical was rated as more attractive (Mealey et al., 1999). In contrast, women find attractive men who appear to be able to protect and nourish them and their children; in modern society, researchers translate this as having good earning potential (Buss, D. M., 1989, 1999; Sprecher, Sullivan, et al., 1994). Evolutionary psychologists have argued that characteristics associated with reproduction are particularly likely to have been shaped by natural selection. Buss, D. M., (1989) asked people in 37 countries to rank order how important they believed 18 different characteristics are in ideal mates. In most respects, men and women valued the characteristics similarly; everybody agreed, for example, that kindness and intelligence are of paramount importance, and that emotional stability, dependability, and a good disposition are important (see also Cramer et al., 1996). Respondents also valued mutual attraction and love. However, men and women did not have identical desires: Men tended to focus on physical attractiveness, whereas women tended to focus on wealth and power. Basing his view on evolutionary theory (Trivers, 1972, 1985), Buss (1994) has argued that women seek characteristics in men that would direct resources to their children, whereas men seek characteristics in women that indicate high fertility.

However, Speed and Gangestad (1997) found slightly different results when they collected less subjective ratings. In their study, they asked members of a sorority and a fraternity house to nominate other members whom they felt scored high on specific qualities such as physical attractiveness and likelihood of financial success. The investigators then examined which of these characteristics predicted the frequency with which those nominated were asked out on dates. Perhaps the most interesting results concerned the men. As expected, romantically popular men were seen by their peers as confident, outgoing, and "trend-setting." However, they were not seen as likely to succeed financially or as the best leaders, both characteristics that would seem to reflect the qualities that evolution is supposed to favor in males.

Evolutionary theorists propose that women are attracted to men who will be good providers and men are attracted to women who have physical attributes associated with fertility. However, not all research supports this view: As women gain more economic power, they become more interested in a man's attractiveness.

Other studies have shown that as women come to have more economic power, their preference in mates becomes more similar to men's—that is, physical attractiveness becomes more important (Eagly & Wood, 1999; Gangestad, 1993). Women's preference for men who make good providers may reflect women's historic economic dependence on men rather than a true biological preference. In general, then, the sex differences are more pronounced in studies that use self-reports versus actual behavior (Feingold, 1990) and in situations in which women have less economic power.

However, evolution is more than natural selection (see Chapters 1 and 2); we have inherited some characteristics not because they are adaptive in themselves but rather because they are associated with other characteristics that are adaptive. Nor are the brain's circuits all dictated from birth: Learning rewires the brain, and development itself allows the environment to shape the way the brain works. Culture obviously

What constitutes an "attractive" body type differs over time and across cultures. Women who today in America would be considered overweight or even obese have a body type that has been and continues to be attractive in some cultures.

plays an important role in shaping mate preferences: What is deemed an attractive body type changes with time (Wolf, 1991). Also, the characteristics that make a man a good provider depend in part on the culture; the properties that make a man a good rancher are not necessarily those of a good stockbroker. In short, it would be a serious error to assume that what people find attractive or unattractive can be entirely explained by analyses of what was useful for mating among our distant ancestors.

How else, then, do psychologists explain why we get into and stay in relationships? Another approach looks for explanations in the immediate situation. **Social exchange theory** offers a rather dry-eyed view, holding that individuals are like accountants, trying to maximize the gains and minimize the losses in their relationships. If the losses outweigh the gains, the relationship is likely to end. In order for a relationship to continue it must be profitable enough for both parties (Kelley, 1979; Sprecher, 1998; Thibaut & Kelley, 1959). But what is "enough"? The profits and losses in a relationship are compared with expectations based on past relationships, or the *comparison level*. Thus, if you have just left an abusive relationship, your comparison level is likely to be low, and a relationship without abuse might be seen as one providing a big profit.

In short, we enter, maintain, and leave relationships for a multitude of reasons. Unless a relationship is arranged for us by others, as it is in some cultures, attractiveness and similarity are two key factors that influence whom we like and whom we love.

Social Organization: Group Rules, Group Roles

If you live with other people, in the same apartment or on the same dorm floor, you might agree that the people in your living unit constitute a group, even if you don't get along. But if you live in a building with a number of apartments, or a residence hall with many floors, would everyone living there be considered part of a larger group, even if they don't all know one another? What, exactly, constitutes a group? Social psychologists have long wrestled with such questions and have come up with a number of definitions. There are some commonalities, though, in the use of the term **group:** regular interaction among members, some type of emotional connection with one another, a common frame of reference, and some type of interdependence (Levine &

The military tries to instill a sense of "groupness" in new recruits: The group's goal, such as a successful military action, is more important than an individual's goal, such as staying alive.

Moreland, 1998). In a group, each of us may feel, think, and act less from the point of view of an individual and more from the point of view of a group member. Military training, such as boot camp, is a dramatic example of the shift from feeling like an individual to feeling like a group member: Loyalties and actions are no longer driven by individual goals but by group goals. In contrast, the use of the Internet for communication, although creating an opportunity to be part of a larger group in cyberspace, may not really promote a sense of interdependence, emotional connection, or "groupness." In one study, researchers examined the use of the Internet among people who did not previously have Internet access. Those who used the Internet more had decreased the size of their social circle from that of their pre-Internet days (and you know from Chapter 12 that social circles can provide a buffer against the harmful effects of stress), had less family communication, and experienced more loneliness and depression (Kraut et al., 1998).

At the other extreme of group experience is **deindividuation**, traditionally defined as the loss of sense of self that occurs when people in a group are literally *anonymous*—their identities are unknown to others in the group. This is often the situation in crowds. With deindividuation, attention is focused on external events, and a high level of arousal is experienced (Diener, 1977). When this occurs, the members of this temporary group respond to external cues and immediate feelings and act on them without monitoring the appropriateness of their behaviors. Violence by fans at European soccer matches has usually been explained by deindividuation. However, a meta-analytic study on deindividuation suggests that loss of self is not the precipitating cause of the behaviors attributed to deindividuation, as has traditionally been thought. Rather, the behaviors result from the sense, shared by members of the crowd, that in this limited circumstance certain behaviors are permissible that would not be acceptable otherwise (Postmes & Spears, 1998).

Recent research suggests that deindividuation may not be so much a loss of sense of self as situation-specific behaviors that are inconsistent with general expectations of appropriate behavior.

As a member of a group, you may at times be faced with the choice of acting in your own interest or in that of the common good. Consider a social dilemma that has been generalized as the *tragedy of the commons* (Hardin, 1968): If herders graze their animals on common pasture, each can gain by being able to feed more animals than could otherwise be maintained on an individual pasture, and so the sizes of the herds can grow. But if all the herders increase their herds, the larger number of animals will overgraze the common pasture, eventually destroying it, and everyone will lose. Social dilemmas such as the tragedy of the commons occur in many situations. Not voting may be in your interest because it saves you the time and trouble of getting to the voting booth. But if everyone follows this course, we all end up without a republic. In serving their interests, factory owners pollute the air; but if all factory owners follow this practice, in the end none of us will be able to breathe. Social organizations, both governmental and private, work to resolve such conflicts and dilemmas. Groups survive, resolve conflict, and exert control over their members with the aid of several organizational elements.

NORMS. The Delany sisters recount that in their hometown of Raleigh, North Carolina, even strangers passing on the street would nod and say good morning or good evening. But when Sadie and Bessie moved to New York City, they discovered that courteous behavior toward strangers did not always end in a pleasant exchange, and they had to learn a new way of behaving in their new social context. Perhaps you, like them on their arrival in New York, have at one time or another been the "new kid on the block"—in school or college, in a new neighborhood, in an already established group of people. Chances are you didn't know the "rules"—how people were supposed to behave toward one another, and especially how you, a new member, were supposed to behave. Once you figured things out by watching other people (Gilbert, 1995)—an obvious case of observational learning—you probably felt more comfortable in the group. And, in fact, groups create such rules and structures to help the group function.

Social exchange theory: A theory that proposes that individuals act to maximize the gains and minimize the losses in their relationships.

Group: A social entity characterized by regular interaction among members, emotional connection, a common frame of reference, and interdependence.

Deindividuation: The loss of sense of self that occurs when people are in a group but are anonymous.

Norms can affect all kinds of behavior, including a cold sufferer's willingness to wear a surgical mask when out in public. This Japanese woman is behaving according to one of her culture's proscriptive norms: It is frowned on for a cold sufferer to go outside without a mask and spread cold germs to others.

The rules that implicitly or explicitly govern members of a group are called **norms.** They are, in essence, shared belief systems that are enforced through the group's use of sanctions, or penalties (Cialdini & Trost, 1998). Just as individuals have attitudes, groups have norms (Wellen et al., 1998). There are two kinds of norms: *prescriptive norms,* which dictate which behaviors are acceptable (such as how much physical affection is allowed in a group), and *proscriptive norms,* which dictate what behaviors are not acceptable (such as passing gas while at a formal restaurant). Some groups or cultures have "perverse" norms, norms that are formally agreed on but rarely enforced. On Boston's streets, for example, a traffic law for cars is that right turns may be made from the right lane only; however, it is not uncommon to see someone turn right from the left-hand lane in full view of police, who do not ticket for the offense. When perverse norms exist, those in authority maintain control by deciding when they are enforced (Dols, 1992, cited in M. Bond & Smith, 1996).

Norms pervade our everyday experience, defining the behaviors that make us good members of a family, friends, neighbors, partners, employees, employers, students, teachers, and so on. Norms may vary from group to group, or by age, sex, race, social class, or geographic region. For example, in the culture of the American South, honor is very important. Male southerners are more likely than northern men to think their reputation is threatened when others swear at them in public, and thus they respond with more aggressive behavior (Cohen et al., 1996). Moreover, Cohen and his colleagues found that southerners in general were more likely than northerners to view such aggressive responses as appropriate. Southern norms of appropriate reactions to an insult are reflected in the more lenient judicial sentences given to certain types of violent offenders (Nisbett & Cohen, 1996).

Although norms can endure over time, even if the members of the group change (Jacobs & Campbell, 1961), norms too can change. This is the case with the use of the title "Ms." When this form of address was introduced, it was seen as a title that would

TABLE 15.6

Personal Attitudes and Perceived Norms

Source: *Adapted from Perkins & Berkowitz (1986).*

What college students *think* are the norms for alcohol use are not necessarily accurate. Most students in a 1986 study had a more conservative view of alcohol use than they thought their peers did, but their peers were similarly conservative. This table shows the percentage of students personally agreeing with each item, and the percentage of students who thought that an item was the "norm" on campus. As you can see, the only time students' personal attitudes were near the perceived norm was in the lack of enthusiasm for total abstinence.

ITEM	PERSONAL ATTITUDES (% of students agreeing)	PERCEIVED NORM
Drinking is never a good thing to do.	1.4	0.1
Drinking is all right, but a student should never get "smashed."	12.7	0.8
An occasional "drunk" is okay as long as it doesn't interfere with grades or responsibilities.	66.0	35.4
An occasional "drunk" is okay even if it does occasionally interfere with grades or responsibilities.	9.3	33.2
A frequent "drunk" is okay if that's what the individual wants to do.	9.5	29.5

be used only by radical feminists. Now, however, Ms. is much more widely used and positively viewed (Crawford et al., 1998). Moreover, as adolescents in India watch Western television shows (and derive what they perceive of as Western norms), their attitudes about drugs, alcohol, and sex change, rejecting the social norms of Indian society and becoming more Western (Varma, 2000).

How we *perceive* norms is important. Even if those perceptions are not necessarily accurate, we still behave in accordance with them. For instance, some antidrug programs emphasize both *why* you should say no to drugs and *how* to say no. But it appears that training students *how* to say no leads them to think that offers of drugs, and drug use in general, are more common than they really are, thereby creating the impression of a pro–drug-use social norm and leading to an increase in drug use. This is particularly true for alcohol use among college students (see Table 15.6; Berkowitz, 1997). Programs that focus only on *why* you should say no appear to be more successful (Botvin, 1995; Cialdini & Trost; 1998; Donaldson, 1995; Hansen et al., 1988). Programs aimed at emphasizing a drug-abstinent norm or a moderate-drinking norm also appear to be effective (Barnett et al., 1996; Berkowitz, 1997).

This problem of falsely perceived norms may explain why eating disorder prevention programs that feature speakers who have recovered from an eating disorder may inadvertently lead students to develop eating disorder symptoms (Carter et al., 1997; Mann et al., 1997): Students inflate the perceived norm of eating disorders on campus after hearing and seeing the speaker and are thus led to change their behavior in the direction of the perceived norm.

ROLES AND STATUS. In contrast to norms, **roles** are the behaviors that members in different positions in a group are expected to perform. Groups often create different roles to fulfill different group functions. Sometimes roles are assigned officially, as when a group votes for a leader; sometimes roles are filled informally, without a specific election or appointment. Roles help a group delineate both responsibility *within* the group and responsibility *to* the group.

In a **status hierarchy,** different roles reflect the distribution of power in a group. The Delany sisters describe the status hierarchy of the South during and after Jim Crow laws: "White men were the most powerful, followed by white women. Colored people were absolutely below them and if you think it was hard for colored men, honey, colored women were on the bottom" (pp. 75–76). You can often tell who has a high-status position in a group from nonverbal cues: High-status members are more likely to maintain eye contact, be physically intrusive (somewhat "in your face"), and stand up straight (Leffler et al., 1982). You can also identify high-status members from what they say and how they say it: They are usually the ones who criticize or interrupt others or tell them what to do. In addition, other members direct their comments to the high-status member (Skvoretz, 1988). Perhaps because of the absence of nonverbal cues, social status differences have been found to be less prominent in groups communicating by e-mail as opposed to face to face (Dubrovsky et al., 1991).

Yielding to Others: Going Along With the Group

In Raleigh when the Jim Crow laws were in effect, black customers in a white-owned shoe store were supposed to sit in the back of the store to try on shoes. On one occasion when Sadie shopped for shoes, she was asked by the white owner, Mr. Heller, to sit in the back. She asked, "Where, Mr. Heller?" And he gestured to the back saying, "'Back there.' And I would say, 'Back *where?*' . . . Finally, he'd say, 'Just sit anywhere, Miss Delany.' And so I would sit myself down in the white section, and smile" (p. 84). What made Sadie able to resist Mr. Heller's request—or his order, backed by law? What made Mr. Heller give up his attempt to have Sadie comply with the law and social convention? What made him call her "Miss Delany" and not "Sadie"? What would you have done? In what circumstances do we go along with the group, do what someone asks of us, obey orders? When do we resist?

Norm: A shared belief that is enforced through a group's use of penalties.

Role: The behaviors that a member in a given position in a group are expected to perform.

Status hierarchy: The distribution of power in a group.

Conformity: A change of beliefs or actions in order to follow a group's norms.

CONFORMITY AND INDEPENDENCE: DOING WHAT'S EXPECTED. Social norms tell us how we ought to behave, and sometimes we change our beliefs or behavior in order to follow these norms. This change in beliefs or behavior because of pressure from others is known as **conformity**. For example, major league baseball players' wives live by an unwritten rule that they not go to the bars in hotels where the team is staying (Ortiz, 1997). The wife of a new player must decide whether to go along with this implicit norm. Similarly, immigrants must decide how much to conform to the norms of their new country and how much to retain the ways of their homeland (Lorenzo-Hernandez, 1998).

When and why do people conform? Suppose you are working in a study group that is trying to solve a complex engineering problem, or that you are part of a medical team trying to agree on a diagnosis of a particularly perplexing case. The majority agree on an answer that doesn't seem right to you. What would make you more likely to go along with the majority view? Research indicates that *task difficulty* increases conformity: The harder the task, the more you are likely to conform—at least in part because you are less sure of yourself. *Social comparison* theory (Festinger, 1950) is consistent with this explanation: All people are driven to evaluate their abilities and opinions. When their abilities or views cannot be measured objectively, they seek out others, particularly people similar to themselves, to serve as a basis of comparison (Morris et al., 1976). Thus, even when we are initially certain, the disagreement of other members of our group can make us doubt (Orive, 1988). This process can ex-

FIGURE 15.5
Asch's Conformity Study

Participants in Asch's classic study on conformity were shown lines similar to these and asked the following type of question: Here are three lines of different lengths and a fourth target line. Which of the three lines matches the target line?

Only two people have yet to give their opinions, but everyone else appears to have given the same incorrect answer. Which would you say was the correct line if you were next in line? Asch (1951, 1955) created this situation with the use of accomplices, and the true participant was the next-to-last person. Although 75% of participants conformed to the incorrect group response at least once, over the entire experiment, two thirds of responses were independent of the majority.

plain why people succumb to the pressure to conform and why group members are ill tempered toward those who do not agree with the majority view (Levine, 1989).

Uncertainty in the face of a difficult task and social comparisons, however, cannot be the only explanations for conformity; people may also conform when tasks are easy, as demonstrated in pioneering research by Solomon Asch (1951, 1955). If you had been a participant in Asch's original study, you would have found yourself in a group with five to seven others asked to perform a task of visual perception. You are all shown a target line and asked to say which of three other lines matches the length of the target line. Each person gives an answer aloud; you are next to last. This sounds like an easy task, as you can see in Figure 15.5, but it soon becomes perplexing. For 12 of the 18 times you are shown the lines, everyone else gives the wrong answer! Will you agree with the answer everyone else is giving?

In fact, in Asch's experiment only one person in the group was the true participant; the others were accomplices playing a role. Seventy-six percent of participants went along with the accomplices at least once, and overall approximately one third of participants' responses conformed with the obviously wrong majority.

Why would these people conform with the norm established by the group? Variations on Asch's original experiment showed that characteristics of the situation are part of the answer. When participants *wrote* their answers instead of announcing them to the group, they gave the correct response 98% of the time, reflecting the fact that participants accurately perceived the lines. *Social support* also influences conformity. If a group member openly disagrees with the group consensus, conformity is less likely (Morris & Miller, 1975). When Asch had one accomplice disagree—that is, give the correct answer—91% of actual participants did not conform with the group answer. Furthermore, the more *cohesive* a group—the more attraction and commitment members have toward it—the more likely members are to conform, as are those who identify more strongly with its norms (Prapavessis & Carron, 1997; Terry & Hogg, 1996). And when a member of a less powerful group, such as a social or political minority, is in a group with more powerful members, the minority member may be more likely to conform (Roll et al., 1996). In general, despite the pressure to conform to group norms, not everyone is equally affected (Trafimow & Finlay, 1996).

One person not given to conformity for its own sake was Sadie and Bessie Delany's maternal grandfather, James Millam. A white man, he fell in love with a free woman, Martha Logan, who was one quarter black; marriage between them was, at the time, illegal. In such situations, it was usual for the man to marry a white woman and establish the black woman as his mistress. Millam refused to conform to this convention; he lived openly with Martha Logan without benefit of marriage. Why would he not conform? Because to go along with the group, to conform, against one's beliefs or better judgment, leads to a loss of choice, of independence. The desire to retain a sense of individuality (Maslach et al., 1987) or control (Burger, 1992; Burger & Cooper, 1979) also provides reasons for not conforming. Thus, to understand someone's choice to conform, you need to look not only at the situation and the group but also at that person's characteristics—such as his or her commitment to the group or desire for individuality.

Were the people in Asch's study typical? All were men, but the results of later studies with women were similar (Eagly & Carli, 1981). However, Asch's original participants may have been influenced by their culture. His experiment has been repeated by many researchers in many countries, and studies in countries with a more collectivist orientation, such as China, found higher levels of conformity than did those in individualistic countries (R. Bond & Smith, 1996). Furthermore, the findings of conformity studies over the years suggest that conformity has decreased since Asch's original work (R. Bond & Smith, 1996). Thus, characteristics of the individual, his or her relationship to the group, characteristics of the group, and the larger culture can all affect conformity and independence.

COMPLIANCE: DOING WHAT YOU'RE ASKED. Even if you don't want to go along with a group's norms, you may be willing to comply with a direct request, as occurs when someone asks, "Could you please tell me how to get to the library?"

Compliance is a change in behavior brought about through a direct request rather than by social norms. When the driver of the car in the next lane gestures to you, asking to be let into your lane in front of you, you will either comply or not.

Without realizing it, you are a target of multiple requests for compliance each day, from television commercials, in conversations with friends, or through questions on a survey form. Skill at getting people to comply is key to success in many occupations, from sales and advertising to lobbying, politics, and health prevention programs. Psychologist Robert Cialdini decided to find out from "compliance professionals"—people in jobs such as advertising, fundraising, and door-to-door sales—exactly what they know about the subject. He inferred that the essence of effective compliance technique lies in six principles (Cialdini, 1994):

1. *Friendship/liking.* People are more likely to comply with a request from a friend than from a stranger.
2. *Commitment/consistency.* The likelihood of compliance increases when the request is consistent with a previous commitment.
3. *Scarcity.* People are more likely to comply with requests related to limited, short-term, rather than open-ended, opportunities.
4. *Reciprocity.* The likelihood of compliance rises when the request comes from someone who has provided a favor.
5. *Social validation.* The likelihood of compliance rises if people think that others similar to themselves would comply.
6. *Authority.* People tend to comply with a request if it comes from someone who appears to be in authority.

To see these principles at work, let's examine a few of the techniques most often used to win compliance. The commitment/consistency principle explains why a classic compliance technique, the **foot-in-the-door technique,** works so often. In this method, first you make an insignificant request; if you meet with compliance, you follow up with a larger request. Consider the study by Freedman and Fraser (1966), who had a male experimenter phone housewives, asking what soap they used. Three days later, the same man telephoned and asked if five or six people could perform a 2-hour inventory of everything in the housewife's cupboards, drawers, and closets. Fifty-three percent of the housewives who had agreed to the simple first request agreed to this much larger second request. In contrast, when housewives did not receive the first request but were asked to allow the inventory, only 22% complied.

The foot-in-the-door technique appears to work, at least in part, because people want to seem consistent. If you agree to the first request, you are being a nice person; declining the second request would call this self-perception into question. The consistency principle also explains the success of an unethical sales technique, the **lowball technique,** which consists of first getting someone to make an agreement, and then increasing the cost of that agreement. Suppose you see an advertisement for some shoes you've been eyeing—for a very low price. You go the store and are told that the shoes are no longer available at that price, but you can get them for a somewhat higher (although still discounted) price. What do you do? Many people would comply with the request to buy the shoes at the higher price.

Turning the foot-in-the-door procedure backward also works; this is the **door-in-the-face technique.** You begin by making a very large request; when it is denied, as expected, you make a smaller request, for what you actually wanted in the first place. For instance, in one study (Cialdini et al., 1975), college students were stopped on campus and asked to serve as unpaid counselors to a group of juvenile delinquents for 2 hours a week for 2 years. Not surprisingly, no one agreed. Then the same students were asked to take the group on a 2-hour field trip. Fifty percent agreed. In contrast, when students were asked only to make the field trip without the larger, first request, only 17% agreed.

The door-in-the-face technique is a staple of diplomacy and labor–management negotiations. Why does it work? The reciprocity principle may hold the answer. If your first request is denied and you then make a smaller one, you appear to be making concessions, and the other party tries to reciprocate.

Compliance: A change in behavior prompted by a direct request rather than social norms.

Foot-in-the-door technique: A technique that achieves compliance by beginning with an insignificant request, which is then followed by a larger request.

Lowball technique: A compliance technique that consists of getting someone to make an agreement and then increasing the cost of that agreement.

Door-in-the-face technique: A compliance technique in which someone makes a very large request; when it is denied, as expected, a second, smaller request (the desired one) is made.

People sometimes go to surprising lengths to comply with a request. Kassin and Kiechel (1996) provided one example in a study that involved the *appearance* that participants had destroyed some data after being explicitly warned not to touch the ALT key on a keyboard. Sixty-nine percent of the participants agreed with a request to sign a confession that they had destroyed data—even though they had done no such thing. Nine percent made up details to support their (false) admission of guilt. You might suspect that something about the laboratory situation created an unnatural, unrealistic result. But Kassin and Kiechel were reproducing a result found in life: Innocent suspects sometimes comply with requests for a false confession to having committed a crime, even one as serious as murder (see Kassin, 1997, for a detailed discussion). Even more surprising, some of those who falsely confessed to a crime came to believe they actually committed it (see Chapter 6 for a discussion of how this can occur).

OBEDIENCE: DOING AS YOU'RE TOLD. If people can be so obliging in response to a polite request, what happens when they receive an order? Compliance with an order is called **obedience.** The nature of obedience attracted intense study in the United States after World War II, when the world heard about atrocities apparently committed in the name of obedience.

The most famous study of obedience was done by Stanley Milgram (1963). Milgram expected that Americans would not follow orders to inflict pain on innocent people. In testing this hypothesis, his challenge was to design a study that gave the appearance of inflicting pain without actually doing so. He hit on the following procedure: Suppose you volunteered to participate in a study of memory. You are asked to act the part of "teacher" (see Figure 15.6). You are paired with a "learner" (an accomplice), who, you are told, was asked to memorize a list of pairs of common words. You, the teacher, are to present one word from each pair and keep track of how well the learner does in correctly remembering the other word. If the learner makes a mistake, you are to administer a shock, increasing the voltage with each successive mistake. Although the shock generator is a phony and no shock at all is administered, you do not know this.

This is precisely what Milgram did; by pre-arrangement, at "120 volts" the learner shouted that the shocks were becoming too painful. At "150 volts" the learner asked to stop. At 180 he screamed that he couldn't stand the pain. At 300 volts he pounded on the wall and demanded to be set free. At 330 volts there was only silence—an "incorrect response" according to the directions of the experimenter, who stood beside the teacher.

How far would you go in obeying the experimenter's instructions? If you were like the participants in Milgram's study, when the learner cried out in pain or refused to go on, you would turn to the

Obedience: Compliance with an order.

FIGURE 15.6
The Milgram Obedience Study

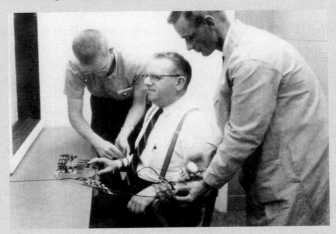

Each participant was paired with another man, having drawn lots to decide who would be the "teacher" and the "learner." In fact, the participant was always the teacher. The learner was always the same 47-year-old accountant who was an accomplice in the study. The man who introduced himself as the experimenter was an actor. The learner was asked to memorize a list of pairs of common words; the teacher was to present the words, keep track of how well the learner did, and punish the learner for incorrect responses. The teacher watched as the learner was brought to a cubicle where the experimenter asked him to sit down and strapped him in a chair to "prevent excess movement." The experimenter attached shock electrodes to his wrist. Throughout the remainder of the study, the teacher could not see the learner, and all communication was via an intercom.

The teacher was seated in front of the shock generator. The generator had 30 switches labeled in 15-volt increments from 15 to 450 volts. A description below each switch ranged from "Slight Shock" to "Danger: Severe Shock." The labels under the last two switches were ominous: "XXX." At the outset the teacher was given a sample shock of 45 volts so that he could know what it felt like.

experimenter for instructions, who would reply that the experiment had to proceed and that he would take full responsibility. Would you obey? When Milgram described the experiment to a group of psychiatrists, they predicted that only a "pathological fringe" of at most 2% of the population would go to the maximum shock level. In fact, much to Milgram's surprise, 65% of the participants went to the highest level. Some of the participants, but apparently not all, felt terrible about what they were doing. But they still continued to administer the shocks.

The willingness of so many of Milgram's participants to obey orders to hurt others disturbed many people. Was there something distinctive about Milgram's participants that could explain the results? In the original studies, the participants were men. Later studies, however, found similar results with women (Milgram, 1965, 1974), as well as with people in Jordan, Germany, and Australia, and with children (Kilham & Mann, 1974; Shanab & Yahya, 1977).

Why did so many participants obey orders to hurt someone else? Were there particular characteristics of the situation that fostered obedience? Compliance research suggests two ways in which the design increased the likelihood of obedience. First, Milgram's experiment applied something like the foot-in-the-door-technique: Participants were first asked to give a trivial amount of shock before going on to give apparently harmful ones. When the participants were allowed to set the punishment voltage themselves, none ever went past 45 volts. Second, additional research indicated that people become more likely to comply with a request if it comes from someone in authority; the same holds true for obedience (Bushman, 1984, 1988). In a variant of the study (Milgram, 1974), when a college student was the one who gave a fellow student the order to shock instead of an older, white-coated experimenter, compliance fell to only 20%. When the experimenters were two authority figures who disagreed with each other, no participants administered further shocks. It appears that when someone in authority gives an order, the person obeying can deny responsibility for his or her actions.

Later variations of Milgram's original study point to other characteristics of the situation that have an important influence on obedience. *Proximity* to the learner is one. When teachers saw the learners while they were being shocked, and even held an electrode directly on the accomplice's skin (with a "special insulating glove"), 30% progressed to the maximum voltage, compared with 65% in the original design. Proximity to the experimenter also matters: When the experimenter telephoned his commands instead of giving face-to-face instructions, obedience dropped to 21%.

Disturbing as Milgram's results were, it is important to remember that not all participants obeyed the experimenter, and in some conditions the great majority did not obey, and that it is the specifics of the situation (such as proximity to the learner) that influences an individual's willingness to obey an order to hurt someone else (Blass, 1999; Gibson, 1991; Miller et al., 1995).

Performance in Groups: Working Together

When Sadie and Bessie went to New York City, they moved into their brother Hubert's apartment, along with another brother and sister. Now there were five Delanys living in a three-room apartment. In such tight quarters, it helped to be very organized and to have clear rules and clear roles. Even though the apartment was Hubert's, and they all participated in making decisions, Sadie would have the final say because she was the oldest. How do groups make decisions? What are the advantages and disadvantages of working as a group?

DECISION MAKING IN GROUPS: PATHS TO A DECISION. After living at Hubert's apartment for a while, Sadie and Bessie got a place of their own in New York, and their mother came to live with them. However, at some point, their mother's health began to fade, and it was no longer safe for her to be home alone all day while her daughters were at work. The situation required that one of them leave her job to stay home with Mrs. Delany (it never occurred to them to hire someone to stay at home with their mother while they were out at work). How did they decide who would stay home? This question faces many families today, and the path to a solution often involves group decision making. Decision making also occurs in other contexts: Political parties, military planners, and athletic teams must decide on strategies; clinical groups must decide who receives what medical treatment and for how long; college admissions officers decide who is accepted and who is not. How are decisions made in groups?

In general, if a group is not initially unanimous in favor of a particular decision, it is likely that the view favored by the majority will prevail (Levine & Moreland, 1998). The larger the majority, the more likely it is that their choice will "win." This path is known as the *majority-win rule,* and it works well when the decision involves judgments or opinions. But there are times—you may have been present at some—when what began as the minority position eventually "wins." When there is an objectively correct answer, the *truth-win rule* works well because its inherent worthiness is recognized by the group (Kirchler & Davis, 1986). In general, groups reach a better decision when one solution can be shown to be correct (Hastie, 1986; Laughlin & Ellis, 1986). Consider the decision the Delany sisters made about caring for their mother: Bessie closed her dental practice and stayed home. Their reasoning was economic. Bessie was self-employed and had neither retirement benefits nor job stability. Sadie, as a teacher employed by a city, had both, as long as she worked until she was eligible for retirement. Thus, it was to the family's long-term financial advantage to have Bessie stay home, even though Sadie would have been more temperamentally suited for the task. In this case, the "truth"—the objectively advantageous long-term financial reality—won.

An interesting facet of group decision making is the way that a group "remembers" information in order to decide what to do. The memory of the group as a whole can in fact be better than the memory of any individual alone. This linking of human memory systems into a group memory system is called *transactive memory* (Wegner, 1995). Groups that learn new information together are more likely to remember the information accurately when together than those whose members learned the information individually, at least on some group tasks (Liang et al., 1995).

A group's heterogeneity may also affect its decision-making process and performance. In general, as a group becomes more heterogeneous, it communicates less effectively (Maznevski, 1994; Zenger & Lawrence, 1989), and subgroups of similar members may form, causing nonsimilar members to feel alienated (Jackson et al., 1991). Some of the negative effects of heterogeneous groups can be minimized in the following ways: education about similarities and differences; recategorization by increasing a sense of the group as a team (creating an "us"); increasing social skills among members; and learning conflict resolution skills (Caudron, 1994). Paradoxically, although heterogeneity can create some group conflict, it can also have a positive effect on the group's performance (McLeod & Lobel, 1992) because of the increased innovation and flexibility that diversity brings to a group (Levine & Moreland, 1998).

Group decision making does not always lead to the best decision. The opinion of a powerful member can shift others' opinions by might rather than right. Group decisions can be marred by **group polarization,** the tendency of members of the group to take more extreme positions (in the same direction as their initial opinions) after discussion (Isenberg, 1986; Levine & Moreland, 1998). Thus, when debating the merits of impeaching President Clinton in 1998 in the House Judiciary Committee, Republicans who may have only moderately favored impeachment likely left the session more strongly in favor. As you may have seen during the impeachment process, this polarization of attitude can last beyond the initial discussion (Liu & Latané, 1998).

One reason why group polarization develops is that some members of the group may give very compelling reasons for their initial views, and more of them. In listening to these reasons, members who are in general agreement may become more convinced of the correctness of that initial assessment and more extreme in their views (Burnstein, 1982). This route to group polarization is more likely to be a factor when an intellectual issue is at stake, or when the group's goal is to make a "correct" or task-oriented decision (Kaplan, 1987). Another reason behind group polarization is that, through discussion, members can figure out the group's "normative" position on the issue and

Group polarization: The tendency of group members' opinions to become more extreme (in the same direction as their initial opinions) after group discussion.

may be tempted to increase their standing in the group (and improve their view of themselves) by taking a more extreme position in accordance with the group norm (Goethals & Zanna, 1979). Thus, seeing that most Republicans were in favor of *some* action against Clinton (the normative attitude), members of the committee began to outdo one another in presenting pro-impeachment arguments. This route to group polarization is likely when the issue requires judgments, and when the group is more focused on group harmony than on correctness (Kaplan, 1987).

Groupthink (see Chapter 7) is another means by which decision making can go awry. The phenomenon of groupthink impels every member to feel that the group's decision must be supported, and consensus becomes more important than the critical appraisal of different positions (Janis, 1982).

When a group as a whole is responsible for a task, some members may work less hard than they would if they were individually responsible for a task. This tendency toward social loafing can be countered by evaluating everyone's performance separately or by making the task attractive.

SOCIAL LOAFING. When responsibility for an outcome is spread among the members of the group, some members may be likely to let other members work harder (Latané et al., 1979), a phenomenon that has been called **social loafing**. One way to prevent social loafing is to instill a sense of importance and responsibility in each person's work, even if the work is boring or if the member's contribution is anonymous (Harkins & Petty, 1982). Making the task attractive also reduces social loafing, as does knowing that individual as well as group performance will be evaluated (Harkins & Szymanski, 1989; Hoeksema-van Orden et al., 1998; Karau & Williams, 1993). If you have lived with other people, you may have experienced the effects of social loafing: When dishes pile up in the sink or the bathroom goes uncleaned for weeks, each member of the household is doing a little social loafing, waiting for somebody else to do the cleaning.

Although working in groups may lead some people to indulge in social loafing, it may lead others to engage in *social compensation*, working harder in a group than they do when they are alone. Social compensation usually occurs when some members of the group see the task to be done as important but don't expect that other members will pull their weight (Williams & Karau, 1991). Social compensation occurs when someone finally washes the dishes or cleans the bathroom: The mess bothers someone enough that he or she cleans it all up. But the one cleaning is doing more than his or her share.

SOCIAL FACILITATION: EVERYBODY LOVES AN AUDIENCE. Sometimes being part of a group, or just being in the presence of other people, can increase performance; this effect is called **social facilitation**. However, usually the presence of others enhances performance only on well-learned simple tasks; on complicated, less well-learned tasks, the presence of others can hinder our performance (Guerin, 1993). The presence of others appears to increase our arousal, which then facilitates our *dominant* response in that situation (Schmitt et al., 1986; Seta & Seta, 1992). Thus, well-learned responses are likely to come to the fore when we are aroused, and we will be less likely to execute complicated or recently learned behaviors. Hence, at a concert a musician may perform an old song better than a new one.

Helping Behavior: Helping Others

When Bessie Delany began her dentistry practice in 1923, both cleanings and extractions were $2 each, and a silver filling cost $5. When she retired in 1950, she charged the same rates and was proud of it. In fact, she treated people regardless of their ability to pay. The Delany family ethic was to help others. This quality is called **altruism**, which has been defined as "the motivation to increase another person's welfare" (Batson, 1998, p. 282). What made Bessie so willing to help others? Why do we help other people? What circumstances encourage altruism?

PROSOCIAL BEHAVIOR. Acting to benefit others, called **prosocial behavior**, includes sharing, cooperating, comforting, and helping (Batson, 1998). Whether or not

Social loafing: The tendency to work less hard when responsibility for an outcome is spread over the group's members.

Social facilitation: The increase in performance that can occur simply by being part of a group or in the presence of other people.

Altruism: The motivation to increase another person's welfare.

Prosocial behavior: Acting to benefit others.

we help someone depends on factors about us and the person we could help. We are more likely to help others if we have certain personality traits, such as a high need for approval, or a predisposition to feeling personal and social responsibility, or an empathic concern for others (Batson et al., 1986; Eisenberg et al., 1989). People who tend to be helpers also have a sense of empathy, belief in a just world, an internal locus of control, and less concern for their own welfare (Bierhoff et al., 1991). Bessie Delany seemed to feel a sense of personal and social responsibility toward others and could empathize with their plights. She also appeared to have less concern for her own welfare; when she was in dental school, a white girl born with syphilis came to the dental clinic—only Bessie volunteered to help her.

Some people in need of assistance are more likely to be helped than others. Who are they? First, we are more likely to help people we view as similar to ourselves. Consider an experiment in which Americans in three foreign cities asked for directions: Residents of those cities who were similar in age to the Americans requesting help were more likely to give directions (Rabinowitz et al., 1997). Second, we are more likely to help friends or people we like (remember, similarity facilitates liking). Third, we are more likely to help people we believe are not responsible for their predicaments, or people who give a socially acceptable justification for their plight (Weiner, 1980). In fact, the more justification the requester gives, the more likely he or she is to receive help (Bohm & Hendricks, 1997).

As in the tragedy of the commons, sometimes we may be faced with a choice between acting in our own personal interest and acting for the common good. When we choose not to act on the group's behalf, our distressing feelings, often resulting from cognitive dissonance, may be assuaged in a number of ways. Some people perform a prosocial act *other than* the one facing them (McMillen & Austin, 1971); others minimize the impact they would have made had they chosen to cooperate—"I probably couldn't have made a difference anyway" (Kerr & Kaufman-Gilliland, 1997).

Group identity also plays a role in prosocial behavior. We are more likely to help and cooperate with other members of our group. Principles of learning (see Chapter 5) are also influential. Through our learning history, we may have been reinforced for helping, or punished for not helping. Parents, teachers, and others were models for observational learning. Thus, in time, we come to reward ourselves for helping, feel good after helping, and punish ourselves or feel guilty when we don't (Batson, 1998).

BYSTANDER INTERVENTION. A great deal has been learned about a specific type of prosocial behavior—bystander intervention—as a result of research inspired by one dreadful incident. At about 3 A.M. on March 13, 1964, a 28-year-old woman named Catherine Genovese—known to her neighbors as Kitty—was brutally murdered in Queens, a borough of New York City, only minutes from her own apartment building. She was coming home from work as a manager of a bar. When her attacker first caught and stabbed her, she screamed for help. The lights came on in several apartments overlooking the scene of the crime, and a man yelled down to her attacker to leave her alone. Her attacker briefly stopped and walked away. The apartment lights went out. The attacker returned and stabbed her again; she screamed again, to no avail, although lights again came on in the surrounding apartments. The attacker left in a car, and Kitty Genovese dragged herself to the lobby of an apartment building near her own. The attacker returned again, and this time he kept stabbing her until she died. The gruesome ordeal took some 35 minutes and was viewed by at least 38 witnesses. Only one person called the police (Rosenthal, 1964).

Darley and Latané (1968) hypothesized that if only a few bystanders had witnessed the crime, those few would have been more likely to help Kitty Genovese. This relationship is known as the **bystander effect:** As the number of bystanders increases, offers of assistance decrease. To test this relationship, Darley and Latané, with the aid of accomplices, created the following situation. Imagine yourself as a participant in a study, taking part in a telephone conference about campus life with a number of others. Each participant speaks without interruption, and when everyone has spoken, the first person gets to speak again, and so on. Suppose another participant mentions that

Bystander effect: The decrease in offers of assistance that occurs as the number of bystanders increases.

FIGURE 15.7
Bystander Intervention

Participants thought they were involved in a study of campus life but instead were exposed to an "emergency" with a varying number of bystanders. Participants went into a private cubicle and were told that they could all hear one another, but only one student would be able to speak during any 2-minute period; when all had spoken, the cycle would start again. They were also told that the experimenter would not be listening. Participants were led to believe that either four, one, or no other students ("bystanders") were listening. In fact, there was only one true participant at a time; the rest of the voices on the intercom were prerecorded tapes.

The crisis came after one (prerecorded) voice confessed to having seizures in stressful situations, subsequently seemed to be having a seizure, and asked for help.

Would participants leave their cubicles to get help? Their responses depended greatly on the perceived number of bystanders. The great majority of participants went to get help when they thought they were the only ones aware of the problem, but they helped less often the more bystanders they thought were aware of the problem.

when stressed he gets seizures; then you hear that person stutter, start to choke, and ask for help. Would you go get aid? If you were like most participants in Darley and Latané's study (1968) (see Figure 15.7), if you believed there were only two people in the telephone conference—you and the person with seizures—you would very likely seek help. But if you had been told there were three participants, you would be less likely to seek help, and even less likely with a total of six. In short, attempts to help rose as the number of apparent bystanders dropped. Thus, when participants thought that they were the only one aware of the "emergency," 85% of them left the cubicle and got the experimenter within the first minute. When they thought there was one other bystander, 65% helped within the first minute. When participants thought there were four other bystanders, only 25% helped within the first minute. At the end of 4 minutes, all in the smallest group helped, as did 85% of those in the mid-size group, but only 60% in the largest group.

From this and other studies, Darley and Latané (1970) described five steps, or "choice points," in bystander intervention.

Step 1. Is an emergency actually noticed by the bystander? If yes, proceed to Step 2. If no, no help is given.

Step 2. Is the bystander correctly perceiving the event as an emergency? If yes, proceed to Step 3. If no, no help is given.

Step 3. Does the bystander assume responsibility to intervene? If yes, proceed to Step 4. If no, no help is given.

Step 4. Does the bystander know what to do, how to be helpful? If yes, proceed to Step 5. If no, no help is given.

Step 5. Is the bystander motivated enough to help, despite possible negative consequences? If yes, then he or she intervenes.

Diffusion of responsibility: The diminished sense of responsibility to help that each person feels as the number of bystanders grows.

At each step, various factors, such as the number of bystanders and characteristics of the bystanders, shape the likelihood that someone will help. For example, consider Step 2, perceiving the event. If a situation is ambiguous, leaving you uncertain about whether the emergency is real, you may hesitate to offer help. If other bystanders are present, your hesitancy may be increased by *evaluation apprehension*—a fear that you might be embarrassed or ridiculed if you try to intervene because there may be no emergency after all. The number of bystanders also influences Step 3, assuming responsibility. The more bystanders there are, the less each one feels responsible to help, creating a **diffusion of responsibility.** Interestingly, once people have learned about the bystander effect, they are subsequently more likely to intervene (Beaman et al., 1978).

LOOKING AT LEVELS

Cults

In 1997 members of the Heaven's Gate cult killed themselves in order to ascend to join an alien spaceship that they believed was hidden behind the Hale–Bopp Comet, which they believed would take them to the next level of existence. How is it that cults exert such a powerful influence on their members? We can best understand how cults function by looking at the phenomenon from the three levels of analysis and their interactions. At the level of the brain, the bodily functions of cult members, such as eating, sleeping, and sexual relations (in those cults that permit them), are carefully monitored. New recruits in many cults are often physically and mentally exhausted after listening to music, chanting, or other auditory stimuli for hours on end (Streiker, 1984), which can induce a meditative or hypnotic-like state that alters brain function as well as the sense of reality.

At the level of the person, many cults try to eliminate members' experience of themselves as individuals. In the Heaven's Gate group, each day was structured down to the minute in order to minimize the sense of self and individual choice. Moreover, members were forbidden to trust their own judgments or to have "inappropriate" curiosity (Bearak, 1997). Members, particularly new ones, were not allowed to be alone, even in the bathroom. These measures, as well as the altered state of consciousness and the exhaustion, can induce a sense of depersonalization (the experience of observing oneself as if from the outside) and derealization (the sense that familiar objects have changed or seem unreal), as well as deindividualization (see Chapter 13).

At the level of the group, the arousal and unpleasant effects of the derealization are calmed by listening to the group and by being cared for by others. This resulting dependency increases the desire to stay within the group. Performing actions at the behest of the group that would otherwise be refused, such as begging for money or having sexual relations (raising issues of compliance and obedience), can induce cognitive dissonance; only a change in attitude can then resolve the discomfort aroused. Moreover, members receive enormous amounts of attention and reinforcement, sometimes called "love-bombing," for behaving in desired ways—in other words, conforming to their expected role and to group norms. Group polarization and groupthink may affect the group's decision making. Perhaps these group processes led to the decision that group suicide was an effective way to join the alien spaceship.

Events at these levels of analysis interact: The unpleasant bodily and psychological states are relieved when desired behaviors are performed, in a process of negative reinforcement; this relief leads to a change in self-concept and a heightened importance of, and dependence on, the group.

CONSOLIDATE!

▶ **1. What psychological principles explain why we like certain people and not others?** If our first impression of someone is positive, we are more apt to like that person with repeated contact, if the person is similar to us and is physically attractive to us. Liking is not the same as loving, which can be passionate or compassionate. According to Sternberg's triangular theory, love has three dimensions: passion, intimacy, and commitment. Relationships reflect different proportions of each dimension, and those proportions change over time. People's attachment styles—secure, avoidant, or anxious–ambivalent—also affect the pattern of relationships they will develop.

▶ **2. Why do all groups have rules for social behavior and organization?** Social norms and roles help a group function, defining appropriate and inappropriate behavior for some or all members; they also help new members learn how to function in the group. The perception of a norm can affect members' behavior, even if that perception is inaccurate, as has been the case with some drug prevention programs. Within a group, a status hierarchy reflects the distribution of power assigned to each role.

▶ **3. Why do we sometimes "go along" with others even when we don't want to? What makes us able to refuse?** We conform to the majority view when the task at hand is difficult; if we hold a minority position, we come to doubt the correctness of our view. Furthermore, as Asch's studies showed, we are more likely to conform to the majority view when we are part of a cohesive group. In contrast, we are less likely to conform to the majority view if another member also does not conform to that position or if we have a strong desire to retain a sense of individuality. Compliance with a request can be maximized when the person making the request is a friend, someone who has pro-

vided a favor in the past, or someone in authority. We are also more likely to comply if we think people similar to ourselves would comply. A number of persuasion techniques make use of these principles, including the foot-in-the-door technique, the lowball technique, and the door-in-the-face technique. Obedience to a command with which we don't agree is more likely when compliance principles are used, as well as when the person issuing commands is nearby. However, not everyone obeys such orders, and the specifics of the situation help determine the level of obedience.

▶ **4. Does being part of a group change our behavior? How do groups make decisions?** Groups can make decisions according to the majority-win or truth-win rule; the latter is more likely when one answer is objectively correct. Although more heterogeneous groups may communicate less effectively, they may also be more innovative and flexible because of their diversity. Examples of group decision making gone awry are found in group polarization and groupthink. Being part of a group can cause people to do less than their share (social loafing) or more than their share (social compensation). Moreover, just being in the presence of others can increase someone's performance of a well-learned task (social facilitation), but have the opposite effect on newly learned skills.

▶ **5. Are some people more helpful than others? Why would we not help other people?** People with certain personality traits are more likely to help others. Those traits include a high need for approval and a feeling of social responsibility. We are more likely to help people who seem similar to ourselves, people we like, or people who have a socially justifiable reason for needing help. The more bystanders on hand (diffusion of responsibility) or the more ambiguous the situation, the less likely we are to help.

A FINAL WORD: ETHICS AND SOCIAL PSYCHOLOGY

The researchers involved in many of the studies described in this chapter did not tell participants about the true nature of the experiments at the outset, and several used accomplices. As discussed in the section on ethics in Chapter 1, many of the classic social psychology studies were carried out before the discipline established rigorous ethical guidelines. In fact, many of the guidelines were formulated *because* these studies raised serious ethical concerns. Keep in mind several issues related to the use of deception in psychology. First, many of the pioneering researchers did not expect to cause psychological distress. For example, Milgram initially did not expect participants to be willing to shock learners at higher "voltage" levels, although he did continue to perform variants of his study after he knew the results of his first study. Second, some psychological phenomena are extremely difficult, if not impossible, to study if the participant knows the true nature of the experiment. For example, could you think of a way to design a study on conformity *without* using deception? Third, at present, in order to receive approval for a study that uses deception, researchers must show that the deception is absolutely necessary (that the information could not be ascertained without deception); that the information is valuable and the deception minimal; and that at the conclusion of the study, the investigators will fully explain to the participants the nature of the study and the reasons for deception. In short, today deception is permitted in research only if it is crystal clear that the participants will not be harmed and important knowledge will be gained.

A DEEPER LEVEL
Recap and Thought Questions

▶ Social Cognition: Thinking About People

Attitudes and stereotypes help lessen the cognitive effort of understanding the social world. Our impressions, attitudes, stereotypes, and attributions affect how we encode, store, and retrieve information. Our attitudes can affect our behavior and are especially likely to do so when they are strong, stable, relevant, and salient. Conflict between attitudes and behavior (or between two attitudes) can lead to cognitive dissonance, which we are then driven to reduce. The human process of categorizing objects (including people) leads to stereotypes, and our stereotypes of others not only affect our behavior but can also affect the way others behave toward us and can lead to prejudice and discrimination. Because stereotypes create biases in the way we process information, our stereotypes often seem more accurate than they really are and thus are difficult to change. Although we are driven to make attributions to understand events, our reasoning about the causes of these events may rely on the fundamental attribution error and other attributional biases, possibly leading us to understand people's behavior in inaccurate ways.

What does social cognition have to do with the Delanys? The Delanys, like all of us, tried to make sense of the social world around them. Rather than actively process every bit of information presented to them, they relied on cognitive shortcuts. Thus, the Delanys developed attitudes about other people (such as New Yorkers walking down the street, or Mr. Heller), which influenced their behavior toward others. In addition, other people's stereotypes of blacks and women affected how they treated the Delanys; negative attitudes (prejudice) may have led to discriminatory behavior; their prejudice toward the sisters may have been unconscious. All these cognitive processes influence the attributions people make to explain the Delany sisters' successes.

Think It Through. If you were to design an anti-smoking campaign based on your knowledge of persuasion and stereotypes, what strategies might you include? If you wanted to help people resist the pull of advertisements or political campaigns, what information would be particularly important to convey? Explain.

▶ Social Behavior: Interacting With People

Psychological factors lead us to behave in certain ways when we are with others. In our intimate relationships, we are more likely to be attracted to, and to like, people we view as similar to ourselves. Love can be understood using Sternberg's triangular model or looking at different styles of attachment. All groups have norms and roles and assign status to members; these factors are used to obtain conformity, compliance, and obedience from the members of the group. The style of a group's decision making depends on the group's goals and on the ways group members articulate their views on an issue before the group. Being in a group can help or harm a given individual's performance. Psychological principles are at work in determining when and whom we help.

How can psychological research results help us understand the Delany sisters' interactions with other people? The Delany sisters' interactions with others were governed by certain principles. For instance, their interactions with strangers on New York City streets were at first determined by their previous experience with the social norms and roles of Raleigh; when the social norms of New York proved different, their behavior changed accordingly. During and after Jim Crow, their behavior generally conformed to the norms (and laws), but not always, as Sadie's experience with Mr. Heller in the shoe store illustrates. Moreover, Bessie's altruism (performing dental work on the syphilitic girl) reflects a strong sense of empathy and social responsibility, traits that are more likely to lead to helping behavior.

Think It Through. Imagine that you have started a new job working in a large corporation. Based on what you have learned, what colleagues are you likely to be attracted to and why? What are you likely to know about the structure of your work group—its norms, roles, and the like—even before your first day? If your boss wants employees to do something "slightly illegal," what factors may make employees less likely to go along with this request (or order)? Will working as a group change the way the work is performed? Why or why not? If an employee is injured at work, what factors may make the employees who witness the incident more likely to help?

APPENDIX A

STATISTICS

Mark Twain once said that there are three kinds of lies: "Lies, damn lies, and statistics." **Statistics** are numbers that summarize or indicate differences or patterns of differences in measurements. Twain's point was that statistics can be used to obscure the facts as easily as to illuminate them. For instance, although the divorce rate in the United States is about 50%, this does not necessarily mean that out of 10 couples only 5 will stay married. If 3 of those 10 couples divorce and remarry, and all 3 of those second marriages end in divorce, that makes 6 divorces out of 13 marriages; and if one of those ex-partners remarries a third time and divorces again, we now have 14 marriages and 7 divorces: a 50% divorce rate, even though 7 of the original 10 couples stayed married from the start. To understand and evaluate reports of psychological research, be they surveys in newspapers or television, or formal research reports in scientific publications, you need to know a few basics about statistics.

There are two major types of statistics: One type describes or summarizes data, whereas the other indicates which differences or patterns in the data are worthy of attention. This is the distinction between descriptive statistics and inferential statistics. **Descriptive statistics** are concise ways of summarizing properties of sets of numbers. You're already familiar with such statistics: They are what you see plotted in bar graphs and pie charts, and presented in tables. Descriptive statistics include measures of *central tendency*, such as the familiar arithmetic average. But descriptive statistics are not limited to figures and tables. For example, in financial news, the Dow Jones Industrial Average is a descriptive statistic, as is the unemployment rate.

Inferential statistics, in contrast, are the results of tests that reveal whether differences or patterns in measurements reflect true differences in the population, or just chance variations. For instance, if you toss a coin 10 times and it lands heads up 7 times, instead of the 5 you would expect purely by chance, does this mean that it is a "trick coin," or an edge is worn away, or could this outcome also arise from just chance? Inferential statistics seek to address this question of whether patterns in a set of data are random, or if they reflect a true underlying phenomenon. A correlation (see Chapter 1) is an example of inferential statistics; if the correlation is high enough (we will discuss what "high enough" means later), it tells you that the scores on one variable do in fact vary systematically with the scores on another variable.

In this appendix we consider both types of statistics, starting with descriptive statistics and the nature of variables and data, then turning to an overview of key inferential statistics. We conclude by exploring how statistics can be used to deceive you, both in printed numbers and in graphs, and how you can use statistics in everyday life.

DESCRIPTIVE STATISTICS

You already know a lot about descriptive statistics, but you may not be aware you know it—and you may not be familiar with the technical vocabulary scientists use to discuss such statistics. This section provides a review of the essential points of descriptive statistics.

Variables and Data

First, you need to learn about variables and data—what they are, how researchers obtain data, and how they use the data to answer the questions posed in their research.

In Chapter 1, a *variable* was defined as an aspect of a situation that is liable to change (or, in other words, that can *vary*). More precisely, a variable is a characteristic of a substance, quantity, or entity that is measurable. *Independent variables* are the characteristics manipulated, and *dependent variables* are those measured, whose values depend on the values of the independent variable. For example, in Chapter 1 you read about an experiment in which golfers were or were not asked to use "mental practice" between games (the independent variable), and their subsequent golfing performance (the dependent variable) was measured by their scores. *Data* are careful observations or numerical measurements of a phenomenon, such as golf scores. In other words, in an experiment, data are the measurements, the values of the dependent variable as it varies. Examples of dependent variables used in psychological research are response time (how fast it takes to press a button after perceiving a stimulus), scores on an intelligence test, and ratings of the severity of depression.

Values of variables can be described in two ways. For example, intelligence could be described numerically by a score (such as 104) or by the category in which a score falls (such as "average intelligence"). **Continuous variables** are those whose values can fall anywhere along the measurement scale, just as measures of length can fall anywhere along a ruler. Continuous variables allow you to perform mathematical operations such as adding or subtracting two or more values. For example, suppose you developed a drug that you think boosts memory. If your drug works as promised, it would be in great demand—from language-learning schools to Wall Street firms. To test the effectiveness of your drug, you ask people to learn a set of words either after taking the drug or, on another day, after taking a placebo. You are interested in whether the participants can later recall more words if they've taken your drug than if they took the placebo; the condition, drug versus placebo, is the independent variable, and the number of words recalled is the dependent variable. Half the participants get the drug first and half get an identical-looking and -tasting placebo first. You've put the pills in coded envelopes so that your assistant doesn't know when she's giving the drug versus the placebo (nor do the participants, because you've used a *double-blind* procedure; see Chapter 1). The comparison, easily accomplished with values from a continuous scale, would be expressed as the number of words remembered following

Statistics: Numbers that summarize or indicate differences or patterns of differences in measurements.

Descriptive statistics: A concise way of summarizing properties of sets of numbers.

Inferential statistics: Results of tests that reveal which differences or patterns in the measurements reflect actual differences in a population, as opposed to those that merely reflect random variations.

Continuous variables: Variables whose values can fall anywhere along the measurement scale.

TABLE A.1

Fictional Data From Drug and Placebo Conditions

NUMBER OF WORDS REMEMBERED

Placebo	Memory drug
15	27
12	34
18	21
21	17
22	31
38	47
28	31
15	23
14	40
17	19

the drug minus the number following the placebo. Ten participants' scores in each condition are shown in Table A.1.

Some data cannot be expressed as continuous variables, such as sex (male versus female), city of residence (Toledo versus Austin), or stage of sleep (Stage 2, 3, 4, or REM). These are examples of **categorical variables,** which assign measurements to discrete classes. Such variables do not change gradually from one to the other, and you can't perform mathematical operations on them. Commonly used categorical variables are sex, race, location, and political party. However, note that continuous measurements can also be classified as categorical variables, such as assigning an IQ score to an "average" category.

Frequency Distributions

It can be useful to treat continuous measures as categorical if you want to get a sense of the way scores are distributed in a population (such as how many college students have above average IQ scores). **Frequency distributions** indicate the number of each type of case that was observed in a set of data. For example, the number of people who voted for a Democratic versus a Republican candidate can be considered for different ages. You could group the ages (making a continuous variable, age, into a categorical variable), perhaps starting with ages 18–30, and then considering each subsequent decade. For each category, you would indicate the number of people who voted Democrat versus Republican. If you were a political strategist trying to determine how best to spend your candidate's campaign money, such a distribution would be helpful: You could decide to target the age ranges that had previously voted your way, or—alternatively—you could figure that they are relatively secure and instead target age ranges that previously were *not* in your camp.

Measures of Central Tendency

When individual measurements are directly presented, they are considered *raw data*; Table A.1 presents raw data. Descriptive statistics are used to summarize characteristics of a set of such data. It is the transformation of raw data into statistical terms that makes the data useful, allowing you to illustrate the relationships among the values or scores. One important type of descriptive statistic is the **central tendency** of the data: the clustering of the most characteristic values, or scores, for a particular group or sample. Central tendency can be expressed three ways. The most common, and probably the one with which you are most familiar, is the arithmetic average, or **mean,** of the scores or values. You calculate a mean by adding up the values in the group or sample, then dividing that sum by the total number of entries you summed. As shown in Table A.2, the mean for the placebo condition is 20 words remembered, and the mean for the drug condition is 29 words remembered.

Categorical variables: Variables whose values are assigned to discrete classes.

Frequency distribution: A distribution that indicates the number of each type of case that was observed in a set of data.

Central tendency: A descriptive statistic that indicates the clustering of the most characteristic values, or scores, for a particular group or sample.

Mean: A measure of central tendency that is the arithmetic average of a set of scores or values.

TABLE A.2

Calculating the Mean

NUMBER OF WORDS REMEMBERED

Placebo Total: 200   **Memory drug** Total: 290

Mean = Total number of words remembered ÷ Number of participants

Mean: 200 ÷ 10 = 20   Mean: 290 ÷ 10 = 29

A second way to specify central tendency is the **median**, which is the score that is the midpoint of the values for the group or sample; half the values fall above the median, and half fall below the median. It is easier to find the median if the data are arranged in order, as shown in Table A.3. The median in the placebo condition is 17.5, halfway between 17 and 18, the fifth and sixth ordered scores. In the memory drug condition, the median is 29.0, halfway between the fifth and sixth ordered scores of 27 and 31.

A third measure of central tendency is the **mode**, the value that appears most frequently in the group or sample. The mode can be any value, from the highest to the lowest. The mode in Table A.3 is 15 for the placebo condition and 31 for the memory drug condition. In addition, you can also use a mode for categorical scales, where the mode would be the most frequent category, such as "children" among all viewers of Sesame Street, or "Saturday night" as the evening most people go to bed the latest.

The mean is the measure of central tendency that is most sensitive to extreme values or scores; if you have a few values at the extreme end of the scale, the mean would change much more than the median (which often will not change at all). The mode does not generally change in response to an extreme score. If you changed the last score in Table A.3 in the placebo condition from 38 to 50, the mean would change from 20 to 21.2, but the median and mode would remain the same.

TABLE A.3	Fictional Data From Drug and Placebo Conditions, Arranged in Order

NUMBER OF WORDS REMEMBERED

Placebo condition	Memory drug condition
12	17
14	19
15	21
15	23
17	27
– – – – Median 17.5	– – – – Median 29.0
18	31
21	31
22	34
28	40
38	47
Mode* = 15	Mode* = 31

Mode = Value that appears most frequently.

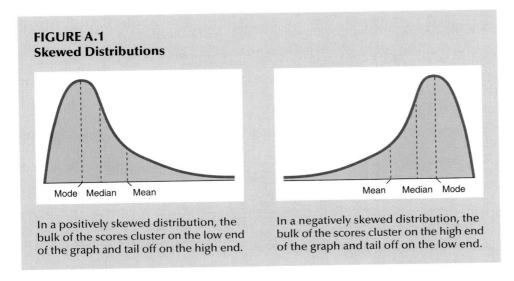

FIGURE A.1
Skewed Distributions

In a positively skewed distribution, the bulk of the scores cluster on the low end of the graph and tail off on the high end.

In a negatively skewed distribution, the bulk of the scores cluster on the high end of the graph and tail off on the low end.

When a set of data has many scores near one extreme value and away from the center, it is said to have a **skewed distribution**. When a set of data has a skewed distribution, the median is often a more appropriate measure of central tendency than the mean (see Figure A.1).

However, the three measures of central tendency generally yield similar results; this is especially likely as the number of observations (data points) becomes larger and if the data follow a normal distribution. As discussed in Chapter 8, the *normal distribution* is the familiar bell-shaped curve, in which most values fall in the midrange of the scale, and scores are increasingly less frequent as they taper off symmetrically toward the extremes (see Figure A.2 on page 596). Normal curves occur many places

Median: A measure of central tendency that is the midpoint score of the values for the group or sample; half the values fall above the median, and half fall below the median.

Mode: A measure of central tendency that is the most frequently occurring value in a group or sample.

Skewed distribution: A set of data that has many scores near one extreme value and away from the center.

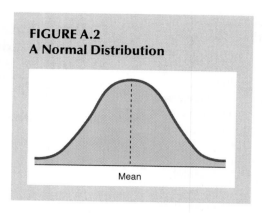

FIGURE A.2
A Normal Distribution

Mean

in nature. For example, look at stone stairs in a very old building: You can usually see that they are worn more deeply in the center, and then less so as you move toward the sides. (If the building isn't old enough, you will see the beginnings of a normal curve, which over the generations will become deeper in the center until it resembles the shape of Figure A.2 upside down.) Or picture your classmates lined up according to height. Probably there are a few very tall or very short students on either end, with most clumping at an intermediate height. The same is true for many psychological qualities, such as scores on intelligence or personality tests.

Measures of Variability

Whereas measures of central tendency convey information about the most common values or scores, measures of *variability* convey information about the spread of the scores. **Range,** the difference obtained when you subtract the smallest score from the largest, is the simplest measure of variability. For the data in Table A.3, for example, the range of scores in the placebo condition is 38 – 12, or 26. The range of scores for the drug condition is 47 – 17, or 30. But the range does not tell you how variable the scores are in general. Suppose you have developed two different drugs for improving memory, and participants who are given either one learn anywhere from 30 to 40 words; thus, both drugs have a range of 10. However, this measure of variability does not tell you that most participants who took drug A remember 37 or 38 words, whereas most of those who received drug B remember only 31 or 32 words. The range is the measure of variability most sensitive to extreme values.

Another method of assessing variability is the *standard deviation*, which is a kind of "average variability" in a set of measurements. In Chapter 8, you saw how important the standard deviation is for understanding IQ. Let's walk through how this important measure is computed:

Step 1: Calculate how much each score differs from the mean of the scores, as shown in Table A.4. Following this, it might be tempting to try to obtain an "aver-

Range: The difference obtained by subtracting the smallest score from the largest; the simplest measure of variability.

TABLE A.4	**Computing the Standard Deviation From the Placebo Condition Data in Table A.3**

Step 1:

(Number of words remembered – Mean)^2 = Deviation score^2

$(12 - 20)^2 = -8^2 = 64$ $(18 - 20)^2 = -2^2 = 4$

$(14 - 20)^2 = -6^2 = 36$ $(21 - 20)^2 = 1^2 = 1$

$(15 - 20) = -5^2 = 25$ $(22 - 20)^2 = 2^2 = 4$

$(15 - 20)^2 = -5^2 = 25$ $(28 - 20)^2 = 8^2 = 64$

$(17 - 20)^2 = -3^2 = 9$ $(38 - 20)^2 = 18^2 = 324$

Step 2: Sum of squares (SS) = Sum of squared deviation scores = 556

Step 3: Variance = SS ÷ Number of deviation scores = 556 ÷ 10 = 55.6

Step 4: Standard deviation = Square root of the variance = $\sqrt{55.6}$ = 7.46

age difference score" directly, by simply computing the average of the differences from the mean. But if you do this, you will get an average score of zero (each difference above the mean will be compensated by one below the mean; otherwise it wouldn't be the mean!). Instead, before taking the average of the deviations from the mean, you square them, which eliminates the plus or minus signs.

Step 2: Find the total of these squared values. This figure is often referred to as the *sum of squares*, or *SS*. As shown in Table A.4, the SS for the placebo condition data recorded in Table A.3 is 556.

Step 3: The sum of squares is then divided by the total number of deviation scores that contributed to this sum. The resulting value is the *variance*. The variance for the placebo condition is 55.6.

Step 4: Finally, because the difference scores were squared in the first step, the variance must be "unsquared" to get a number that conveys meaningful information about the average variability of the scores. The square root of the variance is the *standard deviation*. The *standard deviation* of the placebo condition is 7.46.

Here is a simpler example. Say you want to know which of two Web search engines is likely to be consistently fastest. This means not just which engine has the fastest mean search time, or even the narrowest range of search times, but which has the tightest spread from the mean. The standard deviation is a measure of how consistently scores or values cluster near the mean, in this case how consistently fast a search engine can produce a list of hits for your query. The standard deviation is computed by taking each measured search time and subtracting it from the mean. Say, for simplicity's sake, that you measured the times for three searches of one search engine at 1, 3, and 5 seconds. The average (the mean) is 3 seconds. If you subtract each number from 3, you get −2, 0, and 2. Then, you square each of the differences from the mean (in this case, obtaining 4, 0, and 4), which gets rid of the plus and minus signs, and then sum these squared numbers and take their average (which gives you 8 divided by 3, or 2.67). If you then take the square root of this average (to undo the act of squaring), you have the standard deviation, a bit more than 1.6 seconds. You would do the same thing with the other search engine and compare the results. A smaller standard deviation would mean that the searches are, in general, closer to the average search time. To do this right, however, you would perform many more than three trials with each search engine.

For values that are normally distributed, the standard deviation will tell you the percentage of values that fall at different points on the distribution. For instance, as discussed more precisely in Chapter 8, about 68% of values fall between one standard deviation below the mean and one standard deviation above the mean. And about 95% of the values fall between two standard deviations below the mean and two standard deviations above the mean. Because 99.7% of values fall between three standard deviations below the mean and three standard deviations above the mean, you know that any value greater than three standard deviations is *really* different from the other values. The fact that standard deviations in a normal distribution always have these properties makes it easier to understand the relationship of standard deviations to the rest of the values in the data.

Let's go back to the earlier example of the placebo condition's standard deviation of 7.46 words (for simplicity's sake, we'll round this down to 7 words). What this means is that, with the placebo condition's mean of 20 words, roughly 68% of the participants in the placebo condition will remember somewhere between 13 and 27 words (20 − 7 to 20 + 7). At two standard deviations from the mean, roughly 95% of participants will remember between about 6 and 34 words.

Finally, it is well worth being familiar with the concept of a **confidence interval,** which specifies the range within which the mean of the actual population is likely to fall. The confidence interval is calculated like the standard deviation, but it is adjusted to reflect how the means of samples are distributed, not the individual data points (the details of this adjustment are not crucial here). You are probably already familiar with

Confidence interval: The range within which the mean of the population is likely to occur.

this concept, having heard it referred to in news broadcasts as the "margin of error" that accompanies poll results. For example, you might hear that "Smith is preferred by 51% of the voters and Jones by 40%, with a margin of error of 4—which puts them in a dead heat." A margin of error of 4 is a way of saying "plus or minus 4." That is, Smith is preferred by somewhere between 47% and 55% of the voters—51% plus or minus 4%. The confidence intervals can be set more or less stringently. For example, the most common confidence interval, set at 95%, means that 95% of the time the mean of the population would fall within the range of the upper and lower ends of that confidence interval.

Relative Standing

Sometimes you want to know where a particular score stands relative to other scores. For example, college admissions officers want to know how an applicant's SAT scores stand relative to other applicants' scores. One way to convey this information is in terms of measures of variability. For example, you could specify how many standard deviations a score is from the mean. (This is the way IQ scores are set up, with 15 points on the WAIS indicating a standard deviation.) However, this isn't very useful if you are interested in the specific number or percentage of other cases that fall above or below a particular one. Another way of conveying information about a value relative to other values in a set of measurements is to use a **percentile rank:** the percentage of data that have values at or below a particular value. A value converted to a percentile rank of 50, for example, instantly tells you that 50% of the values in a sample fall at or below that particular score; the median is a percentile rank of 50. *Quartiles* are percentile ranks that divide the group into fourths (25th, 50th, 75th, and 100th percentiles); a score that is at the third quartile signifies that 75% of the group fall at or below that score. *Deciles* are percentile ranks that divide the group into tenths; a score at the sixth decile indicates that 60% of the scores fall at or below that value.

INFERENTIAL STATISTICS

So far the discussion has focused on descriptive statistics. But you now have the tools to understand common inferential statistics.

Correlation: The Relationship Between Two Variables

Suppose you want to know not just about the central tendency and variability of a set of scores, but whether two variables are related to each other. Is a change in one variable accompanied by a change in another? You saw in Chapter 1 that *correlations* show only that two variables vary together, not that a change in one causes a change in the other. A positive relationship (in which increases in one variable are accompanied by increases in another) is indicated by a correlation value that falls between zero and 1.0; a negative relationship (in which increases in one variable are accompanied by decreases in another) is indicated by a correlation that is between zero and −1.0. Zero indicates no relationship between the two variables; they do not vary together. The closer the correlation is to 1.0 or −1.0, the stronger the relationship. So, for instance, you may read that people who exercise moderately don't get as severely depressed as people who don't exercise at all. If this information is based on a correlation, it would be a negative correlation: Increasing exercise is associated with less severe depression. However, concluding that exercise helps prevent severe depression (exercise *causes* less

Percentile rank: The percentage of data that have values at or below a particular value.

severe depression) based on that correlation would be a mistake. Perhaps people who are severely depressed don't have the energy to exercise. If that is true, the direction of causation would be in the other direction (more severe depression *causes* less exercise). With correlation, we know only that the two variables are related, either positively or negatively, not the direction of causality. It is possible that some third variable affects the other two variables. It could be that regularly getting out of the house or office and going to a gym (and therefore having a change of scenery and being around other people) affects the severity of depression, and so it is not the exercise per se but interacting with people that is related to less severe depression.

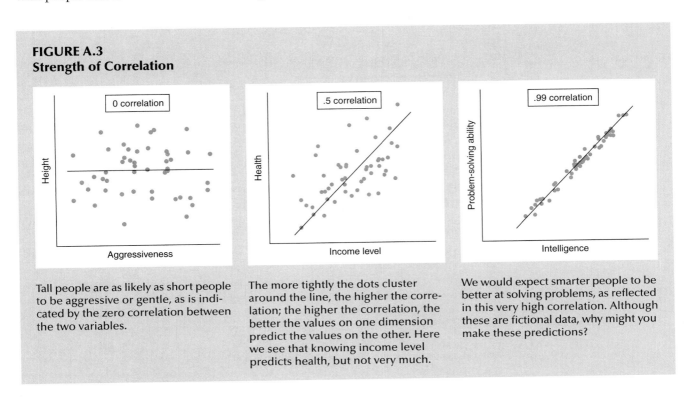

FIGURE A.3
Strength of Correlation

Tall people are as likely as short people to be aggressive or gentle, as is indicated by the zero correlation between the two variables.

The more tightly the dots cluster around the line, the higher the correlation; the higher the correlation, the better the values on one dimension predict the values on the other. Here we see that knowing income level predicts health, but not very much.

We would expect smarter people to be better at solving problems, as reflected in this very high correlation. Although these are fictional data, why might you make these predictions?

To think about how the correlation value is calculated, go back to the idea of a standard deviation. But now, instead of computing the deviations relative to the mean of all the numbers, imagine that you have a line fitting through the data (Figure A.3). The closer the data points hug the line, the higher the absolute value of correlation (that is, the higher the number—ignoring whether it is positive or negative). The *method of least squares* is a way to fit a line to a cloud of points. Again, squared numbers are used to eliminate the signs of the difference values. This method positions the line to minimize the square of the distance of each point from the line.

Correlations and other types of inferential statistics can be *significant* or *not significant*. What does "significant" mean? In statistics, it does not mean "important." Rather, it means that the measured relationship is not simply due to chance. If you correlate any two randomly selected sets of measurements, it is likely that the correlation will not be precisely zero. Say you correlated IQ with ear size and found a correlation of .12. Should you pay attention to this correlation, developing a grand theory to explain it? The size of a correlation needed for statistical significance, to be taken as more than just chance variation, depends on the number of pairs of values analyzed (each represented by a point in Figure A.3). As a general rule, the more observations considered when computing the correlation, the smaller the correlation value needs to be to achieve statistical significance. Why? Imagine that you were randomly throwing darts into a rectangular corkboard on the wall. It is possible that the first few on the left would be lower than those on the right. But as you tossed more and more darts, those initial quirks would be balanced out by quirks later in the process, so after 100 darts, there would no longer be any discernible pattern. The more observations you have, the less influence extreme values will have.

Statistical significance is expressed in terms of the probability (p) that a value (such as the size of a correlation) could be due to chance. For example, $p < .05$ means that the probability that the result was simply due to chance is less than 5 in 100; $p < .001$ means that the probability that it was due to chance is less than 1 in 1,000. By convention, any value with $p < .05$ or smaller is considered significant—not likely to be a result simply of chance variation in the data. You can look up a correlation value in a table to determine its significance, but most computer programs that compute correlation do this for you automatically.

Samples and Populations

Back to the memory-enhancing drug study. Did the drug work? If you had measured every person on the planet, all you would need to do is look at the descriptive statistics. Either the drug resulted in more learning than the placebo or it didn't. But such all-inclusive testing isn't practical. Virtually all research in psychology relies on studying data from a *sample*—a group drawn from the population at large—and the goal is to generalize from the findings with the sample to the larger population. Inferential statistics let you *infer* that the difference found between your samples does in fact reflect a difference in the corresponding populations.

Here's a simple example: Say you wanted to know whether seniors are generally friendlier than freshmen (you theorize that as they gain confidence and a sense of independence, students *do* become friendlier). To find out, you administer a scale your professor has just designed and validated to measure friendliness. If you administered the scale to five freshmen and five seniors, you would probably find a difference. But if you had ten from a single year and randomly assigned them to two groups of five, you would probably also find a difference between the groups! This difference would arise because of how you happened to assign students to groups. No matter how you did it, the groups would be likely to be different. Only if you had a large number of students would assigning them randomly to two groups be likely to result in groups that were very similar. When enough students have been tested, ones who score particularly high or low will be assigned equally often to each group, on average, and thus their disproportionate contributions will cancel out. When you compare freshmen and seniors, you can't know for sure whether you've got enough participants so that any difference between them is "real"—reflecting actual differences between the two classes in general—or is due to **sampling error**, differences that arise from the luck of the draw, not because two samples are in fact representative of different populations. In this example, if differences between freshmen and seniors are due to sampling error, this means that the two classes of students are not different. There are tests that can indicate whether a difference between two groups is due to sampling error or reflects a real difference, although details about such tests are beyond the scope of this appendix.

Generalizing From the Results

Say that a research study found that exercise *per se* really does ward off severe depression. Does that mean that *you* should start exercising when you feel yourself getting depressed? Not necessarily. Generalizing from the results of a study should be done with caution. Consider the following questions before applying the results of this or any study to yourself or anyone else.

1. Are the results *valid*? If the study relied on an experimental design, were the participants randomly assigned? (See Chapter 1 for an explanation of why this is important.) If it used a correlational design, is the study implying that one variable causes another? If so, that conclusion isn't supported by the data. Do

Sampling error: A difference that arises by chance, not because the samples are representative of different populations.

you think the researchers were appropriately assessing the variables they claimed to be assessing? For instance, if they measured depression by simply comparing how slowly participants spoke at the end of the study with their speech speed at the beginning, would that be a valid assessment of depression?

2. If the study involved a new treatment or method of improving some aspect of life, was this method compared with a control group, perhaps a group given a placebo?

3. Did the researchers try to control for possible confounds?

4. Was the study performed with a wide cross-section of people or a small sample? For instance, if a positron emission tomography (PET) study found that people with attention-deficit/hyperactivity disorder (ADHD) had unusual activity levels in a particular part of the brain, you would want to ask the following questions before concluding that the findings generalize beyond the participants in the study: How many participants were involved? What was the gender of the participants? Are there other factors about the participants that make it difficult to generalize to you, to North Americans, or to all people? If the study was restricted to people of a certain geographic region, ethnic group, or those with a particular medical, psychological, or social history, it may not be appropriate to generalize the results, depending on the variable being assessed.

LYING WITH STATISTICS

Statistics can be used or misused. In a famous book entitled *How to Lie with Statistics*, Derrell Huff (1954) demonstrated many ways that people use statistics to distort the pattern of results. This book played a valuable role in inoculating many people against these deceptive techniques, and some of its high points are summarized here. Be on the look out for these manipulations whenever you see statistics.

Selective Reporting

Because different types of statistics convey different information, the same data can be manipulated to "say" different things. Look at Figure A.4 and Table A.5, which present fictitious data for the results of a new type of therapy for people with acrophobia—a

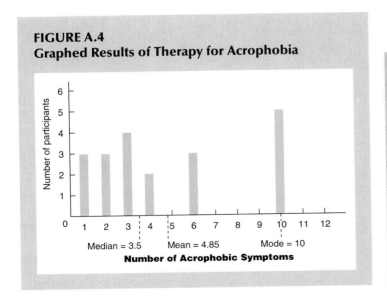

FIGURE A.4
Graphed Results of Therapy for Acrophobia

Median = 3.5   Mean = 4.85   Mode = 10
Number of Acrophobic Symptoms

TABLE A.5

Fictional Results of Therapy for Acrophobia

Mean number of symptoms after therapy for acrophobia

= Total number of symptoms ÷ Total number of participants

$= 1 + 1 + 1 + 2 + 2 + 2 + 3 + 3 + 3 + 3 + 4 + 4 + 6 + 6 + 6 + 10 + 10 + 10 + 10 + 10$

$= 97 ÷ 20 = 4.85$

Median = 3.5

Mode = 10

fear of heights. Before the therapy, participants reported, on average, 9 symptoms of acrophobia; that is, before treatment, the mean number of symptoms was 9. After the therapy, the mean number of symptoms was 4.85, the median was 3.5, and the mode was 10. Proponents of the new therapy make the following claims: On average, symptoms decreased by almost half (based on the mean), and more than 50% of participants had substantial symptom reduction (based on the median). Opponents, however, convey the data differently. A spokeswoman from the pharmaceutical company that manufactures a medication to treat acrophobia makes several counterclaims when she promotes the superiority of her company's medication: The number of symptoms most frequently reported was 10, which shows that the therapy actually made people *more* symptomatic (based on the mode). Also, the therapy achieved mixed results, as indicated by the fact that the number of symptoms after treatment ranged from 1 to 10.

As you can see, both supporters and detractors of the new treatment are correct. They are just presenting different aspects of the data. Thus, when hearing or reading about research or survey results, you should ask several questions before taking the results too seriously.

1. What is the distribution of the results? If they are normally distributed, the measures of central tendency will be similar to each other. If they are skewed, the measures of central tendency will convey different information, and the one presented will be the one that conveys the information the reporter wants you to know about. Do the other measures of central tendency paint a different picture of the results?

2. How variable are the data? What does it mean if the results vary a lot rather than a little?

Lying With Graphs

Many results are presented in graph form. Graphs work largely because of a single principle: *More is more* (Kosslyn, 1994). Larger bars, higher lines, or bigger wedges all stand for greater amounts than smaller bars, lines, or wedges. Our tendency to see more on the page as standing for more of a substance can lead us astray if graphs are constructed to deceive. Be alert to the following tricks.

Shortening the Y (vertical) axis to exaggerate a difference. As you can see in Figure A.5, starting the Y axis at a high value and devoting the Y axis to a small part of the scale make what is in fact a small difference look like a large one. If a difference is significant, it should look that way (and thus shortening the axis may be appropriate). But if it's not, then shortening the axis to exaggerate the difference is deception.

Using an inappropriately large range of values to minimize a difference. The flip side of the coin is illustrated in Figure A.6, in which a difference is made to appear smaller by using a large range in values on the Y axis.

Using three-dimensional graphics to exaggerate size. As shown in Figure A.7, a designer can take advantage of our tendency to impose size constancy (see Chapter 3), so that a bar that is farther away will be seen as *much* larger than a same-size one that is closer. And even if an actual difference exists, this technique can exaggerate its magnitude.

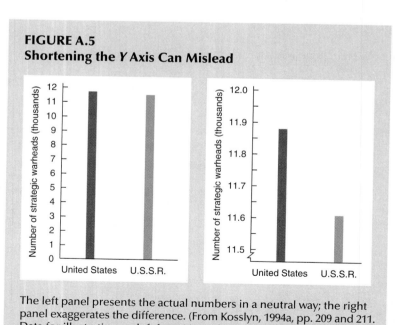

FIGURE A.5
Shortening the Y Axis Can Mislead

The left panel presents the actual numbers in a neutral way; the right panel exaggerates the difference. (From Kosslyn, 1994a, pp. 209 and 211. Data for illustration on left from Natural Resources Defense Council.)

FIGURE A.6
Lengthening the Y Axis Can Mislead

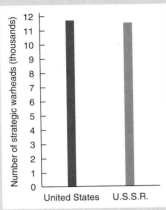

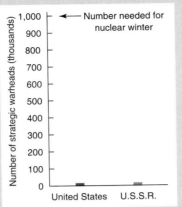

The left panel presents the actual numbers in a neutral way; the right panel minimizes the difference. (From Kosslyn, 1994a, pp. 209 and 211. Data for illustration on left from Natural Resources Defense Council.)

Transforming the data before plotting. Compare the two panels of Figure A.8. The first shows the size of the stock market in three countries over 3 years, the second the percentage increase over two 5-year periods. If you saw only the second, you wouldn't realize that the increases in the U.S. stock market were actually much greater than those in Japan. If the user is trying to sell Japanese stocks, you can bet which display will be preferred.

FIGURE A.7
Size Constancy Can Exaggerate 3-D Bar Size

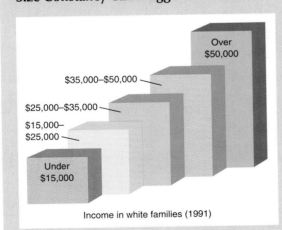

Size constancy leads us to see the bars that are farther away as larger than they are, thereby exaggerating a difference. (From Kosslyn, 1994a, p. 227. Data from Hacker, 1992, p. 98, cited in *Newsweek*, 23 March 1992, p. 61.)

FIGURE A.8
Two Ways of Viewing Changes in Stock Markets

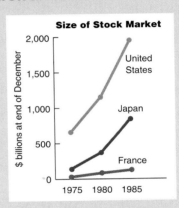

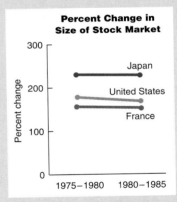

The top panel shows the actual dollar figures, and the bottom shows the percentage change. Clearly, the message conveyed by the two displays is different. Which one is "more honest" depends on the purpose for which the graph is used. (From Kosslyn, 1994a, p. 219. Data from Morgan Stanley Capital International, cited in *The Economist World Atlas and Almanac*, 1989, p. 90.)

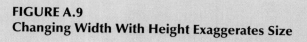

FIGURE A.9
Changing Width With Height Exaggerates Size

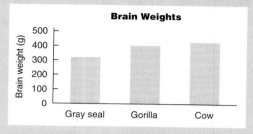

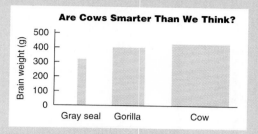

Expanding the bar width conveys the impression that more quantity is being presented than increasing the height alone signals. (From Kosslyn, 1994a, p. 225. Data from Weisberg, 1980, cited in Chambers et al., 1983, p. 371.)

Changing width along with height. As shown in Figure A.9, our visual system does not register height and width separately, but rather we see them simultaneously, as specifying area. So changing the width along with the height gives a much larger impression of amount than is conveyed by changing height alone.

STATISTICS IN DAILY LIFE

You can see that there is nothing magical or mysterious about statistics. Whenever you see a graph in the newspaper, you are seeing statistics; when you hear that a poll is accurate to "plus or minus 3 points," you know that you are being supplied with a confidence interval. The crucial ideas are that there are measures of central tendency (mean, median, and mode), measures of variability (range and standard deviation), and statistical tests that tell you the likelihood that a measured difference is due to chance alone.

What you've learned here is enough to enable you to read and understand many reports of original research in psychology. Appendix B focuses on other aspects of a research study and provides you with tools for analyzing what you read and for writing reports of your own.

APPENDIX B

HOW TO READ, CRITICALLY EVALUATE, AND WRITE RESEARCH PAPERS

Science is a community effort. Only through the cooperation (and competition) of many people does scientific knowledge inch forward. Both to get a sense of what's happening at the cutting edge of the science of psychology and to learn how to write better research papers yourself, you need to read articles published in psychology journals. These articles report new findings and theories and document the latest progress in the field. At first glance, a journal article may seem hopelessly dense and difficult to understand. One goal of this appendix, therefore, is to give you a brief guide to reading such articles, as well as to provide you with pointers on how to evaluate them. In addition, this appendix gives you background and resources that will help you write your own research papers.

USING THE APA FORMAT

Most articles published in psychology, and most of the papers you will be asked to write in psychology classes, are organized according to guidelines provided by the American Psychological Association (APA) in the *Publication Manual of the American Psychological Association* (4th ed., 1994; you can find more detailed information about these guidelines at *http://www.apa.org/apa-style/homepage.html*). This standardized format not only ensures consistency across the scientific community but also helps authors to include all of the crucial information and allows readers to know what to expect. A paper that reports new research findings using the APA format follows this structure:

GENERAL INTRODUCTION. The General Introduction provides the context for the research. It consists of an overview of the topic being researched, describing previous studies on the topic, analyzing their flaws, pointing out gaps in what they examined, and noting contradictory findings. In this section, the authors introduce the general purpose of the study.

STUDY INTRODUCTION. Here, the study is introduced more narrowly, with background information supplied for the particular technique being used. If only one study is reported, this material is presented at the end of the General Introduction.

METHOD. The Method section explains, in detail, what was actually done. The type of method used, of the sort summarized in Chapter 1 (case study, quasi-experiment, and so on), and the specific details of how the study was conducted are provided. The goal is to describe the methodology in enough detail that someone else could repeat the study in precisely the same way. The Method section often has distinct subsections:

Participants (or *subjects*) describes the nature of the people or animals that took part in the study.

Materials describes the stimuli. For example, a questionnaire, words read aloud, pictures shown on a screen—all of these are typical materials in psychology studies.

Apparatus describes the physical props or instruments involved in the study (for example, the type of computer and monitor used to present stimuli, as well as the monitor settings). The apparatus is used to present the stimuli (described in *Materials*) and to record responses.

Procedure describes exactly how the study was conducted, step by step.

RESULTS. The Results section reports what happened. This section includes descriptive statistics (such as means and standard deviations, as described in Appendix A) and inferential statistics (tests to determine which differences in and patterns of responses should be taken seriously; see Appendix A).

DISCUSSION. Whereas the Results section provides just the bare facts, the Discussion section seeks to interpret them, often referring to previous studies or theories.

GENERAL DISCUSSION. One journal article may report several studies. After one General Introduction, separate sections ranging from Study Introduction to Discussion—as described above—are included for each study. After the last study is reported, a General Discussion ties them all together. A General Discussion typically begins with a brief summary of the sum total of the results and often ends with suggestions for additional research that would answer new questions raised by the results.

HOW TO ORGANIZE AND EVALUATE WHAT YOU READ AND WRITE

Once you understand the structure of a journal article, you will find it useful to approach reading and writing such articles armed with what we call the

QALMRI method. This method provides a means for critically evaluating a study in the literature, as well as for organizing your own study, and will help you see the connection between theory and data. That is, it will help you to be clear on what question is being asked, how to answer it, and whether the results really do support the preferred answer. In brief:

Q stands for the **question.** All research begins with a question, and the point of the research is to answer it. For example, we can ask whether a placebo is better than no action in curing depression. The first few paragraphs of the General Introduction should tell the reader what question the article is addressing. In addition, the context provided by the General Introduction's review of previous studies should explain why the question is important, why anybody should care about answering it. The General Introduction should provide the general context, providing the reasons why the question is worthy of consideration.

A stands for **alternatives.** A good report describes at least two possible answers to the question and explains why both are plausible. For example, the possibility that the placebo is better than doing nothing is plausible because beliefs arise from the brain, and brain activity can in turn affect the endocrine system—which could in turn affect mood. And the alternative possibility, that a placebo is no more effective than doing nothing in combating depression, is also plausible.

The General Introduction should also explain what alternatives are being considered. When reading or writing the General Introduction, identify the question and then the alternative answers that will be considered. If the alternatives in a study you read are not spelled out, try to figure out for yourself what they might be; if the study is simply seeking to confirm a theory's prediction, try to get a sense of whether other theories (or just common sense) would make the same prediction. If all the theories make the same prediction, it probably isn't worth testing. When writing your own reports, clearly describe the alternatives and why they are plausible.

L stands for the **logic** of the study. The goal of the study is to discriminate among the alternatives, and the logic is the general idea behind the study—the way the study will distinguish among the alternatives. The logic is typically explained toward the end of a study introduction and has the following structure: *If* alternative 1 (and not alternative 2) is correct, *then* when a particular variable is manipulated, the participant's behavior should change in a specific way. For example, the logic of a study of placebo effectiveness would rest on comparing a group receiving a placebo with a group receiving nothing. (In all other respects, the groups would be treated the same.) The logic would sound like this: *If* the placebo has a curative effect (and doing nothing doesn't), *then* the people receiving it should report fewer symptoms than the people receiving nothing. Notice that the logic depends crucially on the question and alternatives. For example, if we had asked a different question, such as whether a placebo is as effective as antidepressant medication, then the logic would require that we include a group receiving medication—but given the way we have formulated the question, this isn't necessary.

M stands for the **method,** found in the Method section. When reading an article, or writing your own, consider the following. With regard to *participants:* How were they selected? Are they a representative sample of the population in general? If the study involves more than one group, are they equivalent on important variables, such as age and education? For the placebo study, participants in both groups should be of identical age, education, and health status. It is crucial that they have the same level of depression prior to the study and the same prior experiences with medication. *Materials:* If questionnaires are used in the study, have they been shown to be valid (that is, do they measure what they are supposed to measure)? Are they reliable (that is, do they produce consistent results)? Do the materials used in different parts of the study differ inappropriately in important ways? For the placebo study, one key would be the nature of the placebo itself: What did the pill look like? Did it resemble pills that the participants had already taken and knew to be effective? Did it taste like a sugar pill? *Apparatus:* Was a computer used? If so, exactly how did it present the stimuli? What other physical props were used? In the placebo study, were the pills dispensed using a special machine or just given in a bottle? *Procedure:* Try to visualize yourself in the study. Is it clear exactly what was done? How were the pills produced? provided to the participants? Were there proper control groups? Were participants given appropriate instructions (clear, but not leading them on)? For studies using a placebo group, as in all studies, it is crucial that the investigator treat the participants in the two groups exactly the same way; if the investigator is cheerful and friendly to the people in the placebo group but distant and cold to those in the control group, it could be this treatment—and not the presence or absence of placebo—that affects the participants' feelings of depression. Such nuts-and-bolts concerns can make or break a study; if they are not properly handled, the results are ambiguous at best.

R stands for the **results,** found in the Results section. What happened? First, look for (when reading) or report (when writing) measures of central tendency (means, medians, modes) and some measure of the sampling variability (commonly, standard deviations; see Appendix A). The actual results are descriptive. For example, the ratings of depression might be lower for the group receiving a placebo than for the group receiving nothing. Second, not all differences and patterns in the results should be taken seriously—some differences are simply quirks due to chance. Inferential statistics are performed to determine which patterns of variation are unlikely to have arisen due to chance.

For most studies in psychology, inferential statistics are used to assign a probability value to a comparison, noted as $p < .05$ (or $p > .1$, $p < .01$, and so on). As discussed in Appendix A, this number indicates the likelihood that the difference occurred merely due to chance; $p < .05$, for example, means that the probability that the difference occurred due to chance is less than 5 in 100. Usually, any p value of .05 or less means that the result is considered "statistically significant"—you can be reasonably certain that the difference found in the sample reflects an actual difference in the population as a whole. For example, if an inferential test showed that the difference between the placebo and the control group was "significant at $p < .001$," that would mean that the difference would occur by chance less than 1 time in 1,000 if the study were repeated over and over (see Appendix A).

Finally, **I** stands for the **inferences** that can be drawn about the question and alternatives, given the results. The Discussion section usually contains the inferences the authors want to draw from their results. If the study was well designed (the logic sound and the method rigorous), the results should allow you to eliminate at least one of the alternatives. For example, in the placebo study, the results might show that placebo really does help depression more than doing nothing. At this point, take a step back and think about potential *confounds* that could have led to the results. Were any alternative explanations *not* ruled out? And consider any loose ends. For example, perhaps the way the participants were treated when given the placebo is a major variable, and the effects of placebos can be enhanced or reduced by different social interactions with the caregivers.

USING ONLINE SOURCES OF INFORMATION

How do you find research or other relevant material about a topic when writing a paper? For that matter, how do you evaluate the references cited in journal articles? To take advantage of all that the research community has to offer, you should be seeking online as well as print sources of information. Much of this textbook was written using online sources. But as you probably know, the Web has at least as much misleading information as it has correct reporting. Nobody edits it, nobody monitors it, nobody certifies it. It's up to you to sort the wheat from the chaff.

How, then, can you find useful information on the Web, and how can you verify that it should be taken at face value? There are three general ways to use online sources.

Databases

First, if you already know of a likely source of information or a particular article, you can go directly to a specialized database, such as PsychInfo or Medline. PsychInfo is offered through many college libraries, and Medline's search is publicly available at http://www.nlm.nih.gov/medlineplus/searchmedlineplus.html. At a database, you can usually retrieve abstracts of articles simply by entering key terms (including the author's name, if you know it). If you have access only to an abstract, beware: Abstracts sometimes aren't written by the authors themselves, and even when they are, they necessarily simplify the study and its findings. This simplification is sometimes so extreme that the results can be distorted. Thus, we urge you to use abstracts only as a "first pass," to narrow down likely sources. If the results seem important, get the actual paper.

Sometimes you can even obtain an entire paper online. The American Psychological Association offers a site where you can read complete versions of all papers published in APA journals since the late 1980s. The APA continues to enter earlier papers, so the database will have more older articles available over time. This site, however, is available only to members (including student members) of the APA and to schools or organizations that subscribe to the service.

Organizations' Web Sites

If you don't know which database to check, you can try the Web sites of relevant organizations, such as the American Psychological Association (www.apa.org). In this case, the challenge is to think of the most relevant organizations for your topic. In psychology, the two APAs (the American Psychological Association and the American Psychiatric Association) are good places to start. In fact, the American Psychological Association has a special online pamphlet for students—"Library Research in Psychology: Finding It Easily" (http://www.apa.org/science/lib.html)—and the American Psychiatric Association has links to many useful sources (http://www.psych.org/libr_publ/index.html). You can also search the Web sites of other psychological organizations, such as the Society for Research in Child Development (http://www.srcd.org/publica.shtml) and the American Psychological Society (http://www.psychologicalscience.org/). Similarly, for many subfields in psychology, there are relevant national organizations with Web sites, such as the American Association for Mental Retardation (http://www.aamr.org) and the American Society for Clinical Hypnosis (www.asch.net). Links posted on such sites have more credibility than those found through a search engine, given the likelihood that they've been approved by the parent organization. However, the parent organization can't possibly ensure that all information on other sites is correct. So again, don't take what you find at face value. Look before you leap, and think before you quote.

Search Engines

Finally, what do you do if you're forced to cast your search more widely and browse the whole Web? You can simply use a search engine, such as Google (www.google.com) or Excite (www.excite.com). We've found that the best searches have as many specific terms as possible; the more terms you include, the more irrelevant cites will be weeded out. It's instructive to look at a dozen or so of the sites that turn up following a search. You may be shocked to discover how much inconsistency there is; not only can the summaries of the research differ but so can the evaluations and conclusions that are based on it. And sometimes the authors of the secondary sources (which summarize or discuss an original article) just get it wrong—they either describe the study incorrectly or misinterpret the implications of the results.

As a first step in evaluating a site, see whether five or six other researchers reach consistent conclusions. Moreover, evaluate the source of each site. Does it have a reputable host? Are you reading an actual published paper, an unpublished paper, notes used in lectures, or notes used by someone else in writing a paper? In general, the more evaluation that a given paper receives (as happens with published papers, but not student notes), the better. Also consider whether the material is up-to-date. Check the date to make sure that the work reflects the most recent research. This isn't to say, however, that time-honored and well-replicated older studies are any less credible because of their age.

In Sum

Reading Research

When you read a study, remember to read it in terms of both the big picture outlined above and the details. Figure out exactly what question the authors wanted to answer and what alternative answers they've considered. Can you think of others? Always be on the lookout for potential confounds and alternative explanations, and look for features of the study that limit how well its results can be generalized; for example, can you assume that the results necessarily generalize to other ages, races, or cultures? Be sure to read the footnotes. The single most important advice we can give about reading a study is to be an active reader: Think about what the authors are claiming, and think about whether it makes sense.

Writing Your Own Papers

The same principles apply to writing your own research papers. Write the **Introduction** so that the reader clearly understands the question you are addressing, why it is important (in the context of the previously reported studies on the topic), the alternative possible answers you will consider (including, in most cases, your "favorite" one—often called simply the hypothesis), and the logic of the design (the basic idea underlying the study). In the **Method** section, be sure to include enough detail to allow another researcher to repeat, exactly, what you did. In the **Results** section, first present results that bear directly on the question and alternative answers. These results should be measures of central tendency and variability, which are often best presented in a graph. The results that address the question are most important—even if they are not as striking as some of the other findings. If your Introduction is clear, the reader is focused like a laser beam on the question and is waiting to find out which alternative answer is supported by the results. Don't keep the reader in suspense; present the results that speak to the question at the outset of the Results section. Finally, in the **Discussion,** return to the question and alternative answers, and discuss exactly what you can infer from your results. Have you shown that some of the alternatives must be discarded? Is only one viable? What should future research focus on to propel the field even further ahead?

When reading or writing a research report, always put yourself in the place of the intelligent reader. If a report has been written clearly, the reader will glide through it effortlessly, understanding what the author intended to convey, why the research was conducted in a particular way, what the discoveries were, and why the report is interesting and important.

REFERENCES

Aarons, L. (1976). Sleep-assisted instruction. *Psychological Bulletin, 83,* 1–40.

Abel, T., Martin, K. C., Bartsch, D., & Kandel, E. R. (1998). Memory suppressor genes: Inhibitory constraints on the storage of long-term memory. *Science, 279,* 338–341.

Ablon, J. S., & Jones, E. E. (1999). Psychotherapy process in the National Institute of Mental Health Treatment of Depression Collaborative Research Program. *Journal of Consulting and Clinical Psychology, 67,* 64–75.

Abraham, H. D. (1983). Visual phenomenology of the LSD flashback. *Archives of General Psychiatry, 40,* 884–889.

Abramowitz, J. S. (1997). Effectiveness of psychological and pharmacological treatments for obsessive-compulsive disorder: A quantitative review. *Journal of Consulting and Clinical Psychology, 65,* 44–52.

Abrams, L. R., & Jones, R. W. (1994, August). *The contribution of social roles to psychological distress in businesswomen.* Paper presented at the 102nd annual convention of the American Psychological Association, Los Angeles, CA.

Abramson, L. Y., Seligman, M. E., & Teasedale, J. D. (1978). Learned helplessness in humans: Critique and reformulation. *Journal of Abnormal Psychology, 87,* 49–74.

Achter, J., Lubinski, D., & Benbow, C. P. (1996). Multipotentiality among the intellectually gifted: "It was never there and already it's vanishing." *Journal of Counseling Psychology, 43,* 65–76.

Adams, H. E., Wright, W. L., & Lohr, B. A. (1996). Is homophobia associated with homosexual arousal? *Journal of Abnormal Psychology, 105,* 440–445.

Adams, J. (1967). *Human memory.* New York: McGraw-Hill.

Adams, S. H., Cartwright, L. K., Ostrove, J. M., Stewart, A. J., & Wink, P. (1998). Psychological predictors of good health in three longitudinal samples of educated midlife women. *Health Psychology, 17,* 412–420.

Addis, M. E. (1997). Evaluating the treatment manual as a means of disseminating empirically validated psychotherapies. *Clinical Psychology: Science & Practice, 4,* 1–11.

Ader, R. (1976). Conditioned adrenocortical steroid elevations in the rat. *Journal of Comparative and Physiological Psychology, 90,* 1156–1163.

Ader, R., & Cohen, N. (1975). Behaviorally conditioned immunosuppression. *Psychosomatic Medicine, 37,* 333–340.

Ader, R., & Cohen, N. (1985), CNS-immune system interactions: Conditioning phenomena. *Behavioral and Brain Sciences, 8,* 379–394.

Ader, R., & Cohen, N. (1993). Psychoneuroimmunology: Conditioning and stress. *Annual Review of Psychology, 40,* 53–85.

Adler, A. (1956). *The individual psychology of Alfred Adler: A systematic presentation of selections from his writings.* (H. L. Ansbacher & R. R. Ansbacher, Eds.). New York: Basic Books.

Adler, A. (1964). *Social interest: A challenge to mankind.* New York: Capricorn Books. (Original work published 1933).

Adolphs, R., Damasio, H., Tranel, D., & Damasio, A. R. (1996). Cortical systems for the recognition of emotion in facial expressions. *Journal of Neuroscience, 16,* 7678–7687.

af Klinteberg, B., Andersson, T., Magnusson, D., & Stattin, H. (1993). Hyperactive behavior in childhood as related to subsequent alcohol problems and violent offending: A longitudinal study of male subjects. *Personality of Individual Differences, 15,* 381–388.

Agency for Health Care Policy and Research. (1999). Newer antidepressant drugs are equally as effective as older-generation drug treatments, research shows. AHCPR Pub. No. 99-E013. Rockville, MD.

Aglioti, S., Smania, N., Manfred, M., & Berlucchi, G. (1996). Disownership of left hand and objects related to it in a patient with right brain damage. *Neuroreport, 8,* 293–296.

Aguilar-Alonso, A. (1996). Personality and creativity. *Personality and Individual Differences, 21,* 959–969.

Ainsworth, M. D. S., Blehar, M. C., Waters, E., & Wahl, S. (1978). *Patterns of attachment: A psychological study of the Strange Situation.* Hillsdale, NJ: Erlbaum.

Akhtar, N., & Tomasello, M. (1996). Two-year-olds learn words for absent objects and actions. *British Journal of Developmental Psychology, 14,* 79–93.

Akiskal, H. S. (1996). The prevalent clinical spectrum of bipolar disorders: Beyond DSM–IV. *Journal of Clinical Psychopharmacology, 16* (Suppl. 1), 4S–14S.

Alan Guttmacher Institute. (1994). *Sex and America's teenagers.* New York.

Alba, J. W., & Hasher, L. (1983). Is memory schematic? *Psychological Bulletin, 93,* 203–231.

Albert, M. S., Duffy, F. H., & McAnulty, G. B. (1990). Electrophysiologic comparisons between two groups of patients with Alzheimer's disease. *Archives of Neurology, 47,* 857–863.

Albert, M. S., & Moss, M. B. (1996). Neuropsychology of aging: Findings in humans and monkeys. In E. L. Schneider, J. W. Rowe, T. E. Johnson, N. J., Holbrook, & J. H. Morrison, (Eds.), *Handbook of the biology of aging (4th ed.).* San Diego, CA: Academic Press.

Alcock, J. E. (1987). Parapsychology: Science of the anomalous of search for the soul? *Behavioral and Brain Sciences, 10,* 553–565.

Alcoholics Anonymous. (1999). *12 Steps of Alcoholics Anonymous.* URL http://www.addictions.org/aa/steps.htm.

Aldag, R. J., & Fuller, S. R. (1993). Beyond fiasco: A reappraisal of the groupthink phenomenon and a new model of group decision processes. *Psychological Bulletin, 113,* 533–552.

Aldous, J., & Ganey, R. F. (1999). Family life and the pursuit of happiness: The influence of gender and race. *Journal of Family Issues, 20,* 155–180.

Alexander, C. N., Robinson, P., Orme-Johnson, D. W., Schneider, R. H., & Walton, K. G. (1994a). The effects of transcendental meditation compared to other methods of relaxation and meditation in reducing risk factors, morbidity, and mortality. *Homeostasis, 35,* 243–264.

Alexander, C. N., Robinson, P., & Rainforth, M. (1994b). Treating and preventing alcohol, nicotine, and drug abuse through transcendental meditation: A review and statistical meta-analysis of 19 studies. *Alcoholism Treatment Quarterly, Vol. II,* 13–87.

Alexander, D. (1991). Keynote Address. In *President's Committee on Mental Retardation, Summit on the National Effort to Prevent Mental Retardation and Related Disabilities.*

Alexander, F., & French, T. (1946). *Psychoanalytic theory.* New York: Ronald.

Alexander, M. G., Brewer, M. B., & Hermann, R. K. (1999). Images and affect: A functional analysis of out-group stereotypes. *Journal of Personality and Social Psychology, 77,* 78–93.

Alkire, M. T., Haier, R. J., & James, H. F. (1998). Toward the neurobiology of consciousness: Using brain imaging and anesthesia to investigate the anatomy of consciousness. In S. Hameroff, A. Kaszniak, & A. Scott (Eds.) *Toward a Science of Consciousness II.* Cambridge, MA: MIT Press.

Allen, B. (1997). *Personality theories: Development, growth, and diversity.* (2nd ed.). Needham Heights, MA: Allyn & Bacon.

Allen, J. J. B., & Iacono, W. G. (1997). A comparison of methods for the analysis of event-related potentials in deception detection. *Psychophysiology, 34,* 234–240.

Allen, L. S., & Gorski, R. A. (1992). Sexual orientation and the size of the anterior commissure in the human brain. *Proceedings of the National Academy of Sciences of the United States of America, 89,* 7199–7202.

Allison, J. (1970). Respiratory changes during transcendental meditation. *Lancet, 1(7651),* 833–834.

Allyn, J., & Festinger, L. (1961). The effectiveness of unanticipated persuasive communications. *Journal of Abnormal and Social Psychology, 62,* 35–40.

Almor, A., & Sloman, S. A. (1996). Is deontic reasoning special? *Psychological Review, 103,* 374–380.

Alper, C. M., Doyle, W. J., Skoner, D. P., Buchman, C. A., Seroky, J. T., Gwaltney, J. M., & Cohen, S. (1996). Pre-challenge antibodies moderate infection rate, and signs and symptoms in adults experimentally challenged with rhinovirus 39. *Laryngoscope, 106,* 1298–1305.

Altshuler, L. L., Bartzokis, G., Grieder, T., Curran, J., & Mintz, J. (1998). Amygdala enlargement in bipolar disorder and hippocampal reduction in schizophrenia: An MRI study demonstrating neuroanatomic specificity. *Archives of General Psychiatry, 55,* 663–664.

Aluja-Fabregat, A., Colom, R., Abad, F., & Juan-Espinosa, M. (2000). Sex differences in general intelligence defined as *g* among young adolescents. *Personality & Individual Differences, 28,* 813–820.

Amabile, T. M. (1983). *The social psychology of creativity.* New York: Springer-Verlag.

Amabile, T. M. (1985). Motivation and creativity: Effects of motivational orientation on creative writers. *Journal of Personality & Social Psychology, 48,* 393–397.

Amabile, T. M. (1998, September–October). How to kill creativity. *Harvard Business Review,* pp. 76–87.

Amabile, T. M., Hennessey, B. A., & Grossman, B. S. (1986). Social influences on creativity: The effects of contracted-for reward. *Journal of Personality and Social Psychology, 50,* 14–23.

Amat, J., Matus-Amat, P., Watkins, L. R., & Maier, S. F. (1998). Escapable and inescapable stress differentially alter extracellular levels of 5-HT in the basolateral amygdala of the rat. *Brain Research, 812,* 113–120.

Ambady, N., & Rosenthal, R. (1992). Thin slices of expressive behavior as predictors of interpersonal consequences: A meta analysis. *Psychological Bulletin, 111,* 256–274.

Ambady, N., & Rosenthal, R. (1993). Half a minute: Predicting teacher evaluations from thin slices of behavior and physical attractiveness. *Journal of Personality and Social Psychology, 64,* 431–441.

Ambrose, N. G., Yairi, E., & Cox, N. (1993). Genetic aspects of early childhood stuttering. *Journal of Speech & Hearing Research, 36,* 521–528.

Ambuel, B. (1995). Adolescents, unintended pregnancy, and abortion: The struggle for a compassionate social policy. *Current Directions in Psychological Science, 4,* 1–5.

American Association for Mental Retardation (1992). *Mental retardation: Definition, classification, and systems of supports* (9th ed.).

American Foundation for Suicide Prevention. (1996). *http://www.afsp.org/suicide/facts.html.*

American Psychiatric Association (1987). Diagnostic and statistical manual of mental disorders (3rd ed., rev.). Washington, DC: American Psychiatric Association.

American Psychiatric Association. (1994). *Diagnostic and statistical manual of mental disorders, 4th edition.* Washington, DC: American Psychiatric Association.

American Psychological Association (APA). (1992). *Ethical principles of psychologists & code of conduct* [www.document]. URL http://www.apa.org/ethics/code.html.

Ames, A. (1952). *The Ames demonstration in perception.* New York: Hafner.

Amsterdam, B. (1972). Mirror self-image reactions before age two. *Developmental Psychology, 5,* 297–305.

Anand, B. K., & Brobeck, J. R. (1952). Food intake and spontaneous activity of rats with lesions in the amygdaloid nuclei. *Journal of Neurophysiology, 15,* 421–430.

Anastasi, A. (1988). *Psychological testing* (6th ed.). New York: Macmillan.

Anch, A. M., Bowman, C. P., Mitler, M. M., & Walsh, J. K. (1988). *Sleep: A scientific perspective.* Englewood Cliffs, NJ: Prentice-Hall.

Andersen, A. E., & DiDomenico, L. (1992). Diet vs. shape content of popular male and female magazines: A dose response relationship to the incidence of eating disorders? *International Journal of Eating Disorders, 11,* 283–287.

Andersen, B. (1997, July). Psychological interventions for individuals with cancer. *Clinician's Research Digest* (Suppl. bulletin) *16,* 1–2.

Andersen, B. L., Kiecolt-Glaser, K. K., & Glaser, R. (1994). A biobehavioral model of cancer stress and disease course. *American Psychologist, 49,* 389–404.

Andersen, B. L., & Nakayama, K. (1994). Toward a general theory of stereopsis: Binocular matching, occluding contours, and fusion. *Psychological Review, 101,* 414–445.

Anderson, C. A. (1983). Abstract and concrete data in the perseverance of social theories: When weak data lead to unshakable beliefs. *Journal of Experimental Social Psychology, 19,* 930–1108.

Anderson, C. A., & Bushman, B. J. (1997). External validity of "trivial" experiments: The case of laboratory aggression. *Review of General Psychology, 1,* 19–41.

Anderson, C. A., Lepper, M. R., & Ross, L. (1980). Perseverance of social theories: This role of explanation in the persistence of discredited information. *Journal of Personality and Social Psychology, 39,* 1037–1049.

Anderson, J. R. (2000). *Cognitive psychology and its implications* (5th ed.). New York: Worth.

Anderson, M. (1992). *Intelligence and development: A cognitive theory.* Oxford, England: Blackwell.

Anderson, M. C., Bjork, R. A., & Bjork, E. L. (1994). Remembering can cause forgetting: Retrieval dynamics in long-term memory. *Journal of Experimental Psychology: Learning, Memory and Cognition, 20,* 1063–1087.

Anderson, N. A. (1981). *Foundations of information integration theory.* New York: Academic Press.

Anderson, N. B. (1998). Levels of analysis in health science: A framework for integrating sociobehavioral and biomedical research. In S. M. McCann, J. M. Lipton, et al. (Eds.), *Annals of the New York Academy of Sciences: Vol. 840, Neuroimmunomodulation: Molecular aspects, integrative systems, and clinical advances* (pp. 563–576). New York: New York Academy of Sciences.

Anderson, V. L., Levinson, E. M., Barker, W., & Kiewra, K. R. (1999). The effects of meditation on teacher perceived occupational stress, state and trait anxiety, and burnout. *School Psychology Quarterly, 14,* 3–25.

Andreasen, N. C. (1987). Creativity and mental illness: Prevalence rates in writers and their first-degree relatives. *American Journal of Psychiatry, 144,* 1288–1292.

Andreasen, N. C., Nasrullah, H., Dunn, V., Olson, S., Grove, W., Erhardt, J., Coffman, J., & Crosett, J. (1986). Structural abnormalities in the fronal system in schizophrenia. *Archives of General Psychiatry, 43,* 136–144.

Andreasen, N. C., Rezai, K., Alliger, R., Swayze, V., Flaum, M., Kirchner, P., Cohen, G., & O'Leary, D. (1992). Hypofrontality in neuroleptic-naïve patients and in patients with chronic schizophrenia: Assessment with xenon-133 single proton emission computed tomography and the Tower of London. *Archives of General Psychiatry, 49,* 943–958.

Andreasen, N. C., Flashman, L., Flaum, M., Arndt, S., Swayze, V., O'Leary, D. S., Ehrhardt, J. C., & Yuh, W. T. (1994). Regional brain abnormalities in schizophrenia measured with magnetic resonance imaging. *Journal of the American Medical Association, 272,* 1763–1769.

Andrews, H. B., & Jones, S. (1990). Eating behaviour in obese women: A test of two hypotheses. *Australian Psychologist, 25,* 351–357.

Andrews, J. A., Hops, H., Duncan, S. C. (1997). Adolescent modeling of parent substance use: The moderating effect of the relationship with the parent. *Journal of Family Psychology,11,* 259–270.

Angier, N. (1999, September 7). Route to creativity: Following bliss or dots? *New York Times,* F3 (col. 1).

Angleitner, A., Riemann, R., & Strelau, J. (1995). A study of twins using the self-report and peer-report NEO-FFI sclaes. Paper presented at the seventh meeting of the International Society for the Study of Individual Differences, July 15–19, Warsaw, Poland.

Anglin, J. M. (1993). Vocabulary development: A morphological analysis. *Monographs of the Society for Research in Child Development, 58(10,* Serial No. 238).

Angst, J. (1998). The emerging epidemiology of hypomania and bipolar II disorder. *Journal of Affective Disorders, 50,* 143–151.

Anisman, H., Zaharia, M. D., Meaney, M. J., & Merali, Z. (1998). Do early-life events permanently alter behavioral and hormonal responses to stressors? *International Journal of Developmental Neuroscience, 16,* 149–164.

Ankney, C. D. (1992). Sex differences in relative brain size: The mismeasure of women, too? *Intelligence, 16,* 329–336.

Anonymous. (1970). Effects of sexual activity on beard growth in man. *Nature, 226,* 867–870.

Antoch, M. P., Song, E. J., Chang, A. M., Vitaterna, M. H., Zhao, Y., Wilsbacher, L. D., Sangoram, A. M., King, D. P., Pinto, L. H., Takahashi, J. S. (1997, May 16). Functional identification of the mouse circadian Clock gene by transgenic BAC rescue. *Cell, 89(4),* 655–667.

Antonuccio, D. O., Danton, W. G., & DeNelsky, G. Y. (1995). Psychotherapy versus medication for depression: Challenging the conventional wisdom with data. *Professional Psychology: Research & Practice, 26,* 574–585.

Aoyama, N., Kinoshita, Y., Fujimoto, S., Himeno, S., Todo, A., Kasuga, M., & Chiba, T. (1998). Peptic ulcers after the Hanshin-Awaji earthquake: Increased incidence of bleeding gastric ulcers. *American Journal of Gastroenterology, 93,* 311–316.

Aram, D. M., Morris, R., & Hall, N. E. (1992). The validity of discrepancy criteria for identifying children with developmental language disorders. *Journal of Learning Disabilities, 25,* 549–554.

Aranda, M. P., & Knight, B. G. (1997). The influence of ethnicity and culture on the caregiver stress and coping process: A socio-cultural review and analysis. *Gerontologist, 37,* 342–354.

Archer, S. L., & Waterman, A. S. (1988). Psychological individualism: Gender differences or gender neutrality? *Human Development, 31,* 65–81.

Arend, L. (1994). Surface colors, illumination and surface geometry: Intrinsic-image models of human color perception. In A. Gilchrist (Eds.), *Lightness, brightness, and transparency* (pp. 159–213). Hillsdale, NJ: Erlbaum.

Arguin, M., Cavanagh, P., & Joanette, Y. (1994). Visual feature integration with an attention deficit. *Brain and Cognition, 24,* 44–56.

Argyle, M. L., & Lu, L. (1990). Happiness and social skills. *Personality & Individual Differences, 11,* 1255–1261.

Arking, R. (1991). *Biology of aging: Observations and principles.* Englewood Cliffs, NJ: Prentice Hall.

Armstrong, S. L., Gleitman, L. R., & Gleitman, H. (1983). What some concepts might not be. *Cognition, 13,* 263–308.

Arnell, K. M., & Jolicoeur, P. (1999). The attentional blink across stimulus modalities: Evidence for central processing limitations. *Journal of Experimental Psychology: Human Perception and Performance, 25,* 630–648.

Arnett, J. (1992). Reckless behavior in adolescence: A developmental perspective. *Developmental Review, 12,* 339–373.

Arnett, J. J. (1999). Adolescent storm and stress, reconsidered. *American Psychologist, 54,* 317–326.

Arnold, M. B. (1960a). *Emotion and personality: Vol. I, Psychological aspects.* New York: Columbia University Press.

Arnold, M. B. (1960b). *Emotion and personality: Vol. II, Neurological and physiological aspects.* New York: Columbia University Press

Aron, E. N., & Aron, A. (1997). Sensory-processing sensitivity and its relation to introversion and emotionality. *Journal of Personality and Social Psychology, 73,* 345–368.

Aronson, J., Blanton, H., & Cooper, J. (1995). From dissonance to disidentification: Selectivity in the self-affirmation process. *Journal of Personality and Social Psychology, 68,* 986–996.

Asch, S. E. (1951). Effects of group pressure upon the modification and distortion of judgment. In H. Guetzkow (Ed.), *Groups, leadership, and men* (pp. 177–190). Pittsburgh: Carnegie.

Asch, S. E. (1955). Opinions and social pressure. *Scientific American, 193,* 31–35.

Asendorpf, J. B., Warkentin, V., & Baudonniere, P-M. (1996). Self-awareness and other-awareness: II. Mirror self-recognition, social contingency awareness, and synchronic imitation. *Developmental Psychology, 32,* 313–321.

Ashbridge, E., Walsh, V., & Cowley, A. (1997). Temporal aspects of visual search studied by transcranial magnetic stimulation. *Neuropsychologia, 35,* 1121–1131.

Aslin, R. N., Saffran, J. R., & Newport, E. L. (1998). Computation of conditional probability statistics by 8-month-old infants. *Psychological Science, 9,* 321–324.

Atre-Vaidya, N., & Hussain, S. M. (1999). Borderline personality disorder and bipolar mood disorder: Two distinct disorders or a continuum? *Journal of Mental and Nervous Disorders, 187,* 313–315.

Auden, W. H. (1989). *Van Gogh: A self-portrait.* New York: Marlowe.

Avorn, J., & Langer, E. (1982). Induced disability in nursing home patients: A controlled trial. *Journal of the American Geriatrics Society, 30,* 397–400.

Awh, E., Jonides, J., Smith, E. E., Schumacher, E. H., Koeppe, R. A., & Katz, S. (1996). Dissociation of storage and rehearsal in verbal working memory: Evidence from positron emission tomography. *Psychological Science, 7,* 25–31.

Ayton, P., & Wright, G. (1994). Subjective probability: What should we believe? In G. Wright, & P. Ayton. (Eds.), *Subjective Probability* (pp. 163–183). New York: Wiley.

Azar, B. (1995). Timidity can develop in the first days of life. *APA Monitor, 26* (11), 23

Azari, N. P. (1991). Effects of glucose on memory processed in young adults. *Psychopharmacology, 105,* 521–524.

Azrin, N. H., Sisson, R. W., Meyers, R., & Godley, M. (1982). Alcoholism treatment by disulfiram and community reinforcement therapy. *Journal of Behavior Therapy and Experimental Psychiatry, 13,* 105–112.

Babad, E. (1993). Pygmalion—25 years after interpersonal expectations in classroom. In P. D. Blanck (Ed.), *Interpersonal expectations: Theory,* research, and applications (pp. 125–153). Cambridge: Cambridge University Press.

Bachen, E. A., Manuck, S. B., Cohen, S., Muldoon, M. F., Raible, R., Herbert, T. B., & Rabin, B. S. (1995). Adrenergic blockage ameliorates cellular immune responses to mental stress in humans. *Psychosomatic Medicine, 57,* 366–372.

Baddeley, A. (1986). *Working Memory.* Oxford, England: Clarendon.

Baddeley, A. (1992). The magical number seven: Still magic after all these years? *Psychological Review, 101,* 353–356.

Baenninger, M., & Newcombe, N. (1989). The role of experience in spatial test performance: A meta-analysis. *Sex Roles, 20,* 327–344.

Baer, J. (1998). The case for domain specificity of creativity. *Creativity Research Journal, 11,* 173–177.

Baer, L., Ackerman, R., Surman, O., Correia, J., Griffith, J., Alpert, N., & Hackett, T. (1990). PET studies during hypnosis and hypnotic suggestion. In P. Berner (Ed.), *Psychiatry: The state of the art, biological psychiatry, higher nervous activity* (pp. 293–298). New York: Plenum Press.

Bagwell, C. L., Newcomb, A. F., & Bukowski, W. M. (1998). Preadolescent friendship and peer rejection as predictors of adult adjustment. *Child Development, 69,* 140–153.

Bahrick, H. P. (1974). Semantic memory content in permastore: Fifty years of memory for Spanish learned in school. *Journal of Experimental Psychology: General, 120,* 1–31.

Bahrick, H. P., & Phelps, E. (1987). Retention of Spanish vocabulary over eight years. *Journal of Experimental Psychology: Learning, Memory and Cognition, 13,* 344–349.

Bahrick, L. E., Moss, L., & Fadil, C. (1996). Development of visual self-recognition in infancy. *Ecological Psychology, 8,* 189–208.

Bailey, J. M., & Pillard, R. C. (1991). A genetic study of male sexual orientation. *Archives of General Psychiatry, 48,* 1089–1096.

Baillargeon, R. (1993). The object concept revisited: New directions in the investigation of infants' physical knowledge. In C. E. Granrud (Ed.), *Visual perception and cognition in infancy* (pp. 265–315). Hillsdale, NJ: Erlbaum.

Baillargeon, R. (1994). How do infants learn about the physical world? *Current Directions in Psychological Science, 3*(5), 133–140.

Baillargeon, R. (1995). A model of physical reasoning in infancy. In C. K. Rovee-Collier & L. P. Lipsitt (Eds.), *Advances in infancy research* (Vol. 9, pp. 305–371). Norwood, NJ: Ablex.

Baillargeon, R., Graber, M., Devos, J., & Black, J. (1990). Why do young infants fail to search for hidden objects? *Cognition, 36,* 255–284.

Baillargeon, R., Kotovsky, L., & Needham, A. (1995). The acquisition of physical knowledge in infancy. In D. Sperber, D. Premack, & A. J. Premack (Eds.), *Causal understandings in cognition and culture* (pp. 79–116). New York: Oxford University Press.

Baily, C. H., & Chen, M. (1989). Time course of structural changes at identified sensory neuron synapses during long-term sensitization in Aplysia. *Journal of Neuroscience, 9,* 1774–1781.

Baird, J. C. (1982). The moon illusion: II. A reference theory. *Journal of Experimental Psychology, 111,* 304–315.

Baird, J. C., & Wagner, M. (1982). The moon illusion: I. How high is the sky? *Journal of Experimental Psychology, 111,* 296–303.

Baker, R. R. (1980). Goal orientation by blindfolded humans after long-distance displacement: Possible involvement of a magnetic sense. *Science, 210,* 555–557.

Baker, S. C., Dolan, R. J., & Frith, C. D. (1996). The functional anatomy of logic: A PET study of inferential reasoning. *Neuroimage, 3,* S218.

Baldwin, D. A. (2000). Interpersonal understanding fuels knowledge acquisition. *Current Directions in Psychological Science, 9,* 40–45.

Baldwin, J. D., & Baldwin, J. I. (1989). The socialization of homosexuality and heterosexuality in a non-Western society. *Archives of Sexual Behavior, 18,* 13–29.

Ball, D., Hill, L., Eley, T. C., Chorney, M. J., Chorney, K., Thompson, L. A., Detterman, D. K., Benbow, C., Lubinski, D., Owen, M., McGuffin, P., & Plomin, R. (1998). Dopamine markers and general cognitive ability. *NeuroReport, 9,* 347–349.

Ball, T. (1971). *Itard, Seguin, and Kephart: Sensory education—A learning interpretation.* Columbus, OH: Merrill.

Ballus, C. (1997). Effects of antipsychotics on the clinical and psychosocial behavior of patients with schizophrenia. *Schizophrenia Research, 28,* 247–255.

Baltes, P. B. (1987). Theoretical propositions of life-span developmental psychology: On the dynamics between growth and decline. *Developmental Psychology, 23,* 611–626.

Baltes, P. B., Cornelius, S. W., & Nesselroade, J. R. (1979). Cohort effects in developmental psychology. In J. R. Nesselroade & P. B. Baltes (Eds.), *Longitudinal reserach in the study of behavior and development* (pp. 61–87). New York: Academic Press.

Baltes, P. B., Dittmann-Kohli, F., & Dixon, R. A. (1984). New perspectives on the development of intelligence in adulthood: Toward a dual-process conception and a model of selective optimization with compensation. In P. B. Baltes & O. G. Brim, Jr. (Eds.), *Life-span development and behavior* (Vol. 6, pp. 33–76). San Diego, CA: Academic Press.

Banaji, M. R., & Hardin, C. D. (1996). Automatic stereotyping. *Psychological Science, 7,* 136–141.

Bandura, A. (1976). Self-reinforcement: Theoretical and methodological considerations. *Behaviorism, 4,* 135–155.

Bandura, A. (1977a). *Social learning theory.* Englewood Cliffs, NJ: Prentice-Hall.

Bandura, A. (1977b). Self-efficacy: Toward a unifying theory of behavior change. *Psychological Review, 84,* 191–215.

Bandura, A. (1978). The self-system in reciprocal determinism. *American Psychologist, 33,* 344–358.

Bandura, A. (1986). *Social foundations of thought and action: A social-cognitive theory.* Englewood Cliffs, NJ: Prentice-Hall.

Bandura, A., Grusec, J. E., & Menlove, F. L. (1967). Vicarious extinction of avoidance behavior. *Journal of Personality & Social Psychology, 5,* 16–23.

Bandura, A., & Rosenthal, T. L. (1966). Vicarious classical conditioning as a function of arousal level. *Journal of Personality and Social Psychology, 3,* 54–62.

Bandura, A., Ross, D., & Ross, S. A. (1961). Transmission of aggression through imitation of aggressive models. *Journal of Abnomal and Social Psychology, 63,* 575–582.

Bandura, A., Ross, D., & Ross, S. A. (1963). Imitation of film-mediated aggressive models. *Journal of Abnormal & Social Psychology, 66,* 3–11.

Banks, M. S., & Bennett, P. J. (1988). Optical and photoreceptor immaturities limit the spatial and chromatic vision of human neonates. *Journal of the Optical Society of America, 5,* 2059–2079.

Bar, M., & Biederman, I. (1998). Subliminal visual priming. *Psychological Science, 9,* 464–469.

Barabasz, A., & Barabasz, M. (1989) Effects of restricted environmental stimulation: Enhancement of hypnotizability for experimental and chronic pain control. *International Journal of Clinical and Experimental Hypnosis, 37,* 217–231.

Barabasz, A. F., & Lonsdale, C. (1983). Effects of hypnosis on P300 olfactory-evoked potential amplitudes. *Journal of Abnormal Psychology, 92,* 520–523.

Barber, J. (1997). Hypnosis and memory: A cautionary chapter. In G. A. Fraser (Ed.), *The dilemma of ritual abuse: Cautions and guides for therapists.* (pp. 17–29). Washington, DC: American Psychiatric Press.

Barber, J., & Adrian, C. (1982). *Psychological Approaches to the Management of Pain.* New York: Brunner/Mazel Publishers.

Barber, J. P., & Muenz, L. R. (1996). The role of avoidance and obsessiveness in matching patients to cognitive and interpersonal psychotherapy: Empirical findings from the Treatment for Depression Collaborative Research Program. *Journal of Consulting and Clinical Psychology, 64,* 951–958.

Barber, T. X. (1969). An empirically based formulation of hypnotism. *American Journal of Clinical Hypnosis, 12,* 100–130.

Barber, T. X., Spanos, N. P., & Chaves, J. F. (1974) *Hypnosis, Imagination, and Human Potentialities.* New York: Pergamon.

Barbur, J. L., Watson, J. D. G., Frackowiak, R. D. G., & Zeki, S. (1993). Conscious visual perception without V1. *Brain, 116,* 1293–1302.

Barclay, J. R., Bransford, J. D., Franks, J. J., McCarrell, N. S., & Nitsch, K. (1974), Comprehension and semantic flexibility. *Journal of Verbal Learning and Verbal Behavior, 13,* 471–481.

Barefoot, J. C., Dahlstrom, W. G., & Williams, R. B. (1983). Hostility, CHD incidence, and total mortality: A 25-year follow-up study of 255 physicians. *Psychosomatic Medicine, 45,* 59–63.

Barefoot, J., Dodge, K., Peterson, B., Dahlstrom, W., & Williams, R. (1989). The Cook-Medley Hostility Scale: Item content and ability to predict survival. *Psychosomatic Medicine, 51,* 46–57.

Bargh, J. A. (1997). The automaticity of everyday life. In R. S. Eyer, Jr. (Ed.), *Advances in social cognition* (Vol. 10, pp. 1–61). Mahwah, NJ: Erlbaum.

Bargh, J. A., Chen, M., & Burrows, L. (1996). Automaticity of social behavior: Direct effects of trait construct and stereotype activation on action. *Journal of Personality and Social Psychology,71,* 230–244.

Barinaga, M. (1995). Remapping the motor cortex. *Science, 268,* 1696–1698.

Barkham, M., & Shapiro, D. A. (1990). Brief psychotherapeutic interventions for job-related distress: A pilot study of prescriptive and exploratory therapy. *Counseling Psychology Quarterly, 3,* 133–147.

Barkham, M., Shapiro, D. A., Hardy, G. E., & Rees, A. (1999). Psychotherapy in two-plus-one sessions: Outcomes of a randomized controlled trial of cognitive-behavioral and psychodynamic-interpersonal therapy for subsyndromal depression. *Journal of Consulting and Clinical Psychology, 67,* 201–211.

Barkow, J. H., Cosmides, L., & Tooby, J. (Eds.) (1992). *The adapted mind: Evolutionary psychology and the generation of culture.* New York: Oxford University Press.

Barlow, D. H. (1986). Causes of sexual dysfunction: The role of anxiety and cognitive interference. *Journal of Consulting and Clinical Psychology, 54,* 140–148.

Barlow, D. H. (1988). *Anxiety and its disorders.* New York: Guilford Press.

Barlow, D. P. (1995). Gametic imprinting in mammals. *Science, 270,* 1610–1613.

Barnett, L. A., Far, J. M., Mauss, A. L., & Miller, J. A. (1996). Changing perceptions of peer norms as a drinking reduction program for college students. *Journal of Alcohol & Drug Education, 41,* 39–62.

Barnett, M. A., Howard, J. A., King, L. M., & Dino, G. A. (1980). Antecedents of empathy: Retrospective accounts of early socialization. *Personality and Social Psychology Bulletin, 6,* 361–365.

Baron, R., & Byrne, D. (1997). *Social Psychology* (8th ed.). Needham Heights, MA: Allyn & Bacon.

Baron, R. A. (1977). *Human aggression.* New York: Plenum.

Baron, R. A. (1988). Negative effects of destructive criticism: Impact on conflict, self-efficacy, and task performance. *Journal of Applied Psychology, 73,* 199–207.

Baron, R. A. (1993). Criticism (informal negative feedback) as a source of perceived unfairness in organizations: Effects, mechanisms, and countermeasures. In R. Cropanzano (Ed.), *Justice in the workplace: Approaching fairness in human resource management* (pp. 155–170). Hillsdale, NJ: Erlbaum.

Baron, R. B., & Richardson, D. (1994). *Human aggression.* New York: Plenum.

Baron, R. M., & Rodin, J. (1978). Personal control as a mediator of crowding. In A. Baum, J. E. Singer, & S. Valins (eds.), *Advances in environmental psychology, Vol. 1, The urban environment* (pp. 145–190). Hillsdale, NJ: Erlbaum.

Baron, R. S., Vandello, J. A., & Brunsman, B. (1996). The forgotten variable in conformity research: Impact of task importance on social influence. *Journal of Personality and Social Psychology, 71,* 915–927.

Bartlett, F. C. (1932). *Remembering.* Cambridge, England: Cambridge University Press.

Bartoshuk, L. M., & Beauchamp, G. K. (1994). Chemical senses. *Annual Review of Psychology, 45,* 419–449.

Bartoshuk, L. M., Rifkin, B., Marks, L. E., & Bars, P. (1986). Taste and aging. *Journal of Gerontology, 41,* 51–57.

Bartussek, D., Diedrich, O., Naumann, E., & Collet, W. (1993). Introversion-extraversion and event-related potential (ERP): A test of J. A. Gray's theory. *Personality and Individual Differences, 14,* 565–574.

Basic Behavioral Science Task Force of the National Advisory Mental Health Council (1996). Basic behavioral science research for mental health, *American Psychologist, 51,* 722–731.

Bass, B. M. (1990). Bass and Stogdill's handbook of leadership: Theory, reseach, and managerial applications (3rd ed.). New York: Free Press.

Bass, M. B., & Avolio, B. J. (1993). Transformational leadership: A response to critiques. In M. M. Chemers & R. Ayman (Eds.), *Leadership theory and research: Perspectives and directions* (pp. 49–80). San Diego, CA: Academic Press.

Bassili, J. N. (1978). Facial motion in the perception of faces and of emotional expression. *Journal of Experimental Psychology: Human Perception & Performance, 4,* 373–379.

Bates, E., & MacWhinney, B. (1987). Competition, variation, and language learning. In B. MacWhinney (Ed.), *Mechanisms of language acquisition* (pp. 157–193). Hillsdale, NJ: Erlbaum.

Bates, E., Thal, D., Trauner, D., Fenson, J., Aram, D., Eisele, J., & Nass, R. (1997). From first words to grammar in children with focal brain injury. *Developmental Neuropsychology, 13,* 275–343.

Bates, T. C., & Eysenck, H. J. (1993). Intelligence, inspection time, and decision time. *Intelligence, 17,* 523–531.

Batsell, W. R., Jr., & Brown, A. S. (1998). Human flavor-aversion learning: A comparison of traditional aversions and cognitive aversions. *Learning & Motivation, 29,* 383–396.

Batshaw, M., & Perret, Y. (1992). *Children with disabilities: A medical primer.* Baltimore: Brookes.

Batson, C. D. (1998). Altruism and prosocial behavior. In D. T. Gilbert, S. T. Fiske, & G. Lindzey (Eds.), *The handbook of social psychology* (4th ed., pp. 282–316). New York: McGraw Hill.

Batson, C. D., Bolen, M. H., Cross, J. A., & Neuringer-Benefiel, H. E. (1986). Where is the altruism in the altruistic personality? *Journal of Personality & Social Psychology, 50,* 212–220.

Baumeister, R. F., & Boden, J. M. (1998). Aggression and the self: High self-esteem, low self-control, and ego threat. In R. G. Geen and E. Donnerstein (Eds.), *Human aggression: Theories, research, and implications for social policy* (pp. 111–137). San Diego, CA: Academic Press.

Baumeister, R. F., Smart, L., & Boden, J. M. (1996). Relation of threatened egotism to violence and aggression: The dark side of high self-esteem. *Psychological Review, 103,* 5–33.

Baumeister, R. F., Stillwell, A., & Wotman, S. R. (1990). Victim and perpetrator accounts of interpersonal conflict: Autobiographical narratives about anger. *Journal of Personality and Social Psychology, 59,* 994–1003.

Bauserman, R. (1996). Sexual aggression and pornography: A review of correlational research. *Basic & Applied Social Psychology, 18,* 405–427.

Baxter, L. R., Schwartz, J. M., Bergman, K. S., Szuba, M. P., Guze, B. H., Mazziota, J. C., Alazraki, A., Selin, C. E., Ferng, H. K., Munford, P., & Phelps, M. E. (1992). Caudate glucose metabolic rate changes with both drug and behavior therapy for obsessive-compulsive disorder. *Archives of General Psychiatry, 49,* 681–689.

Baxter, L. R., Schwartz, J. M., Guze, B. H., Begman, K., & Szuba, M. P. (1990). Neuroimaging in obsessive-compulsive disorder: Seeking the mediating neuroanatomy. In M. A. Jenike, L. Baer, W. E. Minichiello (Eds.), *Obsessive compulsive disorder: Theory and management* (2nd ed., pp. 167–188). Chicago: Year Book Medical Publishers.

Bayley, N. (1969). *Bayley Scales of Infant Development.* New York: The Psychological Corporation.

Beach, F. A. (1956). Characteristics of masculine "sex drive." In M. Jones (Ed.), *Nebraska Symposium on Motivation* (pp. 1–32). Lincoln, NE: University of Nebraska Press.

Beagley, G. H., & Beagley, W. K. (1978). Alleviation of learned helplessness following septal lesions in rats. *Physiological Psychology, 6,* 241–244.

Beaman, A., Barnes, P. Kletz, B., & McQuirk, B. (1978). Increasing helping rates through information dissemination: Teaching pays. *Personality and Social Psychology Bulletin, 4,* 406–411.

Beaman, A. L., Cole, C. M., Preston, M., Klentz, B., & Steblay, N. M. (1983). Fifteen years of foot-in-the-door research: A meta-analysis. *Personality and Social Psychology Bulletin, 9,* 181–196.

Bearak, B. (1997, March 29). Time of puzzles heartbreak binds relatives left behind. *New York Times,* 1.

Beatty, J. (1995). *Principles of behavioral neuroscience.* Dubuque, IA: Brown & Benchmark.

Bebbington, P. E., Brugha, T., MacCarthy, B., Potter, J., Sturt, E., et al. (1988). The Camberwell Collaborative Depression Study: I. Depressed probands: Adversity and the form of depression. *British Journal of Psychiatry, 152,* 754–765.

Bechara, A., Damasio, H., Tranel, D., & Damasio, A. R. (1997). Deciding advantageously before knowing the advantageous strategy. *Science, 275,* 1293–1294.

Bechara, A., Damasio, H., Tranel, D., Anderson, S. W. (1998). Dissociation of working memory from decision making within the human prefrontal cortex. *Journal of Neuroscience, 18,* 428–437.

Bechara, A. & Van der Kooy, D. (1992). A single brain stem substrate mediates the motivational effects of both opiates and food in nondeprived rats but not in deprived rats. *Behavioral Neuroscience, 106,* 351–363.

Beck, A. T. (1967). *Depression: Causes and treatment.* Philadelphia: University of Pennsylvania Press.

Beck, A. T., Emery, G., & Greenberg, R. L. (1985). *Anxiety disorders and phobias: A cognitive perspective.* New York: Basic Books.

Beck, A. T., Rush, A. J., Shaw, B. F., & Emery, G. (1979). *Cognitive Therapy of depression: A treatment manual.* New York: Guilford Press.

Beck, H. (1976). Neuropsychological servosystems, consciousness, and the problem of embodiment. *Behavioral Sciences, 21,* 139–160.

Beck, J. G., Ohtake, P. J., & Shipherd, J. C. (1999). Exaggerated anxiety is not unique to CO2 in panic disorder: A comparison of hypercapnic and hypoxic challenges. *Journal of Abnormal Psychology, 108,* 473–482.

Beck, R., & Fernandez, E. (1998). Cognitive-behavioral therapy in the treatment of anger: A meta-analysis. *Cognitive Therapy & Research, 22,* 63–74.

Becker, A., & Hamburg, P. (1996). Culture, the media, and eating disorders. *Cross-Cultural Psychiatry, 4,* 163–167.

Bedford, F. L. (1999). Keeping perception accurate. *Trends in Cognitive Sciences, 3,* 4–10.

Beer, M. (1966). *Leadership, employee needs, and motivation* (Monograph No. 129). Columbus, OH: Ohio State University, Bureau of Business Research, College of Commerce.

Beggs, J. M., Brown, T. H., Byrne, J. H., Crow, T., LeDoux, J. E., LeBar, K., & Thompson, R. F (1999). Learning and memory: Basic mechanisms. In M. J. Zigmond, F. E. Bloom, S. G. Landis, J. L. Roberts, & L. R. Squire (Eds.), *Fundamental neuroscience* (pp. 1411–1454). New York: Academic Press.

Behrman, R. E. (Ed.). (1996). *The Future of children: Financing child care* (Vol. 6, No.2). Los Altos, CA: Center for the Future of Children, The David and Lucile Packard Foundation.

Behrmann, M. (2000). The mind's eye mapped onto the brain's matter. *Current Directions in Psychological Science, 9,* 50–54.

Beilin, H. (1996). Mind and meaning: Piaget and Vygotsky on causal explanation. *Human Development, 39,* 277–286.

Belcher, G., & Costello, C. G. (1991). Do confidants of depressed women provide less social support than confidants of nondepressed women? *Journal of Abnormal Psychology, 100,* 516–525.

Bell, A. E. (1977). Heritability in retrospect. *Journal of Heredity, 68,* 297–300.

Beller, M., & Gafni, N. (1996). The 1991 international assessment of educational progress in mathematics and sciences: The gender differences perspective. *Journal of Educational Psychology, 88,* 365–377.

Bellugi, U., Adolphs, R., Cassady, C., & Chiles, M. (1999a). Towards the neural basis for hypersociability in a genetic syndrome. *NeuroReport, 10,* 1653–1657.

Bellugi, U., Birhle, A., Neville, H., Jernigan, T., & Doherty, S. (1992). Language, cognition, and brain organization in a neurodevelopmental disorder. In M. R. Gunnar and A. C. Nelson (Eds.), *Developmental behavioral neuroscience* (pp. 201–232). Hillsdale, NJ: Erlbaum.

Bellugi, U., Lichtenberger, L., Mills, D., Galaburda, A., & Korenberg, J. R. (1999b). Bridging cognition, the brain and molecular genetics: Evidence from Williams syndrome. *Trends in Neurosciences, 22,* 197–207.

Bellugi, U., Poizner, H., & Klima, E. S. (1993). Language, modality, and the brain. In M. Johnson (Ed.), *Brain development and cognition* (pp. 380–388). Cambridge, MA: Blackwell.

Bem, D. J. (1972). Self-perception theory. In L. Berkowitz (Ed.), *Advances in experimental social psychology* (Vol. 6, pp. 1–62). San Diego: Academic Press.

Bem, D. J. (1996). Exotic becomes erotic: A developmental theory of sexual orientation. *Psychological Review, 103,* 320–335.

Bem, D. J. (1998). Is EBE theory supported by the evidence? Is it androcentric? A reply to Peplau et al. *Psychological Review, 108,* 395–398.

Bem, D. J., & Allen, A. (1974). On predicting some of the people some of the time: The search for cross-situational consistencies in behavior. *Psychological Review, 81,* 506–520.

Bem, D. J., & Honorton, C. (1994). Does psi exist? Replicable evidence for an anomalous process of information transfer. *Psychological Bulletin, 115,* 4–18.

Ben-Shakhar, G., & Furedy, J. J. (1990). *Theories and applications in the detection of deception: A psychophysiological and international perspective.* New York: Springer-Verlag.

Benbow, C. P., & Minor, L. L. (1990). Cognitive profiles of verbally and mathematically precocious students: Implications for identification of the gifted. *Gifted Child Quarterly, 34,* 21–26.

Bender, K. J. (1998). "Substance P" antagonist relieves depression. *Psychiatric Times, 15*(11).

Benedict, J. G., & Donaldson, D. W. (1996). Recovered memories threaten all. *Professional Psychology: Research & Practice, 27,* 427–428.

Benes, F. M. (1996, November). Schizophrenia: Altered neural circuits in schizophrenia. *The Harvard Mental Health Letter, 13*(5).

Beninger, R. J. (1983). The role of dopamine in locomotor activity and learning. *Brain Research Reviews, 6,* 173–196.

Beninger, R. J. (1989). Dissociating the effects of altered dopaminergic function on performance and learning. *Brain Research Bulletin, 23,* 365–371.

Beninger, R. J., Mason, S. T., Phillips, A. G., & Fibiger, H. C. (1980). The use of extinction to investigate the nature of neuroleptic-induced avoidance deficits. *Psychopharmacology, 69,* 11–18.

Benjafield, J. G. (1996). *The history of psychology.* Needham, MA: Allyn & Bacon.

Benjamin, J., Li, L., Patterson, C., Greenberg, B. D., Murphy, D. L., & Hamer, D. H. (1996). Population and familial association between the D4 dopamine receptor gene and measure of novelty seeking. *Nature Genetics, 12,* 81–84.

Benson, D. F., & Greenberg, J. P. (1969). Visual form agnosia: A specific deficit in visual recognition. *Archives of Neurology, 20,* 82–89.

Berenbaum, S. A. (1999). Effects of early androgens on sex-typed activities and interests in adolescents with congenital adrenal hyperplasia. *Hormones & Behavior, 35,* 102–110.

Berenbaum, S. A., & Hines, M. (1992). Early androgens are related to childhood sex-typed toy preferences. *Psychological Science, 3,* 203–206.

Berg, S. (1996). Aging, behavior, and terminal decline. In J. E. Birren & K. W. Schaie (Eds.), *Handbook of the psychology of aging* (4th ed.) (pp. 323–337). New York: Academic Press.

Bergeman, C. S., Plomin, R., Pederson, N. L., McClearn, G. E., & Nesselraod, J. R. (1990). Genetic and environmental influences on social support: The Swedish Adoption/Twin Study of Aging (SATSA). *Journal of Gerontology: Psychological Sciences, 45,* P101–P106.

Berk, L. (1989). Eustress of mirthful laughter modifies natural killer cell activity. *Clinical Research, 37,* 115.

Berk, L. E. (1992a). Children's private speech: An overview of theory and the status of research. In R. M. Diaz & L. E. Berk (Eds.), *Private speech:*

From social interaction to self-regulation (pp. 17–53). Hillsdale, NJ: Erlbaum.

Berk, L. E. (1992b). The extracurriculum. In P. W. Jackson (Ed.), *Handbook of research on curriculum* (pp. 1002–1043). New York: Macmillan.

Berk, L. E. (1994a). Vygotsky's theory: The importance of make-believe play. *Young Children, 50,* 30–39.

Berk, L. E. (1994b). Why children talk to themselves. *Scientific American, 271*(5), 78–83.

Berk, L. E. (1997). *Child development* (4th ed.). Boston: Allyn & Bacon.

Berkman, L. F., & Syme, S. L. (1979). Social networks, host resistance, and mortality: A nine year follow-up study of Alameda Country residents. *American Journal of Epidemiology, 109,* 186–204.

Berko, J. (1958). The child's learning of English morphology. *Word, 14,* 150–177.

Berkowitz, A. D. (1997). From reactive to proactive prevention: Promoting an ecology of health on campus. In P. C. Rivers & E. R. Shore (Eds.), *Substance abuse on campus: A handbook for college and university personnel.* Westport, CT: Greenwood Press.

Berkowitz, L. (1983). Aversively stimulated aggression: Some parallels and differences in research with animals and humans. *American Psychologist, 38,* 1135–1144.

Berkowitz, L. (1998). Affective aggression: The role of stress, pain, and negative affect. In R. G. Geen and E. Donnerstein (Eds.), *Human aggression: Theories, research, and implications for social policy* (pp. 49–72). San Diego, CA.: Academic Press.

Berlyne, D. E. (1960). *Conflict, arousal, and curiosity.* New York: Mcgraw-Hill.

Berlyne, D. E. (Ed.). (1974). *Studies in the new experimental aesthetics: Steps toward an objective psychology of aesthetic appreciation.* Washington, DC: Hemisphere.

Berman, S. M., & Noble, E. P. (1995). Reduced visuospatial performance in children with the D2 dopamine receptor A1 allele. *Behavior Genetics, 25,* 45–58.

Bermond, B. N., Fasotti, L., & Schuerman, J. (1991). Spinal cord lesions, peripheral feedback, and intensities of emotional feelings. *Cognition & Emotion, 5,* 201–220.

Bernier, D. (1998). A study of coping: Successful recovery from severe burnout and other reactions to severe work-related stress. *Work & Stress, 12,* 50–65.

Bernstein, I. L., Zimmerman, J. C., Czeisler, C. A., & Weitzman, E. D. (1981). Meal patterns in "free-running" humans. *Physiology & Behavior, 27,* 621–623.

Berridge, K. C. (1996). Food reward: Brain substrates of wanting and liking. *Neuroscience and Biobehavioral Reviews, 20,* 1–20.

Berscheid, E., & Reis, H. T. (1998). Attraction and close relationships. In D. T. Gilbert, S. T. Fiske, & G. Lindzey (Eds.), *The handbook of social psychology* (4th ed., pp. 193–281). New York: McGraw Hill.

Bess, B. E. (1997). Human sexuality and obesity. *International Journal of Mental Health, 26,* 61–67.

Bettencourt, B. A., & Miller, N. (1996). Sex differences in aggression as a function of provacation: A meta-analysis. *Psycholological Bulletin, 119,* 422–447.

Beutler, L. E., Engle, D., Mohr, D., Daldrup, R. J., Bergan, J., Meredity, K., & Merry, W. (1991). Predictors of differential response to cognitive, experiential, and self-directed psychotherapeutic procedures. *Journal of Consulting & Clinical Psychology, 59,* 333–340.

Beutler, L. E., & Hodgson, A. B. (1993). Prescriptive psychotherapy. In G. Stricker & J. R. Gold (Eds.), *Comprehensive Handbook of Psychotherapy Integration* (pp. 151–164). New York: Plenum Press.

Beutler, L. E., Machado, P. P., Engle, D., & Mohr, D. (1993). Differential patient X treatment maintenance among cognitive, experiential, and self-directed psychotherapies. *Journal of Psychotherapy Integration, 3,* 15–31.

Beutler, L. E., Machado, P. P., & Neufeldt, S. A. (1994). Therapist variables. In A. E. Bergin & S. L. Garfield (Eds.), *Handbook of psychotherapy and behavior change,* (4th ed., pp. 229–269). New York: Wiley.

Biederman, I. (1987). Recognition-by-components: A theory of human image understanding. *Psychological Review, 94,* 115–147.

Biederman, I., & Shaffir, M. (1987). Sexing day-old chicks: A case study and expert systems analysis of a difficult perceptual-learning task. *Journal of Experimental Psychology: Learning, Memory, and Cognition, 13,* 640–645.

Bierhoff, H. W., Klein, R., & Kramp, P. (1991). Evidence for the altruistic personality from data on accident research. *Journal of Personality, 59,* 263–280.

Bihrle, A. M., Brownell, H. H., Powelson, J. A., & Gardner, H. (1986). Comprehension of humorous and non-humorous materials by left and right brain-damaged patients. *Brain and Cognition, 5,* 399–411.

Bijeljac-Babic, R., Bertoncini, J., & Mehler, J. (1993). How do 4-day-old infants categorize multisyllabic utterances? *Developmental Psychology, 29,* 711–721.

Bindra, D. (1968). Neuropsychological interpretation of the effects of drive and incentive motivation on general activity and instrumental behavior. *Psychological Review, 75,* 1–22.

Birenbaum, L. K., Stewart, B. J., & Phillips, D. S. (1996). Health status of bereaved patients. *Nursing Research, 45,* 105–109.

Birren, J. E. (1988). Behavior as a cause and a consequence of health and aging. In J. J. F. Schroots, J. E. Birren, & A. Svanborg (Eds.), *Health and aging* (pp. 25–41). New York: Springer.

Birren, J. E., Riegel, K. F., & Morrison, D. F. (1962). Age differences in response speed as a function of controlled variations of stimulus conditions: Evidence of a general speed factor. *Gerontologia, 6,* 1–18.

Bishop, D. V. M. (1983). Linguistic impairment after left hemidecortication for infantile hemiplegia? A reappraisal. *Quarterly Journal of Experimental Psychology, 35A,* 199–207.

Bishop, D. V. M., North, T., & Donlan, C. (1995). Genetic basis of specific language impairment: Evidence from a twin study. *Developmental Medicine and Child Neurology, 37,* 56–71.

Bishop, G. D. (1994). *Health psychology: Integrating mind and body.* Boston, MA: Allyn & Bacon.

Bisiach, E. (1981). Brain and conscious representation of outside reality. *Neuropsychologia, 19,* Pergamon Journals, Ltd.

Bisiach, E., & Luzzatti, C. (1978). Unilateral neglect of representational space. *Cortex, 14,* 129–133.

Bjork, R. A. (1989). Retrieval inhibition as an adaptive mechanism in human memory. In H. L. Roediger, III, & F. I. M. Craik (Eds.), *Varieties of memory and consciousness: Essays in honour of Endel Tulving* (pp. 309–330). Hillsdale, NJ: Erlbaum.

Black, D. W., Noyes, R., Goldstein, R. B., & Blum, N. (1992). A family study of obsessive-compulsive disorder. *Archives of General Psychiatry, 49,* 362–368.

Black, J. E., Jones, T. A., Nelson, C. A., & Greenough, W. T. (1998). Neuronal plasticity and the developing brain. In N. E. Alessi, J. T. Coyle, S. I. Harrison, & S. Eth (Eds.), *Handbook of child and adolescent psychiatry: Vol 6. Basic psychiatric science and treatment* (pp. 31–53). New York: Wiley.

Blais, M. A., Hilsenroth, M. J., & Castlebury, F. D. (1997). Psychometric characteristics of the Cluster B personality disorders under DSM–III—R and DSM–IV. *Journal of Personality Disorders, 11,* 270–278.

Blakeslee, S. (1997). Brain studies tie marijuana to other drugs. *New York Times.* June 27:A16 (col. 4).

Blanchard, R. (1997). Birth order and sibling sex ratio in homosexual versus heterosexual males and females. *Annual Review of Sex Research, 8,* 27–67.

Blanton, H., Gibbons, F. X., Gerrard, M., Conger, K. J., & Smith, G. E. (1997). Role of family and peers in the development of prototypes associated with substance abuse. *Journal of Family Psychology, 11,* 271–288.

Blass, T. (1999). The Milgram Paradigm after 35 years: Some things we now know about obedience to authority. *Journal of Applied Social Psychology, 29,* 955–978.

Bleibtreu-Ehrenberg, G. (1990). Pederasty among primitives: Institutionalized initiation and cultic prostitution. *Journal of Homosexuality, 20,* 13–30.

Bliss, E. L. (1984). Spontaneous self-hypnosis in multiples personality disorder. *Psychiatric Clinics of North America, 7,* 135–148.

Block, J. (1995). A contrarian view of the five-factor approach to personality description. *Psychological Bulletin, 117,* 187–215.

Block, N. (1995). How heritability misleads about race. *Cognition, 56,* 99–128.

Bloom, B. (Ed). (1985). *Developing talent in young people.* New York: Ballantine Books.

Bloom, B. L. (1997). *Planned short-term psychotherapy: A clinical handbook* (2nd ed.). Boston, MA: Allyn & Bacon.

Bloom, B. S. (1985). Generalizations about talent development. In B. S. Bloom (Ed.), *Developing talent in young people* (pp. 507–549). New York: Ballantine Books.

Bloom, F. E., & Lazerson, A. (1988). *Brain, mind, behavior* (2nd ed.). New York: Freeman.

Bloom, J. W. (1998). The ethical practice of WebCounseling. *British Journal of Guidance & Counselling, 26,* 53–59.

Blundell, J. E. (1977). Is there a role for 5-hydroxytryptamine in feeding? *International Journal of Obesity, 1,* 15–42.

Blundell, J. E. (1984). Serotonin and appetite. *Neuropharmacology, 23,* 1537–1551.

Blundell, J. E. (1986). Serotonin manipulations and the structure of feeding behaviour. *Appetite, 7,* 39–56.

Blundell, J. E., & Halford, J. C. G. (1998). Serotonin and appetite regulation: Implications for the pharmacological treatment of obesity. *CNS Drugs, 9,* 473–495.

Bly, B. M., & Kosslyn, S. M. (1997). Functional anatomy of object recognition in humans: Evidence from PET and fMRI. *Current Opinion in Neurology, 10,* 5–9.

Bobo, L. (1983). Whites' opposition to busing: Symbolic racism or realistic group conflict? *Journal of Personality and Social Psychology, 45,* 1196–1210.

Boddy, J. (1992). Comment on the proposed DSM–IV criteria for trance and possession disorder. *Transcultural Psychiatric Research Review, 29,* 323–330.

Boden, M. A. (2000). State of the art: Computer models of creativity. *Psychologist, 13,* 72–76.

Bodenhausen, G. V. (1990). Stereotypes as judgmental heuristics: Evidence of circadian variations in discrimination. *Psychological Science, 1,* 319–322.

Bodenhausen, G. V., Kramer, G. P., & Susser, K. (1994). Happiness and stereotypic thinking in social judgment. *Journal of Personality and Social Psychology, 66,* 621–632.

Boeringer, S. B. (1994). Pornography and sexual aggression: Associations of violent and nonviolent depictions with rape and rape proclivity. *Deviant Behavior, 15,* 289–304.

Bogaert, A. F. (1996). Volunteer bias in human sexuality research: Evidence for both sexuality and personality differences in males. *Archives of Sexual Behavior, 25,* 125–140.

Bohm, J. K., & Hendricks, B. (1997). Effects of interpersonal touch, degree of justification, and sex of participant on compliance with a request. *Journal of Social Psychology, 137,* 460–469.

Boiten, F. (1996). Autonomic response patterns during voluntary facial action. *Psychophysiology, 33,* 123–131.

Boiten, F. A. (1998). The effects of emotional behavior on components of the respiratory cycle. *Biological Psychiatry, 49,* 29–51.

Boivin, D. B., Czeisler, C. A., Dijk, D., Duffy, J. F., Folkard, S., Minors, D. S., Totterdell, P., & Waterhouse, J. M. (1997). Complex interaction of the sleep-wake cycle and circadian phase modulates mood in healthy subjects. *Archives of General Psychiatry, 54,* 145–152.

Bokert, E. (1968). The effects of thirst and a related verbal stimulus on dream reports. *Dissertation Abstracts, Vol. 28(11-B),* 4753. (18192)

Bolger, F., & Harvey, N. (1993). Context-sensitive heuristics in statistical reasoning. *Quarterly Journal of Experimental Psychology, 46A,* 779–811.

Bond, M., & Gardiner, S. T., Christian, H., & Sigel, J. J. (1983). Empirical study of self-rated defense styles. *Archives of General Psychiatry, 40,* 333–338.

Bond, M. H., & Smith, P. B. (1996). Cross-cultural social and organizational psychology. *Annual Review of Psychology, 47,* 205–235.

Bond, R., & Smith, P. B. (1996). Culture and conformity: A meta-analysis of studies using Asch's (1952b, 1956) line judgment task. *Psychological Bulletin, 119,* 111–137.

Booth, R. J., Petrie, K. J., & Pennebaker, J. W. (1997). Changes in circulating lymphocyte numbers following emotional disclosure: Evidence of buffering? *Stress Medicine, 13,* 23–29.

Borg, E., & Counter, S. A. (1989). The middle ear muscles. *Scientific American, 261,* 74–80.

Boring, E. G. (1950). *A history of experimental psychology* (2nd ed.). New York: Appleton-Century-Crofts.

Borman, W. C., Hanson, M. A., & Hedge, J. W. (1997). Personnel selection. *Annual Review of Psychology, 48,* 299–337.

Bornstein, M. H. (1992). Perception across the life span. In M. H. Bornstein & M. E. Lamb (Eds.), *Developmental psychology: An advanced textbook* (pp. 155–209). Hillsdale, NJ: Erlbaum.

Bornstein, M. H., Tal, J., Rahn, C., Galperin, C. Z., et al. (1992). Functional analysis of the contents of maternal speech to infants of 5 and 13 months in four cultures: Argentina, France, Japan, and the United States. *Developmental Psychology, 28,* 593–603.

Bornstein, R. F. (1989). Exposure and affect: Overview and meta-analysis of research, 1968–1987. *Psychological Bulletin, 106,* 265–289.

Bornstein, R. F., & D'Agostino, P. R. (1992). Stimulus recognition and the mere exposure effect. *Journal of Personality and Social Psychology, 63,* 545–552.

Bornstein, R. F., & D'Agostino, P. R. (1994). The attribution and discounting of perceptual fluency: Preliminary tests of a perceptual fluency/attributional model of the mere exposure effect. *Social Cognition, 12,* 103–128.

Bornstein, R. F., Leone, D. R., & Galley, D. (1987). The generalizability of subliminal mere exposure effect: Influence on stimuli perceived without awareness on social behavior. *Journal of Personality and Social Psychology, 53,* 1070–1079.

Bosch, J. A., Brand, H. S., Ligtenberg, A. J. M., Bermond, B., Hoogstraten, J., & Nieuw Amgerongen, A. V. (1998). The response of salivary protein levels and S-IgA to an academic examination are associated with daily stress. *Journal of Psychophysiology, 12,* 384–391.

Bosma, H., Stansfelt, S. A., & Marmot, M. G. (1998). Job control, personal characteristics, and heart disease. *Journal of Occupational Health Psychology, 3,* 402–409.

Bothwell, R. K., & Brigham, J. C. (1983). Selective evaluation and recall during the 1980 Reagan-Carter debate. *Journal of Applied Social Psychology, 13,* 427–442.

Bottini, G., Corcoran, R., Sterzi, R., Paulesu, E., Schenone, P., Scarpa, P., Frackowiak, R. S. J., & Frith, C. D. (1994). The role of the right hemisphere in the interpretation of figurative aspects of language: A positron emission tomography activation study. *Brain, 117,* 1241–1253.

Bottini, G., Paulesu, E., Sterzl, R., Warburton, E., Wise, R. J. S., Vallar, G., Frackowiak, R. S. J., & Frith, C. D. (1995). Modulation of conscious experience by peripheral sensory stimuli. *Nature, 376,* 778–781.

Botvin, G. J. (1995). Drug abuse prevention in school settings. In G. J. Botvin, S. Schinke, & M. A. Orlandi (Eds.), *Drug abuse prevention with multiethnic youth* (pp. 169–192). Newbury Park, CA: Sage.

Botwinick, J. (1984). *Aging and behavior: A comprehensive integration of research findings.* New York: Springer.

Bouchard, T. J. (1983). Do environmental similarities explain the similarity in intelligence of identical twins reared apart? *Intelligence, 7,* 175–184.

Bouchard, T. J. (1991). Identical twins reared apart: What they reveal about human intelligence. Paper presented at the American Association for the Advancement of Science, Washington, DC.

Bouchard, T. J., & McGue, M. (1981). Familial studies of intelligence: A review. *Science, 212,* 1055–1059.

Bouchard, T. J., Jr. (1994). Genes, environment, and personality. *Science, 264,* 1700–1701.

Bouchard, T. J., Jr., Lykken, D. T., McGue, M., Segal, N. L, & Tellegen, A. (1990). Sources of human psychological differences: The Minnesota study of twins reared apart. *Science, 250,* 223–228.

Bourguignon, E. (1973). *Altered States of Consciousness and Social Change.* Columbus: Ohio State University Press.

Bousfeld, W. A. (1953). The occurrence of clustering in the recall of randomly arranged associates. *Journal of General Psychology, 49,* 229–240.

Bouton, M. (1993). Context, time and memory retrieval in the interference paradigms of Pavlovian conditioning. *Psychological Bulletin, 114,* 80–99.

Bouton, M. (1994). Context, ambiguity and classical conditioning. *Current Directions in Psychological Science, 3,* 49–52.

Bovasso, G. B., Eaton, W. W., & Armenian, H. K. (1999). The long-term outcomes of mental health treatment in a population-based study. *Journal of Consulting and Clinical Psychology, 67,* 529–538.

Bower, B. (1996, May 18). Trauma syndrome traverses generations. *Science News, 149,* 315.

Bower, G. H. (1972). Mental imagery and associative learning. In L. Gregg (Ed.), *Cognition and learning and memory* (pp. 51–88). New York: Wiley.

Bower, G. H. (1981). Mood and memory. *American Psychologist, 36,* 129–148.

Bower, G. H. (1992). How might emotions effect learning? In S.-Å. Christianson (Ed.), *The handbook of emotion and memory: Research and theory* (pp. 3–31). Hillsdale, NJ: Erlbaum.

Bower, G. H., Clark, M. C., Lesgold, A. M., & Winzenz, D. (1969). Hierarchical retrieval schemes in recall of categorized word lists. *Journal of Verbal Learning and Verbal Behavior, 8,* 323–343.

Bowlby, J. (1969). *Attachment and loss: Vol. 1, Attachment.* New York: Basic Books.

Bowlby, J. (1980). *Attachment and loss: Vol. 3, Loss.* New York: Basic Books.

Bowman, E. S., & Nurnberger, J. I. (1993). Genetics of psychiatry diagnosis and treatment. In D. L. Dunner (Ed.), *Current psychiatric therapy* (pp. 46–56). Philadelphia: Saunders.

Bowman, M. L. (1999). Individual differences in posttraumatic distress: Problems with the DSM–IV model. *Canadian Journal of Psychiatry, 44,* 21–33.

Boyle, C. A., Decoufle, P., & Yeargin-Allsopp, M. (1994). Prevalence and health impact of developmental disabilities in US children. *Pediatrics, 93,* 399–403.

Bradburn, N. M. (1969). *The structure of psychological well-being.* Chicago: Aldine.

Bradley, M. M., Greenwald, M. K., Petry, M. C., & Lang, P. J. (1992). Remembering pictures: Pleasure and arousal in memory. *Journal of Experimental Psychology: Learning, Memory, and Cognition, 18,* 379–390.

Bradley, M. T., MacLaren, V. V., & Carle, S. B. (1996). Deception and non-deception in Guilty Knowledge and Guilty Actions Polygraph Tests. *Journal of Applied Psychology, 81*, 153–160.

Bradley, M. T., & Warfield, J. F. (1984). Innocence, information, and the Guilty Knowledge Test in the detection of deception. *Psychophysiology, 21*, 683–689.

Bradshaw, G. L., & Anderson, J. R. (1982). Elaborative encoding as an explanation of levels of processing. *Journal of Verbal Learning & Verbal Behavior, 21*, 165–174.

Brannon, L. (1996). *Gender: Psychological perspectives*. Needham Heights, MA: Simon & Schuster.

Bransford, J. D., & Franks, J. J. (1971). The abstraction of linguistic ideas. *Cognitive Psychology, 2*, 331–350.

Brashers-Krug, T., Shadmehr, R., & Bizzi, E. (1996) Consolidation in human motor memory. *Nature, 382*, 252–254.

Braverman, P. K., & Strasburger, V. C. (1993). Adolescent sexual activity. *Clinical Pediatrics, 32*, 658–668.

Brebner, J. (1998). Happiness and personality. *Personality & Individual Differences, 25*, 279–296.

Bregman, A. S. (1990). *Auditory scene analysis: The perceptual organization of sound*. Cambridge, MA: MIT Press.

Bregman, A. S. (1993). Auditory scene analysis: Hearing in complex environments. In S. McAdams & E. Bigand (Eds.), *Thinking in sound: The cognitive psychology of human audition* (pp. 10–36). New York: Oxford University Press.

Bregman, E. O. (1934). An attempt to modify the emotional attitudes of infants by the conditioned response technique. *Journal of Genetic Psychology, 45*, 169–__.

Brehm, J. W. (1966). *A theory of psychological reactance*. New York: Academic Press.

Breiter, H. C., Rauch, S. L., Kwong, K. K., Baker, J. R., Weisskoff, R. M., Kennedy, D. N., Kendrick, A. D., Davis, T. L., Jiang, A., Cohen, M. S., Stern, C. E., Belliveau, J. W., Baer, L., O'Sullivan, R. L., Savage, C. R., Jenike, M. A., & Rosen, B. R. (1996). Functional magnetic resonance imaging of symptom provocation in obsessive-compulsive disorder. *Archives of General Psychiatry, 53*, 595–606.

Breland, K., & Breland, M. (1961). The misbehavior of organisms. *American Psychologist, 16*, 661–664.

Bremner, J. D., Stienberg, M., Southwick, S. M., Johnson, D. R., & Charney, D. S. (1993). Use of the structured clinical interview for DSM-IV dissociative disorders for systemic assessment of dissociative symptoms in posttraumatic stress disorder. *American Journal of Psychiatry, 150*, 1011–1014.

Breslau, N., Kessler, R. C., Chilcoat, H. D. Schultz, L. R., Davis, G. C., & Andreski, P. (1998). Trauma and posttraumatic stress disorder in the community: The 1996 Detroit Area Survey of Trauma. *Archives of General Psychiatry, 55*, 626–632.

Brewer, J. B., Zhao, Z., Desmod, J. E., Glover, G. H., & Gabrielli, J. D. E. (1998). Making memories: Brain activity that predicts how well visual experience will be remembered. *Science, 281*, 1185–1187.

Brewer, K. R., & Wann, D. L. (1998). Observational learning effectiveness as a function of model characteristics: Investigating the importance of social power. *Social Behavior & Personality, 26*,1–10.

Brewer, M. B., & Brown, R. J. (1998). Intergroup relations. In D. T. Gilbert, S. T. Fiske, & G. Lindzey (Eds.), The handbook of social psychology (4th ed., pp. 554–594). New York: McGraw Hill.

Brewer, M. B., & Kramer, R. M. (1986). Choice behavior in social dilemmas: Effects of social identity, group size, and decision framing. *Journal of Personality and Social Psychology, 50*, 543–549.

Brewer, W. F. (1988). Qualitative analysis of the recalls of randomly sampled autobiographical events. In M. M. Gruneberg & P. E. Morris (Eds.), *Practical aspects of memory: Current research and issues, Vol. 1: Memory in everyday life.* (pp. 263–268). New York: John Wiley & Sons.

Britt, T. A., & Shepperd, J. A. (1999). Trait relevance and trait assessment. *Personality and Social Psychology Review, 3*, 108–122.

Broadbent, D. E. (1971). The magic number seven after fifteen years. In A. Kennedy & A. Wilkes (Eds.), *Studies in long-term memory* (pp. 2–18). New York: Wiley.

Brody, J. (1998, April 6). Dealing with sleep deprivation. *International Herald Tribune, 9.*

Brody, N. (1997). Intelligence, schooling, and society. *American Psychologist, 52*, 1046–1050.

Brooks, D. C., & Bouton, M. E. (1993). A retrieval cue for extinction attenuates spontaneous recovery. *Journal of Experimental Psychology: Animal Behavior Processes, 19*, 77–89.

Brooks-Gunn, J., Graber, J. A., & Paikoff, R. L. (1994). Studying links between hormones and negative affect: Models and measures. *Journal of Research on Adolescence, 4*, 469–486.

Brosschot, J. F., Benschop, R. J., Godaert, G. L. R., Olff, M., de Smet., M., Heijnen, C. J., & Ballieux, R. E. (1994). Influence of life stress on im-munological reactivity to mild psychological stress. *Psychosomatic Medicine, 56*, 216–224.

Brown, A. L., & Campione, J. C. (1972). Recognition memory for perceptually similar pictures in preschool children. *Journal of Experimental Psychology, 95*, 55–62.

Brown, A. S., van Os, J., Driessens, C., Hoek, S. W., & Susser, E. S. (1999). Prenatal famine and the spectrum of psychosis. *Psychiatric Annals, 29*, 145–150.

Brown, B. (1999). Optimizing expression of the common human genome for child development. *Current Directions in Psychological Science, 8*, 37–41.

Brown, B. B., Clasen, D., & Eicher, S. (1986). Perceptions of peer pressure, peer conformity dispositions, and self-reported behavior among adolescents. *Developmental Psychology, 22*, 521–530.

Brown, B. B., Lohr, M. J., & McClenahan, E. L. (1986). Early adolescents' perceptions of peer pressure. *Journal of Early Adolescence, 6*, 139–154.

Brown, D. E. (1991). *Human universals*. Philadelphia: Temple University Press.

Brown, I., Jr., & Inouye, D. K. (1978). Learned helplessness through modeling: The role of perceived similarity in competence. *Journal of Personality and Social Psychology, 36*, 900–908.

Brown, J. D. (1991). Staying fit and staying well: Physical fitness as a moderator of stress. *Journal of Personality and Social Psychology, 60*, 555–561.

Brown, J. D., & Rogers, R. J. (1991). Self-serving attributions: The role of physiological arousal. *Personality and Social Psychology Bulletin, 17*, 501–506.

Brown, P. L., & Jenkins, H. M. (1968). Auto-shaping of the pigeon's key peck. *Journal of the Experimental Analysis of Behavior, 68*, 503–507.

Brown, R. (1989). Roger Brown. In G. Lindzey (Ed.), *A history of psychology in autobiography*, Vol. 8 (pp. 37–60). Stanford, CA: Stanford University Press.

Brown, R., & Kulik, J. (1977). Flashbulb memories. *Cognition, 5*, 73–99.

Brown, R., & McNeill, D. (1966). The "tip of the tongue" phenomenon. *Journal of Verbal Learning and Verbal Behavior, 5*, 325–337.

Brown, T. A., & Barlow, D. H. (1997). *Casebook in abnormal psychology*. Pacific Grove, CA: Brooks/Cole.

Brownell, H., Gardner, H., Prather, P., & Martino, G. (1995). Language, communication, and the right hemisphere. In H. S. Kirshner (Ed.), *Handbook of neurological speech and language disorders* (pp. 325–349). New York: Dekker.

Brownell, H. H., Michelow, D., Powelson, J., & Gardner, H. (1983). Surprise but not coherence: Sensitivity to verbal humor in right hemisphere patients. *Brain and Language, 18*, 20–27.

Brownell, H. H., Potter, H. H., Michelow, D., & Gardner, H. (1984). Sensitivity to lexical denotation and connotation in brain-damaged patients: A double dissociation. *Brain and Language, 22*, 253–265.

Brownell, H. H., Simpson, T. L., Bihrle, A. M., Potter, H. H., & Gardner, H. (1990). Appreciation of metaphoric alternative word meanings by left and right brain-damaged patients. *Neuropsychologia, 28*, 375–383.

Brownell, K. D., & Rodin, J. (1992). *Medical, metabolic, and psychological effects of weight cycling*. Unpublished manuscript, Yale University.

Brubaker, R. G., Prue, D. M., & Rycharik, R. G. (1987). Determinants of disulfiram acceptance among alcohol patients: A test of the theory of reasoned action. *Addictive Behaviors, 12*, 43–51.

Brugger, P., Landis, T., & Regard, M. (1990). A "sheep-goat effect" in repetition avoidance: Extrasensory perception as an effect of subjective probability? *British Journal of Psychology, 81*, 455–468.

Brugioni, D. A. (1996). The art and science of photoreconnaissance. *Scientific American*, 78–85.

Brunner, D. P., Dijk, D. J., Tobler, I., & Borbely, A. A. (1990). Effect of partial sleep deprivation on sleep stages and EEG power spectra: Evidence for non-REM and REM sleep homeostasis. *Electroencephalogr. Clin. Neurophysiol., 75*, 492–499.

Bryan, R. N., Wells, S. W., Miller, T. J., Elster, A. D., Jungreis, C. A., Poirier, V. C., Lind, B. K., & Manolio, T. A. (1997). Infarctlike lesions in the brain: Prevalence and anatomic characteristics at MR imaging of the elderly—data from the Cardiovascular Health Study. *Radiology, 202*, 47–54.

Bryant, R. A., & Barnier, A. J. (1999). Eliciting autobiographical pseudomemories: The relevance of hypnosis, hypnotizability, and attributions. *International Journal of Clinical & Experimental Hypnosis, 47*, 267–283.

Buchanan, C. M., Eccles, J., & Becker, J. (1992). Are adolescents the victims of raging hormones? Evidence for activational effects of hormones on moods and behavior at adolescence. *Psychological Bulletin, 111*, 62–107.

Buchkremer, G., Klingberg, S., Holle, R., Schulze-Moenking, H., & Hornung, W. P. (1997). Psychoeducational psychotherapy for schizophrenic patients and their key relatives or care-givers: Results of a 2-year follow-up. *Acta Psychiatrica Scandinavica, 96*, 483–491.

Buckalew, L. W., & Ross, S. (1981). Relationship of perceptual characteristics to efficacy of placebos. *Psychological Reports, 49,* 955–961,

Buckley, K. W. (1982). The selling of a psychologist: John Broadus Watson and the application of behavioral techniques to advertising. *Journal of the History of the Behavioral Sciences,18,* 207–221.

Buckner, R. L., Kelley, W. M., & Petersen, S. E. (1999). Frontal cortex contributes to human memory formation. *Nature Neuroscience, 2,* 311–314.

Buda, R., & Elsayed-Elkhouly, S. M. (1998). Cultural differences between Arabs and Americans: Individualism-collectivism revisited. *Journal of Cross-Cultural Psychology, 29,* 487–492.

Buehler, R., Griffin, D., & Ross, M. (1994). Exploring the "planning fallacy": Why people underestimate their task completion times. *Journal of Personality & Social Psychology, 67,* 366–381.

Buka, S. L., Goldstein, J. M., Seidman, L. J., Zornberg, G. L., Donatelli, J. A., Denny, L. R., & Tsuang, M. T. (1999). Prenatal complications, genetic vulnerability, and schizophrenia: The New England Longitudinal Studies of Schizophrenia. *Psychiatric Annals, 29,*151–156.

Bunce, S. C., Bernat, E., Wong, P. S., & Shevrin, H. (1999). Further evidence for unconscious learning: Preliminary support for the conditioning of facial EMG to subliminal stimuli. *Journal of Psychiatric Research, 33,* 341–347.

Bunney, W. E., & Garland, B. L. (1983). Possible receptor effects of chronic lithium administration. *Neuropharmacology, 22,* 367–372.

Burger, J. M. (1992). *Desire for control: Personality, social, and clinical perspectives.* New York: Plenum.

Burger, J. M., & Cooper, H. M. (1979). The desirability of control. *Motivation and Emotion, 3,* 381–393.

Burger, J. M., Horita, M., Kinoshita, L., Roberts, K., & Vera, C. (1997). Effects of time on the norm of reciprocity. *Basic & Applied Social Psychology, 19,* 91–100.

Burgoon, J. K., Buller, D. B., Hale, J. L., & DeTurck, M. A. (1984). Relational messages associated with nonverbal behaviors. Human Communication Research, 10, 351–378.

Burish, T. G., & Carey, M. P. (1986). Conditioned aversive responses in cancer chemotherapy patients: Theoretical and developmental analysis. *Journal of Counseling and Clinical Psychology, 54,* 593–600.

Burnstein, E. (1982). Persuasion as argument processing. In H. Brandstatter, J. H. Davis, & G. Stocker-Krechgauer (Eds.), *Group decision making* (pp. 103–124). London: Academic Press.

Burton, M. J., Rolls, E. T., & Mora, F. (1976). Effects of hunger on the responses of neurons in the lateral hypothalamus to the sight and taste of food. *Experimental Neurology, 51,* 668–677.

Bushman, B. J. (1984). Perceived symbols of authority and their influence on compliance. *Journal of Applied Social Psychology, 14,* 501–508.

Bushman, B. J. (1988). The effects of apparel on compliance: A field experiment with a female authority figure. *Personality and Social Psychology Bulletin, 14,* 459–467.

Bushman, B. J. (1998). Threatened egotism, narcissism, self-esteem, and direct and displaced aggression: Does self-love or self-hate lead to violence? *Journal of Personality and Social Psychology, 75,* 219–229.

Bushman, B. J., Baumeister, R. F., & Stack, A. D. (1999). Catharsis, aggression, and persuasive influence: Self-fulfilling or self-defeating prophesies? *Journal of Personality and Social Psychology, 76,* 367–376.

Bushman, B. J., & Cooper, H. M. (1990). Effects of alcohol on human aggression: An integrative research review. *Psychological Bulletin, 107,* 1–14.

Bushman, B. J., & Wells, G. L. (1998). Trait aggressiveness and hockey penalties: Predicting hot tempers on the ice. *Journal of Applied Psychology, 83,* 969–974.

Busjahn, A., Faulhaber, H. D., Freier, K., & Luft, F. C. (1999). Genetic and environmental influences on coping styles: A twin study. *Psychosomatic Medicine, 61,* 469–475.

Buss, A. H. (1989). Personality as traits. *American Psychologist, 44,* 1378–1388.

Buss, A. H. (1995). *Personality: Temperament, social behavior, and the self.* Needham Heights, MA: Allyn & Bacon.

Buss, A. H., & Plomin, R. (1975). *A temperament theory of personality development.* New York: Wiley Interscience.

Buss, A. H., & Plomin, R. (1984). *Temperament: Early developing personality traits.* Hillsdale, NJ: Erlbaum.

Buss, D. M. (1989). Sex differences in human mate preferences: Evolutionary hypotheses tested in 37 cultures. *Behavioral and Brain Sciences, 12,* 1–49.

Buss, D. M. (1994). *The evolution of desire: Strategies of human mating.* New York: Basic Books.

Buss, D. M. (1995). Psychological sex differences: Origins through sexual selection. *American Psychologist, 50,* 164–168.

Buss, D. M. (1998). The psychology of human mate selection: Exploring the complexity of the strategic repetoire. In C. B. Crawford & D. L. Krebs (Eds.), *Handbook of evolutionary psychology: Ideas, issues, and applications* (pp. 405–429). Mahwah, NJ: Erlbaum.

Buss, D. M. (1999). *Evolutionary psychology: The new science of the mind.* Boston: Allyn & Bacon.

Buss, D. M., & Craik, K. H. (1984). Acts, dispositions, and personality. In B. A. Maher & W. A. Maher (Eds.), *Progress in experimental personaity research* (Vol. 13). New York: Academic Press.

Buss, D. N. (1995). Psychological sex differences: Origins through sexual selection. *American Psychologist, 50,* 164–168.

Busse, E. W. (1969). Theories of aging. In E. W. Busse & E. Pfeiffer (Eds.), *Behavior and adaptation in later life* (pp. 11–32). Boston: Little, Brown.

Butcher, J. N., & Rouse, S. V. (1996). Personality: Individual difference and clinical assessment. *Annual Review of Psychology, 47,* 87–111.

Butters, N., Heindel, W. C., & Salmon, D. P. (1990). Dissociation of implicit memory in dementia: Neurological implications. *Bulletin of the Psychonomic Society, 28,* 359–366.

Butzlaff, R. L., & Hooley, J. M. (1998). Expressed emotion and psychiatric relapse: A meta-analysis. *Archives of General Psychiatry, 55,* 547–552.

Buunk, B. P., Angleitner, A., Oubaid, V., & Buss, D. M. (1996). Sex differences in jealousy in evolutionary and cultural perspective: Tests from the Netherlands, Germany, and the United States. *Psychological Science, 7,* 359–363

Byrne, D. (1971). *The attraction paradigm.* New York: Academic Press.

Byrne, D. (1982). Prediciting human sexual behavior. In A. G. Kraut (Ed.), *The G. Stanley Hall Lecture Series* (Vol.2). Washingotn, DC: American Psychological Association.

Cabeza, R., & Nyberg, L. (1997). Imaging cognition: An empirical review of PET studies with normal subjects. *Journal of Cognitive Neuroscience, 9,* 1–26.

Cabeza, R., & Nyberg, L. (2000). Imaging cognition II: An empirical review of 275 PET and fMRI studies. *Journal of Cognitive Neuroscience, 12,* 1–47.

Caccioppo, J. T., Gardner, J. T., & Berntson, W. L. (1997). Beyond bipolar conceptualizations and measures: The case of attitudes and evaluative space. *Personality & Social Psychology Review, 1,* 3–25.

Caccioppo, J. T., & Petty, R. E. (1982). The need for cognition. *Journal of Personality & Social Psychology, 42,* 116–131.

Caccioppo, J. T., Petty, R. E., Feinstein, J. A., & Jarvis, W. B. G. (1996). Disposition differences in cognition motivation: The life and times of individuals varying in need for cognition. *Psychological Bulletin, 119,* 197-253.

Caccioppo, J. T., Petty, R. E., & Kao, C. F. (1984). The efficient assessment of need for cognition. *Journal of Personality Assessment, 48,* 306–307.

Caccioppo, J. T., Petty, R. E., Kao, C. F., & Rodriguez, R. (1986). Central and peripheral routes to persuasion: An individual difference perspective. *Journal of Personality & Social Psychology, 51,* 1032–1043.

Caccioppo, J. T., Petty, R. E., Losch, M. E., & Kim, H. S. (1986). Electromyographic activity over facial muscle regions can differentiate the valence and intensity of affective reactions. *Journal of Personality and Social Psychology, 50,* 260–268.

Cadoret, R. J., O'Gorman, T. W., Heywood, E., & Troughton, E. (1995). Genetic and environmental factors in major depression. *Journal of Affective Disorders, 9,* 155–164.

Cahan, S., & Cohen, N. (1989). Age versus schooling effects on intelligence development. *Child Development, 60,* 1239–1249.

Cahill, L., Haier, R. J., Fallon, J., Alkire, M. T., Tang, C., Keator, D., Wu, J., & McGaugh, J. L. (1996). Amygdala activity at encoding correlated with long-term free recall of emotional information. *Proceedings of the National Academy of Sciences, USA, 93,* 8016–8021.

Cahill, L., Prins, B., Weber, M., & McGaugh, J. L. (1994). Adrenergic activation and memory for emotional events. *Nature, 371,* 702–704.

Cailliet, R. (1993). *Pain: Mechanisms and management.* Philadelphia: Davis.

Cain, W. S. (1973). Spatial discrimination of cutaneous warmth. *American Journal of Psychology, 86,* 169–181.

Cain, W. S. (1979). To know with the nose: Keys to odor identification. *Science, 203,* 467–470.

Cain, W. S. (1982). Odor identification by males and females: Predictions and performance. *Chemical Senses, 7,* 129–141.

Cain, W. S., & Gent, J. F. (1991). Olfactory sensitivity: Reliability, generality, and association with aging. *Journal of Experimental Psychology: Human Perception and Performance, 17,* 382–391.

Calder, A. J., Young, A. W., Rowland, D., Perrett, D. I., Hodges, J. R. & Etcoff, N. L. (1996). Face perception after bilateral amygdala damage: Differentially severe impairment of fear. *Cognitive Neuropsychology, 13,* 699–745.

Caldera, Y. M., & Sciaraffa, M. A. (1998). Parent-toddler play with feminine toys: Are all dolls the same? *Sex Roles, 39,* 657–668

Calkins, S. D., Fox, N. A., & Marshall, T. R. (1996). Behavioral and physiological antecedents of inhibited and uninhibited behavior. *Child Development, 67,* 523–540.

Calvert, G. A., Bullmore, E. T., Brammer, M. J., Campbell, R., Williams, S. C. R., McGuire, P. K., Woodruff, P. W. R., Iverson, S. D., & David, A. S. (1997). Activation of auditory cortex during silent lipreading. *Science*, 276, 593–596.

Calvocoressi, L., Lewis, B., Harris, M., Trufan, S. J., et al. (1995). Family accommodation in obsessive-compulsive disorder. *American Journal of Psychiatry*, 152, 441–443.

Cameron, J., & Pierce, W. D. (1994). Reinforcement, reward, and intrinsic motivation: A meta-analysis. *Review of Educational Research, 64*, 363–423.

Campbell, D. T. (1960). Blind variation and selective retention in creative thought as in other knowledge processes. *Psychological Review*, 67, 380–400.

Campbell, F. A., & Ramey, C. T. (1994). Effects of early intervention on intellectual and academic achievement: A follow-up study of children from low-income families. *Child Development*, 65, 684–698.

Campbell, J. I. D., & Charness, N. (1990). Age-related declines in working-memory skills: Evidence from a complex calculation task. *Developmental Psychology*, 26(6), 879–888.

Canli, T., Zhao, Z., Desmond, J. E., Kang, E., Gross, J., & Gabrieli, J. D. E. (in press). An fMRI study of personality influences on brain reactivity to emotional stimuli. *Behavioral Neuroscience.*

Cannon, M., Jones, P., Huttunen, M. O., Tanskanen, A., Huttunen, T., Rabe-Hesketh, S., & Murray, R. M. (1999). School performance in Finnish children and later development of schizophrenia: A population-based longitudinal study. *Archives of General Psychiatry*, 56, 457–463.

Cannon, T. D., Kaprio, J., Lönnqvist, J., Huttunen, M., & Koskenvuo, M. (1998). The genetic epidemiology of schizophrenia in a Finnish twin cohort: a population-based modeling study. *Archives of General Psychiatry, 55*, 67–74.

Cannon, W. B. (1927). The James-Lange theory of emotions: A critical examination and an alternative theory. *American Journal of Psychology*, 39, 106–124.

Cannon, W. B. (1942). Voodoo death. *American Anthropologist, 44*, 169–181.

Canter, S. (1973). Personality traits in twins. In G. Claridge, S. Canter, & W. I. Hume (Eds.). *Personality differences and biological variations* (pp. 21–51). New York: Pergamon.

Cantor, N., & Norem, J. K. (1989). Defensive pessimism and stress and coping. *Social Cognition*, 7, 92–112.

Caramazza, A. (1984). The logic of neuropsychological research and the problem of patient classification in aphasia. *Brain and Language*, 21, 9–20.

Caramazza, A. (1986). On drawing inferences about the structure of normal cognitive systems from the analysis of patterns of impaired performance: The case for single-patient studies. *Brain and Cognition*, 5, 41–66.

Caramazza, A. (1992). Is cognitive neuropsychology plausible? *Journal of Cognitive Psychology*, 4(1), 80–95.

Caramazza, A., McCloskey, M., & Green, B. (1981). Naive beliefs in "sophisticated" subjects: Misconceptions about trajectories of objects. *Cognition*, 9, 117–123.

Caramazza, A., & Zurif, E. B. (1976). Dissociation of algorithmic and heuristic processes in language comprehension: Evidence from aphasia. *Brain & Language*, 3, 572–582.

Carey, M. P., & Burish, T. G. (1988). Etiology and treatment of the psychological side effects associated with cancer chemotherapy: A critical review and discussion. *Psychological Bulletin*, 104, 307–325.

Carey, S. (1978). The child as word learner. In J. Bresnan, G. Miller, & M. Halle (Eds.), *Linguistic theory and psychological reality* (pp. 264–293). Cambridge, MA: MIT Press.

Carey, S. (1985). *Conceptual change in childhood*. Cambridge, MA: Bradford/MIT Press.

Carey, S. (1988). Conceptual differences between children and adults. *Mind and Language* 3, 67–82.

Carey, S. (1995a). Continuity and discontinuity in cognitive development. In E. E. Smith, & D. N. Osherson (Eds.), *Thinking: An invitation to cognitive science* (2nd ed.). Cambridge, MA: MIT Press.

Carey, S. (1995b). On the origin of causal understanding. In D. Sperber, D. Premack, & A. J. Premack (Eds.), *Causal cognition: A multidisciplinary debate* (pp. 268–302). Oxford: Clarendon Press.

Carlson, N. R. (1992). *Foundations of physiological psychology* (2nd ed.). Boston: Allyn & Bacon.

Carlson, N. R. (1994). *Physiology of behavior*. Needham Heights, MA: Allyn & Bacon.

Carlson, R., & Levy, N. (1973). Studies of Jungian typology: I. Memory, social perception, and social action. *Journal of Personality*, 48, 87–94.

Carney, R. M., Freeland, K. E., Veith, R. C., Cryer, P. E., Skala, J. A., Lynch, T., & Jaffe, A. S. (1999). Major depression, heart rate, and plasma norepinephrine in patients with coronary heart disease. *Biological Psychiatry, 45*, 458–463.

Carpenter, P. A., Just, M. A., & Shell, P. (1990). What one intelligence test measures: A theoretical account of the processing in the Raven Progressive Matrices test. *Psychological Review, 97*, 404–431.

Carraher, T. N., Carraher, D. W., & Schliemann, A. D. (1985). Mathematics in the streets and in schools. *British Journal of Developmental Psychology*, 3, 21–29.

Carrington, P. (1977). *Freedom in Meditation*. Garden City, NY: Anchor Press/Doubleday.

Carroll, L. (1992). Alice in wonderland. Authoritative texts of Alice's adventures in wonderland, Through the looking-glass, The hunting of the snark. Backgrounds. *Essays in criticism* (2nd ed.). (D. J. Gray, Ed.). New York: Norton.

Carroll, J. (1993). *Human cognitive abilities: A survey of factor-analytic studies*. New York: Cambridge University Press.

Carskadon, M., Vieria, C., & Acebo, C. (1993). Association between puberty and delayed phase preference. *Sleep*, 16, 258–262.

Carskadon, T. G. (1978). Use of the Myers-Briggs Type Indicator in psychology courses and discussion groups. *Teaching of Psychology*, 5, 140–142.

Carstens, C. B., Huskins, E., & Hounshell, G. W. (1995). Listening to Mozart may not enhance performance on the revised Minnesota Paper Form Board Test. *Psychological Reports*, 77, 111–114.

Carstensen, L. L. (1991). Socioemotional selectivity theory: Social activity in life-span context. In K. W. Schaie & M. P. Lawton (Eds.), *Annual review of gerontology and geriatrics* (Vol. 11, pp. 195–217). New York: Springer.

Carstensen, L. L. (1992). Social and emotion patterns in adulthood: Support for socioemotional selectivity theory. *Psychology and Aging*, 7, 331–338.

Carter, C., & Rice, C. L. (1997). Acquisition and manifestation of prejudice in children. *Journal of Multicultural Counseling and Development, 25*, 185–194.

Carter, C., Robertson, L., Nordahl, T., Chaderjian, M., Kraft, L., & O'Shora-Celaya, L. (1996). Spatial working memory deficits and their relationship to negative symptoms in unmedicated schizophrenia patients. *Biological Psychiatry*, 40, 930–932.

Carter, J. C., Stewart, D. A., Dunn, V. J., and Fairburn, C. G. (1997). Primary prevention of eating disorders: Might it do more harm than good? *International Journal of Eating Disorders*, 22, 167–172.

Carter, M. M., Hollon, S. D., Carson, R., & Shelton, R. C. (1995). Effects of a safe person on induced distress following a biological challenge in panic disorder with agoraphobia. *Journal of Abnormal Psychology*, 104, 156–163.

Cartwright-Hatton, S., & Wells, A. (1997). Beliefs about worry and intrusions: The Meta-Cognitions Questionnaire and its correlates. *Journal of Anxiety Disorders, 11*, 279–296.

Carver, C. S., & Scheier, M. F. (1996). *Perspectives on personality*. Boston: Allyn & Bacon.

Carver, C. S., Scheier, M. F., & Weintraub, J. K. (1989). Assessing coping strategies: A theoretically based approach. *Journal of Personality and Social Psychology*, 56, 267–83.

Casada, J. H., Amdur, R., Larsen, R., & Liberzon, I. (1998). Psychophysiologic responsivity in posttraumatic stress disorder: Generalized hyperresponsiveness versus trauma specificity. *Biological Psychiatry, 44*, 1037–1044.

Case, R. (1977). Responsiveness to conservation training as a function of induced subjective uncertainty, M-space, and cognitive style. *Canadian Journal of Behavioral Sciences*, 9, 12–25.

Case, R. (1978). Intellectual development from birth to adulthood: A neo-Piagetian approach. In R. S. Siegler (Ed.), *Children's thinking: What develops?* (pp. 37–71). Hillsdale, NJ: Erlbaum.

Case, R. (1985). *Intellectual development: A systematic reinterpretation*. New York: Academic Press.

Case, R. (1992a). The role of the frontal lobes in the regulation of cognitive development. *Brain & Cognition*, 20, 51–73.

Case, R. (1992b). *The mind's staircase*. Hillsdale, NJ: Erlbaum.

Case, R. (1992c). The role of the frontal lobes in the regulation of cognitive development. *Brain and Cognition*, 20, 51–73.

Caspi, A. (1998). Personality development across the life course. In W. Damon (Series Ed.) & N. Eisenberg (Vol. Ed.), *Handbook of child psychology: Vol. 3. Social, emotional, and personality development.* (5th ed., pp. 311–388). New York: Wiley.

Caspi, A. (2000). The child is father of the man: Personality continuities from childhood to adulthood. *Journal of Personality and Social Psychology*, 78, 158–172.

Caspi, A., Begg, D., Dickson, N., Harrington, H., Langley, J., Moffitt, T. E., & Silva, P. A. (1997). Personality differences predict health-risk behaviors in young adulthood: Evidence from a longitudinal study. *Journal of Personality and Social Psychology*, 73, 1052–1063.

Caspi, A., & Herbener, E. S. (1990). Continuity and change: Assortative marriage and the consistency of personality in adulthood. *Journal of Personality and Social Psychology*, 58, 250–258.

Cassone, V. M., Warren, W. S., Brooks, D. S., & Lu, J. (1993). Melatonin, the pineal gland and circadian rhythms. *J. Biol. Rhythms, 8* (Suppl.), S73–S81.

Castillo, R. J. (1994). Spirit possession in South Asia, dissociation or hysteria? II. Case histories. *Culture, Medicine & Psychiatry, 18,* 141–162.

Catalan-Ahumeda, M., Dewggouj, N., De Volder, A., Melin, J., Michel, C., & Veraart, C. (1993). High metabolic activity demonstrated by positron emission tomography in human auditory cortex in case of deafness of early onset. *Brain Research, 623,* 287–292.

Cattell, R. B. (1971). *Abilities: Their structure, growth, and action.* Boston: Houghton Mifflin.

Cattell, R. B., Eber, H. W., & Tatsuoka, M. M. (1970). *Handbook for the Sixteen Personality Factor Questionnaire (16PF).* Champaign, IL: Institute for Personality and Ability Testing.

Caudron, S. (1994). Diversity ignites effective work teams. *Personnel Journal, 73,* 54–63.

Cavanagh, P. (1992). Attention-based motion perception. *Science, 257,* 1563–1565.

Cave, C. B. (1997). Very long-lasting priming in picture naming. *American Psychological Society, 8,* 322–325.

Cave, C. B., & Kosslyn, S. M. (1993). The role of parts and spatial relations in object identification. *Perception, 22,* 229–248.

Cave, C. B., & Squire, L. R. (1992). Intact and long-lasting repetition priming in amnesia. *Journal of Experimental Psychology: Learning, Memory, and Cognition, 18,* 509–520.

Cechetto, D. F., & Saper, C. B. (1990). Role of the cerebral cortex in autonomic function. In A. D. Loewy & K. M. Speyer (Eds.), *Central regulation of autonomic function* (pp. 208–223). New York: Oxford University Press.

Ceci, S. J. (1990). *On intelligence . . . more or less: A bio-ecological treatise on intellectual development.* Englewood Cliffs, NJ: Prentice-Hall.

Ceci, S. J. (1991). How much does schooling influence general intelligence and its cognitive components? A reassessment of the evidence. *Developmental Psychology, 27,* 703–722.

Ceci, S. J. (1996). *A bioecological treatise on intellectual development.* Cambridge, MA: Harvard University Press.

Ceci, S. J., & Williams, W. M. (1997). Schooling, intelligence, and income. *American Psychologist, 52,* 1051–1058.

Center for the Advancement of Health (1998). Facts of life: An issue briefing for health reporters. *3*(3), 2.

Centers for Disease Control. (1999, May 5). *http://www.cdc.gov/nchswww/fastats/alcohol.htm,.*

Cerella, J. (1990). Aging and information-processing rate. In J. E. Birren & K. W. Schaie (Eds.), *Handbook of the psychology of aging* (3rd ed., pp. 201–221). San Diego, CA: Academic Press.

Cerella, J., Poon, L., & Williams, D. (1980). Age and the complexity hypothesis. In L. W. Poon (Ed.), *Aging in the 1980's* (pp. 332–340). Washington, DC: American Psychological Association.

Cernoch, J. M., & Porter, R. H. (1985). Recognition of maternal axillary odors by infants. *Child Development, 56,* 1593–1598.

Chabris, C. F. (1998). IQ since "The Bell Curve." *Commentary, 106,* 33–40.

Chabris, C. F. (1999). Prelude or requiem for the "Mozart effect"? *Nature, 400,* 826–827.

Chamberlain, K., & Zika, S. (1990). The minor events approach to stress: Support for the use of daily hassles. *British Journal of Psychology, 81,* 469–481.

Chamberlain, M. C., Nichols, S. L., & Chase, C. H. (1991). Pediatric AIDS: Comparative cranial MRI and CT scans. *Pediatric Neurology, 7,* 357–362.

Chambers, J. M., Cleveland, W. S., Kleiner, B., & Turkey, P. A. (1983). *Graphical methods for data analysis.* Belmont, CA: Wadsworth.

Chambless, D. L., & Gillis, M. M. (1993). Cognitive therapy of anxiety disorders. *Journal of Consulting and Clinical Psychology, 61,* 248–260.

Chan, R. W., Raboy, B., & Patterson, C. J. (1998). Psychosocial adjustment among children conceived via donor insemination by lesbian and heterosexual mothers. *Child Development, 69,* 443–457.

Channouf, A., & Roubah, A. (1995). The effect of non-conscious perception of frequent stimuli on credibility judgement. *International Journal of Psychology, 30(2),* 213–235.

Chao, L. L., & Martin, A. (1999). Cortical regions associated with perceiving, naming, and knowing about colors. *Journal of Cognitive Neuroscience, 11,* 25–35.

Chapman, C. (1989). Giving the patient control of opioid analgesic administration. In C. Hill & W. Fields (Eds.). *Advances in Pain Research and Therapy,* Vol. 11. New York: Raven Press.

Chapman, C. R., & Nakamura, Y. (1999). A passion of the soul: An introduction to pain for consciousness researchers. *Consciousness and Cognition, 8,* 391–422.

Charness, N. (1981). Aging and skilled problem solving. *Journal of Experimental Psychology: General, 110,* 21–38.

Chase, W. G., & Ericsson, K. A. (1981). Skilled memory. In J. R. Anderson (Ed.), *Cognitive skills and their acquisition.* Hillsdale, NJ: Erlbaum.

Chase, W. G., & Simon, H. A. (1973). The mind's eye in chess. In W. G. Chase (Ed.), *Visual information processing* (pp. 215–281). New York: Academic Press.

Chassin, L., Curran, P. J., Hussong, A. M., & Colder, C. R. (1996). The relation of parent alcoholism to adolescent substance use: A longitudinal follow-up study. *Journal of Abnormal Psychology, 105,* 70–80.

Chatterjee, S., Heath, T. B., Milberg, S. J., & France, K. R. (2000). The differential processing of price in gains and losses: The effects of frame and need for cognition. *Journal of Behavioral Decision Making, 13,* 61–75.

Chaves, J. F. (1989). Hypnotic control of clinical pain. In N. P. Spanos & J. F. Chaves (Eds.), *Hypnosis: The cognitive-behavioral perspective,* pp. 242–272. Buffalo, NY: Prometheus Books.

Chen, Y., Levy, D. L., Nakayama, K., Matthysee, S., Palafox, G., & Holzman, P. S. (1998). Dependence of Impaired Eye Tracking on Deficient Velocity Discrimination in Schizophrenia. *Archives of General Psychiatry, 56,*155–161.

Cheour-Luhtanen, M., Alho, K., Sainio, K., Rinne, T., & Reinikainen, K. (1996). The ontogenetically earliest discriminative response of the human brain. *Psychophysiology, 33,* 478–481.

Cherry, E. C. (1953). Some experiments on the recognition of speech with one and two ears. *Journal of the Acoustical Society of America, 25,* 975–979.

Chess, S., & Thomas, A. (1987). *Know your child.* New York: Basic Books.

Chess, S., & Thomas, A. (1996). *Temperament: Theory and practice.* New York: Brunner/Mazel.

Chi, M. T. H. (1978). Knowledge structures and memory development. In R. S. Siegler (Ed.), *Children's thinking: What develops?* (pp. 73–96). Hillsdale, NJ: Erlbaum.

Chi, M. T. H., & Glaser, R. (1985). Problem solving ability. In R. J. Sternberg (Ed.), *Human abilities: An information processing approach* (pp. 227–250). New York: Freeman.

Chi, M. T. H., Glaser, R., & Rees, E. (1982). Expertise in problem solving. In R. J. Sternberg (Ed.), *Advances in the psychology of human intelligence* (Vol. 1, pp. 7–75). Hillsdale, NJ: Erlbaum.

Chilcoat, H. D., & Breslau, N. (1998). Posttraumatic Stress Disorder and Drug Disorders Testing Causal Pathways. *Arch Gen Psychiatry, 55,* 913–917.

Child, I. L. (1985). Psychology and anomalous observations: The question of ESP in dreams. *American Psychologist, 40,* 1219–1230.

Chipuer, H. M., Rovine, M. J., & Plomin, R. (1990). LISREL modeling: Genetic and environmental influences on IQ revisited. *Intelligence, 14,* 11–29.

Choderow, N. (1978). *The reproduction of mothering.* Berkeley: University of California Press.

Chomsky, C. (1969). *The acquisition of syntax in children from 5 to 10.* Cambridge, MA: MIT Press.

Chomsky, N. (1957). *Syntactic Structures* . Mouton: The Hague.

Chomsky, N. (1965). *Aspects of a Theory of Syntax* . Cambridge, MA: MIT Press.

Chomsky, N. (1972). *Language and mind.* New York: Harcourt Brace.

Chomsky, N. (1975). *Reflections on language.* New York: Pantheon.

Chomsky, N. (1976). *Reflections on language.* London: Temple Smith.

Chorney, M. K, Chorney, K., Seese, N., Owen, M. J., Daniels, J., McGufin, P., Thompson, L. A., Detterman, D. K., Benbow, C., Lubinski, D., Eley, T., & Plomin, R. (1998). A quantative trait locus associated with cognitive ability in children. *Psychological Science, 9,* 159–166.

Christensen, K. A., Stephens, M. A. P., & Townsend, A. L. (1998). Mastery in women's multiple roles and well-being: Adult daughters providing care to impaired parents. *Health Psychology, 17,* 163–171.

Christopher J., Murray, L., & Lopez, A. D., Eds. (1998). The global burden of disease: Volume 2 (Global Health Statistics. Cambridge, MA: Harvard University Press.

Chun, M. M. (1997). Types and tokens in visual processing: A double dissociation between the attentional blink and repetition blindness. *Journal of Experimental Psychology: Human Perception and Performance, 23,* 738–755.

Cialdini, R. B. (1979). Interpersonal influence. In S. Shavitt & T. C. Brock (Eds.), *Persuasion* (pp. 195–218). Boston: Allyn & Bacon.

Cialdini, R. B. (1994). Interpersonal influence. In N. S. Shavitt & T. C. Brock (Eds.), *Persuasion: Psychological insights and perspectives* (pp. 195–218). Boston: Allyn & Bacon.

Cialdini, R. B., Eisenberg, N., Green, B. L., Rhoads, K., & Bator, R. (1998). Undermining the undermining effect of reward on sustained interest. *Journal of Applied Social Psychology, 28,* 249–263.

Cialdini, R. B., & Petty, R. (1979). Anticipatory opinion effects. In B. Petty, T. Ostrom, & T. Brock (Eds.), *Cognitive responses in persuasion.* Hillsdale, NJ: Erlbaum.

Cialdini, R. B., Reno, R. R., & Kallgren, C. A. (1990). A focus theory of normative conduct: Recycling the concept of norms to reduce littering in public places. *Journal of Personality and Social Psychology, 58,* 1015–1026.

Cialdini, R. B., & Trost, M. R. (1998). Social influence: Social norms, conformity, and compliance. In D. T. Gilbert, S. T. Fiske, & G. Lindzey (Eds.), *The Handbook of Social Psychology* (4th ed.). New York: McGraw Hill. 151–192.

Cialdini, R. B., Trost, M. R., Newsom, J. T. (1995). Preference for consistency: the development of a valid measure and the discovery of surprising behavioral implications. *Journal of Personality and Social Psychology, 69,* 318–328.

Cialdini, R. B., Vincent, J. A., Lewis, S. K., Catalan, J., Wheeler, D., & Darby, B. L. (1975). Reciprocal concessions procedure for inducing compliance: The door-in-the-face technique. *Journal of Personality and Social Psychology, 31,* 206–215.

Cicero, T. J. (1978). Tolerance to and physiological dependence on alcohol: Behavioral and neurobiological mechanisms. In M. A. Lipton, A. DiMascio, & K. F. Killman (Eds.), *Psychopharmacology.* New York: Raven.

Citron, M., Solomon, P., & Draine, J. (1999). Self-help groups for families of persons with mental illness: Perceived benefits of helpfulness. *Community Mental Health Journal, 35,* 15–30.

Clancy, S. A., McNally, R. J., & Schacter, D. L. (1999). Effects of guided imagery on memory distortion in women reporting recovered memories of childhood sexual abuse. *Journal of Traumatic Stress, 12,* 559–569.

Clapp, G. (1988). *Child study research: Current perspectives and applications.* Lexington, MA: Lexington Books/D. C. Heath and Company.

Clarey, J. C., Barone, P., & Imig, T. J. (1992). Physiology of thalmus and cortex. In A. N. Popper & R. R. Fay (Eds.), *The mammalian auditory pathway: Neurophysiology* (pp. 232–334). New York: Springer-Verlag.

Clark, D. M., Ball, S., & Pape, D. (1991). An experimental investigation of thought suppression. *Behaviour Research and Therapy, 29,* 253–257.

Clark, D. M., Salkovskis, P. M., Hackmann, A., Middleton, H., Anastasiades, P., & Gelder, M. (1994). A comparison of cognitive therapy, applied relaxation and imipramine in the treatment of panic disorder. *British Journal of Psychiatry, 164,* 759–769.

Clark, D. M., Salkovskis, P. M., Hackmann, A., Wells, A., Ludgate, J., & Gelder, M. (1999). Brief cognitive therapy for panic disorder: A randomized controlled trial. *Journal of Consulting and Clinical Psychology, 67,* 583–589.

Clark, E. V. (1983). Meanings and concepts. In P. H. Mussen (Ed.), *Handbook of child psychology: Vol. 3, Cognitive development* (pp. 787–840). New York: Wiley.

Clark, E. V. (1993). *The lexicon in acquisition.* Cambridge: Cambridge University Press.

Clark, E. V. (1995). The lexicon and syntax. In J. L. Miller & P. D. Eimas (Eds.), *Speech, language, and communication* (pp. 303–337). San Diego: Academic Press.

Clark, L. F., & Collins, J. E. (1993). Remembering old flames: How the past affects assessments of the present. *Personality & Social Psychology Bulletin, 19,* 399–408.

Clark, S. A., Allard, T., Jenkins, W. M., & Merzenich, M. M. (1988). Receptive fields in the body-surface map in adult cortex defined by temporally correlated inputs. *Nature, 332,* 444–445.

Clarke, D. J., Boer, H., & Webb, T. (1995). Genetic and behavioural aspects of Prader-Willi syndrome: A review with a translation of the original paper. *Mental Handicap Research, 8,* 38–53.

Clay, R. (1995). Working mothers: happy or haggard? *The APA Monitor, 26 (11),* 1, 37.

Clifford, D. B. (2000). Human immunodeficiency virus-associated dementia. *Archives of Neurology, 57,* 321–324.

Clementz, B. A., & Sweeney, J. A. (1990). Is eye movement dysfunction a biological marker for schizophrenia? A methodological review. *Psychological Bulletin, 108,* 77–92.

Cloninger, R., & Svarkic, D. M. (1997). Integrative psychobiological approach to psychiatric assessment and treatment. *Psychiatry, 60,* 120–141.

Cloninger, R., Svarkic, D. M., & Prysbeck, T. R. (1993). Psychobiological model of temperament and character. *Archives of General Psychiatry, 50,* 975–990.

Cloninger, S. C. (1996). *Personality: Description, Dynamics, and Development.* New York: Freeman.

Clopton, N. A., & Sorell, G. T. (1993). Gender differences in moral reasoning: Stable or situational? *Psychology of Women Quarterly, 17,* 85–101.

Clum, G. A., Clum, G. A., & Surls, R. (1993). A meta-analysis of treatments for panic disorder. *Journal of Consulting & Clinical Psychology, 61,* 317–326.

Coats, E. J., & Feldman, R. S. (1996). Gender differences in nonverbal correlates of social status. *Personality & Social Psychology Bulletin, 22,* 1014–1022.

Coe, W. C. (1978). The credibility of posthypnotic amnesia: A contextualists' view. *International Journal of Clinical & Experimental Hypnosis, 26,* 218–245.

Cohen, D., Nisbett, R. E., Bowdle, B. F., & Schwarz, N. (1996). Insult, aggression, and the southern culture of honor: An "experimental ethnography." *Journal of Personality and Social Psychology, 70,* 945–960.

Cohen, H., Kotler, M., Matar, M. A., Kaplan, Z., Loewenthal, U., Miodownik, J., & Cassuto, Y. (1998). Analysis of heart rate variability in posttraumatic stress disorder patients in response to a trauma-related reminder. *Biological Psychiatry, 44,* 1054–1059.

Cohen, J. D., Peristein, W. M., Braver, T. S., Nystrom, L. E., Noll, D. C., Jonides, J., & Smith, E. E. (1997). Temporal dynamics of brain activation during a working memory task. *Nature, 386,* 604–608.

Cohen, N. J., & Squire, L. R. (1980). Preserved learning and retention of pattern analyzing skill in amnesia: Dissociation of knowing how and knowing that. *Science, 210,* 207–209.

Cohen, S., Doyle, W. J., Skoner, D. P., Rabin, B. S., & Gwaltney, J. M., Jr. (1997). Social ties and susceptibility to the common cold. *Journal of the American Medical Association, 277,* 1940–1944.

Cohen, S., Doyle, W. J., Skoner, D. P., Fireman, P., Gwaltney, J., & Newsom, J. (1995). State and trait negative affect as predictors of objective and subjective symptoms of respiratory viral infections. *Journal of Personality and Social Psychology, 68,* 159–169.

Cohen, S., Evans, F. W., Krantz, D. S., & Stokols, D. S. (1986). *Behavior, health, and environmental stress.* New York: Plenum Press.

Cohen, S., Frank, E., Doyle, W. J., Skoner, D. P., Rabin, B. S., & Gwaltney, J. M., Jr. (1998). Types of stressors that increase susceptibility to the common cold in adults. *Health Psychology, 17,* 214–223.

Cohen, S., & Herbert, T. B. (1996). Health Psychology: psychological factors and physical disease from the perspective of human psychoneuroimmunology. *Annual Review of Psychology, 47,* 113–142.

Cohen, S., Tyrrell, D. A. J., & Smith, A. P. (1991). Psychological stress and susceptibility to the common cold. *New England Journal of Medicine, 325,* 606–612.

Cohen, S., Tyrrell, D. A. J., & Smith, A. P. (1993). Negative life events, perceived stress, negative affect, and susceptibility to the common cold. *Journal of Personality and Social Psychology, 64,* 131–140.

Cohen, S., Tyrrell, D. A. J., & Smith, A. P. (1997). Psychological stress in humans and susceptibility to the common cold. In T. W. Miller (Ed.), *Clinical disorders and stressful life events.* (pp. 217–235). Madison, CT: International Universities Press.

Cohen, S., & Wills, T. (1985). Stress, social support and the buffering hypothesis. *Psychological Bulletin, 98,* 310–357.

Colapinto, J. (2000). *As nature made him: The boy who was raised as a girl.* New York: HarperCollins.

Colby, A., Kohlberg, L., Gibbs, J. C., & Lieberman, M. (1983). A longitudinal study of moral judgment. *Monographs of the Society for Research in Child Development, 48* (1–2, Serial No. 200).

Cole, M. (1990). Cognitive development and formal schooling: The evidence from cross-cultural research. In L. C. Moll (Ed.), *Vygotsky and education* (pp. 89–110). New York: Cambridge University Press.

Cole, M. (1996). *Cultural psychology: A once and future discipline.* Cambridge, MA: Harvard University Press.

Cole, M., & Bruner, J. S. (1971). Cultural differences and inferences about psychological processes. *American Psychologist, 26,* 867–876.

Cole, M., Engestroem, Y., & Vasquez, O. A. (Eds.), (1997). *Mind, culture, and activity: Seminal papers from the Laboratory of Comparative Human Cognition.* New York: Cambridge University Press.

Cole, M., Gay, J., Glick, J. A., & Sharp, D. W. (1971). *The cultural context of learning and thinking.* New York: Basic Books.

Cole, M., & Wertsch, J. V. (1996). Beyond the individual-social antinomy in discussions of Piaget and Vygotsky. *Human Development, 39,* 250–256.

Cole, P. M. (1998). Nepali children's ideas about emotional displays in hypothetical challenges. *Developmental Psychology, 34,* 640–646.

Coleman, P., & Flood, D. (1986). Dendritic proliferation in the aging brain as a compensatory repair mechanism. *Progress in Brain Research, 70,* 227–236.

Collier, B. A. C. (2000). *The library: Quotes.* Retrieved 19 July 2000 from the World Wide Web: http://www.uniblab.com/collie/Quotes/n.html.

Collings, V. B. (1974). Human taste response as a function of locus of stimulation on the tongue and soft palate. *Perception & Psychophysics, 16,* 169–174.

Collins, M. A., & Zebrowitz, L. A. (1995). The contributions of appearance to occupational outcomes in civilian and military settings. *Journal of Applied Social Psychology, 25,* 129–163.

Collins, W. A. (1990). Parent-child relationships in the transition to adolescence: Continuity and change in interaction, affect, and cognition. In R. Montemayor, G. R. Adams, & T. P. Gullota (Eds.), *From childhood to adolescence: A transitional period?* (pp. 85–106). Newbury Park, CA: Sage.

Colom, F., Vieta, E., Martinez, A., Jorquera, A., & Gasto, C. (1998). What is the role of psychotherapy in the treatment of bipolar disorder? *Psychotherapy & Psychosomatics, 67,* 3–9.

Comery, T. A., Shah, R., & Greenough, W. T. (1995). Differential rearing alters spine density on medium-sized spiny neurons in the rat corpus striatum: Evidence for association of morphological plasticity with early response gene expression. *Neurobiology of Learning & Memory, 63,* 217–219.

Compas, B. E., Haaga, D. A. F., Keefe, F. J., Leitenberg, H., & Williams, D. A. (1998). Sampling of Empirically Supported Psychological Treatments From Health Psychology, *Journal of Consulting and Clinical Psychology, 66,* 89–112.

Comstock, G., & Paik, H. (1991). *Television and the American child.* San Diego, CA: Academic Press.

Cone, E. J. (1995). Pharmacokinetics and Pharmacodynamics of Cocaine. *Journal of Analytical Toxicology, 19,* 459–477.

Conger, J. A. (1991). Inspiring others: The language of leadership. *Academy of Management Executive, 5,* 31–45.

Conn, J. H., & Conn, R. N. (1967). Discussion of T. X. Barber's "Hypnosis as a causal variable in present day psychology: A critical analysis." *International Journal of Clinical & Experimental Hypnosis, 15,* 106–110.

Connolly, J. B., Roberts, I. J. H., Armstrong, J. D., Kaiser, K., Forte, M., Tully, T., & O'Kane, C. J. (1996). Associative learning disrupted by impaired Gs signaling in Drosophila mushroom bodies. *Science, 274,* 2104–2107.

Connor, E. M., Sperling, R. S., Gelber, R., Kiselev, P., Scott, G., & Sullivan, M. J. (1995). Reduction of maternal-infant transmission of human immunodeficient virus 1 with zidovudine treatment. *Obstetrical and Gynecological Survey, 50,* 253–255.

Consortium for Longitudinal Studies (Ed.). (1983). *As the twig is bent . . . Lasting effects of preschool programs.* Hillsdale, NJ: Erlbaum.

Conti, R., Coon, H., & Amabile, T. M. (1996). Evidence to support the componential model of creativity: Secondary analyses of three studies. *Creativity Research Journal, 9,* 385–389.

Conway, M. A., & Rubin, D. C. (1993). The structure of autobiographical memory. In A. F. Collins, S. E. Gathercole, M. A. Conway, & P. E. Morris (Eds.), *Theories of memory* (pp. 103–137). Hillsdale, NJ: Erlbaum.

Cook, E. W., III, Hawk, L. W., Davis, T. L., Stevenson, V. E. (1991). Affective individual differences and startle reflex modulation. *Journal of Abnormal Psychology, 100,* 5–13.

Cook, M., & Mineka, S. (1991). Selective Associations in the origins of phobic fears and their implications for behavioar therapy. In P. Martin (Ed.), *Handbook of behavior therapy and psychological science :An integrative approach.* New York: Pergamon Press.

Coons, P. M., Milstein, V., & Marley, C. (1982). EEG studies of two multiple personalities and a control. *Archives of General Psychiatry, 39,* 823–825.

Cooper, J. (1998). Unlearning cognitive dissonance: Toward an understanding of the development of dissonance. *Journal of Experimental Social Psychology, 34,* 562–575.

Cooper, M. L., Shapiro, C. M., & Powers, A. M. (1998). Motivations for sex and risky sexual behavior among adolescents and young adults: A functional perspective. *Journal of Personality and Social Psychology, 75,* 1528–1558.

Cooper, R. P., Abraham, J., Berman, S., & Staska, M. (1997). The development of infants' preference for motherese. *Infant Behavior & Development, 20,* 477–488.

Coplan, J. D., Goetz, R., Klein, D. F., Papp, L. A., Fyer, A. J., Liebowitz, M. R., Davies, S. O., & Gorman, J. M. (1998). Plasma cortisol concentrations preceding lactate-induced panic: Psychological, biochemical, and physiological correlates. *Archives of General Psychiatry, 55,* 130–136.

Corbetta, M., Miezin, F. M., Dobmeyer, S., Shulman, G. L., & Petersen, S. E. (1990). Attentional modulation of neural processing of shape, color, and velocity in humans. *Science, 248,* 1556–1559.

Corbetta, M., Miezin, F. M., Dobmeyer, S., Shulman, G. L., & Petersen, S. E. (1991). Selective and divided attention during visual discriminations of shape, color, and speed: Functional anatomy by positron emission tomography. *Journal of Neuroscience, 11,* 2383–2402.

Corbetta, M., Miezen, F. M., Shulman, G. L., & Petersen, S. E. (1993). A PET study of visuospatial attention. *Journal of Neuroscience, 13,* 1202–1226.

Coren, S. (1996). *Sleep Thieves: An Eye-opening exporation into the science and mysteries of sleep,* New York: Free Press.

Corr, P. J., & Kumari, V. (1997). Sociability/impulsivity and attenuated-dopaminergic arousal: Critical flicker/fusion frequency and procedural learning. *Personality and Individual Differences, 22,* 805–815.

Corr, P. J., Pickering, A. D., & Gray, J. A. (1995). Sociability/impulsivity and caffeine-induced arousal: Critical flicker/fusion frequency and procedural learning. *Personality and Individual Differences, 18,* 713–730.

Corr, P. J., Pickering, A. D., & Gray, J. A. (1997). Personality, Punishment, and Procedural Learning: ATest of J. A. Gray's Anxiety Theory. *Journal of Personality and Social Psychology, 73,* 337–344.

Cosmides, L. (1989). The logic of social exchange: Has natural selection shaped how humans reason? Studies with the Wason selection task. *Cognition, 31,* 187–276.

Cosmides, L., & Tooby, J. (1996). Are humans good intuitive statisticians after all? Rethinking some conclusions from the literature on judgment under uncertainty. *Cognition, 58,* 1–73.

Costa, P. T., & McCrae, R. R. (1988). Personality in adulthood: A six-year longitudinal study of self-reports and spouse ratings on the NEO personality inventory. *Journal of Personality and Social Psychology, 54,* 853–863.

Costa, P. T., & McCrae, R. R. (1995). Primary traits of Eysenck's P-E-N System: Three- and five-factor solutions. *Journal of Personality and Social Psychology, 69,* 308–317.

Costa, P. T., McCrae, R. R., & Dye, D. A. (1991). Facet scales for agreeableness and conscientiousness: A revision of the NEO Personality Inventory. *Personality and Individual Differences, 12,* 887–898.

Costela, C., Tejedor-Real, P., Mico, J. A., & Gilbert-Rahola, J. (1995). Effect of neonatal handling on learned helplessness model of depression. *Physiology and Behavior, 57,* 407–410.

Cotman, C. (1990). The brain: New plasticity/new possibility. In R. N. Butler, M. R. Oberlink, & M. Schechter (Eds.), *The promise of productive aging: From biology to social policy* (pp. 70–84). New York: Springer.

Council, J. R. (1993). Contextual effects in personality research. *Current Directions in Psychological Science, 2,* 31–34.

Council, J. R., Kirsch, I., & Grant, D. L. (1996). Imagination, expectancy and hypnotic responnding. In R. G. Kunzendorf, N. P. Spanos, & B. J. Wallace (Eds.), *Hypnosis and imagination* (pp. 41–65). Amityville, NY: Baywood.

Counts, D. A., & Counts, D. R. (1992). "I'm not dead yet!" Aging and death: Process and experience in Kaliai. In L. A. Platt & V. R. Persico, Jr. (Eds.), *Grief in cross-cultural perspective: A casebook* (pp. 307–343). New York: Garland.

Courtney, S. M., Ungerleider, L. G., Keil, K., & Haxby, J. V. (1997). Transient and sustained activity in a distributed neural system for human working memory. *Nature 386,* 608–611.

Cover, H., & Irwin, M. (1994). Immunity and depression: Insomnia, retardation, and reduction of natural killer cell activity. *Journal of Behavioral Medicine, 17,* 217–223.

Cowan, N. (in press). The magical number 4 in short-term memory: A reconsideration of mental storage capacity. *Brain and Behavioral Sciences.*

Cowan, W. M., Fawcett, J. W., O'Leary, D. D. M., & Stanfield, B. B. (1984). Regressive events in neurogenesis. *Science, 225,* 1258–1265.

Cowey, A., & Stoerig, P. (1995). Blindsight in monkeys. *Nature, 373,* 247–249.

Cox, H. (2000). Personal communication.

Coyne, J. C. (1976). Toward an interactional description of depression. *Psychiatry, 39,* 28–40.

Coyne, J. C., & Downey, G. (1991). Social factors in psychopathology: Stress, social support, and coping processes. *Annual Review of Psychology, 42,* 401–425.

Coyne, J. C., Kessler, R. C., Tal, M., Turnbull, J., Wortman, C., & Greden, J. (1987). Living with a depressed person: Burden and psychological distress. *Journal of Clinical and Consulting Psychology, 55,* 347–352.

Craig, R. L., & Siegel, P. S. (1978). Does negative affect beget positive affect? A test of the opponent-process theory. *Bulletin of the Psychonomic Society, 14,* 404 406.

Craik, F. I., & McDowd, J. M. (1987). Age differences in recall and recognition. *Journal of Experimental Psychology: Learning, Memory, & Cognition, 13,* 474–479.

Craik, F. I. M., Anderson, N. D., Kerr, S. A., & Li, K. Z. H. (1995). Memory changes in normal aging. In A. D. Baddeley, B. A. Wilson, & F. N. Watts (Eds.). *Handbook of memory disorders* (pp. 211–241). New York: Wiley.

Craik, F. I. M., & Lockhart, R. S. (1972). Levels of Processing: A framework for memory research. *Journal of Verbal Learning and Verbal Behavior, 11,* 671–684.

Craik, F. I. M., & Tulving, E. (1975). Depth of processing and the retention of words in episodic memory. *Journal of Experimental Psychology: General, 104,* 268–294.

Craik, F. I. M., & Watkins, M. J. (1973). The role of rehearsal in short-term memory. *Journal of Learning and Verbal Behavior, 12,* 599–607.

Cramer, R. E., Schaefer, J. T., & Reid, S. (1996). Identifying the ideal mate: More evidence for male–female convergence. *Current Psychology: Developmental, Learning, Personality, Social, 16,* 157–166.

Crawford, H. J., Gur, R. C., Skolnick, B., Gur, R. E., & Benson, D. (1993). Effects of hypnosis on regional cerebral blood flow during ischemic pain with and without suggested hypnotic analgesia. *International Journal of Psychophysiology, 15,* 181–195.

Crawford, M., Stark, A. C., & Renner, C. H. (1998). The meaning of Ms.: Social assimilation of a gender concept. *Psychology of Women Quarterly, 22,* 197–208.

Crawford, R. P. (1954). *The technique of creative thinking: How to use your ideas to achieve success.* New York: Hawthorn Books.

Crick, F., & Koch, C. (1995). Are we aware of neural activity in primary visual cortex? *Nature, 375,* 121–123.

Crick, F., & Koch, C. (1998). Consciousness and neuroscience. *Cerebral Cortex, 8,* 97–107.

Crick, F., & Mitchison, F. (1983). The function of dream sleep. *Nature, 304,* 111–114.

Crick, F., & Mitchison, G. (1986). REM sleep and neural nets. *Journal of Mind and Behavior, 7,* 229–250.

Crick, N. R., & Grotpeter, J. K. (1995). Relational aggression, gender, and social-psychological adjustment. *Child Development, 66,* 710–722.

Crisp, A. H., Hsu, L. K., & Harding, B. (1980). The starving hoarder and voracious spender: Stealing in anorexia nervosa. *Journal of Psychosomatic Research, 24,* 225–231.

Critchley, H. D., & Rolls, E. T. (1996). Hunger and satiety modify the responses of olfactory and visual neurons in the primate orbitofrontal cortex. *Journal of Neurophysiology, 75,* 1673–1686.

Crits-Christoph, P. (1992). The efficacy of brief dynamic psychotherapy: A meta-analysis. *American Journal of Psychiatry, 149,* 151–158.

Croizet, J.-C., & Claire, T. (1998) Extending the concept of stereotype and threat to social class: The intellectual underperformance of students from low socioeconimic backgrounds. *Personality & Social Psychology Bulletin, 24,* 588–594.

Cronbach, L. J. (1990). *Essentials of psychological testing.* New York: Harper & Row.

Crowe, R., Noyes, R., Pauls, D., & Slyman, D. (1983). A family study of panic disorder. *Archives of General Psychiatry, 40,* 1065–1069.

Crozier, J. B. (1997). Absolute pitch: Practice makes perfect, the earlier the better. *Psychology of Music, 25,* 110–119.

Csikszentmihalyi, M., & Csikszentmihalyi, I. S. (Eds.). (1988). *Optimal Experience: Psychological studies of flow in consciousness.* New York: Cambridge University Press.

Cuijpers, P. (1997). Bibliotherapy in unipolar depression: A meta-analysis. *Journal of Behavior Therapy & Experimental Psychiatry, 28,* 139–147.

Culbertson, F. M. (1997). Depression and gender: An international review. *American Psychologist, 52,* 25–31.

Cummings, N. (1992). Self-defense training for college women. *Journal of American College Health, 40,* 183–188.

Cunningham, M. R. (1986). Measuring the physical in physical attractiveness: Quasi-experiments on the sociobiology of female facial beauty. *Journal of Personality and Social Psychology, 50,* 925–935.

Cunningham, M. R., Barbee, A. P., & Pike, C. L. (1990). What do women want? Facialmetric assessment of multiple motives in the perception of male facial physical attractiveness. *Journal of Personality and Social Psychology, 59,* 61–72.

Cunningham, M. R., Roberts, A. R., Barbee, A. P., Druen, P. B., & Wu, C. H. (1995). "Their ideas of beauty are, on the whole, the same as ours": Consistency and variability in the cross-cultural perception of female physical attractiveness. *Journal of Personality and Social Psychology, 68,* 261–279.

Cupach, W. P., & Spitzberg, B. H. (1994). *The dark side of interpersonal communication.* Hillsdale, NJ: Erlbaum.

Curtiss, S. (1977). *Genie: A psycholinguistic study of a modern-day "wild child."* New York: Academic Press.

Curtiss, S. (1989). The independence and task-specificity of language. In M. H. Bornstein & J. S. Bruner (Eds.), *Interaction in human development* (pp. 105–137). Hillsdale, NJ: Erlbaum.

Czeisler, C. A., Duffy, J. F., Shanahan, T. L., Brown, E. N., Mitchell, J. F., Rimmer, D. W., Ronda, J. M., Silva, E. J., Allan, J. S., Emens, J. S., Dijk, D. J., & Kronauer, R. E. (1999). Stability, precision, and near-24-hour period of the human circadian pacemaker. *Science, 284,* 2101–2103.

D'Esposito, M., Detre, J. A., Alsop, D. C., Shin, R. K., Atlas, S., & Grossman, M. (1995). The neural basis of the central executive system of working memory. *Nature, 378,* 279–281.

Dadds, M. R., Bovberg, D. H., Redd, W. H., & Cutmore, T. R. H. (1997). Imagery in human classical conditioning. *Psychological Bulletin, 122,* 89–103.

Dai, X. Y., & Lynn, R. (1994). Gender differences in intelligence among Chinese children. *The Journal of Social Psychology, 134,* 123–125.

Dalbert, C., & Yamauchi, L. (1994). Belief in a just world and attitudes toward immigrants and foreign workers: A cultural comparison between Hawaii and Germany. *Journal of Applied Social Psychology, 24,* 1612–1626.

Dalderup, L. M., and Fredericks, M. L. C. (1969). Colour sensitivity in old age. *Journal of the American Geriatic Society, 17,* 388–390.

Dale, R. (1997, November 25). A psychoanalyst's view of Japan's ills. *International Herald Tribune,* 13.

Damasio, A. R. (1985). Disorders of complex visual processing: Agnosias, achromatopsia, Balint's syndrome, and related difficulties of orientation and construction. In M.-M. Mesulam (Ed.), *Principles of behavioral neurology* (pp. 259–288). Philadelphia: Davis.

Damasio, A. R. (1994). *Descartes' error: Emotion, reason, and the human brain.* New York: Grosset/Putnam.

Damasio, A. R. (1996). The somatic marker hypothesis and the possible functions of the prefrontal cortex. *Philosophical Transactions of the Royal Society London Series B, 351,* 1413–1420.

Damasio, A. R. (1999). *The feeling of what happens: Body and emotion in the making of consciousness.* New York: Harcourt Brace.

Damasio, H., Grabowski, T. J., Tranel, D., Hichwa, R. D., & Damasio, A. R. (1996). A neural basis for lexical retrieval. *Nature, 380,* 499–505.

Darley, J. M., & Latané, B. (1968). Bystander intervention in emergencies: Diffusion of responsibility. *Journal of Personality and Social Psychology, 10,* 202–214.

Darley, J. M., & Latané, B. (1970). Norms and normative behavior: Field studies of social interdependence. In J. Macauley and L. Berkowitz (Eds.), *Altruism and helping behavior.* (pp. 83–101). New York: Academic Press.

Darwin, C. (1872). *The expression of the emotions in man and animals.* Chicago: University of Chicago Press, 1965.

Das, A., & Gilbert, C. D. (1995). Long-range horizontal connections and their role in cortical reorganization revealed by optical recording of cat primary visual cortex. *Nature, 375,* 780–784.

Dauncey, K., Giggs, J., Baker, K., & Harrison, K. (1993). Schizophrenia in Nottingham: Lifelong residential mobility of a cohort. *British Journal of Psychiatry, 163,* 613–619.

Davey, G. C. L. (1992). Classical condiotining and the acquisition of human fears and phobias: A review of synthesis of the literature. *Advances in Behavior Research and Therapy, 14,* 29–66.

David, J. P., & Suls, J. (1999). Coping efforts in daily life: Role of Big Five traits and problem appraisals. *Journal of Personality, 67,* 265–294.

Davidson, R. J. (1992a). Emotion and affective style: Hemispheric substrates. *Psychological Science, 3,* 39–43.

Davidson, R. J. (1992b). A prolegomenon to the structure of emotion: Gleanings from neuropsychology. *Cognition and Emotion, 6,* 245–268.

Davidson, R. J. (1993). Parsing affective space: Perspectives from neuropsychology and psychophysiology. *Neuropsychology, 7,* 464–475.

Davidson, R. J. (1994a). Honoring biology in the study of affective style. In P. Ekman & R. J. Davidson (Eds.), *The nature of emotion: Fundamental questions* (pp. 321–328). New York: Oxford University Press.

Davidson, R. J. (1994b). The role of prefrontal activation in the inhibition of negative affect. *Psychophysiology, 31,* S7.

Davidson, R. J. (1998). Affective style and affective disorders: Perspectives from affective neuroscience. *Cognition and Emotion, 12,* 307–330.

Davidson, R. J., Abercrombie, H., Nitschke, J. B., & Putnam, K. (1999). Regional brain function, emotion and disorders of emotion. *Current Opinion in Neurobiology, 9,* 228–234.

Davies, K. A. (1997). Voluntary exposure to pornography and men's attitudes toward feminism and rape. *Journal of Sex Research, 34,* 131–137.

Davis, G. A. (1973). *Psychology of problem solving. Theory and practice.* New York: Basic Books.

Davis, J. D., & Campbell, C. S. (1973). Peripheral control of meal size in the rat: Effects of sham feeding on meal size and drinking rate. *Journal of Comparative & Physiological Psychology, 83,* 379–387.

Davis, J. D., & Levine, M. W. (1977). A model for the control of ingestion. *Psychological Review, 84,* 379–412.

Davis, J. O., Phelps, J. A., & Bracha, H. S. (1995). Prenatal development of monozygotic twins and concordance for schizophrenia. *Schizophrenia Bulletin, 21,* 357–366.

Davis, K. D., Kiss, Z. H., Luo, L., Tasker, R. R., Lozano, A. M., & Dostrovsky, J. O. (1998). Phantom sensations generated by thalamic microstimulation. *Nature, 391,* 385–387.

Davis, M. (1992). The role of the amygdala in conditioned fear. In J. P. Aggleton (Ed.), *The amygdala: Neurobiological aspects of emotion, memory, and mental dysfunction* (pp. 255– 306). New York: Wiley-Liss.

Davis, M. C., Matthews, K. A., McGrath, C. E. (2000). Hostile attitudes predict elevated vascular resistance during interpersonal stress in men and women. *Psychosomatic Medicine, 62,* 17–25.

Davis, M. S. (1973). *Intimate relations.* New York: Free Press.

Dean, H. J., McTaggart, T. L., Fish, D. G., & Friesen, H. G. (1986). Long-term social follow-up of growth hormone deficient adults treated with growth hormone during childhood. in B. Stabler & L. E. Underwood (Eds.), *Slow grows the child: Psychosocial aspects of growth delay.* (pp. 73–82). Hillsdale, NJ: Erlbaum.

Dean, W., Morgenthaler, J., & Fowkes, S. W. (1993). *Smart drugs: II. The next generation: New drugs and nutrients to improve your memory and increase your intelligence (Smart Drug Series, Vol. 2)*. Petaluma, CA: Smart Publications.

Deary, I. J. (1995). Auditory inspection time and intelligence: What is the direction of causation? *Developmental Psychology, 31,* 237–250.

Deary, I. J., & Pagliari, C. (1991). The strength of *g* at different levels of ability: Have Detterman & Daniel rediscovered Spearman's "law of diminishing returns"? *Intelligence 15,* 247–250.

DeCasper, A. J., & Spence, M. J. (1986). Prenatal maternal speech influences newborns' perception of speech sounds. *Infant Behavior and Development, 9,* 133–150.

De Castro, J. M. (1990). Social facilitation of duration and size but not rate of the spontaneous meal intake of humans. *Physiology & Behavior, 47,* 1129–1135.

Deci, E. L., Koestner, R., & Ryan, R. M. (1999a). A meta-analytic review of experiments examining the effects of extrinsic rewards on intrinsic motivation. *Psychological Bulletin, 125,* 627–668.

Deci, E. L., Koestner, R., & Ryan, R. M. (1999b). The undermining effect is a reality after all—Extrinsic rewards, task interest, and self-determination: Reply to Eisenberger, Pierce, and Cameron (1999) and Lepper, Henderlong, and Gingras (1999). *Psychological Bulletin, 125,* 692–700.

Deese, J. (1959). On the prediction of occurrence of particular verbal intrusions in immediate recall. *Journal of Experimental Psychology, 58,* 17–22.

Deffenbacher, J. L., Oetting, E. R., Huff, M. E., Cornell, G. R., & Dalleger, C. J. (1996). Evaluation of two cognitive-behavioral approaches to general anger reduction. *Cognitive Therapy & Research, 20,* 551–573.

DeFries, J. C., Fulker, D. W., & LaBuda, M. C. (1987). Evidence for a genetic aetiology in reading disability of twins. *Nature, 329,* 537–539.

DeFries, J. C., Vogler, G. P., & LaBuda, M. C. (1986). Colorado Family Reading Study: An overview. In J. L. Fuller & E. C. Simmel (Eds.), *Perspectives in behavior genetics* (pp. 29–56). Hillsdale, NJ: Erlbaum.

Degarrod, L. N. (1990). Coping with stress: Dream interpretation in the Mapuche family. *Psychiatric Journal of the University of Ottawa, 15,* 111–116.

DeGroot, A. D. (1965). *Thought and choice in chess.* The Hague: Mouton.

DeGroot, A. D. (1966). Perception and memory versus thought. In B. Kleinmuntz (Ed.), *Problem solving* (pp. 19–50). New York: Wiley.

Dehaene, S. (1997). *The number sense: How the mind creates mathematics.* New York: Oxford.

Dehaene-Lambertz, G., & Dehaene, S. (1994). Speed and cerebral correlates of syllable discrimination in infants. *Nature, 370,* 292–295.

Deiber, M. P., Passingham, R. E., Colebatch, J. G., Friston, K. J., Nixon, P. D., & Frackowiak, R. S. J. (1991). Cortical areas and the selection of movement: A study with positron emission tomography. Experimental Brain Research, 84, 393–402.

Delany, S. L., Delany, A. E., & Hearth, A. H. (1993). *Having Our Say: The Delany Sisters' First 100 Years.* New York: Delta.

Delbridge, M. L., & Graves, J. A. M (1999). Mammalian Y chromosome evolution and the male-specific functions of Y chromosome-borne genes *Reviews of Reproduction, 4,* 101–109.

Delis, D. C., Robertson, L. C., & Efron, R. (1986). Hemispheric specialization of memory for visual hierarchical stimuli. *Neuropsychologia, 24,* 205–214.

DeLisi, L. E. (1999). Structural Brain Changes in Schizophrenia. *Archives of General Psychiatry, 56,* 195.

Delk, J. L., & Fillenbaum, S., (1965). Difference in perceived color as a function of characteristic color. *American Journal of Psychology, 78,* 290–293.

Dell, G. S. (1990). Effects of frequency and vocabulary type on phonological speech errors. *Language & Cognitive Processes, 3,* 17–22.

Dell, G. S., Burger, L. K., & Svec, W. R. (1997). Language production and serial order: A functional analysis and a model. *Psychological Review, 104,* 123–147.

Dell, P. F. (1998). Axis II pathology in outpatients with dissociative identity disorder. *Journal of Nervous & Mental Disease, 186,* 352–356.

DeLoache, J. S., Pierroutsakos, S. L., Uttal, D. H., Rosengren, K. S., & Gottlieb, A. (1998). Grasping the nature of pictures. *Psychological Science, 9,* 205–210.

DeLongis, A., Coyne, J. C., Dakof, G., Folkman, S., & Lazrus, R. S. (1982). Relationship of daily hassles, uplifts, and major life events to health status. *Health Psychology, 1,* 119–136.

DeMann, Jeffrey A. (1994). First person account: The evolution of a person with schizophrenia. *Schizophrenia Bulletin, 20,* 579–582.

Demarais, A. M., & Cohen, B. H. (1998). Evidence for image–scanning eye movement during transitive inference. *Biological Psychology, 49,* 229–247.

De Marchi, N., & Mennella, R. (2000). Huntington's disease and its association with psychopathology. *Harvard Review of Psychiatry, 7,* 278–89.

Demare, D., Briere, J., & Lips, H. M. (1988). Violent pornography and self-reported likelihood of sexual aggression. *Journal of Research in Personality, 22,* 140–153.

Demare, D., Lips, H. M., & Briere, J. (1993). Sexually violent pornography, anti-women attitudes, and sexual aggression: A structural equation model. *Journal of Research in Personality, 27,* 285–300.

Dement, W. C. (1974). *Some must watch while some must sleep.* San Francisco, CA: W. H. Freeman.

DeNeve, K. M., & Cooper, H. (1998). The happy personality: A meta-analysis of 137 personality traits and subjective well-being. *Psychological Bulletin, 124,* 197–229.

Denis, M., & Kosslyn, S. M. (1999). Scanning visual images: A window on the mind. *Current Psychology of Cognition, 18,* 409–465.

Dennehy, E. B., Bulow, P., Wong, F. Y., Smith, S. M., & Aronoff, J. B. (1991). *A test of cognitive fixation in brainstorming groups.* Unpublished manuscript. Department of Psychology, Texas A&M University, College Station, TX.

Dennett, D. C. (1991). *Consciousness Explained.* Boston: Little, Brown & Co.

Dennis, W. (1966). Goodenough scores, art experience, and modernization. *Journal of Social Psychology, 68,* 211–228.

Dennis, W. (1973). *Children of the creche.* New York: Appleton-Century-Crofts.

Department of Health and Human Services: Substance Abuse and Mental Health Services Administration. Preliminary Results from the 1997 National Household Survey on Drug Abuse. Rockville: SAHMSA, 1998.

DePaulo, B. M., Charlton, K., Cooper, H., Lindsay, J. J., & Muhlenbruck, L. (1997). The accuracy-confidence correlation in the detection of deception. *Personality & Social Psychology Review, 1,* 346–357.

DeQuardo, R. (1998). Pharmacologic treatment of first-episode schizophrenia: Early intervention is key to outcome. *Journal of Clinical Psychiatry, 59,* 9–17.

De Renzi, E., Liotti, M., & Nichelli, P. (1987). Semantic amnesia with preservation of autobiographic memory. A case report. *Cortex, 23,* 575–597.

Desimone, R., Albright, T. D., Gross, C. G., & Bruce, C. (1984). Stimulus-selective properties of inferior temporal neurons in the macaque. *Journal of Neuroscience, 8,* 2051–2062.

D'Esposito, M., Detre, J. A., Alsop, D. C., Shin, R. K., Atlas, S., & Grossman, M. (1995). The neural basis of the central executive system of working memory. *Nature, 378,* 279–281.

Detterman, D. K., & Daniel, M. H. (1989). Correlates of mental tests with each other and with cognitive variables are highest for low IQ groups. *Intelligence, 13,* 349–359.

Deutsch, J. A., Young, W. G., & Kalogeris, T. J. (1978). The stomach signals satiety. *Science, 201,* 165–167.

De Valois, R. L., & De Valois, K. K. (1975). Neural coding of color. In E. C. Carterette & M. P. Friedman (Eds.), *Handbook of perception* (pp. 117–166). New York: Academic Press.

De Valois, R. L., & De Valois, K. K. (1988). *Spatial vision.* New York: Oxford University Press.

De Valois, R. L., & De Valois, K. K. (1993). A multi-stage color model. *Vision Research, 33,* 1053–1065.

de Villiers, P. A., & de Villiers, J. G. (1992). Language development. In M. H. Bornstein & M. E. Lamb (Eds.), *Developmental psychology: An advanced textbook* (3rd ed., pp. 337–418). Hillsdale, NJ: Erlbaum.

de Villiers, P. A., & de Villiers, J. G. (1992). Language development. In M. H. Bornstein & M. E. Lamb (Eds.), *Developmental psychology: An advanced textbook* (3rd ed., pp. 337–418). Hillsdale, NJ: Erlbaum.

Devine, P. G., & Monteith, M. J. (1993). The role of discrepancy-associated affect in prejudice reduction. In D. M. Mackie & D. L. Hamilton (Eds.), et al. *Affect, cognition, and stereotyping: Interactive processes in group perception* (pp. 317–344). San Diego, CA: Academic Press.

Devlin, B., Daniels, M., & Roeder, K. (1997). The heritability of IQ. *Nature, 388,* 468–471.

deVries, M. W. (1984). Temperament and infant mortality among the Masai of East Africa. *American Journal of Psychiatry, 141,* 1189–1194.

De Wijk, R. A., & Cain, W. S. (1994). Odor identification by name and by edibility: Life-span development and safety. *Human Factors, 36,* 182–187.

De Wijk, R. A., Schab, F. R., & Cain, W. S. (1995). Odor identification. In F. R. Schab & R. G. Crowder (Eds.), *Memory for odors* (pp. 21–37). Mahwah, NJ: Erlbaum.

Dew, A. M., & Ward, C. (1993). The effects of ethnicity and culturally congruent and incongruent nonverbal behaviors on interpersonal attraction. *Journal of Applied Social Psychology, 23,* 1376–1389.

Dewhurst, S. A., & Conway, M. A. (1994). Pictures, images, and recollective experience. *Journal of Experimental Psychology: Learning, Memory, and Cognition, 20,* 1088–1098.

DeZazzo, J., & Tully, T. (1995). Dissection of memory formation: From behavioral pharmacology to molecular genetics. *Trends in Neuroscience, 18,* 212–218.

Diamond, M. (1997). Sexual identity and sexual orientation in children with traumatized or ambiguous genetalia. *Journal of Sex Research, 34,* 199–211.

Diamond, M., & Sigmundson H. K. (1997). Sex reassignment at birth. Long-term review and clinical implications. *Archives of Pediatrics & Adolescent Medicine, 151,* 298–304.

Diamond, M. C., Rosenzweig, M. R., Bennett, E. L., Lindner, B., & Lyon, L. (1972). Effects of environmental enrichment and impoverishment on rat cerebral cortex. *Journal of Neural Biology, 3,* 47–64.

DiBlasio, F. A., & Benda, B. B. (1990). Adolescent sexual behavior: Multivariate analysis of a social learning model. *Journal of Adolescent Research, 5,* 449–466.

Dickinson, A., & Dawson, G. R. (1987). Pavlovian processes in the motivational control of instrumental performance. *Quarterly Journal of Experimental Psychology: Comparative & Physiological Psychology, 39*(3, Section B), 201–213.

Diehl, M., & Stroebe, W. (1987). Productivity loss in brainstorming groups: Toward the solution of a riddle. *Journal of Personality & Social Psychology, 53,* 497–509.

Diener, E. (1977). Deindividualtion: Causes and consequences. *Social Behavior and Personality, 5,* 143–155.

Diener, E. (2000). Subjective well-being: The science of happiness and a proposal for a national index. *American Psychologist, 55,* 34–43.

Diener, E., and Emmons, R. A. (1984). The independence of positive and negative affect. *Journal of Personality and Social Psychology, 47,* 1105–1117.

Dienstfrey, H. (1991). *Where The Mind Meets The Body.* New York: HarperCollins.

Digman, J. M. (1990). Personality structure: Emergence of the five-factor model. *Annual Review of Psychology, 41,* 417–440.

DiLalla, L. F., Kagan, J., Reznick, J. S. (1994). Genetic etiology of behavioral inhibition among 2-year-old children. *Infant Behavior & Development, 17,* 405–412.

Dill, P. L., & Henley, T. B. (1998). Stressors of college: A comparison of traditional and nontraditional students. *Journal of Psychology, 132,* 25–32.

Dillbeck, M. C., & Orme-Johnson, D. W. (1987). Physiological differences between transcendental meditation and rest. *American Psychologist,* 879–881.

Dimberg, U., & Thunberg, M. (1998). Rapid facial reactions to emotion facial expressions. *Scandinavian Journal of Psychology, 39,* 39–46.

Dinges, D., Pack, F., Williams, K., Gillen, K., Powell, J., Ott, G., Aptowicz, C., & Pack, A. (1997). Cumulative sleepiness, mood disturbance, and psychomotor vigilance performance decrements during a week of sleep restricted to 4–5 hours per night. *Sleep, 20,* 267–277.

Dion, K., Berscheid, E., & Walster, E. (1972). What is beautiful is good. *Journal of Personality & Social Psychology, 24,* 285–290.

Dion, K. L., & Dion, K. K. (1988). Romantic love: Individual and cultural perspectives. In R. J. Sternberg & M. L. Barnes (Eds.), *The psychology of love* (pp. 264–289). New Haven, CT: Yale University Press.

DiPietro, J. A., Hodgson, D. M., Costigan, K. A., Hilton, S. C., & Johnson, T. R. B. (1996). Fetal neurobehavioral development. *Child Development, 67,* 2553–2567.

Ditto, P. H., & Lopez, D. A. (1993). Motivated skepticism: use of differential decision criteria for preferred and nonpreferred conclusions. *Journal Personality and Social Psychology, 63,* 568–584.

Dittrich, W. H., Troscianko, T., Lea, S., & Morgan, D. (1996). Perception of emotion from dynamic point-light displays represented in dance. *Perception, 25,* 727–738.

Dobbins, A. C., Joe, R. M., Fiser, J., & Allman, J. M. (1998). Distance modulation of neural activity in the visual cortex. *Science, 281,* 552–555.

Dobkin, P. L., Tremblay, R. E., Másse, L. C., & Vitaro, F. (1995). Individual and peer characteristics in predicting boys' early onset of substance abuse: A seven-year longitudinal study. *Child Development, 66,* 1198–1214.

Dobson, M., & Markham, R. (1993). Imagery ability and source monitoring: Implications for eyewitness memory. *British Journal of Psychology, 32,* 111–118.

Docter, R. F., & Prince, V. (1997). Transvestism: A survey of 1032 crossdressers. *Archives of Sexual Behavior, 26,* 589–605.

Dodge, K. A., & Newman, J. P. (1981). Biased decision-making processes in aggressive boys. *Journal of Abnormal Psychology, 90,* –379.

Doheny, M. (1993). Effects of mental practice on performance of a psychomotor skill. *Journal of Mental Imagery, 17*(3–4), 111–118.

Dohrenwend, B. P., Levav, I., Shrout, P. E., Schwartz, S., Naveh, G., Link. B. G., Skodol, A. E., & Stueve, A. (1992). Socioeconomic status and psychiatric disorders: The causation-selection issue. *Science, 255,* 946–952.

Dohrmann, R. J., & Laskin, D. M. (1978). An evaluation of electromyographic biofeedback in the treatment of myofascial pain-dysfunction syndrome. *J Am Dent Assoc, 96,* 656–62.

Dolan, B. (1991). Cross-cultural aspects of anorexia nervosa and bulimia: A review. *International Journal of Eating Disorders, 10,* 67–79.

Dolan, R. J., & Fletcher, P. C. (1997). Dissociating prefrontal and hippocampal function in episodic memory encoding. *Nature, 388,* 582–585.

Dolinski, D., & Nawrat, R. (1998). "Fear-then-relief" procedure for producing compliance: Beware when the danger is over. *Journal of Experimental Social Psychology, 34,* 27–50.

Dollard, J., Doob, L. W., Miller, N. E., Mowrer, O. H., Sears, R. R., Ford, C. S., Hovland, C. I., & Sollenberger, R. T. (1939). *Frustration and aggression.* New Haven: Yale Univ. Press.

Domar, A. D., Noe, J. M., & Benson, H. (1987). The preoperative use of the relaxation response with ambulatory surgery patients. *Journal of Human Stress, 13,* 101–107.

Domjan, M. (1992). Adult learning and mate choice: Possibilities and experimental evidence. *American Zoologist, 32,* 48–61.

Donaldson, S. O. (1995). Peer influence on adolescent drug use: A persepctive rom the trench of experimental evauation research. *American Psychologist, 50,* 801–802.

Doty, R. L., Bartoshuk, L. M., & Snow, J. B., Jr. (1991). Causes of olfactory and gustatory disorders. In T. V. Getchell, R. L. Doty, L. M. Bartoshuk, & J. B. Snow, Jr. (Eds.), *Smell and taste in health and disease* (pp. 449–462). New York: Raven.

Doty, R. L., Shaman, P., Applebaum, M. S. L., Gilberson, R., Siksorski, L., & Rosenberg, L. (1984). Smell identification ability: Changes with age. *Science, 226,* 1441–1443.

Dovidio, J. F., Brigham, J. C., Johnson, B. T., & Gaertner, S. L. (1996). Sterepyting, prejudice, and discrimination: Another look. In N. Macrae, C. Stangor, & M Hewston (Eds.), *Stereotypes and stereotyping* (pp. 276–319). New Yuork: Guilford.

Dovidio, J. F., Evans, N., & Tyler, R. B. (1986). Racial stereotypes: The contents of their cognitive representations. *Journal of Experimental Social Psychology, 22,* 22–37.

Dowdall, G. W., Crawford, M., & Wechsler, H. (1998). Binge drinking among American college women: A comparison of single-sex and coeducational institutions. *Psychology of Women Quarterly, 22,* 705–715.

Dowling, J. E. (1992). *Neurons and networks: An introduction to neuroscience.* Cambridge, MA: Harvard University Press.

Downing, J. W., Judd, C. M., & Brauer, M. (1992). Effects of repeated expressions on attitude extremity. *Journal of Personality and Social Psychology, 63,* 17–29.

Draycott, S. G., & Kline, P. (1995). The Big Three or the Big Five—the EPQ—R vs the NEO-PI: A research note, replication and elaboration. *Personality & Individual Differences, 18,* 801–804.

Dreary, I. J. (1995). Auditory inspection time and intelligence: What is the direction of causation? *Developmental Psychology, 31,* 237–250.

Drevets, W. C., Price, J. L., Simpson, J. R., Jr., Todd, R. D., Reich, T., Vannier, M., & Raichle, M. E. (1997). Subgenual prefrontal cortex abnormalities in mood disorders. *Nature 386,* 824–827.

Driskell, J., Copper, C., & Moran, A. (1994). Does mental practice enhance performance? *Journal of Applied Psychology, 79*(4), 481–492.

Druckman, D. & Bjork, R. A. (1994) Learning, Remembering, Believing: Enhancing Human Performance; Washington, D.C.: National Academy Press)

Druckman, D., & Swets, J. A. (Eds.), (1988). *Enhancing human performance: Issues, theories, and techniques.* Washington, D.C.: National Academy Press.

Drummond, S. P. A., Brown, G. G., Gillin, J. C., Stricker, J. L., Wong, E. C., & Buxton, R. B. (2000). *Nature, 403,* 655–657.

Dubrovsky, V. J., Kiesler, S., & Sethna, B. N. (1991). The equalization phenomenon: stauts inequalities in computer-mediated and face-to-face decision-making groups. *Hum.-Comput. Interact., 6,* 119–146.

Duclaux, R., Feisthauer, J., & Cabanac, M. (1973). The effects of eating on the pleasantness of food and nonfood odors in man. *Physiology & Behavior, 10,* 1029–1033.

Duclos, S. E., Laird, J. D., Schneider, E., Sexter, M., Stern, L., & Van Lighten, O. (1989). Emotion-specific effects of facial expressions and postures on emotional experience. *Journal of Personality and Social Psychology, 57,* 100–108.

Dudai, Y. (1996). Consolidation: Fragility on the road to the engram. *Neuron, 17,* 367–370.

Duman, R. S., Heninger, G. R., & Nestler, E. J. (1997). A molecular and cellular theory of depression. *Archives of General Psychiatry, 54,* 597–606.

Duncan, H. F., Gourlay, N., & Hudson, W. (1973). *A study of pictorial perception among Bantu and White primary school children in South Africa.* Johannesburg, South Africa: Witwatersrand University Press.

Duncan, J. (1995). Attention, intelligence, and the frontal lobes. In M. S. Gazzaniga (Ed.), *The cognitive neurosciences.* (pp. 721–733). Cambridge, MA: MIT Press.

Duncan, J., Burgess, P., & Emslie, H. (1995). Fluid intelligence after frontal lobe lesions. *Neuropsychologia, 33,* 261–268.

Duncan, J., Emslie, H., Williams, P., Johnson, R., & Freer, C. (1996). Intelligence and the frontal lobe: The organization of goal-directed behavior. *Cognitive Psychology, 30,* 257–303.

Duncan, R. M., & Pratt, M. W. (1997). Microgenetic change in the quantity and quality of preschoolers' private speech. *International Journal of Behavioral Development, 20,* 367–383.

Duncker, K. (1945). On problem solving. *Psychological monographs, 58* (No. 270).

Dunn, J., & Plomin, R. (1990). *Seperate Lives: Why Siblings Are So Different.* New York: Basic Books, pp. 63, 74–75.

Dunnett, S. B., Lane, D. M., & Winn, P. (1985). Ibotenic acid lesions of the lateral hypothalamus: comparison with 6-hydroxydopamine-induced sensorimotor deficits. *Neuroscience, 14,* 509–518.

Dupuy, B., & Krashen, S. D. (1993). Incidental vocabulary acquisition in French as a foreign language. *Applied Language Learning, 4,* 55–63.

Dusek, D., & Girdano, D. A. (1980). *Drugs: A factual account.* Reading, MA: Addison Wesley.

Dykens, E. M., & Cassidy, S. B.(1999). Prader-Willi syndrome. In S. Goldstein & C. R. Reynolds (Ed). *Handbook of neurodevelopmental and genetic disorders in children.* (pp. 525–554). New York: Guilford.

Eagly, A. (1987). *Sex differences in social behavior: A social-role interpretation.* Hillsdale, NJ: Erlbaum.

Eagly, A. H. (1995). The science and politics of comparing women and men. *American Psychologist, 50* 145–158.

Eagly, A. H., & Carli, L. (1981). Sex of researchers and sex-typed communications as determinants of sex differences in influence-ability: A meta-analysis of social influence studies. *Psychological Bulletin, 90,* 1–20.

Eagly, A. H., & Chaiken, S. (1998). Attitude Structure and Function. In D. T. Gilbert, S. T. Fiske, & G. Lindzey (Eds.), The handbook of social psychology (4th ed.). New York: McGraw Hill. 269–322.

Eagly, A. H., & Crowley, M. (1986). Gender and helping: A meta-analytic review of the social psychological literature. *Psychological Bulletin, 100,* 283–308.

Eagly, A. H., & Johnson, B. T. (1990). Gender and leadership style: A meta-analysis. *Psychological Bulletin, 108,* 309–330.

Eagly, A. H., Karau, S. J., & Makhijani, M. G. (1995). Gender and the effectiveness of leaders: A meta-analysis. *Psychological Bulletin, 1,* 125–145.

Eagly, A. H., Makhijani, M. G., & Klonsky, B. G. (1992). Gender and the evaluation of leaders: A meta-analysis. *Psychological Bulletin, 1,* 3–22.

Eagly, A. H., & Steffen, V. J. (1986). Gender and aggressive behavior: A meta-analytic review of the social psycholgical literature. *Psychological Bulletin, 100,* 309–330.

Eagly, A. H., & Wood, W. (1999). The origins of sex differences in human behavior: Evolved dispositions versus social roles. *American Psychologist, 54,* 408–423.

Eakin, E. (2000, January 15). Bigotry as mental illness or just another norm. *New York Times,* p. A21.

Eals, M., & Silverman, I. (1994). The hunter-gatherer theory of spatial sex differences: Proximate factors mediating the female advantage on recall of object arrays. *Ethology and Sociobiology, 15,* 95–105.

Earle, T. L., Linden, W., & Weinberg, J. (1999). Differential effects of harassment on cardiovascular and salivary cortisol stress reactivity and recovery in women and men. *Journal of Psychosomatic Research, 46,* 125–141.

Earnest, C., & Angst, J. (1983). *Birth order: Its influence on personality.* Berlin: Springer-Verlag.

Eaves, L. J., Eysenck, H. J., & Martin, N. G. (1989). *Genes, culture and personality: An empirical approach.* London: Academic Press.

Ebbinghaus, H. (1885/1964). *Memory: A contribution to experimental psychology.* New York: Dover.

Ebstein, R. P., Novick, O., Umansky, R., Priel, B., Osher, Y., Blaine, D., Bennett, E. R., Nemanoc, L., Katz, M., & Belmaker, R. H. (1996). Dopamine D4 receptor (D4DR) exon III polymorphism associated with the human personality trait of Novelty Seeking. *Nature Genetics, 12,* 78–80.

The Economist World Atlas & Almanac (1989). New York: Prentice Hall.

Eden, D. (1990). Pygmalion without interpersonal contrast effects: Whole groups gain from raising manager expectations. *Journal of Applied Psychology, 75,* 394–398.

Eder, R. A. (1989). The emergent personologist: The structure and content of 3-, 5-, and 7-year-olds' concepts of themselves and other persons. *Child Development, 60,* 1218–1228.

Edgerton, R. B., & Cohen, A. (1994). Culture and schizophrenia: The DOSMD challenge. *British Journal of Psychiatry, 164,* 222–231.

Edwards, E., Kornrich, W., Houtten, P. V., & Henn, F. A. (1992). Presynaptic serotonin mechanisms in rats subjected to inescapable shock. *Neuropharmacology, 31,* 323–330

Effa-Heap, G. (1996). The influence of media pornography on adolescents. *IFE Psychologia: An International Journal, 4,* 80–90

Egbert, L. D., Battit, G. E., Welch, C. E., & Barlett, M. K. (1964). Reduction of postoperative pain by encouragement and instruction of patients. *New England Journal of Medicine, 270,* 825–827.

Ehlers, A., Mayou, R. A., & Bryant, B. (1998). Psychological predictors of chronic posttraumatic stress disorder after motor vehicle accidents. *Journal of Abnormal Psychology, 107,* 508–519.

Eich, E. (1989). Theoretical issues in state dependent memory. In H. L. Roediger, III, & F. I. M. Craik (Eds.), *Varieties of memory and consciousness: Essays in honour of Endel Tulving* (pp. 331–354). Hillsdale, NJ: Erlbaum.

Eich, E. (1995). Searching for mood dependent memory. *Psychological Science, 6,* 67–75.

Eimas, P. D., & Corbit, J. D. (1973). Selective adaptation of linguistic feature detectors. *Cognitive Psychology, 4,* 99–109.

Einstein, A. (1945). A testimonial from Professor Einstein (Appendix II). In J. Hadamard, *An essay on the psychology of invention in the mathematical field* (pp. 142–143). Princeton, NJ: Princeton University Press.

Eisenberg, N., Miller, P. A., Schaller, M., Fabes, R. A., Fultz, J., Shell, R., & Shea, C. L. (1989). The role of sympathy and altruistic personality traits in helping: A reexamination. *Journal of Personality, 57,* 41–67.

Eisenberger, R. (1998). Reward, Intrinsic Interest, and Creativity: New Findings. *American Psychologist, 53,* 676–679.

Eisenberger, R., & Armeli, S. (1997). Can salient reward increase creative performance without reducing intrinsic creative interest? *Journal of Personality and Social Psychology, 72,* 652–663.

Eisenberger, R., Armeli, S., & Pretz, J. (1998). Can the promise of reward increase creativity? *Journal of Personality and Social Psychology, 74,* 704–714.

Eisenberger, R., & Cameron, J. (1996). Detrimental effects of reward: Reality or myth? *American Psychologist, 51,* 1153–1166.

Eisenberger, R., Haskins, F., & Gambleton, P. (1999). Promised reward and creativity: Effects of prior experience. *Journal of Experimental Social Psychology, 35,* 308–325.

Ekman, P. (1980). Biological and cultural contributions to body and facial movement in the expression of emotion. In A. O. Rorty (Ed.), *Explaining emotions.* Berkeley, CA: University of California Press.

Ekman, P. (1984). Expression and the nature of emotion. In K. R. Scherer & P. Ekman (Eds.), *Approaches to emotion* (pp. 319–343). Hillsdale, NJ: Erlbaum.

Ekman, P. (1985). *Telling lies: Clues to deceit in the marketplace, marriage, and politics.* New York: Norton.

Ekman, P. (1992). Facial expressions of emotion: New findings, new questions. *Psychological Science, 3,* 34–38.

Ekman, P. (1993). Facial expression and emotion. *American Psychologist, 48,* 384–392.

Ekman, P., & Davidson, R. J. (1993). Voluntary smiling changes regional brain activity. *Psychological Science, 4,* 342–345.

Ekman, P., & Davidson, R. J. (1994). *The nature of emotion: Fundamental questions.* Cambridge, MA: MIT Press.

Ekman, P., and Friesen, W. (1971). Constants across cultures in the face and emotion. *Journal of Personality & Social Psychology, 17,* 124–129.

Ekman, P., & Friesen, W. V. (1975). *Unmasking the face.* Englewood Cliffs, NJ: Prentice-Hall.

Ekman, P., Davidson, R. J., & Friesen, W. V. (1990). The Duchenne smile: Emotional expression and brain psychology II. *Journal of Personality & Social Psychology, 58,* 342–353.

Ekman, P., O'Sullivan, M., & Frank, M. G. (1999). A few can catch a liar. *Psychological Science, 10,* 263–266.

El-Islam, M. F. (1991). Transcultural aspects of schizophrenia and ICD-10. *Psychiatria Danubina, 3,* 485–494

Elber, T., Pantev, C., Wienbruch, C., Rockstroh, B., & Taub, E. (1995). Increased cortical representation of the fingers of the left hand in string players. *Science, 270,* 305–307.

Eley, T. C., Deater-Deckard, K., Fombone, E., Fulker, D. W., & Plomin, R. (1998). An adoption study of depressive symptoms in middle childhood. *Journal of Child Psychology & Psychiatry & Allied Disciplines, 39,* 337–345.

Elkin, I. (1994). The NIMH treatment of depression colarborative research program: Where we began and where we are. In A. E. Bergin & S. L. Garfield (Eds.), *Handbook of psychotherapy and behavior change, 4th edition* (pp. 114–142). New York: John Wiley & Sons.

Elkin, I., Gibbons, R., Shea, M. T., Sotsky, S. M., Watkins, J. T., Pilkonis, P. A., & Hedeker, D. (1995). Initial severity and differential treatment outcome in the National Institute of Mental Health Treatment of Depression Collaborative Research Program., 63 841–847.

Elkind, D. (1967). Egocentrism in adolescence. *Child Development, 38,* 1025–1034.

Elkind, D., & Bowen, R. (1979). Imaginary audience behavior in children and adolescence. *Developmental Psychology, 15,* 33–44.

Elkins, I. J., McGue, M., & Iacono, W. G. (1997). Genetic and Environmental Influences on Parent-Son Relationships: Evidence for Increasing Genetic Influence During Adolescence. *Developmental Psychology, 33,* 351–363.

Elliot, R., & Dolan, R. J. (1998). Neural resnse during preference and memory judgements for subliminally presented stimuli: a functional neuroimaging study. *Journal of Neuroscience. 18,* 4697–4704.

Elliott, D., Huizinga, D., & Ageton, S. S. (1985). Multiple problem youth: Delinquency, substance use, and mental health problems. New York: Springer-Verlag.

Ellis, A. (1958). Rational psychotherapy: *Journal of General Psycology, 59,* 35–49. Repreinted: New York: Institute for Rational-Emotive Therapy.

Ellis, A. (1994a). The treatment of borderline personalities with rational emotive behavioar therapy. *Journal of Rational-Emotive & Cognitive Behavior Therapy, 12,* 101–119.

Ellis, A. (1994b). Rational emotive behavior therapy approaches to obsessive-compulsive disorder (OCD). *Journal of Rational-Emotive & Cognitive Behavior Therapy, 12,* 121–141.

Ellis, A. W., & Young, A. W. (1987). *Human cognitive neuropsychology.* Hillsdale, NJ: Lawrence Erlbaum.

Ellis, G. J., & Peterson, L. R. (1992). Socialization values and parental control techniques: A cross-cultural analysis of child-rearing. *Journal of Comparative Family Studies, 23,* 39–54.

Ellis, H. C. (1973). Stimulus encoding processes in human learning and memory. In G. H. Bower (Ed.), *The psychology of learning and motivation* (Vol. 7, pp. 124–182). New York: Academic Press.

Ellis, H. C., & Hunt, R. R. (1993). *Fundamentals of Cognitive Psychology* (5th ed.). Dubuque, IA: Brown Communications.

Elman, J. L., Bates, E. A., Johnson, M. H., Karmiloff-Smith, A., et al. (1996). *Rethinking innateness: A connectionist perspective on development.* Cambridge: MIT Press.

Emmelkamp, P. M. G. (1994). Behavior therapy with adults. In A. E. Bergin & S. L. Garfield (Eds.), *Handbook of psychotherapy and behavior change, 4th edition* (pp. 379–427). New York: John Wiley & Sons.

Emmorey, K. (1993). Processing a dynamic visual-spatial language: Psycholinguistic studies of American Sign Language. *Journal of Psycholinguistic Research, 22,* 153–187.

Endler, N. S., & Hunt, J. McV. (1969). Generalizability of contributions from the sources of variance in the S-R inventories of anxiousness. *Journal of Personality, 37,* 1–24.

Engen, T. (1991). *Odor sensation and memory.* New York: Praeger.

Entwisle, D. R. (1972). To dispel fantasies about fantasy-based measures of achievement motivation. *Psychological Bulletin, 77,* 377–391.

Epstein, C. M., Figiel, G. S., McDonald, W. M., Amazon-Leece, J., & Figiel, L. (1998). Rapid rate transcranial magnetic stimulation in young and middle-aged refractory depressed patients. *Psychiatric Annals, 28,* 36–39.

Epstein, H. T. (1980). EEG developmental stages. *Developmental Psychobiology, 13,* 629–631.

Epstein, W., & Franklin, S. (1965). Some conditions of the effect of relative size on perceived distance. *American Journal of Psychology, 78,* 466–470.

Erdelyi, M. H. (1984). The recovery of unconcious (inaccessible) memories: Laboratory studies of hypermnesia. In G. H. Bower (Ed.), *The psychology of learning and motivation; Advances in research and theory* (Vol. 18, pp. 95–127). New York: Academic Press.

Ericsson, K. A., & Charness, N. (1994). Expert performance. *American Psychologist, 49,* 725–747.

Ericsson, K. A., Krampe, R. Th., & Tesch-Ràmer, C. (1993). The role of deliberate practice in the acquisition of expert performance. *Psychological Review, 100,* 363–406.

Eriksen, C. W., & Murphy, T. D. (1987). Movement of attentional focus across the visual field: A critical look at the evidence. *Perception and Psychophysics, 42,* 299–305.

Eriksen, C. W., & St. James, J. D. (1986). Visual attention within and around the field of focal attention: A zoom lens model. *Perception and Psychophysics, 40,* 225–240.

Eriksen, C. W., & Yeh, Y. (1985). Allocation of attention in the visual field. *Journal of Experimental Psychology: Human Perception and Performance, 11,* 583–597.

Erikson, D. H., Beiser, M., & Iacono, W. G. (1998). Social support predicts 5-year outcome in first-episode schizophrenia. *Journal of Abnormal Psychology, 107,* 681–685.

Erikson, E. H. (1950). *Childhood and society.* New York: Norton.

Ernst, C., & Angst, J. (1983). *Birth order: Its influence on personality.* Berlin: Springer-Verlag.

Eskenazi, B. (1993). Caffeine during pregnancy: Grounds for concern? *Journal of the American Medical Association, 270,* 2973–2974.

Eskenazi, B., Stapleton, A. L., Kharrazi, M., & Chee, W. Y. (1999). Associations between maternal decaffeinated and caffeinated coffee consumption and fetal growth and gestational duration. *Epidemiology, 10,* 242–249.

Esser, J. K. (1998). Alive and well after 25 years: A review of groupthink research. *Organizational Behavior & Human Decision Processes, 73,* 116–141.

Esser, J. K., & Lindoerfer, J. S. (1989). Groupthink and the space shuttle Challenger accident: Toward a quantitative case analysis. *Journal of Behavioral Decision Making, 2,* 167–177.

Esses, V., & Zanna, M. P. (1995). Mood and the expression of ethnic stereotypes. *Journal of Personality & Social Psychology, 69,* 1052–1068.

Esterling, B. A., L'Abate, L., Murray, E. J., & Pennebaker, J. W. (1999). Empirical foundations for writing in prevention and psychotherapy: Mental and phsycial health outcomes. *Clinical Psychology Review, 19,* 79–96.

Estes, W. (1976). The cognitive side of probability learning. *Psychological Review, 83,* 37–64.

Evans, G. W., Bullinger, M., & Hygge, S. (1998). Chronic noise exposure and physiological response: A prospective study of children living under environmental stress. *Psychological Science, 9,* 75–77.

Exner, J. E., Jr. (1986). *The Rorschach: A comprehensive system* (Volume 1, 2nd ed.). New York: Wiley: Interscience.

Eyferth, K. (1961). Ein Vergleich der Beurteilung projektiver Tests durch verschiedene Berteiler [A comparison of judging projective tests by different judges]. *Zeitschrift fuer Experimentelle und Angewandte Psychologie, 8,* 329–338.

Eysenck, H. J. (1967). *The Biological Basis of Personality.* Springfield, IL: Charles C. Thomas, Publishers.

Eysenck, H. J. (1977). *Crime and Personality,* St. Albans, England: Paladin Frogmore.

Eysenck, H. J. (1979). The conditioning model of neurosis. *Behavioral and Brain Sciences, 2,* 155–199.

Eysenck, H. J. (1990a). Genetic and environmental contributions to individual differences: The three major dimensions of personality. *Journal of Personality, 58,* 245–261.

Eysenck, H. J. (1990b). Biological dimensions of personality. In L. A. Pervin (Ed.), *Handbook of personality: Theory and research* (pp. 244–276). New York: Guilford.

Eysenck, H. J. (1992). Four ways five factors are *not* basic. *Personality and Individual Differences, 13,* 667–673.

Eysenck, H. J. (1993). The structure of phenotypic personality traits: Comment. *American Psychologist, 48,* 1299–1300.

Eysenck, H. J. (1995). *Genius: The natural history of creativity.* Cambridge, England: Cambridge University Press.

Eysenck, H. J., & Gudjonsson, G. (1989). *The Causes and Cures of Criminality.* New York: Plenum Press.

Eysenck, S. B. G., & Eysenck, H. J. (1967). Salivary response to lemon juice as a measure of introversion. *Perceptional and motor skills, 24,* 1047–1053.

Faber, A., & Mazlish, E. (1987). *Siblings without rivalry.* New York: Norton.

Faber, S. (1981). *Identical twins reared apart.* London: Blackwell.

Fairburn, C. G., Cooper, Z., Doll, H. A., Welch, S. L. (1999). Risk factors for anorexia nervosa: Three integrated case-control comparisons. *Archives of General Psychiatry, 56,* 468–476.

Fairburn, C. G., Doll, H. A., Welch, S. L., Hay, P. J., Davies, B. A., & O'Connor, M. E. (1998). Risk factors for binge eating disorder: A community-based, case-control study. *Archives of General Psychiatry, 55,* 425–432.

Fairburn, C. G., Hay, P. J., & Welch, S. L. (1993). Binge eating and bulimia nervosa: Distribution and determinants. In C. G. Fairburn & G. T. Wilson (Eds.), *Binge Eating: Nature, Assessment, and Treatment* (pp. 123–143). New York: Guilford Press.

Fantino, M., & Cabanac, M. (1980). Body weight regulation with a proportional hoarding response in the rat. *Physiology & Behavior, 24,* 939–942.

Farah, M. J., Soso, M. J., & Dasheiff, R. M. (1992). Visual angle of the mind's eye before and after unilateral occipital lobectomy. *Journal of Experimental Psychology: Human Perception and Performance, 18,* 241–246.

Farde, L., & Gustavsson, E. (1997). D2 dopamine receptors and personality traits *Nature, 385,* 590.

Farhi, P. (1996, February 26). Study finds real harm in TV violence. *Washington Post,* A1.

Farthing, G. (1992) *The psychology of consciousness.* Englewood Cliffs, NJ: Prentice-Hall.

Fatt, I., & Weissman, B. A. (1992). *Physiology of the eye: An introduction to the vegetative functions* (2nd ed.). Boston: Butterworth-Heinemann.

Fava, G. A. Rafanelli, C., Grandi, S., Conti, S., & Belluardo, P. (1998a). Prevention of Recurrent Depression With Cognitive Behavioral Therapy: Preliminary Findings. *Archives of General Psychiatry, 55,* 816–820.

Fava, G. A., Rafanelli, C., Grandi, S., Canestrari, R., & Morphy, M. A. (1998b). Six-year outcome for cognitive behavioral treatmetn of residual symptoms in major depression. *American Journal of Psychiatry, 155,* 1443–1445.

Fawzy, F. I., Fawzy, M. O. Hyun, C. S., Elashoff, R., et al. (1993). Malignant melanoma: effects of an early structured psychiatric intervention, coping, and affective state on recurrence and survival six years later. *Archives of General Psychiatry, 50,* 681–689.

Fawzy, F. I., Kemeny, M. E., Fawzy, N. W., Elashoff, R., Morton, D., Cousins, N., Fahey, J. L. (1990). A structured psychiatric intervention for cancer patients: II. Changes over time in immunological measures. *Archives of General Psychiatry, 47,* 729–735.

Fay, R. E., Turner, C. F., Klassen, A. D., & Gagnon, J. H. (1989). Prevalence and patterns of same-gender sexual contact among men. *Science, 243,* 338–348.

Fazio, R. H., Chen, J., McDonel, E. C., & Sherman, S. J. (1982). Attitude accessibility and the strength of the object-evaluation association. *Journal of Experimental Psychology, 18,* 339–357.

Fazio, R. H., Jackson, J. R., Dunton, B. C., & Williams, C. J. (1995). Variability in automatic activation as an unobstrusive measure of racial attitudes: A bona fide pipeline? *Journal of Personality and Social Psychology, 69,* 1013–1027.

Feather, N. T. (1996). Social comparisons across nations: Variables relating to the subjective evaluation of national achievement and to personal and collective. *Australian Journal of Psychology, 48,* 53–63.

Feingold, A. (1990). Gender differences in effects of physical attractiveness on romantic attraction: A comparison across five research paradigms. *Journal of Personality and Social Psychology, 59,* 981–993.

Feingold, A. (1994). Gender differences in personality: A meta-analysis. *Psychological Bulletin, 116,* 429–456.

Feldman, D. H., & Goldsmith, L. T. (1991). *Nature' s gambit: Child prodigies and the development of human potential.* New York: Teachers College Press.

Feldman, R. S., Coats, E. J., & Spielman, D. A. (1996). Television exposure and children's decoding of nonverbal behavior. *Journal of Applied Social Psychology, 26,* 1718–1733.

Felleman, D. J., & Van Essen, D. C. (1991). Distributed hierarchical processing in the primate cerebral cortex. *Cerebral Cortex, 1,* 1–47.

Fenton, W., & McGlashan, T. (1991). Natural history of schizophrenia subtypes: I. Longitudinal study of paranoid, hebephrenic, and undifferentiated schizophrenia. *Archives of General Psychiatry, 48,* 969–977.

Ferguson, N. B., & Keesey, R. E. (1975). Effect of a quinine-adulterated diet upon body weight maintenance in male rats with ventromedial hypothalamic lesions. *Journal of Comparative & Physiological Psychology, 89,* 478–488.

Fernald, A., Taeschner, T., Dunn, J., Papousek, M., Boysson-Bardies, B., & Fukui, I. (1989). A cross-language study of prosodic modifications in mothers' and fathers' speech to infants. *Child Development, 64,* 637–656.

Ferveur, J.-F., Stoertkuhl, K. F., Stocker, R. F., & Greenspan, R. J. (1995). Genetic feminization of brain structures and changed sexual orientation in male Drosophila. *Science, 267,* 902–905.

Feske, U., & Chambless, D. L. (1995). Cognitive behavioral versus exposure only treatment for social phobia: A meta-analysis. Behavior Therapy, 26, 695–720.

Festinger, L. (1950). Informed social comjmunicano., *Psychological Review, 57,* 271–282.

Festinger, L., & Carlsmith, J. M. (1959). Cognitive consequences of forced compliance. *Journal of Abnormal and Social Psychology, 58,* 203–210.

Ficker, J. H. I., Wiest, G. H., Lehnert, G., Meyer, M., & Hahn, E. G. (1999). Are snoring medical students at risk of failing their exams? *Sleep, 22,* 205–209.

Field, A. E., Camargo, C. A., Jr., Taylor, B., Berkey, C. S., Colditz, G. A. (1999). Relation of peer and media influences to the development of purging behaviors among preadolescent and adolescent girls. *Archives of Pediatric Adolescent Medicine, 153,* 1184–1189.

Field, T., Schanberg, S., Scarfidi, F., Bauer, C., Vega-Lahr, N., Garcia, R., Nystrom, J., & Kuhn, C. (1986). Tactile/kinesthetic stimulation effects on preterm neonates. *Pediatrics, 77,* 654–658.

Field, T. M. (1998). Touch therapy effects on development. *International Journal of Behavioral Development, 22,* 779–797.

Field, T. M., Woodson, R., Greenberg, R., & Cohen, D. (1982). Discrimination and imitation of facial expressions by neonates. *Science, 218,* 179–181.

Figiel, G. S., Epstein, C., McDonald, W. M., Amazon-Leece, J., Figiel, L., Saldivia, A., & Glover, S. (1998). The use of rapid-rate transcranial magnetic stimulation (rTMS) in refractory depressed patients. *Journal of Neuropsychiatry & Clinical Neurosciences, 10,* 20–25.

File, S. E., & Bond, J. A. (1979). Impaired performance and sedation after a single dose of lorazepam. *Psychopharmacologia, 61:* 309–312.).

Finch, A. E., Lambert, M. J., & Brown, G., (2000). Attacking anxiety: A naturalistic study of a multimedia self-help program. *Journal of Clinical Psychology, 56,* 11–21.

Findley, M. J., & Cooper, H. M. (1983). Locus of control and academic achievement: A literature review. *Journal of Personality and Social Psychology, 44,* 49–427.

Finke, R. A. (1996). Imagery, creativity, and emergent structure. *Consciousness & Cognition, 5,* 381–393.

Finke, R. A., & Slayton, K. (1988). Explorations of creative visual synthesis in mental imagery. *Memory & Cognition, 16,* 252–257.

Finke, R. A., Ward, T. B., & Smith, S. M. (1992). *Creative cognition: Theory, research, and applications.* Cambridge, MA: MIT Press.

Finkel, D., Pedersen, N. L., McGue, M., & McClearn, G. E. (1995). Heritability of cognitive abilities in adult twins: Comparison of Minnesota and Swedish data. *Behavioral Genetics, 25,* 421–432.

Fiorentine, R. (1999). After drug treatment: Are 12-step programs effective in maintaining abstinence? *American Journal of Drug and Alcohol Abuse, 25,* 93–116.

Fischer, C., Hatzidimitriou, G., Wlos, J., Katz, J., & Ricaurte, G. (1995). Reorganization of ascending 5-HT axon projections in animals previously exposed to recreational drug 3,4-methelenedioxymetham-phetamine (MDMA, "Ecstasy"). *Journal of Neuroscience, 15,* 5476–5485.

Fisher, P. J., Turic, D., Williams, N. M., McGuffin, P., Asherson, P., Ball, D., Craig, I., Eley, T., Hill, L., Chorney, K., Chorney, M. J., Benbow, C. P., Lubinski, D., Plomin, R., & Owen, M. J. (1999) DNA pooling identifies QTLs on Chromosome 4 for general cognitive ability in children. *Human Molecular Genetics, 8,* 915–922.

Fisher, R. P., & Craik, F. I. M. (1977). The interaction between encoding and retrieval operations in cued recall. *Journal of Experimental Psychology: Human learning and Perception, 3,* 153–171.

Fisher, R. P., & Geiselman, R. E. (1992). *Memory enhancing techniques for investigative interviewing: The cognitive interview.* Springfield: Charles C. Thomas.

Fisher, R. P., Geiselman, R. E., & Amador, M. (1989). Field test of the cognitive interview: Enhancing the recollection of actual victims and witnesses of crime. *Journal of Applied Psychology, 74,* 722–727.

Fiske, S. (1998). Stereotyping, prejudice, and discrimination. In D. T. Gilbert, S. T. Fiske, & G. Lindzey (Eds.), The handbook of social psychology (4th ed.). New York: McGraw Hill. 357–411.

Fitton, A., & Heel, R. C. (1990). Clozapine: A review of its pharacological properties and therapeutic use schizophrenia. *Drugs, 40,* 722–747.

Flavell, J. H. (1999). Cognitive development: Children's knowledge about the mind. *Annual Review of Psychology, 50,* 21–45.

Fletcher, A. C., Elder, G. H. Jr., & Mekos, D. (2000). Parental influences on adolescent involvement in community activities. *Journal of Research on Adolescence, 10,* 29–48.

Fleury, C., Neverova, M., Collins, S., Raimbault, S., Champign, O., Levi-Meyrueis, C., Bouillaud, F., Seldin, M. F., Surwit, R. S., Ricquier, D., & Warden, C. H. (1977). Uncoupling protein-2: A novel candidate thermogenic protein linked to obesity and insulin resistance. *Nature Genetics, 15,* 269–272 .

Flexser, A., & Tulving, E. (1978) Retrieved independence in recognition and recall. *Psychological Review, 85,* 153–171.

Floersch, J., Longhofer, J., & Latta, K. (1997). Writing Amish culture into genes: biological reductionism in a study of manic depression. *Culture, Medicine and Psychiatry, 21,* 137–159.

Flor, H., Elbert, T., Knecht, S., Weinbrunch, C., Pantev, C., Birbaumer, N., Labig, W., & Taub, E. (1995). Phantom-limb pain as a perceptual correlate of cortical reorganization following arm amputation. *Nature, 375,* 482–484.

Floyd, R. L., Rimer, B. K., Giovino, G. A., Mullen, P. D., & Sullivan, S. E. (1993). A review of smoking in pregnancy: Effects on pregnancy outcomes and cessation efforts. *Annual Review of Public Health, 14,* 379–411.

Flynn, J. R. (1980). *Race, IQ and Jensen.* London: Routledge.

Flynn, J. R. (1984). The mean IQ of Americans: Massive gains 1932 to 1978. *Psychological Bulletin, 95,* 29–51.

Flynn, J. R. (1991). *Asian Americans: Achievement beyond IQ.* Hillsdale, NJ: Erlbaum.

Flynn, J. R. (1999a). Massive IQ gains in fourteen nations: What IQ tests really measure. *Psychological Bulletin, 101,* 171–191.

Flynn, J. R. (1999b). Searching for justice: The discovery of IQ gains over time. *American Psychologist, 54,* 5–20.

Flynn, J. R. (in press). IQ trends over time: Intelligence, race and meritocracy. In S. Durlauf, K. Arrow, & S. Bowles (Eds.), *Meritocracy and inequality*. Princeton, NJ: Princeton University Press.

Foa, E. B., Steketee, G., & Olasov-Rothbaum, B. O. (1989). Behavioral/cognitive conceptualization of post-traumatic stress disorder. *Behavior Therapy, 20*, 155–176.

Fodor, J. A. (1968). *Psychological explanation: An introduction to the philosophy of psychology*. New York: Random House.

Fodor, J. A. (1983). *The modularity of mind*. Cambridge, MA: MIT Press.

Fodor, J. A. (2000). Why we are so good at catching cheaters. *Cognition, 75*, 29–32.

Fodor, J. A., Bever, T. G., & Garrett, M. F. (1974). *The psychology of language: An introduction to psycholinguistics and generative grammar*. New York: McGraw-Hill.

Fones, C. S. L., Manfro, G. G., & Pollack, M. H. (1998). Social phobia: An update. *Harvard Review of Psychiatry, 5*, 247–259.

Forbes, E. J., & Pekala, R. J. (1993). Psychophysiological effects of several stress management techniques. *Psychological Reports, 72*, 19–27.

Ford, C. S., & Beach, F. (1951). *Patterns of sexual behavior*. New York: Harper & Row.

Ford, K., & Norris, A. E. (1997). Effects of interviewer age on reporting of sexual and reporductive behavior of Hispanic and African American youth. *Hispanic Journal of Behvioral Sciences, 19*, 369–376.

Ford, K., & Norris, A. E. (1997). Effects of interviewer age on reporting of sexual and reproductive behavior of Hispanic and African American youth. *Hispanic Journal of Behavioral Sciences, 19*, 369–376.

Ford, R. P., Schluter, P. J., Mitchell, E. A., Taylor, B. J., Scragg, R., & Stewart, A. W. (1998). Heavy caffeine intake in pregnancy and sudden infant death syndrome. New Zealand Cot Death Study Group. *Archives of Disease in Childhood, 78*, 9–13

Foreman, J. (1997, January 1). To drift off, work out: Exercise found to enhance sleep. *Boston Globe*, A1.

Forest, K. B. (1995). The role of critical life events in predicting world views: Linking two social psychologies. *Journal of Social Behavior and Personality, 10*, 331–348.

Forgas, J. P. (1998). On being happy and mistaken: Mood effects on the fundamental attribution error. *Journal of Personality and Social Psychology, 75*, 318–331.

Forgas, J. P., Levinger, G., & Moylan, S. (1994). Feeling good and feeling close: Mood effects on the perception of intimate relationships. *Personal Relationships, 2*, 165–184.

Forge, K. L., & Phemister, S. (1987). The erfect of prosocial cartoons on preschool children. *Child Study Journal, 17*, 83–88.

Forgione A. G. (1988). Hypnosis in the treatment of dental fear and phobia. *Dental Clinics of North America, 32*, 745–761.

Forsyth, D. R., Heiney, M. W., & Wright, S. S. (1998). Biases in appraisals of women leaders. *Group Dynamics, 1*, 98–103.

Foulke, E. (1991). Braile. In M. A. Heller & W. Schiff (Eds.), *The psychology of touch* (pp. 219–233). Hillsdale, NJ: Erlbaum.

Fouts, R., & Mills, S. (1997). *Next of kin*. New York: William Morrow.

Fox, C. H. (1994). Cocaine use in pregnancy. *Journal of the American Board of Family Practice, 7*, 225–228.

Fox, P. T., Ingham, R. J., Ingham, J. C., Hirsch, T. B., Downs, J. H., Martin, C., Jerabek, P., Glass, T., & Lancaster, J. L. (1996). A PET study of the neural systems of stuttering. *Nature, 382*, 158–162.

Fox, P. T., Mintun, M. A., Raichle, M. E., Miezin, F. M., Allman, J. M., & Van Essen, D. C. (1986). Mapping human visual cortex with positron emission tomography. *Nature, 323*, 806–809.

Fox, S., & Spector, P. E. (2000). Relations of emotional intelligence, practical intelligence, general intelligence, and trait affectivity with interview outcomes: It's not all just 'G'. *Journal of Organizational Behavior, 21*, 203–220.

Fox, W. M. (1982). Why we should abandon Maslow's Need Hierarchy Theory. *Journal of Humanistic Education and Development, 21*, 29–32.

Fozard, J. (1990). Vision and hearing in aging. In J. E. Birren & K. W. Schaie (Eds.), *Handbook of the Psychology of aging* (3rd ed., pp. 150–170). San Diego: Academic Press.

Frances, A. (1998). Problems in defining clinical significance in epidemiological Studies. *Arch Gen Psychiatry, 55*, 119.

Francis, J. R., & Aronson, H. (1990). Communicative efficacy of psychotherapy research. *Journal of Consulting and Clinical Psychology, 58*, 368–370.

Francis, M. E., & Pennebaker, J. W. (1992). Putting stress into words: The impact of writing on physiological, absentee, and self-reported emotional well-being measures. *American Journal of Health Promotion, 6*, 280–286.

Fraser, J. S. (1996). All that glitters is not always gold: Medical offset effects and managed behavioral health care. Professional Psychology: Research and Practice, 27, 335–344.

Fraser, J. S. (1998). People Who Live in Glass Houses . . . : A response to the critique of the article "all that glitters is not always gold." *Professional Psyhology: Research and Practice, 29*, 624–627.

Frasure-Smith, N., Lesperance, F., Juneau, M., Talajic, M., & Bourassa, M. G. (1999). Gender, depression, and one-year prognosis after myocardial infarction. *Psychosomatic Medicine, 61*, 26–37.

Freedman, J. L., & Fraser, S. C. (1966). Compliance without pressure: The foot-in-the-door technique. *Journal of Personality and Social Psychology, 4*, 195–202.

Freedman, M. S., Lucas, R. J., Soni, B., von Schantz, M., Muñoz, M., David-Gray, Z., & Foster, R. (1999). Regulation of mammalian circadian behavior by non-rod, non-cone, ocular photoreceptors. *Science, 284*, 502–504.

Freeman, D. (1983). *Margaret Mead and Samoa: The making and unmaking of an anthropological myth*. Cambridge, MA: Harvard University Press.

Freeman, H. (1994). Schizophrenia and city residence. *British Journal of Psychiatry, 164* (Suppl. 23), 39–50.

Freeman, L. J., Templer, D. I., & Hill, C. (1999). The relationship between adult happiness and self-appraised childhood happiness and events. *Journal of Genetic Psychology, 160*, 46–54.

Freeman, W. J. (1991). The psychology of perception. *Scientific American, 264*, 78–85.

Freese, J., Powell, B., & Steelman, L. C. (1999). Rebel without a cause or effect: Birth order and social attitudes. *American Sociological Review, 64*, 207–231.

Fresko, B. (1997). Attitudinal change among university student tutors. *Journal of Applied Social Psychology, 27*, 1277–1301.

Freud, A. (1958). Adolescence. *Psychoanalytic Study of the Child, 15*, 255–278.

Freud, S. (1900/1958). *The interpretation of dreams*. New York: Basic Books.

Freud, S. (1910). The origin & development of psychoanalysis. *American Journal of Psychology, 21*, 181–218.

Freud, S. (1927). *The ego and the id*. London: Hogarth Press.

Freud, S. (1933/1965). *New Introductory Lectures on Psychoanalysis*. New York: Norton.

Freud, S. (1937/1964). Analysis terminable and interminable. In J. Strachey (Ed. and Trans.), *The standard edition of the complete psychological works of Sigmund Freud* (Vol. 23, pp. 209–253).

Freud, S. (1938). *The basic writings of Sigmund Freud*. New York: Modern Library (Random House).

Frezza, M., di Padova, C., Pozzato, G., Terpin, M., Baraona, E., & Lieber, C. S. (1990). High blood alcohol levels in women: The role of decreased gastric alcohol dehydrogenase activity and first-pass metabolism. *New England Journal of Medicine, 322*, 95–99.

Fried, P. A., & Makin, J. E. (1987). Neonatal behavioral correlates of prenatal exposure to marijuana, cigarettes, and alcohol in a low risk population. *Neurobehavioral Toxicology and Teratology, 9*, 1–7.

Fried, P. A., & Watkinson, B. (2000). Visuoperceptual functioning differs in 9- to 12-year-olds prenatally exposed to cigarettes and marihuana. *Neurotoxicology & Teratology, 22*, 11–20.

Friedler, G. (1996). Paternal exposures: Impact on reproductive and developmental outcome: An overview. *Pharmacology, Biochemistry & Behavior, 55*, 691–700.

Friedman, M. I. (1991). Metabolic control of calorie intake. In M. T. Friedman, M. G. Tordoff, & M. R. Kare (Eds.), *Chemical senses*. New York: Marcel Dekker.

Friedman, M., & Rosenman, R. (1974). *Type A Behavior and Your Heart*. New York: Knopf.

Friedman, M., Thoresen, C., & Gill, J. (1986). Alteration of Type A behavior and its effect on cardiac recurrence in post-myocardial infarction patients: Summary results of the recurrent coronary prevention project. *American Heart Journal, 112*, 653–665

Friedman, M. I., Tordoff, M. G., & Ramirez, I. (1986). Integrated metabolic control of food intake. *Brain Research Bulletin, 17*, 855–859.

Frischholz, E. J. (1985). The relationship among dissocation, hypnosis, and child abuse in the dvelopment of multiple personality . In R. P. Kluft (Ed.), *Childhood antecedencts of multiples personality* (pp. 99–120). Washington, DC: American Psychiatric Press.

Frye, D., Zelazo, P. D., & Burack, J. A. (1998). Cognitive complexity and control: I. Theory of mind in typical and atypical development. *Current Directions in Psychological Science, 7*, 116–121.

Fryers, T. (1993). Epidemiological thinking in mental retardation: Issues in taxonomy and population frequency. In N. W. Bray (Ed.), *International review of research in mental retardation* (Vol. 19). Novato, Calif: Academic Therapy Publications.

Fuller, R. K., Branchey, L., Brightwell, D. R., Derman, R. M., Emrick, C. D., Iber, F. L., James, K. E., Lacoursiere, R. B., Lee, K. K., Lowenstaum, I., Maany, I., Neiderhiser, D., Nocks, J. J., & Shaw, S. (1986). Disulfiram treatment of alcoholism: A Veterans Administration cooperative study. *Journal of the American Medical Association* 256(11):1449–1455.

Fuller, S. R., & Aldag, R. J. (1998). Organizational Tonypandy: Lessons from a quarter century of groupthink phenomenon. *Organizational Behavior & Human Decision Processes, 73*, 163–184.

Fulton, S., Woodside, B., & Shizgal, P. (2000). Modulation of brain reward circuitry by leptin. *Science, 287*, 125–128.

Funk, S. C., & Houston, B. K. (1987). A critical analysis of the hardiness sale's validity and utility. *Journal of Personality and Social Psychology, 53*, 572–578.

Funtowicz, M. N., & Widiger, T. A. (1999). Sex bias in the diagnosis of personality disorders: An evaluation of the *DSM–IV* criteria. *Journal of Abnormal Psychology, 108*, 195–201.

Fuster, J. M. (1997). Network memory. *Trends in Neuroscience, 20*, 451–459.

Futterman, A. D., Kemeny, M. E., Shapiro, D., Polonsky, W., & Fahey, J. L. (1992). Immunological variability associated with experimentally-induced positive and negative affective states. *Psychological Medicine, 22*, 231–238.

Gabbard, G. O. (1990). *Psychodynamic Psychiatry in Clinical Practice.* Washington, DC: American Psychiatric Press.

Gabrieli, J. D. E. (1996). Memory systems analyses of mnemonic disorders in aging and age-related diseases. *Proceedings of the National Academy of Sciences, USA, 93*, 13534–13540.

Gabrieli, J. D. E., Desmond, J. E., Demb, J. B. Wagner, A. D., Stone, M. V., Vaidya, C. J., & Glover, G. H. (1996). Functional magnetic resonance imaging of semantic memory processes in the frontal lobes. *Psychological Science, 7*, 278–283.

Gabrieli, J. D. E., Fleischman, D. A., Keane, M. M., Reminger, S. L., & Morrell, F. (1995). Double dissociation between memory systems underlying explicit and implicit memory in the human brain. *American Psychological Society, 6*, 76–82.

Gallaher, P. E. (1992). Individual differences in nonverbal behavior. Dimensions of style. *Journal of Personality and Social Psychology, 63*, 133–145.

Gallers, J., Foy, D. W., Donahoe, C. P., & Goldfarb, J. (1988). Post-traumatic stress disorder in Vietnam combat veterans: Effects of traumatic violence exposure with military adjustment. *Journal of Traumatic Stress, 1*, 181–192.

Gallistel, C. R. (1983). Self-stimulation. In J. A. Deutsch (Ed.), *The physiological basis of memory* (pp. 73–77). New York: Academic Press.

Gangestad, S. W. (1993). Sexual selection and physical attraiveness: Implications fo rmating dynamics. *Human Nature, 4*, 205–235.

Garb, H. N. (1997). Race bias, social class bias, and gender bias in clinical judgment. *Clinical Psychology: Science & Practice, 4*, 99–120.

Garcia, J., & Koelling, R. (1966). Realtion of cue to consequence in avoidance learning. *Psychonomic Science, 4*, 123–124.

Garcia-Arraras, J. E., & Pappenheimer, J. R. (1983). Site of action of sleep-inducing muramyl peptide isolated from human urine: Microinjection studies in rabbit brains. *Journal of Neurophysiology, 49*, 528–533.

Gardner, H. (1975). *The shattered mind: The person after brain damage.* New York: Knopf.

Gardner, H. (1985). *The mind's new science: A history of the cognitive revolution.* New York: Basic Books.

Gardner, H. (1993a). *Creating minds: An anatomy of creativity as seen through the lives of Freud, Einstein, Picasso, Stravinsky, Eliot, Graham, and Gandhi.* New York: Basic Books.

Gardner, H. (1993b). *Frames of mind: The theory of multiple intelligences.* New York: Basic Books. (Original work published 1983.)

Gardner, H. (1993c). *Multiple intelligences: The theory in practice.* New York: Basic Books.

Gardner, H. (1995, November). Reflections on multiple intelligences: Myths and messages. *Phi Delta Kappan*, pp. 200–209.

Gardner, H. (1999). *Intelligence reframed: Multiple intelligences for the 21st century.* New York: Basic Books.

Gardner, H., Kornhaber, M. L., & Wake, W. K. (1996). *Intelligence: Multiple perspectives.* Ft. Worth, TX: Harcourt Brace.

Gardner, R. A., & Gardner, B. T. (1969). Teaching sign language to a chimpanzee. *Science, 165*, 664–672.

Garfield, S. L. (1994). Research on client variables in psychotherapy. In A. E. Bergin & S. L. Garfield (Eds.), *Handbook of psychotherapy and behavior change, 4th edition* (pp. 190–228). New York: John Wiley & Sons.

Garfield, S. L., & Bergin, A. E. (1994). Introduction and historical overview. In A. E. Bergin & S. L. Garfield (Eds.), *Handbook of psychotherapy and behavior change, 4th edition* (pp. 3–18). New York: John Wiley & Sons.

Garfinkel, P. E., Goldbloom, D., David, R., Olmsted, M. P., Garner, D. M., & Halmi, K. A. (1992). Body dissatisfaction in Bulimia Nervosa: Relationship to weight and shape concerns and psychological functioning. *International Journal of Eating Disorders, 11*, 151–161.

Garner, D. M. (1997). Psycho educational Principles in Treatment. In D. M. Garner & P. E. Garfinkel (Eds.), *Handbook of Treatment for Eating Disorders* (2nd edition). New York: Guilford Press.

Garrett, M., Bever, T., & Fodor, J. (1966). The active use of grammar in speech perception. *Perception & Psychophysics, 1*, 30–32.

Garris, P. A., Kilpatrick, M., Bunin, M. A., Michael, D., Walker, Q. D., & Wightman, R. M. (1999). Dissociation of dopamine release in the nucleus accumbens from intracranial self-stimulation. *Nature, 398*, 67–69.

Garrison, M., & Bly, M. A. (1997). *Human Relations: Productive Approaches to the Workplace.* Boston: Allyn & Bacon.

Garry, M., & Polaschek, D. L. L. (2000). Imagination and memory. *Current Directions in Psychological Science, 9*, 6–10.

Garvey, C. (1974). Requests and responses in children's speech. *Journal of Child Language, 2*, 41–60.

Gaster, B., & Holroyd, J. (2000). St. John's Wort for depression: A systematic review. *Archives of Internal Medicine, 160*, 152–156.

Gater, R., Tansella, M., Korten, A., Tiemens, B. G., Mavreas, V. G., & Olatawura, M. O. (1998). Report from the World Health Organization Collaborative Study on Psychological Problems in General Health Care. *Archives of General Psychiatry, 55*, 405–413.

Gauthier, I., Tarr, M. J., Anderson, A. W., Skudlarski, P., & Gore, J. C. (1997). Expertise training with novel objects can recruit the fusiform face area. *Society of Neuroscience Abstracts, 23*, 868.5.

Gazzaniga, M. S. (1995). Consciousness and the cerebral hemispheres. In M. S. Gazzaniga (Ed.), *The cognitive neurosciences* (pp. 1391–1400). Cambridge, MA: The MIT Press.

Gazzaniga, M. S., & LeDoux, J. E. (1979). *The integrated mind.* New York: Plenum.

Geary, D. C. (1996a). Sexual selection and sex differences in mathematical abilities. *Behavioral and Brain Sciences, 19*, 229–284.

Geary, D. C. (1996b). The evolution of cognition and the social construction of knowledge. *American Psychologist, 51*, 265–266.

Geary, N., & Smith, G. P. (1985). Pimozide decreases the positive reinforcing effects of sham fed sucrose in the rat. *Pharmacology, Biochemistry, & Behavior, 22*, 787–790.

Geddes, J. R., & Lawrie, S. M. (1995). Obstretric complications and schizophrenia: a meta-analysis. *British Journal of Psychiatry, 67*, 786–793.

Geiselman, R. E., Fisher, R. P., MacKinnon, D. P., & Holland, H. L. (1985). Eyewitness memory enhancement in the police interview. *Cognitive Journal of Applied Psychology, 70*, 401–412.

Gelfand, S. A. (1981). *Hearing.* New York: MarcelDekker.

Gelman, R. (1972). Logical capacity of very young children: Number invariance rules. *Child Development, 43*, 75–90.

George, M. S., Lisanby, S. H., & Sackheim, H. A. (1999). Transcranial Magnetic Stimulation: Applications in neuropsychiatry. *Archives in General Psychiatry, 56*, 300–311.

Gerlai, R. (1996). Gene-targeting studies of mammalian behavior: Is it the mutation of the background genotype? *Trends in Neuroscience, 19*, 177–181.

German, D. C., & Bowden, D. M. (1974). Catecholamine systems as the neural substrate for intracranial self-stimulation: A hypothesis. *Brain Research, 73*, 381–419.

Gershberg, F. B., & Shimamura, A. P. (1995). Impaired use of organizational strategies in free recall following frontal lobe damage. *Neuropsychologia, 33*, 1305–1333.

Gerstmann, J. (1942). Problem of imperception of disease and of impaired body territories with organic lesions. *Archives of Neurology and Psychiatry, 48*, 890–913.

Gerteis, J., & Savage, M. (1998). The salience of class in Britain and America: A comparative analysis. *British Journal of Sociology, 49*, 252–274.

Gesell, A., & Thompson, H. (1938). *The psychology of early growth including norms of infant behavior and a method of genetic analysis.* New York: Macmillan.

Getter, L. (1999, March 1). Cancer risk from air pollution still high, study says. *Los Angeles Times*, p. 0.

Gibbons, F. X. & Gerrard, M. (1995). Predicting young adults' health-risk behavior. *Journal of Personality and Social Psychology, 69*, 505–517.

Gibbs, R. W., Jr., & O'Brien, J. E. (1990). Idioms and mental imagery: The metaphorical motivation for idiomatic meaning. *Cognition, 36*, 35–68.

Gibson, E. J. (1969). Principles of perceptual learning and development. New York: Appleton-Century-Crofts.

Gibson, J. J. (1966). *The senses considered as perceptual systems.* Boston: Houghton Mifflin.

Gibson, J. J., & Walk, R. D. (1960). The "visual cliff." *Scientific American, 202*, 64–71.

Gibson, J. T. (1991). Training people to inflict pain: State terror and social learning. *Journal of Humanistic Psychology, 31*, 72–87.

Gick, M. L., & Holyoak, K. J. (1980). Analogical problem solving. *Cognitive Psychology, 12*, 306–355.

Gick, M. L., & Holyoak, K. J. (1983). Schema induction and analogical transfer. *Cognitive Psychology, 15,* 1–38.

Gidron, Y., Davidson, K., & Bata, I. (1999). The Short-Term Effects of a Hostility-Reduction Intervention on Male Coronary Heart Disease Patients. *Health Psychology, 18,* 416–420.

Gigerenzer, G. (1994). Why the distinction between single-event probabilities and frequencies is relevant for psychology and vice versa. In G. Wright & P. Ayton (Eds.), *Subjective probability* (pp. 129–162). New York: Wiley.

Gigerenzer, G. (1996). On narrow norms and vague heuristics: A reply to Kahneman & Tversky (1996). *Psychological Review, 103,* 592–596.

Gigerenzer, G., & Goldstein, D. G. (1996). Reasoning the fast and frugal way: Models of bounded rationality. *Psychological Review, 103,* 650–669.

Gigerenzer, G., Hell, W., & Blank, H. (1988). Presentation and content: The use of base rates as a continuous variable. *Journal of Experimental Psychology: Human Perception and Performance, 14,* 513–525.

Gigerenzer, G., & Hug, K. (1992). Domain-specific reasoning: Social contracts, cheating, and perspective change. *Cognition, 43,* 127–171.

Gilbert, D. T. (1991). How mental systems believe. *American Psychologist, 46,* 107–119.

Gilbert, D. T. (1995). Attribution and interpersonal perception. In A. Tesser (Ed.), *Advanced Social Psychology*(pp. 99–147). New York: McGraw-Hill.

Gilbert, D. T., & Hixon, J. G. (1991). The trouble of thinking: Activation and application of stereotypic beliefs. *Journal of Personality and Social Psychology, 60,* 509–517.

Gilbert, D. T., & Malone, P. S. (1995). The correspondence bias. *Psychological Bulletin, 117,* 21–38.

Gilger, J. W. (1995). Behavioral genetics: Concepts for research and practice in language development and disorders. *Journal of Speech and Hearing Research, 38,* 1126–1142.

Gilligan, C. (1982). *In a different voice.* Cambridge, MA: Harvard University Press.

Gilmore, J. H., Sikich, L., & Lieberman, J. A. (1997). Neuroimaging, neurodevelopment, and schizophrenia. *Child & Adolescent Psychiatric Clinics of North America, 6(2),* 325–341.

Gladis, M. M. Gosch, E. A., Dishuk, N. M., & Crits-Christoph, P. (1999). Quality of life: Expanding the scope of clinical significance. *Journal of Consulting and Clinical Psychology, 67,* 320–331.

Gladwell, M. (1998, February 2). The pima paradox. *New Yorker,* pp. 44–57.

Glass, D., & Singer, J. (1972). *Urban Stress: Experiments on Noise and Social Stressors.* New York: Academic Press.

Glennon, F., & Joseph, S. (1993). Just world belief, self-esteem, and attitudes towards homosexuals with AIDS. *Psychological Reports, 72,* 584–586.

Glick, J. (1968). Cognitive style among the Kpelle of Liberia. Paper presented at the meeting on Cross-Cultural Cognitive Studies, American Educational Research Association, Chicago.

Glisky, E. L, Polster, M. R, & Routhieaux, B. C. (1995). Double dissociation between item and source memory. *Neuropsychology, 9,* 229–235.

Gloaguen, V., Cottraux, J., Cucherat, M., & Blackburn, I. (1998). A meta-analysis of the effects of cognitive therapy in depressed patients. *Journal of Affective Disorders, 49,* 59–72.

Glynn, S. M. (1990). Token economy approaches for psychiatric patients: Progress and pitfalls over 25 years. *Behavior Modification, 14,* 383–407.

Godden, D. R., & Baddeley, A. D. (1975). Context-dependent memory in two natural environments: On land and underwater. *British Journal of Psychology, 66,* 325–331.

Goedde, H. W., & Agarwal, D. P. (1987). Aldehyde hydrogenase polymorphism: Molecular basis and phenotypic relationship to alcohol sensitivity. *Alcohol & Alcoholism* (Suppl. 1), 47–54.

Goetestam, K. G., & Berntzen, D. (1997). Use of the modelling effect in one-session exposure. *Scandinavian Journal of Behaviour Therapy, 26,* 97–101.

Goethals, G. R., Cooper, J., & Naficy, A. (1979). Role of foreseen, foreseeable, and unforeseeable behavioral consequences in the arousal of cognitive dissonance. *Journal of Personality and Social Psychology, 37,* 1179–1185.

Goethals, G. R., & Zanna, M. P. (1979). The role of social comparison in choice shifts. *Journal of Personality and Social Psychology, 37,* 1469–1185.

Goldberg, L. R. (1981). Language and individual differences: The search for universals in personality lexicons. In L. Wheeler (Ed.), *Review of personality and social psychology* (Vol. 2, pp. 141–165). Beverly Hills, CA: Sage.

Goldberg, P. (1968). Are women prejudiced against women? Transaction, 5, 28–30.

Goldenberg, J., Mazursky, D., & Solomon, S. (1999). Essays on science and society: Creative sparks. *Science, 285,* 1495–1496.

Goldin-Meadow, S., & Mylander, C. (1998). Spontaneous sign systems created by deaf children in two cultures. *Nature, 391,* 279–281.

Golding, J. M., Sanchez, R. P., & Sego, S. A. (1996). Do you believe in repressed memories? *Professional Psychology Research and Practice, 27,* 429–237.

Goldman, W. P., Wolters, N. C. W., & Winograd, E. (1992). A demonstration of incubation in anagram problem solving. *Bulletin of the Psychonomic Society, 30,* 36–38.

Goldman-Rakic, P. S. (1987). Development of cortical circuitry and cognitive function. Child Development, 58, 601–622.

Goldstein, A. (1994). *Addiction: From biology to drug policy.* New York: Freeman.

Goldstein, J. M., Goodman, J. M., Seidman, L. J., Kennedy, D. N., Makris, N., Lee, H., Tourville, J., Caviness, V. S., Jr., Faraone, S. V., & Tsuang, M. T. (1999). Cortical abnormalities in schizophrenia identified by structural magnetic resonance imaging. *Archives of General Psychiatry, 56,* 537–547.

Goldstein, M. D., & Strube, M. J. (1994). Independence revisited: The relation between positive and negative affect in a naturalistic setting. *Personality & Social Psychology Bulletin, 20,* 57–64.

Goldstein, M. J. (1992). Psychosocial strategies for maximizing the effects of psychotropic medications for schizophrenia and mood disorder. *Psychopharmacology Bulletin, 28,* 237–240.

Goleman, D. (1995). *Emotional intelligence.* New York: Bantam Books.

Golombok, S., & Tasker, F. (1996). Do parents influence the sexual orientation of their children? Findings from a longitudinal study of lesbian families. *Developmental Psychology, 32,* 3–11.

Gontkovsky, S. T. (1998). Huntington's disease: A neuropsychological overview. *Journal of Cognitive Rehabilitation, 16,* 6–9.

Goodale, M. A., & Milner, A. D. (1992). Separate visual pathways for perception and action. *Trends in Neurosciences, 15,* 20–25.

Goode, E. (1999a). *New Clues to Why We Dream.* Thursday, November 2, 1999, p. D1. New York Times.

Goode, E. (1999b, December 7). Doctors try a bold move against schizophrenia. *New York Times,* Science Times, p. D1.

Goodfellow, P. N., & Lovell-Badge, R. (1993). SRY and sex determination in mammals. *Annual Review of Genetics, 27,* 71–92.

Goodglass, H. (1976). Agrammatism. In H. Whitaker & H. A. Whitaker (Eds.), *Studies of neurolinguistics.* New York: Academic Press.

Goodie, A. S., & Fantino, E. (1996). Learning to commit or avoid the base-rate error. *Nature, 380,* 247–249.

Goodman, N. (1983). *Fact, fiction, and forecast* (4th edition). Cambridge: Harvard University Press.

Goodman, R. (1988). Are compicaitons of pregnancy and birth causes of schizphrenia? *Developmental Medical Child Neurology, 30,* 391–395.

Goodwin, F. K., & Ghaemi, S. N. (1998). Understanding manic–depressive illness. *Archives of General Psychiatry, 55,* 23–25.

Goodwin, F. K., & Jamison, K. R. (1990). *Manic-depressive illness.* New York: Oxford University Press.

Gopnik, A. (1996). The post-Piaget era. *Psychological Science, 7,* 221–225.

Gopnik, M. (1990). Dysphasia in an extended family. *Nature, 344,* 715.

Gopnik, M. (1997). Language deficits and genetic factors. *Trends in Cognitive Sciences, 1,* 5–9.

Gopnik, M., & Crago, M. (1991). Familial aggregation of a developmental language disorder. *Cognition, 39,* 1–50.

Gorcynski, R. Cited in Dienstfrey, H. (1991). *Where The Mind Meets The Body.* New York: HarperCollins.

Gorman, J. M., & Kent, J. M. (1999). SSRIs and SNRIs: Broad spectrum of efficacy beyond major depression. *Journal of Clinical Psychiatry, 60(Suppl. 4)* 33–39.

Gorman, J. M., Liebowitz, M. R., Fyer, A. J., &Stein, J. (1989). A neuroanatomical hypothesis for panic disorder. *American Journal of Psychiatry, 146,* 148–161.

Gortner, E. T., Gollan, J. K., Dobson, K. S., & Jacobson, N. S. (1998). Cognitive-Behavioral Treatment for Depression: Relapse Prevention. *Journal of Consulting and Clinical Psychology, 66,* 377–384.

Gotlib, I. H., & Robinson, L. A. (1982). Responses to depressed individuals: Discrepancies between self-report and observer rated behavior. *Journal of Abnormal Psychology, 91,* 231–240.

Gottesman, I. I. (1991). *Schizophrenia genesis: The origins of madness.* New York: Freeman.

Gottesman, I. I., Goldsmith, H. H., & Carey, G.. (1997). A developmental and a genetic perspective on aggression. In N. L. Segal, G. E. Weisfeld, C. C. Weisfield (Eds.), *Uniting psychology and biology: Integrative perspectives on human development.* (pp. 107–130). Washington, DC, USA: American Psychological Association.

Gottesman, I. I., & Moldin, S. O. (1998). Genotypes, Genes, Genesis, and pathogenesis in schizophrenia. In M. F. Lenzenweger & R. H. Dworkin (Eds.), *Origins and Development of Schizophrenia: Advances in Exper-*

imental *Psychopathology*. Washington, DC: American Psychological Association. pp. 5–26.

Gottfredson, L. (1997). Why "g" matters: The complexity of everyday life. *Intelligence, 24*, 79–132.

Gottfredson, M. R., & Hirschi, T. (1990). *A general theory of crime*. Stanford, CA: Stanford University Press.

Gottlieb, G. (1998). Normally occurring environmental and behavioral influences on gene activity: From central dogma to probabilistic epigenesis. *Psychological Review, 105*, 792–802.

Gould, E., Tanapat, P., Hastings, N. B., & Shors, T. J. (1999). Neurogenesis in adulthood: A possible role in learning. *Trends in Cognitive Sciences, 3*, 186–192.

Gould, R. (1978). *Transformations*. New York: Simon & Schuster.

Gould, R. A., Buckminster, S., Pollack, M. H., Otto, M. W., & Yap, L. (1997). Cognitive-behavioral and pharmacological treatment for social phobia: A meta-analysis. *Clinical Psychology: Science & Practice, 4*, 291–306.

Gould, R. A., & Clum, G. A. (1993). A meta-analysis of self-help treatment approaches. *Clinical Psychology Review, 13*, 169–186.

Gould, R. A., Otto, M. W., & Pollack, M. H. (1995). A meta-analysis of treatment outcome for panic disorder. *Clinical Psychology Review, 15*, 819–844.

Gould, S. J., & Lewontin, R. C. (1979). The spandrels of San Marco and the Panglossian paradigm: A critique of the adaptationist programme. *Proceedings of the Royal Society of London, Series B, 205*, 581–598.

Gouldner, A. W. (1960). The norm of reciprocity: A preliminary statement. *American Sociological Review, 25*, 161–179.

Graf, P., & Mandler, G. (1984). Activation makes words more accessible, but not necessarily more retrievable. *Journal of Verbal Learning and Verbal Behavior, 23*, 553–568.

Grammer, K. (1990). Strangers meet: Laughter and nonverbal signs of interest in opposite-sex encounters. *Journal of Nonverbal Behavior, 14*, 209–236.

Grammer, K., & Thornhill, R. (1994). Human *(Homo sapiens)* facial attractiveness and sexual selecgtion: The role of symmetry and averageness. *Journal of Comparative Psychology, 108*, 233–242.

Grant, B. F., & Dawson, D. A. (1997). Age at onset of alcohol use and its association with DSM–IV alcohol abuse and dependence: Results from the National Longitudinal Alcohol Epidemiologic Survey. *Journal of Substance Abuse, 9*, 103–110.

Grant, I., Marcotle, T. D., Heaton, R. K., & HNRC Group, San Diego, CA, USA. (1999). Neurocognitive complications of HIV disease. *Psychological Science, 10*, 191–195.

Gray, J. A. (1987). Perspectives on anxiety and implusivesness: A commentary. *Journal of Research in Personality, 21*, 493–509.

Gray, J. A. (1994). The neuropsychology of anxiety and schizophrenia. In M. S. Gazzaniga (Ed.), *The cognitive neurosciences* (pp. 1165–1176). Cambridge, MA: MIT Press.

Gray, J. R. (1999). A bias toward short-term thinking in threat-related negative emotional states. *Personality and Social Psychology Bulletin, 25*, 65–75.

Grayson, B. and Stein, M. I. (1981) Attracting assault: Victims' nonverbal cues. *Journal of Communication 31*, 68–75.

Graziano, W. G., Jensen-Campbell, L. A., & Sullivan-Logan, G. M. (1998). Temperament, Activity, and Expectations for Later Personality Development, *Journal of Persoanlity and Social Psychology, 74*, 1266–1277.

Green, D. E., Walkey, F. H., & Taylor, A. J. W. (1991). The three-factor structure of the Maslach Burnout Inventory: A multicultural, multinational confirmatory study. *Journal of Social Behavior & Personality, 6*, 453–472.

Green, D. M. (1976). *An introduction to hearing*. Hillsdale, NJ: Erlbaum.

Green, D. M., & Swets, J. A. (1966). *Signal detection theory and psychophysics*. New York: Wiley.

Green, J. P. (1999). Hypnosis, context effects, and the recall of early autobiographical memories. *International Journal of Clinical and Experimental Hypnosis, 47*, 284–300.

Green, J. P., Lynn, S. J., & Malinoski, P. (1998). Hypnotic pseudomemories, prehypnotic warnings, and malleability of suggested memories. *Applied Cognitive Psychology, 12*, 431–444.

Green, M. W., Elliman, N. A., & Rogers, P. J. (1997). The effects of food deprivation and incentive motivation on blood glucose levels and cognitive function. *Psychopharmacology, 134*, 88–94.

Green, N. W., Elliman, N. A., & Rogers, P. J. (1995). Lack of effect of short-term fasting on cognitive function. *Journal of Psychiatric Research, 29*, 245–253.

Greenberg, B. D., Altemus, M., & Murphy, D. L. (1997). The role of neurotransmitters and neurohormones in obsessive-compulsive disorder. *International Review of Psychiatry, 9*, 31–44.

Greenberg, J. R., & Mitchell, S. A. (1983). *Object Relations in Psychoanalytic Theory*. Cambridge, MA: Harvard University Press.

Greene, W., Conron, D., Schalch, S., & Schreiner, B. (1970). Psychological correlates of growth hormone and adrenal secretory responses of patients undergoing cardiac catheterization. *Psychosomatic Medicine, 32*, 599–?.

Greenfield, P. (1992, June). *Notes and references for developmental psychology*. Conference on Making Basic Texts in Psychology More Culture-Inclusive and Culture-Sensitive, Western Washington University, Bellingham, WA.

Greenfield, P. M., & Savage-Rumbaugh, S. (1990). Grammatical combination in *Pan paniscus*: Processes of learning and invention in the evolution and development of language. In S. Parker & K. Gibson (Eds.), *"Language" and intelligence in monkeys and apes: Comparative developmental perspectives* (pp. 540–578). New York: Cambridge University Press.

Greenglass, E. R., Burke, R. J., & Konarski, R. (1998). Components of burnout, resources, and gender-related differences. *Journal of Applied Social Psychology, 28*, 1088–1106.

Greeno, J. G. (1989). A perspective on thinking. *American Psychologist, 44*, 134–141.

Greenough, W. T., & Black, J. E. (1992). Induction of brain structure by experience. In M. R. Gunnar & C. A. Nelson (Eds.), *Minnesota symposium on child psychology: Vol. 24. Developmental behavior neuroscience* (pp. 155–200). Hillsdale, NJ: Erlbaum.

Greenough, W. T., Black, J. E., & Wallace, C. S. (1987). Experience and brain development. *Child Development, 58*, 539–559.

Greenough, W. T., Chang, F.-L. F. (1985). Synaptic structural correlates of information storage in mammalian nervous systems. In C. W. Cotman (Ed.), *Synaptic plasticity* (pp. 335–372). New York: Gilford.

Greenough, W. T., Larson, J. R., & Withers, G. S. (1985). Effect of unilateral and bilateral training in a reaching task on dendritic branching of neurons in the rat motor-sensory forelimb cortex. *Behavioral Neural Biology, 44*, 301–314.

Greenwald, A. G., & Banaji, M. R. (1995). Implicit social cognition: Attitudes, self-esteem, and stereotypes. *Psychological Review, 102*, 4–27.

Greenwald, A. G., Draine, S. C., Abrams, R. L. (1996). Three cogntive markers of unconscious semantic activation. *Science, 273*, 1699–1702.

Greenwald, A. G., Spangenberg, E. R., Pratkanis, A. R., & Eskenazi, J. (1991). Double-blind tests of subliminal self-help audiotapes. *Psychological Science, 2*, 119–122.

Gregerson, M. B., Roberts, I. M., & Amiri, M. M. (1996). Absorption and imagery locate immune response in the body. *Biofeedback and Self-regulation, 21*, 149–165.

Gregory, G. D., & Munch, J. M. (1997). Cultural values in international advertising: An examination of familial norms and roles in Mexico. *Psychology & Marketing, 14*, 99–119.

Gregory, R. L. (1961). The brain as an engineering problem. In W. H. Thorpe & O. L. Zangwill (Eds.), *Current problems in animal behaviour*. Cambridge: Cambridge University Press.

Gregory, R. L. (1974). *Concepts and mechanisms of perception*. New York: Scribner.

Grice, H. P. (1975). Logic and conversation. In P. Cole & J. L. Morgan (Ed.), *Syntax and semantics: Vol. 3, Speech acts* (pp. 41–58). New York: Seminar Press.

Griggs, R. A., & Cox, J. R. (1982). The elusive thematic-materials effect in Wason's selection task. *British Journal of Psychology, 73*, 407–420.

Grill-Spector, K., Kushnir, T., Hendler, T., Edelman, S., Itzchak, Y., & Malach, R. (1998). A sequence of object-processing stages revealed by fMRI in the human occipital lobe. *Human Brain Mapping, 6*, 316–328.

Grilly, D. (1994). *Drugs and human behavior, 2nd edition*. Boston: Allyn and Bacon.

Grimes, K., & Walker, E. F. (1994). Childhood emotional expressions, educational attainments, and age at onset of illness in schizophrenia. *Journal of Abnormal Psychology, 103*, 784–790.

Grimshaw, G. M., Adelstein, A., Bryden, M. P., & MacKinnon, G. E. (1998). First-language acquisition in adolescence: Evidence for a critical period for verbal language development. *Brain & Language, 63*, 237–255.

Grisaru, N., Amir, M., Cohen, H., & Kaplan, Z. (1998). Effect of transcranial magnetic stimulation in posttraumatic stress disorder: A preliminary study. *Biological Psychiatry, 44*, 52–55.

Grisaru, N., Chudakov, B., Yaroslavsky, Y., & Belmaker, R. H. (1998). Transcranial magnetic stimulation in mania: A controlled study. *American Journal of Psychiatry, 155*, 1608–1610.

Grissmer, D. W., Kirby, S. N., Bevends, M., & Williamson, S. (1994). *Student achievement and the changing American family*. Santa Monica, CA: RAND.

Groome, L. J., Swiber, M. J., Bentz, L. S., Holland, S. B., et al. (1995). Maternal anxiety during pregnancy: Effect on fetal behavior at 38 to 40 weeks of gestation. *Journal of Developmental & Behavioral Pediatrics, 16*, 391–396.

Gross, J., & Levenson, R. W. (1997). Hiding feelings: The acute effects of inhibiting negative and positive emotion. *Journal of Abnormal Psychology, 106*, 95–103.

Grossarth-Maticek, R., Eysenck, H. J., Boyle, G. J., Heeb, J., Costa, C. D., & Diel, I. J. (2000). Interaction of psychosocial and physical risk factors in the causation of mammary cancer, and its prevention through psychological methods of treatment. *Journal of Clinical Psychology, 56,* 33–50.

Grossberg, S., Mingolla, E., & Ross, W. D. (1997). Visual brain and visual perception: How does the cortex do perceptual grouping? *Trends in Neuroscience, 20,* 106–111.

Grossman, R. P., & Till, B. D. (1998). The persistence of classically conditioned brand attitudes. *Journal of Advertising, 27,* 23–31.

Gudjonsson, G. H. (1991). Suggestibility and compliance among alleged false confessors and resisters in criminal trials. *Medicine, Science, and the Law, 31,* 147–151.

Guerin, B. (1993). *Social faciliatation.* Paris: Cambridge University Press.

Guice, J. (1999, November). Sociologists go to work in high technology. *Footnotes,* p. 8.

Guilford, J. P. (1967). *The nature of human intelligence.* New York: McGraw-Hill.

Guilford, J. P. (1979). Some incubated thoughts on incubation. *Journal of Creative Behavior, 13,* 1–8.

Guilleminault, C., Raynal, D., Takahashi, S., Carskadon, M., & Dement, W. (1976). Evaluation of short-term and long-term treatment of the narcolepsy syndrome with clomipramine hydrochloride. *Acta Neurologica Scandinavica, 54,* 71–87.

Guldner, G. T., & Swensen, C. H. (1995). Time spent together and relationship quality: Long-distance relationships as a test case. *Journal of Social and Personal Relationships, 12,* 313–320.

Gulick, W. L., Gescheider, G. A., & Frisina, R. D. (1989). *Hearing: Physiological acoustics, neural coding, and psychoacoustics.* New York: Oxford University Press.

Gur, R. C., Turetsky, B. I., Matsui, M., Yan, M., Bilker, W., Hughett, P., & Gur, R. E. (1999). Sex differences in brain gray and white matter in healthy young adults: Correlations with cognitive performance. *Journal of Neuroscience, 19,* 4065–4072.

Gureje, O., Mavreas, V., Vazquez-Barquero, J. L., & Janca, A. (1997). Problems related to alcohol use: A cross-cultural perspective. *Culture, Medicine, and Psychiatry, 21,* 199–211.

Gustavson, C. R., Garcia, J., Hankins, W. G., & Rusiniak, K. W. (1974). Coyote predation control by aversive conditioning, *Science, 184,* 581–583.

Gustavson, C. R., Kelly, D. J., & Sweeney, M. (1976). Prey-lithium aversions I: Coyotes and wolves. *Behavioral Biology, 17,* 61–72.

Guthrie, G. M., Guthrie, H. A., Fernandez, T. L., & Esterea, N. O. (1982). Cultural influences and reinforcement stratefies. *Behavior Therapy, 13,* 624–637.

Guttmann, C. R. G., Jolesz, F. A., Kikinis, R., Killiany, R. J., Moss, M. B., Sandor, T., & Albert, M. S. (1998). White matter changes with normal aging, *Neurology, 50,* 972–978.

Gyulai, L., Abass, A., Broich, K., & Reilley, J. (1997). I-123 lofetamine single-photon computer emission tomography in rapid cycling bipolar disorder: A clinical study. *Biological Psychiatry, 41,* 152–161.

Haaga, D. A., & Davison, G. C. (1989). Slow progress in rational-emotive therapy outcome research: Etiology and treatment. *Cognitive Therapy & Research, 13,* 493–450.

Haberlandt, K. (1997). *Cognitive Psychology* (2nd ed.). Needham Heights, MA: Allyn & Bacon.

Hackenberg, T. D., & Hineline, P. N. (1990). Discrimination, symbolic behavior, and the origins of awareness. Unpublished manuscript, Temple University, Philadelphia.

Hacker, A. (1992). *Two nations: Black and white, separate, hostile, unequal.* New York: Scribner's.

Hacking, I. (1995). *Rewriting the soul: Multiple personality and the sciences of memory.* Princeton, NJ: Princeton University Press.

Hadamard, J. (1945). *An essay on the psychology of invention in the mathematical field.* Princeton, NJ: Princeton University Press.

Haddad, A., & Newby, R. (1999, May–June). Members comment on ASA's publication on affirmative action. *Footnotes,* p. 9.

Hahn, R. A. (1997). The nocebo phenomenon: Scope and foundations. In A. Harrington (Ed.). *The Placebo Effect: An Interdisciplinary Exploration.* Cambridge, MA: Harvard University Press.

Haier, R. J., Siegel, B. V., Nuechterlein, K. H., Hazlett, E., Wu, J. C., Paek, J., Browning, H. L., & Buchsbaum, M. S. (1988). Cortical glucose metabolic rate correlates of abstract reasoning and attention studied with positron emission tomography. *Intelligence, 12,* 199–217.

Haier, R. J., Siegel, B., Tang, C., Abel, L., & Buchsbaum, M. S. (1992). Intelligence and changes in regional cerebral glucose metabolic rate following learning. *Intelligence 16,* 415–426.

Haier, R. J., et al. (1984) Evoked potential augmenting-reducing and personality differences. *Personality & Indiv. Differences 5,* 293–301.

Hall, C. S. (1984). "A ubiquitous sex difference in dreams." revisited. *Journal of Personality and Social Psychology, 46,* 1109–1117.

Hall, D. T., & Nougaim, K. E. (1968). An examination of Maslow's need hierarchy in an organizational setting. *Organizational Behavior and Human Performance, 3,* 12–35.

Hall, G. S. (1904). *Adolescence: Its psychology and its relation to physiology, anthropology, sociology, sex, crime, religion, and education* (Vols. I & II). Englewood Cliffs, NJ: Prentice-Hall.

Hall, J. A. (1978). Gender effects in decoding nonverbal cues. *Psychological Bulletin, 85,* 845–875.

Hall, J. A. (1987). On explaining gender differences: The case of nonverbal communication. In P. Shaver & C. Hendrick (Eds.). *Sex and gender.* Newbury Park, Calif.: Sage.

Hall, J. F. (1984). Backward conditioning in Pavlovian type studies: Reevaluation and present status. *Pavlovian Journal of Biological Science, 19,* 163–168.

Hall, J. F. (1989). *Learning and Memory (2nd. Ed.).* Massachusetts: Allyn & Bacon.

Halle, M. (1990). Phonology. In D. N. Osherson, & H. Lasnik (Ed.), *An invitation to cognitive science: Vol. 1, Language* (pp. 43–68). Cambridge, MA: MIT Press.

Hallstrom, T., & Samuelsson, S. (1990). Changes in women's sexual desire in middle life: The longitudinal study of women in Gothenburg. *Archives of Sexual Behavior, 19,* 259–268.

Halmi, K. (1995). Basic Biological overview of eating disorders. IN F. E. Bloom & D. J. Kupfer (Eds.), *Psychopharmacology: The Fourth Generation of Progress.* New York; Raven Press, Ltd.

Halmi, K. (1996). The psychobiology of eating behavior in anorexia nervosa. *Psychiatry Research, 62,* 23–29.

Halpern, A. R. (1988). Mental scanning in auditory imagery for songs. *Journal of Experimental Psychology: Learning, Memory and Cognition, 14,* 434–443.

Halpern, A. R., & Zatorre, R. J. (1999). When that tune runs through your head: A PET investigation of auditory imagery for familiar melodies. *Cerebral Cortex, 9,* 697–704.

Halpern, D. F. (1992). *Sex differences in cognitive ability.* Hillsdale, NJ: Erlbaum.

Halpern, D. F. (1997). Sex differences in intelligence: Implications for education. *American Psychologist, 52,* 1091–1102.

Hamann, S. B., Stefanacci, L., Squire, L. R., Adolphs, R., Tranel, D., Damasio, H., & Damasio, A. (1996). Recognizing facial emotion. *Nature, 379,* 497.

Hamer, D. H., Hu, S., Magnuson, V. L., Hu, N., & Pattatucci, A. M. (1993). A linkage between DNA markers on the X chromosome and male sexual orientation. *Science, 261,* 321–327.

Hamilton, D. L., & Sherman, S. J. (1989). Illusory correlations: Implications for stereotype theory and research. In D. Bar-Tal, C. F. Graumann, A. W. Kruglanski, & W. Stroebe (Eds.), *Stereotyping and prejudice: Changing conceptions* (pp. 59–82). New York: Springer-Verlag.

Hamilton, G. V. (1978). Obedience and responsibility: A jury simulation. *Journal of Personality and Social Psychology, 36,* 126–146.

Hamilton, J. A., Haier, R. J., & Buchsbaum, M. S. (1984). Intrinsic enjoyment and boredom coping scales: Validation with personality, evoked potential and attention measures. *Personality and Individual Differences, 5,* 183–193.

Hamilton, M. E., Voris, J. C., Sebastian, P. S., Singha, A. K., Krejci, L. P., Elder, I. R., Allen, J. E., Beitz, J. E., Covington, K. R., Newton, A. E., Price, L. T., Tillman, E., & Hernandez, L. L. (1998). Money as a tool to extinguish conditioned responses to cocaine in addicts. *Journal of Clinical Psychology, 54,* 211–218.

Hamilton, R. F. (1996). *The social construction of reality.* New Haven, CT: Yale University Press.

Hamilton, V. L., Hoffman, W. S., Broman, C. L., & Rauma, D. (1993). Unemployment, distress, and coping: A panel study of autoworkers. *Journal of Personality and Social Psychology, 65,* 234–247.

Hampson, E. (1990). Estrogen-related variations in human spatial and articulatory motor skills. *Psychoneuroendocrinology, 15,* 97–111.

Hampson, E., & Kimura, D. (1988). Reciprocal effects of hormonal fluctuations on human motor and perceptual-spatial skills. *Behavioral Neuroscience, 102,* 456–459.

Hansen, W. B., Graham, J. W., Wolkenstein, B. H., Lundy, B. Z., Pearson, J., Flay, B. R., & Joshnson, C. A. (1988). Differential impact of three alcohol prevetion curricula on hypothesized mediating variables. *Journal of Drug Educaiton, 18,* 143–153.

Hanson, K. A., & Gidycz, C. A. (1993). Evaluation of a sexual assault prevention program. *Journal of Consulting & Clinical Psychology, 61,* 1046–1052.

Hapidou, E. G., & De Catanzaro, D. (1988). Sensitivity to cold pressor pain in dysmenorrheic and non-dysmenorrheic women as a function of menstrual cycle phase. *Pain, 34,* 277–283.

Haqq, C. M., King, C-Y., Ukiyama, E., Falsafi, S., Haqq, T. N., Donahoe, P. K., & Weiss, M. A. (1994). Molecular basis of mammalian sexual determination: Activation of mullerian inhibiting substance gene expression by SRY. *Science, 266,* 1494–1500.

Haracz, J. L., Minor, T. R., Wilkins, J. N., & Zimmermann, E. G. (1988). Learned helplessness: An experimental model of the DST in rats. *Biological Psychiatry, 23,* 388–396.

Harada, S. (1989). Polymorphism of aldehyde dehydrogenase and its application to alcoholism. *Electrophoresis 10* (8–9), Aug–Sep, pp. 652–655.

Haraldsson, E., & Gissurarson, L. R. (1987). Does geomagnetic activity affect extrasensory perception? *Personality and Individual Differences, 8,* 745–747.

Haraldsson, E., & Houtkooper, J. M. (1992). Effects of perceptual defensiveness, personality and belief on extrasensory perception tasks. *Personality and Individual Differences, 13,* 1085–1096.

Hardin, G. (1968). The tragedy of the commons. *Science, 162* 1243–1248.

Hardy, J. D., & Smith, T. W. (1988). Cynical hostility and vulnerability to disease: Social support, life stress, and physiological response to conflict. *Health Psychology, 7,* 447–459.

Hare, R. D. (1993). *Without conscience: The disturbing world of the psychopaths among us.* New York: Pocket Books.

Harkins, S., & Szymanski, K. (1989). Social loafing and group evaluation. *Journal of Personality and Social Psychology, 56,* 934–941.

Harkins, S. G., & Petty, R. E. (1982). Effects of task difficulty and task uniqueness on social loafing. *Journal of Personality & Social Psychology, 43,* 1214–1229.

Harman, D. (1956). Aging: A theory based on free radical and radiation chemistry. *Journal of Gerontology, 11,* 298–300.

Harris, H. (1976). The false controversy: Clitoral vs. vaginal orgasm. *Psychotherapy: Theory. Research, and Practice, 13,* 99–103.

Harris, J. R. (1995). Where is the child's environment? A group socialization theory of development. *Psychological Review, 102,* 458–489.

Harris, J. R. (1998). *The nurture assumption: Why children turn out the way they do.* New York: The Free Press.

Harris, P. L. (1995). From simulation to folk psychology. In M. Davies & T. Stone (Eds.), *Folk psychology: The case for development* (pp. 207–221). Cambridge, England: Blackwell.

Harris, R. J., Schoen, L. M., & Hensley, D. L. (1992). A cross-cultural study of story memory. *Journal of Cross-Cultural Psychology, 23,* 133–147.

Hart, J., Berndt, R. S., & Caramazza, A. (1985). Category-specific naming deficit following cerebral infarction. *Nature, 316,* 439–440.

Hartman, B. J. (1982). An exploratory study of the effects of disco music on the auditory and vestibular systems. *Journal of Auditory Research, 22,* 271–274.

Hartshorne, H., & May, M. A. (1928). *Studies in deceit.* New York: Macmillan.

Hartung, C. M., & Widiger, T. A. (1998). Gender differences in the diagnosis of mental disorders: Conclusions and controversies of the DSM–IV. *Psychological Bulletin, 123,* 260–278.

Hasher, L., & Zacks, R. T. (1979). Automatic and effortful processes in memory. *Journal of Experimental Psychology: General, 108,* 356–388.

Hasher, L., & Zacks, R. T. (1984). Automatic processing of fundamental information. The case of frequency of occurence. *American Psychologist, 39,* 1327–1388.

Hastie, R. (1986). Review essay: Experimental evidence on group accuracy. In B. Grofman & G. Owen (Eds.), *Information pooling and group decision making* (pp. 129–157). Greenwich, CT: JAI Press.

Hastorf, A. H. & Cantril, H. (1954). They saw a game; a case study. *Journal of Abnormal and Social Psychology, 49,* 129–134.

Hatano, G., & Osawa, K. (1983). Digit memory of grand experts in abacus-derived mental calculation. *Cognition, 15,* 95–110.

Hatfield, E., Brinton, C., & Cornelius, J. (1989). Passionate love and anxiety in young adolescents. *Motivation and Emotion, 13,* 271–289.

Hatfield, E., & Sprecher, S. (1986). Men's and women's preferences in marital partners in the United States, Russia, and Japan. *Journal of Cross-Cultural Psychology. 26,* 728–750.

Haug, H. (1987). Brain sizes, surfaces, and neuronal sizes of the cortex cerebri: A stereological investigation of man and his variability and a comparison with some mammals (primates, whales, marsupials, insectivores, and one elephant). *American Journal of Anatomy, 180,* 126–42.

Haug, H., Barmwater, U., Eggers, R., Fischer, D., Kuhl, S., & Sass, N. L. (1983). Anatomical changes in the aging brain: Morphometric analysis of the human prosencephalon. In J. Cervos-Navarro & H. I. Sarkander (Eds.), *Aging: Vol. 21. Brain Aging: Neuropathology and Neuropharmacology* (pp. 1–22). New York: Raven Press.

Haugtvedt, C. P., & Petty, R. E. (1992). Personality and persuasion: need for cognition moderates the ersistence and resisance of attitude chagnes. *Journal of Personality and Social Psychology, 63,* 308–319.

Hauri, P. (1970). Evening activity, sleep mentation, and subjective sleep quality. *Journal of Abnormal Psychology, 76,* 270–275.

Hauser, M. (1996). *The evolution of communication.* Cambridge, MA: MIT Press.

Havinghurst, R. (1953). *Human development and education.* New York: Longmans, Green.

Hawkins, J. R. (1994). Sex determination. *Human Molecular Genetics, 3,* 1463–1467.

Haxby, J. V., Grady, C. L., Horowitz, B., Ungerleider, L. G., Mischkin, M., Carson, R. E., Hercovitch, P., Schapiro, M. B., & Rapoport, S. I. (1991). Dissociation of object and spatial visual processing pathways in human extrastriate cortex. *Proceedings of the National Academy of Sciences, USA, 88,* 1621–1625.

Haxby, J. V., Horowitz, B., Ungerleider, L. G., Maisog, J. M., Pietrini, P., & Grady, C. L. (1994). The functional organization of human extrastriate cortex: A PET-rCBF study of selective attention to faces and locations. *Journal of Neuroscience, 14,* 6336–6353.

Hayes, A. F., & Dunning, D. (1998). Construal Processes and Trait Ambiguity: Implications for Self-Peer Agreement in Personality Judgment. *Journal of Personality and Social Psychology, 72,* 664–677.

Hayflick, L. (1965). The limited in vitro lifetime of human diploid cell strains. *Experimental Cell Research, 37,* 614–636.

Haynor, A. L., & Varacalli, J. A. (1993). Sociology's fall from grace: The six deadly sins of a discipline at the crossroads. *Quarterly Journal of Ideology: A Critique of Conventional Wisdom, 16* (1 & 2), p. 3–29.

Hazan, C., & Shaver, P. R. (1987). Romantic love conceptualized as an attachment process. *Journal of Personality and Social Psychology, 52,* 511–524.

Hazan, C., & Shaver, P. R. (1990). Love and work: An attachment-theoretical perspective. *Journal of Personality and Social Psychology, 59,* 270–280.

Healey, B., & Wearing, A. (1989). Personality, life events, and subjective well-being: Toward a dynamic equilibrium model. *Journal of Personality and Social Psychology, 57,* 731–739.

Hearth, A. H. (1991, September 22). Two 'maiden ladies' with century-old stories to tell. *New York Times.*

Hearts and minds. (1997). *Harvard Mental Health Letter, 14*(1), 1–4.

Heath, A. C., Cloninger, C. R., & Martin, N. G. (1994). Testing a model for the genetic structure of personality: A comparison of the personality systems of Cloninger and Eysenck. *Journal of Personality and Social Psychology, 66,* 762–775.

Heath, A. C., & Martin, N. G. (1990) Psychoticism as a Dimension of Personality: A multivariate genetic test of Eysenck and Eysenck's Psychoticism construct. *Journal of Personality and Social Psychology, 58,* 11–121.

Heath, A. C., Neale, M. C., Kessler, R. C., Eaves, L. H., & Kendler, K. S. (1992). Evidence for genetic influences on personality from self-reports and informant ratings. *Journal of Personality and Social Psychology, 63,* 85–96.

Hebb, D. W., & Penfield, W. (1940). Human behavior after extensive bilateral removals from the frontal lobes. *Archives of Neurology and Psychiatry, 44,* 421–438.

Hébert, S., & Peretz, I. (1997). Recognition of music in long-term memory: Are melodic and temporal patterns equal partners? *Memory & Cognition, 25,* 518–533.

Hecker, M., Chesney, M. N., Black, G., & Frautsch, N. (1988). Coronary-prone behaviors in the Western Collaborative Group Study. *Psychosomatic Medicine, 50,* 153–164.

Hedges, C. (1997, November 26). Bosnia's factions push their versions of war into the history books. *International Herald Tribune, 5.*

Heider, K. G. (1976). Dani sexuality: A low energy system. *Man, 11,* 188–201.

Heimberg, R. G., Liebowitz, M. R., Hope, D. A., Schneier, F. R., Holt, C. S., Welkowitz, L. A., Juster, H. R., Campeas, R., Bruch, M. A., Cloitre, M., Fallon, B., & Klein, D. F. (1998). Cognitive behavioral group therapy vs phenelzine therapy for social phobia: 12-week outcome. *Archives of General Psychiatry, 55,* 1133–1141.

Heiss, W. D., Pawlik, G., Herholz, K., Wagner, R., & Weinhard, K. (1985). Regional cerebral glucose metabolism in man during wakefulness, sleep, and dreaming. *Brain Research, 327,* 362–366.

Heit, G., Smith, M. E., & Halgren, E. (1988). Neural encoding of individual words and faces by the human hippocampus and amygdala. *Nature, 333,* 773–775.

Held, J. D., Alderton, D. L., Foley, P. P., & Segall, D. O. (1993). Arithmetic reasoning gender differences: Explanations found in the Armed Services Vocational Aptitude Battery. *Learning and Individual Differences, 5,* 171–186.

Hellige, J. B. (1993). *Hemispheric asymmetry: What's right and what's left.* Cambridge, MA: Harvard University Press.

Hellige, J. B., & Michimata, C. (1989). Categorization versus distance: Hemispheric differences for processing spatial information. *Memory & Cognition, 17,* 770–776.

Hellige, J. B., & Sergent, J. (1986). Role of task factors in visual field asymmetries. *Brain and Cognition, 5,* 200–222.

Helms, J. E. (1996). The triple quandary of race, culture, and social class in standardized cognitive ability testing. In D. P. Flanaghan, J. L. Genshaft, & P. L. Harrison (Eds.), *Contemporary intellectual assessment: Theories, test and issues* (pp. 517–532). New York: Builford Press.

Helms, J. E., & Cook, D. A. (1999). *Using race and culture in counseling and psychotherapy: Theory and process*. Needham Heights, MA: Allyn & Bacon.

Helson, H. (1964). *Adaptation-level theory: An experimental and systematic approach to behavior*. New York: Harper & Row.

Hendricks, J., & Hendricks, C. D. (1986). *Aging in mass society: Myth and realities*. Boston: Little, Brown.

Henley, N. M. (1977). *Body politics: Power, sex, and non-verbal communication*. Englewood Cliffs, NJ: Prentice-Hall.

Hennessey, B. A., & Amabile, T. M. (1998). Reward, Intrinsic Motivation, and Creativity. *American Psychologist, 53,* 674–675.

Henry, B., Caspi, A., Moffitt, T. E., & Silva, P. A. (1996). Temperamental and familial predictors of violent and nonviolent criminal convictions: Age 3 to Age 18. *Developmental Psychology, 32,* 614–623.

Henry, J. P. (1977). *Stress, health, and the environment*. New York: Springer-Verlag.

Henry, W. P., Strupp, H. H., Schacht, T. E., & Gaston, L. (1994). Psychodynamic approaches. In A. E. Bergin & S. L. Garfield (Eds.), *Handbook of psychotherapy and behavior change, 4th edition* (pp. 467–508). New York: John Wiley & Sons.

Hensel, H. (1982). *Thermal sensations and thermoreceptors in man*. Springfield, IL: Thomas.

Henslin, J. M. (1999). *Sociology: A down-to-Earth approach* (4th ed.). Needham Heights, MA: Allyn & Bacon.

Henson, R., Shallice, T., & Dolan, R. (2000). Neuroimaging evidence for dissociable forms of repetition priming. *Science, 287,* 1269–1272.

Herbert, T. B., & Cohen, S. (1993a). Depression and immunity: A meta-analytic review. *Psychological Bulletin, 113,* 472–486.

Hermann, J. A., deMontes, A. I., Dominguez, B., Montes, F., & Hopkins, B. L. (1973). Effects of bonuses for punctuality on the tardiness of industrial workers. *Journal of Applied Behavior Analysis, 4,* 267–272.

Herrnstein, R. J. (1963). *IQ in the meritocracy*. Boston: Little, Brown.

Herrnstein, R. J., & Loveland, D. H. (1964), Complex visual concept in the pigeon. *Science, 146,* 549–551.

Herrnstein, R. J., & Murray, C. (1994). *The bell curve: Intelligence and class structure in American life*. New York: Free Press.

Hershberger, S. L., Lichtenstein, P., & Knox, S. S. (1994). Genetic and environmental influences on perceptions of organizational climate. *Joiurnal of Applied Psychology, 79,* 24–33.

Hershman, D. J., & Lieb, J. (1988). *The key to genius/manic-depression and the creative life*. New York: Prometheus Books.

Hershman, D. J., & Lieb, J. (1998). *Manic depression and creativity*. New York: Prometheus Books.

Hertzog, C., & Schaie, K. W. (1988). Stability and change in adult intelligence: 2. Simultaneous analysis of longitudinal means and covariance structures. *Psychology and Aging, 3,* 122–130.

Herz, R. S., & Cahill, E. D. (1997). Differential use of sensory information in sexual behavior as a function of gender. *Human Nature, 8,* 275–286.

Herzog, T. A., Abrams, D. B., Emmons, K. M., Linnan, L. A., & Shadel, W. G. (1999). Do Processes of Change Predict Smoking Stage Movements? A Prospective Analysis of the Transtheoretical Model. *Health Psychology, 18,* 369–375.

Hess, E. E. (1975). The role of pupil size in communication. *Scientific American, 233,* 110–119.

Huerta, P. T., Scearce, K. A., Farris, S. M., Empson, R. M., & Prusky, G. T. (1996). Preservation of spatial learning in fyn tryosine kinase knockout mice. *Neuroreport, 7,* 1685–1689.

Hierholzer, R., Munson, J., Peabody, C., & Rosenberg, J. (1992). Clinical presentation of PTSD in World War II combat veterans. Hospital and Community Psychiatry, 43, 816–820.

Higgenbotham, H. N., West, S., & Forsyth, D. (1988). *Psychotherapy and behavior change: Social, cultural and methodological perspectives*. New York: Pergamon.

Higgens, S. T., & Morris, E. K. (1984). Generality of free-operant avoidance conditioning to human behavior. *Psychological Bulletin, 96,* 247–272.

Higgins, E. T. (1996). Knowledge activation: Accessibility, applicability, and salience. In E. T. Higgins & A. Kruglanski (Eds.), *Social psychology: Handbook of basic principles* (pp. 133–168). New York: Guilford.

Higgins, E. T. (1997). Beyond pleasure and pain. *American Psychologist, 52,* 1280–1300.

Hilgard, E. R. (1979). Consciousness and control: Lessons from hypnosis. *Australian Journal of Clinical & Experimental Hypnosis, 7,* 103–115.

Hilgard, E. R. (1965). *Hypnotic susceptibility*. New York: Harcourt, Brace & World.

Hilgard, E. R. (1992). Dissociation and Theories of Hypnosis. In E. Fromm and M. R. Nash (Eds.). *Contemporary Hypnosis Research,* New York: Guilford Press, p. 69–101.

Hilgard, E. R., & Hilgard, J. R. (1999). *Hypnosis in the relief of pain*. New York: Brunnel/Mazel.

Hilgard, E. R., Hilgard, J. R., Macdonald, J., Morgan, A. H., & Johnson, L. S. (1978). Covert pain in hypnotic analgesia: Its reality as tested by the real-simulator design. *Journal of Abnormal Psychology, 87,* 239–246.

Hill, J. O., & Peters, J. C. (1998). Environmental contributions to the obesity epidemic. *Science, 280,* 1371–1374.

Hill, L., Craig, I. W., Asherson, P., Ball, D., Eley, T., Ninomiya, T., Fisher, P. J. Turic, D., McGuffin, P., Owen, M. J., Chorney, K., Chorney, M. J., Benbow, C. P., Lubinski, D., Thompson, L. A., & Plomin, R. (1999). DNA pooling and dense marker maps: A systematic search for genes for cognitive ability. *Neuroreport, 10,* 843–848.

Hines, M., & Kaufman, F. R. (1994). Androgen and the development of human sex-typical behavior: Rough-and-tumble play and sex of preferred playmates in children with congenital adrenal hyperplasia (CAH). *Child Development, 65,* 1042–1053.

Hirsch, J. (1971). Behavior-genetic analysis and its biosocial consequences. In R. Cancro (Ed.), *Intelligence: Genetic and environmental influences* (pp. 88–106). New York: Grune & Stratton.

Hirsch, J. (1997). The triumph of wishful thinking over genetic irrelevance. *Cahiers de Psychologie Cognitive/Current Psychology of Cognition, 16,* 711–720.

Hirschfeld, R. M. A. (1997). Long-term drug treatment of unipolar depression. *International Clinical Psychopharmacology, 11,* 211–217.

Hobson, J. A. (1995). *Sleep*. New York: Scientific American Library.

Hobson, J. A. (1996, February). How the brain goes out of its mind. *Harvard Mental Health Newsletter, 3.*

Hobson, J. A., & McCarley, R. W. (1977). The brain as a dream state generator: An activation-synthesis hypothesis of the dream process. *American Journal of Psychiatry, 134,* 1335–1348.

Hobson, J. A., Pace-Schott, E., & Stickgold, R. (2000). Dreaming and the Brain: Toward a Cognitive Neuroscience of Conscious States. *Behavioral and Brain Sciences,* 23, in press.

Hochschild, A. (1989). *The Second Shift: Working Parents and the Revolution at Home*. NewYork: Viking.

Hoeksema-van Orden, C. Y. D., Gaillard, A. W. K., & Buunk, B. P. (1998). Social loafing under fatigue. *Journal of Personality and Social Psychology, 75,* 1179–1190 .

Hofer, M., Wolff, C., Friedman, S., & Mason, J. (1972). A psychoendocrine study of bereavement. I: 17-hydroxycorticosteroid excretion rates of parents following death of their children from leukemia *Psychosomatic Medicine, 34,* 481–491.

Hoffart, A. (1998). Cognitive and guided mastery therapy of agoraphobia: Long-term outcome and mechanisms of change. *Cognitive Therapy and Research,22,* 195–207.

Hoffman, D. D., & Richards, W. A. (1984). Parts of recognition. *Cognition, 18,* 65–96.

Hoffman, L. W. (1991). The influence of the family environment on personality: Accounting for sibling differerences. *Psychological Bulletin, 110,* 187–203.

Hogan, J., & Hogan, R. T. (1993). Ambiguities of conscientiousness. Presented at 10th Annual Meeting of Society Industrial and Organizational Psychology, Orlando, FL.

Hohlstein, L. A., Smith, G. T., & Atlas, J. G. (1998). An application of expectancy theory to eating disorders: Development and validation of measures of eating and dieting expectancies. *Psychological Assessment, 10,* 49–58.

Hohman, G. W. (1966). Some effects of spinal cord lesions on experienced emotional feelings. *Psychophysiology, 3,* 143–156.

Holahan, C. K., Holahan, C. J., & Belk, S. S. (1984). Adjustment in aging: The roles of life stress, hassles, and self-efficacy. *Health Psychology, 3,* 3315–328.

Holden, C. (1980). Identical twins reared apart. *Science, 207,* 1323–1328.

Holland, A. J., Sicotte, N., & Treasure, J. (1988). Anorexia nervosa: Evidence for a genetic basis. *Journal of Psychosomatic Research, 32,* 561–571.

Hollerman, J. R., & Schultz, W. (1998). Dopamine neurons report an error in the temporal prediction of reward during learning. *Nature Neuroscience, 1,* 304–309.

Hollerman, J. R., Tremblay, L., & Schultz, W. (1998). Influence of reward expectation on behavior-related neuronal activity in primate striatum. *Journal of Neurophysiology, 80,* 947–963.

Hollis, K. L. (1997). Compenory reserch on pavlovian conditioning: A 'new' functional analysis. *American Psychologist, 52,* 956–965.

Hollon, S. D., & Beck, A. T. (1994). Cognitive and cognitive-behavioral therapies. In A. E. Bergin & S. L. Garfield (Eds.), *Handbook of psycho-*

therapy and behavior change, 4th edition (pp. 428–466). New York: John Wiley & Sons.

Holmes, D. S. (1984). Meditation and somatic arousal reduction. A review of the experimental evidence. American Psychologist, 39, 1–10.

Holmes, N. (1984). Designer's guide to creating charts & diagrams. New York: W. H. Freeman.

Holmes, T. H., & Rahe, R. H. (1967). The social readjustment rating scale. Journal of Psychosomatic Research, 11, 213–218.

Holyoak, K. J., & Thagard, P. (1997). The analogical mind. American Psychologist, 52, 35–44.

Holzman, P. S., Chen, Y., Nakayama, K., Levy, D. L., & Matthysse, S. (1998). How are deficits in motion perception related to eye-tracking dysfunction in schizophrenia? In M. F. Lenzenweger & R. H. Dworkin (Eds.), Origins and Development of Schizophrenia: Advances in Experimental Psychopathology (pp. 161–184). Washington, DC: American Psychological Association.

Holzman, P. S., Kringlen, E., Matthysse, S., Flanagan, S. D., Lipton, R. B., Cramer, S., Levin, S., Lange, K., & Levy, D. L. (1988). A single dominant gene can account for eye tracking dysfunctions and schizophrenia in offspring of discordant twins. Archives of General Psychiatry, 45, 641–647.

Honeybourne, C., Matchett, G., & Davey, G. C. (1993). Expectancy models of laboratory preparedness effects: A UCS-expectancy bias in phylogenetic and ontogenetic fear-relevant stimuli. Behavior Therapy, 24, 253–264.

Honeycutt, J. M. Cantrill, J. G., Kelly, P., & Lambkin, D. (1998). How do I love thee? Let me consider my options: Cognition, verbal strategies, and the escalation of intimacy. Human Communication Research, 25, 39–63.

Honig, A., Hofman, A., Rozendaal, N., & Dingemans, P. (1997). Psychoeducation in bipolar disorder: Effect on expressed emotion. Psychiatry Research, 72, 17–22.

Honorton, C. (1997). The Ganzfeld novice: Four predictors of initial ESP performance. Journal of Parapsychology, 61, 143–158.

Hooley, J. M., & Licht, D. M. (1997). Expressed emotional and causal attributions in the spouses of depressed patients. Journal of Abnormal Psychology, 106, 298–306.

Hooper, F. H., Hooper, J. O., & Colbert, K. K. (1984) Personality and memory correlates of intellectual functioning: Young adulthood to old age. Basel, Switzerland: Karger.

Horesh, N., Amir, Marianne, Kedem, P., Goldberger, Y., & Kotler, M. (1997). Life events in childhood, adolescence and adulthood and the relationship to panic disorder. Acta Psychiatrica Scandinavica, 96, 373–378.

Horn, J. (1985). Remodeling old models of intelligence. In B. B. Wolman (Ed.), Handbook of intelligence (pp. 267–300). New York: Wiley.

Horn, J. (1989). Models of intelligence. In R. L. Linn (Ed.), Intelligence: Measurement, theory, and public policy (pp. 29–73). Urbana, IL: University of Illinois Press.

Horn, J., & Cattell, R. B. (1966). Refinement and test of the theory of fluid and crystallized general intelligences. Journal of Educational Psychology, 57, 253–270.

Horn, J. L. (1986). Intellectual ability concepts. In R. J. Sternberg (Ed.), Advances in the psychology of human intelligence, Vol. 3 (pp. 35–77). Hillsdale, NJ: Erlbaum.

Horn, J. L. (1994). Theory of fluid and crystallized intelligence. In R. J. Sternberg (Ed.), The encyclopedia of human intelligence, Vol. 1 (pp. 443–451). New York: Macmillan.

Horn, J. L., & Noll, J. (1994). A system for understanding cognitive capabilities: A theory and the evidence on which it is based. In D. K. Detterman (Ed.). Current topics in human intelligence, Volume 4: Theories of Intelligence. Norwood, NJ: Ablex.

Horney, K. (1937). Neurotic personality of our times. New York: Norton.

Horowitz, M. J. (1998). Personality disorder diagnoses. American Journal of Psychiatry, 155, 1464.

Hortacsu, N. (1997). Family- and couple-initiated marriages in Turkey. Genetic, Social, and General Psychology Monographs, 123, 325–342.

Horwitz, W. A., Kestenbaum, C., Person, E., & Jarvik, L. (1965). Identical twin—"idiot savants"—calendar calculators. American Journal of Psychiatry, 121, 1075–1079.

House, J., Landis, K., & Umberson, D. (1988). Social relationships and health. Science, 241, 540–545.

House, R. J., & Podsakoff, P. M. (1994). Leadership effectiveness: Past perspectives and future directions for research. In J. Greenberg (Ed.), Organizational behavior: The state of the science (pp. 45–82). Hillsdale, NJ: Erlbaum.

Hovland, C. I., & Weiss, W. (1951). The influence of source credibility on communication effectiveness. Public Opinion Quarterly, 15, 635–650.

Howard, K. I., Kopta, S. M., Krause, M. S., & Orlinsky, D. E. (1986). The does-effect relationship in psychotherapy. American Psychologist, 41, 159–164.

Howell, J. M., & Frost, P. J. (1989). A laboratory study of charismatic leadership. Organizational Behavior & Human Decision Processes, 43, 243–269.

Hsee, C. K., Elaine, H., Carlson, J. G., & Chemtob, C. (1990). The effect of power on susceptibility to emotional contagion. Cognition & Emotion, 4(4), 327–340.

Hubel, D. H., & Wiesel, T. N. (1965). Receptive fields of neurons in two nonstriate visual areas (18 and 19) of the cat. Journal of Neurophysiology, 28, 229–289.

Huddy, L., & Virtanen, S. (1995). Subgroup differentiation and subgroup bias among Latinos as a function of familiarity and positive distinctiveness. Journal of Personality and Social Psychology, 68, 97–108.

Hudspeth, A. J. (1983). The hair cells of the inner ear. Scientific American, 248, 54–64.

Huerta, P. T., Scearce, K. A., Farris, S. M., Empson, R. M., & Prusky, G. T. (1996). Preservation of spatial learning in fyn tryosine kinase knockout mice. Neuroreport, 7, 1685–1689.

Huesmann, L. R., & Eron, L. D. (1986). Television and the aggressive child: A cross-national comparison. Hillsdale, NJ: Erlbaum.

Huesmann, L. R., & Miller, L. S. (1994). Long-term effects of repeated exposure to media violence in childhood. In L. R. Huesmann (Ed.) et al. Aggressive behavior: Current perspectives. (pp. 153–186). New York, NY: Plenum Press.

Huff, D. (1954). How to lie with statistics. New York: Norton.

Hugdahl, K. (1995a). Classical conditioning and implicit learning: The right hemisphere hypothesis. In R. J. Davidson & K. Hugdahl (Eds.), Brain asymmetry, (pp. 235–267). Cambridge, MA: MIT Press.

Hugdahl, K. (1995b). Psychophysiology: The mind-body perspective. Cambridge, MA: Harvard University Press.

Hui, C. H., & Triandis, H. C. (1986). Individualism-collectivism: A study of cross-cultural researchers. Journal of Corss-cultural psychology, 17, 225–248.

Hull, J. G., Van Treuren, R. R., & Virnelli, S. (1987). Hardiness and health: A critique and alternative approach. Journal of Personality & Social Psychology, 53, 518–530.

Hultman, C. M., Wieselgren, I., & Oehman, A. (1997). Relationships between social support, social coping and life events in the relapse of schizophrenic patients. Scandinavian Journal of Psychology, 38, 3–13.

Hummel, J. E., & Biederman, I. (1992). Dynamic binding in a neural network for shape recognition. Psychological Review, 99, 480–517.

Hummel, J. E., & Holyoak, K. J. (1997). Distributed representations of structure: A theory of analogical access and mapping. Psychological Review, 104, 427–466.

Humphreys, G. W., Riddoch, M. J., & Price, C. J. (1997). Top-down processes in object identification: Evidence from experimental psychology, neuropsychology and functional anatomy. Philosophical Transactions of the Royal Society, London, 352, 1275–1282.

Hunt, E. (1995). Will we be smart enough? A cognitive analysis of the coming workforce. New York: Russell Sage.

Hunt, M. (1993). The Story of Psychology. New York: Doubleday.

Hunter, J. E. (1983). A casual analysis of cognitive ability, job knowledge, job performance, and supervisor ratings. In F. Landy, S. Zedeck, & J. Cleveland (Eds.), Performance measurement and theory (pp. 257–266). Hillsdale, NJ: Erlbaum.

Hurvich, L. M., & Jameson, D. (1957). An opponent-process theory of color vision. Psychological Review, 64, 384–404.

Huttenlocher, J. (1968). Constructing spatial images: A strategy in reasoning. Psychological Review, 75(6), 550–560.

Huttenlocher, J., Higgins, E. T., Milligan, L., & Kaufman, B. (1970). The mystery of the "negative equative" construction. Journal of Verbal Learning and Verbal Behavior, 9, 334–341.

Huttenlocher, P. (in press). Neural plasticity. Cambridge, MA: Harvard University Press.

Huttenlocher, P. R. (1990). Morphometric study of human cerebral cortex development. Neuropsychologia, 28(6), 517–527.

Hyde, T. S., & Jenkins, J. J. (1973). Recall for words as a function of semantic, graphic, and syntactic orientation tasks. Journal of Verbal Learning and Verbal Behavior, 12, 471–480.

Hyman, A., Mentzer, T., & Calderone, L. (1979). The contribution of olfaction to taste discrimination. Bulletin of Psychonomic Society, 13, 359–362.

Hyman, I. E., & Billings, F. J. (1998). Individual differences and the creation of false childhood memories. Memory, 6, 1–20.

Hyman, I. E., & Pentland, J. (1996). The role of mental imagery in the creation of false childhood memories. Journal of Memory and Language, 35, 101–117.

Hyman, S. (1998). Personal communication.

Iacono, W. G., Moreau, M., Beiser, M., Fleming, J. A. E., & Lin, T. Y. (1992). Smooth-pursuit eye movement dysfunction and liability for schizophrenia: Implications for genetic modeling. *Journal of Abnormal Psychology, 101,* 104–116.

Iansek, R., & Porter, R. C. (1980). The monkey globus pallidus: Neuronal discharge properties in relation to movement. *Journal of Physiology, 301,* 439–455.

Imber, S. D., Pilkonis, P. A., Sotsky, S. M., Elkin, I., Watkins, J. T., Collins, J. F., Shea, M. T., & Leber, S. R. (1991). Mode-specific effects among three treatments for depression. *Journal of Consulting and Clinical Psychology, 58,* 352–359.

Ingledew, D. K., Hardy, L., & Cooper, C. L. (1997). Do resources bolster coping and does coping buffer stress? An organizational study with longitudinal aspect and control for negative affectivity. *Journal of Occupational Health Psychology, 2,* 118–133.

Inman, D. J., Silver, S. M., & Doghramji, K. (1990). Sleep disturbance in Post-Traumatic Stress Disorder: A comparison with non-PTSD insomnia. *Journal of Traumatic Stress, 3,* 429–437.

Insel, T. R. (1992). Toward a neuroanatomy of obsessive-compulsive disorder. *Archives of General Psychiatry, 49,* 739–744.

Inui, A. (1999). Feeding and body-weight regulation by hypothalamic neuropeptides—mediation of the actions of leptin. *Trends in Neurosciences, 22,* 62–67.

Ironson, G., Wynings, C., Schneiderman, N., Baum, A., Rodriguez, M., Greenwood, D., Benight, C., Antoni, M., LaPerriere, A., Huang, H., Klimas, N., & Fletcher, M. A. (1997). Posttraumatic stress symptoms, intrusive thoguhts, loss, and immune function after Hurricane Andrew. *Psychosomatic Medicine, 59,* 128–141.

Irwin, M., Lacher, U., & Caldwell, C. (1992). Depression and reduced natural killer cytotoxicity: a longitudinal study of depressed patients and control subjects. *psychological Medicine, 22,* 1045–50.

Isenberg, D. J. (1986). Group polarization: A critical review and meta-analysis. *Journal of Personality & Social Psychology, 50,* 1141–115?.

Ivry, R. B., & Robertson, L. C. (1998). *The two sides of perception.* Cambridge, MA: The MIT Press.

Ivy, G., MacLeod, C., Petit, T., & Markus, E. (1992). A physiological framework for perceptual and cognitive changes in aging. In F. I. M. Craik & T. A. Salthouse (Eds.), *The handbook of aging and cognition* (pp. 273–314). Hillsdale, NJ: Erlbaum.

Izard, C. E. (1971). *The face of emotion.* New York: Appleton-Century-Crofts.

Jacklin, C. N., & Reynolds, C. (1993). Gender and childhood socialization. In A. E. Beall & R. J. Sternberg (Eds.), *The psychology of gender* (pp. 197–214). New York: Guilford Press.

Jackson, N., & Butterfield, E. (1986). A conception of giftedness designed to promote research. In R. J. Sternberg & J. E. Davidson (Eds.), *Conceptions of giftedness* (pp. 151–181). New York: Cambridge University Press.

Jackson, P., & Delehanty, H. (1995). *Sacred hoops : spiritual lessons of a hardwood warrior.* New York: Hyperion.

Jackson, S. E., Brett, J. F., Sessa, V. I., Cooper, D. M., Julin, J. A., & Peyronnin, K. (1991). Some differences make a difference: Indivdiual dissimilarity and group hertergeneity as correlates of recruitment, promotion, and turnover. *Jouranl fo Applied Psychology, 76,* 675–689.

Jacobs, R. C., & Campbell, D. T. (1961). The perpetuation of an arbitrary tradition through several generations of a laboratory microculture. *Journal of Abnormal and Social Psychology, 62,* 649–648.

Jacobsen, A., & Gilchrist, A. (1988a). Hess and Pretori revisited: Resolution of some old contradictions. *Perception & Psychophysics, 43,* 7–14.

Jacobsen, A., & Gilchrist, A. (1988b). The ratio principle holds over a million-to-one range of illumination. *Perception & Psychophysics, 43,* 1–6.

Jacobsen, P. B., Bovbjerg, D. H., Schwartz, M. D., & Andrykowski, M. A. (1994). Formation of food aversions in patients receiving repeated infusions of chemotherapy. *Behavior Research & Therapy, 38,* 739–748.

Jacobson, B. H., Aldana, S. G., Goetzel, R. Z., Vardell, K. D., et al (1996). The relationship between perceived stress and self-reported illness-related absenteeism. *American Journal of Health Promotion, 11,* 54–61.

Jacobson, E. (1925). Progressive Relaxation. *American Journal of Psychology, 36,* 73–87.

Jacobson, N. S., & Christensen, A. (1996). Studying the effectiveness of psychotherapy: How well can clinical trials do the job? *American Psychologist, 51,* 1031–1039.

Jacobson, N. S., Dobson, K. S., Truax, P. A., Addis, M. E., Koerner, K., Gollan, J. K., Gortner, E., & Prince, S. E. (1996). A Component Analysis of Cognitive-Behavioral Treatment for Depression. *Journal of Consulting and Clinical Psychology, 64,* 295–304.

Jacoby, L. L., & Dallas, M. (1981). On the relationship between autobiographical memory and perceptual learning. *Journal of Experimental Psychology: General, 110,* 306–340.

Jadack, R. A., Hyde, J. S., Moore, C. F., & Keller, M. L. (1995). Moral reasoning about sexually transmitted diseases. *Child Development, 66,* 167–177.

Jakobson, R., & Halle, M. (1956). *Fundamentals of language* . The Hague: Mouton.

James, L. E., Burke, D. M., Austin, A., & Hulme, E. (1998). Production and perception of "verbosity" in younger and older adults. *Psychology and Aging, 13,* 355–367.

James, W. (1884). What is emotion? *Mind, 9,* 188–205.

James, W. (1890/1950). *Principles of psychology.* New York: Dover.

Jamison, K. R. (1989). Mood disorders and patterns of creativity in British writers and artists. *Psychiatry, 52,* 125–134.

Jamison, K. R. (1993). *Touched With Fire: Manic-Depressive Illness and the Artistic Temperament.* New York: Free Press.

Jamison, K. R. (1995). *An Unquiet Mind: A Memoir of Moods and Madness.* New York: Vintage Books, p. 67.

Jamison, K. R., Gerner, R. H., Hammen, C., & Padesky, C. (1980). Clouds and silver linings: Positive experiences associated with primary affective disorders. *American Journal of Psychiatry, 137,* 198–202.

Jamner, L. D., & Leigh, H. (1999). Repressive/defensive coping, endogen fous opioids and health: How a life so perfect can make you sick. *Psychiatry Research, 85,* 17–31.

Jamner, L. D., Schwartz, G. E., & Leigh, H. (1988). The relationship between repressive and defensive coping styles and monocyte, eosinophile, and serum glucose levels: Support for the opioid peptide hypothesis of repression. *Psychosomatic Medicine, 50,* 567–575.

Jancke, L., & Steinmetz, H. (1994). Interhemispheric-transfer time and corpus callosum size. *Neuroreport, 5,* 2385–2388.

Jang, K. L. (1993). *A behavioral genetic analysis of personality, personality disorder, the environment, and the search for sources of nonshared environmental influences.* Unpublished doctoral dissertation, University of Western Ontario, London, Ontario.

Jang, K. L., Livesley, W. J., & Vernon, P. A. (1996). Heritability of the Big Five personality dimensions and their facets: A twin study. *Journal of Personality, 64,* 577–91.

Janis, I. L. (1954). Personality correlates to susceptibility to persuasion. *Journal of Personality, 22,* 504–518.

Janis, I. L. (1972). *Victims of groupthink.* Boston: Houghton Mifflin.

Janis, I. L. (1982). *Victims of groupthink* (2nd ed.). Boston: Houghton Miffin.

Janowiak, J. J. (1994). Meditation and college students' self-actualization and rated stress. *Psychological Reports, 75,* 1007–1010.

Janowsky, J. S., Oviatt, S. K., & Orwoll, E. S. (1994). Testosterone influences spatial cognitin in older men. *Behavioral Neuroscience, 108,* 325–332.

Jansma, L. L., Linz, D. G., Mulac, A., & Imrich, D. J. (1997). Men's interactions with women after viewing sexually explicit films: Does degradation make a difference? *Communication Monographs, 64,* 1–24

Jarvis, W. B. G., & Petty, R. E. (1996). The need to evaluate. *Journal of Personality and Social Psychology, 70,* 172–194.

Jeannerod, M. (1994). The representing brain: Neural correlates of motor intention and imagery. *Behavioral & Brain Sciences, 17,* 187–245.

Jeannerod, M. (1995). Mental imagery in the motor context. *Neuropsychologia, 33,* 1419–1432.

Jenike, M. (1984). Obsessive-comulsive disorder: A question of a neurologic lesion. *Compr. Psychiatry, 25,* 298–304.

Jenkins-Hall, K., & Sacco, W. P. (1991). Effects of client race and depression on evaluations by white therapists. *Journal of Social Clinical Psychology, 10,* 322–333.

Jensen, A. R. (1969). How much can we boost IQ and scholastic achievement? *Harvard Educational Review, 39,* 1–123.

Jensen, A. R. (1980). *Bias in mental testing.* New York: Free Press.

Jensen, A. R. (1987). Psychometric g as a focus of concerted research effort. *Intelligence, 11,* 193–198.

Jensen, A. R. (1991). General mental ability: From psychometrics to biology. Paper presented at the Annual Meeting of the American Association for the Advancement of Science, Washington, DC.

Jensen, A. R. (1993). Why is reaction time correlated with psychometric g? *Current Directions in Psychological Science, 2,* 53–56.

Jensen, A. R. (1998). *The g factor: The science of mental ability.* Westport, CT: Praeger.

Jensen, J. P., Bergin, A. E., & Greaves, D. W. (1990). The meaning of eclecticism: New survey and analysis of commponents. *Professional Psychology: Research and Practice, 21,* 124–130.

Jevning, R., Wallace, R. K., & Beidebach, M. (1992). The physiology of Meditation: A review. A wadeful hypnometabolic integrated response. *Neuroscience and Biobehavioral Reviews, 16,* 415–424.

Johnson, J. A. (2000). Predicting observers' ratings of the Big Five from the CPI, HPI, and NEO-PI-R: A comparative validity study. *European Journal of Personality, 4,* 1–19.

Johnson, J. A., Germer, C. K., Efran, J. S., & Overton, W. F. (1988). Personality as the basis of theoretical predilections. *Journal of Personality and Social Psychology, 55*, 824–835.

Johnson, J. D., Noel, N. E., & Sutter, J. (in press). Alcohol and male sexual aggression: A cognitive disruption analysis. *Journal of Applied Social Psychology.*

Johnson, L. S., & Wright, D. G. (1975). Self-hypnosis versus heterohypnosis: Experiential and Behavioral Comparisons. *Journal of Abnormal Psychology, 85*, 523–526.

Johnson, M. K., Hashtroudi, S., & Lindsy, D. S. (1993). Source monitoring. *Psychological Bulletin, 114*, 3–28.

Johnson, M. K., Nolde, S. F., Mather, M., Kounios, J., Schacter, D. L., & Curran, T. (1997). The similarity of brain activity associated with true and false recognition memory depends on test format. *Psychological Science, 8*, 250–257.

Johnson, M. K., & Raye, C. L. (1981). Reality monitoring. *Psychological Review, 88*, 67–85.

Johnson, M. R., & Lydiard, B. (1995). Personality disorders in social phobia. *Psychiatric Annals, 25*, 554–563.

Johnson, S. (2000). The recognition of mentalistic agents in infancy. *Trends in Cognitive Sciences, 4*, 22–28.

Johnson, S. C., & Carey, S. (1998). Knowledge enrichment and conceptual change in folkbiology: Evidence from Williams syndrome. *Cognitive Psychology, 37*, 156–200.

Johnson, S. D., & Bechler, C. (1998). Examining the relationship between listening effectiveness and leadership emergence: Perceptions, behaviors, and recall. *Small Group Research, 29*, 452–471.

Johnson, S. L., & Miller, I. (1997). Negative life events and time to recovery from episodes of bipolar disorder. *Journal of Abnormal Psychology, 106*, 449–457.

Johnson, S. M., & Roberts, J. E. (1995). Life events and bipolar disorder: Implications from biological theories. *Psychological Bulletin, 117*, 434–449.

Johnson-Laird, P. N. (1983). *Mental models.* Cambridge, MA: Harvard University Press.

Johnson-Laird, P. N. (1995). Mental models, deductive reasoning, and the brain. In M. S. Gazzaniga (Ed.), *The cognitive neurosciences* (pp. 999–1008). Cambridge, MIT Press.

Johnson-Laird, P. N., & Oatley, K. (1989). The language of emotions: An analysis of a semantic field. *Cognition and Emotion, 3*, 81–123.

Johnson-Laird, P. N., and Oatley, K. (1992). Basic emotions, rationality and folk theory. *Cognition and Emotion, 6*, 201–223.

Johnston, L. C., & Macrae, C. N. (1994). Changing social stereotypes: The case of the information seeker. *European Journal of Social Psychology, 24*, 581–592.

Johnston, L. D., O'Malley, P. M., & Bachman, J. G. (1994). *National survey results on drug use from the Monitoring the Future study, 1975–1993* (NIH Publication No. 94–3810). Washington, DC: U.S. Government Printing Office.

Johnstone, E. C. (1998). Predictive symptomatology, course, and outcome in first-episode schizophrenia. *International Clinical Psychopharmacology, 13*, S97–S99

Joiner, T. E. (1994). Contagious depression: Existence, specificity to depressed symptoms, and the role of reassurance seeking. *Journal of Personality and Social Psychology, 67*, 287–296.

Jolicoeur, P. (1998). Modulation of the attentional blink by on-line response selection: Evidence from speeded and unspeeded Task 1 decisions. *Memory & Cognition, 26*, 1014–1032.

Jones, C. J., & Meredith, W. (1996). Patterns of personality change across the life span. *Psychology and Aging, 11*, 57–65.

Jones, D., & Hill, K. (1993). Criteria of facial attractiveness in five populations. *Human Nature, 4*, 271–296.

Jones, E. E., & Nisbett, R. E. (1971). *The actor and the observer: Divergent perceptions of the causes of behavior.* Morristown, NJ: General Learning Press.

Jones, M. C. (1924a). The elimination of children's fears. *Journal of Experimental Psychology, 7*, 383–390.

Jones, M. C. (1924b). A laboratory study of fear: The case of Peter. *Journal of Genetic Psychology, 31*, 308–315.

Jones, M. K., & Menzies, R. G. (1995). The etiology of fear of spiders. *Anxiety, Stress & Coping: An International Journal, 8*, 227–234.

Jones, N. A., Field, T., & Davalos, M. (1998). Massage therapy attenuates right frontal EEG asymmetry in one-month-old infants of depressed mothers. *Infant Behavior & Development, 21*, 527–530.

Jones, T. A., & Greenough, W. T. (1996). Ultrastructural evidence for increased contact between astrocytes and synapses in rats reared in a complex environment. *Neurobiology of Learning and Memory, 65*, 48–56.

Jonides, J., Schumacher, E. H., Smith, E. E., Koeppe, R. A., Awh, E., Reuter Lorenz, P. A., Marshuetz, C., & Willis, C. R. (1998). The role of parietal cortex in verbal working memory. *Journal of Neuroscience, 18*, 5026–5034.

Jonides, J., Schumacher, E. H., Smith, E. E., Lauber, E. J., Awh, E., Minoshima, S., & Koeppe, R. A. (1997). Verbal working memory load affects regional brain activation as measured by PET. *Journal of Cognitive Neuroscience, 9*, 462–475.

Jonides, J., Smith, E. E., Koeppe, R. A., Awh, E., Minoshima, S., Mintin, M. A. (1993) Spatial working memory in humans as revealed by PET. *Nature, 363*, 623–625.

Joseph, S., Williams, R., & Yule, W. (1995). Psychosocial perspectives on post-traumatic stress disorder. *Clinical Psychology Review, 15*, 515–544.

Judd, C. M., Ryan, C. S., & Parke, B. (1991). Accuracy in the judgment of in-group and out-group variability. *Journal of Personality and Social Psychology, 61*, 366–379.

Judd, L. L., Akiskal, H. S., . Maser, J. D., Zeller, P. J., Endicott, J., Coryell, W., Paulus, M. P., Kunovac, J. L., Leon, A. C., Mueller, T. I., Rice, J. A., & Keller, M. B. (1998). A Prospective 12–Year Study of Subsyndromal and Syndromal Depressive: Symptoms in Unipolar Major Depressive Disorders. *Archives of General Psychiatry, 55*, 694–700.

Jusczyk, P. W. (1995). Language acquisition: Speech sounds and phonological development. In J. L. Miller & P. D. Eimas (Eds.), *Handbook of perception and cognition: Vol. 11. Speech, language, and communication* (pp. 263–301). Orlando, FL: Academic Press.

Kaas, J. H. (1995). The reorganization of sensory and motor maps in adult mammals. In M. S. Gazzaniga (Ed.), *The cognitive neurosciences* (pp. 51–71). Cambridge, MA: MIT Press.

Kabat-Zinn, J., Wheeler, E., Light, T., Skillings, A., Scharf, M. J., Copley, T. G., Hosmer, D., & Bernhard, J. D. (1998). Influence of a mindfulness meditation-based stress reduction intervention on rates of skin clearing in patients with moderate to severe psoriasis undergoing phototherapy (UVB) and photochemotherapy (PUVA). *Psychosomatic Medicine, 60*, 625–632.

Kagan, J. (1989a). Temperamental contributions to social behavior. *American Psychologist, 44*, 668–674.

Kagan, J. (1989b). *Unstable ideas: Temperament, cognition, and self.* Cambridge, MA: Cambridge University Press.

Kagan, J. (1992). Behavior, biology, and the meanings of temperamental constructs. *Pediatrics, 90*, 510–513.

Kagan, J. (1994a). *Galen's prophecy.* New York: Basic Books.

Kagan, J. (1994b). On the nature of emotion. *Monographs of the Society for Research in Child Development, 59*, 7–24, 250–283.

Kagan, J. (1996). Three pleasing ideas. *American Psychologist, 51*(9), 901–908.

Kagan, J., & Snidman, N. (1991). Temperamental factors in human development. *American Psychologist, 46*, 856–862.

Kagan, J., Kearsley, R. B., & Zelazo, P. R. (1978). *Infancy: Its place in human development.* Cambridge, MA: Harvard University Press.

Kagan, J., Reznick, J. S., & Snidman, N. (1988). Biological bases of childhood shyness. *Science, 240*, 167–171.

Kagan, J., Snidman, N., & Arcus, D. (1998). Childhood derivatives of high and low reactivity in infancy. *Child Development, 69*, 1483–1493.

Kagan, J., Snidman, N., Arcus, D., & Reznick, J. S. (1994). *Galen's prophecy: Temperament in human nature.* New York: Basic Books.

Kagan, R. M., & Reid, W. J. (1986). Critical factors in the adoption of emotionally disturbed youths. *Child Welfare, 65*, 63–73.

Kahn, P. H., Jr. (1992). Children's obligatory and discretionary moral judgments. *Child Development, 63*, 416–430.

Kahneman, D., & Knetsch, J. (1993). *Strong influences and shallow inferences: An analysis of some anchoring effects.* Unpublished manuscript, University of California, Berkeley.

Kahneman, D., & Tversky, A. (1996). On the reality of cognitive illusions: A reply to Gigerenzer's critique. *Psychological Review, 103*, 582–591.

Kail, R. (1988). Developmental functions speeds of cognitive processes. *Journal of Experimental Child Psychology, 45*, 339–364.

Kail, R. (1991). Processing time declines exponentially during childhood and adolescence. *Developmental Psychology, 27*, 259–266.

Kalimo, R., Tenkanen, L., Haermae, M., Poppius, E., & Heinsalmi, P. (2000). Job stress and sleep disorders: Findings from the Helsinki Heart Study. *Stress Medicine, 16*, 65–75.

Kalish, R. A., & Reynolds, D. K. (1977). The role of age in death attitudes. *Death Education, 1*, 205–230.

Kalivas, P. W., & Nakamura, M. (1999). Neural systems for behavioral activation and reward. *Current Opinion in Neurobiology, 9*, 223–227.

Kameda, T., & Sugimori, S. (1993). Psychological entrapment in group decision making: An assigned decision rule and a groupthink phenomenon. *Journal of Personality and Social Psychology, 65*, 282–292.

Kamin, L. (1969). Predictability, surprise, attention and conditioning. In B. A. Camppbell and R. M. Church (Eds.), *Punishment and aversive behavior.* New York: Appleton-Century-Crofts.

Kaniasty, K., & Norris, F. H. (1992). Social support and victims of crime: Matching event, support, and outcome. *American Journal of Community Psychology*, 20, 211–241.

Kaniasty, K. Z., Norris, F. H., & Murrell, S. A. (1990). Received and perceived social support following natural disaster. *Journal of Applied Psychology*, 20, 85–114.

Kanner, A. D., Coyne, J. C., Schaefer, C., & Lazarus, R. S. (1981). Comparison of two modes of stress management: Daily hassles and uplifts versus major life events. *Journal of Behavioral Medicine, 4*, 1–39.

Kanwisher, N. (1991). Repetition blindness and illusory conjunctions: Errors in binding visual types with visual tokens. *Journal of Experimental Psychology: Human Perception and Performance*, 17, 404–421.

Kanwisher, N. G. (1987). Repetition blindness: Type recognition without token individuation. *Cognition*, 27, 117–143.

Kaplan, F. (1997, January 19). Looks count. *Boston Sunday Globe*, E1.

Kaplan, H. S. (1979). *Disorders of sexual desire*. New York: Brunner/Mazel

Kaplan, H. S. (1981). *The New Sex Therapy: Active Treatment of Sexual Dysfunctions*. New York: Brunner/Mazel.

Kaplan, M. F. (1987). The influencing procedss in group decision making. In C. Hendrick (Ed.), *Review of Personality and Social Psychology* (Vol. 8, pp. 189–212). Newbury Park, CA: Sage.

Karacan, I., Goodenough, D. R., Shapiro, A., & Starker, S. (1966). Erection cycle during sleep in relatin to dream anxiety. *Archives of General Psychiatry*, 15, 183–189.

Karau, S. J., & Williams, K. D. (1993). Social loafing: A meta-analytic review and theoretical integration. *Journal of Personality and Social Psychology, 65*, 681–706.

Karayiorgou, M., Altemus, M., Galke, B. L., Goldman, D., Murphy, D. L., Ott, J., & Gogos, J. A. (1997). Genotype determining low catechol-O-methyltransferase activity as a risk factor for obsessive-compulsive disorder. *Proceedings of the National Academy of Sciences, 94*, 4572–4575.

Karkowski, L. M., & Kendler, K. S. (1997). An examination of the genetic relationship between bipolar and unipolar illness in an epidemiological sample. *Psychiatric Genetics, 7*, 159–163.

Karni, A., & Bertini, G. (1997). Learning perceptual skills: Behavioral probes into adult cortical plasticity. *Current Opinion in Neurobiology, 7*, 530–535.

Karni, A., & Sagi, D. (1993). The time course of learning a visual skill. *Nature, 365*, 250–252.

Karni, A., Tanne, D., Rubenstein, B. S., Askenasi, J. J. M., & Sagi, D. (1994). Dependence on REM sleep of overnight improvement of a perceptual skill. *Science, 265*, 679–682.

Karpov, Y. V., & Haywood, H. C. (1998). Two ways to elaborate Vygotsky's concept of mediation. *American Psychologist, 53*, 27–36.

Karuza, J., & Carey, T. O. (1984). Relevance preference and adaptiveness of behavioral blame for observers of rape victims. *Journal of Personality, 52* 249–262.

Kass, S. (1999). Breast cancer intervention group aids physical healing, research find. *APA Monitor*, October, p. 7.

Kassin, S. M. (1997). The psychology of confession evidence. *American Psychologist, 52*, 221–233.

Kassin, S. M., & Kiechel, K. L. (1996). The social psychology of false confessions: Compliance, internatlization, and confabulation. *Psychological Science, 7*, 125–128.

Kassin, S. M., & Wrightsman, L. S. (1981). Coerced confessions, judicial instruction, and mock juror verdicts. *Journal of Applied Social Psychology, 11*, 489–506.

Katchadourian, H. (1977). *The biology of adolescence*. San Francisco: Freeman.

Katigbak, M. S., Church, A. T., & Akamine, T. X. (1996). Cross-Cultural generalizability of personality dimensions: Relating indigenous and imported dimensions in two cultures. *Journal of Personality and Social Psychology, 70*, 99–114.

Katz, J., Beach, S. R. H., & Joiner, T. E. (1999). Contagious depression in dating couples. *Journal of Social & Clinical Psychology, 18*(1), 1–13.

Kaufman, L., & Kaufman, J. H. (2000). Explaining the moon illusion. *Proceedings of the National Academy of Sciences, USA, 97*, 500–505.

Kaufman, L., & Rock, I. (1962). The moon illusion, I. *Science, 136*, 953–961.

Kaufman, M. H. (1997). The teratogenic effects of alcohol following exposure during pregnancy, and its influence on the chromosome constitution of the pre-ovulatory egg. *Alcohol & Alcoholism, 32*, 113–128.

Kaufmann, G. (1990). Imagery effects on problem solving. In P. J. Hampson, D. E. Marks, & J. T. E. Richardson (Eds.), *Imagery: Current developments* (pp. 169–197). London and New York: Routledge.

Kavanagh, D. J. (1992). Recent developments in expressed emoition in schizophrenia. *British Journal of Psychiatry, 148*, 601–620.

Kaye, W. H. (1995). Neurotransmitters and anorexia nervosa. In K. D. Brownell & C. G. Fairburn (Eds.), *Eating Disorders and Obesity: A Comprehensive Handbook* (pp. 255–260). New York: Guilford Press.

Kazdin, A. E. (1994). Methodology, design, and evaluation in psychotherapy research. In A. E. Bergin & S. L. Garfield (Eds.), *Handbook of psychotherapy and behavior change, 4th edition* (pp. 19–71). New York: John Wiley & Sons.

Keane, R. M., Kolb, L. C., Kaloupek, D. G., Orr, S. P., Blanchard, E. B., Thomas, R. G., Hsieh, F. Y., & Lavori, P. W. (1998). Utility of psychophysiology measurement in the diagnosis of posttraumatic stress disorder: Results from a department of Veteran's Affairs cooperative study. *Journal of Consulting and Clinical Psychology*, 914–923.

Keane, T. M., Zimering, R. T., & Caddell, J. M. (1985). A behavioral formulation of post-traumatic stress disorder in Vietnam veterans. *The Behavior Therapist, 8*, 9–12.

Keefe, R. S. E., Silva, S. G., Perkins, D. O., & Lieberman, J. A. (1999). The effects of atypical antipsychotic drugs on neurocognitive impairment in schizophrenia: A review and meta-analysis. *Schizophrenia Bulletin, 25*, 201–222.

Keeton, W. T., Larkin, T. S., & Windsor, D. M. (1974). Normal fluctuations in the earth's magnetic field influence pigeon orientation. *Journal of Comparative Physiology, 95*, 95–103.

Keil, F. C. (1989a). *Concepts, kind, and cognitive development*. Cambridge, MA: MIT Press.

Keil, F. C. (1989b). The origins of an autonomous biology. In M. R. Gunnar & M. Marstsos (Eds.), *The Minnesota symposium on child psychology: Vol. 25. Modularity and constraints in language and cognition* (pp. 103–137). Hillsdale, NJ: Erlbaum.

Keil, F. C., & Silberstein, C. S. (1996). Schooling and the acquisition of theoretical knowledge. In D. R. Olson & N. Torrance (Eds.), *Handbook of education and human development: New models of learning, teaching and schooling*. Cambridge, MA: Blackwell.

Keith, P. M., & Schafer, R. B. (1991). *Relationships and well-being over the life stages*. New York: Praeger.

Keitner, G. I., Solomon, D. A., Ryan, C. E., Miller, I. W., & Mallinger, A. (1996). Prodromal and residual symptoms in bipolar I disorder. *Comprehensive Psychiatry, 37*, 362–367.

Kelleher, R. T. (1956). Intermittant reinforcement in chimpanzees. *Science, 124*, 679–680.

Kelleher, R. T. (1957). Conditioned reinforcement in chimpanzees. *Journal of Comparative and Physiological Psychology, 49*, 571–575.

Kelleher, R. T. (1958). Fixed-ratio schedules of conditioned reinforcement with cimpanzees. *Journal of the Experimental Analysis of Behavior, 1*, 281–289.

Keller, A., Ford, L. H., & Meacham, J. A. (1978). Dimensions of self-concept in preschool children. *Developmental Psychology, 14*, 483–489.

Kelley, H. H. (1972). Attribution in social interaction. In E. E. Jones , D. E. Kanouse, H. H. Kelley, R. E. Nisbett, S. Vahns, & B. Weiner (Eds.), *Attribution: Perceiving the causes of behavior*. Morristown, NJ: General Learning Press.

Kelley, H. H. (1979). *Personal relationships: Their structures and processes*. Hillsdale, NJ: Erlbaum.

Kelley, H. H., & Michela, J. L. (1980). Attribution theory and research. *Annual Review of Psychology, 31*, 57–501.

Kelley, T. (1998, October 1). To surf, perchance to dream. *New York Times*, E1, E5.

Kelley, W. M., Miezin, F. M., McDermott, K. B., Buckner, R. L., Raichle, M. E., Cohen, N. J., Ollinger, J. M., Akbudak, E., Conturo, T. E., Znyder, A. Z., & Petersen, S. E. (1998). Hemispheric specialization in human dorsal frontal cortex and medial temporal lobe for verbal and nonverbal memory encoding. *Neuron, 20*, 927–936.

Kelling, G. L., & Coles, C. M. (1996). *Fixing Broken Windows: Restoring order and reducing crime in our communities*. New York: Touchstone.

Kellogg, W. N., & Kellogg, L. A. (1933). *The ape and the child*. New York: McGraw-Hill.

Kelman, H. (1997). Group processes in the resolution of international conflicts. *American Psychologist, 52*, 212–220.

Kelsey, B. L. (1998). The dynamics of multicultural groups: Ethnicity as a determinant of leadership. *Small Group Research, 29*, 602–623.

Kelsey, J. E., & Baker, M. D. (1983). Ventromedial septal lesions in rats reduce the effects of inescapable shock on escape performance and analgesia. *Behavioral Neuroscience, 97*, 945–961.

Kemp, D. T. (1978). Stimulated acoustic emissions from within the human auditory system. *Journal of the Acoustical Society of America, 64*, 1386–1391.

Kemp, D. T. (1979). Evidence of mechanical nonlinearity and frequency selective wave amplification in the cochlea. *Archives of Otology, Rhinology, and Laryngology, 224*, 37–45.

Kendler, K. S., & Diehl, S. R. (1993). The genetics of schizophrenia: A current genetic-epidemiologic perspective. *Schizophrenia Bulletin, 19*, 87–112.

Kendler, K. S., & Gardner, C. O. (1998). Boundaries of major depression: An evaluation of DSM–IV criteria *American Journal of Psychiatry, 155,* 172–177.

Kendler, K. S., Gardner, C. O., & Prescott, C. A. (1999). Clinical Characteristics of Major Depression That Predict Risk of Depression in Relatives. *Archives of General Psychiatry, 56,* 322–327.

Kendler, K. S., MacLean, C., Neale, M., Kessler, R. C., Heath, A. C., & Eaves, L. J. (1991). The genetic epidemiology of bulimia nervosa. *American Journal of Psychiatry, 148,* 1627–1637.

Kendler, K. S., Neale, M. C., Kessler, R. C., Heath, A. C., & Eaves, L. J. (1993). A twin study of recent life events and difficulties. *Archives of General Psychiatry, 50,* 789–796.

Kendler, K. S., Neale, M., Kessler, R. C., Heath, A., & Eaves, L. (1992). The genetic epidemiology of phobias in women: The interrelationship of agoraphobia, social phobia, situational phobia and simple phobia. *Archives of General Psychiatry, 49,* 273–281.

Kennedy, M. M. (1979). *The mystery of hypnosis.* New York: Contemporary Perspectives.

Kennedy, S. H., Javanmard, M., Franco, J., & Vaccarino, F. J. (1997). A review of functional neuroimaging in mood disorders: Positron Emission Tomography and Depression. *Canadian Journal of Psychiatry, 42,* 467–475.

Kenny, D. A., & LaVoie, L. (1982). Reciprocity of attraction: A confirmed hypothesis. *Social Psychology Quarterly, 45,* 54–58.

Kenrick, D. T., & Stringfeld, D. O. (1980). Personality traits and the eye of the beholder: Crossing some traditional philosophical boundaries in search for consistency in all the people. *Psychological Review, 87,* 88–104.

Kerr, M., Lambert, W. W., Stattin, H., & Klackenberg-Larsson, I. (1994). Stability of inhibition in a Swedish longitudinal sample. *Child Development, 65,* 138–146.

Kerr, N. L., & Kaufman-Gilliland, C. M. (1997). " . . . and besides, I probably couldn't have made a difference anyway": Justification of social dilemma defection via perceived self-inefficacy. *Journal of Experimental Social Psychology, 33,* 211–230.

Kertesz, A. (1981). Anatomy of jargon. In J. Brown (Ed.), *Jargonaphasia* (pp. 63–112). New York: Academic Press.

Keshavan, M. S., Anderson, S., & Pettigrew, J. W. (1994). Is schizophrenia due to excessive synaptic pruning in the prefrontal cortex? The Feinberg hypothesis revisited. *Journal of Psychiatry Research, 28,* 239–265.

Kessler, R. C., & Frank, R. G. (1997). The impact of psychiatric disorders on work loss days. *Psychological Medicine, 27,* 861–873.

Kessler, R. C., Kendler, K. S., Heath, A., Neale, M. C., & Eaves, L. J. (1992). Social support, depressed mood, and the adjustment to stress: A genetic epidemiologic investigation. *Journal of Personality and Social Psychology, 62,* 257–272.

Kessler, R. C., McGonagle, K. A., Zhao, S., Nelson, C. B., Hughes, M., Eshelman, S., Whittchen, H. N., & Dendler, K. S. (1994). Lifetime and 12-month prevalence of DSM–III—R psychiatric disorders in the United States: Results from the National Comorbidity Study. *Archives of General Psychiatry, 51,* 8–19.

Kessler, R. C., Rubinow, D. R., Holmes, C., Abelson, J. M., & Zhao, S. (1997). The epidemiology of DSM–III-R bipolar I disorder in a general population. *Psychological Medicine, 27,* 1079–1089.

Kessler, R. C., Stang, P. E., Wittchen, H., Ustun, T., Bedirhan, R., Burne, P. P., & Walters, E. E. (1998). Lifetime panic-depression comorbidity in the National Comorbidity Survey. *Archives of General Psychiatry, 55,* 801–808.

Kessler, R. C., Stein, M. B., & Berglund, P. (1998). Social phobia subtypes in the National Comorbidity Survey. *American Journal of Psychiatry, 155,* 613–619.

Kety, S. (1974). Biochemical and neurochemical effects of electroconvulsive shock. In M. Fink, S. Kety, J. McGaugh, & T. A. Williams (Eds.), *Psychobiology of Convulsive Therapy* (pp. 285–294). Washington, DC: Winston.

Kety, S. S. (1974). From rationalization to reason. *American Journal of Psychiatry, 131,* 957–963.

Keverne, E. B. (1997). Genomic imprinting in the brain: Commentary. *Current Opinion in Neurobiology, 7,* 463–468.

Keys, A., Brozek, J., Henschel, A., Mickelsen, O., & Taylor, H. L. (1950). *The biology of human starvation.* Minneapolis: University of Minnesota Press.

Khwaja, A. (1997). Use and abuse in the countertransference. *Psychoanalytic Psychotherapy, 11,* 101–117.

Kidd, K. K. (1993). Associations of disease with genetic markers: Déjà vu all over again. *Neuropsychiatric Genetics, 48,* 71–73.

Kiecolt-Glaser, J., Garner, W., Speicher, C., Penn, G., & Glaser, R. (1984). Psychosocial modifiers of immuno-competence in medical students. *Psychosomatic Medicine, 46,* 7–14.

Kiecolt-Glaser, J., Glaser, R., Strain, E., Stout, J., Tarr, K., Holliday, J., & Speicher, C. (1986). Modulation of cellular immunity in medical students. *Journal of Behavioral Medicine, 9,* 5–?.

Kiecolt-Glaser, J. K., Kennedy, S., Malkoff, S., Fisher, L., Speicher, C., & Glaser, R. (1988). Marital discord and immunity in males. *Psychosomatic Medicine, 50,* 213–229.

Kiecolt-Glaser, J. K., Marucha, P. T., Malarky, W. B., Mercado, A. M., & Glaser, R. (1995). Slowing of wound healing by psychological stress. *The Lancet, 346,* 1194–1196.

Kiecolt-Glaser, J. K., Page, G. G., Marucha, P. T., MacCallum, R. C., & Glaser, R. (1998). Psychological Influences on Surgical Recovery Perspectives From Psychoneuroimmunology. *American Psychologist, 53,* 1209–1218.

Kiepenheuer, J. (1982). The effect of magnetic anomalies on the homing behavior of pigeons: An attempt to analyze the possible factors involved. In F. Papi & H. G. Wallraff (Eds.), *Animal navigation* (pp. 120–128). Berlin: Springer-Verlag.

Kiepenheuer, J. (1986). A further analysis of the orientation behavior of homing pigeons released within magnetic anomalies. In G. Maret, N. Boccara, & J. Kiepenheuer (Eds.), *Biophysical effects of steady magnetic fields* (pp. 148–153). Berlin: Springer-Verlag.

Kiesler, C. A., & Kiesler, S. B. (1969). *Conformity.* Reading, MA: Addison-Wesley.

Kihlstrom, J. F. (1985). Hypnosis. *Annual Review of Psychology, 36,* 385–418.

Kihlstrom, J. F. (1987). The cognitive unconscious. *Science, 273,* 1445–1452.

Kilham, W., & Mann, L. (1974). Level of destructive obedience as a function of transmitter and executant roles in the Milgram obedience paradigm. *Journal of Personality and Social Psychology, 29,* 696–702.

Killen, J. D., Hayward, C., Wilson, D. M., Haydel, K. F., Robinson, T. N., Taylor, C. B., Hammer, L. D., & Varady, A. (1996). Predicting onset drinking in a community sample of adolescents: The role of expectancy and temperament. *Addictive Behaviors, 21,* 473–480.

Kim, J., Lim, J., & Bhargava, M. (1998). The role of affect in attitude formation: A classical conditioning. *Journal of the Academy of Marketing Science, 26,* 143–152.

Kim, K. H. S., Relkin, N. R., Lee, K., & Hirsch, J. (1997). Distinct cortical areas associated with native and second languages. *Nature, 388,* 171–174.

Kim, M., & Kim, H. (1997). Communication goals: Individual differences between Korean and American speakers. *Personality & Individual Differences, 23,* 509–517.

Kimble, G. A. (1981). *Biological and cogntive constraints of learning.* In L. T. Benjamin, Jr. (Ed.) *The G. Stanley Hall Lecture Series* (Vol. 1). Washington, DC: American Psychological Associatoin.

Kimmel, M. S., & Linders, A, (1996). Does censorship make a difference? An aggregate empirical analysis of pornography and rape. *Journal of Psychology & Human Sexuality, 8,* 1–20.

Kimura, D. (1994). Body asymmetry and intellectual pattern. *Personality and Individual Differences, 17,* 53–60.

King, A. C., Oman, R. F., Brassington, G. S., Bliwise, D. L., & Haskell, W. L. (1997). Moderate-Intensity Exercise and Self-rated Quality of Sleep in Older Adults: A Randomized Controlled Trial. *Journal of the American Medical Association.277,*32–37

King, D. W., King, L. A., Foy, D. W., Keane, T. M., & Fairbank, J. A. (1999). Posttraumatic stress disorder in a national sample of female and male Vietnam veterans: Risk factors, war-zone stressors, and resilience-recovery variables. *Journal of Abnormal Psychology, 108,* 164–170.

King, L. A., King, D. W., Fairbank, J. A., Keane, T. M., & Adams, G. A. (1998). Resilience-Recovery Factors in Post-Traumatic Stress Disorder Among Female and Male Vietnam Veterans: Hardiness, Postwar Social Support, and Additional Stressful Life Events. *Journal of Personality and Social Psychology, 74,* 420–434.

King, M. L., Jr. (1963, August 28). I have a dream. Speech delivered at the Lincoln Memorial, Washington, DC.

King, S. A., Engi, S., & Poulos, S. T. (1998). Using the internet to assist family therapy. *British Journal of Guidance and Counselling, 26,* 43–52.

Kintsch, W. (1998). *Comprehension: A paradigm for cognition.* New York: Cambridge University Press.

Kipnis, D. (1993). Unanticipated consequences of using behavior technology. *Leadership Quarterly, 4,* 149–171.

Kirby, K. C., Marlowe, D. B., Festinger, D. S., Lamb, R. J., & Platt, J. J. (1998). Schedule of Voucher Delivery Influences Initiation of Cocaine Abstinence. *Journal of Consulting and Clinical Psychology, 66,* 761–767.

Kirby, K. N. (1994). Probabilities and utilities of fictional outcomes in Wason's four-card selection task. *Cognition, 51,* 1–28.

Kirchler, E., & Davis, J. H. (1986). The influence of member status differences and task type on group consensus and member position change. *Journal of Personality and Social Psychology, 51,* 83–91.

Kirkness, E. F., & Durcan, M. J. (1992). Genomic imprinting: Parental origin effects on gene expression. *Alcohol Health & Research World, 16*(4), 312–316.

Kirkpatrick, L. A., & Locke, E. A. (1991). Leadership: Do traits matter? *Academy of Management Executive, 5,* 48–60.

Kirsch, I., & Council, J. R. (1992). SItuational and personality correlates of hypnotic responsiveness. In E. Fromm and M. R. Nash (Eds.). *Contemporary Hypnosis Research* (pp. 267–291). New York: Guilford.

Kirsch, I., & Lynn, S. J. (1999). Automaticity in Clinical Psychology. *American Psychologist, 54,* 504–515.

Kisilevsky, B. S., & Low, J. A. (1998). Human fetal behavior: 100 years of study. *Developmental Review, 18,* 1–29.

Kitchener, R. F. (1996). The nature of the social for Piaget and Vygotsky. *Human Development, 39,* 243–249.

Kitzmann, K. M. (2000). Effects of marital conflict on subsequent triadic family interactions and parenting. *Developmental Psychology, 36,* 3–13.

Kivlighan, D. M., Jr., Multon, K. D., & Patton, M. J. (2000). Insight and symptom reduction in time-limited psychoanalytic counseling. *Journal of Counseling Psychology, 47,* 50–58.

Kleemeier, R. W. (1962). Intellectual changes in the senium. *Proceedings of the American Statistical Association, 1,* 290–295.

Klein, D. F. (1993). False suffocation alarms, spontaneous panics, and related conditions: An integrative hypothesis. *Archives of General Psychiatry, 50,* 306–317.

Klein, E., Kreinin, I., Chistyakov, A., Koren, D., Mecz, L., Marmur, S., Ben-Shachar, D., & Feinsod, M. (1999). Therapeutic Efficacy of Right Prefrontal Slow Repetitive Transcranial Magnetic Stimulation in Major Depression: A Double-blind Controlled Study. *Archives of General Psychiatry, 56,* 315–320.

Kleinke, C. L., & Taylor, C. (1991). Evaluation of opposite-sex person as a function of gazing, smiling, and forward lean. *Journal of Social Psychology, 131,* 451–453.

Kleinknecht, R. A., & Lenz, J. (1989). Blood/injury fear, fainting and avoidance of medical treatment: A family correspondence study. *Behaviour Research and Therapy, 27,* 537–547.

Kleinman, A. (1978). Clinical relevance of anthropological and cross-cultural research: Concepts and strategies. *American Journal of Psychiatry, 135,* 427–431.

Klima, E. S., & Bellugi, U. (1979). *The signs of language.* Cambridge, MA: Harvard University Press.

Klinkenborg, V. (1997, January 5). Awakening to sleep. *Sunday New York Times Magazine,* 26.

Klinteberg, B., Andersson, T., Magnusson, D., & Stattin, H. (1993). Hyperactive behavior in childhood as related to subsequent alcohol problems and violent offending: A longitudinal study of male subjects. *Personality and Individual Differences, 15,* 381–388.

Klosko, J. S., Barlow, D. H., Tassinari, R., & Cerny, J. A. (1990). A comparison of alprazolam and behavior therapy in treatment of panic disorder. *Journal of Consulting and Clinical Psychology, 58,* 77–84.

Knapp, S., & VandeCreek, L. (1996). Risk management for psychologists: Treating patients who recover lost memories of childhood abuse. *Professional Psychology Research and Practice, 27,* 452–459.

Knauth, P. (1997). Changing schedules: Shiftwork. *Chronobiology International, 14,* 159–171.

Knobloch, H., & Pasamanick, B. (Eds.). (1974). *Gessell and Amatruda's developmental diagnosis.* Hagerstown, MD: Harper & Row.

Kobasa, S. C. (1979). Stressful life events, personality and health: An inquiry into hardiness. *Journal of Personality and Social Psychology, 37* 1–11.

Kobasa, S. C., Maddit, S. R., & Kuhn, S. (1982). Hardiness and health: A prospective study. *Journal of Personality and Social Psychology, 42,* 168–177.

Koestler, A. (1964). *The act of creation.* New York: Macmillan.

Koffka, K. (1935). *Principles of Gestalt psychology.* New York: Harcourt Brace.

Kohlberg, L. (1969). Stage and sequence: The cognitive-developmental approach to socialization. In D. S. Goslin (Ed.), *Handbook of socialization theory and research* (pp. 347–480). Chicago: Rand McNally.

Kohlberg, L. (1981). *Essays on moral development. Vol. 1. The philosophy of moral development: Moral stages and the idea of justice.* San Francisco: Harper & Row.

Kohler, P. F., Rivera, V. J., Eckert, E. D., Bouchard, T. J., Jr., & Heston, L. L. (1985). Genetic regulation of immunoglobulin and specific antibody levels in twins reared apart. *Journal of Clinical Investigation, 75,* 883–888.

Kohler, S., Kapur, S., Moscovitch, M., Winocur, G., & Houle, S. (1995). Dissociation of pathways for object and spatial vision: A PET study in humans. *Neuroreport, 6,* 1865–1868.

Köhler, W. (1925/1956). *The mentality of apes.* New York: Vintage.

Kohn, A. (1996). By all available means: Cameron and Pierce's defense of extrinsic motivators. *Review of Educational Research, 66,* 1–4.

Kohn, M. L., & Schooler, C. (1973). Occupational experience and psychological functioning: An assessment of reciprocal effects. *American Sociological Review, 38,* 97–118.

Kohut, H. (1977). *The restoration of self.* New York: International Universities Press.

Kolata, G. (1997, January 14). Which comes first: Depression or heart disease? *New York Times,* C1.

Kolb, F. C., & Braun, J. (1995). Blindsight in normal observers. *Nature, 377,* 336–338.

Konishi, M. (1993). Listening with two ears. *Scientific American, 268,* 66–73.

Koob, G. F. (1999). Drug reward and addiction. In M. J. Zigmond, F. E. Bloom, S. C. Landis, J. L. Roberts, & L. R. Squire. *Fundamental neuroscience* (pp. 1261–1279). San Diego: Academic Press.

Koob, G. F., & Bloom, F. E. (1988). Cellular and molecular mechanisms of drug dependence. *Science, 242,* 715–723.

Kosslyn, S. M. (1975). On retrieving information from visual images. In R. Schank & B. Nash-Webber (Eds.), *Theoretical issues in natural language processing.* Arlington, VA: Association for Computational Linguistics.

Kosslyn, S. M. (1976). Can imagery be distinguished from other forms of internal representation? Evidence from studies of information retrieval times. *Memory and Cognition, 4,* 291–297.

Kosslyn, S. M. (1978). Measuring the visual angle of the mind's eye. *Cognitive Psychology, 10,* 356–389.

Kosslyn, S. M. (1980). *Image and mind.* Cambridge, MA.: Harvard University Press.

Kosslyn, S. M. (1994a). *Elements of graph design.* New York: Freeman.

Kosslyn, S. M. (1994b). *Image and brain: The resolution of the imagery debate.* Cambridge, MA: MIT Press.

Kosslyn, S. M., & Hugdahl, K. (1999). Effects of mood on mental rotation and deductive reasoning. Harvard University manuscript.

Kosslyn, S. M., & Intriligator, J. M. (1992). Is cognitive neuropsychology plausible? The perils of sitting on a one-legged stool. *Journal of Cognitive Neuroscience, 4,* 96–106. (Translated into Italian and reprinted in *Sistemi Intelligenti, 6,* 181–205, 1994)

Kosslyn, S. M., & Koenig, O. (1995). *Wet mind: The new cognitive neuroscience.* New York: Free Press.

Kosslyn, S. M., Alpert, N. M., Thompson, W. L., Maljkovic, V., Weise, S. B., Chabris, C. F., Hamilton, S. E., & Buonano, F. S. (1993). Visual mental imagery activates topographically organized visual cortex: PET investigations. *Journal of Cognitive Neuroscience, 5,* 263–287.

Kosslyn, S. M., Ball, T. M., & Reiser, B. J. (1978). Visual images preserve metric spatial information: Evidence from studies of image scanning. *Journal of Experimental Psychology: Human Perception and Performance, 4,* 47–60.

Kosslyn, S. M., Daly, P. F., McPeek, R. M., Alpert, N. M., Kennedy, D. N., & Caviness, V. S. (1993). Using locations to store shape: An indirect effect of a lesion. *Cerebral Cortex, 3,* 567–582.

Kosslyn, S. M., Digirolamo, G. J., Thompson, W. L., & Alpert, N. M. (1998). Mental rotation of objects versus hands: Neural mechanisms revealed by positron emission tomography. *Psychophysiology, 35,* 151–161.

Kosslyn, S. M., Koenig, O., Barrett, A., Cave, C. B., Tang, J., & Gabrieli, J. D. E. (1989). Evidence for two types of spatial representations: Hemispheric specialization for categorical and coordinate relations. *Journal of Experimental Psychology: Human Perception and Performance, 15,* 723–735.

Kosslyn, S. M., Pascual-Leone, A., Felician, O., Camposano, S., Keenan, J. P., Thompson, W. L., Ganis, G., Sukel, K. E., & Alpert, N. M. (1999). The role of area 17 in visual imagery: Convergent evidence from PET and rTMS. *Science, 284,* 167–170.

Kosslyn, S. M., Segar, C., Pani, J., & Hillger, L. A. (1990). When is imagery used in everyday life? A diary study. *Journal of Mental Imagery. 14,* 131–152.

Kosslyn, S. M., Thompson, W. L., & Alpert, N. M. (1997). Neural systems shared by visual imagery and visual perception: A positron emission tomography study. *NeuroImage, 6,* 320–334.

Kosslyn, S. M., Thompson, W. L., Costantini-Ferrando, M. F., Alpert, N. M., & Spiegel, D. (2000). Hypnotic visual illusion alters brain color processing. *American Journal of Psychiatry.*

Kosslyn, S. M., Thompson, W. L., Kim, I. J., & Alpert, N. M. (1995). Topographical representations of mental images in primary visual cortex. *Nature, 378,* 496–498.

Kosslyn, S. M., Thompson, W. L., Kim, I. J., Rauch, S. L., & Alpert, N. M. (1996). Individual differences in cerebral blood flow in area 17 predict the time to evaluate visualized letters. *Journal of Cognitive Neuroscience, 8,* 78–82.

Koutstaal., W., & Schacter, D. L. (1997). Inaccuracy and inaccessibility in memory retrieval: Contributions from cognitive psychology and cognitive neuropsychology. In P. S. Appelbaum, L. Uyehara, & M. Elin (Eds.),

Trauma and memory: Clinical and legal controversies (pp. 93–137). New York: Oxford University Press.

Kovacs, I. (1996). Gestalten of today: Early processing of visual contours and surfaces. *Behavioural Brain Research, 82*, 1–11.

Kovacs, I., & Julesz, B. (1993). A closed curve is much more than an incomplete one: Effect of closure in figure-ground segmentation. *Proceedings of the National Academy of Sciences, USA, 90*, 7495–7497.

Kowalski, U., Waltschko, R., & Fuller, E. (1998). Normal fluctuations of the geomagnetic field may affect initial orientation of pigeons. *Journal of Comparative Physiology, 163*, 593–600.

Kozak, M. J., Liebowitz, M. R., & Foa, E. B. (2000). Cognitive behavior therapy and pharmacotherapy for obsessive-compulsive disorder: The NIMH-sponsored collaborative study. In W. K. Goodman, M. V. Rudorfer, & J. D. Masur (Eds.). *Obsessive-compulsive disorder: Contemporary issues in treatment* (pp. 501–530). Mahwah, NJ: Erlbaum.

Kozhevnikov, M., Hegarty, M., & Mayer, R. (1998, August). Visual/spatial abilities in problem solving in physics. *Proceedings of the Thinking with Diagrams 98 Conference*, The University of Wales, Aberystwyth.

Kraepelin, E. (1921). Ueber Entwurtzelung [Depression]. *Zietschrift fuer die Gasamte Neurologie und Psychiatrie, 63*, 1–8.

Krafft, K. C., & Berk, L. E. (1998). Private speech in two preschools: Significance of open-ended activities and make-believe play for verbal self-regulation. *Early Childhood Research Quarterly, 13*, 637–658.

Kramer, M. S., Cutler, N., Feighner, J., Shrivastava, R., Carman, J., Sramek, J. J., et al. (1998). Distinct mechanism for antidepressant activity by blockade of central substance P receptors. *Science, 281*, 1640–1645.

Kranzler, J. H., & Jensen, A. R. (1989). Inspection time and intelligence: A meta-analysis. *Intelligence, 13*, 329–347.

Kraut, R., Patterson, M., Lundmark, V., Kiesler, S., Mukophadhyay, T., & Scherlis, W. (1998). Internet paradox: A social technology that reduces social involvement and psychological well-being? *American Psychologist, 53*, 1017–1031.

Kring, A. M., & Gordon, A. H. (1998). Sex differences in emotion: Expression, experience, and physiology. *Journal of Personality & Social Psychology, 74*, 686–703.

Kroon, M. B. R., van Kreveld, D., & Rabbie, J. M. (1992). Group versus individual decision making: Effects of accountability on gender and groupthink. *Small Group Research, 23*, 427–458.

Krueger, J. (1996). Personal beliefs and cultural stereotypes about racial characteristics. *Journal of Personality and Social Psychology, 71*, 536–548.

Krueger, L. E. (1992). The word-superiority effect and phonological recoding. *Memory & Cognition, 20*, 685–694.

Krug, R., Pietrowsky, R., Fehm, H. L., & Born, J. (1994). Selective influence of menstrual cycle on perception of stimuli with reproductive significance. *Psychosomatic Medicine, 56*, 410–417.

Kruglanski, A. W., & Webster, D. M. (1996). Motivated closing of the mind: "Seizing" and "freezing." *Psychological Review, 103*, 263–283.

Krumhansl, C. L. (2000). Rhythm and pitch in music cognition. *Psychological Bulletin, 126*, 159–179.

Krumhansl, C. L., (1991). Music perception: Tonal structures in perception and memory. *Annual Review of Psychology, 42*, 277–303.

Krupnick, J. L., Sotsky, S. M., Simmens, S., Moyer, J., Elkin, I., Watkins, J., & Paulinis, P. A. (1996). The role of the therapeutic alliance in psychotherapy and pharmacotherapy outcome: Findings in the National Institute of Mental Health Treatment of Depression Collaborative Research Program. *Journal of Consulting & Clinical Psychology, 64*, 532–539.

Kübler-Ross, E. (1969). *On death and dying.* New York: Macmillan.

Kuhl, P. K. (1989). On babies, birds, modules, and mechanisms: A comparative approach to the acquisition of vocal communication. In R. J. Dooling & S. H. Husle (Eds.), *The comparative psychology of audition: Perceiving complex sounds* (pp. 379–419). Hillsdale, NJ: Erlbaum.

Kuhl, P. K., Williams, K. A., Lacerda, F., Stevens, K. N., et al. (1992). Linguistic experience alters phonetic perception in infants by 6 months of age. *Science, 255*, 606–608.

Kuipers, E., Fowler, D., Garety, P. Chisholm, D., Freeman, D., Dunn, G., Bebbington, P., & Hadley, C. (1998). London-East Anglia randomised controlled trial of cognitive-behavioural therapy for psychosis. III: Followup and economic evaluation at 18 months. *British Journal of Psychiatry, 173*, 61–68.

Kuipers, E., Garety, P., Fowler, D., Dunne, G., Bebbington, P., Freeman, D., & Hadley, C. (1997). London-East Anglia randomised controlled trial of cognitive-behavioural therapy for psychosis. I: Effects of the treatment phase. *British Journal of Psychiatry, 171*, 319–327.

Kunda, Z., & Oleson, K. C. (1995). Maintaining stereotypes in the face of disconfirmation: Constructing grounds for subtyping deviants. *Journal of Personality and Social Psychology, 68*, 565–579.

Kunz, G., Beil, D., Deininger, H., Einspanier, A., Mall, G., & Leyendecker, G. (1997). The uterine peristaltic pump. Normal and impeded sperm transport within the female genital tract. *Advances in Experimental Medicine and Biology, 424*, 267–277.

Kushner, M., Riggs, D., Foa, E., & Miller, S. (1992). Perceived controllability and the development of posttraumatic stress disorder (PTSD) in crime victims. *Behaviour Research and Therapy, 31*, 105–110.

Kushnir, T., Malkinson, R., & Ribak, J. (1998). Rational thinking and stress management in health workers: A psychoeducational program. *International Journal of Stress Management, 5*, 169–178.

Kutchinsky, B. (1991). Pornography and rape: Theory and practice? Evidence from crime data in four countries where pornography is easily available. *International Journal of Law & Psychiatry, 14*, 47–64.

Kvale, G., & Hugdahl, K. (1994). Cardiovascular conditioning and anticipatory nausea and vomiting in cancer patients. *Behavioral Medicine, 20*, 78–83.

Lachman, H. M., Papolos, D. F., Boyle, A., Sheftel, G., Juthani, M., Edwards, E., & Henn, F. A. (1993). Alterations in glucocorticoid inducible RNAs in the limbic system of learned helpless rats. *Brain Research. 609*, 110–116.

Lachman, M. E., & Weaver, S. L. (1998). The sense of control as a moderator of social class differences in health and well-being. *Journal of Personality and Social Psychology, 74*, 763–773.

Lacks, P., & Morin, C. M. (1992). Recent advances in the assessment and treatment of insomnia. *Journal of Consulting & Clinical Psychology, 60*, 586–594.

Lafuente, M. J., Grifol, R., Segarra, J., Soriano, J., Gorba, M. A., & Montesinos, A. (1997). Effects of the Firstart method of prenatal stimulation on psychomotor development: The first six months. *Pre- & Peri-Natal Psychology Journal, 11*, 151–162.

Laird, J. D. (1974). Self-attribution of emotion: The effects of expressive behavior on the quality of emotional experience. *Journal of Personality & Social Psychology, 29*, 475–486.

Laird, J. D. (1984). The real role of facial response in the experience of emotion: A reply to Tourangeau and Ellsworth, and others. *Journal of Personality & Social Psychology, 47*, 909–917.

Laird, J. D., Alibozak, T., Davainis, D., Deignan, K., Fontanella, K., Hong, J., Levy, B., & Pacheco, C. (1994). Individual differences in the effects of spontaneous mimicry on emotional contagion. *Motivation and Emotion, 18*, 231–247.

Lakey, B., & Dickenson, L. G. (1994). Antecedents of perceived support: Is perceived family environment generalized to new social relationships? *Cognitive Therapy and Research, 18*, 39–53.

Lakey, B., & Heller, K. (1988). Social support form a friend, perceived support, and social problem solving. *American journal of Community Psychology, 16*, 811–824.

Lakey, B., & Lutz, C. J. (1996). Social Support and Preventative and therapeutic interventions. In G. R. Pierce, B. R. Sarason, & I. G. Sarason (Eds.), *Handbook of social support and the family.* New York: Plenum Press.

Lakey, B., Moineau, S., & Drew, J. B. (1992). Perceived social support and individual differences in the interpretation and recall of support behavior. *Journal of Social and Clinical Psychology, 11*, 336–348.

Lakey, B., Ross, L. T., Butler, C., & Bentley, K. (1996). Making social support judgments: The role of similarity and conscientiousness. *Journal of Social and Clinical Psychology, 15*, 283–304.

Lalumiere, M. L., & Quinsey, L. (1998). Pavlovian conditioning of sexual interests in human males. *Archives of Sexual Behavior, 27*, 241–252.

Lam, R. W., Bartley, S., Yatham, L. N., Tam, E. M., & Zis, A. P. (1999). Clinical predictors of short-term outcome in electroconvulsive therapy. *Canadian Journal of Psychiatry, 44*, 158–163.

Lam, S. K., Hui, W. M., Shiu, L. P., Ng, M. M. (1995). Society stress and peptic ulcer perforation. *Journal of Gastroenterology and Hepatology, 10*, :570–576.

Lambert, A. J. (1995). Stereotypes and social judgment: The consequences of group variability. *Journal of Personality and Social Psychology, 68*, 388–403.

Lambert, M. J. (1983). Introduction to assessment of psychotherapy outcome: Historical perspective and current issues. In M. J. Lambert, E. R. Christensen, & S. S. DeJulio (Eds.), *The assessment of psychotherapy outcome* (pp. 3–32). New York: Wiley-Interscience.

Lambert, M. J. (1999). Are differential treatment effects inflated by researcher therapy allegiance? Could Clever Hans count? *Clinical Psychology: Science & Practice, 6*, 127–130.

Lambert, M. J., & Bergin, A. E. (1994). The effectiveness of psychotherapy. In A. E. Bergin & S. L. Garfield (Eds.), *Handbook of psychotherapy and behavior change, 4th edition* (pp. 143–189). New York: John Wiley & Sons.

Land, E. H. (1959). Experiments in color vision. *Scientific American, 200*, 84–99.

Land, E. H. (1977). The retinex theory of color vision. *Scientific American, 237*, 108–128.

Land, E. H. (1983). Recent advances in retinex theory and some implications for cortical computations: Color vision and the natural image. *Proceedings of the National Academy of Sciences, USA, 80*, 5163–5169.

Landauer, T., & Whiting, J. (1964). Infantile stimulation and adult stature of human males. *American Anthropologist, 66*, 1007–1028.

Lane, H. (1976). *The wild boy of Aveyron*. Cambridge, MA: Harvard University Press.

Lane, R. D., Reiman, E. M., Ahern, G. L., & Schwartz, G. E. (1997a). Neuroanatomical correlates of happiness, sadness, and disgust. *American Journal of Psychiatry, 154*, 926–933

Lane, R. D., Reiman, E. M., Bradley, M. M., Lang, P. J., Ahern, G. L., Davidson, R. J., and Schwartz, G. E. (1997b). Neuroanatomical correlates of pleasant and unpleasant emotion. *Neuropsychologia, 35*, 1437–1444.

Lang, P. J. (1994). The varieties of emotional experience: A meditation on the James-Lange theory. *Psychological Review: Special Issue: The Centennial Issue of the Psychological Review, 101*, 211–221.

Lang, P. J. (1995). The emotion probe: Studies of motivation and attention. *American Psychologist, 50*, 372–385.

Lang, P. J., Bradley, M. M., Cuthbert, B. N. (1990). Emotion, attention, and the startle reflex. *Psychological Review, 97*, 377–395.

Lange, C. (1887). *Uber gemuthsbewegungen*. Leipzig: Theodor Thomas.

Langer, E. J., & Rodin, J. (1976). The effects of choice and enhanced personal responsibility for the aged: A field experiment in an institutional setting. *Journal of Personality & Social Psychology, 34*, 191–198.

Langevin, R., Lang, R. A., Wright, P., Handy, L., Frenzel, R. R., & Black, E. L. (1988). Pornography and sexual offences. *Annals of Sex Research, 1*, 335–362.

La Piere, R. T. (1934). Attitude and actions. *Social Forces, 13*, 230–237.

Lapsley, D. K. (1990). Egocentrism theory and the "new look" at the imaginary audience and personal fable in adolescence. In R. M. Lerner, A. C. Petersen, & J. Brooks-Gunn (Eds.), *The encyclopedia of adolescence* (pp. 281–286). New York: Garland.

Lapsley, D. K., Jackson, S., Rice, K., & Shadid, G. (1988). Self-monitoring and the "new look" at the imaginary audience and personal fable: An ego-developmental analysis. *Journal of Adolescent Research, 3*, 17–31.

Lapsley, D. K., Milstead, M., Quintana, S. M., Flannery, D., & Buss, R. (1986). Adolescent egocentrism and formal operations: Tests of a theoretical assumption. *Developmental Psychology, 22*, 800–807.

Larimer, M. E., Irvine, D. L., Kilmer, J. R., & Marlatt, G. A. (1997). College drinking and the Greek system: Examining the role of perceived norms for high-risk behavior. *Journal of College Student Development, 38*, 587–598.

Larkin, T., & Keeton, W. T. (1976). Bar magnets mask the effect of normal magnetic disturbances on pigeon orientation. *Journal of Comparative Physiology, 110*, 227–231.

Larson, J. A. (1932). *Lying and its detection: A study of deception and deception tests*. Chicago, IL: University of Chicago Press.

Larson, R., & Richards, M. H. (1994). *Divergent realities: The emotional lives of mothers, fathers, and adolescents*. New York: Basic Books.

Laruelle, M., Ai-Dargham, A., Casanova, M., Toti, R., Weinberger, D., & Kleinman, J. (1993). Selective abnormalities of prefrontal serotonergic receptors in schizophrenia. *Archives of General Psychiatry, 50*, 810–818.

Lassiter, G. D., Apple, K. J., & Slaw, R. D. (1996). Need for cognition and thought-induced attitude polarization: Another look. *Journal of Social Behavior & Personality, 11*, 647–665.

Latané, B., & Darley, J. M. (1968). Group inhibition of bystander intervention. *Journal of Personality and Social Psychology, 10*, 215–221.

Latané, B., & Darley, J. M. (1970). *The unresponsive bystander: Why doesn't he help?* New York: Appletone-Crofts.

Latané, B., Williams, K., & Harkins, S. (1979). Many hands make light the work: The causes and consequences of social loafing. *Journal of Personality and Social Psychology, 37*, 822–832.

Laughlin, P. R., & Ellis, A. L. (1986). Demonstrability and social combination processes on mathematical intellective tasks. *Journal of Experimental Social Psycology, 22* 177–189.

Laursen, B., Coy, K. C., & Collins, W. A. (1998). Reconsidering changes in parent-child conflict across adolescence: A meta-analysis. *Child Development, 69*, 817–832.

Lautrey, J., & Caroff, X. (1996). Variability and cognitive development. *Polish Quarterly of Developmental Psychology, 2*, 71–89.

Lavergne, G. M. (1997). A sniper in the tower: The Charles Whitman murders. Denton, TX: University of North Texas Press.

Lawless, H. T. (1984). Oral chemical irritation: Psychophysical properties. *Chemical Senses, 9*, 143–155.

Lazarus, R. S. (1984). On the primacy of cognition. *American Psychologist, 39*, 124–129.

Lazarus, R. S., & Folkman, S. (1984). *Sstress, appraisal, and coping*. New York: Springer.

Lazev, A. B., Herzog, T. A., & Brandon, T. H. (1999). Classical conditioning of environmental cues to cigarette smoking. *Experimental and Clinical Psychopharmacology, 7*, 56–63.

Leary, W. (1997, December 18). Responses of alcoholics to therapists seem similar. *New York Times*, A17.

Leask, M. J. M. (1977). A physicochemical mechanism for magnetic field detection by migrating birds and homing pigeons. *Nature, 267*, 144–145.

Leavitt, F. (1997). False attribution of suggestibility to explain recovered memory of childhood sexual abuse following extended amnesia. *Child Abuse & Neglect, 21*, 265–272.

LeBihan, D., Jezzard, P., Turner, R., Cuenod, C. A., Pannier, L., & Prinster, A. (1993). Practical problems and limitations in using z-maps for processing of brain function MR images. *Abstracts of the 12th Meeting of the Society of Magnetic Resonance in Medicine, 1*, 11.

Leccese, A. P. (1991). *Drugs and society: Behavioral medicines and abusable drugs*. Englewood Cliffs, NJ: Prentice-Hall, Inc.

LeDoux, J. E. (1994). Emotion, memory, and the brain. *Scientific American, 270*, 50–57.

LeDoux, J. E. (1995). Emotion: Clues from the brain. *Annual Review of Psychology, 46*, 209–235.

LeDoux, J. E. (1996). *The emotional brain: The mysterious underpinnings of emotional life*. New York: Simon & Schuster.

LeDoux, J. E., Ruggiero, D. A., & Reis, D. J. (1985). Projections to the subcortical forebrain from anatomically defined regions of the medial geniculate body in the rat. *Journal of Comparative Neurology, 242*, 182–213.

LeDoux, J. E., Wilson, D. H., & Gazzaniga, M. S. (1977). A divided mind: Observations on the conscious properties of the separated hemispheres. *Annals of Neurology, 2*, 417–421.

Lee, A. M., & Lee, S. (1996). Disordered eating and its psychosocial correlates among Chinese adolescent females in Hong Kong. *International Journal of Eating Disorders, 20*, 177–183.

Lee, E. S. (1951). Negro intelligence and selective migration: A Philadelphia test of the Klineberg hypothesis. *American Sociological Review, 16*, 227–233.

Lee, S. (1996). Clinical lessons from the cross-cultural study of anorexia nervosa. *Eating Disorders Review, 7*(3), 1

Lee, S., & Tedeschi, J. T. (1996). Effects of norms and norm-violations on inhibition and instigation of aggression. *Aggressive Behavior, 22*, 17–25,

Leedy, C., & Dubeck, L. (1971). Physiological changes during tournament chess. *Chess Life and Review*, 708.

Leffler, A., Gillespie, D. L., & Conaty, J. C. (1982). The effects of status differentiation on non-verbal behavior. *Social Psychology Quarterly, 45*, 153–151.

Lehman, A. F., & Steinwachs, D. M. (1998). Translating research into practice: The Schizophrenia Patients Outcome Research Team (PORT) Treatment Recommendations. *Schizophrenia Bulletin, 24*, 1–10.

Lehman, D. R., & Nisbett, R. E. (1990). A longitudinal study of the effects of undergraduate training on reasoning. *Developmental Psychology, 26*, 952–960.

Lehrl, S., & Fischer, B. (1990) A basic information psychological parameter (BIP) for the reconstruction of concepts of intelligence. *European Journal of Personality, 4*, 259–286.

Leibowitz, H. W. (1971). Sensory, learned and cognitive mechanisms of size perception. *Annals of the New York Academy of Sciences, 188*, 47–62.

Leitenberg, H., Rosen, J. C., Gross, J., Nudelman, S., & Vara, L. (1988). Exposure plus response-prevention treatment of bulimia nervosa. *Journal of Consulting and Clinical Psychology, 56*, 535–541.

Lemme, B. H. (1995). *Development in adulthood*. Needham Heights, MA: Allyn & Bacon.

Lenneberg, E. H. (1967). *Biological foundations of language*. New York: Wiley.

Lennon, R., & Eisenberg, N. (1987). Gender and age differences in empathy and sympathy. In N. Eisenberg & J. Strayer (Eds.), *Empathy and its development* (pp. 195–217). New York: Cambridge University Press.

Leo, R. A. (1992). From coercion to deception: The changing nature of police interrogation in America. *Crime, Law, and Social Change, 18*, 35–39.

Leone, C., & Ensley, E. (1986). Self-generated attitude change: A person by situation analysis of attitude polarization and attenuation. *Journal of Research in Personality, 20*, 434–446.

Leopold, D. A., & Logothetis, N. K. (1996). Activity changes in early visual cortex reflect monkeys' percepts during binocular rivalry. *Nature, 379*, 549–553.

Lepper, M. R., Greene, D., & Nisbett, R. E. (1973). Undermining children's intrinsic interest with extrinsic reward: A test of the "overjustification" hypothesis. *Journal of Personality and Social Psychology, 28*, 129–137.

Lepper, M. R., Henderlong, J., & Gingras, I. (1999). Understanding the effects of extrinsic rewards on intrinsic motivation—Uses and abuses of meta-analysis: Comment on Deci, Koestner, and Ryan (1999). *Psychological Bulletin, 125*, 669–676.

Leproult, R., Copinschi, G., Buxton, O., & Van Cauter, E. (1997). Sleep loss results in an elevation of cortisol levels the next evening. *Sleep, 20*, 865–870.

Leproult, R., Van Reeth, O., Byrne, M. M., Sturis, J., & Van Cauter, E. (1997). Sleepiness, performance, and neuroendocrine function during sleep deprivation: Rffects of exposure to bright light or exercise. *Journal of Biological Rhythms, 12*, 245–258.

Lerner, M. J. (1980). *The belief in a just world: A fundamental illusion.* New York: Plenum Press.

Lesch, K-P., Bengel, D., Heils, A., Sabol, S. Z., Greenberg, B. D., Petri, S., Benjamin, J., Müller, C. R., Hamer, D. H., & Murphy, D. L. (1996). Association of anxiety-related traits with a polymorphism in the serotonin transporter gene regulatory region. *Science, 274*, 1527–1531.

Leserman, J., Stuart, E. M., Mamish, M. E., & Benson, H. (1989). The efficacy of the relaxation response in preparing for cardiac surgery. *Behavioral Medicine, 15*, 111–117.

Leshner, A. I., & Segal, M. (1979). Fornix transection blocks "learned helplessness" in rats. *Behavioral & Neural Biology, 26*, 497–501.

Leslie, A. (1994) TOMM, ToBy, and agency: Core architecture and domain specificity. In L. A. Hirschfeld & S. A. Gelman (Eds.). *Mapping the mind: Domain specificity in cognition and culture.* (pp. 119–148). New York: Cambridge University Press.

Leslie, A. (1999). The innate capacity to acquire a 'theory of mind': Synchronic or diachronic modularity? *Mind & Language, 17*, 141–155 (1999)

LeVay, S. (1991). A difference in hypothalamic structure between heterosexual and homosexual men. *Science, 253*, 1034–1037.

LeVay, S., & Hamer, D. (1994). Evidence for a biological influence in male homosexuality. *Scientific American, 270*, 44–49.

Levenson, R. W. (1992). Autonomic nervous system differences among emotions. *Psychological Science, 3*, 23–27.

Levenson, R. W, Ekman, P., and Friesen, W. V. (1990). Voluntary facial action generates emotion-specific autonomic nervous system activity. *Psychophysiology, 27*, 363–384.

Leventhal, G. S., Singer, R., & Jones, S. (1965). The effects of fear and specificity of recommendation upon attitudes and behavior. *Journal of Personality and Social Psychology, 2*, 20–29.

Levie, W. H., & Lentz, R. (1982). Effects of text illustrations: A review of research. *Educational Communication and Technology Journal, 30*, 195–232.

Levin, J. R., Anglin, G. J., & Carney, R. N. (1987). On empirically validating functions of pictures in prose. In D. M. Willows & H. A. Houghton (Eds.), *The psychology of illustration: I. Basic research* (pp. 51–85). New York: Springer-Verlag.

Levin, R. J. (1994). Human male sexuality: Appetite and arousal, desire and drive. In C. R. Legg & D. Booth (Eds.), *Appetite: Neural and behavioral bases.* (pp. 127–164). New York: Oxford University Press.

Levin, R. S. (1980). The physiology of sexual function in women. *Clinics in Obstetrics and Gynaecology, 7*, 213–252.

Levine, D. N. (1982). Visual agnosia in monkey and man. In D. J. Ingle, M. A. Goodale, & R. J. W. Mansfield (Eds.), *Analysis of Visual Behavior* (pp. 629–670). Cambridge: MIT Press.

Levine, J. A., Eberhardt, N. L., & Jensen, M. D. (1999). The role of non-exercise activity thermogenesis in resistance to fat gain in humans. *Science, 283*, 212–214.

Levine, J. M. (1989). Reaction to opinion deviance in small groups. In P. B. Paulus (Ed.), *Psychology of group influence* (2nd ed., pp. 187–231).

Levine, J. M., & Moreland, R. L. (1998). Small groups. In D. T. Gilbert, S. T. Fiske, & G. Lindzey (Eds.), The handbook of social psychology (4th ed., pp. 415–469). New York: McGraw Hill..

Levine, R. L., & Bluni, T. D. (1994). Magnetic field effects on spatial discrimination learning in mice. *Physiology and Behavior, 55*, 465–467.

Levine, R. L., & Stadtman, E. R. (1992). Oxidation of proteins during aging. *Generations, 16*(4), 39–42.

Levinson, D. J. (1977). The mid-life transition: A period in adult psychosocial development. *Psychiatry: Journal for the Study of Interpersonal Processes, 40*, 99–112.

Levinson, D. J. (1978). Eras: The anatomy of the life cycle. *Psychiatric Opinion, 15*, 10–11, 39–48.

Levinson, D. J. (1986). A conception of adult development. *American Psychologist, 41*, 3–13.

Levinson, D. J. (1990). A theory of life structure development in adulthood. In C. N. Alexander & E. J. Langer (Eds.), *Higher stages of human development: Perspectives on adult growth* (pp. 35–53). New York: Oxford University Press.

Levinson, D. J., & Levinson, J. D. (1997). *The seasons of a woman's life.* New York: Ballantine.

Levinson, D., Darrow, C., Klein, E. Levinson, M., & Braxton, M. (1978). *The seasons of a man's life.* New York: Ballantine.

Levitas, A. (2000). Fragile X syndrome. *Journal of the American Academy of Child and Adolescent Psychiatry, 39*, 398–399.

Levitt, A. G., & Wang, Q. (1991). Evidence for language-specific rhythmic influences in the reduplicative babbling of French- and English-learning infants. *Language and Speech, 34*, 235–249.

Levitt, M. J., Weber, R. A., & Guacci, N. (1993). Convoys of social support: An intergenerational analysis. *Psychology and Aging, 8*, 323–326.

Levy, S. M., Herberman, R. B., Lippman, M. N., & d'Angelo, T. (1987). Correlation of stress factors with sustained depression of natural killer cell activity and predicted prognosis in patients with breast cancer. *Journal of Clinical Oncology, 5*, 348–353.

Levy, S. M., Herberman, R. B., Maluish, A. M., Schlien, B., & Lippman, M. (1985). Prognostic risk assessment in primary breast cancer by behavioral and immunological parameters. *Health Psychology, 4*, 99–113.

Levy, S. M., Lee, J., Bagley, C., & Lippman, M. (1988). Survival hazards analysis in first year recurrent breast cancer patients: Seven-year follow-up. *Psychosomatic Medicine, 50*, 520–528.

Lewin, K., Lippitt, R., & White, R. K. (1939). Patterns of aggressive behavior in experimentally created "social climates." *Journal of Social Psychology, 10*, 271–299.

Lewinsohn, P. M., Mischel, W., Chaplin, W., & Barton, R. (1980). Social competence and depression: The role of illustory self-perceptions. *Journal of Abnormal Psychology, 89*, 203–212.

Lewinsohn, P. M., Rohde, P., Seeley, J. R., & Fischer, S. A. (1993). Age-cohort changes in the lifetime occurrence of depression and other mental disorders. *Journal of Abnormal Psychology, 102*, 110–120.

Lewis, B., & Thompson, L. A. (1992). A study of developmental speech and language disorders in twins. *Journal of Speech and Hearing Research, 35*, 1086–1094.

Lewis, D. O., Yeager, C. A., Swica, Y., Pincus, J. H., & Lewis, M. (1997). Objective documentation of child abuse and dissociation in 12 murderers with dissociative identity disorder. *American Journal of Psychiatry, 154*, 1703–1710.

Lewis, F. M., & Daltroy, L. H. (1990). How causal explanations influence health behavior: Attribution theory. In K. Glanz, F. M. Lewis, & B. K. Rimer (Eds.), *Health education and health behavior: Theory, research, and practice* (pp. 92–114). San Francisco, CA: Jossey-Bass.

Lewis, M., & Brooks-Gunn, J. (1979). *Social cognition and the acquisition of self.* New York: Plenum.

Lewontin, R. C. (1976a). Further remarks on race and the genetics of intelligence. In N. J Block & G. Dworkin (Eds.), *The IQ controversy* (pp. 107–112). New York: Pantheon Books.

Lewontin, R. C. (1976b). Race and intelligence. In N. J. Block & G. Dworkin (Eds.), *The IQ controversy* (pp. 78–92). New York: Pantheon Books.

Liang, D. W., Moreland, R., & Argote, L. (1995). Group versus individual training and group performance: The mediating factor of transactive memory. *Personality & Social Psychology Bulletin, 21*, 384–393.

Liddell, C. (1997). Every picture tells a story—or does it? Young South African children interpreting pictures. *Journal of Cross-Cultural Psychology, 28*, 266–282.

Lidsky, A. S., Ledley, F. D., DiLella, A. G., Kwok, S. C., Daiger, S. P., Robson, K. J., & Woo, S. L. (1985). Extensive restriction site polymorphism at the human phenylalanine hydroxylase locus and the application of prenatal diagnosis of phenylketonuria. *American Journal of Human Genetics, 37*, 619–634.

Lifton, P. D. (1985). Individual differences in moral development: The relation of sex, gender, and personality to morality. *Journal of Personality, 53*, 306–334.

Light, L. (1991). Memory and aging: Four hypotheses in search of data. *Annual Review of Psychology, 42*, 333–376.

Lilenfeld, L. R., Kaye, W. H., Greeno, C. G., Merikangas, K. R., Plotnicov, K., Pollice, C., Raol, R., Strober, M., Bulik, C. M., & Nagy, L. (1998). A controlled family study of anorexia nervosa and bulimia nervosa: Psychiatric disorders in first-degree relatives and effects of proband comorbidity. *Archives of General Psychiatry, 55*, 603–610.

Lillard, A. S. (1999). Developing a cultural theory of mind: The CIAO approach. *Current Directions in Psychological Science, 8*, 57–61.

Lindemann, E. (1991). The symptomatology and management of acute grief. *American Journal of Psychiatry, 144*, 141–148.

Lindley, R. H., Wilson, S. M., Smith, W. R., & Bathurst, K., (1995). Reaction time (RT) and IQ: Shape of the task complexity function. *Personality and Individual Differences, 18*, 339–345.

Lindsay, D. S., & Johnson, M. K. (1989). The eyewitness suggestibility effect and memory for source. *Memory & Cognition, 17*, 349–358.

Linehan, M. M. (1993). *Skills training manual for treating borderline personality disorder.* New York: Guilford.

Linner, B. (1972). *Sex and society in Sweden.* New York: Harper Colophon Books.

Linnoila, M., Virkkunen, M., Scheinin, M., Nuutila, A., Romin, R., & Goodwin, F. K. (1983). Low cerebrospinal fluid 5-hydroxindoleacetic acid concentration differentiates impulsive from non-impulsive violent behavior. *Life Sciences, 33,* 2609–2614.

Linville, P. W., & Fischer, G. W. (1993). Exemplar and abstraction models of perceived group variability and stereotypicality. *Social Cognition, 11,* 92–125.

Lipkus, I. M., & Siegler, I. C. (1993). The belief in a just world and perceptions of discrimination. *Journal of Psychology, 127,* 465–474.

Lipkus, I. M., Dalbert, C., & Siegler, I. C. (1996). The importance of distinguishing the belief in a just world for self versus for others: Implications for Psychological Well-being. *Personality and Social Psychology Bulletin, 22,* 666–677.

Lipsey, M. W., & Wilson, D. B. (1993). The efficacy of psychological, educational, and behavioral treatment: Confirmation from meta-analysis. *American Psychologist, 48,* 1181–1209.

Liu, D., Diorio, J., Tannenbaum, B., Caldji, C., Francis, D., Freedman, A., Sharma, S., Pearson, D., Plotsky, P. M., & Meaney, M. J. (1997). Maternal care, hippocampal glucocorticoid receptors, and hypothalamic-pituitary-adrenal responses to stress. *Science, 277,* 1659–1662.

Liu, J. H., Campbell, S. M., & Condie, H. (1995). Ethnocentrism in dating preferences for an American sample: The ingroup bias in social context. *European Journal of Social Psychology, 25,* 95–115.

Liu, J. H., & Latané, B. (1998). Extremitization of attitudes: Does thought- and discussion-induced polarization cumulate? *Basic & Applied Social Psychology, 20,* 103–110.

Livesley, W. J. (1998). Suggestions for a framework for an empirically based classification of personality disorder. *Canadian Journal of Psychiatry 43,* 137–147.

Livingstone, M. S., & Hubel, D. H. (1984). Anatomy and physiology of a color system in the primate visual cortex. *Journal of Neuroscience, 4,* 309–356.

Lobaugh, N. J., Cole, S., & Rovet, J. F. (1998). Visual search for features and conjunctions in development. *Canadian Journal of Experimental Psychology, 52,* 201–212.

Locke, S. E., Kraus, L., Leserman, J., Hurst, M. W., Heisel, J. S., & Williams, R. M. (1984). Life change stress, psychiatric symptoms, and natural killer-cell activity. *Psychosomatic Medicine, 46,* 441–453.

Loehlin, J. C. (1989). Partitioning environmental and genetic contributions to behavioral development. *American Psychologist, 44,* 1285–1292.

Loehlin, J. C. (1992). *Genes and environment in personality development.* Newbury Park, CA: Sage.

Loehlin, J. C. (1997). A test of J. R. Harris' theory of peer influences on personality. *Journal of Personality and Social Psychology, 72,* 1197–1201.

Loehlin, J. C., Horn, J. M., & Willerman, L. (1981). Personality resemblance in adoptive families. *Behavior Genetics, 11,* 309–330.

Loehlin, J. C., Willerman, L., & Horn, J. M. (1985). Personality resemblances in adoptive families when the children are late-adolescent or adult. *Journal of Personality and Social Psychology, 48,* 376–392.

Loehlin, J. C., Willerman, L., & Horn, J. M. (1987). Personality resemblance in adoptive families: A 10-year follow-up. *Journal of Personality and Social Psychology, 53,* 961–969.

Loewenstein, R. J. (1994). Diagnosis, epidemiology, clinical course, treatment, and cost effectiveness of treatment for dissociative disorders and MPD: Report submitted to the Clinton Administration Task Force on Health Care Financing Reform. *Dissociation: Progress in the Dissociative Disorders, 7,* 3–11.

Loftus, E. F. (1993). The reality of repressed memories. *American Psychologist, 48,* 518–537.

Loftus, E. F., & Hoffman, H. G. (1989). Misinformation and memory: The creation of new memories. *Journal of Experimental Psychology: General, 118,* 100–114.

Loftus, E. F., Miller, D. G., & Burns, H. J. (1978). Semantic integration of verbal information into a visual memory. *Journal of Experimental Psychology: Human Learning and Memory, 4,* 19–31.

Loftus, E. F., & Palmer, J. C. (1974). Reconstruction of automobile destruction: An example of the interaction between language and memory. *Journal of Verbal Learning and Verbal Behavior, 13,* 585–589.

Loftus, E. F., & Pickrell, J. E. (1995). The formation of false memories. *Psychiatric Annals, 25,* 720–725.

Loftus, G. R. (1972). Eye fixations and recognition memory for pictures. *Cognitive Psychology, 3,* 525–551.

Loftus, G. R. (1983). Eye fixations on text and scenes. In K. Rayner (Ed.), *Eye movements in reading* (pp. 359–376). New York: Academic Press.

Logie, R. H., & Baddeley, A. D. (1990). Imagery and working memory. In P. J. Hampson & D. F. Marks (Eds.), *Imagery: Current developments.* (pp. 103–128). London: Routledge.

Logie, R. H., & Marchetti, C. (1991). Visuo-spatial working memory: Visual, spatial or central executive? In R. H. Logie & M. Denis, (Eds.), *Mental images in human cognition* (pp.105–115). Amsterdam: North-Holland.

Logie, R. H. (1986). Visuo-spatial processing in working memory. *Quarterly Journal of Experimental Psychology, 80,* 229–247.

Lohmann, K. J., & Lohmann, C. M. (1994). Detection of magnetic inclination angle by sea turtles: A possible mechanism for determining latitude. *Journal of Experimental Biology, 194,* 23–32.

Lohmann, K. J., & Lohmann, C. M. F. (1996). Detection of magnetic field intensity by sea turtles. *Nature, 380,* 59–61.

Loke, W., & Song, S. (1988). Central and peripheral visual processing in hearing and non-hearing individuals. *Bulletin of Psychonomic Society, 29,* 437–440.

Lonetto, R., & Templer, D. (1986). *Death anxiety.* New York: Hemisphere.

Loomis, A. L., Harvey, E. N., & Hobart, G. A. (1937). Cerebral states during sleep as studied by human potentials. *Journal of Experimental Psychology, 21,* 127–144.

Looren de Jong, H. (1996). Levels: Reduction and elimination in cognitive neuroscience. In C. W. Tolman, F. Cherry, et al. (Eds.), *Problems of theoretical psychology* (pp. 165–172). North York, ON, Canada: Captus Press.

Lord, K. R. (1994). Motivating recycling behavior: A quasiexperimental investigation of message and source strategies. *Psychology & Marketing, 11,* 341–358.

Lorenzo-Hernandez, J. (1998). How social categorization may inform the study of Hispanic immigration. *Hispanic Journal of Behavioral Sciences, 20,* 39–59.

Losch, M., & Cacioppo, J. (1990). Cognitive dissonance may enhance sympathetic tonis, but attitudes are changed to reduce negative effect rather than arousal. *Journal of Experimental Social Psychology, 26,* 289–304.

Lott, B. (1996) Politics or science? The question of gender sameness/difference. *American Psychologist, 51,* 153–154.

Lou, H. C., Hansen, D., Nordentoft, M., Pryds, O., et al. (1994). Prenatal stressors of human life affect fetal brain development. *Developmental Medicine & Child Neurology, 36,* 826–832.

Lovibond, P. F., Siddle, D. A., & Bond, N. W. (1993). Resistance to extinction of fear-relevant stimuli: Preparedness or selective sensitization? *Journal of Experimental Psychology: General, 122,* 449–461.

Lowe, C. F. (1979). Determinants of human operant behaviour. In M. D. Zeiler and P. Harzem (Eds.), *Advances in analysis of behavior (Vol. 1). Reinforceemnt and the organziation of behavior.* New York: Wiley.

Lowe, P. (1999, May 2). Alike and different. *Denver Post.*

Lu, L. (1999). Personal or environmental causes of happiness: A longitudinal analysis. *Journal of Social Psychology, 139,* 79–90.

Lu, L., & Shih, J. B. (1997a). Sources of happiness: A qualitative approach. *Journal of Social Psychology, 137,* 181–188.

Lu, L., & Shih, J. B. (1997b). Personality and happiness: Is mental health a mediator? *Personality & Individual Differences, 22,* 249–256.

Lu, L., Shih, J. B., Lin, Y. Y., & Ju, L. S. (1997). Personal and environmental correlates of happiness. *Personality & Individual Differences, 23,* 453–462.

Lubin, A. J. (1972). *Stranger on the Earth: Vincent van Gogh.* New York: Da Capo Press.

Luborsky, L., Diguer, L., Seligman, D. A., Rosenthal, R., Krause, E. D., Johnson, S., Halperin, G., Bishop, M., Berman, J. S., & Schweizer, E. (1999). The researcher's own therapy allegiances: A "wild card" in comparisons of treatment efficacy. *Clinical Psychology: Science & Practice 6,* 95–106.

Luborsky, L., Singer, B., & Luborsky, L. (1975). Comparative studies of psychotherapies: Is it true that "everyone has won and all must have prizes"? *Archives of General Psychiatry, 32,* 995–1008.

Lucas, R. J., Freedman, M. S., Muñoz, M., Garcia-Fernandez, J-M., & Foster, R. G. (1999). Regulation of the mammalian pineal by non-rod, non-cone, ocular photoreceptors. *Science, 284,* 505–507.

Luce, G. G. (1971). Biological rhythms in human and animal physiology. New York: Dover.

Luck, S. J., Vogel, E. K., & Shapiro, K. L. (1996). Word meanings can be accessed but not reported during the attentional blink. *Nature, 383,* 616–618.

Lunzer, E. A. (1978). Formal reasoning: A reappraisal. In B. Z. Presseisen, D. Goldstein, & M. H. Appel (Eds.), *Topics in cognitive development: Vol. 2. Language and operational thought* (pp. 47–76). New York: Plenum.

Luparello, T. J., Lyons, H. A., Bleecker, E. R., & McFadden, E. R. (1968). Influences of suggestion on airway reactivity in asthmatic subjects. *Psychosomatic Medicine, 30,* 819–825.

Lush, J. L. (1937). *Animal breeding plans.* Ames, IA: Collegiate Press

Lydon, J. E., Jamieson, D. W., & Zanna, M. P. (1988). Interpersonal similarity and the social and intellectual dimensions of first impressions. *Social Cognition, 6,* 269–286.

Lydon, J. E., Zanna, M. P., & Ross, M. (1988). Bolstering attitudes by auto-biographical recall: Attitude persistence and selective memory. *Personality and Social Psychology Bulletin, 14,* 78–86.

Lykken, D., Bouchard, T. J., Jr., McGue, M., & Tellegen, A. (1993). Heritability of Interests: A twin study. *Journal of Applied Psychology, 78,* 649–661.

Lykken, D., & Tellegen, A. (1996). Happiness is a stochastic phenomenon. *Psychological Science, 7,* 186–189.

Lykken, D. T. (1959). The GSR in the detection of guilt. *Journal of Applied Psychology, 43,* 385–388.

Lykken, D. T. (1960). The validity of the guilty knowledge technique: The effects of faking. *Journal of Applied Psychology, 44,* 258–262.

Lynch, E. D., Lee, M. K., Morrow, J. E., Welsch, P. L., Leon, P. E., & King, M. C. (1997). Nonsyndromic deafness DFNA1 associated with mutation of human homolog of the Drosophila gene diaphanous. *Science, 278,* 1315–1318.

Lynn, R. (1990). The role of nutrition in secular increases in intelligence. *Personality & Individual Differences, 11,* 273–285.

Lynn, R., & Martin, T. (1997). Gender differences in extraversion, neuroticism, and psychoticism in 37 nations. *Journal of Social Psychology, 137,* 369–373.

Lyons, E. A., & Levi, C. S. (1994). Sperm are not like salmon: Altered myometrial contractility is significant in unexplained infertility rates. *Radiology, 193[P],* 144.

Lyons, M. J., Eisen, S. A., Goldberg, J., True, W. Lin, N., Meyer, J. M., Toomey, R., Faraone, S. V., Merla-Ramos, M. A., &Tsuang, M. T. (1998). A Registry-Based Twin Study of Depression in Men. *Archives of General Psychiatry, 55,* 468–472.

Lyons, M. J., Goldberg, J., Eisen, S. A., True, W., Tsuang, M. T., Meyer, J. M., & Henderson, W. G. (1993). Do genes influence exposure to trauma: A twin study of combat. *American Journal of Medical Genetics (Neuropsychiatric Genetics), 48,* 22–27.

Lytton, H., & Romney, D. M. (1991). Parents' differential socialization of boys and girls: A meta-analysis. *Psychological Bulletin, 109,* 267–296.

Lyubomirsky, S., & Tucker, K. L. (1998). Implications of individual differences in subjective happiness for perceiving, interpreting, and thinking about life events. *Motivation & Emotion, 22,* 155–186.

Maas, J. B. (1998). *Power sleep.* New York: Harper Perennial.

Maass, A., Salvi, D., Arcuri, L., & Semin, G. (1989). Language use in intergroup contexts: The linguistic intergroup bias. *Journal of Personality and Social Psychology, 57,* 981–993.

Macaskill, N. D., & Macaskill, A. (1996). Rational-emotive therapy plus pharmacotherapy versus pharmacotherapy alone in the treatment of high cognitive dysfunction depression. *Cognitive Therapy & Research, 20,* 575–592.

Maccoby, E. E. (1988). Gender as a social category. *Developmental Psychology, 26,* 755–765.

Maccoby, E. E. (1990). Gender and relationships: A developmental account. *American Psychologist, 45,* 513–520.

Maccoby, E. E. (1991). Gender and relationships: A reprise. *American Psychologist, 46,* 538–539.

Maccoby, E. E., & Jacklin, C. N. (1987). Gender segregation in childhood. In H. W. Reese (Ed.), *Advances in child development and behavior* (Vol. 20, pp. 239–288). New York: Academic Press

MacGregor, A. J., Griffiths, G. O., Baker, J., & Spector, T. D. (1997). Determinants of pressure pain threshold in adult twins: Evidence that shared environmental influences predominate. *Pain, 73,* 253–257.

Mackie, D. M. (1986). Social identificaiton effects in group polarization. *Journal of Personality and Social Psychology, 50,* 720–728.

Macklin, M. L., Metzger, L. J., Litz, B. T., McNally, R. J., Lasko, N. B., Orr, S. P., & Pitman, R. K. (1998). Lower precombat intelligence is a risk factor for posttraumatic stress disorder. *Journal of Consulting & Clinical Psychology, 66,* 323–326.

MacLean, C. R. K., Walton, K. G., Winneberg, S. R., Levitsky, D. K., Manderino, J. V., Waziri, R., Hillis, S. L., & Schneider, R. H. (1997). Effects of the Transcendental Meditation program on adaptive mechanisms: Changes in hormone levels and responses to stress after 4 months of practice. *Psychoneuroendocrinology, 22,* 277–295.

Macmillan, M. (1992). Inhibition and the control of behavior: From Gall to Freud via Phineas Gage and the frontal lobes. *Brain & Cognition, 19,* 72–104.

Macmillan, M. B. (1986). A wonderful journey through skull and brains: The travels of Mr. Gage's tamping iron. *Brain & Cognition, 5,* 67–107.

MacPhillamy, D. J., & Lewinsohn, P. M. (1974). Depression as a function of levels of desired and obtained pleasure. *Journal of Abnormal Psychology, 83,* 651–657.

Macrae, C. N., Bodenhausen, G. V., Milne, A. B., & Jetten, J. (1994). Out of mind but back in sight: Stereotypes on the rebound. *Journal of Personality and Social Psychology, 67,* 808–817.

Macrae, C. N., Hewstone, M., & Griffiths, R. G. (1993). Procesing load and memory for stereotype-based information. *European Journal of Social Psychology, 23,* 77–87.

Maddi, S. R. (1989). *Personality Theories: A Comparative Analysis.* (Fifth Ed.), Chicago: Dorsey Press.

Maddi, S. R. (1998). The effectiveness of hardiness training. *Consulting Psychology Journal: Practice and Research, 50,* 78–86.

Madison, L. S., George, C., & Moeschler, J. B. (1986). Cognitive functioning in the fragile-*x* syndrome: A study of intellectual, memory and communication skills. *Journal of Mental Deficiency Research, 30,* 129–148.

Maguire, E. A., Gadian, D. G., Johnsrude, I. S., Good, C. D., Ashburner, J., Frackowiak, R. S. J., & Frith, C. D. (2000). Navigation-related structural change in the hippocampi of taxi drivers. *Proceedings of the National Academy of Sciences, USA,* 10.1073/pnas.070039597.

Maher, B. A. (1966). *Principles of psychopathology: An experimental approach.* New York: McGraw-Hill.

Mahler, H. I. M., & Kulik, J. A. (1998). Effects of preparatory videotapes on self-efficacy beliefs and recovery from coronary bypass surgery. *Annals of Behavioral Medicine, 20,* 39–46.

Mair, R. G., Harrison, L. M., & Flint, D. L. (1995). The neuropsychology of odor memory. In F. R. Schab & R. G. Crowder (Eds.), *Memory for odors* (pp. 39–69). Mahwah, NJ: Erlbaum.

Malan, D. H. (1976). *The frontier of brief psychotherapy: An example of the convergence of research and clinical practice.* New York: Plenum Medical Book Co.

Malina, R. M., & Bouchard, C. (1991). *Growth, maturation, and physical activity.* Champaign, IL: Human Kinetics Books.

Malkoff-Schwartz, S., Frank, E., Anderson, B., Sherrill, J. T., Siegel, L., Patterson, D., & Kupfer, D. J. (1998). Stressful Life Events and Social Rhythm Disruption in the Onset of Manic and Depressive Bipolar Episodes: A Preliminary Investigation. *Archives of General Psychiatry, 55,* 702–707.

Manabe, T., Noda, Y., Mamiya, T., Katagirl, H., Houtani, T., Nishi, M., Noda, T., Takahashi, T., Sugimoto, T., Nabeshima, T., & Takeshima, H. (1998). Facilitation of long-term potentiation and memory in mice lacking nociceptin receptors. *Nature, 394,* 577–581.

Mandler, G. (1967). Organization in memory. In K. W. Spence & J. T. Spence (Eds.), *The psychology of learning and motivation* (Vol. 1, pp. 327–372). San Diego: Academic Press.

Manfro, G. G., Otto, M. W., McArdle, E. T., Worthington, J. J., III, Rosenbaum, J. F., & Pollack, M. H. (1996). Relationship of antecedent stressful life events to childhood and family history of anxiety and the course of panic disorder. *Journal of Affective Disorders, 41,* 135–139.

Manke, B., McGuire, S., Reiss, D., Hetherington, E. M., & Plomin, R. (1995). Genetic contributions to children's extrafamilial social interactions: Teachers, friends, and peers. *Social Development, 4,* 238–256.

Mann, T., Nolen-Hoeksema, S., Huang, K., Burgard, D., Wright, A., & Hanson, K. (1997). Are Two Interventions Worse than None? Joint Primary and Secondary Prevention of Eating Disorders in College Females. *Health Psychology, 16,* 3.

Mansour, C. S., Haier, R. J., & Buchsbaum, M. S. (1996). Gender comparisons of cerebral glucose metabolic rate in healthy adults during a cognitive task. *Personality and Individual Differences, 20,* 183–191.

Mantzoros, C. S. (1999). The role of leptin in human obesity and disease: A review of current evidence. *Annals of Internal Medicine, 130,* 651–657.

Manuck, S. B., Cohen, S., Rabin, B. S., Muldoon, M. F., & Bachen, E. A. (1991). Individual differences in cellular immune response to stress. *Psychological. Science, 2,* 111–115.

Marcel, A. J. (1980). Conscious and preconscious recognition of polysemous words: Locating the selective effects of prior verbal context. In R. S. Nickerson (Ed.), *Attention and performance VIII.* Hillsdale, NJ: Erlbaum.

Marcel, A. J. (1983). Conscious and unconscious perceptions: Experiments on visual masking and word recognition. *Cognitive Psychology, 15,* 197–237.

Marcus, G. F., Vijayan, S., Rao, S. B., & Vishton, P. M. (1999). Rule learning by seven-month-old infants. *Science, 283,* 77–80.

Markham, R., & Wang, L. (1996). Recognition of emotion by Chinese and Australian children. *Journal of Cross-Cultural Psychology, 27,* 616–643.

Markovic, B. M., Dimitrijevic, M., & Jankovic, B. D (1993). Immunomodulation by conditioning: Recent developments. *International Journal of Neuroscience, 71*(1–4) 231–249.

Marks, I. (1997). Behaviour therapy for obsessive-compulsive disorder: A decade of progress. *Canadian Journal of Psychiatry, 42,* 1021–1027.

Marks, I., Lovell, K., Noshirvani, H., Livanou, M., & Sian, T. (1998). Treatment of Posttraumatic Stress Disorder by Exposure and/or Cognitive Restructuring: A Controlled Study. *Archives of General Psychiatry, 55,* 317–325.

Marks, I. M. (1969). *Fears and phobias.* New York: Academic Press.

Markson, L., & Bloom, P. (1997). Evidence against a dedicated system for word learning in children. Nature, 385, 813–815.

Markus, H. R., & Kitayama, S. (1991). Culture and the self: Implications for cognition, emotion, and motivation. *Psychological Review, 98,* 224–253.

Marmot, M. G. (1998). Improvement of social environment to improve health. *Lancet, 331,* 57–60.

Marmot, M. G., & Syme, S. L. (1976). Acculturation and coronary heart disease in Japanese-Americans. *American Journal of Epidemiology, 104,* 225–247.

Marr, D. (1982). *Vision: A computational investigation into the human representation and processing of visual information.* New York: Freeman.

Marsh, H. W. (1990). The structure of academic self-concept: The Marsh/Shavelson model. *Journal of Educational Psychology, 82,* 623–636.

Marsh, R. L., Landau, J. D., & Hicks, J. L. (1997). Contributions of inadequate source monitoring unconscious plagiarism during idea generation. *Journal of Experimental Psychology: Learning, Memory, and Cognition, 23,* 886–897.

Marshall, D. S. (1971). Sexual behavior on Mangaia. In D. S. Marshall & R. C. Suggs (Eds.), *Human sexual behavior* (pp. 103–162). New York: Basic Books.

Martin, A., Wiggs, C. L., Ungerlieder, L. G., & Haxby, J. V. (1996). Neural correlates of category-specific knowledge. *Nature, 379,* 649–652.

Martin, N. G., Eaves, L. J., Heath, A. C., Jardine, R., Feingold, L. N., & Eysenck, H. J. (1986). Transmission of social attitudes. *Proceedings of the National Academy of Sciences, 83,* 4364–4358.

Martin, R. A. (1996). The Situational Humor Response Questionnaire (SHRQ) and Coping Humor Scale (CHS): A decade of research findings. *Humor: International Journal of Humor Research, 9,* 251–272.

Martin, R. A., & Dobbin, J. P. (1988). Sense of humor, hassles, and immunoglobulin A: Evidence for a stress-moderating effect of humor. *International Journal of Psychiatry in Medicine, 18,* 93–105.

Martin, W. G., & Beittel, M. (1998) Toward a Global Sociology: Evaluating Current Conceptions, Methods, and Practices. *Sociological Quarterly, 39*(1), pp. 139–161.

Martindale, C. (1990). *The clockwork muse: The predictability of artistic styles.* New York: Basic Books.

Marucha, P. T., Kiecolt-Glaser, J. K., & Favagehi, M. (1998). Mucosal wound healing is impaired by examination stress. *Psychosomatic Medicine, 60,* 362–365.

Masataka, N. (1996). Perception of motherese in a signed language by 6-month-old deaf infants. *Developmental Psychology, 32,* 874–879.

Maslach, C., Santee, R. T., & Wade, C. (1987). Individuation, gender role, and dissent: Personality mediators of situational forces. *Journal of Personality and Social Psychology, 53,* 1088–1194.

Maslow, A. H. (1954). *Motivation and personality.* New York: Harper.

Maslow, A. H. (1968). *Toward a psychology of being* (2nd ed.). New York: Van Nostrand.

Maslow, A. H. (1970). *Motivation and personality* (2nd ed.). New York: Harper and Row.

Master mimics. (1996, December 30). *Boston Globe,* C1, C3.

Masters, W. H., & Johnson, V. E. (1966). *Human sexual response.* Boston: Little, Brown.

Matarazzo, J. D. (1972). *Wechsler's measurement and appraisal of adult intelligence.* Baltimore: Williams & Wilkins.

Mather, M., Henkel, L. A., & Johnson, M. K. (1997). Evaluating characteristics of false memories: Remember/know judgments and memory characteristics questionnaire compares. *Memory & Cognition, 25,* 826–837.

Matsumae, M., Kikinis, R., Mórocz, I. A., Lorenzo, A. V., Sándor, T., Albert, M. S., Black, P. M., & Jolesz, F. A. (1996). Age-related changes in intracranial compartment volumes in normal adults assessed by magnetic resonance imaging. *Journal of Neurosurgery, 84,* 982–992.

Matt, G. E., Navarro, A. M. (1997). What meta-analyses have and have not taught us about psychotherapy effects: A review and future directions. *Clinical Psychology Review, 17,* 1–32.

Matthews, B. A., Shimoff, E., Catania, A. C., & Sagvolden, T. (1977). Uninstructed human responding: Sensitivity to ratio and interval contingencies. *Journal of the Experimental Analysis of Behavior, 27,* 453–467.

Matthews, G., & Amelang, M. (1993). Extraversion, arousal theory and performance: A study of individual differences in the EEG. *Personality and Individual Differences, 14,* 347–363.

Matthews, G., & Gilliland, K. (1999). The personality theories of H. J. Eysenck and J. A. Gray: A comparative review. *Personality and Individual Differences, 26,* 583–626.

Mauro, R. (1988). Opponent processes in human emotions? An experimental investigation of hedonic contrast and affective interactions. *Motivation & Emotion, 12,* 333–351.

Mayer, J. D., & Salovey, P. (1997). What is emotional intelligence? In P. Salovey & D. J. Sluyter (Eds.), *Emotional development and emotional intelligence.* New York: Basic Books.

Mayer, R. E. (1997). *Thinking, problem solving, cognition.* New York: Freeman.

Mayes, A. R., & Downes, J. J. (Eds.). (1997). *Theories of organic amnesia.* Hove, England: Psychology Press/Erlbaum (UK) Taylor & Francis.

Maynard, R. A. (Ed.). (1996). *Kids having kids: A Robin Hood Foundation special report on the costs of adolescent childbearing.* New York: Robin Hood Foundation.

Maznevski, M. L. (1994). Understanding our differences: Performance in decision—making groups with diverse members. *Human Relations, 47,* 531–552.

McBride, J. (1999). *Steven Spielberg: A biography.* New York: Da Capo.

McCarlet, R. W., & Hobson, J. A. (1977). The neurobiological origins of psychoanalytic dream theory. *American Journal of Psychiatry, 134,* 1211–1221.

McCarley, R. W., & Hobson, J. A. (1975). Neuronal excitability modulation over the sleep cycle: A structural and mathematical model. *Science, 189,* 58–60.

McCartney, K., Harris, M. J., & Bernieri, F. (1990). Growing up and growing apart: A developmental meta-analysis of twin studies. *Psychological Bulletin, 107,* 226–237.

McCauley, C. R., Jussim, L. J., & Lee, Y. (1995). Stereotype accuacy: Toward appreciatig group differenfecs. In Y. Lee, L. J. Jussim, & C. R. McCauley (Ed.), *Stereotype acuracy: Toward appreciating group differences* (pp. 293–312). Washington DC: American Psychological Association.

McClearn, G. E., Johansson, B., Berg, S., Pedersen, N. L., Ahern, F., Petrill, S. A., & Plomin, R. (1997). Substantial genetic influence on cognitive abilities in twins 80 or more years old. *Science, 276,* 1560–1563.

McClelland, D. C., & Atkinson, J. W. (1953). *The achievement motive.* New York: Appleton-Century-Crofts.

McClelland, D. C., Koestner, R., & Weinbereger, J. (1989). How do self-attributed and implicit motives differ? *Psychological Review, 96,* 690–702.

McClelland, J. L., & Rumelhart, D. E. (1981). An interactive activation model of context effects in letter perception: Part 1. An account of basic findings. *Psychological Review, 88,* 375–407.

McClelland, J. L., & Rumelhart, D. E. (1986). *Parallel distributed processing: Explorations in the microstructure of cognition.* Cambridge: MIT Press.

McClintock, M. K. (1971). Menstrual synchrony and suppression. *Nature, 229,* 244–245.

McClintock, M. K., & Herdt, G. (1996). Rethinking puberty: The development of sexual attraction. *Current Directions in Psychological Science, 5,* 178–183.

McCloskey, M., Caramazza, A., & Green, B. (1980). Curvilinear motion in the absence of external forces: Naive beliefs about motion of objects. *Science, 210,* 1139–1141.

McCloskey, M, & Zaragoza, M. (1985). Misleading postevent information and memory for events: Arguments and evidence against memory impairment hypotheses. *Journal of Experimental Psychology: General, 114,* 1–16.

McCornack, S. A., & Parks, M. R. (1990). What women know that men don't: Sex differences in determining the truth behind deceptive messages. *Journal of Social and Personal Relationships, 7,* 107–118.

McCrae, R. H., & Costa, P. T. Jr. (1989a). Reinterpreting the Myers-Briggs type indicator from the perspective of the five-factor model of personality *Journal of Personality, 57,* 17–40.

McCrae, R. H., & Costa, P. T., Jr. (1989b). Different points of view: Self-reports and ratings in the assessment of personality. In J. P. Forgas & J. M. Innes (Eds.), *Recent Advance in Social Psychology: An International perspective* (pp. 429–439). Amsterdam: Elsevier North-Holland.

McCrae, R. H., & Costa, P. T., Jr. (1987). Validation of the five-factor model of personality across instruments and observers. *Journal of Personality and Social Psychology, 52,* 81–90.

McCrae, R. H., & Costa, P. (1984). *Emerging lives, enduring dispositions: Personality in adulthood.* Boston: Little, Brown.

McCrae, R. H., & Costa, P. T. (1997). Personality trait structure as a human universal. *American Psychologist, 52,* 509–516.

McCrae, R. H., Costa, P. T., Jr., DelPilar, G. H. Rolland, J. P., & Parker, W. D. (1998). Cross-cultural assessment of the five-factor model: The Revised NEO Personality Inventory. *Journal of Cross-Cultural Psychology, 29,* 171–188.

McDaniel, M. A., & Einstein, G. O. (1986). Bizarre imagery as an effective memory aid: The importance of distinctiveness. *Journal of Experimental Psychology: Learning, Memory, & Cognition, 12,* 54–65.

McDaniel, M. A., & Einstein, G. O., DeLosh, E. L., & May, C. P. (1995). The bizarreness effect: It's not surprising, it's complex. *Journal of Experimental Psychology: Learning, Memory, & Cognition, 21,* 422–435.

McDermott, K. B, & Roediger, H. L., III. (1998). Attempting to avoid illusory memories: Robust false recognition of associates persists under conditions of explicit warnings and immediate testing. *Journal of Memory and Language, 39,* 508–520.

McDougall, W. (1908/1960). *Introduction to social psychology.* New York: Barnes & Noble.

McEwen, B. S. (1997). Possible mechanisms for atrophy of the human hippocampus. *Molecular Psychiatry, 2,* 255–262.

McEwen, B. S., Biron, C. A., Brunson, K. W., Bulloch, K., Chambers, W. H., Dhabhar, F. S., Goldfarb, R. H., Kitson, R. P., Miller, A. H., Spencer, R. L., & Weiss, J. M. (1997). The role of adrenocorticoids as modulators of immune function in health and disease: Neural, endocrine and immune interactions. *Brain Research Review, 23,* 79–133.

McEwen, B. S., & Schmeck, H. M., Jr. (1994). *The Hostage Brain.* New York: Rockefeller University Press.

McFadden, D. (1982). *Tinnitus: Facts, theories and treatments.* Washington, DC: National Academy Press.

McFadden, D., & Pasanen, E. G. (1999). Spontaneous otoacoustic emissions in heterosexuals, homosexuals, and bisexuals. *Journal of the Acoustical Society of America, 105,* 2403–2413.

McFadden, D., & Plattsmier, H. S. (1983). Aspirin can potentiate the temporary hearing loss induced by intense sounds. *Hearing Research, 9,* 295–316.

McFadyen, R. G. (1998). Attitudes toward the unemployed. *Human Relations, 51,* 179–199.

McGaugh, J. L., & Herz, M. J. (1972). *Memory Consolidation.* San Francisco, CA: Albion.

McGoldrick, M., Giordano, J., Pearce, J. K. (Eds.) (1996). *Ethnicity and family therapy (2nd ed.).* New York: Guilford Press.

McGorry, P. D., & Edwards, J. (1998). The feasibility and effectiveness of early intervention in psychotic disorders: The Australian experience. *International Clinical Psychopharmacology,* 13(Suppl 1), S47–S52.

McGraw, K., Hoffman, R. I., Harker, C., & Herman, J. H. (1999). The development of circadian rhythms in a human infant. *Sleep, 22,* 303–310.

McGraw, M. B. (1943). *The neuromuscular maturation of the human infant.* New York: Columbia University Press.

McGue, M., & Lykken, D. T. (1992). Genetic influence on the risk of divorce. *Psychological Science, 3,* 368–373.

McGue, M., Bouchard, T. J., Jr., Iacono, W. G., & Lykken, D. T. (1993). Behavioral genetics of cognitive ability: A life-span perspective. In R. Plomin & G. E. McClearn (Eds.). *Nature, nurture & psychology* (pp. 59–76). Washington, DC, USA: American Psychological Association.

McGuffin, P., & Gottesman, I. I. (1985). Genetic influences on normal and abnormal development. In M. Rutter & L. Hersov (Eds.), *Child and Adolescent Psychiatry: Modern Approaches.* (2nd edition, pp. 17–33). Oxford: Blackwell Scientific.

McGuffin, P., Katz, R., Aldrich, J., & Bebbington, P. (1988). The Camberwell Collaborative Depression Study. II. Investigation of family members. *British Journal of Psychiatry, 152,* 766–774.

McGuffin, P., Katz, R., & Rutherford, J. (1991). Nature, nurture, and depression: A twin study. *Psycholoogical Medicine, 21,* 329–335.

McHale, S. M., Crouter, A. C., McGuire, S. A., & Updegraff, K. A. (1995). Congruence between mothers' and fathers' differential treatment of siblings: Links with family relations and children's well-being. *Child Development, 66,* 116–128.

McHugh, T. J., Blum, K. I., Tsien, J., Tonegawa, S., & Wilson, M. (1996). Impaired hippocampal representation of space in CA1-specific NMDAR1 knockout mice. *Cell, 87,* 1339–1349.

McIntosh, W. D., Martin, L. L., & Jones, J. B., III (1997). Goal beliefs, life events, and the malleability of people's judgments of their happiness. *Journal of Social Behavior & Personality, 12,* 567–575.

McKellar, P. (1965). The investigation of mental images. In S. A. Bartnet & A. McLaren (Eds.), *Penguin science survey B (biological sciences)* (pp. 79–94). New York: Penguin Books.

McKenna, R. J. (1972). Some effects of anxiety level and food cues on the eating behavior of obese and normal subjects: A comparison of the Schachterian and psychosomatic conceptions. *Journal of Personality and Social Psychology, 22,* 311–319.

McKoon, G., Ratcliff, R., & Dell, G. S. (1986). A critical evaluation of the semantic-episodic distinction. *Journal of Experimental Psychology: Learning, Memory, and Cognition, 12,* 295–306.

McLaughlin, S., & Margolskee, R. F. (1994). The sense of taste. *American Scientist, 82,* 538–545.

McLean, A. A. (1980). *Work stress.* Reading, MA: Addison-Wesley.

McLean, D. F., Timajchy, K. H., Wingo, P. A., & Floyd, R. L. (1993). Psychosocial measurement: Implications of the study of preterm delivery in black women. *American Journal of Preventive Medicine, 9,* 39–81.

McLeod, P. L., & Lobel, S. A. (1992). The effects of ethinic diversity on idea generation in small groups. *Academy of Management Best Paper Proceedings, 22,* 227–231.

McMillen, D. L., & Austin, J. B. (1971). Effect of positivev feedback on complaince following transgression. *Psychonomic Science, 24,* 59–61.

McNeil, T. F., Cantor-Graae, E., & Weinberger, D. R. (2000). Relationship of obstetric complications and differences in size of brain structures in monozygotic twin pairs discordant for schizophrenia. *American Journal of Psychiatry, 157,* 203–212.

McNicol, D. (1972). *A primer of signal detection theory.* London: Allen & Unwin.

McRoberts, C., Burlingame, G. M., & Hoag, M. J. (1998). Comparative efficacy of individual and group psychotherapy: A meta-analytic perspective. *Group Dynamics, 2,* 101–117.

Mead, M. (1928). *Coming of age in Samoa.* New York: Morrow.

Mealey, L., Bridgestock, R., & Townsend, G. C. (1999). Symmetry and perceived facial attractiveness: A monozygotic co-twin comparison. *Journal of Personality and Social Psychology, 76,* 151–158.

Meaney, M. J., Mitchell, J. B., Aitken, D. H., Bhatnagar, S., Bodnoff, S. R., Iny, L. J., & Sarrieau, A. (1991). The effects of neonatal handling on the development of the adrenocortical response to stress: Implications for neuropathology and cognitive deficits in later life. *Psychoneuroendocrinology, 16,* 85–103.

Medin, D. L., Lynch, E. B., & Solomon, K. O. (2000). Are there kinds of concepts? In S. T. Fiske, D. L. Schacter, & C. Zahn-Waxler (Eds.), *Annual Review of Psychology, 51,* 121–147.

Medin, D. L., & Schaffer, M. M. (1978). A context theory of classification learning. *Psychological Review, 85,* 207–238.

Mednick, S. (1962). The associative basis of the creative process. *Psychological Review, 69,* 220–232.

Mednick, S. A., Gabrielli, W. F., & Hutchings, B. (1984). Genetic factors in criminal behavior: Evidence from an adoption cohort. *Science, 224,* 891–893.

Mednick, S. A., Watson, J. B., Huttunen, M., Cannon, T. D., Katila, H., Machon, R., Mednick, B., Hollister, M., Parnas, J., Schulsinger, F., Sajaniemi, N., Voldsgaard, P., Pyhala, R., Gutkind, D., & Wang, X. (1998). A two-hit workikng model of the etiology of schizophrenia. In M. F. Lenzenweger & R. H. Dworkin (Eds.), *Origins and Development of Schizophrenia: Advances in Experimental Psychopathology.* Washington, DC: American Psychological Association. pp. 27–66.

Meehl, P. (1960). The cognitive activity of the clinician. *American Psychologist, 15,* 19–27.

Mehl, L. E. (1994). Hypnosis and conversion of the breech to the vertex position. *Archives of Family Medicine, 3,* 881–887l.

Mehler, J., Jusczyk, P. W., Lambertz, G., Halsted, N., Bertoncini, J., & Amiel-Tison, C. (1988). A precursor of language acquisition in young infants. *Cognition, 29,* 143–178.

Melchert, T. P. (1996). Childhood memory and a history of different forms of abuse. *Professional Psychology Research and Practice, 27,* 438–446.

Melding, P. S. (1995). How do older people respond to chronic pain? A review of coping with pain and illness in elders. *Pain Review, 2,* 65–75.

Mellet, E., Petit, L., Mazoyer, B., Denis, M., & Tzourio, N. (1998). Reopening the mental imagery debate: Lessons from functional neuro-anatomy. *NeuroImage, 8,* 129–139.

Mellet, E., Tzourio, N., Denis, M., & Mazoyer, B. (1998). Cortical anatomy of mental imagery of concrete nouns based on their dictionary definition. *Neuroreport, 9,* 803–808.

Mello, C., Nottebohm, F., & Clayton, D. (1995). Repeated exposure to one song leads to a rapid and persistent decline in an immediate early gene's response to that song in zebra finch telencephalon. *Journal of Neuroscience, 15,* 6919–6925.

Mello, C. V., Vicario, D. S., & Clayton, D. F. (1992). Song presentation induces gene expression in the songbird forebrain. *Proceedings of the National Academy of Science, USA, 89,* 6818–6822.

Melson, G. F., Windecker-Nelson, E., & Schwarz, R. (1998). Support and stress in mothers and fathers of young children. *Early Education & Development, 9,* 261–281.

Meltzoff, A. N., & Moore, M. K. (1977). Imitation of facial and manual gestures by human neonates. *Science, 198,* 75–78.

Melzack, R., & Wall, P. D. (1982). *The challenge of pain.* New York: Basic Books.

Menard, M. T., Kosslyn, S. M., Thompson, W. T., Alpert, N. M., & Rauch, S. L. (1996). Encoding words and pictures: A positron emission tomography study. *Neuropsychologia, 34,* 185–194.

Menyuk, P., Liebergott, J. W., & Schultz, M. C. (1995). *Early language development in full-term and premature infants.* Hillsdale, NJ: Erlbaum.

Menzies, R. G., & Clarke, J. C. (1993). The etiology of childhood water phobia. *Behaviour Research & Therapy, 31,* 499–501.

Menzies, R. G., & Clarke, J. C. (1995a). The etiology of acrophobia and its relationship to severity and individual response patterns. *Behaviour Research & Therapy, 33,* 795–803.

Menzies R. G., & Clarke, J. C. (1995b). The etiology of phobias: A non-associative account. *Clinical Psychology Review, 15,* 23–48.

Mercer, R. T., Nichols, E. G., & Doyle, G. C. (1989). *Transitions in a woman's life: Major life events in developmental context*. New York: Springer.

Meredith, L. S., Wells, K. B., Kaplan, S. H., & Mazel, R. M. (1996). Counseling typically provided for depression. Role of clinican specialty and payment system. *Arch Gen Psychiatry, 53*, 905–12 .

Merrick, E. N. (1995). Adolescent childbearing as career "choice": Perspective from an ecological context. *Journal of Counseling & Development, 73*, 288–295.

Merzenich, M. M., Jenkins, W. M., Johnston, P., Shreiner, C., Miller, S. L., & Tallal, P. (1996). Temporal processing deficits of language-learning impaired children ameliorated by training. *Science, 271*, 77–81.

Merzenich, M. M., Kaas, J. H., Wall, J. T., Sur, M., Nelson, R. J., & Felleman, D. J. (1983). Progression of change following median nerve section in the cortical representation of the hand in areas 3b and 1 in adult owl and squirrel monkeys. *Neuroscience, 10*(3), 639–665.

Merzenich, M. M., Kaas, J. H., Wall, J., Nelson, R. J., & Sur, M. (1983). Topographic reorganization of somatosensory cortical areas 3b and 1 in adult monkeys following restricted deafferentation. *Neuroscience, 8*, 33–55.

Messinger, S. M. (1998). Pleasure and complexity: Berlyne revisited. *Journal of Psychology, 132*, 558–560.

Metalsky, G. I., Joiner, T. E., Hardin, T. S., Abramson, L. Y. (1993). Depressive reactions to failure in a naturalistic setting: A test of the hopelessness and self-esteem theories of depression. *Journal of Abnormal Psychology, 103*, 101–109.

Metcalfe, J. (1986). Premonitions of insight predict impending error. *Journal of Experimental Psychology: Learning, Memory, and Cognition, 12*, 623–634.

Metcalfe, J., & Wiebe, D. (1987). Intuition in insight and non-insight problem solving. *Memory and Cognition, 15*, 238–246.

Meunier, M., Hadfield, W., Bachevalier, J., & Murray, E. A. (1996). Effects of rhinal cortex lesions combined with hippocampectomy on visual recognition memory in rhesus monkeys. *Journal of Neurophysiology, 75*, 1190–1205.

Meyer, D. E., & Schvaneveldt, R. W. (1971). Facilitation in recognizing pairs of words: Evidence of a dependence between retrieval operations. *Journal of Experimental Psychology, 90*, 227–234.

Meyer, S-L., Murphy, C. M., Cascardi, M., & Birns, B. (1991). Gender and relationships: Beyond the peer group. *American Psychologist, 46*, 537.

Meyers, A. W., Stunkard, A. J., & Coll, M. (1980). Food accessibility and food choice: A test of Schachter's externality hypothesis. *Archives of General Psychiatry, 37*, 1133–1135.

Micheli, R. (1985, June). Water babies. *Parents, 60*(6), 8–13.

Michener, W., & Rozin, P. (1994). Pharmacological versus sensory factors in the satiation of chocolate craving. *Physiology & Behavior, 56*, 419–422.

Mickelson, K. D., Kessler, R. C., & Shaver, P. R. (1997). Adult attachment in a nationally representative sample. *Journal of Personality & Social Psychology, 73*, 1092–1106.

Miklowitz, D. J., Goldstein, M. J., Nuechterlein, K. H., Snyder, K. S., & Mintz, J. (1988). Family factors and the course of bipolar affective disorder. *Archives of General Psychiatry, 45*, 225–231.

Mikulincer, M. (1994). *Human learned helplessness: A coping perspective*. New York: Plenum.

Mikulincer, M., Florian, V., & Weller, A. (1993). Attachment styles, coping strategies, and posttraumatic psychological distress: The impact of the Gulf War in Israel. *Journal of Personality & Social Psychology, 64*, 817–826 .

Mikulincer, M., & Horesh, N. (1999). Adult attachment style and the perception of others: The role of projective mechanisms. *Journal of Personality and Social Psychology, 76*, 1022–1034.

Miles, L. E. M., Raynal, D. M., & Wilson, M. A. (1977). Blind man living in normal society has circadian rhythms of 24.9 hours. *Science, 198*, 421–423.

Miles, W. F. S. (1993). Hausa dreams. *Anthropologica, 35*, 105–116.

Milgram, S. (1963). Behavioral study of obedience. *Journal of Abnormal and Social Psychology, 67*, 371–378.

Milgram, S. (1965). Some conditions of obediencce and disobedience to authority. *Human Relations, 18*, 57–76.

Milgram, S. (1974). *Obedience to authority: An experimental view*. New York: Harper & Row.

Miller, A. G., Collins, B. E., Brief, D. E. (1995). Perspectives on obedience to authority: The legacy of the Milgram experiments. *Journal of Social Issues, 51*, 1–19.

Miller, G. A. (1956). The magical number seven, plus or minus two: Some limits on our capacity for processing information. *Psychological Review, 63*, 81–97.

Miller, G. E., Dopp, J. M., Stevens, S. Y., & Fahey, J. L. (1999). Psychosocial predictors of natural killer cell mobilzation during marital conflict. *Health Psychology, 18*, 262–271.

Miller, I. W., Keitner, G. E., Whisman, M. A., Ryan, C. E., Epstein, N. B., & Bishop, D. S. (1992). Depressed patients with dysfunctional families: Description and course of illness. *Journal of Abnormal Psychology, 101*, 637–646.

Miller, J. G. (1997). A cultural-psychology perspective on intelligence. In R. J. Sternberg & E. Grigorenko (Eds.), *Intelligence, heredity, and environment* (pp. 269–302). New York: Cambridge University Press.

Miller, J. M., Boudreaux, M. C., & Regan, F. A. (1995). A case-control study of cocaine use in pregnancy. *American Journal of Obstetrics and Gynecology, 172*, 180–185.

Miller, M. G., & Ross, M. (1975). Self-serving biases in attribution of causality: Fact or fiction? *Psychological Bulletin, 82*, 313–325.

Miller, N., Maruayama, G., Beaber, R. J., & Valone, K. (1976). Speed of speech and persuasion. *Journal of Personality and Social Psychology, 34*, 615–624.

Miller, N. E. (1959). Liberalization of basic S-R concepts: Extensions to conflict behavior, motivation, and social learning. In S. Koch (Ed.), *Psychology: A study of sicience: Vol. 2*. New York: McGraw –Hill.

Miller, T. Q., Smith, T. W., Turner, C. W., Guijarro, M. L., & Hallet, A. J. (1996). A meta-analytic review of research on hostility and physical health. *Psychological Bulletin, 119*, 322–348.

Miller, W. B., Pasta, D. J., MacMurray, J., Chiu, C., Wu, H., & Comings, D. E. (1999). Dopamine receptor genes are associated with age at first sexual intercourse. *Journal of Biosocial Science, 31*, 43–54.

Mills, D. L., Coffey-Corina, S., & Neville, H. J. (1997). Language comprehension and cerebral specialization from 13 to 20 months. *Developmental Neuropsychology, 13*, 397–445.

Milner, A. D., & Goodale, M. A. (1995). *The visual brain in action*. Oxford University Press.

Milner, B., Corkin, S., & Teuber, H. L. (1968). Further analysis of the hippocampal amnesic syndrome: 14-year followup study of H. M. *Neuropsychologia, 6*, 215–234.

Milton, J., & Weisman, R. (1999a). Does psi exist? Lack of replication of an anomalous process of information transfer. *Psychological Bulletin, 125*, 387–391.

Milton, J., & Weisman, R. (1999b). A meta-analysis of mass-media tests of extrasensory perception. *British Journal of Psychology, 90*, 235–240.

Minckler, T. M., & Boyd, E. (1968). Physical growth. In J. Minckler (Ed.), *Pathology of the nervous system* (Vol. 1, pp. 98–122). New York: McGraw-Hill.

Mineka, S., Davison, M., Cook, M., & Keir, R. (1984). Observational conditioning of snake fear in Rhesus monkeys. *Journal of Abnormal Psychology, 93*, 355–372.

Minton, H. L. (1988). Charting life history: Lewis M. Terman's study of the gifted. In J. G. Morawski (Ed.). *The rise of experimentation in American psychology* (pp. 138–162). New Haven, CT: Yale University Press.

Minuchin, S. (1974). *Families and Family Therapy*. Cambridge, MA: Harvard University Press.

Minuchin, S., & Fishman, H. C. (1981). *Family Therapy Techniques*. Cambridge, MA: Harvard University Press.

Mirsky, A. F., & Quinn, O. W. (1988). The Genain quadruplets. *Schizophrenia Bulletin, 14*, 595–612.

Mischel, W. (1984). Convergences and challenges in the search for consistency. *American Psychologist, 39*, 351–364.

Mischel, W., & Peake, P. K. (1982). Beyond déjà vu in the search for cross-situational consistency. *Psychological Review, 90*, 394–402.

Mischel, W., Shoda, Y., & Rodriguez, M. L. (1989). Delay of gratification in children. *Science, 244*, 933–938.

Mishkin, M. (1982). A memory system in the monkey. *Philosophical Transactions of the Royal Society of London Series B, 298*, 85–95.

Mishkin, M., & Appenzeller, T. (1987). The anatomy of memory. *Scientific American, 256*, 80–89.

Mishkin, M., Ungerleider, L. G., & Macko, K. A. (1983). Object vision and spatial vision: Two cortical pathways. *Trends in Neurosciences, 6*, 414–417.

Miyazaki, K. (1993). Absolute pitch as an inability: Identification of musical intervals in a tonal context. *Music Perception, 11*, 55–71.

Modell, J. (1996). Family niche and intellectual bent. [Review of *Born to Rebel* by Frank J. Sulloway]. *Science, 275*, 624.

Modell, J., Mountz, J., Curtis, G., & Greden, J. (1989). Neurophysiologic dysfunction in basal ganglia/limbic striatal and thalamocortical circuits as a pathogenetic mechanisms of obsessive-compulsive disorder. *Journal of Neuropsychiatry, 1*, 27–36.

Mogilner, A., Grossman, J. A., Ribary, U., Joliot, M., Volkman, J., Rapaport, D., Beasley, R. W., & Llinas, R. R. (1993). Somatosensory cortical plasticity in adult humans revealed by magnetoencephalography. *Proceedings of the National Academy of Sciences, USA, 90*(8), 3593–3597.

Mojtabai, R., Nicholson, R. A., & Carpenter, B. N. (1998). Role of psychosocial treatments in management of schizophrenia: A meta-analytic review of controlled outcome studies. *Schizophrenia Bulletin, 24*, 569–587.

Money, J. (1975). Ablatio penis: normal male infant sex-reassigned as a girl. *Archives of Sexual Behavior, 4,* 65–71.

Monk, T. H., Buysse, D. J., Reynolds, C. F., Berga, S. L., Jarrett, D. B., Begley, A. E., & Kupfer, D. J. (1997). Circadian rhythms in human performance and mood under constant conditions. *Journal of Sleep Research, 6,* 9–18.

Monroe, S. M., & Depue, R. A. (1991). Life stress and depression. In J. Becker & A. Kleinman (Eds.), Psychosocial aspects of depression (pp. 101–130). Hillsdale, NJ: Erlbaum.

Monteith, M. J. (1996). Affective reactions to prejudice-related discrepant responses: The impact of standard salience. *Personality and Social Psychology Bulletin, 22,* 48–59.

Montgomery, G. H., & Bovbjerg, D. H. (1997). The development of anititpatory nausea in patients receiving adjuvant chemotherapy for breast cancer. *Physiology & Behavior, 5,* 737–741.

Montgomery, G. H., & Sheehan, J. (1998). Surreptitious observation of responses to hypnotically suggested hallucinations: A test of the compliance hypothesis. *International Journal of Clinical & Experimental Hypnosis, 46,* 191–203.

Montreys, C. R., & Borod, J. C. (1998). A preliminary evaluation of emotional experience and expression following unilateral braiin damage. *International Journal of Neuroscience, 96,* 269–283.

Moody, D. B., Stebbins, W. C., & May, B. J. (1990). Auditory perception of communication signals by Japanese monkeys. In W. C. Stebbins & M. A. Berkley (Eds.), *Comparative perception: Complex signals* (pp. 311–343). New York: Wiley.

Moore, B. C. J. (1982). *Introduction to the psychology of hearing* (2nd ed.). New York: Academic Press.

Moore, K. L., & Persaud, T. V. N. (1993). *Before we are born* (4th ed.). Philadelphia: Saunders.

Moore-Ede, M. (1982). *The clocks that time us: Physiology of the circadian timing system.* Cambridge, MA: Harvard University Press.

Mooren, J. H., & Van Krogten, I. A. (1993). Contributions to the history of psychology: CXII. Magda B. Arnold revisited: 1991. *Psychological Reports, 72,* 67–84.

Moorhead, G., Ference, R., & Neck, C. P. (1991). Group decision fiascoes continue: Space shuttle Challenger and a revised groupthink framework. *Human Relations, 44,* 539–550.

Moran, P. (1999). The epidemiology of antisocial personality disorder. *Social Psychiatry & Psychiatric Epidemiology, 34,* 231–242.

Moreland, R. L., Argote, L., & Krishnan, R. (1996). Socially shared cognition at work: Transactive memory and group performance. In J. L. Nye & M. Bower (Eds.), *What so social about social cognition? Social cognition in small groups* (pp. 57–84). Newbury Park, CA: Sage.

Moreland, R. L., & Zajonc, R. B. (1982). Exposure effects in person perception: Familiarity, similarity, and attraction. *Journal of Experimental Social Psychology, 18,* 395–415.

Morgan, A. H. (1973). The heritability of hypnotic susceptibility in twins. *Journal of Abnormal Psychology, 82,* 55–61.

Morgan, J. L., & Demuth, K. D. (1996). *Signal to syntax: Bootstrapping from speech to grammar in early acquisition.* Hillsdale, NJ: Erlbaum.

Morgane, P. J., Austin-LaFrance, R., Bronzino, J., Tonkiss, J., Diaz-Cintra, S., Cintra, L., Kemper, T., & Galler, J. R. (1993). Prenatal malnutrition and development of the brain. *Neuroscience and Biobehavioral Reviews, 17,* 91–128.

Mori, H., Kamada, M., Maegawa, M., Yamamoto, S., Aono, T., Futaki, S., Yano, M., Kido, H., & Koide, S. S. (1998). Enzymatic activation of immunoglobulin binding factor in female reproductive tract. *Biochemical and Biophysical Research Communications, 246,* 409–413.

Morin, R. (1997, November 6). Skewering the perpetrators of science's most improbable research. *International Herald Tribune,* Thursday, Nov. 6, 1977, p. 1.

Morris, C. D., Bransford, J. D., & Franks, J. J. (1977). Levels of processing versus transfer-appropriate processing. *Journal of Verbal Learning and Verbal Behavior, 16,* 519–533.

Morris, J. S., Oehman, A., & Dolan, R. J. (1998). Conscious and unconscious emotional learning in the human amygdala. *Nature, 393,* 460–470.

Morris, M. W., & Peng, K. (1994). Culture and cause: American and Chinese attributions for social and physical events. *Journal of Personality and Social Psychology, 67,* 949–971.

Morris, R. (1984). Developments of a water-maze procedure for studying spatial learning in the rat. *Journal of Neuroscience Methods, 11,* 47–60.

Morris, S. (1979) *The Book of Strange Facts and Useless Information.* Garden City, NY: Doubleday.

Morris, W., & Miller, R. (1975). The effects of consensus-breaking and consensus preempting partner onreduction in conformity. *Journal of Experimental Social Psychology, 11,* 215–23.

Morris, W. N., Worchel, S., Bois, J. L., Pearson, J. A., Rountree, C. A., Samaha, G. M., Wachtler, J., & Wright, S. I. (1976). Collective coping with stress: Group reactions to fear, anxiety, and ambiguity. *Journal of Personality and Social Psychology, 33,* 674–679.

Morrison, E. W., & Bies, R. J. (1991). Impression management in the feedback-seeking process: A literature review and research agenda. *Academy of Management Review, 16,* 322–341.

Morse, D. R., Martin, J. S., Furst, M. L., & Dubin, L. L. (1977). A physiological and subjective evaluation of meditation, hypnosis, and relaxation. *Psychosomatic Medicine, 39,* 304–324.

Mortensen, P. B., Pedersen, C. B., Westergaard, T., Wohlfahrt, J., Ewald, H., Mors, O., Andersen, P. K., & Melbye, M. (1999). Effects of family history and place and season of birth on the risk of schizophrenia. *New England Journal of Medicine, 340,* 603–608.

Moscovitch, M., & Craik, F. I. M. (1976). Depth of processing, retrieval cues, and uniqueness of encoding as factors in recall. *Journal of Verbal Learning and Verbal Behavior, 15,* 447–458.

Moser, M., Lehofer, M., Hoehn-Saric, R., McLeod, D. R., Hildebrandt, G., Steinbrenner, B., Voica, M., Liebmann, P., & Zapotoczky, H. (1998). Increased heart rate in depressed subjects in spite of unchanged autonomic balance. *Journal of Affective Disorders, 48,* 115–124.

Moskowitz, D. S. (1993). Dominance and friendliness: On the interaction of gender and situation. *Journal of Personality, 61,* 387–409.

Mowrer, O. H. (1939). A stimulus-response analysis of anxiety and its role as a reinforcing agent. *Psychological Review, 46,* 553–565.

Muczyk, J. P., & Reimann, B. C. (1987). The case for directive leadership. *Academy of Management Review, 12,* 647–687.

Muehlenhard, C. L., & Linton, M. A. (1987). Date rape and sexual aggression in dating situations: Incidence and risk factors. *Journal of Counseling Psychology, 34,* 186–196.

Mueser, K. T., Goodman, L. B., Trumbetta, S. L., Rosenberg, S. D., Osher, F. C., Vidaver, R., Auciello, P., & Foy, D. W. (1998). Trauma and posttraumatic stress disorder in severe mental illness. *Journal of Consulting & Clinical Psychology, 66,* 493–499.

Mullen, B., Anthony, T., Salas, E., & Driskell, J. E. (1994). Group cohesiveness and quality of decision making: An integration of tests of the groupthink hypothesis. *Small Group Research, 25,* 189–204.

Mullen, B., & Johnson, C. (1990). Distinctiveness-based illusory correlations and stereotyping: A meta-analytic integration. *British Journal of Social Psychology, 29,* 11–28.

Mullen, B., Symons, C., Hu, L., & Salas, E. (1989). Group size, leadership, behavior, and subordinate satisfaction. *Journal of General Psyuchology, 116,* 155–170.

Murphy, C. (1986). Taste and smell in the elderly. In H. L. Meiselman & R. S. Rivlin (Eds.), *Clinical measurement of taste and smell* (pp. 343–371). New York: Macmillan.

Murphy, C. (1995). Age-associated differences in memory for odors. In F. R. Schab & R. G. Crowder (Eds.), *Memory for odors* (pp. 109–131). Mahwah, NJ: Erlbaum.

Murphy, L. J., & Mitchell, D. L. (1998). When writing helps to heal: e-mail as therapy. *British Journal of Guidance and Counseling, 26,* 21–32.

Murray, C. J. L., and Lopez, A. D. (Eds.). (1996). *The global burden of disease. A comprehensive assessment of mortality and disability from diseases, injuries, and risk factors in 1990 and projected to 2020.* Cambridge, MA: Harvard School of Public Health.

Murray, E. A. (1996). What have ablation studies told us about the neural substrates of stimulus memory? *Seminars in Neuroscience, 8,* 13–22.

Murray, E. J., Lamnin, A., & Carver, C. (1989). Emotional expression in written essays and psychotherapy. *Journal of Social and Clinical Psychology, 8,* 414–429.

Murray, I. R., Arnott, J. L., & Rohwer, E. A. (1996). Emotional stress in synthetic speech: Progress and future directions. *Speech Communication, 20,* 85–91.

Murray, S. L., Holmes, J. G., & Griffin, D. W. (1996a). The benefits of positive illusions: Idealization and the construction of satisfaction in close relationships. *Journal of Peresonaltiy and Social Psychology, 70,* 78–98.

Murzynski, J. & Degelman, D. (1996). Body language of women and judgments of vulnerability to sexual assault. *Journal of Applied Social Psychology 26,* 1617–1626.

Myers, C. E., McGlinchey-Berroth, R., Warren, S., Monti, L., Brawn, C. M., & Gluck, M. A. (2000). Latent learning in medial temporal amnesia: Evidence for disrupted representational but preserved attentional processes. *Neuropsychology, 14,* 3–15.

Myers, D. G. (1993). *The pursuit of happiness : Discovering the pathway to fulfillment, well-being, and enduring personal joy.* New York: Avon Books.

Myers, D. G. (2000). The funds, friends, and faith of happy people. *American Psychologist, 55,* 56–67.

Myers, M. B., & McCaulley, M. H. (1985). *Manual: A guide to the development and the use of the Myers-Briggs Type Indicator.* Palo Alto, CA: Consulting Psychologists Press.

Nadel, L., & Moscovitch, M. (1997). Memory consolidation, retrograde amnesia and the hippocampal complex. *Current Opinion in Neurobiology, 7*, 217–227.

Nader, K., Bechara, A., & van der Kooy, D. (1997). Neurobiological constraints on behavioral models of motivation. *Annual Review of Psychology, 48*, 85–114.

Nagel, E. (1979). *The structure of science: Problems in the logic of scientific explanation* (2nd ed.). Indianapolis: Hackett.

Naigles, L. G., & Gelman, S. A. (1995). Overextensions in comprehension and production revisited: Preferential-looking in a study of dog, cat, and cow. *Journal of Child Language, 22*, 19–46.

Nakayama, K., He, Z. J., & Shimojo, S. (1995). Visual surface representation: A critical link between lower-level and higher-level vision. In S. M. Kosslyn & D. N. Osherson (Eds.), *Visual cognition: An invitation to cognitive science, Vol. 2* (2nd ed) (pp. 1–70). Cambridge, MA: MIT Press.

Nakayama, K., & Mackeben, M. (1989). Sustained and transient components of focal visual attention. *Vision Research, 29*, 1631–1647.

Nasby, W., Hayden, B., & DePaulo, B. M. (1979). Attributional bias among aggressive boys to interpret unambiguous social stimuli as displays of hostility. *Journal of Abnormal Psychology 89*, 459–468.

Nathans, J. (1994). In the eye of the beholder: Visual pigments and inherited variations in human vision. *Cell, 78*, 357–360.

Nathawat, S. S., Singh, R., & Singh, B. (1997). The effect of need for achievement on attributional style. *Journal of Social Psychology, 137*, 55–62.

National Alliance for Caregiving, and the American Association of Retired Persons. (1997). *Family Caregiving in the U.S.: Findings from a National Study.*

National Center on Addiction and Substance Abuse at Columbia University. (1994). *Cost of substance abuse to America's health care system; Report 2: Medicare Hospital Costs.*

National Institute on Drug Abuse (1998). Slide Teaching Packet I, For Health Practitioners, Teachers and Neuroscientists. Section III: Introduction to Drugs of Abuse: Cocaine, Opiates (Heroin) and Marijuana (THC).

National Institute on Drug Abuse. (1997). Monitoring the Future Study: Drug use among high school Seniors. *http://www.whitehousedrugpolicy. gov/drugfact/factsheet/druguse.html.*

National Opinion Research Center. (1994). *General social surveys, 1972–1994: Cumulative codebook.* Chicago: Author, pp. 881–889.

National Sleep Foundation. (1998). *Omnibus sleep in America poll.* www.sleepfoundation.org/publications/1998poll.html.

Nauta, M. C. E. & Vorst, H. C. M. (1994). A meta-analysis on the treatment of obsessive-compulsive disorder: A comparison of antidepressants, behavior, and cognitive therapy. *Clinical Psychology Review, 14*, 359–381.

Neel, R. G., Tzeng, O. C., & Baysal, C. (1986). Need achievement in a cross-cultural contact study. *International Review of Applied Psychology, 35*, 225–229.

Neeper, S. A., Gómez-Pinilla, F., Choi, J., & Cotman C. (1995). Exercise and brain neurotropins. *Nature, 373*, 109.

Neeper, S. A., Gómez-Pinilla, F., Choi, J., & Cotman C. W. (1996). Physical activity increases mRNA for brain-derived neurotrophic factor and nerve growth factor in rat brain. *Brain Research, 726*, 49–56.

Neimeyer, G. J., MacNair, R., Metzler, A. E., & Courchaine, K. (1991). Changing personal beliefs: Effects of forewarning, argument quality, prior bias, and personal exploration. *Journal of Social & Clinical Psychology, 10*, 1–20.

Neisser, U. (1967). *Cognitive psychology.* New York: Appleton-Century-Crofts.

Neisser, U. (1982). *Memory observed: Remembering in natural contexts.* San Francisco: Freeman.

Neisser, U., Boodoo, G., Bouchard, T. J., Jr., Boykin, A. W., Brody, N., Ceci, S. J., Halpern, D. F., Loehlin, J. C., Perloff, R., Sternberg, R. J., & Urbina, S. (1996). Intelligence: Knowns and unknowns. *American Psychologist, 51*, 77–101.

Neisser, U., & Harsch, N. (1992). Phantom flashbulbs: False recollections of hearing news about *Challenger.* In E. Winograd & U. Neisser (Eds.), *Affect and accuracy in recall: Studies of "flashbulb memories"* (pp. 9–31). Cambridge, UK: Cambridge University Press.

Neitz, J., Neitz, M., & Jacobs, G. H. (1993). More than three different cone pigments among people with normal color vision. *Vision Research, 33*, 117–122.

Neitz, J., Neitz, M., & Kainz, P. M. (1996). Visual pigment gene structure and the severity of color vision defects. *Science, 274*, 801–804.

Neitz, M., & Neitz, J. (1995). Numbers and ratios of visual pigment genes for normal red-green color vision. *Science, 267*, 1013–1016.

Nelson, C. A. (1999). Human plasticity and human development. *Current Directions in Psychological Science, 8*, 42–45.

Nelson, C. B., Heath, A. C., & Kessler, R. C. (1998). Temporal progression of alcohol dependence symptoms in the U.S. household population: results from the National Comorbidity Survey. *Journal of Consulting & Clinical Psychology, 66,3*, 474–483.

Nelson, K. (1981). Individual differences in language development: Implications for development and language. *Developmental Psychology, 17*, 170–187.

Nelson, K. E. (1989). Strategies for first language teaching. In M. L. Rice & R. L. Schiefelbusch (Eds.), *The teachability of language* (pp. 263–310). Baltimore: Paul H. Brookes.

Nelson, M. D., Saykin, A. J., Flashman, L. A., & Riordan, H. J. (1998). Hippocampal Volume Reduction in Schizophrenia as Assessed by Magnetic Resonance Imaging: A Meta-analytic Study (1998). *Archives of General Psychiatry, 55*, 433–440.

Nemeroff, C., & Rozin, P. (1989). "You are what you eat": Applying the demand-free "impressions" technique to an unacknowledged belief. *Ethos, 17*, 50–69.

Nemeroff, C. J., Stein, R., Diehl, N. S., & Smilach, K. M. (1994). From the Cleavers to the Clintons, Role choices and body orientation as reflected in magazine article content. *International Journal of Eating Disorders, 16*, 167–176.

Nemeth, P. (1979). *An investigation into the relationship between humor and anxiety.* Unpublished doctoral dissertation. University of Maryland, College Park.

Nestler, E. J. (1997). Schizophrenia: An emerging pathophysiology. *Nature, 385*, 578–579.

Nettelbeck, T. (1987). Inspection time and intelligence. In P. A. Vernon (Ed.), *Speed of information processing and intelligence.* Norwood, NJ: Ablex.

Neuman, J. H., & Baron, R. A. (1998). Workplace violence and workplace aggtression: Evbidence concerning specific forms, potential causes, and preferred targets. *Journal of Management, 3*, 391–419.

Neumann, C., & Walker, E. F. (1996). Childhood neuromotor soft signs, behavior problems, and adult psychopathoology. In: T. Ollendick & R. Prinz (Eds.), *Advances in Clinical Child Psychology.* New York: Plenum Press.

Nevid, J., Rathus, S., & Rubenstein, H. (1998). *Health in the new millennium.* New York: Worth.

Neville, H. J. (1988). Cerebral organization for spatial attention. In J. Stiles-Davis, M. Kritchevsky, & U. Bellugi (Eds.), *Spatial cognition. Brain bases and development.* Hillsdale, NJ: Erlbaum.

Neville, H. J. (1990). Intermodal competition and compensation in development. *Annals of the New York Academy of Sciences, 608*, 71–91.

Neville, H. J., & Lawson, D. (1987). Attention to central and peripheral visual space in movement detection tasks: An event-related and behavioral study: II. Congenitally deaf adults. *Brain Research, 405*, 268–283.

Neville, H. J., Schmidt, A., & Kutas, M. (1983). Altered visual-evoked potentials in congenitally deaf adults. *Brain Research, 266*, 127–132.

Newcombe, N. S., Drummey, A. B., Fox, N. A., Lie, E, & Ottinger-Alberts, W. (2000). Remembering early childhood: How much, how, and why (or why not). *Current Directions in Psychological Science, 9*, 55–58.

Newcomer, J. W., Selke, G., Melson, A. K., Hershey, T., Craft, S., Richards, K., & Alderson, A. L. (1999). Decreased Memory performance in healthy humans induced by stress-level cortisol treatment. *Archives of General Psychiatry, 56*, 527–533.

Newell, A. (1990). *Unified theories of cognition.* Cambridge, MA: Harvard University Press.

Newell, A., & Simon, H. A. (1972). *Human problem solving.* Englewood Cliffs, NJ: Prentice-Hall.

Newman, E. A., & Zahs, K. R. (1998). Modulation of neuronal activity by glial cells in the retina. *Journal of Neuroscience, 18*, 4022–4028.

Newman, J., Rosenbach, J. H., Burns, K. L., Latimer, B. C. Matocha, H. R. & Vogt, E. R. (1995). An experimental test of "The Mozart effect": Does Listening to his music improve spatial ability? *Perceptual and Motor Skills, 81*, 1379–1387.

Newman, L. S., Duff, K. J., & Baumeister, R. F. (1997). A New Look at Defensive Projection: Thought Suppression, Accessibility, and Biased Person Perception. *Journal of Personality and Social Psychology, 72*, 980–1001.

Newman, M. G., Kenardy, J., Herman, S., & Taylor, C. B. (1997). Comparison of Palmtop-Computer-Assisted Brief Cognitive-Behavioral Treatment to Cognitive-Behavioral Treatment for Panic Disorder. *Journal of Consulting and Clinical Psychology, 65*, 178–183.

Newton, P. M. (1970). Recalled dream content and the maintenance of body image. *Journal of Abnormal Psychology, 76*, 134–139.

Nezu, A. M., Nezu., C. M., & Blissett, S. E. (1988). Sense of humor as a moderator of the relationship between stressful events and psychological distress: A prospective study. *Journal of Personality and Social Psychology, 54*, 520–525.

NICHD Early Child Care Research Network. (1997). The effects of infant child care on infant-mother attachment security: Results of the NICHD study of early child care. *Child Development, 68*, 860–879.

NICHD Early Child Care Research Network. (1999). Child care and mother–child interaction in the first 3 years of life. *Developmental Psychology, 35*, 1309–1413.

Nichelli, P., Grafman, J., Pietrini, P., Alway, D., Carton, J. J., & Miletich, R. (1994). Brain activity in chess playing. *Nature, 369*, 191.

Nichols, R. C. (1978). Twin studies of ability, personality, and interests. *Homo, 29*, 158–173.

Nickerson, R. S., & Adams, M. J. (1979). Long-term memory for a common object. *Cognitive Psychology, 11*, 287–307.

Nigg, J. T., & Goldsmith, H. H. (1994). Genetics of personality disorders: Perspectives from personality and psychopathology research. *Psychological Bulletin, 115*, 346–380.

NIH Technology Assessment Panel. (1996). Integration of Behavioral and relaxation approaches into the threatment of chornic pain and insomnia. *Journal of the American Medical Association, 276*, 313–318.

Niles, S. (1998). Achievement goals and means: A cultural comparison. *Journal of Cross-Cultural Psychology, 29*, 656–667.

Nilsson, L., & Hamberger, L. (1990). *A child is born.* New York: Delacorte.

Nilsson, T., Ericsson, M., Poston, W. S. C., Linder, J., Goodrick, G. K., & Foreyt, J. P. (1998). Is the assessment of coping capacity useful in the treatment of obesity? *Eating Disorders: The Journal of Treatment & Prevention, 6*, 241–251.

Nisbett, R. E. (1972). Hunger, obesity, and the ventromedial hypothalamus. *Psychological Review, 79*, 433–453.

Nisbett, R. E. (1996). *Race, genetics, and IQ.* In C. Jencks & M. Phillips (Eds.), *The black-white test score gap* (pp. 86–102). Washington, DC: Brookings Institution.

Nisbett, R. E., & Cohen, D. (1996). *Culture of Honor: The Psychology of violence in the South.* Boulder, CO: Westview.

Nisbett, R. E., & Kanouse, D. E. (1969). Obesity, food deprivation, and supermarket shopping behavior. *Journal of Personality & Social Psychology, 12*, 389–294.

Nolan, S. A., & Mineka, S. (1997, November). Verbal, nonverbal, and gender-related factors in the interpersonal consequences of depression and anxiety. Presented at the annual meeting of the Association for the Advancement of Behavior Therapy, Miami Beach, FL.

Nolde, S. F., Johnson, M. K., & Raye, C. L. (1998). The role of prefrontal cortex during tests of episodic memory. *Trends in Cognitive Sciences, 2*, 399–406.

Nolen-Hoeksema, S. (1987). Sex differences in unipolar depression: Evidence and theory. *Psychological Bulletin, 101*, 259–282.

Nolen-Hoeksema, S., & Davis, C. G. (1999). "Thanks for sharing that": Ruminators and their social support networks. *Journal of Personality and Social Psychology, 77*, 801–814.

Nolen-Hoeksema, S., & Morrow, J. (1993). Effects of rumination and distraction on naturally occurring depressed mood. *Cognition & Emotion, 7*, 561–570.

Norman, D. (1988). *The psychology of everyday things.* New York: Basic Books.

Norman, K. A., & Schacter, D. L. (1997). False recognition in younger and older adults: Exploring the characteristics of illusory memories. *Memory & Cognition, 25*, 838–848.

Northcraft, G. B, & Neale, M. A. (1987). Experts, amateurs, and real estate: An anchoring-and-adjustment perspective on property pricing decisions. *Organizational Behavior & Human Decision Processes, 39*, 84–97.

Nowakowski, R. S. (1987). Basic concepts of CNS development. *Child Development, 58*, 568–595.

Nozick, R. (in preparation). *The structure of the objective world.* Cambridge, MA: Harvard University Press.

Nurmi, J. E., & Salmela-Aro, K. (1997). Social Strategies and loneliness: A prospective study. *Person. Individ. Diff., 23*, 205–215.

Nurnberger, J. I., & Hingtgen, J. N. (1973). Is symptom substitution an important issue in behavior therapy? *Biological Psychiatry, 7*, 221–236.

Nyberg, L., Cabeza, R., & Tulving, E. (1996). PET studies of encoding and retrieval: The HERA model. *Psychonomic Bulletin & Review, 3*, 134–148.

Nyberg, L., McIntosh, A. R., Houle, S., Nilsson, L. G., & Tulving, E. (1996). Activation of medial temporal structures during episodic memory retrieval. *Nature, 380*, 715–717.

Nye, R. D. (1992). *Three Psychologies: Perspectives from Freud, Skinner, and Rogers.* California: Brooks-Cole.

Nyklicek, I., Vingerhoets, A. J. J. M., Van Heck, G. L., & Van Limpt, M. C. A. M. (1998). Defensive coping in relation to casual blood pressure and self-reported daily hassles and life events. *Journal of Behavioral Medicine, 21*, 145–161.

Oaksford, M., & Chater, N. (1994). A rational analysis of the selection task as optimal data selection. *Psychological Review, 101*, 608–631.

O'Connor, W. E., Morrison, T. G., McLeod, L. D., & Anderson, D. (1996). A meta-analytic review of the relationship between gender and belief in a just world. *Journal of Social Behavior and Personality, 11*, 141–148.

Oden, M. H. (1968). The fulfillment of promise: Forty-year follow-up of the Terman gifted group. *Genetic Psychology Monographs, 77*, 3–93.

Oei, T. P. S., & Yeoh, A. E. O. (1999). Pre-existing antidepressant medication and the outcome of group cognitive-behavioural therapy. *Australian & New Zealand Journal of Psychiatry, 33*, 70–76.

Ogden, J. A. (1988). Language and memory functions after long recovery periods in left-hemispherectomized subjects. *Neuropsychologia, 26*, 645–659.

Ohman, A., Fredrikson, M., Hugdahl, K., & Rimmo, P.-A. (1976). The premise of equipotentiality in human classical conditioning: Conditioned electrodermal responses to potentially phobic stimuli. *Journal of Experimental Psychology: General, 105*, 313–337.

Ohzawa, I., DeAngelis, G. C., & Freeman, R. D. (1990). Stereoscopic depth discrimination in the visual cortex: Neurons ideally suited as disparity detectors. *Science, 249*, 1037–1041.

Ojemann, G. A. (1983). Brain organization for language from the perspective of electrical stimulation mapping. *Behavioral and Brain Sciences, 6*, 189–230.

Ojemann, G. A., Ojemann, J., Lettich, E., & Berger, M. (1989). Cortical language localization in left, dominant hemisphere. *Journal of Neurosurgery, 71*, 316–326.

Okonkwo, R. U. N. (1997). Moral development and culture in Kohlberg's theory: A Nigerian (Igbo) evidence. *IFE Psychologia: An International Journal, 5*, 117–128.

Okubo, Y., Suhara, T., & Suzuki, K., Kobayashi, K., Inoue, O., Teraski, O., Someya, Y., Sassa, T., Sudo, Y., Matsushima, E., Iyo, M., Tateno, Y., & Toru, M. (1997). Decreased prefrontal dopamine D1 receptors in schizophrenia revealed by PET. *Nature, 385*, 634–636.

Olczak, P. V., Kaplan, M. F., & Penrod, S. (1991). Attorneys' lay psychology and its effectiveness in selecting jurors: Three empirical studies. *Journal of Social Behavior and Personality, 6*, 431–452.

Olds, J., & Milner, P. (1954). Positive reinforcement produced by electrical stimulation of septal area and other regions of rat brain. *Journal of Comparative & Physiological Psychology, 47*, 419–427.

Olton, R. M. (1979). Experimental studies of incubation: Searching for the elusive. *Journal of Creative Behavior, 13*, 9–22.

Oppenheim, J. S., Skerry, J. E., Tramo. M. J., & Gazzaniga, M. S. (1989). Magnetic resonance imaging morphology of the corpus callosum in monozygotic twins. *Annals of Neurology, 26*, 100–104.

O'Regan, J. K. (1992). Solving the "real" mysteries of visual perception: The world as an outside memory. *Canadian Journal of Psychology, 46*, 461–488.

Organ, D. W., & Ryan, K. (1995). A meta-analytic review of attitudinal and dispositional predictors of organizational citizenship behavior. *Personnel Psychology, 48*, 775–802.

Orive, R. (1988). Social projection and social comparison of opinions. *Journal of Personality and Social Psychology, 54*, 953–964.

Orlans, H. (1999, May–June). Members comment on ASA's publication on affirmative action. *Footnotes*, p. 8.

Ornish, D., Scherwitz, L. W., Billings, J. H., Gould, K. L., Merritt, T. A., Sparler, S., Armstrong, W. T., Ports, T. A., Kirkeeide, R. L., Hogeboom, C., & Brand, R. J. (1998). Intensive lifestyle changes for reversal of coronary heart disease. *Journal of the American Medical Association, 280*, 2001–2007.

Ornstein, R. (1986). *Multimind: A new way of looking at human behavior.* Boston: Houghton Mifflin.

Ortiz, S. M. (1997). Traveling with the ball club: A code of conduct for wives only. *Symbolic Interaction, 20*, 225–249.

Osborn, A. F. (1953). *Applied imagination.* New York: Scribner's.

Osherson, D., Perani, D., Cappa, S., Schnur, T., Grassi, F., & Fazio, F. (1998). Distinct brain loci in deductive versus probabilistic reasoning. *Neuropsychologia, 36*, 369–376.

Osherson, D. N., & Markman, E. M. (1975). Language and the ability to evaluate contradictions and tautologies. *Cognition, 2*, 213–226.

O'Sullivan, C. S, & Durso, F. T. (1984). Effects of schema-incongruent information on memory for stereotypical attributes. *Journal of Personality and Social Psychology, 47*, 55–70.

Otto, M. W., Gould, R. A., & Pollack, M. H. (1994). Cognitive-behavioral treatment of panic disorder: Considerations for the treatment of patients over the long term. *Psychiatric Annals, 24*, 307–315.

Overmeier, J. B., & Seligman, M. E. P. (1967). Effects of inescapable shock upon subsequent escape and avoidance responding. *Journal of Comparative and Physiological Psychology, 63*, 28–33.

Ozer, D. J., & Reise, S. P. (1994). Personality Assessment. *Annual Review of Psychology, 45,* 357–88.

Páez, D., Velasco, C., & González, J. L. (1999). Expressive writing and the role of alexythimia as a dispositional deficit in self-disclosure and psychological health. *Journal of Personality and Social Psychology, 77,* 630–641.

Pagano, R. R., Rose, R. M., Stivers, R. M., & Warrenburg, S. (1976). Sleep during transcendental meditation. *Science, 191,* 308–309.

Page, D. C., Mosher, R., Simpson, E. M., Fisher, E. M. C., Mardon, G., Pollack, J., McGillivray, B., de la Chapelle, A., & Brown, L. G. (1987). The sex-determining region of the human Y chromosome encodes a finger protein. *Cell, 51,* 1091–1104.

Page, S. (1990). The turnaround on pornography research: Some implications for psychology and women. *Canadian Psychology, 31,* 359–367.

Paivio, A. (1971). *Imagery and verbal processes.* New York: Holt, Rinehart & Winston.

Paivio, S. C., & Greenberg, L. S. (1995). Resolving "Unfinished Business": Efficacy of Experiential Therapy Using Empty-Chair Dialogue. *Journal of Consulting and Clinical Psychology, 63,* 419–425.

Palace, E. M. (1999). Response expectancy and sexual dysfunction. In I. Kirsch (Ed.), *How expectancies shape experience* (pp. 173–196). Washington, DC: American Psychological Association.

Palmer, S. E. (1975). The effects of contextual scenes on the identification of objects. *Memory & Cognition, 3,* 519–526.

Palmer, S. E. (1992a). Modern theories of Gestalt perception. In G. W. Humphreys (Ed.), *Understanding vision: An interdisciplinary perspective* (pp. 39–70). Oxford: Blackwell.

Palmer, S. E. (1992b). Common region: A new principle of perceptual grouping. *Cognitive Psychology, 24,* 436–447.

Papi, F., Meschini, E., & Baldacinni, N. E. (1983). Homing behavior of pigeons released after having been placed in an alternating magnetic field. *Comparative Biochemistry & Physiology, 76A,* 673–682.

Papolos, D. F., Yu, Y-M., Rosenbaum, E., & Lachman, H. M. (1996). Modulation of learned helplessness by 5-hydroxytrptamine-2A receptor antisense oligodeoxynucleotides. *Psychiatry Research, 63,* 197–203.

Papp, L. A., Klein, D. F., & Gorman, J. M. (1993). Carbon dioxide hypersensitivity, hyperventilation, and panic disorder. *American Journal of Psychiatry, 150,* 1149–1157.

Papp, L. A., Martinez, J. M., Klein, D. F., Coplan, J. D., Norman, R. G., Cole, R., de Jesus, M. J., Ross, D., Goetz, R., & Gorman, J. M. (1997). Respiratory psychophysiology of panic disorder: Three respiratory challenges in 98 subjects. *American Journal of Psychiatry, 154,* 1557–1565.

Park, S., & Holzman, P. S. (1992). Schizophrenics show spatial working memory deficits. *Archives of General Psychiatry, 49,* 975–982.

Park, S., & Holzman, P. S. (1993). Associatoin of working memory deficit and eye tracking dysfunction in schizophrenia. *Schizophrenia Research, 11,* 55–61.

Park, S., Holzman, P. S., & Goldman-Rakic, P. (1995). Spatial working memory deficits in the relatives of schizophrenics. *Archives of General Psychiatry, 52,* 821–828.

Parker, A., & Gellatly, A. (1997). Movable cues: A practical method for reducing context-dependent forgetting. *Applied Cognitive Psychology, 11,* 163–173.

Parkin, A. J. (1987). *Memory and amnesia: An introduction.* Oxford, England: Basil Blackwell.

Parkin, A. J., & Walter, B. M. (1992). Recollective experience, normal aging, and frontal dysfunction. *Psychology and Aging, 7,* 290–298.

Parks, M. R., & Eggert, L. L. (1991). The role of social context in the dynamics of personal relationships. In W. H. Jones & D., Perlman (Eds.), *Advances in Personal Relationships* (Vol. 2, pp. 1–34). London: Jessica Kingsley.

Parks, M. R., & Roberts, L. D. (1998). "Making MOOsic": The development of personal relationships on line and a comparison to their off-line counterparts. *Journal of Social & Personal Relationships, 15,* 517–537.

Parsons, L. M. (1987). Imagined spatial transformation of one's body. *Journal of Experimental Psychology: General, 116,* 172–191.

Parsons, L. M. (1994). Temporal and kinematic properties of motor behavior reflected in mentally simulated action. *Journal of Experimental Psychology: Human Perception & Performance, 20,* 709–730.

Parsons, L. M., & Fox, P. T. (1998). The neural basis of implicit movements used in recognising hand shape. *Cognitive Neuropsychology, 15,* 583–615.

Pascalis, O., de Haan, M., Nelson, C. A., & de Schonen, S. (1998). Long-term recognition memory for faces assessed by visual paired comparison in 3- and 6-month-old infants. *Journal of Experimental Psychology: Learning, Memory, & Cognition, 24,* 249–260.

Pascual-Leone, A., Grafman, J., Cohen, L. G., Roth, B. J., & Hallett, M. (1997). Transcranial magnetic stimulation. A new tool for the study of higher cognitive functions in humans. In J. Grafman & F. Boller (Eds.), *Handbook of neuropsychology* (Vol. 11). Amsterdam: Elsevier B.V.

Pascual-Leone, A., Tormos, J. M., Keenan, J., Tarazona, F., Cañete, C., & Catalá, M. D. (1998). Study and modulation of human cortical excitability with transcranial magnetic stimulation. *Journal of Clinical Neurophysiology, 15,* 333–343.

Pascual-Leone, J. (1970). A mathematical model for the transition rule in Piaget's developmental stages. *Acta Psychologia, 32,* 301–345.

Patterson, G. R. (1986). Performance models for antisocial boys. *American Psychologist, 41,* 432–444.

Patterson, G. R., DeBaryshe, B. D., & Ramsey, E. (1989). A developmental perspective on antisocial behavior. *American Psychologist, 44,* 329–335.

Patterson, R., & Martin, W. L. (1992). Human stereopsis. *Human Factors, 34,* 669–692.

Patterson, T. L., Semple, S. J., Shaw, W. S., Yu, E., He, Y., Zhang, M. Y., Wu, W., & Grant, I. (1998). The cultural context of caregiving: A comparison of Alzheimer's caregivers in Shanghai, China and San Diego, California. *Psychological Medicine, 28,* 1071–1084.

Paulesu, E., Frith, C. D., & Frackowiak, R. S. J. (1993). The neural correlates of verbal component of working memory. *Nature, 362,* 342–345.

Paulesu, E., Harrison. J., Baron-Cohen, S., Watson, J. D. G., Goldstein, L., Heather, J., Frackowaik, R. S. J., & Frith, C. D. (1995). The physiology of coloured hearing: A PET activation study of colour-word synaesthesia. *Brain, 118,* 661–676.

Paulhus, D. L., & Bruce, M. N. (1992). The effect of acquaintanceship on the validity of personality impressions: a longitudinal study. *Journal of Personality and Social Psychology, 63,* 816–824.

Paulus, P. B., Seta, C. E., & Baron, R. A. (1996). *Effective Human Relations.* (3rd edition). Boston: Allyn & Bacon.

Paunonen, S. V. (1998). Hierarchical Organization of Personality and Prediction of Behavior. *Journal of Personality and Social Psychology, 74,* 538–556.

Paunonen, S. V., & Ashton, M. C. (1998). The structured assessment of personality across cultures. *Journal of Cross-Cultural Psychology, 29,* 150–170.

Paunonen, S. V., Zeidner, M., Engvik, H. A., Oosterveld, P., & Maliphant, R. (2000). The nonverbal assessment of personality in five cultures. *Journal of Cross-Cultural Psychology, 31,* 220–239.

Paus, T. (1996). Location and function of the human frontal eye-field: A selective review. *Neuropsychologia, 34,* 475–483.

Pavlov, I. P. (1927). *Condtioned reflexes* (G. V. Anrep, Trans.). London: Oxford University Press.

Payne, D. G. (1987). Hypermnesia and reminiscence in recall: A historical and empirical review. *Psychological Bulletin, 101,* 5–27.

Pearson, S. E., & Pollack, R. H. (1997). Female response to sexually explicit films. *Journal of Psychology & Human Sexuality, 9,* 73–88.

Pederson, N. L., Plomin, R., McClearn, G. E., & Friberg, L. (1988) Neuroticism, extraversion and related traits in adult twins reared apart and reared together. *Journal of Personality and Social Psychology, 55,* 950–957.

Peeck, J. (1987). The role of illustrations in processing and remembering illustrated text. In H. A. Houghton & D. M. Willows (Eds.), *The psychology of illustration,* Vol. 2 (pp. 115–152). New York: Springer-Verlag.

Peltonen, L. (1995). Schizophrenia: All out for chromosome six. *Nature, 378,* 665–666.

Penfield, W. (1955). The permanent record of the stream of consciousness. *Acta Psychologica, 11,* 47–69.

Penfield, W., & Perot, P. (1963). The brain's record of auditory and visual experience. *Brain, 86,* 595–696.

Penfield, W., & Rasmussen, T. (1950). *The cerebral cortex of man: A clinical study of localization of function.* New York: Macmillan.

Pengilly, J. W., & Dowd, E. T. (1997). Hardiness and social support as moderator of stress in college students. Paper presented at the 1997 annual convention of the Association for the Advancement of Behavior Therapy, Miami Beach, FL.

Pennebaker, J. W. (1989). Confession, inhibition and disease. In L. Berkowitz (Ed.), Advances in experimental social psychology (Vol. 22, pp. 211–244). New York: Academic Press.

Pennebaker, J. W. (1993). Social mechanisms of constraint. In D. M. Wegner & J. W. Pennebaker (Eds.), *Handbook of mental control* (pp. 200–219). Englewood Cliffs, NJ: Prentice Hall.

Pennebaker, J. W., Colder, M., & Sharp, L. K. (1990). Accelerating the coping process. *Journal of Personality and Social Psychology, 58,* 528–537.

Pennebaker, J. W., & Francis, M. E. (1996). Cognitive, emotional, and language processes in disclosure. *Cognition & Emotion, 10,* 601–626.

Pennebaker, J. W., Kiecolt-Glaser, J. K., & Glaser, R. (1988). Disclosures of trauma and immune function: health implications for psychotherapy. *Journal and Consulting and Clinical Psychology, 56,* 239–245.

Peplau, L. A., & Gordon, S. L. (1985). Women and men in love: Gender differences in close heterosexual relatonships. In V. E. O'Leary, R. K. Unger, & B. S. Wallston (Eds.). *Women, gender, and social psychology* (pp. 257–291). Hillsdale, NJ: Erlbaum.

Perdue, C. W., Dovidio, J. F., Gurtman, M. B., & Tyler, R. B. (1990). Us and them: Social categorization and the process of intergroup bias. *Journal of Personality and Social Psychology,59*, 475–486.

Perera, S., Sabin, E., Nelson, P., & Lowe, D. (1998). Increases in salivary lysozyme and IgA concentrations and secretory rates independent of salivary flow rates following viewing of a humorous videotape. *International Journal of Behavioral Medicine, 5*, 118–128.

Perkins, D. N., & Grotzer, T. A. (1997). Teaching intelligence. *American Psychologist, 52*, 1125–1133.

Perkins, H. W., & Berkowitz, A. D. (1986). Perceiving the community norms of alchol use among students.: Some research implications for campus alcohol education programming. *International Journal of the Addictions, 21*, 961–976.

Perkins, H. W., & Wechsler, H. (1996). Variation in perceived college drinking norms and its impact on alcohol abuse: A nationwide study. *Journal of Drug Issues, 26*, 961–974.

Perlmutter, M. (1988). Cognitive potential throughout life. In J. E. Birren & V. L. Bengtson (Eds.), *Emergent theories of aging* (pp. 247–267). New York: Springer.

Perls, F. S. (1969). *Gestalt therapy verbatim.* Lafayette: CA: Real People Press.

Perrett, D. I., Lee, K. J, Penton-Voak, I., Rowland, D., Yoshikawa, S., Burt, D. M., Henzi, S. P., Castles, D. L., & Akamatsu, S. (1998). Effects of sexual dimorphism on facial attractiveness. *Nature, 394*, 884–887.

Perrett, D. I., Smith, P. A. J., Potter, D. D., Mistlin, A. J., Head, A. S., Milner, A. D., & Jeeves, M. A. (1985). Visual cells in the temporal cortex sensitive to face view and gaze direction. *Proceedings of the Royal Society of London, Series B: Biological Sciences, 223*, 293–317.

Perry, B. D., Pollard, R. A., Blakley, T. L., Baker, W. L., & Vigilante, D. (1995). Childhood trauma, the neurobiology of adaptation, and "use-dependent" development of the brain: How "states" become "traits." *Infant Mental Health Journal, 16*, 271–291.

Perugini, E. M., Kirsch, I, Allen, S. T., Coldwell, E., Meredith, J., Montgomery, G. H., & Sheehan, J. (1998). Surreptitious observation of responses to hypnotically suggested hallucinations: A test of the compliance hypothesis. *International Journal of Clinicacl and Experimental Hypnosis, 46*, 191–203.

Petersen, A. C., Compas, B. E., Brooks-Gunn, J., Stemmler, M., Ey, S., & Grant, K. E. (1993). Depression in adolescence. *American Psychologist, 48*, 155–168.

Petersen, R. C. (1977). Marihuana research findings: 1976: Summary. *NIDA Research Monograph, Jul (14)*, 1–37.

Petersen, R. C. (1979). Importance of inhalation patterns in determining effects of marihuana use. *Lancet, 31*, 727–728.

Peterson, C. (2000). The future of optimism. *American Psychologist, 55*, 44–55.

Peterson, C., & Seligman, M. E. (1984). Causal explanations as a risk factor for depression: Theory and evidence. *Psychological Review, 91*, 347–374.

Petitto, L. A., & Marentette, P. F. (1991). Babbling in the manual mode: Evidence for the ontogeny of language. *Science, 251*, 1493–1496.

Petrides, M., Alivisatos, B., Meyer, E., & Evans, A. C. (1993). Functional activation of the human frontal cortex during the performance of verbal working memory tasks. *Proceedings of the National Academy of Sciences, USA, 90*, 878–882.

Petrie, K. J., Booth, R. J., & Pennebaker, J. W. (1998). The immunological effects of thought suppression. *Journal of Personality and Social Psychology, 75*, 1264–1272.

Petrie, K. J., Booth, R. J., Pennebaker, J. W., Davison, K. P., & Thomas, M. G. (1995). Disclosure of Trauma and Immune Response to a Hepatitis B Vaccination Program. *Journal of Consulting and Clinical Psychology, 63*, 787–792.

Petrill, S. A., Ball, D., Eley, T., Hill, L., Plomin, R., McClearn, G. E., Smith, D. L., Chorney, K., Chorney, M., Hershz, M. S., Detterman, D. K., Thompson, L. A., Benbow, C., Lubinski, D., Daniels, J., Owen, M. J., & McGuffin, P. (1997a). Failure to replicate a QTL association between a DNA marker identified by EST00083 and IQ. *Intelligence, 25*, 179–184.

Petrill, S. A., Plomin, R., Berg, S., Johansson, B., Pedersen, N. L., Ahern, F., & McClearn, G. E. (1998). The genetic and environmental relationship between general and specific cognitive abilities in twins age 80 and older. *Psychological Science, 9*, 183–189.

Petrill, S. A., Plomin, R., McClearn, G. E., Smith, D. L., Vignetti, S., Chorney, M. J., Chorney, K., Thompson, L. A., Detterman, D. K., Benbow, C., Lubinski, D., Daniels, J., Owen, M., & McGuffin, P. (1997a). No association between general cognitive ability and the A1 allele of the D2 dopamine receptor gene. *Behavior Genetics, 27*, 29–31.

Petrill, S. A., Plomin, R., McClearn, G. E., Smith, D. L., Vignetti, S., Chorney, M. J., Chorney, K., Thompson, L. A., Detterman, D. K., Benbow, C., Lubinski, D., Daniels, J., Owen, M., & McGuffin, P. (1997b). No association between general cognitive ability and the A1 allele of the D2 dopamine receptor gene. *Behavior Genetics, 27*, 29–31.

Petrill, S. A., Thompson, L. A., & Detterman, D. K. (1995). The genetic and environmental variance underlying elementary cognitive tasks. *Behavior Genetics, 25*, 199–209.

Pettigrew, T. F. (1969). Racially separate or together? *Journal of Social Issues, 24*, 43–69.

Pettigrew, T. F. (1981). Extending the stereotype concept. In D. L. Hamilton (Ed.), *Cognitive processes in stereotyping and intergroup behavior* (pp. 303– 331). Hillsdale, NJ: Erlbaum.

Pettigrew, T. F., & Meertens, R. W. (1995). Subtle and blatant prejudice in western Europe. *European Journal of Social Psychology, 25*, 57–75.

Petty, F., Kramer, G., Wilson, L., & Jordan, S. (1994). In vivo serotonin release and learned helplessness. *Psychiatry Research, 52*, 285–293.

Petty, R. E., & Cacioppo, J. T. (1981). *Attitudes and persuasion: Classic and contemporary approaches.* Dubuque, IA: Wm. C. Brown.

Petty, R. E., & Krosnick, J. A. (1996). *Attitude strength: Anetecedents and consequences.* Hillsdale, NJ: Erlbaum.

Petty, R. E., & Wegener, D. T. (1998). Attitude Change: multiple roles for persuasion variables. In D. T. Gilbert, S. T. Fiske, & G. Lindzey (Eds.), *The handbook of social psychology* (4th ed.). New York: McGraw Hill. 323–390.

Pezdek, K., Finger, K., & Hodge, D. (1997). Planting false childhood memories: The role of event plausibility. *Psychological Science, 8*, 437–441.

Pfaffmann, C. (1978). The vertebrate phylogeny, neural code, and integrative processes of taste. In E. C. Carterette & M. P. Friedman (Eds.), *Handbook of perception* (pp. 51–123). New York: Academic Press.

Phelps, J. A., Davis, J. O., & Schartz, K. M. (1997). Nature, nurture, and twin research strategies. *Current Directions in Psychological Science, 6*, 117–121.

Phillips, D. P., & Smith, D. G. (1990). Postponement of death until symbolically meaningful occasions. *Journal of the American Medical Association, 263*, 1947–1951.

Phillips, D. P., Van Voorhees, C. A., & Ruth, T. E. (1992). The birthday: Lifeline or deadline. *Psychosomatic Medicine, 54*, 532–542.

Phillips, J. B. (1986a). Two magnetoreception pathways in a migratory salamander. *Science, 233*, 765–767.

Phillips, J. B. (1986b). Magnetic compass orientation in the Eastern red-spotted newt (*Notophthalmus viridescens*). *Journal of Comparative Physiology, 158*, 103–109.

Phillips, J. B. (1996). Magnetic navigation. *Journal of Theoretical Biology, 180*, 309–319.

Phillips, K., & Matheny, A. P., Jr. (1995). Quantitative genetic analysis of injury liability in infants and toddlers. *American Journal of Medical Genetics (Neuropsychiatric Genetics), 60*, 64–71.

Phillips, S. D., & Imhoff, A. R. (1997). Women and career development: A decade of research. *Annual Review of Psychology, 48*, 31–59.

Piaget, J. (1954). *The construction of reality in the child.* New York: Free Press.

Piaget, J. (1962). *Play, dreams, and imitation in childhood.* New York: W. W. Norton.

Piaget, J. (1969). *The mechanisms of perception.* (G. N. Seagrim, Trans.). New York: Basic Books.

Piazza, C. C., Hanley, G. P., Fisher, W. W., Ruyter, J. M., & Gulotta, C. S. (1998). On the establishing and reinforcing effects of termination of demands for destructive behavior maintained by positive and negative reinforcement. *Research in Developmental Disabilities, 19*, 395–407.

Pickles, J. O. (1988). *An introduction to the physiology of hearing* (2nd ed.). London: Academic Press.

Pierce, C. A. (1992). *The effects of physical attractiveness and height on dating choice: A meta-analysis.* Unpublished masters thesis, University at Albany, State University of New York, Albany, NY.

Pietromonaco, P. R., Manis, J., & Frohardt-Lane, K. (1986). Psychological consequences of multiple social roles. *Psychology of Women Quarterly, 10*, 373–381.

Pinel, J. P. J. (1993). *Biopsychology (2nd ed.).* Boston: Allyn & Bacon.

Pinhey, T. K., Rubinstein, D. H., & Colfax, R. S. (1997). Overweight and happiness: The reflected self-appraisal hypothesis reconsidered. *Social Science Quarterly, 78*, 747–755.

Pinker, S. (1994). *The language instinct: How the mind creates language.* New York: Morrow.

Pinker, S. (1997). *How the mind works.* New York: Norton.

Pirke, K. M. (1995). Physiology of bulimia nervosa. In K. D. Brownell & C. G. Fairburn (Eds.), *Eating Disorders and Obesity: A Comprehensive Handbook.* New York: Guilford Press, 261–265.

Pitman, D. L., Natelson, B. H., Ottenmiller, J. E., McCarty, R., Pritzel, T., & Tapp, W. N. (1995). Effects of exposure to stressors of varying predictability on adrenal function in rats. *Behavioral Neuroscience, 109*, 767–776.

Plato. (1956). Meno (Menon). In R. H. D. Rouse (Trans.), *Great dialogues of Plato.* New York: New American Library.

Platt, L. A., & Persico, V. R., Jr. (Eds.) (1992). *Grief in cross-cultural perspective: A casebook*. New York: Garland.

Plomin, R. (1988). The nature and nurture of cognitive abilities. In R. J. Sternberg (Ed.), *Advances in the psychology of human intelligence* Vol. 4 (pp. 1–33). Hillsdale, NJ: Erlbaum.

Plomin, R. (1990). *Nature and nurture : An introduction to human behavioral genetics*. Pacific Grove, CA: Brooks/Cole.

Plomin, R. (1995). Genetics and children's experiences in the family. *Journal of Child Psychology and Psychiatry, 36*, 33–68.

Plomin, R., & Bergeman, C. S. (1991). The nature of nurture: Genetic influences on "environmental" measures. *Behavioral and Brain Sciences, 14*, 373–427.

Plomin, R., Chipuer, H. M., & Loehlin, J. C. (1990). Behavioral genetics and personality. In L. A. Pervin (Ed.), *Handbook of personality: Theory and research* (pp. 225–243). New York: Guilford.

Plomin, R., Corley, R., Caspi, A., Fulker, D. W., & DeFries, J. (1998). Adoption Results for Self-Reported Personality: Evidence for Nonadditive Genetic Effects? *Journal of Personality and Social Psychology 75*, 211–218.

Plomin, R., Corley, R., DeFries, J. C., & Fulker, D. W. (1990). Individual Differences in television viewing in early childhood: Nature as well as nurture. *Psychological Science, 1*, 371–377.

Plomin, R., & DeFries, J. C. (1998). The genetics of cognitive abilities and disabilities: Investigations of specific cognitive skills can help clarify how genes shape the components of intellect. *Scientific American, 278*, 40–47.

Plomin, R., DeFries, J. C., & Loehlin, J. C. (1977). Genotype-environment interaction and correlation in the analysis of human behavior. *Psychological Bulletin, 84*, 309–322.

Plomin, R., DeFries, J. C., McClearn, G. E., & Rutter, M. (1997). *Behavioral genetics* (3rd ed.). New York: Freeman.

Plomin, R., & Foch, T. T. (1980). A twin study of objectrively assessed personality in childhood. *Journal of Personality and Social Psychology, 39*, 680–688.

Plomin, R. Lichtenstein, P., Pedersen, N. L., McClearn, G. E., & Nesselroade, J. R. (1990b). Genetic influence on life events during the last half of the life span. *Psycology and Aging, 5*, 25–30.

Plomin, R., Pedersen, N. L., Lichtenstein, P., & McClearn, G. E. (1994). Variability and stability in cognitive abilities are largely genetic later in life. *Behavior Genetics, 24*(3), 207–215.

Plomin, R., Scheier, M. F., Bergeman, C. S., Pederson, N. L., Nesselroade, J. R., & McClearn, G. E. (1992). Optimism, pessimism and mental health: A twin/adoption analysis. *Personality and Individual Differences., 13*, 921–930.

Plotkin, H. (1994). *The nature of knowledge: Concerning adaptations, instinct and the evolution of intelligence*. New York: Allen Lane/Viking Penguin.

Plotkin, H. (1997). *Evolution in mind: An introduction to evolutionary psychology*. Cambridge, MA: Harvard University Press.

Plucker, J. A. (1998). Beware of simple conclusions: The case for content generality of creativity. *Creativity Research Journal, 11*, 179–182.

Plucker, J. A. (1999). Reanalyses of student responses to creativity checklists: Evidence of content generality. *Journal of Creative Behavior, 33*, 126–137.

Plutchik, R. & Kellerman, H. (1980). *Emotions: A psychoevolutionary synthesis*. New York: Harper Row.

Poizner, H., & Kegl, J. (1992). Neural basis of language and motor behavior: Perspectives from American Sign Language. *Aphasiology, 6*, 219–256.

Poizner, H., Klima, E. S., & Bellugi, U. (1987). *What the hands reveal about the brain*. Cambridge, MA: MIT Press.

Polivy, J., & Herman, C. P. (1993). Etiology of binge eating: Psychological mechanisms. In *Binge Eating: Nature, Assessment, and Treatment*. In C. G. Fairburn & G. T. Wilson (Eds.), New York: Guilford Press. 173–205.

Pollard, C. A., Pollard, H. J., & Corn, K. J. (1989). Panic onset and major events in the lives of agoraphobics: A test of contiguity. *Journal of Abnormal Psychology, 98*, 318–321.

Pollock, V. E., Briere, J., Schneider, L., Knop, J., Mednick, S. A., & Goodwin, D. H. (1990). Childhood antecedents of antisocial behavior: Parental alcoholism and physical abusiveness. *American Journal of Psychiatry, 147*, 1290–1293.

Ponomarenko, V. V., & Kamyshev, N. G. (1997). Genetic aspects of the mechanisms of learning. *Neuroscience and Behavioral Physiology, 27*, 245–249.

Pope, K. S. (1996). Memory, abuse, and science: Questioning claims about the false memory syndrome epidemic. *American Psychologist, 51*, 957–974.

Porter, D., & Neuringer, A. (1984). Music discrimiinations by pigeons. *Journal of Experimental Psychology: Animal Behavior Processes, 10*, 138–148.

Porter, R. H. (1991). Human reproduction and the mother-infant relationship: The role of odors. In T. V. Getchell, R. L. Doty, L. M. Bartoshuk, & J. B. Snow, Jr. (Eds.), *Smell and taste in health and disease* (pp. 429–442). New York: Raven.

Porter, R. H., Cernoch, J. M., & Balogh, R. D. (1985). Odor signatures and kin recognition. *Physiology & Behavior, 24*, 445–448.

Porter, R. H., Cernoch, J. M., & McLaughlin, F. J. (1983). Maternal recognition of neonates through olfactory cues. *Physiology & Behavior, 30*, 151–154.

Porter, R. H., Makin, J. W., Davis, L. B., & Christensen, K. M. (1992). An assessment of the salient olfactory environment of formula-fed infants. *Physiology & Behavior, 50*, 907–911.

Posner, M. I., DiGirolamo, G. J., & Fernandez-Duque, D. (1997). Brain mechanisms of cognitive skills. *Consciousness and Cognition, 6*, 267–290.

Posner, M. I., & Raichle, M. (1994). *Images of mind*. New York: Freeman.

Post, R. M. (1992). Transdirection of psychosocial stress into the neurobiology of recurrent affective disorder. *American Journal of Psychiatry, 149*, 999–1010.

Postmes, T., & Spears, R. (1998). Deindividuation and antinormative behavior: A meta-analysis. *Psychological Bulletin, 123*, 238–259.

Poston, W. S. C., Ericsson, M., Linder, J., Nilsson, T., Goodrick, G. K., & Foreyt, J. P. (1999). Personality and the prediction of weight loss and relapse in the treatment of obesity. *International Journal of Eating Disorders, 25*, 301–309.

Poulton, R., Menzies, R. G., Craske, M. G., Langley, J. D., & Silva, P. A. (1999). Water trauma and swimming experiences up to age 9 and fear of water at age 18: A longitudinal study. *Behaviour Research & Therapy, 37*, 39–48.

Powell, M. C., & Fazio, R. H. (1984). Attitude accedssibility as a function of repeatred attitudinal expression. *Personality and Social Psychology Bulletin, 10*, 139–148.

Powers, P. C., & Green, R. G. (1972). Effects of the behavior and perceived arousal of a model on instrumental aggression. *Journal of Personality and Social Psychology, 23*, 175–184.

Prabhakaran, V., Smith, J. A. L., Desmond, J. E., Glover, G. H., & Gabrieli, J. E. (1997). Neural substrates of fluid reasoning: An fMRI study of the neocortical activation during performance of the Raven's Progressive Matrices Test. *Cognitive Psychology, 33*, 43–63.

Practice Directorate (1998). *How to find help through psychotherapy*. Washington DC: American Psychological Association.

Prapavessis, H., & Carron, A. V. (1997). Sacrifice, cohesion, and conformity to norms in sport teams. *Group Dynamics: Theory, Research, and Practice, 1*, 231–240.

Prasada, S. (2000). Acquiring generic knowledge. *Trends in Cognitive Science, 4*, 66–72.

Prechtl, H. F. R., & Beintema, D. (1965). *The neurological examination of the full-term newborn infant*. London: Heinemann.

Prescott, C. A., Johnson, R. C., & McArdle, J. J. (1991). Genetic contributions to television viewing. *Psycho9logical Science, 2*, 430–431.

Pressley, M., Brown, R. El-Dinary, P. B., & Allferbach, P. (1995). The comprehension instruction that students need: Instruction fostering constructively responsive reading. *Learning Disabilities Research & Practice, 10*, 215–224.

Pressman, E. K., DiPietro, J. A., Costigan, K. A., Shupe, A. K., & Johnson, T. R. B. (1998). Fetal neurobehavioral development: Associations with socioeconomic class and fetal sex. *Developmental Psychobiology, 33*, 79–91.

Prien, R. F., & Kocsis, J. H. (1995). Long term treatment of mood disorders. In F. E. Bloom & D. J. Kupfer (Eds.), *Psychopharmacology: The Fourth Generation of Progress*. (pp. 1067–1080). New York: Raven Press.

Priester, J. R., & Petty, R. E. (1995). Source attributions and persuaion: Perceived honesty as a determinant of message scrutiny. *Personality and Social Psychology Bulletin, 21*, 637–654.

Privette, G., & Landsman, T. (1983). Factor analysis of peak performance: The full use of potential. *Journal of Personality and Social Psychology, 44*, 195–200.

Prochaska, J. O., Norcross, J. C., & DiClemente, C. C. (1994). *Changing for Good*. New York: William Morrow & Co.

Prochaska, J. O., Velicer, W. F., Rossi, J. S., Goldstein, M. G., Marcus, B. H., Rakowski, W., Fiore, C., Harlow, L. L., Redding, C. A., Rosenbloom, D., & Rossi, S. R. (1994). Stages of change and decisional balance for 12 problem behaviors. *Health Psychology, 13*, 39–46.

Proctor, R. W., & Van Zandt, T. (1994). *Human Factors In Simple And Complex Systems*. Boston: Allyn & Bacon.

Project MATCH Research Group National Institute on Alcohol Abuse and Alcoholism Bethesda, MD (1997). Project MATCH secondary a priori hypotheses. *Addiction, 92*, 1671–169.

Project on the Status and Education of Women (1987). Association of American Colleges, 1818 R St. NW, Washington, DC 20009, 202/387–1300.

Przybyla, D. P., & Byrne, D. (1984). The mediating role of cognitive processes in self-reported sexual arousal. *Journal of Research in Personality, 18,* 54–63.

Pujol, R., Lavigne-Rebillard, M., & Uziel, A. (1990). Physiological correlates of development of the human cochlea. *Seminars in Perinatology, 14,* 275–280.

Puka, B. (Ed.) (1994). *Kohlberg's original study of moral development.* New York: Garland.

Putnam, F. W. (1989). *Diagnosis and treatment of Multiple Personality Disorder.* New York: Guilford Press.

Putnam, F. W., Helmers, K., Horowitz, L. A., & Trickett, P. K. (1995). Hypnotizability and dissociativity in sexually abused girls. *Child Abuse and Neglect, 19,* 645–655.

Putnam, H. (1973). Reductionism and the nature of psychology. *Cognition, 2,* 131–146.

Quadrel, M. J., Fischhoff, B., & Davis, W. (1993). Adolescent (in)vulnerabilty. *American Psychologist, 48,* 102–116.

Quay, H. C. (1965). Psychopathic personality as pathological stimulus-seeking. *American Journal of Psychiatry, 122,* 180–183.

Quinn, J. G. (1991). Encoding and maintenance of information in visual working memory. In R. H. Logie & M. Denis (Eds.), *Mental images in human cognition.* (pp. 95–104). Amsterdam: North-Holland.

Raag, T., & Rackliff, C. L. (1998). Preschoolers' awareness of social expectations of gender: Relationships to toy choices. *Sex Roles, 38,* 685–700.

Rabin, M. D., & Cain, W. S. (1986). Determinants of measured olfactory sensitivity. *Perception & Psychophysics, 39,* 281–286.

Rabinowitz, F. E., Sutton, L., Schutter, T., Brow, A., Krizo, C., Larsen, J., Styn, J., Welander, A., Wilson, M., & Wright, S. (1997). Helfulness to lost tourists. *Journal of Social Psychology, 137,* 502–509.

Rachman, S. (1997). A cognitive theory of obsessions. *Behaviour Research & Therapy, 35,* 793–802.

Radvansky, G. A. (1999). Aging, memory, and comprehension. *Current Directions in Psychological Science, 8,* 49–53.

Räikkönen, K., Matthews, K. A., Flory, J. D., & Owens, J. F. (1999). Effects of Hostility on Ambulatory Blood Pressure and Mood During Daily Living in Healthy Adults. *Health Psychology, 18,* 44–53.

Raine, A., Venables, P. H., & Wiliams, M. (1990). Relationships between central and autonomic measures of arousal at age 15 years and criminality at age 24 years. *Archives of General Psychiatry, 47,* 1003–1007.

Rainville, P., Duncan, G. H., Price, D. D, Carrier, B., & Bushnell, M. C. (1997). Pain affect encoded in human anterior cingulate but not somatosensory cortex. *Science, 277,* 968–971.

Rakic, P. (1975). Timing of major ontogenetic events in the visual cortex of the rhesus monkey. In N. Buchwald & M. Brazier (Eds.), *Brain mechanisms in mental retardation* (pp. 3–40). New York: Academic Press.

Rakic, P., Bourgeois, J-P., & Goldman-Rakic, P. S. (1994). Synaptic development of the cerebral cortex: Implications for learning, memory, and mental illness. In J. van Pelt, M. A. Corner, H. B. M. Uylings, & F. H. Lopes da Silva (Eds.), *Progress in brain research: Vol. 102. The self-organizing brain: From growth cones to functional networks* (pp. 227–243). Amsterdam: Elsevier.

Ramachandran, V. S. (1993). Behavioral and magnetoencephalographic correlates of plasticity in the adult human brain. *Proceedings of the National Academy of Sciences, 90,* 10413–10420.

Ramachandran, V. S., Rogers-Ramachandran, D., & Cobb, S. (1995). Touching the phantom limb. *Nature, 377,* 489–490.

Ramachandran, V. S., Rogers-Ramachandran, D., & Stewart, M. (1992). Perceptual correlates of massive cortical reorganization. *Science, 258,* 1159–1160.

Ramey, C. T., & Ramey, S. L. (1998). Early intervention and early experience. *American Psychologist, 53*(2), 109–120.

Ramirez, M., III. (1999). *Mulitcultural Psychotherapy: An approach to invidividual and cultural differences (2nd edition).* Needham Heights, MA: Allyn & Bacon.

Ranieri, D. J., & Zeiss, A. M. (1984). Induction of depressed mood: A test of opponent-process theory. *Journal of Personality & Social Psychology, 47,* 1413–1422.

Rao, S. C., Rainer, G., & Miller, E. K. (1997). Integration of what and where in the primate prefrontal cortex. *Science, 276,* 821–834.

Rapee, R. M., & Heimberg, R. G. (1997). A cognitive-behavioral model of anxiety in social phobia. *Behaviour Research & Therapy, 35,* 741–756.

Rauch, S. L., Jenike, M. A., Alpert, N. M., Baer, L., Breiter, H. C. R., Savage, C. R., & Fischman, A. J. (1994). Regional cerebral blood flow measured during symptom provocation in obsessive-compulsive disorder using oxygen 15-labeled carbon dioxide and poitron emission tomography. *Archives of General Psychiatry, 51,* 62–70.

Rauch, S. L., van der Kolk, B. A., Risler, R. E., Alpert, N. M., Orr, S. P., Savage, C. R., Fischman, A. J., Jenike, M. A., & Pitman, R. K. (1996). A symptom provocation study of posttraumatic stress disorder using positron emission tomography and script-driven imagery. *Archives of General Psychiatry, 53,* 380–387.

Raudenbush, S. W. (1984). Magnitude of teacher expectancy effects on pupil IQ as a function of the credibility of expectancy induction: A synthesis of findings from 18 experiments. *Journal of Educational Psychology, 76,* 85–97.

Rauscher, F. H. (1999). Prelude or requiem for the "Mozart effect"? *Nature, 400,* 827–828.

Rauscher, F. H., Shaw, G. L., & Ky, K. N. (1993). Music and spatial task performance. *Nature, 365,* 611.

Raven, B. (1998). Groupthink, Bay of Pigs, and Watergate reconsidered. *Organizational Behavior & Human Decision Processes, 73,* 352–361.

Raven, J. C. (1965). *Advanced progressive matrices: Sets I and II.* London: Lewis.

Raven, J. C. (1976). *Standard progressive matrices: Sets A, B, C, D & E.* Oxford: Oxford Psychologists Press.

Ray, J., & Sapolsky, R. (1992). Styles of male social behavior and their endocrine correlates among high-ranking wild baboons. *American Journal of Primatology, 28,* 231–250.

Ray, W. J., Sabsevitz, D., DePascalis, V., Quigley, K., Aikens, D., & Tubbs, M. (2000). Cardiovascular reactivity during hypnosis and hypnotic susceptibility: Three studies of heart rate variability. *International Journal of Clinical & Experimental Hypnosis, 48,* 22–31.

Raymond, J. E., Shapiro, K. L., & Arnell, K. M. (1992). Temporary suppression of visual processing in an RSVP task: An attentional blink? *Journal of Experimental Psychology: Human Perception and Performance, 18,* 849–860.

Razran, G. H. S. (1940). Conditioned response changes in rating and appraising sociopolitical solutions. *Psychological Bulletin, 37,* 481.

Rechtschaffen, A., Gilliland, M. A., Bergmann, B. M., & Winter, J. B. (1983). Physiological correlates of prolonged sleep deprivation in rats. *Science, 221:* 182–4.

Redd, W. H., Dadds, M. R., Futterman, A. D., Taylor, K. L., & Bovbjerg, D. J. (1993). Nausea induced by mental images of chemotherapy. *Cancer, 72,* 629–636.

Reed, T. E., & Jenson, A. R. (1990). Choice reaction time and visual pathway nerve conduction velocity both correlate with intelligence but appear not to correlate with each other: Implications for information processing. *Intelligence, 17,* 191–203.

Regan, D. T., & Fazio, R. H. (1977). On the consistency between attitudes and behavior: Look to the method of attitude formation. *Journal of Experimental Psychology, 13,* 38–45.

Regan, P. C. (1996). Rhythms of desire: The association between menstrual cycle phases and female sexual desire. *Canadian Journal of Human Sexuality, 5,* 145–156.

Regier D. A., & Kaelber, C. T. (1995). The Epidemiologic Catchment Area (ECA) program: studying the prevalence and incidence of psychopathology. In: M. T. Tsuang, M. Tohen, G. E. P. Zahner (Eds.), *Textbook in Psychiatric Epidemiology* (pp. 133–157). New York: John Wiley & Sons Inc.

Regier, D. A., Narrow, W. E., Rae, D. S., Manderscheid, R. W., Locke, B. Z., & Goodwin, F. K. (1993). The de facto US mental and addictive disorders service system. Epidemiologic Catchment Area prospective 1-year prevalence rates of disorders and services. *Archives of General Psychiatry, 50,* 85–94.

Reicher, G. M. (1969). Perceptual recognition as a function of meaningfulness of stimulus material. *Journal of Experimental Psychology, 81,* 275–280.

Reid, J. E. (1947). A revised questioning technique in lie-detection tests. *Journal of Criminal Law & Criminology, 37,* 542–547.

Reid, R. C. (1999). Vision. In M. J. Zigmond, F. E. Bloom, S. C. Landis, J. L. Roberts, & L. R. Squire (Eds.), *Fundamental neuroscience* (pp. 821–851). New York: Academic Press.

Reifman, A., & Windle, M. (1995). Adolescent suicidal behaviors as a function of depression, hopelessness, alcohol use, and social support: A longitudinal investigation. *American Journal of Community Psychology, 23,* 329–354.

Reiman, E. M., Lane, R. D., Ahern, G. L., Schwartz, G. E., Davidson, R. J., Friston, K. J., Yun, L-S., & Chen, K. (1997). Neuroanatomical correlates of externally and internally generated human emotion. *American Journal of Psychiatry, 154,* 918–925.

Reinberg, A., Vieux, N., Andlauer, P., & Smolensky, M. (1983). Tolerance to shift work" A chronobiological approach. In J. Mendlewicz & H. M. van Praag (eds.), *Biological Rhythms and Behavior Advances in Biological Psychiatry,* vol. 2, pp. 20–34. Basel, Switzerland: S. Karger.

Reinisch, J. M., & Sanders, S. A. (1992). Prenatal hormonal contributions to sex differences in human cognitive and personality development. In A. A. Gerall, H. Moltz, & I. I. Ward (Eds.), *Sexual differentiation: Vol. II. Handbook of behavioral neurobiology* (pp. 221–243). New York: Plenum.

Reis, H. T., & Shaver, P. (1988). Intimacy as an interpersonal process. In S. W. Duck (Ed.), *Handbook of basic principles* (pp. 367–389). Chichester, England: Wiley.

Rende, R., & Plomin, R. (1992). Diathesis-stress models of psychopathology: A quantitative genetic perspective. *Applied & Preventative Psychology. 1*, 177–182.

Rensink, R. A., O'Regan, J. K., & Clark, J. J. (1997). To see or not to see: The need for attention to perceive changes in scenes. *Psychological Science, 8*, 368–373.

Repetti, R. L. (1993). Short-term effects of occupational stressors on daily mood and health complaints. *Health Psychology, 12*, 125–131.

Rescorla, R. A. (1966). Predictability and number of pairings in Pavolvian fear condiitong. *Psychonomic Science, 4*, 383–385.

Rescorla, R. A. (1967). Pavlovian conditioning and its proper control procedures. *Psychological Review, 74*, 71–80.

Resnick, H. S., Kilpatrick, D. G., Dansky, B. S., Saunders, B., & Best, C. L. (1993). Prevalence of civilian trauma and posttraumatic stress disorder in a representative national sample of women. *Journal of Consulting and Clinical Psychology, 61*, 984–991.

Rest, J. R. (1979). *Development in judging moral issues*. Minneapolis: University of Minnesota Press.

Rest, J. R. (1986). *Moral development: Advances in research and theory*. New York: Praeger.

Retsinas, J. (1988). A theoretical reassessment of the applicability of Kübler-Ross's stages of dying. *Death Studies, 12*, 207–216.

Reynolds, C. F., III., Frank, E., Perel, J. M., Imber, S. D., Cornes, C., Miller, M. D., Mazumdar, S., Houck, P. R., Dew, M. A., Stack, J. A., Pollock, B. G., & Kupfer, D. J. (1999). Nortriptyline and interpersonal psychotherapy as maintenance therapies for recurrent major depression: A randomized controlled trial in patients older than 59 years. *Journal of the American Medical Association, 281*,:39–45.

Reynolds, S., Stiles, W. B., Barkham, M., Shapiro, D. A., Hardy, G. E., & Rees, A. (1996). Acceleration of changes in session impact during contrasting time-limited psychotherapies. *Journal of Consulting & Clinical Psychology, 64*, 577–586.

Reznick, J. S., & Goldfield, B. A. (1992). Rapid change in lexical development in comprehension and production. *Developmental Psychology, 28*, 406–413.

Rhine, J. B. (1934). *Extra-sensory perception*. Boston: Boston Society for Psychic Research.

Rhine, L. E. (1967). *ESP in life and lab: Tracing hidden channels*. New York: Macmillan.

Rhodewalt, F., & Davison, J., Jr. (1983). Reactance and the coronary-prone behavior pattern: The role of self-attribution in response to reduced behavioral freedom. *Journal of Personality and Social Psychology, 44*, 220–228.

Rice, G., Anderson, C., Risch, N., & Ebers, G. (1999). Male homosexuality: Absence of linkage to microsatellite markers at Xq28. *Science, 284*, 665–667.

Rice, M. E., & Grusec, J. E. (1975). Saying and doing: Effects on observer performance. *Journal of Personality and Social Psychology, 32*, 584–593.

Richards, J. C., Edgar, L. V., & Gibbons, P. (1996). Cardiac acuity in panic disorder. *Cognitive Therapy and Research, 20*, 361–376.

Richardson, A. (1994). *Individual differences in imaging: Their measurement, origins, and consequences*. Amityville, NY: Baywood.

Richert, E. S. (1997). Excellence with equity in identification and programming. In N. Colangelo & G. A. Davis (Eds.), *Handbook of gifted education* (2nd ed.), (pp. 75–88). Boston: Allyn & Bacon.

Ridgeway, C. L. (1991). The social construction of status calue: Gender and other nominal characteristics. *Social Forces, 70*, 367–386.

Rijsdijk, F. V., & Boomsma, D. I. (1997). Genetic meditation of the correlation between peripheral nerve conduction velocity and IQ. *Behavior Genetics, 27*, 87–98.

Rinn, W. E. (1984). The neuropsychology of facial expression: A review of the neurological and psychological mechanisms for producing facial expressions. *Psychological Bulletin, 95*, 52–77.

Riordan-Eva, P. (1992). Blindness. In D. Vaugh, T. Ashbury, & P. Riordan-Eva (Eds.), *General opthalmology* (pp. 404–409). Norwalk, CT: Appleton & Lange.

Rips, L. J., & Marcus, S. L. (1977). Supposition and the analysis of conditional sentences. In M. A. Just & P. A. Carpenter (Eds.), *Cognitive processes in comprehension* (pp. 185–220). Hillsdale, NJ: Erlbaum.

Rips, L. J., Shoben, E. J., & Smith, E. E. (1973). Semantic distance and the verification of semantic relations. *Journal of Verbal Learning and Verbal Behavior, 12*, 1–20.

Rivera-Arzola, M., & Ramos-Grenier, J. (1997). Anger, ataques de nervios, and la mujer puertorriquena: Sociocultural considerations and treatment implications. In J. G. Garcia & M. C. Zea (Eds.), *Psychological interventions and research with Latino populations*. Boston, MA: Allyn & Bacon, Inc.

Robbins, T. W., & Everitt, B. J. (1998). Motivation and reward. In M. J. Zigmond, F. E. Bloom, S. C. Landis, J. L. Roberts, and L. R. Squire (Eds.), *Fundamental neuroscience*. New York: Academic Press, pp. 1245–1260.

Robbins, T. W., & Everitt, B. J. (1999). Motivation and reward. In M. J. Zigmond, F. E. Bloom, S. C. Landis, J. L. Roberts, & L. R. Squire (Eds.), *Fundamental neuroscience* (pp. 1245–1260). San Diego: Academic Press.

Roberts, A. H., Kewman, D. G., Mercier, L., & Hovell, M. (1993). The power of nonspecific effects in healing: implications for psychosocial and biological treatments. *Clinical Psychology Review, 13*, 375–391.

Roberts, B. W., & DelVecchio, W. F. (2000). The rank-order consistency of personality traits from childhood to old age: A quantitative review of longitudinal studies. *Psychological Bulletin, 126*, 3–25.

Roberts, P., & Newton, P. M. (1987). Levinsonian studies of women's adult development. *Psychology and Aging, 2*, 154–163.

Robertson, L. C., & Delis, D. C. (1986). "Part-whole" processing in unilateral brain damaged patients: Dysfunction of hierarchical organization. *Neuropsychologia, 24*, 363–370.

Robertson, L. C., Lamb, M. R., & Knight, R. T. (1988). Effects of lesions of temporal-parietal junction on perceptual and attentional processing in humans. *Journal of Neuroscience, 8*(10), 3757–3769.

Robins, L. N., & Regier, D. A. (1991). *Psychiatric disorder s in America: The epidemiological catchment area study*. New York: The Free Press.

Robinson, J. L., Kagan, J., Reznick, J. S., & Corley, R. (1992). The heritability of inhibited and uninhibited behavior: A twin study. *Developmental Psychology, 28*, 1030–1037.

Robinson, N. M., Abbott, R. D., Berninger, V. W., & Busse, J. (1996). The structure of abilities in math-precocious young children: Gender similarities and differences. *Journal of Educational Psychology, 88*, 341–352.

Robinson, V. (1977a). *Humor and the health professions*. Thorofare, NJ: Slack.

Robinson, V. (1977b). Humor in nursing. In C. Carlson & B. Blackwell (Eds.), *Behavioral Concepts and Nursing Interventions*. Philadelphia: Lippincott.

Robinson-Whelen, S., Kim, C., MacCallum, R. C., & Kiecolt-Glaser, J. K. (1998). Distinguishing optimism from pessimism in older adults: Is it more important to be optimistic or not to be pessimistic? *Journal of Personality and Social Psychology, 73*, 1345–1353.

Rochat, P., & Hespos, S. J. (1997). Differential rooting response by neonates: Evidence for an early sense of self. *Early Development & Parenting, 6*, 105–112.

Rock, I. (1983). *The logic of perception*. Cambridge, MA: MIT Press.

Rock, I., & Ebenholtz, S. (1959). The relational determination of perceived size. *Psychological Review, 66*, 387–401.

Rodda, G. H. (1984). The orientation and navigation of juvenile alligators: Evidence of magnetic sensitivity. *Journal of Comparative Physiology, 154*, 649–658.

Rodier, P. (1980). Chronology of neuron development. *Developmental Medicine and Child Neurology, 22*, 525–545.

Rodin, J. (1981). Current status of the internal/external hypothesis for obesity: What went wrong? *American Psychologist, 36*, 361–372.

Rodin, J., & Langer, E. J. (1977). Long-term effects of a control-relevant intervention with the institutionalized aged. *Journal of Personality & Social Psychology, 35*, 897–902.

Roe, A. W., Pallas, S. L., Hahm, J. O., & Sur, M. (1990). A map of visual space induced in primary auditory cortex. *Science, 250*, 818–820.

Roediger, H. L., & Thorpe, L. A. (1978). The role of recall time in producing hypermnesia. *Memory & Cognition, 6*, 296–305.

Roediger, H. L., III (1980). Memory metaphors in cognitive psychology. *Memory & Cognition, 8*, 231–246.

Roediger, H. L., III, & McDermott, K. B. (1993). Implicit memory in normal human subjects. In F. Bohler & J. Grafman (Eds.), *Handbook of Neuropsychology* (Vol. 8, pp. 63–131). Amsterdam: Elsevier.

Roediger, H. L., III, & McDermott, K. B. (1995). Creating false memories: Remembering words not presented in lists. *Journal of Experimental Psychology: Learning, Memory, and Cognition, 21*, 803–814.

Roggman, L. A., Langlois, J. H., Hubbs-Tait, L., & Rieser-Danner, L. A. (1994). Infant day-care, attachment, and the "file drawer problem." *Child Development, 65*, 1429–1443.

Roland, P. E., & Seitz, R. J. (1989). Mapping of learning and memory functions in the human brain. In D. Ottoson (Ed.), Visualization of brain functions. London: Stockton Press, pp. 141–151.

Roll, S., McClelland, G., & Abel, T. (1996). Differences in susceptibility to influence in Mexican American and Anglo females. *Hispanic Journal of Behavioral Sciences, 18*, 13–20.

Rollman, G. B. (1987). The detectability, discriminability, and perceived magnitude of painful electrical shock. *Perception & Psychophysics, 42*, 257–268.

Rollman, G. B. (1991). Pain responsiveness. In M. A. Heller & W. Schiff (Eds.), *The psychology of touch* (pp. 91–114). Hillsdale, NJ: Erlbaum.

Rollman, G. B., & Harris, G. (1987). The detectability, discriminability, and perceived magnitude of painful electrical shock. *Perception & Psychophysics, 42,* 257–268.

Rolls, B. J., Rolls, E. T., Rowe, E. A., & Sweeney, K. (1981). Sensory specific satiety in man. *Physiology & Behavior, 27,* 137–142.

Rolls, B. J., Rowe, E. A., Rolls, E. T., Kingston, B., Megson, A., & Gunary, R. (1981). Variety in a meal enhances food intake in man. *Physiology & Behavior, 26,* 215–221.

Rolls, E. T. (1992). Neurophysiology and functions of the primate amygdala. In J. P. Aggleton (Ed.), *The amygdala: Neurobiological aspects of emotion, memory, and mental dysfunction* (pp. 143–165). New York: Wiley-Liss.

Rolls, E. T., & Cooper, S. J. (1974). Connection between the prefrontal cortex and pontine brain-stimulation reward sites in the rat. *Experimental Neurology, 42,* 687–699.

Romach, M. K., & Sellers, E. M. (1991). Management of the alcohol withdrawal syndrome. *Annual Review of Medicine, 42,* 323–340.

Romani, G. L., Williamson, S. J., & Kaufman, L. (1982). Tonotopic organization of the human auditory cortex. *Science, 216,* 1339–1340.

Romero, A. A., Agnew, C. R., & Insko, C. A. (1996). The cognitive mediation hypnothesis revisted. *Perosnality and Social Psychology Bulletin, 22,* 1001–1012.

Romero, A. A., Agnew, C. R., & Insko, C. A. (1996). The cognitive mediation hypothesis revisited: An empirical response to methodological and theoretical criticism. *Personality & Social Psychology Bulletin, 22,* 651–665.

Romero, L., & Sapolsky, R. (1996). Patterns of ACTH secretagog secretion in response to psychological stimuli. *Journal of Neuroendocrinology, 8,* 243–258.

Rosch, E. (1973). Natural categories. *Cognitive Psychology, 4,* 328–350.

Rosch, E. (1975). The nature of mental codes for color categories. *Journal of Experimental Psychology: Human Perception and Performance, 1,* 303–322.

Rosch, E. (1978). Principles of categorization. In E. Rosch, & B. B. Lloyd (Ed.), *Cognition and categorization* (pp. 27–48). Hillsdale, NJ: Erlbaum.

Rosch, E., Mervis, C. B., Gray, W. D., Johnson, D. M., & Boyes-Braem, P. (1976). Basic objects in natural categories. *Cognitive Psychology, 8,* 382–439.

Rosen C. M. (1987). The eerie world of reunited twins. *Discover, 8,* 36–46.

Rosenbaum, M., & Leibel, R. L. (1999). The role of leptin in human physiology. *New England Journal of Medicine, 341,* 913–915.

Rosenbaum, M. E. (1986). The repulsion hypothesis: On the nondevelopment of relationships. *Journal of Personality and Social Psychology, 51,* 1156–1166.

Rosenberg, M. (1979). *Conceiving the self.* New York: Basic Books.

Rosenfarb, I. S., Goldstein, M. J., Mintz, J., & Nuechterlein, K. H. (1995). Expressed emotion and subclinical observable within transactions between schizophrenia patients and their family members. *Journal of Abnormal Psychology, 104,* 259–267.

Rosenhan, D. L. (1973). On being sane in insane places. *Science, 179,* 250–258.

Rosenheim, M. K., & Testa, M. F. (Eds.) (1992). *Early parenthood and coming of age in the 1990s.* New Brunswick, NJ: Rutgers University Press.

Rosenthal, A. M. (1964). *Thiry-eight witnesses.* New York: McGraw-Hill.

Rosenthal, D. (1963). *The Genain Quadruplets.* New York: Basic Books.

Rosenthal, R. (1976). *Experimenter effects in behavioral research.* New York: Irvington.

Rosenthal, R. (1986). Meta-analytic procedure and the nature of replication: The Ganzfeld debate. *Journal of Parapsychology, 50,* 316–336.

Rosenthal, R. (1991). *Meta-analytic procedures for social research.* Beverly Hills, CA: Sage.

Rosenthal, R. (1993) Interpersonl expectations: Some antecedents and some consequences. In P. D. Blanck (Ed.), *Interpersonal expectations: Theory, research, and applications* (pp. 3–24). Cambridge: Cambridge University Press.

Rosenthal, R. (1994). Interpersonal expectancy effects: A 30-year perspective. *Current Directions in Psychological Sciences, 3,* 176–179.

Rosenthal, R., & Jacobson, L. (1968). *Pygmalion in the classroom.* New York: Holt, Rinehart & Winston.

Roskill, M. (1963). *The letters of Vincent van Gogh.* London: William Collins.

Ross, C. A. (1991). Epidemiology of multiple personality disorder and dissociation. *Psychiatric Clinics of North America, 14,* 503–517.

Ross, C. A., Miller, S. D., Bjornson, L., Reagor, P., & Fraser, G. A. (1991). Abuse histories in 102 cases of multiple personality disorder. *Canadian Journal of Psychiatry, 36,* 97–101.

Ross, C. E. (1995). Reconceptualizing marital status as a continuum of social attachment. *Journal of Marriage & the Family, 57,* 129–140.

Ross, H. E., & Ross, G. M. (1976). Did Ptolemy understand the moon illusion? *Perception, 5,* 377–385.

Ross, L., Greene, D., & House, P. (1977). The false consensus effect: An egocentric bias in social perception and attribution processes. *Journal of Experimental Social Psychology, 13,* 279–301.

Rossi, E. L., & Cheek, D. B. (1988). *Mind-Body Therapy,* New York: Norton.

Rothman, A. J., Salovey, P., Antone, C., Keough, K., & Martin, C. (1993). The influence of message framing on intentions to perform health behaviors. *Journal of Experimental Social Psychology, 29,* 408–433

Rotter, J. B. (1966). Generalized expectancies for internal versus extrnal control of reinforcement. *Psychological Monographs, 80* (1, Whole No. 609).

Rouhana, N. N., & Bar-Tal, D. (1998). Psychological Dynamics of Intractable ethnonational conflicts: The Israeli-Palestinian case. *American Psychologist, 53,* 761–770.

Rouillon, F. (1997). Epidemiology of panic disorder. *Human Psychopharmacology Clinical & Experimental, 12*(Suppl. 1), S7–S12.

Rowatt, W. C., Cunningham, M. R., & Druen, P. B. (1998). Deception to get a date. *Personality and Social Psychology Bulletin, 24,* 1228–1242.

Rowe, J. W., & Kahn, R. L. (1998). *Successful aging.* New York: Pantheon.

Rozin, P. (1982). "Taste-smell confusions" and the duality of the olfactory sense. *Perception and Psychophysics, 31,* 397–401.

Rozin, P. (1990). Getting to like the burn of chili pepper: Biological, psychological and cultural perspectives. In B. G. Green, J. R. Mason, & M. R. Kare (Eds.), *Chemical senses: Volume 2, Irritation* (pp. 231–269). New York: Marcel Dekker.

Rozin, P., & Fallon, A. (1986). The acquisition of likes and dislikes for foods. In National Research Council et al., *What is America eating?: Proceedings of a symposium.* Washington, DC: National Academy Press.

Rozin, P., & Jonides, J. (1977). Mass reaction time: Measurement of the speed of the nerve impulse and the duration of mental processes in class. *Teaching of Psychology, 4,* 91–94.

Rozin, P., Ashmore, M., & Markwith, M. (1996). Lay American conceptions of nutrition: Dose insensitivity, categorical thinking, contagion, and the monotonic mind. *Health Psychology, 15,* 438–447.

Rozin, P., Dow, S., Moscovitch, M., & Rajaram, S. (1998). What causes humans to begin and end a meal? A role for memory for what has been eaten, as evidenced by a study of multiple meal eating in amnesic patients. *Psychological Science, 9,* 392–396.

Rozin, P., Levine, E., & Stoess, C. (1991). Chocolate craving and linking. *Appetite, 17,* 199–212

Rozin, P., Lowery, L., & Ebert, R. (1994). Varieties of disgust faces and the structure of disgust. *Journal of Personality & Social Psychology, 66,* 870–881.

Rozin, P., Lowery, L., Imada, S., & Haidt, J. (1999). The CAD triad hypothesis: A mapping between three moral emotions (contempt, anger, disgust) and three moral codes (community, autonomy, divinity). *Journal of Personality & Social Psychology, 76,* 574–586.

Rozin, P., Millman, L., & Nemeroff, C. (1986). Operation of the laws of sympathetic magic in disgust and other domains. *Journal of Personality & Social Psychology, 50,* 703–712.

Rubin, L. J. (1996). Childhood sexual abuse: False accusations of "False memory"? *Professional Psychology Research and Practice, 27,* 447–451.

Rubin, Z. (1970). Measurement of romantic love. *Journal of Personality and Social Psychology, 16,* 265–273.

Rumelhart, D. E. (1975). Notes on schema for stories. In D. G. Bobrow & A. M. Collins (Eds.), *Representations and understanding: Studies in cognitive science* (pp. 211–236). New York: Academic Press.

Rumelhart, D. E., & McClelland, J. L. (1986). *Parallel distributed processing: Explorations in the microstructure of cognition: Volume 1, Foundations* (2nd Ed.), Cambridge, MA: MIT Press.

Runco, M. A., & Albert, R. S. (1986). The threshold theory regarding creativity and intelligence: An empirical test with gifted and nongifted children. *Creative Child & Adult Quarterly, 11,* 212–218.

Rushton, J. P. (1975). Generosity in children: Immediate and long-term effects of modeling, preaching, and moral judgement. *Journal of Personality and Social Psychology, 31,* 459–466.

Rushton, J. P. (1980). *Altruism, socializaion and society.* Englewood Cliffs, NJ: Prentice Hall.

Rushton, J. P. (1995). *Race, evolution and behavior: A life-history perspective.* New Brunswick, NJ: Transaction.

Rushton, J. P., & Ankney, C. D. (1996). Brain size and cognitive ability: Correlations with age, sex, social class, and race. *Psychonomic Bulletin & Review, 3,* 21–36.

Rushton, J. P., Jackson, D. N., & Paunonen, S. V. (1981). Personality: Nomothetic or idiographic? A response to Kenrick and Stringfield. *Psychological Review, 88,* 582–589.

Russell, M. J. (1976). Human olfactory communication. *Nature, 260,* 520–522.

Russell, M. J., Switz, D. M., & Thompson, K. (1980). Olfactory influences on the human menstrual cycle. *Pharmacology, Biochemistry, & Behavior, 13,* 737–8.

Russo, J. F., & Schoemaker, P. J. H. (1989). *Decision traps.* New York: Doubleday.

Rustemli, A., Mertan, B., & Ciftci, O. (2000). In-group favoritism among native and immigrant Turkish cypriots: Trait evaluations of in-group and out-group targets. *Journal of Social Psychology, 140,* 26–34.

Ruzyla-Smith, P, Barabasz, A., Barabasz, M., & Warner, D. (1995) Effects of hypnosis on the immune response: B cells, T cells, helper and suppressor cells. *American Journal of Clinical Hypnosis, 38,* 72–79.

Ryan, R. M., & Deci, E. L. (1996). When paradigms clash: Comments on Cameron and Pierce's claim that rewards to not undermine intrinsic motivation. *Review of Educational Research, 66,* 33–38.

Ryan, R. M., & Deci, E. L. (2000). Self-determination theory and the facilitation of intrinsic motivation, social development, and well-being. *American Psychologist, 55,* 68–78.

Rymer, R. (1993). *Genie: An abused child's flight from silence.* NY: HarperCollins.

Ryner, L. C., Goodwin, S. F., Castrillon, D. H., Anand, A., Villella, A., Baker, B. S., Hall, J. C., Taylor, B. J., & Wasserman, S. A. (1996). Control of male sexual behavior and sexual orientation in Drosophila by the fruitless gene. *Cell, 87,* 1079–1089.

Ryska, T. A. (1998). Cognitive-behavioral strategies and precompetitive anxiety among recreational athletes. *Psychological Record, 48,* 697–708.

Sabourin, M. E., Cutcomb, S. D., Crawford, H. J., & Pribram, K. (1990–1991). EEG correlates of hypnotic susceptibility and hypnotic trance: Spectral analysis and coherence. *International Journal of Psychophysiology, 10,* 125–142.

Sachdev, I., & Bourhis, R. Y. (1991). Power and status differentials in minority and majority relations. *European Journal of Social Psychology, 21,* 1–24.

Sachs, J. S. (1967). Recognition memory for syntactic and semantic aspects of connected discourse. *Perception and Psychophysics, 2,* 437–442.

Sackett, P. R. (1994). Integrity testing for personnel selection. *Current Directions in Psychological Science, 3,* 73–76.

Sackeim, H. A., Devanand, D. P., & Nobler, M. S. (1995). Electroconvulsive therapy. In F. E. Bloom & D. J. Kupfer (Eds.), *Psychopharmacology: The Fourth Generation of Progress.* New York: Raven Press. pp. 1123–1141.

Sacks, O. (1995). *An anthropologist on Mars: Seven paradoxical tales.* New York: Knopf.

Sadato, N., Pascual-Leone, A., Grafman, J., Ibanez, V., Deiber, M. P., Dold, G., & Hallett, M. (1996). Activation of the primary visual cortex by Braille reading in blind subjects. *Nature, 380,* 526–528.

Sadler, T. W. (1995). *Langman's medical embryology* (7th ed.). Baltimore: Williams & Wilkins.

Sadowski, C. J., & Guelgoez, S. (1996). Elaborative processing mediates the relationship between need for cognition and academic performance. *Journal of Psychology, 130,* 303–307.

Saffran, E. M., & Schwartz, M. F. Of Cabbages and things: Semantic memory from a neuropsychological perspective—a tutorial review. In D. Meyer & S. Cornblum (Eds.), *International symposium on attention and performance performance XV* (pp. 507–536). Cambridge, MA: MIT Press.

Saffran, J. R., Aslin, R. N., & Newport, E. L. (1996). Statistical learning by 8-month-old infants. *Science, 274,* 1926–1928.

Saffran, J. R., Aslin, R. N., & Newport, E. L. (1996). Statistical learning by 8-month-old infants. *Science, 274,* 1926–1928.

Saggino, A. (2000). The Big Three or the Big Five? A replication study. *Personality & Individual Differences, 28,* 879–886.

Sagie, A., Elizur, S., & Hirotsugu, Y. (1996). The structure and strength of achievement motivation: A cross-cultural comparison. *Journal of Organization Behavior, 17,* 431–444.

Saldana, H. N., & Rosenblum, L. D. (1993). Visual influences on auditory pluck and bow judgments. *Perception & Psychophysics, 54,* 406–416.

Salkovskis, P. M. (1985). Obsessional-compulsive problems: A cognitive-behavioral analysis. *Behaviour Research and Therapy, 23,* 571–583.

Sallis, J., Johnson, C., Treverow, T., Kaplan, R., & Hovell, M. (1987). The relationship between cynical hostility and blood pressure reactivity. *Journal of Psychosomatic Research, 31,* 111–116.

Salmon, C. A. (1998). The Evocative Nature of Kin Terminology in Political Rhetoric. *Politics and the Life Sciences 17,* 51–57.

Salmon, C. A. (1999). On the impact of sex and birth order on contact with kin. *Human Nature, 10,* 183–197.

Salmon, C. A., & Daly, M. (1998). Birth order and familial sentiment: middleborns are different. *Evolution and Behavior, 19,* 299–312.

Salmon, D. P., & Butters, N. (1995). Neurobiology of skill and habit learning. *Current Opinion in Neurobiology, 5,* 184–190.

Salovey, P., & Mayer, J. D. (1990). Emotional intelligence. *Imagination, Cognition, and Personality, 9,* 185–211.

Salthouse, T. A. (1984). Effects of age and skill in typing. *Journal of Experimental Psychology: General, 113,* 345–371.

Salthouse, T. A. (1985). Speed of behavior and its implications for cognition. In J. E. Birren & K. W. Schaie (Eds.), *Handbook of the psychology of aging* (2nd ed., pp. 400–426). New York: Van Nostrand Reinhold.

Salthouse, T. A. (1991a). Cognitive facets of aging well. *Generations, 15*(1), 35–38.

Salthouse, T. A. (1991b). *Theoretical perspectives on cognitive aging.* Hillsdale, NJ: Erlbaum.

Salthouse, T. A. (1996). The processing-speed theory of adult age differences in cognition. *Psychological Review, 103,* 403–428.

Salthouse, T. A., & Somberg, B. L. (1982). Skilled performance: Effects of adult age and experience on elementary processes. *Journal of Experimental Psychology: General, 111,* 176–207.

Sameroff, A. J., & Haith, M. M. (Eds.) (1996). *The five to seven year shift: The age of reason and responsibility.* Chicago, IL: University of Chicago Press.

Samoluk, S. B., & Stewart, S. H. (1998). Anxiety sensitivity and situation-specific drinking. *Journal of Anxiety Disorders, 12,* 407–419.

Sanbonmatsu, D. M., & Fazio, R. H. (1990). The Role of Attitudes in Memory-Based Decision Making. *Journal of Personality and Social Psychology, 59,* 614–622.

Sand, G., & Miyazaki, A. D. (2000). The impact of social support on salesperson burnout and burnout components. *Psychology & Marketing, 17,* 13–26.

Sandman, C. A., Wadhwa, P., Hetrick, W., Porto, M., & Peeke, H. V. S. (1997). Human fetal heart rate dishabituation between thirty and thirty-two weeks gestation. *Child Development, 68,* 1031–1040.

Sandvik, E., Diener, E., & Larsen, R. J. (1985). The opponent process theory and affective reactions. *Motivation & Emotion, 9,* 407–418.

Sanna, L. J. (1996). Defensive pessimism, optimism, and simulating alternatives: Some ups and downs of prefactual and counterfactual thinking. *Journal of Personality and Social Psychology, 71,* 1020–1036.

Sansone, C. & Harackiewicz, J. M. (1998). "Reality" is complicated. *American Psychologist, 53,* 673–674.

Sapolsky, R. M. (1992). *Stress, the aging brain, and the mechanisms of neuron death.* Cambridge, MA: MIT Press.

Sapolsky, R. M. (1996). Why stress is bad for your brain. *Science, 273,* 749–750.

Sapolsky, R. M. (1997). *Why Zebras Don't Get Ulcers.* New York: Freeman.

Sapp, D. D. (1992). The point of creative frustration and the creative process: A new look at an old model. *The Journal of Creative Behavior, 26,* 21–28.

Sarbin, T. R. (1995). On the belief that one body may be host to two or more personalities. *International Journal of Clinical & Experimental Hypnosis, 43,* 163–183.

Sarbin, T. R., & Coe, W. C. (1972). *Hypnosis: A social psychological analysis of influence communication.* New York: Holt, Rinehart, & Winston.

Sargent, P. A., Sharpley, A. L., Williams, C., Goodall, E. M., & Cowen, P. J. (1997). 5-HT-sub(2C) receptor activation decreases appetite and body weight in obese subjects. *Psychopharmacology, 133,* 309–312.

Satcher, D. (1999). *Mental health: A report of the Surgeon General.* Washington, DC: Department of Health and Human Services.

Saudino, K. J., Gagne, J. R., Grant, J., Ibatoulina, A., Marytuina, T., Ravich-Scherbo, I., & Whitfield, K. (1999). Genetic and environmental influences on personality in adult Russian twins. *International Journal of Behavioral Development, 23,* 375–389.

Saudino, K. J., Pedersen, N. L., Lichtenstein, P., McClearn, G. E., & Plomin, R. (1997). Can personality explain genetic influences on life events? *Journal of Personality and Social Psychology, 72,* 196–206.

Savage-Rumbaugh, S., McDonald, K., Sevcik, R. A., Hopkins, W. D., & Rubert, E. (1986). Spontaneous symbol acquisition and communicative use by pygmy chimpanzees (*Pan paniscus*). *Journal of Experimental Psychology: General, 112,* 211–235.

Saxe, G. B. (1988). Candy selling and math learning. *Educational Research. 17,* 14–21.

Scarr, S. (1976). An evolutionary perspective on infant intelligence: Species patterns and individual variations. In M. Lewis (Ed.), *Origins of intelligence* (pp. 165–197). New York: Plenum.

Scarr, S. (1987). Personality and experience: Individual encounters with the world. In J. Aronoff, A. I. Rabin, and R. A. Zucker (Eds.), *The mergence of personality* (pp. 49–78). New York: Springer.

Scarr, S. (1997). Why child care has little impact on most children's development. *Current Directions in Psychological Science, 6*(5), 143–148.

Scarr, S. (1998). American child care today. *American Psychologist, 53*(2), 95–108.

Scarr, S., & McCartney, K. (1983). How people make their own environments: A theory of genotype-environment effects. *Child Development, 54,* 424–435.

Scarr, S., & Weinberg, R. A. (1983). The Minnesota Adoption Studies: Genetic differences and malleability. *Child Development, 54,* 260–267.

Schab, F. R. (Ed.), (1995). *Memory and odors.* Mahwah, NJ: Erlbaum.

Schachter, S. (1968). Obesity and eating. *Science, 16,* 751–756.

Schachter, S. (1971). Some extraordinary facts about obese humans and rats. *American Psychologist, 26,* 129–144.

Schachter, S., & Gross, L. P. (1968). Manipulated time and eating behavior. *Journal of Personality & Social Psychology, 10,* 98–106.

Schacter, D. (1987). Implicit memory: History and current status. *Journal of Experimental Psychology: Learning, Memory, and Cognition, 13,* 501–518.

Schacter, D. L. (1996). *Searching for memory: The brain, the mind, and the past.* New York: Basic Books.

Schacter, D. L. (1999). The seven sins of memory: Insights from psychology and cognitive neuroscience. *American Psychologist, 54,* 182–203.

Schacter, D. L., Kaszniak, A. K., Kihlstrom, J. F., & Valdiserri, M. (1991). The relation between source memory and aging. *Psychology and Aging, 6,* 559–568.

Schacter, D. L., Koutstaal, W., & Norman, K. A. (1997). False memories and aging. *Trends in Cognitive Sciences, 1,* 229–236.

Schacter, D. L., Osowiecki, D., Kaszniak, A. W., Kihlstrom, J. F., & Valdiserri, M. (1994). Source memory: Extending the boundaries of age-related deficits. *Psychology and Aging, 9,* 81–89.

Schacter, D. L., Reiman, E., Curran, T., Yun, L. S., Bandy, D., McDermott, K. B., & Roediger, H. L., III (1996). Neuroanatomical correlates of veridical and illusory recognition memory: Evidence from positron emission tomography. *Neuron, 2,* 267–274.

Schacter, D. L., & Wagner, A. D. (1999). Medial temporal lobe activations in fMRI and PET studies of episodic encoding and retrieval. *Hippocampus, 9,* 7–24.

Schacter, S., & Latané, B. (1964). Crime, cognition, and the autonomic nervous system. In D. Levine (Ed.), *Nebraska Symposium on Motivation* (Vol. 12, pp. 221–273). Lincoln: University of Nebraska Press.

Schacter, S., & Singer, J. (1962). Cognitive, social and physiological determinants of emotional state. *Psychological Review, 69,* 379–399.

Schaffner, K. F. (1967). Approaches to reduction. *Philosophy of Science, 34,* 137–147.

Schaie, K. W. (1983). The Seattle longitudinal study: A twenty-one-year exploration of psychometric intelligence in adulthood. In K. W. Schaie (Ed.), *Longitudinal studies of adult psychological development* (pp. 64–135). New York: Guilford.

Schaie, K. W. (1989). Individual differences in rate of cognitive change in adulthood. In V. L. Bengtson & K. W. Schaie (Eds.), *The course of later life: Research and reflections* (pp. 65–85). New York: Springer.

Schaie, K. W. (1990a). Intellectual development in adulthood. In J. E. Birren & K. W. Schaie (Eds.), *Handbook of the psychology of aging* (3rd ed., pp. 291–309). San Diego, CA: Academic Press.

Schaie, K. W. (1990b). The optimization of cognitive functioning in old age: Predictions based on cohort-sequential and longitudinal data. In P. B. Baltes & M. M. Baltes (Eds.), *Successful aging: Perspectives from the behavioral sciences* (pp. 94–117). Cambridge, England: Cambridge University Press.

Schaie, K. W., & Willis, S. L. (1993). Age difference patterns of psychometric intelligence in adulthood: Generalizability within and across ability domains. *Psychology and Aging, 8,* 44–55.

Schaller, M. (1994). The role of statistical reasoning in the formation, preservation and prevention of group stereotypes. *British Journal of Social Psychology, 33,* 47–61.

Schaller, M., Asp, C. H., Rosell, M. C., & Heim, S. J. (1996). Training in statistical reasoning inhibits the formation of erroneous group stereotypes. *Personality and Social Psychology Bulletin, 22,* 829–844.

Schank, R. C., & Abelson, R. P. (1977). *Scripts, plans, goals, and understanding.* Hillsdale, NJ: Erlbaum.

Scharf, B., & Houtsma, A. J. M. (1986). Audition II. In K. R. Boff, L. Kaufman, & J. P. Thomas (Eds.), *Handbook of perception and human performance* (pp. 15.1–15.60). New York: Wiley.

Scheflin, A., & Brown, D. (1996). Repressed memory or dissociative amnesia: What science says. *Journal of Psychiatry and Law, 24,* 143–188.

Scheier, M. F., & Carver, C. S. (1985). Optimism, coping, and health: Assessment and implications of generalized outcome expectancies. *Health Psychology, 4,* 219–247.

Scheier, M. F., & Carver, C. S. (1993). On the power of positive thinking: The benefits of being optimistic. *Current Directions in Psychology Science, 2,* 26–30.

Scheier, M. F., Matthews, K. A., Owens, J. F., Magovern, G. J., Lefebvre, R. C., Abbott, R. A., & Carver, C. S. (1989). Dispositional optimism and recovery from coronary artery bypass surgery: The beneficial effects on physical and psychological well-being. *Journal of Personality and Social Psychology, 57,* 1024–1040.

Scheier, M. F., Matthews, K. A., Owens, J. F., Schulz, R., Bridges, M. W., Magovern, G. J., & Carver, C. S. (1999). Optimism and rehospitalization after coronary artery bypass graft surgery. *Archives of Internal Medicine, 159,* 829–835.

Schellenberg, E. G., & Trehub, S. E. (1996). Natural musical intervals: Evidence from infant listeners. *Psychological Science, 7,* 272–277.

Schiavi, R. C., White, D., Mandeli, J., & Levine, A. C.(1997). Effect of testosterone administration on sexual behavior and mood in men with erectile dysfunction. *Archives of Sexual Behavior, 26,* 231–241

Schiffman, S. S. (1992). Aging and the sense of smell: Potential benefits of fragrance enhancement. In S. Van Toller & G. H. Dodd (Eds.). *Fragrance: The psychology and biology of perfume.* (pp. 51–62). London: Elsevier.

Schiffman, S. S., Graham, B. G., Sattely-Miller, E. A., & Warwick, Z. S. (1999). Orosensory perception of dietary fat. *Current Directions in Psychological Science, 7,* 137–143.

Schilder, P. (1938). Psychoanalytic remarks on Alice in Wonderland and Lewis Carroll. *Journal of Nervous & Mental Disease, 87,* 159–168.

Schizophrenia: Two roads to schizophrenia. (1996, September). *Harvard Mental Health Letter, 1.*

Schlaug, G., Jancke, L., Huang, Y., & Steinmetz, H. (1995). In vivo evidence of structural brain asymmetry in musicians. *Science, 267,* 699–701.

Schlegel, A., & Barry, H., III. (1991). *Adolescence: An anthropological inquiry.* New York: Free Press.

Schlenker, B. R. (1980). *Impression management: The self-concept, social identity, and interpersonal relations.* Belmont, CA: Brooks/Cole.

Schmidt, N. B., Lerew, D. R., & Jackson, R. J. (1997). The Role of Anxiety Sensitivity in the Pathogenesis of Panic: Prospective Evaluation of Spontaneous Panic Attacks During Acute Stress. *Journal of Abnormal Psychology, 106,* 355–364.

Schmidt, N. B., Lerew, D. R., & Jackson, R. J. (1999). Prospective evaluation of anxiety sensitivity in the pathogenesis of panic: Replication and extension. *Journal of Abnormal Psychology, 108,* 532–537.

Schmitt, B. H., Gilovich, T., Goore, N., & Joseph, L. (1986). Mere presence and social facilitation: One more time. *Journal of Experimental Social Psychology,22,* 242–248.

Schmolck, H., Buffalo, E. A., & Squire, L. R. (2000). Memory distortions develop over time: Recollections from the O. J. Simpson trial verdict after 15 and 32 months. *Psychological Science, 11,* 39–45.

Schneider, B. S., Goldstein, H. W., & Smith, D. B. (1996). The ASA framework: an update. *Personality and Psychology, 48,* 747–773.

Schneider, B., Smith, D. B., Taylor, S., & Fleenor, J. (1998). Personality and Organizations: A Test of the Homogeneity of Personality Hypothesis. *Journal of Applied Psychology, 83,* 462–470.

Schneider, L. H., Davis, J. D., Watson, C. A., & Smith, G. P. (1990). Similar effect of raclopride and reduced sucrose concentration on the microstructure of sucrose sham feeding. *European Journal of Pharmacology, 186,* 61–70.

Scholnick, E. K. (1995, Fall). Knowing and constructing plans. *SRCD Newsletter,* pp. 1–2, 17.

Schrof, J. M., & Schultz, S. (1999). Melencholy Nation. U.S. News and World Report. March 8., *126(9),* p. 56–63.

Schuckit, M. A. (1999). New Findings in the Genetics of Alcoholism. *Journal of the American Medical Association, 281,* 1875–1876.

Schul, R., Slotnick, B. M., & Dudai, Y. (1996). Flavor and the frontal cortex. *Behavioral Neuroscience, 110,* 760–765.

Schulberg, H. C., Magruder, K. M., & deGruy, F. (1996). Major depression in primary medical care practice: Research trends and future priorities. *General Hospital Psychiatry, 18,* 395–406.

Schulenberg, J., Wadsworth, K. N., O'Malley, P. M., Bachman, J. G., & Johnston, L. D. (1996). Adolescent risk factors for binge drinking during the transition to young adulthood: Variable- and pattern-centered approaches to change. *Developmental Psychology, 32,* 659–674.

Schultz, W. (1997). Dopamine neurons and their role in reward mechanisms. *Current Opinion in Neurobiology, 7,* 191–197.

Schultz, W., Dayan, P., & Montague, P. R. (1997). A neural substrate of prediction and reward. *Science, 275,* 1593–1599.

Schwartz, B. (1984). *Psychology of learning and behavior* (2nd ed.) New York: Norton.

Schwartz, C. E., Snidman, N., & Kagan, J. (1996). Early childhood temperament as a determinant of externalizing behavior in adolescence. *Development & Psychopathology, 8,* 527–537.

Schwartz, D. L., & Black, T. (1999). Inferences through imagined actions: Knowing by simulated doing. *Journal of Experimental Psychology: Learning, Memory & Cognition, 25,* 116–136.

Schwartz, J. E., Neale, J., Marco, C., Shiffman, S. S., & Stone, A. A. (1999). Does trait coping exist? A momentary assessment approach to the evaluation of traits. *Journal of Personality and Social Psychology, 77,* 360–369.

Schwartz, J. M., Stoessel, P. W., Baxter, L. R., Martin, K. M., Phelps, M. E. (1996). Systematic changes in cerebral glucose metabolic rate after successful behavior modification treatment of obsessive-compulsive disorder. *Archives of General Psychiatry, 53,* 109–113.

Schwartz, N., & Bless, H. (1992). Constructing reality and its alternatives: An inclusion/exclusion model of assimilation and contrast effects in social judgment. In L. L. Martin & A. Tesser (Eds.), *The construction of social judgments* (pp. 217–245). Hillsdale, NJ: Erlbaum.

Schwartz, T. (1999, January 10). The test under stress. *New York Times Magazine,* pp. 30–63.

Schwartzwald, J., Amir, Y., & Crain, R. L. (1992). Long-term effects of school desegregation experiences on interpersonal relations in the Israeli defense forces. *Personality and Social Psychology Bulletin, 18,* 357–368.

Schwarz, N. (1999). Self-reports: How the questions shape the answers. *American Psychologist, 54,* 93–105.

Schyns, P. (1998). Crossnational differences in happiness: Economic and cultural factors explored. *Social Indicators Research, 43,* 3–26.

Sclafani, A. & Aravich, P. F. (1983). Macronutrient self-selection in three forms of hypothalamic obesity. *American Journal of Physiology, 244,* R686–R694.

Sclafani, A., Aravich, P. F., & Xenakis, S. (1983). Macronutrient preferences in hypothalamic hyperphagic rats. *Nutrition & Behavior, 1,* 233–251.

Scogin, F., Bynum, J., Stephens, G., & Calhoon, S. (1990). Efficacy of self-administered treatment programs: Meta-analytic review. *Professional Psychology: Research & Practice, 21,* 42–47.

Scott, B., & Melin, L. (1998). Psychometric properties and standardised data for questionnaires measuring negative affect, dispositional style and daily hassles: A nation-wide sample. *Scandinavian Journal of Psychology, 39,* 301–307.

Scott, S. K., Young, A. W., Calder, A. J., Hellawell, D. J., Aggleton, J. P. & Johnson, M., (1997) Impaired auditory recognition of fear and anger following bilateral amygdala lesions. *Nature, 385,* 254–257.

Scott, T. R., & Plata-Salaman, C. R. (1991). Coding of taste quality. In T. V. Getchell, R. L. Doty, L. M. Bartoshuk, & J. B. Snow, Jr. (Eds.), *Smell and taste in health and disease* (pp. 345–368). New York: Raven.

Sears, R., Maccoby, E., & Levin, H. (1957). *Patterns of child rearing.* New York: Harper & Row.

Seay, B., Alexander, B. K., & Harlow, H. F. (1964). Maternal behavior of socially deprived rhesus monkeys. *Journal of Abnormal and Social Psychology, 69,* 345–354.

Seeman, R. E., Berkman, L. F., Blazer, D., & Rowe, J. W. (1994). Social ties and support and neuroendocrine function: The MacArthur studies of successful aging. *Annals of Behavioral Medicine, 16,* 95–106.

Segal, N. L. (1999). *Entwined lives: Twins and what they tell us about human behavior.* New York: Dutton/Penguin Books.

Segal, Z. V., Gemar, M., & Williams, S. (1999). Differential cognitive response to a mood challenge following successful cognitive therapy or pharmacotherapy for unipolar depression. *Journal of Abnormal Psychology, 108,* 3–10.

Segerstrom, S. C., Taylor, S. E., Kemeny, M. E., & Fahey, J. L. (1998). Optimism is associated with mood, coping, and immune change in response to stress. *Journal of Personality and Social Psychology, 74,* 1646–1655.

Segerstrom, S. C., Taylor, S. E., Kemeny, M. E., Reed, G. M., & Visscher, B. R. (1996). Causal attributions predict rate of immune decline in HIV-seropositive gay men. *Health Psychology, 15,* 485–493.

Segrin, C., & Abramson, L. Y. (1994). Negative reactions to depressive behaviors: A communication theory analysis. *Journal of Abnormal Psychology, 103,* 655–668.

Segrin, C., Dillard, J. P. (1992). The interactional theory of depression: A meta-analysis of the research literature. *Journal of Social & Clinical Psychology, 11*(1), 43–70.

Seligman, C., Fazio, R. H., & Zanna, M. P. (1980). Effects of salience of extrinsic rewards on liking and loving. *Journal of Personality and Social Psychology, 38,* 453–460.

Seligman, M. E. P. (1971). Phobias and preparedness. *Behavior Therapy, 2,* 307–320.

Seligman, M. E. P. (1995). The effectiveness of psychotherapy: The Consumer Reports study. *American Psychologist, 50,* 965–974.

Seltzer, J., & Numeroff, R. E. (1988). Supervisory leadership and subordinate burnout. *Academy of Management Journal, 31,* 439–446.

Selye, H. (1976). *The Stress of Life.* New York: McGraw Hill.

Semenov, L. A., Chernova, N. D., & Bondarko, V. M. (2000). Measurement of visual acuity and crowding effect in 3–9-year-old children. *Human Physiology, 26,* 16–20.

Sensky, T., Turkington, D., Kingdon, D., Scott, J. L., Scott, J., Siddle, R., O'Carroll, M., & Barnes, T. R. E. (2000). A randomized controlled trial of cognitive-behavioral therapy for persistent symptoms in schizophrenia resistant to medication. *Archives of General Psychiatry, 57,* 165–172.

Seppa, N. (1996). What qualities make a good president? *APA Monitor, 27* (11), p. 1.

Sereny, G., Sharma, V., Holt. J., and Gordis, E. (1986). Mandatory supervised Antabuse therapy in an outpatient alcoholism program: A pilot study. Alcoholism (NY) 10:290–292.

Sergent, J., & Hellige, J. B. (1986). Role of input factors in visual-field asymmetries. *Brain and Cognition, 5,* 174–199.

Serpell, R. (1979). How specific are perceptual skills? A cross-cultural study of pattern reproduction. *British Journal of Psychology, 70,* 365–380.

Seta, J. J., & Seta, C. E. (1992). Increments and decrements in mean arterial pressure as a function of audience composition: An averaging and summation analysis. *Personality and Social Psychology Bulletin, 18,* 173–181.

Settersten, R. A., Jr. (1998). A time to leave home and a time never to return? Age constraints on the living arrangements of young adults. *Social Forces, 76,* 1373–1400.

Seuling, B. (1975). *You can't eat peanuts in church and other little-known laws.* New York: Doubleday.

Seuling, B. (1976). *The loudest screen kiss and other little-known facts about the movies.* New York: Doubleday.

Seuling, B. (1978). *The last cow on the White House lawn and other little-known facts about the Presidency.* New York: Doubleday.

Seuling, B. (1982). *You can't show kids in underwear and other little-known fact about television.* New York: Doubleday and Co., Inc.

Seuling, B. (1986). *You can't sneeze with your eyes open and other freaky facts about the human body.* New York: Ballantine Books.

Seuling, B. (1988). *It is illegal to quack like a duck and other freaky laws.* New York: Dutton.

Seuling, B. (1991). *The man in the moon is upside down in Argentina and other freaky facts about geography.* New York: Ballantine Books.

Shadish, W. R., Matt, G. E., Navarro, A. M., Siegle, G., Crits-Cristophe, P., Hazelrigg, M. D., Jorm, A. F., Lyons, L. C., Nietzel, M. T., Robinson, L., Prout, H. T., Smith, M. L., Svartberg, M., & Weiss, B. (1997). Evidence that therapy works in clincally representative conditions. *Journal of Consulting & Clinical Psychology, 65,* 355–365.

Shafir, E., & Tversky, A. (1995). Decision making. In E. E. Smith & D. N. Osherson (Eds.), *An invitation to cognitive science: Thinking* (pp. 77–100). Cambridge, MA: MIT Press.

Shafran, R., Thordarson, D. S., & Rachman, S. (1996). Thought-action fusion in obsessive compulsive disorder. *Journal of Anxiety Disorders, 10,* 379–391.

Shah, J., Higgins, E. T., & Friedman, R. S. (1998). Performance incentives and means: How regulatory focus influences goal attainment. *Journal of Personality and Social Psychology, 74,* 285–293.

Shalev, A. Y., Peri, T., Brandes, D., Freedman, S., Orr, S. P., & Pitman, R. K. (2000). Auditory startle response in trauma survivors with posttraumatic stress disorder: A prospective study. *American Journal of Psychiatry, 157,* 255–261.

Shalev, A. Y., Sahar, T., Freedman, S., Peri, T., Glick, N., Brandes, D., Orr, S. P., & Pitman, R. K. (1998). A Prospective Study of Heart Rate Response Following Trauma and the Subsequent Development of Posttraumatic Stress Disorder. *Archives of General Psychiatry, 55,* 553–559.

Shallenberger, R. S. (1993). *Taste chemistry.* New York: Blackie Academic.

Shallice, T. (Vol. Ed.). (1988). *From neuropsychology to mental structure* (2nd ed.). Cambridge: Cambridge University Press.

Shallice, T., Fletcher, P., Frith, C. D., Grasby, P., Frackowiak, R. S. J., & Dolan, R. J. (1994). Brain regions associated with acquisition and retrieval of verbal episodic memory. *Nature, 368,* 633–635.

Shallice, T., & Warrington, E. K. (1980). Single and multiple component central dyslexic syndromes. In M. Coltheart, K. E. Patterson, & J. C. Marshall (Eds.), *Deep dyslexia* (pp. 119–145). London: Routledge.

Shanab, M. E., & Yahya, K. A. (1977). A behavioral study of obedience in children. *Journal of Personality and Social Psychology, 35,* 530–536.

Shapira, B., Tubi, N., Drexler, H., Lidsky, D., Calev, A., & Lerer, B. (1998). Cost and benefit in the choice of ECT schedule: Twice versus three times weekly ECT. *British Journal of Psychiatry, 172,* 44–48.

Shapiro, A. K. (1964). Factors cfontributing to the placebo effect: Their significance for psychotherapy. *American Journal of Psychotherapy, 18,* 73–88.

Shapiro, A. K., & Morris, L. A. (1978). The placebo effect in medical and psychological therapies. In S. L. Garfield & A. E. Bergin (eds.), *Handbook of Psychotherapy and Behavior Change: An empirical analysis* (2nd ed.). New York: Wiley.

Shapiro, D. A., & Shapiro, D. (1982). Meta-analysis of comparative therapy outcome studies: A replication and refinement. *Psychological Bulletin, 92,* 581–604.

Shapiro, D. H. (1982). Overview: Clinical and physiological comparison of meditation with other self-control strategies. *American Journal of Psychiatry, 139,* 267–274.

Shapiro, D. H. Jr., Schwartz, C. E., & Astin, J. A. (1996). Controlling ourselves, controlling our world: Psychology's role in understandinf positive and negative consequences of seeking and gaining control. *American Psychologist, 51,* 1213–1230.

Shapley, R., Kaplan, E., & Purpura, K. (1993). Contrast sensitivity and light adaptation in photoreceptors or in the retinal network. In R. Shapley & D. M.-K. Lam (Eds.), *Contrast sensitivity: Proceedings of the Retina Research Foundation Symposia* (pp. 103–116). Cambridge, MA: MIT Press.

Sharfstein, S. S., Muszynski, S., & Myers, E. S. (1984) *Health insurance and psychiatric care: Update and apraisal.* Washinton, DC: American Psychiatric Press.

Shaver, P. R., & Hazan, C. (1994). Attachment. In *Perspectives on Close Relationships.* A. L. Weber & J. H. Harvey (Eds.). Boston: Allyn & Bacon.

Shaw, J. B., & Riskind, J. H. (1981 or 1983). Predicting job stress using data from the position analysis questionnaire. *Journal of Applied Psychology, 68,* 253–261.

Shaw, P. J., Bergmann, B. M., & Rechtschaffen, A. (1998). Effects of paradoxical sleep deprivation on thermoregulation in the rat. *Sleep, 21,* p. 7–17.

Shaywitz, B. A., Shaywitz, S. E., Pugh, K. R., Constable, R. T., Skudlarski, P., Fulbright, R. K., Bronen, R. A., Fletcher, J. M., Shankweller, D. P., Katz, L., & Gore, J. C. (1995). Sex differences in the functional organization of the brain for language. *Nature, 373,* 607–611.

Shea, J. D., Burton, R., & Girgis, A. (1993). Negative affect, absorption, and immunity. *Physiological Behavior, 53,* 449–457.

Shea, M. T., Elikin, I., Imber, S. D., Sotsky, S. M., Watkins, J. T., Collins, J. F., Pilkonis, P. A., Beckham, E., Glass, D. R., Dolan, R. T., & Parloff, M. B. (1992). Course of depressive symptoms over follow-up: Findings from the National Institute of Mental Health Treatment of Depression Collaborative Research Program. *Archives of General Psychiatry, 49,* 782–787.

Sheehan, P. W. (1988). Memory distortion in hypnosis. *International Journal of Clinical Experimental Hypnosis, 36,* 296–311.

Shekelle, R., Raynor, W., Ostfeltd, A., Garron, D., Bieliauskas, L., Liu, S., Maliza, C., & Paul, O. (1981). Psychological depression and 17-year risk of death from cancer. *Psychosomatic Medicine, 43,* 177–?

Shekim, W. O., Bylund, D. B., Frankel, F., Alexson, J., Jones S. B., Blue, L. D., Kirby, J., & Corchoran, C. (1989). Platelet MAO activity and personality variations in normals. *Psychiatry Research, 27,* 81–88.

Sheldon, K. M., Ryan, R., & Reis, H. T. (1996). What makes for a good day? Competence and autonomy in the day and in the person. *Personality & Social Psychology Bulletin, 22,* 1270–1279.

Shelton, J. R., & Caramazza, A. (1999). Deficits in lexical and semantic processing: Implications for models of normal language. *Psychonomic Bulletin & Review, 6,* 5–27.

Shepard, R. N. (1967). Recognition memory for words, sentences and pictures. *Journal of Verbal learning and Verbal Behavior, 6,* 156–163.

Shepard, R. N., & Cooper, L. A. (1982). *Mental images and their transformations.* Cambridge, MA: MIT Press/Bradford Books.

Shepherd, G. M. (1999). Information processing in dendrites. In M. J. Zigmond, F. E. Bloom, S. C. Landis, J. L. Roberts, & L. R. Squire (Eds.), *Fundamental neuroscience* (pp. 363–388). New York: Academic Press.

Shepherd, M. D., Schoenberg, M., Slavich, S., Wituk, S., Warren, M., & Meissen, G. (1999). Continuum of professional involvement in self-help groups. *Journal of Community Psychology, 27,*39–53.

Sherif, M. (1966). *Group conflict and co-operation: Tgheir social psychology.* London: Routledge & Kegen Paul.

Sherif, M., Harvey, O. J., White, B. J., Hood, W. R., & Sherif, C. W. (1961). *Intergroup conflict and cooperation: The robber's cave experiment.* Norman, OK: The University Book Exchange.

Sherif, M., & Sherif, C. W. (1953). *Groups in harmony an dtension: An integration of sstudies on intergroup relations.* New York: Octagon.

Sherman, J. J. (1998). Effects of psychotherapeutic treatments for PTSD: A meta-analysis of controlled clinical trials. *Journal of Traumatic Stress, 11,* 413–435.

Sherman, S. S. (1980). On the self-erasing nature of errors of prediction. *Journal of Personality and Social Psychology, 16,* 388–403.

Shibahara, H., Shigeta, M., Toji, H., & Koyama, K. (1995). Sperm immobilizing antibodies interfere with sperm migration from the uterine cavity through the fallopian tubes. *American Journal of Reproductive Immunology, 34,* 120–124.

Shields, S. A. (1987). Women, men, and the dilemma of emotion. In P. Shaver & C. Hendrick (Eds.), *Sex and gender* (pp. 229–250). Newbury Park, Calif.: Sage.

Shin, L. M., Kosslyn, S. M., McNally, R. J., Alpert, N. M., Thompson, W. L., Raush, S. L., Macklin, M. L., & Pitman, R. K. (1997). Visual imagery and perception in posttraumatic stress disorder: A positron emission tomographic investigation. *Archives of General Psychiatry, 54,* 233–241.

Shortridge, J. R. (1993). The Great Plains. In M. K. Cayton, E. J. Gorn, & P. W. Williams (Eds.), *Encyclopedia of American Social History* (Vol. 2, pp. 1001–1015). New York: Scribner.)

Shouksmith, G., & Taylor, J. E. (1997). The interaction of culture with general job stressors in air traffic controllers. *International Journal of Aviation Psychology, 7,* 343–352.

Shulman, S., Elicker, J., & Sroufe, L. A. (1994). Stages of friendship growth in preadolescence as related to attachment history. *Journal of Social & Personal Relationships, 11,* 341–361.

Shweder, R. A., Much, N. C., Mahapatra, M. & Park, L. (1997). The "big three" of morality (autonomy, community, divinity) and the "big three" explanations of suffering. In A. M. Brandt & P. Rozin (Eds.), *Morality and health* (pp. 119–169). New York: Routledge.

Siegel, J. L., & Longo, D. L. (1981). The control of chemotherapy induced emesis. *Annals of Internal Medicine, 95,* 352–359.

Siegel, M., Brisman, J., & Weinshel, M. (1988). *Surviving an Eating Disorder: Strategies for Family and Friends.* New York: Harper and Row.

Siegel, S. (1988). State dependent learning and morphine tolerance. *Behavioral Neuroscience, 102,* 228–232.

Siegel, S., Hinson, R. E., Krank, M. D., & McCully, J. (1982). Heroin "overdoes" death: Contribution of drug-associated environmental cues. *Science, 216,* 436–437.

Siegler, R. S. (1989). Mechanisms of cognitive development. *Annual Review of Psychology, 40,* 353–379.

Sifneos, P. E. (1992). *Short-term anxiety-provoking psychotherapy: A treatment manual.* New York: Basicbooks, Inc.

Silverman, L. (1976). Psychoanalytic theory: The reports of my death are greatly exaggerated. *American Psychologist, 31,* 621–637.

Silverman, L. K. (1993a). Counseling families. In L. K. Silverman (Ed.), *Counseling the gifted and talented* (pp. 43–89). Denver: Love.

Silverman, L. K. (1993b). A developmental model for counseling the gifted. In L. K. Silverman (Ed.), *Counseling the gifted and talented* (pp. 51–78). Denver: Love.

Simmons, J. A., & Chen, L. (1989). The acoustic basis for target discrimination by FM echolocating bats. *Journal of the Acoustical Society of America, 86,* 1333–1350.

Simon, H. A., & Chase, W. G. (1973). Skill in chess. *American Scientist, 61,* 394–403.

Simon, L., Greenberg, J., & Brehm, J. (1995). Trivialization: The forgotten mode of dissonance reduction. *Journal of Personality and Social Psychology, 68,* 247–260.

Simons, D. J. (1999). Current approaches to change blindness. *Visual Cognition, 7,* 1–15.

Simons, D. J., & Levin, D. T. (1997). Change blindness. *Trends in Cognitive Sciences, 1,* 261–267.

Simonton, D. K. (1984). *Genius, creativity, and leadership: Historiometric inquiries.* Cambridge, MA: Harvard University Press.

Simonton, D. K. (1988). Creativity, leadership, and chance. In R. J. Sternberg (Ed.), *The nature of creativity* (pp. 386–436). New York: Cambridge University Press.

Simonton, D. K. (1990). Political pathology and societal creativity. *Creativity Research Journal, 3,* 85–99.

Simonton, D. K. (1994). *Greatness: Who makes history and why.* New York: Guilford.

Simonton, D. K. (1995). Foresight in insight? A Darwinian answer. In R. J. Sternberg & J. E. Davidson (Eds.), *The nature of insight* (pp. 465–494). Cambridge, MA: MIT Press.

Simonton, D. K. (1997). Creative productivity: A predictive and explanatory model of career trajectories and landmarks. *Psychological Review, 104,* 66–89.

Simpson, M. (1996). Suicide and religion. *American Sociological Review, 63,* pp. 895–896.

Singh, D., Meyer, W., Zambarano, R. J., & Hurlbert, D. F. (1998). Frequency and timing of coital orgasm in women desirous of becoming pregnant. *Archives of Sexual Behavior, 27,* 15–29.

Singh, V. N. (1995). Human uterine amylase in relation to infertility. *Hormone and Metabolic Research, 27,* 35–36.

Siomi, M. C., Zhang, Y., Siomi, H., & Dreyfuss, G. (1996). Specific sequences in the fragile X syndrome protein FMR1 and the FXR proteins mediate their binding to 60S ribosomal subunits and the interactions among them. *Molecular and Cellular Biology, 16,* 3825–3832.

Sireteanu, R. (2000). Texture segmentation, "pop-out," and feature binding in infants and children. In C. Rovee-Collier & L. P. Lipsitt (Eds.), *Progress in infancy research, Vol. 1* (pp. 183–249). Mahwah, NJ: Erlbaum.

Skinner, B. F. (1938). *The behavior of organisms: An experimental analysis.* New York: Appleton-Century.

Skinner, B. F. (1953). *Science and human behavior.* New York: MacMillan.

Skinner, B. F. (1956). A case history in scientific method. *American Psychologist, 11,* 221–233.

Skinner, B. F. (1961, November). Teaching Machines. *Scientific American,* 91–102.

Skinner, B. F. (1983). Can the experimental analysis of behavior rescue psychology? *Behavior Analyst, 6,* 9–17.

Skinner, B. F. (1989). Teaching Machines. *Science, 243,* 1535.

Skuder, P., Plomin, R., McClearn, G. E., Smith, D. L., Vignetti, S., Chorney, M. J., Chorney, K., Kasarda, S., Thompson, L. A., Detterman, D., Petrill, S. A., Daniels, J., Owen, M. J., & McGuffin, P. (1995). A polymorphism in mitochondrial DNA associated with IQ? *Intelligence, 21,* 1–11.

Skvoretz, J. (1988). Models of participation in status-differentiated groups,. *Social Psychollogy Quarterly, 51,* 43–57.

Slater, A., Brown, E., & Badenoch, M. (1997). Intermodal perception at birth: Newborn infants' memory for arbitrary auditory-visual pairings. *Early Development & Parenting, 6,* 99–104.

Sleek, S. (1997, November). Online therapy services raise ethical questions. *APA Monitor,* p. 1, 38.

Slep, A. M. S., & O'Leary, S. G. (1998). The effects of maternal attributions on parenting: An experimental analysis. *Journal of Family Psychology, 12,* 234–243.

Slimp, J. C., Hart, B. L., & Goy, R. W. (1978). Heterosexual, autosexual and social behavior of adult male rhesus monkeys with medial preoptic-anterior hypothalamic lesions. *Brain Research, 142,* 105–122.

Slob, A. K., Bax, C. M., Hop, W. C. J., Rowland, D. L., & van der Werff ten Bosch, J. J. (1996). Sexual arousability and the menstrual cycle. *Psychoneuroendocrinology, 21,* 545–558.

Small, B. J., & Bäckman, L. (2000). Time to death and cognitive performance. *Current Directions in Psychological Science, 6,* 168–172.

Smeets, M. A. M., Smit, F., Panhuysen, G. E. M., & Ingleby, J. D. (1997). The influence of methodological differences on outcome of body size estimation studies in anorexia nervosa. *British Journal of Clinical Psychology, 36,* 263–277.

Smeets, M. A. M., Smit, F., Panhuysen, G. E. M., & Ingleby, J. D. (1997). The influence of methodological differences on the outcome of body size estimation studies in anorexia nervosa. *British Journal of Clinical Psychology, 36,* 263–277.

Smith, D. (1982). Trends in counseling and psychotherapy. *American Psychologist, 37,* 802–809.

Smith, D. V., & Frank, M. E. (1993). Sensory coding by peripheral taste fibers. In S. A. Simon & S. D. Roper (Eds.), *Mechanisms of taste transduction* (pp. 295–338). Boca Raton, FL: CRC Press.

Smith, E. E. (1988). Concepts and thought. In R. J. Sternberg & E. E. Smith (Eds.), *The psychology of human thought* (pp. 19–49). New York: Cambridge University Press.

Smith, E. E. (2000). Neural bases of human working memory. *Current Directions in Psychological Science, 9,* 45–49.

Smith, E. E., & Jonides, J. (1997). Working memory: A view from neuroimaging. *Cognitive Psychology, 33,* 5–42.

Smith, E. E., & Jonides, J. (1999). Storage and executive processes in the frontal lobes. *Science, 283,* 1657–1661.

Smith, E. E., Jonides, J., & Koeppe, R. A. (1996). Dissociating verbal and spatial working memory using PET. *Cerebral Cortex, 6,* 11–20.

Smith, E. E., & Medin, D. L. (1981). *Categories and concepts* . Cambridge, MA: Harvard University Press.

Smith, E. E., Patalano, A. L., & Jonides, J. (1998). Alternative strategies of categorization. *Cognition, 65,* 167–196.

Smith, E. R. (1998). Mental Representation and memory. In D. T. Gilbert, S. T. Fiske, & G. Lindzey (Eds.), The handbook of social psychology (4th ed.). New York: McGraw Hill. Vol. 1, pp. 391–445.

Smith, G. E. (1996). Framing in advertising and the moderating impact of consumer education. *Journal of Advertising Research. 36,* 49–64.

Smith, J. T., Barabasz, A., & Barabasz, M. (1996) Comparison of hypnosis and distraction in severely ill children undergoing painful medical procedures. *Journal of Counseling Psychology, 43,* 187–195.

Smith, M. E. (1993). Television violence and behavior: a research summary. ERIC Digest. Syracuse, NY: Educational Resources Information Center Clearinghouse on Information and Technology. ED 366 329.

Smith, M. L., & Glass, G. V. (1977). Meta-analysis of psychotherapy outcome studies. *American Psychologist, 32,* 752–760.

Smith, R. E., Leffingwell, T. R., & Ptacek, J. T. (1999). Can people remember how they coped? Factors associated with discordance between same-day and retrospective reports. *Journal of Personality and Social Psychology, 76,* 1050–1061.

Smith, S. M. (1988). In G. M. Davies, & D. M. Thompson (Eds.), *Memory in Context: context in memory* (pp. 13–34). Chichester, UK: Wiley.

Smith, S. M., & Blankenship, S. E. (1989). Incubation effects. *Bulletin of the Psychonomic Society, 27,* 311–314.

Smith, S. M., & Blankenship, S. E. (1991). Incubation and the persistence of fixation in problem solving. *American Journal of Psychology, 104,* 61–87.

Smith, S. M., & Levin, I. P. (1996). Need for cognition and choice framing effects. *Journal of Behavioral Decision Making, 9,* 283–290.

Smith, S. M., & Shaffer, D. R. (1991). Celerity and cajolery: Rapid speech may promote or inhibit persuasion through its impact on message elaboration. *Personality and Social Psychology Bulletin, 17,* 663–669.

Smolucha, F. C. (1992). A reconstruction of Vygotsky's theory of creativity. *Creativity Research Journal, 5,* 49–67.

Smyth, J. M., Stone, A. A., Hurewitz, A., & Kaell, A. (1999). Effects of writing about stressful experiences on symptom reduction in patietns with asthma or rheumatoid arthritis. *Journal of the American Medical Association, 281,* 1304–1329.

Snidman, N., Kagan, J, Riordan, L., & Shannon, D. C. (1995). Cardiac function and behavioral reactivity during infancy. *Psychophysiology, 32,* 199–207.

Snodgrass, S. E. (1985). Women's intuition: The effect of subordinate roel on interpersonal sensitivity. *Journal of Personality and Social Psychology, 49,* 146–155.

Snow, C. E. (1991). The language of the mother–child relationship. In M. Woodhead & R. Carr (Eds.), *Becoming a person* (pp. 195–210). London: Routledge.

Snow, C. E. (1999). Social perspectives on the emergence of language. In B. MacWhinney (Ed.), *The emergence of language* (pp. 257–276). Mahwah, NJ: Erlbaum.

Snow, C. E. (in press). Second language learners' contributions to our understanding of languages of the brain. In A. M. Galaburda, S. M. Kosslyn, & Y. Christen (Eds.), *Languages of the brain.* Cambridge, MA: Harvard University Press.

Snow, R., & Yalow, R. (1982). Education and intelligence. In R. J. Sternberg (Ed.), *Handbook of human intelligence* (pp. 493–585). New York: Cambridge University Press.

Snyder, C. R., & Larson, G. R. (1972). A further look at student acceptance of general personality interpretations. *Journal of Consulting and Clinical Psychology, 38,* 384–388.

Snyder, M. (1984). When belief creates reality. In L. Berkowitz (Ed.), *Advances in experimental social psychology* (Vol. 25, pp. 67–114). San Diego, CA: Academic Press.

Snyder, M. (1992). Motivational foundations of behavioral confirmation. In M. P. Zanna (Ed.), *Advances in experimental social psychology* (Vol. 18, pp. 248–306). New York: Academic Press.

Snyder, M., & Ickes, W. (1985). Personality and social behavior. In G. Lindzey & E. Aronson (Eds.), *Handbook of social psychology* (3rd ed.) (Vol. 2, pp. 883–947). New York: Random House.

Snyder, M., Tanke, E. D., & Berscheid, E. (1977). Social perception and interpersonal behavior: On the self-fulfilling nature of social stereotypes. *Journal of Personality and Social Psychology, 35,* 656–666.

Snyderman, M., & Herrnstein, R. J. (1983). Intelligence tests and the Immigration Act of 1924. *American Psychologist, 38,* 986–995.

Soli, S. D. (1994). Hearing aids: Today and tomorrow. *Echoes: The newsletter of the Acoustical Society of America, 4,* 1–5.

Solms, M. (1997). *The neuropsychology of dreams: A clinico-anatomical study.* Mahwah, NJ: Erlbaum.

Solomon, D. A., Keller, M. B., Leon, A. C., Mueller, T. I., Lavori, P. W., Shea, M. T., Coryell, W., Warshaw, M., Turvey, C., Maser, J. D., & Endicott, J. (2000). Multiple recurrences of major depressive disorder. *American Journal of Psychiatry, 157,* 229–233.

Solomon, R. L. (1980). The opponent-process theory of acquired motivation: The costs of pleasure and the benefits of pain. *American Psychologist, 35,* 691 712.

Solomon, R. L., & Corbit, J. D. (1973). An opponent-process theory of motivation: II. Cigarette addiction. *Journal of Abnormal Psychology, 81,* 158–171.

Solomon, R. L., & Corbit, J. D. (1974a). An opponent-process theory of motivation: I. Temporal dynamics of affect. *Psychological Review, 78,* 3–43.

Solomon, R. L., & Corbit, J. D. (1974b). An opponent-process theory of motivation: I. Temporal dynamics of affect. *Psychological Review, 81,* 119–145.

Sommers, E. K., & Check, J. V. (1987). An empirical investigation of the role of pornography in the verbal and physical abuse of women. *Violence & Victims, 2,* 189–209.

Soper, B., Milford, G. E., & Rosenthal, G. T. (1995). Belief when evidence does not support the theory. *Psychology & Marketing, 12,* 415–422.

Sosik, J. J., Kahai, S. S., & Avolio, B. J. (1998). Transformational leadership and dimensions of creativity: Motivating idea generation in computer-mediated groups. *Creativity Research Journal, 11,* 111–121.

Sowell, E. R., Thompson, P. M., Holmes, C. J., Jernigan, T. L., & Toga, A. W. (1999). In vivo evidence for post-adolescent brain maturation in frontal and striatal regions. *Nature Neuroscience, 2,* 859–61.

Spangler, D. L., Simons, A. D., Monroe, S. M., & Thase, M. E. (1997). Relationships Between Cognitive Constructs and Cognitive Diathesis-Stress Match. *Journal of Abnormal Psychology, 106,* 395–403.

Spangler, W. D. (1992). Validity of questionnaire and TAT measures of need for achievement: Two meta-analyses. *Psychological Bulletin, 112,* 140–154.

Spearman, C. (1927). *The abilities of man.* New York: Macmillan.

Speed, A., & Gangestad, S. (1997). Romantic popularity and mate preferences: A peer-nomination study. *Personality & Social Psychology Bulletin, 23,* 928–935.

Speisman, J. C., Lazarus, R. S., Mordkoff, A., & Davison, L. (1964). Experimental reduction of stress based on ego-defense theory. *Journal of Abnormal and Social Psychology, 68,* 367–380.

Spelke, E. S. (1991). Physical knowledge in infancy: Reflections on Piaget's theory. In S. Carey & R. Gelman (Eds.), *The epigenesis of mind: Essays on biology and cognition* (pp. 133–169). Hillsdale, NJ: Erlbaum.

Spelke, E. S., Breinlinger, K., Jacobson, K., & Phillips, A. (1993). Gestalt relations and object perception: A developmental study. *Perception, 22,* 1483–1501.

Spelke, E. S., Breinlinger, K., Macomber, J., & Jacobson, K. (1992). Origins of knowledge. *Psychological Review, 99,* 605–632.

Spence, M. J., & DeCasper, A. J. (1987). Prenatal experience with low-frequency maternal voice sounds influences neonatal perception of maternal voice samples. *Infant Behavior and Development, 10,* 133–142.

Spencer, W. D., & Raz, N. (1995). Differential age effects on memory for content and context: A meta-analysis. *Psychology and Aging, 10,* 527–539.

Sperber, D., Cara, F., & Girotto, V. (1995). Relevance theory explains the selection task. *Cognition, 57,* 31–95.

Sperling, G. (1960). The information available in brief visual presentations. *Psychological Monographs, 74,* 1–29.

Spiegel, D (1994). *Living beyond limits: new hope and help for facing life-threatening illness.* New York: Ballantine/Fawcett.

Spiegel, D. (1993). Social support: how friends, family and groups can help. In *Mind Body Medicine* (eds.), D. Goleman and J. Gurin. New York: Consumer Reports Books.

Spiegel, D. (1997). Psychosocial aspects of breast cancer treatment. *Seminars in Oncology, 24,* S1-36–S1-47.

Spiegel, D. (1999). Personal communication.

Spiegel, D., & Cardeña, E. (1991). Disintegrated experience: The dissociated disorders revisited. *Journal of Abnormal Psychology, 100,* 366–378.

Spiegel, D., & King, R. (1992). Hypnotizability and CSF HVA levels among psychiatric patients. *Biological Psychiatry, 31,* 95–98.

Spiegel, D., Bierre, P., & Rootenberg, J. (1989). Hypnotic alteration of somatosensory perception. *American Journal of Psychiatry, 146,* 749–754.

Spiegel, D., Bloom, J., & Kraemer, H. (1989). Effect of psychosocial treatment on survival of patients with metastatic breast cancer. *The Lancet, 2,* 888–891.

Spiegel, D., Cutcomb, S., Ren, C., & Pribram, K. (1985). Hypnotic hallucination alters evoked potentials. *Journal of Abnormal Psychology, 94,* 249–255.

Spiegel, D., Sephton, S., Terr, A., & Stites, D. (1998). Effects of psychosocial treatment in prolonging cancer survival may be mediated by neuroimmune pathways. In S. McCann, J. Lipton, E. Sternberg, et al. (Eds.), *Neuroimmunomodulation: Molecular aspects, integrative systems, and clinical advances* (pp. 674–683). New York: New York Academy of Sciences.

Spitzer, H., Desimone, R., & Moran, J. (1988). Increased attention enhances both behavioral and neuronal performance. *Science, 240,* 338–340.

Sprecher, S. (1989). The importance of males and females of physical attractiveness, earning potential and expressiveness in intial attraction. *Sex Roles, 21,* 591–607.

Sprecher, S. (1998). The effect of exchange orientation on close relationships. *Social Psychology Quarterly, 61,* 220–231.

Sprecher, S. (1999). "I Love You More Today Than Yesterday": Romantic Partners' Perceptions of Changes in Love and Related Affect Over Time. *Journal of Personality and Social Psychology,76,* 46–53.

Sprecher, S., Aron, A., Hatfield, E., Cortese, A., Potapova, E., & Levitskaya, A. (1994). Love: American style, Russian style and Japanese style. *Personal Relationships, 1,* 349–369.

Sprecher, S., Sullivan, Q., & Hatfield, E. (1994). Mate selection preferences: Gender differences examined in a national sample. *Journal of Personality and Social Psychology, 66,* 1074–1080.

Springer, S. P., & Deutsch, G. (1994). *Left brain, right brain.* New York: Freeman.

Springer, S. P., & Deutsch, G. (1998). *Left brain, right brain: Perspectives from cognitive neuroscience (5th ed.).* New York: W. H. Freeman.

Sprock, J., & Yoder, C. Y. (1997). Women and depression: An update on the report of the APA Task Force. *Sex Roles, 36,* 269–303.

Spyraki, C., Fibiger, H. C., & Phillips, A. G. (1982). Dopaminergic substrates of amphetamine-induced place preference conditioning. *Brain Research, 253* (1-sup-2), 185–193.

Squire, L. R. (1987). *Memory and the brain.* New York: Oxford University Press.

Squire, L. R. (1992). Memory and the hippocampus: A synthesis from findings with rats, monkeys, and humans. *Psychological Review, 99,* 195–231.

Squire, L. R., Ojemann, J. G., Miezin, F. M., Petersen, S. E., Videen, T. O., & Raichle, M. E. (1992). Activation of the hippocampus in normal humans: A functional anatomical study of memory. *Proceedings of the National Academy of Sciences, USA, 89,* 1837–1841.

Sroufe, L. A., & Fleeson, J. (1986). Attachment and the construction of relationships. In W. W. Hartup and Z. Rubin (Eds.), *Relationships and development* (pp. 51–71). Hillsdale, NJ: Erlbaum.

Stack, S., & Eshleman, J. R. (1998). Marital status and happiness. *Journal of Marriage and the Family, 60,* 527–536.

Stager, C. L., & Werker, J. F. (1997). Infants listen for more phonetic detail in speech perception than in word-learning tasks. *Nature, 388,* 381–382.

Stalder, D. R., & Baron, R. S. (1998). Attributional Complexity as a Moderator of Dissonance-Produced Attitude Change. *Journal of Personality and Social Psychology, 75,* 449–455.

Stallone, D. D., & Stunkard, A. J. (1994). Obesity. In A. Frazer & P. B. Molinoff (Eds.), *Biological bases of brain function and disease* (pp. 385–403). New York: Raven Press.

Stanbury, J. B. (1992). Iodine and human development. *Medical Anthropology, 13,* 413–423.

Stanley, M. A., Beck, J. G., Averill, P. M., & Balwin, L. E., Deagle, R. A., III, & Stadler, J. G. (1996). Patterns of change during cognitive behavioral treatment for panic disorder. *Journal of Nervous & Mental Disease, 184,* 567–572.

Stanley, M. A., & Turner, S. M. (1995). Current status of pharmacological and behavioral treatment of obsessive-compulsive disorder. *Behavior Therapy, 25,* 153–186.

Stanton, M. D. (1981). Strategic approaches to family therapy. In A. S. Gurman & D. P. Kniskern (Eds.), *Handbook of Family Therapy.* (pp. 361–402). New York: Brunner/Mazel.

Starker, S. (1988). Psychologists and self-help books: Attitudes and prescriptive practices of clinicians. *American Journal of Psychotherapy, 42,* 448–455.

Stayman, D. M., & Kardes, F. R. (1992). Spontaneous inference processes in advertising: Effects of need for cognition and self-monitoring on inference generation and utilization. *Journal of Consumer Psychology, 1,* 125–142.

Steele, C., & Aronson, J. (1995). Stereotype threat and the intellectual test performance of African Americans. *Journal of Personality and Social Psychology, 69,* 797–812.

Steele, C., & Josephs, R. A. (1990). Alcohol Myopia: Its prized and dangerous effects. *American Psychologist, 45,* 921–933.

Steele, C. M. (1997). A threat in the air: How stereotypes shape intellectual identity and performance. *American Psychologist, 52,* 613–629.

Steele, C. M., & Aronson, J. (1995). Stereotype threat and the intellectual test performance of African Americans. *Journal of Personality & Social Personality, 69,* 797–811.

Steele, C. M., Critchlow, B., & Liu, T. J. (1985). Alcohol and Social Behavior II: The Helpful Drunkard. *Journal of Personality and Social Psychology, 48,* 35–46.

Steele, C. M., & Southwick, L. (1985). Alcohol and Social Behavior I: The Psychology of Drunken Excess. *Journal of Personality and Social Psychology, 48,* 18–34.

Steele, K. M., Ball, T. N., & Runk, R. (1997). Listening to Mozart does not enhance backwards digit span performance. *Perceptual and Motor Skills, 84,* 1179–1184.

Steele, K. M., Bella, S. D., Peretz, I., Dunlop, T., Dawe, L. A., Humphrey, G. K., Shannon, R. A., Kirby, J. L., Jr., & Olmstead, C. G. (1999). Prelude or requiem for the "Mozart effect"? *Nature, 400,* 827–828.

Steele, R. L. (1992). Dying, death, and bereavement among the Maya Indians of Mesoamerica: A study in antropological psychology. In L. A. Platt & V. R. Persico, Jr. (Eds.), *Grief in cross-cultural perspective: A casebook* (pp. 399–424). New York: Garland.

Steinberg, M. (1994). Systematizing dissociation: Symptomatology and diagnostic assessment. In D. Spiegel (Ed.), *Dissociation: Culture, mind, and body* (pp. 59–90). Washington, DC: American Psychiatric Press.

Steketee, G., & White, K. (1990). *When Once Is Not Enough: Help for Obsessive-Compulsives.* Oakland, CA: New Harbinger Publications, Inc.

Stelmack, R. M. (1990). Biological bases of extraversion: Psychophysiological evidence. *Journal of Personality, 58,* 293–311.

Stephan, W. G., Stephan, C. W., & de Vargas, M. C. (1996). Emotional expression in Costa Rica and the United States. *Journal of Cross-Cultural Psychology, 27*, 147–160.

Stephens, T. A., & Burroughs, W. A. (1978). An application of operant conditioning to absenteeism in a hospital setting. *Journal of Applied Pychilogy, 63*, 518–521.

Steptoe, A., Lipsey, Z., & Wardle, J. (1998). Stress, hassles and variations in alcohol consumption, food choice and physical exercise: A diary study. *British Journal of Health Psychology, 3*, 51–63.

Sterling-Smith, R. S. (1976). A special study of drivers most responsible in fatal accidents. Summary for Management Report, Contract DOT HS 310-3-595. Washington, DC: Department of Transportation.

Stern, K., & McClintock, M. K. (1998). Regulation of ovulation by human pheromones. *Nature, 392*, 177–179.

Sternbach, R. A. (1978). Psychological dimensions and perceptual analyses, including pathologies of pain. In E. C. Carterette & M. P. Friedman (Eds.), *Handbook of perception* (pp. 231–261). New York: Academic Press.

Sternberg, R. J. (1985). *Beyond IQ: A triarchic theory of human intelligence*. Cambridge: Cambridge University Press.

Sternberg, R. J. (1986a). A triangular theory of love. *Psychological Review, 93*, 119–135.

Sternberg, R. J. (1986b). *What is intelligence?* Norwood, NJ: Ablex.

Sternberg, R. J. (1988a). *The triangle of love.* New York: Basic Books.

Sternberg, R. J. (1988b). *The triarchic mind: A new theory of human intelligence.* New York: Viking.

Sternberg, R. J. (1990). *Metaphors of mind: Conceptions of the nature of intelligence.* New York: Cambridge University Press.

Sternberg, R. J. (1997). Educating intelligence: Infusing the triarchic theory into school instruction. In R. J. Sternberg & E. L. Grigorenko (Eds.), *Intelligence, heredity, and environment* (pp. 343–362). New York: Cambridge University Press.

Sternberg, R. J., & Detterman, D. K. (Eds.). (1986). *What is intelligence? Contemporary viewpoints on its nature and definition.* Norwood, NJ: Ablex.

Sternberg, R. J., & Wagner, R. K. (1993). The g-ocentric view of intelligence and job performance is wrong. *Current Directions in Psychological Science, 2*, 1–5.

Sternberg, R. J., Wagner, R. K., & Okagaki, L. (1993). Practical intelligence: The nature and role of tacit knowledge in work. In J. M. Puckett, H. W. Reese, et al. (Eds.), *Mechanisms of everyday cognition.* Hillsdale, NJ: Erlbaum.

Stevens, L. E., & Fiske, S. T. (1995). Motivation and cognition in social life: A social survival perspective. *Social Cognition, 13*, 189–214.

Stevens, W. K. (1995, September 18). Scientists say earth's warming could set off wide disruptions. *New York Times,* p. ?.

Stevens, W. K. (1998a, August 18). As Alaska melts, scientists consider the reasons why. *New York Times,* p. ?.

Stevens, W. K. (1998b, August 10). Linking health effects to changes in climate. *New York Times,* p. ?.

Stevens, W. K. (1998c, April 22) Science academy disputes attack on global warming. *New York Times,* p. ?.

Stevenson, H., Lee, S., & Stigler, J. (1986). Mathematics achievement of Chinese, Japanese, and American children. *Science, 231*, 693–699.

Stewart, D., & Winser, D. (1942, February 28). Incidence of perforated peptic ulcer: Effect of heavy air-raids. *The Lancet, 259*–260.

Stickgold, R., Rittenhouse, C. D., & Hobson, J. A. (1994). Dream splicing: A new technique for assessing thematic coherence in subjective reports of mental activity. *Consciousness & Cognition: An International Journal, 3*, 114–128.

Stoel-Gammon, C., & Otomo, K. (1986). Babbling development of hearing-impaired and normally hearing subjects. *Journal of Speech and Hearing Disorders, 51*, 33–41.

Stokes, J. P., Damon, W., & McKirnan, D. J. (1997). Predictors of movement toward homosexuality: A longitudinal study of bisexual men. *Journal of Sex Research, 34*, 304–312.

Stone, A. A., Nele, J. M., Cox, D. S., Napoli, A., Valdimarsdottir, H., & Kennedy-Morre, E. (1994). Daily events are associated with a secretory immune response to an oral antigen in men. *Health Psychology, 13*, 440–446.

Stone, J., Cooper, J., Wiegand, A. W., & Aronson, E. (1997). When Exemplification Fails: Hypocrisy and the Motive for Self-Integrity. *Journal of Personality and Social Psychology, 72*, 54–65.

Stone, J., Lynch, C. I., Sjomeling, M., & Darley, J. M. (1999). Stereotype threat effects on black and white athletic performance. *Journal of Personality and Social Psychology, 77*, 1213–1227.

Stoolmiller, M. (1999). Implications of the restricted range of family environments for estimates of heritability and nonshared environment in behavior-genetic adoption studies. *Psychological Bulletin, 125*, 392–409.

Stoolmiller, M. (in press). Correcting estimates of shared environmental variance for range restriction in adoption studies using a truncated multivariate normal model. *Behavioral Genetics.*

Stough, C., Kerkin, B., Bates, T., & Mangan, G. (1994). Music and spatial IQ. *Personality and Individual Differences, 17*, 695.

Strack, F., Martin, L. L., & Stepper, S. (1988). Inhibiting and facilitating conditions of the human smile: A nonobtrusive test of the facial feedback hypothesis. *Journal of Personality & Social Psychology, 54*, 768–777.

Strakowski, S. M., Lonczak, H. S., Sax, K. W., West, S. A., Crist, R. M., & Thienhaus, O. J. (1995). The effects of race on diagbosis and disoposition from a psychiatric emergency service. *Journal of Clinical Psychiatry, 56*, 101–107.

Strakowski, S. M., Shelton, R. C., Kolbrener, M. L. (1993). The effects of race and comorbidity on clinical diagnosis in patients with psychosis. *Journal of Clinical Psychiatry, 54*, 96–102.

Straus, M. A. (1980). Social stress and marital violence in a national sample of American families. *Annals of the New York Academy of Sciences, 347,*229–250.

Straus, M. A., & Gelles, R. J. (1980). *Behind closed dorrs: Violence in the American family.* New York: Anchor/Doubleday.

Straus, M. A., & McCord, J. (1998). Do physically punished children become violent adults? In S. Nolen-Hoeksema (Ed.). *Clashing views on abnormal psychology: A Taking Sides custom reader.* (pp. 130–155). Guilford, CT: Dushkin/Mcgraw-Hill (1998) xi, 272 pp.

Streiker, L. D. (1984). Mind-Bending: Brainwashing, Cults, and Deprogramming in the '80s. Garden City, New York: Doubleday &

Streissguth, A. P., Barr, H. M., Bookstein, F. L., Sampson, P. D., & Olson, H. C. (1999). The long-term neurocognitive consequences of prenatal alcohol exposure: A 14-year study. *Psychological Science, 10*, 186–190.

Streissguth, A. P., Barr, H. M., Sampson, P. D., Darby, B. L., & Martin, D. C. (1989). IQ at age 4 in relation to maternal alcohol use and smoking during pregnancy. *Developmental Psychology, 25*, 3–11.

Streufert, S., & Swezey, R. W. (1986). *Complexity, managers, and organizations.* Orlando, FL: Academic Press.

Stricker, E. M., Swerdloff, A. F., & Zigmond, M. J. (1978). Intrahypothalamic injections of kainic acid produce feeding and drinking deficits in rats. *Brain Research, 158*, 470–473.

Stricker, G. (1993). The current status of psychotherapy integration. In *Comprehensive Handbook of Psychotherapy Integration.* pp. 533–545. G. Stricker & J. R. Gold (Eds.), New York: Plenum Press.

Striegel-Moore, R. H. (1993). Etiology of binge eating: A developmental perspective. In *Binge Eating: Nature, Assessment, and Treatment.* In C. G. Fairburn & G. T. Wilson (Eds.), New York: Guilford Press. 144–172.

Strober, M. (1995). Family-genetic perspective on anorexia nervosa and bulimia nervosa. In C. G. Fairburn & K. Brownell (eds.), *Comprehensive textbook of eating disorders and obesity* (pp. 212–218). New York: Guilford Press.

Strom, S. (2000, January 4). Tradition of equality fading in new Japan, *New York Times.*

Stromswold, K., Caplan, D., Alpert, N., & Rauch, S. (1996). Localization of syntactic comprehension by positron emission tomography. *Brain and Language, 52*, 452–473.

Stroop, J. R. (1935). Studies of interference in serial verbal reactions. *Journal of Experimental Psychology, 28*, 643–662.

Strupp, H. H. (1997). Research, practice, and managed care. *Psychotherapy, 34*, 91–94.

Strupp, J. J., & Binder, J. L. (1984). *Psychotherapy in a new key: A guide to time-limited dynamic psychotherapy.* New York: Basic Books.

Strupp, H. H., & Hadley, S. W. (1977). A tripartite model of mental health and therapeutic outcomes: With special reference to negative effects in psychotherapy. *American Psychologist. 32,* . 187–19.

Stuckey, J., Marra, S., Minor, T. & Insel, T. R. (1989). Changes in mu opiate receptors following inescapable shock. *Brain Research, 476*, 167–169.

Stunkard, A. J. (1982). Anorectic agents lower a body weight set point. *Life Science, 30*, 2043–2055.

Stuss, D. T., Alexander, M. P., Palumbo, C. L., Buckle, L., et al. (1994). Organizational strategies with unilateral or bilateral frontal lobe injury in word learning tasks. *Neuropsychology, 8*, 355–373.

Suarez, E., & Williams, R. (1989). Situational determinants of cardiovascular and emotional reactivity in high and low hostile men. *Psychosomatic Medicine, 51*, 404–?.

Suarez, E. C., Kuhn, C. M., Schanberg, S. M., Williams, R. B., Jr., & Zimmermann, E. A. (1998). Neuroendocrine, cardiovascular, and emotional responses of hostile men: The role of interpersonal challenge. *Psychosomatic Medicine, 60*, 78–88.

Subrahmanyam, K., & Greenfield, P. M. (1994). Effect of video game practice on spatial skills in girls and boys [Special issue]. *Journal of Applied Developmental Psychology, 15*, 13–32.

Sue, S., Zane, N., & Young, K. (1994). Research on psychotherapy with culturally diverse populations. In A. E. Bergin & S. L. Garfield (Eds.),

Handbook of psychotherapy and behavior change, 4th edition (pp. 783–820). New York: John Wiley & Sons.

Suga, N. (1990). Biosonar and neural computation in bats. *Scientific American, 262*, 60–68.

Sullins, E. S. (1991). Emotional contagion revisited: Effects of social comparison and expressive style on mood convergence. *Personality & Social Psychology Bulletin, 17*(2), 166–174.

Sullivan, H. S. (1953). *The interpersonal theory of psychiatry.* New York: Norton.

Sullivan, L. (1999). Looking at vision: Reflections on the role of religious vision in the project of visual truth. In M. Zyniewicz (Ed.), *The papers of the Henry Luce III fellows in theology, Vol. 3* (pp. 115–140). Atlanta: Scholars Press.

Sullivan, R. (1999, June). Dad again. *Life,* pp. 66–68.

Sulloway, F. J. (1996). *Born to rebel: Birth order, family dynamics, and creative lives.* New York, NY: Pantheon Books.

Sulloway, F. J. (1997). *Born to Rebel: Birth Order, Family Dynamics, and Creative Lives.* New York: Vintage.

Sulloway, F. J. (1998). Sensationalism as scientific radicalism: A reply to Judith Harris. *www.edge.org*

Sulloway, F. J. (in press). Birth order, sibling competition, and human behavior. In P. S. Davies & H. R. Holcomb III (Eds.), *The Evolution of Minds: Psychological and Philisophical Perspectives.* Boston: Kluwer Academic Publishers.

Suls, J., & Fletcher, B. (1985). The relative efficacy of avoidant and nonavoidant coping strategies: A meta-analysis. *Health Psychology, 4,* 249–288.

Sutker, P., Davis, J. M., Uddo, M., & Ditta, S. (1995). War zone stresses, personal resources, and PTSD in Persian Gulf returnees. *Journal of Abnormal Psychology, 59,* 704–714.

Suzuki, L. A., & Valencia, R. R. (1997). Race-ethnicity and measured intelligence: Educational implications. *American Psychologist, 52,* 1103–1114.

Svanborg, P., Gustavsson, J. P., & Weinryb, R. M. (1999). What patient characteristics make therapists recommend psychodynamic psychotherapy or other treatment forms? *Acta Psychiatrica Scandinavica, 99,* 87–94.

Svartberg, M., & Stiles, T. C. (1991). Comparative effects of short-term psycnodynamic psychotherapy: A meta-analysis. *Journal of Consulting & Clinical Psychology, 59,* 704–714.

Svartberg, M., & Stiles, T. C. (1993). Efficacy of brief dynamic psychotherapy. *American Journal of Psychiatry, 150,* 684.

Swap, W. C. (1977). Interpersonal attraction and repeated exposure to rewarders and punishers. *Personality and Social Psychology Bulletin, 3,* 248–251.

Swedo, S. E, Leonard, H. L., Garvey, M., Mittleman, B. Allen, A. J., Perlmutter, S., Dow, S., Zamkoff, J., Dubbert, B. K., & Lougee, L. (1998). Pediatric Autoimmune Neuropsychiatric Disorders Associated With Streptococcal Infections: Clinical Description of the First 50 Cases. *Am J Psychiatry, 155,* 264–271.

Swedo S. E., Leonard, H. L., Mittleman, B. B., Allen, A. J., Rapoport, J. L., Dow, S. P., Kanter, M. E., Chapman, F., & Zabriskie, J. (1997). Identification of children with pediatric autoimmune neuropsychiatric disorders associated with streptococcal infections by a marker associated with rheumatic fever. *American Journal of Psychiatry, 154*(1), 110–112.

Swica, Y., Lewis, D. O., & Lewis, M. (1996). Child Abuse and Dissociative Identity Disorder/Multiple Personality Disorder: The Documentation of Childhood Maltreatment and the Corroboration of Symptoms. *Child & Adolescent Psychiatric Clinics of North America, 5,* 431–447.

Swinney, D. A. (1979). Lexical access during sentence comprehension: (Re)consideration of context effects. *Journal of Verbal Learning and Verbal Behavior, 18,* 645–659.

Syvalathi, E. K. G. (1994). Biological factors in schizophrenia: Structural and functional aspects. *British Journal of Psychiatry, 164* (Suppl. 23), 9–14.

Szasz, T. S. (1961). *The myth of mental ilness: Foundations of a theory of personal conduct.* New York: Hoeber-Harper.

Tafarodi, R. W., & Swann, W. B., Jr. (1996). Individualism-collectivism and global self-esteem: Evidence for a cultural trade-off. *Journal of Cross-Cultural Psychology, 27,* 651–672.

Tajfel, H. (1970, November). Experiments in intergroup discrimination. *Scientific American, 223,* 96–102.

Tajfel, H. (1982). *Social identity and intergroup relations.* Cambridge, England: Cambridge University Press.

Takahashi, K. (1990). Are the key assumptions of the "Strange Situation" procedure universal? A view from Japanese research. *Human Development, 33,* 23–30.

Takahashi, Y. (1990). Is multiple personality disorder really rare in Japan? *Dissociation, 3,* 57–59.

Takano, Y., & Noda, A. (1993). A temporary decline of thinking ability during foreign language processing. *Journal of Cross-Cultural Psychology, 24,* 445–462.

Takeuchi, A. H., & Hulse, S. H. (1993). Absolute pitch. *Psychological Bulletin, 113,* 345–361.

Tallal, P., Miller, S. L., Bedi, G., Byma, G., Wang, X., Nagarajan, S. S., Schreiner, C., Jenkins, W. M., & Merzenich, M. M. (1996). Language comprehension in language-learning impaired children improved with acoustically modified speech. *Science, 271,* 81–84.

Tanaka, K. (1997). Mechanisms of visual object recognition: Monkey and human studies. *Current Opinion in Neurobiology, 7,* 523–529.

Tang, S., & Hall, V. C. (1994). The overjustification effect: A meta-analysis. *Journal of Applied Cognitive Psychology, 9,* 365–404.

Tang, S., & Hall, V. C. (1995). Even with problems, meta-analysis contributes. *Applied Cognitive Psychology, 9,* 423–424.

Tang, Y.-P., Shimizu, E., Dube, G. R., Rampon, C., Kerchner, G. A., Zhuo, M., Liu, G., & Tsien, J. Z. (1999). Genetic enhancement of learning and memory in mice. *Nature, 401,* 63–69.

Tanner, J. M. (1990). *Foetus into man* (2nd ed.). Cambridge, MA: Harvard University Press.

Taris, T. W. (2000). Dispositional need for cognitive closure and self-enhancing beliefs. *Journal of Social Psychology, 140,* 35–50.

Tarr, M. J., & Beulthoff, H. H. (1995). Is human object recognition better described by geon structural descriptions or by multiple views? Comment on Biederman and Gerhardstein (1993). *Journal of Experimental Psychology: Human Perception and Performance, 212,* 1494–1505.

Tarrier, N., Pilgrim, H., Sommerfield, C., Faragher, B., Reynolds, M., Graham, E., & Barrowclough, C. (1999). A randomized trial of cognitive therapy and imaginal exposure in the treatment of chronic posttraumatic stress disorder. *Journal of Consulting and Clinical Psychology, 67,* 13–18.

Tarrier, N., Yusupoff, L., Kinney, C., McCarthy, E., Gledhill, A., Haddock, G., & Morris, J. (1998). Randomised controlled trial of intensive cognitive behaviour therapy for patients with chronic schizophrenia. *British Medical Journal, 317,* 303–307.

Tarter, R. E., Jones, B. M., Simpson, C. D., & Vega, A. (1971). Effects of task complexity and practice on performance during acute alcohol intoxication. *Perceptual & Motor Skills, 33,* 307–318.

Tavris, C. (1991). The mismeasure of woman: Paradoxes and perspective in the study of gender. In J. D. Goodchilds (Ed.), *Psychological perspectives on human diversity in America* (pp. 89–136). Washington, DC: American Psychological Association.

Taylor, M. G. (1996). The development of children's beliefs about social and biological aspects of gender differences. *Child Development, 67,* 1555–1571.

Taylor, S. (1996). Meta-analysis of cognitive-behavioral treatment for social phobia. *Journal of Behavior Therapy & Experimental Psychiatry, 27,* 1–9.

Taylor, S. W., Repetti, R. L., & Seeman, T. (1997). Health psychology: What is an unhealthy environment and how does it get under the skin? *Annual Review of Psychology, 48,* 411–447.

Tecott, L. H., Sun, L. M., Akana, S. F., Strack, A. M., Lowenstein, D. H., Dallman, M. F., & Julius, D. (1995). Eating disorder and epilepsy in mice lacking 5-HT2C serotonin receptors. *Nature, 374,* 542–546.

Tedlock, B. (1992). The role of dreams and visionary narratives in Mayan cultural survival. *Ethos, 20,* 453–476.

Teigen, K. H. (1994). Variants of subjective probabilities: Concepts, norms, and biases. In G. Wright & P. Ayton (Eds.), *Subjective probability.* New York: Wiley.

Tein, J. Y., Sandler, I. N., & Zautra, A. J. (2000). Stressful life events, psychological distress, coping, and parenting of divorced mothers: A longitudinal study. *Journal of Family Psychology, 14,* 27–41.

Teitelbaum, P., & Stellar, E. (1954). Recovery from the failure to eat produced by hypothalamic lesions. *Science, 120,* 894–895.

Telch, M. J., Lucas, J. A., & Nelson, P. (1989). Nonclinical panic in college students: An investigation of prevalence and symptomatology. *Journal of Abnormal Psychology, 98,* 300–306.

Tellegen, A., & Atkinson, G. (1974). Openness to absorbing and self-altering experiences ("absorption"), a trait related to hypnotic susceptibility. *Journal of Abnormal Psychology, 83,* 268–277.

Tellegen, A., Lykken, D. T., Bouchard, T. J., Wilcox, K. J., Segal, N. L., & Rich, S. (1988). Personality similarity in twins reared apart and together. *Journal of Personaltiy and Social Psychology, 54,* 1031–1039.

Teri, L., & Lewinsohn, P. M. (1985). Group intervention for unipolar depression. *Behavior Therapist, 8,* 109–111, 123.

Terman, L. M., & Oden, M. H. (1959). *Genetic studies of genius: Vol. IV; The gifted group of midlife.* Stanford, CA: Stanford University Press.

Terrace, H. S. (1979, November). How Nim Chimpsky changed my mind. *Psychology Today,* 23–28.

Terrace, H. S., Pettito, L. A., & Bever, T. G. (1976). *Project Nim, progress report I.* New York: Columbia University Press.

Terry, D. J., & Hogg, M. A. (1996). Group norms and the attitude-behavior relationship: A role for group identification. *Personality & Social Psychology Bulletin, 22*, 776–793.

Tesser, A. (1993). The importance of heritability of psychological research: the case of attitudes. *Psychological Review, 100*, 129–142.

Tetlock, P. E., Peterson, R. S., McGuire, C., Chang, S., & Feld, P. (1992). Assesing political group dynmaics: A test of the groupthink model. *Journal of Personality and Social Psychology, 63*, 403–425.

Tew, J. D., Jr., Mulsant, B. H., Haskett, R. F., Prudic, J., Thase, M. E., Crowe, R. R., Dolata, D., Begley, A. E., Reynolds, C. F., III, & Sackheim, H. A. (1999). Acute efficacy of ECT in the treatment of major depression in the old-old. *American Journal of Psychiatry, 156*, 1865–1870.

Thalbourne, M. A. (1989). Psychics and ESP: A reply to Grimmer and White. *Australian Psychologist, 24*, 307–310.

Thapar, A., Petrill, S. A., & Thompson, L. A. (1994). The heritability of memory in the Western Reserve twin project. *Behavior Genetics, 24*, 155–160.

Thase, M. E., Greenhouse, J. B., Frank, E., Reynolds, C. F. III, Pilkonis, P. A., Hurley, K., Grochocinski, V., & Kupfer, D. J. (1997). Treatment of major depression with psychotherapy or psychotherapy-pharmacotherapy combinations. *Archives of General Psychiatry, 54*, 1009–1015.

Thatcher, R. W. (1994). Cyclic cortical reorganization: Origins of human cognitive development. In G. Dawson & K. W. Fischer (Eds.), *Human behavior and the developing brain* (pp. 232–266). New York: Guilford.

The Arc. (1998). Introduction to Mental Retardation. Available: *http://thearc.org/faqs/mrqa.html*

The National Center on Addiction and Substance Abuse at Columbia University (CASA). (1998). *http://www.casacolumbia.org/pubs/feb95/sa_resum.htm.*

The National Sleep Foundation. (1998). Omnibus Sleep in America Poll. Cited in Center for the Advancement of Health (1998). Facts of Life: An Issue Briefing for Health Reporters. 3(3): p. 3. www.sleepfoundation.org

The Role of Avoidance and Obsessiveness in Matching Patients to Cognitive and Interpersonal Psychotherapy: Empirical Findings From the Treatment for Depression Collaborative Research Program

Theeuwes, J., Kramer, A. F., Hahn, S., & Irwin, D. E. (1998). Our eyes do not always go where we want them to go: Capture of the eyes by new objects. *Psychological Science, 9*, 379–385.

Thelen, E. (1983). Learning to walk is still an "old" problem: A reply to Zelazo. *Journal of Motor Behavior, 15*, 139–161.

Thelen, E. (1995). Motor development: A new synthesis. *American Psychologist, 50*, 79–95.

Thelen, E., & Ulrich, B. D. (1991). Hidden skills: A dynamic systems analysis of treadmill stepping during the first year. *Monographs of the Society for Research in Child Development, 56 (1, Serial No. 223).*

Thibaut, J. W., & Kelley, H. H. (1959). *The social psychology of groups.* New York: Wiley.

Thomas, A., & Chess, S. (1996). *Temperament: Theory and practice.* New York: Brunner/Mazel.

Thompson, P. M., Giedd, J. N., Woods, R. P., MacDonald, D., Evans, A. C., & Toga, A. W. (2000). Growth patterns in the developing brain detected by using continuum mechanical tensor maps. *Nature, 404*, 190–193.

Thompson, R. F. (1993). *The brain, a neuroscience primer* (2nd ed.). New York: Freeman.

Thompson, R. F., and Krupa, D. J. (1994). Organization of memory traces in the mammalian brain. *Annual Review of Neuroscience, 17*, 519–549.

Thompson, W. L., & Kosslyn, S. M. (2000). Neural systems activated during visual mental imagery: A review and meta-analyses. In A. W. Toga & J. C. Mazziotta (Eds.), *Brain mapping: The systems.* San Diego, CA: Academic Press.

Thorn, B. L., & Gilbert, L. A. (1998). Antecedents of work and family role expectations of college men. *Journal of Family Psychology, 12*, 259–267.

Thorndike, E. L. (1927). The law of effect. *American Journal of Psychology, 39*, 212–222.

Thorndike, E. L. (1933). A proof of the law of effect. *Science, 77*, 173–175.

Thorndike, E. L. (1949). The law of effect. in E. L. Thorndike, *Selected writings from a connectionist's psychology* (pp. 13–26). New York: Appleton-Century-Crofts. (Original work published 1933).

Thorndike, R. L., Hagen, E. P., & Sattler, J. M. (1986). *Stanford-Binet Intelligence Scale* (4th ed.). Itasca, IL: Riverside.

Thornhill, R., & Gangestad, S. W. (1993). Human facial beauty: Averageness, symmetry, and parasite resistance. *Human Nature, 4*, 237–269.

Thurlow, W. R. (1971). Audition. In J. W. Kling & L. A. Riggs (Eds.), *Woodworth and Schlosberg's experimental psychology* (pp. 223–271). New York: Holt, Rinehart & Winston.

Thurstone, L. L. (1938). *Primary mental abilities.* Chicago: University of Chicago Press.

Thurstone, L. L., & Thurstone, T. G. (1941). *Factorial studies of intelligence.* Chicago: University of Chicago Press.

Tidwell, M. O., Reis, H. T., Shaver, P. R. (1996). Attachment, attractiveness, and social interaction: A diary study. *Journal of Personality & Social Psychology, 71*, 729–745.

Tiernari, P. (1991). Interaction between genetic vulnerability and family environment: The Finnish adoptive family study of schizophrenia. *Acta Psychiatrica Scandinavica, 84*, 460–465.

Till, B. D., & Priluck, R. L. (2000). Stimulus generalization in classical conditioning: An initial investigation and extension. *Psychology & Marketing, 17*, 55–72.

Timmerman, I. G. H., Emmelkamp, P. M. G., & Sanderman, R. (1998). The effects of a stress-management training program in individuals at risk in the community at large. *Behaviour Research & Therapy, 36*, 863–875.

Tingey, H., Kiger, G., & Riley, P. J. (1996). Juggling multiple roles: Perceptions of working mothers. *Social Science Journal, 33*, 183–191.

Tinker, J. E., & Tucker, J. A. (1997). Motivations for weight loss and behavior change strategies associated with natural recovery from obesity. *Psychology of Addictive Behaviors, 11*, 98–106.

Tinney, W. J., Jr. (1999, May–June). Members comment on ASA's publication on affirmative action. *Footnotes*, pp. 8–9.

Tkachuk, G. A. (1999). Exercise therapy for patients with psychiatric disorders: Research and clinical implications. *Professional Psychology: Research and Practice, 30*, 275–282.

Tohen, M., & Grundy, S. (1999). Management of acute mania. *Journal of Clinical Psychology, 60*(Supplement 5), 31–34.

Tolman, E. C. and Honzik, C. H. (1930a). "Insight" in rats. *University of California Publications in Psychology, 4*, 215–232.

Tolman, E. C., & Honzik, C. H. (1930b). Degrees of hunger, reward and non-reward, and maze learning in rats. *University of California Publications in Psychology, 4*, 241–256.

Tolman, E. C., & Honzik, C. H. (1930c). Introduction and removal of reward, and maze performance in rats. *Univeristy of California Publications in Psychology, 4*, 257–275.

Tom, G., & Rucker, M. (1975). Fat, full, and happy: Effects of food deprivation, external cues, and obesity on preference ratings, consumption, and buying intentions. *Journal of Personality & Social Psychology, 32*, 761–766.

Tomasello, M. (1996). Piagetian and Vygotskian approaches to language acquisition. *Human Development, 39*, 269–276.

Tomkins, S. S. (1962). *Affect, imagery, consciousness, Vol I. The positive affects.* New York: Springer-Verlag.

Tootell, R. B. H., Hadjikhani, N. K., Vanduffel, W., Lui, A. K., Medola, J. D., Sereno, M. I., & Dale, A. M. (1998). Functional analysis of primary visual cortex (V1) in humans. *Proceedings of the National Academy of Sciences, USA, 95*, 811–817.

Tootell, R. B. H., Mendola, J. D., Hadjikhani, N. K., Ledden, P. J., Liu, A. K., Reppas, J. B., Serano, M. I., & Dale, A. M. (1997). Functional analysis of V3A and related areas in human visual cortex. *The Journal of Neuroscience, 17*, 7060–7078.

Torgersen, S. G. (1983). Genetic factors in anxiety disorders. *Archives of General Psychiatry, 40*, 1085–1089.

Torrance, E. P. (1980). Creativity and style of learning and thinking characteristics of adaptors and innovators. *Creative Child and Adult Quarterly, 5*, 80–85.

Torrey, E. F. (1988). *Nowhere to go: The tragic odyssey of the homeless mentally ill.* New York: Harper & Row.

Torrey, E. F., Miller, J., Rawlings, R., & Yolken, R. H. (1997). Seasonality of births in schizophrenia and bipolar disorder: A review of the literature. *Schizophrenia Research, 28*, 1–38.

Trafimow, D., & Finlay, K. (1996). The importance of subjective norms for a minority of people: Between-subjects and with-subjects analyses. *Personality and Social Psychology Bulletin, 22*, 820–828.

Tramo, M. J., Loftus, W. C., Stukel, T. A., Green, R. L., Weaver, J. B., & Gazzaniga, M. S. (1998). Brain size, head size, and intelligence quotient in monozygotic twins. *Neurology, 50*, 1246–1252.

Tramo, M. J., Loftus, W. C., Thoman, C. E., Green, R. L., Mott, L. A., & Gazzaniga, M. S. (1995). Surface area of human cerebral cortex and its gross morphological subdivisions: *In vivo* measurements in monozygotic twins suggest differential hemisphere effects of genetic factors. *Journal of Cognitive Neuroscience, 7*, 292–301.

Treisman, A. M. (1964a). Monitoring and storage of irrelevant messages in selective attention. *Journal of Verbal Learning and Verbal Behavior, 3*, 449–459.

Treisman, A. M. (1964b). Selective attention in man. *British Medical Bulletin, 20*, 12–16.

Treisman, A. M., & Gormican, S. (1988). Feature analysis in early vision: Evidence from search asymmetries. *Psychological Review, 95*, 15–48.

Treisman, A. M., & Schmidt, H. (1982). Illusory conjunctions in the perception of objects. *Cognitive Psychology, 14*, 107–141.

Treisman, A. M., & Souther, J. (1985). Search asymmetry: A diagnostic for preattentive processing of separable features. *Journal of Experimental Psychology: General, 114,* 285–310.

Trevethan, S. D., & Walker, L. J. (1989). Hypothetical versus real-life moral reasoning among psychopathic and delinquent youth. *Development and Psychopathology, 1,* 91–103.

Triandis, H. C., Bontempo, R. Villareal, M. J., Asai, M., & Lucca, N. (1988). Individualism and collectivism: Cross-cultural perspectives on self-ingroup relationships. *Journal of Prsonality and Social Psychology, 54,* 323–338.

Triandis, H. C., McCusker, C., & Hui, C. H. (1990). Multimethod probes of individualism and collectivism. *Journal of Personality and Social Psychology, 59,* 1006–1020.

Trimpop, R., & Kirkcaldy, B. (1997). Personality predictors of driving accidents. *Personality & Individual Differences, 23,* 147–152.

Trivedi, N., & Sabini, J. (1998). Volunteer bias, sexuality, and personality. *Archives of Sexual Behavior, 27,* 181–195.

Trivers, R. (1972). Parental investment and sexual selection. In B. Campbell (Ed.), *Sexual selection and the descent of man, 1871–1971* (pp. 136–179). Chicago: Aldine.

Trivers, R. (1985). *Social evolution.* Menlo Park, CA: Benjamin/Cummings.

True, W. R., Rice, J., Eisen, S. A., Heath, A. C., Phil, D., Goldberg, J., Lyons, M., & Nowak, J. (1993). A twin study of genetic and environmental contributions to liability for posttraumatic stress symptoms, *Archives of General Psychiatry, 50,* 257–264.

Tryphon, A., & Vonèche, J. (Eds.). (1996). *Piaget-Vygotsky: The social genesis of thought.* East Sussex, England: Psychology Press.

Tsien, J. Z., Chen, D. F., Gerber, D., Tom, C., Mercer, E. H., Anderson, D. J., Mayford, M., Kandel, E. R., & Tonegawa, S. (1996). Subregion- and cell type-restricted gene knockout in mouse brain. *Cell, 87,* 1317–1326.

Tsuang, M. T., Lyons, M. J., Eisen, S. A., True, W. T., Goldberg, J., & Henderson, W. (1992). A twin study of drug exposure and intitiation of use. *Behavior Genetics, 22,* 756 (abstract).

Tucker, G. J. (1998). Putting DSM-IV in Perspective. *Am J Psychiatry 155:2,* February 1998, pp. 159–161

Tulving, E. (1972). Episodic and semantic memory. In E. Tulving & W. Donaldson (Eds.), *Organization and memory* (pp. 381–403). New York: Academic Press.

Tulving, E. (1985). How many memory systems are there? *American Psychologist, 40,* 395–398.

Tulving, E., Kapur, S., Craik, F. I. M., Moscovitch, M., & Houle, S. (1994). Hemispheric encoding/retrieval asymmetry in episodic memory: Positron emission tomography findings. *Proceedings of the National Academy of Science, USA, 91,* 2016–2020.

Tulving, E., & Markowitsch, H. J. (1997). Memory beyond the hippocampus. *Current Opinion in Neurobiology, 7,* 209–216.

Tulving, E., Schacter, D. L., & Stark, H. (1982). Priming effects in word-fragment completion are independent of recognition memory. *Journal of Experimental Psychology: Learning, Memory, and Cognition, 8,* 336–342.

Turkheimer, E., & Waldron, M. (2000). Nonshared environment: A theoretical, methodological, and quantitative review. *Psychological Bulletin, 126,* 78–108.

Turner, A. M., & Greenough, W. T. (1985). Differential rearing effects on rat visual cortex synapses. I. Synaptic and neuronal density and synapses per neuron. *Brain Research, 329,* 195–203.

Turvey, M. T. (1990). Coordination. *American Psychologist, 4,* 938–953.

Tversky, A., & Kahneman, D. (1974). Judgment under uncertainty: Heuristics and biases. *Science, 185,* 1124–1131.

Twisk, J. W. R., Snel, J., Kemper, H. C. G., & van Mechelen, W. (1999). Changes in daily hassles and life events and the relationship with coronary heart disease risk factors: A 2-year longitudinal study in 27–29-yr-old males and females. *Journal of Psychosomatic Research, 46,* 229–240.

Tykocinksi, O., Higgens, E. T., & Chaiken, S. (1994). Message framing, self-discrepancies, and yielding to persuasive messages: The motivational significance of psychological situations. *Personality & Social Psychology Bulletin, 20,* 107–115.

Tzeng, O. C., Ware, R., & Chen, J. (1989). Measurement and utility of continuous unipolar ratings for the Myers-Briggs Type Indicator. *Journal of Personality, 53,* 727–738.

Ubell, E. (1995). New devices can help you hear. *Parade Magazine,* Jan. 15, pp. 14–15.

Udwin, O., & Yule, W. (1990). Expressive language of children with Williams syndrome. *American Journal of Medical Genetics Supplement, 6,* 108–114.

Udwin, O., & Yule, W. (1991). A cognitive and behavioral phenotype in Williams syndrome. *Journal of Clinical and Experimental Neuropsychology, 13,* 232–244.

Ullman, S. (1996). *High-level vision.* Cambridge: MIT Press.

Ulrich, R. (1984). View through a window may influence recovery from surgery. *Science, 224,* 420.

Ulrich, R. E., Stachnik, T. J., & Stainton, N. R. (1963). Student acceptance of generalized personality interpretations. *Psychological Reports, 13,* 831–834.

Ungerleider, L. G. (1995). Functional brain imaging studies of cortical mechanisms for memory. *Science, 270,* 769–775.

Ungerleider, L. G., & Haxby, J. V. (1994). "What" and "where" in the human brain. *Current Opinion in Neurology, 4,* 157–165.

Ungerleider, L. G., & Mishkin, M. (1982). Two cortical visual systems. In D. J. Ingle, M. A. Goodale, & R. J. W. Mansfield (Eds.), *Analysis of visual behavior* (pp. 549–586). Cambridge, MA: MIT Press.

United Nations. (1991). *The world's women 1970–1990: Trends and statistics.* New York: United Nations.

Ursin, H., Baade, E., & Levine, S. (1978). *Psychobiology of Stress.* San Diego: Academic Press.

U.S. Office of Technology Assessment. (1991). *Adolescent health: Vol. 3, Crosscutting issues in the delivery of health and related services.* (Publication No. OTA-H-467). Washington, DC: U.S. Congress.

Vaillancourt, M. (1996). Campaigns try to soften image. *The Boston Globe.* Monday, October 7, 1996, p. B1.

Vaillant, G. (1977). *Adaptation to life.* Boston: Little, Brown.

Vajk, F. C., Craighead, W. E., Craighead, L. W., & Holley, C. (1997). Risk of major depression as a function of response styles to depressed mood. Poster presented at the annual meeting of the Association for the Advancement of Behavior Therapy, November, Miami Beach, FL.

Valenstein, E. T. (1973). *Brain control.* New York: Wiley.

Valins, S. (1966). Cognitive effects of false heart-rate feedback. *Journal of Personality & Social Psychology, 4,* 400–408.

van Balkom, A. J. L. M., van Oppen, P., Vermeulen, A. W. A., Nauta, N. C. E., Vorst, H. C. M., & van Dyck, R. (1994). A meta-analysis on the treatment of obsessive-compulsive disorder: A comparison of antidepressants, behaviour and cognitive therapy. *Clinical Psychology Review, 14,* 359–381.

Van Cauter, E., & Turek, F. W. (in press). Roles of sleep-wake and dark-light cycles in the control of endocrine, metabolic, cardiovascular and cognitive function. In B. S. McEwen, Ed.). *Coping with the environment: Handbook of Physiology Series. Part. 2: Environmental regulation of states and functions of the organism.*

Van der Hart, O. (1990). "Is multiple personality disorder really rare in Japan?": Commentary. *Dissociation: Progress in the Dissociative Disorders, 3,* 66–67.

van der Veer, R. (1996). Vygotsky and Piaget: A collective monologue. *Human Development, 39,* 237–242.

Van Essen, D. C. (1997). A tension-based theory of morphogenesis and compact wiring in the central nervous system. *Nature, 385,* 313–318.

Van Goozen, S. H. M, Cohen-Kettenis, P. T., Gooren, J. J. G., Frijda, N. H., & Van De Poll, N. E. (1995). Gender differences in behaviour: Activating effects of cross-sex hormones. *Psychoneuroendocrinology, 20,* 343–363.

Van Goozen, S. H., Wiegant, V. M., Endert, E., Helmond, F. A., & Van de Poll, N. E. (1997). Psychoendocrinological assessment of the menstrual cycle: The relationship between hormones, sexuality, and mood. *Archives of Sexual Behavior, 26,* 359–382.

van Reekum, R., Black, S. E., Conn, D., & Clarke, D. (1997). Cognition-enhancing drugs in dementia: A guide to the near future. *Canadian Journal of Psychiatry, 42,* suppl 1, 35S–50S.

Vandello, J. A., & Cohen, D. (1999). Patterns of individualism and collectivism across the United States. *Journal of Personality and Social Psychology, 77,* 279–292.

Vanni, S., Revonsuo, A., Saarinen, J., & Hari, R. (1996). Visual awareness of objects correlates with activity of right occipital cortex. *Neuroreport, 8,* 183–186.

Vargha-Khadem, F., Isaacs, E. B., Papaleloudi, H., Polkey, C. E., & Wilson, J. (1991). Development of language in 6 hemispherectomized patients. *Brain, 114,* 473–495.

Vargha-Khadem, F., Watkins, K., Alcock, K., Fletcher, P., & Passingham, R. (1995). Praxic and nonverbal cognitive deficits in a large family with a genetically transmitted speech and language disorder. *Proceedings of the National Academy of Sciences, USA, 92,* 930–933.

Varma, A. (2000). Impact of watching international television programs on adolescents in India. *Journal of Comparative Family Studies, 31,* 117–126.

Vasterling, J., Jenkins, R. A., Tope, D. M., & Burish, T. G. (1993). Cognitive distraction and relaxation training for the control of side effects due to cancer chemotherapy. *Journal of Behavioral Medicine, 16,* 65–80.

Vaughan, S. C. (1997). *The Talking Cure: The Science Behind Psychotherapy.* New York: Putnam & Sons.

Vaughn, C., & Leff, J. (1976). Measurement of expressed emotion in the families of psychiatric patients. *British Journal of Social and Clinical Psychology, 15,* 1069–1177.

Vehmanen, L., Kaprio, J., & Loennqvist, J. (1995). Twin studies on concordance for bipolar disorder. *Psychiatria Fennica, 26,* 107–116.

Velakoulis, D., Pantelis, C., McGorry, P. D., Dudgeon, P., Brewer, W., Cook, M., Desmond, P., Bridle, N., Tierney, P., Murrie, V., Singh, B., & Copolov, D. (1999). Hippocampal Volume in First-Episode Psychoses and Chronic Schizophrenia: A High-Resolution Magnetic Resonance Imaging Study. *Archives of General Psychiatry, 56,* 133–140.

Ventura, J., Nuechterlein, K. H., Lukoff, D., & Hardesty, J. P. (1989). A prospective study of stressful life events and schizophrenic relapse. *Journal of Abnormal Psychology, 98,* 407–411.

Verhaeghen, P., Marcoen, A., & Goosens, L. (1992). Improving memory performance in the aged through mnemonic training: A meta-analytic study. *Psychology and Aging, 7,* 242–251.

Vernon, P. A., Jang, K. L., Harris, J. A., & McCarthy, J. M. (1997). Environmental Predictors of Personality Differences: A Twin and Sibling Study. *Journal of Personality and Social Psychology, 72,* 177–183.

Verwey, W. B., & Zaidel, D. M. (2000). Predicting drowsiness accidents from personal attributes, eye blinks and ongoing driving behaviour. *Personality & Individual Differences, 28,* 123–142.

Vickers, K. S., & Vogeltanz, N. D. (2000). Dispositional optimism as a predictor of depressive symptoms over time. *Personality and Individual Differences, 28,* 259–272.

Vieweg, R., & Shawcross, C. R. (1998). A trial to determine any difference between two and three times a week ECT in the rate of recovery from depression. *Journal of Mental Health (UK), 7,* 403–409.

Vincent, K. R. (1991). Black/White IQ differences: Does age make the difference? *Journal of Clinical Psychology, 47,* 266–270.

Viney, W. (1994). *A history of psychology: Ideas and context.* Needham Heights, MA: Allyn & Bacon.

Vogel, G. (1996). School achievement: Asia and Europe top in the world, but reasons are hard to find. *Science, 274,* 1296.

Vogel, G. (1997). Cocaine wreaks subtle damage on developing brains. *Science, 278,* 38–39.

Volkmar, F. R., Klin, A., Siegel, B., et al. (1994). Field trial for autistic disorder in DSM-IV. *American Journal of Psychiatry, 151,* 1361–1367.

von der Heydt, R., & Peterhans, E. (1989). Mechanisms of contour perception in monkey visual cortex. I. Lines of pattern discontinuity. *Journal of Neuroscience, 9,* 1731–1748.

von der Heydt, R., Peterhans, E., & Baumgartner, G. (1984). Illusory contours and cortical neuron responses. *Science, 224,* 1260–1262.

von Zerssen, D., Leon, C. A. Moller, H., Wittchen, H., Pfister, H., & Sartorius, N. (1990). Care strategies for schizophrenic patients in a transcultural comparison. *Comprehensive Psychiatry, 31,* 398–408.

Vonk, R., & van Knippenberg, A. (1995). Processing attitude statements from in-group and out-group members: Effects of within-group and within-person inconsistencies on reading times. *Journal of Personality and Social Psychology, 68,* 215–227.

Voth, H. M., & Orth, M. H. (1973). *Psychotherapy and the role of the environment.* New York: Behavioral Press.

Voudouris, N. J., Peck, C. L., & Coleman, G. (1985). Conditioned Placebo Responses. *Journal of Personality and Social Psychology, 48,* 47–53.

Vrana, S. R. & Lang, P. J. (1990). Fear imagery and the startle-probe reflex. *Journal of Abnormal Psychology, 99,* 181–189.

Vrana, S. R., Spence, E. L., & Lang, P. J. (1988). The startle probe response: A new measure of emotion? *Journal of Abnormal Psychology, 97,* 487–491.

Vrugt, A., & Luyerink, M. (2000). The contribution of bodily posture to gender stereotypical impressions. *Social Behavior & Personality, 28,* 91–104.

Vurpillot, E. (1968). The development of scanning strategies and their relation to visual differentiation. *Journal of Experimental Child Psychology, 6,* 632–650.

Vygotsky, L. S. (1962). On inner speech. In E. Hanfman & G. Vakar (Eds. and Trans.), *Thought and language* (pp. 130–138). Cambridge, MA: MIT Press.

Vygotsky, L. S. (1978). *Mind in society: The development of higher mental processes.* Cambridge, MA: Harvard University Press. (Original works published 1930, 1933, and 1935)

Vygotsky, L. S. (1986). (A. Kozulin, Trans.). *Thought and language.* Cambridge, MA: MIT Press (originally published 1934).

Vygotsky, L. S. (1988). On inner speech. In M. B. Franklin & S. S. Barten (Eds.), *Child language: A reader* (pp. 181–187). New York: Oxford University Press.

Waddell, C. (1998). Creativity and mental illness: Is there a link? *Canadian Journal of Psychiatry, 43,* 166–172.

Wade, T., Martin, N. G., & Tiggemann, M. (1998). Genetic and environmental risk factors for the weight and shape concerns characteristic of bulimia nervosa. *Psychological Medicine, 28,* 761–771.

Wagner, A. D., Schacter, D. L., Rotte, M., Koutstaal, W., Maril, A., Dale, A. M., Rose, B. R., & Buckner, R. L. (1998). Building memories: Remembering and forgetting of verbal experiences as predicted by brain activity. *Science, 281,* 1188–1191.

Wagner, J. A. (1995). Studies of individualism-collectivism: Effects on cooperation in groups. *Academy of Management Review, 38,* 152–172.

Wagner, R. K. (1997). Intelligence, training, and employment. *American Psychologist, 52,* 1059–1069.

Wagner, R. K., & Sternberg, R. J. (1986). Tacit knowledge and intelligence in the everyday world. In R. J. Sternberg & R. W. Wagner (Eds.), *Practical intelligence: Nature and origins of competence in the everyday world.* Cambridge, England: Cambridge University Press.

Wahba, M. A., & Bridwell, L. G. (1976). Maslow reconsidered: A review of research on the need hierarchy theory. *Organizational Behavior & Human Decision Processes, 15,* 212–240.

Wahba, M. A., & Bridwell, L. G., (1976). Maslow reconsidered: A review of research on the need hierarchy theory. *Organizational Behavior and Human Performance, 15,* 212–240.

Walker, E. F., & Diforio, D. (1997). Schizophrenia: A neural diathesis-stress model. *Psychological Review, 104,* 667–685.

Walker, E. F., Grimes, K. E., Davis, D., & Smith, A. (1993). Childhood precursors of schizophrenia: Facial expressions of emotion. *American Journal of Psychiatry, 150,* 1654–1660.

Walker, E. F., Logan, C. B., & Walder, D. (1999). Inidcators of neurdevelopmental abnormality in schizotypcal personality disorder. *Psychiatric Annals, 29,* 132–136.

Walker, E. F., Savoie, T., Davis, D. (1994). Neuromotor precursors of schizophrenia. *Schizophrenia Bulletin, 148,* 661–666.

Walker, L. J. (1995). Sexism in Kohlberg's moral psychology? In W. M. Kurtines & J. L. Gewirtz (Eds.), *Moral development: An introduction* (pp. 83–107). Boston: Allyn & Bacon.

Walker, L. J., & Taylor, J. H. (1991). Stage transitions in moral reasoning: A longitudinal study of developmental processes. *Developmental Psychology, 27,* 330–337.

Wallace, R. K. (1970). Physiological effects of transcendental meditation. *Science, 167,* 1751–1754.

Wallace, R. K., Benson, H., & Wilson, A. F. (1971). A wakeful hypometabolic physiologic state. *American Journal of Physiology, 221,* 795–799.

Wallas, G. (1926). *The art of thought.* New York: Harcourt, Brace.

Waller, N. G., Kojetin, B. A., Bouchard, T. J., Jr, Lykken, D. T., & Tellegen, A. (1990). Genetic and environmental influences on religious interests, attitudes, and values: A study of twins reared apart and together. *Psychological Science, 1,* 138–142.

Waller, N. G., & Shaver, P. R. (1994). The importance of non-genetic influences on romantic love styles: A twin family study. *Psychological Science, 5,* 268–274.

Wallis, G., & Bülthoff, H. (1999). Learning to recognize objects. *Trends in Cognitive Sciences, 3,* 22–30.

Walsh, B. T. (1993). Binge eating in bulimia nervosa. In *Binge Eating: Nature, Assessment, and Treatment.* In C. G. Fairburn & G. T. Wilson (Eds.), New York: Guilford Press. 37–49.

Walsh, V., & Cowey, A. (1998). Magnetic stimulation studies of visual cognition. *Trends in Cognitive Sciences, 2,* 103–111.

Walster, E., Walster, G. W., & Berscheid, E. (1978). *Equity: Theory and research.* Needham Heights, MA: Allyn & Bacon.

Walters, E. E., Neale, M. C., Eaves, L. H., Health, A.., Kessler, R. C., & Kendler, K. S. (1992). Bulimia nervosa and major depression: A study of common genetic and environmental factors. *Psychological Medicine, 22,* 617–622.

Walters, J., & Gardner, H. (1985). The development and education of intelligences. In F. Link (Ed.), *Essays on the intellect* (pp. 1–21). Washington, DC: Curriculum Development Association/Association for Supervision and Curriculum Development.

Wandell, B. A. (1995). *Foundations of vision.* Sunderland, MA: Sinauer.

Wang, A. Y., & Hguyen, H. T. (1995). Passionate love and anxiety: A cross-generational study. *The Journal of Social Psychology, 135,* 459–470.

Wang, G., Tanaka, K., & Tanifuji, M. (1996). Optical imaging of functional organization in the monkey inferotemporal cortex. *Science, 272,* 1665–1668.

Wang, T., Hartzell, D. L., Rose, B. S., Flatt, W. P., Hulsey, M. G., Menon, N. K., Makula, R. A., & Baile, C. A. (1999). Metabolic responses to intracerebroventricular leptin and restricted feeding. *Physiology & Behavior, 65,* 839–848.

Wang, X., Merzenich, M. M., Sameshima, K., & Jenkins, W. (1995). Remodelling of hand representation in adult cortex determined by timing of tactile stimulation. *Nature, 378,* 71–75.

Wang, X., Merzenich, M. M., Sameshima, K., & Jenkins, W. M. (1995). Remodeling of hand representation in adult cortex determined by timing of tactile stimulation. *Nature, 378*, 71–75.

Wanska, S. K., & Bedrosian, J. L. (1995). Conversational structure and topic performance in mother–child interaction. *Journal of Speech and Hearing Research, 28*, 579–584.

Wanska, S. K., & Bedrosian, J. L. (1996). Topic and communicative intent in mother–child discourse. *Journal of Child Language, 13*, 523–535.

Ward, C. (Ed.) (1989). *Altered states of consciousness and mental health: A cross-cultural perspective.* Newbury Park, CA: Sage.

Ward, C. (1994). Culture and altered states of consciousness. I *Psychology and Culture.* (Eds.) Lonner, W. J., & Malpass, R. S. Boston: Allyn & Bacon.

Wark, G. R., & Krebs, D. L. (1996). Gender and dilemma differences in real-life moral judgment. *Developmental Psychology, 32*, 220–230.

Warren, R. M., & Warren, R. P. (1970). Auditory illusions and confusions. *Scientific American, 223*, 30–36.

Warrington, E. K., & McCarthy, R. (1987). Categories of knowledge: Further fractionation and an attempted integration. *Brain, 110*, 1273–1296.

Warrington, E. K., & McCarthy, R. A. (1988). The fractionation of retrograde amnesia. *Brain and Cognition, 7*, 184–200.

Warrington, E. K., & Shallice, T. (1984). Category-specific semantic impairments. *Brain, 107*, 829–854.

Washburne, C. (1956). Alcohol, self and the group. *Quarterly Journal of Studies on Alcohol, 17*, 108–123.

Wason, P. C., & Johnson-Laird, P. N. (1972). *Psychology of Reasoning: Structure and content.* Cambridge, MA: Harvard University Press.

Wasserman, E. A. Comparative cognition: Toward a general understanding of cognition in behavior. *Psychological Science, 4*, 156–161.

Watson, D., & Hubbard, B. (1996). Adaptation style and dispositional structure: Coping in the context of the five-factor model. *Journal of Personality, 64*, 737–774.

Watson, J., & Raynor, R. (1920). Conditioned emotional reactions. *Journal of Experimental Psychology, 3*, 1–14.

Watson, J. B. (1913). Psychology as a behaviorist views it. *Psychological Review, 20*, 158–177.

Watson, M., Greer, S., Rowden, L., Gorman, C., Robertson, B., Bliss, J. M., & Tunmore, R. (1991). Realtionships between emotional control, adjustment to cancer, and depression and anxiety in breast cancer patients. *Psychological Medicine, 21*, 51–57.

Watt, C. A, & Morris, R. L. (1995). The relationship among performance on a prototype indicator of perceptual defence/vigilance, personality, and extrasensory perception. *Personality and Individual Differences, 19*, 635–648.

Waxman, S. R. (1992). Linguistic and conceptual organization. *Lingua, 92*, 229–257.

Wayne, S. J., & Ferris, G. R. (1990). Influence tactics and exchange quality in supervisor-subordinate interactions: A laboratory experiment and field study. *Journal of Applied Psychology, 75*, 487–499.

Wayne, S. J., & Liden, R. C. (1995). Effects of impression management on performance ratings: A longitudinal study. *Academy of Management Journal, 38*, 232–260.

Webb, W. B. (1982). Some theories about sleep and their clinical implications. *Psychiatric Annals, 11*, 415–422.

Webb, W. B., & Cartwright, R. D. (1978). Sleep and dreams. *Annual Review of Psychology, 29*, 223–252.

Webster, M. J., Bachevalier, J., & Ungerleider, L. G. (in press). Development and plasticity of visual memory circuits. In B. Julesz & I. Kovacs (Eds.), *Maturational windows and cortical plasticity in human development: Is there reason for an optimistic view?* Reading, MA: Addison-Wesley.

Wechsler, D. (1958). *The measurement and appraisal of adult intelligence* (5th ed.). Baltimore: Williams & Wilkins.

Wechsler, H., Dowdall, G. W., Maenner, G., Gledhill-Hoyt, J., & Lee, H. (1998). Changes in binge drinking and related problems among American college students between 1993 and 1997. *Journal of American College Health, 47*, 57–68.

Wechsler, H., Fulop, M., Padilla, A., Lee, H., & Patrick, K. (1997). Binge drinking among college students: A comparison of California with other states. *Journal of American College Health, 45*, 273–277.

Weerasinghe, J., & Tepperman, L. (1994). Suicide and happiness: Seven tests of the connection. *Social Indicators Research, 32*, 199–233.

Wegner, D. M. (1995). A computer network model of human transactive memory. *Social Cognition, 13*, 319–339.

Wegner, D. M., Erber, R., & Raymond, P. (1991). Transactive memory in close relationships. *Journal of Personality and Social Psychology, 61*, 923–929.

Wegner, D. M., & Gold, D. B. (1995). Fanning old flames: Emotional and cognitive effects of suppressing thoughts of a past relationship. *Journal of Personality and Social Psychology, 68*, 782–792.

Wegner, D. M., Schneider, D. J., Carter, S. R., & White, T. L. (1987). Paradoxical effects of thought suppression. *Journal of Personality & Social Psychology, 53*, 5–13.

Wegner, D. M., & Zanakos, S. (1994). Chronic thought suppression. *Journal of Personality, 62*, 615–640.

Wehr, T. A., Turner, E. H., Shimada, J. M., Clark, C. H., Barker, C., & Liebenluft, E. (1998). Treatment of a rapidly cycling bipolar patient by using extended bedrest and darkness to stabilize the timing and duration of sleep. *Biological Psychiatry, 43*, 822–828.

Weinberg, R. A. (1989). Intelligence and IQ: Landmark issues and great debates. *American Psychologist, 44*, 98–104.

Weinberger D. R. (1987). Implications of normal brain development for the pathogenesis of schizophrenia. Arch Gen Psychiatry. 1987; 44:660–669.

Weinberger, D. R., & Lipska, B. K. (1995). Cortical maldevelopment, antipsychotic drugs, and schiophrenia: a search for common ground. *Schizophrenia Research, 16*, 87–110.

Weiner, B. (1980). A cognitive (attribution) emotion-action model of motivated behavior: An analysis of judgments of help-giving. *Journal of Personality and Social Psychology, 39*, 186–200.

Weiner, B., & Kukla, A. (1970). An attributional analysis of achievement motivation. *Journal of Personality & Social Psychology, 15*, 1–20.

Weingarten, H. P., Chang, P., & McDonald, T. J. (1985). Comparison of the metabolic and behavioral disturbances following paraventricular- and ventromedial-hypothalamic lesions. *Brain Research Bulletin, 14*, 551–559.

Weinstein, N. D. (1984). Why it won't happen to me: Perceptions of risk factors and susceptibility. *Health Psychology, 3*, 431–457.

Weinstein, N. D. (1993). Optimisitic biases about perosnal risks. *Science, 155*, 1232–1233.

Weinstein, S. (1968). Intensive and extensive aspects of tactile sensitivity as a function of body part, sex, and laterality. In D. R. Kenshalo (Ed.), *The skin senses* (pp. 195–218). Springfield, IL: Thomas.

Weinstock, M. (1997). Does prenatal stress impair coping and regulation of hypothalamic-pituitary-adrenal axis? *Neuroscience & Biobehavioral Reviews, 21*, 1–10.

Weisberg, R. W. (1994). Genius and madness?: A quasi-experimental test of the hypothesis that manic-depression increases creativity. *Psychological Science, 5*, 361–367.

Weisberg, R. W., & Alba, J. W. (1981). An examination of the alleged role of "fixation" in the solution of several "insight" problems. *Journal of Experimental Psychology: General, 110*, 169–192.

Weiskrantz, L. (1986). *Blindsight: A case study and implications.* New York: Oxford University Press.

Weisman, A. D., & Hackett, T. P. (1961). Predilection to death: Death and dying as a psychiatric problem. *Psychosomatic Medicine, 23*, 232–256.

Weiss, R. L., & Heyman, R. E. (1990). Observation of marital interaction. In F. D. Fincham &T. N. Bradbury (Eds.), *The psychology of marriage: Basic issues and applications* (pp. 87–117). New York: Guilford.

Weiss, R. S. (1986). Continuities and transformations in social relationships from childhood to adulthood. In W. W. Hartup and Z. Rubin (Eds.), *Relationships and development* (pp. 95–110). Hillsdale, NJ: Erlbaum.

Weiss, V. (1995) The advent of a molecular genetics of general intelligence. *Intelligence, 20*, 115–124.

Weissman, D. E., Griffie, J., Gordon, D. B., & Dahl, J. L. (1997). A role model program to promote institutional changes for management of acute and cancer pain. *Journal of Pain & Symptom Management, 14*, 274–279.

Weissman, M. M., Bland, R. C., Canino, G. J., Greenwald, S., Hwu, H., Lee, C. K., Newman, S., Oakley-Brown, M. A., Rubio-Stipec, M., Wickramartne, P., Wittchen, H. U., & Yeh, E. K. (1994). The cross national epidemiology of obsessive compulsive disorder: The Cross National Collaborative Group. *Journal of Clinical Psychiatry, 55*(3, Suppl.), 5–10.

Weissman, M. M., Bruce, M. L., Leaf, P. J., Florio, L., & Holzer, C. (1991). Affective disorders. In L. N. Robins & D. A. Regier (Eds.), *Psychiatric disorders in America* (pp. 53–80). New York: The Free Press.

Wellen, J. M., Hogg, M. A., & Terry, D. J. (1998). Group norms and attitude-behavior consistency: The role of group salience and mood. *Group Dynamics: Theory, Research, and Practice, 2*, 48–56.

Wellman, H. M. (1990). *The child's theory of mind.* Cambridge, MA: Bradford/MIT Press.

Wender, P. H., Kety, S. S., Rosenthal, D., Schulsinger, F., Ortmann, J., & Luhde, I. (1986). Psychiatric disorders in the biological and adoptive families of adopted individuals with affective disorders. *Archives of General Psychiatry, 43*, 923–929.

Werner, C., Brown, B., & Altman, I. (1997). Environmental Psychology. In J. W. Berry, M. H. Segall, & C. Kagitçibasi (Eds.), Cross-Cultural Psychology, Volume 3: Social Behavior and Applications. 255–290

Wertheimer, M. (1923). Untersuchungen zur Lehre von der Gestalt, II. (Translated as Laws of organization in perceptual forms.). In W. D. Ellis

(Ed.), *A source book of Gestalt psychology* (pp. 71–88). London: Routledge & Kegan Paul.

Werthemimer, M. (1912/1938). Uber das Denken des Naturvolker. In W. D. Ellis (Trans.), *A source book of Gestalt psychology* (pp. 265–273). New York: Harcourt Brace.

Westen, D. (1998). The scientific legacy of Sigmund Freud. Toward a psychodynamically informed psychological science. *Psychological Bulletin, 124,* 333–371.

Westen, D. (1999). The scientific status of unconscious processes: Is Freud really dead? *Journal of the American Psychoanalytic Association, 47,* Supplement, 1–45.

Westman, M., & Eden, D. (1997). Effects of a Respite From Work on Burnout: Vacation Relief and Fade-Out. *Journal of Applied Psychology, 82,* 516–527.

Whalen, P. J., Rauch, S. L., Etcoff, N. L., McInerney, S. C., Lee, M. B., & Jenike, M. A. (1998). Masked presentations of emotional facial expressions modulate amygdala activity without explicit knowledge. *Journal of Neuroscience, 18,* 411–418.

Wheeler, L., & Kim, Y. (1997). What is beautiful is culturally good: The physical attractiveness stereotype has different content in collectivistic cultures. *Personality and Social Psychology Bulletin, 23,* 795–800.

Wheeler, M. D. (1991). Physical changes of puberty. *Endocrinology and Metabolism Clinics of North America, 20,* 1–14.

White, A., & Hardy, L. (1995). Use of different imagery perspectives on the learning and performance of different motor skills. *British Journal of Psychology, 86*(2), 169–180.

White, J. M., & Ryan, C. F. (1996). Pharmacological properties of ketamine. *Drug & Alcohol Review, 15,* 145–155.

White, S. H. (1965). Evidence for a hierarchical arrangement of learning processes. In L. P. Lipsitt & C. C. Spiker (Eds.), *Advances in child development and behavior, Vol 2* (pp.187–220). New York: Academic Press.

Whitehouse, W. G., Dinges, D. F., Orne, E. C., Keller, S. E., Bates, B. L., Bauer, N. K., Morahan, P., Haupt, B. A., Carlin, M. M., Bloom, P. B., Zaugg, L., & Orne, M. T. (1996). Psychosocial and immune effects of self-hypnosis training for stress management throughout the first semester of medical school. Psychosomatic Medicine, 58, 249–263.

Whiting, J. W. M., Burbank, V. K., & Ratner, M. S. (1986). The duration of maidenhood across cultures. In J. B. Lancaster & B. Hamburg (Eds.), *School-age pregnancy and parenthood: Biosocial dimensions* (pp. 273–302). New York: Aldine De Gruyter.

Whittal, M. L., Agras, W. S., & Gould, R. A. (1999). Bulimia nervosa: A meta-analysis of psychosocial and pharmacological treatments. *Behavior Therapy, 30,* 117–135.

Whorf, B. (1956). *Language, thought, and reality.* Cambridge, MA: MIT Press.

Whyte, G. (1998). Recasting Janis's groupthink model: The key role of collective efficacy in decision fiascoes. *Organizational Behavior & Human Decision Processes, 73,* 185–209.

Wickramasekera, I., Davies, T. E., & Davies, S. M. (1996). Applied psychophysiology: A bridge between the biomedical model and the biopsychosocial model in family medicine. *Professional Psychology: Research & Practice, 27,* 221–233.

Wiebe, D. J., & McCallum, D. M. (1986). Health practices and hardiness as mediators in the stressllness relationship. *Health Psychology, 5,* 425–438.

Wiedemann, G., Pauli, P., Dengler, W., Lutzenberger, W., Birbaumer, N., & Buchkremer, G. (1999). Frontal Brain Asymmetry as a Biological Substrate of Emotions in Patients With Panic Disorders. *Arch Gen Psychiatry, 56,* 78–84.

Wiggins, J. S. (1992). Have model, will travel. *Journal of Personality, 60,* 527–532.

Wiggins, J. S., & Pincus, A. L. (1992). Conceptions of personality disorders and dimensions of personality. *Psychological Assessment: Journal of Consulting and Clinical Psychology, 1,* 305–316.

Wilder, D. A., Simon, A. F., & Faith, M. (1996). Enhancing the impact of counterstereotypic information: Dispositional attributions for deviance. *Journal of Personality and Social Psychology, 71* 276–287.

Wilkins, L. & Richter, C. P. (1940). A great craving for salt by a child with cortico-adrenal insufficiency. *Journal of the American Medical Association, 114,* 866–868.

Wilkinson, D. J. C., Thompson, J. M., Lambert, G. W., Jennings, G. L., Schwarz, R. G., Jefferys, D., Turner, A. G., & Esler, M. D. (1998). Sympathetic Activity in Patients With Panic Disorder at Rest, Under Laboratory Mental Stress, and During Panic Attacks. *Archives of General Psychiatry, 55,* 511–520.

Willer, J. C., Le, B. D., & De, B. T. (1990). Diffuse noxious inhibitory controls in man: Involvement of an opioidergic link. *European Journal of Pharmacology, 182,* 347–355.

Williams, J. E., Paton, C. C., I. C., Eigenbrodt, M. L., Nieto, F. J., & Tyroler, H. A. (2000). Anger proneness predicts coronary heart disease risk:

Prospective analysis from the atherosclerosis risk in communities (ARIC) study. *Circulation, 101,* 2034–2039.

Williams, K. D., & Karau, S. J. (1991). Social loafing and social compensation: The effects of expectations of coworker performance. *Journal of Personality and Social Psychology, 61,* 570–581.

Williams, L. M. (1994). Recall of childhood trauma: A prospective study of women's memories of child sexual abuse. *Journal of Consulting and Clinical Psychology, 62,* 1167–1176.

Williams, R., Barefoot, J., Califf, R., Haney, T., Saunders, E., Pryor, D., Hlatky, M., Siefler, I., & Mark, D. (1992). Prognostic importance of social and economic resources among patients with angiographically documented coronary artery disease. *Journal of the American Medical Association, 267,* 520–?.

Williams, R. B., Barefoot, J. C., Blumenthal, J. A., Helms, M. J., Luecken, L., Pieper, C. F., Siegler, I. C., & Suarez, E. C. (1997). Psychosocial correlates of job strain in a sample of working women. *Archives of General Psychiatry, 54,* 543–548.

Williams, S., & Luthans, F. (1992). The impact of choice of rewards and feedback on task performance. *Journal of Organizational Behavior, 13,* 653–666.

Williams, W. (1998). Are we raising smarter kids today? School-and-home-related influences on IQ. In U. Neisser (Ed.), *The rising curve: Long-terms gains in IQ and related measures* (pp. 125–154). Washington, DC: American Psychological Association.

Wilson, D. K., Kaplan, R. M., Schneiderman, L. (1987). Framing of decisions and selections of alternatives in health care. *J. Social Behaviour, 2,* 51–59.

Wilson, J. Q., & Kelling, G. L. (1982). Broken Windows, *The Atlantic Monthly,* March,*249 (3),* 29–38.

Wilson, T. D., Houston, C. E., Etling, K. M., & Brekke, N. (1996). A new look at anchoring effects: Basic anchoring and its antecedents. *Journal of Experimental Psychology: General, 125,* 387–402.

Wilson, T. L., & Brown, T. L. (1997). Reexamination of the effect of Mozart's music on spatial-task performance. *Journal of Psychology, 131,* 365–370.

Wiltschko, W., Munro, U., Beason, R., Ford, H., & Wiltschko, R. (1994). A magnetic pulse leads to a temporary deflection in the orientation of migratory birds. *Experientia, 50,* 697–700.

Winderickx, J., Battisti, L., Hibiya, Y., Motulsky, A. G., & Deeb, S. S. (1993). Haplotype diversity in the human red and green opsin genes: Evidence for frequent sequence exchange in exon 3. *Human Molecular Genetics, 2,* 1413.

Winderickx, J., Lindsey, D. T., Sanocki, E., Teller, D. Y., Motulsky, A. G., & Deeb, S. S. (1992). Polymorphism in red photopigment underlies variation in colour matching. *Nature, 356,* 431–433.

Winer, G. A., & Cottrell, J. E. (1996). Does anything leave the eye when we see? Extramission beliefs of children and adults. *Current Directions in Psychological Science, 5,* 137–142.

Winer, G. A., Cottrell, J. E., Karefilaki, K. D., & Gregg, V. R. (1996). Images, words and questions: Variables that influence beliefs about vision in children and adults. *Journal of Experimental Child Psychology, 63,* 499–525.

Winick, C., & Evans, J. T. (1996). The relationship between nonenforcement of state pornography laws and rates of sex crime arrests. *Archives of Sexual Behavior, 25,* 439–453.

Winner, E. (1996). *Gifted children: Myths and realities.* New York: Basic Books.

Winner, E. (1997). Exceptionally high intelligence and schooling. *American Psychologist, 52,* 1070–1081.

Winner, E. (2000). The origins and ends of giftedness. *American Psychologist, 55,* 159–169.

Winter, A. (1998). *Mesmerized: Powers of mind in victorian Britain.* Chicago: University of Chicago Press.

Winzelberg, A. (1997). The analysis of an electronic support group for individuals with eating disorders. *Computers in Human Behavior, 13,* 393–407.

Winzelberg, A., & Humphreys, K. (1999). Should patients' religiosity influence clinicians' referral to 12-step self-help groups? Evidence from a study of 3,018 male substance abuse patients. *Journal of Consulting and Clinical Psychology,67,* 790–794.

Wise, P. M., Krajnak, K. M., & Kashon, M. L. (1996). Menopause: The aging of multiple pacemakers. *Science, 273,* 67–70.

Wise, R. A. (1982). Neuroleptics and operant behavior: The anhedonia hypothesis. *Behavioral & Brain Sciences, 5,* 39–87.

Wise, R. A. (1996). Addictive drugs and brain stimulation reward. *Annual Review of Neuroscience, 19,* 319–340.

Wisniewski, H. M., & Terry, R. D. (1976). Neuropathology of the aging brain. In R. D. Terry & S. Gershod (Eds.), *Neurobiology of aging* (pp. 65–78). New York: Raven.

Witelson, S. F., Kigar, D. L., & Harvey, T. (1999). The exceptional brain of Albert Einstein. *Lancet, 353,* 2149–2153.

Witt, S. D. (1997). Parental influence on children's socialization to gender roles. *Adolescence, 32,* 253–259.

Wixted, J. T., & Ebbesen, E. B. (1991). On the form of forgetting. *Psychological Science, 2,* 409–415.

Wixted, J. T., & Ebbesen, E. B. (1997). Genuine power curves in forgetting: A quantitative analysis of individual subject forgetting functions. *Memory & Cognition, 25,* 731–739.

Wojciulik, E., Kanwisher, N., & Driver, J. (1998). Covert visual attention modulates face-specific activity in the human fusiform gyrus: An fMRI study. *Journal of Neurophysiology, 79,* 1574–1578.

Wolf, A., & Thatcher, R. (1990). Cortical reorganization in deaf children. *Journal of Clinical and Experimental Neuropsychology, 12,* 209–221.

Wolf, N. (1991). *The Beauty Myth.* New York: Anchor Books, Doubleday.

Wolfe, B. E., & Maser, J. D. (Eds.). (1994). *Treatment of panic disorder: A consensus development conference.* Washington, DC: American Psychiatric Press, Inc.

Wolff, C., Friedman, S., Hofer, M., & Mason, J. (1964). Relationships between psychological defenses and mean urinary 17-hydroxycorticosteroid excretion rates. I. A predictive study of parents of fatally ill children. *Psychosomatic Medicine, 26,* 576.

Wolpe, J. (1958). *Psychotherapy by reciprocal inhibition.* Stanford: Stanford University Press.

Wolpe, J. (1973). *The practice of behavior therapy* (2nd ed.). New York: Pergamon.

Wolpe, J. (1982). *The practice of behavior therapy.* New York: Pergamon.

Wolpe, J. (1997). Thirty years of behavior therapy. *Behavior Therapy, 28,* 633–635.

Wolpe, J., & Rachman, S. (1960). Psychoanalytic evidence: A critique of Freud's case of little Hans. *Journal of Nervous and Mental Diseases, 130,* 198–220.

Wood, P. (1963). Dreaming and social isolation. *Dissertation Abstracts, Vol. 23,* 4749–4750.(9609).

Woods, S. C., Schwartz, M. W., Baskin, D. G., & Seeley, R. J. (2000). Food intake and the regulation of body weight. *Annual Review of Psychology, 51,* 255–277.

Woodward, A. L. (1998). Infants selectively encode the goal object of an actor's reach. *Cognition, 69,* 1–34.

World Health Organization. (1948). *Charter.* Geneva, Switzerland: United Nations.

Worthington, T. S. (1979). The use in court of hypnotically enhanced testimony. *International Journal of Clinical & Experimental Hypnosis, 27,* 402–416.

Wright, R. (1998, August 24). Viewpoint: The power of their peers. *Time,* 67.

Wu, J., Kramer, G. L., Kram, M., Steciuk, M., Crawford, I. L., & Petty, F. (1999). Serotonin and learned helplessness: A regional study of 5-HT-sub(1A), 5-HT-sub(2A) receptors and the serotonin transport site in rat brain. *Journal of Psychiatric Research, 33,* 17–22.

Wurtzel, E. (1995). *Prozac Nation: A Memoir.* New York: Riverhead Books.

Wyatt, R. J., Damiani, L. M., & Henter, I. D. (1998). First-episode schizophrenia: Early intervention and medication discontinuation in the context of course and treatment. *British Journal of Psychiatry, 172,* 77–83.

Wyatt, R. J., Green, M. F., & Tuma, A. H. (1997). Long-term morbidity associated with delayed treatment of first admission schizophrenic patients: A re-analysis of the Camarillo state hospital data. *Psychological Medicine, 27,* 261–268.

Wyer, N. A., Sherman, J. W., & Stroessner, S. J. (2000). The roles of motivation and ability in controlling the consequences of stereotype suppression. *Personality & Social Psychology Bulletin, 26,* 13–25.

Xerri, C., Merzenich, M. M., Jenkins, W., & Santucci, S. (1999). Representational plasticity in cortical area 3b paralleling tactual motor skill acquisition in adult monkeys. *Cerebral Cortex, 9,* 264–276.

Yagueez, L., Nagel, D., Hoffman, H., Canavan, A., Wist, E., & Hoemberg, V. (1998). A mental route to motor learning: Improving trajectoral kinematics through imagery training. *Behavioral and Brain Research, 90,* 95–106.

Yamadori, A. (1997). Body awareness and its disorders. In M. Ito & Y. Miyashita (Eds.), *Cognition, computation, and consciousness* (pp. 169–176). Oxford, England: Oxford University Press.

Yang, K., & Bond, M. H. (1990). Exploring implicit personliaty theories with indigenous or imported constructs: The Chinese case. *Journal of Personality and Social Psychology, 58,* 1087–1095.

Yates, A. (1996). Eating disorders in women athletes. *Eating Disorders Review, 7(4),* p. 1.

Yazigi, R. A., Odem, R. R., & Polakoski, K. L. (1991). Demonstration of specific binding of cocaine to human spermatozoa. *Journal of the American Medical Association, 266,* 1956–1959.

Yehuda, R., McFarlane, A. C., & Shalev, A. Y. (1998). Predicting the development of posttraumatic stress disorder from the acute response to a traumatic event. *Biological Psychiatry, 44,* 1305–1313.

Yeomans, M. R., & Gray, R. W. (1997). Effects of naltrexone on food intake and changes in subjective appetite during eating: evidence for opioid involvement in the appetizer effect. *Physiology & Behavior, 62,* 15–21.

Yeshurun, Y., & Carrasco, M. (1998). Attention improves or impairs visual performance by enhancing spatial resolution. *Nature, 396,* 72–75.

Yeshurun, Y., & Carrasco, M. (1999). Spatial attention improves performance in spatial resolution tasks. *Vision Research, 39,* 293–306.

Yin, J. C. P., Del Vecchio, M., Zhou, H., & Tully, T. (1995). CREB as a memory modulator: Induced expression of a dCREB2 activator isoform enhances long-term memory in Drosophila. *Cell, 81,* 107–115.

Yokosuka, M., Xu, B., Pu, S., Kalra, P. S., & Kalra, S. P. (1998). Neural substrates for leptin and neuropeptide Y (NPY) interaction: Hypothalamic sites associated with inhibition of NPY-induced food intake. *Physiology & Behavior, 64,* 331–338.

Yost, W. A., & Dye, R. H. (1991). Properties of sound localization by humans. In R. A. Altschuler, R. P. Bobbin, B. M. Clopton, & D. W. Hoffman (Eds.), *Neurobiology of hearing: The central auditory system* (pp. 389–410). New York: Raven.

Young, A. W., Hellawell, D. J., Van De Wal, C., & Johnson, M. (1996). Facial expression processing after amygdalotomy. *Neuropsychologia, 34,* 31–39.

Young, F. A. (1981). Primate myopia. *American Journal of Optometry and Physiological Optics, 58,* 560–566.

Zaccaro, S. J., Foti, R. J., & Kenny, D. A. (1991). Self-monitoring and trait-based variance in leadership: An investigation of leader flexibility across multiple group situations. *Journal of Applied Psychology, 76,* 308–315.

Zaharia, M. D., Kulczycki, J., Shanks, N., Meaney, M. J., & Anisman, H. (1996). The effects of early postnatal stimulation on Morris water-maze acquisition in adult mice: Genetic and maternal factors. *Psychopharmacology, 128,* 227–239.

Zajonc, R. (1970). Brainwash: Familiarity breeds comfort. *Psychology Today, 3,* 32–35, 60–64.

Zajonc, R. B. (1968). Attitudinal effects of mere exposure. *Journal of Personality & Social Psychology, 9(2, Pt. 2),* 1–27.

Zakowski, S., Hall, M. H., & Baum, A. (1992). Stress, stress management, and the immune system. *Applied and Preventative Psychology, 1,* 1–13.

Zane, N. W. S., Sue, S., Hu, L., & Kwon, J. H. (1991). Asian-American assertion: A social learning anyalysis of cultural differences. *Journal of Counseling Psychology, 38,* 63–70.

Zatorre, R. J., & Halpern, A. R. (1993). Effect of unilateral temporal-lobe excision on perception and imagery of songs. *Neuropsychologia, 31,* 221–232.

Zebrowitz, L. A., Andreoletti, C., Collins, M. A., Lee, S. Y., & Blumenthal, J. (1998). Bright, bad, babyfaced boys: Appearance stereotypes do not always yield self-fulfilling prophecy effects. *Journal of Personality & Social Psychology, 75,* 1300–1320.

Zeki, S. M. (1978). Functional specialisation in the visual cortex of the rhesus monkey. *Nature, 274,* 423–428.

Zeki, S. M. (1993). *Vision of the brain.* London: Blackwell.

Zelazo, P. R., Zelazo, N. A., & Kolb, S. (1972). "Walking" in the newborn. *Science, 177,* 1058–1059.

Zenger, T. R., & Lawrence, B. S. (1989). Organizational demography: The differential effect of age and tenure distributions on technical communication. *Academy of Management Journal, 32,* 353–376.

Zentner, M. R., & Kagan, J. (1996). Perception of music by infants. *Nature, 383,* 29.

Zentner, M. R., & Kagan, J. (1998). Infants' perception of consonance and dissonance in music. *Infant Behavior & Development, 21,* 483–492.

Zhdanova, I., & Wurtman, R. (June, 1996). "How does Melatonin affect sleep? Harvard Mental Health Newsletter, p. 8

Zhou, J-N., Hofman, M. A., Gooren, L. J. G., & Swaab, D. F. (1995). A sex difference in the human brain and its relation to transsexuality. *Nature, 378,* 68–70.

Zhou, J., Oldham, G. R., & Cummings, A. (1998). Employee reactions to the physical work environment: The role of childhood residential attributes. *Journal of Applied Social Psychology, 28,* 2213–2238.

Zhukov, D. A., & Vinogradova, E. P. (1998). Agonistic behavior during stress prevents the development of learned helplessness in rats. *Neuroscience & Behavioral Physiology, 28,* 206–210.

Zihl, J., von Cramon, D., & Mai, N. (1983). Selective disturbance of movement vision after bilateral brain damage. *Brain, 106,* 313–340.

Zimmer, E. Z., Fifter, W. P., Young-Ihl, K., Rey, H. R., Chao, C. R., & Myers, M. M. (1993). Response of the premature fetus to stimulation by speech sounds. *Early Human Development, 33,* 207–215.

Zimmerman, M. A., Salem, D. A., & Maton, K. I. (1995). Family structure and psychosocial correlates among urban African-American adolescent males. *Child Development, 66*, 1598–1613.

Zlotnick, C. (1999). Antisocial personality disorder, affect dysregulation and childhood abuse among incarcerated women. *Journal of Personality Disorders, 13*, 90–95.

Zoccolillo, M., Price, R., Ji, T., & Hwu, H. (1999). Antisocial personality disorder: Comparisons of prevalence, symptoms, and correlates in four countries. In P. Cohen, C. Slomkowski et al. (Eds.). *Historical and geographical influences on psychopathology.* (pp. 249–277). Mahwah, NJ: Erlbaum.

Zola-Morgan, S., Squire, L. R., & Amaral, D. G. (1986). Human amnesia and the medial temporal region: Enduring memory impairment following a bilateral lesion limited to field CA1 of the hippocampus. *Journal of Neuroscience, 6*, 2950–2967.

Zornberg, G. L., Buka, S. L., & Tsuang, M. T. (2000). Hypoxic-ischemia-related fetal/neonatal complications and risk of schizophrenia and other nonaffective psychoses: A 19-year longitudinal study. *American Journal of Psychiatry 157*, 196–202.

Zuckerman, M. (1979). *Sensation seeking: Beyond the optimal level of arousal.* Hillsdale, NJ: Erlbaum.

Zuckerman, M. (1991). *Psychobiology of Personality.* Cambridge: Cambridge University Press.

Zuckerman, M. (1995). Good and bad humors: Biochemical bases of personality and its disorders. *Psychological Science, 6*, 325–332.

Zuckerman, M., DePaulo, B. M., & Rosenthal, R. (1981). Verbal and nonverbal communication of deception. In L. Berkowitz (Ed.), *Advances in experimental social psychology* (Vol. 14) (pp. 1–59). New York: Academic Press.

Zuckerman, M., Kuhlman, D. M., & Camac, C. (1988). What lies beyond E and N? Factor analyses of scales believed to measure basic dimensions of personality. *Journal of Personality and Social Psychology, 54*, 96–107.

Zurek, P. M. (1981). Spontaneous narrowband acoustic signal emitted by human ears. *Journal of Acoustical Society of America, 69*, 514–523.

Zurek, P. M. (1985). Acoustic emissions from the ear: A summary of results from humans and animals. *Journal of the Acoustical Society of America, 78*, 340–344.

Zurif, E. B., Caramazza, A., & Myerson, R. (1972). Grammatical judgments of agrammatic aphasics. *Neuropsychologia, 10*, 405–417.

Zwicker, E., & Schloth, E. (1984). Interrelation of different oto-acoustic emissions. *Journal of Acoustical Society of America, 75*, 1148–1154.

GLOSSARY

Absolute pitch: The ability to identify a particular note by itself, not simply in relation to other notes.

Absolute threshold: The smallest amount of a stimulus needed in order to detect that the stimulus is present.

Absorption: The capacity to concentrate totally on external material.

Academic psychologist: The type of psychologist who focuses on conducting research and teaching.

Accommodation: In Piaget's theory, the process that results in schemas' changing as necessary to cope with a broader range of situations. The automatic adjustment of the eye that occurs when muscles change the shape of the lens so that it focuses light on the retina from objects at different distances.

Acquisition: The technical name given to the initial learning of the conditioned response (CR).

Action potential: A shifting change in charge that moves down the axon to the end, causing the terminal buttons to release a chemical signal.

Activation-synthesis hypothesis: The theory that dreams arise from random bursts of nerve cell activity, which may affect brain cells involved in hearing and seeing; the brain attempts to make sense of this hodgepodge of stimuli, resulting in the experience of dreams.

Active interaction: Occurs when people choose, partly based on genetic tendencies, to put themselves in specific situations and to avoid others.

Activity: A temperament characterized by the general expenditure of energy; activity has two components—vigor (intensity of the activities) and tempo (speed of the activities).

Actor–observer effect: A person's inclination to attribute his or her own behavior to external factors but to attribute others' behavior to internal factors.

Acute stressor: A stressor of short-term duration.

Adaptation: A characteristic that increases "fitness" for an environment.

Adolescence: The period between the onset of puberty and, roughly, the end of the teenage years.

Adoption study: Study of related or unrelated children who were separated at or near birth and raised in the same versus different households.

Affirming the consequent: A reasoning error that occurs because of the assumption that if a result is present, a specific cause must also be present.

Afterimage: The image left behind by a previous perception.

Aggression: Behavior directed toward harming another living being who is motivated to avoid such treatment.

Agonist: A chemical that mimics the effects of a neurotransmitter (sometimes by preventing reuptake).

Agoraphobia: A condition in which people fear or avoid places that might be difficult to leave should a panic attack occur.

Alarm phase: The first phase of the GAS, in which a stressor is perceived and a fight-or-flight response is activated.

Alcohol myopia: Impaired ability, when drinking, to process information and perceive situational cues.

Algorithm: A set of steps that, if followed methodically, will guarantee the solution to a problem.

All-or-none law: States that if the neuron is sufficiently stimulated, it fires, sending the action potential all the way down the axon and releasing chemicals from the terminal buttons; either the action potential occurs or it doesn't.

Altered state of consciousness (ASC): State of awareness that is other than the normal waking state.

Altruism: The motivation to increase another person's welfare.

Amnesia: A loss of memory over an entire time span resulting from brain damage from an accident, infection, or stroke.

Amphetamines: Synthetic stimulants.

Amplitude: In vision and audition, the height of light or pressure waves, registered as lightness (or brightness, if the object emits light) or volume, respectively.

Amygdala: A subcortical structure that plays a special role in fear and is involved in other sorts of emotions, such as anger.

Androgens: Male hormones, which cause many male characteristics such as beard growth and a low voice.

Anorexia nervosa: An eating disorder characterized by the refusal to maintain even a low normal weight and an intense fear of gaining weight.

Antagonist: A chemical that blocks the effect of a neurotransmitter (sometimes by blocking a receptor or enhancing the reuptake mechanism).

Anterograde amnesia: Amnesia that leaves consolidated memories intact but prevents new learning.

Antipsychotic medication: Medication that reduces psychotic symptoms.

Antisocial personality disorder: A long-standing pattern of disregard for others to the point of violating other people's rights.

Anxiety disorder: A disorder whose hallmark is intense and pervasive anxiety and fear, or extreme attempts to avoid these feelings.

Aphasia: A disruption of language caused by brain damage.

Applied psychologist: The type of psychologist who studies how to improve products and procedures and conducts research to help solve specific practical problems.

Approach–approach conflict: The internal predicament that occurs when competing alternatives are equally positive.

Approach–avoidance conflict: The internal predicament that occurs when a course of action has both positive and negative aspects.

Archetype: A Jungian concept of symbols that represent basic aspects of the world.

Artificial intelligence (AI): The field devoted to building smart machines.

Assimilation: In Piaget's theory, the process that allows use of existing schemas to take in new sets of stimuli and respond accordingly.

Associative priming: Priming that makes related information more easily accessed in the future.

Atherosclerosis: A medical condition characterized by plaque buildup in the arteries.

Attachment: An emotional bond that leads us to want to be with someone and to miss him or her when we are separated.

Attention: The act of focusing on particular information, which allows it to be processed more fully than what is not attended to.

Attentional blink: A rebound period in which a person cannot pay attention to one thing after having just paid attention to another.

Attitude: An overall evaluation about some aspect of the world.

Attribution: An explanation for the cause of an event or behavior.

Attributional bias: A cognitive shortcut for determining attribution that generally occurs outside our awareness.

Attributional style: A person's characteristic way of explaining life events.

Autism: A condition of intense self-involvement to the exclusion of external reality; about three quarters of autistic people are mentally retarded.

Autonomic nervous system (ANS): Controls the smooth muscles in the body, some glandular functions, and many of the body's "self-regulating" activities such as digestion and circulation.

Availability heuristic: The heuristic that the easier events or objects are to bring to mind, the more likely, common, or frequent they are judged to be.

Avoidance–avoidance conflict: The internal predicament that occurs when competing alternatives are equally unpleasant.

Avoidance learning: In classical conditioning, learning that occurs when a CS is paired with an unpleasant UCS that leads the organism to try to avoid the CS. In operant conditioning, the process by which an organism learns to avoid an unpleasant consequence by emitting a particular response.

Axon: The sending end of the neuron, or the long cable extending from the cell body, which affects other neurons.

Basal ganglia: Subcortical structures that play a role in planning and producing movement.

Base-rate rule: The rule stating that if something is sampled at random, the chances of obtaining a particular type are directly proportional to its percentage in the set from which the sample is taken.

Basic emotion: An innate emotion that is shared by all humans, such as surprise, happiness, anger, fear, disgust, and sadness.

Basic level: A level of specificity, which is usually the most likely to be applied to an object.

B cell: A type of white blood cell that matures in the bone marrow.

Behavior: The outwardly observable acts of an individual, alone or in a group.

Behavioral genetics: The field in which researchers attempt to determine how much of the differences among people are due to their genes and how much to the environment.

Behaviorism: The school of psychology that focuses on how a specific stimulus (object, person, or event) evokes a specific response (behavior in reaction to the stimulus).

Behavior modification: A category of therapeutic techniques for changing behavior based on operant conditioning principles. A technique that brings about therapeutic change in behavior through the use of secondary reinforcers.

Behavior therapy: A type of therapy, based on well-researched principles of learning, that focuses on observable, measurable behaviors.

Belief in a just world: An attributional bias that assumes people get what they deserve.

Benzodiazepine: A type of antianxiety medication that affects the target symptoms within 36 hours and does not need to be taken for more than a week to be effective.

Bereavement: The experience of missing a loved one and longing for his or her company.

Bias: In signal detection theory, a person's willingness to report noticing a stimulus. Occurs when previous beliefs, expectations, or habits alter the participants' responses or affect the design or conduct of a study.

Bibliotherapy: The use of self-help books and tapes for therapeutic purposes.

"Big Five": Five superfactors of personality—extraversion, neuroticism, agreeableness, conscientiousness, and openness—determined by factor analysis.

Binaural cues: Differences in the stimuli reaching the two ears that are used to localize the sources of sounds.

Binocular cues: Cues to the distance of an object that arise from both eyes working together.

Binocular disparity: The difference between the images striking the retinas of the two eyes.

Biological preparedness: A built-in readiness for certain conditioned stimuli to elicit certain conditioned responses so that less learning is necessary to produce conditioning.

Bipolar disorder: A mood disorder marked by one or more episodes of either mania or hypomania.

Bisexual: A person who is sexually attracted to members of both sexes.

Blackout: Loss of memory for events that transpired while intoxicated.

Bottom-up processing: Processing that is initiated by stimulus input.

Brain circuit: A set of neurons that affect one another.

Brainstem: The set of neural structures at the base of the brain, including the medulla and pons.

Breadth of processing: Processing that organizes and integrates information into previously stored information, often by making associations.

Brightness and color constancy: Seeing objects as having the same lightness, brightness, or color in different viewing situations.

Broca's aphasia: Problems with producing language following brain damage (typically to the left frontal lobe).

Bulimia nervosa: An eating disorder characterized by recurrent episodes of binge eating, followed by some attempt to prevent weight gain.

Burnout: A work-related state characterized by chronic stress, accompanied by physical and mental exhaustion and a sense of low accomplishment.

Bystander effect: The decrease in offers of assistance that occurs as the number of bystanders increases.

Case study: A scientific study that examines a single instance of a situation in detail.

Castration anxiety: A boy's anxiety-laden fear that, as punishment for loving mother and hating father, his father will cut off his penis (the primary zone of pleasure).

Categorical perception: Identifying sounds as belonging to distinct categories that correspond to the basic units of speech.

Categorical variables: Variables whose values are assigned to discrete classes.

Cell body: The middle part of a cell, which contains the nucleus.

Cell membrane: The skin of a cell.

Central executive: The set of processes that operates on information in one or another STM; part of working memory.

Central nervous system (CNS): The spinal cord and the brain.

Central tendency: A descriptive statistic that indicates the clustering of the most characteristic values, or scores, for a particular group or sample.

Cerebellum: A large structure at the base of the brain that is concerned in part with physical coordination, estimating time, and paying attention.

Cerebral cortex: The convoluted pinkish-gray surface of the brain, where most mental processes take place.

Cerebral hemisphere: A left or right half-brain, roughly half a sphere.

Channels: Sets of neurons in the visual system that pick up shape variations at different levels of resolution. Small holes in the outer skin of cells that can open and close.

Chemical senses: Taste and smell, which rely on sensing the presence of specific chemicals.

Child-directed speech (CDS): Speech to babies that relies on short sentences with clear pauses, careful enunciation, exaggerated intonation, and a high-pitched voice; also known as *motherese*.

Chronic stressor: A stressor of long-term duration.

Chunk: A unit of information, such as a digit, letter, or word.

Circadian rhythms: The body's daily physiological fluctuations in response to the dark and light cycle, which affects blood pressure, pulse rate, body temperature, blood sugar level, hormone levels, and metabolism.

Classical conditioning: A type of learning that occurs when a neutral stimulus becomes paired (associated) with a stimulus that causes a reflexive behavior and, in time, is sufficient to produce that behavior.

Client-centered therapy: A type of insight-oriented therapy that focuses on people's potential for growth and the importance of an empathic therapist. Therapy developed by Rogers that focuses on the client's potential for growth and the therapist's role as provider of unconditional support.

Clinical psychologist: The type of psychologist who provides psychotherapy and is trained to administer and interpret psychological tests.

Cocktail party phenomenon: The effect of not being aware of other people's conversations until your name is mentioned, and then suddenly hearing it.

Code: A mental representation; an internal "re-presentation" of a stimulus or event.

Cognitive dissonance: The uncomfortable state that arises because of a discrepancy between an attitude and behavior or between two attitudes.

Cognitive distortion: Irrational thoughts that arise from a systematic bias in the way a person thinks about reality.

Cognitive engineering: The field devoted to using theories of human information processing to guide the design of products and devices.

Cognitive learning: The acquisition of information that often is not immediately acted on but is stored for later use.

Cognitive neuroscience: A blending of cognitive psychology and neuroscience (the study of the brain) that aims to specify how the brain stores and processes information.

Cognitive psychology: The approach in psychology that attempts to characterize how information is stored and operated on internally.

Cognitive restructuring: The process of helping clients shift their thinking away from the focus on automatic, dysfunctional thoughts to more realistic ones.

Cognitive therapy: Therapy that focuses on the client's thoughts rather than his or her feelings or behaviors.

Cohort: A group of people who were born at about the same time and thus move through life together and share many experiences.

Collectivist culture: A culture that emphasizes the rights and responsibilities of the group over those of the individual.

Color blindness: An inability, either acquired (by brain damage) or inherited, to perceive hue.

Common factor: A curative factor of therapy common to all types of treatment.

Compassionate love: A type of love marked by very close friendship, mutual caring, liking, respect, and attraction.

Complex inheritance: The transmission of characteristics that depends on joint actions of genes working together; in general, when a characteristic varies continuously, it reflects complex inheritance.

Compliance: A change in behavior prompted by a direct request rather than social norms.

Compulsion: A repetitive behavior or mental act that an individual feels compelled to perform in response to an obsession.

Computer-assisted tomography (CT, formerly CAT): A neuroimaging technique that produces a three-dimensional image of brain structure using X rays.

Concentrative meditation: A form of meditation in which the meditator restricts attention and concentrates on one stimulus while disregarding everything else.

Concept: An unambiguous, sometimes abstract, internal representation that defines a grouping of a set of objects (including living things) or events (including relationships).

Concrete operation: In Piaget's theory, a (reversible) manipulation of the mental representation of perceived events and actions that corresponds to the actual physical manipulation.

Conditioned emotional response (CER): An emotional response elicited by a previously neutral stimulus.

Conditioned response (CR): A response that depends, or is conditional, on pairings of the conditioned stimulus with an unconditioned stimulus; the conditioned response occurs in response to the CS alone.

Conditioned stimulus (CS): An originally neutral stimulus that acquires significance through the "conditioning" of repeated pairings with an unconditioned stimulus (UCS).

Conduction deafness: Deafness caused by a physical impairment of the external or middle ear.

Cones: Retinal cells that respond most strongly to one of three wavelengths and that play a key role in producing color vision.

Confidence interval: The range within which the mean of the population is likely to occur.

Confirmation bias: A tendency to seek information that will confirm a rule, and not to seek information that is inconsistent with the rule.

Conflict: The emotional predicament experienced when making difficult choices.

Conformity: A change of beliefs or actions in order to follow a group's norms.

Confound (or **confounding variable**): Independent variable that varies along with the one of interest and could affect what is measured.

Consciousness: A person's awareness of his or her own existence, sensations, and cognitions.

Conservation: The principle that certain properties of objects remain the same even when their appearance changes, provided that nothing is added or removed.

Consolidation: The process of converting information stored dynamically in long-term memory into a structural change in the brain.

Continuous reinforcement: Reinforcement given for each desired response.

Continuous variables: Variables whose values can fall anywhere along the measurement scale.

Contrapreparedness: A built-in disinclination (or even an inability) for certain conditioned stimuli to elicit particular conditioned responses.

Control condition: Like a control group, but administered to the same participants who receive the experimental condition.

Control group: A group that is treated exactly the same way as the experimental group, except for the one aspect of the situation under study—the independent variable—and so holds constant, or controls, all of the other variables.

Convergent thinking: Thinking that involves focusing on a particular approach and following a series of steps to converge on a solution.

Coping: Taking a course of action regarding the stressor, its effects, or the person's reaction to it.

Cornea: The transparent covering over the eye, which serves partly to focus the light onto the back of the eye.

Corpus callosum: The huge band of nerve fibers that connects the two halves of the brain.

Correlation: An index of how closely interrelated two measured variables are; the higher the correlation, the better the values of one variable predict the values of the other.

Cortisol: A hormone produced by the outer layer of the adrenal glands that helps the body cope with the extra energy demands of stress by breaking down and converting protein and fat to sugar.

Counseling psychologist: The type of psychologist who is trained to help people with issues that naturally arise during the course of life.

Countertransference: The therapist's own response to the patient, stemming from the therapist's own transference-related issues.

Crack: Cocaine in crystalline form, usually smoked in a pipe (free-basing) or rolled into a cigarette.

Creativity: The ability to produce something original of high quality or to devise effective new ways of solving a problem.

Critical period: A narrow window of time when certain types of learning are possible.

Cross-sectional study: A study in which different groups of people are tested, with each group at a different age.

Crystallized intelligence: According to Cattell and Horn, the kind of intelligence that relies on knowing facts and having the ability to use and combine them.

Cues: Stimuli that trigger or enhance remembering; reminders.

Curative factor: A therapy-related factor that helps make clients better.

Cybertherapy: Therapy over the Internet.

Dark adaptation: The process whereby exposure to darkness causes the eyes to become more sensitive, allowing for better vision in the dark.

Data: Careful observations or numerical measurements.

Debriefing: An interview after a study to ensure that the participant has no negative reactions as a result of participation and understands why the study was conducted.

Decay: The fading away of memories with time because the relevant connections between neurons are lost.

Deductive reasoning: Reasoning that applies the rules of logic to a set of assumptions (stated as premises) to discover whether certain conclusions follow from those assumptions; deduction goes from the general to the particular.

Defense mechanism: An unconscious psychological means by which a person tries to prevent unacceptable, id-based thoughts or urges from reaching conscious awareness.

Deindividuation: The loss of sense of self that occurs when people are in a group but are anonymous.

Delayed reinforcement: Reinforcement given some period of time after the desired behavior is exhibited.

Deliberate practice: Practice that is motivated by the goal of improving performance, usually by targeting specific areas of weakness and working to improve them.

Delusions: Entrenched false beliefs that are often bizarre.

Dendrite: A twiggy part of a neuron that receives messages from the axons of other neurons.

Deoxyribonucleic acid, or DNA: The molecule that contains genes.

Dependent variable: The aspect of the experimental situation that is measured as an independent variable is changed; the value of the dependent variable *depends on* the value of the independent variable.

Depressant: Class of substances, including barbiturates, alcohol, opiates, and antianxiety drugs, that depress the central nervous system, decreasing the user's behavioral activity and level of awareness; also called *sedative-hypnotic drugs*.

Deprived reward: Reward that occurs when a biological need is filled.

Depth of processing: The number and complexity of the operations involved in processing information, expressed in a continuum from shallow to deep.

Descriptive statistics: A concise way of summarizing properties of sets of numbers.

Diathesis–stress model: A predisposition to a given disorder (diathesis) and specific factors (stress) that combine with the diathesis to trigger the onset of the disorder.

Difference threshold: The difference needed to notice a stimulus change half the time.

Diffusion of responsibility: The diminished sense of responsibility to help that each person feels as the number of bystanders grows.

Discrimination: The ability to distinguish between the desired response and a similar but undesirable one.

Discriminative stimulus: The cue that tells the organism whether a specific response will lead to the expected reinforcement.

Disinhibition: Occurs when depressants cause the inhibition of inhibitory neurons, which make other neurons (the ones that are usually inhibited) more likely to fire.

Display rule: A culture-specific rule that indicates when, to whom, and how strongly certain emotions can be shown.

Dissociation: The sense of being split off from the normal level of awareness.

Dissociative amnesia: An inability to remember important personal information, often experienced as memory "gaps."

Dissociative disorder: A disorder marked by a disruption in the usually integrated functions of consciousness, memory, or identity.

Dissociative fugue: An abrupt, unexpected departure from home or work, combined with an inability to remember some or all of the past.

Dissociative identity disorder (DID): A disorder in which a person has two or more distinct personalities that take control of the individual's behavior.

Distributed practice: Studying in small chunks of time, spread out over time.

Divergent thinking: Thinking that involves taking different perspectives on a problem and exploring different approaches to a solution.

Dizygotic: From different eggs and sharing only as many genes as any pair of brothers or sisters—on average, half.

Door-in-the-face technique: A compliance technique in which someone makes a very large request; when it is denied, as expected, a second, smaller request (the desired one) is made.

Double blind design: An experimental procedure in which the participant is "blind" to (unaware of) the predictions of the study (and so cannot try, consciously or unconsciously, to produce the predicted results), and the experimenter is "blind" to the condition assigned to the participant (and so cannot induce the predicted results).

Double pain: The sensation that occurs when an injury first causes a sharp pain, and later a dull pain; the two kinds of pain arise from different fibers sending their messages at different speeds.

Down syndrome: A type of retardation that results from the creation of an extra chromosome during conception; it is genetic but not inherited.

Dream analysis: A technique used in psychoanalysis and psychodynamic therapies in which the therapist examines the content of dreams to gain access to the unconscious.

Drive: A motivation that pushes an animal to reach toward a particular goal.

Dysthymia: A mood disorder similar to major depressive disorder, but less intense and longer lasting.

Eating disorder: A disorder involving a severe disturbance in eating behavior.

Effect: The difference in the dependent variable that is due to changes in the independent variable.

Efficacy expectancy: The sense of being able to follow through and produce the behaviors one would like to perform.

Ego: A Freudian psychic structure, developed in childhood, that tries to balance the competing demands of the id, superego, and reality.

Egocentrism: In Piaget's theory, the inability to take another person's point of view.

Elaborative encoding: Encoding that involves great breadth of processing.

Electroconvulsive therapy (ECT): A controlled brain seizure, used to treat people with certain psychological disorders such as psychotic depression or those for whom medication has not been effective or recommended.

Electroencephalogram: A recording from the scalp of electrical activity over time, which produces a tracing of pulses at different frequencies.

Electroencephalograph (EEG): A machine that records electrical current produced by the brain.

Emotion: A positive or negative reaction to a perceived or remembered object, event, or circumstance, accompanied by a subjective feeling.

Emotional intelligence (EI): The ability to understand and regulate emotions effectively.

Emotionality: A temperament characterized by an inclination to become physiologically aroused in situations in which the predominant emotions are distress, fear, and anger.

Emotion-focused coping: Coping focused on changing the person's emotional response to the stressor.

Empiricism (approach to language): The approach that views language as entirely the result of learning.

Empty chair technique: A Gestalt therapy technique in which the client imagines talking to a particular person (parent, friend) who is "sitting" in an empty chair in the room.

Enacted social support: The specific supportive behaviors provided by others.

Encoding: The process of organizing and transforming incoming information so that it can be entered into memory, to be either stored or compared to previously stored information.

Encoding failure: A failure to process to-be-remembered information well enough to begin consolidation.

Endorphins: Painkilling chemicals produced naturally in the brain.

Episodic memories: Memories of events that are associated with a particular context—a time, place, and circumstance.

Estrogen: The female hormone that causes many female characteristics, such as breast development and the bone structure of the female pelvis, and is involved in the menstrual cycle.

Evocative (or reactive) interaction: Occurs when genetically influenced characteristics draw out behaviors from other people.

Evolution: Gene-based changes in the characteristics of members of a species over successive generations.

Evolutionary psychology: The approach in psychology that assumes that certain cognitive strategies and goals are so important that natural selection has built them into our brains.

Exhaustion phase: The final stage of the GAS, in which the continued stress response itself becomes damaging to the body.

Expectancies: Expectations that have a powerful influence on behavior, thoughts, feelings, and in turn personality.

Experimenter expectancy effects: Occurs when an investigator's expectations lead him or her (consciously or unconsciously) to treat participants in a way that induces the expected results.

Explicit (or declarative) memories: Memories that can be retrieved at will and represented in STM; verbal and visual memories are explicit if the words or images can be called to mind.

Exposure with response prevention: A behavior therapy technique that, in a planned, programmatic way, exposes the client to an anxiety-provoking object and prevents the usual maladaptive response.

External attribution: An explanation of behavior that focuses on the situation; also called *situational attribution.*

Extinction: In classical conditioning, the process by which a CR comes to be eliminated through repeated presentations of the CS without the presence of the UCS. In operant conditioning, the fading out of a response following an initial burst of a behavior after the withdrawal of reinforcement.

Extrasensory perception (ESP): The ability to perceive and know things without using the ordinary senses.

Extrinsic motivation: Motivation that leads a person to want to engage in an activity for external reasons.

Facial feedback hypothesis: The idea that emotions arise partly as a result of the position of facial muscles.

Factor analysis: A statistical method that uncovers the particular attributes (factors) that make scores more or less similar; the more similar the scores, the more attributes they should have in common.

False memory: Memory for an event that did not actually occur.

Family therapy: A therapy modality in which a family (or certain members of a family) is seen for treatment.

Fetal alcohol syndrome: A type of retardation caused by excessive drinking of alcohol by the mother during pregnancy.

Figure: In perception, a set of characteristics (such as shape, color, texture) that corresponds to an object.

Fixed interval schedule: Reinforcement schedule in which reinforcement is given for a response emitted after a fixed interval of time.

Fixed ratio schedule: Reinforcement schedule in which reinforcement is given after a fixed ratio of responses.

Flashback: Hallucination that recurs without the use of a drug.

Flashbulb memory: An unusually vivid and accurate memory of a dramatic event.

Flow: The experience of complete absorption in and merging smoothly into an activity and losing track of time.

Fluid intelligence: According to Cattell and Horn, the kind of intelligence that underlies the creation of novel solutions to problems.

Flynn effect: Increases in IQ in the population with the passage of time.

Food aversion (taste aversion): A classically conditioned avoidance of a certain food or taste.

Foot-in-the-door technique: A technique that achieves compliance by beginning with an insignificant request, which is then followed by a larger request.

Forebrain: The cortex, thalamus, limbic system, and basal ganglia.

Forgetting curve: A graphic representation of the rate at which information is forgotten over time: recent events are recalled better than more distant ones, but most forgetting occurs soon after learning.

Formal operation: In Piaget's theory, a mental act that can be performed (and reversed) even with abstract concepts.

Fovea: The small, central region of the retina with the highest density of cones and the highest resolution.

Fragile X syndrome: A type of retardation that affects the X chromosome; it is both genetic and inherited.

Free association: A technique used in psychoanalysis and psychodynamic therapies in which the patient says whatever comes to mind and the train of thoughts reveals the patient's issues and ways of dealing with them.

Frequency: In vision and audition, the rate at which wave peaks arrive; higher frequencies of electromagnetic waves are seen as more toward the violet end of the spectrum, whereas higher frequencies of sound waves are heard as higher tones.

Frequency distribution: A distribution that indicates the number of each type of case that was observed in a set of data.

Frequency theory: The theory that higher frequencies produce higher rates of neural firing.

Frontal lobe: The brain lobe located behind the forehead; the seat of planning, memory search, motor control, and reasoning, as well as numerous other functions.

Functional fixedness: When solving a problem, getting stuck on one interpretation of an object or one part of the situation.

Functionalism: The school of psychology that sought to understand the ways that the mind helps individuals *function,* or adapt to the world.

Functional magnetic resonance imaging (fMRI): A type of MRI that usually detects the amount of oxygen being brought to a particular place in the brain.

Fundamental attribution error: The strong tendency to interpret other people's behavior as due to internal (dispositional) causes rather than external (situational) ones.

g: "General factor," a single intelligence that underlies the positive correlations among different tests of intelligence.

Gate control of pain: The top-down inhibition of interneurons that regulate the input of pain signals to the brain.

Gender identity: A person's belief that he or she is male or is female.

Gender roles: The culturally determined appropriate behaviors of males versus females.

Gene: A stretch of DNA that produces a specific protein, which in turn forms the building blocks of our bodies (including our brains) or drives the processes that allow us to live.

General adaptation syndrome (GAS): The technical name for the three phases of the body's response to stress.

Generalization: The ability to generalize both to similar stimuli and from the desired response to a similar response.

Generalized reality orientation fading: A tuning out of external reality during hypnosis.

Gestalt laws of organization: A set of rules describing the circumstances under which marks will be grouped into perceptual units, such as proximity, good continuation, similarity, closure, and good form.

Gestalt psychology: An approach to understanding mental processes that focuses on the idea that the whole is more than the sum of its parts.

Gestalt therapy: A type of insight-oriented therapy that helps clients experience their authentic, spontaneous needs and desires by expanding their moment-to-moment awareness of their bodies, feelings, and thoughts.

Gifted: People who have IQs of at least 135, but more commonly between 150 and 180.

Glial cell: A cell that fills the gaps between neurons, influences the communication among them, and generally helps in the care and feeding of neurons.

Glove anesthesia: Hypnotically induced anesthesia of the hand.

Glucocorticoids: A type of hormone that is released when the stress response is triggered. Glucocorticoids have anti-inflammatory properties.

Grammar: The rules that determine how words that belong to different parts of speech can be organized into acceptable sentences.

Grief: The emotion of distress that follows the loss of a loved one.

Ground: In perception, the background, which must be distinguished in order to pick out figures.

Group: A social entity characterized by regular interaction among members, emotional connection, a common frame of reference, and interdependence.

Group polarization: The tendency of group members' opinions to become more extreme (in the same direction as their initial opinions) after group discussion.

Group therapy: A therapy modality in which a number of clients with similar needs meet together with one or two therapists.

Gyrus: A bulge between sulci in the cerebral cortex that forms a crease.

Habit: A well-learned response that is carried out automatically (without conscious thought) when the appropriate stimulus is present.

Hair cells: Cells with stiff hairs along the basilar membrane of the inner ear that, when moved, produce nerve impulses that are sent to the brain; these cells are the auditory equivalent of rods and cones.

Hallucinations: Mental images so vivid that they seem real.

Hallucinogen: A substance that induces hallucinations.

Hardy personality: The constellation of personality traits associated with health; these include commitment, control, and challenge.

Heritability: The degree to which variability in a characteristic is due to genetics.

Heterosexual: A person who is sexually attracted to members of the opposite sex.

Heuristic: A rule of thumb that does not guarantee the correct answer to a problem but offers a likely shortcut to it.

Hidden observer: A part of the self that experiences (and can record) what the part of the self responding to hypnotic trance does not "consciously" experience.

High expressed emotion: An emotional style in families that are critical, hostile, and overinvolved.

Hindbrain: The medulla, pons, and cerebellum.

Hippocampus: A subcortical structure that plays a key role in allowing new information to be stored in the brain's memory banks.

Homeostasis: The process of maintaining a steady state, a constant level of a bodily substance or condition.

Homosexual: A person who is sexually attracted to members of the same sex.

Hormone: A chemical produced by glands that can act as a neuromodulator.

Hostile attribution bias: The propensity to misread the intentions of others as negative.

Hostility: The personality trait associated with heart disease, characterized by mistrust, an expectation of harm and provocation by others, and a cynical attitude.

Humanistic psychology: The school of psychology that assumes people have positive values, free will, and deep inner creativity, the combination of which leads them to choose life-fulfilling paths to personal growth.

Hypermnesia: Memory that improves over time without feedback, particularly with repeated attempts to recall.

Hypnogogic sleep: Characterized by the experience of gentle falling or floating, or "seeing" flashing lights and geometric patterns; describes Stage 1 sleep.

Hypnosis: A state of mind characterized by a focused awareness on vivid, imagined experiences and decreased awareness of the external environment.

Hypnotic induction: The procedure used to attain a hypnotic trance state.

Hypomania: A mood state similar to mania, but less severe, with fewer and less intrusive symptoms.

Hypothalamus: A brain structure that sits under the thalamus and plays a central role in controlling eating and drinking, and in regulating the body's temperature, blood pressure, and heart rate.

Hypothesis: A tentative idea that might explain a set of observations.

Id: A psychic structure, proposed by Freud, that exists at birth and houses sexual and aggressive drives and physical needs.

Identification: Your ability to perceive an object and know facts that are associated with it.

Imitation: Mimicking another person's actions based purely on observing them.

Immediate reinforcement: Reinforcement given immediately after the desired behavior is exhibited.

Immune system: The system that protects the body from disease by developing chemicals and specific types of cells to fight against foreign organisms.

Implicit memories: Memories that cannot be voluntarily called to mind, but nevertheless influence behavior or thinking in certain ways.

Implicit motive: A need or want that unconsciously directs behavior.

Impression formation: The process of developing impressions of others.

Impression management: A person's efforts to control the type of impression he or she creates.

Impulsivity: A temperament characterized by the propensity to respond to stimuli immediately, without reflection or concern for consequences.

Incentive: A stimulus that draws a person toward a particular goal, in anticipation of a reward.

Incidental learning: Learning that occurs without intention.

Incongruence: According to client-centered therapy, a mismatch between a person's *real self* and his or her *ideal self*.

Incubation: Improved thinking following a period of not consciously working on solving a problem or performing a task.

Independent variable: The aspect of the experimental situation that is intentionally varied.

Individualist culture: A culture that emphasizes the rights and responsibilities of the individual over those of the group.

Individual therapy: A therapy modality in which one client is treated by one therapist.

Inductive reasoning: Reasoning that uses examples to figure out a rule; induction goes from the particular (examples) to the general (a rule).

Inferential statistics: Results of tests that reveal which differences or patterns in the measurements reflect actual differences in a population, as opposed to those that merely reflect random variations.

Inferiority complex: The experience that occurs when inferiority feelings are so strong that they hamper striving for superiority.

Informed consent: The requirement that a potential participant in a study be told what he or she will be asked to do and possible risks and benefits of the study before agreeing to take part.

Ingroup: An individual's own group.

Inhibitory conflict: A response that is both strongly instigated and inhibited.

Insight: A new way to look at a problem that implies the solution.

Insight learning: Learning that occurs when a person suddenly grasps what something means and incorporates that new knowledge into old knowledge.

Insight-oriented therapy: Therapy that aims to remove distressing symptoms by leading people to understand their causes through deeply felt personal insights.

Insomnia: Repeated difficulty falling asleep, difficulty staying asleep, or waking up too early.

Instinct: An inherited tendency to produce organized and unalterable responses to particular stimuli.

Insulin: A hormone that stimulates the storage of food molecules in the form of fat.

Intelligence: The ability to solve problems well and to understand and learn complex material.

Intelligence quotient (IQ): A score on an intelligence test, originally based on comparing mental age to chronological age but later based on norms.

Intentional learning: Learning that occurs as a result of trying to learn.

Interactionism: A view of personality in which both traits and situations are believed to affect behavior, thoughts, and feelings.

Interference: The disruption of the ability to remember one piece of information by the presence of other information.

Internal attribution: An explanation of someone's behavior that focuses on the person's beliefs, goals, or other dispositions; also called *dispositional attribution*.

Interneuron: A neuron that is connected to other neurons, not to sense organs or muscles.

Interpretation: A technique used in psychoanalysis and psychodynamic therapies in which the therapist deciphers the patient's words and behaviors, assigning unconscious motivations to them.

Interval schedule: Partial reinforcement schedule based on time.

Intrinsic motivation: Motivation that leads a person to want to engage in an activity for its own sake.

Introspection: The process of "looking within."

Ion: An atom that has a positive or negative charge.

Iris: The circular muscle that adjusts the size of the pupil.

Islands of excellence: Areas in which retarded people perform remarkably well.

Just-noticeable difference (JND): The size of the difference in a stimulus property needed for the observer to notice a change has occurred.

Kinesthetic sense: The sense that registers the movement and position of the limbs.

Korsakoff's syndrome: A disorder, related to alcoholism, in which the brain's mammillary bodies are destroyed, damaging learning and memory abilities.

Language acquisition device (LAD): An innate mechanism, hypothesized by Chomsky, that contains the grammatical rules common to all languages and allows language acquisition.

Language comprehension: The ability to understand language.

Language production: The ability to speak or otherwise use language to send information.

Latent content: The symbolic content and meaning of a dream.

Latent learning: Learning that occurs without obvious evidence.

Law of effect: Actions that subsequently lead to a "satisfying state of affairs" are more likely to be repeated.

Learned helplessness: The condition that occurs after an animal has an aversive experience in which nothing it does can affect what happens to it, and so it simply gives up and stops trying to change the situation or to escape.

Learning: A relatively permanent change in behavior that results from experience.

Lens: The flexible disk under the cornea that focuses light onto the back of the eye.

Lesion: A region of impaired tissue.

Level of the brain: Events that involve the structure and properties of the organ itself—brain cells and their connections, the chemical soup in which they exist, and the genes.

Level of the group: Events that involve relationships between people (e.g., love, competition, cooperation), relationships among groups, and culture. Events at the level of the group are one aspect of the environment; the other aspect is the physical environment itself (the time, temperature, and other physical stimuli).

Level of the person: Events that involve the nature of beliefs, desires, and feelings—the *content* of the mind, not just its internal mechanics.

Limbic system: A set of brain areas, including the hippocampus, amygdala, and other areas, that has long been thought of as being involved in fighting, fleeing, feeding, and sex.

Linguistic relativity hypothesis: The idea that perceptions and thoughts are shaped by language, and thus people who speak different languages think differently.

Lobes: The four major parts of each cerebral hemisphere—occipital, temporal, parietal, and frontal.

Locus of control: The source perceived to be the center of control over life's events.

Logic: The process of applying the principles of correct reasoning to reach a decision or evaluate the truth of a claim.

Longitudinal study: A study in which the same people are tested repeatedly, at different ages.

Long-term memory (LTM): A memory store that holds a huge amount of information for a long time (from hours to years).

Long-term potentiation (LTP): A receiving neuron's increased sensitivity to input from a sending neuron, resulting from previous activation.

Lowball technique: A compliance technique that consists of getting someone to make an agreement and then increasing the cost of that agreement.

Magnetic resonance imaging (MRI): A technique that uses magnetic properties of atoms to take sharp pictures of the structure of the brain.

Magnetoencephalography (MEG): Measurement of the magnetic waves emitted during brain activity.

Major depressive disorder (MDD): A disorder characterized by at least 2 weeks of depressed mood or loss of interest in nearly all activities, along with sleep or eating disturbances, loss of energy, and feelings of hopelessness.

Manic episode: A period of at least 1 week during which an abnormally elevated, expansive, or irritable mood persists.

Manifest content: The obvious, memorable content of a dream.

Massed practice: Studying all in one session, or cramming.

Maturation: The developmental process that produces genetically programmed changes with increased age.

Mean: A measure of central tendency that is the arithmetic average of a set of scores or values.

Means–ends analysis: A heuristic in which a problem is divided into a set of smaller problems, each of which includes an end (goal) and the means for getting to it.

Median: A measure of central tendency that is the midpoint score of the values for the group or sample; half the values fall above the median, and half fall below the median.

Meditation: An altered state of consciousness characterized by a sense of deep relaxation and loss of self-awareness.

Medulla: The lowest part of the lower brainstem, which plays a central role in automatic control of breathing, swallowing, and blood circulation.

Memory store: A set of neurons that serves to retain information over time.

Mendelian inheritance: The transmission of characteristics by individual dominant and recessive elements acting separately.

Meninges: The covering of the brain.

Mental images: Internal representations like those that arise during perception, but based on stored information rather than immediate sensory input.

Mentally retarded: Having an IQ of 70 or less and experiencing significant limitations in at least two aspects of everyday life since childhood.

Mental model: An image or description of a specific situation used to reason about abstract entities.

Mental processes: What the brain does when a person stores, recalls, or uses information, or has specific feelings.

Mental simulation: The technique of operating on a represented object as if it were real, "seeing" what would happen in the corresponding actual situation.

Meta-analysis: A technique that combines the results from different studies to discover patterns in the data.

Metabolism: The sum of the chemical events in each of the body's cells, events that convert food molecules to the energy needed for the cells to function.

Microelectrode: A tiny probe inserted into the brain to record electrical activity.

Microenvironment: The environment created by a person's own presence, which depends partly on appearance and behavior.

Midbrain: Brainstem structures that connect the forebrain and hindbrain, including the reticular formation.

Mindfulness meditation: A combination of concentrative and opening-up meditation in which the meditator focuses on whatever is most prominent at the moment; also known as *awareness meditation*.

Minnesota Multiphasic Personality Inventory-2 (MMPI-2): A personality inventory primarily used to assess psychopathology.

Misattribution of arousal: The failure to interpret signs of bodily arousal correctly, which leads to the experience of inappropriate emotions.

Mnemonic devices: Strategies that improve memory, typically by using effective organization and integration.

Modality: A form of therapy.

Modality-specific memory stores: Memory stores that retain input from a single sense, such as vision or audition, or from a specific processing system, such as language.

Mode: A measure of central tendency that is the most frequently occurring value in a group or sample.

Monaural cues: Cues to the location of the source of a sound (such as volume) that do not depend on two ears.

Monoamine oxidase inhibitor (MAOI): A type of antidepressant medication that requires strict adherence to a diet free of tyramine-based foods.

Monocular static cues: Information that specifies the distance of an object that can be picked up with one eye without movement of the object or eye.

Monozygotic: From the same egg and having identical genes.

Mood disorder: A condition marked by persistent or episodic disturbances in affect that interfere with normal functioning in at least one realm of life.

Moon illusion: The fact that the moon appears larger near the horizon than it does high in the sky.

Moral dilemmas: Situations in which there are moral pros and cons for each of a set of possible actions.

Morpheme: The smallest unit of meaning in a language.

Motion cues: Information that specifies the distance of an object on the basis of its movement.

Motivation: The requirements and desires that lead animals (including humans) to behave in a particular way at a particular time and place.

Motor neurons of spinal cord: Neurons in the front inside part of the spinal cord that carry commands from the brain to the muscles to control movement.

Motor strip: The gyrus, located immediately in front of the central sulcus, that controls fine movements and is organized by body part; also called *primary motor cortex*.

Mutation: A physical change of a gene.

Myelin: A fatty substance that helps impulses travel down the axon more efficiently.

Narcolepsy: Sudden attacks of extreme drowsiness.

Narcotic analgesic: A class of strongly addictive drugs, such as heroin, that relieve pain.

Nativist (approach to language): The approach that views crucial aspects of language as innate.

Natural killer (NK) cell: A type of T-cell that destroys damaged or altered cells, such as precancerous cells.

Natural selection: Changes in the frequency of genes in a population that arise because genes allow an organism to have more offspring that survive.

Need: A condition that arises from the lack of a requirement; needs give rise to drives.

Negative reinforcement: Occurs when an unpleasant event or circumstance is removed following a desired behavior, thereby increasing the probability of the behavior's occurring again.

Negative symptom: A diminution or loss of normal functions, such as a restriction in speech.

Nerve deafness: A type of deafness that typically occurs when the hair cells are destroyed by loud sounds.

Neural network: A computer program whose units interact via connections that imitate (roughly) the way the brain works.

Neuroendocrine system: The system regulated by the CNS, that makes hormones that affect many bodily functions; also provides the CNS with information.

Neuroimaging: Brain scanning techniques that produce a picture of the structure or functioning of neurons.

Neuromodulator: A chemical that alters the effects of neurotransmitters.

Neuron: A cell that receives signals from other neurons or sense organs, processes these signals, and sends the signals to other neurons, muscles, or bodily organs; the basic unit of the nervous system.

Neurosis: An abnormal behavior pattern relating to a conflict between the ego and either the id or the superego.

Neurotransmitter: A chemical that sends signals from the terminal buttons on one neuron to the dendrites or cell body of another.

Nightmare: A dream with strong negative emotion.

Night terrors: Vivid and frightening dreams; the sleeper may appear to be awake during the experience but has no memory of it the following day.

Nocebo effect: A variation of the placebo effect in which the subject expects a negative outcome instead of a positive outcome.

Nondeprived reward: Reward that occurs even when a requirement is not being met.

Nonverbal communication: Facial expressions and body language that allow others to infer an individual's internal mental state.

Norm: A shared belief that is enforced through a group's use of penalties.

Normal consciousness: State of awareness that occurs during the usual waking state; also called *waking consciousness*.

Normal curve: A particular distribution of scores, in which most fall in the middle, and symmetrically fewer toward the extremes; also known as a *bell curve*.

Norming: The process of setting the mean score and standard deviation of a test, based on results from a standardized sample.

Obedience: Compliance with an order.

Object permanence: The understanding that objects (including people) continue to exist even when they cannot be immediately perceived.

Observational learning: Learning that occurs through watching others, not through reinforcement.

Obsession: A recurrent and persistent thought, impulse, or image that feels intrusive and inappropriate, and is difficult to suppress or ignore.

Obsessive-compulsive disorder (OCD): A disorder marked by the presence of obsessions, and sometimes compulsions.

Occipital lobe: The brain lobe at the back of the head; concerned entirely with different aspects of vision.

Opening-up meditation: A form of meditation in which the meditator focuses on a stimulus but also broadens that focus to encompass the whole of his or her surroundings.

Operant conditioning: The process by which a behavior becomes associated with its consequences.

Opiate: A narcotic, such as morphine, derived from the opium poppy.

Opponent cells: Cells that pit the colors in a pair, notably blue/yellow or red/green, against each other.

Opponent process theory of color vision: The theory that if a color is present, it causes cells that register it to inhibit the perception of the complementary color (such as red versus green).

Optic nerve: The large bundle of nerve fibers carrying impulses from the retina into the brain.

Outcome research: Research that asks whether, after psychotherapy, the client is feeling better, functioning better, living more independently, or has fewer symptoms.

Outgroup: A group different than a person's own.

Overextension: An overly broad use of a word to refer to a new object or situation.

Overregularization error: A speaking error that occurs because the child applies a rule even to cases that are exceptions to the rule.

Panic attack: An episode of intense fear or discomfort accompanied by physical and psychological symptoms such as palpitations, breathing difficulties, chest pain, fear of impending doom or doing something uncontrollable, and a sense of unreality.

Panic disorder: A disorder whose hallmark is panic attacks.

Paradoxical cold: A phenomenon that occurs when stimulation of nerves by something hot produces the sensation of cold.

Paradoxical intention: A family therapy technique that encourages a behavior that seems contradictory to the desired goal.

Paradoxical sleep: Another name for REM sleep, used to emphasize the marked brain activity.

Parasympathetic nervous system: Part of the ANS that is "next to" the sympathetic system and that tends to counteract its effects.

Parietal lobe: The brain lobe at the top, center/rear of the head, involved in registering spatial location, attention, and motor control.

Partial reinforcement: Reinforcement given only intermittently.

Passionate love: An intense feeling that involves sexual attraction, a desire for mutual love and physical closeness, arousal, and a fear that the relationship will end.

Passive interaction: Occurs when the parents' or sibling's genetically shaped tendencies produce an environment that is passively received by the child.

Perceived social support: The subjective sense that support is available should it be needed.

Percentile rank: The percentage of data that have values at or below a particular value.

Perception: The act of organizing and interpreting sensory input as signaling a particular object or event.

Perceptual constancy: The perception of characteristics that occurs when an object or quality (such as shape or color) looks the same even though the sensory information striking the eyes changes.

Peripheral nervous system (PNS): The autonomic nervous system and the skeletal system.

Personality: A consistent set of characteristics that people display over time and across situations, and that distinguish individuals from each other.

Personality disorder: Relatively stable personality traits that are inflexible and maladaptive, causing distress or difficulty with daily functioning.

Personality inventory: A pencil-and-paper method for assessing personality that requires the test-taker to read statements and indicate whether each is true or false about themselves.

Personality trait: A relatively consistent characteristic exhibited in different situations.

Persuasion: Attempts to change people's attitudes.

Phenylketonuria (PKU): A genetic form of retardation that can be treated with dietary supplements if detected early in life.

Pheromones: Chemicals that function in some ways like hormones but are released outside the body (in urine and sweat).

Phobia: A fear and avoidance of an object or situation extreme enough to interfere with everyday life. An irrational fear of a specific object or situation.

Phoneme: The basic building block of speech sounds.

Phonology: The structure of the sounds that can be used to produce words in a language.

Pitch: How high or low a sound seems; higher frequencies of pressure waves produce the experience of higher pitches.

Pituitary gland: So-called "master gland" that regulates other glands but is itself controlled by the brain, primarily via connections from the hypothalamus.

Placebo: An inert substance that nevertheless seems to have medicinal effects.

Place theory: The theory that different frequencies activate different places along the basilar membrane.

Planning fallacy: The tendency to underestimate the time it takes to accomplish a task.

Polygraph: A machine that monitors the activity of the sympathetic and parasympathetic nervous systems, particularly changes in skin conductance, breathing, and heart rate. These machines are used in attempts to detect lying.

Pons: A bridge between the brainstem and the cerebellum that plays a role in functions ranging from sleep to control of facial muscles.

Pop-out: A phenomenon that occurs when a stimulus is sufficiently different from the ones around it that it is immediately evident.

Population: A group of people who share certain characteristics, such as age, sex, or other relevant variables. The entire set of relevant people or animals.

Positive reinforcement: Occurs when a desired reinforcer is presented after a response, thereby increasing the likelihood of a recurrence of that response.

Positive symptom: An excess or distortion of normal functions, such as a hallucination.

Positron emission tomography (PET): A neuroimaging technique that uses small amounts of radiation to track blood or energy consumption in the brain.

Posthypnotic suggestion: A suggestion regarding a change in perception, mood, or behavior that will occur *after* leaving the hypnotic state.

Posttraumatic stress disorder (PTSD): A disorder experienced by some people after a traumatic event, whose symptoms include an unwanted re-experiencing of the trauma, avoidance of anything associated with the trauma, and heightened arousal.

Pragmatics: The way that language conveys meaning indirectly, by implying rather than asserting.

Prediction: Expectation about specific events that should occur in particular circumstances if a theory or hypothesis is correct.

Prejudice: An attitude (generally negative) toward members of a group.

Primacy effect: Increased memory for the first few stimuli in a set.

Primary mental abilities: According to Thurstone, seven fundamental abilities that are not outgrowths of other abilities.

Primary prevention: A type of program that focuses on eliminating sociocultural causes of psychological disorders.

Primary reinforcer: An event or object that is inherently reinforcing, such as food, water, or relief from pain.

Priming: The result of having just performed a task that facilitates repeating the same or an associated task.

Private speech: The use of language in planning or in prompting oneself to behave in specific ways.

Proactive interference: Interference that occurs when previous knowledge makes it difficult to learn something new.

Problem: An obstacle that must be overcome to reach a goal.

Problem-focused coping: Coping focused on changing the environment itself, or how the person interacts with the environment.

Prodigies: People who early in life demonstrate immense talent in a particular domain, such as music or mathematics, but who are normal in other domains.

Progressive muscle relaxation: A relaxation technique whereby the person relaxes muscles sequentially from one end of the body to the other.

Projective test: A method used to assess personality and psychopathology that involves asking the test-taker to make sense of an ambiguous stimulus.

Propositional representation: A mental sentence that asserts the unambiguous meaning of a statement.

Prosocial behavior: Acting to benefit others.

Prototype: A representation of the most typical example of a category.

Pruning: A process whereby certain connections among neurons are eliminated.

Pseudoimitation: Mimicking another person's actions only when those actions are ones the mimicker (baby) has just performed.

Pseudopsychology: Theories or statements that look like psychology but are in fact superstition or unsupported opinion pretending to be science.

Psychiatric nurse: A nurse who holds a master's degree in nursing as well as a certificate of clinical specialization in psychiatric nursing (M.S.N., C.S.), and who provides psychotherapy and works with medical doctors to monitor and administer medications.

Psychiatrist: A physician who focuses on mental disorders; unlike psychologists, psychiatrists can prescribe drugs, but they are not trained to administer and interpret psychological tests, nor are they trained to interpret and understand psychological research.

Psychoanalysis: An intensive form of therapy, originally developed by Freud, based on the idea that people's psychological difficulties are caused by conflicts among the id, ego, and superego.

Psychodynamic theory: A theory of how thoughts and feelings affect behavior; refers to the continual push-and-pull interaction among various conscious and unconscious forces.

Psychodynamic therapy: A less intensive form of psychoanalysis.

Psychoeducation: The process of educating clients about therapy and research findings pertaining to their disorders or problems.

Psychological determinism: The view that all behavior, no matter how mundane or insignificant, has a psychological cause.

Psychological disorder: A constellation of symptoms marked by an individual's significant distress or impairment in work, school, family, relationships, or daily living.

Psychology: The science of mental processes and behavior.

Psychopharmacology: The use of medication to treat psychological disorders and problems.

Psychophysics: The study of the relation between physical events and the corresponding experience of those events.

Psychosexual stages: Freud's developmental stages based on erogenous zones; the specific needs of each stage must be met for its successful resolution.

Psychosis: An obvious impairment in the ability to perceive and comprehend events accurately and a gross disorganization of behavior.

Psychosocial development: The effects of maturation and learning on personality and relationships.

Psychotherapy: Talking and listening to patients about their problems and helping them to see the causes and—more important—to find solutions.

Psychotherapy integration: The use of techniques from different theoretical orientations with an overarching understanding of how the different techniques will be used to achieve the goals of treatment.

Puberty: The time when hormones cause the sex organs to mature and secondary sexual characteristics appear, such as breasts for women and a beard for men.

Punishment: An unpleasant event that occurs as a consequence of a behavior, thereby decreasing the probability of the recurrence of the behavior.

Pupil: The opening in the eye through which light passes.

Range: The difference obtained by subtracting the smallest score from the largest; the simplest measure of variability.

Ratio schedule: Partial reinforcement schedule based on a specified number of emitted responses.

Raven's Progressive Matrices: A nonverbal test that assesses fluid intelligence and *g*.

Reaction range: The range of possible reactions to environmental events that is set by the genes.

Reality monitoring: An ongoing awareness of perceptual and other properties that distinguish real from imagined stimuli.

Recall: The act of intentionally bringing explicit information to awareness, which requires transferring the information from LTM to STM.

Recategorization: A means of reducing prejudice by shifting the categories of "us" and "them" so that the two groups are no longer distinct entities.

Recency effect: Increased memory for the last few stimuli in a set.

Receptor: A site on the dendrite or cell body where a messenger molecule attaches itself; like a lock that is opened by one key, a receptor receives only one type of neurotransmitter or neuromodulator.

Reciprocal determinism: The interactive relationship between the environment, cognitive/personal factors, and behavior.

Recognition: The act of encoding an input and matching it to a stored representation. Your awareness when you perceive an object and simply know that it is familiar.

Reflex: An automatic response to an event.

Reframing: A therapy technique in which the therapist offers a new way of conceptualizing, or "framing," the problem.

Rehearsal: The process of repeating information over and over to retain it in STM.

Reinforcement: The process by which consequences lead to an increase in the likelihood that the response will occur again.

Reinforcer: Any object or event that follows the desired response and changes the likelihood of the recurrence of that response.

Reliability: A study is reliable if it yields the same results when repeated.

REM rebound: The higher percentage of REM sleep following a night's sleep deprived of REM.

REM sleep: Stage of sleep characterized by rapid eye movements and marked brain activity.

Repetition blindness: The inability to see the second occurrence of a stimulus that appears twice in succession.

Repetition priming: Priming that makes the same information more easily accessed in the future.

Replicate: To repeat a study and obtain the same results as were found previously.

Representation problem: The challenge of how best to formulate the nature of a problem.

Representativeness heuristic: The heuristic that the more similar something is to a prototype stored in memory, the more likely it is to belong to the prototype's category.

Repressed memories: Real memories that have been pushed out of consciousness because they are emotionally threatening.

Repression: A defense mechanism that occurs when the unconscious prevents threatening thoughts, impulses, and memories from entering consciousness.

Resistance: A reluctance or refusal to cooperate with the therapist, which can range from unconscious forgetting to outright refusal to comply with a therapist's request.

Resistance phase: The second phase of the GAS, in which the body mobilizes its resources to attain equilibrium, despite the continued presence of the stressor; also called the *adaptation phase*.

Response bias: A tendency to respond in a particular way regardless of knowledge or beliefs relevant to performing the task correctly.

Response contingency: The relationship that occurs when a consequence is dependent on the organism's emitting the desired behavior.

Reticular formation: Two-part structure in the brainstem; the "ascending" part plays a key role in keeping a person awake and alert; the "descending" part is important in producing autonomic nervous system reactions.

Retina: A sheet of tissue at the back of the eye containing cells that convert light to neural impulses.

Retroactive interference: Interference that occurs when new learning impairs memory for something learned earlier.

Retrograde amnesia: Amnesia that disrupts previous memories.

Reuptake: The process by which surplus neurotransmitter is reabsorbed back into the sending neuron so that the neuron can effectively fire again.

Rods: Retinal cells that are very sensitive to light but register only shades of gray.

Role: The behaviors that a member in a given position in a group is expected to perform.

Rorschach test: A projective test consisting of a set of inkblots that people are asked to "interpret."

s: "Specific factors," or aspects of performance that are particular to a given kind of processing—and distinct from *g*.

Sample: The group from which a researcher obtains measures or observations.

Sampling bias: Occurs when the participants or items are not chosen at random, so that an attribute is over- or underrepresented.

Sampling error: A difference that arises by chance, not because the samples are representative of different populations.

Schema: A collection of concepts that specify necessary and optional aspects of a particular situation. A mental structure that organizes perceptual input and connects it with the appropriate responses.

Schizophrenia: A psychotic disorder in which the patient's affect, behavior, and thoughts are profoundly altered.

Scientific method: The scientific method involves specifying a problem; systematically observing events; forming a hypothesis of the relation between variables; collecting new observations to test the hypothesis; using such evidence to formulate and support a theory; and finally, testing the theory.

Secondary prevention: A type of program that seeks to intervene with those at risk for developing a disorder to prevent its occurrence.

Secondary reinforcer: A event or object that does not inherently satisfy a physical need, such as attention, praise, money, good grades, or a promotion.

Selective serotonergic reuptake inhibitor (SSRI): A type of antidepressant medication that affects only *selective* serotonin receptors, with fewer side effects.

Selective serotonin-reuptake inhibitor (SSRI): A chemical that blocks the reuptake of the neurotransmitter serotonin.

Self-actualization: An innate motivation to attain the highest possible emotional and intellectual potential.

Self-concept: The beliefs, desires, values, and attributes that define a person to himself or herself.

Self-help group: A group whose members focus on a specific disorder or event and do not usually have a clinically trained leader; also called a *support group*.

Self-monitoring techniques: Behavioral techniques that help the client identify the antecedents, consequences, and patterns of a targeted behavior.

Self-perception theory: The theory that people come to understand themselves by making inferences from their behavior and the events surrounding their behavior, much like those they would make about another person's behavior.

Self-serving bias: A person's inclination to attribute his or her own failures to external causes and successes to internal causes, but to attribute other people's failures to internal causes and their successes to external causes.

Semantic memories: Memories of the meanings of words, concepts, and general facts about the world.

Semantics: The meaning of a word or sentence.

Sensation: The immediate experience of basic properties of an object or event that occurs when a receptor is stimulated.

Sensitive period: A window of time when a particular type of learning is *easiest*, but not the only time it can occur.

Sensitivity: In signal detection theory, the threshold level for distinguishing between a stimulus and noise; the lower the threshold, the greater the sensitivity.

Sensory memory (SM): The "lowest" level of memory, which holds a large amount of perceptual input for a very brief time, typically less than one second.

Sensory neuron: A neuron that responds to input from sense organs.

Sensory neurons of spinal cord: Neurons in the back of the spinal cord that carry information about touch and the state of internal organs to the brain.

Separation anxiety: Fear of being away from the primary caregiver.

Serotonergic/noradrenergic reuptake inhibitor (SNRI): A newer antidepressant that affects both serotonin and noradrenergic neurotransmitter systems.

Set point: The particular body weight that is easiest for an animal (including a human) to maintain.

Sexual response cycle (SRC): The stages the body passes through during sexual activity, now characterized as including sexual attraction, desire, excitement, and performance (which includes plateau, orgasm, and resolution).

Shape constancy: Seeing objects as having the same shape even when the image on the retina changes.

Shaping: The gradual process of reinforcing an organism for behavior that gets closer to the desired behavior.

Short-term memory (STM): A memory store that holds relatively little information (typically 5 to 9 items) for a few seconds (but perhaps as long as 30 seconds); people are conscious only of the current contents of STM.

Signal detection theory: A theory explaining why people detect signals, which are always embedded in noise, in some situations but not in others.

Situationism: A view of personality that regards behavior as mostly a function of the situation, not of internal traits.

Size constancy: Seeing an object as being the same size when viewed at different distances and visual angles.

Skeletal system: Consists of nerves that are attached to striated muscles and bones.

Skewed distribution: A set of data that has many scores near one extreme value and away from the center.

Sleep: The naturally recurrent experience during which normal consciousness is suspended.

Sleep apnea: Difficulty breathing accompanied by loud snoring during sleep.

Sociability: A temperament characterized by a preference to be in other people's company rather than alone.

Social categorization theory: The theory that people are driven to divide the world automatically into categories of "us" versus "them."

Social causation: The chronic psychological and social stresses of living in an urban environment that may lead to an increase in the rate of schizophrenia (especially among the poor).

Social cognition: The area of social psychology that focuses on how people attend to, store, remember, and use information about other people and the social world.

Social desirability: A bias in responding to questions such that people try to make themselves "look good" even if it means giving untrue answers.

Social exchange theory: A theory that proposes that individuals act to maximize the gains and minimize the losses in their relationships.

Social facilitation: The increase in performance that can occur simply by being part of a group or in the presence of other people.

Social loafing: The tendency to work less hard when responsibility for an outcome is spread over the group's members.

Social phobia: A type of phobia involving fear of public humiliation or embarrassment and the ensuing avoidance of situations likely to arouse this fear.

Social psychology: The field of psychology pertaining to how people think about other people and interact in relationships and groups.

Social selection: The tendency of the mentally disabled to drift to the lower economic classes; also called *social drift*.

Social support: The help and support gained through interacting with others.

Social worker: A mental health professional who helps families (and individuals) with psychotherapy and helps clients use the social service systems in their communities.

Sociological role theory: The view that a person in a trance enacts the role of a hypnotized person as he or she understands it, which leads to behaviors believed to be produced by hypnosis.

Somasthetic senses: Senses that have to do with perceiving the body and its position in space—specifically, kinesthetic sense, vestibular sense, touch, temperature sensitivity, pain sense, and possibly magnetic sense.

Somatosensory strip: The gyrus, located immediately behind the central sulcus, that registers sensation on the body and is organized by body part.

Source amnesia: A failure to remember the source of information.

Specific factor: A curative factor related to the specific type of therapy being employed.

Specific language impairment: A specific problem in understanding grammar and complex words that is not related to more general cognitive deficits.

Specific phobia: A type of phobia involving persistent and excessive or unreasonable fear triggered by a specific object or situation, along with attempts to avoid the feared stimulus.

Speech segmentation problem: The problem of organizing a continuous stream of speech into separate parts that correspond to individual words.

Spinal cord: The flexible rope of nerves that runs inside the backbone, or spinal column.

Split-brain patient: A person whose corpus callosum has been severed for medical reasons, so that neuronal impulses no longer pass from one hemisphere to the other.

Spontaneous recovery: In classical conditioning, the process by which the CS will again elicit the CR after extinction has occurred. In operant conditioning, the process by which an old response reappears if there is a break after extinction.

Spoonerisms: Transpositions of speech sounds, as in "tons of soil" instead of "sons of toil."

St. John's wort: An herbal remedy for mild to moderate depression.

Standard deviation: A measure of the degree to which individual scores deviate from the mean.

Standardized sample: A random selection of people, drawn from a carefully defined population.

State-dependent retrieval: Recall that is better if it occurs in the same psychological state as when the information was first encoded.

Statistics: Numbers that summarize or indicate differences or patterns of differences in measurements.

Status hierarchy: The distribution of power in a group.

Stereopsis: The process that registers depth on the basis of binocular disparity.

Stereotype: A belief (or set of beliefs) about people in a particular social category.

Stimulant: A class of substances that excite the central nervous system, leading to increases in behavioral activity and heightened arousal.

Stimulus control: A behavior therapy technique that involves controlling the exposure to a stimulus that elicits a conditioned response, so as to decrease or increase the frequency of the response.

Stimulus discrimination: The ability to distinguish among similar conditioned stimuli and to respond only to actual conditioned stimuli.

Stimulus generalization: A tendency for the CR to be elicited by neutral stimuli that are like, but not identical to, the CS; in other words, the response *generalizes* to similar stimuli.

Strategy: An approach to solving a problem, determined by the type of representation used and the processing steps to be tried.

Stress: The general term describing the psychological and bodily response to a stimulus that alters a person's state of equilibrium.

Stressor: A stimulus that throws the body's equilibrium out of balance.

Stress response: The physiological changes that occur to help people cope with a stressor; also called the *fight-or-flight response*.

Stroke: A result of the failure of blood (with its life-giving nutrients and oxygen) to reach part of the brain, causing neurons in that area to die.

Structuralism: The school of psychology that sought to identify the basic elements of experience and to describe the rules and circumstances under which these elements combine to form mental *structures*.

Subcortical structure: An "inner brain" organ that contains gray matter, located under the cerebral cortex.

Substance abuse: Drug or alcohol use that leads to legal difficulties, causes distress or difficulty functioning in major areas of life, or occurs in dangerous situations.

Substance dependence: Chronic substance abuse that is characterized by seven symptoms, the two most important being tolerance and withdrawal.

Successive approximations: The series of smaller behaviors involved in shaping a complex behavior.

Sulcus: A fold in the cerebral cortex.

Superego: A Freudian psychic structure that is formed during early childhood and houses the sense of right and wrong, based on the internalization of parental and cultural morality.

Superstitious behavior: A behavior that depends on an accidental association between two things, even though one is not a consequence of the other.

Suprachiasmatic nucleus (SCN): A small part of the hypothalamus just above the optic chiasm that registers changes in light, which lead to production of hormones that regulate various bodily functions.

Survey: A set of questions, typically about beliefs, attitudes, preferences, or activities.

Sympathetic nervous system: Part of the ANS that readies an animal to fight or to flee by speeding up the heart, increasing breathing rate to deliver more oxygen, dilating the pupils, producing sweat, increasing salivation, inhibiting activity in the stomach, and relaxing the bladder.

Synapse: The place where an axon of one neuron meets the membrane (on a dendrite or cell body) of another neuron.

Synaptic cleft: The gap between the axon of one neuron and the membrane of another, across which communication occurs.

Syntax: The internal grammatical structure of a sentence, determined by how words that belong to different parts of speech are organized into acceptable arrangements.

Systematic desensitization: A behavior therapy technique that teaches people to be relaxed in the presence of a feared object or situation.

Systems therapy: A type of therapy that views a client's symptoms as occurring in a larger context, or system (the family and subculture), in which a change in one part of the system affects the rest of the system.

Tardive dyskinesia: An irreversible movement disorder in which the person involuntarily smacks his or her lips, displays facial grimaces, and exhibits other symptoms, caused by traditional antipsychotic medication.

Task-motivation theory: The view that some people are predisposed to attend and respond to suggestions made by a hypnotist and are more motivated to perform the requested task.

Taste buds: Microscopic structures on the bumps on the tongue surface, at the back of the throat, and inside the cheeks; the four types of taste buds are sensitive to sweet, sour, salty, and bitter tastes.

T cell: A type of white blood cell that matures in the thymus.

Technical eclecticism: The use of specific techniques that may benefit a particular client, without regard for an overarching theory.

Telegraphic speech: Speech that packs much information into few words.

Temperament: Innate inclinations to engage in a certain style of behavior.

Temporal lobe: The brain lobe under the temples, in front of the ears, where sideburns begin to grow down; among its many functions are visual memory and hearing.

Teratogen: Any chemical, virus, or type of radiation that can cause damage to the zygote, embryo, or fetus.

Terminal button: A structure at the end of axons that, when the neuron is triggered, releases chemicals into the space between neurons.

Tertiary prevention: A type of program that tries to decrease the severity, duration, and frequency of a psychological disorder once it has developed.

Test bias: Test design features that lead a particular group to perform well or poorly and that thus invalidate the test.

Testosterone: The hormone that causes males to develop facial hair and other sex characteristics and to build up muscle volume.

Texture gradients: Progressive changes in texture that signal distance.

Thalamus: A subcortical region that receives inputs from sensory and motor systems and plays a crucial role in attention; often thought of as a switching center.

Theory: A statement of a set of underlying principles that are supposed to explain a set of observations.

Theory of causal attribution: Rules for deciding whether to attribute a given behavior to a person's enduring traits or to the situation.

Theory of mind: A theory of other people's mental states (their beliefs, desires, and feelings) that allows prediction of what other people can understand and how they will react in a given situation.

Theory of multiple intelligences: Gardner's theory of eight distinct types of intelligence, which can vary separately for a given individual.

Thought suppression: The coping strategy that involves purposefully trying not to think about something emotionally arousing or distressing.

Threshold: The point at which stimulation is strong enough to be noticed.

Tinnitus: A form of hearing impairment signaled by a constant ringing or noise in the ears.

Token economy: A treatment program that uses secondary reinforcers (tokens) to bring about behavior modification.

Tolerance: The condition of requiring more of a substance to achieve the same effect (or the usual amount providing a diminished response).

Tonotopic organization: The use of distance along a strip of cortex to represent differences in pitch.

Top-down processing: Processing that is initiated by knowledge, expectation, or belief.

Trance logic: An uncritical acceptance of incongruous, illogical events during a hypnotic trance.

Trance state: A hypnotically induced altered state of consciousness in which awareness of the external environment is diminished.

Trance theory: The view that a person in a trance experiences an altered, dissociated state of consciousness characterized by increasing susceptibility and responsiveness to suggestions.

Transcranial magnetic stimulation (TMS): An experimental treatment for psychological disorders involving the use of electromagnetic stimulation. Researchers stimulate the brain from the outside, by putting a wire coil on a person's head and delivering a magnetic pulse. The magnetic fields are so strong that they make neurons under the coil fire.

Transduction: The process whereby physical energy is converted by a sensory neuron into neural impulses.

Transfer appropriate processing: Processing that transfers to a task that requires similar processing.

Transference: The process by which patients may relate to their therapists as they did to some important person in their lives.

Triangular model of love: A theory of love marked by the dimensions of (1) passion (including sexual desire), (2) intimacy (closeness), and (3) commitment.

Trichromatic theory of color vision: The theory that color vision arises from the combinations of neural impulses from three different kinds of sensors, each of which responds maximally to a different wavelength.

Tricyclic antidepressant (TCA): A common set of antidepressant medications named for the three rings in the chemical compound.

Twin study: Study that compares identical and fraternal twins to determine the relative contribution of genes to variability in a behavior or characteristic.

Typicality: The degree to which an entity is representative of its category.

Unconditional positive regard: Acceptance without any conditions. The stance taken by a client-centered therapist that conveys positive feelings for the client, regardless of the client's thoughts, feelings, or actions.

Unconditioned response (UCR): The reflexive response elicited by a particular stimulus.

Unconditioned stimulus (UCS): A stimulus that elicits an automatic response (UCR), without requiring prior learning.

Unconscious: Outside conscious awareness and not able to be brought to consciousness at will.

Validation: A therapy technique in which the therapist conveys his or her understanding of the client's feelings and wishes.

Validity: A measure is valid if it does in fact measure what it is supposed to measure.

Variable: An aspect of a situation that can vary, or change.

Variable interval schedule: Reinforcement schedule in which reinforcement is given for a response emitted after a variable interval of time.

Variable ratio schedule: Reinforcement schedule in which reinforcement is given after a variable ratio of responses.

Ventricle: A hollow area in the center of the brain that stores fluid.

Vestibular sense: The sense that provides information about the body's orientation relative to gravity.

Volume: The strength of a sound; pressure waves with greater amplitude produce the experience of louder sound.

Want: A condition that arises when you have an unmet goal that will not fill a requirement; wants turn goals into incentives.

Wavelength: The distance between the peaks of light or sound waves; thus, the higher the frequency, the shorter the wavelength.

Weber's law: The rule that a constant percentage of a magnitude change is necessary to detect a difference.

Wechsler Adult Intelligence Scale (WAIS): The most widely used intelligence test; consists of both verbal and performance subtests.

Wernicke's aphasia: Problems with comprehending language following brain damage (typically to the left posterior temporal lobe).

Withdrawal symptoms: The onset of uncomfortable or life-threatening effects when the use of a substance is stopped.

Working memory (WM): The system that includes specialized STMs and the "central executive" processes that operate on them.

Zeitgebers: Environmental cues for sleeping and waking.

Zygote: A fertilized ovum (egg).

NAME INDEX

Note: Page numbers followed by f *indicate figures; page numbers followed by* t *indicate tables.*

SUBJECT INDEX

Note: Page numbers followed by f *indicate figures; those followed by* t *indicate tables;* **bold-face** *type indicates key terms and the pages where they are defined.*

Distinctiveness, causal attribution and, 568
Distress, 470
Distributed practice, 213
Divergent thinking, 303
Dizygotic, 82
DNA (deoxyribonucleic acid), 77, 78f, 389
Dodo bird verdict, 542
Dominant traits, 288, 389
Door-in-the-face technique, 582
Dopamine, 52, 187
Dopamine hypothesis of schizophrenia, 495
Double-blind design, 35, 593
Double pain, 123
Down, J. Langdon, 298
Down syndrome, 298
Dream analysis, 515
Dreaming, 134–136
reasons for, 135–136
triggers for, 134–135
Drive, 325, 325–326
Drug abuse. *See* Substance abuse
DSM (*Diagnostic and Statistical Manual of Mental Disorders*), 473–474, 474t, 475t
Dual codes, 211–212
Dynamic memory, 212
Dysthymia, 485

Eardrum, 114
Early processing, 91
Eating disorder, 501, 501–505
explanations for, 503–504
Ebbinghaus, Hermann, 203
Echoic memory, 202
ECT (electroconvulsive therapy), 537
EEG (electroencephalograph), 72
Effect, 28–29, 29
Efficacy expectancy, 374, 375
Ego, 367
Egocentrism, 402
adolescent, 415–416
Ego ideal, 367
EI (emotional intelligence), 283
Einstein, Albert, 285–286, 330, 372
Elaborative encoding, 213
Electra complex, 369
Electroconvulsive therapy (ECT), 537
Electroencephalogram, 72, 72–73, 73f
Electroencephalograph (EEG), 72
Electromganetic radiation, range of, 97, 97f
Ellis, Albert, 18, 526
Emotion(s), 312, 312–324. *See also specific emotions*
approach and withdrawal, 315
basic, 312–314, 313f
causes of, 315–319, 316f
cognitive interpretation of, 318f, 318–319

combinations of, 314, 314f
conditioned, 168–170
decision making and, 268
expression of, 320–322, 520–521
lie detection and, 322–324
memory and, 214–215
physiological aspects of, 316–317
separate, 315
Emotional arousal, 447
Emotional intelligence (EI), 283
Emotionality, 362, 363
Emotion-focused coping, 449, 450t, 450–451
Empathy, in client-centered therapy, 518
Empiricism (approach to language), 238
Empty chair technique, 519
Enacted social support, 459, 459–460
Encoding, 210, 210–212
elaborative, 213
Encoding failure, 223
Endocrine glands, 68–69, 69f
Endorphins, 123
Environment
inheritance and, 289–291, 290f
mental retardation and, 300
prenatal development and, 392–393
Epilepsy, 62
Episodic memory, 205, 420
Erikson, Erik, 422
Escher, Maurits, 105
ESP (extrasensory perception), 36, 124
Estrogen, 68, 340
Ethic of care, 410
Ethics, 38–41
in clinical practice, 39–40, 40t
in research, 38–39, 41
Evaluation apprehension, 589
Evocative (or reactive) interaction, 81
Evolution, 82
brain and, 82–83
Evolutionary psychology, 18, 18–20, 20t
Excitatory effects, 51
Excitement stage of sexual response, 339
Exhaustion phase, 434
Existential intelligence, 281
Expectancies, 373, 373–376
Expectations
experimenter expectancy effects and, 35
hearing and, 117–118
vision and, 109–110
Experiment(s), natural, 71–72
Experimental design, 28f, 28–29, 33t
Experimenter expectancy effects, 35
Expertise, problem solving and, 260–261
Explicit (or declarative) memories, 206, 206–207, 207f
Exposure with response prevention, 524, 524–525

External attribution, 567, 567t
External cues, 230
Extinction, 170, 183
Extrasensory perception (ESP), 36, 124
Extraversion, 360
Extrinsic motivation, 327
Eye, 98f, 98–99, 99f
Eye blink reflex, 394t

Facial expressions, emotions and, 312–314, 313f
Facial feedback hypothesis, 317
Factor analysis, 279
Fallacies, planning, 267
False alarms, 478
False lives, 519
False memory, 221, 221–222
distinguishing fact from fiction and, 222
implanting, 221f, 221–222, 222f
Family therapy, 533, 533–534, 534f
Fear, 319–320
Fechner, Gustav Theodor, 92
Female arousal dysfunction, 344
Fetal alcohol syndrome, 300
Fetishes, 344
Fetoscopes, 391
Figure, 102, 103–105, 105f
First words, 242f, 242–243
Five Factor Model of personality, 353–355, 354t
Fixations, 368
Fixed interval schedule, 185
Fixed ratio schedule, 185, 185–186
Flashback, 160
Flashbulb memory, 215
Flat affect, in schizophrenia, 492
Flow, 372
Fluid intelligence, 279, 420
Flynn effect, 294–295, 295, 421
fMRI (functional magnetic resonance imaging), 76
Food aversion (taste aversion), 173, 173–175, 174f
Foot-in-the-door technique, 582
Ford, Gerald, 134
Forebrain, 64
Foreshortening, 106
Forewarning, persuasion failure and, 561
Forgetting, 223f, 223–224. *See also* Amnesia
decay and, 223
interference and, 224
Forgetting curve, 223, 223f
Formal operation, 402
Fovea, 98, 98f
Fox, Michael J., 52
Fragile X syndrome, 298
Free association, 515
Frequency, 97
Frequency distribution, 594

Hz (Hertz), 114

Id, 366, 366–367
Ideal self, real self versus, 517–518
Identity
    of children, 408
    gender, 408–409
Identity confusion or alteration, 499
Identity versus role confusion stage, 423t
Illusory correlation, 563
Images, interactive, 228
Imaginary audience, 415–416
Imitation, 401
Immediate reinforcement, 182
Immune system, 69
    conditioning of, 175
    stress and, 443f, 443–444
Implicit memories, 206, 206–207, 207f
Implicit motive, 328
Impotence, 344
Impression formation, 555
Impression management, 555
Imprinting, genomic (gametic), 390
Impulsivity, 362, 363
Incentive, 326–328, 327
Incidental learning, 214
Incongruence, 517, 517–518
Incubation, 259
Independent variable, 28, 593
Individualist culture, 331
Individual therapy, 532, 532–533
Inductive reasoning, 265, 265–266
Industrial/organizational (I/O) psychologists, 24, 24t
Industry versus inferiority stage, 423t
Infantile amnesia, 225
Infants and children, 396–412
    cognitive development of, 399–405, 400t, 401f, 403f
    gender role development in, 411
    newborn infants, 393–396
    perceptual development of, 298f, 397–399
    physical and motor development of, 396–397
    social and emotional development of, 406–411
Inferential statistics, 592–593, 593, 598–601
Information processing, 18
    neural development and, 404–405
Inferiority complex, 371
Informed consent, 38, 38–39
Ingroup, 563
Ingroup differentiation, 563
Inhibitory conflict, 155
Inhibitory effects, 51
Initialisms, 229
Initiative versus guilt stage, 423t
Inner speech, 405
Insanity, 469

Insight, 259, 259–260, 260f
Insight learning, 191
Insight-oriented therapy, 514, 514–521
    expression of emotion in, 520–521
    humanistic, 517–520
    psychodynamic, 515–517
    techniques of, 514–515
Insomnia, 140, 140–141
Instinct, 325
Institutional Review Board (IRB), 39
Insulin, 335
Integrity versus despair stage, 422, 423t
Intellectualization, 370t
Intelligence, 272–309, 274
    in adulthood, 420–422, 421f
    analytic, 282
    boosting, 294–296
    brain size and, 285–286
    creative, 282
    creativity and. See Creativity
    crystallized, 279, 420–421
    emotional, 283
    environment and, 289–291, 290f
    existential, 281
    fluid, 279, 420
    general, 421
    genes and, 287–289, 289f
    giftedness and, 300–301
    group differences in, 291–294
    mental retardation and, 297–300, 299t
    practical, 282
    single versus multiple intelligences and, 278–283
    working memory and, 286–287, 287f
Intelligence quotient (IQ), 274, 274–278
    achievement and, 277–278
    Flynn effect and, 294–295, 421
    scoring IQ tests and, 276f, 276–277
    single versus multiple intelligences and, 278–279, 280t
    testing, 274–276, 275t
    test stress and, 283–284
Intentional learning, 214
Interactionism, 353
Interactive images, 228
Interference, 224
Intermediate processing, 91
Internal attribution, 567, 567t
Internal conflict, stress and, 436–437
Interneuron, 46
Interpersonal therapy, effectiveness of, 547, 548
Interpretation, 516
    in psychodynamic therapy, 516–517
Interval schedule, 184, 185
Interviews, for personality assessment, 355
Intimacy versus isolation stage, 422, 423t
Intrinsic motivation, 327, 327–328

Introspection, 13
Introversion, 360
Intuition, 268
Inventories, for personality assessment, 355–356, 356f
Ion, 48
    flow of, 48, 49f
I/O (industrial/organizational) psychologists, 24, 24t
IQ. See Intelligence quotient (IQ)
IRB (Institutional Review Board), 39
Islands of excellence, 298

Jackson, Phil, 150
James, William, 14
James-Lange theory of emotion, 316, 317, 319
Jefferson, Thomas, 443
Jet lag, 142
JNDs (just-noticeable differences), 92
Johnson, Virginia, 339
Jordan, David Starr, 224
Jung, Carl, 369–370
Just-noticeable differences (JNDs), 92

Kasparov, Garry, 261, 262, 268
Kaysen, Susanna, 472
K-complex, 132
Kennedy, John F., 286
Ketamine, 159, 160
Kinesthetic sense, 122
Kinsey, Alfred, 339
Klebold, Dylan, 455
Knock-out mice, 208–209
Kohler, Wolfgang, 191
Korsakoff's syndrome, 157
Kulpe, Oswald, 14

Labeling, abnormal behavior and, 472f, 472–473
Language, 236–248
    bilingualism and, 246
    brain damage and, 70
    genes for, 246–247
    phonology and, 237
    pragmatics and, 240–241
    semantics and, 239–240
    shaping of thought by, 249
    syntax and, 238f, 238–239
Language acquisition device (LAD), 238
Language comprehension, 237
Language development
    critical period for, 243–244
    first words and, 242f, 242–243
    foundations of language and, 241–242
Language production, 236, 236–237
Latency period, 369
Latent content, 135
Latent learning, 190, 190–191
Late processing, 91
Lateral geniculate nuclei (LGN), 65

Law of Effect, 178
Learned alarms, 478
Learned helplessness, **331**, 331–332, 332f, 436
Learning, 164–197, **167**
  associative, 166
  avoidance, 181
  cognitive, 166, 189–191, 190f
  conditioning and. *See* Classical conditioning; Operant conditioning
  incidental, 214
  insight, 191
  intentional, 214
  latent, 190–191
  from models, 193–195
  observational, 191–195, 192f
Lens, 98, 98f
Leptin, 337
Lesioning studies, 72
Lesion, 71
Level of the brain, 10, 10f, 11, 12
Level of the group, 10–11, **11**, 12
Level of the person, 10, 11, 12
Levels of analysis, 9–12
Levine, James, 422
LGN (lateral geniculate nuclei), 65
Lie detection, 322–324
Life hassles, as stressors, 437
Life structure, 423–424
Light, 97, 97f
Lightness, 101
Liking, 572–573
Limbic system, 67
Lincoln, Abraham, 372
Linear perspective, 106
Linguistic relativity hypothesis, 249
Lithium, 536
Little Albert, 169, 171
Lobes, 57, 57–58, 58f
Locus of control, 374, 375
Logan, Martha, 581
Logic, 264, 264–265, 265f
Longitudinal study, 420
Long-term memory (LTM), 202, 202–204, 203f, 404
  storage in, 211
Long-term potentiation (LTP), 208, 208–209
Loving, 573f, 573–574
Lowball technique, 582
LSD (lysergic acid diethylamide), 159, 160
LTM (long-term memory), 202, 202–204, 203f, 404
  storage in, 211
LTP (long-term potentiation), 208, 208–209
Lysergic acid diethylamide (LSD), 159, 160

MA (mental age), 275
Magic Eye drawings, 105

Magnetic resonance imaging (MRI), 75, 76
Magnetic sense, 123
Magnetoencephalography (MEG), 73
Magritte, René, 105
Major depressive disorder (MDD), 484, 484t, 484–486, 486t
Majority-win rule, 585
Male erectile dysfunction, 344
Managed care, 538–539
Mandalas, 148–149
Manic episodes, 486, 486t
Manifest content, 135
Mantras, 149
MAO (monoamine oxidase), 31
MAOIs (monoamine oxidase inhibitors), 536
Marijuana, 159, 160
Maslow, Abraham, 17, 372
Massed practice, 213
Masters, William, 339
Mating preferences, 575–576
Maturation, 389
McKinley, Ida, 62
McKinley, William, 62, 193
MDD (major depressive disorder), 484, 484t, 484–486, 486t
MDMA, 158
Mead, Margaret, 415
Mean, 594, 594t
Medial geniculate nuclei (MGN), 65
Median, 595
Medication. *See also specific drugs and types of drugs*
  psychotherapy versus, 544–546
Meditation, 148, 148–151
  benefits of, 149–150
  in groups, 150–151
  physiology of, 150
  relaxation versus, 150
  types of, 148–149
Medline, 609
Medulla, 67, 67–68
MEG (magnetoencephalography), 73
Melatonin, 99
  sleep and, 136
Memory, 198–233
  in adulthood, 419–420
  amnesia and, 224–225
  autobiographical, 205
  creation of memories and, 210–215, 211f
  culture and, 219–220
  dynamic, 212
  echoic, 202
  emotionally charged, 214–215
  episodic, 205, 420
  exlicit (declarative), 206–207, 207f
  false memories and, 221–222
  flashbulb, 215
  forgetting and, 223f, 223–224
  genes and, 208–209

hypnosis and, 230–231
iconic, 201–202
implicit, 206–207, 207f
improving, 227–231
long-term, 202–204, 203f, 205–207, 211, 404
neurons and, 208
remembering and, 215–219
repressed memories and, 225–226
retrieval of, improving, 229–230
semantic, 205, 420
sensory, 201f, 201–202, 404
short-term, 202–204, 203f, 211
stores and, 200–205
stress and, 209–210
structural, 212
transactive, 585
for truth of statements, 226
working, 204f, 204–205, 286–287, 287f, 404
Memory store, **201**, 201f, 201–202
  modality-specific, 205
Mendel, Gregor, 287
Mendelian inheritance, **287**, 287–288
Meninges, **57**
Meningitis, 57
Menopause, 418
Mental age (MA), 275
Mental disengagement, 450
Mental images, **249**, 249–252
  brain and, 251–252
  mental space and, 250f, 250–251
Mental model, **265**
Mental processes, **8**, 8–9
Mental retardation, **297**, 297–300
  environment and, 300
  genes and, 298–300
Mental simulation, **258**, 258f
Mere exposure effect, 25, 560–561
Mescaline, 159
Meta-analysis, **32**, 32–33, 33t
Metabolism, **336**
Method of least squares, 599
Method of loci, 228
MGN (medial geniculate nuclei), 65
Microelectrodes, **73**
Microenvironment, **290**
Midbrain, **68**
Midlife crises, 424
Midlife transition, 424
Millan, James, 581
Mind-body interventions, for stress management, 460–461
Mindfulness meditation, **149**
Minnesota Multiphasic Personality Inventory-2 (MMPI-2), 356, 357
Minnesota Study of Twins Reared Apart (MISTRA), 363
Misattribution of arousal, **318**
Mnemonic devices, 227–229, **228**
Modality, **532**, 532–535
Modality-specific memory stores, **205**

Prototype, 252–253, **253**, 253f, 255
    alcohol abuse and, 255
Proximity, 104
Pruning, 79
Pseudoimitation, 401
Pseudopsychology, 35, 35–36
Psilocybin, 159
Psychiatric nurse, 22
Psychiatrist, 22
PsychInfo, 609
Psychoanalysis, 16, 515, 515–517
Psychodynamic theory, 15, 15–16, 20t
Psychodynamic therapy, 515–517, 516,
    520t
    effectiveness of, 547
Psychoeducation, 529
Psychokinesis (PK), 124
Psychological determinism, 366
Psychological disorder, 466–511, 470.
    See also specific disorders and
    types of disorders
    categorizing, 473–474, 474t, 475t
    defining, 469–470
    diagnosis of, 509
    explanations for, 470–473
    treatment for. *See* Treatment; *specific*
    treatments
Psychology, 8
    definition of, 8–9
    evolution of, 13–20
Psychoneuroimmunology, 69
Psychopharmacology, 535
Psychophysics, 92, 92f, 92–93
    signal detection and, 93
    thresholds and, 92–93
Psychosexual stages, 367, 367t,
    367–369
Psychosis, 368, 469, 470
    treatment of, 535–536
Psychosocial development, 422
    in adulthood, 422–425, 423t
Psychotherapists, picking, 549
Psychotherapy, 21
    medication versus, 544–546
    research on, 541–549
Psychotherapy integration, 538
Psychoticism, 360–361
PTSD (posttraumatic stress disorder),
    444, 480–482, 481
Puberty, 413
Punishment, 180, 180t, 180–181
    of rapists, 570
Pupil, 98, 98f
    attention and, 95–96
Purging. *See* Eating disorders

QALMRI method, 607–608
Qualitative overload, 439
Qualitative underload, 439
Quantitative overload, 439
Quantitative underload, 439
Quartiles, 598

Quasi-experimental design, 29–30, 33t

Racial bias, abnormal behavior and,
    473
Racial differences, in intelligence,
    292–293
Range, 596
Rapid eye movement (REM) sleep,
    133, 134, 136
Rapists, punishment of, 570
RAS (reticular activating system), 68
Rational-emotive therapy (RET),
    526–529
    techniques of, 527–529, 528f
    theory behind, 526–527, 527t
Rationalization, 370t
Ratio schedule, 184, 185–186
Raven's Progressive Matrices, 287
Raw data, 594
Reactance, persuasion failure and, 561
Reaction formation, 370t
Reaction range, 291
Reactive interaction, 81
Realistic conflict theory, 564f, 564–565
Reality monitoring, 222
Reality principle, 367
Real self, ideal self versus, 517–518
Reasoning
    deductive, 264, 265
    improving, 267–268
    inductive, 265–266
    rhythms in, 268–269
Rebound effect, 451
Recall, 216
Recategorization, 566
Recency effect, 203, 203–204
Receptor, 50–51, 51
Recessive traits, 288
Reciprocal determinism, 375
Recognition, 108–109, 109f, 216,
    216–217, 217f
Reflex, 54, 393, 394t
Refractory period, 340
Reframing, 534
Rehearsal, 202
Reinforcement, 17, 178, 178–180
    immediate versus delayed, 182
    negative, 179–180, 180t
    positive, 179, 180t
    schedules of, 184–186, 185f
Reinforcer, 179
    primary and secondary, 181
Relapses, 447
Relational aggression, 454
Relationships, 572–576
    in adulthood, 425
    liking and, 572–573
    loving and, 573f, 573–574
    mating preferences and, 575–576
Relative standing, 598
Relaxation, meditation versus, 150
Relevant/irrelevant technique (RIT), 322

Reliability, 33
Religion
    hallucinations and delusions and, 470
    meditation and, 149
Remembering, 215–219
REM rebound, 138
REM (rapid eye movement) sleep, 133,
    134, 136
    sleep disorders and, 140
Repetition blindness, 111
Repetition priming, 207
Replicate, 26
Representation problem, 256, 257
Representativeness heuristic, 266,
    266–267
Repressed memory, 225, 225–226
Repression, 369, 370t
Repressors, 457
Research, 26–33
    case study, 31–32, 33t
    correlational, 30f, 30–31, 33t
    ethics in, 38–39, 41
    experimental design for, 28f, 28–29,
        33t
    generalization of results of, 600–601
    genetic, 81–82. *See also* Adoption
        studies; Twin studies
    on intelligence, 288–291, 289f, 290f,
        421–422
    on mental process and physical
        health, 36–37
    meta-analysis and, 32–33, 33t
    naturalistic observation for, 31, 33t
    on obvious situations, 24–25
    outcome, 542–544
    on personality, 362–364, 363f, 363t
    on psychotherapy, 541–549
    quasi-experimental design for, 29–30,
        33t
    scientific method and, 26–28
    split-brain, 62f, 62–63, 63f
    statistics and. *See* Statistics
    survey, 32, 33t
Research papers
    APA format for, 606
    evaluating, 607–608
    online information sources for,
        608–610
    reading, 610
    writing, 610–611
Resistance, 517
Resistance phase, 434
Resistant attachment, 406–407
Resolution stage of sexual response,
    339
Response bias, 35
Response contingency, 179
Responsibility, diffusion of, 589
RET (rational-emotive therapy),
    526–529
    techniques of, 527–529, 528f
    theory behind, 526–527, 527t

CREDITS

TEXT AND ILLUSTRATIONS

Figure 1, p. 3: From *Elements of Graphic Design* by Stephen M. Kosslyn. © 1994 by W.H. Freeman and Company. Used with permission.

Figure 2, p. 4: Based on a chart by Nigel Holmes from *Designer's Guide to Creating Charts and Diagrams,* 1984. Reprinted with permission.

Figure 1.4, p. 30: From *Introduction to the Practice of Statistics,* Second Edition, by David S. Moore and George P. McCabe. © 1993 by W.H. Freeman and Company. Used with permission.

Table 1.5, p. 40: Abridgment and adaptation of Code of Ethics, American Psychological Association, www.apa.org/ethics/cod.html. Copyright by the American Psychological Association. Reprinted with permission.

Figure 2.1, p. 47: Figure from Dowling, J. E. (1992). *Neurons and Networks: An Introduction to Neuroscience.* Reprinted by permission of Cajal Institute, CSIC, Madrid, Spain.

Figure 2.13, p. 61: Reprinted from Bisiach et al., "Brain and conscious representation of outside reality," *Neuropsychologia, 19.* Copyright 1981, with permission from Elsevier Science.

Figure 2.15, p. 63: From Gazzaniga, M. S., and LeDoux, J. E. *The Integrated Mind.* New York: Plenum Press, 1978. Reprinted by permission.

Figure 3.1, p. 91: From *Psychology,* Third Edition, by Peter Gray. © 1991, 1994, and 1999 by Worth Publishers. Used with permission.

Figure 3.6, p. 99: From Dowling, J. E., & Boycott, B. B. (1966). *Proceedings of the Royal Society* (London), B166, 80–111, Figure 7. Reprinted by permission.

Figure 3.9, p. 102: From *Elements of Graphic Design* by Stephen M. Kosslyn. © 1994 by W.H. Freeman and Company. Used with permission.

Figure 4.2, p. 133: From *Sleep* by J. Allan Hobson © 1989 by Scientific American Library. Used with the permission of W.H. Freeman.

Figure 4.3, p. 134: Reprinted with permission from Roffwarg, H. P., Muzio, J. N., & Dement, W. C., "Ontogenetic development of human sleep-dream cycle," *Science, 152,* 604–619. Copyright 1996 American Association for the Advancement of Science.

Figure 5.4, p. 171: From Brooks, D. C., & Bouton, M. E., "A retrieval cue for extinction attentuates spontaneous recovery," *Journal of Experimental Psychology: Animal Behavior Processes, 19,* 77–89. Copyright © 1993 by the American Psychological Association. Adapted with permission.

Figure 5.5, p. 172: Illustration by Roberto Osti from J. E. LeDoux, "Emotion, memory and the brain," *Scientific American,* June 1994, Vol. 270, p. 56. Reprinted by permission of Roberto Osti.

Figure 5.12, p. 185: Figure from "Teaching machines" by B. F. Skinner, *Scientific American,* 1961. Reprinted by permission of the Estate of Mary E. and Dan Todd.

Figure 5.13, p. 190: From Tolman, E. C., & Honzik, C. H., *Introduction and Removal of Reward and Maze Performance in Rats.* Copyright © 1930 The Regents of the University of California.

Figure 6.2, p. 203: Figure adapted from Glanzer, M., & Cunitz, A.R., "Two storage mechanisms in free recall," *Journal of Verbal Learning and Verbal Behavior, 5,* 351–360, 1996. Reprinted by permission of the author.

Figure 6.3, p. 204: From Baddeley, Alan (1986), *Working Memory.* Oxford: Clarendon Press. Reprinted by permission of Oxford University Press.

Figure 6.4, p. 207: Reprinted with permission from Squire, L. R., & Zola-Morgan, S., 1991, "The medical temporal lobe memory system" *Science, 253:* 1380–1386. Copyright © 1991 American Association for the Advancement of Science.

Figure 6.6, p. 214: Figure from "Hierarchical retrieval schemes in recall of categorized word list" by Bower, G. H., Clark, M. C., Lesgold, A. M., & Winzenz, D. in *Journal of Verbal Learning and Verbal Behavior*, Vol. 8, 323–343, copyright © 1969 by Academic Press. Reproduced by permission of the publisher and the author.

Figure 7.2, p. 242: Figure from Reznick, J. S., & Goldfield, B. A., "Rapid change in lexical development in comprehension and production," *Developmental Psychology*, 28, 406–413. Copyright © 1992 by the American Psychological Association. Reprinted with permission.

Figure 7.3, p. 250 (top left and bottom left): From Kosslyn, S. M., Ball, T. M., & Reiser, B. J., "Visual images preserved metric spatial information: Evidence from studies of image scanning," *Journal of Experimental Psychology: Human Perception and Performance*, 4, 47–60. Copyright © 1978 by the American Psychological Association. Reprinted with permission.

Figure 7.8, p. 258: From "Visual/Spatial Abilities in Problem Solving in Physics" by Kozhevnikov, M., Hegarty, M., & Mayer, R., *Thinking with Diagrams '98*, The University of Wales, Aberystwyth, United Kingdom, August 22–23, 1998. Reprinted by permission of Maria Kozhevnikov.

Figure 7.10, pp. 260, 262: Figures by Janet Metcalfe from *Journal of Experimental Psychology: Learning, Memory and Cognition*, 12, 623–634. Copyright © 1986 by the American Psychological Association. Reprinted with permission.

Figure 8.2, p. 287: Figure from "Neural substrates of fluid reasoning: An fMRI study of the neocortical activation during performance of the Raven's Progressive Matrices Test" by Prabhakaran, V., Smith, J. A. L,. Desmond, J. E., Glover, G. H., & Gabrieli, J. E. in *Cognitive Psychology*, Vol. 33, 43–63, copyright © 1997 by Academic Press. Reproduced by permission of the publisher. All rights reserved.

Figure 8.3, p. 289: From *Behavior Genetics* by R. Plomin, J. C. DeFries, G. E. McClearn, and M. Rutter. © 1997 by W.H. Freeman and Company. Used with permission.

Figure 8.6, p. 303: From Finke, R. A., & Slayton, K. (1988), "Explorations of creative visual synthesis in mental imagery," *Memory and Cognition*, 16, 252–257. Reprinted by permission.

Figure 9.2, p. 314: From *Emotion: A Psychoevolutionary Synthesis* by Robert Plutchik. Copyright 1980 by Robert Plutchik. Reprinted by permission of Addison-Wesley Educational Publishers, Inc.

Figure 9.3, p. 316: From Lefton, Lester A., *Psychology*, Seventh Edition. Copyright © 2000 by Allyn & Bacon. Reprinted by permission.

Figure 9.9, p. 341: Figure from Cooper, M. L., Shapiro, C. M., & Powers, A. M., "Motivations for sex and risky sexual behavior among adolescents and young adults: A functional perspective," *Journal of Personality and Social Psychology*, 75, 1528–1558. Copyright © 1998 by the American Psychological Association. Reprinted with permission.

Figure 9.10, p. 343: From Levin, R. J. (1994), "Human male sexuality: Appetite and arousal, desire and drive," *Appetite: Neural and Behavioral Bases* edited by Charles R. Legg and David Booth, pp. 127–164. © European Brain and Behavior Society, 1994. Reprinted by permission of Oxford University Press.

Figure 10.1, p. 356: Adapted from Cattell, Eber, & Tatsuoka. Copyright © 1970 by the Institute for Personality and Ability Testing Inc. Reproduced by permission. "16PF" is a trademark belonging to IPAT, Inc.

Figure 10.3, p. 359: From H. J. Eysenck, *The Biological Basis of Personality*, 1967. Courtesy of Charles C. Thomas, Publisher, Ltd., Springfield, Illinois.

Figure 10.5, p. 366: From *New Introductory Lectures on Psycho-Analysis* by Sigmund Freud, translated by James Strachey. Copyright © 1965, 1964 by James Strachey. Used by permission of W. W. Norton & Company Inc. Sigmund Freud © Copyrights, The Institute of Psycho-Analysis and The Hogarth Press for permission to quote from *The Standard Edition of the Complete Psychological Works of Sigmund Freud,* translated and edited by James Strachey.

Figure 10.7, p. 382: Figure from Vandello, J. A., & Cohen, D. (1999), "Patterns of individualism and collectivism across the United States," *Journal of Personality and Social Psychology*, 77, 279–292. Copyright © 1999 by the American Psychological Association. Reprinted with permission.

Figure 11.4, p. 403: Figure from Baillargeon, Renee (1994) "How do infants learn about the physical world?" *Current Directions in Psychological Science*, 3(5), 133–140. Reprinted by permission of Blackwell Publishers.

Figure 11.5, p. 421: From Schaie, K. W. (1989), "Individual differences in rate of cognitive change in adulthood," in V. L. Bengtson & K. W. Schaie, *The Course of Later Life: Research and Reflections*. Used by permission of Springer Publishing Company, Inc., New York, 10012.

Figure 12.1, p. 433: From Selye, Hans (1978). *The Stress of Life,* Second Edition. Copyright 1976. Reprinted with permission of The McGraw-Hill Companies.

Figure 12.5, p. 446: Figure from *Changing for Good* by James O. Prochaska, John C. Norcross, and Carlo C. Diclemente. Copyright © 1994 by James O. Prochaska, John C. Norcross, and Carlo C. Dicelemente. Reprinted by permission of HarperCollins Pubishers, Inc.

Table 13.5, p. 486: Excerpt adapted from "Common Misconceptions About Suicide" from www.save.org. Reprinted by permission.

Table 14.4, p. 535: The "Twelve Steps" are reprinted with permission of Alcoholics Anonymous World Services, Inc. (A.A.W.S.) Permission to reprint the "Twelve Steps" does not mean that A.A.W.S. has reviewed or approved the contents of this publication, or that A.A.W.S. necessarily agrees with the views expressed herein. A.A. is a program of recovery from alcoholism *only*—use of the "Twelve Step" in connection with programs and activities that are patterned after A.A., but that address other problems, or in any other non-A.A. context, does not imply otherwise.

Figure 15.4, p. 573: Sternberg's Triangular Theory of Love. Reprinted by permission of Robert Sternberg.

PHOTOS

3: Gerald Davis/Woodfin Camp & Associates; 8: AP/Wide World Photos; 12: H. Gans/The Image Works; 16: THE FAR SIDE © 1986 FARWORKS, INC. Used by permission. All rights reserved.; 21: David Young Wolff/PhotoEdit; 22: Brian Smith/Stock Boston; 23: David Young Wolff/Stone; 27: C/B Productions/The Stock Market; 29: Mary Evans Picture Library; 36: Mary Evans Picture Library; 39: © 1996 Jane Tyska/Stock Boston; 57: A. Glauberman/Photo Researchers, Inc.; 61 (Fig. 2.13): Reprinted with permission from Bisiach et al. (1981). Brain and conscious representation of outside reality. *Neuropsychologia, 19,* © 1981, Pergamon Journals Ltd.; 61 (bottom): Reprinted with permission from Damasio, H., Grabowsk, T., Frank, R., Galaburda, A. M., & Damasio, A. R.: The return of Phineas Gage: Clues about the brain from a famous patient. *Science,* 264: 1102–1105, © 1994. American Association for the Advancement of Science. Photo courtesy of H. Damasio, Human Neuroanatomy and Neuroimaging Laboratory, Department of Neurology, University of Iowa.; 73: Will and Deni McIntyre/Science Source/Photo Researchers, Inc.; 74 (right): Scott Camazine/Photo Researchers, Inc.; 74 (left): © Susie Leavines/Photo Researchers, Inc.; 75 (left): Will and Deni McIntyre/Photo Researchers, Inc.; 75 (right): Courtesy of Marcus E. Raichle, M.D., Washington University School of Medicine; 80 (top): © 1994 Gail Shumway/FPG International; 80 (bottom): David Madison/Stone; 95: © VCG 1998/FPG International; 98: S. R. Maglione/Photo Researchers, Inc.; 101: Robert Harbison; 103: All artwork by Bev Doolittle has been reproduced with the permission of The Greenwich Workshop, Inc. For information on limited edition fine art prints contact The Greenwich Workshop, Inc. One Greenwich Place, Shelton, CT 06484.; 104 (top): Reprinted with permission from Tootell, R. B. H., Silverman, M. S., Switkes, E., & DeValors, R. L., 1982. Deoxyglucose analysis of retinotopic organization in primate striate cortex. *Science,* Vol. 218, 26 November 1982. pg. 902. © 1982 American Association for the Advancement of Science.; 104 (bottom): M.C. Escher. Dutch. 1898–1972. Sky and Water 1. M.C. Escher Heirs.

Cordon Art, Baarn, Holland; 105: © 2000 Magic Eye, Inc. www.magiceye.com; 106: Bill Lyons/The Liaison Agency; 109: Hulton Getty/Liaison Agency; 111: Corel, Courtesy of Ron Rensink; 112: Perrett, D. I., et al., (1998). *Nature,* Vol. 394, August 27, 1998. p. 885. Effects of sexual dimorphism on facial attractiveness. 884–887. Courtesy of Perception Laboratory/University of St. Andrews.; 117: Jack K. Clark/The Image Works; 132: Michael Heron/Woodfin Camp & Associates; 134: DENNIS THE MENACE ® used by permission of Hank Ketcham and © by North America Syndicate; 135: Theo Allofs/Stone; 140: Mary Evans Picture Library; 147: Bettmann/Corbis; 149: Robert Fried/Stock Boston; 150: Reuters/Gary Hershorn/Archive Photos; 159: Mary Evans Picture Library; 179: William Johnson/Stock Boston; 181: "Illustrations" by Kimberly Ann Coe, from SIBLINGS WITHOUT RIVALRY: HOW TO HELP YOUR CHILDREN LIVE TOGETHER SO YOU CAN TOO by Adele Faber and Elaine Mazlish. Copyright © 1987 by Adele Faber and Elaine Mazlish. Used by permission of the author and W. W. Norton & Company, Inc.; 186: Bonnie Kamin/PhotoEdit; 191: Corbis; 194: Monkmeyer/Kopstein; 201: Alex Hermant/Liaison Agency; 204: Reprinted with permission from Smith, E. E., & Jonides, J., Storage and executive processes in the frontal lobes, *Science,* Vol. 283, 12 March 1999. pp. 1657–1661. © 1999 American Association of the Advancement of Science.; 212: Le Penseur; Rodin, Auguste Christie's Images/SuperStock; 215: David Young Wolff/PhotoEdit; 217: *Young Frankenstein,* Gene Wilder and Peter Boyle, 1974. 20th Century Fox/Motion Picture and Television Photo Archives; 224: Everett Collection, Inc.; 228: PhotoDisc; 230: Tony Freeman/PhotoEdit; 244: AP/Wide World Photos; 245: Courtesy of Language Research Center Staff/GSU; 249: Corbis; 261: AP/Wide World Photos; 275: Bob Daemmrich Photography; 281 (top right): Lawrence Migdale/Stock Boston; 281 (top left): David Young Wolff/Stone; 281 (bottom): Tony Freeman/PhotoEdit; 282: Will Hart; 293: © Material World/Kirk McCoy; 300: © Andy Levin/Photo Researchers, Inc.; 304: AP/Wide World Photos; 305: Carol Ann DeSimine for Creative Competitions, Inc.; 313: Reprinted by permission of the Human Interaction Laboratory/Japanese and Caucasian Facial Expressions of Emotion, Matsimoto & Ekman, 1988; 321: Michael Dick/Animals Animals; 323: Mark C. Burnett/Photo Researchers, Inc.; 327: Adam Woolfitt/Corbis; 331: M. Granitsas/The Image Works; 334: © Nathan Benn/Woodfin Camp & Associates; 335: © Ramage, A./Animals Animals; 336: Bob Daemmrich/Stock Boston; 337: AP/Wide World Photos; 344 (top): Hans Pfletschinger/Peter Arnold, Inc.; 344 (bottom): Martin Harvey/NHPA/Photo Researchers, Inc.; 350: Everett Collection, Inc.; 352 (left): Reuters/Ray Stubblebine/Archive Photos; 352 (right): Richard Ellis/Sygma; 356: Monkmeyer/Merrim; 362 (top): Corbis; 362 (bottom): Bob Sacha Photography; 373: Cindy Charles/PhotoEdit; 374:

Everett Collection, Inc.; **381:** Joe Cavanaugh/DDB Stock Photo; **389:** Dr. Dennis Kunkel/Phototake; **394** (top): © 1998 Laura Dwight; **394** (**middle**): Monkmeyer/Conklin; **394** (**bottom**): E. Crews/The Image Works; **397:** Monkmeyer/Birnbach; **399:** Monkmeyer/Anderson; **400:** Michael Newman/PhotoEdit; **402:** Reprinted with permission from A. N. Meltzoff & M. K. Moore, 1977, "Imitation of facial and manual gestures by human neonates," *Science, 198*, p. 75, © 1977 American Association for the Advancement of Science.; **406:** University of Wisconsin, Animal Science Dept.; **407:** © Mark Wexler/Woodfin Camp & Associates, Inc.; **408:** Michael Newman/PhotoEdit; **411:** © Kit Walling/Folio, Inc.; **413:** © Bob Daemmrich/Stock Boston; **415:** James Darell/Stone; **418:** © Larry Mulvehill/Science Source/Photo Researchers, Inc.; **419:** Tom Prettyman/PhotoEdit; **422:** © Timothy Greenfield-Sanders/Corbis Outline; **425** (**top left**): Sergei Milansky/ RPG/Sygma; **425** (**top right**): Joe Caputo/Liaison Agency; **425** (**bottom**): © Photonews/Liaison Agency; **434:** B. Stitzer/PhotoEdit; **436:** Archive Photos; **438** (**left**): © Bill Horsman/Stock Boston; **438** (**right**): Monkmeyer/Gish; **439:** Reuters/Kimimasa Mayama/Archive Photos; **441:** Bob Daemmrich; **443:** © Meckes/Ottawa/Photo Researchers, Inc.; **444:** AP/Wide World Photos; **452:** AP/Wide World Photos; **453:** AP/Wide World Photos; **455** (**background**): © Mark Leffingwell/Boulder Daily Camera; **455** (**inset left**): Reuters/Ho/Archive Photos; **455** (**inset right**): Reuters/Ho/Archive Photos; **456:** Nancy Richmond/The Image Works; **459:** Network Productions/The Image Works; **461:** Kolvoord/The Image Works; **469:** Musee d'Orsay, Paris France, © Erich Lessing/Art Resource, NY; **473:** Suzanne Tenner/Everett Collection, Inc; **477:** Everett Collection, Inc.; **480:** Culver Pictures, Inc.; **482:** Margaret Ross/Stock Boston; **485:** Painting by Kate Monson, Courtesy of Sistare; **494:** Courtesy of D. R. Weinberger, National Institute of Mental Health, Saint Elizabeth's Hospital, Washington, DC; **497:** Edna Morlock; **500:** © Dale St. Hilaire; **502:** Lara Jo Regan/Liaison Agency; **507:** Reuters/HO/Archive Photos; **515** (**left**): Rhoda Sidney/Stock Boston; **515** (**right**): Zigy Kaluzny/Stone; **518:** R. Lord/The Image Works; **533:** Bob Daemmrich/Stock Boston; **536:** Michael P. Gadomski/Photo Researchers, Inc.; **538:** Julian Keenan; **539:** David Young Wolff /PhotoEdit; **545:** David Young Wolff/PhotoEdit; **549:** Chuck Fishman/Woodfin Camp & Associates; **555** (**right**): Reuters/Sam Mircovich/Archive Photos; **555** (**left**): Reuters/Archive Photos; **560:** Canadian Press CP; **565:** Culver Pictures, Inc.; **566:** AP/Wide World Photos; **567:** Melinda Sue Gordon/Everett Collection, Inc.; **575:** Jason Laure/Woodfin Camp & Associates; **576** (**top**): Kunsthistorisches Museum, Gemaeldegalerie, Vienna, Austria, © Erich Lessing/Art Resource, NY; **576:** David Wells/The Image Works; **577:** Reuters/Yannis Behrakis/Archive Photos; **578:** Burbank/The Image Works; **583:** Alexandra Milgram; **586:** James Nubile/The Image Works.